POLITICAL
PROFILES
☆ ☆ ☆
The
Eisenhower
Years

POLITICAL PROFILES

☆ ☆ ☆

The Eisenhower Years

EDITOR:

Eleanora W. Schoenebaum, Ph.D., Columbia University

ASSOCIATE EDITOR:
Michael L. Levine, Ph.D., Rutgers University

Facts On File, Inc.
119 West 57th Street, New York, N.Y. 10019

POLITICAL PROFILES
The Eisenhower Years

Library of Congress Catalog Card No. 76-20897
ISBN 0-87196-452-3
9 8 7 6 5 4 3 2 1

PRINTED IN THE UNITED STATES OF AMERICA

Contents

Preface

The Eisenhower Years is the third volume in the *Political Profiles* series. It contains biographies of 501 men and women who played a significant role in U.S. politics during the 1950s. When completed, *Political Profiles* will consist of six volumes which include detailed biographies of those individuals prominent in American politics since the end of World War II. Each volume, with the exception of *The Nixon/Ford Years,* will cover a single presidency and will profile the several hundred figures who were most influential in shaping public life during that period.

As in the case of the profiles in *The Kennedy Years* and *The Johnson Years,* each entry is a detailed account of the individual's career during a particular presidential administration. It also includes his social and political background, his early career and major accomplishments as well as an assessment of his impact on the social, political or cultural life of the nation. Individuals with long careers, such as Orville Freeman, Hubert Humphrey and George Meany, appear in several volumes of the series. In these cases each volume's entry briefly summarizes his entire career but concentrates on his activities during the administration under consideration. For example, Sen. William Fulbright's profile in *The Eisenhower Years* focuses on the role he played in the downfall of Sen. Joseph R. McCarthy. His entry in *The Kennedy Years* emphasizes his demands for a reorientation of U.S. policy toward the Soviet Union. Fulbright's profile in *The Johnson Years* traces his growing opposition to the Vietnam war. This unique organizational structure enables us to update the series by tracing an individual's career through *The Truman Years* to *The Carter Years* if necessary. It provides a richness of detail and historical perspective unavailable in other biographical reference works.

Each entry begins with a headnote giving the individual's name, date and place of birth and death, and major offices held during the period covered in the volume. In the case of men and women in political office the years—and if important the months—in office are given. We have chosen to list the date of Senate confirmation as the beginning of service to maintain consistency. Thus, Charles E. Wilson is listed in

this volume as "Secretary of Defense, January 1953–October 1957."
Arthur Miller, however, is recorded simply as "Playwright."

The body of the entry then follows, its size commensurate with the
individual's importance or the significance of the issue he or she was
involved in. If the individual is profiled in another volume this is indicated in a bracketed notation in the text. The notation [q.v.] (ie. quod
vide) follows the names of other men and women who have entries in
the same volume. (The notation does not follow the names of Presidents.) Each profile concludes with the initials of the author and, in
many instances, brief suggestions for further reading.

One of the most difficult tasks in compiling a new biographical
reference work is choosing the individuals to be covered. A large portion of the entries are self-evident: the President and Vice President,
members of the Supreme Court and cabinet, and chairmen of important congressional committees. Beyond these individuals we have
been guided by two questions: Did the man or woman have a lasting
impact on politics broadly defined? Or, did the individual capture the
political attention of the nation? We have, therefore, included not only
political officeholders but also influential business and labor leaders,
journalists and intellectuals as well as civil rights activists.

Because of the importance of the executive branch during the
postwar period, we have included important figures in the executive
departments, particularly Defense and State, as well as the President's
aides and advisers. We have been more selective in choosing members
of Congress. Only those associated with a major issue or interest have
been included. Because of the importance of the Southern reaction to
the Supreme Court's desegregation decisions, a large number of
Southern governors have been included.

Choosing among the numerous journalists and intellectuals of the
period has been one of the most difficult tasks. We have included a
number of those, such as Hannah Arendt, Will Herbert, C. Wright
Mills, Daniel Bell, William F. Buckley and Peter Viereck, who had an
influence on the general body politic. Left out are those academics
who, while important in their fields, are little-known to the general
public. Finally, we have profiled a number of figures who achieved
brief fame or notariety. These include Irving Peress, the Army dentist
attacked by McCarthy, Francis Gary Powers, the U-2 spy plane pilot
and Morton Sobell, the convicted espionage agent.

Because *Political Profiles* deals with those individuals who
dominated the visible surface of public affairs during the postwar period, we have not attempted to provide a political or ethnic balance.
The selection of individuals included reflects the nature of national
politics under each President. *The Eisenhower Years* contains very
few women and blacks. Most of those profiled in this volume are white
males, many with connections to big business, living in Washington,
D.C., New York or a handful of other cities.

Our series does not purport to be a reference work on the American
political and economic elite. There has been little attempt to profile

members of the so-called American establishment who may have had a profound influence on policy but who chose to work behind the scenes. Similarly, while we have profiled business leaders such as Frank Pace and Crawford Greenewalt who played a role in politics during the period, *The Eisenhower Years* contains no representatives of the Mellon or DuPont dynasties.

Almost all of the entries in this volume were researched and written by trained historians, either graduate students or Ph.D's. A distinguished editorial board helped us select those profiled. Edward W. Knappman, executive editor of Facts on File, conceived the series and reviewed most profiles included in the volume. Howard Langer provided valuable assistance on many of the entries. Martin Goldberg undertook the arduous task of compiling the index and assemblying the appendix.

The Eisenhower Years contains several useful appendixes. It had a complete chronology of the period, the membership list of the 83rd–86th Congresses, a list of the Eisenhower cabinet, the Supreme Court and the membership of the most important regulatory agencies. The volume also contains an extensive bibliography covering the Eisenhower era. We thought it useful to include a topical index for the convenience of those seeking information on individuals in similar fields. The volume also contains an extensive index.

The Eisenhower Years:
An Introduction

Dwight D. Eisenhower came to office in 1953 at a time of disillusionment and bitter division. Retiring President Harry S. Truman had lost the confidence of many Americans who blamed him and his Administration for the problems at home and abroad. Having been assured that peace would follow the defeat of the Axis powers, the U.S. found itself fighting an unpopular "police action" in Korea with its military leaders forced to accept a stalemate. Cold War tensions continued unabated. The Soviet Union maintained control of Eastern Europe as a result of what some thought was President Franklin D. Roosevelt's sell-out of that area at Yalta. In China, Communists, led by Mao Tse-tung, had driven Chiang Kai-shek from the mainland.

On the domestic scene, the trials of Alger Hiss and Julius and Ethel Rosenberg revealed possible Communist subversion in government. Sen. Joseph R. McCarthy (R, Wisc.) had begun a crusade against domestic Communism. Through innuendo, overstatement and lies, he had created a climate of fear in many segments the country. Labor and management conflict continued unabated. Most dramatically, the Supreme Court limited the implied powers of the presidency when it ruled that Truman's 1952 seizure of the steel mills was unconstitutional. Investigations of official corruption revealed what came to be called "that mess in Washington." Several of Truman's top aides were implicated in conflict-of-interest scandals and a number of high-ranking members of the Bureau of Internal Revenue were discovered willing to "fix" tax cases.

Americans were prosperous, but there was a political restlessness captured by the Republican Party's 1952 proclamation, "It's Time for a Change." In an editorial discussing the problem, Louis B. Seltzer of the *Cleveland Press* asked, "What is wrong with us? . . ." "We have everything. We abound with all of the things that make us comfortable. . . . Yet . . . something is not there that should be—something we once had. . . ."

Eisenhower's 1952 landslide was the result of the American people's belief that the General could lead a "great crusade" to return the U.S.

to its traditional values and recover that undefinable "something." He was the man who appeared able to restore morality in government and reestablish domestic tranquility. He could give the country peace and end the frustration of the world's greatest power unable to achieve its own destiny. "The people want another George Washington," wrote Harry A. Bullis to Eisenhower, "They really think you are the man who can best help them keep their liberty and their freedom." After the inaugural one minister began his prayer, "Now that virtue has been restored to high places. . . ."

Eisenhower's character was well suited to the nation's mood. He was a man untainted by political strife, who in the late-1940s had turned down presidential bids because he believed that career soldiers should not become involved in partisan politics. He had, in fact, decided to run only because he had become convinced that the nation needed him. His genial, fatherly personality and his lack of pretense impressed the American people. He once remarked during campaign, "It's all a bit overwhelming to me to see a great crowd like this. My memory goes back to the barren Kansas prairie and . . . little boys running around barefooted in the dust. I never got over my astonishment that you would want to know what I think." He was a man who made a virtue of his lack of intellectual background and his adherence to traditional American values. Eisenhower, the general who had led the Allies to victory against the Axis powers, appeared to have the leadership qualities needed to end the Korean conflict and deal forcefully with the Soviet Union.

Eisenhower had a formalist view of this office, particularly in domestic affairs. He saw himself primarily as a leader giving direction to the Administration. With what historian William Leuchtenburg has termed his "chairman-of-the-board-stance," he left specific policy formulation to his subordinates, particularly in such areas as labor and economics in which he had little interest. Anxious to uphold the image of a man above politics and maintain the dignity of this office, Eisenhower refused to take part in the bickering and maneuvering that were necessary to achieve passage of his programs.

Eisenhower's appointments reflected his conservative, business oriented philosophy. Only four of the 53 highest appointments went to professional politicians. With the exception of labor leader Martin Durkin, who left after a short period, Eisenhower's cabinet was composed of either conservative lawyers or leaders of business. *The New Republic* described it as "Eight millionaires and a plumber." Two, John Foster Dulles and Herbert Brownell, were members of prestigious law firms, while Ezra Taft Benson was one of the Quorum of Twelve Apostles, the ruling body of the Mormon church. The remainder were mostly self-made individuals who had risen to key posts in the business world. Postmaster General Arthur Summerfield and Secretary of the Interior Douglas McKay had made fortunes as auto dealers. George Humphrey had been head of Mark Hanna and Co. Many of Eisenhower's key advisers headed companies with large numbers of government contracts. Air Force Secretary Harold Talbott was associated with Chrysler and North American Aviation; Navy Secretary Robert Anderson was closely tied to oil interests. Secretary of Defense Charles Wilson, former President of General Motors, held 39,470 shares of GM stock, worth over $2.5 million, in the company which had over $5 billion in defense contracts.

Liberals questioned the close connection between business and the Administration, but neither the President nor his advisers saw any danger or possible conflict of interest in the relationship. The new Secretary of Defense seemed to speak for the Administration when he said, "What was good for our country was good for General Motors, and vice versa." The phrase was immediately repeated as "What's good for General Motors is good for the country," a statement which prompted Democrats to object to "government by Big Business." Nevertheless, polls indicated that the majority of Americans expressed confidence in this type of leadership and believed the former business leaders could provide direction for defense, make the government more efficient and work for world peace.

The President came to office with a desire to give the nation a period of respite and repose from the activist years of the 1930s and 1940s. Eisenhower and his advisers were, according to his description, spokesmen for the "Practical Right." They realized they could not turn back the clock to the 1920s, particularly in the area of social welfare, and they accepted many New and Fair Deal programs. However, they believed these programs should be implemented on what they thought was a fiscally sound basis. Eisenhower described his Administration as one "of dynamic conservatism" implying that he would be "conservative when it comes to money and liberal when it comes to human beings."

The Administration closely tied its economic theory with its ideas of national defense. In the eyes of the President and Secretary of the Treasury Humphrey, who was the Administration's foremost economic policy formulator, a healthy economy, along with fighting strength, were the two pillars of American power. They believed that the economy could be strengthened by limiting the government's role. Only in one area, maintaining the stability of the dollar, did the federal government have a prime responsibility. The dollar could be protected by reducing inflationary pressures through budget cutting. In all other areas, government regulation was to be kept at a minimum. Even before taking office the President's economic advisers, Humphrey and Sinclair Weeks, recommended removing Truman's wage and price controls on the grounds that they would distort and impede production efforts. A healthy economy was to be maintained by a series of tax reductions aimed primarily at business and the wealthy. This conservative policy was designed to stimulate equity financing and capital spending and thus ultimately benefit low-income families by creating jobs and bringing over-all prosperity.

The Administration was cautious about using traditional New Deal remedies even in a recession. It opposed deficit financing and large-scale public works projects. Eisenhower accepted some government spending (on projects too large to be handled by state and private enterprise), easier credit, tax cuts and depreciation allowances to ease recovery. However, he emphasized that he preferred to rely on public confidence in the fact that he would act if the situation worsened to regenerate the economy.

Six months after taking office, the President declared that the Republican Party "had instituted what amounts almost to a revolution in the federal government as we have known it in our time, trying to make it smaller rather than bigger and finding things it could stop doing instead of new things for it to do." The Administration attempted to drastically limit the size of the bureaucracy and to cut the number of federal contracts. During 1953 the Secretary of Defense pared his immediate staff by 700; the Secretary of Commerce by 1,000. Eisenhower trimmed the fiscal 1954 budget by $7.3 billion. The Administration also attempted to limit government action in several fields. Eisenhower kept his campaign promise to return ownership of offshore oil deposits to the states by signing the submerged lands bill of 1953. Secretary of Agriculture Ezra Taft Benson tried to reduce aid to agriculture and move it closer to the free market system. Secretary of Labor James P. Mitchell convinced the President to keep the White House out of major labor disputes.

One of the primary areas in which the Administration moved to limit federal intervention was in the area of power development. It supported state development of hydroelectric power along the St. Lawrence Seaway and granted a private utility the right to build generating facilities at Hell's Canyon on the Snake River in Idaho. It failed, however, when it tried to circumscribe the Tennessee Valley Authority by negotiating a contract with the Mississippi Valley Generating Co., headed by Edgar Dixon and Eugene Yates. The circumstances surrounding the negotiation of the contract were so controversial that the government was forced to cancel the agreement in 1955 as "contrary to public policy."

Occasionally Administration desires to prevent government intervention went to extremes. In 1953 Secretary of Commerce Weeks fired Dr. Allen Austin, head of the Bureau of Standards, because he had shown no awareness of the "business point of view" in refusing to permit the marketing of a useless product. Weeks thought that no product should be "denied an opportunity in the market place" because government tests showed it to have no value. He was eventually forced to reinstate Austin. In 1955 Secretary of Health Education and Welfare Oveta Culp Hobby opposed the free distribution of the newly-developed Salk polio vaccine as a move toward socialized medicine "through the back door." The resulting furor eventually led to her resignation.

Although the Administration did little to develop federal programs, it did acknowledge the government's obligations in the area. In 1954 it pushed the St. Lawrence Seaway Project through Congress, where it had been stalled for over three decades, and the following year it began a joint state-federal highway program designed to create over 40,000 miles of controlled access roads to link major American cities.

Eisenhower and his advisers did little to turn back the clock in the area of social welfare and often pushed for modest improvements in this area. During the decade Social Security coverage was expanded and the minimum wage raised. Programs in housing, medical care and education were also increased. However, when defense expenditures rose during the latter part of the decade, the President, intent on balancing the budget, vetoed further housing, public works, area redevelopment and anti-pollution legislation.

Support for the Administration's legislative program came from a coalition of moderate Republicans and Democrats. In 1952 the Republicans gained control of Congress and a large number of liberal urban Democrats lost their seats. The Democratic congressional delegation was composed of moderates and conservative Southerners many of whom had been on Capitol Hill since the Roosevelt Administration. These men, often powerful chairmen of important committees, had opposed government expansion and the economic theories of the New Deal. Such senators as Richard Russell (D, Ga.), chairman of the Armed Services Committee, A. Willis Robertson (D, Va.), of the Banking and Currency Committee and Harry F. Byrd (D, Va.) of the Finance Committee, as well as such representatives as Clarence Cannon (D, Mo.) of the Appropriations Committee and Howard W. Smith (D, Va.) of the Rules Committee supported Eisenhower's modest social programs and his emphasis on fiscal integrity.

The Democratic Party was led by Sen. Lyndon B. Johnson (D, Tex.) and Rep. Sam Rayburn (D, Tex.), prominent supporters of the New Deal, who became more conservative during the 1950s. They refused to take a strong stand in opposition to the Administration and instead offered "responsible cooperation." The Democrats staged a holding action against much Administration legislation, not advancing large-scale projects but differing with the President over the amount of money to be spent on existing ones. Despite the fact that the Democrats regained control of Congress in 1954, they failed to develop viable policy alternatives. Power remained in the conservative coalition of Republicans and Southern Democrats. Liberal Democrats, helpless in the face of such strength, termed the Eisenhower presidency "years in the wilderness."

Eisenhower's major opposition came from the right wing of the Republic Party, led by Sens. William Jenner (R, Ind.), Joseph McCarthy, Styles Bridges, (R, N.H.), John Bricker (R, Ohio), Karl Mundt (R, S.D.), and Herman Welker (R, Ida.). Frustrated by years out of power, they hoped to use the Republican majority to undo much of the New and Fair Deal legislative programs. More conservative than Eisenhower on economic affairs, they pushed for early tax cuts to aid business. The move, led by Rep. Daniel Reed (R, N.Y.), was defeated only with the help of House Speaker Joseph Martin (R, Mass.). The conservatives were particularly concerned with foreign affairs. They objected strenuously to the wartime agreements with the Soviet Union, which many argued had led to the Soviet takeover of Eastern Europe. Angered by the secret diplomacy these agreements represented, in 1953 Sen. John Bricker offered an amendment that would have limited the President's treaty-making powers. The move, which Eisenhower considered the most serious threat to his presidency, was defeated by only one vote in the Senate. Conservatives also had a potent voice in the formation of U.S. policy toward Communist China. As the result of pressure from members of the congressional China bloc, led by Sens. Jenner, William Knowland (R, Calif.), Alexander Wiley (R, Wisc.), and Rep. Walter Judd (R, Ohio) and from the Committee for One Million Against the Admission of Communist China to the U.N., the Administration was forced to maintain a hard-line against Communist China. The U.S. refused to recognize the regime and vetoed its admission to the U.N. while supporting Chiang Kai-shek and offering military and economic support to Taiwan.

The right was not primarily interested in legislation but in probes of domestic subversion. The belief that American problems were a result of Communist infiltration was not new to the 1950s but reached its peak during that period in a series of spectacular congressional investigations. The anti-Communist crusade was personified by Sen. Joseph McCarthy. Through a series of dramatic probes of government agencies such as the Voice of America and the International Information Agency and a campaign of innuendo and insinuations, he created a climate of fear that gripped government, colleges and other institutions. The Senator's suggestion that an individual was connected with leftist groups could jeopardize his career. In the case of John Carter Vincent, John Patton Davies and John Service, it led to their forced resignations. Under McCarthy's direction, aides Roy Cohn and G. David Schine traveled throughout Europe looking for subversive literature in overseas libraries. Some books were burned by diplomats who feared for their jobs. McCarthy was joined in his campaign by Rep. Harold Velde, chairman of the House Un-American Activities Committee, who conducted probes of subversion in public schools and in the motion picture industry. William Jenner held hearings on possible Communist influence in the U.N. Rep. Francis Walter (D, Pa.) investigated private foundations, denouncing such fund executives as Dean Rusk and Robert Hutchins for supporting leftist groups and what he thought were un-American projects.

Initially the Administration did little to stop McCarthy's excesses. Despite the fact that Eisenhower drew some of his electoral support from those who hoped he would stop McCarthy and Jenner, the President did not take a firm stand against them. Eisenhower made only two overt moves against the Senator in 1953. He pointedly denounced "book burners" and castigated McCarthy aide J. B. Matthews for suggesting that the Protestant clergy was infiltrated by Communists. Although privately deploring McCarthy, he ignored the advice of such aides as James Hagerty and Gabriel Hauge and refused to "get into the gutter with that guy."

The Administration was drawn into the fight against subversion both as a result of Eisenhower's own anti-Communism and pressure from the right. In April 1953 the President issued Executive Order 10450, tightening security procedures in executive departments. Federal employment became contingent upon whether retention was "clearly consistent with the interests of national security." Under these directions the Administration fired men and women because of questionable associations and personal habits. The purges of the State Department were most highly publicized, but there were also dismissals in other executive agencies. The Department of Agriculture fired respected agricultural expert Wolf Ladejinsky on the grounds that he was a security risk even after the State Department had granted him security clearance. In one of his most controversial moves, Eisenhower ordered the Atomic Energy Commission to suspend Dr. Robert Oppenheimer's security clearance in December 1953 because of suspicions that he had been closely associated with Communists.

The reasons for the rise of McCarthyism, as the fear of domestic subversion became known, were debated by contemporaries and historians. Daniel Bell and Seymour Martin Lipset suggested that it was the result of a status anxiety on the part of Wasps losing their place in the social hierarchy, newly wealthy uneasy about how their acquired their money, and certain ethnics who felt they needed to establish their patriotism as a result of World War II. Conservatives such as Peter Viereck and Will Herberg viewed it as an indication of a resurgence of radical populism. Vierick termed it the "same old isolationist, Anglophobe, Germanophile revolt of radical populists, lunatic-fringers against the Wester-education anglicized elite."

Historians have tended to play down the role of status, pointing out that social mobility has always been a major characteristic of American society. Scholars such as William Leuchtenburg have suggested that McCarthyism was a result of the fears of the late-1940s. Belief in a Communist conspiracy was reinforced by the Cold War and the spectacular trials of Anger Hiss and Julius and Ethel Rosenberg. They have pointed to a sense of impotence America felt at being the most powerful country in the world and yet unable to impose its view of order on other nations. Historians such as Michael Rogin, Robert Griffith and Earl Latham have suggested that McCarthyism was a product of a fear of radical Communist ideology that predated World War II and a result of the frustrations of a political party long out of power. They have shown that support for the anti-Communist crusade was strongest in areas which opposed the New Deal. Still another contributing factor might have been a deep distrust of Eastern seaboard patricians. Those "selling the nation out" were often described as "the bright young men who were born with silver spoons in their mouths."

Recent studies have indicated that McCarthy's beleaguered opponents exaggerated the Senator's popular following. Although domestic Communism was one of the major issues raised by candidates in the 1952 campaign, polls showed that only 1% of the people considered it a serious issue. Following the GOP victory, McCarthy was credited with being a major force behind the defeat of such senators as William Benton. However, careful analysis has suggested that the desire for change and not the aid of McCarthy was responsible for these defeats. As late as 1953 polls revealed that most of those surveyed disapproved of McCarthy. Even in 1954, when the Senator's popularity reached its height, only 50% of those questioned were worried about Communism in government.

McCarthy's crusade reached a climax in 1954, after he charged that the Army was harboring subversives. At the suggestion of the White House the Army countered with evidence that he had attempted to get special treatment for his aide, G. David Schine, recently inducted into the Armed Forces. After a vicious attack on Gen. Ralph Zwicker, the Administration took action against the Senator. Vice President Richard Nixon denounced him in a speech during March. Eisenhower backed Stevens's refusal to continue testifying in light of McCarthy's harassment. In a precedent setting move, the President refused to give McCarthy documents for his probe, citing executive privilege.

The Army-McCarthy hearings, carried on national television in the spring, gave Americans their first close look at the Senator and his techniques—his bullying, insinuations and intrusions. In one of the most famous confrontations of the hearings, Army Council Joseph Welch, outraged that McCarthy had charged one of his associates with having had Communist connections, asked, "Have you no sense of decency, sir, at long last?" His question won the applause of the audience.

McCarthy rapidly lost support after the hearings. During the summer of 1954 a bipartisan group of senators, led by Ralph Flanders (R, Vt.), initiated a campaign to censure the Wisconsin Republican. In August the Senate voted to establish a committee, headed by Arthur Watkins (R, Utah), to investigate the charges. The panel unanimously recommended censure. McCarthy was "condemned" at the end of the year not because of his reckless charges or insult to justice but because of his affronts to the dignity of the Senate. After that the question of domestic subversion faded from the national limelight. McCarthy, despite his crusade, never had exposed Communists in government, instead he chose to prey on those who had left government or on men whose policies he disapproved.

The Administration's foreign policy was molded on the belief that the Western world faced a continuous threat from expansionist, monolithic Communism. Largely formulated by Secretary of State John Foster Dulles, who viewed the struggle against the Soviet Union as a conflict between good and evil, it asked the nation to wage a moral crusade against Communism. The Secretary denounced the Truman Administration's containment policy and instead called for a roll-back of the Communist sphere in Eastern Europe. In early 1953 he said, "It is only by keeping alive the hope of liberation, by taking advantage of whatever opportunity arises, that we will end the terrible peril which dominates the world, which imposes upon us such terrible sacrifices and so great a fear for the future." Despite his military background,

Eisenhower precluded war as a policy option; he continued to search for ways of diminishing tensions between nations. "Against the dark background of the atomic bomb," he said in 1953, "the U.S. does not wish merely to present strength, but also the desire and hope for peace." From 1953 to 1961 U.S. policy was formulated by the give and take between these two men, one pushing for action and the other asking for restraint.

Although Eisenhower had promised a new direction in foreign policy, his actions were merely a modification of Truman's approach. Under Dulles the U.S. moved beyond its traditional sphere of focus in Western Europe, the Western Hemisphere and the Pacific, to establish a network of mutual security treaties to contain Communism. This "pactomania," as critics called it, eventually encompassed over 50 nations. Large-scale alliances such as the Southeast Asia Treaty Organization and the Central Treaty Organization were created in Indochina and the Middle East, while mutual security treaties were signed with nations such as Nationalist China and Japan. These pacts were supplemented by military aid, thus enabling U.S. allies to supply conventional forces which Americans were reluctant to commit in cases of limited warfare.

As under Truman, the Administration's policy was centered on Europe, which Dulles termed "the world's worst fire hazard." There the U.S. continued to press for a unified front to Communist expansion through the development of economic and military alliances. American policymakers supported the development of the Common Market and pushed for the acceptance of the European Defense Community (EDC). Dulles put such a great emphasis on the EDC that he threatened France with an "agonizing reappraisal of American policy" if the plan was not accepted. His threat proved useless; the proposal was defeated. Nevertheless, the Administration succeeded in strengthening the North Atlantic Treaty Organization with the inclusion of West Germany as a full member.

Dulles believed that the U.S. had a special mission to lead the postwar world and so often attempted to dictate to American allies. His attitude created tension between the U.S. and France and Britain. He did not consult the two nations before suggesting joint action in Vietnam during 1954 and making policy recommendations during the Suez crisis of 1956. The latter incident precipitated a temporary schism in the Western alliance. Although relations with Great Britain gradually improved during the latter part of the decade as that nation followed America's policy recommendations, relations between the U.S. and France remained strained because of Charles de Gaulle's decision to pursue an independent foreign policy.

The major difference between Eisenhower's foreign policy and that of Truman was in Dulles's use of "brinksmanship" to achieve his goals. On several occasions the Secretary took the nation to the edge of war in order to force concessions from opponents. Nowhere was this policy more apparent than in the manner the Administration ended the Korean war and handled the 1954 crisis in the Formosa Straits. In both cases the Administration hinted that nuclear weapons should be used unless the crisis was successfully resolved. Yet Dulles's brinksmanship was often restrained by Eisenhower's attempts to use diplomacy to settle international disputes. In 1954 he overrode the suggestion of Dulles and the Joint Chiefs of Staff, led by Adm. Arthur Radford, to employ American air power in support of the French in Vietnam. Instead he looked to an international convention to arrive at a peaceful solution to the problem.

The Administration was divided on its policy toward the Soviet Union. Dulles refused any attempt at conciliation, believing it would encourage Communist expansion. He opposed a public response to the Soviet peace overtures of 1953 and counseled Eisenhower not to attend the 1955 summit conference. As late as 1959 he believed that nuclear war might be necessary to defend Berlin. Eisenhower, backed by such men as Harold Stassen, was optimistic about possible coexistence. He and several of his advisers believed that as the two nations reached nuclear parity some accommodation would be necessary. No breakthrough was achieved, but the Administration did begin to develop concrete positions for a discussion of differences, particularly in the area of disarmament.

The Administration's bipolar view of the world seriously affected its relations with third world nations, many of whom attempted to pursue a neutral course. Both Eisenhower and Dulles viewed neutrality as anti-American. This attitude crippled American diplomacy in the Middle East, where a Pan-Arab movement was growing under the leadership of Gamal Abdul Nasser. The Secretary proved unable to comprehend Nasser's determination not to become involved in the Cold War and his willingness to receive economic aid from both the Soviet Union and the United States. When the Administration refused to grant Egypt arms and canceled discussions of possible aid for the construction of the Aswan Dam, Nasser nationalized the Suez Canal, precipitating events that eventually led to the Middle Eastern War in the fall of 1956. Similarly, the State Department's refusal to accept the neutral government of Prince Souvanna Phouma, despite the advice of Assistant Secretary of State Graham Parsons and Ambassador Winthrop Brown, precipitated a crisis in Laos in 1960.

Although Eisenhower was adverse to the use of force to contain Communist expansion, he was not skeptical about intervention per se. In 1958 he sent U.S. troops to Lebanon, at the request of President Camille Chamoun, to prevent a possible overthrow of the pro-Western government there. Under Eisenhower the Central Intelligence Agency (CIA) became a prime instrument of American foreign policy. It helped overthrow unfriendly governments in Iran in 1953, in Guatemala in 1954 and made an unsuccessful attempt to do so in Indonesia in 1958. It helped install pro-American governments in Laos and in South Vietnam, where the Administration sent Edward Lansdale to help Ngo Dinh Diem consolidate power. The CIA also began organizing an expedition of Cuban refugees to overthrow the Castro regime.

Despite his limited view of a President's role in domestic policies, Eisenhower had an expansionist interpretation of presidential authority in foreign affairs. Under his direction presidential power grew tremendously. As a result of the passage of the Formosa Resolution in 1955 and the Eisenhower Doctrine in 1957, Congress gave the President prior authorization to use military force in the Formosa Straits and the Middle East. These actions proved the basis for a continual expansion of presidential power in the 1960s and 1970s.

One of the major components of the Administration's foreign policy was a strong military capable of dealing immediately with aggression. America's defense policy was based principally on "massive retaliation," the willingness to use strategic nuclear weapons as the nation's primary deterrent. Eisenhower supported the policy for several reasons. He was determined to reduce military spending and was reluctant commit American men to a ground war. By lowering the number of costly troops and relying on nuclear weapons, he could achieve both ends. In addition, Eisenhower assumed that the U.S. would never start a war and so placed emphasis on deterrence rather than fighting capacity. America's nuclear strike force was to be a diplomatic instrument as well as a weapon for military use.

The acceptance of massive retaliation was accompanied by the "New Look" in defense planning, developed by Radford. In a radical departure from the Truman Administration, Eisenhower rejected the notion that the nation had to build maximum strength for a specific date at which a Soviet attack was expected. Instead, he advocated planning for the long haul. With no emergency target date, costs could be decreased and the military made more efficient through effective business methods. In the words of the Administration, the U.S. would get "more bang for the buck."

While the Administration was focusing on defense and foreign policy needs, events were taking place that had a long-term effect on American social and political life. During the decade the momentum for civil rights increased as organizations such as the NAACP carried on a campaign to end discrimination through court action. Initially civil rights groups had accepted separation but demanded absolute equality. However, during the 1950s they challenged the concept of separateness itself. This struggle culminated in *Brown v. Board of Education*, argued before the Supreme Court in 1952–53. In that case NAACP counsel Thurgood Marshall attacked the principle of separateness per se, offering evidence that segregation was emotionally harmful to both black and white children and that classification by race was a violation of the 14th Amendment guaranteeing due process and equal protection under the law.

In May 1954 a unanimous court accepted Marshall's argument. Reversing *Plessy v. Ferguson*, the Court stated that the doctrine of separate but equal was unconstitutional. Separating children by race, the Court stated, "generated a feeling of inferiority as to their status in the community that may affect their hearts and minds in a way unlikely ever to be undone." Realizing the social effects of the decision, the Court later required compliance "with all deliberate speed."

During the ensuing years the South wages a campaign of "massive resistance" to the decision. Through the use of "interposition," the insertion of state power between the federal courts and the local school boards, state governments hoped to prevent implementation of the decision. School boards were authorized to transfer their property to private hands. Pupil assignment laws were passed requiring students changing schools to receive written permission from both institutions, and state constitutions were modified repealing provisions requiring a public school system. State legislatures passed laws requiring governments to take control of these desegregated schools, shut them down and stop state funds. Some officials spoke of nullifying the Court's decision. Southerners formed White Citizens Councils to preserve segregation. In March 1956, 101 Southern members of Congress signed the "Southern Manifesto" denouncing the *Brown* decision and vowing to reverse it by lawful means. As the South moved to the right in 1956 and 1957, even moderate governors such as Mississippi's James Coleman, who had urged compliance with the law no matter how distasteful, were pushed into opposition to the ruling.

The Administration did little to promote compliance with the order. Anxious not to overstep the bounds of his constitutional authority and skeptical of the use of coercion, Eisenhower preferred to ignore the problem. Only when Arkansas Gov. Orval Faubus challenged federal authority in 1957 by refusing to obey a court order to desegregate Little Rock's Central High School did the President act. On the day before classes were to begin, Faubus used the National Guard to bar blacks. Although he removed them at the insistence of the federal government, violence continued. Eisenhower federalized the Arkansas National Guard and sent U.S. paratroopers to ensure desegregation. The troops remained there throughout the year. By 1959 a series of Court decisions ended massive resistance. Yet during the decade the government achieved only token integration. As late as 1964 only 1% of the black students in the South went to integrated schools.

Congress took only limited action to ensure black rights despite the prompting of liberals and civil rights leaders such as Clarence Mitchell. During 1955 and 1956 New York Rep. Adam Clayton Powell, Jr. attempted to attach anti-segregation riders to various appropriation measures, particularly education legislation. Even liberals opposed these efforts, fearing that they would delay needed educational funding. In 1956 and 1957 the Administration presented a proposal drawn up by Attorney General Herbert Brownell. The measure would have granted the Attorney General the right to institute suits in a broad range of cases where blacks were denied their civil rights. When signed into law in September 1957, the proposal was far more limited in scope. It dealt only with voting rights and was restricted further by an amendment granting jury trials to those charged with violating the law. Nevertheless, the Civil Rights Act of 1957 was hailed as epicmaking, the first time since 1875 that Congress had enacted a rights statute.

A second law was passed in 1960 strengthening the government's authority to ensure suffrage.

During the decade a new chapter was born in the civil rights struggle as blacks began using mass action to demand their rights. In 1955 Montgomery, Ala., blacks, under the leadership of young Rev. Martin Luther King Jr., boycotted the city's bus system to protest segregated transit. The struggle ended in victory in November of 1956, when the Supreme Court supported a lower court ruling invalidating Alabama's segregation statute. The nonviolent resistant movement was used again in 1960 when four blacks sat-in at a Woolworth lunch counter in Greensboro, N.C., to demand service. The movement gained momentum, and soon 50,000 were staging sit-ins at various public facilities. By the end of 1960 lunch counters in 126 cities were desegregated.

The major governmental force for change during the 1950s was the Supreme Court. Under the direction of Chief Justice Earl Warren, appointed by Eisenhower in 1953, the once conservative body became an instrument of social action. Warren's influence was clearly shown in the unanimity of *Brown v. Board of Education*, which was the result of his efforts. Although no decision had the major impact of *Brown*, a number reflected Warren's pragmatism and desire to make the Court a positive force for change.

During the middle of the decade, the Court moved cautiously to expand civil liberties, particularly in domestic subversion investigations. In 1956 it issued three decisions broadening protection granted political dissenters. In *Pennsylvania v. Nelson*, the Court invalidated state sedition laws, ruling that legislation in that field was the province of the federal government. In *Solchower v. Board* it overturned the dismissal of a professor who had pleaded the Fifth Amendment before a congressional committee. The Court also invalidated actions taken by the Subversive Activities Control Board on the basis of perjured testimony. In 1958, in a series of three decisions (*Yates v. United States*, *Watkins v. United States* and *Sweezy v. New Hampshire*), the Court limited prosecution under the Smith Act and curbed the power of congressional and state committees to punish witnesses refusing to answer questions.

The Court also expanded defendants' rights in criminal proceedings. In *Griffin v. Illinois* in 1956 it ruled that states had to furnish indigent persons with copies of trial transcripts for appeal or in issues of due process. The following year, in *Jencks v. United States*, it held that the accused had the right to see government files, including all FBI reports. In one of its most controversial actions, the Mallory decision of 1957, it upset the conviction of a black for the rape of a white woman because there had been a delay in arraignment.

By 1958 criticism of the Court had mounted, and "Impeach Earl Warren" billboards appeared at various places throughout the nation. Congress made several unsuccessful attempts to limit the Court's appellate jurisdiction in sedition cases and to overturn the Mallory ruling. As a result of these actions, the Court seemed to backtract, delivering decisions in 1958–59 that permitted the House Un-American Activities Committee to continue its investigations and upheld the Smith Act. However, legal historian Walter F. Murphy observed it was "a tactical withdrawal not a rout." The decisions of the middle of the decade formed the basis for continued liberal rulings during the 1960s.

By 1957 the Eisenhower equilibrium had broken down, and there were increased signs of discontent with the President's lack of forceful leadership. Eisenhower, once immune from personal attack, was increasingly criticized for his golfing vacations and failure to push his legislative program. In addition, a series of conflict-of-interest scandals forced to resign as Secretary of the Air Force, and Peter Strobel stepped down as Commissioner of the Public Building Service. The following year Edward Mansure, head of the General Services Administration, also left office under a cloud. By 1958 congressional committees were probing regulatory agencies. The scandals touched the White House, and the President's chief aide, Sherman Adams, was forced to resign in September as a result of implications of influence peddling.

The President was not the only leader to come under fire. Liberal Democrats elected in 1958 revolted against Rayburn and Johnson and demanded a clear alternative to the Administration's legislative program. The Democratic Study Group, formed in 1957 to increase liberal influence in Congress, became increasingly impatient with Rayburn's inability to deal with the intransigence of Southern committee chairmen who dominated major panels. It demanded changes in procedures governing the Rules Committee and more effective leadership support for social welfare programs. Rayburn and Johnson, however, remained reluctant to act.

One of the primary catalysts for change was the Soviet launching of *Sputnik* in October 1957. The event rocked American complacency about its defense and brought into question its vaunted technological superiority. The nation's self-esteem fell as it watched an American satellite fall, and its sense of security weakened as it thought of the possibility of Soviet satellites armed to destroy the U.S. The launching precipitated a major debate within government over the continuation of Eisenhower's New Look defense policy. Such military leaders as Gen. Curtis LeMay, Adm. Arleigh Burke and Gen. Maxwell Taylor openly opposed Eisenhower's limited defense budget and called for increased spending for conventional as well as atomic weapons. In Congress powerful Senators such as Stuart Symington and Henry Jackson criticized the Administration for the low priority it had given missile development and maintained that a "missile gap" was developing between the U.S. and the USSR. The Administration sent officials such as Donald Quarles to Congress in an unsuccessful attempt to justify the budget and to warn of the economic dangers of a crash missile program. Eisenhower was able to prevent a weapons race such as that which developed in the 1960s, but he was forced to increase defense spending.

The reluctant President was pushed into beginning an all-out effort to overtake the Russians in the space race. Over the opposition of the Armed Forces, he put the program under the direction of a civilian agency. In July 1958 Congress created the National Aeronautics and Space Administration (NASA) to coordinate nonmilitary space efforts. NASA began with a modest annual budget of $340 million in 1959 but six years later had increased its budget to over $5 billion.

Sputnik had a great impact upon American education. After the Soviet success in outer space, the Administration was criticized for the low priority it had put on basic research. Demands rose for a reorientation of American education to basic mathematics and sciences. The controversial developer of the nuclear submarine, Adm. Hyman Rickover, urged increased sums for education and federal standards for teachers. In September 1958 Congress approved the National Defense Education Act to provide funds for laboratory facilities, graduate studies and the training of science, mathematics and language specialists.

The Administration's fiscal policies also came under fire. Eisenhower's critics maintained that the nation's rate of economic growth had been unsatisfactory and pointed out that it did not equal that of the Soviet Union. They charged that as a result of the President's policies the growth rate had dropped by almost 50% from that of the previous decade. The three recessions during the Administration hindered continued development and resulted in a rise in unemployment to almost 8% in 1960. Democrats, led by Adlai Stevenson, charged that the Administration's insistence on a balanced budget resulted in a "private opulence and public squalor."

By 1959 critics were charging that the nation had "lost its sense of national purpose." In response the President appointed a commission to develop national goals for the next decade. Many of its conclusions were in conflict with Eisenhower's views. Assuming the continuation of the Cold War, the panel supported larger military expenditures. It also called for a more activist role by the federal government in stimulating domestic and foreign economic growth, improving education, supporting basic research in natural sciences, uplifting the arts, and above all, insuring all Americans the right to vote.

Throughout his tenure Eisenhower had conceived of himself as a man above party who assumed the presidency to restore domestic tranquility and return the nation to peace. In terms of these goals, Eisenhower's presidency was a success. With his remarkable political instinct, he knew what the American people wanted and how they wished to achieve their goals. Although criticism of the President had grown during the later years of his second term, no one doubted that he could have been reelected if he had been eligible to run in 1960. He had reunified the nation by serving as a conciliator between diverse factions. Eisenhower prevented the powerful ultra-conservative wing from taking control of the Republican Party and forced a larger segment of it to acknowledge the federal government's responsibility in social welfare. By 1961 Republican isolationism was dead, and in the years to come Eisenhower's successors would find much of the support for their internationalist policies coming from the GOP. Although he never won liberal approval, he maintained the backing of Democratic moderates who supported his desire for an era of consolidation.

In foreign affairs Eisenhower succeeded in restoring peace and preventing an arms race with the Soviet Union. Because of his stature he was able to convince Congress and the American people to accept an armistice rather than a total victory in Korea. This would have been extremely difficult for any Democratic President to achieve in light of Truman's unpopularity and the power of the conservative bloc in Congress. He shrewdly used Dulles's bellicose rhetoric to placate the right while refusing to approve military commitments supported by many on his staff.

Yet Eisenhower failed to achieve some of his goals. Despite his attempts at budget cutting and reducing the size of the federal government, the bureaucracy grew. During the decade the administrative budget rose from $39.5 billion in 1950 to $76.5 billion in 1960 and the national debt from $266 billion in 1953 to $286 billion in 1960. By the end of fiscal 1959, the nation was running the highest deficit ever accumulated in peacetime. The federal government remained committed to a large number of social welfare and public development projects. Despite his limited view of the presidency, Eisenhower bequeathed his successors an expanded office. His refusal to permit Sen. McCarthy to examine executive records proved one of the precedents for President Richard Nixon's rejection of Watergate Committee requests for tapes. In foreign affairs he set a precedent for the Tonkin Gulf Resolution of 1964 when he received prior congressional authorization to use American troops in the Middle East and the Formosa Straits.

Contemporaries and scholars disagreed in their evaluation of the Eisenhower presidency. Some have called it a period of postponement, when problems such as civil rights were ignored, leaving Eisenhower's successors a bitter heritage. Others have praised it as an era of peace and prosperity in which Americans were permitted to recover from the traumas of the preceding decades. Herbert Parmet summed up the thinking of many modern historians: "To label [Eisenhower] a good or even a weak President misses the point. He was merely necessary."

POLITICAL PROFILES
The Eisenhower Years

ABERNATHY, RALPH D(AVID)
b. March 11, 1926; Linden, Ala.
Financial Secretary-Treasurer, Southern Christian Leadership Conference, 1957-65; Vice-President, 1965-68; President, 1968-

Born on his parents' 500-acre farm in Marengo Co., Ala., Ralph Abernathy was the 10th of 12 children. He received a B.S. from Alabama State College in 1950 and an M.A. in sociology from Atlanta University in 1951. Ordained a Baptist minister in 1948, Abernathy became pastor of the First Baptist Church in Montgomery, Ala. in 1951.

Active in civic affairs and a member of the NAACP, Abernathy readily agreed to help organize a boycott of Montgomery's racially segregated bus system following the arrest of Rosa Parks [q.v.], a black seamstress, on Dec. 1, 1955 for violation of the city's bus segregation ordinance. Abernathy helped contact other black ministers, set up planning meetings and prepared for the boycott, which began on Dec. 5. He urged the formation of a permanent organization to manage the protest and suggested the name Montgomery Improvement Association (MIA) for the body, which was established on the first day of the boycott. Martin Luther King, Jr. [q.v.], a young Baptist minister relatively new to Montgomery, was chosen to lead the MIA. Abernathy was named to the executive board and the program committee.

Abernathy and King had already become close friends by the time the Montgomery boycott started. "From the beginning of the protest," King later declared, "[Abernathy] was my closest associate and most trusted friend. We prayed together and made important decisions together. His ready good humor lightened many tense moments." A member of the MIA's negotiating committee, Abernathy rose to King's defense at a meeting with city and bus company officials in mid-December, when several of the whites present challenged King's leadership position. He took charge of much MIA business when King was out of town, was a close adviser to King throughout the 381-day boycott and organized regular mass meetings of Montgomery's blacks.

On Nov. 13, 1956 the Supreme Court ruled that bus segregation in Montgomery was unconstitutional. Abernathy then helped organize a program of mass training in nonviolent techniques to prepare the black community for integration. On Dec. 21, 1956, the day after the Supreme Court's desegregation order arrived in Montgomery, Abernathy and King rode on an integrated bus. A month of retaliatory violence by whites followed. In the early hours of Jan. 10, 1957, while King and Abernathy were in Atlanta for a meeting, Abernathy's home and church, along with three other black churches and the home of another minister, were bombed.

The historic Montgomery boycott marked the beginning of an era of nonviolent direct action by Southern blacks against racial segregation and discrimination. It also inaugurated a partnership between King and Abernathy. Early in 1957 the two helped found the Southern Christian Leadership Conference (SCLC). Abernathy was appointed financial secretary-treasurer, while

King was named president. Under the auspices of the SCLC, the two ministers preached a philosophy of nonviolent resistance to Jim Crow practices and began organizing nonviolent training institutes and voter registration drives among Southern blacks. The burly Abernathy was regarded as less intellectual than King and as having more of a common touch in his preaching and speaking, but the two became alter egos. Beginning with Montgomery, King consulted Abernathy before making any important decision. In 1961, at King's urging, Abernathy moved to Atlanta in order to be closer to King, who had moved there the year before, and to the SCLC's Atlanta headquarters.

During the next seven years Abernathy remained King's chief aide and confidant, helping him direct desegregation and voter registration campaigns in Albany, Ga., in 1962, Birmingham, Ala., in 1963 and Selma, Ala., in 1965. Abernathy was with King when he was assassinated in Memphis, Tenn., on April 4, 1968. He succeeded King as president of the SCLC and led a Poor People's Campaign in Washington, D.C. in the spring and summer of 1968. [See KENNEDY, JOHNSON, NIXON/FORD Volumes]

[CAB]

ACHESON, DEAN G(OODERHAM)
b. April 11, 1893; Middletown, Conn.
d. Oct. 12, 1971; Silver Springs, Md.
Foreign policy critic.

Following his graduation from Harvard Law School in 1918, Acheson became private secretary to Supreme Court Justice Louis Brandeis. He then entered law practice in Washington with the prestigious firm of Covington and Burling. In 1933 he was appointed undersecretary of the treasury but resigned after a few months in a disagreement with the Administration over economic policy. Acheson returned to public service in 1941 as assistant secretary of state. From 1944 to 1947 he served as undersecretary of state, the Department's second-ranking post, and from 1949 to 1952 he was Secretary of State.

While at the State Department Acheson helped formulate the early American response to the Cold War. Believing that the Soviet Union was bent on world conquest, he thought that attempts to negotiate with the Russians from a position of equality were useless. Instead, Acheson recommended that the U.S. give immense amounts of economic, political and military aid to countries on the rim of the Communist bloc to prevent or "contain" future Soviet expansion. In his view Germany played a key role in the redevelopment of Europe. Acheson's ideas were reflected in the Marshall Plan of 1947.

Acheson firmly believed that America should negotiate from a position of overwhelming military strength maintained by a strong nuclear strike force, a large conventional Army and a series of regional alliances designed to rim the Communist bloc. Faced with such awesome power, the Soviet Union, he believed, would be willing to negotiate differences. As Secretary of State, Acheson was instrumental in the creation of the North Atlantic Treaty Organization (NATO), the rebuilding and rearming of Germany and the development of atomic policy. Although he believed that the North Atlantic community represented the peak of man's cultural and political growth and therefore made it the focus of his diplomacy, Acheson spent a large portion of his time on Asian affairs. Following the fall of Chiang Kai-shek, Acheson pursued a nonrecognition policy toward Communist China. During his last years in the State Department, he also worked to prevent the widening of the Korean war.

Despite his vigorous anti-Communism, Acheson was attacked as being "soft on Communism" for his defense of Alger Hiss, for what rightists termed his "appeasement" of the Soviet Union and for his "loss" of China. Acheson left office at the end of the Truman Administration to return to his private law practice. [See TRUMAN Volume]

During the Eisenhower Administration Acheson attempted to defend his record against criticism by Secretary of State John Foster Dulles [q.v.] and the right wing of the Republican Party while trying to articulate an alternative foreign policy for the Democratic Party. Acheson charged that the Administration's reliance on "massive retaliation," the use of strategic nuclear weapons as America's prime deterrent, "was a fraud upon words and upon facts." It produced "doubts, fears and loss of confidence in our leadership." To him, massive retaliation implied unilateralism. It was a reversion to isolationism, for Dulles's threat that the U.S. would retaliate "by means and places of our own choosing" precluded any consultation with American allies. This pledge, Acheson argued, showed that the U.S. would recklessly gamble its allies' future to win diplomatic victories.

Acheson maintained that massive retaliation was irrelevant to the past and future skirmishes of the Cold War. Only unified ground action had checked Communist advances in Korea. During the 1956 presidential campaign, he charged that the Republican foreign policy of "bluff and bluster" did not save Dien Bien Phu or prevent Nasser from seizing the Suez Canal. He said that Eisenhower and Dulles could have continued Truman's foreign policy but, instead, had become "the prisoners of the primitive propaganda and slogans of the McCarthy-Taft-Knowland forces." Acheson recommended the return to a proper balance between conventional and nuclear weapons, the end of empty rhetorical threats and the willingness to work with NATO to repair the alleged damage done to American prestige during Eisenhower's first term.

When the Communist Chinese resumed shelling the offshore islands of Quemoy and Matsu in 1958, Acheson denounced Eisenhower's foreign policy once again. He observed that the U.S. seemed to be "drifting, either dazed or indifferent, to war with China." Rejecting Dulles's position that Quemoy was crucial to the defense of Formosa, he maintained that the island traditionally belonged to the mainland. Its population was minimal and it had no strategic value. Acheson warned that Chiang Kai-shek was interested in the island only as a staging area to attack the Communists and would use the crisis to embroil the U.S. in a conflict with the Communist Chinese.

Maintaining his strong mistrust of the Communists into the 1950s, the former Secretary was skeptical of Eisenhower's attempts to relax tensions between the U.S.

and the Soviet Union. He counseled the nation to be ever vigilant to meet any Soviet challenge and be cautious of being lured into making premature agreements that could be harmful in the future. He discounted the efficacy of summit conferences with the Soviets, writing in 1958 that the U.S. had nothing to negotiate with the Soviet Union. He opposed George Kennan's [q.v.] call for negotiations on American and Soviet withdrawal from Eastern and Western Europe and the reunification and neutralization of Germany. Acheson thought neutralization would eventually push Germany into the Soviet camp, while withdrawal of American troops would leave NATO countries vulnerable to Communist infiltration. As late as 1959 he opposed summit meetings, where he thought the Soviet Union would possess all the advantages. Soviet Premier Nikita Khrushchev, he believed, would endeavor to obtain concessions from the West on Berlin and try to obtain American endorsement of the status quo in Eastern Europe. To make such an agreement, Acheson wrote, would be tantamount to "Munich."

During the late 1950s Acheson served as chairman of the Democratic Advisory Council's foreign policy committee. He spoke for the hard-line faction, which saw little possibility for accommodation with the Soviets. In contrast, such notable Democrats as Eleanor Roosevelt [q.v.] and Chester Bowles [q.v.] advocated closer relations with the USSR.

In the 1960s Dean Acheson advised President John F. Kennedy during the Cuban missile crisis and President Lyndon B. Johnson on policy in Vietnam. Following the Tet offensive of early 1968, Johnson asked Acheson to make an independent study of U.S. involvement in Vietnam. Acheson concluded that the U.S. could not win the war without another major troop buildup, which the American people would not support. He advised the President to get out of Vietnam as soon as possible. His recommendation was a leading factor in Johnson's decision to de-escalate the war in March 1968. Acheson died in October 1971. [See KENNEDY, JOHNSON Volumes]

[JB]

ADAMS, JOHN G(IBBONS)
b. March 23, 1912; Ashland, Ky.
General Counsel, Department of the
Army, 1953-56.

After earning a law degree from the University of South Dakota in 1935, John Adams worked for the South Dakota department of justice and served as vice president of the Young Republican National Federation. At the same time he owned and operated an oil company in Sioux Falls, S.D. In 1947 Adams moved to Washington as a clerk for the Senate Committee on Armed Services, and two years later, he became assistant general counsel for the Department of Defense. In 1953 he was named general counsel of the Department of the Army. That year the Senate Government Operations Committee's Permanent Investigations Subcommittee, chaired by Sen. Joseph McCarthy (R, Wisc.) [q.v.], intensified its investigations of alleged subversive activity in the Army. Adams soon came into conflict with the panel over what he regarded as its interference in Army affairs.

In March 1954 the Army released a report, which Adams had helped draft, accusing the Investigations subcommittee counsel, Roy Cohn [q.v.], of trying to force the Army to give special privileges to Pvt. G. David Schine [q.v.], a former special investigator for the subcommittee and a close friend of Cohn. Schine had been drafted in November 1953 and assigned to Ft. Dix, N.J. McCarthy then called a press conference at which he accused Adams of trying to use Schine as a hostage to force him to call off his probe of Communists in the Army. He added that Adams had encouraged him to investigate the Navy and Air Force instead. On March 16 the subcommittee voted to hold hearings on the dispute. In April Adams, was named, along with Army Secretary Robert T. Stevens [q.v.] and Assistant Defense Secretary H. Struve Hensel [q.v.], in formal charges filed by McCarthy.

During the Army-McCarthy hearings in April, May and June, Adams was temporarily replaced as Army counsel by Joseph N. Welch [q.v.]. In testimony offered in May on the "abuse and pressure" he had received from Cohn on Schine's behalf, Adams alleged that Cohn had persistently sought to have his friend assigned to New York and had threatened to "wreck the Army" if Schine were given overseas duty. Cohn and McCarthy testified that Adams had tried to blackmail them into dropping their investigations at Ft. Monmouth, N.J., by threatening to circulate an embarrassing report about Cohn. Other testimony indicated that Adams had gone to great lengths to satisfy Cohn's demands. In the subcommittee's report, released in August, the Republican majority concluded that the charge of "improper influence" by McCarthy on behalf of Schine "was not established" and that Adams and Stevens had tried "to terminate or influence" the Ft. Monmouth probe. Subcommittee Democrats, however, sharply condemned the actions of Cohn and McCarthy. In addition, they accused Stevens and Adams of following a "policy of appeasement" and of "weakness and lack of propriety."

In 1956 Adams became a consultant and staff member with the Atomic Energy Commission. From 1965 to 1971 he was a member of the U.S. Civil Aeronautics Board, and in 1970, he became a lecturer in law at the American University in Washington, D.C.

[TLH]

ADAMS, SHERMAN
b. Jan. 8, 1899; East Dover, Vt.
Assistant to the President, January 1953-
September 1958.

The son of a grocery store owner, Adams served in the Marine Corps during World War I and received a B.A. from Dartmouth College in 1920. He then began a career in the lumber industry, starting as a clerk and scaler in southern Vermont and ultimately becoming general manager of a lumber company in Lincoln, N.H. Following a 1938 hurricane that leveled many trees in New Hampshire, Adams was selected to tour the state urging an emergency salvage effort. His success encour-

inet officers (with the exception of Secre-
y of State John Foster Dulles [q.v.]), could
  the President without making arrange-
nts with Adams, who was grudging and
ective in alloting the chief executive's time.
 also determined what the President read.
ly very important problems were brought
 Eisenhower's desk. They were accom-
nied by a one page summary written by
ams. Consequently, Adams had a great but
direct influence on policy.

Adams generally stood with the liberal wing
 the Republican Party. Soon after Sen.
eph McCarthy (R, Wisc.) [q.v.] began his
acks on the Administration in 1953, Adams
ged Eisenhower to prepare a counteroffen-
e. He reportedly was the first to suggest
at the Army compile a record of its disputes
th McCarthy. The resulting dossier was
ed in the Army-McCarthy hearings. During
senhower's first term Adams opposed the
nservative bloc within the Administration,
d by Secretary of the Treasury George
umphrey [q.v.], that stressed budget-
lancing. He defended the Department of
ealth, Education and Welfare in its battles
th Humphrey for additional funds and sup-
rted expanded social security and housing
ograms, federal aid for school construction
d high levels of foreign aid. After the Presi-
nt's reelection in 1956, Adams played a key
le in replacing Humphrey with the more
eral Robert B. Anderson [q.v.]. At the
me time he also had a hand in replacing
nservatives such as Secretary of Defense
arles E. Wilson [q.v.] and Undersecretary
 State Herbert Hoover, Jr. [q.v.], with
oderates Neil H. McElroy [q.v.] and Chris-
n Herter [q.v.], respectively. In 1957
lams backed the President's civil rights
gislation and played a key role in the Ad-
inistration's reaction to the desegregation
isis in Little Rock, Ark.

Eisenhower had used alleged corruption in
e Truman Administration as a major Repub-
an issue during the 1952 campaign. He as-
rted that public officials must be untainted
 unethical as well as illegal activities. Adams
peared to be a strict enforcer of the Presi-
nt's standards. A 1955 investigation by the
ouse Judiciary Committee's Antitrust and
onopoly Subcommittee revealed that Peter
robel [q.v.], commissioner of the Public

Buildings Service, had approved contracts
awarded to companies that were clients of his
private firm. Although subcommittee chairman Rep. Emanuel Celler (D, N.Y.) [q.v.]
decided that Strobel had not acted illegally,
Adams forced the commissioner to resign. In
February 1958 the House Interstate and
Foreign Commerce Committee's Legislative
Oversight Subcommittee discovered that
Federal Communications Commission member Richard A. Mack [q.v.] had received
financial assistance from a friend seeking a
license to operate a Miami television station.
Adams immediately demanded Mack's resignation, which was tendered on March 3.

During 1958 serious questions arose concerning Adams's own public ethics. A congressional probe of his activities created the
biggest scandal of the Administration and
culminated in Adams's resignation. In February 1958 the Legislative Oversight Subcommittee discovered that five years earlier
Adams had apparently intervened with the
Civil Aeronautics Board (CAB) on behalf of
Murray Chotiner [q.v.], former campaign
manager for Vice President Nixon and, in
1953, counsel for North American Airlines.
Adams asked CAB chairman Herman B.
Denny how the airline could delay the implementation of a Board ruling revoking
North American's operating license.

This matter was overshadowed in June and
July 1958 when the panel probed the relationship between Adams and his old friend
Bernard Goldfine [q.v.], a Boston textile
magnate. Subcommittee staff members and
witnesses charged that Adams received gifts
from Goldfine during the early and mid
1950s while at the same time intervening
on his friend's behalf with the Federal
Trade Commission (FTC) and the Securities
and Exchange Commission (SEC).

Goldfine, it was alleged, had paid over
three thousand dollars in hotel bills for Adams
between 1953 and 1958 and had given him a
vicuna coat, two suits and a $2,400 oriental
rug. Meanwhile, Goldfine was facing FTC
mislabeling charges against his textile firms.
FTC officials testified that in 1954 Adams had
asked the Commission chairman about the
charges and the following year arranged a
meeting between Goldfine and agency
officials. In February 1957 the FTC merely

aged him to wage a campaign for the New Hampshire House of Representatives in 1940. He won the race and was reelected two years later. During his second term he became Speaker of the House.

In 1944 Adams was elected to the U.S. House of Representatives. There he compiled a moderately conservative domestic record. He did not establish a clear pattern of voting in foreign affairs. In 1946 Adams lost the New Hampshire Republican gubernatorial primary by 157 votes and returned to private life.

Two years later Adams waged a successful gubernatorial campaign; he was reelected in 1950. As governor he consolidated government departments to promote efficiency and attempted to reduce the budget. To set an example of austerity, Adams arrived at his office at dawn and in the winter walked to and from work on snowshoes.

On Sept. 30, 1951 Adams joined five other Republicans at the annual Governors Conference in endorsing Dwight D. Eisenhower for their party's presidential nomination. The first primary was held in New Hampshire, and under Adams's leadership the Eisenhower forces won all the state's delegates to the Republican National Convention. With his home state's primary over, Adams campaigned for Eisenhower throughout the country. At the July Convention he was the candidate's floor leader. He impressed Eisenhower with his penchant for hard work, mastery of detail and skill in behind-the-scenes political combat.

Meeting for the first time near the end of the Convention, Eisenhower asked Adams to be his campaign manager. The Governor accepted, and accompanied Eisenhower during the entire race. Adams decided when and where the candidate would speak and helped make major strategy decisions. After the revelation that vice presidential nominee Richard M. Nixon [q.v.] had use of an alleged slush fund, Adams advocated the middle-of-the-road course adopted by Eisenhower. He recommended waiting for public reaction before deciding whether to dump the candidate. Adams's endorsement of the proposal that Eisenhower pledge to go to Korea was an important factor in the presidential nominee's acceptance of the idea. Shortly after the election Eisenhower asked Adams to come to

Washington as the President's ch
Adams's job had been created b
order during the Truman Adm
Under President Eisenhower its
panded tremendously. As a form
officer Eisenhower was accustome
ing through channels of delegate
and had been relieved of many of
highly competent chiefs of
thermore, he disliked performing
of administrative work, sought t
conflict involved in the formulati
and tried to stay out of partisan pc
other matter that might create
wards himself. As a result Adams
of the most powerful appointed
modern American history.

Adams was often given the t
hower preferred not to do. A
President directed patronage pc
Adams who dispensed jobs, m
enemies both within and without
lican Party among disappointed o
and their sponsors. In 1953, for
offended Walter Reuther [q.v.]
the latter's candidate for assistant
labor. He was also influential in
government officials and was beli
had a significant role in the d
Secretary of Health, Education
Oveta Culp Hobby [q.v.] in
Secretary of the Interior Dou
[q.v.] in 1956. Even when he di
hand in a dismissal, he was ofter
convey the news to the individu

Eisenhower avoided partisan p
on Democrats and frequently tu
over to Adams. In reply Democr
nounced him rather than the
Adams also put pressure on mem
gress to advance Administration
Adams preformed the unpleasa
Eisenhower did not want to do, t
tial assistant's public image was th
Eisenhower's. The President wa
fatherly, genial man above part
Adams, on the other hand, was
cold-blooded, ruthless partisan.
referred to as "Great Stone Fa
Administration's "Abominable N

Eisenhower made Adams a sc
which most of his contact with tl
side his office was filtered. No c

issued a cease-and-desist order against Goldfine, although agency lawyers had recommended a civil suit. In 1956 the SEC had considered action against Goldfine for not filing required financial reports on his real estate operations. After Adams had directed an inquiry on the matter to the SEC, proceedings against Goldfine were dropped.

The presidential assistant appeared before the legislative oversight panel on June 17. He acknowledged the payment of his hotel bills by Goldfine and the receipt of the coat, suits and rug. (He stated that the rug was a loan, not a gift.) However, he contended that the gifts were merely tokens of a longstanding friendship. Adams said that his efforts on behalf of Goldfine had been routine responses to requests and that he had not used his influence on his friend's behalf. He conceded, however, that unfavorable implications could be drawn from his actions and that "if I had the decisions before me to make, I believe I would have acted a little more prudently."

President Eisenhower steadfastly defended Adams, but the presidential assistant received little additional support. He got backing from some Republican senators who were not up for reelection. However, the great majority of Republican congressmen running for office in 1958 believed that their candidacies would be damaged by Adams's presence in the White House, particularly since the Administration had prided itself on its ethical standards. Adams's position was further damaged when, on July 2, Goldfine's attorney revealed that the textile magnate had charged off the hotel bills and the rug as business expenses.

In late August GOP National Chairman Meade Alcorn [q.v.] told the President that almost all Party leaders and major financial backers believed Adams had to go. With great reluctance Eisenhower finally agreed. The defeat of Sen. Frederick Payne (R, Me.), who had been implicated in the Goldfine-Adams scandal, in the early Maine elections of Sept. 8 merely confirmed this decision.

On Sept. 22 Adams submitted his resignation. Later that day he made a national television and radio address. He charged that he had been the victim of a "campaign of vilification" and asserted that he had "never influenced nor attempted to influence" any agency on any matter. Adams remained on the White

House payroll into October to help the President's staff through its transition period. In late October he flew home to Lincoln, N.H.

Adams became a part owner of a New Hampshire ski resort. In 1961 he published *First-Hand Report: The Story of the Eisenhower Administration*, detailing his years at the White House.

[MLL]

For further information:
Sherman Adams. *First-Hand Report: The Story of the Eisenhower Administration* (New York. 1961).
Louis W. Koenig. *The Invisible Presidency* (New York. 1960).

AIKEN, GEORGE D(AVID)
b. Aug. 30, 1892; Dummerston, Vt.
Republican Senator, Vt., 1941-75;
Chairman, Agriculture and Forestry
Committee, 1953-55.

Raised on his father's farm near Brattleboro, Vt., Aiken had a strong interest in agriculture and joined the local branch of the National Grange while in high school. Subsequently he became a leading expert in the commercial cultivation of wildflowers. In 1930 Aiken was elected to the state House of Representatives and was chosen speaker of that body in 1933. He ran successfully for lieutenant governor in 1935 and for governor in 1937 and 1939. A moderate Republican, Aiken gained national attention in 1937, when he wrote an open letter to his party's national committee urging abandonment of a "hate-Roosevelt" policy for a more positive program.

Aiken was elected to the U.S. Senate in 1940. He gained a reputation for integrity and independence and won each of his subsequent reelection bids with over 65% of the vote. During the 1940s Aiken opposed the use of subsidies to lower farm prices and sought to revive the food stamp program of the 1930s. He was an active proponent of the St. Lawrence Seaway project and backed federal aid to education and minimum wage legislation. In June 1950 Aiken joined Sen. Margaret Chase Smith (R, Me.) [q.v.] and five other senators in signing a "Declaration of Conscience," denouncing Sen. Joseph R. McCarthy's (R, Wisc.) [q.v.] use of "fear, bigotry, ignorance and intolerance" in his investigations of domestic Communists. [See TRUMAN Volume]

One of the leaders of the congressional farm bloc, Aiken served as chairman of the Agriculture and Forestry Committee from 1953 to 1955. In 1953 he backed President Dwight D. Eisenhower's reorganization plan for the Agriculture Department, which strengthened the authority of Secretary of Agriculture Ezra Taft Benson [q.v.]. When Sen. Wayne Morse (Ind., Ore.) [q.v.] said that the measure might create a one-man "super legislature," Aiken replied that the farmers had "no better friend on earth" than Benson. The following year Aiken endorsed the Administration's omnibus farm program, which proposed to replace fixed price supports with lower, flexible supports to discourage overproduction.

Concerned with promoting the welfare of farm areas, Aiken introduced the Water Facilities Act of 1954. The measure provided federal aid to rural communities seeking to develop an adequate power supply. Aiken believed that this measure was essential for the prosperity of rural America, and he regarded its adoption as one of his most important achievements. During the same year he sponsored the Small Watershed Act, which authorized the Secretary of Agriculture to cooperate with state and local authorities in implementing projects for improving methods of soil conservation.

In 1958 Aiken opposed an amendment to a farm surplus disposal bill, offered by Sens. William E. Jenner (R, Ind.) [q.v.] and Styles Bridges (R, N.H.) [q.v.], that would have barred the sale of farm surpluses to Communist countries. He commented that the Jenner-Bridges amendment would give the USSR "an iron-clad guarantee that we'll never attempt to win any satellite away from her." Aiken supported the farm surplus law of 1959, which provided for the distribution of excess farm products through a food stamp program and other means. Aiken broke with his more conservative Republican colleagues on a number of issues. In January

1954 he and Sen. Smith were the only Republicans who opposed Robert E. Lee's confirmation as a member of the Federal Communications Commission. Lee was a conservative allegedly indebted to Sen. McCarthy for his appointment. During the same year he joined Sens. John J. Williams (R, Del.) [q.v.] and Herbert H. Lehman (D, N.Y.) [q.v.] in an unsuccessful effort to cut oil and gas depletion allowances from 27.5% to 15%.

In 1960 Aiken and seven other Republican senators offered a voluntary federal-state health insurance program for all Americans over 65. Under the plan the state would have contracted with private firms for the coverage and subscribers would have made payments based on income, with the federal and state governments sharing the remaining costs. Aiken's proposal was more liberal than the Administration plan, which limited aid to single elderly persons with adjusted gross incomes of up to $2,500 a year and married couples with annual incomes up to $3,800. The plan finally adopted in August contained most of the basic features of Aiken's proposal but required a means test and permitted each state to determine the type and extent of medical assistance provided.

Aiken backed the Kennedy Administration's 1961 minimum wage and school aid programs but voted against medicare in 1962. During the late 1960s he received national attention for his opposition to the Johnson Administration's Vietnam war policies. In 1970 he supported the Cooper-Church amendment barring the use of American troops in Cambodia. Aiken announced his retirement in 1974. [See KENNEDY, JOHNSON, NIXON/FORD Volumes]

[MLL]

ALBERT, CARL (BERT)
b. May 10, 1908; McAlaster, Okla.
Democratic Representative, Okla., 1947-77; House Majority Whip, 1955-62.

Albert was the son of a poor farmer and coal miner in southeastern Oklahoma. An extremely able student, he graduated Phi

Beta Kappa from the University of Oklahoma in 1931 and won a Rhodes Scholarship to study at Oxford, where he earned two law degrees. Upon his return to the U.S. in 1934, Albert worked as a law clerk, accountant and lawyer until 1941, when he enlisted in the Army. In 1946 Albert, bucking a Republican tide, won a seat in the U.S. House of Representatives by a narrow 329-vote margin. He backed President Harry S. Truman's foreign policy and generally supported the Administration's liberal domestic programs. However, he opposed the anti-poll tax bill in 1947 and voted to override Truman's vetoes of the Taft-Hartley bill in 1947 and the Communist-control bill in 1950. [See TRUMAN Volume]

Albert consistently backed the House's Democratic leadership. From the beginning of his congressional tenure he carefully scrutinized the operations of the lower chamber to acquaint himself with its procedures and with the voting patterns of its members. Because of his loyalty and diligence, his Democratic colleagues tapped him for leadership positions. In August 1954 he became cochairman of the Party's speakers committee for the forthcoming congressional campaign. The Democrats captured control of the House in the November elections, and in January 1955 Reps. Sam Rayburn (D, Tex.) [q.v.] and John W. McCormack (D, Mass.) [q.v.], the new Speaker and majority leader respectively, chose him to serve as majority whip.

As whip Albert's functions were to familiarize himself with the sentiments of the Democratic members of the House, persuade wavering representatives to vote as the leadership wished and make certain that the Democrats were on the floor for major votes. An undemonstrative, modest man, he worked behind the scenes using persuasion and compromise rather than threats to win support for leadership proposals. Although some journalists described Albert as an effective bridge between Northern liberals and Southern conservatives, some congressional liberals viewed his desire to compromise as an indication of ineffective leadership. Reacting to their complaints, not only about Albert but also about McCormack and Rayburn, the

Democratic National Committee announced in 1956 its intention to appoint an advisory committee of non-congressional liberals to help shape the Party's legislative program. However, when the Democratic congressional leadership refused to cooperate with the plan, it was dropped.

As a representative of a predominantly rural state, one of Albert's major concerns was farm policy. Using his power as majority whip, member of the Agriculture Committee and, beginning in 1955, chairman of its Wheat Subcommittee, he opposed the Eisenhower Administration's program of reduced and flexible price supports. Soon after becoming majority whip, Albert predicted that the new Democratic House majority would vote to reestablish high, rigid supports. In May 1955 the lower chamber passed a bill supporting major crops at 90% of parity, but the measure did not reach the Senate floor that year. A similar bill, passed by both houses in 1956, was vetoed by the President. In 1959 Albert backed a bill offering wheat growers the alternative of reducing their acreage by 25% and receiving 90% of parity price support or receiving 50% of parity with no production controls. Eisenhower also vetoed this measure.

In January 1963, shortly after the death of Speaker Rayburn, Albert became majority leader. Nine years later he succeeded McCormack as Speaker. Albert retired in 1977.

[MLL]

ALCORN, (HUGH) MEADE (JR.)
b. Oct. 20, 1907; Suffield, Conn.
Chairman, Republican National Committee, 1957-59.

The son of a distinguished Connecticut Republican jurist, Meade Alcorn attended Dartmouth College and Yale University School of Law, where he received his LL.B. degree in 1933. That year Alcorn was admitted to the Connecticut bar and joined his father's law firm. He immediately became active in Republican politics, joining the Suffield Republican Committee. Alcorn served as a Republican representative in the Connecticut General Assembly from 1936 to 1942. He was then appointed state attorney for Hartford Co., a post he held for six years. Alcorn ran unsuccessfully for lieutenant governor on the Republican ticket in 1948. He served as state chairman of the Connecticut "Eisenhower for President" committee in 1952 and was a delegate to the Republican National Convention, where he assisted Eisenhower floor leader Sherman Adams [q.v.] in rounding up votes.

In 1953 Alcorn and other liberal Eisenhower supporters won election to the Republican National Committee. Two years later national chairman Leonard Hall [q.v.] chose him to assist in making arrangements for the 1956 Republican National Convention. Together with Hall, Alcorn backed retention of Richard Nixon [q.v.] as vice president despite criticism of his right-wing stands. Alcorn denounced Democratic attacks on the Vice President and quieted Republican fears about his popularity by pointing to a Gallup poll showing that an Eisenhower-Nixon ticket would win in November. That fall Alcorn worked hard for the Republican national ticket in Connecticut.

In a January 1957 news conference, President Eisenhower spoke of Alcorn as one of the Party leaders responsible for "modern Republicanism." Alcorn described this as "enlightened conservatism" that favored government services without government restriction of individual liberty. When Leonard Hall resigned in January 1957, Eisenhower enthusiastically supported Alcorn for national chairman. He took office immediately.

The new chairman announced that his first priority was to elect a Republican Congress in 1958. Signs were unfavorable for the Republicans, however. Inflation and discontent about Eisenhower's lack of leadership reduced his popularity in the spring of 1957. Sensing a rightward drift, Alcorn attempted to focus attention on charges that the Democrats had been the party of corruption and treason during the late-1940s and early-1950s. His charges backfired. In March 1958 Federal Communications Commission head Richard Mack [q.v.], accused of taking bribes, was forced to resign

under pressure from the White House. Alcorn's assertion that Mack was a Democrat did not change the fact that he had been a Republican appointee. Three months later White House special assistant Sherman Adams was accused of accepting gifts while in office. The scandal grew throughout the summer, and financial contributions to the National Committee dropped off sharply. In August Alcorn conducted a secret survey of the Republican National Committee and Finance Committee that indicated all members favored Adams's dismissal. Alcorn carried this information to the President, who turned the job of firing his aide over to the national chairman. Adams resigned in September.

That month an election in normally Republican Maine saw Democratic Gov. Edmund Muskie swamp his Republican opponent. Alcorn's worst fears were realized in the congressional elections eight weeks later. Republicans lost 47 seats in the House and 13 in the Senate, a rout unmatched since the 1930s. In April 1959 Meade Alcorn resigned. He returned to private law practice and continued representing Connecticut on the Republican National Committee until 1961.

[MJS]

ALDRICH, WINTHROP W(ILLIAMS)
b. Nov. 2, 1885; Providence, R.I.
d. Feb. 25, 1974; New York, N.Y.
Ambassador to Great Britain, February 1953-February 1957.

Descended from Pilgrims and theologian Roger Williams, Aldrich was the son of powerful conservative Sen. Nelson W. Aldrich (R, R.I.). After receiving a B.A. degree from Harvard in 1907 and an LL.B. from that institution three years later, he joined a prominent New York law firm. Aldrich served in the Naval Reserve during World War I. In 1919 he joined the law firm of Murray, Prentice and Howland and became a specialist in finance and banking. In perhaps his most significant case, he successfully represented the Rockefeller family interests in their fight for control of

Standard Oil of Indiana. In 1930 he became president of the Chase National Bank; four years later he rose to chairman of the board.

During World War II Aldrich directed Allied relief efforts. As president of the International Chamber of Commerce during the Truman Administration, he helped win conservative support for the Marshall Plan and the President's foreign aid proposals. Aldrich was an early supporter of Gen. Dwight D. Eisenhower for President. In 1951 he helped survey potential Eisenhower support in Texas and reportedly raised large sums of money for the General during the 1952 election campaign.

Eisenhower named the millionaire ambassador to Great Britain shortly after his election. The Senate confirmed the appointment in February 1953. As ambassador, Aldrich took little part in policy formulation. He served primarily as a spokesman for the Administration. During the mid-1950s he was particularly involved in discussions on the Middle East. After Egypt seized the Suez Canal and closed it to international shipping in July 1956, Aldrich attempted to forestall war between Great Britain and France (the major investors in the canal) and Egypt. He warned that the U.S. would not back military efforts to re-open the waterway. His efforts failed; during late October the British and French joined Israel in attacking Egypt.

British public opinion deplored the American failure to join in the invasion. Aldrich vigorously sought to reestablish good will between the U.S. and Great Britain, but strained relations between the two nations compelled him to announce his retirement in December 1956. At a farewell dinner for Aldrich in February 1957, Prime Minister Harold Macmillan praised him for playing "a remarkable and indeed historic role during those weeks of anxious strain." Because of Aldrich's efforts, the Prime Minister asserted, the British government looked forward to re-establishing relations with the U.S. "on the old level."

Upon returning to the U.S., Aldrich resumed his business activities. He died in 1974 at the age of 88.

[RJB]

ALLEN, GEORGE V(ENABLE)
b. Nov. 3, 1903; Durham, N.C.
d. July 11, 1970; Durham, N.C.
Ambassador to India and Nepal, March 1953-January 1955; Assistant Secretary of State for Near Eastern, South Asian and African Affairs, January 1955-January 1958; U.S. Information Agency Director, January 1958-November 1960.

After graduating from Duke University in 1924, Allen taught high school in Buncombe Co., N.C., for four years and simultaneously was a reporter for the *Asheville (N.C.) Times*. In 1930 he joined the Foreign Service. Prior to World War II, he held posts in Kingston, Shanghai, Athens and Cairo. Recalled to Washington in 1938, Allen became assistant chief of the State Department's New Eastern division in 1942; two years later he advanced to chief of the Middle Eastern division. Allen was a member of the first U.S. delegation to the U.N. in 1945. The following year he was appointed ambassador to Iran. He served as assistant secretary of state for public affairs from 1948 to 1950 and was ambassador to Yugoslavia from 1950 to 1953. President Dwight D. Eisenhower nominated him to succeed Chester Bowles [*q.v.*] as ambassador to India and Nepal in February 1953.

During his two years in India, Allen attempted to allay fears that the Eisenhower Administration was pursuing a pro-Pakistan policy at the expense of India. He was also called upon to explain the 1954 India-Communist Chinese mutual nonaggression agreement to the House Foreign Affairs Committee. Allen observed that India regarded Communist China with an uneasy mixture of fear and admiration. The U.S., Allen urged the Committee, should respond by increasing its aid to India to help make it "a source of strength to the free world."

In January 1955 President Eisenhower nominated Allen to be assistant secretary of state for Near Eastern, South Asian and African affairs. He was confirmed that month. In September Allen undertook his most important mission for the Eisenhower Administration. During the spring of 1955

Egyptian Premier Gamal Abdel Nasser had sent the U.S. several requests for military aid to strengthen Egypt against any armed threat from Israel. However, for some reason never entirely explained, the State Department failed to answer his pleas. Finally, in June 1955 Nasser threatened to ask the USSR for weapons. The State Department did not consider the threat seriously. By late September the deal appeared all but consummated and Secretary of State John Foster Dulles [q.v.] hurriedly sent the Central Intelligence Agency's Middle Eastern expert, Kermit Roosevelt [q.v.], to urge Nasser to reconsider the Soviet arms deal. However, Roosevelt was unable to head off the arms accord, which the Soviets and the Egyptians formally signed on Sept. 27, 1955.

The next day Dulles sent Allen to Cairo in a final effort to turn Nasser around and discuss the ramifications of the pact. Allen believed his mission ill-conceived. As far as he was concerned, it could only appear to the Arab world as an American ultimatum to Nasser.

Allen's visit to Cairo was, according to historian Townsend Hoopes, "a reasonably cordial exercise in futility." At first Allen was something less than candid, explaining to Nasser that while the U.S. could understand Egypt's policy of neutrality, it surely was not neutral to accept weapons from a single source. At this point Nasser recounted his frustrations in getting a clear reply to his frequent pleas for U.S. arms. The Egyptian ruler further emphasized his country's need to maintain a military balance vis-a-vis Israel. Allen warned Nasser that Soviet arms would mean the introduction of Soviet technicians and advisers and argued that their presence might endanger Egyptian sovereignty. Nasser dismissed the threat. Leaving Cairo, Allen told reporters that while the U.S. regretted the Egyptian-Soviet arms deal, it firmly believed that Nasser's sole purpose was to defend his country. Nevertheless, relations between the two nations remained severely strained.

Allen remained assistant secretary until October 1957, when the White House announced his appointment as director of the U.S. Information Agency (USIA). Taking over the Agency at a time when its prestige and budget were at an all-time low, Allen attempted to change its often-criticized image. To counter charges that the USIA was naive and propaganda-oriented, he attempted to adapt Agency information to the needs and viewpoints of the recipient nations. This policy brought him into frequent conflict with his State Department superiors.

In 1961 Allen left the State Department and became president of the Tobacco Institute. During the next few years he defended the tobacco industry against the early reports linking cigarette smoking to lung cancer. In 1966 President Lyndon Johnson named Allen a career ambassador and appointed him head of the Foreign Service Institute. He retired in 1969 and died the following year.

[RJB]

For further information:
Herman Finer, *Dulles Over Suez: The Theory and Practice of His Diplomacy* (Chicago, 1964).
Townsend Hoopes, *The Devil and John Foster Dulles* (Boston, 1973).

ALLEN, LEO E(LWOOD)

b. Oct. 5, 1898: Elizabeth. Ill.
d. Jan. 19, 1973: Galena, Ill.
Republican Representative, Ill., 1933-61; Chairman, Rules Committee, 1947-49, 1953-55.

Allen received a B.A. degree from the University of Michigan in 1923 and the following year became a clerk in the Jo Daviess Co., Ill., Circuit Court. Admitted to the Illinois bar in 1929, he began practicing law in Galena the next year. Allen won election to the U.S. House of Representatives in 1932, where he established a record as an isolationist and opponent of New Deal domestic programs. After the Republicans gained control of the House in the 1946 elections, he served as chairman of the Rules Committee. In that post he attempted to block universal military training legislation but failed to defeat the Selective

Service Act of 1948. During the Truman Administration Allen compiled a consistently conservative record, backing the Taft-Hartley Act of 1947, the Internal Security Act of 1950 and the McCarran Act of 1952. [See TRUMAN Volume]

Allen again became chairman of the Rules panel in 1953, following the Republican electoral sweep of the preceding year. As head of the Committee he defended Eisenhower's tax proposals against the attacks of Ways and Means Committee chairman Rep. Daniel Reed (R, N.Y.) [q.v.]. Early in 1953 Reed's panel blocked an Administration bill to extend an excess profits tax on corporations. In June the Rules Committee, under Allen's leadership, took the unusual step of reporting the bill to the floor without a favorable vote from the Ways and Means panel. At about the same time, Allen blocked a Reed bill to cut income taxes, a measure opposed by the Administration.

Still conservative in his voting during the 1950s, Allen opposed a $1 minimum wage in 1955. He claimed that it would harm "2.5 million subnormals and elderly people" whom employers would not be willing to pay eight dollars a day. During the same year he favored the deregulation of natural gas prices.

As a member of the Rules Committee, Allen formed part of the Southern Democratic-Republican coalition that prevented many social welfare measures from reaching the House floor. In 1959 his vote helped produce a tie in the Committee that blocked the progress of a $1 billion housing bill. The following year he and the panel's other conservatives succeeded in stalling another housing bill, with Allen commenting that "once these extravagant schemes start, they never stop." During the same year they were also able to stop an aid-to-education measure. However, Allen and most of the other Committee Republicans broke with the Southern Democrats in 1957 and 1960 to enable the Administration's civil rights bills to go to the House floor.

In 1960 Allen declined to run for reelection. He died in Galena, Ill., on Jan. 19, 1973.

[MLL]

ALLISON, JOHN M(OORE)
b. April 7, 1905; Holton, Kan.
Assistant Secretary of State for Far Eastern Affairs, February 1952-April 1953; Ambassador to Japan, April 1953-January 1957; Ambassador to Indonesia, January 1957-March 1958; Ambassador to Czechoslovakia, March 1958-May 1960.

After graduating from the University of Nebraska in 1927, Allison went to Japan to teach English. In 1930 he began his diplomatic career as a clerk in the American consulate in Shanghai. Between 1932 and 1941 Allison was alternately stationed in China and Japan. He was interned by the Japanese for six months following the attack on Pearl Harbor. Allison spent the remainder of World War II in London, where he participated in negotiations for shipping and transportation agreements. He returned to Washington in 1947 to become chief of the State Department's division of Far Eastern affairs. In 1950 he served as special assistant to John Foster Dulles [q.v.] in preliminary negotiations for the Japanese peace treaty. The treaty was signed in 1951.

Allison was appointed ambassador to Japan in March 1953 and confirmed by the Senate the following month. His chief problem in the post was the issue of Japanese rearmament. Allison was under strong pressure from Dulles to convince Japan to rearm itself as a primary bulwark against Communist expansion in the Pacific. However, the Japanese were solidly opposed to the plan. They had not only accepted Gen, Douglas MacArthur's postwar idea that Japan should become the "Switzerland of Asia" but had also written it into a strongly anti-war constitution. Consequently, Japanese constitutional experts argued that any military establishment would be unconstitutional. In addition, the Japanese faced severe economic problems well into the 1950s and thus maintained that the nation could not afford a strong defense force. Allison took a stand against the Secretary of State on the rearmament issue. He strongly believed that Japan, as an autonomous nation, should not be reduced to a forward bastion of American strategic strength.

Allison's sympathy for the Japanese position considerably aided negotiations. On March 8, 1954 the two nations signed a mutual defense agreement. The U.S. agreed to give at least $100 million in finished weapons, industrial subsidies to munitions makers and other types of economic aid. In return, Japan promised to rebuild its armed forces under U.S. guidance and make a "full contribution to the strength of the anti-Communist world." Allison disliked the provision permitting the U.S. to intervene in the Japanese budgetary process to guarantee $155 million annually for the support of American troops there. In April 1955 he reached an agreement with Prime Minister Shigeru Yoshida that the U.S. would assume one-third of the Japanese burden for American troops, in return for which Japan would spend more on its airfields and armed forces. However, Dulles disavowed the agreement in August.

Allison faced a more emotional problem in March 1954, when a Japanese fishing boat was contaminated with radioactive ash from an American nuclear bomb test in the South Pacific. One crew member died as a result. Allison was widely praised for the way he handled the delicate situation, which resulted in an American settlement of $2 million in January 1955.

Allison was appointed ambassador to Indonesia in April 1957. During the early years of the decade he had been a strong anti-Communist. However, by the time of this appointment, he had come to believe that foreign relations should not be defined simply in terms of anti-Communist ideology. He maintained that nations generally acted on self-interest rather than political doctrine, and so he was not overly concerned with President Achmed Sukarno's left-wing tendencies. Because Washington feared Sukarno's overtures to the Soviet Union, Allison was unable to acquire the U.S. support he felt necessary to prevent a further drift to the left. When he recommended that the U.S. back Sukarno's bid for a U.N. resolution calling for Indonesian control over Western New Guinea, Washington recommended that the Ambassador

encourage regional uprisings against Sukarno.

Finding his advice disregarded by the State Department, Allison offered his resignation in September 1957. In a final attempt to influence policy, he sent a telegram in November recommending that the U.S. support the transfer of Western New Guinea to Indonesia after five years in exchange for economic concessions to the Dutch, who still owned the territory. The concessions included Indonesian adherence to the ANZUS Pact; a pledge from Sukarno to "control strictly" Communist activity and "accept American assistance and guidance in anti-subversive activities"; and increased U.S. aid to Indonesia. The State Department rejected the proposal when it was opposed by Australia and the Netherlands.

Allison was appointed ambassador to Czechoslovakia in March 1958. He served there until 1960, when he resigned from the Foreign Service because of his wife's ill health. Allison retired to Honolulu, where he taught at the University of Hawaii.

[JPL]

For further information:
John M. Allison, *Ambassador from the Prairie, or Allison Wonderland* (Boston, 1973).

ALLOTT, GORDON (LLEWELLYN)
b. Jan. 2, 1907; Pueblo, Colo.
Republican Senator, Colo., 1955-73.

Son of a federal meat inspector, Allott graduated from the University of Colorado Law School and was admitted to the bar in 1929. He then set up a legal practice in Lamar, Colo., a wheat-belt trading center. During the 1930s and 1940s Allott was active on state and national Republican committees. In 1950 he won election as lieutenant governor.

Allott was a close friend of former Minnesota Gov. Harold Stassen [q.v.] and backed Stassen's unsuccessful bid for the presidential nomination at the 1952 Chicago Republican National Convention. In 1954 he ran for the U.S. Senate on a platform supporting the Eisenhower Administration's farm policy. With strong support from the state's farm sections, he won an upset victory against the popular Democrat, John Carroll.

Allott voted as a conservative Republican on most issues during the Eisenhower Administration. However, he supported the Civil Rights Acts of 1957 and 1960. As a member of the Interior and Insular Affairs Committee, Allott helped win Senate approval of the Upper Colorado River Project in 1955. The Project was one of the largest and most important federal reclamation efforts up to that time. Conservationists, however, objected to the Allott-backed proposal to flood much of the Dinosaur National Monument in Colorado and Utah. This provision was deleted from the final version of the bill as passed by the House in 1956.

During the 1960s Allott opposed most of the Democratic Administrations' domestic legislative programs. In 1969 he won the chairmanship of the powerful Senate Republican Conference Committee. Allott lost his reelection bid in 1972. [See KENNEDY, JOHNSON, NIXON/FORD Volumes]

[TLH]

ALMOND, J(AMES) LINDSAY, JR.
b. June 15, 1898; Charlottesville, Va.
Governor, Va., 1958-62.

After earning his LL.B. at the University of Virginia in 1923, J. Lindsay Almond practiced law in Roanoke for the next nine years. In 1932 he was elected judge of Roanoke's Hustings Court and served until 1945. He then successfully ran as a Democrat to fill a House seat vacated by the resignation of Clifton A. Woodrum (D, Va.). Reelected to a full term in 1946, Almond compiled a generally conservative record, voting to extend the draft and override President Harry S. Truman's veto of the Taft-Hartley bill. He resigned from Congress in April 1948 to complete a term as state attorney general after the occupant died in office.

Almond campaigned for a four-year term as attorney general in 1949 on a platform supporting an amendment that would have repealed the poll tax and placed increased restrictions on the right to vote. Although the amendment was defeated, Almond won

handily. As attorney general, he expected to be the Byrd organization candidate for governor, but in January 1953 he withdrew his name at Sen. Harry F. Byrd's (D. Va.) [q.v.] request. He was elected to a second term as attorney general in November.

During 1952 Almond pleaded the state's case in *Davis v. County School Board of Prince Edward County*. The suit had been brought by blacks demanding that the state law requiring segregated schools be struck down. Although privately conceding that blacks had received an inferior education in the state, Almond opposed demands for school integration and rejected the NAACP's contention that separate but equal facilities were inherently discriminatory. Instead, he supported a "separated equality" and recommended the use of funds to equalize black facilities. A three-member federal court upheld the constitutionality of the Virginia statute but ordered the unequal facilities remedied. The case was later taken to the Supreme Court, where it became one of several argued as *Brown v. Board of Education*. Almond helped present Virginia's case before the high tribunal. In May 1954 the Supreme Court unanimously declared segregated schools unconstitutional.

In the wake of the decision, Virginia Gov. Thomas B. Stanley [q.v.] appointed a commission, headed by Garland Gray, to seek means to preserve the status quo in Virginia's schools. The Gray Commission's November 1955 report recommended that local authorities be permitted to close public schools threatened with integration. The state would then pay tuition for private schooling. These recommendations were approved in a March 1956 referendum. Interpreting approval of local option as total support for segregation, Sen. Byrd called for "massive resistance" to the Supreme Court decision through a policy of interposition. The state would close schools threatened with integration regardless of local feeling. During the dispute over the *Brown* decision, Almond maintained a moderate stand, in April 1956 stating that interposition had no legal validity. While such prominent Southerners as Texas Gov. Alan Shivers [q.v.] were recommending a regional candidate for President in 1956 and the Byrd machine remained neutral, Almond worked for the 1956 Democratic national ticket.

When Almond announced for governor in late 1956, Byrd concluded he could not stop the attorney general and so endorsed him. Running as the organization candidate, and recognizing a rightward drift in public sentiment, Almond campaigned on a massive resistance platform. Yet, he remained skeptical of that position and surprised segregationists in October 1957 by saying there would be a degree of forced integration under federal mandate. Despite the statement, Almond went on to win the governorship two-to-one over Republican Ted Dalton the following month.

In his inaugural address Almond gave unqualified support for opposition to the *Brown* decision. "Against massive attacks," he stated, "we must marshall massive resistance." He warned that "integration anywhere means destruction everywhere." Sensing rising segregationist sentiment, in April Almond sponsored legislation consolidating state control of pupil assignments and strengthening the governor's school closing authority. In September Almond closed nine schools that were under court order to integrate.

During the fall of 1958 moderate forces began demanding a change of position on school integration. In October the Virginia Parent-Teacher Association urged abandonment of interposition and adoption of local option. Shortly thereafter city newspapers began to withdraw support for massive resistance. By Dec. 29 leading industrialists were sufficiently alarmed by declining out-of-state investment to call on Almond and urge him to drop interposition. Attempting to stall until the direction of public opinion was clear, Almond refused to invoke laws that permitted him to reopen closed schools as segregated institutions. He also directed his attorney general to prepare a test case for the Virginia courts. According to historian Numan Bartley, Almond presumed that federal courts would strike down massive resistance and felt it would be better received if the decision came from a state court. On Jan. 19, 1959 both a federal district court and the Virginia Supreme Court of Appeals ruled closing schools and withholding state funds from integrated institutions unconstitutional.

While denouncing the decision, the Governor maneuvered Virginia toward compliance with the order. He called a special session of the legislature in January and cautiously sounded a retreat from massive resistance. Closed schools were reopened and three city systems began at least token desegregation. In the legislature Almond prevented a resurgence of extremist forces led by the Byrd organization. A report by the Perrow Commission, packed with Almond appointed moderates, recommended a 15-bill program to develop a policy of local option that held integration to token levels. In April the legislature enacted the measures dispite bitter opposition.

During the remaining years of his term, the breech between Almond and Byrd hardened, and the Governor purged Byrd supporters at every opportunity. Forbidden by law to succeed himself, Almond ran his own anti-organization candidate for governor in the July 1961 Democratic primary. His effort failed, and Byrd maintained control of the statehouse. In 1962 Almond was appointed a judge of the Federal Patents Court, where he served until his retirement in 1973.

[MJS]

For further information:
Numan Bartley, *The Rise of Massive Resistance* (Baton Rouge, 1969).

ALSOP, JOSEPH W(RIGHT), JR.
b. Oct. 11, 1910; Avon, Conn.
Journalist, author.

Joseph Alsop was the eldest son of one of the most socially prominent families in Connecticut. His father was an insurance executive and both his parents served several terms in the state legislature. Alsop attended the prestigious Groton School and graduated from Harvard *magna cum laude* in 1932. Family influence gained him a job as a reporter for the *New York Herald*

Tribune. Alsop quickly proved to be one of the paper's top feature writers and in 1936 was sent to Washington to cover the capital news. Alsop soon established a secure position for himself in the Washington political and social scene. From 1937 to 1940 he coauthored with Robert E. Kintner a syndicated column entitled "The Capitol Parade," which was distributed to almost 100 newspapers throughout the country. During the same period he collaborated on several books dealing with various aspects of both domestic and foreign affairs.

Although an isolationist during the 1930s, Alsop adopted a strong interventionist stance well before America's entry into World War II. In 1940 he initiated lobbying efforts which proved decisive in convincing Roosevelt to honor Britain's urgent request for American warships. Alsop served briefly in the Navy during World War II but soon resigned his commission in order to become an adviser and supporter of Gen. Claire Chennault and Generalissimo Chiang Kai-shek in wartime China. Alsop's experience left him a strong supporter of Nationalist China and a vigorous anti-Communist.

In 1946 Alsop resumed his work as a columnist, this time collaborating with his brother Stewart [q.v.]. Through their column, "Matter of Fact," they built a joint reputation as leading commentators of the day on foreign affairs. In both 1950 and 1952 they were cited by the Overseas Press Club for "the best interpretation of foreign news." The Alsops took a strong stand against McCarthyism, maintaining that the real threat to the U.S. was not internal Communist subversion, but external Communist attack. [See TRUMAN Volume]

During the Eisenhower Administration the Alsops took a pessimistic view of world events. The column's doom-crying refrain was primarily the responsibility of Joseph Alsop. His New Year's message in 1954 was simply, "All is lost." In general, his favorite descriptions of the 1950s depicted an era poised dangerously on "the edge of the abyss."

In the autumn of 1953 Alsop journeyed to Asia where he wrote ominously of the great power of Communist China and the harmful effects of the armistice in Korea. In November he called upon the American government to take a more active role in Vietnam. He warned that if the French pulled out, all of Indochina would soon fall under Communist control. Alsop returned to Southeast Asia a number of times, always writing of its imminent collapse.

In 1956 Alsop turned his attention to the Middle East. He described the problems of Arab nationalism, growing Soviet involvement and the plight of Palestinian refugees. He viewed the situation as so tense that several months before the Suez crisis he wrote, "finding a way out is so urgent that it may not be just a matter of days, but even of hours." The following year he found himself in the Soviet Union. There he described the enormous strength of Soviet industry and what he thought was the illusory nature of de-Stalinization. "While somewhat more supple than their late master," he said, "Stalin's heirs have actually proven somewhat more adventurous."

In 1954 the brothers collaborated on a book entitled *We Accuse!*, which denounced the Atomic Energy Commission, and Commission head Lewis Strauss [q.v.] in particular, for refusing to reinstate J. Robert Oppenheimer's [q.v.] security clearance. They defended Oppenheimer's prewar connections with left-wing organizations as a "brand of political folly that was a common highbrow reaction to the menace of Nazism." The Alsops pointed out that the scientist had quickly renounced the ties and had become what they saw as a prominent cold warrior, a position they both lauded. "Oppenheimer," they said, "became the only truly eminent American outside the Armed Services . . . who was willing to discuss dispassionately the idea of preventive war to save the world from Communist tyranny." The two writers maintained that Oppenheimer had been brought to trial not because of his left-wing connections but because of his opposition to the development of the hydrogen bomb. The Alsops termed the Administration's security system "inherently repugnant in its present standards and procedures to every high tradition of the American past." The two brothers predicted that if the system was not reformed quickly "lasting harm will begin to be done."

In March 1958 the Alsop brothers ended their 12-year partnership when Stewart took a job as a contributing editor for the *Saturday Evening Post*. Their reputation was then at its height. The column was distributed to almost 200 newspapers throughout the world. Several months earlier *Newsweek* had called the brothers "possibly the most influential and provocative columnists in the business. After they ended their partnership they collected a number of their articles into a book, *The Reporter's Trade*, which they introduced with a plea for the government to be more open with the press. They also praised Eisenhower for bringing the McCarthy era to a close but criticized him for not pouring enough money into the national defense effort. Joseph Alsop continued to write "Matter of Fact" alone, focusing on the Cold War struggle between the U.S. and the USSR. During the last years of the decade he was one of several prominent Americans to warn of a growing "missile gap" between the U.S. and the USSR.

Alsop was a firm supporter of the Vietnam war. In 1964 he wrote what some critics thought was his best book, *From the Silent Earth*, a study of the Greek bronze age. Alsop retired in 1974 soon after his brother's death.

[JPL]

ALSOP, STEWART (JOHONNOT) (OLIVER)

b. May 17, 1941; Avon, Conn.
d. May 26, 1974; Bethesda, Md.
Journalist, author.

Alsop was born into a Connecticut family with a history of government service. His mother was a niece of Theodore Roosevelt and a cousin of both Franklin and Eleanor Roosevelt. Stewart Alsop attended Groton and then Yale University, where he graduated in 1936. He became an editor for the Doubleday Doran publishing company in New York. Following the U.S. entry into World War II, he attempted to enlist in the Army but was rejected on medical grounds.

He then went to England and joined the rifle corps. In 1944 he was transfered to the U.S. Army. Alsop served in the Office of Strategic Services and parachuted into occupied France shortly after D-day. On his return to the U.S. Stewart collaborated with his brother Joseph [*q.v.*] on a syndicated column, "Matter of Fact." The partnership lasted until 1958.

In 1950 and 1952 both Alsops were cited by the Overseas Press Club for the "best interpretation of foreign news." In 1954 they joined forces to write *We Accuse!*, a defense of J. Robert Oppenheimer [*q.v.*] against security-risk charges investigated by the Atomic Energy Commission. The book won an award by the Author's Guild in 1955 for its contribution to civil liberties. When Stewart Alsop accepted a job as a contributing editor for the *Saturday Evening Post* in 1958, the brothers ended what had often been described as a "stormy partnership." Later that year they published *The Reporter's Trade*, a collection of their columns introduced by a plea for government candor with the press.

In contrast to his brother, Stewart Alsop was a family man, a cautious writer and a cheerful personality. Although he generally agreed with his brother's positions, he freely conceded that "Joe can play the organ of gloom better than I." During their partnership, his main contribution was a series of articles on ballistic missiles. He was the first to point out that the Air Force planned to fire an intercontinental ballistic missile (ICBM) in 1957 and the first to report the Soviet ICBM tests.

Alsop had announced his support for Eisenhower as a presidential candidate as early as April 1950. However, soon after Eisenhower took office, Alsop joined his brother in criticizing the President for placing budgetary considerations above defense requirements. They expressed this view in an early series of attacks on George Humphrey [*q.v.*], Eisenhower's first Secretary of the Treasury. In his *Nixon and Eisenhower*, published in 1960, Alsop repeated the charge that the Eisenhower Administration had failed "to maintain a genuine balance of power with the Communist bloc." However, he offset the charge with his judgement that "the Eisenhower years have been a settling-down period, a time of adjustment and stabilization after an era of enormous change."

Alsop continued working for the *Saturday Evening Post* until its close in 1968, when he began writing a weekly column for *Newsweek*. Although he was slow in advocating American withdrawal from Vietnam, he did not give the war the kind of support his brother did. In 1973 he wrote *Stay of Execution* about his impending death from leukemia. He continued his work for *Newsweek* until the eve of his death in the spring of 1974. His last articles expressed his concern over Watergate and his loss of faith in Richard Nixon, whom he had long admired.

[JPL]

ANASTASIA, ALBERT
b. Sept. 26, 1902; Tropea, Italy
d. Oct. 29, 1957; New York, N.Y.
Organized crime figure.

Umberto Anastasia joined the Mafia while in Italy. He jumped ship in New York in 1919 but later reentered the U.S. legally. Encouraged by official laxity, Anastasia and his three brothers subverted the Brooklyn longshoremen's union. He changed his name to Albert Anastasia in 1921, following his arrest for the murder of a fellow longshoreman. Anastasia spent 18 months on Death Row until, in what was to become a familiar gangland pattern, a new trial was granted on a technicality and a key prosecution witness disappeared. Arrested again in 1923, he served two years for carrying a gun. Between 1921 and 1954 he was arrested 10 times, five for murder.

Anastasia joined Louis (Lepke) Buchalter in terrorizing unions in New York's garment district, often extorting "sweetheart contracts" at gunpoint. Between 1931 and 1940 Buchalter and his gang, known as Murder Inc., allegedly committed 63 murders. Buchalter was convicted of murder and sent to the electric chair in 1941. However, Anastasia went free when Brooklyn District Attorney William O'Dwyer, who had connections to organized crime, declined to

prosecute him after the mysterious death of a leading witness in O'Dwyer's custody. O'Dwyer was censured by a grand jury for his conduct. From 1942 to 1944 Anastasia served in the Army. After his discharge he bought a dress factory in order to establish a legitimate front.

During the 1950s Anastasia's activities were the subject of two highly publicized congressional hearings. In 1950 and 1951 Sen. Estes Kefauver (D, Tenn.) [q.v.] and his Senate Crime Investigating Committee probed what they thought was a massive crime conspiracy aided by official corruption. Anastasia was called to testify and was cited for contempt of Congress when he refused to tell the Committee how he earned his living. The Kefauver Committee report accused O'Dwyer, who was then ambassador to Mexico, of aiding crime by not prosecuting Anatasia. Despite the publicity generated by Kefauver's campaign and the widespread belief that a criminal network had extended its power throughout the nation, the federal government took little action against organized crime. The FBI did not officially recognize the existence of a national crime syndicate. Director J. Edgar Hoover [q.v.] shunned Mafia cases. They were difficult to prosecute and did not result in a high rate of conviction.

In May 1956 Anastasia was questioned by Robert Kennedy [q.v.], chief counsel of the Senate Permanent Investigations Subcommittee, about racketeer domination of companies producing military uniforms under government contract. No action was taken on the matter. Later Kennedy outlined another instance of Anastasia's penetration of labor. In 1955 private garbage collectors in New York formed an employer's association. According to Kennedy, Anastasia took control of this through Teamster Local 813 and maneuvered to monopolize the garbage industry through the employers' "adviser" Jimmy Squillante. Anastasia was shot to death in October 1957.

The following month 58 known hoodlums were arrested in Appalachin, N.Y., at the largest Mafia conference ever held. Of these 22 said their businesses dealt with labor-management relations. All were released for lack of evidence. It was later learned that Vito Genovese [*q.v.*] had called the conclave to ratify his control of America's largest Mafia "family" following the death of Anastasia and the retirement of Frank Costello [*q.v.*].

Appalachin marked the beginning of an effort by the federal government against organized crime. Eisenhower's Attorney General, William T. Rogers [*q.v.*], established a special group within the Justice Department to investigate organized crime without asking Hoover. The section lasted only two years but provided a focus for anti-crime activity. In the 1960s the Attorney General Robert Kennedy pressed for new wiretap legislation and encouraged a new policy of prosecuting mobsters under any and all available laws.

[MJS]

ANDERSON, CLINTON P(RESBA)
b. Oct. 23, 1895; Centerville, S.D.
d. Nov. 11, 1975; Albuquerque, N.M.
Democratic Senator, N.M., 1949-73;
Chairman, Joint Congressional Committee on Atomic Energy, 1955, 1959-60.

A native of rural South Dakota, Anderson studied at Dakota Wesleyan University from 1913 to 1915. After completing a year of pre-law studies at the University of Michigan, he attempted to enter military service but was rejected because of a tubercular condition. He then moved to New Mexico, where the climate helped him improve his health. From 1918 to 1922 he worked for the *Albuquerque Journal*, where he helped uncover evidence relating to the Teapot Dome scandal. He began a career in insurance in 1922, eventually becoming president of his own firm. Anderson was appointed treasurer of New Mexico in 1933, and throughout the 1930s he helped administer various New Deal relief programs in the state.

In 1940 Anderson won election to the U.S. House as a representative at large. There he led a congressional probe of national food shortages and blackmarketing in the meat industry. President Harry S. Truman was so impressed by Anderson's investigations that he appointed the Con-

gressman Secretary of Agriculture in 1945. In 1948 Anderson was elected to the Senate. [See TRUMAN Volume]

From the beginning of his Senate tenure, Anderson consistently voted with the Democratic liberals. An advocate of federal control of natural resources, he fought the Eisenhower concept of federal-state "partnership." In early 1953 the Administration overturned Truman's designation of offshore oil lands as a Navy reserve, thereby giving control of these fields back to the states. Anderson and other liberals staged an unsuccessful filibuster to protest the move and press for federal control. Administration backers succeeded in passing a bill supporting state ownership, but the Supreme Court eventually ruled in favor of limited control by those states whose colonial charters stipulated it.

Best known as an effective defender of New Mexico's interests, Anderson sponsored legislation that brought his state large sums of federal money for defense installations, land reclamation and water resources. As chairman of the Joint Congressional Committee on Atomic Energy, he was particularly influential in bringing the nuclear power industry to New Mexico. He consistently supported programs for nuclear power projects and later contended that they had not been adequately funded by the government. In 1956 Anderson served as floor manager of the Upper Colorado River Storage project, a plan to divert Colorado River water to New Mexico, particularly to Indian lands. Because of his efforts the Senate raised the Administration's suggested initial appropriation from $8 to $13 million.

In 1959 Anderson led the fight against confirmation of Lewis Strauss [*q.v.*] as Secretary of Commerce. An advocate of public power development, the Senator opposed Strauss because he had backed the 1954 Dixon-Yates contract giving a private combine, rather than the Tennessee Valley Authority, the right to supply power to Atomic Energy Commission installations in the Tennessee Valley area. Anderson also objected to Strauss's refusal to support J. Robert Oppenheimer [*q.v.*] during the latter's 1954 security hearings. Partly as a result of Anderson's opposition, Strauss was the first cabinet appointee to be rejected by the Senate since 1925.

Anderson played a prominent role in the 1960s in both atomic affairs and the U.S. space program. In his final term in the Senate he won the Goddard Memorial Trophy for "outstanding contributions to space flight programs that promoted American leadership in astronautics." He retired from the Senate in 1973 and died in New Mexico three years later. [See KENNEDY, JOHNSON Volumes]

[TGD]

ANDERSON, ROBERT B(ERNARD)
b. June 4, 1910; Burleson, Tex.
Secretary of the Navy, February 1953-March 1954; Deputy Secretary of Defense, April 1954-August 1955; Secretary of the Treasury, July 1957-January 1961.

Born and raised on a farm in the cotton and cattle region of Texas, Anderson graduated from Weatherford College in 1927. To finance his law studies he taught Spanish, history and mathematics in 1929 at a local high school. He was elected to the state legislature the same day he graduated from the University of Texas Law School in 1932. Named state tax commissioner in 1934, Anderson successfully introduced a bill to organize the first social security agency in Texas. Three years later he became general attorney for the vast W.I. Waggoner ranch, at that time the second richest in the nation. Appointed general manager four years later, he increased its holdings and introduced modern ranching methods.

During World War II Anderson served as a civilian aide to the Secretary of the Army. In the 1940s he was associated with several large business organizations among them the American Petroleum Institute. Anderson was one of the oil industry's most effective witnesses before Congress. In 1949 he became chairman of the Texas State Board of Education.

President-elect Eisenhower designated Anderson Secretary of the Navy in December 1952. Shortly after the appointment Anderson came under criticism from Rep. Adam Clayton Powell (D, N.Y.) [q.v.]. In June 1953 Powell notified the White House that Anderson was

guilty of "insubordination" for blocking federal efforts to end segregation at shipyards in Charleston, S.C., and Norfolk, Va. In response the Secretary ordered the complete integration of civilian employes at 43 Navy shore stations. He informed all members of naval districts practicing segregation that the federal government would condone only equal treatment of personnel and asked each commander to draw up desegregation plans sensitive to local conditions. The operation was accomplished without resistance. In November 1953 Eisenhower announced that the policy had been "completely effective." Powell sent Anderson an apology for his statements.

Anderson was appointed deputy secretary of defense in March 1954. During his tenure he helped Eisenhower formulate his Open Skies proposal delivered at the 1955 Geneva summit conference. The plan was designed to give the Administration the psychological offensive following the Soviet Union's disarmament overture of May. It suggested that the U.S. and USSR exchange military blueprints and allow mutual air reconnaissance over their military installations. The proposal was eventually rejected by the Kremlin.

Anderson left his post in August 1955 to return to business, but Eisenhower called him into government service again in 1956 as his personal emissary to the Middle East. The former Secretary attempted to initiate direct discussions between Israeli Prime Minister David Ben Gurion and Egyptian President Gamal Abdel Nasser in an effort to resolve outstanding differences over the Suez Canal. However, his efforts failed, and in October Israel attacked Egypt.

Eisenhower had great political plans for Anderson. The President found the deeply religious, conservative, mild-mannered Anderson the ideal man to implement his own ideas for America and urged him to be his running mate in the 1956 campaign. Eisenhower also felt that Anderson, a Southerner and a Democrat, would improve Republican chances in the South. However, Anderson refused, pleading inexperience in partisan politics. Eisenhower confided to Emmet J. Hughes [q.v.] before the 1960 election that he considered Anderson his number one choice for the presidency. Of all the possible candidates, "the only one who has the broadest range—best in experience and sense and the right age—it's that Bob Anderson. Boy, I'd like to fight for him in 1960."

Anderson replaced George Humphrey [q.v.] as Secretary of the Treasury in July 1957. In fiscal and monetary policy he was as conservative as his predecessor. He stood firmly behind the Administration's desire to pare the size of government and balance the budget in order to cut inflation and invigorate private enterprise. Anderson differed with Humphrey, however, in his more relaxed attitude toward increased defense spending and his more liberal approach to foreign economic policy.

Anderson's concern with preventing inflation was reflected in his treatment of the recession of 1957-58. Convinced that the recession would be short-lived, he opposed tax cuts to stimulate the economy because he believed they would be inflationary. His popularity with Democratic congressional leaders Rep. Sam Rayburn (D, Tex.) [q.v.] and Sen. Lyndon B. Johnson (D, Tex.) [q.v.] helped him maintain this policy. In March 1958 he made a "gentleman's agreement" with Rayburn, pledging that each would consult the other before moving to reduce taxes. Anderson surprised critics when he floated a long-term bond issue at the recession's trough but justified his move by saying that short-term financing was inflationary.

The budget for fiscal 1959 reflected Anderson's continued fear of inflation. In the wake the Soviet launching of *Sputnik* in October 1957, demands grew for increased military spending. Anderson supported the action but insisted that the budget be tightened elsewhere. As a result, the 1959 budget put a ban on flood control and reclamation projects, reduced agricultural subsidies and implemented a cutback on federal grants for urban renewal and welfare programs. However, increases in military spending, together with a small decline in revenue caused by the recession, produced a deficit of $12.5 billion, the largest during Eisenhower's presidency.

Conflict between the Secretary of the Treasury and the Democratic Congress over economic policy came to a head in August 1959. The President's request to raise interest rates on government bonds was shelved by the House Ways and Means Committee. Anderson called the Committee's decision "a matter of great concern." He argued that the only alternative to the repeal of interest rate ceilings was to force more of the national debt into inflationary short-term securities, to which the ceilings did not apply. Intent on exploiting the issue, the Democrats in the Senate lashed out against the move, stating that it would raise interest rates for all borrowers. Anderson refused to yield to the criticism, saying "the government, in the management of the debt, can actively contribute to inflationary pressures by being confined to short-term financing, which the shorter it gets, is more nearly like money." Congress refused to raise the rate on long-term obligations.

With the retirement and death of Secretary of State John F. Dulles [q.v.], Anderson, in the words of *New York Times* correspondent James Reston [q.v.], became the cabinet "strongman." He used his position to fight for a balanced budget and persuaded Eisenhower to oppose Secretary of State Christian Herter's [q.v.] attempts to arrange long-term financing of the Development Loan Fund. Anderson also convinced the President to insist that recipients of development loans spend their dollars in the U.S. To reduce the balance of payment deficit, he insisted that the allies remove their quotas against the importation of American goods and take on a greater share of the cost of defending their territories.

During the Kennedy Administration Anderson was a partner in the investment house of Loeb, Rhodes & Co. and a member of the presidential panel formed to study the U.S. foreign aid program. Anderson served as an informal consultant to President Johnson and advised him to pursue a conservative fiscal policy. [See JOHNSON Volume]

[ACD]

ARENDS, LES(LIE) C(ORNELIUS)
b. Sept. 27, 1895; Melvin, Ill.
Republican Representative, Ill., 1935-74.

After studying at Oberlin College for two years, Arends entered the Army during World War I and received his discharge in

1919. Following in his father's footsteps, Arends became a farmer and banker in 1920. Seeking public office for the first time in 1934, he was elected to the U.S. House of Representatives from a prosperous agricultural region south of Chicago. Arends was a critic of what he believed was the dangerous centralization of power under the New Deal. He became Republican minority whip in 1943 and served as majority whip for two years after the Republican electoral victory of 1946. [See TRUMAN Volume]

Arends again became majority whip after the 1952 election. His major functions were to line up Republican support for positions favored by the White House and the Party's congressional leadership, make sure that Republican representatives were present for important votes and ascertain the views of rank-and-file Republican representatives. After the 1954 election he again became assistant minority leader, performing essentially the same duties.

A conservative and a supporter of President Eisenhower's policies, Arends defended the Administration's program to eliminate security risks from the government. In January 1954 Eisenhower maintained that under his program more than 2,200 Communists had left the federal payroll. Congressional critics charged that Eisenhower was attempting to mislead the public into believing that all of these employes were Communists, whereas many were social rather than political deviates. In February 1954 Sen. Wayne Morse (Ind. Ore.) [q.v.] charged the President with responsibility for a "fascist big lie technique" and asked for a breakdown on how many of the security risks were Communists. Two days later Arends said there was no reason for a classification of the causes of the employes' dismissals and charged that Morse had "impeached the honesty and integrity" of the President.

In 1955 Arends denounced an unsuccessful Democratic effort to introduce a bill ending the Administration's program of flexible farm price supports and restoring rigid supports at 90% of parity. Arends charged that "political considerations, not economic, bring this [bill] before us. . . . The sole objective of this bill is to try to embarrass the Eisenhower Administration."

Arends was a strong supporter of private enterprise, and he sought to minimize government intervention in the workings of the market economy. In 1955 he defended the sale of government-owned synthetic rubber plants to the highest-bidding private companies against Democratic charges that the sale might promote monopoly. Two years later he unsuccessfully attempted to delete from a military public works bill a provision giving Congress a veto over the transfer of Defense Department work to private industry. However, the final bill that emerged from the House-Senate conference did not include that provision.

The second-ranking Republican on the Armed Services Committee through 1956 and subsequently the senior Republican on the panel, Arends was a staunch defender of large military appropriations. In 1957 he declared that "if there is one thing the American people demand, it is that we make certain we have the proper national defense. Anyone who votes against a national defense need is certain to have to make an accounting with the people he represents."

Arends generally opposed Kennedy and Johnson Administration domestic programs, although he voted for the 1964 Civil Rights Act. He also backed the Johnson Administration's Vietnam war policy. Arends announced in 1974 that he would not seek reelection. He retained his post as minority leader until his retirement. [See KENNEDY, JOHNSON, NIXON/FORD Volumes]

[MLL]

ARENDT, HANNAH
b. Oct. 14, 1906; Hanover, Germany.
d. Dec. 4, 1975; New York, N.Y.
Philosopher, political scientist.

Born into a German-Jewish family, Arendt earned a doctorate at the age of 22 from the University of Heidelberg. She studied under the existentialist philosopher Karl Jaspers, who remained a lifelong source of inspiration for her. In 1933 she fled Hitler's Germany and went to Paris, where she worked for a Jewish refugee center. In 1940, before the Nazi occupation of France, she moved to the United States. Arendt settled in New York and became director for the Conference on Jewish Relations. In 1946 she became chief editor of Schocken Books, while also writing articles on diverse themes. From 1949 to 1952 she served as executive secretary of Jewish Cultural Reconstruction, Inc. She professed no personal religious affiliation, but always participated in Jewish cultural activities.

Arendt's first book in English was *The Origins of Totalitarianism* (1951), a study of fascism and Communism, which attempted to trace both back to a common origin in 19th-century imperialism and anti-Semitism. The book established her reputation and won her several university teaching positions. In 1953 she delivered the Christian Gauss lectures at Princeton University and in 1959 she was the first woman to be appointed a full professor at Princeton. She also held positions at Columbia, the University of Chicago, and for a number of years before her death, at the New School for Social Research. [See TRUMAN Volume]

In articles written in the 1950s and published primarily in *Partisan Review*, Arendt struggled with the broad concepts of history and freedom, tradition and authority. Her work culminated in a lecture series given at the University of Chicago in 1956 and published as *The Human Condition* in 1958. The central theme of the work was that modern society was founded on an ethic of labor which precluded true contributions to political life and the creation of lasting objects of value. Because automation was progressively liberating people from the need to labor for survival, she believed a major crisis could soon develop. Arendt, in effect, warned the free world that its materialistic values could create the conditions of a totalitarianism as pernicious as that found in Nazi Germany and Stalinist Russia. Her primary value was the expression of human freedom through political activity. Her fear was that the world would soon make such activity impossible.

Reviews of her work were mixed. Many acknowledged its importance as a philosophical structure for understanding the contemporary political situation but complained of its obscurity. Arendt made her position much clearer in the epilogue to the 1958 edition of the *The Origins of Totalitarianism*, which she wrote in response to the 1956 revolt in Hungary. She hailed the revolt as "the first and yet unique instance of a people's uprising against total domination." It was important as a display of man's insuppressible freedom, his ability to act in the public realm even under the most intolerable circumstances. However, she did not see revolt as a portent of future uprisings. She attributed it to the temporary thawing of Soviet opression, indicating that where oppression was total, rebellion might be impossible. The thaw left no room for optimism, since, according to Arendt, the period of de-Stalinization represented only a tactical maneuver on the part of the Soviet hierarchy and would be followed by a renewal of totalitarian policies. As evidence she cited the heavy-handed reaction to the Hungarian uprising and Khruschev's declarations that the Soviet Union had no need to fear the consequences of nuclear warfare.

In 1963 Arendt became the focus of extensive controversy with the publication of *Eichmann in Jerusalem*. She argued that the evil of Eichmann's crimes lay less in his personal guilt than in the Nazi bureaucracy which allowed him to view his actions as a mechanical fulfillment of duty. Arendt developed this appraisal of bureaucracy into a deeply pessimistic evaluation of the modern world. America's involvement in Vietnam and the circumstances surrounding the Watergate affair only served to make her evaluation more severe. When she died in 1975, Arendt was praised as a great thinker, a courageous woman, and a true stoic. [See KENNEDY Volume]

[JPL]

ARMOUR, NORMAN
b. Oct. 14, 1887; Brighton, England.
Ambassador to Guatemala, December 1954-May 1955.

Born in England of American parents, Armour was educated in the United States, receiving a B.A. from Princeton in 1909, an

LL.B. from Harvard in 1913 and an M.A. from Princeton in 1915. He entered the Foreign Service that same year. Assigned to Russia both prior to and during the Russian Revolution, he rescued a princess whom he later married. Armour was appointed ambassador to Chile in 1938 and served as ambassador to Argentina and Spain during World War II. He retired in 1945 only to be recalled by President Harry S. Truman in 1948 to become ambassador to Venezuela, where the U.S. was carrying on delicate oil negotiations. He retired again in 1951.

During the opening days of the Eisenhower Administration, Armour joined other Foreign Service officers in protesting Sen. Joseph R. McCarthy's (R, Wisc.) [q.v.] attacks on the State Department. In March 1953, when Senate conservatives challenged Charles Bohlen's [q.v.] nomination as ambassador to the USSR because of his ties to Truman's foreign policy, Armour and other career Foreign Service officers sent a letter to the Senate Foreign Relations Committee in support of Bohlen. In January 1954 Armour joined four other career diplomats in publicly deploring the "sinister" effects of McCarthy's "flimsy" attacks on the Foreign Service. The diplomats complained that the Administration's loyalty-security and personnel policies might produce "a Foreign Service competent to serve a totalitarian government."

Armour was once again called out of retirement in 1954 to become ambassador to Guatemala. He arrived in that country just after the Central Intelligence Agency had helped overthrow the leftist regime of Jacobo Arbenz. Armour's task was to aid the rightist government in restoring the Guatemalan economy and to oversee the vast amounts of American economic aid given that country. Approaching 70 at the time of his recall to duty, Armour again retired in early May 1955, announcing that he intended "to give some attention to my own personal affairs," and stressing that the post-revolutionary economic recovery of Guatemala was well under way.

In October 1956 Sen. J. William Fulbright (D, Ark.) [q.v.], chairman of a special Senate subcommittee investigating foreign aid, appointed Armour to a panel making on-the-spot studies of the program. Assigned to observe activities in Greece, Turkey and Iran, Armour reported back to the Committee in March 1957 that new foreign aid efforts were needed. Estimates by the North Atlantic Treaty Organization of Turkey's military capabilities were probably "overly optimistic," he said, while U.S. security interests in Greece were jeopardized because of unsettled relations between Greece and Cyprus. The U.S., he warned, needed to provide "substantial assistance" for Iran to resist any Soviet aggression in the years ahead.

Armour retired from public life after his Mediterranean fact-finding mission.

[RJB]

ASHMORE, HARRY S(COTT)
b. July 27, 1916; Greenville, S.C.
Executive Editor, *Arkansas Gazette*, 1948-59.

Harry Ashmore was the son of a Greenville merchant whose ancestors served in the Confederate Army. Ashmore became acquainted with the plight of the Southern black when, as a teenager, he worked on a cotton farm during the summer. In 1937 he graduated from Clemson Agricultural College and began a career in journalism, covering the local courthouse for the Greenville *Piedmont*. In the late 1930s he toured poverty areas above the Mason-Dixon line to do a series on Northern "Tobacco Roads." Following service in the Army during World War II, Ashmore was named associate editor of the Charlotte, N.C., *News*. He wrote editorials advocating two-party politics in the South, racial and religious tolerance and the enfranchisement of blacks. The *Arkansas Gazette* hired Ashmore as editor in 1947. He became executive editor the following year.

In 1953 the Ford Foundation commissioned Ashmore to head a team of scholars studying biracial education in the U.S. The report, entitled *The Negro and the School* (1954), was published the day before the Supreme Court handed down its decision in *Brown v. Board of Education* outlawing segregation in public schools. The Ashmore study revealed that blacks in segregated schools were getting an inferior education; it also noted that a gap existed in the North between the quality of education blacks were getting compared to whites. The report cautioned that desegregation was an explosive issue because of Americans' intense interest in education. It pointed to community attitudes as the most important factor in integration but noted that gradual desegregation had often proved more volatile than immediate integration. The study was used by both integrationists and segregationists to support their positions.

In September 1957, when Arkansas Gov. Orval Faubus [q.v.] ordered National Guardsmen to Little Rock to prevent the integration of Central High School, Ashmore endorsed President Eisenhower's use of federal troops to ensure desegregation. In an editorial he wrote, "We are going to have to decide what kind of people we are—whether we obey the law only when we approve of it, or whether we obey it no matter how distasteful we find it." By mid-October Ashmore had written more than 40 pro-integration editorials and appeared on television and radio pleading for compliance. Faubus denounced him as an "ardent integrationist" while the White Citizens' Councils branded him "Public Enemy No. 1." In December 1957 segregationists attempted a boycott of *Gazette* advertisers to induce a change in the paper's editorial policies. Its circulation did drop for a short time, but throughout the incident Hugh B. Patterson, Jr., the paper's publisher, backed Ashmore. In May 1958 Ashmore received the Pulitzer Prize for editorial writing. The *Gazette* also received a Prize for carrying his work.

Ashmore's book, *An Epitaph for Dixie* (1958), appeared following the Little Rock crisis. As the title indicated, he argued that the old South was dying. He predicted that its reliance on agriculture, its one-party political system and its racial policies would crumble in the face of the demands of a growing, Northern-oriented, industrialized society. Ashmore observed that a developing industrial elite would replace the old agrarian-based Southern high society. These new leaders, anxious for immediate economic growth, would realize that a prosperous black citizenry was essential for Southern prosperity and therefore would accept integration. Segregation, with all its political, social and economic consequences, must end so that blacks could be integrated into the new system. Ashmore also predicted that, in the future, blacks would be more aggressive in demanding their rights.

From 1955 to 1956 Ashmore took a leave of absence to work in Adlai Stevenson's [q.v.] presidential campaign. In September 1959 he left the *Gazette* to become a director of the Center for the Study of Democratic Institutions. At the Center he concentrated his attention on race relations and the press, defending the growing militancy of the civil rights movement in the mid-1960s. He was also a prominent critic of the Johnson Administration's Vietnam policy. Ashmore left the Center in 1974 amidst a financial crisis which curbed its activities. [See JOHNSON Volume]

[JB]

AVERY, SEWELL (LEE)
b. Nov. 4, 1874; Saginaw, Mich.
d. Oct. 31, 1960; Chicago, Ill.
Chairman of the Board, Montgomery Ward & Company, 1932-55.

The son of a wealthy lumberman, Avery managed one of his father's businesses, a plaster works, following his graduation from the University of Michigan in 1894. The plaster works was soon combined with other companies to form U.S. Gypsum Co. The enterprising Avery became its president at the age of 30. Twenty-eight years later, at the initiative of J.P. Morgan & Co., Avery assumed the board chairmanship of Montgomery Ward & Co. Avery turned the debt-ridden mail and retail department store chain into an again viable competitor. Operating in a highly autocratic fashion, he recruited the best marketers and upgraded Ward's merchandise line. By 1939 Ward's sales approached 75% of those of Sears Roebuck & Co., the field leader and the only department store chain surpassing Ward's in annual sales.

Politically, Avery was an extreme conservative. A frequent critic of the Roosevelt New Deal, he engaged in a long struggle during World War II over the recognition of a retail employe's union. In a dramatic climax President Roosevelt utilized special war powers in December 1943 and ordered the Army to seize Ward's Chicago building. Army police removed the intransigent Avery bodily from his offices.

Following the War Avery dictated company policy in anticipation of another imminent Great Depression. This fear led him to suspend all expansion; between 1941 and 1957 Ward opened no new stores. Even store modernization was kept to a minimum in the interest of maintaining high liquidity. Ward's earnings per share plummeted from $5.59 in 1950 to $2.62 in 1955. Its optimistic rival, Sears, expanded and increased its market share.

Ward suffered in other ways as a result of Avery's continued one-man rule. While Sears decentralized, Ward consolidated its management structure. Avery dominated its management past his 80th birthday. Subordinates quit or were fired at an unusually rapid rate: in August 1953 Avery caused the resignation of his 32nd vice president.

Avery's domination began to end in mid-1954. Between then and Ward's May 1955 annual shareholders' meeting, Florida investor Louis E. Wolfson [q.v.] tried to buy controlling interest in Ward to exercise effective management. Wolfson planned to replace Avery. "Among the most widely publicized corporate skirmishes of the century," as *Financial World* described it in 1959, the battle ended with Wolfson's failure to secure more than 1% of Ward stock. Yet the Wolfson campaign itself placed enormous pressures on Avery, who at one point asked Teamster Union president James Hoffa [q.v.] to purchase shares on his behalf. Anti-Wolfson forces among the major shareholders forced Avery's resignation at the 1955 annual meeting. His successor, John A. Barr, soon inaugurated an ambitious capital expansion program and decentralized operations on the Sears model. Despite Barr's initiatives, however, Ward's sales and earnings lagged through the decade.

[JLB]

BARDEN, GRAHAM A(RTHUR)
b. Sept. 26, 1896; Sampson Co., N.C.
d. Jan. 29, 1967; New Bern, N.C.
Democratic Representative, N.C., 1935-61; Chairman, Education and Labor Committee, 1950-61.

Barden served in the Navy during World War I and then studied at the University of North Carolina at Chapel Hill, where he received an LL.B. in 1920. He practiced law in New Bern, N.C., while serving as judge of the Craven Co. Court from 1920 to 1924. Barden represented the County in the North Carolina General Assembly in 1933.

The following year Barden was elected to the U.S. House of Representatives, where he was known as a conservative and an opponent of organized labor. However, he did sponsor vocational rehabilitation and education bills. In 1949, as chairman of a subcommittee of the Education and Labor Committee, he introduced a school-aid bill that provided no assistance for either parochial schools or schools for racial minorities. Francis Cardinal Spellman [q.v.] of New York attacked Barden as a "new apostle of bigotry," and Rep. John Lesinski (D, Mich.), chairman of the Education and Labor Committee, charged that the bill "dripped with bigotry and racial prejudice." In 1950, following Lesinski's death, Barden became chairman of the Education and Labor Committee.

Barden expressed his conservative views in his assertion that he "never knew the Republic to be endangered by a bill that was not passed." Because of this belief and his desire to control the education and labor panel, he called few meetings of the Committee. To further enhance his dominance, he decided personally which subcommittee would receive each bill. By 1955, however, the number of liberals on the panel had increased sufficiently to cause a revolt against the chairman. Barden agreed to establish a regular schedule of Committee meetings and to create subcommittees with specified areas of jurisdiction. He rejected the liberals' request that subcommittee chairmen be appointed on the basis of seniority. In practice, however, Barden did appoint chairmen on that basis with the exception of Rep. Adam Clayton Powell, Jr., (D, N.Y.) [q.v.], a black, whom he refused to appoint. Barden contended that his objections to Powell were of a personal rather than a racial nature.

In 1955 Barden backed an Administration bill to raise the minimum wage from 75 to 90 cents. During Committee hearings he opposed a greater increase, asserting that with a $1 minimum rate many firms might have to "turn their employes loose to join the unemployment rolls." However, the Committee passed a $1 minimum wage bill which became law in August. In 1960 another minimum wage bill failed to pass in part because Barden, the chairman of the House delegation in a Senate-House conference, insisted upon the $1.15 minimum voted by the House instead of the $1.25 minimum in the Senate version.

In 1960 the Education and Labor Committee considered a bill to legalize common-site picketing, which would have permitted unions to picket a firm at a construction site even if the effect was to stop the work of other firms at the same location. Barden opposed the measure, stating that employers on a construction site generally did not act as partners. He also said that it would have a "devastating effect . . . on the health and welfare of a community, or upon our national defense effort." The bill passed the Education and Labor Committee but was blocked by the Rules Committee.

In 1955 the Education and Labor Committee passed a school-construction aid bill. Barden backed the measure and sponsored it on the House floor the following year. However, he withdrew his sponsorship after the chamber adopted an amendment, offered by Rep. Powell, barring federal funds for segregated schools. Two years later he opposed a scholarship provision, designed to meet the Soviet technological threat, in a school-aid bill. Barden claimed the measure was based on the "idea that all you have to do is put a million dollars in the slot and have a scientist drop out." The scholarship plan cleared the Committee but was stricken on the House floor. The fol-

lowing year Barden opposed a school-construction aid bill, which was passed by the panel but blocked by the Rules Committee. In 1960 he attacked a Senate-passed measure eliminating the non-Communist affidavit requirement from the National Defense Education Act of 1958. The bill was pigeonholed in the Education and Labor Committee.

In January 1960 Barden announced that he would not seek reelection. He died of cancer in New Bern, N.C., seven years later.

[MLL]

BATES, DAISY (GATSON)
b. 1922; Huttig, Ark.
President, Arkansas NAACP, 1953-61.

Daisy Gatson grew up on farms in eastern Arkansas. She attended Philander Smith College and Shorter College in Little Rock, Ark., and in 1941 founded the Arkansas *State Press* with her husband, L.C. Bates, to advance the cause of black rights. Daisy Bates first became known in the civil rights movement in 1946, when she was found guilty on contempt charges in circuit court for criticizing the trial of a black defendant. This conviction was overturned by the Arkansas Supreme Court.

When the U.S. Supreme Court ruled public school segregation unconstitutional in May 1954, a number of Arkansas school districts desegregated voluntarily. This process was supported by Gov. Francis A. Cherry [q.v.], who promised compliance with the law. In November 1954 Orval Faubus [q.v.] was elected governor, pledging not to "force" integration on those communities who opposed it. Several attempts to delay integrating Little Rock schools were challenged by Mrs. Bates and the NAACP and nullified in federal court.

Little Rock's school board prepared to integrate Central High School in September 1957. Nine black students were selected by the NAACP and coached in Daisy Bates's home on nonviolent reaction to expected segregationist abuse. Beginning in August 1957 and for the next two years, Daisy Bates was regarded as the driving force behind Little Rock's integration effort. Her life was repeatedly threatened. In September Gov. Faubus uttered his famous warning that "blood will run in the streets" if integration were attempted, and he called out the National Guard to keep black students from entering Central. Later in the month President Dwight D. Eisenhower federalized the Arkansas Guard. He dispatched federal troops to maintain order and escort the blacks through hostile mobs to Central High. Central was forcibly integrated, but in October Little Rock's City Council ordered the arrest of Daisy Bates and other civil rights activitists on charges of failing to register as NAACP members under a new law. The defendants were convicted and fined in municipal court in December 1957. This conviction was overturned by the Supreme Court in 1960.

Little Rock remained under court order to desegregate all of its schools. Faubus closed all Little Rock high schools in September 1958. As they prepared to reopen on an integrated basis, Daisy Bates's home was bombed in July 1959. She escaped injury and wired Attorney General William P. Rogers [q.v.] requesting federal protection. When this was denied she telegraphed President Eisenhower, who referred her back to the Justice Department. All Little Rock's high schools reopened on an integrated basis in September 1959, and the tide of violence began to ebb.

Daisy Bates told her story in a book, *The Long Shadow of Little Rock* (1962). She continued to be an activist and 10 years later denounced President Richard Nixon's [q.v.] cutoff of Office of Economic Opportunity funds for an Arkansas community as "economic genocide." In 1974 Bates was honored for her role in Little Rock by the National Black Political Convention. She remained a trustee of the NAACP. [MJS]

BATTLE, JOHN S(TEWART)
b. July 11, 1890; New Bern, N.C.
d. April 9, 1972; Charlottesville, Va.
Member, U.S. Civil Rights Commission, 1958-59.

John S. Battle, the son of a Baptist minister, received his LL.B. at the University of Virginia in 1913. A member of the conser-

vative Democratic Byrd machine in Virginia politics, he served 19 years in the House of Delegates and state Senate, where he became chairman of the Finance Committee. In 1949 Sen. Harry Byrd (D, Va.) [q.v.] picked the state Senator as the organization's candidate for governor. He won the August 1950 primary against the strongest liberal Democratic challenge to Byrd dominance in decades and went on to win the general election in November. Fiscally liberal by Byrd machine standards, Battle pioneered a $75 million public school building program.

Battle gained prominence at the 1952 Democratic National Convention, when he led three rebellious Southern delegations from Virginia, Louisiana and South Carolina, in refusing to sign a loyalty oath. The oath required delegates to support the Convention's presidential ticket, a pledge politically anathema in some Southern states because of the fear that the Convention would choose a civil rights supporter. Battle insisted the defiant delegates be seated. They were, and he went home a hero to support the Convention nominee, Adlai Stevenson [q.v.], while Virginia's Democratic Party remained neutral.

Although Battle was a firm segregationist, he refused Sen. Byrd's call for "massive resistance" to school desegregation. Fully formulated by 1957, Byrd's resistance program called for states to block federal integration orders they deemed illegal. Some states declared the Supreme Court's desegregation decision itself null and void. Battle's position was apparently noticed by President Eisenhower. In August 1957 Congress created a six-member Civil Rights Commission to investigate voting rights violations as part of that year's Civil Rights Act. Trying to include a broad range of opinion, Eisenhower appointed Battle to the Commission in November. During Senate confirmation hearings in February 1958, the former North Carolina Governor described his job as exclusively fact-finding. The Committee approved his appointment to the post at the beginning of March.

During the Commission's first public hearings, Battle clashed with Alabama officials attempting to obstruct its work. Six Montgomery registrars refused to produce subpoenaed voting records, and Judge George Wallace threatened to jail registrars who complied. Battle assailed the officials, warning of new federal rights legislation if the defiance continued. He then joined the Commission in asking U.S. Attorney General William P. Rogers [q.v.] to take appropriate legal action.

Battle dissented from the Civil Rights Commission's first report to Congress, presented in the summer of 1959. It offered specific legislation to assure equal voting, educational and housing rights. He thought this exceeded the Commission's mandate. Insisting present civil rights guarantees were sufficient and should be enforced, Battle urged only the investigation of voting rights and did not favor sending federal registrars into the South. Battle concluded that the Commission's report was not factual and impartial as Congress had intended. The former North Carolina Governor maintained that the document was only "an argument in advocacy of preconceived ideas in race relations."

Noting that the Commission had completed its two-year term, Battle resisted Eisenhower's plea to stay on and resigned his position in October 1959. He returned to his law practice in Charlottesville, Va. Battle died there on April 9, 1972.

[MJS]

BEAM, JACOB D(YNELEY)
b. March 24, 1908; Princeton, N.J.
Deputy Director, State Department Policy Planning Staff, June 1953-June 1957; Ambassador to Poland, June 1957-December 1961.

Beam, the son of a university professor, attended the Kent School in Connecticut and Princeton University, from which he graduated in 1929. Following a year of graduate study at Cambridge University, he served as a clerk at the U.S. consulate in Geneva. From 1934 to 1940 he was assigned to the American embassy in Berlin. Beam served as secretary to the ambassador to Great Britain, John J. Winant, during

World War II. From 1945 to 1947 he worked on the staff of the U.S. political adviser in Germany. Beam became consul general in Java in 1949, and during the early 1950s he was a U.S. Information Service Officer in Belgrade. Beam temporarily headed the embassy in Moscow after Ambassador George F. Kennan [q.v.] had been declared persona non grata in October 1952. He remained there through the tense period of Stalin's death, leaving in April 1953, when Charles Bohlen [q.v.] became ambassador. Beam became deputy director of the State Department's policy planning staff that June.

President Eisenhower appointed Beam ambassador to Poland in June 1957. Along with his embassy responsibilities, the new American ambassador was given the task of negotiating with Communist China in the only official contact the U.S. then had with that country. The primary issue under discussion was the mainland Chinese shelling of the offshore islands of Quemoy and Matsu, held by Nationalist China.

At talks held during the fall of 1958, Beam and his Chinese counterpart, Wang Ping-nan, found themselves deadlocked. Beam demanded an immediate ceasefire after which the U.S. would negotiate to have the islands neutralized through a gradual Nationalist withdrawal. Wang, on the other hand, maintained that the ceasefire did not concern the U.S. because its troops were not under attack. He demanded Nationalist withdrawal from the islands and the removal of U.S. troops from Formosa. Although the Communists did gradually stop the shelling, Beam and Wang failed to come to an agreement on the subject. The diplomat continued his contacts with the Chinese until he left his post in December 1961, when he was appointed deputy director of the U.S. Disarmament Agency.

President Lyndon B. Johnson appointed Beam ambassador to Czechoslovakia in 1968. The following year President Richard M. Nixon appointed him ambassador to the Soviet Union. Beam held this post until his retirement in 1973. [See NIXON/FORD Volume]

[JB]

BECK, DAVE
b. June 16, 1894; Stockton, Calif.
President, International Brotherhood of
Teamsters, 1952-57.

The son of a carpet cleaner, Beck was
forced to leave high school before graduation because of his family's financial difficulties. He went to work in a laundry and
then became a laundry wagon driver. In
1917 he became a charter member of Seattle, Wash., Local 566 of the International
Brotherhood of Teamsters (IBT). During
World War I Beck was a machinist's mate
with the Naval Aviation Service. He resumed work as a laundry driver after the
War; in 1923 he was elected to the executive board of his local and two years later
became secretary-treasurer. Beck was chosen president of the local in 1927.

During the 1930s and 1940s, Beck moved
up through the ranks of the IBT to become
one of the most powerful Teamster leaders
in the nation. Acknowledging his work in
organizing the West Coast, the IBT elected
him to the newly created position of executive vice president in 1947. When IBT
president Dan Tobin retired in 1952, Beck
was elected Teamster president. He also sat
on the Executive Council of the American
Federation of Labor (AFL) and became one
of its vice presidents in 1953.

Described as a practical man with a
"business rather than a social philosophy,"
Beck began a program to expand and consolidate the Teamsters' power. Under Tobin
the union had been composed of a series of
locals with leaders interested only in their
own affairs. When Beck took over he employed the techniques he had used on the
West Coast to forge a centralized structure.
He formed regional conferences and
merged small locals to centralize power
groups. Along with the conferences Beck
established 15 trade divisions that sought
contracts on an area-wide basis. Beck promised to double union membership by 1960
and alienated such labor leaders as Walter
Reuther [q.v.] by his willingness to raid
other unions. By 1955 the Teamsters controlled the nation's truck drivers in a
tightly centralized organization guided by

Beck and his right-hand man, Jimmy Hoffa
[q.v.]. In addition to trucking, the IBT
represented workers in municipal government, canneries, breweries and the taxi
industry. Reflecting the union's national
importance, in 1956 Beck moved its headquarters to Washington into a plush $5
million building facing the Capitol.

Beck had grave reservations about the
merger of the AFL and the Congress of Industrial Organizations (CIO) in 1955. Although he headed the largest AFL union,
he refused to take part in negotiations on
the merger and was away "on Teamster
business" when the pact was ratified. In a
press conference Beck maintained that the
merger had proceeded too quickly and that
many large problems remained. One of the
major issues unresolved between Reuther,
George Meany [q.v.] and Beck was the
Teamster leader's refusal to sign the organization's no-raiding pact. Beck, pushing to
increase his membership, hoped to achieve
his goal through a series of alliances in a
trade-union center apart from the AFL-
CIO.

During 1956 Beck became the focus of a
congressional investigation of union corruption. Robert Kennedy [q.v.], chief counsel
of the Senate Permanent Investigations
Subcommittee, learned that the union president had used $150,000 from the union
treasury to improve his vast estate and had
then sold his home to the IBT to repay the
loan while arranging to live in it rent free
for the rest of his life. Beck had also used
Teamster funds for personal purchases. In
January and February 1957 Beck avoided
testifying before the Select Committee on
Improper Activities in the Labor or
Management Field, first claiming to be sick
and then leaving the country on winter
cruises. On March 26 he finally appeared
before the panel, headed by Sen. John
McClellan (D, Ark.) [q.v.], to answer the
charges. Beck took the Fifth Amendment
90 times. Sen. McClellan accused him of
showing "flagrant disregard and disrespect
for honest and reputable unionism and for
the best interests and welfare of the laboring people of the country." The AFL-CIO
expelled Beck from its Executive Council
for refusing to answer the Committee's

questions. As a result of pressure from the IBT, Beck did not seek reelection that year.

Following his retirement Beck became involved in a series of legal cases dealing with the charges aired before the Committee. In 1957 he was convicted of embezzling $1,900 for the sale of a union-owned Cadillac. Two years later he was indicted on charges of having violated the Taft-Hartley Act by borrowing $200,000 from trucking industry representatives, but he was acquitted in 1962. Between 1962 and 1965 he served a 30-month prison term after being convicted for filing a false federal income tax return. After his release Beck became a successful real estate promoter in Seattle.

[JB]

BELL, DANIEL
b. May 10, 1919; New York, N.Y.
Sociologist.

The son of Polish-Jewish garment workers, Bell grew up on New York's Lower East Side. A precocious student, Bell was soon attracted to the socialist movement. Following his graduation from City College in 1938, he edited the Social Democratic *New Leader*. In 1945 he briefly held the job of managing editor at *Common Sense*. Bell left journalism in the fall of 1945 to become an instructor in social sciences at the University of Chicago. Three years later he became labor editor of *Fortune*. He continued in that post until 1958 while maintaining ties to the academic community as a part-time instructor at Columbia University. He assumed full-time teaching at Columbia in 1959, gradually rising to the rank of professor by 1962.

During the 1950s Bell was an articulate spokesmen for the growing centrist movement among postwar intellectuals. In a series of essays, Bell extolled the diversity of contemporary American society and politics. His most influential work of the decade was his introduction to *The New American Right* (1955), a collection of articles by scholars which publicized the view that McCarthyism was heir to the radical populist and agrarian agitation of an earlier

time. Bell thought McCarthyism was a manifestation of the social tensions of the postwar period. McCarthy's attack on Communists afforded an outlet for the "status anxieties" of various social groups. These included: the "new middle class" of German and Irish-Americans which felt it had to prove its patriotism in light of World War II; the "soured patricians," members of old upper classes who saw their power diminishing; and the "new rich," uneasy with the way they acquired their wealth. Combined with an inbred American populism, "with its insistence on disclosure and leveling," these status anxieties produced impressive support for McCarthy.

Bell argued that McCarthyism was unique in American life because it injected ideology into the mainstream of American politics. Previously, he said, it had been confined to such tangential issues as prohibition and Sunday blue laws. Bell feared that the divisions it produced were inherently irreconcilable and not amenable to the traditional American way of compromise. "The tendency to convert issues into ideologies, to invest them with moral color and high emotional charge, invites conflicts which can only derange a society," Bell warned. "The new divisions created by status anxieties of new middle class groups pose a new threat. The rancor of McCarthyism was one of its ugly excesses." Bell's remedy was to return to the pragmatic, issue-oriented politics of the pre-New Deal age and a political system divorced from the intervention of moral issues.

In 1960 Bell published *The End of Ideology: On the Exhaustion of Political Ideas in the Fifties*. The work was soon acclaimed as a classic, for many summing up the political consensus of the period. Reviewing the developments of the twentieth century, Bell argued that the Depression, the World Wars and the emergence of the welfare state had destroyed radical faith in mass movements for social change. He urged intellectuals to take the responsibility for defining and working toward limited, empirical social goals. During the 1960s Bell, in his book *The Radical Right*, continued to stress the effect of status anxiety in the development of American conservatism. Toward the end of the decade, he grew increasingly pessimistic about government's ability to produce beneficial social change. In 1969 Bell left Columbia's sociology department for Harvard. [See KENNEDY Volume]

[AES]

For further information:
Daniel Bell, *The New American Right* (New York, 1955).
—————, *The End of Ideology* (New York, 1960).
"Daniel Bell," *Current Biography Yearbook, 1973* (New York, 1974), pp. 40-42.

BENNETT, WALLACE F(OSTER)
b. Nov. 13, 1898; Salt Lake City, Utah.
Republican Senator, Utah, 1951-75.

Born into a Mormon family, Bennett attended a church high school and received a B.A. from the University of Utah in 1919. Shortly afterwards he entered his father's paint and glass firm. When his father died in 1938, Bennett became president and general manager of the business. In December 1948 he was elected president of the National Association of Manufacturers. The Mormon emphasis upon hard work and individual responsibility shaped his conservative political views. He opposed extensive social welfare programs and what he regarded as excessive government regulation of the economy. In 1950 he won a U.S. Senate seat by defeating the incumbent, liberal Sen. Elbert Thomas (D, Utah), with 53.9% of the vote.

Serving on the Banking and Currency and Finance Committees, Bennett was a leading spokesman for the Eisenhower Administration on matters of taxation and finance. He supported a 1954 Administration tax revision bill that was criticized by many Democrats for allegedly providing more tax relief to big business than to individual taxpayers. When Democrats unsuccessfully attempted to reduce personal income taxes the following year, Bennett defended the 1954 measure as "carefully balanced to bring some measure of relief to every part of our economy" and denounced the

Democratic proposal as "the height of fiscal irresponsibility."

An opponent of strong federal controls over the economy, in May 1955 Bennett dissented from a majority report of the Banking and Currency Committee that recommended tightening existing regulations of the stock market and investigating the possibility of fraud and manipulation in the sharp rise of stock prices during the preceding 15 months. Bennett, along with Sens. Homer E. Capehart (R, Ind.), [q.v.], John W. Bricker (R, Ohio) [q.v.] and J. Glenn Beall (R, Md.), denounced the majority for attempting "to disturb the economy" and "to weaken the confidence of the people in the Administration. . . ."

A persistent critic of social welfare programs, in 1957 Bennett successfully offered a floor amendment to a housing bill to retain the federal contribution to slum clearance and urban renewal at two-thirds of the cost rather than raising it to three-quarters, as proposed by the Banking and Currency panel. In both 1958 and 1959 he was among the minority on the Committee that voted against reporting out area redevelopment bills to aid regions suffering from chronic unemployment.

Bennett supported legislation to promote the economic growth of his state. In 1955 he backed a billion-dollar program to construct water storage facilities in the Upper Colorado River Basin, an important project for promoting agriculture and the production of minerals in Utah. The measure became law the following year. In 1956 he contributed an amendment to the Defense Production Act that directed the government to promote the geographical dispersal of defense-related industries. He contended that dispersal was "one of the best ways to insure the survival of this nation in the event of an attack. . . ." Tax incentives resulting from the amendment played a major role in attracting the missile industry to Utah.

During the early 1960s Bennett helped defeat a truth-in-lending proposal in the Banking and Currency Committee. He voted against most of the Kennedy Administration's social welfare programs, including the aid-to-education bill in 1961, medicare in 1962 and mass transit aid in

1962 and 1963. During the Johnson presidency Bennett opposed the bulk of the Administration's Great Society programs but supported its civil rights measures. He was a strong backer of the Vietnam war. In 1974 Bennett announced that he would not seek reelection. [See KENNEDY, JOHNSON, NIXON/FORD Volumes]

[MLL]

BENSON, EZRA TAFT
b. Aug. 4, 1899; Whitney, Idaho.
Secretary of Agriculture, January 1953-January 1961.

Descended from Mormon pioneers who accompanied Brigham Young on the 1847 westward trek, Benson grew up on an Idaho farm and attended Utah State Agricultural College. He performed the required Mormon missionary service in Europe during 1922-23 and then returned to work on his father's farm while continuing his agricultural studies. He received a B.S. degree in 1926 from Brigham Young University. Benson took an M.S. degree in agricultural economics at Iowa State College the following year. In the early 1930s he worked as a county agricultural agent for the University of Idaho Extension Service and later helped organize the Idaho Cooperative Council, of which he was secretary from 1933 to 1939. In the latter year he went to Washington to assume the post of executive secretary of the National Council of Farm Cooperatives, a position in which he represented 4,600 member cooperatives whose annual business approximated $1.3 billion. Although Benson served with many government agencies during his Washington tenure, including the National Farm Credit Committee and the National Agricultural Advisory Commission, he was a sharp critic of President Franklin Roosevelt's activist farm policies. In 1943 Benson gave up his influential job when he was selected to become the youngest member of the Quorum of Twelve Apostles, the ruling group of the Mormon Church. Despite his church work, Benson served as director of the Farm Foundation from 1946 to 1950 and remained in the spotlight with zealous attacks on "paternalistic government" and calls to the cooperative movement to propagate the "free enterprise" system.

After Dwight D. Eisenhower's victory in November 1952, observers thought that he would name his brother, Milton S. Eisenhower [q.v.], to head the Department of Agriculture (USDA). But Milton was not interested in the job. Many prominent names were discussed until the President-elect settled on Benson, a relatively unknown figure nationally but highly recommended by farm leaders. At the time the appointment was interpreted as a concession to the conservative wing of the Republican Party led by Sen. Robert A. Taft (R, Ohio) [q.v.]. Nonetheless, Eisenhower assured Benson that he was in agreement with the new Secretary's plans to decrease government interference in agriculture and to make research, education and market development the USDA's prime responsibilities.

Farm policy constituted one of the most complex and intractable problems in postwar American politics. Despite a steady decline in farm population, advanced technology concentrated in ever larger farm units produced crops at a rate greater than the rise in demand, resulting in enormous surpluses. Democratic administrations bought and stored the farmers' surplus at a high cost to the taxpayers. In combination with production controls this policy sought to ensure farmers incomes at or near parity with the non-farm population by subsidizing high prices in the market. Because of the relatively high demand created by postwar reconstruction and the Korean war, the surplus problem did not assume extraordinary proportions until the advent of the Eisenhower Administration, when prices declined. At the same time the price of manufactured goods purchased by farmers rose.

Secretary Benson believed that a return to the free market of supply and demand offered the best solution to the problems of overproduction and declining farm income. He argued that without artificial controls market prices would at first decline, thus encouraging farmers to cut production. Government price supports had encouraged overproduction, Benson said. Without supports agriculture could be more efficient, and lower prices would stimulate consumption and ensure a higher standard of living for the general population. In addition, he felt that continued dependence on the federal government would prove morally corrupting to the farmer. In response to critics who noted that laissez-faire would drive smaller, less efficient farmers out of business—and thus destroy the cherished family farm ideal—Benson argued that through education and marketing research some small farmers could find new markets while others could find non-farm work in their region. Besides, he pointed out, it was the giant commercial farm, not the small family unit, which benefited most from existing price support policies.

President Eisenhower asked Benson to move slowly in his goal to reinstate the free market in American agriculture because of the considerable opposition radical changes in USDA policy would evoke in Congress and the farm states. In his election campaign Eisenhower had been intentionally ambiguous about whether he would continue to support 90% of parity price supports after the law establishing that level expired in 1954. Benson aroused the ire of a number of farm-belt Republican senators in his January 1953 confirmation hearings when he refused to commit the Administration to an extension of 90% of parity price supports for the six basic crops (wheat, corn, cotton, rice, peanuts and tobacco) for three additional years. Criticism of Benson increased when, in his first public speech as Secretary, he told a February meeting of cattle raisers concerned about falling beef prices that they should produce for a free market and consider price supports only as "disaster insurance" rather than as an encouragement to "uneconomic production." Democrats and some Republicans immediately seized upon the speech as an insult to stockmen.

Benson's reorganization of the USDA with the aid of the interim National Agricultural Advisory Commission established by President Eisenhower in July 1953 irritated Republican farm-bloc leaders whom Benson neglected to consult about new appointments. Granted greater powers than his predecessors, Benson angered Democrats in November by abolishing the Production and Marketing Administration (PMA), a New Deal stronghold, and the Bureau of Agricultural Economics (BAE) and also by substantially reducing the authority of the Soil Conservation Service. In place of the PMA and the BAE, he set up the Commodity Stabilization Service to handle production control and price support functions and the Agricultural Marketing Service to handle marketing functions. Because of his desire to enlarge agricultural exports, Benson fostered the creation of the Foreign Agricultural Service to develop markets abroad. Finally, the Secretary reorganized the USDA into four branches, each headed by an assistant secretary: federal-state relations, marketing and foreign agriculture, agricultural stabilization and agricultural credit.

Benson's public statements and reorganization program as well as a steady decline in farm prices accelerated by the close of the Korean war elicited widespread calls for his resignation. President Eisenhower publicly declared his confidence in the Secretary, but privately cautioned Benson to moderate his attacks on high price supports.

In 1954 Benson presented Congress with a new farm package intended for implementation in 1955. He wanted to set aside a certain part of government surpluses so that they could be eliminated from price support computations. More importantly, he favored a new system of flexible price supports for basic commodities that could be gradually related to supply. Speaking before the Senate Agriculture and Forestry Committee in April 1954, Benson said that the current program had become unmanageable because even the acreage allotments, marketing quotas and cross-compliance which he had long criticized were being circumvented for reasons of political expediency. As expected, many of Benson's recommendations were assailed by farm-bloc congressmen, but they won the approval of a group of urban liberal Democrats.

In order to ensure the farm bill's passage,

President Eisenhower took the Benson plan to the public, pointing out that a change from rigid to flexible price supports would affect less than one-fourth of the income received by farmers. In June 1954 Benson and Vice President Richard Nixon [q.v.] appeared on national television to inform the American people that a flexible price support program would merely implement legislation passed in 1949. Benson explained that after World War II the nation "stopped all-out production of munitions and ships [but] we didn't put a stop to all-out production of surplus food."

In August the Agricultural Act of 1954 was finally passed after prolonged debate. Flexible price supports ranged from 82.5% to 90% of parity for basic crops—Benson had desired a minimum level of 75%—in 1955 and thereafter from 75% to 90% depending upon market prices. Of the six basic crops only tobacco, which had no surplus problem, had a mandatory 90% support level. Commodity Credit Corporation (CCC) surplus holdings were set aside, as Benson had requested, to be used for foreign and domestic disaster relief, school lunch programs, research and other purposes. Benson's victory was marred, however, when in September the White House, concerned about the November elections, overruled his stringent controls on wheat acreage allotments. Nonetheless, the perception of Benson as a political liability seemed to be refuted by the elections, in which pro-Benson congressmen ran better than his critics in the farm belt.

The success of a flexible price support policy depended in large part upon unloading surpluses abroad. The Agricultural Trade Development and Assistance Act, passed in July 1954, met some of Benson's policy goals. The bill authorized the sale of surpluses abroad in exchange for foreign currencies with a provision allowing the CCC to take a $700 million annual loss in such transactions. The President could also send needy nations up to $300 million worth of surpluses over a three-year period. Another provision allowed the government to barter food for goods essential to national security.

The disposal of surpluses abroad was politically complicated. If sold at price-supported domestic prices, most U.S. commodities could not compete with foreign producers in the world market. On the other hand, any dumping might violate the General Agreement on Tariffs and Trade (GATT) and disturb the equilibrium of international trade. Despite these difficulties Benson undertook a series of foreign tours to Latin America, Canada and Europe in 1955 in order to promote U.S. farm products. However, his agressive trade expansion program was opposed by Secretary of State John Foster Dulles [q.v.], who did not wish to weaken the economies of American allies. The Dulles policy yielded some markets to allies and nonaligned nations in the interest of national security. In addition, the State Department steadfastly opposed trade with Communist-bloc nations, thereby eliminating a potentially important market for American farmers. Benson, a fierce anti-Communist, was not inclined to confront Dulles on this particular issue, but expansion of exports remained one of the most consistent and possibly one of the most successful themes of his tenure. The Secretary frequently traveled abroad on trade missions.

By the late fall of 1955 Republicans were already worried about the 1956 elections. The decline in farm income by 20% since the peak of the Korean war, with no upturn in sight, was one of the major causes for concern. In 1955 a new protest movement, the National Farm Organization (NFO), was established. The NFO demanded 100% of parity and advocated collective bargaining for farmers. It was clear to leading Republicans that the Administration needed a new agricultural program to win farmer confidence. Benson refused to repudiate his price support policy, but he responded in December 1955 with the Soil Bank, a land-retirement program that had been promoted by both Democrats and Republicans in the past. Under the plan the government would pay farmers either to retire a specified amount of land from production or to devote the land to conservation practices. Production of basics could then be reduced while giving farmers financial incentives to improve the soil. Some of Benson's conservative supporters, opposed to federal subsidies, criticized the Soil Bank, while his opponents attacked it as insufficient to bring farm income up to nonfarm levels. Nonetheless, Benson believed the Soil Bank could help stem overproduction, and he had been in the Administration long enough to recognize its political value.

In January 1956 President Eisenhower offered Congress the "Soil Bank" as the cornerstone of his farm program, stressing the contribution the Bank could make to conservation rather than its economic benefits to farmers. In addition, the President asked Congress to expand surplus disposal programs. But Eisenhower also clearly indicated his intention to reduce surpluses by either tightening acreage controls or lowering price supports.

Debate on the new farm package was spirited. In March Rep. Wayne Hays (D, Ohio) [q.v.] recommended that Benson be impeached, if, as had been reported, the Secretary had offered to make a deal with three Democratic senators to raise price supports for cotton in exchange for their votes in favor of flexible price supports. The three Senators in question, James Eastland (D, Miss.) [q.v.], John Stennis (D, Miss.) [q.v.] and Carl Hayden (D, Ariz.) [q.v.], had, in fact, supported the Administration, but nothing came of the Hays charge.

In April Congress passed an omnibus farm bill that included most of the President's recommendations but also restored 90% supports for basics, higher supports for dairy products, two-price plans for wheat and rice and other costly measures. President Eisenhower took Benson's advice and vetoed the bill. Efforts by the majority of Democrats and some farm-belt Republicans to override the veto failed. The Agricultural Act signed in May was a compromise. Administration plans to pay farmers in advance of their Soil Bank contracts—and, therefore, before the November elections—failed, but the Soil Bank itself was established and the surplus disposal provisions approved. The opposition won floors on cotton and rice acreage, a cotton export program and a two-price plan for rice. It also gained mandatory supports for small grains

and a temporary freeze on transitional parity.

Benson's reputation now rested largely on the performance of the Soil Bank. He knew there was little chance that it would be an immediate success. The program was expensive, and farmers might cultivate their reduced acreage more intensively. Through 1957 production continued to outstrip demand, farm income fell and USDA spending exceeded its budget. Despite the surplus disposal program high production kept CCC holdings constant.

The only major bill Benson presented to Congress in 1957 proposed to allow corn farmers to expand their acreage allotments and still remain eligible for price supports, provided they agreed to participate in the Soil Bank. Since the bill was considered too favorable to the corn area, a coalition of Southern and urban congressmen combined to defeat the plan in March. In May Benson suggested that the parity floors for price supports be lowered or the Secretary be given the authority to set levels at anywhere from zero percent to 90 percent of parity. The recommendation made clear his refusal to cease pressing for more flexible price supports.

Meanwhile, the Secretary directed criticism at another area of congressional inaction. Speaking at the University of Tennessee in June 1957, he charged that congressional unwillingness to fund the Rural Development Program (RDP), established in 1955, prejudiced the future of the family farm that figured so prominently in congressional rhetoric. Benson said that the program could alleviate rural poverty by teaching either modern farming techniques or non-farm skills and by providing easier credit and health services. An ambitious RDP, Benson implied, could cope with the dislocations that might be caused by the end of price supports. Rural development, however, did not receive substantial funding until the 1960s.

In 1958 Benson persisted in his efforts to move toward a free market. He and President Eisenhower proposed lowering the support scale for basics and dairy products from 70% to 90% of parity. The Secretary predicted that lower prices and increased sales would result and that production controls could be eased or perhaps eliminated for corn. But the Democratic Congress passed a freeze on price supports and acreage restrictions, prompting a presidential veto in March. The Agricultural Act of 1958, enacted in August, was another compromise. Benson and the Administration got an eventual reduction of price support floors for corn, upland cotton and rice from 75% to 65% of parity, while various congressional groups won removal of limits on corn production and a bar to further large cutbacks in rice and cotton allotments.

Despite a slight increase in farm income in 1958, overproduction continued and discontent was widespread in the farm belt. On Feb. 30 farm-bloc Republican congressmen had requested Benson's resignation, stating that his farm policies would cost the Republicans 20 to 25 House seats in the elections. As in the past Eisenhower stood by Benson. But although Benson campaigned vigorously in the farm states, defending his program and asking voters whether they wanted "a truly American or a left-wing dominated Congress for the next two critical years," the Democrats won impressive gains in both the House and Senate. Democratic dominance ensured that Benson could not hope to maintain the limited successes he had achieved.

However, Benson persuaded the President to propose his most far-reaching agricultural program yet: abandonment of both the parity concept and the idea of a statutory price-support floor based on parity. In his January 1959 message to Congress, Eisenhower suggested that price supports be used to prevent precipitate price drops rather than to sustain farm prices against long-range market trends. The President recommended that either supports for a commodity in a given year be fixed at some percentage of its average market prices during the three years preceding or that supports be made discretionary, to be fixed by the Secretary at zero percent to 90% of parity. Not surprisingly, Congress ignored the Benson proposals.

In October 1959 Benson made a trip to the Soviet Union, where he delivered a sermon to a Moscow Baptist congregation, advising it to "love all mankind [and] strive for peace." On his return the Secretary said that he was more convinced than ever of the "superiority of our system of privately owned family-sized farms, the profit system, freedom for the farmer to decide what to grow and market, and competitive markets."

Some conservative Republicans tried to persuade Benson to run for the 1960 presidential nomination. The Secretary, however, did not want to remain in public life. Furthermore, it was clear that Vice President Nixon was the favorite to capture the nomination and that Benson was too unpopular in the Party to be nominated. The Democrats were preparing the most comprehensive farm platform in history, which sought to capitalize on anti-Benson feeling, promising farmers full parity of income with the non-farm population. Fearing the effect of the Benson legacy on the 1960 elections, several farm-belt members of the Republican National Committee got GOP National Chairman Sen. Thruston B. Morton (R, Ky.) [q.v.] to ask for Benson's resignation in December 1959. Nixon tried to dissociate himself from Benson and successfully persuaded Eisenhower to moderate his final farm message to Congress. Yet he had generally supported Benson, and his 1960 campaign platform advocated a continuation of the Secretary's policies. Benson had hoped to campaign for the Nixon ticket, but he was sidelined by the Republican nominee. Nonetheless, the Secretary was able to get his views across by circulating a personal statement, "Where We Stand," at the GOP National Convention and with publication of his book, *Freedom to Farm*.

Benson returned to Salt Lake City in January 1961 to resume his work with the Quorum of Twelve Apostles. He continued his interest in agriculture, and in the mid-1960s he was a vigorous defender of the John Birch Society.

[JCH]

For further information:
Edward L. Schapsmeier and Frederick H. Schapsmeier, *Ezra Taft Benson and the Politics of Agriculture: The Eisenhower Years, 1953-1961* (Danville, Ill., 1975).

BENTON, WILLIAM (BURNETT)
b. April 1, 1900; Minneapolis, Minn.
d. March 18, 1973; New York, N.Y.
Democratic Senator, Conn., 1949-53.

The descendant of a family which first settled in Connecticut during the seventeenth century, Benton was born and raised in Minneapolis. After service in the Army during World War I, he entered Yale and received his degree in 1921. Benton turned down a Rhodes Scholarship for a job as advertising copywriter with the George Batten agency in New York. During the 1920s he rose in the advertising world, and in 1929, he helped found the firm of Benton and Bowles with his Yale schoolmate Chester Bowles [q.v.]. The agency prospered inspite of, or some say because of, the Depression, pioneering in such fields as consumer surveys and sponsorship of soap operas.

In 1936 Benton left the advertising business to become vice president of the University of Chicago, then under the leadership of Robert Hutchins [q.v.]. He remained there for eight years, helping the University pioneer in the use of educational radio and movies. Benton also urged the University of Chicago to publish the *Encyclopedia Britainnica* and provided the necessary working capital for the venture. In 1943 he became chairman of the *Encyclopedia Britainnica*.

Benton served as assistant secretary of state from 1945 to 1947, supervising the Department's overseas information program. At that post he helped establish the United Nation's Education, Scientific and Cultural Organization (UNESCO) and organized the Voice of America broadcasts. In 1949 Chester Bowles, then governor of Connecticut, appointed his former advertising partner to fill a Senate seat vacated by the retiring Raymond Baldwin. He won reelection to the remainder of the term in 1950 by a bare 1,100 margin. During his short career Benton gained a reputation as one of the upper chamber's most liberal members.

The freshmen Senator quickly emerged as a major opponent of Sen. Joseph R. McCarthy (R, Wisc.) [q.v.]. Angered at

McCarthy's role in the 1950 Maryland senatorial campaign, during which McCarthy campaigned against Millard Tydings (D, Md.) [one of his most vocal critics] Benton began a personal crusade against the right-wing Senator. He was also disturbed by what he believed were McCarthy's outright lies in claiming knowledge of Communist subversion and by the Senator's denunciation of George Marshall as a Communist sympathizer.

In August Benton presented a resolution asking for an investigation of McCarthy's actions in order to decide if he should be expelled. The following month Benton presented a lengthy, biting indictment of the Senator on the Senate floor. In words that even his lawyers thought libelous, he excoriated McCarthy for his charges against Marshall, saying that if the Senator believed his "towering lies," this Congress "might investigate the precedent of an expulsion proceeding against a Senator thought to be of unsound mind." The Privileges and Elections Subcommittee reluctantly voted to investigate Benton's charges as well as McCarthy's countercharges. The Wisconsin Republican maintained that Benton had shielded security risks and had failed to report a $600 donation as part of his campaign funds. McCarthy refused to answer Benton's charges and testified before the panel only on his allegations against Benton.

In January 1954 the panel issued its report. It contained no recommendations but said that the probe raised questions about McCarthy's activities and charged that McCarthy had deliberately "set out to thwart the committee." (The Senator's conduct before the Committee proved the basis for one of the counts upon which he was later condemned in December.) The panel criticized Benton for accepting the $600 contribution but took no action. The Justice Department also cleared him of campaign irregularities.

While the probe was going on Benton, hoping to bring his crusade to court, had waived congressional immunity on his Senate speech against McCarthy. McCarthy then instituted a $2 million libel suit. The case, carried on during 1952 and 1953, proved inconclusive. In March 1954 McCarthy announced he had dropped the suit because his lawyers could find no one to testify that they believed Benton's charges. Benton's allies launched a campaign to gather signatures of "Believers"; 14,000 responded.

Benton lost his Senate seat in the 1952 election as a result of Dwight D. Eisenhower's victory in Connecticut. Out of office he criticized the Eisenhower Administration. In 1956 he charged that the GOP had failed to keep a 1952 campaign pledge to revise immigration restrictions and said the U.S. had been fortunate to "avoid disaster" under the Eisenhower Administration's foreign policy.

Benton attempted a political comeback in 1958. During the spring he ran for the Democratic senatorial nomination against his liberal friend Chester Bowles and conservative Thomas Dodd [q.v.]. Despite polls showing Bowles far in the lead and his friend's warning that his candidacy would split the liberal faction, Benton refused to drop out. At the convention Dodd won the nomination. Bowles attributed Benton's stubborn stand in part to pressure from Gov. Abraham Ribicoff [q.v.], who was up for reelection. According to Bowles, the Governor feared that having the controversial ex-Governor on the ticket would undermine his election strength. After his defeat Benton returned to his business. From 1963 to 1968 he was the U.S. member of the Executive board of UNESCO. Benton died in 1973.

[EWS]

BETHE, HANS A(LBRECHT)
b. July 2, 1906; Strasbourg, Alsace-Lorraine.
Member, President's Science Advisory Committee, 1956-60.

The son of a distinguished physiologist, Bethe was educated in Germany, where he received his doctorate in physics in 1928. He taught at various German universities, but because of his part-Jewish ancestry, fled the country in 1933. After a year in England he settled in the U.S. and joined the faculty of Cornell University, where his

research into celestial energy aided scientists in developing the hydrogen bomb. From 1943 to 1946 Bethe worked on the Manhattan Project under the direction of J. Robert Oppenheimer [q.v.]. Although the project's primary goal was to build an atomic or fission bomb, work also proceeded on the development of the hydrogen bomb. The latter project was blocked in 1944 because of technical problems.

Bethe and Oppenheimer became leading spokesmen for "finite containment" in the postwar debate over continuation of research on the hydrogen bomb. These scientists believed that a large stockpile of American nuclear arms was necessary to contain Soviet aggression. However they maintained that further technological advances would bring the supply of weapons to dangerous levels unwarranted by strategic considerations. Declaring that the Soviet Union was "largely imitative" in its atomic energy programs, they maintained that the U.S. could forego the hydrogen weapon without incurring a serious security risk. Instead, they suggested that work on the bomb be conducted only at a theoretical level. President Harry Truman rejected their advice, and reacting to recommendations of Edward Teller [q.v.], authorized production of the weapon in 1950. It was first exploded in November 1952. [See TRUMAN Volume]

During the early years of the Eisenhower Administration, Bethe became a leading defender of Oppenheimer, who had been suspended from his post as an Atomic Energy Commission (AEC) consultant in 1953 as an alleged security risk. In part, this suspension was based on his failure to endorse a "crash" program for the development of the hydrogen bomb. When the suspension and subsequent hearings were publicized in April 1954, Bethe was among the many outstanding scientists who declared their confidence in Oppenheimer and testified on his behalf. Following the AEC's decision not to reinstate Oppenheimer despite its finding that he was "loyal," Bethe released a statement by the American Physical Society denouncing the ruling as based on differences over nuclear weapons policy rather than on actual security risk.

In 1956 Bethe was appointed to the President's Science Advisory Committee. Two years later he became chairman of a special panel formed to study the possible effects of a nuclear test ban agreement between the U.S. and the Soviet Union and to research the efficiency of various methods of detecting atomic blasts. Bethe testified before the Senate Disarmament Subcommittee in April 1958 that the U.S. would gain "considerably" from a test ban if it included "a good inspection system with all the trimmings." He rejected Teller's testimony that the Soviet Union would benefit more than the U.S. and that adequate detection was impossible. Bethe maintained that if tests continued the USSR "will surely attain the same level of capability as we. . . . It is more advantageous to stop when . . . you are still ahead." He did, however, suggest that any ban include provisions for continued high altitude tests to gain information on such explosions.

Bethe attended the 1958 U.S.-Soviet disarmament talks in Geneva, where the two delegations agreed that any test ban accord would include acoustical, radiological, seismic and electromagnetic detection systems. A year later, in secret testimony before the Senate Disarmament Subcommittee, he recommended that a treaty also provide for satellite monitoring of explosions in outer space. The advocates of finite containment won a major victory in March 1960, when the U.S. and the USSR agreed to negotiate a ban on nuclear tests except for small underground ones considered unverifiable.

Bethe continued to serve as a presidential adviser in the Kennedy Administration. During his career he won many scientific honors, including the Max Planck Medal, West Germany's highest scientific honor, for his research on celestial energy. He received the AEC's Enrico Fermi Award in 1961 and the Nobel Prize in physics in 1967. Bethe continued to teach at Cornell through the 1970s.

[MDB]

For further information:
Robert Gilpin, *American Scientists and Nuclear Weapons Policy* (Princeton, 1962).

BIBLE, ALAN D.

b. Nov. 20, 1909; Lovelock, Nev.
Democratic Senator, Nev., 1954-75.

A protege and former law partner of Sen. Patrick McCarran (D, Nev.) [*q.v.*], Bible was attorney general of Nevada from 1942 to 1950. Following McCarran's death in 1954 Bible was elected to serve out the remainder of his term. He won reelection for a full six-year term in 1956.

During the Eisenhower Administration Bible voted as a moderately conservative Democrat, backing the party leadership in the Senate. He supported the Civil Rights Act of 1957 but only after voting for the elimination of a provision authorizing the Attorney General to institute civil action for preventive relief in civil rights cases. He also voted to remove a similar enforcement provision from the Civil Rights Act of 1960. By the late 1950s Bible was identified by *Congressional Quarterly* as one of a small number of Northern and Western Democrats who voted more than half the time with the conservative coalition of Southern Democrats and Republicans.

As a representative of a state heavily dependent on mining, Bible continued McCarran's efforts to raise lead and zinc tariffs. Calling attention to the depressed condition of the domestic minerals industry, Bible advocated the establishment of a national minerals policy to protect the industry from foreign competition. Under the plan domestic mining would be protected by a combination of subsidies, import limitations and other forms of aid. However, the Administration feared that heavy tariff increases would hurt foreign countries whose economies the U.S. wished to aid. When Eisenhower presented a minerals plan in 1957 providing for low sliding-scale import taxes on lead and zinc and limiting government assistance for mining exploration, Bible called it a "joke." Eisenhower imposed import quotas on lead and zinc in 1958. The move was widely interpreted as a trade-off in exchange for the support of Western congressmen for the Administration's reciprocal trade program. Bible never succeeded in getting the comprehensive subsidy program he had long desired.

During the Kennedy and Johnson Administrations, Bible's numerous committee assignments attested to his great influence. He sat on the Appropriations, Interior and Insular Affairs and Select Small Business Committees as well as the Special Committee on Aging and the Democratic Steering Committee. He was chairman of the District of Columbia Commitee from 1957 to 1968. Bible's record of support for the liberal legislation of the 1960s was mixed. [See KENNEDY, JOHNSON, NIXON/FORD Volumes]

[TLH]

BIEMILLER, ANDREW J(OHN)
b. July 23, 1906; Sandusky, Ohio.
Director, Department of Legislation, AFL-CIO, 1956- .

Born of Quaker parents, Andrew Biemiller graduated from Cornell University in 1926. He then taught history, specializing in the British trade union movement, at Syracuse University and the University of Pennsylvania. In 1932 he became a reporter for the Milwaukee *Leader*. From 1932 to 1942 he was labor-relations counselor and organizer for the Milwaukee Federation of Trade Councils and the Wisconsin State Federation of Labor. Biemiller was elected as a Socialist-Progressive to the Wisconsin legislature in 1936, serving there until 1942, when he became assistant to the vice-chairman for labor production of the War Production Board. Elected to Congress as a Democrat from Wisconsin's fifth district in 1944, he served from 1945 to 1946 and from 1949 to 1950. He was defeated for reelection in that traditionally Republican state in 1946 and 1952.

During 1951 and 1952 Biemiller was a special assistant to the Secretary of the Interior and a Washington public relations counselor. In 1953 he joined the American Federation of Labor (AFL) as a legislative lobbyist. There he helped AFL President George Meany [q.v.] negotiate the merger with the Congress of Industrial Organizations (CIO) that led to the creation of the AFL-CIO in 1955. Biemiller became director of the organization's department of legislation the following year.

As the AFL-CIO's chief lobbyist, Biemiller often opposed Eisenhower Administration measures on Capitol Hill. In 1957 he challenged Eisenhower's minimum wage bill, extending coverage to 2.5 million additional workers, as "too little too late." Instead he backed Rep. A. B. Kelley's (D, Pa.) unsuccessful measure that would have extended coverage to 9.7 million workers and raised the hourly wage to $1.25. Biemiller and the AFL-CIO favored medicare financed through Social Security rather than Eisenhower's voluntary health insurance proposals, and he worked with House Speaker Sam Rayburn (D, Tex.) [q.v.] to defeat the Administration program in 1957. The following year he supported increased school construction as a means of combating the recession and attacked Eisenhower's failure to mention the proposal in his anti-recession message to Congress. In 1959 he called Eisenhower's four-year, $1 billion housing program inadequate and condemned his lack of action on unemployment. That year Biemiller focused his attention on defeating the Landrum-Griffin bill, which contained provisions limiting secondary boycotts. His actions earned him the wrath of North Carolina Democratic Rep. Graham A. Barden [q.v.], who charged that he, Jimmy Hoffa [q.v.] and other labor leaders were trying to intimidate the members of the House of Representatives. Despite Biemiller's efforts, the measure was signed into law in September.

During the 1950s Biemiller became involved in the question of atomic energy control. He was chairman of the AFL-CIO's committee on atomic energy and a member of the labor-management advisory committee of the Atomic Energy Commission. Testifying before a congressional committee in May 1954, he supported Eisenhower's "Atoms-for-Peace" plan and recommended that Asian nations be included within its provisions for atomic energy development under U.N. control. Biemiller was concerned with the possibility of private monopolies of nuclear power and told Congress in 1955 that the government should prohibit them. The following year he warned against the hazards of nuclear reactors, charging that the Atomic Energy Commission underestimated their dangers and that it had muzzled press reports of accidents.

Disappointed at Sen. Lyndon B. Johnson's (D, Tex.) [q.v.] failure to oppose the Landrum-Griffin Act, Biemiller supported Sen. John F. Kennedy (D, Mass.) [q.v.] for the Democratic presidential nomination in 1960. Biemiller maintained close contact with the White House during the Kennedy and Johnson Administrations. He testified on Capitol Hill in support of Kennedy's manpower retraining, education and foreign aid bills and lobbied for Johnson's Great Society legislation. Biemiller also supported the Administration's Vietnam policy. During the Nixon Administration he played an important role in blocking the appointment of conservative Southern judges Clement F. Haynsworth and G. Harrold Carswell to the U.S. Supreme Court. [See KENNEDY, JOHNSON, NIXON/FORD Volumes]

[AES]

BISSELL, RICHARD M(ERVIN), JR.
b. Sept. 18, 1909; Hartford, Conn.
Special Assistant to the Director of Central Intelligence, 1954-58; Deputy Director of Plans, Central Intelligence Agency, 1959-62.

Bissell attended the elite Groton School and then went to Yale, where he graduated in 1932. From 1932 to 1933 he studied at the London School of Economics. He then returned to Yale as an instructor and eventually assistant professor in economics. Bissell received his Ph.D. from that university in 1939. He was appointed assistant administrator of the Marshall Plan in 1948 and served there until 1951.

In 1954 Bissell joined the Central Intelligence Agency (CIA) as special assistant to Director Allen W. Dulles [q.v.]. He was one of the few high-ranking members of the Agency who had no background in wartime intelligence work. Bissell's major responsibility was to develop techniques for obtaining information on the strategic capabilities of the Soviet Union. He sided with Dulles in advocating the use of modern technology rather than operatives to gather data. He conceived and supervised the program of U-2 flights over the Soviet Union and helped develop the SR-71 high altitude surveillance plane. He was also an early advocate of spy satellites. Bissell's U-2 program became public in May 1960, when pilot Francis Gary Powers [q.v.] was shot down over Soviet territory. The U.S. defended the mission and announced that it would continue over-flights to prevent Communist expansion.

In 1959 Bissell became deputy director for plans, responsible for coordinating covert operations. According to the report of the Senate Select Committee on Intelligence Activities, issued in 1975, at this post Bissell supervised plans to assassinate Congolese leader Patrice Lumumba and Cuban Premier Fidel Castro and his brother Raul. In September 1960 a CIA scientist, Sidney Gottlieb, acting on orders from Bissell, obtained poison and hypodermic needles from Army stockpiles and flew to Leopoldville with instructions for CIA station officer Victor Hedgman to kill Lumumba. When this failed, Bissell asked a senior CIA officer, Michael Mulroney, to undertake the assignment. Mulroney refused to assassinate Lumumba, but he flew to the Congo and got two other CIA agents to attempt the assassination. However, before the CIA could make further attempts, Lumumba was killed by Congolese opponents.

According to the Senate Select Committee report, during the summer of 1960 Bissell sanctioned attempts on the lives of Raul and Fidel Castro. The decision to kill Raul was reversed before action could be taken, but an attempt was authorized on the life of the Premier. The plan involved CIA cooperation with organized crime leaders Sam Giancana and John Roselli, who were given CIA money, poison and electronic gear to give to hired assassins. Although the plan was never put into operation, the CIA made several other attempts on Castro's life during the early 1960s.

The origin of the orders to assassinate Lumumba and Castro were never clearly determined because the system of executive command in the Agency was purposefully ambiguous to permit "plausible denial." Bissell testified in 1975 that he had assumed he had the authority of Eisenhower and Dulles to engage in such activities. He also said he had interpreted Dulles's original order to eliminate Castro as including possible assassination. The Committee, however, was never able to discover Dulles's role in the action. It did conclude that Bissell had exceeded his delegated authority by engaging in the projects.

On March 17, 1960 Eisenhower ordered the CIA to help unify opposition to the Castro regime and overthrow the government. Dulles turned the task over to Bissell, who proposed to train guerrillas in Guatemala to infiltrate Cuba and organize a popular revolt. When infiltration proved unworkable, Bissell proposed a full-scale invasion of the island by refugees trained and armed by the U.S. Bissell organized the project in Guatemala. The plan called for not only the development of camps for training guerrillas but also the construction of air strips. These would provide a base for CIA planes, piloted by Americans, which would drop arms to guerrillas already in Cuba and provide cover for the invasion. Shortly after the 1960 election President-elect John F. Kennedy approved continuation of the project.

The disastrous invasion took place on April 17, 1961. By April 19 the invasion force was defeated. Discredited, Bissell resigned in February 1962. Shortly thereafter he became head of the Institute for Defense Analysis. He remained there until 1964, when he became an executive of the United Aircraft Corp. [See KENNEDY Volume]

[JB]

BLACK, EUGENE R(OBERT)
b. May 1, 1898; Atlanta, Ga.
President, International Bank for Reconstruction and Development, 1949-63.

Born and raised in Atlanta, Black received his B.A. from the University of Georgia in 1918 and served as an ensign in the Navy during World War I. Black joined an Atlanta-based New York investment house in 1931 and two years later associated himself with the Chase National Bank of New York, where he became an expert on the bond market. From 1933 to 1947 Black was involved in Chase's international activities. He briefly served as undersecretary of the treasury in 1936. In 1947 President Harry S. Truman appointed Black an executive director of the International Bank for Reconstruction and Development (World Bank). The appointment of the conservative Black was welcomed by Wall Street, which disapproved of the Bank's earlier liberal loan policies. In 1949 Black become president of the World Bank. [See TRUMAN Volume]

During Black's presidency the Bank turned from an emphasis on European redevelopment loans to a stress on projects in underdeveloped nations. Black was alert to the economics of development, which, he once remarked, involve "most of technical skills and a complex of behavior patterns that took centuries to evolve in the industrial world of today." Therefore, he emphasized education and the development of technological knowledge in directing the Bank's investments. Under Black the Bank tried to avoid high-risk projects and instead opted for the development of "economies of scale," such as transportation facilities, power installations, irrigation and land reclamation projects—prerequisites for increased productivity in many sectors of the borrowing nations's economies. To prevent political pressures, the Bank usually made loans only where they could be entrusted to a quasi-autonomous authority, not to the government of a recipient nation.

Black became deeply involved in the negotiations for financing the Aswan High Dam in 1955-56. A Bank study, made in 1953-54, showed that the project was both technically sound and economically feasible. Black reported directly to President Dwight D. Eisenhower that the construction of the dam was Egypt's highest economic and social priority and recommended joint financing by Great Britain, the U.S. and the World Bank. He then attempted to counter

President Gamal Abdel Nasser's fear that the agreement would infringe upon Egypt's sovereignty and to convince him to accept the plan. He also had to persuade Secretary of State John Foster Dulles [q.v.] to agree to the measure despite Egypt's increasing closeness to the USSR.

Black's task became more difficult in May 1956, when Nasser's recognition of Communist China and rumors of Egypt's increased arms and financial dealings with the Russians further cooled Administration sentiment. He continued to promote the proposal, cautioning that the U.S. would lose a public relations battle and push Nasser into the arms of the Soviets if it refused aid. In his words, "All hell would break loose" if the U.S. abandoned the plan. Nevertheless, Dulles decided to withdraw American support for the project in July.

Black also served as a mediator in disputes arising from the Suez conflict of 1956. In December 1958 he left for Cairo to negotiate a settlement of the British-French claims arising from Nasser's 1956 nationalization of the canal. Black's efforts ended triumphantly in February 1959 with the signing of an Anglo-Egyptian accord outlining terms of compensation to British property owners.

The Kennedy Administration also used Black as mediator in the 1962 India-Pakistan conflict. In 1963 Black retired from the World Bank, but maintained close contacts both with the business community. That year he served on the Clay Committee, formed to study the nation's foreign aid program. During the Johnson Administration Black served as presidential adviser on Southeast Asian economic affairs [See KENNEDY, JOHNSON Volumes]

[ACD]

BLACK, HUGO L(AFAYETTE)
b. Feb. 27, 1886; Harlan, Ala.
d. Sept. 25, 1971; Bethesda, Md.
Associate Justice, U.S. Supreme Court, 1937-71

Born and raised in rural Clay Co., Ala., Hugo Black received a law degree from the University of Alabama in 1906. He built a successful law practice in Birmingham and held several local offices there before winning election to the U.S. Senate in 1926. Reelected in 1932, Black quickly became an outspoken supporter of the New Deal. President Roosevelt selected the Alabaman as his first nominee to the Supreme Court in August 1937. Shortly after the Senate confirmed the appointment on Aug. 17, a Pittsburgh newspaper published evidence of Black's membership in the Ku Klux Klan. The furor died down only after Black made a brief radio speech on Oct. 1 stating that he had joined the Klan in 1923 but had resigned from it in 1925.

On the bench Black favored expanded government power over the economy, and he voted to sustain the New Deal's economic and social welfare legislation. However, he opposed government intrusion on individual liberties guaranteed by the Bill of Rights and gradually emerged as one of the foremost defenders of civil liberties on the Court. Black insisted that the provisions of the Bill of Rights were absolutes which could not be abridged by the government. He also contended that the 14th Amendment had made the first eight Amendments fully applicable to the states as well as the federal government. The Justice gave a special position to the First Amendment, for he believed the rights of free speech, press and assembly were the foundation of a free government. He argued that the Amendment unequivocally barred all government interference with individual thought and expression, Black was especially ardent in its defense during the McCarthy era, when a majority of the Court often restricted the rights of free speech and association in loyalty-security cases. In a famous dissent in the 1951 *Dennis* case, for example, Black asserted that the Smith Act, which made it illegal to teach or advocate violent overthrow of the U.S. government, violated the First Amendment. [See TRUMAN Volume]

During the Eisenhower years Black continued to express his absolutist views of the First Amendment. When the Court reconsidered the Smith Act in June 1957 and interpreted it in a manner that gave greater scope to freedom of speech, but not declaring it unconstitutional, Black wrote a separate opinion. He again arguing that the statute was unconstitutional under the First Amendment. The Justice also opposed legislative investigations into subversion that probed individual beliefs. He repeatedly voted to overturn the contempt convictions of witnesses who refused to answer committee questions about their political ideas and associations. He joined the majority in two June 1957 decisions setting limits on congressional and state investigative powers and dissented when the Court retreated from this position in two June 959 cases.

In a dissenting opinion in one of the latter suits, Black contended that the chief aim of the House Un-American Activities Committee was to expose and try witnesses who were suspected Communists and to punish them by humiliation and public scorn. As a result, the Committee was not only violating individual rights of free association and expression, but also was also illegally exercising a judicial function which the Constitution had assigned to the courts. Justice Black did get to speak for the majority in two May 1957 cases placing limits on the legal profession's power to regulate admission to its ranks. He overturned the refusal of state bar associations to admit candidates with actual or alleged Communist backgrounds as a denial of due process of law. Throughout this period Black opposed all government attempts to regulate obscenity. Justice Black maintained that even obscene expression was protected by the First Amendment.

Black's absolutist views generally led him to give wide scope to the criminal rights guarantees in the Bill of Rights. He continually insisted that the states as well as the federal government must supply counsel to all indigent criminal defendants. In an April 1956 opinion, he ruled that the states must also supply an indigent defendant with a free trial transcript if it was essential to appeal a criminal conviction. Black believed the Fifth Amendment's privilege against self-incrimination was beyond the reach of government. He dissented from a February 1954 Court judg-

ment upholding a state gambling conviction because he thought the defendant's Fifth Amendment rights had been denied. The Justice also wrote the majority opinion in a well-known March 1960 case, *Thompson v. City of Louisville* which held it a denial of due process to convict an individual of loitering or vagrancy when there was no evidence to support the charge.

Black was fully in accord with Court rulings overturning racial segregation and discrimination. He joined in the Court's May 1954 *Brown* decision holding segregated public schools unconstitutional. Black wrote the majority opinion in a December 1960 case ruling segregation in restaurants at interstate bus terminals a violation of the Interstate Commerce Act.

During the 1960s a liberal majority emerged on the Court which adopted many of the positions Black had long advocated. That development ensured Black's profound impact on constitutional law, and legal scholars have rated him as one of the most influential justices in the Court's history. Black also won praise for his devotion to individual liberties and for the integrity he demonstrated in adhering to his principles during periods when they were rejected by a majority of the members of the Supreme Court and were unpopular with the public. Justice Black showed, according to legal scholar Norman Dorsen, an "important capacity for lonely and persistent dissent." "At the end, much of what he professed was accepted" by the Court. [See KENNEDY, JOHNSON, NIXON/FORD Volumes]

[CAB]

For further information:
Hugo Black, *A Constitutional Faith* (New York, 1968).
———, *One Man's Stand for Freedom: Mr. Justice Black and the Bill of Rights*, ed., Irving Dilliard (New York, 1963).
"Mr. Justice Black; Thirty Years in Retrospect," *UCLA Law Review*, 14 (1967), pp. 397-552.
John P. Frank, "Hugo L. Black," in Leon Friedman and Fred L. Israel, eds., *The Justices of the United States Supreme Court, 1789-1969* (New York, 1969), Vol. 3.
Stephen P. Strickland, ed., *Hugo Black and the Supreme Court* (New York, 1967).

BLAKE, EUGENE CARSON
b. Nov. 7, 1906; St. Louis, Mo.
President, National Council of
Churches of Christ in the U.S.A.,
1954-57.

The son of a Presbyterian elder, Eugene
Carson Blake received his A.B. degree with
honors in philosophy at Princeton in 1928.
He then studied at Edinburgh University
and was awarded a Th.B. from Princeton
Theological Seminary in 1932. During the
next two decades Blake held pulpits in Albany, N.Y., Pasadena, Calif., and New
York, N.Y. He was a delegate to the conference establishing the World Council of
Churches in 1948. The organization was
founded to foster cooperation between 163
different Protestant and Orthodox denominations. Two years later Blake helped form
the National Council of Churches of Christ
in the U.S.A. (NCCC), an organization of
Protestant and Orthodox churches formed
to promote ecumenism and coordinate
church welfare programs, social research
and charity. He was elected stated elder of
the United Presbyterian Church in the
U.S. in 1951 and president of the NCCC in
1954.

During the 1950s Blake was in the forefront of what church historian Harvey Cox
called the "New Breed" of clergymen, social activists who led the struggle for civil
liberties and civil rights. In December 1953
the General Council of the United Presbyterian Church in the U.S. sent a letter
to its congregations decrying "assaults on
basic human rights" in the U.S. Defending
the message, Blake pointed to two serious
threats to religion in America: "anti-
intellectualism . . . which tends to blur all
distinctions except those of white and black"
and the forces of "totalitarianism, Communism and fascism."

The following year Black chaired a subcommittee of the NCCC which called for
the adoption of procedural reforms in congressional investigating committees to protect individual freedom. Reacting to the
probes stemming from Sen. Joseph R.
McCarthy's (R, Wisc.) [q.v.] anti-
Communist crusade, the NCCC also called

for a single joint congressional committee to
investigate subversive activity.

In February 1960 it was revealed that an
Air Force training manual contained
charges that the NCCC was Communist infiltrated. Six Protestant leaders, including
Blake, demanded apologies from Air Force
Secretary Dudley C. Sharp and Rep. Francis E. Walter (E, Pa.) [q.v.], chairman of
the House Un-American Acitivities Committee (HUAC), and assurances that the
manual containing the allegations would not
be reissued. Walter offered to let the six
testify before the Committee on the accuracy of the charges, but they refused on the
grounds that HUAC was not the proper
forum for discussing their protest. They
maintained that there were other committees charged with the oversight of government operations. The leaders said they
would be happy to cooperate with those
panels to "reveal the facts of military actions that might jeopardize the First
Amendment." The manual was withdrawn
without any determination as to the
charges.

Blake was also active in the growing civil
rights movement. In 1956 he sent a telegram to the Rev. Solomon S. Seay in
Montgomery, Ala., assuring blacks that he
supported the Montgomery bus boycott.
Two years later he issued a statement declaring that desegregation in the South
should be enforced "with troops and tanks
if necessary." The view was rejected by
Philip Howerton, moderator of the Presbyterian Church in the U.S. (Southern
Presbyterian Church), who warned that
force would result in "nothing but chaos."

In 1960 Blake was one of 13 prominent
Protestant clergymen who, in an open letter to fellow pastors, condemned the use of
anti-Catholicism in the presidential primary
campaign. They urged ministers to preach
"charitable moderation" lest "the forces of
hate and uninformed hostility" be based in
America. "We should think it unjust to discount any [candidate] . . . because of his
chosen faith," they wrote.

Blake maintained his involvement in civil
rights throughout the 1960s and continued
to champion the union of Protestant denominations. He also emerged as a promi-

nent opponent of the Vietnam war. Blake became secretary-general of the World Council of Churches in 1966; he served at that post until 1972. [See KENNEDY, JOHNSON, NIXON/FORD Volumes]

[SY]

BLATNIK, JOHN A(NTON)
b. Aug. 17, 1911; Chisholm, Minn.
Democratic Representative, Minn., 1947-75.

A former high school chemistry teacher and a state senator from 1940 to 1946, Blatnik was elected to Congress in 1946 from the ore-mining region of the northeastern Minnesota. In the House he compiled a liberal record, supporting the labor and civil rights legislation of the Truman and Eisenhower Administrations. A descendant of Slovene immigrants, Blatnik was particularly concerned with the loss of American influence in Yugoslavia following World War II. He denounced Eisenhower's foreign policy, describing it as based "almost entirely on armament" rather than economic aid and cultural exchange.

By the early 1950s the high-grade iron ores that had made Blatnik's district the iron capital of the world were becoming seriously depleted, and steel manufacturers were turning to cheaper foreign sources. In an effort to counteract this trend, Blatnik fought for the long-postponed St. Lawrence Seaway Project, which he viewed as a means of opening the isolated region to industrial development. In 1954 Congress finally authorized the construction of a deep-water navigation channel in the St. Lawrence River, making it possible for large ships to sail the 2,300-mile distance from the Atlantic Ocean to Duluth, Minn., at the western end of the Great Lakes.

During the Eisenhower years Blatnik also became known as a crusader for clean water legislation. As chairman of the Public Works Committee's Rivers and Harbors Subcommittee, he sponsored the Federal Water Pollution Control Act of 1956, steering it skillfully through the pro-industry Committee and a hostile Congress. The Act authorized federal grants for the construc-

tion of local sewage treatment plants and established a Water Pollution Control Advisory Board within the Public Health Service. Federal investigators were empowered to force polluting industries or cities to clean up rivers and streams but only in cases of interstate pollution. Moreover, they were not given the legal right to inspect industrial plants or municipal waste treatment facilities. Although these jurisdictional limitations weakened the law, the Act was hailed as a landmark in the fight for clean water. Through 1961 Blatnik was the principal sponsor of congressional efforts to strengthen the federal program.

During the 1960s Blatnik maintained his liberal record on most issues, but he ceased to be a vigorous proponent of pollution-control legislation. The reasons for this about-face were not clear, but critics suggested that it was a result of the Federal Water Quality Control Administration's attempt to stop the Reserve Mining Co., the largest employer in Blatnik's district, from dumping industrial wastes into Lake Superior. Blatnik retired from Congress in 1975. [See JOHNSON, NIXON/FORD Volumes]

[TLH]

For further information:
David Zwick, *Water Wasteland* (New York, 1971).

BLOSSOM, VIRGIL T(RACEY)
b. 1906 (?); Brookfield, Mo.
d. Jan. 15, 1965; San Antonio, Tex.
Superintendent of Schools, Little Rock, Ark., 1953-58.

A product of schools of the upper South, Blossom graduated from Missouri Valley College as an outstanding athlete. He quickly found a job coaching athletics and teaching social science at the Fayetteville, Ark., high school. Blossom served there first as head coach and then as principal before being promoted to school superintendent. In the spring of 1953 he became superintendent of Little Rock schools while continuing his work at Fayetteville. Following the Supreme Court's May 1954 ruling declaring segregated schools unconstitutional, Blossom desegregated Fayetteville without incident. The following September he took up his post in Little Rock on a full-time basis. He pursued his duties so energetically that in 1955 Little Rock citizens named him "Man of the Year."

Blossom was a moderate on civil rights. While not welcoming integration he did not encourage violent opposition to it. Instead, he advocated a plan for voluntary compliance with the Court decision. Because of NAACP legal opposition to that plan, Blossom worked out another program during 1955 calling for token desegregation of grade schools. During the year, however, Blossom changed his proposal. The superintendent decided to support the token integration of Central High School, which drew its pupils from lower and middle-class white families, ignoring the fact that their racial feelings were strongest. Integration was to take place during the fall 1957 term.

Opposition to the plan began to develop during the summer of 1957 and increased steadily during the days before school was to open. Gov. Orval Faubus [q.v.], campaigning for reelection, refused Blossom's requests to support peaceful integration. Surreptitiously Faubus appealed to the Justice Department to enlist federal support for the desegregation plan, but when his efforts became known, the Governor, attempting to maintain a broad political base, came out strongly for segregation. On Sept. 2, Faubus ordered the National Guard to Central High School to prevent desegregation. For three weeks Blossom stood by while Faubus fought a spectacular series of court battles and blacks were refused admittance to the school. On Sept. 20 the Governor withdrew the National Guard in response to a court injunction. Central High School was finally desegregated on Sept. 23. The following day President Eisenhower federalized the National Guard and sent Army paratroops to Little Rock to ensure peaceful compliance with the Court's decision.

Blossom remained the target of local extremists. He was nearly assassinated by a sniper and had his telephone disconnected to stem the tide of threatening calls. In September 1958, after failing to get a court order to halt further integration, Gov. Faubus closed Little Rock's secondary schools completely. Five of the six school board members friendly to Blossom resigned. Newly elected segregationists then fired the superintendent. Blossom moved to San Antonio, Tex., where he guided a rural school district through a period of expansion into a position of excellence. He died of a heart attack at the age of 58.

[MJS]

For further Information:
Virgil T. Blossom, *It Has Happened Here* (New York, 1959).
Corinne Silverman, *The Little Rock Story* (University, Ala., 1959).

BLOUGH, ROGER M(ILES)
b. Jan. 19, 1904; Riverside, Pa.
Chairman, United States Steel Corporation, 1955-69.

The son of a truck farmer, Roger Blough grew up in Pennsylvania and attended Susquehanna University. After graduating in 1925, he taught history in high schools briefly before deciding to take up law. Earning an LL.B. from Yale in 1931, he became a corporate lawyer with the Wall Street firm of White and Case. Blough's association with U.S. Steel began in the late 1930s, when he served as an associate counsel for the corporation during congressional investigations of the steel industry. In 1952 he joined the board of directors as an executive vice-president. A close confidante of U.S. Steel president Benjamin Fairless [q.v.], Blough steadily rose in the firm's hierarchy. In 1952 he helped plead the corporation's case before the U.S. Supreme Court against President Truman's seizure of the steel mills. The Court ruled that Truman's action was unconstitutional, and the mills were returned to their owners. In July 1953 Blough assumed the position of general counsel, and in May 1955 he succeeded the retiring Fairless as chairman of the board and chief executive of the giant firm.

The world's largest steel-making enterprise and the producer of one-third of the nation's total steel capacity, U.S. Steel had total sales of $3.5 billion at the time of Blough's ascendancy. As the industry's pace-setter in determining steel prices, the company contributed greatly to the rise of prices throughout the American economy in the 1950s. After mid-decade, however, U.S. Steel, along with the rest of the industry, was afflicted by a slowdown in orders for military hardware, autos, business construction and, after 1957, exports.

As corporation head, Blough supervised negotiations with the United Steel Workers of America (USW). In 1955 talks were held under the wage-reopening clause of a two-year pact signed in 1954. At midnight on June 30 steelworkers went on strike, but the next morning Blough hastened to sign an agreement granting an average hourly wage increase of 15 cents. The contract also provided the union with protection against the unilateral introduction of labor-saving machinery by the company.

With the basic steel agreements due to expire in 1959, U.S. Steel went on the offensive, conducting a lavish public relations and advertising campaign that claimed USW demands were directly responsible for inflation. The union, on the other hand, pointed out that company profits were high as a result of several price increases since 1955, which outstripped by far increases in labor costs. The USW's insistence upon retaining a voice in determining the pace of technological change was also an issue in the dispute, since the company's shutdown of older plants in 1957 and 1958 resulted in layoffs for thousands of steelworkers.

The 1959 strike lasted 116 days and required Eisenhower's intervention to settle. The contract, finally signed in January 1960, granted workers raises and other benefits costing 41 cents a hour over a 2½ year period. The benefits included increased and broadened pensions, continued supplemental unemployment benefits and creation of a human relations research committee to study wage adjustment, job classification, incentive pay and other problems. The U.S. Steel leader maintained that the cost of the new wage package would be "well over one billion dollars."

In 1962 Blough was at the center of a major confrontation between U.S. Steel and the Kennedy Administration. After an unprecedented campaign of presidential pressure to role back a steel price increase, which sent shock waves through the business community, Blough backed down. U.S. Steel was also involved in antitrust litigation and inquiries into secret price-fixing during the 1960s. Blough retired as chairman of the board in 1969. [See KENNEDY Volume]

[TLH]

BOGGS, J(AMES) CALEB
b. May 15, 1909; Cheswold, Del.
Governor, Del., 1953-60.

Boggs, the product of an old, established Delaware family, received his A.B. degree from the University of Delaware in 1931 and an LL.B. from Georgetown University six years later. He set up law practice in Dover, Del. and later helped found the Wilmington firm of Logan, Duffy and Boggs. Following service in the Army during World War II, Boggs was elected Delaware's representative at large in 1946. On Capitol Hill he took a stand against what he termed the "waste and duplication" of the Truman Administration, which he thought was "drifting towards socialism."

In November 1952 Boggs defeated the Democratic incumbent, Elbert N. Carvel, to be elected Delaware's governor. He continued to maintain his position against the growth of federal power and increased spending, declaring that "the amount of money spent is less important than the way it is spent." During his first year in office, Boggs signed a bill requiring all Communists and members of organizations appearing on the Attorney General's subversive list who lived in or passed through Delaware to register with the state police. The law proved unenforceable. In 1953 Boggs attempted civil service reform but was blocked by the state legislature. Three years later he had considerably more success in getting through a program of extensive executive and judicial reform, school consolidation and increased salaries for teachers.

Boggs received national attention in 1954, when he requested Delaware's Board of Education to comply with the Supreme Court's *Brown* decision outlawing segregation in public schools. His action made Delaware the scene of the first of many confrontations over the desegregation issue. Although integration proceeded smoothly in the northern, industrialized sector of the state, it met with stiff resistance in the southern section. In September Boggs was forced to intervene when a plan bringing 11 black children into an all-white school in Milford, Del. resulted in a much publicized boycott. He put a temporary halt to the desegregation effort and ordered the arrest of Bryant W. Bowles, self-styled founder and president of the National Association for the Advancement of White People, whom Boggs alleged had come to the state specifically to organize the boycott. He justified the arrest as being directed against "organized mob rule and mass hysteria," though the State Supreme Court subsequently declared Bowles innocent.

Boggs was reelected governor in 1956, and in 1959 he served as chairman of the U.S. Governors Conference. He won election to the U.S. Senate in 1960, where he compiled a generally conservative record. He was a strong supporter of the 1964 Civil Rights Act. In 1965 Boggs was appointed to the White House Conference on International Cooperation and in the same year joined Sen. Mike Mansfield (D, Mont.) [q.v.] on a fact-finding tour of Asia, which resulted in a plea for a negotiated settlement in Vietnam. Boggs was defeated for reelection in 1972 and returned to his old law firm.

[JPL]

BOGGS, T(HOMAS) HALE
b. Feb. 15, 1914; Long Beach, Miss.
d. Oct. 16, 1972; Alaska.
Democratic Representative, La., 1947-72.

Boggs, the descendant of a colonial family, received a law degree from Tulane University in 1937 and then entered private practice in New Orleans. In 1939 he helped form the People's League of Independent Voters, an organization of business and professional men established to combat the state Democratic machine. In the 1940 Democratic House primary, Boggs ran successfully against the machine-backed incumbent and went on to win the general election. However, the former incumbent defeated him in the 1942 primary. Boggs joined the U.S. Naval Reserve in November 1943.

In 1946 Boggs was again elected to the House from New Orleans. A political protege of Democratic leader Rep. Sam Rayburn (D, Tex.) [q.v.], he was appointed to the influential Ways and Means Committee. Boggs became head of the panel's Subcommittee on Narcotics in 1951, and during that year, he successfully sponsored a bill to stiffen the penalties for violations of federal narcotics and marijuana laws. In January 1952 he lost the Louisiana Democratic gubernatorial primary. [See TRUMAN Volume]

Boggs, a moderate Southern Democrat, often broke with his more liberal party colleagues. In July 1953 he joined with Ways and Means Committee conservatives in an unsuccessful attempt to block an Administration-sponsored effort to extend an excess-profits tax on corporations. Boggs voted against the Civil Rights Acts of 1957 and 1960. In March 1959, as a member of the Joint Economic Committee, he dissented from a report of the panel's Democratic majority urging a stress upon the expansion of production and employment rather than the containment of inflation. In March 1960 Boggs voted with a Ways and Means Committee majority opposing the Forand bill, which would have provided medical care for the aged under Social Security.

The sugar industry was an important element of Louisiana's economy, and in March and April 1955 Boggs and Sen. Allen J. Ellender (D, La.) [q.v.] introduced a sugar quota bill to enable American growers to benefit more substantially from the expanding U.S. market for sugar. It proposed to enlarge the domestic producers' share of excess market demand above estimated annual American consumption. A modified version of this measure became law in May 1956.

In 1957 Boggs became chairman of the Ways and Means Committee's Foreign Trade Policy Subcommittee, where he advocated liberal foreign trade programs. That December he backed Eisenhower's request for a five-year extension of the Reciprocal Trade Agreements granting the President authority to cut tariffs by as much as 25%. In August 1958 Eisenhower signed a four-year extension bill permitting cuts up to 20%. Boggs's subcommittee began hearings on American investment in underdeveloped areas in December 1958. A month later he introduced a bill to encourage investment in those regions by permitting investors to defer payment of U.S. corporation taxes on foreign earnings until the funds were returned to America. A modified version of this proposal passed the House in May 1960 but was rejected by the Senate Finance Committee. Another provision of Boggs's 1959 bill liberalized the terms by which U.S. firms with investments abroad could take credit for their foreign tax payments in computing their U.S. tax liability. The measure was introduced as a separate bill early in 1960. Sen. Albert Gore (D, Tenn.) [q.v.], a leading advocate of tax reform and an opponent of the foreign tax credit, denounced the proposal in May 1960 as an attempt to expand an already unjustified loophole. However, the bill passed both chambers and was signed into law in September.

In 1962 Boggs succeeded Rep. Carl Albert (D, Okla.) [q.v.] as majority whip. During the mid-1960s his voting record became more liberal. He opposed the 1964 Civil Rights Act but supported the Voting Rights Act of 1965 and the 1968 Civil Rights Act. Boggs also voted for antipoverty legislation. In 1971 he became majority leader following the retirement of House Speaker John McCormack (D, Mass.) [q.v.]. He was a passenger in a plane that disappeared over Alaska on Oct. 16, 1972. The craft was not located, and Boggs was presumed to have died in a crash. [See KENNEDY, JOHNSON Volumes]

[MLL]

BOHLEN, CHARLES E(USTIS)
b. Aug. 30, 1904; Clayton, N.Y.
d. Jan. 1, 1974; Washington, D.C.
Ambassador to the Soviet Union, March 1953-April 1957; Ambassador to the Philippines, May 1957-October 1959.

The son of a well-to-do sportsman and a descendant of the first U.S. ambassador to France, Bohlen was educated at St. Paul's School and Harvard University. Two years after his graduation in 1927, he joined the Foreign Service and was posted as vice-consul in Prague. He remained there until 1931, when he was assigned to Paris as vice-consul and language officer. While in France he took extensive courses in Russian history, language and culture in preparation for a specialization in Soviet affairs. Upon the recommendation of William Bullitt, ambassador to the Soviet Union, Bohlen was made part of the first American mission to the USSR in 1934. He served there intermittently until 1939, when he was posted to Tokyo. Bohlen was at the embassy during the Japanese attack on Pearl Harbor and, like the other members of the mission, was interned by the Japanese for six months after the attack. Upon his return to Washington he became acting chief of the State Department's division of Eastern European affairs.

During World War II Bohlen was an adviser and chief interpreter at the Teheran Conference of 1943 and the Yalta and Potsdam Conferences of 1945. He also worked as liaison officer between the State Department and the White House. In 1947 Bohlen became personal adviser to Secretary of State George C. Marshall. He played an important role in developing the Marshall Plan and molding the Truman policy of containment of the Soviet Union. Bohlen became counselor of the Paris embassy in 1949. Two years later he returned to Washington and served as an aide to John Foster Dulles [q.v.] at the Japanese peace conference in San Francisco. [See TRUMAN Volume]

President Eisenhower nominated Bohlen as ambassador to the Soviet Union in 1953. The appointment was bitterly opposed by conservatives, led by Sens. Joseph McCarthy (R, Wisc.) [q.v.] and Patrick McCarran (D, Nev.) [q.v.], who claimed that Bohlen was too closely associated with Truman's foreign policy to properly represent the Republican administration. They also charged that, based on Bohlen's FBI record, the State Department could not recommend the appointment. Although the Senators were never able to reveal specific instances of disloyalty, their charges seriously jeopardized confirmation. For many individuals in the State Department, the Bohlen case became a "symbol of the foreign service at bay" and a test of the new Administration's willingness to defend the beleaguered Department against McCarthy's continuing attacks.

At the confirmation hearings Dulles supported the appointment fully and denied that Bohlen had security problems. He conceded that the two men did not often agree on policy and specifically viewed the Yalta agreements in different lights. Nevertheless, he reminded the Foreign Relations Committee that as ambassador Bohlen would have little influence in policymaking. Eisenhower, too, defended the nomination, although he apparently had been asked by a high-ranking official, never identified, to withdraw it. McCarthy's attempt to prevent the appointment failed when several important conservatives, led by Sen. Robert Taft (R, Ohio) [q.v.], rejected the Wisconsin Senator's contention that Dulles had lied in defending Bohlen's security record. Bohlen was confirmed in March 1953.

As ambassador, Bohlen's task was to inform the Kremlin of official U.S. positions and to gather as much information as possible about Soviet leadership and policy changes. During his tenure he reported on the changes of leadership following Stalin's death in 1953 and on the Soviet reaction to the Suez crisis and the Hungarian revolt of 1956. These reports often contained policy recommendations, but, according to Bohlen, Secretary of State Dulles rarely heeded them. In summing up his four years in the Soviet Union, the Ambassador wrote, "I cannot say I accomplished much during my four years . . . nor can I think of any serious mistakes we made at the embassy."

In 1957 Dulles, apparently as a result of a commitment to appoint Llewellyn Thompson [q.v.] ambassador to the Soviet Union, announced that Bohlen had decided to give up his position. Bohlen, who had not considered this, thought of resigning from the Foreign Service. Instead he accepted a post as ambassador to the Philippines. Despite Bohlen's protestations, rumors persisted that he was being "exiled" to the Philippines because of policy disagreements with Dulles. During his tour Bohlen settled Philippine war claims against the U.S. and unsuccessfully attempted to convince Congress to give the Philippines jurisdiction over the prosecution of crimes committed by U.S. military personnel off U.S. bases.

In 1959 Secretary of State Christian Herter [q.v.] appointed Bohlen his special assistant for Soviet affairs. Plans to make him a counselor or assistant secretary were dropped because of fear that conservative senators would oppose confirmation. As Herter's assistant, he was an adviser and interpreter at the abortive May 1960 summit conference.

During the 1960s Bohlen served as a presidential adviser to both John Kennedy and Lyndon Johnson. He was named ambassador to France in 1962 and remained at that post until the end of 1967, when he was appointed deputy undersecretary of state for political affairs. Bohlen retired in January 1969 and died five years later. [See KENNEDY, JOHNSON Volumes]

[EWS]

For further information:
Charles Bohlen, *Witness to History, 1929-1969* (New York, 1973).

BOLTON, FRANCES P(AYNE BINGHAM)
b. March 29, 1885; Cleveland, Ohio
d. March 9, 1977; Lyndhurst, Ohio.
Republican Representative, Ohio, 1940-69.

Born to one of Cleveland's oldest and wealthiest families, Frances Bingham married steel executive Chester C. Bolton in 1907.

She devoted both time and money to a variety of philanthropic enterprises, notably the Tuskegee Institute. With particular interest in nursing, Bolton persuaded the War Department, then headed by fellow Clevelander Newton D. Baker, to create the Army School of Nursing during World War I. Beginning in 1928 she participated in her husband's usually successful campaigns for the House. Upon her husband's death Bolton succeeded to his seat in a special 1940 election.

One of the few women members of the House in the 1940s, Bolton fought for an end to discriminatory practices by the Armed Services. During World War II she called for the desegregation, both by race and sex, of military nursing units. In 1949 she argued for the inclusion of women in the Selective Service System.

Throughout her House career Bolton served on the Foreign Affairs Committee. She led efforts that resulted in the restructuring of committee procedure. A frequent defender of the United Nations, she also advocated independence for colonial Africa in the late 1940s. Although a mild isolationist prior to Pearl Harbor, Bolton assumed positions more internationalist than those of most of her fellow Midwestern Republicans. [See TRUMAN Volume]

In February 1954 Bolton declined to join some GOP members of Congress in criticizing a plan—presented by Secretary of State John Foster Dulles [q.v.]—for an April conference at Geneva, which would have included a delegation from Communist China. Senate Majority Leader William F. Knowland, Jr. (R, Calif.) [q.v.] led an assault upon Dulles's qualified support for Communist China's representation at talks on Indochina and Korea. Bolton, Sen. Walter F. George (D, Ga.) [q.v.], Reps. James P. Richards (D, S.C.), and Franklin D. Roosevelt, Jr. (D, N.Y.) supported Dulles; they argued that China's presence at the discussions would not indicate American recognition of the Communist regime.

Bolton consistently supported foreign policy legislation favored by the White House. During the 84th Congress (1955-56) she voted for 93% of the foreign policy measures endorsed by the President, as measured by *Congressional Quarterly*. The House Repub-

lican average was 70%. She similarly led her fellow Republicans 79% to 56% in the 85th Congress (1957-58).

By the 1960s Bolton was both the ranking woman representative and the ranking GOP member on the Foreign Affairs Committee. Her oldest son, Oliver P. Bolton, served three terms in the House from the nearby 11th District; they represented the only mother-son team in the lower chamber. Bolton encountered little opposition in winning reelection until 1968, when at age 83, she lost her seat due to redistricting. Bolton died in 1977 at the age of 91. [See JOHNSON Volume]

[JLB]

BONNER, HERBERT C(OVINGTON)
b. May 16, 1891; Washington, N.C.
d. Nov. 7, 1965; Washington, D.C.
Democratic Representative, N.C., 1940-65; Chairman Merchant Marine and Fisheries Committee, 1955-65.

Bonner worked as a salesman and a farmer until enlisting in the Army during World War I. In 1924 he became secretary to Assemblyman Lindsay Warren. When Warren was elected to the U.S. House of Representatives, Bonner accompanied him to Washington. In 1940 he was elected to fill Warren's unexpired term, vacated when the Congressman became controller general. In Congress Bonner represented an eastern North Carolina district of small towns and textile mills until his death in 1965. During the 1940s he led a number of congressional investigations, including one into postwar profiteering and another on waste in military installations.

While on Capitol Hill Bonner compiled a conservative record as an opponent of labor and civil rights legislation. He voted against the Civil Rights Acts of 1957 and 1960 and was paired for the Landrum-Griffin Act of 1959. Bonner also opposed federally financed public housing and measures to aid education. A conservative on foreign policy, he voted against lower tariffs requested by President Dwight D. Eisenhower and most foreign aid bills except those specifically designed to curb Communist aggression. Bonner was a strong anti-Communist and supported measures, such as the 1957 Eisenhower Doctrine, that were designed to give the President the power to act swiftly against Communist aggression throughout the world.

Bonner's major concern in Congress was the U.S. maritime industry. As chairman of the Merchant Marine and Fisheries Committee, he criticized what he thought were excessive union demands and the failure of management to modernize shipping. He also pleaded for increased federal aid to the industry. During 1956 Bonner was responsible for defeating amendments to the "50-50 law." This law, supported by the industry, required that at least half of all agricultural surpluses shipped as foreign aid be moved in American ships. In February Bonner's Committee issued a report concluding that the law did not impair the success of the aid program and was "vitally necessary" to American shipping.

Bonner was a vocal supporter of the construction of a nuclear powered merchant vessel. However, he objected to Eisenhower's proposal that the vessel be used as a "peace ship," carrying "practical knowledge of the usefulness of [atomic] science." Bonner called the President's plan "an international side-show, a Mississippi River Showboat" and proposed development of a second "practical" vessel. The final bill, signed into law in July 1956, combined Eisenhower's and Bonner's proposals. The first nuclear ship, the *Savannah*, was launched in 1962.

During the 1960s Bonner pushed for compulsory arbitration in the shipping industry and increased federal subsidies for ship building. Bonner died in 1965. [See KENNEDY Volume]

[EWS]

BOULWARE, LEMUEL (RICKETTS)
b. June 3, 1895; Springfield, Ky.
Vice-President in Charge of Employe, Community and Union Relations, General Electric Company, 1947-57.

A 1916 graduate of the University of Wisconsin, Lemuel Boulware taught business administration briefly before embarking on a career as an industrial executive.

During World War II he joined the War Production Board as an operations vice chairman and met Charles E. Wilson [q.v.] of the General Electric Co. (GE). When Wilson became president of GE after the War, he brought Boulware into the Company as a vice president.

GE's union relations had been relatively amicable from the mid-1930s through the War years. After a major strike victory for the United Electrical Workers in 1946, however, the company sought to restrict future union gains by adopting a firmer bargaining approach. Boulware was charged with devising an aggressive employe-relations policy, which came to be known as "Boulwarism" after its inauguration in 1947. GE proceeded to carry out what its opponents called one of the best-financed, most highly organized and longest antiunion campaigns in corporate history.

The principal element in the Boulware formula was what the company called "truthful offers." In an effort to end what Boulware described as "eastern bazaar haggling" and to deny unions the opportunity to claim that they had forced the company to raise its contract offers, GE put on the bargaining table everything it was willing to give. As a result, the company's first offer was usually its last. Unions charged that GE was thus bargaining by ultimatum. However Boulware denied that the company attempted to drive a bargain less favorable to its employes than could be achieved by the more conventional negotiating approach used by most large businesses.

Boulwarism also featured the extensive use of advertising and mass-marketing techniques. Fearing that unless the company communicated its proposals by every means available, employes and the public would learn only the unions' version of events, GE produced regular plant bulletins, sent management representatives to public gatherings and placed full-page advertisements in the press of all communities in which its plants were located. With the aid of a large research staff, Boulware applied the techniques of market research to merchandise GE's "product"—its contract offers—on all fronts in order to make the most effective "sale" to employes and local communities.

Although several unions competed for jurisdiction over GE workers after 1949, the International Union of Electrical Workers (IUE) was the largest by far, and its president, James Carey [q.v.], was GE's principal adversary during the 1950s. At the yearly contract rounds between 1950 and 1955, Carey usually failed to move the company from its initial bargaining position. He was also unable to gain his membership's strike support in the face of effective GE publicity. As a result, the IUE repeatedly ended up accepting GE's offer long after the expiration of each previous year's contract.

In 1955, with market forecasters predicting a long-term boom, GE planned new investments in plant, equipment, manpower and research and prepared to expand into the atomic power and computer fields. In a temporary departure from Boulwarism, the company also offered a five-year contract package in 1955, including quarterly cost-of-living adjustments, a comprehensive medical insurance program and an informal pledge not to launch any anti-union campaigns during the contract's annual escape periods. Three years later, however, the agreement was renegotiated after GE's utility apparatus, industrial equipment and appliance departments were severely hit by the 1957 recession. Talks ended in a stalemate when the company refused the IUE's demands for supplemental unemployment benefits and joint union-management automation committees.

Boulware retired as head of union relations in 1957. However, Boulwarism was revived after 1958 as GE prepared for a confrontation with the Electrical Workers Union. The 1960 strike, which was marked by company-organized back-to-work movements, widely-publicized plant openings and occasional use of police force, was called off by the IUE after three weeks. It proved a major defeat for Carey and his union in what *New York Times* labor editor A.H. Raskin called "the worst setback any union has received in a nationwide strike since World War II."

[TLH]

BOWIE, ROBERT R(ICHARDSON)
b. Aug. 24, 1909; Baltimore, Md.
Director of Policy Planning, Department of State, 1953-55; Assistant Secretary of State for Policy Planning, 1955-57.

Robert R. Bowie graduated from Princeton in 1931 and, after receiving a law degree from Harvard three years later, returned to Baltimore to begin legal practice. He served as assistant director of the Maryland Legislative Council from 1940 to 1941 and as assistant attorney general of Maryland from 1941 to 1942. After service in the Army during World War II, Bowie became professor of law at Harvard, where he remained intermittently until 1955. During the Truman Administration he was special assistant to the deputy military governor of Germany from 1945 to 1946 and served as director of the task force of the Hoover Commission on the Reorganization of the Federal Government in 1948. Bowie returned to Germany as general counsel and special adviser to the U.S. high commissioner in 1950 and 1951.

In 1953 Secretary of State John Foster Dulles [q.v.] appointed Bowie director of policy planning in the State Department. Dulles frequently consulted Bowie, who often opposed the Secretary's uncompromising anti-Communism. Yet, despite Dulles's respect for him, Bowie never exerted much influence over the Secretary, and the planning staff wielded far less power than it had during the Truman Administration.

At a series of conferences held in the spring and fall of 1953, Bowie helped formulate the Administration's policy of "massive retaliation." Under this plan the U.S. relied on strategic nuclear weapons rather than conventional warfare to prevent Soviet expansion and guard against Russian nuclear attack. The Department reiterated its support of "containment" of Communism in Eastern Europe and upheld the use of nuclear weapons to prevent Communist subversion in non-aligned nations. However, the Administration rejected suggestions of "liberating" Eastern Europe by force.

Bowie was critical of Dulles's belligerent

policy over Quemoy and Matsu in the spring of 1954 and disliked his willingness to discuss possible use of nuclear weapons against Communist China. Relying heavily on information supplied him by Chairman of the Joint Chiefs of Staff Adm. Arthur Radford [q.v.], Dulles claimed that tactical nuclear weapons could "destroy military targets without endangering unrelated civilian centers." Astonished by Dulles's statements, Bowie gave him Central Intelligence Agency estimates that civilian casualties on the Chinese mainland would reach 12 to 14 million even if the U.S. dropped tactical atomic bombs on only military targets.

In August 1955 President Eisenhower appointed Bowie assistant secretary of state for policy planning. The appointment was opposed by Republican Senate Policy Committee Chairman Styles Bridges (R, N.H.) [q.v.], who accused Bowie of favoring Communist China's admission to the U.N. However, the Senate Foreign Relations Committee approved Bowie after he swore he had never advocated Communist China's replacement of Taiwan in the organization. The Senate confirmed Bowie's appointment in February 1956.

Following his retirement from the State Department in May 1957, Bowie returned to Harvard, where he taught international relations and served as director of the Center for International Affairs from 1957 to 1972. In 1960 Bowie wrote a report for the Senate Foreign Relations Committee entitled "Ideology and Foreign Affairs." In it he contended that the U.S. should remain on guard against the Soviet Union despite an apparent thaw in relations between the two countries and rising Russian living standards which might lead the USSR to an accommodation with the U.S. However, his report advocated adoption of "wider perspectives than those stimulated by the continuous clash with the USSR" and recommended a less direct competition between the two countries for the allegiance of the uncommitted nations. Bowie held the post of counselor to the State Department from 1966 to 1968.

[AES]

BOWLES, CHESTER
b. April 5, 1901; Springfield, Mass.
Foreign policy critic; Democratic Representative, Conn., 1959-61.

The product of a well-to-do Yankee family, Chester Bowles graduated from Yale University in 1924. He then worked for a short time as a journalist for his hometown newspaper, the *Springfield Republican*. In 1925 he moved to New York to accept a copywriter position in an advertising agency. Four years later he and a partner, William Benton, founded their own agency which prospered despite or even perhaps because of the Depression.

With the outbreak of World War II, Bowles, a Connecticut resident, administered his state's rationing program. His success impressed President Franklin D. Roosevelt, who invited him to Washington to serve as director of the Office of Price Administration in 1943. President Harry S. Truman appointed him Director of Economic Stabilization two years later. Bowles also represented the U.S. at the first conference of the United Nations Education, Scientific and Cultural Organization in 1946 and served as special assistant to U.N. Secretary General Trygve Lie.

In 1948 Bowles was elected governor of Connecticut. When Bowles lost his reelection campaign in 1950, President Truman named him ambassador to India. There he defended the neutralist policies of Prime Minister Jawharlal Nehru against criticism by American conservatives who equated neutralism with pro-Communism. Supporting Adlai Stevenson's [q.v.] statement that "a full belly is the best enemy of Communism," Bowles joined other liberals in urging a shift from military to economic aid. Bowles retired from government service at the end of the Truman Administration. [See TRUMAN Volume]

During the early years of the Eisenhower Administration, Bowles wrote numerous articles and books, including *The New Dimensions of Peace* (1953), *Africa's Challenge to America* (1956) and *Ideas, People and Peace* (1958), which established his reputation as a leading critic of American policy toward developing nations, particularly in the area of foreign aid. Bowles deplored the refusal of colonial powers to grant their territories independence. This, he maintained, led to discontent which proved a fertile ground for Communist subversion. He argued that foreign aid was America's best deterrent against the spread of Communism. Bowles charged that the Eisenhower Administration's foreign aid program was stingy and its emphasis on military aid misguided. The small amount of foreign aid offered, he stated, was designed not to improve living standards but to gain support for the U.S. in the United Nations and win a popularity contest with the Soviet Union. Quite often the programs failed to meet such expectations. This, in turn, disillusioned Congress which then slashed foreign aid. The State Department's role in dispensing aid also drew Bowles's fire. He deplored officials' ignorance of the cultures and languages of developing countries and charged that bureaucrats were more concerned with the political effects of the dollars given than in aiding the population.

At a time when many liberals, defensive about their past connections with the Left, become cold warriors, Bowles stood apart from them. According to journalist David Halberstam, "the Cold War had never taken place" for Bowles. He downgraded the Soviet threat and stressed the world dangers of poverty and hunger. However, his plans for a successful foreign aid program did have some anti-Soviet overtones.

In 1958 Bowles began his political comeback by seeking the Democratic nomination for a Senate seat from Connecticut. Ironically, his old advertising partner, William Benton [q.v.], who previously served in the Senate, entered the race along with Rep. Thomas Dodd (D, Conn.) [q.v.]. Benton had the backing of state party chairman John Bailey and Gov. Abraham Ribicoff [q.v.], who feared that Bowles's controversial stands on foreign policy would weaken the ticket which he headed. At the Party's convention in June, Benton and Bowles split the liberal vote permitting Dodd to win the nomination. Bowles then ran for a House seat in his traditionally Republican home district and won by a large margin. During his one term in Congress, he lobbied for improvements in foreign aid programs.

In 1959 many liberals mentioned Bowles as a dark-horse candidate for the Democratic presidential nomination. However, his controversial stands limited his appeal. In late 1959 presidential aspirant Sen. John F. Kennedy (D, Mass.) [q.v.] elicited Bowles's support in the belief that his endorsement would aid him in a struggle with Adlai Stevenson. Bowles did endorse Kennedy, but his refusal to campaign for the Senator against his old friend, Sen. Hubert Humphrey (D, Minn.) [q.v.], alienated many Kennedy supporters. Bowles served as Kennedy's foreign policy adviser during the 1960 general election campaign.

When Kennedy became President, Bowles was appointed undersecretary of state. As a result of clashes with Attorney General Robert F. Kennedy [q.v.] and many powerful members of the State Department and Congress, Bowles was forced to resign in November 1961. Kennedy then appointed him special adviser on Asian, African and Latin American affairs. In December 1962 Bowles once again became ambassador to India. During the 1960s Bowles lobbied for more foreign aid for that nation but had little success in convincing Presidents Kennedy and Johnson to follow his recommendations. Bowles retired in 1969.

[JB]

For further information:
Chester Bowles, *Promises to Keep* (New York, 1971).

BRADEN, SPRUILLE
b. March 13, 1894; Elkhorn, Mont.
Chairman, Crime Committee of Greater New York, February 1951-December 1956.

Born into a mining family—his father founded the Braden Copper Co.—Spruille Braden studied mining engineering at Yale University. After receiving a Ph.B. in 1914, Braden worked in a number of South American mining ventures and married the daughter of a prominent Chilean physician. During the 1920s he advised South American governments in loan negotiations, participated in inter-American financial conferences and served as an official of several large corporations.

Braden turned to a diplomatic career in

1933, when he was appointed U.S. delegate to the Seventh International Conference of American States. From 1935 to 1939 he headed the U.S. team at the Chaco Peace Conference, where he negotiated the settlement of the war between Bolivia and Paraguay. Ambassador to Colombia from 1939 to 1942, he then became ambassador to Cuba. In 1945 he was made Ambassador to Argentina and in six months was promoted to assistant secretary of state for American republic affairs. During the postwar period Braden recommended a "hard-line" policy against all forms of dictatorship. His widely publicized efforts to pressure Argentine dictator Juan Domingo Peron to restore constitutional liberties, deliver over to the U.S. Nazi agents hiding in Argentina and abide by the provisions of inter-American defense commitments disturbed State Department officials eager to restore friendly relations with a government that had had close ties to the Axis. He also made enemies in the Pentagon with his opposition to large military aid programs to Latin American nations, arguing that such programs wasted U.S. taxpayers' money and encouraged military adventurism among the Latins. Braden left government service in July 1947, believing that his anti-Communist, anti-fascist policies had been sabotaged by pro-Communist, incompetent employes of the State Department. He then settled in New York City and worked as a lecturer and as a consultant to a number of large corporations, including Anaconda Copper, American Foreign Power, Lone Star Cement and United Fruit. In February 1949 Braden was named president of the American Arbitration Association. [See TRUMAN Volume]

Reacting to the growing concern over the activities of organized crime and corruption in government, in January 1951 a group of prominent citizens formed the New York City Anti-Crime Committee. They asked Braden, who had frequently spoken out against the breakdown of social morality and the threat of Communist subversion, to act as the Committee's unpaid chairman. Supported by the municipal government, the Anti-Crime Committee concentrated its investigations on organized crime's infiltration into labor, business and politics. In February 1953 the panel issued its first report, citing evidence of organized crime in the city's food, garment-trucking and building industries. Its investigation of crime on the waterfront was instrumental in influencing the American Federation of Labor to expel the International Longshoremen's Association and set up a new union in September 1953. Organized crime's role on the docks became a national issue, and the situation in the port of New York was dramatized in the successful 1954 film, *On the Waterfront*. In July 1955 Braden warned that racketeers planned to take over the trucking industry and strongly criticized Teamsters President David Beck [q.v.] for failure to take action against his vice president, James Hoffa [q.v.]. The Anti-Crime Committee suspended its operations in December 1956 for lack of funds. Braden, however, was satisfied with the Committee's work and believed that it had encouraged the public to demand more vigorous prosecution of official corruption.

During the 1950s Braden was closely identified with some of the most right-wing elements in public life. In November 1954 he helped organize "10 Million Americans Mobilizing for Justice," an organization designed to oppose the Senate's proposed censure of Sen. Joseph McCarthy (R, Wisc.) [q.v.]. Braden also cooperated with the Senate Internal Security Subcommittee's investigations into Communist subversion in the U.S. government. In December 1953 he told the subcommittee that Communism could not be eliminated from Latin America until "insidious groups" and "bad characters" were removed from the State Department. He asserted that the official actions of Alger Hiss were "down the Communist line" and noted that his own reports warning of Communism were missing from the State Department files. Although Braden said that he had no personal knowledge of Harry Dexter White, a Treasury Department official accused of being a Soviet agent, he argued that White's wartime financial plan for Cuba would have bankrupted the country, thus abetting Communist interests on the island. Testifying before the subcommittee again in November 1954, Braden stated that pro-Communists were apparently still influencing State Department policy as they had during World War II.

In his retirement Braden continued to

speak out publicly on foreign affairs. He defended U.S. private investments in Latin America, arguing that, overall they helped rather than exploited the Latin American people. In addition, he believed that the U.S. had the responsibility to intervene in hemisphere nations to protect U.S. businesses and to suppress Communism. Finally, Braden was a leading opponent of American foreign aid programs. In June 1957 testimony against the Eisenhower foreign aid package before the House Foreign Affairs Committee, Braden said that the U.S. was "going broke, committing suicide, by uselessly giving away billions of dollars to the rest of the world."   [JCH]

For further information:
Spruille Braden, *Diplomats and Demagogues: The Memoirs of Spruille Braden* (New Rochelle, 1971).

BRENNAN, WILLIAM J(OSEPH), JR.
b. April 25, 1906; Newark, N.J.
Associate Justice, U.S. Supreme Court, 1956-   .

The son of Irish immigrants, Brennan received a B.S. from the Wharton School of Finance of the University of Pennsylvania in 1928. He won a degree from Harvard law school in 1931 and then joined a Newark, N.J., law firm, where he became a partner in 1937 and a labor law specialist. A leader of a group of young attorneys who successfully promoted reform and streamlining of the New Jersey judicial system, Brennan was named a judge on the state Superior Court in 1949. The next year he was appointed to the Appellate Division of the Superior Court and in 1952 to the New Jersey Supreme Court.

President Eisenhower announced Brennan's appointment to the U.S. Supreme Court to replace retiring Justice Sherman Minton [q.v.] on Sept. 29, 1956. Although a Democrat, Brennan had not been politically active, and he had the judicial experience and high standing within the legal profession that Eisenhower said he wanted in a Supreme Court candidate. Brennan began serving on the Court under a recess appointment on Oct. 16. The Sen-

ate confirmed his nomination on March 19, 1957. Only Sen. Joseph R. McCarthy (R, Wisc.) [q.v.], whose methods Brennan had criticized in two speeches in the mid-1950s, voted against him.

By the end of his first term on the Court, Brennan had clearly aligned himself with the liberals on the bench. In June 1957 his majority opinion in the highly controversial *Jencks* case ruled that in federal criminal trials the government must let the defense examine relevant reports previously made to the government by prosecution witnesses. On the same day Brennan's opinion for the Court in the *E.I. du Pont de Nemours & Co.* case held that the Clayton Antitrust Act applied to vertical as well as to horizontal mergers. Therefore duPont, which manufactured many automotive products, was in violation of the law by its ownership of a controlling share of General Motors Corp. stock. Later in the month he voted in two important cases to reverse the contempt convictions of witnesses who had refused to answer questions during congressional and state investigations of Communism.

Though he had joined the Court's libertarian wing in his votes, Brennan remained largely independent of it in his judicial philosophy. Unlike Justice Hugo Black [q.v.], for example, Brennan did not consider First Amendment guarantees absolute but believed that these rights must be balanced against government interests. He insisted, however, that only a real and very substantial government need justified any curtailment of individual rights and thus usually favored the individual in loyalty-security cases. Brennan dissented, for example, when the majority in two June 1958 cases upheld the dismissal of municipal employes in Philadelphia and New York because they had refused to answer questions from superiors about their political activities. The Justice declared there had been no demonstration in either suit of a government security interest sufficient to justify the denial of the appellants' free speech rights. Brennan again dissented in two cases, decided a year later, in which the majority sustained the contempt convictions of witnesses who had failed to provide information during congressional and state investigations into possible subversion. The record in both cases, he asserted, showed the investigations had no valid legislative purpose but only the impermissible goal of exposure for exposure's sake. In the realm of obscenity law, Brennan emerged as the primary spokesman for the Court in the June 1957 *Roth* case. His opinion held that since obscene expression was "utterly without redeeming social importance," it was not protected by the First Amendment's guarantees of free speech and free press. He also defined the test of obscenity as whether to the average person, applying contemporary community standards, the dominant theme of the material taken as a whole appealed to prurient interest. In later cases Brennan made it clear he believed strict procedural standards must be followed in determining obscenity in order to prevent the suppression of non-obscene and thus constitutionally protected materials.

In criminal rights cases Brennan generally took a liberal stance. He favored extending the right to counsel in state court criminal cases, and he voted in March 1960 to overturn the espionage conviction of Soviet Col. Rudolf I. Abel because he believed the evidence used against Abel had been illegally obtained. In two March 1959 cases, however, Brennan was part of a majority that decided that an individual could be tried in both federal and state courts for the same offense without any violation of the prohibition against double jeopardy.

After Brennan's first two years on the high bench, Court analyst Daniel Berman wrote that the Justice "almost unfailingly revealed the fundamental attitudes of a judicial liberal: a desire to protect the rights of the accused rather than to expand the powers of the police; a willingness to employ judicial power to repel attacks on the dignity and freedom of the individual; and a preference for liberty over order."

During the heyday of the Warren Court in the 1960s, Brennan became an even more staunch liberal who believed the judiciary was constitutionally vested with the job of protecting the integrity and privacy of the individual from unnecessary government interference. He remained the Court's main spokesman in the troublesome area of obscenity, wrote significant opinions for the Court in cases involving reapportionment, freedom of the press and the Fourteenth Amendment, and won a reputation as a justice who was firmly committed to individual civil liberties and to the guarantees of procedural due process. [See KENNEDY, JOHNSON, NIXON/FORD Volumes]

[CAB]

For further information:
David Brennan, "Mr. Justice Brennan: A Preliminary Appraisal," *Catholic University of America Law Review*, VII (January, 1958), pp. 1-15.
Stephen J. Friedman, "William J. Brennan," in Leon Friedman and Fred L. Israel, eds., *The Justices of the U.S. Supreme Court, 1789-1969* (New York, 1969), Vol. 4.

BREWSTER, FRANK W.
b. 1898; Seattle, Wash.
Vice President, International Brotherhood of Teamsters, 1953-58.

The son of a postman, Brewster got his first job in 1913 driving a dray team. After serving two years in the Army during and after World War I, he became recording secretary of his Teamsters Union local. When the Western Conference of Teamsters was formed in 1937, Brewster became its secretary. He succeeded Dave Beck [*q.v.*] as president in 1953. During 1956 Brewster was involved in a dispute with Beck, then president of the International Brotherhood of Teamsters (IBT) and James R. Hoffa [*q.v.*], a vice president, over a mutual aid pact between the Teamsters and the International Longshoremen's Association. Beck and Hoffa favored the pact. However, Brewster wanted no part of the "racketeering and Communism of the longshore unions on both coasts."

During the opening months of 1957, the Senate Government Operations Committee's Permanent Investigations Subcommittee probed charges of racketeering and illegal use of union funds in the IBT. Over a three-month period subcommittee counsel Robert F. Kennedy [*q.v.*] revealed evidence that Brewster had been engaged in a variety of illegal activities. Brewster was charged with having used union funds to pay his personal bills (including several for maintenance of his racing stable and traveling expenses for his jockey). Testimony also revealed Brewster's links to organized crime. According to gambler James B. Elkins, Brewster had invited two alleged racketeers to Portland to take over and expand the rackets there. Elkins also implied that Brewster had a great deal of influence within Portland municipal government.

Brewster initially refused to testify before the subcommittee and was cited for contempt of Congress in February. The following month he appeared before the panel. He swore that he had "never conspired" to engage in any racket and knew of no "official or employe of the Teamsters who [had]." Brewster declared that Elkins had lied when he accused the union leader of "mastermining a plan to take over Portland rackets." He refused to admit that he had used union funds to pay personal bills. However, he acknowledged that he had ordered his secretary to spend union money for plane tickets for his jockey. He said he had intended to pay it back—although he had not yet done so.

In March officials of the Western Conference gave Brewster a vote of confidence. They charged that the Senate investigation was being used by employers to prevent unions from obtaining the best possible hours, wages and working conditions. Brewster was convicted of contempt of Congress in June 1957. The conviction was reversed in April 1958, when an appeals court ruled that the Senate committee had exceeded its jurisdiction in investigating rackets. In June Brewster was deposed as head of the Western Conference in a power struggle with Jimmy Hoffa.

[SY]

BRICKER, JOHN W(ILLIAM)
b. Sept. 6, 1893; Madison Co., Ohio.
Republican Senator, Ohio, 1947-59;
Chairman, Senate Commerce Committee, 1953-55.

John W. Bricker grew up in rural Madison Co., Ohio, and received his B.A. from Ohio State University in 1916. During World War I he served as an Army chaplain. Bricker returned to Ohio State and earned a law degree. He then held several local elective offices as a Republican. He won election for state attorney general in 1932 but lost a reelection bid. Bricker was elected governor in 1938. A white-maned, handsome man, an effective speaker and efficient administrator, "Honest John" won reelection in 1940 and 1942 by wide margins. After a brief try for the 1944 Republican presidential nomination, Bricker agreed to run for vice president. The GOP ticket lost in November. Two years later, Bricker won election to the U.S. Senate. There, he stood with the Party's conservative "Old Guard." In 1952, as in 1940 and 1948, Bricker backed the fellow Ohioan, Sen. Robert A. Taft (R, Ohio) [q.v.] for the Republican presidential nomination. Running for reelection in 1952 Bricker defeated Democratic nominee Michael V. DiSalle [q.v.] by a comfortable margin. [See TRUMAN Volume]

Few members of the Old Guard created more problems for the Eisenhower Administration than Bricker did between 1953 and 1954. In March 1953 he joined conservative Republicans voting against confirmation of Charles E. Bohlen [q.v.] as ambassador to the Soviet Union. Bricker also initiated efforts to cut the Administration's foreign aid requests. In January 1954 he opposed funding for the St. Lawrence Seaway, despite its expected benefits to Ohio's Lake Erie ports. That December he voted against the censure, quietly sought by the White House, of Sen. Joseph R. McCarthy, (R, Wisc.) [q.v.].

Yet no position more aggravated Eisenhower than did Bricker's sponsorship of an amendment to restrict the federal government's treaty-making powers. He had advocated such a proposal since the Truman Administration. As reported by the Judiciary Committee in June 1953, the Bricker amendment first voided any provision of treaties which conflicted with the Constitution. Second, it stipulated that treaties, executive agreements and international organizations could not determine domestic policy (i.e., a body such as the U.N. could not make social policy) without accompanying federal or state legislation. Known as the "which clause," this section raised the possibility that a single state could nullify an international compact. More importantly, the amendment delimited Congress's powers. Because of a 1920 Supreme Court ruling, Congress appeared empowered to extend its authority over states in enacting social legislation whenever it was carrying out the obligations of a treaty. Bricker's article would have prevented Congress from passing laws—as argued, for example, by some civil rights advocates—on the basis of that court precedent. Finally, the amendment made all executive understandings with foreign powers subject to Senate ratification. Bricker and other Republican nationalists had condemned Franklin D. Roosevelt's secret World War II agreements with the Soviet Union. They identified undisclosed, undebated understandings with Russian expansion into Eastern Europe immediately after the War. The Ohioan had long been a foe of those he called "One Worlders," generally liberal easterners like Eleanor Roosevelt [q.v.], who promoted international agreements in social and economic policy. Repeatedly, Bricker worked against American funding of the U.N.'s International Labor Organization or its International Atomic Energy Commission. The U.N.'s Covenant on Human Rights particularly incensed Bricker. This covenant, under negotiation between 1948 and 1954, included provisions that suspended such rights as freedom of speech during times of national emergency.

The fight for the Bricker amendment quickly evolved into a mass crusade. Many associations had long advocated a clarification of the statuatory effect of treaties and world organizations upon domestic law. The 1952 Republican platform had endorsed Bricker's article, as had Taft, the American Bar Association (ABA) and especially its past president, Frank E. Holman. Besides the ABA, pro-amendment associations included the American Farm Bureau, American Legion and the Daughters of the American Revolution. Special committees like the Vigilant Women for the Bricker Amendment organized spontaneously. View-ing it as a defense of states rights, Southerners opposed to federal civil rights legislation overwhelmingly backed the proposal.

The most pronounced critics of the measure tended to be liberal, long-standing internationalists. Championing a strong chief executive, they deemed the Bricker amendment a hazardous weakening of presidential powers. Amendment foes also viewed the mass movement for the article as "new isolationism," a variation of that stand more widely held in the 1920s and 1930s.

Mindful of a growing public debate that threatened party unity, Eisenhower initially refused to take a stand on the issue. His biographer Emmet J. Hughes [q.v.] claimed that the Bricker matter upset the President more than any other single crisis of his presidency. The amendment, Eisenhower complained one day, "is a damn thorn in our side." Secretary of State John Foster Dulles [q.v.] who had called for "some" sort of treaty-making amendment in 1952, urged Eisenhower to oppose Bricker's proposal.

In January 1954 the Administration declared itself opposed to the Bricker amendment. Eisenhower stated publicly in January that ratification would signal America's intention "to withdraw from its leadership in world affairs." His chief aide, Sherman Adams [q.v.], recalled that the President had become "thoroughly disgusted with what he now considered a direct attempt to undermine the constitutional structure of the executive branch." The Administration assigned at least one lobbyist for each Republican senator.

The Administration beat Bricker but barely. On Feb. 26, 1954, a milder version, sponsored by Sen. Walter F. George (D, Ga.) [q.v.] and also opposed by the White House, fell one vote short of the required two-thirds majority. One day earlier, Bricker's original amendment had lost 42-50. Bricker inexplicably abandoned his crusade thereafter; though he reintroduced the article in 1955, he never again labored strenuously for it.

On domestic policy Bricker figured prominently first as chairman (1953-55) and then as the ranking Republican (1955-59) of the Commerce Committee. Early in the fall of

1953, he acknowledged that he had accepted monies from his Columbus law firm, which represented the Pennsylvania Railroad; he had done so even though his panel oversaw transportation policy. Bricker attacked the two then dominant television networks in February 1955 as a monopoly. In June 1956, however, he defended the major automobile manufacturers on the same charges during Judiciary Committee hearings. That July Bricker blocked floor consideration of a new price discrimination bill that policed the pricing policies of major producers.

In 1958 Bricker unexpectedly lost his Senate seat. He had originally planned to retire from politics, but Eisenhower, despite the amendment quarrel, urged him to seek a third term. Bricker agreed. However, his victory was jeopardized when a group of Ohio business leaders met in June and determined to place a "right-to-work" (RTW) referendum on the November ballet. The RTW proposal would have prevented "union shop" labor contracts (those compelling employes to join unions after being hired.) At the businessmen's gathering in June, Bricker objected vehemently to the initiative. The Ohio GOP would lose badly, he predicted, because it would invariably be identified with the pro-business RTW forces and against organized labor. "I may go down myself," Bricker cried. And "Honest John" did. Although he evaded the RTW issue, he lost to a token Democratic opponent, Stephen M. Young, by just over 100,000 votes. But for the RTW issue, Bricker felt later, he might have won by between 250,000 and 500,000 votes. Bricker quit active politics to practice law in Columbus.

[JLB]

BRIDGES, HARRY (ALFRED) (RENTON)

b. July 28, 1901; Melbourne, Australia.
President, International Longshoremen's and Warehousemen's Union, 1937-77.

Bridges, the son of a prosperous Melbourne realtor, spent five years as a seaman before beginning work on the San Francisco docks in 1922. During this period he was a member of the Industrial Workers of the World and in the early 1930s was close to the Communist Party. In 1934 Bridges emerged as the leader of the San Francisco dock strike that triggered the city's general strike that year. Bridges organized Pacific Coast and Hawaiian longshoremen, and in 1937 he led a group of locals out of the American Federation of Labor (AFL) and into the International Longshoremen's and Warehousemen's Union (ILWU) affiliated with the new Committee for Industrial Organization (CIO). During the 1940s Bridges became one of the most powerful labor figures on the West Coast, and his ILWU became an important base of Communist strength in the CIO.

Beginning in 1939 Bridges was the target of a 16-year effort by the federal government to denaturalize and deport him. Although the CIO expelled the ILWU in 1949 because of Communist domination, the Justice Department never proved Bridges was a Communist. However, in 1950 he was convicted of perjury. A jury ruled that he had obtained his U.S. citizenship in 1945 by fraud when he had denied he had ever been a Communist. The Federal Appeals Court upheld the conviction in 1952, but in 1953 the Supreme Court ruled that Bridges had been indicted after the statute of limitations had run out. [See TRUMAN Volume]

Long an opponent of congressional investigations of alleged subversion, Bridges threatened in 1955 to shut down all of Hawaii's industries in a protest strike against a four-day hearing Sen. James O. Eastland (D, Miss.) [q.v.] had planned to investigate subversion on the islands. Only 3,000 of Hawaii's 24,000 ILWU members walked off their jobs in November, when the probe began. At the hearings, Gov. Samuel W. King testified that ILWU leaders, including Bridges, were the core of the territory's Communist problem. He expressed hope that the probe might lead to the ILWU being "listed as Communist-infiltrated "under the Communist Control Act of 1954 and that Hawaiian industry consequently would be freed "from the necessity of recognizing such organizations as legitimate labor unions. . . ." The power of Bridges's union was regarded as one of the obstacles to Hawaiian statehood.

In 1959 Bridges was called to testify on possible Communist Party affiliation before the House Un-American Activities Committee. He invoked the Fifth Amendment, saying he had been cleared of such charges in the past. In answering questions on the union's attitude toward China, Bridges said he personally would "object in every way I could" to shipment of U.S. arms to Nationalist China for the invasion of the Chinese mainland. He said he regarded Nationalist leader Chiang Kai-shek as a "bum." However, he asserted it would be up to union members to decide whether the ILWU would boycott such shipments. He denied having joined Teamster president James R. Hoffa [q.v.] in plans for a worldwide transport workers' union or having conferred with foreign Communists during a trip abroad on how to institute a worldwide shipping boycott.

In October 1959 Bridges became the first labor leader to defy the Landrum-Griffin Act, when he refused to comply with Secretary of Labor James P. Mitchell's [q.v.] request that he report on Communists and ex-convicts in the ILWU. Bridges maintained that the law "violates . . . at least the First and Fifth Amendments" and said he found nothing in it that authorized Mitchell to request such reports or that required Bridges to respond or "to undertake the various investigations which might be necessary. . . ."

Bridges continued as president of the ILWU during the 1960s and 1970s. In 1960 he signed a five-and-one-half-year collective bargaining contract with the Pacific Maritime Association. Known as the M & M Agreement, it had a far-reaching impact on the nature of longshore work and the character of the industry. Bridges retired as head of the union in 1977. [See KENNEDY, JOHNSON, NIXON/FORD Volumes]

[SY]

For further information:
Charles P. Larrowe, *Harry Bridges: the Rise and Fall of Radical Labor in the United States* (New York, 1972).

BRIDGES, (HENRY) STYLES
b. Sept. 9, 1898; West Pembroke, Me.
d. Nov. 26, 1961; Concord, N.H.
Republican Senator, N.H., 1937-61.

Bridges was raised and educated in Maine, where he received a degree in agriculture from the state university in 1918. In 1921 he moved to New Hampshire as a member of the extension staff of the University of New Hampshire. From 1924 to 1930 he served as secretary of the New Hampshire Farm Bureau Federation, edited the *Granite Monthly* and was director and secretary of the New Hampshire Investment Co. He was appointed to the New Hampshire Public Service Commission in 1930. Four years later Bridges was elected governor, the youngest in the state's history. He was elected to the U.S. Senate in 1936.

Bridges was known from the beginning of his tenure as a vigorous conservative and anti-Communist. He assailed many of Franklin D. Roosevelt's New Deal domestic policies but supported Roosevelt's efforts early in World War II to supply the Allied powers. He was a foe of Secretary of State Dean Acheson [q.v.] and led the "Asia-firsters" in denouncing the Administration's refusal to give large-scale aid to Chiang Kai-shek as a "sellout" to the Communists. [See TRUMAN Volume]

Bridges, called the Gray Eminence of the Republican Party, became the senior member of the GOP and its floor leader in the Senate in 1952. With the introduction of a Republican Administration in 1953, he was named President Pro Tempore of the Senate and chairman of the Appropriations Committee, from which post he frequently pressed for cuts in the federal budget.

Bridges remained a strident anti-Communist throughout the Eisenhower Administration. When President Dwight D. Eisenhower nominated Charles Bohlen [q.v.] to be ambassador to the Soviet Union in February 1953, Bridges joined other conservatives in attempting to block the appointment. He seized the moment to attack the Yalta agreements of 1945, which Bohlen had helped negotiate, as a traitorous mishandling of American foreign policy and denounce Bohlen as an "appeaser" of Communists. Despite conservative efforts, the Senate confirmed Bohlen in March.

Bridges was a strong supporter of Sen. Joseph R. McCarthy's (R, Wisc.) [q.v.] attacks on alleged subversives in government, disdaining Republican moderates' misgivings about McCarthy's tactics in the hearing room and use of the press. When, in September 1954, the Senate Select Committee to Study Censure Charges, filed a report recommending censure of McCarthy for his contempt of the Senate and his abuse of Gen. Ralph Zwicker [q.v.], Bridges began attempts to either dilute the resolution or defeat it entirely. First he pressured to delay the full Senate hearings on the resolution until after the November elections. With that objective accomplished, he used the period of Senate inactivity to attempt to win moderate Republican support for McCarthy. With GOP backing he hoped to approach Democratic leaders and offer a compromise resolution so that the censure did not appear to be a partisan Democratic move. The support did not materialize; McCarthy was condemned by the Senate in December. One of 22 Republicans to vote against the measure, Bridges denounced the action as a blow against patriotic anti-Communism.

Undaunted, Bridges carried his anti-Communist battle to the White House. When President Eisenhower agreed to U.S. participation in a Geneva summit conference in 1955, Bridges avowed that all international conferences held the dangers of "appeasement, compromise and weakness"—particularly those conferences that included the USSR. Eisenhower, who had been threatened with the Bricker amendment that sought to curb his treaty-making power, promised Bridges and other Republican leaders that he would take no actions without congressional approval. In 1956 Bridges introduced amendments that would have cut off all aid to Yugoslavia. He reasoned, "What have we got in exchange for the $1 billion we gave to Tito? . . . We get a Tito honeymoon staged in Moscow. . . ." He also ridiculed the neutralist positions of Prime Minister Jawaharlal Nehru and wanted to decrease U.S. assistance to India.

Bridges was a prominent political strategist in the Republican hierarchy, particularly as the chairman of the GOP Policy Committee from 1955 to 1961. Eisenhower's heart attack in 1955 occasioned major concerns within the party: the possibility of his death in office, the delegation of his responsibilities during the illness and the status of the Republican ticket in 1956. Fully aware of the importance of the vice presidency, some conservatives, displeased with Richard Nixon [q.v.] because of his association with Eisenhower's moderate policies, hoped to advance Bridges as a candidate for the office. Bridges, however, strongly supported Nixon's remaining on the ticket. During Eisenhower's illnesses Bridges advocated Nixon's assumption of some presidential duties, but he found his suggestions blocked by White House chief aide Sherman Adams [q.v.]. The New Hampshire Senator believed Nixon to be a strong candidate for President in 1960.

Bridges won a fifth term in the Senate in 1960. He supported those Kennedy Administration actions he believed challenged Communism and advised a resumption of U.S. nuclear testing in 1961. That same year he died in his home state. [See KENNEDY Volume]

[TGD]

For further information:
Robert Griffith, *The Politics of Fear* (Lexington, 1970).

BROWN, CLARENCE
b. July 14, 1893; Blanchester, Ohio.
d. Aug. 23, 1965; Washington, D.C.
Republican Representative, Ohio, 1939-65.

As a boy Brown sold popcorn and newspapers from a baby carriage and served as a janitor in a bank. He studied at Washington and Lee University law school from 1913 to 1915. Rather than practice law, he became a newspaper publisher. In 1918 Brown was elected lieutenant governor of Ohio and served two two-year terms. He won the election for secretary of state in 1926. In 1932 he lost the Republican gubernatorial primary. Two years later he was defeated in the general election. Brown headed Frank Knox's campaign for the vice presidency in 1936.

Brown was elected to a seat in the U.S. House of Representatives in 1938. Before World War II he generally opposed legislation aimed at reversing American neutrality. After the War he opposed aid to Greece and Turkey on grounds of economy but was paired in favor of the Marshall Plan. Brown compiled a consistently conservative domestic record. He supported the establishment of the Un-American Activities Committee on a permanent basis in 1945, the Taft-Hartley Act in 1947 and the Internal Security Act in 1950. However, he backed an anti-poll tax bill in 1944 and the Fair Employment Practices Act of 1950.

In 1952, as in 1940 and 1948, Brown actively supported Sen. Robert A. Taft (R, Ohio) [q.v.], for the Republican presidential nomination. He served as one of Taft's campaign managers and was one of the Ohio Senator's major strategists in the struggle over contested delegate seats at the Republican National Convention. At the first session of the Convention, he moved to exclude, on a technicality, Taft's Louisiana delegates from the provisions of the "Fair Play" amendment. This rule stipulated that contested delegates could not vote on any challenges to delegates' credentials. The defeat of Brown's proposal was an early signal that Taft's nomination bid had failed. Taft and many others regarded Brown's proposal as a major tactical error because it appeared to be a crude, unprincipled attempt to strengthen the Ohioan's forces.

Brown was appointed to the Commission on Organization of the Executive Branch of the Government, unofficially known as the Second Hoover Commission. An opponent of what he regarded as government encroachment in business, he concurred with the Committee's 1955 report, urging substantial cutbacks in government activity. Its major proposals, echoing the general theme "get government out of business," included

the transfer of federal lending agencies and power installations to private hands and the elimination of federal medical services. Testifying before the Government Operations Committee's Intergovernmental Relations Subcommittee in 1954, he criticized military commissaries as presenting "a real threat to free enterprise" because of their competition with private business.

Brown was a member of the Rules Committee, which had the power to block legislation on the way from its committee of original jurisdiction to the House floor. He generally joined the Southern Democratic-Republican conservative coalition on the panel in their often successful efforts to kill liberal social welfare measures. He helped block housing bills in 1955, 1959 and 1960 and school aid and minimum wage bills in the latter year. However, in 1957 and 1960 he backed successful liberal efforts to clear civil rights bills for floor consideration.

As a member of the Rules panel, Brown was a leading opponent of President John F. Kennedy's liberal domestic legislation. Brown died of uremic poisoning in Washington, D.C., in August 1965. [See KENNEDY Volume]

[MLL]

For further information:
James T. Patterson, Mr. Republican—A Biography of Robert A. Taft (Boston, 1972).

BROWN, EDMUND G(ERALD)
b. April 21, 1905; San Francisco, Calif.
Governor, Calif., 1959-67.

The son of Gold Rush settlers, "Pat" Brown attended San Francisco public and parochial schools. Lacking the money to attend college, he worked in his father's cigar store-poker room establishment while studying law at night. He received his LL.B. from the San Francisco law school in 1927 and opened a private practice in San Francisco. In 1928 Brown entered politics as an unsuccessful Republican candidate for the California Assembly. He switched parties during the New Deal and in 1943 won the first of two terms as San Francisco district attorney. Brown was elected state attorney general in 1950 and again in 1954. As the only Democrat holding statewide office, he was the titular head of the state Democratic Party. During his eight years in office he earned a reputation as a progressive but tough criminal investigator.

In 1958 Brown entered the state's gubernatorial race against conservative Republican Sen. William F. Knowland [q.v.]. In contrast to Knowland's extreme conservatism, Brown was able to seize the center of the political spectrum, describing himself as a "responsible" liberal and advocating more ambitious state programs to keep pace with California's demographic and physical growth. Backed strongly by organized labor, which mobilized its ranks to help Brown and defeat a right-to-work initiative backed by his opponent, the Democrat won the November election by more than one million votes. He was the state's second Democratic governor in the century. Brown also swept Democrats into all the top state offices except one and carried the first Democratic majorities in both houses of the legislature since 1889.

As governor, Brown undertook an ambitious bipartisan legislative program which easily passed the legislature. He took action on air pollution, old age problems, prisons, highway safety and atomic energy. Brown also established a state economic development commission, a consumers' council and the state's first fair employment practices commission. The Governor developed $200 million in new tax revenues and abolished the state's troublesome cross-filing primary election system, which allowed a voter to participate in any primary he chose, regardless of his registration. Brown also brought northern and southern California interests together to approve the $1.7 billion California Water Project in 1960. The project, the most costly in U.S. history, was designed to provide water from the northern part of the state for the burgeoning population of the south and the irrigated farmlands of the Central Valley.

At the time Brown's water plan was lauded as a spectacular achievement. However, by the 1970s observers concluded that the plan had become unnecessary because of the slowdown in California's population increase and had caused ecological damage to northern rivers. A Ralph Nader research group charged that the water project was a "special interest boondoggle" that had ultimately cost close to $10 billion and placed greater burdens on the individual taxpayer than on the largest industrial and corporate farm users of the water.

During his early years as governor, Brown made a number of important enemies, who continued to plague him throughout his career. His unsuccessful effort to pass a tax on oil alienated California's powerful oil lobby. His attempts to subject unions to state regulations failed and weakened organized labor's support for his future political ambitions.

Brown's inconsistent position on the fate of Caryl Chessman [q.v.], a convicted rapist, hurt his standing both among conservatives and a large segment of liberal Democrats. Chessman, who had spent over a decade on San Quentin's Death Row, had become an international *cause celebre* through repeated protestations of his innocence and publication of four popular books. In October 1959 Brown rejected a plea for clemency, but Chessman's life was spared for the seventh time by a U.S. Supreme Court stay of execution. In February 1960 Brown reprieved Chessman 10 days before his eighth scheduled date of execution because, Brown said, the State Department had informed him that President Eisenhower's visit to Uruguay might be disturbed by hostile demonstrations if Chessman were executed. In addition, Brown argued that he wanted the California legislature to consider abolition of the death penalty. Chessman was finally executed in May 1960 after Brown refused to grant another reprieve. Demonstrators at the execution attacked the Governor as "the hangman of California."

Brown's power within the California Democratic Party declined after 1961 as President Kennedy looked to the Democratic Speaker of the Assembly, Jesse Unruh, as his chief political operative in the state. Nonetheless, Brown won a spectacular reelection victory in November 1962 over former Vice President Richard Nixon [q.v.]. Brown's second term coincided with the Berkeley student revolt, the 1965 Watts riot and the growing farmworker movement. Conservative Republicans benefited most from these developments and held Brown's "soft" liberalism partly responsible. In 1966 Brown lost his bid for a third gubernatorial term to Ronald Reagan, a former movie star and conservative spokesman. Following his defeat Brown served as head of the National Commission for the Reform of Federal Criminal Laws. [See KENNEDY, JOHNSON Volumes]

[JCH]

BROWN, WITHROP G(ILMAN)
b. July 12, 1907; Seal Harbor, Me.
Ambassador to Laos, July 1960-June 1962.

Brown attended Yale law school, and after receiving his degree in 1929, practiced in New York. He joined the staff of the Lend-Lease Administration in 1941. Over the next five years he represented the agency in missions in London and New Delhi. Brown was director of the Office of International Trade Policy from 1947 to 1950 and of the Office of International Materials Policy from 1950 to 1952. During the 1950s he served as minister for Economic Affairs in London and New Delhi. In July 1960 he became an ambassador to Laos.

Brown arrived at his assignment shortly before an Aug. 9 coup, led by Laotian Air Force Capt. Kong Le, toppled the pro-American government of Gen. Phoumi Nosavan. Brown sympathized with Le, whom he considered a sincere nationalist disturbed by Phoumi's corruption. The Ambassador did not think Le a potential ally of the Communist Pathet Lao, which controlled a large portion of the countryside, and he saw no danger to American interests from the new regime. Despite State Department requests that he take steps to have Le removed, Brown did not act, preferring to see how the situation developed.

Kong Le turned administrative power over to neutralist Prince Souvanna Phouma, who formed a government composed of opponents of Phoumi's pro-Western stance.

Phoumi refused to accept Souvanna's offer of a position in the new regime. Instead, he decided to use his control of the Royal Laotian Army to retake the government by force.

Brown respected Souvanna and soon threw his support behind the neutralist leader. He questioned the possibility of developing a pro-Western government in light of the corruption of the previous regime and growing national feelings in the country. However, many high State Department officials feared that Souvanna would make an alliance with the Left, and they demanded his replacement.

Because of the growing opposition to Souvanna in Washington, Brown was anxious to promote a rightist-neutralist coalition that would exclude pro-Communists. At the same time, he attempted to prevent Phoumi from reestablishing his control through military action. Brown was unsuccessful in his efforts because the Central Intelligence Agency continued to supply Phoumi with troops and material.

Souvanna, unable to get U.S. military aid or assurances of diplomatic backing, formed an alliance with the Pathet Lao in September. Hoping to reverse Souvanna's stand, Brown asked the State Department to grant him assistance. Washington did give both Souvanna and Phoumi loans but granted military aid only to Phoumi. Nevertheless Brown still pushed for a reorientation of American policy. He risked his own diplomatic position by returning instructions to Washington and asking for clarification. In this way he hoped to maintain a discussion of policy options.

By November Brown and Washington were pursuing opposite policies. The State Department openly backed Phoumi, who had begun his military campaign against Souvanna. Brown opposed this action and asked for U.S. air support to reinforce Souvanna's troops, led by Kong Le. By the end of the month he was able to persuade Washington to cut off aid to Phoumi. However, by that time the General had driven Souvanna to exile and Kong Le into an alliance with the Communists.

Brown remained at his post into the Kennedy Administration. Unlike his predecessor, John F. Kennedy supported a neutralist government in Laos, It was formed in June 1962. Brown, however, had little part in the negotiations leading to its creation. During the Johnson Administration he served as ambassador to Korea and special assistant to the Secretary of State. He was appointed deputy assistant secretary of state for East Asian and Pacific affairs in 1968. Brown retired from the Foreign Service two years later. [See KENNEDY Volume]

[EWS]

For further information:
Charles A. Stevenson, *The End of Nowhere, American Policy Toward Laos since 1954* (Boston, 1972).

BROWNELL, HERBERT, JR.
b. Feb. 20, 1904; Peru, Neb.
Attorney General, January 1953-October 1957.

The son of a university teacher, Herbert Brownell, Jr., grew up in Nebraska and attended the University of Nebraska, where he edited the college newspaper. He earned his law degree from Yale law school in 1927 and began his career at a New York firm. In 1929 he joined the firm of Lord, Day and Lord, with which he was associated for the next five decades. Brownell's specialty was hotel and restaurant law. He also served as counsel for New York's 1939 World's Fair.

Brownell became active in New York Republican politics early in his career. From 1933 to 1937 he represented a Manhattan district in the New York State Assembly. Brownell became politically prominent with the help of Manhattan District Attorney Thomas E. Dewey. He managed Dewey's unsuccessful bid for the governorship in 1938 as well as his successful campaign in 1942. Accompanying Dewey to Albany, Brownell handled patronage but refused a cabinet post. He was manager of Dewey's unsuccessful presidential campaigns in 1944 and 1948, and he also served as chairman of the Republican National Committee during 1944-45.

During the 1952 campaign Brownell was one of Gen. Dwight D. Eisenhower's key advisers. He played a major role in the formulation of convention strategy, most notably in his recommendation that Eisenhower forces support a "Fair Play Amendment," under which many delegates backing Sen. Robert Taft (R, Ohio) [*q.v.*] were unseated. Brownell also urged Eisenhower to select Sen. Richard Nixon (R, Calif.) [*q.v.*] as his running mate. After Eisenhower's election in November Brownell continued in his crucial advisory role, proposing cabinet nominees and overseeing patronage. According to presidential assistant Sherman Adams [*q.v.*], "Eisenhower at that time had more confidence in Brownell's political advice than he had in anyone else's." On Nov. 21 the President-elect designated Brownell as his Attorney General.

During Brownell's first year in office the hot political debate over the issue of Communists in government continued to rage. A vigorous anti-Communist, Brownell generated controversy on his own on Nov. 6, 1953, when he resurrected the Harry Dexter White case of the Truman years. (White, an assistant secretary of the Treasury appointed by President Harry S. Truman to be executive director of the International Monetary Fund [IMF] in 1946, had been accused in 1948 of spying for the Soviet Union; he died on Aug. 16, 1949.)

Speaking before the Executives' Club of Chicago, Brownell declared that "Harry Dexter White was known to be a Communist agent by the very people who appointed him to the most sensitive position he ever held in government service." He charged that White had smuggled secret documents to the Soviets and that Truman had received FBI reports detailing White's espionage activities but had appointed him anyway.

Truman vehemently denied Brownell's charges. He and other prominent Democrats accused Brownell of making the charges in order to offset recent electoral reverses suffered by Republicans. On Nov. 10 Truman denounced "fake crusaders who dig up and distort records of the past to distract the attention of people from political failures of the present." He castigated the Attorney General for lying and "shameful demagoguery" and charged that the Administration had embraced "McCarthyism."

On Nov. 11 President Eisenhower said that he did not think Truman had knowingly appointed a Communist to high office or had consciously damaged the interests of the U.S. Eisenhower said it was reckless and un-American to make accusations from a favored position without being prepared to make evidence available, but he maintained that FBI files should not be released. He said he would permit Brownell to handle the case in his own way. He also rejected suggestions that Brownell had impugned President Truman's loyalty. On the same day Brownell modified his original charge, stating that he was exposing the "laxity" of the previous Administration but had no intention of questioning the loyalty of any Truman Administration official.

On Nov. 16 Truman outlined his role in the White case. Acknowledging receipt of an FBI report on White in February 1946, after White's confirmation for the IMF post by the Senate, he said the FBI's charges were "impossible to prove." Truman maintained that he had allowed White's appointment to proceed so as not to disrupt any of the FBI's parallel investigations into security risks or to alert White to the fact that he was under suspicion. The next day Brownell and FBI Director J. Edgar Hoover [q.v.] appeared before the Senate Internal Security Subcommittee to rebut Truman's version of events. Hoover testified that he had advised Truman's Attorney General, Tom Clark [q.v.], that the White appointment was "unwise"; he also stated that the FBI's investigation was "hampered" by White's appointment because the IMF's premises were "extraterritorial" and FBI agents could not enter them. Brownell dismissed Truman's claim and declassified the 1945-46 FBI reports on White to buttress his case. The Senate subcommittee took no action. Truman refused to answer a subpoena issued by the House Committee on Un-American Activities, and little more was said in public on the White affair.

On other issues involving Communists and suspected subversives, Brownell consis-

tently followed a hard line. In June 1953 he filed an immediate protest when Supreme Court Justice William O. Douglas [q.v.] granted a stay of execution to convicted spies Julius and Ethel Rosenberg [q.v.]. The full Court soon reversed the order. After the execution defense attorney Emanuel Bloch blamed Brownell along with President Eisenhower and J. Edgar Hoover for "the murder of the Rosenbergs." Brownell asked Congress in April 1954 to permit the death penalty for peacetime spying as well as wartime espionage.

In August 1953 Brownell declared that U.S. Communists were "a greater menace now than at any time [because they] have gone underground since the Smith Act trials started. They are better organized and detection is more difficult." In line with his pledge to "utterly destroy all" Communist Party activities in the United States, Brownell from 1953 to 1955 proposed a body of anti-Communist legislation for congressional enactment. He sought legislation to compel witnesses to testify if granted immunity from criminal prosecution. He requested a "greatly needed" amendment to the perjury law to make "willful giving of contradictory statements under oath" a crime. Existing law required the government to prove one of the statements false. He recommended increasing penalties for seditious conspiracy and advocating the forcible overthrow of the government to a maximum of 20 years imprisonment; he also sought authority for the government to revoke the citizenship of persons convicted of such offenses. Under his existing authority Brownell added scores of left-wing organizations to the Attorney General's list of subversive groups, a number that exceeded 300 by 1955.

The Attorney General personally intervened in a split within the Justice Department in 1955 over a case involving the right of a fired government employe to confront his accuser. The Department's brief, urging the Supreme Court to uphold the 1951 U.S. Public Health Service's dismissal of Dr. John Peters on loyalty grounds, was signed by Brownell instead of Solicitor General Simon Sobeloff [q.v.] who normally represented the government before the Supreme Court. Sobeloff and other department lawyers argued that Peter's dismissal violated the Fifth Amendment's ban on depriving a person of liberty or property without due process of law, while Brownell maintained that the due process clause did not cover government jobs, since government security programs depended on undercover agents and secret informers. In June 1955 the Court overturned Peters's dismissal. The Court decided the case on procedural grounds relating to the Loyalty Review Board having exceeded its authority; it did not rule on the constitutional question of whether he had been denied due process of law.

Brownell singled out labor unions for special attention in his anti-Communist offensive. Denying in an August 1953 interview that Communists were "concentrated in the clergy," he said, "I suppose there are more in labor unions than anywhere else." In July 1955 he asked that the striking Union of Mine, Mill and Smelter Workers be stripped of its privileges before the National Labor Relations Board on the grounds that it was Communist-dominated. In December he urged the Subversive Activities Control Board to declare the striking United Electrical, Radio and Machine Workers (UE) "Communist-infiltrated." UE President Albert Fitzgerald denied Brownell's accustaion and denounced him as "the nation's No. 1 strikebreaker."

In the area of antitrust policy, the Justice Department under Brownell differed in a number of ways from its Democratic predecessors. In June 1953 Brownell pledged that the Eisenhower Administration would tolerate "no winking" at antitrust violations but would emphasize civil rather than criminal actions. He attempted to hire only top law school graduates for the Department and the antitrust division under the so-called Honors Program. He promulgated a firm rule whereby ex-division lawyers could not represent firms being sued by the division for a two-year period after leaving the Justice Department. He also sought legislation raising from $5,000 to $50,000 the maximum fine for antitrust violations and enabling the government to sue for actual damages resulting from violations, since the government was the nation's "largest single purchaser of goods" and its losses could be substantial.

Among the firms prosecuted for antitrust violations by Brownell's department were the Westinghouse Electric Co. and the Aluminum Company of America (Alcoa). Perhaps the most ambitious suit filed during his tenure was against the General Motors Corp. (GM). The suit charged that GM, which sold 84% of all new buses in 1955, had conspired with four bus operating companies to maintain its monopoly.

Brownell's antitrust policy differed in a number of ways from his Democratic predecessors. In June 1953 he pledged grand jury proceedings against several large international oil companies which allegedly formed a cartel to control distribution and prices. "The highest considerations of national security," was the explanation given for the dismissal.

In January 1956 the Justice Department signed a famous consent decree with the American Telephone and Telegraph Co. (AT&T). The original Justice Department suit, filed in 1949, had charged AT&T with monopolizing the telephone market via its control of the Western Electric Co., the leading manufacturer of telephone equipment, and called for the separation of the two companies. On taking office Brownell met privately with AT&T's general counsel to discuss ways of ending the litigation without damaging AT&T. The 1956 settlement allowed AT&T to keep Western Electric and continue their previous arrangements. AT&T consented to license patents to all applicants at reasonable royalties. Brownell called the decree "a major victory" for the government, but *Business Week* commented that the " 'major victory' turned out on second look to be hardly more than a slap on the wrist for the biggest corporation in the world." Frederick Kappel, president of Western Electric, directed his executives, "Don't brag about having won victory or getting everything we wanted."

Within the Eisenhower cabinet Brownell was the most active proponent of expanding the role of the federal government in protecting civil rights. In December 1953 he filed an *amicus curiae* brief in the landmark

Brown v. Board of Education case before the Supreme Court. The brief supported the Court's authority to declare school segregation unconstitutional, as the Court eventually ruled in 1954. (The new Chief Justice, Earl Warren [*q.v.*] had been chosen by President Eisenhower upon Brownell's recommendation.)

Brownell was the key Administration figure behind the origination and passage of the Civil Rights Act of 1957. The proposed bill, put together by Justice Department lawyers early in 1956, would have created a Civil Rights Commission and a new civil rights division within the Justice Department. Its third section would have armed the government with injunctive power against civil rights violations and enabled the Attorney General to join civil suits against individuals infringing on others' right to vote. Despite an unenthusiastic attitude on the part of Eisenhower and the rest of the cabinet, Brownell won official backing for the proposals and defended them before the Judiciary Committees in Congress in the spring of 1956. The legislation made little progress during that year. Brownell was later accused of concealing the sweeping import of the bill's third section in order to get the measure past the White House.

Brownell played an active part in the Senate battle over the bill in the spring of 1957. He argued strongly against an amendment initiated by Southern senators to require jury trials for persons charged with contempt of court for violating injunctions against interfering with individuals' civil rights. The Administration's version left contempt decisions up to the discretion of a fedaral judge. It was widely assumed that Southern juries would refuse to convict accused violators of civil rights laws. Brownell warned that the jury trial amendment guaranteed the "practical nullification" of the bill's effectiveness by "seriously weakening" the courts' power to enforce their orders. He pointed out that under "traditional rules of procedure" a "defendant is not entitled to jury trial in contempt proceedings" when the government sued for "preventive relief."

The Senate passed the jury trial amend-

ment, nevertheless, and also deleted the bill's controversial Part III. In the debates Southern senators attacked Brownell as the author of these allegedly punitive section. The final bill retained the Civil Rights Commission and the new civil rights division for the Justice Department, but it restricted the government's enforcement powers in civil rights cases to those protecting voting rights. The House version of the bill, which the Senate ultimately accepted, restricted jury trials to cases in which the judge imposed a sentence of more than 30 days or a fine of more than $300.

Brownell also played a vital advisory role in the September 1957 school integration crisis in Little Rock, Ark. Arkansas Gov. Orval Faubus [*q.v.*] had precipitated the crisis when he ordered the Arkansas National Guard to prevent black students from entering the city's Central High School as part of a court-ordered integration plan. Acting on Brownell's advice, President Eisenhower dispatched regular Army paratroopers to Little Rock to enforce the federal court's integration order.

Brownell resigned as Attorney General in October 1957 and returned to the law firm of Lord, Day & Lord.

[TO]

For further information:
J. W. Anderson, *Eisenhower, Brownell and the Congress* (University, Ala., 1964).

BRUCE, DAVID K(IRKPATRICK) E(STE)
b. Feb. 12, 1898; Baltimore, Md.
Observer to the European Defense Community Interim Commission and Special Representative to the European Coal and Steel Community, February 1953-January 1955; Ambassador to Germany, February 1957-November 1959.

Born into a politically and socially prominent Baltimore family, David Bruce was the son of William Cabell Bruce, U.S. senator from Maryland from 1923 to 1929 and author of a Pulitzer prize-winning biography of Benjamin Franklin. He briefly attended Princeton University before serving in the

Army during World War I. Bruce earned a law degree from the University of Maryland in 1921 and practiced law in Baltimore. Bruce served briefly in the Virginia House of Delegates and the Foreign Service before leaving in 1927 to join the Bankers Trust Co. He later worked for W. A. Harriman and Co. At one time he was the director of 25 corporations. Between 1926 and 1945 Bruce was married to Ailsa Mellon, the daughter of Andrew Mellon and reputedly the richest woman in the United States.

During World War II Bruce directed the Office of Strategic Services' sabotage and espionage activities in Europe. In June 1947 he became assistant secretary of commerce under his friend and business associate, W. Averell Harriman [q.v.]. He went to Paris to administer the Marshall Plan in 1948 and became ambassador to France one year later. In April 1952 Bruce was named undersecretary of state and also assumed the posts of alternate governor of the International Monetary Fund and governor of the International Bank for Reconstruction and Development (World Bank). [See TRUMAN Volume]

In February 1953 President Eisenhower appointed Bruce observer at the Interim Commission of the European Defense Community (EDC) and special representative to the European Coal and Steel Community (ECSC). Bruce had long been a proponent of European integration and was an originator of the concept of a European army. In addition, he was well acquainted with European political leaders, particularly the French, whose consent was vital for the establishment of the EDC. Because he was a liberal and a leading financial contributor to the Democratic Party, conservative Republicans disapproved of the nomination, but he was easily confirmed by the Senate.

Bruce's Paris based operation was established to convince Europeans of the merits of political, economic and military integration. Political analyst Theodore White credited Bruce with mobilizing American diplomacy behind the EDC. By the end of 1953 the six member-nations had created a single market for coal and steel. Despite early production difficulties and conflicts among the members, the economic union progressed, and in 1958 it gave way to the European Economic Community.

Bruce found the EDC negotiations more difficult. He traveled throughout Western Europe seeking support for a supranational army capable of resisting Soviet aggression without a heavy U.S. commitment. He concentrated most of his attention, however, on France. Although he had considerable popularity in that country during his ambassadorial tenure, Bruce was criticized there for conducting a high-pressure lobbying campaign for the EDC among members of the French National Assembly. Opponents of EDC, including Communists, Gaullist nationalists and those fearful of German rearmament, combined to reject the EDC in the Assembly in August 1954. The defeat of EDC was a personal setback for Bruce and effectively concluded his special role in Europe.

Bruce left the State Department in February 1955 but agreed to serve as a consultant. In August 1956 President Eisenhower named him to an eight-member board of consultants that periodically reviewed foreign intelligence activities. Six months later he returned to full-time diplomatic work as ambassador to West Germany. Less popular in Germany than in France, Bruce nonetheless succeeded in cultivating an extremely close relationship with Chancellor Konrad Adenauer, although he neglected other West German politicians and trade union leaders.

Bruce resigned his diplomatic post in November 1959 to serve as a foreign policy adviser to the Democratic Party during the 1960 presidential election. In February 1961 President Kennedy named him ambassador to Great Britain. Bruce thus became the first U.S. diplomat to hold the three most important European ambassadorships. He remained in London until February 1969. After a brief retirement, Bruce was appointed U.S. representative to the Vietnam peace talks in Paris in 1970, and in 1972 he went to Peking as liaison officer to the People's Republic of China. [See KENNEDY, JOHNSON, NIXON/FORD Volumes]

[JCH]

BRUCKER, WILBER M(ARION)
b. June 23, 1894; Saginaw, Mich.
d. Oct. 28, 1968; Detroit, Mich.
Secretary of the Army, June 1955-January 1961.

The son of a judge and Democratic congressman, Brucker worked his way through the University of Michigan, from which he received a law degree in 1916. Admitted to the Michigan bar that year, he served as state attorney general from 1928 to 1930 and as governor from 1930 to 1932. From the 1930s until the early 1950s, Brucker worked in a Detroit law firm and was active in Republican politics.

Brucker left private law practice upon his nomination as general counsel of the Defense Department in 1954. He gained publicity during the Army-McCarthy hearings of that year by laughing at Sen. Joseph R. McCarthy's (R, Wisc.) [q.v.] accusation that President Eisenhower was conducting "a conspiracy of silence" about military security. However, Brucker called for legislation to keep subversives out of defense plants and supervised the development of a Pentagon program to screen and review all defense personnel. In 1955 the Army security program was attacked by Norman Thomas [q.v.] and other civil libertarians for issuing less than honorable discharges to military personnel based on pre-induction activities.

Appointed Secretary of the Army in June 1955, Brucker initially supported the Administration's "New Look" policy, which stressed massive nuclear retaliation as the nation's primary defense. However, by 1957 he joined Army Chief of Staff Maxwell D. Taylor [q.v.] in opposing the budget reductions the policy entailed. During testimony before the Senate Appropriations Committee, Brucker argued that the cutbacks would reduce troop strength, lower service standards and limit research in biological and chemical warfare. Taking a vigorous stand in opposition to the emphasis on nuclear weapons, he stated that modern warfare would require the development of tactics to meet limited types of conflict. At the meeting of the Associa-

tion of the U.S. Army in 1958, Brucker argued that as nuclear stalemate was reached between the U.S. and the USSR, the possibilities of limited wars would be "most likely." A year later he told members of Congress that the Communists had been involved in 18 limited wars since 1945 and described the Soviet Army as "modern, mobile and menacing." Before leaving office Brucker initiated an Army reorganization plan to enable it to adapt to either atomic or conventional war on any scale.

In 1957, after President Eisenhower issued an executive order placing the Arkansas National Guard under federal control and Secretary of Defense Charles E. Wilson [q.v.] ordered 1,000 troops into Little Rock, Ark., Brucker supervised the government's enforcement of the integration of Central High School. Brucker returned to private law practice following John F. Kennedy's inauguration in 1961. He died in 1968.

[FJD]

BRUNDAGE, PERCIVAL F(LACK)
b. April 2, 1892; Amsterdam, N.Y.
Director, Bureau of the Budget, April 1956-March 1958.

The son of a Protestant minister, Percival Brundage graduated from Harvard in 1914 with a B.A. in the classics. He then took a job as an office boy with an accounting firm in New York. Following a night course in accounting, he joined another firm, Price, Waterhouse & Co. Brundage remained with Price, Waterhouse for the next 38 years, advancing from staff accountant to partner in 1930 and senior partner by 1944. He joined the Eisenhower Administration in May 1954 as deputy director of the Budget; in April 1956 he was sworn in as successor to director Rowland Hughes [q.v.].

As budget director, Brundage spearheaded the Administration's drive to get the government out of competition with private industry. In May 1956 the Budget Bureau reported that the federal government was operating 19,321 commercial and industrial facilities. At the end of October Brundage disclosed that 492 of those facilities had been dropped or curtailed on the principle that "the government has ordinarily no right to compete in a private enterprise economy," even if "the apparent cost" to the government would be increased by shifting to private production. Brundage also announced that the government had sold over $1 billion of the assets of the liquidated Reconstruction Finance Corp.

Throughout 1957 Brundage was at the center of a controversy over the budget for fiscal 1958, the first he prepared. Presented in January 1957, the 1958 budget placed estimated expenditures at $71.8 billion, the highest ever in peacetime. Over the next few months Brundage was in the paradoxical position of defending the Administration's budget while President Eisenhower and Secretary of the Treasury George Humphrey [q.v.] were inviting Congress to make cuts.

In January Brundage appeared before the Joint Economic Committee and characterized his budget as a "good budget and a fair compromise between demands for increased federal spending and demands for cutbacks in federal services." In May, after months of congressional criticism, he said the budget had been "examined, analyzed and evaluated" and could be cut no further. However, some fiscal conservatives were still unsatisfied. Sen. Harry Byrd (D, Va.) [q.v.], chairman of the Senate Finance Committee, said that Brundage did not know there was "such a word in the dictionary as economy." Byrd called on President Eisenhower to replace Brundage with someone "dedicated to economy instead of . . . finding new ways to spend more money."

Brundage was also an adversary of congressional proposals for tax cuts, which he steadfastly opposed through 1957. In October he argued that the projected surplus of $1.5 billion for fiscal 1958 was too small to allow for tax reductions. Ultimately, the recession of 1958 wiped out the expected surplus, and the 1958 budget instead ended up with a $2.8 billion deficit.

Brundage left the Budget Bureau in March 1958 and returned to Price, Waterhouse as a consultant.

[TO]

BUCKLEY, WILLIAM F(RANK), JR.
b. Nov. 24, 1925; New York, N.Y.
Editor-in-chief, *National Review*,
1955- .

The sixth of 10 children of an oil millionaire, William F. Buckley, Jr., followed his father's strong Catholicism and doctrinaire conservative politics. He attended private schools in England and spent less than a year at the University of Mexico before entering the Army in 1944. Following military service he enrolled at Yale University, where he also taught Spanish and stood out as a debater and as chairman of the *Yale Daily News*.

One year after his 1950 graduation, Buckley won quick prominence with the publication of his first book, *God and Man at Yale*. It was a vehement attack against the schools of thought he considered ascendent at his *alma mater* and a rejection of liberal education as an academic ideal. He argued that Yale professors preached atheism, secularism and collectivism and slighted religion and free market economics. Deriding "the superstitions of academic freedom" and dismissing neutral, independent inquiry as a goal of higher education, Buckley called upon Yale's conservative alumni to assert control over the institution and make sure that their values were inculcated in the University's students.

Buckley was a member of the Central Intelligence Agency from July 1951 to April 1952. In 1954 he stirred up another controversy with his second book, *McCarthy and His Enemies*, the most important defense of McCarthyism to appear in print during the period. Buckley and his co-author, L. Brent Bozell, combined a spirited justification of the charges of the Wisconsin Senator with sharp thrusts at the supposed inconsistencies and unfair tactics of his opponents. Although acknowledging that McCarthy had been guilty of blunders and misconduct, they endorsed his contention that there was widespread Communist subversion of the U.S. government. Concluding that "on McCarthyism hang the hopes of America for effective resistance to Communist infiltration," Buckley and

Bozell praised the movement as one "around which men of good will and stern morality can close ranks."

In 1955 Buckley founded the *National Review*, which before long became the leading intellectual organ of American conservatism. In the "Publisher's Statement" of its inaugural issue, Buckley declared, *"National Review* is out of place in the sense that the United Nations and the League of Women Voters and the *New York Times* and Henry Steele Commager are in place." It "stands athwart history, yelling Stop!" Among the magazine's editors and contributors, many of them ex-Communists, were the luminaries of the intellectual Right: Russell Kirk [*q.v.*], James Burnham [*q.v.*], Willmoore Kendall, Max Eastman [*q.v.*] and Whittaker Chambers [*q.v.*].

As editor-in-chief, Buckley orchestrated their weekly denunciations of the manifestations of modern liberalism: big government, social welfare programs, civil rights laws, unbalanced budgets, containment, foreign aid and contemporary mores. Its contributors ranged from libertarian to conservative to reactionary, but all shared a fierce anti-Communism and an abhorrence of the welfare state. Buckley himself emerged as the premier polemicist of American right-wing politics. Moving across a broad field of issues, he used wit, mockery, and verbal refinement to prick the hides of liberal targets, both institutional, such as Social Security and the United Nations, and personal, such as Eleanor Roosevelt [*q.v.*] and Arthur Schlesinger, Jr. [*q.v.*].

In 1959 Buckley published his only substantial exposition of his credo, *Up from Liberalism.* He criticized the materialistic limits of liberal thought and registered alarm at the centralization of power in the state to accomplish liberalism's social ends. He deplored "liberalism's total appetite for power" and "the root assumptions of liberal economic theory . . . that, economically speaking, the people are merely gatherers of money which is the right and duty of a central intelligence to distribute." Buckley's prescription for social progress derived from classical economics: "It is to maintain and wherever possible enhance the freedom of the individual to acquire property and dispose of that property in ways he decides on." He defined conservatism as "the tacit acknowledgement that all that is finally important in human experience is behind us; that the crucial explorations have been undertaken, and that it is given to man to know what are the great truths that emerged from them. Whatever is to come cannot outweigh the importance to man of what has gone before."

Buckley reached a wider audience with his syndicated newspaper column, beginning in 1962. After 1966 he was the host of *Firing Line*, a television program on which he interviewed and debated guests in his provocative style. In 1965 Buckley ran for mayor of New York City as the candidate of the Conservative Party and lost with 13.4% of the vote. [See KENNEDY, JOHNSON, NIXON/FORD Volumes]

[TO]

For further information:
Charles L. Markmann, *The Buckleys: A Family Examined* (New York, 1973).
George H. Nash, *The Conservative Intellectual Movement in America Since 1945* (New York, 1976).

BUNCHE, RALPH J(OHNSON)
b. Aug. 7, 1904; Detroit, Mich.
d. Dec. 9, 1971; New York, N.Y.
Director, United Nations Department of Trusteeship, 1948-54; United Nations Undersecretary, 1954-58, United Nations Undersecretary for Special Political Affairs, 1958-71.

A descendant of slaves and American Indians, Ralph Bunche worked his way through the University of California at Los Angeles, graduating Phi Beta Kappa in 1927. After receiving an M.A. from Harvard University in 1928, he taught political science at Howard University. Bunche received his Ph.D. from Harvard in 1934, writing a dissertation comparing government in African colonies and League of Nations mandates. From 1938 to 1940 he served as Swedish sociologist Gunnar Myrdal's chief aide in gathering materials for Myrdal's massive study of U.S. race relations, *An American Dilemma* (1944).

During World War II Bunche served in the Office of Strategic Services as senior social science analyst and expert on Africa and the Far East. Joining the State Department in 1944 as a colonial specialist, Bunche drew up the trusteeship section of the United Nations Charter at the Dumbarton Oaks Conference of 1944. He attended the first U.N. conference at San Francisco in 1945. From 1945 to 1947 Bunche was associate chief of the State Department's division of dependent area affairs.

At the request of U.N. Secretary General Trygve Lie, Bunche became director of the U.N.'s trusteeship division in 1947. That year he sat on the Special Committee on Palestine, which recommended creation of a Jewish national state. During 1948 and 1949 Bunche mediated the Arab-Israeli war, an effort that earned him the Nobel Peace Prize in 1950. [See TRUMAN Volume]

In response to growing rightist criticism of the American delegation at the U.N., Ambassador Henry Cabot Lodge [*q.v.*] began a loyalty investigation of the personnel, including Bunche, in 1953. The plan had the full support of Secretary General Lie, who authorized non-American employes to provide information to the FBI. When Dag Hammarskjold replaced Lie in April, he ordered the FBI off U.N. territory. In response, the Eisenhower Administration created the International Organizations Employes Loyalty Board to continue the probe. Despite attempts to keep its efforts secret, news leaked out in May 1954 that the Board was investigating Bunche. Eisenhower opposed the probe and sent presidential assistant Maxwell Rabb to warn Bunche about FBI reports and the Board's queries and to offer his support. Bunche, however, decided to stand alone. At the hearing he was confronted by two ex-Communist witnesses on the payroll of the Justice Department, who charged him with Communist connections. After two days of testimony, board chairman Pierce J. Geraty announced on May 28, 1954 that Bunche had been unanimously cleared of all charges.

Bunche was appointed undersecretary of the U.N. in August 1954, the highest post ever held by an American in the organization. Following the 1956 Israeli-Egyptian war, he was made a member of the three-man committee supervising the ceasefire. As such, Bunche was criticized for siding with the Egyptians and denounced by Israeli Prime Minister David Ben Gurion as a "dictator."

In April 1958 Bunche headed a special commission that successfully settled an Israeli-Jordanian dispute over Israel's Mt. Scopus enclave in Jordanian Jerusalem. After meeting in May with officials from both countries, Bunche persuaded the Jordanian government to lift a blockade of Israeli convoys to the Jewish community. The following month he was promoted to undersecretary for special political affairs, serving as Hammarskjold's principal troubleshooter.

Bunche played a major role in the Congo crisis of 1960. Four days after the declaration of Congolese independence in June 1960, President Joseph Kasavubu and Premier Patrice Lumumba, facing civil war with breakaway Katanga province, petitioned for U.N. troops to preserve order and prevent unilateral intervention by Belgium. On July 14 the U.N. voted to send a force, and Bunche was assigned to organize the effort. He then remained in the Congo as Hammarskjold's personal representative.

In the post Bunche helped negotiate the agreement, disclosed on July 18, for Belgian officials in the Congo to accept U.N. Force orders and to limit their troops' actions to "the security needs of Belgian nationals." At the beginning of August Bunche met with Premier Moise Tshombe, head of breakaway Katanga, to try to convince him to permit U.N. troops to enter the province to oust Belgian troops in the area. The Undersecretary was unable to persuade Tshombe that the force would not be used as an advance guard for his rival, Lumumba, and advised Hammarskjold against pressing the issue for fear of bloodshed.

During the summer Bunche became embroiled in a dispute between the commanders of the U.N. Force, Gen. Henry Alexander, commander of Ghanaian U.N.

troops, and Gen. Carl von Horn, U.N. force commander. In August Alexander protested that von Horn was "unprepared to exercise any military authority at all, thus putting Ghanaian and other U.N. troops in an impossible position." Alexander's protest implied that Hammarskjold and Bunche bore responsibility for the U.N. command's weakness. Bunche maintained that Alexander's criticisms were invalid because the General could not "comprehend the nature of an international peace force." Nevertheless, he was replaced as Hammarskjold's representative that month. U.N. officials denied that the move was connected with the dispute.

Bunche continued to advise Hammarskjold on the Congo until the Secretary General's death in September 1961. That month he became temporary head of the organization, serving until the installation of U Thant as secretary general in November. Bunche served as U.N. troubleshooter in Yemen during 1963 and Cyprus during 1964. He also lent his prestige to the American civil rights movement. However, during the mid-1960s he opposed attempts to link the civil rights movement with opposition to the Vietnam war. [See KENNEDY, JOHNSON Volumes]

[AES]

BURKE, ARLEIGH A(LBERT)
b. Oct. 19, 1901; Boulder, Colo.
Chief of Naval Operations, June 1955-August 1961.

Of Swedish and Pennsylvania Dutch ancestry, Burke was raised on a farm near Boulder, Colo. Intent on a naval career while still a child, Burke entered the U.S. Naval Academy at Annapolis and graduated in 1923. He served five years sea duty and then returned to the U.S. to study ordnance engineering at Annapolis. He received his M.S. in engineering from the University of Michigan in 1931. During the 1930s Burke continued his career as an ordnance officer. He served in the Pacific during World War II, where he gained a reputation for the speed at which he carried squadrons into combat.

Burke was head of the research and development division of the Bureau of Ordnance in 1945. Three years later he was promoted to an assistant to the chief of naval operations in the organizational research and policy division. Burke participated in the so-called Admiral's revolt of 1949, opposing the emphasis on the B-36 Air Force bomber in the Armed Forces unification plan. Reportedly because of his part in the action, Capt. Burke's promotion to rear admiral was postponed until July 1950. During the summer of 1951 Burke served as a member of the U.N. Military Armistice Commission in Korea. In July 1951 he was named director of strategic plans of naval operations, the second highest post in the Navy hierarchy. After a brief stint as commander of the Atlantic Fleet from November 1954 to June 1955, he was appointed chief of naval operations. In choosing Burke, Eisenhower passed over 38 admirals with more seniority.

Burke initially supported Eisenhower's "New Look" defense policy. This had been established as a result of a desire to limit the defense budget and prevent debilitating ground wars such as those in Korea. The policy focused on planning for the "long push." It placed a lid on the defense budget and emphasized the need for services to use their resources more efficiently. The policy placed primary emphasis on "massive retaliation," the use of nuclear weapons delivered by Air Force strategic bombers or missiles as America's major deterrent against aggression. In testimony before a Senate Appropriations subcommittee in 1957, Burke vigorously endorsed the President's fiscal 1958 budget, maintaining that it would "give us the maximum in naval power for every dollar requested."

The launching of the Soviet satellite *Sputnik* in the fall of 1957 opened a debate on defense strategy among different branches of the military and between the military and the Administration. Burke joined Army Gens. Maxwell Taylor [*q.v.*] and James Gavin [*q.v.*] in urging the Administration to reorient its defense policies. They pointed out that with the two superpowers gradually reaching nuclear parity, general warfare would be replaced by limited wars. Burke cautioned that the Soviet Union was still bent on "engulfing the whole world," but because it had been thwarted by American nuclear power, it would not stage a large-scale attack. Instead it would adopt a "piecemeal approach to world domination." Burke opposed Air Force demands for an emphasis on missiles, and he pointed to the need to develop conventional forces such as the Navy to meet the challenge of limited war. Anxious to preserve the twin roles of his service, he maintained that the Navy could fight both limited and full-scale wars with the use of such weapons as aircraft carriers and submarines equiped with missiles.

Burke opposed the Administration's defense budget and urged major increases to prepare the Armed Forces to fight both nuclear and limited wars. He alleged that the Administration's continuous desire for budget reviews had forced the Navy to submit smaller budget requests than needed.

Burke's call for a more varied defense strategy met with little action until the Kennedy Administration, when emphasis was placed on "flexible response." Burke continued at his post until August 1961, when he retired from the Navy. [See KENNEDY Volume]

[EWS]

BURNHAM, JAMES
b. Nov. 22, 1905; Chicago, Ill.
Journalist, writer.

The son of a railroad executive, Burnham received his B.A. from Princeton University in 1927 and attended Oxford University, earning a B.A. in 1929 and an M.A. in 1932. From 1929 to 1953 he was professor of philosophy at New York University. He coedited the left-wing literary and philosophical review *The Symposium* from 1930 to 1933 and in 1934 became coeditor of the *New International*, a journal of American Trotskyists. Although he had once supported the concept of "the dictatorship of the proletariat," Burnham criticized Stalin's "exploitive and imperialist" policies and eventually opposed Trotsky's belief that

the USSR was a "progressive workers" state, which must be defended despite Stalin's actions. Quitting the *New International* in 1940, he forcefully broke away from Trotsky and renounced his former pro-Soviet sympathies.

Burnham was still viewed by many as a leftist, albeit anti-Communist, when he wrote *The Managerial Revolution* in 1941. In the book he predicted the replacement of the ruling capitalist powers not with the working class but with a new, elite class of managers who controlled the means of production in a society incapable of democracy. He predicted the fall of the USSR and Great Britain and the rise to dominance of Germany, Japan and the U.S., all destined to endless power struggles.

Six years later Burnham wrote *The Struggle for the World*. In it he maintained the greatest threat to world stability was Communism's implacable goal of world conquest, a plan made all the more ominous by the USSR's nuclear capability. An influential theorist for conservative views after 1945, he advised a concentrated attack on Communism through interventionist policies toward other nations, widespread efforts at propaganda, foreign aid to allies and a dismissal of the facile rhetoric of peace in a world of irreconcilable political differences. [See TRUMAN Volume]

In *Containment or Liberation?* (1953) Burnham focused his criticism on U.S. foreign policy toward the Communist bloc. He believed the Truman Administration's policy of "containing" Soviet influence in Eastern Europe had been weak and defeatist. Instead, he favored a policy of "liberation," for Eastern Europe which he viewed as the most vital theater of confrontation. He proposed aggressive, well-funded programs aimed at "freeing the enslaved" peoples of Communist nations through use of governments-in-exile, militarily trained refugees and the threat of force from non-Communist allies.

In 1954 Burnham published *The Web of Subversion*, a discussion of what he believed was Communist infiltration in government since the 1930s. Focusing mainly on foreign policy, it sketched a web of massive Communist influence in the

State Department which permitted the Soviet takeover of Eastern Europe, the increased infiltration of Third World independence movements and the fall of mainland China to the Communists.

Burnham claimed to be without bias for or against Sen. Joseph R. McCarthy (R, Wisc.) [q.v.] and his anti-Communist crusade. However, in November 1954 he did oppose Senate moves to censure McCarthy. He believed, in retrospect, that McCarthyism had a larger significance than the question of Communism in government. Burnham used the issue to introduce one of the major elements in postwar conservative thought: the criticism of the liberal ideal of an open society. He wrote, "The issue was philosophical, metaphysical: what kind of community are we. And the Liberals were correct in labeling McCarthy The Enemy, and in destroying him. From the Liberal standpoint—secularist, egalitarian, relativist—the line is now drawn, Relativism must be Absolute."

Burnham revised his advocacy of the liberation of Eastern Europe after the Hungarian uprising of 1956. He remained conspicuously silent while the U.S. watched the USSR crush the Hungarian rebels and only later claimed that a properly timed U.S. ultimatum would have dissuaded the Russians from intervening. But Burnham had to admit that the time for a policy of liberating Communist nations had passed. According to Burnham, with Soviet hegemony in Eastern Europe firmly established, the West could only employ those tactics it had already applied under a containment policy. To the disappointment of his conservative colleagues, he now suggested a mutual withdrawal of North Atlantic Treaty Organization and Warsaw Pact divisions from Europe.

When William F. Buckley, Jr., [q.v.] organized the conservative National Review in 1955, Burnham became one of the original members of the editorial board. He contributed to the magazine in a regular column throughout the next two decades, his area of commentary still the battle against Communism. Burnham supported the Vietnam war but was highly critical of what he perceived as a no-win policy. The

war could and should be won, he believed, by intensified destruction of military and civilian targets, through bombing and "biological or chemical means."

[TGD]

For further information:
John P. Diggins, *Up from Communism: Conservative Odysseys in American Intellectual History* (New York, 1975).

BURNS, ARTHUR F(RANK)
b. April 27, 1904; Stanislau, Austria-Hungary.
Chairman, Council of Economic Advisers, August 1953-November 1956.

Born in Eastern Europe, Arthur Burns emigrated to America with his parents and grew up in Bayonne, N.J. He worked his way through Columbia University, earning his B.A. and M.A. in economics in 1925 and his Ph.D. in 1934. Burns began teaching at Rutgers University in 1927; by 1943 he had become a full professor. The following year he joined the Columbia faculty as a full professor.

In addition to teaching Burns produced studies for the National Bureau of Economic Research, a private organization engaged in statistical research on economic issues. Through his work with the National Bureau, of which he became director of research in 1948, he became an acknowledged expert on business cycles. Among his studies were *Production Trends in the United States Since 1870* (1934), his doctoral dissertation, and *Measuring Business Cycles* (1946), written in collaboration with Wesley Mitchell, whom Burns regarded as the principal influence on his thought.

In 1946 Burns published a critique of Keynesian economics. In general Burns's economics were moderately conservative: he favored a free market and increased competition but also recognized that government must play a role in fostering economic stability and leveling business cycles. In 1951 he praised the existing distribution of income in America and said that any future redistribution should not come by transferring income from the rich to the poor but by increasing the productivity of those at the bottom through encouragement of increased competition and small business. Burns was also a critic of the "free money" policies of the Truman Administration.

In March 1953 President Eisenhower appointed Burns a member of the Council of Economic Advisers. That August Burns became Council chairman. At the outset of his tenure he had to defend the very existence of the Council against congressional Republicans who had grown hostile toward the six-year-old agency during the Truman years. Burns managed to maintain the Council and its staff intact, and he exercised a key role in the making of economic policy during Eisenhower's first term.

According to presidential assistant Sherman Adams [q.v.] in *First Hand Report: The Story of the Eisenhower Administration,* "Arthur Burns turned out to be a pleasant surprise. He and Eisenhower got along fine. They shared the same outlook and philosophy. Far from being the abstract and impractical professor, Burns had his feet planted solidly on the ground and had no difficulty in more than holding his own in arguments at the cabinet table with such hard-headed protagonists as [George] Humphrey [q.v.] and [Joseph] Dodge [q.v.]."

In 1953 Burns correctly predicted that the restrictive credit policies being pursued by the Treasury and the Federal Reserve would contribute to an economic slowdown. During the recession of 1953-54 he recommended the remedies subsequently applied by the Administration: liberalization of credit combined with tax cuts. The Administration allowed the expiration of the excess profits tax and the Korean war increases in the personal income and excise rates. These reductions added $7.4 billion to disposable income and helped fuel the prosperity of 1954-55.

In general, Burns favored monetary over fiscal stimulation of the economy. "The more you can get out of monetary policy," he said, "the less you need to get out of fiscal policy, with its headaches about deficits, the public debt, and the like." Burns sought, with mixed success, to get the Federal Reserve to ease up on credit restrictions, particularly in the area of hous-

ing. He also backed a liberalization of Federal Housing Authority lending rules in order to stimulate housing starts and home modernization. To guard against inflation, however, Burns sometimes favored credit restrictions, as in January 1956, when he unsuccessfully argued at a cabinet meeting in favor of controls on consumer credit.

Burns, on the whole, was more willing than President Eisenhower's conservative advisers to resort to public works to promote economic expansion. He supported the idea of an ambitious highway-building program. In 1955 he helped prepare a plan to aid chronically depressed areas such as New England textile towns and the Appalachian coal country. The plan called for the formation of an area redevelopment agency within the Commerce Department to extend capital improvement loans to depressed communities. President Eisenhower originally favored the idea but withdrew his support when Democrats in Congress expanded the proposal. Area redevelopment legislation remained stymied throughout the 1950s.

Burns left the Eisenhower Administration in November 1956, returning to his work at Columbia University and the National Bureau of Economic Research. He continued to advise the Administration, as in March 1960 when he warned Vice-President Richard Nixon [q.v.] that the Republicans would lose the November election unless the Administration cut taxes to combat the current recession. Nixon took Burns's counsel to a cabinet meeting, but the President was reluctant to add to the already sizeable deficit and ruled out a tax reduction. The recession continued to the end of the year, and Nixon lost the presidential contest by a narrow margin to Sen. John F. Kennedy (D, Mass.) [q.v.].

Burns served on Kennedy's Advisory Committee on Labor-Management Policy. During the Kennedy-Johnson years he frequently spoke out on economic policy, often in opposition to the fiscal activism of Democratic economic policymakers. Burns's version of economic stimulus called for a revision of progressive tax laws to lower rates on corporations and people with high incomes. He argued that this approach would provide more investment capital and generate more jobs. He steadily advocated less government spending to curb inflation and annual tax cuts to spur economic growth.

In January 1969 President Nixon named Burns counselor to the President and in October nominated him to succeed William McChesney Martin [q.v.] as chairman of the Board of Governors of the Federal Reserve System. Confirmed by the Senate in December, Burns took office on Feb. 1, 1970. [See NIXON/FORD, CARTER Volumes]

[TO]

BURTON, HAROLD H(ITZ)
b. June 22, 1888; Jamaica Plain, Mass.
d. Oct. 28, 1964; Washington, D.C.
Associate Justice, U.S. Supreme Court, 1945-58.

Harold H. Burton graduated from Bowdoin College in 1909 and from Harvard law school in 1912. After Army service in World War I, he practiced law in Cleveland and became a member of the Ohio House of Representatives in 1929. Elected mayor of Cleveland in 1935 as a reform candidate, Burton was twice reelected by wide margins. A Republican, he ran successfully for the U.S. Senate in 1940 despite opposition from the state party leadership. In the Senate Burton was an internationalist in foreign policy and a moderate on domestic issues. He served as a member of the Senate committee, headed by Harry S. Truman (D, Mo.), that investigated the defense effort in World War II. President Truman chose Burton as his first Supreme Court nominee in September 1945.

On the bench Burton displayed a conservative orientation. He generally favored judicial self-restraint and usually voted to uphold government power, especially in loyalty-security cases. Burton did occasionally join the Court's more liberal justices to overturn some aspect of a government anti-Communist program, but he based these decisions on narrow statutory or procedural grounds. [See TRUMAN Volume]

Burton adhered to this pattern during his years on the Warren Court. He dissented from an April 1956 decision upsetting state sedition laws and from a June 1957 ruling placing limits on state subversion investigations. The Justice also objected to a June 1958 judgment holding the denial of passports to members of the Communist Party illegal. In the same month Burton spoke for a five-man majority which upheld the dismissal of a public school teacher for incompetency after he had refused to tell school authorities whether he had once been an officer in a Communist organization.

Burton wrote the majority opinion in a June 1953 case setting aside the perjury conviction of labor leader Harry Bridges [q.v.] for allegedly having sworn falsely at his 1945 naturalization hearing that he was not a Communist. The Justice based his decision on the ground that the statute of limitations had run out before Bridges was indicted. He concurred in a June 1957 decision overturning the convictions of California Communist Party leaders under the Smith Act. However, he opposed the majority opinion that the Act did not outlaw the advocacy of the forcible overthrow of the government "as an abstract doctrine." Burton also took the narrow ground in another case that month in which the majority ruled that a federal criminal defendant was entitled to see statements government witnesses made to the FBI before trial. In a separate opinion he said the trial judge should examine the statements before they were turned over to defense counsel and withhold those containing national security information.

Justice Burton also tended to uphold government power in criminal rights cases. He frequently voted to sustain convictions in which a defendant alleged that he had been denied the right to counsel or that his confession was coerced. Although Burton usually favored the government position in antitrust cases, he wrote the dissenting opinion in an important June 1957 case in which the majority held that the DuPont Co.'s acquisition of General Motors stock in 1917-19 violated the Clayton Antitrust Act. After his first term on the Court, Burton repeatedly voted to outlaw racial segregation and discrimination. He joined in the Court's May 1954 *Brown* decision, which ruled public school segregation unconstitutional.

Burton retired from the Supreme Court in October 1958 because of ill health. He was considered then and later to have been a largely conservative jurist but one with a certain flexibility and independence. A very conscientious and hard-working man, Burton had a reputation both on and off the Court for having a judicial temperament because of his capacity to keep an open mind on issues and to maintain an emotional distance from cases. Nonetheless, most legal scholars have ranked him as, at best, an average justice. Burton did not play a leading role on the Court; he was neither a great scholar nor an original thinker. Although his opinions improved during his years on the Court, they remained rather lackluster and tedious. Burton died in Washington in October 1964.

[CAB]

For further information:
Richard Kirkendall, "Harold Burton," in Leon Friedman and Fred L. Israel, eds., *The Justices of the U.S. Supreme Court, 1789-1969* (New York, 1969), Vol. 4.

BUSH, PRESCOTT S(HELDON)
b. May 15, 1895; Columbus, Ohio.
d. Oct. 8, 1972; New York, N.Y.
Republican Senator, Conn., 1952-63.

Bush grew up in Columbus, Ohio, where his father was a steel manufacturer. He received a B.A. from Yale University in 1917. After service in World War I, Bush worked for a St. Louis hardware firm and the United States Rubber Co. He then became a vice president of W.A. Harriman and Co., a New York City investment firm, in 1926. When Brown Brothers merged with Harriman in 1930, Bush became a partner in the new firm.

From 1935 to 1952 Bush was the moderator of the Representative Town Meeting in Greenwich, Conn. During World War II he served as campaign chairman for the United Service Organizations (USO) and the National War Fund, Inc. Because of his success as a fundraiser, he was chosen chairman of the Connecticut Republican State Finance Committee in 1947. Three years later Bush ran unsuccessfully for the U.S. Senate.

In 1952 Bush opposed Rep. Abraham Ribicoff (D, Conn.) [*q.v.*] in a contest to fill the remainder of the term of the late Sen. Brien McMahon (D, Conn.). During the contest Bush criticized Sen. Joseph R. McCarthy (R, Wisc.) [*q.v.*], stating that there were "many, like myself, who approve heartily of his goals but hold reservations at times concerning his methods." He defeated Ribicoff in November by 30,000 votes. In 1956 Bush won a full term by defeating Rep. Thomas J. Dodd (D, Conn.) [*q.v.*] by 128,000 votes.

As a senator, Bush was a flexible conservative. In 1954 he defended the Dixon-Yates contract, stating that it was time for Congress to "contain" the Tennessee Valley Authority and prevent "this sprawling giant" from "groping its way across the country." In 1955 Bush attacked a public highways bill for, among other things, imposing new controls upon the states in the areas of highway construction and operation. In 1956 Bush opposed public power development at Niagara Falls. He signed a minority report of the Public Works Committee that described the approval of public development as "tantamount to saying that all public resources must be publicly developed." Bush voted against a 1958 area redevelopment bill to aid economically distressed regions on the grounds that "it would create a new channel into which to pour vast amounts of federal dollars in futile attempts" to cure unemployment.

On a number of issues Bush broke with many of his conservative colleagues. In 1954 he offered a uniform code of committee behavior to prevent McCarthy's continued abuse of investigating committees; later that year he voted to condemn the Wisconsin Senator. In 1955 he expressed regret that a housing bill did not provide for a larger number of public housing units. Bush was a strong backer of President Eisenhower's civil rights bills. In 1957 he opposed an effort by Southern senators to weaken an Administration measure by guaranteeing a jury trial to those accused of contempt for trying to prevent blacks from voting. Three years later Bush and seven other Republicans joined Northern Democrats in an unsuccessful effort to end a Southern civil rights filibuster by invoking cloture.

During his years in Congress Bush gained a reputation as an expert on government finance and the national economy. Because of his banking background he was named to Eisenhower's Commission on Foreign Economic Policy in 1953. Bush concurred with most of the panel's recommendations, including those urging an early termination of economic aid in the form of grants, continuation of a vigorous technical assistance program without huge expenditures, encouragement of U.S. private investment abroad by reducing taxes on income from such investment, and extension of reciprocal trade legislation.

In 1954 Bush, as chairman of the Banking and Currency Committee's Subcommittee on Securities, backed the panel's bill amending the Securities Exchange Act. Enacted in August, it permitted a wider dissemination of information about securities before their sale and simplified the procedures involved in the registration of securities issues with the Securities and Exchange Commission. In 1957 he succeeded in amending a Banking and Currency Committee banking bill to require disclosure of the names of only those persons owning at least 5% of the outstanding stock of banks. Three years later Bush supported an Administration bill to remove the statutory ceiling of 4¼% on government bond interest rates. When Democrats blocked the measure, Bush denounced them for playing politics with the nation's credit. He asserted that, while interest rates had declined somewhat because of a slight recession in business, rates would rise again as the economy picked up steam.

Bush served as chairman of the Republican National Platform Committee in 1956. Four years later he was chairman of the subcommittee that wrote the planks on business, labor and the economy in the National Platform.

Bush generally opposed President John F. Kennedy's domestic policies. He criticized the Administration's 1962 Trade Expansion Act, which gave the President increased power to cut tariffs through reciprocal agreements. In May 1962 Bush announced that he would not seek reelection for health reasons. He returned to Brown Brothers, Harriman and Co. Bush died in New York City in 1972.

[MLL]

BUSH, VANNEVAR
b. March 11, 1890; Everett, Mass.
d. June 28, 1974, Belmont, Mass.
President, Carnegie Institution of Washington, 1939-55; Chairman, Massachusetts Institute of Technology Corporation, 1957-59.

The son of a Universalist minister, Bush earned both his B.S. and M.S. degrees from Tufts College in 1913 and received his Ph.D. in engineering jointly from Harvard and the Massachusetts Institute of Technology (MIT) in 1916. The following year he worked in a special Navy anti-submarine laboratory. Bush joined MIT's faculty in 1919, becoming the Institute's vice president and dean of its school of engineering in 1932. A prolific inventor, he designed a number of advanced mathematical analyzing instruments, including the differential analyzer, the forerunner of the computer. In 1939 he became the president of the Carnegie Institution of Washington.

In 1940 Bush served as chairman of the National Defense Research Committee (NDRC), formed at his suggestion to direct war-related scientific research. The following year he became chairman of the Office of Scientific Research and Development (OSRD) which included the NDRC. Bush made no technical contribution to the war effort, but as an administrator he was responsible for the development of an array of new weapons, including radar, amphibious vehicles and the atomic bomb. In June 1945 he advised President Harry S. Truman to use the atomic bomb against Japan without prior warning.

After the War Bush continued to serve on government policy committees. He prepared recommendations on ways in which wartime research could be applied to peace. The report, "Science, the Endless Frontier," urged massive government support for basic research. His recommendations resulted in the establishment of the National Science Foundation in 1950. Bush opposed the development of the hydrogen bomb and urged negotiations to end the arms race. [See TRUMAN Volume]

In the 1950s Bush was a vocal critic of abuses in security investigations, which he thought had retarded weapons research by undermining scientists' morale. He was particularly alarmed by the 1954 Oppenheimer security hearings. J. Robert Oppenheimer [q.v.] had directed the development of the atomic bomb and had served as chairman of the Atomic Energy Commission's (AEC) General Advisory Committee (GAC) in the early postwar period. Because of Oppenheimer's prewar involvement with leftist groups and his postwar reservations about the development of the hydrogen bomb, President Dwight D. Eisenhower ordered his security clearance suspended in late 1953 pending a hearing. Bush objected to the charges, urging that they be "redrafted in such a way as to remove all implication that Oppenheimer was being tried for his opinions."

Following the AEC's decision that clearance remain suspended, Bush wrote in the *New York Times*, " . . . there should be no insistence that any individual cease his thinking at any time, or that he suppress his honest opinion in order slavishly to follow a policy abstractly laid down." Referring to proponents of hydrogen bomb development, Bush further contended that Oppenheimer had run afoul of "a group so obsessed with the utter necessity for maximum progress toward a single goal that they have been willing to brush aside or push aside any opinions which would tend to emphasize other matters in connection with the country's defense." In an address to the American Association for the Advancement of Science in December 1954, he declared that "useful men" were "denied the opportunity to contribute to our scientific efforts because of their youthful indiscretions." In an apparent reference to

Sen. Joseph R. McCarthy (R, Wisc.) [q.v.], he accused "ruthless, ambitious men" of using "our loyalty procedures for political purposes."

In 1957 Bush became chairman of the MIT Corporation and in 1959 its honorary chairman. He continued to write and lecture on national defense through the 1960s. In 1970 he and James Conant [q.v.] received the Atomic Pioneers Award from the AEC. Bush suffered a stroke in 1974 and died of pneumonia shortly afterward at the age of 84.

[MDB]

For further information:
Vannevar Bush, *Pieces of the Action* (New York, 1970).
John Major, *The Oppenheimer Hearing* (New York, 1971).

BUTLER, PAUL M(ULHOLLAND)

b. June 15, 1905; South Bend, Ind.
d. Dec. 30, 1961; Washington, D.C.
Chairman, Democratic National Committee, 1954-60.

Butler received an LL.B. degree from Notre Dame law school in 1927 and established a legal practice in South Bend, Ind. During the 1930s and 1940s he gradually rose in the state Democratic Party ranks. In 1952 he ousted Frank McHale, a friend of President Harry S. Truman, as Democratic National Committeeman from Indiana. At the Democratic National Convention that year, Butler was one of Illinois Gov. Adlai E. Stevenson's [q.v.] principal supporters.

In 1954 Butler was elected chairman of the Democratic National Committee over Truman's strenuous opposition. The Committee's functions were normally limited to raising money, organizing presidential nominating conventions and providing assistance in the management of campaigns. However, in the absence of a Democratic President, Butler sought to transform the panel into an instrument of national party leadership. To accomplish this, he advocated more aggressive political attacks on the Eisenhower Administration and pushed for the adoption of a clear-cut, liberal national platform.

The day after his election as chairman, Butler directly attacked President Eisenhower for failing to unite the nation. Until then most Democrats had criticized only the men around the President. In 1956 Butler urged the Party to adopt a strong civil rights platform and to endorse the Supreme Court's 1954 school desegregation decision. His strong stand earned him the enmity of Southern leaders, who accused him of having dared the South to bolt the Party.

Immediately after the 1956 presidential election, Butler asserted that Senate Majority Leader Lyndon B. Johnson (D, Tex.) [q.v.] and Speaker Sam Rayburn (D, Tex.) [q.v.] were too moderate and too conciliatory towards the Administration. He charged that the congressional Democrats had not played "the true role of an opposition party from 1952 up to the [1956] presidential campaign." On Nov. 27, 1956 the National Committee voted to create the Democratic Advisory Council to enable Northern liberals to circumvent those leaders in the formulation of Democratic legislative programs. Johnson and Rayburn refused to join the Council, although Stevenson and Truman participated in its efforts.

Under Butler's chairmanship the National Committee took several other measures to centralize and unify the Party under its direction. It appointed six regional representatives to coordinate state and national programs, created a program for training precinct workers and inaugurated executive leadership conferences for state and county party officials.

In 1960 the uneasy truce between Truman and Butler was broken when the former President charged Butler with rigging the National Convention in favor of Sen. John F. Kennedy (D, Mass.) [q.v.]. Truman resigned as a Missouri delegate before the gathering convened. Following Kennedy's nomination Butler announced that he would not seek another term as Committee chairman. At the candidate's behest the Committee chose Sen. Henry M. Jackson (D, Wash.) [q.v.] to succeed Butler.

Butler retired to law practice in Washington, D.C., where he died of a heart attack in December 1961.

[MLL]

For further information:
Sidney Hyman, "The Collective Leadership of Paul Butler," *The Reporter* (Dec. 24, 1959), pp. 8-12.

BYRD, HARRY F(LOOD)
b. June 10, 1887; Martinsburg, W.Va.
d. Oct. 20, 1966; Berryville, Va.
Democratic Senator, Va., 1933-66; Chairman, Joint Committee on Reduction of Nonessential Federal Expenditures, 1941-66; Finance Committee, 1955-66.

Harry Byrd was the scion of a Virginia line dating back to 1674. His father was a lawyer, newspaper publisher and one-time speaker of the Virginia House of Delegates. Byrd left school at the age of 15 to restore his father's paper, the Winchester *Star*, to solvency. He established his own newspaper at the age of 20 in Martinsburg, W. Va., and in 1923 acquired the Harrisonburg (Va.) *News-Record*. Byrd also became involved in apple growing. His chain of orchards in the Shenandoah Valley grew to one of the largest in the world.

Byrd entered the Virginia State Senate in 1915 and within a decade was the dominant figure in Virginia politics. He remained so for the next 40 years. A master political technician, Byrd built a durable personal fiefdom out of the existing Democratic machine based on farmers, rural businessmen, county courthouse cliques and the virtual disenfranchisement of most black citizens. He won prominence by his key role in the defeat of a bond issue for roads in 1923. The "pay-as-you-go" principle of government finance became the trademark of Byrd's political career. He served as Virginia's governor from 1926 to 1930, and his frugal regime was considered innovative and successful. Appointed to the Senate in 1933 at the urging of President Franklin D. Roosevelt, Byrd ironically became one of the most bitter opponents of the New Deal.

With his installment as chairman of the newly created Joint Committee on Reduction of Nonessential Federal Expenditures in 1941, he attained a forum for his sallies against unbalanced budgets and social welfare programs. [See TRUMAN Volume]

In the 1950s Byrd was one of the Senate's most influential members, possessing two decades of experience and senior positions on the powerful Armed Services Committee and the Finance Committee. (He became chairman of the latter in 1955.) In the presidential election of 1952, he refused to endorse the Democratic ticket headed by Adlai Stevenson [q.v.]. Virginia's 12 electoral votes went to the Republican candidate, Dwight D. Eisenhower. The new Administration was more committed than its Democratic predecessors to the fiscal conservatism espoused by Byrd.

Byrd's unflagging pursuit of economy in government frequently placed him in an adversary position vis-a-vis the Eisenhower Administration as well as his fellow Democrats. He often voted against public works bills, including the great public works projects of the decade, the St. Lawrence Seaway and the national highway program. He consistently fought to eliminate all economic assistance from foreign aid packages. In 1955 Byrd opposed a salary increase for members of Congress and a $20 tax cut for lower income families. In 1957 he called upon President Eisenhower to make $5 billion in budget cuts and to replace Budget Director Percival F. Brundage [q.v.] for not pruning aggressively enough. Byrd also worked to block enactment of his Democratic colleagues' social measures. In 1960 he opposed federal aid to education, federal aid for areas beset by chronic unemployment, an increase in the minimum wage from $1 to $1.25 an hour and medicare.

In the wake of the Supreme Court's 1954 ruling banning school segregation, Byrd moved to the forefront of the Southern crusade to maintain segregation and states rights. His February 1956 call for "massive resistance" became a rallying cry for those determined to oppose even token desegregation. In March he helped mobilize the signing of the "Southern Manifesto," a rhetorical defiance of the Court signed by 101 Southern members of Congress.

Within Virginia the Byrd organization was the backbone of the legislative effort to frustrate school desegregation. In 1956 the Virginia legislature enacted laws requiring the governor to close a public school rather than allow it to be integrated and providing tuition grants to students attending segregated private schools in their place. In September 1958 Gov. J. Lindsay Almond [q.v.] ordered the closing of several public schools. Byrd characterized the situation as "the gravest crisis since the War Between the States." The forces of integration are "working on the theory that if Virginia can be brought to her knees, they can march through the rest of the South singing *Hallelujah*." In January 1959 the courts invalidated Virginia's massive resistance laws. Almond permitted the schools to reopen, but Byrd remained in adamant opposition.

A national symbol of unbudging resistance to integration, deficit-spending and the welfare state, Byrd received demonstrations of support in the presidential elections of 1956 and 1960. Although not a declared candidate, he won 134,157 votes for President in 1956. In the election of 1960 he received the electoral votes of Mississippi, Alabama and one Oklahoma Republican elector for a total of 15.

The crumbling of massive resistance speeded the atrophy of the Byrd machine. The growth of the state's urban areas and the decline in the state's agricultural population gradually undermined its rural foundation, while legislative reapportionment and the repeal of the poll tax in the 1960s ended the systematic weakening and exclusion of potential contending groups that had insulated the Byrd organization for half a century. Declining in influence and in failing health, Byrd resigned from the Senate in November 1965; his son, Harry F. Byrd, Jr., was appointed his successor. The elder Byrd died of a brain tumor on Oct. 20, 1966. [See KENNEDY, JOHNSON Volumes]

[TO]

For further information:
J. Harvie Wilkinson III, *Harry Byrd and the Changing Face of Virginia Politics, 1945-1966* (Charlottesville, 1968).

BYRD, ROBERT C(ARLYLE)
b. Jan. 15, 1918; North Wilkesboro, N.C.
Democratic Representative, W. Va., 1953-59; Democratic Senator, W. Va., 1959- .

Orphaned at the age of 10 months, Byrd was raised in West Virginia by his uncle, a poor coal miner. After graduating from high school Byrd worked as a butcher. During World War II he was employed in Maryland and Florida shipyards. In 1942 he was an active organizer for the Ku Klux Klan (KKK) but left the group after about a year. Byrd won a seat in the West Virginia House of Delegates in 1946 and was reelected in 1948. Two years later he ran a successful campaign for the state Senate.

In 1952 Byrd sought a seat in the U.S. House of Representatives from his state's sixth congressional district, a coal mining region that included the city of Charleston. Byrd won the primary, but during the general election campaign, his opponent revealed that in 1946 Byrd had expressed a renewed interest in the Klan in a letter to its Imperial Wizard. Gov. Okey Patteson demanded that he abandon the race, and the Democratic Party withdrew its backing. Byrd, however, renounced the KKK, continued his campaign and defeated his Republican opponent with 55.6% of the vote.

As a representative, Byrd was most vocal in matters affecting coal miners and the coal industry, the major interest groups of his district. Having won election with labor's backing, he supported a House proposal to repeal the Taft-Hartley Act in 1953. Byrd also devoted considerable attention to protecting the coal industry against competition from alternate forms of energy. In 1953 and 1955 he unsuccessfully attempted to add oil import quotas to bills extending reciprocal trade laws. In June 1957 Byrd warned against importing natural gas from Canada, asserting that it "would create a serious impact upon the economy of the coal regions of West Virginia and neighboring states."

Byrd ran for the Senate in 1958. Making the recession the major issue in his campaign, he defeated the Republican incumbent, Sen. Chapman Rivercomb, with 59.2% of the vote. A moderate Democrat, Byrd voted with the upper chamber's Southern Democratic-Republican conservative coalition on 42% of key roll calls in 1959 and 1960. In January 1959 he opposed a liberal effort to modify Senate Rule 22 to facilitate the invoking of cloture against Southern filibusters. He voted for the Civil Rights Act of 1960 after opposing attempts to expand the scope of its coverage.

Byrd backed Sen. Lyndon B. Johnson's (D, Tex.) [q.v.] 1960 presidential bid, but when Johnson declined to enter the May West Virginia primary, he supported Sen. Hubert H. Humphrey (D, Minn.) [q.v.]. He denied the contention of some critics that his endorsement was influenced by Sen. John F. Kennedy's (D, Mass.) [q.v.] Catholicism.

Byrd, an energetic and tireless worker, moved up in the Senate Democratic hierarchy during the 1960s and early-1970s. In 1971 he became majority whip. Byrd succeed John McCormack (D, Mass) [q.v.] as majority leader in 1977. [See KENNEDY, JOHNSON NIXON/FORD CARTER Volumes]

[MLL]

BYRNES, JAMES F(RANCIS)
b. May 2, 1879; Charleston, S.C.
d. April 9, 1972; Columbia, S.C.
Governor, S.C., 1951-55.

The son of Irish immigrants, Byrnes was apprenticed as a law clerk at the age of 14. He became a court stenographer at 21, studied law in his spare time and was admitted to the South Carolina bar in 1903. That year he bought the *Aiken (S.C.) Journal and Review*, which he edited until 1907. A Democrat, Byrnes was elected solicitor of the second judicial circuit in 1908 and two years later to the U.S. House of Representatives, where he served until 1925. He ran unsuccessfully for the Senate in 1924 but won a seat six years later.

Following Roosevelt's election in 1932, Byrnes served as one of the President's chief legislative tacticians and the de facto leader of congressional Democrats. After 1936 Byrnes joined the Southern Democratic opposition to the New Deal. However, with the advent of World War II in 1939, he muted his differences with the President to help repeal the Neutrality Act and pass the lend-lease bill. In 1941 Roosevelt appointed Byrnes associate justice of the Supreme Court. He stepped down 16 months later to head the Office of Economic Stabilization. In 1943 Byrnes became director of the Office of War Mobilization, where he supervised the production of war and civilian goods. Roosevelt described him as "assistant President on the home front."

Byrnes accompanied Roosevelt to the Yalta Conference in 1945 and after Roosevelt's death became Secretary of State. He was one of Truman's closest advisers, helping make the decision to drop the atomic bomb on Japan and formulating policy toward the Soviet Union. As Secretary of State, Byrnes sought a postwar settlement that would prevent Soviet control over Eastern Europe and retain the American atomic monopoly. Byrnes resigned in 1947 in a disagreement with Truman over his domestic program, particularly civil rights. After a period of silence he denounced Truman's domestic policies and the movement toward a strong, centralized government. [See TRUMAN Volume]

In January 1950 Byrnes was elected governor of South Carolina on a states rights platform. While in office he pushed through the legislature a school administration reorganization plan, an anti-masking bill aimed at the Ku Klux Klan, a right-to-work law forbidding compulsory union membership and a statute increasing support for state colleges. Vowing to upgrade mental hospitals, he took legislators on a tour of the state's deteriorated facilities and obtained immediate approval for a new mental health bond issue.

Byrnes's primary focus was on the restoration of states rights, particularly what he believed was their right to maintain segregation. The Governor felt three things were necessary to restore those rights: increased state responsibility toward blacks to give them equal facilities and services without integration; a determined stand by states to prevent further federal inroads, particularly in civil rights and school segregation; and, cooperative action by Southern states to prevent the continued growth of federal power. As part of this program Byrnes proposed and the legislature passed a 3% sales tax and a $75 million school bond issue to upgrade black facilities in 1951.

While developing his school equalization program, Byrnes had the legislature enact measures to counter possible federal intervention to desegregate local schools. School boards were authorized to transfer their property to private hands. A pupil assignment law was passed requiring students switching schools to receive written permission from both institutions. Byrnes created the first segregation strategy-mapping group in the South, headed by state Sen. L. Marion Gressette. The Gressette Committee suggested South Carolina drop the state constitutional provision requiring free public schools. Byrnes approved and called for action on the proposal in January 1952. The legislature responded, and voters ratified the amendment in the November 1952 elections.

Byrnes denounced the Supreme Court's 1954 *Brown v. Board of Education* ruling, which declared segregated school facilities unconstitutional. The ruling directly affected South Carolina schools because a challenge to its Clarendon Co. system had been part of the *Brown* case. The Governor maintained that the validity of the Constitution was ageless and that Court precedent supporting segregation should not be overturned. That year he supported segregationist Lt. Gov. George Bell Timmerman [*q.v.*] for the Democratic gubernatorial nomination. In 1957, when Eisenhower sent troops into Little Rock, Ark., to desegregate its Central High School, Byrnes denounced the action. "Whenever the tanks and guns are removed," he said, "there will remain the same determination on the part of the white people to resort to every legal means to prevent the mixing of the races." Byrnes maintained that "sensible Negroes" "know that when integration occurs, there will cease to be education for either the white or colored child."

In response to his desire to revive regional unity, Byrnes urged the South to become independent of the Democratic Party. In major addresses before the Virginia and Georgia legislatures in 1952, he denounced the growth of federal power under Truman, particularly its intrusion into the area of civil rights, and called on the South to put principle before party. When Eisenhower won the Republican nomination, Byrnes openly supported him and was responsible for the General's doing better in the South than any other Republican candidate since Reconstruction. In September 1953 National Democratic Chairman Stephen A. Mitchell [q.v.] read Byrnes out of the Party. In March 1956 Byrnes, Timmerman and Sen. Strom Thurmond (D, S.C.) [q.v.) tried to force South Carolina to break with the national Democrats. When this movement collapsed in October, Byrnes endorsed Sen. Harry F. Byrd (D, Va.) [q.v.] for President. Following Eisenhower's reelection, Byrnes accused Attorney General Herbert Brownell [q.v.] of persuading the President to support black demands in return for votes.

Unable to serve a second term because of South Carolina law, Byrnes retired in 1955. Throughout the remainder of the 1950s he lent prestige and dignity to the segregationist cause. He supported conservative Sen. Barry M. Goldwater (R, Ariz.) [q.v.] for President in 1964 and Richard Nixon [q.v.] in 1968. Byrnes died in Columbia, S.C., on April 9, 1972.

[MJS]

BYRNES, JOHN W(ILLIAM)
b. June 12, 1913; Green Bay, Wisc.
Republican Representative, Wisc., 1945-73.

John Byrnes received his B.A. from the University of Wisconsin in 1936 and his law degree two years later. In 1938 he was appointed special deputy commissioner of banking for Wisconsin. He stayed in that post until his election to the state Senate as a Republican in 1940. In 1943 he became majority leader and the next year won election to the U.S. House of Representatives.

A fiscal conservative, Byrnes was a vocal opponent of Democratic social welfare programs and deficit-spending and an advocate of economy in government. Named to the Ways and Means Committee in 1947, he gradually rose to prominence in the House as a Republican spokesman on tax and fiscal policy.

During the 1950s Byrnes was a Republican Party loyalist and usually a faithful supporter of the Eisenhower Administration. In February 1953 he was one of only four members of the Ways and Means Committee to vote against an income tax cut being pushed by Committee Chairman Rep. Daniel Reed (R, N.Y.) [q.v.]. The tax cut was opposed by the Eisenhower Administration.

Byrnes generally favored tax measures designed to benefit specific sectors of business, such as the oil depletion allowance and the credit for stock dividend income. In 1954 the House passed his motion to give working parents a tax deduction of up to $600 for child care expenses. Four years later, however, Byrnes opposed the Keogh Plan, a proposal to allow self-employed individuals to set up tax-sheltered retirement plans. He said that it provided no relief for millions of other persons who contributed to the social security system and were not permitted to deduct their contributions from their taxable income.

Byrnes was often in the forefront of conservative efforts to curb federal spending. When the Eisenhower Administration requested a $5 billion increase in the national debt ceiling in January 1958, Byrnes put forth a proposal to limit the rise to $3 billion. The House rejected Byrnes's measure, 275-114. In April he again led the economy bloc in a battle over a Democratic bill expanding unemployment benefits. His proposal to limit benefits to workers currently insured lost in the Ways and Means Committee, 14-7. Byrnes castigated the Democratic plan as "a dole, pure and simple, that goes beyond the wildest dream of the Fair and New Deal, with no basis in need or anything else." In 1960 he opposed the Democrats' medicare plan and opposed a 7½% pay increase for federal workers.

In 1959 Byrnes became chairman of the

House Republican Policy Committee after helping Rep. Charles A. Halleck (R, Ind.) [*q.v.*] depose Rep. Joseph W. Martin (R, Mass.) [*q.v.*] as House minority leader. Over the next decade Byrnes led Republican opposition to Kennedy and Johnson Administration social legislation and fiscal activism while working closely with Ways and Means Committee chairman Rep. Wilbur Mills (D, Ark.) [*q.v.*] to round up a bipartisan consensus on tax measures. Byrnes retired in 1973. [See KENNEDY, JOHNSON, NIXON/FORD Volumes]

[TO]

CABOT, JOHN M(OORS)
b. Dec. 11, 1901; Cambridge., Mass.
Assistant Secretary of State for Inter-American Affairs, February 1953-February 1954; Ambassador to Sweden, February 1954-April 1957; Ambassador to Colombia, April 1957-May 1959; Ambassador to Brazil, May 1959-August 1961.

A member of the prominent Cabot family of Boston, John Moors Cabot graduated from Harvard in 1923 and went on to further studies at Oxford. He began his diplomatic career in 1927 as vice-consul in Callao, Peru. Thereafter, he held a variety of diplomatic posts, mainly in Latin America. In February 1953 President Eisenhower named Cabot assistant secretary of state for inter-American affairs.

In his first month in office, Cabot led the U.S. delegation at the Inter-American Economic and Social Conference in Caracas, Venezuela. There Cabot outlined what all assumed was the official Eisenhower policy for the hemisphere. He recommended continued U.S. technical assistance, considerable movement of federal and particularly private funds to Latin America and equitable trade relations. Speaking later in the United States, Cabot warned that import curbs on Latin American products damaged the ideals of Pan Americanism and could only abet Communist subversion in the hemisphere. He argued that to deal effectively with the Communists, the U.S. had

to cut its ties with reactionary regimes and seize the leadership of social reform in Latin America.

Cabot failed to realize his designs. His efforts to make more use of the Export-Import Bank for long-term development loans were vetoed by Secretary of the Treasury George Humphrey [*q.v.*], who wanted to restrict the bank's role and favored loans for short-term purposes only. The Administration also imposed import restrictions on many Latin American products. His conflicts with Humphrey led to Cabot's resignation in February 1954.

Cabot was immediately named ambassador to Sweden. He was a popular figure in Sweden, setting up meetings with Swedish citizens in which he attempted to explain U.S. foreign policy. He became ambassador to Colombia in April 1957 and remained there until May 1959, when he was transferred to Brazil.

Cabot arrived there at a period when Brazilian-American relations were strained by growing nationalist feelings and the belief that the U.S. was insensitive to Latin American needs. Although he frequently spoke before Brazilian student groups to reduce hostility toward the U.S., he could not restrain the government's development of an independent foreign policy.

President John F. Kennedy asked Cabot to stay on in Brazil because of the Ambassador's sympathy for his Administration's Latin American policy. However, Cabot's difficulties with the new Brazilian president forced him to leave his post in August 1961. He was ambassador to Poland from December 1961 to August 1965 and then had a brief teaching career before his retirement. [See KENNEDY Volume]

[JCH]

CAMPBELL, JOSEPH
b. March 25, 1900; New York, N.Y.
Member, Atomic Energy Commission, 1953-54; U.S. Controller General, 1954-55.

Campbell received an A.B. degree from Columbia University in 1924 and then began a career in accounting with the firm of Lingley, Baird and Dixon. He established his own firm nine years later. During the 1940s he served as assistant treasurer of Columbia University and in 1949 was appointed treasurer and vice president.

President Dwight D. Eisenhower appointed Campbell to the five-man Atomic Energy Commission (AEC) in 1953. During his year on the panel, he was involved in two major controversies of the early Eisenhower Administration: the decision to deny scientist J. Robert Oppenheimer [q.v.] security clearance and the decision to approve the Dixon-Yates contract. In June 1954 Campbell voted with the four-man majority to deny Oppenheimer security clearance. The majority did not find him a security risk but nevertheless voted to deny clearance because of "fundamental defects" in character. It also found that "his association with . . . Communists had extended far beyond the tolerable limits of prudence . . . expected of one holding high government position."

Campbell joined AEC Chairman Lewis Strauss [q.v.] in backing the Dixon-Yates contract in 1954. This agreement provided for a private utility to construct a hydroelectric plant near West Memphis, Ark. The company would then have sold power to AEC installations in the area, replacing the Tennessee Valley Authority (TVA) as the supplier. The contract aroused a storm of protest from public-power advocates who opposed the replacement of the government operated TVA. The contract was canceled in June 1955 after the Democrats had regained control of Congress and after revelations of possible improprieties in the negotiation of the contract.

In January 1955 Campbell was appointed to a 15-year term as Controller General. The position was a non-political one involving no policymaking functions. The Controller advised Congress on legislative matters, audited government programs and offered recommendations designed to make government operations more efficient and effective. During the Eisenhower Administration Campbell testified against the President's highway program of 1955, warning that the moral obligation bonds Eisenhower intended to use to finance the project were

illegal under existing laws. Several years later he scored the Air Force's management of the $2 billion intercontinental ballistic missile program because the service had shifted responsibility for the project to private industry.

In December 1960 Campbell attempted to cut off funds to the State Department Inspector General's office for withholding from Congress information on U.S. aid to Latin America. The Administration, terming the data confidential, supported the State Department. Eisenhower ordered Secretary of State Christian Herter [q.v.] to ignore Campbell's order.

Campbell resigned his post in 1965, before his term expired.

[TLH]

CANNON, HOWARD W(ALTER)
b. Jan. 26, 1912; St. George, Utah
Democratic Senator, Nev., 1959- .

The son of a banker and rancher, Cannon received a law degree from the University of Arizona in 1937 and opened a practice in Utah the following year. After service in the Air Force during World War II, he became a partner in a Las Vegas legal firm. He was elected Las Vegas city attorney in 1949 and occupied that post for eight years. In 1956 he lost the Democratic primary in a bid for U.S. House seat.

Two years later Cannon entered the Nevada senatorial race against incumbent Republican Sen. George W. Malone. The campaign pitted Cannon, whose ties were with the new, growing industrial concerns of southern Nevada, against the conservative Malone, allied with the mining interests of the north and west. Scoring the Republican as an isolationist and conservative, Cannon won the race with 56% of the vote. The nationwide Democratic trend was credited with his success, but equally important was the backing of organized labor and Las Vegas residents. These provided Cannon's political base throughout his career.

During his first two years in the Senate, Cannon compiled a moderately liberal record. In 1959 he supported two housing bills vetoed by President Eisenhower, who contended they were extensive. The following year Cannon voted to override a presidential veto of an area redevelopment bill providing federal aid to depressed regions. In June 1959 he joined a majority of senators in rejecting the nomination of former Atomic Energy Commission Chairman Lewis L. Strauss [q.v.] as Secretary of Commerce on the ground that he had been excessively influenced by private business.

In 1959 Cannon opposed a liberal effort to ease the Senate filibuster rules. These required a two-thirds vote of the entire Senate to stop debate and provided that debate could not be shut off on proposals to consider changes in Senate rules. Liberals wanted to permit imposition of cloture by majority vote of the entire chamber and by 60% of those voting. Instead, Cannon backed a revision introduced by Senate Majority Leader Lyndon B. Johnson (D, Tex.) [q.v.] that would have permitted two-thirds of those voting to shut off debate on all measures, including rules changes.

A member of the Armed Services and Aeronautical and Space Committees, Cannon was a strong backer of military spending and the space program in the 1960s. He also supported President Johnson's Vietnam policies. Cannon first received significant national attention in 1973 when, as chairman of the Rules and Administration Committee, he led its hearings on President Richard Nixon's nomination of Rep. Gerald Ford (R, Mich.) [q.v.] for vice president. During the fall of the following year, he chaired the panel's consideration of Nelson Rockefeller [q.v.] for the vice presidency. [See KENNEDY, JOHNSON, NIXON/FORD Volumes]

[MLL]

CAPEHART, HOMER E(ARL)
b. June 6, 1897; Algiers, Ind.
Republican Senator, Ind., 1945-63.

The son of a tenant farmer, Capehart successfully sold farm machinery, popcorn machines and jukeboxes throughout the Midwest during the 1920s and 1930s. During the Depression he turned an unprofitable piano company into a profit-making record concern. Capehart won election to the U.S. Senate from Indiana in 1944 and quickly emerged as one of the chamber's more conservative anti-Communist Republicans. [See TRUMAN Volume]

When Republicans took control of Congress in 1953, Capehart became chairman of the Senate Banking and Currency Committee. During the early weeks of the Administration, Capehart opposed Eisenhower's plan for ending wage and price controls without provision for standby measures. Fearing a recurrence of the inflation that gripped the nation following the end of controls after World War II, Capehart maintained that it was an ideal time for Congress to review the subject closely "free as it is, from the stress, strains and tensions of a great national emergency." He immediately introduced a bill to set up emergency control machinery. The measure narrowly passed the Senate but died in the House.

Capehart was assigned to the Foreign Relations Committee in 1954. That February he voted for the Bricker amendment, which limited the President's treaty-making powers. It was defeated by one vote. In 1955 Capehart scored a resolution by Sen. Joseph R. McCarthy (R, Wisc.) [q.v.] requiring Eisenhower to condition his participation in the Geneva summit conference on a Soviet agreement to put a discussion of Eastern Europe on the agenda. He also attacked Sen. Lyndon B. Johnson (D, Tex.) [q.v.] and Sen. Walter George (D, Ga.) [q.v.] for permitting the resolution to emerge from the Foreign Relations Committee, saying it should "have been thrown into the trash can." The measure was defeated on the floor of the Senate.

Following his reelection in 1956, Capehart became an increasingly strong supporter of Administration policy. He backed the Civil Rights Act of 1957, which guaranteed voting rights to blacks. The following year he supported President Eisenhower's decision to retain presidential assistant Sherman Adams [q.v.] in the face of conflict-of-interest charges. Capehart also supported the permanent establishment of the Small Business Administration and backed statehood for Alaska.

In 1959 a vice president of Wurlitzer Inc., testifying before the Senate Committee on Improper Relations in the Labor or Management Field, charged that Capehart had been forced to deal with racketeers when he sold jukeboxes to that company in the 1930s. The Senator strongly refuted this. He joined other conservatives in voting down a national commission to deal with organized crime in 1960.

Capehart opposed most Kennedy Administration legislation. He gained national prominence in 1962, when he scored the Administration's Cuban policy and warned of a Soviet buildup in the island. Capehart lost an upset election that year to Democrat Birch Bayh. He retired to farming, manufacturing and investment pursuits. [See KENNEDY Volume]

[MJS]

CAREY, JAMES B(ARRON)
b. Aug. 12, 1911: Philadelphia, Pa.
d. Sept. 11, 1973: Silver Springs, Md.
President, International Union of Electrical, Radio and Machine Workers, 1949-65.

The son of a civil servant, James Carey began working in a local factory at the age of 14. Following graduation from high school he got a job at the Philco Radio Co. in Philadelphia. In 1933 Carey and a group of supporters took over a company union at Philco and led a successful strike of the plant's 3,800 employes. Shortly afterwards he left his job to become an organizer in the radio industry for the American Federation of Labor (AFL). Carey favored industrial unionism, however, and he soon came into conflict with the Federation's policy of assigning workers to separate craft brotherhoods. In March 1936 he helped organize a meeting of 28 AFL locals representing 30,000 electrical workers, which formed an independent union, the United Electrical, Radio and Machine Workers of America (UE). Six months later Carey led the UE into the new Committee for Industrial Organization (CIO). In 1938 he was elected CIO national secretary, and in 1942 he became secretary-treasurer.

A liberal anti-Communist, Carey nevertheless ran the UE after 1936 in cooperation with Communists. Following the Stalin-Hitler Pact in 1939, he broke with these elements, and in 1941 he was ousted from the union presidency by a coalition of Communists and more conservative members. Thereafter Carey led the anti-Communist opposition within the UE, and with Walter Reuther [q.v.] of the United Auto Workers, he spearheaded a drive to purge the CIO of Communist influence.

After World War II Carey worked with the State Department and various European labor leaders to create the anti-Communist International Confederation of Free Trade Unions. In 1949 the UE was expelled from the CIO, and the CIO presented Carey with a charter for a new union, the International Union of Electrical, Radio and Machine Workers (IUE). A long period of jurisdictional warfare followed between the UE, the IUE and several AFL craft unions. During that time the IUE won collective bargaining rights in a majority of plants in the electrical equipment industry. [See TRUMAN Volume]

Carey was a member of the unity committee that negotiated the merger of the AFL and CIO in 1955. He was elected a vice-president of the new organization and general secretary of its industrial union department. He often represented the AFL-CIO at international labor functions during the 1950s.

At the same time, however, continuing jurisdictional conflict and employer resistance steadily weakened Carey's own union. In 1955 the IUE struck the Westinghouse Corp. after the company attempted to extend a three-year contract, negotiated in the previous year, to five years. The strike, which lasted six months and eventually involved more than 70,000 workers throughout the country, was the longest and most bitterly contested dispute in a major industry since 1941. Clashes between striking and non-striking employes and police intervention also marked the strike as a notable exception to the relatively peaceful pattern of labor-management relations established in mass-production industries after the War.

his union was the victim of continuing unfair labor practices on the part of the General Electric Co. IUE members termed the Company's bargaining policy "Boulwarism," after the name of a GE vice president, or "bargaining by ultimatum," since the Company's first offer was its last. In 1960 Carey called a three-week strike against GE that proved disastrous for the union. In the following period the IUE lost 10 important plant elections affecting several thousand workers.

In 1965 Carey was defeated as IUE president by rank-and-file insurgents. Shortly afterwards he left the union to become a labor representative of the United Nations Association, a position which he held until his retirement in 1972. Carey died in Silver Springs, Md., on Sept. 11, 1973. [See KENNEDY, JOHNSON Volumes]

[TLH]

CARLSON, FRANK
b. Jan. 23, 1893; Concordia, Kan.
Republican Senator, Kan., 1950-69.

Carlson, the son of Swedish immigrants, attended Kansas State College. He became a farmer following service in the Army during World War I. He was elected to the state legislature in 1929 and 1931. In 1935 Carlson won a seat in the U.S. House of Representatives from Kansas's sixth district. During the 1930s he backed high parity for farmers but generally opposed New Deal measures. Carlson was elected governor of Kansas in 1946 on a platform that denounced the Truman Administration for continuing New Deal policies. He was reelected in 1948. Two years later he took a seat in the U.S. Senate.

Closely associated with the liberal Eastern wing of the Republican Party, Carlson was an early supporter of Gen. Dwight D. Eisenhower for the 1952 Republican presidential nomination. After the Republican Convention he acted as an intermediary between the Eisenhower forces and Sen. Robert A. Taft (R, Ohio) [q.v.] in an effort to unite the Party. Eisenhower appointed him a special adviser during the campaign.

In August 1954 Carlson served on the committee of six "neutral" senators, known as the Select Committee to Study Censure, created to study charges of misconduct against Sen. Joseph R. McCarthy (R, Wisc.) [q.v.]. That November he joined in its unanimous recommendation for censure. On Nov. 12, during floor debate on the panel's report, Carlson charged that McCarthy had violated Senate rules by his attacks on the Committee's conduct and motives.

First as chairman, and after 1955 as senior Republican, of the Post Office and Civil Service Committee, Carlson attempted to limit the salaries, benefits and promotions of federal Civil Service workers. During the summer of 1954 he succeeded in placing restrictions on the number of permanent employes, promotions and transfers in the federal service. The following year he unsuccessfully offered a floor amendment to reduce pay increases for classified employes from 10%, as provided by a Committee bill, to 6%. In 1957 he opposed another pay raise, again without success, charging that it would require a supplemental appropriation of half a billion dollars.

A supporter of 100% price supports for wheat farmers, Carlson opposed the Administration's 1954 omnibus farm bill, which established flexible price supports. Two years later he successfully introduced a proposal to give the Secretary of Agriculture discretionary authority to support wheat for domestic human consumption at 100% parity if two-thirds of the wheat growers approved in a 1957 crop referendum. However, the President vetoed the bill to which the proviso was attached.

Carlson generally supported the Administration's positions. In 1955, as a member of the three-man Post Office and Civil Service Committee's Government Employes Security Program Subcommittee, he defended President Eisenhower's security program against charges that its procedures failed to adequately protect the rights of federal employees and job applicants. The following year Carlson criticized the Committee report, which recommended that the scope of the program's coverage be reduced from six million to

1.5 million employes. He supported the extension of the Reciprocal Trade Agreements Act in 1955, opposed Sen. Richard B. Russell's (D, Ga.) [q.v.] amendment to the Administration's version of the 1957 Eisenhower Middle East Doctrine, which proposed the elimination of its authorization for economic aid, and voted against a medical insurance system financed through social security in 1960.

Carlson opposed most New Frontier programs in the early 1960s but backed the Kennedy Administration's foreign policies. Subsequently, he was critical of the bulk of President Johnson's Great Society programs, but he supported the Demonstration Cities plan in August 1966. Carlson was not a critic of the Vietnam war. However, from time to time he called for negotiations. In 1968 he decided not to seek reelection. Carlson was a favorite-son candidate at the August 1968 Republican National Convention. [See JOHNSON Volume]

[MLL]

CARR FRANCIS P.
b. 1917; Newport, R.I.
Executive Director, Permanent Investigations Subcommittee of the Senate Government Operations Committee, 1953-54.

Carr graduated from Brown University and received a law degree from the University of Pennsylvania in 1942. He then entered the FBI. As head of the New York field division's security matters section in the late-1940s, he directed the investigation of prominent Communist Party leaders. Carr resigned from the FBI in 1953 and was appointed executive director of the staff of the Senate Permanent Investigations Subcommittee, headed by Sen. Joseph R. McCarthy (R, Wisc.) [q.v.].

During 1954 Carr became embroiled in the dispute between the Army and McCarthy. In March 15, 1954 Secretary of the Army Robert T. Stevens [q.v.] charged that Carr, McCarthy and subcommittee counsel Roy Cohn [q.v.] had exerted pressure on the Army to obtain special treatment for Pvt. G. David Schine [q.v.], a former McCarthy aide.

On March 16 the Permanent Investigations Subcommittee voted to investigate the accusation. Carr was cleared of the charges in May on a straight party vote and was exempted from appearing before the panel. Subcommittee Democrats opposed the action, maintaining it had been taken to help Carr avoid testifying.

On June 14 Carr voluntarily testified. He maintained that, in an effort to stop the McCarthy probe, Stevens had offered preferential treatment to Schine. Carr also testified that the Secretary had been willing to reveal "some homosexuals" in the Air Force in return for information about the next McCarthy investigation.

The subcommittee issued its report on the probe in August. The Democrats denounced McCarthy's conduct, while the Republicans mildly criticized him. Stevens likewise was rebuked more severely by Democrats than by Republicans for submitting to McCarthy's pressure. Members of both parties found no evidence of wrong doing on Carr's part. In a dissenting opinion, Sen. Charles E. Potter (D, Mich.) [q.v.] said he was not entirely blameless. After the hearings Carr faded from public view.

[SY]

CARROLL, JOHN A(LBERT)
b. July 30, 1901; Denver, Colo.
Democratic Senator, Colo. 1957-63.

Carroll served in the Army during World War I and then went on to receive a law degree from Westminster Law College. During the 1930s he served as assistant district attorney for Denver. He was regional attorney for the Office of Price Administration in 1942 and 1943. Carroll saw action in the European theatre during World War II. He won a seat in the U.S. House of Representatives in 1946 and served there until 1951. He was elected to the U.S. Senate in 1956. During his one term Carroll established a liberal record as a supporter of education, medical, social and civil rights legislation. Carroll voted for the Civil Rights Act of 1957 and joined liberals in an unsuccessful attempt to strengthen the civil rights bill of 1960.

As a congressman from a Western state, Carroll was deeply concerned with resource development and conservation. He supported the controversial Hell's Canyon Dam Project, which provided for federal construction and operation of a massive dam on the Snake River. In 1957 he sponsored a bill authorizing funds for the Fryingpan-Arkansas Project, a multiple purpose reclamation effort designed to divert surplus water from the Colorado River Basin to the Arkansas River Basin. The project was vital to the development of southeastern Colorado. An early environmentalist, Carroll supported unsuccessful efforts to limit billboards on highways.

During 1958 Carroll became a major defender of the Supreme Court, then under attack for its controversial decisions on civil liberties. During the mid-1950s the Court had limited the power of both state and local government in subversion cases and strengthened the rights of individuals under arrest. In August 1958 Carroll opposed conservative attempts to strip the Court of the power to review subversion cases. His motion to recommit killed an amendment declaring that "no act of Congress . . . should be construed by the Courts as nullifying state laws on the same subject unless Congress so specified or there was an unreconcilable difference between state and federal law." On a point of order, Carroll defeated a bill reversing the Mallory decision that same month. The decision had invalidated the confession of a confessed rapist because of delays in his arraignment.

Carroll was defeated for reelection in 1962 by a group of conservative Republicans who gained control of Colorado politics that year. [See KENNEDY Volume]

[EWS]

CASE, CLIFFORD P(HILIP)
b. April 16, 1904; Franklin Park, N.J.
Republican Representative, N.J., 1945-53; Republican Senator, N.J., 1955- .

The son of a Dutch Reformed minister, Case attended Rutgers University, where he graduated in 1925. He received an LL.B. from Columbia University in 1928 and joined the Wall Street law firm of Simpson, Thacher and Bartlett the same year. He was a member of the firm from 1939 to 1953. From 1938 to 1942 Case served on the Common Council of Rahway, N.J.

In 1944 Case was elected to the U.S. House of Representatives. There he gained a reputation as a liberal Republican who frequently crossed party lines to support civil rights, education and welfare legislation. He favored an anti-poll tax measure in 1945, opposed the establishment of a permanent Un-American Activities Committee in 1945, supported the creation of a Fair Employment Practices Commission in 1950, and voted against overriding President Harry S. Truman's veto of the McCarran immigration bill in 1952. On the other hand, he voted to override the President's veto of the Taft-Hartley bill in 1947 and helped draft the Communist-control bill in 1948. Dissatisfied with the lack of significant influence of all but the most senior members of the House, Case resigned his seat in August 1953. He became president of the Ford Foundation's Fund for the Republic, established to defend civil liberties against cold war pressures for conformity.

In March 1954 Case resigned that post to run for the U.S. Senate. During the campaign he faced opposition from labor, Old Guard Republicans and supporters of Sen. Joseph R. McCarthy (R, Wisc.) [q.v.], who labeled him a "left-wing socialist" and "darling of the Americans for Democratic Action." Stressing his opposition to McCarthy, Case narrowly defeated his liberal Democratic opponent in November.

As a senator, Case remained a member of the small bloc of Northeastern liberal Republicans in Congress. In November 1956 he urged revision of the McCarran Immigration Act to eliminate "the senseless and serious discriminations against nationalities of Southern and Southeastern Europe." A strong supporter of civil rights, in 1957 Case opposed Southern attempts to weaken the Administration's civil rights bill by requiring a jury trial for contempt cases involving persons who had attempted to prevent blacks from voting. In March 1960

Case was one of eight Republicans who joined liberal Democrats in an unsuccessful effort to end a Southern filibuster against another Administration civil rights bill. The following year he was paired in favor of overriding President Eisenhower's veto of an area redevelopment bill.

Case did not uniformly vote with the Senate's liberal Democrats. In 1959 he backed a $2.1 billion housing bill but declined to support an effort to override President Eisenhower's veto. The same year he voted to confirm Lewis Strauss [q.v.] as Secretary of Commerce, a choice opposed by liberals on the ground that Strauss had been too close to private business interests as chairman of the Atomic Energy Commission.

Case continued his liberal record during the 1960s, backing most civil rights and social welfare legislation. He was also a leading spokesman for financial disclosure legislation for all three branches of the federal government. Case opposed the growth of ultra right-wing influence in the Republican Party, and in 1964 he fought the nomination of conservative Sen. Barry Goldwater (R, Ariz.) [q.v.] for President. During the later part of the decade, Case was also a critic of President Lyndon B. Johnson's Vietnam policies. [See KENNEDY, JOHNSON, NIXON/FORD Volumes]

[MLL]

CELLER, EMANUEL
b. May 6, 1888; Brooklyn, N.Y.
Democratic Representative, N.Y., 1923-73; Chairman, Judiciary Committee, 1949-53, 1955-73.

The son of a liquor distiller, Celler graduated from Columbia University in 1910 and received his LL.B. there two years later. In 1922 he won election to Congress from New York's 10th congressional district, a predominately middle-class Jewish section of Brooklyn. In the House Celler established a strong liberal record, introducing measures to curb big business abuses and advocating the liberalization of the immigration laws. Celler was a fervent supporter of the New Deal and a strong de-

fender of civil liberties. In 1945 he backed an unsuccessful anti-poll tax bill and opposed a measure making the Un-American Activities Committee a standing committee.

Celler maintained his liberal record during the Truman Administration. He opposed the Taft-Hartley bill of 1947. Two years later he became chairman of the Judiciary Committee, a position he held for the duration of his congressional tenure (except for 1953-55, when a Republican majority interrupted the Democrats' control of the House). In 1949 Celler used his post as chairman of the Judiciary Committee to establish the Subcommittee on Antitrust and Monopoly. From 1949 to 1951 the panel conducted a series of well-publicized investigations into insurance companies, the steel industry and monopoly practices in baseball. In 1950 Celler helped steer the Celler-Kefauver anti-merger bill through Congress. Celler was also a vocal opponent of Sen. Joseph R. McCarthy's (R, Wisc.) [q.v.] anti-Communist crusade. [See TRUMAN Volume]

During the 1950s Celler continued to be a leading congressional defender of civil liberties. He cast one of two votes against appropriations for the House Un-American Activities Committee in 1953 and 1954. He opposed the Judiciary Committee's reporting of a witness immunity bill, brought to the floor of the House in August 1954. The bill, formulated as a tool in the anti-Communist crusade, allowed Congress to grant immunity to congressional witnesses under certain conditions. Liberal critics maintained it had the effect of forcing witnesses to testify or face jail sentences. In a minority statement directed at McCarthy and his supporters, Celler and three other Democrats on the Judiciary Committee denounced the action saying, "There is presently an unbecoming shrillness, fed into hysteria by political would-be saviours, in our approach to problems of internal Communism." Despite his strong stand on the rights of witnesses in loyalty-security hearings, Celler did not oppose a 1954 bill banning the Communist Party. Although he described the measure as "palpably unconstitutional," he voted for it.

In May and June of 1955 Celler's antitrust subcommittee held hearings on government policy toward mergers. The subcommittee's report maintained that the "third great merger movement" in U.S. history was already in progress and warned that previous periods of intensive merger activity had been followed by "devastating business collapse." Celler opposed a proposal to grant antitrust immunity to companies involved in defense production, asserting that defense needs could be met "within the traditional framework of our antitrust laws." However, the bill was passed by both houses in August 1955.

Celler was the principal architect of the 1957 Civil Rights Act. In February 1957 the House Judiciary Committee reported a major proposal emphasizing voting rights. The bill called for creation of an executive commission on civil rights, the addition of an assistant attorney general for civil rights to the Justice Department, authorization for the Attorney General to seek an injunction for an individual deprived of his right to vote, and fines for those convicted of violating the measure. Although the bill incorporated proposals made by the Administration, Celler was critical of President Eisenhower's lukewarm support of the measure. He chided the President for making "some pontifical declarations on civil rights," adding, "You need elbow grease to get such legislation passed." Celler was instrumental in defeating a conservative amendment guaranteeing a jury trial to all persons accused of tampering with the voting rights of others. He argued that "juries in at least five states will be composed exclusively of those who are qualified to vote while those individuals or groups who are denied the vote or who fail to qualify, perhaps by the very action of the defendants, will be denied the right to be on a jury list." The final version of the bill, whose passage Celler helped secure in August, allowed the judge to decide whether a jury trial should be granted in cases of voting rights obstruction.

In 1959 Celler introduced the House version of a measure calling for financial aid for school desegregation and authorization for the Department of Health, Education and Welfare to develop desegregation plans.

However, the proposal died in committee. He also failed to get the proposals included in the Civil Rights Act of 1960. Celler participated in the successful drive for a strong civil rights plank in the 1960 Democratic platform. The plank called for federal aid to desegregated school districts, federal authority to file civil injunction suits to prevent any denial of civil rights and a federal Fair Employment Practices Commission.

Celler continued to play an important role in civil rights legislation during the 1960s. He sponsored the 24th Amendment, ratified in 1964, which abolished the poll tax in federal elections, and was a principal author of the 1964 Civil Rights Act. He also helped secure passage of the 1965 Voting Rights Act, the Immigration and Naturalization Act of 1965 and the 1968 Civil Rights Act. After 50 years in the House, Celler was defeated in the 1972 Democratic congressional primary by Elizabeth Holtzman, a young Brooklyn lawyer. [See KENNEDY, JOHNSON, NIXON/FORD Volumes]

[MDB]

For further information:
Steven F. Lawson, *Black Ballots: Voting Rights in the South, 1944-69* (New York, 1976).

CHAMBERS, (JAY) (DAVID) WHITTAKER
b. April 1, 1901: Philadelphia, Pa.
d. July 9, 1961: Westminster, Md.
Journalist.

After attending Columbia University, Chambers joined the Communist Party in 1925. From 1925 to 1938 he served first as a writer, contributing to the *Daily Worker*, *New Masses* and other publications, and then as a secret party agent. He also translated foreign language books, including a version of *Bambi*. Chambers quit the Party in 1938 and joined Time, Inc. in 1939, where he worked as a senior editor until 1948.

In an appearance before the House Un-American Activities Committee in August 1948, Chambers gave testimony that implicated Alger Hiss as a Communist conspirator within the State Department and revealed his own past activities as a Communist agent. When Hiss sued Chambers for libel, Chambers produced government documents—including the so-called Pumpkin Papers—allegedly given him by Hiss when they both worked for the Communist Party. Chambers's evidence was later used to convict Hiss. [See TRUMAN Volume]

After the Hiss case Chambers retired from the public arena to give occasional congressional testimony and work on his farm in Maryland. In 1952 he wrote *Witness,* an autobiography in which he brooded about the massive Communist threat to the West, the concurrent battle between atheism and religion and the more insidious danger of secular liberalism. The book was immediately praised as a contemporary spiritual and political testament by the American Right.

Chambers served as a prominent conservative spokesman during the 1950s. He sympathized with Sen. Joseph R. McCarthy's (R, Wisc.) [*q.v.*] fight against Communism but deplored the Senator's style, and he refused to be aligned with McCarthy's faction. Chambers viewed the Senator as one who "simply knows that somebody threw a tomato and the general direction from which it came," a man who united the Left through fear and divided the Right. Later Chambers's *Witness* was among those books removed from State Department libraries under pressure from Sen. McCarthy. Chambers was an early supporter of Vice President Richard Nixon [*q.v.*], whom he termed an "elusive strategist" with a great chance of defeating the Communists. However, by 1960 he wrote that Nixon, though "the best there is," would likely be crushed by the Communists if elected President.

In August 1957 Chambers joined the staff of *National Review.* He continued to write about the Communist threat and attacked American liberals as spiritually bankrupt, "man-mind oriented, rather than God-soul trusting" theorists who destroyed Western civilization from within. He also argued that the Right, and particularly the Republican Party, had not formed a cohesive philosophy that could either attract the populace or offer solutions for an "anti-conservative," technology-dominated Amercapitalism. Until his retirement from the *National Review* in December 1958 because of illness, Chambers was respected by the Right as a brilliant martyr redeemed from Communism. John Dos Passos described him as an existential hero, a man who recognized his sin of self-deception and fought back to gain his ideals.

Chambers made his final public pronouncement on the Hiss case in 1959. He supported Hiss's attempt to secure a passport but still demanded that Hiss finally confess the truth. In Chambers's words, "Hiss's defiance perpetuates and keeps a fracture in the community as a whole."

In 1959 Chambers enrolled as an undergraduate at Western Maryland College, where he studied Russian, French and economics. He was still a student when he died in 1961 of a heart attack. A collection of his writings, *Cold Friday,* was published posthumously in 1964.

[TGD]

For further information:
William F. Buckley, Jr., *Odyssey of a Friend: Whittaker Chambers. Letters to William F. Buckley, Jr., 1954-61* (New York, 1969).

CHANDLER, A(LBERT) B(ENJAMIN)
b. July 14, 1898; Corydon, Ky.
Governor, Ky., 1935-39, 1955-59

Raised in rural poverty, Chandler worked in laundries and restaurants to earn his tuition for Transylvania College in Lexington. After taking his B.A. degree in 1921, he studied one year at Harvard law school but left Cambridge and earned his LL.B in 1924 from the University of Kentucky in Lexington. He then moved to Versailles, Ky., to practice law and play professional baseball. After terms as a state senator from 1929 to 1931 and lieutenant governor for the next four years, he was elected governor in 1935. Nicknamed "Happy" because of his ever-present smile, the gregarious, back-slapping Chandler mixed a down-home campaign style with a brand of politics that vacillated between populist and arch-conservative. He was credited with bringing about the much-needed reorganization of state government and removing a $20 million budget deficit, but his abolition of the state sales tax, coupled with his other restrained fiscal policies, prevented the rapid development of community welfare programs. He was widely criticized by labor leaders for directing National Guardsmen to bring order to the Harlan Co. United Mine Workers' strikes of 1939.

After an unsuccessful attempt to win a Senate seat in 1938, Chandler resigned the governorship in 1939 to have himself appointed to fill the Senate term of a deceased incumbent. He won election in his own right in 1942, but he resigned his seat to become the commissioner of baseball in 1945. After receiving an insufficient vote of confidence from baseball owners, he resigned his post in 1951 and returned to Versailles to practice law, edit his newspaper, the Woodford *Sun*, and prepare for re-entry into political life.

In 1955 Chandler organized his political allies for a run for the governorship against a candidate supported by his long-time foe, Sen. Earl Clements, and by the state Democratic Party. A mixture of grass-roots campaigning and old friends proved stronger than the party organization and the ex-Governor won the primary by a slim margin. In the general election a campaign style of "backslapping, barbecues, and bombast," as described in the *New York Times*, helped Happy Chandler amass the largest plurality ever for a Kentucky governor. His inauguration was marked by banners carrying such slogans as "Happy for President in 1956 if Mama says yes."

Chandler's presidential campaign in early 1956 developed little momentum. Strongly suspected of Dixiecrat sympathies in the 1948 election and clearly visible as a supporter of presidential aspirant Sen. Richard B. Russell (D, Ga.) [*q.v.*] in 1952, he found scant support in Democratic Party ranks. The Governor solicited the endorsement of ex-President Harry Truman but was refused. He entered the National Convention with only his own state's 30 delegates and left it with 36½ votes.

Chandler, who had been accused by his 1955 Democratic gubernatorial primary opponent of equivocating on his school integration position, clarified his stance to the nation during the presidential campaign, He stated that Kentucky was abiding by the Supreme Court's desegregation decision. In the fall of 1956, when disorders interrupted the integration of schools in several Kentucky cities, Gov. Chandler sent out National Guardsmen to keep the peace. He committed the state to obedience to the law and threatened to declare martial law if further disturbances warranted it. Not until 1966, however, did Kentucky pass major civil rights legislation in the areas of employment and housing.

As governor in his second term, Chandler continued the Kentucky state government's tradition of blatant political patronage, contrary to his campaign promise to replace "buddy" employment practices with a fairer merit system. In 1958 he refused to support proposed merit-system legislation, arguing that state government was "not ready" for the change. He infuriated not only his enemies but also many allies when, in 1956, he allegedly ordered 20,000 state employes to vote and work for him in state and county presidential conventions or be dismissed if they refused. Chandler faced accusations of corruption throughout his various political administrations: in the 1955 gubernatorial election his opponent resurrected lingering allegations that Chandler had accepted gifts from contractors and favors from the state's "liquor trust." Political scientist Neal Peirce wrote that "major questions remain to this day [1975] as to how much Chandler benefited personally from his governorship."

Forbidden by Kentucky state law from running for a second consecutive term, Chandler retired from the statehouse and waited for the next election in four years. In the interim, however, he lost his charm with the voters, and he was defeated in the Democratic gubernatorial primaries of 1963, 1967 and 1971. After his last defeat, he declared his permanent retirement from politics.

[TGD]

CHAVEZ, DENNIS
b. April 8, 1888; Los Chavez, N.M.
d. Nov. 18, 1962; Washington, D.C.
Democratic Senator, N.M., 1935-62.

One of eight children, Chavez dropped out of school in the eighth grade and worked at menial jobs. He served as an interpreter for Sen. A. A. James (D, N.M.) during the 1916 election and, as a result, was given a job as a clerk in the U.S. Senate. While working in the upper house, Chavez passed a special entrance examination to attend Georgetown University. In 1920 he received his LL.B. and returned to Albuquerque, N.M., to practice law. He served in the New Mexico House of Representatives and in 1931 won a seat in the U.S. House. Appointed to fill a Senate vacancy in May 1935, Chavez won election in his own right in 1936. He was the Senate's first Spanish surnamed member.

In the Senate Chavez supported New and Fair Deal programs. He actively promoted Franklin D. Roosevelt's Good Neighbor Policy and sought to improve conditions in Puerto Rico. Chavez frequently voiced support for civil rights and fair employment practice measures, and in 1943 he cosponsored an amendment granting equal rights for women. He was one of 10 senators who voted against overriding President Harry S. Truman's veto of the internal security bill of 1950. [See TRUMAN Volume]

Chavez's reelection in 1952 was contested by Patrick J. Hurley, who charged voting fraud. The following year a Senate elections subcommittee recommended, by a two-to-one vote, that 20,000 votes cast for Chavez and 10,000 for Hurley be invalidated "for lack of secrecy" in voting places. The recommendation would have resulted in Chavez's defeat, but the Senate rejected the suggestion in March 1954.

During the Eisenhower Administration Chavez, as chairman of the Senate Defense Appropriations Subcommittee, opposed Administration attempts to reduce the military budget. In 1956 he recommended increasing Eisenhower's proposed Air Force budget by $1.6 billion to speed up production of B-52 long-range bombers. In 1960

Chavez emphasized that his subcommittee's first responsibility was to provide the monies needed to "keep America strong" in the light of recent events, particularly the Soviet Union's satellite launchings. Remarking that economy was of secondary importance, the Senator implicitly scored the Administration's desire to put budgetary considerations over security needs. He sided with the Joint Chiefs of Staff in demanding increased spending, asking Chairman of the Joint Chiefs Gen. Nathan Twining [q.v.] to "tell us what you want" and his panel would not deprive him of "one dime if it is necessary for our national security."

Chavez had a mixed record of support for the Administration on domestic issues. As chairman of the Public Works Committee, he initially opposed Eisenhower's plan for the construction of a highway system creating some 42,000 miles of controlled access roads. The system was to be funded jointly by the state and federal government with Washington paying 90% of the costs. The Senator preferred Sen. Albert Gore's (D, Tenn.) [q.v.] more modest proposal, which would have increased funds allocated for primary and secondary roads and the National Highway System. Gore's project would have been paid for from the general Treasury funds, thus putting a lesser burden on the states. Nevertheless, Chavez agreed to cosponsor the Eisenhower measure, which became law in 1956.

The Senator supported the Civil Rights Act of 1957. However, he voted against the Administration's initial proposal, which would have given the Attorney General broad powers to seek injunctions in any type of civil rights case with or without the consent of an alleged victim. As enacted, the law dealt only with voting rights.

Chavez favored statehood for Alaska and Hawaii. He was a warm supporter of the massive public housing bill of 1959 and the aid-to-depressed areas bill of 1960. He voted to override Eisenhower's veto in each case.

Chavez supported most of the Kennedy Administration's social welfare legislation including medicare. He died of cancer in November 1962.

[AES]

CHERRY, FRANCIS
b. Sept. 5, 1908; Fort Worth, Tex.
d. July 15, 1965; Washington, D.C.
Governor, Ark., 1953-55; Member,
Subversive Activities Control Board,
October 1955-July 1965.

The youngest of five children of a poor railroad conductor, Francis Cherry graduated from Oklahoma Agricultural and Mechanical College in 1930. He worked at odd jobs for three years to earn tuition money for the University of Arkansas law school, where he obtained his LL.B. in 1936. In 1937 Cherry entered private practice and a short time later became a commissioner for the Workman's Compensation Commission. Five years later he was elected chancellor and probate judge of the 12th chancery district in Northeast Arkansas. He was the youngest man ever to hold that post.

Waiving his judicial deferment, Cherry was commissioned in the Navy in 1944 and served for two years. He returned to the bench in 1946 and won reelection to another six-year term in 1948. He ran for the Arkansas Democratic gubernatorial nomination in 1952. Cherry was given little chance of success against the incumbent, but through the use of radio he won the primary and the general election.

Upon taking office Cherry promoted a legislative program designed to encourage the economic development of the state. He pressed for the adoption of measures establishing a new state fiscal code and revising the Revenue Stabilization Act covering major expenditures. He also supported a constitutional amendment for revision of the property tax system. In addition, he encouraged industrial development. In an interview in the *Christian Science Monitor*, Cherry described his action as a "revolution." "An entire state is pulling itself out of the mire by its own bootstraps," he maintained.

Following the Supreme Court's May 1954 ruling outlawing school desegregation, Cherry announced that he would comply with the decision. He stated, "Obviously it will take a good deal of time to work it out. I only hope that what has happened does not set back the advances Negroes have made in Arkansas in the past several years." He planned to appoint a governor's committee on segregation as a first step toward compliance. Cherry, however, had little role in Arkansas's desegregation battles. In August 1954 he was defeated in the Democratic primary by Orval Faubus [q.v.].

The following year Eisenhower appointed Cherry to the Subversive Acitivities Control Board (SACB). The SACB was established in 1950 to determine if organizations were Communist-affiliated. Under the 1950 Internal Security Act, which established the Board, Communist groups were required to register with the SACB. The registration issue was highly debated during the 1950s as the Supreme Court limited the scope of anti-Communist legislation. In 1958 Cherry supported continued registration.

In 1961 Cherry recommended that the International Mine, Mill and Smelter Workers be declared a Communist-affiliated organization. The findings were upheld by the full Board in 1962. Cherry was appointed chairman of the SACB in 1963 and died of a heart ailment two years later. [See KENNEDY Volume]

[RB]

CHESSMAN, CARYL W(HITTIER)
b. May 17, 1921; Mich.
d. May 2, 1960; San Quentin, Calif.
Convicted felon.

Caryl Chessman was born in Michigan but grew up in Los Angeles. After a childhood scarred by the crippling of his mother and two suicide attempts by his father, Chessman began stealing food at age 15. He later served two terms in California prisons for armed robbery. In January 1948 Chessman was arrested, charged with robbery, kidnapping, sexual abuses and attempted rape. Serving as his own counsel and claiming mistaken identity, Chessman was convicted on 17 counts and sentenced to die for kidnapping.

Chessman appealed the verdict on the grounds that he had been deprived of counsel and that his trial record was faulty. Over the next 12 years his case went to the Supreme Court 16 times. Eleven rehearings were held in state and federal courts. By 1960 Supreme Court Justice William O. Douglas [*q.v.*] said, "The conclusion is irresistible that Chessman is playing a game with the Courts." Chessman was not idle on Death Row. He wrote four books in the 1950s. The first, *Cell 2455, Death Row*, was a best-seller.

Chessman's case generated worldwide attention from many who opposed the death penalty and saw the series of stays followed by proposed dates of execution as cruel. Pleas that his life be spared came from such diverse individuals as Albert Schweitzer, Pablo Casals and Brigitte Bardot and from newspapers such as the Vatican's *L'Osservatore Romano*. The case also prompted anti-American demonstrations.

On February 1960, just 10 hours before he was to die, California Gov. Edmund G. Brown [*q.v.*] granted Chessman his eighth stay of execution. The Governor announced he had taken the action because Assistant Secretary of State Roy R. Rubottom, Jr., in a telegram to Brown, had relayed a Uruguayan government statement warning of possible hostile demonstrations there during President Eisenhower's visit should Chessman be executed. Brown, a foe of capital punishment, also wanted the state legislature to consider ending California's death penalty. Sen. Clair Engle (D, Calif.) [*q.v.*] protested Brown's decision on the ground that justice to an individual should be based on the facts of the case and not "rest on international reaction." Senate Foreign Relations Committee Chairman J. William Fulbright (D, Ark.) [*q.v.*] denounced the State Department for interfering in the affairs of a sovereign state. In March 1960 Secretary of State Christian A. Herter [*q.v.*] said the case had been exploited by anti-American groups in Latin America and pledged that in the future such controversies would be resolved through regular diplomatic channels.

While crowds kept vigil outside San Quentin, Chessman was executied on May 2, 1960. In many high schools and colleges, students observed a minute of silence in his memory. Chessman denied his guilt to the end.

[MJS]

CHOTINER, MURRAY M.
b. Oct. 4, 1909; Pittsburgh, Pa.
d. Jan. 30, 1974; Washington, D.C.
Republican political adviser, 1952-56.

Murray Chotiner graduated from the University of California in 1926. At the age of 20 he received an LL.B. degree from Southwestern University and was admitted to the California bar in 1931. Following World War II Chotiner became a prominent criminal lawyer and political public relations man associated with California Republican Gov. Earl Warren [*q.v.*]. Richard Nixon [*q.v.*], making his first run for the House against Rep. Jerry Voorhis (D, Calif.) in 1946, retained Chotiner as his adviser. The lawyer suggested Nixon associate Voorhis with the "Communist principles" of a few radical Democrats. Nixon used the technique, defeated Voorhis, and in 1950 hired Chotiner to manage his Senate campaign against Rep. Helen Gahagan Douglas (D, Calif.). Amplifying his 1946 approach, Chotiner had Nixon call Douglas "soft on Communism." Applying media technique to politics, he printed her voting record on pink paper for distribution. Nixon won the general election in November.

In 1952 Nixon asked Chotiner to manage his campaign for the vice presidency. The lawyer played his most crucial role in September 1952, when Nixon was accused of illegally maintaining a "secret" political fund for his personal use. Although independent investigation soon established that the fund was neither secret nor illegal, Republican presidential nominee Gen. Dwight D. Eisenhower did not spring to Nixon's defense. There was talk of dropping him from the ticket. Chotiner advised his client to explain his side of the affair. Under no circumstances was Nixon to accept chastisement from Eisenhower. Chotiner boosted Nixon's spirits by asserting he would call a press conference to reveal pressures on Nixon to resign from the ticket if his candidate was dropped. Nixon's reply was the "Checker's speech," which proved to be a landmark in American politics. The candidate bought time on television and proclaimed himself innocent of wrong-doing. Nixon, feeling his speech had failed, then wrote a telegram to Eisenhower resigning from the Republican ticket, but Chotiner destroyed the message before transmission. Following the speech Nixon's popularity rose, and Eisenhower publicly reaffirmed his support.

At the same time he was managing Nixon's campaign, Chotiner advised Sen. William F. Knowland (R, Calif.) [q.v.] in his successful reelection bid. Between 1952 and 1955 Chotiner worked with the Republican National Committee while continuing his law practice. In September 1955 Chotiner lectured GOP state chairmen at a national committee "school" on successful campaign techniques. He advised successful candidates to attack and deflate the opposition at the outset of a political campaign.

Chotiner's career suffered a serious setback in 1956. He was subpoenaed by the Senate Government Operations Committee's Permanent Investigations Subcommittee in April and questioned as to whether he had improperly used his White House influence at the Justice Department. It was alleged Chotiner had asked officials to set aside the fraud conviction of two garment manufacturers accused of stealing U.S. clothing material. Chotiner denied this. He stated that on "one one or two occasions" he had asked White House aides Maxwell Rabb and Charles Willis to obtain information for him in an airlines case but denied ever using "the name of the Vice President in connection with . . . any client." Following Chotiner's testimony presidential Press Secretary James C. Hagerty [q.v.] said there was "nothing wrong" with Chotiner's contacting the aides on behalf of the airlines. President Eisenhower reaffirmed this; Vice President Nixon refused to comment. Nevertheless, Republican National Chairman Leonard Hall [q.v.] dispensed with Chotiner's services in June.

Chotiner charged Senate Democrats with conducting an undirected, scattershot investigation of his law practice in hopes of uncovering damaging information about his professional activities. When Investigations Subcommittee Chairman Sen. John McClel-

lan (D, Ark.) [q.v.] asked Chotiner for a list of his clients since 1953. Chotiner protested this "most dangerous precedent" and wrote letters to every lawyer in Congress. McClellan said he had "reason to believe" Attorney General Herbert Brownell [q.v.] had ordered the Justice Department to "deal . . . cautiously" with Chotiner.

Further light was cast on Chotiner's role in the airlines intervention in February 1958. Testifying before the House Subcommittee on Legislative Oversight, Bernard Schwartz [q.v.] charged that presidential assistant Sherman Adams [q.v.] had improperly intervened at the Civil Aeronautics Board in 1953 on behalf of Chotiner's client, North American Airlines. In June President Eisenhower said that since the case had finally been decided against North American, no government influence was evident. Chotiner's visible influence in the Eisenhower Administration ended in 1958.

Chotiner was President-elect Nixon's first choice as Republican National Chairman in 1969. When opposition to the appointment developed, Chotiner took an obscure job as government counsel for trade negotiations. He died as result of an automobile accident in 1974. [See NIXON/FORD Volume]

[MJS]

CHURCH, FRANK (FORRESTER)
b. July 25, 1924; Boise, Ida.
Democratic Senator, Ida., 1957- .

Frank Church was born into a pioneer Idaho family that had settled in the state shortly after the Civil War. A debate champion in high school and college, he became a Democrat in order to hold his own in dinner-table arguments with his staunchly Republican father. After completing military service in World War II, Church attended Stanford law school, where he earned an LL.B. in 1950. While at Stanford he married the daughter of a former governor of Idaho who had long been prominent in the state's Democratic Party. Upon returning to Boise to practice law, he was encouraged by his father-in-law to launch a political career.

In 1956 Church became a candidate for the Democratic nomination for the Senate seat occupied by Herman Welker (R, Ida.) [*q.v.*]. During the campaign Church was bitterly opposed by the Idaho Power Co. and other private utility concerns for his vigorous advocacy of public power development, a crucial issue throughout the Far West during the 1950s. Church promised to fight for federal construction of a single high dam at Hell's Canyon near the Idaho-Oregon border to generate low-rate hydroelectric power for the entire area. Welker, backed by the Eisenhower Administration, proposed instead that the Idaho Power Co. go through with its plans to build three smaller privately financed dams. Aided by substantial contributions from out-of-state liberal groups and from the Senate Democratic Campaign Committee, Church upset Welker by a margin of 14%, although the Republican ticket carried the state in the presidential election that year. He was only 32 when he took his seat and the fourth youngest man in the history of the Senate.

In June 1957 Church cosponsored a bill authorizing the Hell's Canyon dam that passed the Senate but was subsequently sidetracked in a House committee. The same bill had been defeated the year before in the upper house by a coalition of Southern Democrats and pro-private power Republicans. Some political observers explained its subsequent passage as the result of a trade engineered by Majority Leader Lyndon B. Johnson (D, Tex.) [*q.v.*]. According to Johnson's biographers, Rowland Evans and Robert Novak, the Majority Leader convinced Church to cosponsor a jury-trial amendment weakening the Civil Rights Act of 1957 in exchange for Southern support for the Hell's Canyon project. The provision, requiring jury trials under certain conditions, was expected to cripple the ability of the courts and the Justice Department to protect voting rights, since it was assumed that Southern juries would not convict in civil rights contempt cases. The amendment was passed by the upper chamber on Aug. 2 by a vote of 51-42. Its passage represented a victory for Southern senators who, aware that they did not have

the votes to prevent passage of the bill itself, had adopted a strategy aimed at modifying it as much as possible.

In 1959 Church again lined up with Johnson in opposing an attempt by Northern liberals to substantially overhaul the Senate filibuster rule by permitting the imposition of cloture by majority vote. Instead, he supported a slight revision of the rule, sponsored by Johnson and a bipartisan leadership group, enabling two-thirds of the senators present and voting (rather than two-thirds of the entire Senate membership) to shut off debate. The following year, however, Church joined the liberal bloc in an unsuccessful effort to strengthen the Civil Rights Act of 1960 by empowering the Attorney General to enter private suits for school desegregation. On most issues Church voted as a liberal during his freshman term in the Senate.

A talented orator, Church was selected to give the keynote speech at the 1960 Democratic National Convention. He condemned the slow rate of economic growth under President Dwight D. Eisenhower and called for increased military outlays so that the U.S. could negotiate with the USSR from a position of strength.

During the 1960s Church compiled a strong liberal record, voting for civil rights, school aid, minimum wage and medicare bills. As a member of the Interior and Insular Affairs Committee, his name was frequently linked with conservation measures. Church emerged as one of the earliest and strongest Senate critics of President Lyndon B. Johnson's Southeast Asia policies. In 1970 he coauthored a measure prohibiting President Richard M. Nixon from sending U.S. combat troops into Cambodia without the consent of Congress.

In 1975 Church headed a much publicized investigation of alleged abuse of power by the Central Intelligence Agency and the FBI. Partly on the strength of the publicity he gained as a result of these proceedings, he entered the presidential primaries in 1976 but withdraw from the race before the Democratic National Convention. [See KENNEDY, JOHNSON, NIXON/FORD Volumes]

[TLH]

CLARK, JOSEPH S(ILL), JR.
b. Oct. 21, 1901; Philadelphia, Pa.
Mayor, Philadelphia, Pa., 1952-56;
Democratic Senator, Pa., 1957-69.

A member of a prominent and well-to-do
Philadelphia family, Clark attended the
Middlesex School and Harvard, where he
received a B.S. degree in 1923. Three years
later he obtained an LL.B. degree from the
University of Pennsylvania and began
practicing law in Philadelphia.

In 1928 Clark broke with his family's
long-standing Republican allegiance to endorse Al Smith for the presidency. Six years
later he made an unsuccessful race for the
Philadelphia City Council. In 1934 and
1935 he was deputy attorney general of
Pennsylvania. Clark served in the Air Force
during World War II.

During the postwar years Clark and
Richardson Dilworth [q.v.] led a Democratic reform movement, which sought to end
the Republican machine's longtime dominance of Philadelphia government. Clark
managed Dilworth's unsuccessful Democratic mayoral candidacy in 1947. After serving
as chairman of the Philadelphia chapter of
Americans for Democratic Action (ADA),
Clark was elected city controller in 1949. In
that post he investigated official scandals
and set the stage for a 1951 mayoral race.
He won the election and became Philadelphia's first Democratic mayor in 67 years.

As mayor, Clark tried to bring professional, dedicated men into government
without regard for party. He was known for
his strict enforcement of civil service laws,
a policy that enabled many blacks to get
city jobs for the first time. However, critics
charged that requiring competitive examinations for all promotions discouraged
talented people from entering public service because they could not be promised
anything beyond their entry-level positions.

Clark focused much of his attention upon
the revival of Philadelphia's economy,
which had suffered as a result of corrupt
government and the migration of textile
manufacturers to the South. Under his administration Philadelphia became a pioneer
in planning designed to economically and

architecturally revive the decaying core
city. Clark often used quasi-public corporations to achieve this goal. In February 1955
the nonprofit Food Distribution Center
Corp., with both businessmen and city
officials on its board, was chartered to erect
a new food market. In 1958 another quasi-
public corporation was formed to begin
construction on an industrial park. The
Mayor also supported purely private attempts to revive the area. He backed the
Pennsylvania Railroad's plan for an office
building-shopping center complex on the
site of its old station, and he worked, with
limited success, to improve its design.

To facilitate economic growth, Clark established the Urban Traffic and Transportation Board (UTTB) to devise a plan for a
balanced system of mass and highway
transit. The UTTB's report, submitted in
December 1955, stressed the need for mass
transit and urged the establishment of a regional organization to develop an integrated
transportation network. Clark's successor,
Richardson Dilworth, implemented the
plan.

Clark also tried to deal with the problems
of the poor. He initiated some low-income
housing projects and established the post of
housing coordinator. He unsuccessfully attempted to procure a state law permitting
the city to use its own crews to correct
housing violations. Clark added an economist to his staff to deal with unemployment.
He tried but failed to get federal funds for job
training.

In 1956 Clark decided to run for the Senate. Campaigning on a liberal platform, he
defeated the incumbent, Sen. James Duff
(R, Pa.), by a slim margin. In the Senate
Clark was a leading advocate of civil rights
legislation. He described the opponents of
the 1957 civil rights bill as "defending a
caste system." Three years later, after
Southern Democrats had weakened another
civil rights measure by eliminating school
desegregation and equal job opportunity
provisions, he declared that "in this battle
on the Senate floor the roles of Grant and
Lee at Appomattox have been reversed."

Clark criticized the Administration's
housing programs, asserting in 1957 that
the legislation of that year did not

provide housing for those who really needed it. A strong backer of federal aid to education, he unsuccessfully sought to create a loan fund for the construction of college teaching facilities in 1960. During the same year Clark and Sen. Mike Monroney (D, Okla.) [q.v.] succeeded in amending a Senate bill to double the amount of aid provided to public schools. In January 1960 Clark joined 11 colleagues in the Senate Democratic Conference in an unsuccessful bid to take power away from Majority Leader Lyndon B. Johnson (D, Tex.) [q.v.] and give the liberal Senate Democratic Policy Committee a greater role in formulating policy on legislation.

Clark was a floor manager for many of President John F. Kennedy's liberal proposals. During the mid-1960s he sought to improve Senate efficiency and promote ethics legislation for Congress. In the later part of the decade, he became an outspoken critic of the Johnson Administration's Vietnam policies. Clark was defeated in his 1968 reelection bid. Between 1969 and 1971 he was president of the United World Federalists, U.S.A., and after 1969 he served as chairman of the Coalition on National Priorities and Military Policy.

[MLL]

For further information:
Kirk R. Petshek, *The Challenge of Urban Reform* (Philadelphia, 1973).
Neal R. Peirce, *The Megastate of America* (New York, 1972).

CLARK, MARK W(AYNE)
b. May 1, 1896; Madison Barracks, N.Y.
Commander-in-Chief, U.S. Army Forces in the Far East and UN Command in Korea, 1952-53.

The son of an Army colonel, Mark Clark received a B.S. from the U.S. Military Academy at West Point in 1917. After more than a decade of further military education and minor Army posts, he was promoted to lieutenant colonel in 1940. Clark rose to chief of staff of the Army ground forces in May 1942 and commanded all U.S. infantry

in Europe for the remainder of World War II. Following the War Clark headed occupation forces in Austria. He was named deputy secretary of state in 1947.

This dual military and diplomatic experience prepared Clark for his appointment as commander of U.S. and U.N. forces in Korea in April 1952. When President-elect Dwight D. Eisenhower flew to Korea in December 1952, he was briefed by Clark, who favored a decisive victory over the North Korea. The U.N. Commander advanced three proposals: bombarding the enemy with air and artillery without advancing; destroying Chinese supply bases in Manchuria; or, simultaneously using air power against Manchuria while advancing ground forces to the Chinese border.

Anxious to end the war, Eisenhower followed none of these plans. He relied instead on diplomatic effort coupled with threats of massive American intervention and nuclear warfare. Clark was the conduit for the diplomatic advances and threats. When North Korea stalled peace talks at Panmunjom in May 1953, Clark, acting on instructions, proposed that in the future the peace commission decide disputes by majority vote. This plan would give the neutral Indian delegate the decisive voice. If North Korea rejected this he was prepared to terminate negotiations and resume the war "in new ways never yet tried in Korea." North Korea accepted, and the following month Clark informed Washington that an armistice was near.

The intense anti-Communist nationalism of South Korea's President Syngman Rhee was an obstruction to a final agreement. In June Rhee threatened to reject the truce and attack North Korea without U.N. support. Clark convinced him of the futility of such an action. At the same time he guaranteed Rhee's adherence to truce terms in a letter to North Korea. Clark was denounced for this action by Sen. Ralph Flanders (R, Vt.) [q.v.], but Rhee capitulated. The Korean armistice was signed in July 1953.

Clark retired from the military the following month and advocated the use of nuclear weapons if North Korea broke the truce. Testifying before the Senate Internal Security Subcommittee one year later, Clark recommended that diplomatic relations with Russia be severed and that the USSR and its satellites be ousted from the U.N. Eisenhower disavowed this position.

The U.S. failure to anticipate the 1950 Korean conflict was widely regarded as an intelligence failure. After the war there were allegations of Communist infiltration and gross inefficiency within the Central Intelligence Agency (CIA). Congress called for a full investigation. In July 1954 former President Herbert Hoover [q.v.] announced that Clark would head a Hoover Commission task force studying the "structure and administration" of the CIA. This headed off an independent investigation threatened by by Sen. Joseph McCarthy (R, Wisc.) [q.v.]. Clark said he would search out subversives but that he was primarily concerned with improving the Agency's operating procedures. In June 1955 his task force's findings were presented to the President and Congress in the Hoover Commission Report.

Clark expressed concern at the lack of adequate intelligence data from behind the Iron Curtain but dismissed charges of Communist infiltration. Instead he accused the State Department of intelligence-gathering "timidity." To correct "administrative flaws" within the CIA and insure that the Agency operate within democratic limits, Clark proposed creating a permanent watchdog commission made up of U.S. senators, representatives and presidential appointees. By implication he criticized excessive reliance on spying and other covert action and called on the Agency to strengthen its intelligence-gathering functions. The Clark report was the most critical evaluation made of the CIA until the 1970s. The Hoover Commission weakened Clark's watchdog committee proposal in its final report. President Eisenhower joined the CIA in opposing it in any form, and the proposal died. Clark served as president of The Citadel Military College from 1954 to 1966.

[MJS]

For further information:
U.S. Senate, Select Committee on Intelligence Activities, *Final Report* (Washington, 1976).

CLARK, TOM C(AMPBELL)

b. Sept. 23, 1889; Dallas, Tex.
d. June 13, 1977; New York, N.Y.
Associate Justice, U.S. Supreme Court, 1949-67.

Tom Clark received his law degree from the University of Texas in 1922. Over the next 15 years he built a successful practice in Dallas and from 1927 to 1933 served as county civil district attorney. In 1937 Clark went to work for the Justice Department. He became an assistant attorney general in 1943 and cooperated with Sen. Harry Truman's (D, Mo.) investigation of the defense effort. In 1945 Truman appointed him Attorney General.

In his four years as Attorney General, Clark instituted over 160 antitrust suits and had a major part in the development of the Administration's anti-Communist campaign. He urged the establishment of loyalty programs both in and out of government, drafted the first Attorney General's list of dangerous political organizations and initiated the prosecution of the leaders of the American Communist Party in 1948. When Truman nominated Clark to the Supreme Court in July 1949, there was considerable liberal opposition to the appointment, but Clark was soon confirmed by the Senate. Clark's accession to the bench helped create a five-man conservative bloc, which dominated the Court for the next four years. During this time Clark generally placed the needs of government ahead of individual liberties, especially in loyalty-security cases. [See TRUMAN Volume]

In the mid-1950s Clark entered strong objections when the Court began placing limits on government anti-Communist efforts. He wrote the majority opinion in an April 1956 case holding that a teacher at a municipal college could not be fired without notice or hearing solely because he had invoked the Fifth Amendment before a congressional committee. However, he usually voted to give the government broad powers in loyalty-security cases. Clark dissented from a decision holding that under federal law a government employe could be summarily dismissed as a security risk only if he held a sensitive job. In his opinion he accused the majority of robbing the government of its most potent weapon in the battle against subversion. He again dissented from a June 1957 ruling that a defendant charged with filing a false non-Communist affidavit under the Taft-Hartley Act had to be allowed to see certain secret FBI documents material to his case. The Justice objected to two other decisions that month placing limits on congressional and state investigations into subversion. He was a sole dissenter in another case in which the Court significantly narrowed the scope of the Smith Act. In June 1959 Clark finally spoke for the majority to sustain the contempt conviction of a minister who had refused to turn over to New Hampshire's attorney general the guest list of a summer camp suspected of being a Communist meeting place. The Justice ruled that the state's interest in discovering the presence of possible subversives outweighed any individual rights of privacy or association involved. Later that month Clark once again dissented when the Court overturned a government industrial security program on the ground that neither the President nor Congress had authorized certain of the procedures used in the program.

In criminal rights cases Clark also tended to uphold government power against individual claims. In February 1954, for example, he voted to sustain a state gambling conviction based on illegally seized evidence. He joined the majority in two March 1959 cases ruling that persons tried for the same offense in both federal and state courts had not been subjected to double jeopardy. But Clark was more flexible in this area than in loyalty-security matters and often voted in support of defendants' rights. In April 1956 he was part of a five-man majority that held that states must, under certain circumstances, supply indigent defendants with free trial transcripts on appeal.

Clark joined in the major Supreme Court decisions outlawing racial segregation, including the landmark *Brown* ruling of May 1954. With a strong background in anti-trust matters developed during his Justice Department days, he wrote a large number of important opinions in this field while on the Court.

During the 1960s Clark remained a conservative in loyalty-security cases but took a liberal position in several important criminal rights cases. He concurred in a March 1962 decision holding that courts could rule on legislative apportionment and wrote the opinion of the Court in a case sustaining the public accommodations section of the 1964 Civil Rights Act. When he resigned from the Court in 1967, Clark was generally rated as an able jurist who had grown during his 18 years on the bench and had become a very productive member of the Court. According to some analysts, his achievements were marred by his strong fear of a Communist conspiracy. Clark, historian Richard Kirkendall has written, "brought to the Court a Cold War point of view" and as a result joined in numerous decisions that "imposed or tolerated undesirable restrictions upon freedom of expression and association." [See KENNEDY, JOHNSON Volumes]

[CAB]

For further information:
Richard Kirkendall, "Tom C. Clark," in Leon Friedman and Fred L. Israel, eds., *The Justices of the United States Supreme Court, 1789-1969* (New York, 1969), Vol. 4.

CLAY, LUCIUS D(uBIGNON)
b. April 23, 1897; Marietta, Ga.
Presidential adviser.

The son of a politically prominent family, Clay attended West Point and, following his graduation in 1918, served as an Army engineer. During World War II he coordinated the production and procurement of Army supplies as director of material. In 1944 Clay was appointed deputy director for war programs and general administrator in the Office of War Mobilization and Reconversion.

Upon Gen. Dwight D. Eisenhower's recommendation, Clay became deputy military governor of occupied Germany in April 1945. At that post he helped establish the four occupation zones and undertook the reconstruction of the American sector. In January 1947 Clay became military governor of the American zone and commanding general of U.S. forces in Europe. During the Soviet blockade of Berlin in 1948, Clay oversaw the airlift that supplied the city for over a year. He also supervised German currency reform and the drafting of the West German constitution. Clay retired from the Army in 1949 and a year later became chairman of the board and chief officer of the Continental Can Co. Under his leadership the company prospered, becoming the largest manufacturer of containers in the U.S. [See TRUMAN Volume]

Clay, an old friend of Eisenhower, played an important role in the General's 1952 election effort. In 1951, when Eisenhower was still commander of the North Atlantic Treaty Organization, Clay sought to convince him to run for the Republican presidential nomination. He then acted as liaison between the General and professional politicians compaigning for him in the U.S. Following Eisenhower's nomination Clay backed the choice of Richard Nixon [q.v.] as the vice presidential candidate. He urged the General to steer a middle course during the race to attract "the vital center"—the independent voter.

In the post-election period Clay was one of the men, along with Herbert Brownell [q.v.], who aided Eisenhower in searching out and screening people for high executive positions. The process resulted in the appointment of many conservative businessmen to high posts. Among his recommendations were the appointments of John Foster Dulles [q.v.] as Secretary of State, George Humphrey [q.v.] as Secretary of the Treasury and Joseph Dodge [q.v.] as Director of the Budget. During this period he also helped organize the meetings between Commerce Secretary-designate Sinclair Weeks [q.v.] and financial leaders that led to the decision to remove wage and price controls.

Clay continued to serve as a presidential adviser during the Eisenhower Administration. In late 1954 and early 1955 he headed a presidential commission formed to plan a national highway modernization program. The panel's report, issued in January 1955,

called for a 42,000-mile interstate highway network to be built at a cost of $101 billion. The system was to be constructed in cooperation with the states but would rely heavily on federal funding. The report formed the basis for Eisenhower's legislative proposals, adopted in modified form as the Federal Highways Aid Act of 1956.

During the Kennedy Administration Clay served as a presidential adviser on Berlin. In 1962 he headed a committee formed to study U.S. foreign aid policy. In the late 1960s Clay was a supporter of Lyndon Johnson's Vietnam policy. He retired as chairman of the board of Continental Can in 1970. [See KENNEDY Volume]

[EWS]

CLEMENT, FRANK G(OAD)
b. June 2, 1920: Dickson, Tenn.
d. Nov. 4, 1969: Nashville, Tenn.
Governor, Tenn. 1953-59, 1963-66.

The son of a lawyer, Clement was educated at Cumberland University in Lebanon, Tenn., and at Vanderbilt University, where he received his LL.B. degree in 1942. After spending a year in Chicago as a special agent for the FBI, he joined the Army in 1943 and served within the U.S. throughout the War. In 1946 Clement was appointed general counsel for the Tennessee Railroad and Public Utilities Commission, where he earned a reputation as an outstanding attorney and a "champion of the people." He became involved in Democratic politics and, in 1952, was elected governor of Tennessee.

During the campaign Clement's Bible-thumping, evangelical style of political oratory won him a degree of national attention. As governor he strove primarily to enact educational reform. By March 1953 Clement had gained legislative approval of a $5 million bond issue to provide public school children with free textbooks. He won reelection in 1954 under a new law granting the governor a four-year term (with the condition that he not seek immediate reelection). During his second term Clement pushed through the legislature an annual appropriation of $20 million for increased aid to education. He also won legislative approval of a comprehensive public power policy, a new retirement system for state employes and major reforms in mental health services. To pay for these programs Clement had the state sales tax increased from 2 to 3%.

Much of Clement's tenure was devoted to the issue of school desegregation, raised after the 1954 Supreme Court decision outlawing segregated schools. Clement made no secret of his own segregationist attitudes but swore to uphold the law. Thus, in 1955 he vetoed segregation bills passed by the state legislature. When riots broke out in Clinton, Tenn., in the fall of 1956 over the admission of blacks to previously all-white schools, he responded by calling out the National Guard in an attempt to preserve order. Clement refused to intervene on the segregation issue itself, stating that the matter should be left in the hands of the courts and the local districts. Although he signed a 1957 segregation bill passed by the legislature, Clement asserted that the state would ultimately have to comply with the Supreme Court's ruling. One explanation offered for his attempt to play down the issue was that he was fighting to keep alive his national political prospects.

Clement delivered the keynote address at the 1956 Democratic National Convention, attacking the Republicans for fostering economic recession and favoring big business over the rights of the common man. However, the speech was most memorable for its portrayal of Secretary of State John Foster Dulles [q.v.] as "the greatest unguided missile in the history of American diplomacy" and its characterization of the Eisenhower-Nixon Administration as "the vice-hatchet man slinging slander and spreading half-truths while the top man peers down the green fairways of indifference."

After his term as governor expired in 1959, Clement turned over the office to Buford Ellington, his handpicked successor. In 1962 Clement was elected to another term as governor. His national ambitions were finally destroyed when he ran unsuccessfully for the Senate in 1964 and again in 1966. In 1969 he died in a car accident in Nashville. [See JOHNSON Volume]

[JPL]

COHN, ROY M(ARCUS)
b. Feb. 20, 1927; New York, N.Y.
Chief Counsel, Permanent Investigations Subcommittee of the Senate Government Operations Committee, 1953-54.

The son of a New York State Supreme Court judge and protege of the boss of the Bronx Co. Democratic machine, Cohn attended the Fieldston School, managed by the Ethical Culture Society, and entered Columbia at age 16. He received his LL.B. in 1947. The following year he was admitted to the New York state bar. With the help of political connections he had acquired through his father, he was immediately hired as an assistant U.S. attorney for the southern district of New York. Over the next four years Cohn specialized in the prosecution of subversive activities, working as a staff lawyer in the William Remington perjury trial of 1950-51 and the espionage trial of Julius and Ethel Rosenberg [q.v.] in 1951.

In September Cohn was transferred to Washington, D.C., where he served for four months as a special assistant to the U.S. Attorney General. There Cohn drew up the perjury indictment of Owen Lattimore, whom Sen. Joseph R. McCarthy (R, Wisc.) [q.v.] had charged in 1950 with heading a subversive ring in the State Department. Cohn also conducted a grand jury probe of subversion among employes of the United Nations Secretariat. This probe brought him to the attention of Sen. McCarthy, chairman of the Permanent Investigations Subcommittee, who hired him as chief counsel of the panel in January 1953.

During 1953 Cohn's role in the subcommittee's senational investigations of Communist influence in government agencies was second only to that of McCarthy himself. A brash young man, he was known to pay little attention to the wishes of anyone on the subcommittee except McCarthy. The two worked closely together in coordinating publicity, scheduling hearings and interrogating witnesses. The Wisconsin Senator once remarked that Cohn was "as indispensable as I am."

Energetic and forceful, Cohn was a shrewd strategist with a sharp, retentive mind and a photographic memory. His interrogation of witnesses was relentless and often scornful. Many critics of McCarthy found the chief counsel at least as distasteful as the Senator himself and regarded him as an arrogant thug with little or no regard for the ethics of his profession. At a subcommittee hearing in March 1953, McCarthy stated that the American Civil Liberties Union (ACLU) had been cited as a Communist-front organization. Journalist Richard Rovere [q.v.] charged that Cohn, who was sitting next to McCarthy at the time, had given the Senator the signal to make that incorrect statement although the chief counsel had himself addressed the ACLU three weeks earlier.

In April 1953 Cohn and subcommittee chief consultant G. David Schine [q.v.] went on a 17-day, seven-country tour of Europe in search of pro-Communist literature in the State Department's overseas libraries. The trip received extensive publicity in both the American and European press. At the Vienna library they asked that *The American Legion Magazine* be placed on the shelves. Then, after finding the works of Mark Twain at the Soviet Culture Center, they went back to the State Department library to see if it had the same books. In Munich reporters overheard one of them telling a hotel clerk that they wanted separate rooms since they did not work for the State Department, an allusion to alleged homosexuality among State employes. Reporters also claimed that in Munich Schine chased Cohn in a hotel lobby with a rolled-up magazine. (Cohn and Shine denied this report.) Critics of the McCarthy panel charged the two men with distasteful, childish and farcical behavior deleterious to America's reputation abroad. The tour prompted President Eisenhower to issue an oblique warning against "book burners" in a June 1953 commencement address.

In the fall of 1953 McCarthy and Cohn began hearings on Communist infiltration in the Army. Meanwhile, the Senator and his chief counsel, learning that Schine was to be drafted, tried to procure a commission for him. After Schine was inducted into the Army in November 1953 as a private, Cohn frequently contacted high-level Army figures to obtain passes and easy assignments for the former subcommittee consultant. McCarthy seemed to have little personal interest in Schine's fortunes, and his participation in or tolerance of these activities indicated the extent of Cohn's influence upon the Senator.

On March 11, 1954, after McCarthy had escalated his attack on the Army for allegedly tolerating the presence of subversive elements within its ranks, the Army released a chronology of the efforts of McCarthy, Cohn and other subcommittee staff members on Schine's behalf. According to its account, Cohn had threatened to discredit the Army through the subcommittee investigation unless Schine received special treatment. McCarthy quickly counterattacked by alleging that the Army was holding Schine as a "hostage" to block his panel's probe.

In April 1954 the Investigations Subcommittee began the so-called Army-McCarthy hearings to examine the charges and countercharges. Since Cohn was a principal in the investigation, he temporarily withdrew as the panel's counsel. During the hearings Cohn was heard to threaten to "get" minority subcommittee member Sen. Henry M. Jackson (D, Wash.) [q.v.] (while brandishing a folder marked "Jackson's record") for attacking McCarthy. On June 14, near the end of the investigation, Cohn unsuccessfully tried to prevent McCarthy from mentioning the fact that a member of Army Counsel Joseph Welch's [q.v.] law firm had once belonged to a pro-Communist group. (Cohn and McCarthy's lawyer, Edward Bennett Williams, had agreed not to raise the matter.) Welch turned the incident into a confrontation between himself and McCarthy that severely damaged the Senator's cause.

In August the subcommittee's Republican majority issued a report stating that Cohn had been "unduly aggressive and insistent" in the Schine matter. The Democratic minority went further, insisting that he had "misused and abused the powers of his office and brought disrepute to the Committee." In the meantime Cohn, under strong pressure from Senate Republicans, resigned his subcommittee position on July 19.

Cohn entered a New York City law firm and specialized in divorce cases. In 1957 he became a professor of law at the New York Law School. Cohn invested in many corporations, including Lionel and Fifth Avenue Coach. During the early 1960s he promoted boxing matches between Sonny Liston and Floyd Patterson. At that time he claimed to be a millionaire.

In 1963 Cohn was indicted by a federal grand jury for perjury and conspiracy in a stock fraud case. The following year he was acquitted after a mistrial. Cohn was the author of *McCarthy* (1968), a defense of the Wisconsin Senator.

[TLH]

Richard H. Rovere. "The Adventures of Cohn and Schine. *The Reporter* (July 21. 1953). pp. 9-16.

COLEMAN, JAMES P(LEMON)
b. Jan. 9, 1914; Ackerman, Miss.
Governor, Miss., 1956-60.

Born on a red dirt farm, James P. Coleman worked his way through the University of Mississippi and George Washington University law school. He received his LL.B. in 1939. While in Washington Coleman worked as secretary to Rep. Aaron L. Ford (D, Miss.) and became friends with Rep. Lyndon B. Johnson (D, Tex.) [q.v.]. Coleman returned to Mississippi and served first as a district attorney and then a circuit judge between 1939 and 1950. In October 1950 he was elected state attorney general. Coleman served as Democratic national committeeman in 1952 and kept the Mississippi delegation from bolting the Democratic National Convention over a proposed requirement that delegates promise to support the Convention's ticket regardless of its stand on civil rights.

Following the May 1954 Supreme Court decision outlawing segregation in public schools, Coleman asked for restraint. He cautioned against adoption of a strategy of "massive resistance," which called for the interposition of state power to prevent enforcement of the decision. Coleman avoided Negro-baiting and restored stability after the murder of Emmett Till [q.v.] in August 1955. On Sept. 1 U.S. Attorney General Herbert Brownell [q.v.] announced an inquiry into alleged intimidation of black voters in Mississippi. Coleman denied any violations. In the tense atmosphere following Till's murder and Brownell's inquiry, Coleman's approach was cool and legalistic. He told a White Citizens' Council meeting that eliminating segregation through court action would take the government 2,000 years. In 1955 Coleman ran for governor on a platform pledging continued segregation by legal means. He was unopposed in the November election. When the Interstate Commerce Commission decreed an end to segregated terminals the same month, he announced a $50 fine for mixing races in the depots.

Coleman's attempts to maintain moderation met with only limited success in the face of an increasing rightward trend. The Governor was therefore pushed to adopt a more segreationist position. He endorsed interposition in a January 1956 conference convened by Virginia's Gov. Thomas Stanley [q.v.] but refused to join a call for nullification. The following month Coleman obtained legislative approval for a $78 million school budget—the largest in state history—to upgrade black schools and silence Northern critics. He also urged a bill to keep blacks out of white society by giving businesses the right to choose their customers and providing segregated waiting rooms in intrastate travel.

The segregation laws failed to allay fears of integration, and the Governor faced a restive state Party divided over political strategy in the 1956 presidential election. In May the Association of Citizens' Councils, a group of white supremacist organizations, formulated a resolution demanding that the state delegation to the Democratic National Convention accept only a presidential candidate who supported interposition. Coleman continued to counsel moderation. He insisted that the South concentrate on finding a solution to the school desegregation dilemma in private meetings and avoid public quarrels which would force delegates into rigid positions. Coleman predicted that this attitude would encourage compromise. Supported by Sen. John Stennis (D, Miss.) [q.v.], he won his pleas for an unpledged delegation. Coleman's stand became the basis for Southern convention strategy and resulted in the Democrats adoption of a moderate civil rights platform.

In keeping with his desire to use "friendly persuasion" to convince critics of the validity of Mississippi's moderate stand and prevent racial hysteria, Coleman created a State Sovereignty Commission in June 1956. The Commission was given virtually blank-check authority to "perform any . . . acts . . . necessary and proper to protect the sovereignty of the State of Mississippi." It was granted unlimited powers of investigation and authorized to prevent "provocations," such as desegregation petitions, and to dispel the atmosphere created by the Citizens' Councils.

Coleman's public relations effort bore fruit. Reporters from 18 New England newspapers toured the state writing generally sympathetic accounts of social conditions. However his attempts to lead Mississippi into the mainstream of American life met with deepening suspicion. When he supported a new constitution that did not mention race, it was narrowly defeated in the legislature. He prevented white Citizens' Councils from obtaining tax money and in April 1959 called in the FBI after the lynching of Mack Parker. At the end of his term, Coleman supported Sen. John F. Kennedy (D, Mass.) [q.v.] for President. A more rigidly segregationist governor followed him. In a 1963 gubernatorial comeback attempt, Coleman was called a Kennedy liberal and was defeated im the primary. President Lyndon Johnson appointed him a judge on the U.S. Court of Appeals in 1965.

[MJS]

For further information:
Numan V. Bartley, *The Rise of Massive Resistance* (Baton Rouge, 1969).

COLEMAN, JOHN S(TRADER)
b. Oct. 12, 1897; Charleston, W. Va.
d. April 13, 1958; Detroit, Mich.
President, U.S. Chamber of Commerce, March 1956-March 1957;
Chairman, Board of Directors, March 1957-April 1958.

The son of a West Virginia hardware merchant, John S. Coleman attended Washington, D.C.'s Emerson Institute and worked at the Guaranty Trust Corp. of New York before World War I. He served in the Army during the War. Coleman joined the sales staff of the Burroughs Adding Machine Corp. in 1920, while studying law at night at Georgetown University. He received his LL.B. from that institution in 1924. After obtaining a million-dollar contract with the government for Burroughs, he rose rapidly through the company hierarchy, eventually becoming president in 1946. He greatly improved efficiency at Burroughs, doubling the number of workers and increasing production. Under Coleman's leadership, Burroughs Adding Corp. smoothly made the transition from adding machine production to more diversified operations and did pioneering work in the construction of computers.

A conservative who advocated less government regulation and interference in business affairs, he nevertheless urged greater cooperation between labor, management and government. Burroughs attempted to apply "human engineering" to his organization, maintaining that "the function of management is to operate a successful organization both economically and humanly . . . to give every man a sense of function. Men will strive, but they must see the significance of their striving."

Coleman was an ardent advocate of free trade. During the 1940s he directed a 10-year study for the Detroit Board of Commerce, which concluded in November 1952 that all U.S. tariffs should be abolished. However, he modified his position at the Chicago World Trade Conference in February 1953, merely calling for a gradual reduction of duties. Coleman saw the election of Dwight D. Eisenhower in 1952 as an opportunity for business to exercise its responsibility to the world by cooperating with the President to prevent another depression.

In March 1956 Coleman was elected president of the U.S. Chamber of Commerce; the following year he became chairman of the board. During his two years in office, Coleman served as spokesman for the organization's conservative business philosophy. In a statement in February 1957, he proposed cuts in the federal budget, maintaining that $5 billion could be eliminated by reducing federal aid to education, college housing loans, funds to fight juvenile delinquency and welfare grants. He charged that Secretary of Health, Education and Welfare Marion Folsom [q.v.] had overestimated the national classroom shortage. Coleman contended the problem would be solved by 1960 given the present rate of school construction and claimed that the federal government sought to provide aid as a way of controlling public schools. His position was backed by the National Association of Manufacturers, which represented smaller businessmen. Coleman also demanded that foreign aid and farm programs be scaled down. He wished to "get our derailed train back on the track," hoping the U.S. could "turn back the clock" of foreign aid largesse.

Coleman died of a heart attack in April 1958.

[AES]

COLLINS, J(OSEPH) LAWTON
b. May 1, 1896; New Orleans, La.
U.S. Special Representative in Vietnam, November 1954-May 1955.

J. Lawton Collins, the son of Irish-Catholic parents, was born in New Orleans. After graduating from the United States Military Academy in 1917, Collins commanded a battalion of the occupation forces in Germany during 1919. Collins served in various military capacities in the 1920s and 1930s, and by the outbreak of World War II, he had achieved the rank of brigadier general. During World War II he saw active duty in

the Pacific, where he helped reorganize American defenses on Hawaii, and in France, where he spearheaded a series of crucial Allied combat victories in 1944. After the War Collins was assigned to the Pentagon and from 1948 to 1953 served as Army Chief of Staff. In 1953 President Eisenhower appointed him U.S. representative to the North Atlantic Treaty Organization.

Following the partition of Vietnam in 1954, Collins became prominently involved in the policy debate over U.S. support of South Vietnam Premier Ngo Dinh Diem, appointed as a result of pressure from the U.S. Collins spoke out forcefully against continuing to back Diem, whom he thought totally incapable of leading South Vietnam. However, leading American officials, spurred by Col. Edward Lansdale [q.v.], the principal American intelligence agent in Vietnam, prevailed upon Eisenhower to pledge his support to Diem. To reinforce the Administration's position, Eisenhower dispatched Collins to Vietnam in November 1954 as his personal representative bearing the rank of ambassador.

Arriving in Saigon convinced that a strong pro-Western government in South Vietnam was important to prevent Communist expansion throughout Southeast Asia, Collins began a systematic program of aiding Diem in establishing security, in starting a military training program for the South Vietnamese Army and in paving the way for agrarian reforms. Shortly after his arrival Collins helped the Vietnamese leader exile his major rival, Gen. Nguyen Van Hinh, who commanded the loyalty of the well-equipped South Vietnamese Army and of the Saigon police. However, Collins proved unable to establish a close relationship with Diem. The Vietnamese leader repeatedly refused to listen to what Collins considered to be sound military and political advice. For his part, Diem found Collins insufferably arrogant and condescending.

By March 1955 Collins and other U.S. officials in both Saigon and Washington, distressed by Diem's refusal to institute suggested reforms, began to reconsider U.S. support for the Premier. The issue stirring up the most hostility was the Premier's refusal to reorganize the government to include representatives from South Vietnam's powerful political-religious sects. When Diem turned down the sects' demands for a coalition government in late March 1955, fighting broke out in the streets of Saigon between government forces and the sects, principally the Binh Xuyen. Recalled to Washington in early April, Collins implored Eisenhower to withdraw U.S. support from Diem. Impressed by Collins's arguments and by reports he was receiving from the State Department, the President agreed to approve whatever Collins recommended. The State Department recommended a compromise that would retain Diem as a national symbol while real political power passed to Dr. Phan Huy Quat of the Dai Viet party. Collins accepted the suggestion, but before it could be implemented, Diem's forces crushed the sects. Eisenhower and Secretary of State John Foster Dulles [q.v.] then reversed American policy to full support of Diem.

Collins, who symbolized American opposition to Diem, was soon replaced. The General returned to Washington in May 1955 and shortly thereafter resumed his duties as U.S. representative to NATO.

Retiring in 1957, he served until 1969 as a director of Charles Pfizer and Co., Inc., and as vice president of Pfizer International Subsidiaries until 1972. Throughout these years Collins remained skeptical about U.S. policy in Vietnam and, as one of a small group of "dovish generals," opposed the continual escalation of American involvement in Southeast Asia.

[RJB]

COLLINS, (THOMAS) LeROY
b. March 10, 1909: Tallahassee, Fla.
Governor, Fla., 1955-61.

A grocer's son, Leroy Collins grew up in his native Tallahassee. After high school he studied at the Eastman School of Business in Poughkeepsie, N.Y., and spent a year at the Cumberland Law School in Lebanon, Tenn. Admitted to the Florida bar, Collins started his own practice in Tallahassee and clerked part-time for the Works Progress Administration. He won election to the Florida House of Representatives in 1934 and to the state Senate in 1940. Except for two years in the Navy during World War II, Collins served continuously in the legislature until 1954. In the Senate he earned a reputation for moderate progressivism. A Florida journalists' poll twice named him the state's "most valuable senator."

Beginning in 1952 Collins's own political future became linked with that of Democratic Gov. Dan McCarty, who led a reform coalition of urban voters and minority groups supporting improvements in state services and the continuation of diversified economic development. Following McCarty's death in September 1953, Collins assumed the leadership of his party faction.

In 1954 Collins ran for election to fill out the remaining two years of McCarty's term. In the Democratic primary he defeated the appointed successor, Gov. Charley E. Johns, commonly identified with the Party's powerful, arch-conservative wing. Although Collins condemned Johns's failure to support a 1951 anti-Ku Klux Klan bill while he had been a state legislator, race relations were only a minor issue in the campaign. Collins won election in November without Republican opposition.

As governor, Collins fit the image-conscious, growth-oriented mold of what historians of the modern South term "business progressivism." He improved state services, upgraded Florida's educational systems and reduced patronage through the extension of the civil service system. He also attempted to reapportion the state to give the growing urban centers more equitable representation, but his efforts failed.

Much of Collins's time was devoted to the issue of civil rights. Collins was cautious in his reaction to the 1954 *Brown* decision, outlawing segregation in public schools. Although he said he favored segregated schools, he warned against "hysteria and political demagoguery," and in April 1955 he told the legislature no new laws were needed to protect segregation. Instead, he suggested that the legislators throw the state's weight behind orderly efforts to reverse the decision. Ignoring the Governor, the legislature passed three segregationist measures, which Collins criticized but signed. They provided for the assignment of students to schools on the basis of health, safety and education and not race.

During the 1956 gubernatorial campaign, in which the Governor was opposed by militant segregationist Sumter Lowry, Collins became a more vocal advocate of the status quo, but he urged that it be maintained by lawful and peaceful means. In his campaign Collins announced that he refused to "have the state torn asunder by rioting and disorder and violence and the sort of thing that [Lowry] is seeking to invite." Collins won the election handily. However, Florida's Democratic Party became even more fragmented by region and race, with Collins's strength in his native northern Florida declining sharply while rising in urban and black districts.

Following the Supreme Court's May 1956 ruling that local school authorities had the duty to implement integration, Collins called the legislature into session to enact a program to counter the decision. It passed a pupil placement law permitting appeals from decisions of local school boards and gave the Governor emergency power to call out the militia to prevent or suppress violence. The legislature also adopted a resolution condemning the Supreme Court and asserting the state's right to regulate education. However, Collins opposed more radical antisegregation legislation. He scored a 1957 joint legislative resolution that nullified recent antisegregation Supreme Court edicts, announcing "it is anarchy and rebellion against the nation which must remain 'indivisible under God' if it is to survive. I decry it as an evil thing, whipped up by the demagogues and carried in the hot and erratic words of passion, prejudice and hysteria." Collins also lobbied against other extreme measures, and in June 1957 he vetoed a local option school closing law.

During the 1957 Little Rock, Ark., schools crisis, Collins pleaded for moderation in settling the desegregation issue. Before the Southern Governors Conference in late September, he asked that Southerners consider Supreme Court rulings "the law of the land and insist that ours must be a land of the law." The Southerner, he said,

"must not sanction violence, defiance and disorder and, above all, he must abhor hate." The speech earned him widespread praise and contributed ot his image as a leading Southern moderate.

In his last years as governor, Collins acted increasingly like a national, rather than sectional, leader. He headed the National Governors Conference in May 1958, visited with Soviet Premier Nikita S. Khrushchev in July 1959 and was the first Southern governor since the Civil War to serve as permanent chairman at the Democratic National Convention in July 1960. A few observers considered him a possibility for national office in 1960. Yet Collins's professed aspirations for national office were hurt by Florida's still slow adjustment to racial equality. In *Candidates 1960*, Robert L. Riggs wrote that "Northern Democrats have decided that Collins is a man who talks a lot about leading his people into compliance with the Supreme Court," but he "has accomplished less toward integration in Florida than has been achieved in Virginia against all the force of massive resistance."

As an elected public official, Collins's career ended with his second term. Between 1961 and 1964, Collins was president of the National Association of Broadcasters. During the Johnson Administration Collins served in the Commerce Department, first as the director of the Community Relations Service (created to expedite enforcement of the 1964 Civil Rights Act) and then as undersecretary. Branded "Liberal Leroy" by his conservative Republican opponent, Collins failed to win election to the U.S. Senate in November 1968. He returned to Tallahassee to practice law.

[JLB]

CONANT, JAMES B(RYANT)

b. March 26, 1893; Dorchester, Mass.
High Commissioner for West Germany, January 1953-May 1955, Ambassador to the Federal Republic of Germany, May 1955-January 1957.

Conant graduated from Harvard in 1913 and received his Ph.D. in chemistry there in 1916. During World War I he supervised the production of poisonous gas for the Chemical Warfare Service. Returning to Harvard after the War, Conant won recognition for his research in organic chemistry as well as for his influence as an educator. In 1933 he became president of Harvard, a post he retained until 1953. During his tenure Conant emphasized the need for general education for undergraduates and reformed the system of faculty promotion.

As chairman of the National Defense Research Committee in 1940 and, from 1941 to 1946, as deputy director of the Office of Scientific Research and Development, Conant coordinated war-related scientific research, particularly that involving the development of the atomic bomb. In 1945 he served on the presidential advisory committee that recommended deploying the atomic bomb against Japan without prior warning.

Between 1947 and 1950 Conant served on the General Advisory Committee (GAC) of the Atomic Energy Commission (AEC). During the period he emerged as the panel's strongest, most outspoken opponent of the development of the hydrogen bomb. With the majority of Committee members, he signed a statement denouncing the weapon for strategic as well as political reasons, saying that it could only be a "weapon of genocide." [See TRUMAN Volume]

Conant served as U.S. high commissioner for Germany from 1953 to 1955. His major tasks were to prepare West Germany for full independence, begin steps for its inclusion in the North Atlantic Treaty Organization and protect U.S. claims of free access to the Russian sector, particularly in Berlin. Following the formal establishment of the Federal Republic of Germany in 1955, Conant was named U.S. ambassador there. He resigned the post in January 1957 and declined an offer to become ambassador to India.

During the early 1950s Conant frequently criticized anti-Communist investigations in schools and government. In his final report as president of Harvard, he warned that the damage done by such investigations was "far greater than any conceivable harm" a Communist teacher might do. He was most alarmed about the possible ramifications of the 1954 Oppenheimer security hearing. J. Robert Oppenheimer [q.v.], the director of the wartime atomic bomb project, had had his security clearance suspended in late 1953 because of his prewar left-wing politics and his postwar ambivalence about the development of the hydrogen bomb. During the security hearing Conant testified that Oppenheimer had been "thoroughly loyal," and he pointed out that he, too, had opposed the bomb's development. However, the AEC voted to maintain the suspension. The verdict disturbed Conant, who said that the ruling implied "that anybody who opposed the development of the hydrogen bomb was not eligible for employment on atomic energy work later."

During the late-1950s Conant devoted himself to educational projects. In March 1957 he received a Carnegie Corp. grant to make a thorough study of U.S. secondary education. His report, released in 1960 as *The American High School Today*, affirmed the soundness of U.S. schools while stressing the need to study "solid" academic subjects, including languages. It also noted the need for "guidance of the more able girls." In February 1960 Eisenhower appointed Conant to the Commission on National Goals. The Commission report, issued that November, concluded that to respond to the "Sino-Soviet threat" and the dangers of the nuclear age, the U.S. should strengthen itself domestically by ensuring individual freedoms. The report called on the federal government to "stimulate changes in attitude" concerning race and act against discriminatory voting practices.

Conant continued to write and lecture on education and foreign policy through the 1960s. In 1964 he wrote *Slums and Suburbs*, which described inner city schools as "social dynamite." Advocating decentralization of urban school administrations, he called on the federal government to provide greater employment opportunities for minority youth. Conant was a vocal supporter of the Johnson Administration's conduct of the Vietnam war.

[MDB]

COOPER, (LEON) JERE
b. July 20, 1893; Dyer County, Tenn.
d. Dec. 18, 1957; Bethesda, Md.
Democratic Representative, Tenn.,
1929-57; Chairman, Ways and Means
Committee, 1955-57.

Born on a West Tennessee farm, Cooper
received an LL.B. degree from Cumberland University in Lebanon, Tenn., in
1914. He was admitted to the state bar the
same year and began practicing law in
Dyersburg. After Army service in World
War I, Cooper was elected to the
Dyersburg City Council and in 1920 was
appointed the town's attorney.

In 1928 Cooper was elected to the House
of Representatives, where he backed most
New Deal and Fair Deal measures. He was
also one of the leading congressional supporters of Secretary of State Cordell Hull's
reciprocal trade program. In 1932 he became a member of the Ways and Means
Committee and seven years later became
chairman of the panel's subcommittee on
taxation. Cooper was known as an expert on
tax matters and played a key role in establishing the system of withholding taxes.

As the ranking minority member of the
Ways and Means Committee during the
first two years of the Eisenhower Administration, Cooper was a leading critic of the
President's 1954 tax bill. With many other
Democrats he denounced it for giving more
relief to the wealthy than to the poor. On
the floor of the House, he attacked the
bill's dividend tax relief provision, stating
that he "objected to the principle of providing more favorable treatment for unearned
income than for earned income." Appearing
on television with House Speaker Sam
Rayburn (D, Tex.) [q.v.] and Sen. Walter
George (D, Ga.) [q.v.] to answer the President's plea for passage of the tax bill,
Cooper said Democrats would oppose the
dividend tax relief proposal as a measure
that would give a multi-million dollar advantage to those "fortunate enough" to own
stock. Democratic efforts, backed by
Cooper, to replace the dividend relief provision with a personal exemption increase
were defeated in both houses.

In 1955 Cooper became Ways and Means
chairman as well as chairman of the Joint
Internal Revenue Taxation Committee.
Under his leadership the Ways and Means
panel appended to a corporate and excise
tax extension measure a $20 income tax re-
duction for all persons entitled to a personal
exemption. The Senate, however, rejected
the proposal. Cooper led the House delegation in a joint House-Senate conference on
the bill and demanded reinstatement of the
reduction. However, because of what he
termed the government's need for revenue
from corporate and excise taxes, he reluctantly struck the tax credit.

Cooper strongly backed the Administration's 1953 request for extension of reciprocal trade legislation. Representing a
largely rural constituency, he asserted that
"if there should be a decline in the exports
of farm products so as to increase the supply available to our domestic market by
only 7 or 8%, farm prices would fall as
much as one-third. . . ." However, he opposed a provision of the bill expanding the
Tariff Commission from six to seven members, charging it was an attempt to pack the
panel with opponents of the legislation. The
bill passed with the expansion provision.
Two years later, as chairman of the Ways
and Means Committee, Cooper introduced
and successfully pressed for a measure to
again extend the reciprocal trade law with a
new proviso permitting the President to cut
tariffs by 5% during each of the three years
of the extension period.

Cooper died of a heart attack in
Bethesda, Md., on Dec. 18, 1957.

[MLL]

COOPER, JOHN S(HERMAN)
b. Aug. 23, 1901; Somerset, Ky.
Republican Senator, Ky., 1946-48,
1952-54, 1956-72; Ambassador to India
and Nepal, February 1955-November
1956.

Cooper graduated from Yale and received
his law degree there in 1923. After postgraduate work at Harvard he returned to
Kentucky, where he was elected to the
state legislature in 1928. He sat as a county

judge from 1930 until 1938. Cooper served in the Army during World War II, and in the immediate postwar period, he helped reorganize the German judicial system in Bavaria.

Following a brief stint as a circuit judge in Kentucky in 1946, Cooper was elected to fill a two-year Senate vacancy. When the term ended he joined the U.S. delegation to the U.N. General Assembly. In 1950 he became a consultant to Secretary of State Dean Acheson [q.v.]. Cooper again won a special Senate election in 1952, this time for a three-year term. In 1955 President Dwight D. Eisenhower appointed him ambassador to India and Nepal. The following year Cooper won his first full Senate term.

Cooper quickly established himself as one of the Senate's most liberal, independent Republicans. A critic of Sen. Joseph R. McCarthy's [q.v.] anti-Communist campaign, Cooper chided the Wisconsin Republican in May 1954 for "rash and immoderate statements" regarding the loyalties of British Prime Minister Clement Attlee and Secretary of State Acheson. Cooper was among the first Republicans to endorse McCarthy's censure.

During the 1950s Cooper spoke frequently on international affairs and opposed the vehement anti-Communist position of many of his colleagues as dangerously extreme. In January 1953 he was the only Republican who voted against the unsuccessful Bricker amendment, which would have limited the President's treaty-making powers. He described the proposal, generated by the belief that Franklin D. Roosevelt and Harry S. Truman had used their executive powers to appease the Soviet Union, as "based on fears which have not materialized." Two months later Cooper opposed Sen. William F. Knowland's (R, Calif.) [q.v.] proposal that the U.S. blockade the coast of China and have the Soviet Union condemned in the U.N. as a "supporter of aggression in the Far East." In July 1958 he protested Eisenhower's landing of U.S. troops in Lebanon.

Cooper was one of the few Republican defenders of the Tennessee Valley Author-

ity (TVA), and he advocated its expansion. In July 1954 he cast the sole Republican vote against Eisenhower's omnibus atomic energy bill, which included the Dixon-Yates contract providing for a private utility to replace the TVA as the Atomic Energy Commission's chief energy supplier in the Memphis, Tenn., region. Cooper also voted for a Democratic area redevelopment bill introduced in March 1959. The measure, which called for federal funds to stimulate business in economically depressed areas, was vetoed by Eisenhower, who sent Cooper a letter suggesting other methods of developing the region. However, Cooper maintained his original position and supported the unsuccessful attempt to override the veto in May 1960.

The Senator was among the strongest Republican supporters of civil rights legislation. In January 1957 he voted for a proposal to ease cloture proceedings, an unsuccessful effort by civil rights advocates to skirt the filibuster tactics used by Southern civil rights opponents. Cooper opposed a Southern attempt to weaken the Civil Rights Act of 1957 by guaranteeing a jury trial to persons accused of obstructing the voting rights of others. An amendment he proposed in July 1957 to let the Attorney General decide whether or not to grant a jury trial in such cases was rejected by the Senate, 81-8. He was also among congressional liberals who favored the expansion of the 1957 and 1960 Civil Rights Acts to include school desegregation provisions. The final versions of both acts failed to include these proposals.

Republican liberals nominated Cooper for Senate Republican leader in December 1958, but he was defeated by Sen. Everett Dirksen (R, Ill.) [q.v.]. In 1960 Cooper joined seven other Republican senators in offering a voluntary federal-state health insurance program for all Americans over 65. Under the plan the state would have contracted with private firms for the coverage, and subscribers would have made payments based on income, with the federal and state governments sharing the remaining costs. Cooper's proposal was more liberal than the Administration plan, which limited aid to single elderly persons with adjusted gross incomes of up to $2,500 a year and married couples with annual incomes up to $3,800. The plan finally adopted in August contained most of the basic features of Cooper's proposal. However, it required a means test and permitted each state to determine the type and extent of medical assistance provided.

During the 1960s Cooper continued to support civil rights legislation. He became a leading Republican critic of the Johnson Administration's conduct of the Vietnam war and in 1970 cosponsored an amendment prohibiting the use of U.S. troops in Cambodia. Cooper retired from the Senate in 1972 at the age of 71. [See KENNEDY, JOHNSON, NIXON/FORD Volumes]

[MDB]

CORSI, EDWARD
b. Dec. 29, 1896; Abruzzi, Italy.
d. Dec. 13, 1964; Kingston, N.Y.
Special Assistant to the State Department for Refugee and Immigration Problems, January 1955-April 1955.

Corsi immigrated to the U.S. from Italy at the age of seven. His family settled on New York's Lower East Side, and Corsi attended both public and parochial schools. He also became active in Haarlem House, a settlement house in New York's Little Italy. Corsi worked his way through Fordham law school, from which he graduated in 1922. He then began a career as a journalist for *Outlook* magazine and the *New York World*. President Herbert Hoover appointed him immigration commissioner at Ellis Island in 1931, where he improved and humanized procedures for handling immigrants. He served in that post until 1934, when New York Mayor Fiorello La Guardia appointed him director of emergency relief. The next year he became deputy city welfare director. Gov. Thomas E. Dewey appointed him state industrial commissioner in 1943. A lifelong Republican, Corsi ran unsuccessfully for a U.S. Senate seat in 1938 and for New York City mayor in 1950.

In December 1954 Secretary of State John Foster Dulles [q.v.] appointed Corsi a State Department consultant to help increase immigration under the 1953 Refugee Relief Act. Announcing the move, he called Corsi "the best qualified man in the U.S." for the position. Corsi was to work with Scott McLeod [q.v.], State Department security director, to process the entry of 214,000 over-quota refugees into the U.S. in three years. McLeod and Corsi repeatedly clashed over the administration of the program. The security director insisted on a thorough security check of all entrants, thus slowing down arrivals. Corsi, on the other hand, had elaborate plans to recruit refugees, facilitate the entry process and shortcut the Act's delaying provisions. In addition, the two men fought over authority; Corsi refused to be McLeod's assistant.

On Feb. 28 Rep. Francis E. Walter (D, Pa.) [q.v.], chairman of the House Immigration Subcommittee, charged that Corsi had been associated with two allegedly left-wing organizations: the National Lawyers Guild and the American Committee for the Protection of the Foreign Born. Corsi denied the charges. On March 1 Walter admitted his error on the Lawyers Guild charge but maintained his position on the other. Walter supported McLeod on his clash with Corsi and in a letter to Dulles demanded Corsi's ouster "forthwith." On March 16 McLeod offered Corsi the choice of being his deputy or heading an insignificant project surveying immigration in Latin America. Corsi did not respond.

At the beginning of April Dulles notified Corsi that his appointment had been a 90-day assignment and would not be renewed. The Secretary stressed that he did not question Corsi's loyalty and, in token of this, again offered him the job in Latin America. Corsi refused it, charging that his dismissal had been the result of pressure from Walter and McLeod.

Corsi's ouster was denounced by congressional liberals who demanded an investigation of the incident. In press conferences and in testimony before a Senate Judiciary subcommittee, Dulles and McLeod defended their action. They maintained that Corsi had tried to bypass some provisions of the Refugee Relief Act and was incapable of administering the program. McLeod denied that he had known of Walter's demand when he made Corsi the Latin America job offer. Corsi, in turn, charged that the administration of the act was a national scandal. The law's administration was "wholly dominated by the psychology of security," Corsi declared. He said "refugees are investigated to death" because "the police job is the thing, not the admission of the refugees—that is just incidental."

New York Gov. Averell Harriman [q.v.] appointed Corsi to the New York State Unemployment Insurance Board in 1958. Corsi also served as a director of the New York World's Fair. He practiced law in New York until his death in an automobile accident in December 1964.

[JB]

COSTELLO, FRANK
b. Jan. 26, 1891; Cosenza, Italy.
d. Feb. 1, 1973; New York, N.Y.
Organized crime figure.

Born Francesco Castiglia in southern Italy, Frank Costello came to the U.S. in 1896 and settled in predominantly Italian East Harlem. He became aware early of ethnic power politics in Tammany Hall and changed his name to the Irish Costello in 1914. Arrested twice by the age of 21, in 1915 he was sentenced to one year in prison for carrying a gun.

Costello became prominent as a bootlegger and controller of New York City slot machines during the early 1920s. He was a close friend of such rising organized crime figures as Albert Anastasia [q.v.] and Lucky Luciano. Unlike these two, he preferred manipulation to violence, and during the 1930s and 1940s, he cultivated Democratic leaders in Tammany Hall. Costello's rackets encountered little official opposition except during the administration of Mayor Fiorello LaGuardia, who drove slot machines out of New York in 1935. Costello then moved his machines to New Orleans at the invitation of Sen. Huey E. Long (D, La.) who promised to legalize them. In 1936, after Luciano went to prison and Mafia leader Vito Genovese [q.v.] fled to Italy, Costello found himself head of the New York syndi-

cate. During the next 10 years he controlled Manhattan's organized crime. In 1939 federal authorities tried Costello in New Orleans for tax evasion but lost the case because of lack of evidence.

In 1951 the extent of Costello's racketeering and political influence was publicized during the Senate Crime Investigating Committee's probe of organized crime. For eight days in February and March, Costello testified before the panel, led by Sen. Estes Kefauver (D, Tenn.) [q.v.] on his role in New York City politics. Kefauver made public wiretaps documenting Costello's role in the Democratic nomination of Thomas Aurelio for the State Supreme Court in 1943. Costello's influence over Tammany leaders also enabled William O'Dwyer to win the nomination and election for mayor in 1945.

No formal charges were brought against Costello because much of the evidence had been gained by wiretaps, legally inadmissible in court. However, when Costello walked out of the hearing room on March 15, on the grounds that he had a sore throat, the Committee cited him for contempt of Congress. Kefauver concluded that Costello was part of a national axis of crime including racketeers Meyer Lansky and Joe Adonis. In 1952 Costello was convicted on the contempt charge and sentenced to 18 months in prison and a $5,000 fine. He went free pending appeal. Later that year the federal government began proceedings to revoke his citizenship on the grounds that he had lied about his occupation on naturalization papers.

In 1953 Costello was indicted, and in May 1954, he was convicted of evasion of $73,714 in income taxes. He received a five-year sentence and a $2,000 fine but was freed on bail in 1957. Publicity, time spent in prison and legal appeals weakened Costello within the Mafia. Vying for leadership, Vito Genovese attempted to have him assassinated in May 1957, but Costello survived. After the killing of Anastasia in October, Costello retired. In February 1961 the Supreme Court upheld his loss of citizenship.

In June 1961 Costello was released from prison. During the remaining years of his life, he stayed out of the public eye. However, according to the *New York Times*, Costello came out of retirement after the death of Vito Genovese in 1969 to lead the New York underworld. He was involved in long-range planning and mediation of disputes rather than day-to-day operations. Costello died in 1973 of natural causes.

[MJS]

For further information:
George Wolff, *Frank Costello: Prime Minister of the Underworld* (New York, 1974).

COTTON, NORRIS
b. May 11, 1900; Warren, N.H.
Republican Representative, N.H.,
1947-54; Republican Senator, N.H.,
1954-75.

Cotton graduated from Wesleyan University in 1922 and was elected to the New Hampshire House of Representatives the following year. From 1924 to 1928 he served as secretary to U.S. Sen. George H. Moses (R, N.H.) while attending George Washington law school. Cotton was admitted to the New Hampshire bar in 1928. From 1933 to 1939 he was district attorney for Grafton Co., and from 1939 to 1944 he sat as a justice in the municipal court of Lebanon. He again served in the state House of Representatives in 1943 and 1945. In 1946 Cotton was elected to the U.S. House of Representatives. There he compiled a conservative record, voting to override President Harry S. Truman's veto of the Taft-Hartley bill in 1947, to support the subversive activities control bill in 1948, and to oppose the Administration's long-term housing bill in 1949.

Cotton won a special election to fill a Senate vacancy in 1952. He continued his conservative voting pattern in the upper house, fighting measures extending the power of the federal government. In April 1955 he opposed a federal highway program financed through general Treasury funds on the grounds that it would increase taxes and the public debt and would impose federal controls in areas previously left to the states. The proposal, passed by the Senate

but rejected by the House, was a substitute for an Eisenhower plan to finance highway construction through a federal bond issue.

In 1956 Cotton opposed a public power project at Niagara Falls, stating that "it is simply a question of private versus government enterprise, and I believe in private enterprise." He voted against the area redevelopment bill of 1958, asserting that "when the long arm of the federal government reaches out and helps one section [of the country], it is bound to have an adverse effect on other sections."

Cotton supported the Eisenhower Administration's federal employe security program. In June 1956 the Supreme Court ruled that under a 1950 law the President's executive order of April 1953, which permitted the dismissal of any federal employe for doubtful loyalty, could apply only to persons in sensitive positions. Following the decision Cotton and Sens. Karl E. Mundt (R, S.D.) [q.v.], Edward Martin (R, Pa.) [q.v.] and William F. Knowland (R, Calif.) [q.v.] introduced a bill amending the 1950 act to extend the program to all government employes regardless of position. The measure was not reported to the Senate floor.

In June 1958 the House Interstate and Foreign Commerce Committee's Legislative Oversight Subcommittee began an investigation into the relationship between Boston industrialist Bernard Goldfine [q.v.] and presidential assistant Sherman Adams [q.v.], a probe that culminated in Adams's resignation. The following month Goldfine acknowledged that he had paid hotel bills for Cotton and Sens. Frederick Payne (R, Me.) and Styles Bridges (R, N.H.) [q.v.]. No action was taken against the legislators.

Cotton consistently opposed the domestic legislation of the Kennedy and Johnson Administrations. A militant anti-Communist, he backed American involvement in Vietnam throughout the 1960s. During the early 1970s, however, he became disenchanted with the war. He opposed U.S. military intervention in Cambodia and American support of the Saigon regime in Vietnam. Cotton declined to run for reelection in 1974. [See KENNEDY Volume]

[MLL]

CROSS, HUGH
b. Aug. 24, 1896; Jerseyville, Ill.
Member, Interstate Commerce Commission, April 1949-July 1955; Chairman, July 1955-November 1955.

The son of early Illinois pioneers, Cross received his law degree from the University of Illinois in 1921 and began legal practice in Jerseyville, Ill. In 1932 he won election as a Republican to the Illinois General Assembly, where he served four successive two-year terms. In 1939 he was elected Speaker of the House. Cross was lieutenant governor from 1940 to 1948. In April 1949 President Harry S. Truman appointed him to serve out an unexpired term on the Interstate Commerce Commission (ICC). In December 1950 he was reappointed to a full seven-year term. The Commission rotated its chairmanship, and on the basis of his seniority, Cross became chairman in July 1955.

In November 1955 the Senate Permanent Investigations Subcommittee began closed hearings on possible conflict of interest involving Cross. Testimony revealed that Cross had contacted the heads of three railroads in an effort to secure for Railroad Transfer Service, Inc. a contract to haul passengers and baggage between the city's eight railroad stations. John Keeshin, a long-time friend of Cross, headed Railroad Transfer.

Paul E. Feucht, president of one of the lines, told the panel that Cross had telephoned him saying he was "very much interested in seeing that Keeshin got the new contract with the railroad." Even more damaging was the testimony of two other presidents who reported having heard rumors that Cross was unhappy in Washington and would resign his post to head Railroad Transfer if the company were awarded the contract. Keeshin told the subcommittee that he had discussed business with Cross but denied that he had offered the Commissioner a job. Cross, too, denied charges that Keeshin had promised him a job in return for his favors. The subcommittee concluded that, although there was no evidence that Cross had acted cor-

ruptly or illegally, he had "behaved in an unwise manner involving impropriety." Both Democratic and Republican members of the panel agreed not to pursue the investigation if Cross resigned. On Nov. 23, 1955 he sent a letter of resignation to President Eisenhower. Cross stated that he would have liked to defend himself "against the baseless charges" but was resigning because of his own and his wife's health. Although rumors persisted that Cross had resigned as a result of Administration pressure, the White House denied this.

Reporters across the country protested the manner in which the Cross case was handled. Pointing to the subcommittee's decision not to follow up the investigation, the *St. Louis Post-Dispatch* asked if the subcommittee's apathy did not suggest "a cover-up of some kind." William S. White of the *New York Times* reminded his readers that government officials "not only must be above any suggestion of lawbreaking but also must operate with unblemished ethical records." Despite calls for action neither Congress nor the Justice Department attempted to pursue the investigation.

[ACD]

For further information:
David Frier, *Conflict of Interest in the Eisenhower Administration* (Ames, Iowa, 1969).

COUSINS, NORMAN
b. June 24, 1915; Union Hill, N.J.
Editor, *Saturday Review*, 1942-71.

Cousins graduated from Teachers College at Columbia University in 1933, and the following year he was hired as an editor on the *New York Post*. After subsequently working as a book critic for *Current History*, he became the editor of the *Saturday Review of Literature* (later the *Saturday Review*), a liberal literary weekly, in 1942. Cousins expanded the magazine's format to include feature articles on current events and his own editorials on political and cultural problems, in addition to book reviews.

Although a supporter of American involvement in World War II, Cousins became a peace activist as a result of the atomic bombing of Hiroshima. On the night of August 6, 1945, when the bomb was dropped, he composed a famous editorial for the *Review* entitled "Modern Man is Obsolete," in which he declared that human survival had become absolutely dependent on man's ability to avoid a new war. Believing that nuclear destruction could be averted only by the establishment of a new international order, Cousins helped found the United World Federalists in 1947, an organization which advocated transforming the United Nations into a world government with the authority to enforce disarmament.

During the late-1950s Cousins played an important role in the protest against the atmospheric testing of nuclear bombs. In 1957 he helped organize the National Committee for a Sane Nuclear Policy (SANE), a coalition of pacifists and non-pacifists concerned with peace work, which called for the immediate cessation of nuclear testing. With Cousins as cochairman, SANE began by publicizing the threat of genetic damage and contamination of the food supply from atomic fallout. After the U.S. and the Soviet Union both suspended testing in 1958, the organization, which had grown to about 25,000 members, broadened its aims to include general disarmament. At the same time SANE continued to work for a permanent test ban treaty, organizing mass demonstrations in support of this proposal throughout the country in 1959 and 1960.

In May 1960, one week after an overflow rally in New York's Madison Square Garden, Sen. Thomas Dodd (D, Conn.) [*q.v.*] charged that SANE was infiltrated by Communists. Cousins responded by suspending the organizer of the rally, who had been named by Dodd as one of the "infiltrators," and proposing a resolution, adopted by SANE's national board, restricting membership in the organization to those "whose support is not qualified by adherence to Communist or other totalitarian doctrine." Dodd later claimed that Cousins had agreed to supply his Senate Internal Security Subcommittee with the names of alleged Communists in SANE, but Cousins denied having offered to coop-

erate with an investigation. Cousins's actions were condemned by several leading peace activists as a capitulation to McCarthyism, and many resigned from SANE in protest.

In the following years Cousins continued to work for a nuclear test ban treaty and to advocate disarmament through a world rule of law. During the late 1960s he was active in the campaign for a negotiated settlement of the Vietnam war. In November 1971 Cousins resigned his post at the *Saturday Review* because of an editorial dispute with its new owners. The following year he founded *World* magazine. In 1973 Cousins bought the then bankrupt *Saturday Review* and combined it with his new publication to form *Saturday Review/World*. [See KENNEDY Volume]

[TLH]

For further information:
Lawrence Wittner, *Rebels Against War: The American Peace Movement, 1941-1960* (New York, 1969).

CURRAN, JOSEPH E(DWIN)

b. March 1, 1906; New York, N.Y.
President, National Maritime Union, 1937-73.

The son of a cook, Joseph Curran went to sea at the age of 16. In 1935 he joined the International Seamen's Union (ISU) and sailed on the S.S. *California*. Discovering that West Coast seamen's wages and conditions were better than those on the East Coast, Curran led the crew of the *California* in a wildcat strike to obtain pay parity. Secretary of Labor Frances Perkins assured Curran that if the strike were ended, the crew's grievances would be heard. Instead, 64 seamen were fired. Curran then began a major East Coast strike. He refused to accept a settlement negotiated by the ISU. Instead, he broke away from the union to form the National Maritime Union (NMU), taking 35,000 ISU members with him. The new organization became part of the Congress of Industrial Organizations (CIO). At that time the CIO was a more leftist association than its rival, the American Federation of Labor (AFL). The 31-year old Curran was elected the first NMU president in 1937.

During World War II Curran worked closely with Communist Party members in leading the union, although he himself was not a member of the Party. In 1946 he joined a group of radicals, recently expelled from the Communist Party, in a successful drive to oust Communists from the NMU. He then turned against his former supporters. In a bitter struggle, which culminated in violence, the followers of his rival, David Drummond, were expelled from the union. [See TRUMAN Volume]

Although the NMU joined the AFL-CIO in 1955, Curran was often at odds with the organization's president, George Meany [q.v.]. In 1956 he voted to recommend AFL-CIO endorsement of the Democratic presidential ticket despite Meany's desire to have the organization remain neutral in the election. That year he also gave his support to the International Longshoremen's Association's (ILA) organizing drive, despite the ILA's expulsion from the AFL because of corruption and the establishment of a rival group, the International Brotherhood of Longshoremen, by Meany. Curran refused to support the expulsion of the Teamsters Union from the AFL-CIO and repeatedly attempted to have it reinstated. In 1958 he joined the Teamsters and the ILA in sponsoring a Conference on Transportation Unity under the chairmanship of James Hoffa [q.v.], despite Meany's objections. Curran did, however, agree to abide by an AFL-CIO Executive Council order not to enter into any formal or informal agreements with the Teamsters.

Curran was one of the American labor leaders who met Premier Nikita Khrushchev during the Soviet leader's visit to the U.S. in 1959. While most labor leaders denounced Khrushchev personally and scored the Communist system, he refused to condemn the Premier. In 1960 he visited the Soviet Union and had an apparently cordial interview with the Soviet leader.

In 1960 the Department of Labor challenged Curran's reelection as president of the NMU on the grounds of election irregularities. These included illegal disqualification of candidates; electioneering at the polls; promotion of candidacies with union funds; and, failure to provide secret ballots. The suit was a major test of the provisions of the Landrum-Griffin Act of 1959. The case was later dropped in return for Curran's admission of guilt on some charges and an agreement to conduct future elections according to the provisions of the law.

During the 1950s and 1960s the NMU was threatened by a decline in jobs caused by ships registering under foreign flags and by lack of government subsidies to maintain U.S. supremacy in shipping. Although Curran gained higher wages and better working conditions and benefits for union members, his attempts to win increased government subsidy for shipping were unsuccessful.

Curran remained in office until his retirement in 1973, but in the late-1960s a growing opposition movement within the union challenged his authority, and charges of irregularities forced a 1969 rerun of the 1966 union election. [See KENNEDY, JOHNSON, NIXON/FORD Volumes]

[SY]

CURTICE, HARLOW H(ERBERT)
b. Aug. 15, 1893; Eaton Rapids, Mich.
d. Nov. 3, 1962; Flint, Mich.
President, General Motors Corporation, 1953-58.

Curtice began working at General Motors in 1914 as a bookkeeper for the AC Spark Plug Division. Within a year he was named comptroller. By 1930 he had risen to president of the division. Transferring to the Buick Motor Division in 1933 as its president and general manager, he led the ailing section to produce GM's fourth largest-selling car in the prewar years. He became a vice president of the General Motors Corp. in 1940 and left Buick to become executive vice president in 1948.

When GM President Charles Wilson [q.v.] went to Washington in 1953 as Secretary of Defense, Curtice succeeded him. During his tenure Curtice maintained GM's position as the leading manufacturer in the automotive industry. By announcing a $1 billion expansion program early in 1954, he increased the company's postwar capital investment to $3 billion. Amid conflicting reports of recession and prosperity, he initiated this plan to offset increasing consumer needs and to "underwrite its [G.M.'s] confidence in continuing prosperity." In the middle of 1955 G.M. announced another $500 million expansion, bringing postwar investment to $4 billion. Predicting "another record year for business generally," in January 1956 Curtice announced a further $1 billion growth expenditure.

Curtice testified before the Senate Banking and Currency Committee in March 1955 during its probe of rising stock market prices. Chairman J. William Fulbright (D., Ark.) [q.v.] was attempting to ascertain whether GM could force competitors out of business by lowering prices. Curtice stated that the automotive industry "is even more competitive today than at anytime . . . ." The hearings were recessed indefinitely on March 23.

GM was attacked directly in December 1955 during an investigation by the Antitrust and Monopoly Subcommittee of the Senate Judiciary Committee. The company was accused of monopolistic practices and coercion of dealers. GM dealers charged that the company used "almost diabolical pressure" to increase sales, including threats of eviction upon expiration of their short-term leases. Curtice responded by offering dealers a five-year franchise instead of the existing one-year contracts.

Two bills resulted from these hearings. One measure allowed car dealers to sue in federal court to recover damages from companies not acting in good faith in carrying out the terms of dealer contracts. It was signed by President Eisenhower in August 1956. The other bill, which would have authorized Federal Trade Commission regulation of unfair trade practices in the automobile distributing industry, died in the Senate.

In July 1956 Attorney General Herbert Brownell [q.v.] accused GM and four bus companies of conspiracy to monopolize bus sales. Curtice denied the charge, saying that GM "engaged in no discrimination as regards prices, terms and conditions in the sales of its buses."

In 1957 Curtice opposed Michigan Gov. G. Mennen Williams' [q.v.] request for increased taxes on corporation profits in the state. Curtice warned that GM already had located several new plants outside of Michigan because of tax considerations. After being criticized for his statement, Curtice denied that it had been intended as a threat to remove GM from Michigan.

Disputes between the auto industry and United Auto Workers President Walter P. Reuther [q.v.] raged during contract negotiations in 1957 and 1958. The Big Three auto companies—General Motors, Ford and Chrysler—rejected outright a proposal made in August of 1957 by Reuther to reduce 1958 prices as an anti-inflationary measure. Of the three company heads Curtice particularly was opposed to a later Reuther suggestion of profit sharing to counter a recession. He called it "a radical scheme . . . foreign to the concepts of the American free enterprise system." The contract disputes continued after Curtice's retirement.

Curtice resigned as GM's president and chief executive on Sept. 1, 1958, at the age of 65, under the company's automatic retirement plan. He died on Nov. 3, 1962 of heart failure.

[RB]

CURTIS, CARL T(HOMAS)
b. March 15, 1905; Kearney County, Neb.
Republican Representative, Neb., 1938-54; Republican Senator, Neb., 1955- .

A descendant of early settlers and farmers in Nebraska, Curtis attended the University of Nebraska and Nebraska Wesleyan University. After a brief teaching career he was admitted to the bar and set up private practice in Minden, Neb. From 1931 to 1934 Curtis served as Kearney Co. attorney. In 1938 he ran successfully for the House of Representatives. A Republican from the most Republican state in the nation, Curtis compiled one of the most conservative records in Congress. Except on civil rights, he voted with Southern Democrats on most economic and social issues. In 1959, according to *Congressional Quarterly*,

Curtis voted more consistently with the Senate's conservative coalition than any other Republican.

During his years in the House, Curtis became increasingly interested in the problems of the Social Security system, and in 1947 he called for the "blanketing in" of all aged persons not receiving benefits, especially self-employed professionals, business owners and employes of state and local governments. In 1953, as chairman of a special Social Security subcommittee of the Ways and Means Committee, he helped draw up legislation embodying the new Administration's proposals to extend old-age insurance coverage to 10 million additional persons. The Curtis plan, modeled on one put forward by the U.S. Chamber of Commerce, proposed replacing the insurance principle of the system, by which each worker built up a retirement fund for his old age, with a pay-as-you-go policy, by which currently employed persons would support the aged with their payroll taxes. Opponents such as Secretary of Health, Education and Welfare Oveta C. Hobby [q.v.] described the plan as a "criminal raid on the Social Security Trust Fund" built up by contributions from individual earnings. The bill, passed in August 1954, was modified at the suggestion of the President to provide for greater coverage without drastically reforming the system.

After his election to the Senate in 1954, Curtis focused on what he viewed as the coercive role of labor unions in American society. As a member of the Rules and Administration Committee's Subcommittee on Elections, he participated in the drive to close loopholes in the campaign spending laws that permitted unions to use dues and manpower for partisan purposes under the guise of "education and information" programs. In May 1957 he replaced the deceased Sen. Joseph McCarthy (R, Wisc.) [q.v.] on the Select Committee on Improper Activities in the Labor or Management Field. Eight months later the AFL-CIO singled out Curtis and Sens. Barry Goldwater (R, Ariz.) [q.v.] and Karl Mundt (R, S.D.) [q.v.] as having "demonstrated their anti-labor bias and . . . forfeiting any claim . . . of conducting themselves in a

spirit of fairness or objectivity." Curtis and Mundt constantly pressed the Committee to investigate the crime and violence associated with United Auto Workers (UAW) strikes. In August 1959 they finally succeeded in holding hearings on the UAW over the protest of Committee counsel Robert F. Kennedy [q.v.]. When the Committee's final report was issued in 1960, Curtis joined other Republicans in denouncing the probe. They criticized its failure to investigate cases deeply, to fix responsibility for criminal action or to recommend reform. The Senator's attributed this inaction to what they termed a close alliance between UAW President Walter Reuther [q.v.] and the Democratic Party.

By the late 1950s Curtis and his fellow-Nebraskan, Sen. Roman Hruska (R) [q.v.], had made their state an essential element in the powerful Senate bloc of Southern Democrats and conservative Republicans. In 1963 Curtis sat on five legislative committees—more than any other senator. He rejected most of the social welfare programs of the Kennedy and Johnson Administrations and was a staunch supporter of President Nixon through the Watergate scandals. [See KENNEDY, JOHNSON, NIXON/FORD Volumes]

[TLH]

CURTIS, THOMAS B(RADFORD)
b. May 14, 1911; St. Louis, Mo.
Republican Representative, Mo., 1951-69.

The son and grandson of lawyers, Thomas Curtis attended Dartmouth College. He received an LL.B. degree from Washington University in 1935 and joined his father's law firm the same year. Curtis made a number of unsuccessful bids for public office before his election to Congress in 1950 as a Republican from suburban St. Louis Co. In the House, Curtis emerged as a fiscal conservative who favored ending price controls and cutting military spending and foreign aid.

With the opening of the Republican-controlled 83rd Congress in 1953, Curtis was assigned to the powerful House Ways and Means Committee. During the Eisenhower Administration he gradually established himself as a leading Republican spokesman on economic policy and revenue matters. A resolute foe of social welfare and defense measures he believed contributed to an unbalanced budget, Curtis was often a lone dissenter on appropriations votes. Occasionally his opposition to federal spending led him to take positions that were considered extreme even by other fiscal conservatives. For example, in 1953 he suggested that Social Security be turned over to private industry. Curtis modified his conservative voting record by strongly supporting civil rights legislation. He voted for the Civil Rights Acts of 1957 and 1960 and opposed a Republican coalition with segregationist Southern Democrats.

Curtis attracted attention in 1958 when he came to the defense of presidential assistant Sherman Adams [q.v.], charged with securing favored treatment from federal regulatory agencies for Boston industrialist Bernard Goldfine [q.v.]. Curtis declared that the Interstate and Foreign Commerce Committee's Legislative Oversight Subcommittee, which was investigating the matter, had taken defamatory testimony. He moved that the subcommittee be censured. This motion was ruled out of order by Speaker Sam Rayburn [q.v.]. Later Curtis was one of only eight representatives who voted against citing Goldfine for contempt of Congress for his refusal to answer questions before the subcommittee.

As the senior Republican on the Joint Economic Committee and the second-ranking Republican on the Ways and Means Committee, Curtis maintained his record of fiscal conservatism during the Kennedy and Johnson Administrations. He was particularly active in fighting tax increases and medicare. [See KENNEDY, JOHNSON Volumes]

Curtis left the House in 1969 after an unsuccessful bid for a Senate seat. In 1972 President Richard M. Nixon appointed him chairman of the Corporation for Public Broadcasting, a board set up to control the allocation of federal funds to public radio and television stations.

[TLH]

DALEY, RICHARD J(OSEPH)
b. May 15, 1902; Chicago, Ill.
d. Dec. 20, 1976; Chicago, Ill.
Mayor, Chicago, Ill., 1955-76.

The grandson of Irish immigrants and son of a sheet metal worker, Daley grew up in the predominantly Irish Bridgeport section of Chicago's South Side. He graduated from the Christian Brothers' De La Salle Institute, a commercial high school, in 1919. Later he studied in the evening at DePaul University and received a law degree in 1934.

At the age of 21 Daley became a precinct captain in the city's Democratic organization. After the Democrats won the municipal elections in 1923, he got a job as a clerk for the City Council. During the same period Daley became president of the Hamburg Social and Athletic Club, a sometimes violent neighborhood gang that was politically influential in his ward. When the ward boss was elected treasurer of Cook Co. (which included Chicago and its suburbs) in 1931, Daley became a clerk in the treasurer's office. He was elected to the Illinois House of Representatives in 1936 and ran successful races for the state Senate in 1938 and 1942. Daley lost a race for county sheriff in 1946.

Following Adlai E. Stevenson's [q.v.] election as governor in 1948, Daley was appointed state director of revenue and served as the Governor's representative to the legislature. During these years he received significant press coverage, gaining a reputation as a young, reformist Democrat of the Stevenson type. In 1950 he left his post and ran a successful campaign for Cook Co. clerk.

Daley assumed the leadership of the Chicago party organization in July 1953, when he became chairman of the Cook Co. Democratic Central Committee. The Party's electoral strength was based upon the work of precinct captains and their assistants in the wards. In exchange for their services these party workers received patronage positions from their ward leaders. As county chairman, Daley controlled these leaders by personally determining the patronage each would receive. To preserve his patronage power Daley minimized the number of civil service officeholders chosen by merit. He did this by making many temporary appointments. Daley also selected the party's candidates for local offices.

As chairman of the Democratic Committee, Daley had little difficulty in securing the organization's endorsement for mayor in December 1954. In the February 1955 local Democratic primary, he defeated the incumbent Democratic mayor, Martin Kennelly, who had offended many party leaders by his efforts to combat municipal corruption. Two months later Daley won the general election by a vote of 708,000 to 589,000.

Daley's major goal during his first term was to revitalize Chicago's downtown business area through the construction of expressways, parking garages and docking facilities and by the enlarging of O'Hare Airport to accommodate commercial traffic. He also attempted to stem the middle and upper class exodus to the suburbs by encouraging the construction of highrise luxury apartments along the lakefront. Daley was able to fund his projects through the use of bonds and by procuring greater taxing authority for the city from the state legislature in the summer of 1955.

The Mayor's critics contended that corruption was rampant under his administration and that he was doing little to alleviate the plight of slum dwellers or to halt the declining quality of the schools and the public transportation system. They also noted that his construction plans failed to stop the suburban exodus. However, backed by his machine and with the support of the downtown business community and organized labor, he won reelection in the spring of 1959 with 71.4% of the vote.

Later in the year the city government was tarnished by scandals involving corruption in the traffic and municipal courts. In January 1960 these were overshadowed by revelations that policemen were participating in burglaries. Daley moved dramatically to repair the image of the city government. He fired the police commissioner and replaced him in February with Orlando W. Wilson, a professional criminologist from California. Daley granted Wilson far greater independence from City Hall than police commissioners traditionally had possessed, and the new chief began a major reorganization of his department.

Daley emerged as a major figure in national Democratic politics during his first six years as mayor. At the Party's 1956 Convention he received his first national publicity by rounding up support in the Illinois delegation for Stevenson, who had backed Daley's bid for the mayoralty the previous year. In 1960 he rejected Stevenson's appeal for support in his third bid for the party nomination. At the Convention Daley, who controlled about three-quarters of the state delegation, delivered the bulk of the Illinois votes for Sen. John F. Kennedy (D, Mass.) [q.v.] to help him win a first-ballot victory.

In November 1960 a heavily Democratic Cook Co. vote overcame the traditional downstate Republican majority and enabled Kennedy to carry Illinois's crucial electoral votes by a narrow margin of 10,000 ballots. Many observers believed that Daley's machine, through widespread electoral fraud, had stolen the White House from the Republican candidate, Vice President Richard M. Nixon [q.v.]. Over six hundred polling-place workers and Democratic precinct captains were charged with allowing ineligible voters to cast ballots in the name of deceased persons, permitting individuals to vote more than once and other offenses. Most of the charges were eventually dropped. Mike Royko, in *Boss: Richard J. Daley of Chicago*, attributed the dismissal of charges to the fact that the judge in the case was a loyal organization Democrat. A recount in the 900 Cook Co. precincts using paper ballots significantly reduced the margins of defeat for some state and local Republican candidates, particularly in the case of Benjamin Adamowski, the Republican state's attorney who was seeking reelection. Adamowski had initiated investigations of corruption in the Chicago city government, and Royko contended that capturing his post and other state and local offices were Daley's primary goals. The recount did not substantially affect the presidential tally, and the Republicans did not press for further retabulations. None of the election results, including Adamowski's defeat, were overturned.

Expanded federal aid to cities during the 1960s enabled Daley to strengthen his political base, and he continued to win reelection easily. He dispensed urban renewal contracts to friendly builders and used antipoverty programs as an additional source of patronage. But increasing social discontent throughout the country was felt in Chicago during the summer of 1966, when black open housing demonstrations in white ethnic neighborhoods were marked by violence. Two years later Daley was the focus of considerable criticism when the Chicago police were charged with brutal attacks upon anti-war demonstrators at the Democratic National Convention. Daley's prestige suffered again in 1976, when his handpicked gubernatorial candidate was soundly defeated by a Republican who, as a U.S. attorney, had successfully prosecuted a number of the Mayor's political allies. Daley died of a heart attack on Dec. 20, 1976. [See KENNEDY, JOHNSON, NIXON/ FORD Volumes]

[MLL]

For further information:
Mike Royko, *Boss: Richard J. Daley of Chicago* (New York, 1971).

DANIEL, (MARION) PRICE
b. Oct. 10, 1910: Dayton, Tex.
Democratic Senator, Tex., 1953-56;
Governor, Tex., 1956-63.

Price Daniel studied journalism and law at Baylor University. He received his LL.B. in 1932 and was admitted to the Texas bar the same year. Daniel began a law practice in Liberty that year and became a member of the speakers' bureau of the Democratic national campaign. In 1938 Daniel won election to the Texas House of Representatives as a moderate New Deal Democrat. He served in the Army from 1943 to 1946 and then returned to Texas, where he was elected attorney general without opposition. While in office Daniel established a reputation as a rackets-buster

and champion of state claims to offshore oil. In 1952 he ran for the U.S. Senate on a platform supporting Texas's oil claims and opposing President Harry S. Truman's liberal stand on civil rights. He secured 72% of the votes in the July 1952 Democratic primary and won election without opposition in November.

In the Senate Daniel emerged as a moderate conservative who opposed government expansion and control of the economy except in agriculture. He voted against the St. Lawrence Seaway Project in 1954 and the Administration's 1956 highway bill. Daniel supported the 1954 Bricker amendment, limiting the President's treaty-making powers but opposed foreign aid bills. The Senator also backed Eisenhower's proposal to deregulate the price of natural gas and voted against congressional salary increases in 1955.

A states rights advocate and supporter of segregation, Daniel opposed the Supreme Court's 1954 *Brown* decision outlawing segregation in public schools but refused to take an extreme stand on the issue. He was instrumental in rewriting and moderating the "Southern Manifesto" of 1956. Early drafts of the document, as originally conceived by Sen. Strom Thurmond (D, S.C.) [q.v.], contained passages branding the ruling unconstitutional and approving interposition, the use of state power to nullify the decision. However, several legislators refused to accept these drafts and a committee was formed to modify it. The five-member panel, which included Thurmond, Sens. Richard Russell (D, Ga.) [q.v.], John Stennis (D, Miss.) [q.v.], J. William Fulbright (D, Ark.) [q.v.] and Daniel, drew up a far less dramatic document than the original. It denounced "the unwarranted decision of the Supreme Court" as a substitution of "naked power for established law" and backed the states "which have declared their intention to resist forced integration by any lawful means."

Daniel was one of the leaders of the centrist wing of the Texas Democratic Party. This conservative group refused to follow Gov. Allan Shiver's [q.v.] call to split the state Democrats from the national Party. Daniel supported Adlai Stevenson [q.v.]

for President in 1956 and joined centrists at the September state convention in blocking "Shivercrats" and liberals from positions of power. That year he ran for governor. After barely winning the Democratic primary against liberal Ralph Yarborough, Daniel won election in November.

During his tenure Daniel attempted to maintain his moderate stand on segregation. Texas refused to comply with the desegregation decision but also opposed joining the interposition crusade. In late 1956 a Shivers appointed committee on segregation submitted a hard-line report, including proposals for the state to return to a completely segregated school system. The panel also recommended a pupil placement bill, an interposition resolution and a referendum prohibiting desegregation unless 20% of the voters petitioned for it and a majority approved it. Daniel was not enthusiastic about the report, but legislative pressure and majority support for a return to white supremacy eventually forced him to support certain portions of it. In 1957, when the legislature passed the assignment and referendum bills, Daniel signed both. Four interposition resolutions remained stalled in the legislature. The two laws stemmed the progress of desegregation, which until that time, had proceeded more rapidly in Texas than in any other Southern state.

Daniel won reelection in 1958 and 1960. In 1962 he was defeated in the Democratic primary by John Connally. Price Daniel retired from government in 1962 and resumed his private law practice.

[MJS]

DAVIES, JOHN PATON, JR.
b. April 6, 1908; Kiating, China
Foreign Service officer.

The son of a Baptist missionary, Davies spent his early years in China. He studied at the University of Wisconsin and Yenching University before receiving his degree from Columbia in 1931. He then entered the Foreign Service. Davies served as a consul in a number of Chinese cities and, during the late-1930s and early-1940s, was adviser to Col. Joseph Stilwell.

As one of the highest ranking Foreign Service officials in China, Davies issued frequent reports and policy recommendations on the Chinese civil war. He described Chiang Kai-shek's corruption and decadence and predicted that, because of his refusal to reform, the Communists would defeat him. Davies rejected the assertions of Roosevelt's representative, Gen. Patrick Hurley, that the U.S. give unqualified support to the Nationalists, believing that the statements weakened the American position. He recommended that the U.S. ignore ideology and deal with the Communists not only because it would prevent the formation of a Sino-Soviet bloc but also because the U.S. would eventually have no other choice.

In 1945 Davies was appointed first secretary of the embassy in Moscow; from 1947 to 1951 he was a member of the State Department's policy planning staff. He then served with the U.S. High Commission in Germany and was director of political affairs at the U.S. mission from 1951 to 1953. In 1953-54 he was a counselor and charge d'affaires in Lima, Peru.

During the late-1940s and early-1950s Sen. Joseph R. McCarthy (R, Wisc.) [q.v.] made Davies a frequent target for attack because of his foreign policy views. The Wisconsin Senator denounced him as a pro-Communist and charged him with the responsibility for "losing China." As a result of these and subsequent charges, Davies underwent eight security investigations from 1948 to 1953. He was cleared in each case. [See TRUMAN Volume]

In 1953 McCarthy resumed his attacks on Davies. In response, Secretary of State John Foster Dulles [q.v.] suspended the diplomat and ordered a special security board to review his case. At the hearing Gen. Hurley testified that Davies was one of the men who had sabotaged a Nationalist Chinese victory. The board recommended Davies's removal in August.

Four months later Dulles dismissed Davies on the grounds that he lacked "judgment, discretion and reliability." Dulles said that neither he nor the board had found Davies disloyal but that, under Eisenhower's security orders, "complete and unswerving loyalty was not enough. He must be reliable, trustworthy, of good character and conduct."

The Secretary said that the board had recommended Davies's ouster because "his observation and evaluation of the facts [in reporting to superiors], his policy recommendations, his attitude with respect to existing policy and his disregard of proper forbearance and caution in making known his dissents . . . were not in accordance with the standard required of Foreign Service officers. . . ." Dulles later let it be known that he would furnish Davies a character reference if needed.

Following the dismissal Davies suggested that "a prudent young man who enters the Foreign Service should know another trade." He and his family remained in Lima, where he opened a furniture business. In 1964 Davies returned to Washington and requested a review of his case. His name was cleared by the Johnson Administration in November 1968.

Davies's dismissal was one of a series that purged many China experts from the State Department. Critics such as George Kennan [q.v.] charged that the firings had a long-range detrimental effect on the Department. In his opinion, they dissuaded talented individuals from entering the State Department because of the threat of dismissal at any time for disloyalty. Those men and women who remained became more cautious. Realizing that men had been fired for voicing their expert opinions, they based their recommendations on approved anti-Communist ideology rather than on their knowledge and personal assessment of the situation. Over a decade later David Halberstam pointed to Davies's firing and the purge as an underlying cause for U.S. inability to handle problems in Southeast Asia.

[JB]

DAVIS, JIMMIE H(OUSTON)
b. Sept. 11, 1904; Jackson Parish, La.
Governor, La, 1960-64.

The son of a poor sharecropper, Jimmie Davis worked his way through college and graduate school singing and composing country-western music. After earning a B.A. from Louisiana College and an M.A. from Louisiana State University, he taught history at Dodd College. Davis entered politics in his home city of Shreveport, La., and made his way up the political ladder by winning friends and generating good will. He almost never took a determined stand on issues, preferring to "live and let live." In 1938 he won the race for safety commissioner after a campaign in which he said nothing against his opponent but sang songs that he had composed. He was elected the Democratic governor of Louisiana in 1944. Again he did not run on issues, but rather he sang his compositions during the campaign. By the time of his campaign they included such national hits as "You Are My Sunshine," "Bed Bug Blues," "Bear Cat Poppa," "High Powered Mama" and "Get Yourself a Car."

Davis accomplished little as governor, preferring to put decisions off as long as possible. When forced to make a decision, he would often leave the state for long periods of time, occasionally going to Hollywood to work in movies. Louisiana law prohibited the Governor from succeeding himself. After his term expired he resumed his singing career.

Davis tried for a political comeback in the 1959 December Democratic gubernatorial primary. His leading opponent, deLesseps Morrison [q.v.], ran on his record as an efficient mayor of New Orleans. In contrast, Davis once again sang songs and campaigned on platitudes. Another candidate, State Sen. Willie Rainach, ran on a pro-segregationist platform. Morrison won the primary but was forced to face Davis on a run-off in January 1960. With Rainach out of the race, Davis attempted to appeal to the pro-segregationist vote. He charged Morrison with being soft on integration and labeled him an "NAACP candidate." Davis also took advantage of Morrison's sophisticated appearance to win the state's rural vote. He once said that Morrison "looks right taking Zsa Zsa Gabor to tea [but] looks all wrong to those Rednecks up in hill country." Davis won the run-off and went on to win the election.

In May 1960 Federal Judge J. Skelly

Wright [*q.v.*] ended years of delay by ordering New Orleans to desegregate its schools at the beginning of the fall term. The following month the New Orleans School Board asked the Governor to "interpose state sovereignty" between the judiciary and the school system to prevent integration. At first Davis refused but as a result of pressure from staunch segregationists, he began action. Terming the order an unwarranted intrusion of the federal government in intrastate affairs, Davis pledged to resist the order even at the risk of going to jail. He then worked with the legislature to pass a series of anti-integration laws. These included bills barring state funds for integrated schools, permitting the Governor to close integrated schools and allowing the Governor to close schools to prevent violence.

On Aug. 17 Davis assumed administration of New Orleans schools and appointed his own superintendent. Ten days later the federal court issued a temporary restraining order blocking Davis's action. It also struck down the segregation laws. This act strengthened the moderate faction on the New Orleans School Board, which acknowledged the inevitability of integration and was willing to move slowly on it. Judge Wright then granted this group their request to postpone desegregation until November. On Nov. 4 New Orleans schools were integrated as four blacks entered previously all-white schools amid taunting, jeering mobs. Four days later the state legislature once again gave Gov. Davis the right to close the schools. However, Judge Wright struck down the law. By the spring of 1961 the resistance had broken down as the schools resumed normal operations. Davis continued to back segregation, calling it "the most noble cause that had ever arisen during the lifetime of any man living in the world to date."

After Davis left office, he resumed his singing and business career. He tried a political comeback in November 1971, running for governor in the crowded Louisiana primary, but he did poorly in the race.

[JB]

DAVIS, JOHN (WILLIAM)
b. April 13, 1873; Clarksburg, W. Va.
d. March 24, 1955; Charleston, W. Va.
Attorney.

Born in Clarksburg, W. Va., Davis obtained his B.A. from Washington and Lee University in 1892 and took his law degree there in 1895. Following admission to the bar, he entered practice with his father in Clarksburg. Davis served a term in the West Virginia House of Delegates in 1899 and ran successfully for the U.S. House of Representatives in 1910. Woodrow Wilson appointed him solicitor general in 1913. During the next five years Davis defended a large amount of progressive legislation before the Supreme Court, eventually earning a reputation as one of America's greatest solicitor generals. In 1918 he was named ambassador to Great Britain and served as an adviser to Wilson at Versailles.

Davis became head of the Wall Street firm of Stetson, Jennings and Russell in 1921. Over the next few decades he achieved prominence as a corporation counsel who argued against the expansion of government power into the commercial sector. From 1922 to 1924 he was the president of the American Bar Association. In 1924 the deadlocked Democratic National Convention made Davis the presidential nominee on the 103rd ballot. He was badly defeated by Calvin Coolidge in November, winning only 136 electoral votes, all from the South.

Although he supported Franklin D. Roosevelt in 1932, Davis soon became disenchanted with the expansion of federal power under the New Deal and helped organize the anti-New Deal Liberty League in 1934. As a member of the Lawyers Vigilance Committee, he argued against the constitutionality of much New Deal legislation in the higher courts.

Davis was a deep believer in states rights and strict construction as well as a strong civil libertarian. During the 1940s and 1950s he argued many important cases in the interest of his conservative principles. He battled for the rights of conscientious objectors during World War II and supported Alger Hiss in the postwar period. In 1952 he successfully argued before the Supreme Court against the constitutionality of President Truman's seizure of the steel mills. [See TRUMAN Volume]

During 1952-53 Davis defended South Carolina's school segregation in in a series of cases known as *Brown* v. *Board of Education.* He rejected Thurgood Marshall's [*q.v.*] premise that the 14th Amendment had outlawed segregation and that separate schools were not equal because they produced a sense of inferiority in black children. Citing historical precedent, Davis maintained that the framers of the Amendment had never intended it to be used to support integration. He believed that if segregation were to be outlawed, it had to be done either by an act of Congress or by amending the Constitution. To undo state laws by judicial fiat, Davis insisted, would destroy the separation-of-powers concept of the Constitution and would be an unconstitutional intrusion by the federal government into the affairs of the states.

Davis then challenged Marshall's contention that segregation would lead to feelings of inferiority. He raised the question of whether having "three white children with 27 blacks would prevent the psychological distress segregation was charged with doing." Racism, suggested Davis, had been around for centuries. "You recognize differences," he declared, "which race implants in the human animal." Concluding, the elderly lawyer said that South Carolina "is convinced that the happiness, the progress and the welfare of these children is best promoted in segregated schools." In May 1954 the Supreme Court unanimously ruled that segregated schools were unconstitutional. Davis remarked that the decision was "unworthy of the Supreme Court" and predicted that turmoil would result in the South following the decision.

In 1954 Davis defended J. Robert Oppenheimer [*q.v.*] against Administration charges that he was a security risk. When the Atomic Energy Commission review board refused to clear Oppenheimer, Davis called the ruling not simply "unjust" but "silly."

During the course of his long legal career, Davis appeared before the Supreme Court 104 times, more than any other twentieth century lawyer. He was commonly ranked with Robert Jackson [*q.v.*] as one of the finest advocates of the era. Davis died in 1955 at the age of 82.

[JB]

For further information:
William H. Harbaugh, *Lawyer's Lawyer: The Life of John W. Davis* (New York, 1973).
Richard Kluger, *Simple Justice* (New York, 1975).

DAWSON, WILLIAM L(EVI)
b. April 26, 1886; Albany, Ga.
d. Nov. 9, 1970; Chicago, Ill.
Democratic Representative, Ill., 1943-70; Chairman, Government Operations Committee, 1955-70; Chairman, Committee on Executive Expenditures, 1949-70.

After graduating *magna cum laude* from Fisk University in 1909, Dawson attended Kent College and Northwestern University law school. Following service in the Army during World War I, he began practicing law in Chicago. In 1928 Dawson ran unsuccessfully as a Republican candidate for the U.S. House of Representatives. From 1933 to 1939 he served as alderman from Chicago's South Side. He became a Democrat in 1939 in part because his largely black constituency had switched its allegiance to the party of Franklin D. Roosevelt.

Dawson used his position to build a political machine that controlled politics in the black ghetto. In 1942 he ran for the U.S. House against the wishes of Democratic Mayor Edward Kelly, who had aided his political career. Using his ward position, Dawson won the race and continued to win election from the first congressional district until the time of his death. In Chicago's black ghetto Dawson was the man to see for patronage jobs; he chose or appointed the aldermen of six wards. [See TRUMAN Volume]

Dawson could often determine the fate of white as well as black office holders.

Angered by alleged police brutality and attempts to arrest petty gamblers, he determined to oppose Mayor Martin Kennelly's reelection in 1953. However, because he could find no alternative candidate, he did not openly break with the Mayor. In 1955 he threw his support to Richard Daley [q.v.]. With Dawson's support Daley defeated Kennelly in the primary and went on to win the general election. In three of Dawson's pocket wards, Daley won by an almost four-to-one margin and in the black 24th ward he won by 18 to 1. Dawson's support proved to be the most important element in the Daley victory.

In Congress Dawson was a strong supporter of New and Fair Deal legislation and during the 1940s worked to outlaw the poll tax and segregation in the armed forces. However, during the 1950s he became increasingly alienated from the emerging civil rights movement. He provided only lukewarm backing for civil rights legislation and refused to actively support an anti-lynching bill. In 1956 Dawson opposed an amendment by Rep. Adam Clayton Powell, Jr. (D, N.Y.) [q.v.] to an aid-to-education bill denying federal funds to segregated schools. The Congressman believed that the amendment would kill the proposal, a prediction confirmed when the measure was defeated in July.

Dawson's apathy toward civil rights measures earned him the anger of local NAACP president Willoughby Abner, who called him "soft" on civil rights. In reaction Dawson used his patronage power to gain control of the NAACP chapter. In 1957 his hand-picked candidate, Theodore Jones, took the presidency from Abner in an election dominated by the new "Dawson members."

During the Kennedy and Johnson years, Dawson joined other Northern urban Democrats in support of the Administrations' social welfare legislation. Throughout the decade young blacks, dissatisfied with Dawson's civil rights stand, attempted to unseat him, but he defeated all primary challengers by margins of at least two to one. At his death at 84 he was unbeaten.
[See KENNEDY, JOHNSON Volumes]

[AES]

DEAN, ARTHUR H(OBSON)
b. Oct. 16, 1898; Ithaca, N.Y.
State Department negotiator.

Dean worked his way through Cornell University and, following service in the Army during World War I, he received his law degree there in 1923. The same year he joined the law firm of Sullivan and Cromwell, in which John Foster Dulles [q.v.] was a senior partner. He worked on cases involving American and British banking interests and became a partner in 1929. During World War II Dean served as a Coast Guard instructor in navigation and piloting. Dean was a member of the Institute of Pacific Relations in the early 1950s but resigned in 1952 after a Senate subcommittee report said that the effect of the institute's activities on public opinion had "served Communist interests."

At the behest of Secretary of State Dulles, Dean went to Korea in October 1953 to prepare for peace negotiations with the North Koreans and the Chinese Communists. Dean opposed North Korean and Chinese suggestions that nations not involved in the war, including the USSR, be represented. Reiterating the U.N.'s resolution of August 1953, he stressed that the peace conference should be attended only by the countries participating in the fighting. The Soviet Union was not a neutral but a belligerent that could sit in if it desired. In December 1953 the Communist Chinese delegate accused the U.S. of perfidy in allowing South Korea to "release" 21,000 non-Communist North Korean and Communist Chinese prisoners of war into U.N. custody instead of sending them home. Reacting to the charge, Dean temporarily suspended negotiations.

In January 1954, after Dean was reported to have told the *Providence Journal* that the U.S. should recognize the People's Republic of China, Sen. Herman Welker (R, Ida.) [q.v.] accused Dean of supporting "appeasement" and of collaboration with Communist China. He also assailed Dean as the former "official spokesman" of the Institute of Pacific Relations. In March Dulles asked Dean to resign from the Korean negotiations. However, the Secretary still asked him to go to South Korea and review the political situation with President Syngman Rhee a week before the negotiations opened in Geneva in April 1954.

Dean continued to recommend recognition of Communist China during the Quemoy-Matsu crisis of 1955. In an article in *Foreign Affairs*, he maintained that recognition would improve the U.S.'s international position. He recommended consideration of Great Britain's two-China idea, which would recognize Communist rule on the mainland and Nationalist rule on Formosa. "As things are going," he said, "we face the inevitable defection of friends in the U.N., and when that happens it may be too late to negotiate a ceasefire."

During the spring of 1958 Dean represented the U.S. in Geneva at the 87-nation Conference on the Law of the Sea. Upholding the traditional U.S. position, he initially called for a three-mile limit on national claims to the coastal sea. This stand was opposed by the USSR, Iceland and several South American nations which favored at least a 12-mile limit. In an attempt to break the deadlock, on April 15 Dean proposed that territorial limits be extended to six miles. He also asked for the establishment of an additional six-mile zone from which all foreign fishermen could be excluded except those who had fished the area regularly for 10 years preceding the signing of a new sea law convention. The proposal was voted down on April 28, and Dean gave formal notice that the U.S. would continue to observe the three-mile limit.

During the Kennedy Administration Dean represented the U.S. at the Geneva talks on ending nuclear weapons tests and advised the President on disarmament. In 1968 he became a member of the Senior Advisory Group on Vietnam, convened to consider the military's request for over 200,000 more troops for Vietnam. The panel recommended rejection of the request and the de-escalation of the war. [See KENNEDY Volume]

[RSG]

DeLOACH, DEKE (CARTHA) (DEKLE)
b. July 20, 1920; Claxton, Ga.
FBI official.

Born into a poor Georgia family, DeLoach worked his way through Stetson University, from which he graduated in 1942. He joined the FBI and worked as an agent carrying out investigations of Communist Party members in Norfolk, Toledo and Akron. Dissatisfied with the work, he left the agency in 1944 to join the Navy. Following the War he returned to the Bureau.

Assigned to FBI headquarters, DeLoach carried out security checks of potential employes in atomic energy projects. Later he served as liaison between the FBI and various U.S. intelligence agencies. In 1951 DeLoach attended an international conference on intelligence matters and wrote Director J. Edgar Hoover [*q.v.*] a report on the meeting. Hoover was impressed by the young man, and the two quickly became close friends. According to his historian Sanford Ungar, "As their relationship became closer many FBI colleagues observed that DeLoach seemed to fulfill the role of a son to Hoover; others thought it was more like that of a hatchet man." Hoover quickly promoted DeLoach to inspector and gave the young man sensitive special assignments, mainly disciplining agents who failed to comply with the Bureau's stiff code of personal behavior. He disciplined agents for major offenses such as trying to persuade Communists to become FBI informers and allowing these overtures to be leaked. On other occasions DeLoach punished agents for sexual infidelity. In 1953 DeLoach became a special assistant in the office of Clyde Tolson, Hoover's right-hand man.

That year Hoover asked DeLoach to join the American Legion and guide the group's anti-Communist crusade. Hoover did not object to the spirit of the Legion's campaign. However, he opposed Legion demands for investigating specific groups and individuals, preferring to choose the Bureau's targets himself. He resented amateur attempts to compete with his organization. DeLoach took his task seriously, and using his FBI credentials, he became a post commander, department commander, vice commander and eventually national vice commander. At one point he thought of running for national commander, but Hoover vetoed the proposal as "too political." DeLoach became chairman of the organization's public relations committee in 1958. There, Ungar maintains, he exercised great influence over the organization's internal policy as well as public relations. The American Legion was a strong source of support for Hoover, and over the next 20 years, it often mobilized its forces to defend the Director's controversial actions.

In 1959 DeLoach became assistant director of the crime records division which, despite its title, was responsible for public and congressional relations. He became one of the Bureau's leading speakers, articulating a hard-hitting conservative view of the Communist threat and the FBI's role in combating it. The personable DeLoach maintained a close relationship with Congress and worked with such powerful members of Congress as John J. Rooney (D, N.Y.) [q.v.] to further the interests of the Bureau. DeLoach also improved relations with the press. He had access to the FBI's massive files containing personal information on members of Congress. To advance the Bureau's reputation he often leaked information on individual congressmen to favorite reporters.

In December 1965 DeLoach became assistant to the Director and assumed charge of all the Bureau's investigative activities. He developed a close relationship with President Lyndon B. Johnson, who often preferred to communicate with DeLoach rather than Hoover. DeLoach had hoped to succeed Hoover as Director. When it became apparent that Hoover was unwillling to retire, he accepted a lucrative offer to become an executive with Pepsico, Inc. He left the Bureau in June 1970. [See JOHNSON Volume]

[JB]

For further information:
Sanford J. Ungar. *FBI* (Boston. 1975).

DeSAPIO, CARMINE G(ERALD)
b. Dec. 10, 1908; New York, N.Y.
Chairman, New York County
Democratic Committee, 1949-61.

The son of an Italian immigrant, DeSapio was born on New York City's lower West Side. He attended local parochial schools and studied law at Fordham University. However, he was forced to give up his studies because of an attack of rheumatic fever. The illness resulted in an eye inflammation requiring him to wear the tinted glasses that became his trademark. While still attending high school DeSapio became interested in politics and joined the local Democratic club. A loyal member of New York's Tammany Hall, he worked his way up in the Democratic machine until he won a seat on its executive committee in 1943. He was elected to the city-wide Board of Elections in 1946 and the following year was part of the four-man group that took over effective leadership of Tammany Hall. In 1949 he was chosen leader of the organization.

During the next five years DeSapio expanded his control throughout New York City's five boroughs and amassed great power in the state. In 1953 he broke with Mayor Vincent Impellitteri over questions of patronage and charges that the Mayor had been connected with organized crime. He instead backed Robert F. Wagner, Jr. [q.v.], for the Democratic mayoral nomination. Wagner, the son of a popular liberal senator, was a favorite of New York liberals. With DeSapio's help Wagner defeated Impellitteri in the primary and went on to win the general election.

During the 1950s DeSapio sought to make Tammany Hall a force for liberalism while at the same time continuing to function as a political machine. He championed housing reform and health care legislation. Indebted to DeSapio for his election, Wagner turned patronage over to him. Under his guidance city appointments and elected offices were opened to minorities, and many qualified individuals were appointed to city positions. He democratized the organization's process of electing local political leaders and sought to sever Tammany's ties with organized crime. Unlike many traditional bosses, DeSapio relished public exposure and acclaim. He lectured in colleges, published articles, consented to be interviewed by the media and enjoyed mingling openly with the powerful.

In 1954 DeSapio supported W. Averell Harriman [q.v.] for New York governor. The former ambassador was opposed by such liberals as Thomas Finletter [q.v.] and Eleanor Roosevelt [q.v.], who favored the nomination of Franklin D. Roosevelt, Jr. Using his control of the New York State Democratic Party, DeSapio pushed the nomination through the Democratic convention. With Harriman's victory at the polls, DeSapio emerged as the most powerful Democratic Party leader in the state. To add to his prestige and power, Harriman appointed him secretary of state and consulted him on patronage and other political matters. In addition, DeSapio served as an unofficial lobbyist for New York City in Albany and Washington.

DeSapio's power began to wane during 1957. In July he unwittingly left an envelope containing $11,200 in large bills in a taxi. Although he denied the money was his, the cab driver publicly identified him as the source. Wagner's personal triumph in the election of 1957 released the Mayor from obligations to his former sponsor, and the two men became rivals. At the same time reform stirrings in his own district eroded DeSapio's power at its source. Most importantly, the gubernatorial and senatorial elections proved disastrous for DeSapio. Over the objections of reformers DeSapio pushed the nomination of Frank Hogan [q.v.] for the Senate through the state convention. When Hogan and Harriman lost the November election, DeSapio lost his upstate power base. His dictatorial conduct at the convention served as a catalyst for New York City reformers to organize to unseat DeSapio's supporters from elected positions.

In 1961 Wagner broke openly with DeSapio and accepted the support of the reform movement for his reelection bid. Running on the issue of bossism, Wagner defeated DeSapio's candidate, Arthur Levitt,

in the Democratic primary. DeSapio himself was defeated for his district leadership. Because only district leaders were eligible to serve as county leaders, DeSapio lost all his state and local posts. He attempted a political comeback in 1964 and 1965 but failed in both cases. In 1969 a federal jury convicted DeSapio of having conspired to induce a public official to misuse his office in return for a bribe. After serving a 17-month sentence, he was released in December 1972. [See KENNEDY Volume]

[JB]

For further information:
Warren Moscow, *The Last of the Big Time Bosses: The Life and Times of Carmine DeSapio and the Decline and Fall of Tammany Hall* (New York, 1971).

DILLON, C(LARENCE) DOUGLAS
b. Aug. 21, 1909; Geneva, Switzerland. Ambassador to France, January 1953-Janaury 1957; Deputy Undersecretary of State for Economic Affairs, January 1957-July 1958; Undersecretary of State for Economic Affairs, July 1958-April 1959; Undersecretary of State, April 1959-January 1961.

C. Douglas Dillon grew up amid affluence in New York City suburbs. He attended Groton and Harvard and in 1931 was given a seat on the New York Stock Exchange by his father. Seven years later he became vice president of Dillon, Read and Co., the investment banking firm founded by his father. Dillon followed the firm's president, James V. Forrestal, into the Navy Department in 1940. During World War II he saw action in the Pacific as a Navy air operations officer. After the War Dillon became board chairman of Dillon, Read. There he supervised the firm's far-flung foreign and domestic holdings and doubled its investment portfolio in six years.

A prominent Republican, Dillon worked with John Foster Dulles [q.v.] in Gov. Thomas Dewey's 1948 presidential campaign. In December 1951 he initiated the "draft Eisenhower" movement in New Jersey and became a large financial contributor to the 1952 Republican presidential campaign.

President Eisenhower named Dillon ambassador to France in January 1953. Dillon frequently represented Secretary of State Dulles at the 1954 Geneva Conference on Indochina and assisted Special Ambassador David Bruce [q.v.] in attempting to persuade the French to accept European economic and military unity. The French, fearful of German rearmament and of sacrificing their sovereignty to a supranational army, rejected the European Defense Community in August 1954. However, at the end of the year, they agreed to a compromise solution: the admission of West Germany into the North Atlantic Treaty Organization under the aegis of the Western European Union.

In January 1957 Dillon became deputy undersecretary of state for economic affairs. During the course of the year, he was given supervisory authority over the entire U.S. foreign aid program. In April he was named alternate governor of the International Monetary Fund (IMF), and in December, he was appointed to the Development Loan Fund (DLF). Dillon was promoted to undersecretary of state for economic affairs in July 1958. His increased power reflected Secretary of State Dulles's belief that the State Department should play a more positive role in implementing foreign policy. It was also an indication of the Eisenhower Administration's desire to devise a more ambitious and coherent foreign aid program. Vice President Richard M. Nixon [q.v.] was instrumental in choosing Dillon for the job of coordinating foreign aid, believing that Dillon could ably argue the case for increased expenditures before a skeptical Congress.

With his new authority Dillon sought to revamp foreign aid policy, arguing that Communist technical advances demanded more rapid development of the Western world's economic strength. The U.S., he asserted, could no longer grant foreign aid on an emergency basis. Speaking in November 1957 he advocated a five-year extension of the Reciprocal Trade Agreements Act and more money for the DLF, especially for African and Asian nations. He also urged Congress to approve U.S. membership in the Organization for Trade Cooperation, an agency designed to administer the 38-nation General Agreement on Tariffs and Trade. Finally, he recommended more private investment and greater use of the Export-Import Bank to help the underdeveloped nations.

Dillon's ambitious designs met with considerable success. In September 1957 the Inter-American Economic Conference called for a reduction of trade restrictions among member nations, increased efforts to stimulate investment capital and intergovernmental cooperation on the problems of raw material producers. Dillon encouraged the creation of regional common markets in Latin America, although he pointed out that the U.S. could not join because of conflicting agreements with other parts of the world. In August 1958 Dillon announced U.S. support of the Inter-American Development Institution, formed to provide development loans to Latin American countries.

In April 1959 Dillon became undersecretary of state, the second-ranking post in the State Department. He retained his authority over economic affairs and achieved two of his most notable successes in the last year of the Eisenhower Administration. In September 1960 Dillon submitted a $500 million program to the Inter-American Economic Conference meeting in Bogota, Colombia. Despite Cuban denunciations of the Act of Bogota, all the other nations agreed to the proposal. The social development plan, a forerunner of President Kennedy's Alliance for Progress, was to be financed by the Unites States but administered by the Inter-American Development Bank. With its aims of modernizing Latin American economies, improving standards of living and fostering land and tax reform, Dillon hoped that the plan could help democratize Latin America and thus make the rest of the Hemisphere immune to Communist revolution. In December 1960 Dillon's persistent efforts to convince the Western Europeans to develop more ambitious foreign aid programs led to the establishment of the Organization for Economic Cooperation and Development (OECD). The OECD, consisting of the U.S., Canada and 18 European nations, succeeded the Organization for European Economic Cooperation and marked the beginning of a coordinated foreign aid policy by the developed nations.

Although Dillon was a large contributor to the 1960 Nixon presidential campaign, President-elect Kennedy asked him to join his cabinet as Secretary of the Treasury. Dillon accepted Kennedy's offer and became the most important economic policymaker during the Kennedy Administration. He continued at his post under the Johnson Administration. Unable to achieve a rapport with Johnson, Dillon left the Treasury in March 1965. In February 1967 he became president of the U.S. and Foreign Securities Corp. [See KENNEDY, JOHNSON Volumes]

[JCH]

DILWORTH, RICHARDSON
b. Aug. 29, 1898; Pittsburgh, Pa.
Mayor, Philadelphia, Pa., 1956-62.

Dilworth was born into a patrician Pittsburgh family. After serving in the Marine Corps during World War I, he attended Yale, where he received his A.B. in 1921. Five years later he earned his law degree from the same institution. Dilworth then began law practice in Philadelphia. The colorful, outgoing trial lawyer also became involved in reform politics as a Democrat. Over the next 40 years Dilworth opposed the entrenched Republican machine, which had dominated Philadelphia politics since the end of the nineteenth century.

In 1947 Dilworth ran for mayor on a platform denouncing municipal corruption. He lost to the GOP machine candidate, Mayor Bernard Samuels, by approximately 90,000 votes. However, over the next two years revelations of wholesale municipal corruption were uncovered, and in 1949 Dilworth was elected city treasurer. In 1951 he became district attorney at the same time that his political ally and friend, Joseph Clark

[q.v.], became mayor. The men received their support from a broad based coalition of ethnic minority leaders, ideological liberals and patrician Philadelphia families. Dilworth became mayor in 1956, when Clark went to the U.S. Senate.

During the 1950s the two men ushered in what journalist Neal Peirce called "Philadelphia's modern Golden Age." Under the Clark-Dilworth administrations Philadelphia reorganized its government and reformed its civil service. It began a reform of its transit system, encouraged industrial development and undertook a large-scale public housing program.

The two men developed one of the largest urban renewal projects in the nation. It was designed to rejuvenate the city's waterfront and rehabilitate the aging downtown area. Parks were created and the city's historic sites renovated. Dilworth often used public interest corporations to coordinate and guide renewal efforts. These groups, independent of but close to municipal government, were composed not only of corporate and banking officials but also of members of various interest groups. The businessmen on the board provided investors with confidence in the stability of projects while civic group participation gave the efforts a broad political base.

Dilworth was a liberal on many issues. He opposed segregation in private schools and defended the rights of organized labor. He endorsed federal aid for housing and in 1959 protested Eisenhower's veto of a $1.5 billion housing bill. The Mayor urged the development of a progressive national transportation policy. He recommended that commutter railroads be subsidized by low-interest loans, that rail taxation policies be coordinated among state, local and federal governments and that mass transit facilities be improved.

Dilworth resigned as mayor to run for governor in 1962. He lost to William Scranton but continued in public service as president of the Philadelphia Board of Education. Dilworth resigned from the school board in 1971 to continue actively campaigning for progressive reforms. [See KENNEDY Volume]

[SY]

DIRKSEN, EVERETT McKINLEY
b. Jan. 4, 1895; Pekin, Ill.
d. Sept. 7, 1969; Washington, D.C.
Republican Senator Ill., 1959-69; Senate Minority Leader, 1959-69.

Everett McKinley Dirksen grew up on his family's central Illinois farm. After attending the University of Minnesota, he served in the Army balloon corps during World War I. He returned to Pekin after the War, and in 1932 he won election to the House of Representatives as a Republican. Serving there until 1948, Dirksen generally supported his Party's Eastern internationalist wing. He endorsed Franklin D. Roosevelt's foreign policy on the eve of Pearl Harbor and played an important role in the passage of the first Marshall Plan appropriations in 1947. Dirksen won an upset victory for the U.S. Senate in 1950, changing his politics to match those of the Party's more nationalist "Old Guard." [See TRUMAN Volume]

Dirksen figured prominently in the battle for the 1952 Republican presidential nomination. A leading supporter of Sen. Robert A. Taft (R, Ohio) [q.v.], he twice spoke for the Taft forces before the National Convention, and he nominated the Senator. Dirksen wanted the vice presidential spot and hoped that Taft would choose him as his running mate. From the rostrum he rhetorically attacked the GOP's 1944 and 1948 presidential nominee, Gov. Thomas E. Dewey, who opposed Taft. Pointing to Dewey, seated before him, he cried, "We followed you before, and you took us down the path to defeat!" The Convention fell into pandemonium. Despite Dirksen's histrionics, Dewey's candidate, Dwight D. Eisenhower, won the nomination. The General did not seriously consider Dirksen for the vice presidency despite Taft's strong recommendation.

In the next three years Eisenhower commanded only marginal loyalty from the Illinois Republican. During the fall 1952 campaign, Dirksen gave Eisenhower only lukewarm support. In the 83rd (1953-54) Congress, Taft, then majority leader, rewarded Dirksen with three important committee assignments: Appropriations, Judiciary and Government Operations. Yet, neither Taft nor Eisenhower could count on Dirksen for crucial votes. In March 1953 he voted against the nomination of Charles E. Bohlen [q.v.] to be ambassador to the Soviet Union, despite Taft's support for the appointment. The following month he joined Taft in criticizing Eisenhower's first budget because defense appropriations proved larger than hoped. Dirksen favored the Bricker amendment, which would have curbed the President's treaty-making powers. Long after Sen. John W. Bricker (R, Ohio) [q.v.] had all but abandoned the cause, he reintroduced the measure in early 1956. His initiative failed. In 1954 Dirksen reversed himself and supported Eisenhower's foreign aid and St. Lawrence Seaway proposals.

Dirksen also opposed the Eisenhower Administration during the Army-McCarthy hearings of 1954. From the time of the 1950 campaign for the Senate, Dirksen had been a vociferous proponent of Sen. Joseph R. McCarthy's (R, Wisc.) [q.v.] anti-Communist investigations. Assigned to McCarthy's Permanent Investigation's Subcommittee, he generally backed the Wisconsin Senator's ambitious investigation of subversion in the Army and in 1954 attempted to forestall an open clash between McCarthy and the White House over the issue. In one last attempt to heal the growing breach between the Army and McCarthy, Dirksen hosted a luncheon for Army Secretary Robert E. Stevens [q.v.] and Republican senators in February. No lasting compromise was reached on the issues dividing them. In May, after hearings had begun, Dirksen, wishing to speed up proceedings, unsuccessfully sought to limit subcommittee testimony to only McCarthy and Stevens. He also proposed to close the hearings, but his motion failed, four-to-three, and the press, the public and television cameras observed McCarthy and his adversaries. In June Dirksen motioned, again unsuccessfully, to end the hearings after one additional week of testimony. By then, however, McCarthy had all but destroyed his credibility.

of testimony. By then, however, McCarthy had all but destroyed his credibility.

Dirksen stood by McCarthy through the Senate vote that condemned him. In July 1954 he implored the Senate not to discipline McCarthy and to act like "a judicial body and not a mob." He worked to alter the wording of the resolution from "censure" to "deplore." Visiting McCarthy during the fall, he asked his colleague to sign one of three letters of apology he had drafted; McCarthy refused. In December the Senate condemned McCarthy by a 67-22 vote; Dirksen joined 19 other GOP senators in voting against the motion. Dirksen received severe criticism from his colleagues and the national press for his advocacy of McCarthy's case. The Senator's biographer described December 1954 as the "nadir of Dirksen's career."

Dirksen's political fortunes rose spectacularly within two years after McCarthy's fall. Although erratic in his support for Eisenhower up to 1955, thereafter the Senator identified his interests closely with those of the President. Up for reelection the same year as Eisenhower, Dirksen needed the popular President's endorsement. In addition, Dirksen's former sponsor, the very conservative owner of the Chicago *Tribune*, Robert McCormick, died in April 1955. By early 1956 Dirksen stood apart from the Party's "Old Guard," managing the Administration's plan to sell old Air Force planes to Yugoslavia. Minority Leader William F. Knowland (R, Calif.) [*q.v.*] and the conservative stalwarts prevented the Yugoslav arms sale through an amendment that passed in July. Dirksen also led Administration forces backing a 1956 civil rights bill (to guarantee voting rights), a modified version of which passed the House in August. Eisenhower warmly endorsed Dirksen for his labors, and in the fall both men carried Illinois easily.

In January 1957 Dirksen became minority whip, Knowland's chief assistant. He assumed more and more of his chief's responsibilities as Knowland began his 1958 California gubernatorial campaign. Unlike Knowland, Dirksen established cordial relations with Eisenhower. During the 85th Congress, the once rebellious Dirksen ranked first in *Congressional Quarterly's* listing of senators voting in support of the Administration. Dirksen even defended presidential aide Sherman Adams [*q.v.*] on the eve of his ouster for conflict of interest.

Dirksen succeeded Knowland as minority leader in January 1959. Most Senate Republican moderates opposed his succession as one engineered by the Old Guard and its powerful leader, Styles Bridges (R, N.H.) [*q.v.*]. The moderate's candidate, John Sherman Cooper (R, Ky.) [*q.v.*], lost to Dirksen in a 20-14 party caucus vote. After his victory Dirksen made the liberal Thomas Kuchel (R, Calif.) [*q.v.*], minority whip. As demanded by the younger caucus members, he redistributed at least one important committee assignment to each senator, no matter how low his seniority. Through these moves, his mastery of legislative detail, compromise and cajolery, Dirksen moulded the once fragmented Republican minority into a cohesive unit.

Dirksen worked for the Administration with some success against overwhelming odds. The Democrats made spectacular gains in the 1958 elections; the Democratic Senate edge climbed from 48-47 to 64-34. Despite Republican losses Dirksen and the President, working in concert, frustrated an ambitious legislative program promoted by Majority Leader Lyndon B. Johnson (D, Tex.) [*q.v.*]. Twice, for example, strong Republican support for presidential vetoes killed the Democrats' 1959 housing bill. Congress ultimately passed a measure acceptable to Eisenhower.

Dirksen served as minority leader through the 1960s. His national stature increased markedly when the GOP lost control of the executive branch after 1960. By the mid-1960s Dirksen had earned much praise for his bipartisan support of Kennedy and Johnson Administration civil rights and foreign policy proposals. A colorful, dramatic speaker and story-teller, Dirksen enjoyed a national constituency which long remembered his oratorical flights. By 1967, however, his control over the Senate minority began to wane. Dirksen died in Washington in 1969. [See KENNEDY, JOHNSON, NIXON/FORD Volumes]

[JLB]

DiSALLE, MICHAEL V(INCENT)
b. Jan. 6, 1908; New York, N.Y.
Governor, Ohio, 1959-63.

The son of Italian immigrants, Michael DiSalle grew up in Toledo, Ohio. After earning a law degree at Georgetown University in 1931, DiSalle entered Toledo Democratic politics and in 1947 was appointed mayor. Three years later he lost the primary campaign for the Democratic Senate nomination. In December 1950 President Harry S. Truman appointed him director of price stabilization. DiSalle left Washington in 1952 to again to return to Ohio and campaign for the U.S. Senate. Running ahead of the national ticket, he nonetheless lost to the popular Republican incumbent, John W. Bricker [q.v.]. DiSalle returned to Washington in early December to serve as administrator of the Economic Stabilization Agency for the remaining six weeks of the Truman presidency. [See TRUMAN Volume]

Out of power after 1953, DiSalle nevertheless commanded the loyalty of many state and national Democrats who were dissatisfied with Ohio Democratic Gov. Frank J. Lausche's [q.v.] leadership on partisan issues. In December 1954 DiSalle received 19 votes for the chairmanship of the Democratic National Committee.

DiSalle played a major role in the 1956 Democratic vice presidential nomination. After Adlai E. Stevenson [q.v.] opened the vice presidential nomination to the Convention, DiSalle agreed to nominate Sen. Estes Kefauver (D, Tenn.) [q.v.]. In so doing he ignored Sen. John F. Kennedy (D, Mass.) [q.v.], Kefauver's main opponent. DiSalle's action effectively committed 58 of Ohio's 64 votes to Kefauver, who narrowly defeated the Massachusetts Senator on the second ballot.

In the fall of 1956 DiSalle again ran for Ohio governor. During the campaign he devoted several weeks trying to reinvigorate the state party organization and allotted still more time to touring rural counties, expecting to gain from farmers' unhappiness over Eisenhower's agriculture policies. The strategy failed as Eisenhower swept all parts of the state. Republican gubernatorial nominee Attorney General C. William O'Neill won 56% of the vote.

DiSalle's opportunity came two years later. Poorly staffed, indecisive and ill, O'Neill proved an ineffective governor. In a monumental political error, O'Neill warmly endorsed a business coalition that placed on the November 1958 ballot a "right-to-work" proposal banning union shops. The referendum evoked vehement, well-organized union opposition and failed to engender expected support from Catholics and non-union laborers. It lost by one million votes. Attempting to buck a nationwide Democratic trend, both O'Neill and Sen. Bricker lost their reelection campaigns. DiSalle was the first Democratic governor clearly identifiable with the politics of the national party since 1920.

DiSalle's sense of triumph proved short-lived. His predecessor's policy of borrowing to meet expenses (the state ran a $100 million budget deficit in 1958) forced DiSalle to raise corporate and sales taxes in 1959, an immensely unpopular decision. Yet, despite the increased revenues, DiSalle alienated union officials and liberal Democrats by delaying action on the expansion of social services. He gained nothing in popularity by opposing capital punishment and employing convicted murderers to work at the governor's mansion.

Still smarting from his narrow 1956 convention defeat, Kennedy maneuvered a reluctant DiSalle into endorsing his presidential candidacy in January 1960. Kennedy won the nomination and, with DiSalle's encouragement, selected Senate majority leader Lyndon B. Johnson (D, Tex.) [q.v.] as his running mate.

The Democratic ticket lost Ohio, a defeat historian Theodore H. White said was Kennedy's greatest disappointment of the fall campaign. Surveys later suggested that Kennedy's Catholicism hurt him, but most experts and DiSalle himself blamed the showing on the Governor's 1959 tax increase. The Republicans recaptured control of the legislature and made the Governor's last two years in office difficult.

DiSalle lost his 1962 reelection campaign by a then record margin of 555,669 votes. He returned to law practice in Columbus and remained active in Democratic politics. However, he never again sought elective office. [See KENNEDY Volume]

[JLB]

For further information:
Michael V. DiSalle. *Second Choice* (New York. 1966).
John H. Fenton. "The Right-To-Work Vote in Ohio," *Midwest Journal of Political Science* 3 (August. 1959). pp. 241-53.
Thomas A. Flinn. "How Mr. Nixon Took Ohio." *Western Political Quarterly* 15 (June. 1962). pp. 274-79.

DIXON, EDGAR H.

b. Dec. 16, 1904; Hackensack, N.J.
d. Aug. 3, 1962; New York, N.Y.
President, Middle Southern Utilities, Inc., 1949-59.

Dixon's formal schooling ended with graduation from Hackensack High School in 1922. Starting at Electric Bond and Share Co. as a $70-a-month clerk, he took night courses in English and accounting at New York University. By 1934 Dixon was serving as financial clerk and assistant treasurer of a number of Electric Bond subsidiaries. He was secretary-treasurer and director of Electric Power and Light Corp. from 1935 to 1944 and served as president from 1944 to 1949. Dixon became the first president of Middle Southern Utilities, Inc., in 1949, doubling its profits over the next 10 years.

In 1954 Middle Southern Utilities joined the Southern Co., headed by Eugene Yates, to form the Mississippi Valley Generating Co. Their purpose was to construct a plant at West Memphis, Ark., to sell the Atomic Energy Commission (AEC) 600,000 kilowatts of power annually. Dixon's firm owned 80% of Mississippi Valley and Yates's 20%.

Under the terms of the proposed Dixon-Yates contract, power would be fed into the Tennessee Valley Authority (TVA) system for distribution to consumers, including the AEC. It marked the first time in its history that the TVA would act as a power distributor rather than power generator. Previous contracts between the agency and private companies had been un-

successful. The companies had exceeded agreed-upon costs and had not delivered the required power.

Dixon and Yates started negotiating with the AEC and the Bureau of the Budget in June 1954. Haste was required because President Eisenhower had promised a 600,000-kilowatt reduction in TVA commitments by 1957. The two government agencies, therefore, solicited no other bids. They ignored a proposal by Walter von Tresckow, head of an alternate power syndicate in New York, as well as a TVA suggestion that it could supply the power for $5 million less than private sources. The TVA was not told the terms of the Dixon-Yates contract until after it had been negotiated.

Democratic senators denounced the agreement as an attempt to undermine the TVA. In late 1954 they uncovered possible violations of the Holding Company Act by Dixon's and Yates's southern subsidiaries. In February 1955 Sen. Lister Hill (D, Ala.) [q.v.] discovered that Adolphe H. Wenzell, a vice president of the First Boston Corp., which was arranging financing for Dixon-Yates, was a consultant to the Bureau of the Budget at the time negotiations were in progress. His name was absent from a list that the AEC had released revealing the names of those who had worked on the contract. Questioned by Sen. Estes Kefauver (D, Tenn.) [q.v.] in hearings held by the Judiciary Committee's Subcommittee on Antitrust and Monopoly in July 1955, Director of the Budget Rowland Hughes [q.v.] stated he thought Wenzell's role too insignificant to mention.

After Wenzell openly acknowledged his dual role and stated he had worked with Hughes, the President canceled the contract in July 1955. His action followed an announcement by Memphis that it intended to build a $100 million municipally owned power plant. The following year Dixon and Yates brought suit against the U.S. for $3 million in reported expenditures. In June 1959 the U.S. Claims Court awarded the Mississippi Valley Generating Co. $1.8 million. The decision was reversed by the Supreme Court in January 1961. Throughout the controversy and thereafter, Dixon defended the contract. He remained one of the most sought-after utilities executives in the United States.

[MJS]

For further information:
Jason L. Finkle, *The President Makes a Decision: A Study of Dixon-Yates* (Ann Arbor, 1960).
David A. Frier, *Conflict of Interest in the Eisenhower Administration* (Ames, Iowa, 1969).
Aaron Waldavsky, *Dixon-Yates: A Study in Power Politics* (New Haven, 1962).

DODD, THOMAS J(OSEPH)

b. May 15, 1907; Norwich, Conn.
d. May 24, 1971; Old Lyme, Conn.
Democratic Representative, Conn., 1953-57; Democratic Senator, Conn., 1959-71.

Dodd received a Bachelor of Philosophy degree from Providence College in 1930 and an LL.B. degree from the Yale law school in 1933. From 1933 to 1935 he was a special agent with the FBI. In 1935 Dodd organized the National Youth Administration in Connecticut, and from 1938 to 1945 he served as an assistant to the Attorney General. During the postwar period Dodd was executive trial counsel at the Nuremberg war crimes trials. He unsuccessfully sought the Connecticut Democratic gubernatorial nomination in 1946 and 1948.

In 1952 Dodd won election to the U.S. House of Representatives, where he proved to be one of Congress's staunchest anti-Communists. In 1953 Dodd was named to the seven-man Select Committee to Investigate Soviet Seizure of the Baltic Countries, which held hearings in 1953 and early 1954. The following year he was assigned to that panel's successor, the nine-member Select Committee on Communist Aggression. The Committee's report, in August 1954, recommended that the U.S. call a conference of "free world" nations for the purpose of breaking off trade and diplomatic relations with Communist countries. During the same year he chaired a special subcommittee probing alleged incarceration and abuse of American citizens in Com-

munist China. In November Dodd suggested that the U.S. retaliate by urging the West to apply a trade embargo against mainland China. Two years later he successfully amended a farm surplus disposal bill to restrict surplus transactions to "friendly countries."

Although Dodd was a strong anti-Communist, in 1954 he criticized a bill recommended by Attorney General Herbert Brownell [q.v.], permitting the Attorney General to order wiretapping in suspected cases of espionage, sabotage and other threats to national security. He warned that "if this bill is passed, the abuses which have [existed] for many years in this country will go right on. . . . This bill is a supreme example of government by man instead of by law." He voted for the bill only after the addition of an amendment requiring federal court approval for a tap. Dodd voted against a bill giving Congress and U.S. district courts authority to grant immunity to congressional and court witnesses. The measure was aimed at witnesses taking the Fifth Amendment against self-incrimination in hearings involving national security. Under the bill's provisions such persons would have the alternatives of either testifying or going to jail. Dodd stated that "many of us feel that the present bill has been poorly drawn and that it presents grave constitutional implications." On the other hand, he backed the Communist Control Act of 1954, which outlawed the Communist Party.

Dodd compiled a generally liberal record on domestic issues. A strong supporter of civil rights, in 1956 he backed a controversial amendment offered by Rep. Adam Clayton Powell, Jr. (D, N.Y.) [q.v.] to a school construction aid bill. The Powell amendment would have barred aid to states operating racially segregated schools. Dodd voted both for the amendment, which was adopted, and the final bill, which was defeated. In 1956 he also supported an Administration bill aimed against racial discrimination, particularly in voting.

In 1956 Dodd unsuccessfully ran for the U.S. Senate. The following year he represented three members of the Teamsters Union in an unsuccessful suit to block

James R. Hoffa's [q.v.] accession to the presidency of the organization. In 1958 he again ran for the Senate on a platform stressing the need for a strengthened military and a program to combat unemployment and inflation. He won by 146,000 votes.

Dodd maintained his strong anti-Communist stance as a senator. In a letter to President Eisenhower in January 1959, he warned against a bilateral conference with the Soviet Union on the ground that it would divide the U.S. from its allies. In 1960 he was a leader of opposition to the ratification of the Antarctic Treaty with the Soviet Union and 10 other nations. The purpose of the pact was to ensure that Antarctica would be used for peaceful purposes, but opponents maintained that it did not have guarantees against Soviet military operations on that continent.

In 1960 Dodd and Sen. Kenneth B. Keating (R, N.Y.) [q.v.], as members of the Judiciary Committee's Internal Security Subcommittee, introduced a four-part internal security bill. The measure widened the definition of illegal espionage and of foreign agents under the 1958 Foreign Agents Registration Act. It defined the 1940 Smith Act prohibition against forming a group advocating the violent overthrow of the government as applying to the organization's ongoing activities as well as its initial formation. This represented an effort to overturn the Supreme Court's 1957 interpretation of the Smith Act, which held that the statute did not outlaw advocacy of forcible overthrow as an abstract doctrine. In addition, the bill permitted the Secretary of State to declare certain areas off limits for travel and, after a hearing, to deny passports to Communists and Communist sympathizers whom he believed might endanger U.S. security. The House passed a similar bill, but the Senate did not act. Most of the Dodd-Keating proposals, however, became law in 1961 and 1962.

As chairman of the Internal Security Subcommittee, in 1960 Dodd conducted an investigation into alleged Communist influence in the nuclear test ban movement. He ordered Nobel Prize-winning chemist Dr. Linus C. Pauling [q.v.] to produce the names of persons who helped him circulate a 1957 petition calling for a test-ban agreement, but Pauling declined to do so.

Dodd backed most social welfare and civil rights legislation during his first two years in the Senate. He voted to override Eisenhower's vetoes of housing legislation in 1959 and of an area redevelopment bill in 1960. Dodd supported a boost in the minimum wage from $1 to $1.25, a federal school aid bill, a health care program for the aged funded by social security and the Administration's civil rights bill in 1960.

During the early 1960s Dodd, as chairman of the Judiciary Committee's Juvenile Delinquency Subcommittee, conducted a probe of the influence of television upon juvenile delinquency. Subsequently he was a strong supporter of the Vietnam war and of gun control legislation. In 1967 the Senate censured him for misuse of campaign funds. Dodd unsuccessfully ran for reelection as an independent in 1970. He died on May 24, 1971. [See KENNEDY, JOHNSON Volumes]

[MLL]

DODGE, JOSEPH M(ORRELL)

b. Nov. 18, 1890; Detroit, Mich.
d. Dec. 2, 1964; Detroit, Mich.
Director of the Budget, January 1953-April 1954.

Following his graduation from high school in 1908, Joseph Dodge worked as a bank messenger and in various clerical positions before becoming a bank examiner for the Michigan State Banking Commission in 1911. In 1917 he joined a Dodge (no relation) auto dealership as general manager. He remained until 1932, when he returned to banking as vice president of the First National Bank of Detroit. The next year he became president of the Bank of Detroit.

During World War II Dodge held a number of posts with government agencies, the most important of which was chairman of the War Contracts Board. At the War's end he went to Germany as financial adviser to Gen. Lucius Clay [q.v.], commander of the Allied military government. Returning to the Bank of Detroit in 1946,

Dodge was summoned by President Harry S. Truman in 1949 to play a similar role under Gen. Douglas MacArthur in Japan. Dodge's program of fiscal austerity helped stabilize the Japanese currency and rebuild the country's shattered economy.

In November 1952 Dodge was named budget director by President-elect Dwight D. Eisenhower, who shared the Detroit banker's conservative fiscal views. Dodge's first public statement, on Jan. 6, 1953, warned against expecting any "60-day miracle" in the way of budget cuts, but he devoted himself to reducing government spending during his 15-month tenure. He directed all federal agencies to submit revised estimates of expenditures by driving "for greater efficiency and reduced costs" in order to cut the budget deficit of $9.9 billion projected by the outgoing Truman Administration for fiscal 1954. Under Dodge the deficit for that year was trimmed to $3.1 billion, although the total budget did not fall under $70 billion as President-elect Eisenhower had pledged it would. Among Dodge's methods for raising revenues and cutting costs were increased rents in public housing and admissions to national parks and curtailed use of government automobiles. He also promoted economy in defense spending and opposed plans by Republican members of Congress to cut taxes on 1953 income.

Dodge resigned as budget director in April 1954 to return to his Detroit bank. Later that year he became involved in the congressoinal investigation of the controversial Dixon-Yates affair. Edgar Dixon [q.v.] and Eugene Yates were utility executives seeking a government subsidy and contract to supply power to the Atomic Energy Commission. Dodge had originally suggested having a private company supply the power instead of the Tennessee Valley Authority and had named Adolphe Wenzell of the First Boston Corp, to study the matter. The choice of Wenzell became a subject of controversy when it was revealed that his bank was to finance the Dixon-Yates combine. Testifying before the Senate Subcommittee on Antitrust and Monopoly, Dodge maintained that Wenzell had not influenced his decision on the contract.

In the fall of 1954 Dodge returned to government as a special assistant to President Eisenhower on foreign economic policy. In January he became chairman of the Administration's Council on Foreign Economic Policy, which had been set up at his recommendation. He served in this post until July 1956. His major task was coordinating the disparate activities of the dozens of U.S. agencies involved in international economic affairs. Dodge died in December 1964 at the age of 74.

[TO]

DOERFER, JOHN C(HARLES)
b. Nov. 30, 1904; Milwaukee, Wisc.
Commissioner, Federal Communications Commission, April 1953-March 1960; Chairman July 1957-March 1960.

The son of a German immigrant, John C. Doerfer worked his way through the University of Wisconsin, where he graduated in 1928. He received a law degree from Marquette in 1934 and then opened a private law practice in a Milwaukee suburb. From 1940 to 1949 he served as Milwaukee city attorney; in 1949 he became chairman of the state's Public Service Commission.

President Eisenhower named Doerfer to a one-year vacancy on the Federal Communications Commission (FCC) in 1953 and to a full seven-year term in 1954. At the time some liberals denounced the appointment as a White House effort to placate the then powerful Sen. Joseph R. McCarthy (R, Wisc.) [q.v.] The Senate, however, confirmed Doerfer in April.

Doerfer showed his support for McCarthy's anti-Communist crusade in 1953 by promoting an FCC investigation of an Erie, Pa., TV station license owned by Edward Lamb [q.v.], a wealthy Toledo attorney with a leftist past. FCC hearings in 1954-55 proved embarrassing to Lamb's opponents. Four government witnesses who had told of Lamb's Communist connections confessed to committing perjury at the request of an FCC attorney. Even McCarthy, initially enthused over the affair, admitted by early

1955 that the FCC had no case. In December 1955 FCC examiner Herbert Sharfman exonerated Lamb and recommended the Erie license's renewal.

Like other regulatory commissioners of the Eisenhower Administration, Doerfer sought to minimize governmental interference with business. He did so despite a simultaneous mass communications revolution that made TV an integral part of American life. Doerfer repeatedly expressed doubts about legislation which would have granted the FCC authority to regulate the national networks. Rather, he believed competition between networks would eventually improve program content. Under his chairmanship the FCC issued and renewed station licenses without regard to earlier FCC precedents requiring "public interest," locally-oriented news and cultural programming.

In February 1957 the FCC announced plans for testing a subscription television service (PAY-TV) in selected markets. This action aroused the opposition of the major networks and Congress. Championing the cause of "free TV," House Judiciary Committee Chairman Emanuel Celler (D, N.Y.) [q.v.] denied in a July 1957 letter to Doerfer that the FCC had the power to conduct PAY-TV tests. Popular commercial programs occasionally ended with an announcement predicting the show's demise of PAY-TV became an actuality. At first Doerfer stood firm with the 6-to-1 FCC majority favoring the tests. But in January 1958 he told a House committee that he did not favor PAY-TV if it threatened to replace free TV. By July 1958 Doerfer relented to the pressure, and the FCC delayed indefinitely authorization of the tests.

Early in 1958 newspaper columnist Drew Pearson [q.v.] and House Commerce Committee counsel Bernard Schwartz [q.v.] accused Doerfer of conflict of interest. Pearson and Schwartz related that during a 1954 visit, Doerfer had allowed an Oklahoma City TV station to pay his air fare and hotel costs. He then had the FCC reimburse his personal account for the same trip. Further inquiries by Schwartz showed that the Commissioner's Spokane, Ore., hotel bill had been paid by the National Association of Radio and Television Broadcasters (NARTB). The NARTB had also loaned Doerfer $575. For the five-day visit, it spent $1,080 on Doerfer. Schwartz revealed other improprieties in January and February 1958. FCC members had received free color TV sets from industry executives. (Doerfer defended the gifts as necessary "tools of the trade.") In August 1955 George Storer, owner of 13 radio and TV stations, had provided his private plane and home for Doerfer's use and covered other expenses relating to a Doerfer trip to Miami.

Doerfer survived criticism stemming from the exposes. The press largely ignored the revelations. A 1952 amendment to the FCC law, liberally interpreted by Doerfer and the conptroller general, permitted commissioners to accept honorariums. Hence, Eisenhower refused to remove his designated FCC chief. Schwartz's tactics, both as an investigator and interrogator, also offended many and created sympathy for Doerfer. Attention soon turned away from Doerfer's hearings to another, more serious, conflict-of-interest scandal involving FCC Commissioner Richard A. Mack [q.v.]. Nevertheless, the House Commerce Committee warned Doerfer not to continue his close fraternization with the industry.

Subsequently the FCC chairman had to deal with a series of scandals in the television industry. In the fall of 1959 several contestants on TV quiz shows (once the highest rated programs) confessed to having been given questions and answers in advance. The quiz show scandals shocked the nation and created demands for the producers' criminal prosecution and over-all program reform. In October Doerfer denied any FCC responsibility for "policing" the shows. Rumors concerning their irregularities had reached FCC in July 1958. The Commission had asked the three networks about them but the networks disclaimed knowledge of the alledged practices. Doerfer told a House Commerce subcommittee that the best response to all "objectionable programming" would be "greater incentive for the exercise of self-regulatory restraints."

Early in March 1960, the *New York*

Herald Tribune reported that Doerfer had spent a portion of his previous month's vacation aboard George Storer's yacht. Before the House Commerce Committee a day later. Doerfer admitted to and defended accepting Storer's hospitality. He had not clearly violated the law, but he had acted against the subcommittee's 1958 recommendation that he discontinue his close and renumerative contacts with broadcasting executives. This time Eisenhower immediately requested and secured his resignation. Doerfer accepted a management position with the Storer Broadcasting Co. Congress later in the year passed new, stringent regulations on FCC honorariums.

[JLB]

For further information:
David Frier. *Conflict of Interest in the Eisenhower Administration* (Ames. Iowa, 1969).

DORFMAN, PAUL
b. 1902 (?)
d. March 12, 1971; Chicago, Ill.
Labor figure.

A former prizefighter, member of the Al Capone mob, and associate of such underworld figures as John Dioguardi (Johnny Dio), Paul "Red" Dorfman took over the Waste Materials Handlers Federated Labor Union in 1949, following the murder of its president. That same year he established the Union Casualty Agency with his stepson, Allan, and his wife as the principal agents. Already a leading crime figure in Chicago, Dorfman sought to expand his power through his close personal relationship with Jimmy Hoffa [*q.v.*].

In late January 1959 the Senate Committee on Improper Relations in the Labor or Management Field, chaired by Sen. John McClellan (D, Ark.) [*q.v.*], investigated an insurance scheme ostensibly fashioned by Dorfman and Hoffa to swindle members of the Teamster's Union. According to the Committee, shortly after Dorfman established the Union Casualty Agency, the company bid to handle the welfare pension fund of the huge Central States Drivers Council and Local 1031 of the International

Brotherhood of Electrical Workers. Hoffa arranged for Dorfman's company to obtain the contract. Through testimony it was shown that the Dorfman family made $4 million in commissions and fees as a result of the deal. At the same time the Teamster's benefits were reduced and their premiums raised in 1952. The Committee counsel, Robert F. Kennedy [*q.v.*], revealed that a Chicago Internal Revenue agent had been discharged for having given his personal approval to Allan Dorfman's income tax returns.

Paul Dorfman repeatedly took the Fifth Amendment when he appeared in front of the Committee on Jan. 30, 1959. Robert Kennedy asked him whether the contract that Hoffa gave him was a reward for Dorfman's aid in enabling the Teamster leader to amass power in the Chicago area. Although Dorfman refused to answer this question, the McClellan Committee claimed that a Hoffa-Dorfman deal did occur.

The Committee also charged that Dorfman had helped Hoffa increase his power in New York City. Dorfman persuaded his friend Anthony Doria, an official in the United Automobile Workers-American Federation of Labor (there was another group associated with the Congress of Industrial Organizations) to issue a charter for a new local in New York organized by Sam Zachman, a friend of Dorfman who had ties with organized crime. Involved in the actual setting up of the local was Johnny Dio, one of Hoffa's operatives and another close friend of Dorfman. Dio eventually pushed Zachman out and took over the union himself. He organized additional locals, staffed them with ex-convicts, and he then became the union's regional director. The employes of the businesses organized were forced to join the union. Mostly blacks and Puerto Ricans; they paid a $25 initiation fee and a $3.50 a month dues; the companies paid them the minimum wage with no benefits. By setting up this extortion operation, Dorfman and Dio provided Hoffa with a power base in the New York area.

In December 1958 George Meany placed Dorfman's union under AFL-CIO trusteeship. The federation president then removed Dorfman in August 1959 from his office as secretary-treasurer and from the union itself. Meany based his decision on the fact that the Dorfman family had derived personal advantage from union funds deposited in their insurance company.

Revelations of the activities of union officials such as Paul Dorfman led to a public demand for legislation to prevent such abuses. In September 1959, Congress passed the Landrum-Griffin Act. The law's anticorruption provision subjected union officials found guilty of misusing funds to stiff fines and prison terms. It also prohibited certain types of criminal offenders from holding union offices. However, it soon proved difficult to enforce.

Following the McClellan Committee's revelations, the Dorfman insurance company was reorganized, allegedly to hide its activities. Paul Dorfman devoted most of his time to that business. In 1964 a San Francisco grand jury indicted him and his son on a charge of extorting $100,000 from a San Francisco insurance man. The jury acquitted them on the charge. Allan Dorfman was tried with Jimmy Hoffa in 1964 on a jury tampering charge and was acquitted. Paul Dorfman died in March 1971.

[JB]

For further information:
Walter Sheridan. *The Fall and Rise of Jimmy Hoffa* (New York. 1972)

DOUGLAS, PAUL H(OWARD)
b. March 26, 1892; Salem, Mass.
d. Sept. 24, 1976; Washington, D.C.
Democratic Senator, Ill. 1949-67

Reared on a farm in northern Maine, Paul Douglas worked his way through Bowdoin College, graduating in 1913. He obtained an M.A. and a Ph.D. in economics from Columbia University and taught economics at a number of colleges before joining the prestigious University of Chicago faculty in 1920. Douglas won professional renown for his scholarly works, the most notable of which were *Wages of the Family* (1925), *Real Wages in the United States, 1890-1926* (1930) and *Theory of Wages* (1934). He entered the political arena in 1929, when he undertook an investigation of Chicago utilities magnate Samuel Insull, then at the peak of his power. Persistent in the face of harsh opposition from the financial and political establishment, Douglas displayed the doggedly independent liberalism that became his trademark as a political figure.

During the Depression Douglas influenced public policy through his service on a variety of commissions and committees. In 1930 he was a secretary to the Pennsylvania Commission on Unemployment and the New York Committee to Stabilize Employment. From 1931 to 1933 he was a member of the Illinois Housing Commission, and he helped to formulate the state's Utilities Act of 1933, Old Age Pension Act of 1935 and Unemployment Insurance Act of 1937. He also participated in the drafting of the national Social Security Act of 1935.

In 1938 Douglas won election as a Chicago alderman with the support of intellectuals and upper middle class reformers from the Hyde Park area as well as the Democratic machine. In office he alienated the regular organization with his exposures of graft and corruption and lost the 1942 Democratic nomination for U.S. senator to a machine-backed candidate. Immediately following his defeat Douglas enlisted in the Marine Corps as a private, despite his age (50) and his Quaker faith. (He had been a pacifist at the time of World War I.) He was assigned to the Pacific theater and was wounded at Okinawa. Douglas again ran for the Senate in 1948 on a platform advocating a federal housing program, federal aid to education, repeal of the Taft-Hartley Act and support of President Truman's foreign policy. He defeated the Republican incumbent by 400,000 votes. [See TRUMAN Volume]

Douglas soon became a leader of the Senate's small liberal bloc. His voting record consistently won the approval of the AFL-CIO and the Americans for Democratic Action. During the Eisenhower Administration Douglas called for legislative offensives along numerous domestic fronts, including civil rights, tax reform, stimulative economics and social welfare. He frequently pointed out military waste and public works extravagance. He was frustrated as much by his Democratic colleagues in Congress as by the Republican Administration. Douglas frequently stood alone in a crusade or in the company of a handful of fellow liberals.

Douglas was one of the Senate's most outspoken proponents of civil rights legislation. He persistently and unsuccessfully sought to pave the way for such laws by amending the Senate's Rule 22, which Southerners used to filibuster civil rights proposals to death. Under Rule 22 debate could be ended only by a two-thirds vote, a proportion civil rights supporters could not achieve. Douglas's efforts to substitute cloture by a simple majority consistently failed as did moderate revisions, such as cloture by a three-fifths vote or after 15 days of debate.

During the first term of the Eisenhower Administration, civil rights proposals got nowhere in the Senate. In August 1956 Douglas led a group of northern liberals who tried and failed to put a strong civil rights plank into the Democratic platform. Douglas was disinclined to moderate civil rights goals in order to mollify Southern Democrats. Commenting in the fall of 1957 on reports that forced school desegregation might lead Southern segregationists to form a third party, he said he "would welcome it" because "it would mean getting the Dixiecrats out of our party."

Douglas supported the Civil Rights Act of 1957, although it was not as far-reaching as his own proposals. He fought unsuccessfully against an amendment mandating a jury trial in cases in which a court injunction had been violated. He voted for the final bill in spite of its dilution because it contained some protections for voting rights and established a civil rights division within the Justice Department. "The bill was indeed weak," he later said, "but it gave the possibility of federal aid to hard-pressed Negroes who, lacking money and at the bottom of the social totem pole, could not adequately defend their rights through expensive suits after the offense had been committed."

In January 1959 Douglas headed a 15-member Senate group that introduced a measure empowering the Attorney General to initiate lawsuits to halt illegal bias and providing $40 million a year to help finance school districts trying to desegregate in the face of state opposition. The bill failed to pass at the time, but its major provisions were included in the omnibus Civil Rights Act of 1964.

In economic affairs Douglas was a vocal and knowledgeable spokesman for liberal Senate Democrats. He was defeated several times in his attempts to legislate sizable tax cuts to stimulate the stagnant economy and reduce unemployment. Douglas was the Senate's foremost critic of tax loopholes, or "truckholes" as he called them. Named to the Finance Committee in 1956 after being kept off several years, Douglas and Sen. Albert Gore (D,Tenn.) [q.v.] were frequently a minority of two protesting the Committee's enactment of tax preferences for corporations and wealthy individuals. Douglas's chief target was the 27½% oil depletion allowance. His efforts to reduce or eliminate this provision were easily defeated in the Committee and on the Senate floor.

Douglas enjoyed more success in his promotion of area redevelopment legislation. Parallel to his continuous criticism of "pork barrel" public works projects that he considered expensive and unnecessary, he conceived and gathered support for an ambitious federal program to reinvigorate the economies of chronically depressed regions. The principal featues of Douglas's area redevelopment plan were public works, technical assistance and long-term credit for local industry and the retraining of jobless workers. Douglas first introduced his measure in 1955 with the textile and coal-producing areas of the Northeast in mind; in 1956 he broadened its scope to reach the depressed agricultural regions of the South as well.

Area redevelopment passed the Senate, 60-30, in 1956 but remained bottled up in the House Rules Committee when the 84th Congress adjourned. Congress passed it in 1958 and 1960. Both times it was vetoed by President Eisenhower, who objected to the breadth of the measure and said that it would "greatly diminish local responsibility." The Area Redevelopment Act was signed into law by President John F. Kennedy in 1961. Douglas listed it as his greatest achievement during his over 20 years in Congress.

A vigorous anti-Communist, Douglas was a member of the Committee of One Million Against the Admission of Communist China to the U.N. In 1954 he called for U.S. intervention on the side of France in the Indochina war. He later supported Secretary of State John Foster Dulles's [q.v.] efforts to build the Southeast Asia Treaty Organization. During Soviet Premier Nikita S. Khrushchev's visit to America in 1959, Douglas joined several other members of Congress on the Committee for Freedom of All Peoples, which called for Americans to observe Premier Khrushchev's visit with a period of mourning for victims of Communist oppression.

Douglas was reelected in 1960 by a margin of 420,000 votes. In the next six years he actively supported the Kennedy and Johnson Administrations' social welfare programs: aid to depressed areas, education, and the poor. The Senator continued his personal battles for tax reform and truth-in-lending legislation. In 1966 he lost his Senate seat to Republican Charles Percy. [See KENNEDY, JOHNSON Volumes]

[TO]

For further information:
Paul H. Douglas, *In the Fullness of Time* (New York, 1971).

DOUGLAS, WILLIAM O(RVILLE)
b. Oct. 16, 1898: Maine, Minn.
Associate Justice, U.S. Supreme Court, 1939-75.

The longest tenured justice in the history of the Supreme Court, William O. Douglas grew up in Yakima, Wash., and worked his way through Columbia law school, graduating second in his class in 1925. He worked briefly for a major Wall Street law firm and then taught at Columbia and Yale law schools, where he developed a reputation for his studies of bankruptcy. Named a member of the Securities and Exchange Commission in January 1936 and its chairman in 1937, Douglas pushed the reorganization of stock exchanges and instituted various reforms to protect investors. President Franklin Roosevelt appointed Douglas to the Supreme Court in March 1939. Douglas was confirmed as an associate justice the following month.

In his earliest years on the Court, Douglas joined a majority of his colleagues in sanctioning the expansion of federal government power over the economy and in sustaining various New Deal regulatory measures. A recognized expert in financial and corporate law, the Justice wrote many influential Court opinions in these areas. Yet, Douglas became best known as an ardent defender of individual liberties, one whose commitment to personal freedoms grew over the years. In both his voting pattern and his judicial philosophy, he was closely aligned with Justice Hugo Black [q.v.], but in their last years on the Court together, Douglas, according to many observers, surpassed even Black in consistently safeguarding individual freedoms against government interference. [See TRUMAN volume]

Throughout Douglas's career changes in his views were in the direction of giving greater scope to constitutional liberties. He long regarded First Amendment freedoms, for example, as essential to the maintenance of a free and democratic society. During the 1950s Douglas shifted from the view that government could restrict free speech under extreme circumstances to the position that government could regulate a person's actions, but could not prohibit any form of free expression. In June 1958, for example, he wrote the majority opinion in a decision overturning the State Department's policy of denying passports to members of the Communist Party. Douglas stated that the Department did not have congressional authorization for this practice. In addition, he ruled that the right to travel was protected by the Fifth Amendment's due process clause. That same month Douglas wrote a dissenting opinion in two cases where the Court upheld the dismissal of public employes who had refused to answer questions about possible Communist Party affiliations.

Though he gave a special place to First Amendment rights, Justice Douglas was hardly less solicitous of other guarantees of individual rights. He generally interpreted the criminal procedure guarantees in the Bill of Rights broadly to the benefit of the individual. Throughout the 1950s, for example, he favored extending the right to counsel to all. In March 1956 the Justice wrote a dissenting opinion when the Court upheld a federal law under which the government could force a witness to testify in security cases by promising him immunity from prosecution. Douglas asserted that the Fifth ᵒAmendment made it unconstitutional for Congress to compel anyone to confess to a crime, even with an immunity guarantee. His opinion for the Court in a November 1959 case held that mere suspicion that someone had committed a felony was not sufficient grounds for his arrest. Douglas was also a strong supporter of the right of equal protection under the law, and he unhesitatingly voted with his colleagues in May 1954 to hold racial segregation a violation of the 14th Amendment.

Often a controversial figure, Douglas became a center of conflict in June 1953, when he granted convicted atomic spies Julius and Ethel Rosenberg [q.v.] a stay of execution. The month before the Court had refused for the third time to review the Rosenbergs' conviction. Nevertheless, Douglas granted the stay when new legal arguments were presented on their behalf. Chief Justice Fred Vinson [q.v.] then called the Court into special session. After hearing arguments the Court vacated Douglas's stay. On June 17 Rep. William M. Wheeler (D, Ga.) introduced a resolution to impeach Douglas for his action, but the House Judiciary Committee killed the resolution in July.

One of the more colorful justices on the Court, Douglas was a vigorous and seemingly tireless man who always disagreed with his colleagues' assertions that the Court's workload was too great. He used his spare time to travel widely and to explore the outdoors. The Justice became known to the public as an enthusiastic woodsman and conservationist as well as a judge. A prolific author, Douglas wrote dozens of articles and books on his travels, environmental concerns and the law and was occasionally outspoken on current affairs.

In the 1960s a liberal Court majority gradually adopted many of Douglas's views on criminal rights. The Justice continued to oppose antisubversive measures, maintained his absolutist views on the First Amendment and helped move the Court to new legal frontiers with rulings involving state anticontraceptive laws and the rights of illegitimate children. He retired from the Court in November 1975 after suffering a debilitating stroke. [See KENNEDY, JOHNSON, NIXON/FORD Volumes]

Though all commentators agreed on Douglas's brilliance, his critics over the years charged him with being too doctrinaire in his approach to legal issues. They also disliked Douglas's opinions, which were often brief and colloquial and without much formal legal analysis. The Justice's defenders, however, pointed to the remarkable range of his mind and interests and argued that his decisions reflected a legal realism that attempted to make the law responsive to the new problems and needs of a changing society. Douglas, according to law professor Michael Sovern, insisted that "the law must be shaped to bear witness to the moral development of society" and sought "a simple and uncompromising focus on basic values" in Court decisions. As a result, he achieved "an original and profound vision of the role of law in society."

[CAB]

For further information:
Vern Countryman, *The Judicial Record of Justice William O. Douglas* (Cambridge, Mass. 1974).
John P. Frank, "William O. Douglas," in Leon Friedman and Fred L. Israel, eds., *The Justices of the United States Supreme Court, 1789-1969* (New York, 1969), Vol. 4.
"Mr. Justice William O. Douglas," *Columbia Law Review*, 74 (April, 1974), pp. 341-411.
"Mr. Justice William O. Douglas," *Washington Law Review*, 39 (Spring, 1964), pp. 1-114.
"William O. Douglas," *Yale Law Journal*, 73 (May, 1964), pp. 915-998.

DOWLING, WALTER C(ECIL)

b. Aug. 4, 1905; Atkinson, Ga.
Ambassador to South Korea, May
1956-October 1959; Ambassador to
West Germany, January 1960-April
1963.

Following his graduation from Mercer University in 1925, Dowling worked as a bank clerk. He joined the Foreign Service in 1932 and over the next 12 years served as vice consul in Oslo, Lisbon, Rome and Rio de Janeiro. In 1945 he was transferred to the office of the U.S. representative to the Advisory Council for Italy. The following year Dowling was assigned to the State Department's division of South European affairs and by 1947 was its associate director. In 1949 he was appointed counselor of legation in Vienna. Three years later Dowling became deputy U.S. high commissioner for Austria; in 1953 he represented the Secretary of State in negotiations for an Austrian peace treaty, eventually signed in 1955. Dowling was appointed deputy U.S. high commissioner for Germany in July 1953 and in 1955 became minister-counselor of the American Embassy at Bonn.

Eisenhower appointed Dowling ambassador to South Korea in May 1955. Six months later the U.S. and South Korea signed a treaty of friendship, commerce and navigation designed to further development of economic relations between the two countries. Relations between the U.S. and Korea became strained at the end of the decade because of repressive measures pushed through the South Korean Parliament. In January 1959 Dowling was called to Washington to protest the tactics used in the passage of the Korean National Security Act. The law was one of two measures abolishing local elections and suppressing opposition newspapers. The statutes had been passed in December 1958 after specially hired guards had forceably removed members of the opposition party from Parliament.

In February 1959 the State Department ordered Dowling to return to Seoul to mediate a dispute between South Korea and Japan. Japan's plan to return thousands of Koreans living in that country to Communist North Korea incensed South Korean President Syngman Rhee, who threatened to use military force to prevent the move. Dowling helped bring the two nations to the conference table. As a result, although thousands of Koreans were repatriated to North Korea, the condition of those remaining in Japan improved considerably, as did the relations between the two nations. According to the *New York Times*, "In his dealings with the government of President Syngman Rhee [Dowling] established a reputation for patience, tact and skill in one of the more difficult and challenging assignments in the Foreign Service."

After a stint as assistant secretary of state for European affairs during the fall of 1959, Dowling became ambassador to West Germany. His primary task was to be spokesman for the U.S. position on Berlin and to serve as a symbol of America's commitment to the city in the face of increased Soviet pressure.

In November 1958 Soviet Premier Nikita Khrushchev had announced that the Soviet Union had decided "to renounce the remnants of the occupation regime in Berlin." He demanded that the three Western powers, the U.S., France and Great Britain, withdraw 10,000 men from their occupation zones, declare Berlin a demilitarized free city and negotiate directly with East Germany on access to the city. He threatened that if the Western allies did not comply within six months, the USSR would give the East German government control of Western military supply routes to the city. The U.S. refused Khrushchev's demand that Berlin be made a "free city" independent of control by either East or West. It opposed recognition of East Germany and announced that, as one of the Allied occupation powers, it had and would maintain its access rights to all sectors of Berlin.

Immediately after assuming office Dowling traveled to West Berlin to reassure the people of continued American support. He reiterated the U.S. stand more dramatically in September 1960, when he forced East German border police to back down in their attempt to bar him from the Soviet sector of Berlin because he was not accredited to the East German government. In a special session of the West Berlin city assembly the following month, Dowling stressed that the U.S. would never acknowledge the right of the Soviet Union to transfer its responsibilities in Berlin to East Germany.

Dowling retired from the Foreign Service in 1963 because of poor health. In 1969 he became a visiting professor of political science at Mercer University and served there until his death.

[ACD]

DRUCKER, PETER F(ERDINAND)
b. Nov. 19, 1909; Vienna, Austria.
Author.

The son of a lawyer and university professor, Peter Drucker grew up in Vienna. After receiving a doctorate in law from the University of Frankfort in 1931, he taught international law and constitutional history at the University while writing on finance and foreign affairs for the city's daily newspaper. Soon after Adolf Hitler came to power in 1933, Drucker left Germany for England and took a job with a merchant bank. In 1937 he moved to the United States, where he made his living over the next 40 years as an author, teacher and consultant to business enterprises. He taught first at Sarah Lawrence College and from 1942 to 1948 and then at Bennington College. In 1950 he became professor of management at New York University.

In 1939 Drucker published *The End of Economic Man*, a critique of totalitarianism and a forecast of what it portended for the future of mankind. He offered a dismal vision in which no hope lay in either capitalism or socialism because they failed to satisfy man's need for noneconomic fulfillment. Fascism was a fraud, Drucker asserted, but it had succeeded because it gave individuals status and the illusion that their actions had heroic significance.

In *The Future of Industrial Man* (1942)

Drucker continued to argue that individuals must be given status and functions if a free industrial society were to survive. In his analysis this could only be accomplished within an institution. To Drucker the essential institution of future America would be the corporation, which he considered the representative social phenomenon of the era. He applauded corporate managers: "There has never been a more efficient, a more honest, a more capable and conscientious group of rulers than the professional managers of the great American corporations today."

Drucker gave a more detailed picture of modern business enterprise in *The Concept of the Corporation* (1946), which he undertook as a study of the General Motors Corp. (GM). Drucker held that workers should have no role in the management of the corporation; their sense of status and function might be enhanced by greater participation in activities peripheral to their jobs, such as community services, but not in the making of company policy. Drucker praised bigness as conducive to efficiency and social stability. He generally approved of GM's famous decentralized organization but placed emphasis on the exercise of leadership by top management and the generation of *esprit de corps*.

By the 1950s Drucker's books, his prolific magazine writing, and his successful consulting ventures had established him as an important theorist of corporate capitalism and a seminal contributor to the study of management. His celebration of the corporation fused with the decade's dominant strain of thought. Drucker criticized the popular "organization man" idea. He warned against placing a premium on conformity which could turn the corporate structure into an ossified bureaucracy. He maintained that a good manager understood the need for risk-taking.

Drucker frequently decried the growth of government into a "swollen monstrosity," calling the proliferation of new agencies a cancer on the political system. During the 1960s and 1970s he maintained his steady output of articles and books, including *The Effective Executive* (1967), *The Age of Discontinuity: Guidelines to Our Changing So-*

ciety (1969) and *The Unseen Revolution: How Pension Fund Socialism Came to America* (1976). In his characteristic fashion Drucker mixed philosophic speculation on business, government and society with practical analysis of managerial problems.

[TO]

For further information:
John J. Tarrant. *Drucker: The Man Who Invented the Corporate Society* (New York, 1976).

DRYDEN, HUGH L(ATIMER)
b. July 2, 1898; Pocomoke City, Md.
d. Dec. 2, 1965; Washington, D.C.
Director, National Advisory Committee for Aeronautics, 1949-58; Deputy Administrator, National Aeronautics and Space Administration, July 1958-December 1965.

The son of a streetcar conductor, Dryden grew up in Baltimore and attended the city's public schools. He received his B.A. from Johns Hopkins in 1916 and his Ph.D. there three years later. He then took a job as the director of the aeronautics section of the National Bureau of Standards, where he had conducted research as a student. During the 1920s Dryden made a significant scientific breakthrough by using wind tunnels to determine what the flow around airplane wings would be at speeds approaching and beyond the speed of sound. This work, together with studies of wind turbulence carried out in the 1930s, made him one of the key figures behind the revolutionary strides taken in aircraft design during the 1930s and 1940s. During World War II Dryden headed a project that developed the first self-guided missile used in combat. He was appointed associate director of the Bureau of Standards in 1946 but resigned the following year to join the National Advisory Committee for Aeronautics (NACA), an agency geared toward civilian research in aviation design. In 1949 Dryden became director of the agency.

As director Dryden was often called upon to justify research projects before congressional committees. In April 1953 he appeared before a House Appropriations subcommittee to explain projects carried out by NACA, the Air Force and the Atomic Energy Commission to link a nuclear reactor to a comparatively conventional jet engine. Two years later, after it became known that the Soviet Union was working on an atomic-powered airplane, Dryden went before a Senate Armed Services subcommittee to request funds to expand NACA's facilities for the same research.

In response to the Soviet Union's successful launching of *Sputnik*, man's first satellite, in October 1957 and to the Gaither Report, warning of increasing Soviet advances in military-technology and scientific knowledge, Eisenhower called for the creation of a National Space and Aeronautics Agency in April 1958. This agency, which would absorb the functions of NACA, was designed to direct U.S. activities relating to all non-military aspects of outer space. Dryden played a major role in drafting the legislation and presenting the proposal to Congress. The measure was signed into law in July.

Dryden, himself, had a conservative vision of the goals of the agency. He reported that its initial project would be the orbiting of a star-gazing satellite and urged the development of satellites that could be used either for communications purposes or for the scientific investigation of the moon. When questioned about the feasibility of sending men into space, Dryden dismissed the idea as a circus stunt, "like shooting a lady out of a cannon." Because of his limited view of the agency's goals, he did not oppose NASA's modest budget.

Dryden was appointed deputy administrator of NASA. He was initially shaken by his failure to receive the top post, but this disappointment waned when he learned that his position would permit him to concentrate on the technical aspects of space research. Despite his initial caution, Dryden came to express his full confidence that the U.S. could quickly develop a program of manned space exploration. Pointing to the complexity of the factors involved, he suggested that the best way to meet the goal lay in international cooperation.

Dryden continued at his post during the

Kennedy Administration and the early years of the Johnson presidency. He died in December 1965. [See KENNEDY Volume]

[EF]

DUBINSKY, DAVID
b. Feb. 22, 1892; Brest-Litovsk, Russian Poland (now USSR).
President, International Ladies Garment Workers Union, 1932-66.

David Dubinsky's family moved to Lodz, Poland, when he was very young. In order to work in his father's bakery, Dubinsky had to join the city's semi-legal baker's union. He then led a strike against the bakers, including his father, at the age of 15. Arrested as a labor agitator, he was exiled to Siberia, but he managed to escape en route and emigrated to the U.S. in 1911. In New York Dubinsky learned the cloak-cutting trade, joined the International Ladies Garment Workers Union (ILGWU) and was active in the Socialist Party. In 1922 he became a member of the Union's executive board. Dubinsky tightly controlled his cutters' local and waged a successful 10-year battle with Communists in the union. He became acting president in 1927 and was elected president in 1932. He became a vice president of the American Federation of Labor (AFL) in 1935.

In 1935 Dubinsky joined John L. Lewis [q.v.] and other industrial union advocates to form the Committee (later Congress) for Industrial Organization (CIO). Dubinsky vigorously backed CIO organizing drives among workers in mass production industries but opposed its permanent formation as an alternative to the more conservative, craft-union oriented AFL. For a short time Dubinsky pulled his union out of the AFL in protest against its treatment of the CIO, but he rejoined it in 1940.

An enthusiastic supporter of Franklin D. Roosevelt's New Deal, Dubinsky joined Sidney Hillman and Alex Rose [q.v.] in forming the American Labor Party (ALP) to support the New Deal nationally while remaining outside the Democratic Party, which they thought dominated by urban bosses and Southern conservatives. Because of growing Communist strength in the ALP, Dubinsky, Hillman and Rose left in 1944 to found New York State's Liberal Party. Dubinsky helped form Americans for Democratic Action three years later. By the onset of the Cold War, he had repudiated his Socialist past. Starting with Harry S. Truman in 1948, Dubinsky and the Liberal Party supported every Democratic candidate for President.

Dubinsky also played a major role in the AFL's international activities, helping to organize the International Federation of Trade Unions. Following World War II, the ILGWU spent $3 million abroad, much of it in Israel and Italy, where Dubinsky helped facilitate the merger of Catholic and Socialist trade unions into one federation. [See TRUMAN Volume]

By the 1950s ILGWU welfare programs were among the most extensive of any union in the country. The Union had established its own health centers, radio stations, a major cooperative housing project on New York City's Lower East Side and extensive recreational facilities. Dubinsky continued to extend the benefits throughout the decade. Following a 1958 strike the Union obtained severance pay for those workers whose companies closed down or moved out of New York. This was of crucial importance because many small clothing manufacturers were fleeing the Northeast to the union-free South. Dubinsky also persuaded the employers to sew the famous "union label" into their garments. Both union and management hoped that labeling would persuade Americans to buy union-made garments. Their objective was to fight cheap imports and, just as importantly, hurt many of the non-unionized shops protected from ILGWU organizers through alliances with organized crime. The 1958 strike settlement included provisions to equalize wages for workers outside the Northeast.

Dubinsky's leadership often earned the praise of his opponents at the bargaining table. ILGWU special teams cooperated with industry to encourage efficiency, and many employers acknowledged that the benefits Dubinsky won for his workers made them into a stable, contented workforce. Stability of employment became common in the 1950s for many ILGWU members for the first time. When negotiating Dubinsky often took into consideration the financial status of an industry plagued with price-cutting competition from imports and non-union shops in the South. Finally, many employers admired Dubinsky's campaign against labor racketeers.

In the 1920s and 1930s Dubinsky waged a battle to purge his union of corrupt officials, who were often tied to organized crime. Although he was never completely successful in his campaign, by the late 1930s the ILGWU had purged most criminal elements from its ranks. Dubinsky also sought to pressure the AFL, and after 1955 the AFL-CIO, to deal more forcefully with the criminal elements in member unions. In 1952 he successfully initiated the AFL's expulsion of the racketeer-infested International Longshoremen's Association. Dubinsky sat on the AFL-CIO's Committee on Ethical Practices that expelled the Teamsters Union in December 1957. That year the Senate Select Committee on Improper Activities in the Labor or Management Field heard testimony that Dubinsky had cooperated with criminals to aid his union's past organization drives. Dubinsky denied the accusations.

In the 1960s Dubinsky remained active in Liberal Party politics and aided John V. Lindsay's mayoral campaigns in 1965 and 1969. Dubinsky retired as ILGWU president in 1966. [See KENNEDY Volume]

[JB]

For further information:
David Dubinsky and A. H. Raskin, *David Dubinsky* (New York, 1977).

DULLES, ALLEN W(ELSH)

b. April 7, 1893; Watertown, N.Y.
d. January 29, 1969; Washington, D.C.
Director of Central Intelligence, 1953-61.

Dulles's family had a background in diplomatic service. His grandfather, John W. Foster, served as Benjamin Harrison's Secretary of State. His uncle, Robert Lansing, held the same post in the Wilson Administration; another uncle, John Walsh, had been minister to England. Dulles's father, however, was a Presbyterian minister who imbued his sons with a strong belief in the conflict of good and evil. Dulles attended private schools in upstate New York and Paris and then earned his B.A. and M.A. degrees at Princeton University.

Beginning in 1916 Dulles served in a number of posts in the diplomatic service, including an assignment with the U.S. delegation to the Versailles Peace Conference of 1918-19. From 1922 to 1926 he was the chief of the State Department's division of Near Eastern affairs. After receiving his LL.B. from George Washington University in 1926, he resigned from government work and joined a Wall Street law firm with his brother, John Foster [*q.v.*].

With the outbreak of World War II, Dulles returned to government service as director of the Office of Strategic Services. He supervised espionage activities against Germany and played an important role in the surrender of German troops in Italy in 1945. After the War he helped draft the National Security Act of 1947, which established the Central Intelligence Agency (CIA), and in 1948 he headed a three-man committee that studied the intelligence functions of the organization. In 1951 Dulles left his law practice to become the deputy director of the CIA, in charge of covert operations. [See TRUMAN Volume]

In 1953 President Dwight D. Eisenhower appointed Dulles Director of Central Intelligence, a position that gave him power not only to run the CIA but also to oversee all U.S. intelligence activities. Dulles's personal style quickly became the public's image of the CIA and its formal standard of behavior. Pipe-smoking, urbane and educated in the Ivy League like many early CIA officials, Dulles was able to impress upon his listeners in public and government circles the need for absolute secrecy in CIA operations. During his tenure there was little outside oversight of his agency, largely because of his close relationship with Eisenhower and powerful congressional leaders who shared his views on secrecy.

During the Eisenhower Administration

the CIA and State Department worked harmoniously because of the closeness of Allen Dulles and his brother, Secretary of State John Foster Dulles. The two men shared the view that the Cold War was a moral crusade against Communism. Foster utilized diplomacy as his weapon, while Allen employed subversion and manipulation. Both used their belief in the need and right of democracy to triumph over totalitarianism to justify their policies.

Under Dulles the CIA helped overthrow several left-wing governments and establish regimes supporting U.S. policy. The CIA's first major success occurred in Iran in 1953, when operatives, directed by Kermit Roosevelt [q.v.], helped topple the leftist government of Prime Minister Mohammed Mossadegh. When questioned about CIA involvement in the coup, Dulles demonstrated his characteristically evasive style. He replied, "I can say that the statement that we spent many dollars doing that [inciting street riots] is utterly false."

Two years later Dulles helped plot the overthrow of Guatemalan President Jacobo Arbenz, whose leftist government had initiated land reform programs that threatened the interests of the powerful American-owned United Fruit Co. In June a small army of exiled Guatemalans, trained and financed by the CIA, crossed the Honduras-Guatemala border to overthrow Arbenz. A secret CIA-organized air force, piloted by Americans, provided the army with necessary air cover. When the invasion faltered Dulles convinced Eisenhower to send additional American planes to the small, crippled air force. As a result of the attack, Guatemalan army officials deserted Arbenz, and he was forced to capitulate. With CIA guidance, negotiations brought the rightist Col. Carlos Castillo-Armas into power. In 1957 Castillo-Armas was assassinated after he closed down a gambling casino dominated by American financial interests. The CIA also backed anti-Communist regimes with little popular support. In South Vietnam, for example, the Agency helped President Ngo Dinh Diem solidify his hold on the central government despite opposition from military and sect leaders.

During Dulles's tenure intelligence-gathering operations were expanded and new technological means of surveillance, such as the U-2 and SR-71 spy planes, were developed. Emphasis was put on the use of technology rather than traditional operatives in collecting data.

In 1975 the Senate Select Committee to Study Intelligence Activities (the Church Committee) reported that during Dulles's tenure the CIA formulated a complicated system of responsibility for departmental actions. By issuing vague but suggestive instructions to subordinates, highly placed officials under examination could legitimately claim "plausible denial" of culpability in covert operations. The Committee, therefore, had difficulty in determining Dulles's role in some of the CIA's more controversial projects. It found evidence that he authorized the assassination of Congolese leader Patrice Lumumba and said he may have received suggestive, if not direct, encouragement for such action from President Eisenhower. Dulles sent the following message to the CIA station in Leopoldville in 1960: "We wish every possible support in eliminating Lumumba from any possibility of resuming a governmental position. . . ." CIA operatives, headed by Richard Bissell [q.v.], interpreted the cable as authorization for a death plot. Local Congolese, however, killed Lumumba before the CIA operation could materialize. In addition, the Select Committee revealed that Dulles and Eisenhower had urged the overthrow of Rafael Trujillo, the rightist dictator of the Dominican Republic.

Investigations by the Church Committee and by the Rockefeller Committee on CIA Activities within the U.S. revealed that during the Dulles years some U.S. businesses, small foundations and organizations were used as fronts for CIA activities. From 1952 to 1973, beginning with Dulles's approval of a "New York mail program," CIA officials intercepted, screened, opened and sometimes photocopied millions of mailed items from selected countries, primarily Communist controlled. Presumably with the tacit approval of three Postmasters General, the Agency monitored the correspondence of those on their "watch list," which included such individuals as Victor Reuther and scientist Linus Pauling [*q.v.*].

Former CIA agent Victor Marchetti and ex-State Department official John D. Marks claimed in their book, *The CIA and the Cult of Intelligence*, that in 1959 Dulles had revised the content of a CIA intelligence report describing Cuban Premier Fidel Castro's rise to power as a natural development in the face of the excesses of the Batista regime and had sent Eisenhower a much darker analysis predicting Castro would use extreme measures to solidify his power. In 1960 the President authorized Dulles to begin the training of an army of Cuban refugees to liberate the island from Communist rule. Dulles, in turn, gave Bissell responsibility for handling the operation.

Bissell devised two strategies for removing Castro. One called for the use of exiles, trained at CIA bases in Guatemala, to infiltrate the island and overthrow the regime. When that proved unfeasible he developed a plan to invade the island. Assuming the endorsement of Dulles, Bissell also enlisted the aid of organized crime figures in an unsuccessful effort to assassinate Castro. The Senate Select Committee reported that "it is not entirely certain that Dulles was ever made aware of the true nature of the underworld plot." In his Senate testimony, however, Bissell claimed that Dulles was aware of the plan.

The disastrous Bay of Pigs invasion took place in April 1961. Reportedly President John F. Kennedy intended to remove Dulles even before the affair, but after the fiasco Kennedy moved quickly to replace him. In September 1961 Dulles resigned and returned to his law practice. He served on the Warren Commission studying the Kennedy assassination. Dulles died in Washington in January 1969. [See KENNEDY Volume]

[JB, TCD]

For further information:
Allen Dulles, *The Craft of Intelligence* (New York, 1963).
U.S. Senate, Select Committee to Study Intelligence Activities, *Alleged Assassination Plots Involving Foreign Leaders* (Washington, 1975).

DULLES, JOHN FOSTER
b. Feb. 25, 1888; Washington, D.C.
d. May 24, 1959; Washington, D.C.
Secretary of State, January 1953-April 1959.

Dulles was descended from a family of diplomats and clergymen. His maternal grandfather, John W. Foster, served as ambassador to Russia, Spain and Mexico and was Secretary of State under Benjamin Harrison. Dulles's paternal grandfather, John Welch Dulles, was a Presbyterian missionary in China. His father, Allen Dulles, taught philosophy at Auburn Theological Seminary and was a Presbyterian minister in Watertown, N.Y., where Foster grew up.

Dulles graduated from Princeton University in 1908 and spent a year studying at the Sorbonne. Although he had expressed an interest in entering the ministry, he decided to become a lawyer. He received his degree from George Washington University in 1911 and began a long association with the prestigious New York law firm of Sullivan & Cromwell. Dulles served as a special agent for the State Department in Central America in 1917. During World War I he worked with the Army intelligence service and was an assistant to the chairman of the War Trade Board.

At the request of his uncle, Robert Lansing, Dulles served as President Woodrow Wilson's staff at the Versailles Peace Conference of 1919. He was head of the U.S. delegation to the Reparations Committee and earned high praise for convincing the British and French to lower reparation demands. Dulles returned from Paris to become a partner in his law firm. An austere man and compulsive worker, during the next 30 years he earned a distinguished record as a specialist in international law.

Throughout the 1930s Dulles lectured and wrote on foreign affairs. His reactions to the growth of fascism and the impending war in Europe were presented in *War, Peace and Change*, published in 1939. Devoid of the moral tone that would later typify his work, the book was a systematic, legalistic inquiry into the reasons men go to war. Dulles ascribed the troubled situation in Europe to the failure of the Treaty of Versailles. By insisting on the maintenance of the status quo, the victorious Allies had forced Germany to take violent action to achieve needed change. Dulles saw the threat to peace coming from the system of nation-states advancing their self-interest. He suggested that war could be avoided through the creation of "international mechanisms" (which he did not clearly define) to manage change.

Dulles was deeply disturbed by the war in Europe and believed the United States could avoid entering the struggle by developing a moral solution to the crisis. In 1940 he assumed the chairmanship of the Federal Council of Churchs' Commission on a Just and Durable Peace. Dulles's major goal was to create a successor to the League of Nations without its weaknesses. In May 1943 he set down an abstract plan for preventing war in a report entitled "The Six Pillars of Peace." In contrast to his early works, it contained a strong moral theme. Dulles believed that peace could be achieved only when nations were acting in conjunction with moral law. The U.S. had a particular moral obligation in guiding the postwar world and in forming the international organization that would maintain peace.

During the 1944 presidential campaign Dulles served as a foreign policy adviser to Republican candidate New York Gov. Thomas Dewey. A supporter of a bipartisan foreign policy, Dulles also undertook several diplomatic assignments for the Roosevelt and Truman Administrations. In 1945 he was a member of the U.S. delegation to the U.N. Conference in San Francisco. From 1946 to 1950 he was a delegate to the U.N. General Assembly and an adviser to the State Department. Dulles served as Dewey's adviser during the 1948 presidential campaign and backed the candidate's decision not to attack strongly Truman's foreign policy. During the immediate postwar period Dulles endorsed the Truman Doctrine, the Marshall Plan and the North Atlantic Treaty, as well as the President's conduct of the Korean war.

In the last half of the decade Dulles's as-

sessment of the world situation changed. No longer did he see peace threatened by the system of nation-states and the selfishness of all countries. Instead, it was jeopardized by the evil intentions and ideologies of specific states, particularly the Soviet Union. In a 1946 *Life* article he warned that the Soviet Union would continue its expansionist policy. Dulles called for military measures to meet the threat, but more importantly, he preached a need for a spiritual rebirth and a recommitment to American institutions to counter the threat. Despite his hatred of Communism, he urged a more conciliatory attitude toward the USSR, believing it might lift the Iron Curtain and permit the entrance of beneficent Western influence.

In 1949 Dewey appointed Dulles to fill an unexpired Senate term. He was defeated when he ran as a Republican for a full term in 1950. Dulles became a consultant for State Department and in 1950-51 negotiated the U.S.-Japanese peace treaty. This agreement restored Japan's sovereignty and allowed U.S. bases to remain in that nation. [See TRUMAN Volume]

During the early 1950s Dulles, by then the Republican Party's most prominent foreign policy figure, became increasingly conservative. Historians such as Walter LeFeber have attributed this movement to the rise of McCarthyism and Dulles's hope that a Republican victory in the 1952 presidential election would result in his selection as Secretary of State.

Dulles outlined his new stand in a *Life* article in 1952. He contended that Truman's policy of containment had been only partly successful in preventing Communist expansion and had, in fact, failed to roll back the Communist sphere of influence in Eastern Europe and China. Containment offered the American people only the status quo. Instead, Dulles suggested a policy of liberation for nations of the Eastern bloc. Dulles opposed Truman's reliance on convential weapons, maintaining it would bankrupt the nation. He recommended that the U.S. use nuclear weapons when necessary. In his words, the primary way of countering Communist aggression was "for the free world to develop the will and organize the means to retaliate instantly against open aggression by Red Armies, so that, if it occurred anywhere we could and would strike back, where it hurt, by means of our own choosing."

Dulles's ideas impressed both moderate and conservative Republicans. In 1952 he was asked to draft the foreign policy plank in the Republican platform. There he condemned containment as "negative, futile and immoral" because it abandoned "countless human beings to despotic and godless terror." The Party promised the liberation of Eastern Europe. Dulles campaigned vigorously for the Eisenhower ticket but was rarely seen with the General or asked for his advice. The reasons for the candidate's coldness remain uncertain, but historian Townsend Hoopes suggested it was the result of Eisenhower's reluctance to associate himself with Dulles's policy of liberation.

The press widely assumed that Dulles would be chosen Eisenhower's Secretary of State. However, several of his close aides maintained that the President-elect had ambivalent feelings about the man. According to C. D. Jackson [q.v.], Eisenhower contemplated naming John J. McCloy, a man interested in managing a bureaucracy as well as formulating foreign policy, to head the Department. Dulles, who showed no interest in management, was to have been chief foreign policy adviser. Eisenhower contacted McCloy with the suggestion, but he rejected it. Dulles was named Secretary of State in late November.

Relations between the men were initially extremely formal. The aloof Dulles had difficulty dealing with the President. Eisenhower, in turn, found his Secretary of State dull, verbose and legalistic in his discussions. Yet the two men gradually developed a close relationship. Eisenhower spoke to Dulles daily. The Secretary was the one member of the Cabinet who did not have to go through presidential assistant Sherman Adams [q.v.] to see the President.

Over the decade the two men molded a foreign policy that reflected a moralistic view of the Cold War. Eisenhower often gave Dulles a free hand in shaping and carrying out policy. He consequently became

one of the most powerful Secretaries of State in U.S. history. Yet the President was not Dulles's cypher as critics claimed. Dulles initiated and gave shape to policy, but Eisenhower continually modified it, often softening his Secretary's hard-line attitudes.

Dulles considered himself primarily the President's personal foreign policy adviser, and he jealously guarded his position within the White House. He objected to independent foreign policy initiatives by such advisers as Harold Stassen [q.v.] in the field of disarmament and Nelson Rockefeller [q.v.] in the field of Latin American relations. Each of these men resigned, in part, because the Secretary frustrated their plans.

Because he thought of himself as an adviser, Dulles was not concerned with the administration of the State Department. His many trips were, in part, a result of the desire to escape the problems of department management. Dulles rarely consulted his staff on policy. His contacts were most often for facts with which to support his stand. According to George Kennan [q.v.], this policy weakened morale within the Department and destroyed creativity into the 1960s.

Dulles entered office well aware of the need for good relations with Congress. During his early life he had seen Woodrow Wilson's dream of American participation in the League of Nations destroyed by his inability to deal with Congress. After World War II he saw Dean Acheson [q.v.] hampered by the same failure. Dulles was particularly concerned with maintaining good relations with the powerful Republican Right, led by such senators as William Jenner, (R, Ind.) [q.v.], Styles Bridges (R, N.H.) [q.v.] and Joseph McCarthy (R, Wisc.) [q.v.].

Very early in his career he became involved in attempts to placate the Wisconsin Republican, who had charged that the State Department harbored subversives. Dulles instituted strict security reviews under the direction of Scott McLeod [q.v.], a McCarthy supporter. Over the next few years investigations resulted in the dismissal or forced resignation of several hundred State Department employes as security risks or because of drunkenness, homosexuality, incompetence or "incompatibility." The last reason was used for those whose policy judgments displeased the Republican Right.

Among those removed were John P. Davies [*q.v.*] and John Carter Vincent [*q.v.*], China experts under attack as pro-Communist because they opposed all-out aid to Chiang Kai-shek during the 1940s. Dulles, reviewing their files, found no security violations. Nevertheless, he refused to support these men and asked for their resignations on the grounds of lack of judgment, discretion and reliability.

Dulles did, however, support the nomination of Charles E. Bohlen [*q.v.*] to be ambassador to the USSR. The diplomat was accused of being a security risk and was attacked because of his role in the formation of the Yalta agreements. The appointment was confirmed, but while the Senate debate was in progress, Dulles insisted that he not be seen too frequently in Bohlen's company. Bohlen left Washington with the impression that Dulles was a man with "one obsession: to remain Secretary of State."

Dulles entered his office with the desire to implement a policy of boldness and action. No longer would the U.S. simply react to Communist challenge; it would take the offensive against the adversary. Although he had no long-range plans to implement this idea, his policy initially dealt with four considerations: ending the Korean war without changing the status quo in the rest of Asia; developing anti-Communist alliances in the Middle East; unifying Western Europe; and, maintaining the Cold War against the Soviets.

Shortly after the inauguration Dulles and Eisenhower took steps to end the Korean war. They intensified the pressure on China to accept a compromise agreement. In his State of the Union message, Eisenhower announced he would remove the Seventh Fleet from the Formosa Straits, thus "unleashing" Chiang Kai-shek for a possible attack on the mainland. The Administration also revealed plans to increase U.S. air power in Korea, enlarge the South Korean Army and place nuclear weapons on Okinawa. At the same time Dulles firmly pushed South Korea into accepting an armistice by refusing to give in to President Syngman Rhee's demands for resumption of the war if Korean unification was not achieved within three months of an armistice. The agreement was signed on July 27, 1953.

In the Mideast Dulles attempted to forestall Communist expansion through the establishment of pro-Western governments and the formation of a military alliance similar to the North Atlantic Treaty Organization (NATO). The leftist government of Iranian Premier Mohammed Mossadegh was overthrown in August 1953 with the help of the Central Intelligence Agency (CIA). A pro-Western regime loyal to the Shah took its place. In attempting to form alliances, the Secretary was frustrated by growing nationalism in Arab nations, particularly Egypt. Reacting to years of British colonial rule, Egyptian leader Gamal Abdel Nasser refused to accept membership in any mutual defense organization giving Britain or any other colonial power the right to return to Egypt if strategic interests were threatened. Nasser did not perceive the Communist threat as serious and attempted to maintain a policy of neutrality to prevent domination by either the Western or Soviet bloc. In 1954 the British succeeded in forming the Bagdad Pact, a military alliance with Turkey, Iran, Iraq and Pakistan. Dulles, however, was reluctant to recognize the alliance, not wanting to be associated with colonial powers. Fearing that American membership would antagonize Arab leaders, he sent an "observer" rather than an ambassador to the new organization.

As Secretary of State, Dulles was particularly concerned with American policy in Western Europe, which he thought would be the major battlefield of the Cold War. Throughout his tenure he attempted to promote European unification, maintaining that Europe, "the world's worst fire hazard," could not be rebuilt on the old system of nation-states. The Secretary supported such moves toward economic unification as the formation of the European Iron and Steel Community, and he wanted them complemented by steps toward military unification. By the time Dulles came to office, an agreement on the formation of the European Defense Community (EDC), establishing an inter-European army, had already been initialed by the governments concerned: France, Germany and Benelux. However, popular opposition to the plan, particularly in France, which feared German rearmament, endangered ratification. During the early months of 1953, Dulles flew to various European capitals in an attempt to increase support for the EDC. Intent upon gaining acceptance, he suggested that a defeat of the proposal would result in "an agonizing reappraisal" of American commitments in Europe. However, his efforts failed. The proposal died in August 1954, when the French Assembly refused to consider the plan.

Dulles was particularly upset by the defeat because he felt it necessary to integrate West Germany into the mainstream of European politics as quickly as possible lest the nation make an accommodation with the Soviet bloc. However, the U.S. allies were angered at Dulles's strident stand during the debate over the EDC, and the Secretary was forced to leave the negotiation of the German issue to the British. Over the next few months Foreign Minister Anthony Eden laid the groundwork for the introduction of Germany into NATO while placing constraints on German rearmament to please the French. Dulles supported the plan, approved at a foreign minister's conference convened in London in September.

A strident cold warrior, Dulles opposed any attempt at conciliation with the Soviet Union. When the Soviet leadership made a series of peace overtures following the death of Stalin in March 1953, he recommended no public acknowledgement. He dismissed them as a "tactical retreat" and suggested that the U.S. take advantage of the confused situation in the Kremlin to begin a diplomatic and propaganda offensive against the Communists. When Eisenhower determined to respond publicly to the gesture, Dulles recommended that the speech contain a list of "deeds," including political self-determination for Eastern Europe, to test the sincerity of the Russian proposals. These were included in the President's statement, which despite Dulles's advice, suggested the possibility of accommodation.

Dulles also opposed a summit conference in 1955. He believed that the meeting would accomplish nothing substantial and would antagonize the powerful Republican Right. The Secretary insisted that the U.S. require the USSR to begin withdrawal from Eastern Europe before serious talks began. Eisenhower, however, ignored his Secretary's advice and accepted an invitation to meet with the Soviet leaders in July. Although Dulles had advised him to wear an "austere countenance" when photographed with Premier Nikolai Bulganin, the President conducted himself in a warm, friendly manner. The conference resolved none of the issues dividing the nations—Germany and disarmament—but the fact that the leaders of the two super-powers had discussed differences gave hope of improved chances for peace and led to the "Spirit of Geneva," a thaw in the Cold War.

Dulles, however, had a pessimistic assessment of the meeting. He remained convinced that the Soviet Union had called the summit to gain strategic respite. The Secretary believed that the Soviets had overextended themselves in the arms race and were hence forced toward conciliation with the West. He conceded that the new Soviet policy "might assume the force of an irreversible trend" which should be encouraged. However, he refused to accept the current situation in Europe and warned that Russian actions did not justify "the free world relaxing its vigilance or substantially altering its programs for collective security."

Although Dulles and his defenders hailed his policies as a departure from those of the Truman Administration, they were in essence continuations of containment. The major innovation was the introduction of the "New Look" defense policy with its reliance on strategic deterrence or "massive retaliation" as it became known. Fashioned chiefly by Adm. Arthur Radford [q.v.], chairman of the Joint Chiefs of Staff, the New Look was based on a desire to hold down defense costs and prevent debilitating ground wars such as those in Korea. It called for the movement away from the use of both conventional forces and nuclear weapons toward the acceptance of nuclear weapons delivered by bombers or missiles as a primary deterrent against aggression. Although its origins could be traced to Dulles's 1952 *Life* article, "The Policy of Boldness," the Secretary had very little to do with the actual formulation. In military matters he was content to rely on the Pentagon. Yet the Secretary was given the task of explaining the New Look to the American people. In a speech before the Council on Foreign Relations during January, Dulles told the audience that the use of conventional forces had traditionally given the enemy the initiative. He recommended that local defenses be strengthened with the further deterrent of massive retaliatory power. The Secretary promised that the U.S. could "depend upon a great capacity to retaliate instantly by means and at places of our own choosing."

Foreign policy observers had difficulty trying to understand what Dulles meant by this ambiguous statement. Many thought the Secretary promised nuclear war for any Soviet infraction of the status quo. Dulles attempted to clarify the use of the term, but his several attempts at explanation confused the issue further. Walter Lippmann [q.v.] wrote that "official explanations of the New Look have become so voluminous that it is almost a career to keep up with them." That concept with its ambiguity played an important role in the development of Dulles's foreign policy. The Secretary saw the threat of deterrence as a potent diplomatic weapon to brandish before the Communists.

Dulles's use of his new weapon was tested twice during 1954: in Vietnam and in the Formosa Straits. During the spring of 1954 the French asked for direct American intervention in Vietnam to relieve their garrison at Dien Bien Phu, then under attack by the Communist Vietminh. The French confided in Dulles their desire to reach a settlement in the Indochina war and told him they would restrict military operations to achieve that goal. The Secretary opposed the French decision, believing it would further the expansion of Com-

munism in Southeast Asia. He also rejected Radford's call for bombing raids to relieve the fort, because the proposal was too narrow in scope. Instead, he proposed using the deterrence doctrine to achieve not a compromise settlement but the defeat of Communism in Southeast Asia. On March 29, in a major policy address at the Overseas Press Club, Dulles articulated his policy: "The United States feels that the possibility of Communist control should not be passively accepted, but should be met with united action."

Over the next month Dulles attempted to generate congressional and allied support for his plan. Congress, however, turned down his request for a resolution allowing American intervention because the allies had not been consulted. The British and French, too, refused his overture. They were angered at Dulles's presumption that he could speak for Europe and were wary of a military commitment in light of the implications of his "massive retaliation" speech. In addition, both nations felt that, though the Secretary had emphasized deterrence, Dulles intended to commit the allies to a ground war in Asia to prevent a French withdrawal. His proposal, therefore, would have prevented a peaceful compromise settlement.

Dulles entered the Geneva Conference on Indochina in April 1954 opposed to a negotiated settlement. Reacting to pressure from the Republican Right and to his own anti-Communism, he refused to acknowledge the Communist Chinese delegation. The Secretary remained at the Conference for only one week while he tried to convince the British and French to join the U.S. in an alliance that would influence the outcome of the meeting. When this failed, he returned to Washington. During the substantive sessions, Undersecretary of State Walter Bedell Smith [q.v.] represented the U.S. but on Dulles's order took virtually no part in the discussion.

On July 21 the Geneva Conference reached an agreement on Vietnam. Under the Accords, as the agreement was known, Vietnam was temporarily divided along the 17th parallel with the Communists, led by Ho Chi Minh, controling the north and a pro-Western government, headed by Ngo Dinh Diem, in the south. The nation was to be reunified through free elections scheduled for 1956. On Dulles's order the U.S. refused to sign the treaty but "took note" of it. In a statement after the agreement had been reached, Smith announced that the U.S. "would view any renewal of the aggression in violation of the aforesaid agreements with grave concern and as seriously threatening international peace and security." Thus Dulles committed the U.S. to support a pro-Western government in Southeast Asia.

Over the next few months Dulles worked to prevent Communist expansion in Vietnam. In September eight nations (the U.S., Great Britain, France, Australia, New Zealand, Pakistan, Thailand and the Philippines) formed the Southeast Asia Treaty Organization, pledged to resist Communist aggression in the area. That fall Dulles announced that the U.S. would give both economic and military aid to the Diem government. American military advisers such as Edward Lansdale [q.v.] were sent to Vietnam to help Diem solidify his position. In a shift from his massive retaliation philosophy, the Secretary began backing reliance on "local defense" to counter Communist aggression. At Dulles's behest, Diem resisted British and French pleas to meet with representatives of the Vietminh to set up consultations on the proposed all-Vietnam elections. The elections were never held.

During the fall of 1954 Communist Chinese artillery began shelling the Nationalist held islands of Quemoy and Matsu off the mainland coast. Members of the Administration differed on how to interpret the action. Dulles believed it was a possible prelude for an invasion of Formosa; but several military leaders questioned the Communists' military capacity to stage such an action. The Secretary joined Radford and most of the Joint Chiefs of Staff (except Gen. Matthew Ridgway [q.v.]) in proposing that Eisenhower permit Chiang to bomb the mainland. If Peking retaliated, they suggested the U.S. send bombers to help the Nationalists. Eisenhower, however, rejected the proposal,

preferring to work out a diplomatic solution to the crisis. To prevent military action by the Nationalist Chinese, he sent Dulles to negotiate a mutual security treaty between the two countries. This agreement, signed in December 1954, reflected both Eisenhower's desire that the U.S. commitment be limited to the defense of Taiwan and Dulles's and the congressional right wing's desire to defend the offshore islands. The treaty focused on Taiwan, but accompanying documents extended the commitment to "such other territories as may be determined by a mutual agreement."

The bombing continued into the spring of 1955. Eisenhower still held firm, arguing that the islands were not worth fighting for, but he permitted Dulles to publicly threaten Peking with nuclear reprisals. Vice President Richard Nixon [q.v.] joined Dulles in this stand, and Eisenhower, himself, refused to rule out the possibility of bombing military targets. In April the crisis died down as the Chinese tapered off shelling. Dulles was quick to credit the threat of nuclear attack for the change.

As the 1956 presidential campaign approached, Dulles began defending his controversial policies. In a *Life* interview, he suggested that his successes resulted from the art of what came to be called "brinksmanship." "We were brought to the brink of war," he said, "the ability to get to the verge without getting into the war is the necessary art. If you can't master it you inevitably get into war . . . . we walked to the brink, and we looked it in the face. We took strong action." Yet Adlai Stevenson, [q.v.] the Democratic presidential candidate, and other liberals pointed out that Dulles's threats were useless because nations knew that the U.S. would not be the first to use nuclear weapons.

Dulles's tendency to think in terms of Communism versus anti-Communism limited his response to the growing nationalism in the Middle East. Following Israeli attacks on Egypt in 1955, Nasser turned to the U.S. for arms to repulse further aggression. Dulles, however, denied him the help, believing that the U.S. should not become involved in an arms race in the area. Instead, the U.S. offered Egypt assistance in building the Aswan High Dam. Nasser reluctantly turned to the Soviet bloc for military aid. Although Nasser did not wish to become closely allied with the USSR, Dulles viewed the arms deal as a dangerous drift to the left. Egyptian recognition of Communist China strengthened his belief. Angered at Nasser's conduct (which he thought was an attempt to play one side against the other in the Cold War) and prompted by domestic opposition to the dam, on July 19 Dulles terminated negotiations on the project.

In retaliation Nasser seized the Suez Canal one week later, promising to use the toll money to build the dam. The seizure threatened British and French interests in the Middle East. Both nations began drawing up military plans to regain control of the waterway, but Dulles advocated a negotiated settlement of the issue. At the London Conference, called at his behest in September, he proposed that the U.N. supervise canal operations. Several weeks later he suggested forming an association of canal users to collect tolls and direct piloting. The organization would then give Egypt what it considered a fair share of canal revenues. Dulles's proposals angered both Egypt and the European nations. The British and French resented the fact that they had not been consulted before the proposals were presented. Egypt disliked the plans because they would take control of the Canal out of its hands.

As the negotiations dragged on, the allies became impatient with U.S. leadership. In the fall French and British troops seized the Canal, while the Israeli Army invaded the Sinai. Dulles turned on the British and French for what he considered to be an immoral breach of the peace. With Eisenhower's approval, he joined the Soviet Union at the U.N. to pass a resolution calling for the withdrawal of the invading forces from Egypt. Faced with unanimous world opinion and the prospect of Russian involvement, Britain, France and Israel withdrew. Dulles's refusal to back the military action strained U.S. relations with the allies for months, and in the case of France, years.

Following the Suez crisis the Soviet Union's prestige grew in the Middle East. To prevent the further erosion of the American position there, Dulles and Eisenhower asked Congress to provide them with a joint resolution granting the President authority to send troops to the area if a pro-Western government required assistance against Communist subversion. Congress approved this request, known as the Eisenhower Doctrine, in January 1957. In 1958 the pro-Western Lebanese government, fearing a pro-Nasser revolt which it believed was infiltrated by Communists, asked for American assistance, Eisenhower sent troops to quell the insurrection.

Dulles's activities during the second Eisenhower Administration were curtailed by his bout with cancer. Nevertheless, he continued to expound his hard-line policies in light of a changing world situation. The Secretary still opposed accommodation with the Soviet Union despite Soviet parity in nuclear weapons, and he resisted advocates of nuclear disarmament. He continued to oppose neutralism in the Third World, while young diplomats saw it as a means of preserving peace and depolarizing the world situation.

Dulles, however, did oversee a change in American policy on Quemoy and Matsu. In August 1958 the Communist Chinese resumed heavy shelling of the islands. The Secretary again threatened nuclear reprisal but soon found he had no support for this policy at home or abroad. In September Premier Nikita Khrushchev reminded Eisenhower that the Soviet Union could also employ nuclear weapons in a crisis. Dulles then made a major shift in policy. He stated that Chiang was "rather foolish" in stationing a large garrison on Quemoy and acknowledged that the U.S. had made no guarantees to defend the islands. He visited Taipei to persuade Chiang to thin out his Quemoy garrison. In addition, the U.S. initiated contacts with Communists. Using the American embassy in Warsaw, headed by Ambassador Jacob Beam [q.v.], the two nations discussed the problem, preventing an open rupture in the Formosa Straits.

Dulles faced his last crisis in November 1958, when Khrushchev demanded the

West withdraw its troops from West Berlin and make it an autonomous city. If this did not occur within six weeks, he warned, he would then turn the access routes over to the East Germans and force the West to negotiate with them. Dulles approached the crisis as he had in the past. He viewed the Soviet action as reckless and urged the West not to negotiate under duress. Although he confided that the crisis could be surmounted without going to war, he urged the West to be ready to use nuclear warfare if necessary to protect Berlin. Western strategy had not been agreed upon at the time of Dulles's resignation on April 15. On May 24 Dulles died in his sleep.

[JB]

For further information:
John Robinson Beal. *John Foster Dulles: A Biography* (New York, 1957).
Richard Goold-Adams. *The Time of Power: A Reappraisal of John Foster Dulles* (Boston, 1962).
Michael Guhin. *John Foster Dulles: A Statesman and His Times* (New York, 1972).
Townsend Hoopes. *The Devil and John Foster Dulles* (Boston, 1973).
Hans Morgenthau. "John Foster Dulles," in Norman Graebner, ed., *An Uncertain Tradition: American Secretaries of State in the Twentieth Century* (New York, 1961).

DURKIN, MARTIN P(ATRICK)

b. March 18, 1894; Chicago, Ill.
d. Nov. 13, 1955; Washington, D.C.
Secretary of Labor, January 1953-September 1953.

After four years as an apprentice steam fitter, Durkin became a journeyman plumber in Chicago Local 597 of the United Association of Journeymen and Apprentices of the Plumbing and Pipe Fitting Industry of the U.S. and Canada (UA). He served in the Army during World War I. In 1922 Durkin became business manager of the largest local of the plumbers' union, Local 597, and in 1927 was made vice president of the Chicago Building Trades Council.

Appointed Illinois state director of labor in 1933 by Democratic Gov. Henry Horner, Durkin served in that post until 1941. As director he streamlined his department and gained recognition as an administrator. He successfully pushed through legislation establishing unemployment compensation and a state employment service, developing new safety rules for employes and regulating minimum wages and maximum hours for women and children. Durkin went to Washington in 1941 as secretary-treasurer of the national office of the UA. In 1943 he succeeded George Meany [q.v.] as its president.

Eisenhower announced Durkin's appointment as Secretary of Labor in December 1952. The selection received less personal attention from the President-elect than any other cabinet appointment. Lacking any prior experience with labor, he delegated the job of finding a Labor Secretary to Lucius Clay [q.v.] and Herbert Brownell [q.v.]. On the recommendation of Harold Stassen [q.v.], the two men chose Durkin because he fit the criteria they set for the post: he was a Catholic, necessary in a cabinet composed almost entirely of Protestants; he headed a powerful union; and he was known as an effective leader.

The nomination prompted an angry response from Republicans. As a Democrat Durkin had voted for Adlai E. Stevenson [q.v.] against Eisenhower. Completely unprepared for the Durkin nomination, Sen. Robert Taft (R, Ohio) [q.v.] called it "incredible" and "an affront to millions of union members and officers who had the courage to deny the edict of officers like Mr. Durkin that they vote for Stevenson." Sherman Adams [q.v.], Eisenhower's chief aide, saw the appointment as "an experiment doomed from the start to failure."

Described as a plumber in a cabinet of eight millionaires, Durkin and his pro-labor views found little sympathy in the Administration. The Secretary's primary goal was to revise the Taft-Hartley Act, opposed by labor because of its restrictions on unions. Eisenhower, himself, while rejecting total repeal of the measure, had supported amending the legislation to eliminate those provisions that could be used to "smash unions." However, once in the White House, Eisenhower did not encourage Durkin's efforts or back him in clashes with other departments.

Durkin initially set up a committee of representatives of the public, business and labor to study ways of revising the Taft-Hartley Act. However quarrels over voting procedure led him to recess the panel. He blamed the employer members for the committee's inability to function.

The Secretary's problems with revising the statute soon narrowed to a clash between the Labor Department and the Commerce Department, headed by Sinclair Weeks [q.v.]. Durkin wanted to drop the Act's provision for union leaders to sign non-Communist affadavits and abolish "right-to-work" laws. He also wanted to give labor more control over membership and liberalize the freedom to engage in secondary boycotts. Most importantly he wanted to minimize the jurisdiction of state courts in labor disputes. Weeks, on the other hand, refused to concede anything above what Eisenhower had vaguely promised and wished to emphasize the power of states in disputes.

Because the two executive departments could not come to an agreement, presidential assistants Bernard Shanley [q.v.] and Gerald Morgan [q.v.] drew up a memorandum suggesting an Administration position; most of its 19 points were concessions to Durkin. Their memorandum eventually became the basis for a draft message the President was to make to Congress. It was to have been forwarded to the legislature on July 31. However, Sen. Taft died that day, and because Taft had co-authored the original legislation, the White House felt it would be tactless to submit the amendments. Durkin was assured, however, that they would be publicly released shortly.

In the meantime Weeks and his friends maneuvered behind the scenes to kill the message. Vice President Richard Nixon [q.v.] also intervened and, according to the New York Times, was primarily responsible for preventing the amendments from going to Congress. Both men convinced Eisenhower that alienating business and states rights advocates would be political suicide. On Aug. 2 the Wall Street Journal ran an expose on the message under the headline " . . . They Favor the Unions." The provision, recognizing federal over state

rights in certain labor disputes, could have nullified the "right-to-work" laws. It provoked an uproar in management circles. Despite the furor Eisenhower assured Durkin that the 19 points still stood. However, on Sept. 8 the President informed the Secretary that he could no longer accept them. Durkin immediately resigned and returned to the presidency of the UA. He died in Washington on Nov. 13, 1955 after operations for a brain tumor.

[ACD]

DWORSHAK, HENRY C(LARENCE)
b. Aug. 29, 1894; Duluth, Minn.
d. July 23, 1962; Washington, D.C.
Republican Representative, Ida., 1939-46; Republican Senator, Ida., 1946-49, 1949-62.

After serving in the Army during World War I, Dworshak became manager of a printer supply business. In 1929 he began publishing a newspaper in Idaho. Dworshak won election to the U.S. House of Representatives in 1938, and in 1946 he was elected to complete a Senate term expiring in January 1949. He lost his bid for a full term in 1948, but after his successful Democratic opponent died in October 1949, Dworshak was appointed to fill the seat. The following year he was elected to complete the final four years of the term.

Dworshak was one of the most conservative Republicans in Congress. In 1953 he joined 11 other Republicans voting against the confirmation of Charles Bohlen [q.v.] as ambassador to the Soviet Union. They maintained Bohlen he was associated with President Harry S. Truman's foreign policy, which allegedly was "soft on Communism."

Dworshak was a strong supporter of Sen. Joseph R. McCarthy (R. Wisc.) [q.v.]. In April 1954 McCarthy, with the consent of the Government Operations Committee's Permanent Investigations Subcommittee, chose Dworshak to replace him as chairman during the Army-McCarthy hearings. Dworshak generally favored McCarthy during the probe. In late May he introduced a motion that had the effect of removing

Francis Carr [*q.v.*], the subcommittee's staff director, as a witness. Carr was one of the McCarthy staff members accused by the Army of attempting to secure special favors for Pvt. G. David Schine [*q.v.*], former subcommittee consultant. Despite the pleas of Army counsel Joseph L. Welch [*q.v.*], who wanted to question Carr, the Dworshak motion passed on a straight party vote. The following December Dworshak voted against the Senate's condemnation of McCarthy.

An advocate of a balanced budget, in 1953 Dworshak pressed for cuts in Post Office and Public Housing Administration appropriations. He favored defense budget reductions in 1954 and 1957. Dworshak criticized the foreign aid program. In 1957 the Senator declared that "goodwill and friendship cannot be bought by American dollars alone."

In 1956 Dworshak opposed a bill, sponsored by Sen. Wayne Morse (D, Ore.) [*q.v.*], authorizing federal construction of the Hell's Canyon Dam. Nevertheless, the Interior and Insular Affairs Committee reported out the measure. Dworshak signed the panel's minority report, which stated that private erection of the dam was in the national interest and that there was no need to insist on a federal project when private construction could achieve similar benefits. The committee bill was defeated on the Senate floor, and the project was privately built.

Dworshak was a staunch opponent of President Kennedy's domestic policies. The Idaho Senator died of a heart attack in Washington, D.C. on July 23, 1962.

[MLL]

EASTLAND, JAMES O(LIVER)

b. Nov. 28, 1904; Doddsville, Miss.
Democratic Senator, Miss., 1941, 1943- ; Chairman, Judiciary Committee, 1956- .

Eastland, the son of a well-to-do and influential district attorney, was born in Sunflower Co., Miss. He studied law at Vanderbilt University and the University of Alabama and began a private legal practice

after his admission to the Mississippi bar in 1927. From 1928 to 1932 Eastland served in the Mississippi House of Representatives. He then retired from politics and, beginning in 1934, took over the management of his family's cotton plantation in Ruleville.

In June 1941 Gov. Paul B. Johnson appointed Eastland to a vacant U.S. Senate seat. The following year he won a full term. An unswerving opponent of measures aimed at eliminating racial discrimination, Eastland denounced an anti-poll tax measure in 1944 and charged that "the driving force behind this bill is a bunch of Communists." Four years later he backed the states rights presidential candidacy of Gov. Strom Thurmond [*q.v.*]. Eastland devoted a major share of his activity in the Senate to defending Mississippi's cotton interests. During the 1940s he introduced bills to ban the import of foreign cotton and to withhold government cotton from the domestic market. He consistently opposed liberal social welfare legislation and favored a strongly anti-Communist foreign policy.

During the 1950s Eastland, as a member of the Agriculture and Forestry Committee, attempted to protect the cotton planters of the Deep South against competition from new growers in the Southwest. In 1953 Congress was considering reductions in acreage allotments to reduce cotton surpluses. California and Arizona planters requested special protection for new cotton growers in the form of an acreage reduction ceiling of 25% for their states. Eastland played a key role in working out a compromise, passed in January 1954, that gave California and Arizona bonus acreage but apportioned basic allotments among the states according to past production figures. In 1955 the Agriculture and Forestry Committee, with Eastland's support, reported out a bill to enlarge acreage allotments, with the biggest increases going to small farms. The bill favored the Deep South states, which had more small cotton farms than the states of the Southwest. Opposition from senators of the latter region helped kill the measure in its original form.

Eastland continued his unrelenting opposition to civil rights during the 1950s. In

1955 he denounced the Supreme Court school desegregation decision of the previous year, asking, "Who is obligated morally or legally to obey a decision whose authorities rest not on law but upon the writings and teachings of pro-Communist agitators?" That year he played a major role in the formation of the Federation for Constitutional Government, a short-lived attempt to unite the white Citizens' Councils and other local white supremacist groups. He was a frequent and popular speaker before those organizations.

After becoming chairman of the Judiciary Committee in March 1956, Eastland posed a formidable obstacle to the passage of civil rights bills, which were within the jurisdiction of that panel. The Administration's 1957 civil rights measure was passed only after the Senate, in June, voted to bypass the Committee and place the measure on the chamber's calendar. Throughout 1959 Eastland delayed another civil rights bill in committee. Liberals pressed Majority Leader Lyndon B. Johnson (D, Tex.) [q.v.] and Minority Leader Everett M. Dirksen (R, Ill.) [q.v.] to bring the measure to the floor, and the leaders announced in September that they would act early the following year to bring the legislation up for debate. On March 24, 1960 the Senate, over Eastland's opposition, voted to require the panel to report the measure by March 30. The bill became law the following May. During 1960 Eastland bottled up an anti-poll tax amendment to the Constitution. He asserted in January that "a person who does not care enough for the franchise to desire to pay a poll tax as a qualification should not be permitted to vote. . . ."

Although Eastland did not publicly support Sen. Joseph R. McCarthy (R, Wisc.) [q.v.] and voted for the censure of the Wisconsin Senator in December 1954, his emphasis upon the threat of domestic Communist subversion was as pronounced as McCarthy's. Eastland became chairman of the Judiciary Committee's Internal Security Subcommittee in 1955. In June and July of that year, the panel began an investigation of Communist penetration in the press and radio. Several newspapers fired reporters who invoked the Fifth Amendment when asked by the subcommittee about their alleged Communist affiliations or about Communist activity at their places of employment. On Jan. 3, 1956, the day before the subcommittee was to resume its investigation, Eastland replied to an American Civil Liberties Union statement criticizing the dismissals. He said that the press must be free from control of the Communist Party or "any other conspiracy against the government of the United States" and stated that no one had the right to associate with a group seeking to overthrow the state by force.

Eastland opposed a June 1956 Supreme Court ruling that President Eisenhower had gone beyond the intent of a 1950 law that established the basis for the federal employe security program. The Court declared that the law was meant to exclude persons of doubtful loyalty only from "sensitive" positions affecting national security. Eastland unsuccessfully introduced a bill to apply the act to all federal jobs.

Disturbed by Supreme Court rulings in civil rights, internal security and other areas, Eastland joined Southerners and anti-Communists who sought to restrict its power. In 1956 he introduced a constitutional amendment providing that "there shall be no limitation upon the power of any state to regulate health, morals, education, marriage and good order in the state." No floor action was taken on the proposal. Eastland claimed that Communist influence on the Court was extensive, and in 1958 he asserted that Justices Hugo Black [q.v.], William Douglas [q.v.] and Felix Frankfurter [q.v.] had taken a "pro-Communist" position in the great majority of cases involving subversive activities. In 1959, after the Court overturned a New York State ban on exhibition of the movie *Lady Chatterley's Lover*, Eastland offered a constitutional amendment barring infringement upon the right of a state "to decide on the basis of its own public policy questions of decency [and] morality." No action was taken on the proposed amendment.

Eastland opposed most of the Kennedy Administration's social welfare programs, including the minimum wage and school aid bills in 1961 and medicare in 1962.

Through the Judiciary Committee he was able to delay Senate confirmation of Thurgood Marshall [q.v.], a black jurist, to a circuit court judgeship for almost a year in 1961 and 1962. Eastland refused to endorse Lyndon Johnson's presidential candidacy in 1964. He opposed all of the Johnson Administration's civil rights proposals and almost all of its domestic welfare programs while endorsing the President's policy in Vietnam. [See KENNEDY, JOHNSON, NIXON/FORD Volumes]

[MLL]

EASTMAN, MAX F(ORRESTER)
b. Jan. 4, 1883; Canandaigua, N.Y.
d. March 25, 1969; Bridgetown, Barbados.
Journalist, writer.

The son of two Congregational ministers, Max Eastman graduated from Williams College in 1905. He completed his doctoral work at Columbia University while teaching philosophy there, but he did not accept his Ph.D. degree because of his dislike for titles. As editor of *The Masses* from 1913 to 1917, he rapidly became a leader of the Greenwich Village left, a collection of individuals who combined revolutionary political and historial philosophies with equally radical artistic ideas. Because *The Masses* opposed U.S. entry into World War I, Eastman and the other editors were tried twice for sedition. Both trials ended in hung juries.

In 1918 Eastman and his sister Crystal formed *The Liberator* and continued to speak out against U.S. foreign policy. After spending 1922-24 in the Soviet Union, Eastman lived in France, where he continued writing as a sympathetic translator of Trotsky and a critic of Stalinist policies. Eastman's disillusionment with Stalin and what he thought was the unscientific Marxism of the Bolshevik experience in the Soviet Union resulted in a retreat from Marxism in 1933. Thereafter he served as a conservative commentator. He began a long career as roving editor with *Reader's Digest* in 1941.

Eastman gained more notoriety for his political views, but he believed—and other critics concurred—that his major achievements were in literary studies. His *The Enjoyment of Poetry* (1913) was long used as a standard college text. *The Literary Mind: Its Place in an Age of Science* (1931) was later praised by Edmund Wilson for its incisive analysis of "the larger relations of art and science to one another, and of both to the society behind them." He also published volumes of his own verse.

A brilliant and sometimes contradictory personality, Eastman in the 1950s was as vociferous a spokesman for the Right as he had been for the Left in the 1910s and 1920s. His reaction to Sen. Joseph R. McCarthy's (R, Wisc.) [q.v.] anti-Communist crusade was similar to that of many conservative intellectuals of the period. He believed McCarthy was clumsy, intemperate and embarassing to the Right, but he wholeheartedly supported a full, public attack on the dangers of Communism. He said he would gladly suffer McCarthyism's minor assaults on civil liberties for its usefulness in rooting out Communists from the government. Eastman reserved his greatest contempt for liberalism. Liberals counterattacked McCarthy, he said, because of their guilt over idealizing Communism in the past. He believed that liberalism, with its support of a growing welfare state and a declining free marketplace, might well destroy Western democracy before Communism could. While confessing an incomplete understanding of economics, he advocated strict laissez-faire capitalism and decentralization of government.

In 1955 Eastman published *Reflections on the Failure of Socialism*, in which he analyzed what he believed were fallacies of Marxist and socialist thinking. The book was widely praised by conservatives as an indictment of leftist philosophies. Eastman attacked socialists for their naive, utopian visions of society that were predicated on the destruction of individual liberties. Fearing collectivism in all forms, he selectively cited historical movements in which democracy was ultimately destroyed by planned economies. He criticized Marxism for an inadequate incorporation of Darwinian and

Freudian theories emphasizing individual, instinctual drives and subconscious behavior unrelated to class.

Eastman accepted William F. Buckley, Jr.'s [q.v.] invitation in 1955 to join the *National Review* as a member of the board of directors and a contributor. He continued to attack Communism, but his avowedly non-religious perspective isolated him from many other conservatives on the staff. Throughout his life Eastman, an atheist, deeply distrusted organized religion and its potential for "ecclesiastical authoritarianism." He earlier had abhorred Communism when he believed it to be a religion, and now he disagreed with conservatives such as Whittaker Chambers [q.v.] who viewed the Cold War as a battle of religion versus atheism. For Eastman, the fight had to be won without the invocation of a deity. He resigned from *National Review* in 1958, although he contributed articles until 1964.

Eastman continued to publish books and essays throughout the 1960s. Commenting on the "young rebels" of that period in an interview with Alden Whitman of the *New York Times*, he said that though they shared some of the intensity of feeling of his own Greenwich Village rebels of the 1910s and 1920s, they "have no ultimate purpose." He described them as apart from the working class, "the bohemian wing of the bourgeoisie." Eastman was working on another book when he died in 1969.

[TGD]

For further information:
John P. Diggins, *Up from Communism: Conservative Odysseys in American Intellectual History* (New York, 1975).

EATON, CYRUS S(TEPHEN)
b. Dec. 27, 1883; Pugwash Junction, Canada.
Industrialist.

A descendant of New England Loyalists who emigrated to Canada in 1782, Cyrus Eaton was the son of a village storekeeper. Starting as a protege of John D. Rockefeller and a trouble-shooter for Rockefeller's East Ohio Gas Co., Eaton went on to establish hundreds of gas and electric utilities throughout the Midwest and Southwest. In the 1920s he moved into the rubber and steel industries, buying up virtual control of the Goodyear Rubber Co. and organizing the Republic Steel Co. out of smaller acquisitions. By 1929 Eaton had accumulated a personal fortune of some $100 million, most of which he lost in the stock market crash.

Over the next few decades Eaton regained his fortune. His base of operations was his Cleveland investment banking firm, Otis & Co., and his strategy was to underbid established Wall Street bankers as an underwriter for offerings of railroad and utilities securities. He gradually acquired extensive holdings in the iron ore and steel industries. In 1954 he became chairman of the board of the Chesapeake & Ohio Railroad and also the West Kentucky Coal Co. Over the years Eaton fought and won a series of protracted legal battles with business competitors, the Securities and Exchange Commission and the Internal Revenue Service.

Beginning in the mid-1950s Eaton became a crusader for world peace and rapprochement between the Soviet Union and the United States. The chief media for his advocacy were the Pugwash Conferences, assemblies hosted by Eaton and attended by leading nuclear scientists and intellectuals from East and West who discussed the perils of nuclear weapons. The conferees at the Second Pugwash Conference in April 1958 urged that nations either ban nuclear tests completely or at least establish radioactivity tests and weapons production quotas.

Eaton's public pronouncements were unique at the time for a businessman of his stature. He excited controversy with his May 1958 statement, "The only people in the U.S. who believe that Communism is a menace to the U.S. are the boys on the payroll of the FBI." "Our proper posture," he said in *The Nation* in January 1959, "is not anti-Communism, but enlightened capitalism." Eaton denounced Secretary of State John Foster Dulles [q.v.], who "blithely courts the ultimate world catastrophe of the bomb without consulting even the Senate Foreign Relations Committee and the House Foreign Affairs Committee." He proposed that the U.S. recognize Communist China, halt the nuclear arms race and sign a treaty of peace and friendship with the Soviet Union.

Russian leaders treated Eaton cordially during his visit to the Soviet Union in September 1958. He spoke for an hour-and-a-half with Premier Nikita Khrushchev at the Kremlin. On several future occasions the Soviets singled out Eaton for honors: in January 1959 First Deputy Premier Anastas Mikoyan presented Eaton with a troika carriage and three-horse team as a gift from Khrushchev, and in July 1960 Soviet envoys awarded Eaton the Lenin Peace Prize.

Within the U.S. there were some hostile reactions to the Cleveland industrialist's praise for Soviet accomplishments and publicized meetings with Communist leaders. After Eaton had met briefly with Khrushchev in May 1960 at Paris's Orly Airport following the collapse of the Paris summit meeting, Sen. Thomas Dodd (D, Conn.) [q.v.] called for prosecution of Eaton under the Logan Act. The measure, passed in 1799, barred private citizens from dealing with foreign governments on U.S. policy matters. However, no action was taken on his demand.

Throughout the 1960s and 1970s Eaton continued to promote and finance the cause of world peace and was a vigorous opponent of the Vietnam war. [See KENNEDY Volume]

[TO]

EATON, FREDERICK M(cCURDY)
b. May 21, 1905; Akron, Ohio.
Chairman, U.S. Delegation, Ten-Nation Committee on Disarmament, March 1960-July 1960.

Frederick Eaton received a B.A. from Harvard University in 1927 and obtained a degree from its law school three years later. He was admitted to the New York bar in 1930 and joined the New York law firm of Shearman and Sterling. During World War II Eaton was general counsel to the War Production Board and a member of the Combined Raw Materials Board and Combined Production and Resources Board. After the War he became a director of the New York Life Insurance Co. In 1954 he was appointed a director of the New York City Bank Farmers Trust Co.

Eaton served as chairman of the U.S. delegation to the 10-nation Committee on Disarmament in 1960. When the panel first met on March 15, he served as spokesman for the Western nations—the U.S., Great Britain, France, Italy and Canada. He presented a joint proposal for conventional and nuclear disarmament enforced by an international disarmament organization with the right of on-site inspection. Reflecting the Western nations' most immediate concern, it called for a total prohibition of orbiting satellites carrying nuclear weapons.

Soviet delegate Valerian A. Zorin rejected the plan on the grounds that it would require a prolonged study of the technical problems of inspection and put off practical disarmament indefinitely. The Soviets opposed early inspection measures as "espionage" and preferred enforcing disarmament controls after each phase of the plan was completed. Zorin refused to give priority to the satellite agreement and insisted that the U.S. agree to remove its military bases from Europe before discussing the issue. The Soviets, in turn, offered a plan for total disarmament within four years. Eaton denounced the plan as a "grand but hollow design" and an "unenforceable scheme."

In an attempt to break the deadlock, Eaton offered on April 14 to terminate Western production of nuclear weapons and allow international inspection of Western atomic plants. In a dramatic move he made public a list of U.S. atomic plants, challenging the Soviets to do the same. Eaton then proposed a joint U.S.-USSR inspection team be formed to check manpower reductions in the armed forces of the two nations. The USSR rejected the proposal.

On July 7 the Soviet Union presented still another proposal calling for the evacuation of foreign military bases in Europe simultaneously with the demolition of nuclear delivery systems as the first stage in disarmament. Eaton rejected the plan. He claimed that, because of Russia's large conventional forces in Eastern Europe, the proposal would leave the small Western nations at the mercy of the USSR. Charging that the U.S. sought only "unilateral military advantages," the Communist delegations withdrew from the Committee on June 27, effectively ending negotiations.

Following the failure of the disarmament conference, Eaton returned to private business. Testifying on disarmament before the Senate Foreign Relations Committee in August 1961, he voiced his support for the creation of the Arms Control and Disarmament Agency.

[AES]

EGAN, WILLIAM ALLEN
b. Oct. 8, 1914; Valdez, Alaska.
Governor, Alaska, 1959-66, 1970-74.

The son of a goldminer, William Egan graduated from Valdez High School in 1932 and worked at odd jobs before buying a general store. He was elected to Alaska's House of Representatives in 1941 and, with the exception of service in the Army from 1943 to 1946, remained there until 1953. He entered the territorial Senate in 1953 and became territorial speaker in 1955.

Egan championed Alaskan statehood throughout his career. Pointing to Alaska's lack of adequate civil government and to its exploitation by the salmon industry, he felt that these problems could be solved only after the territory was admitted to the Union. In 1941 he cosponsored the first bill to submit the issue of statehood to Alaskan voters, but it was defeated. Five years later a majority of Alaskans voted for a statehood referendum. When a coalition of Republicans and Southern Democrats defeated statehood bills in the U.S. Congress during 1950, 1954 and 1955, the territorial legislature decided to force the issue. It called a constitutional convention, which met in 1955 and 1956. Egan, who was elected president of the body, was the principal architect of the constitution, signed in February 1956 and ratified by the voters in

April. The document provided for only two elected statewide officials—the governor and secretary of state. The governor appointed all department heads and judges subject to legislative or judicial council approval. The size of the legislature was increased, and it met annually.

The convention also voted for the so-called Tennessee Plan. Used by Tennessee and six other states, the proposal called for the election of a state delegation of two senators and one representative to go to Washington and lobby for statehood. Egan was elected as part of the all-Democratic delegation in October. Despite Republican fears that Alaska would remain a Democratic state, Congress voted for statehood in July 1958. The following month Alaskans approved statehood five to one.

In November 1958 Egan was elected governor, defeating his Republican opponent by a large margin. Much of Egan's political success could be traced to his personal warmth, in contrast to the impersonal coldness Alaskans had associated with government by the federal bureaucracy. Sworn into office in January 1959, a few months after statehood was proclaimed, Egan fell ill and was unable to assume his duties until April. During the early months of his administration, he presented a budget that increased aid for education, health and welfare. He also ended the issuance of licenses for salmon traps, which he felt reduced the salmon crop and aided corporate fishing interests.

Egan supported Sen. John F. Kennedy (D, Mass.) [q.v.] for President in 1960. The Governor was himself defeated by Republican Walter Hickel in 1966. He again served as governor from 1970 to 1974. [See NIXON/FORD Volume]

[MJS]

EINSTEIN, ALBERT
b. March 14, 1879; Ulm, Germany.
d. April 18, 1955; Princeton, N.J.
Theoretical physicist.

The son of non-religious German-Jewish parents, Einstein moved to Switzerland as a young man and renounced his German citizenship. He graduated from the Federal Institute of Technology in Zurich in 1900, and failing to obtain a teaching position, he was employed as a patent office clerk in Berne. Finding that he could complete a day's work in half the time, Einstein secretly worked on problems in theoretical physics. In 1905 he published a series of papers which were to revolutionize modern physics. Perhaps the most famous of these dealt with his theory of special relativity, which Einstein used to conclude that matter and energy were physically equivalent, in effect interconvertible. This result, stated mathematically $E = mc^2$, furnished an explanation for the liberation of energy in atomic explosions. The other papers dealt with Brownian motion as a final proof of the molecular nature of matter and the photoelectric effect, an important advance in quantum mechanics, which founded the photon theory of light.

Einstein received his doctorate from the University of Zurich in 1909 and taught at Zurich, Prague and Leyden before accepting an offer to direct the Kaiser Wilhelm Institute of Sciences in Berlin in 1913. In 1921 he received the Nobel Prize for his work on the photoelectric effect. During the 1920s Einstein became an active Zionist, traveling extensively to raise funds for Jewish settlement in Palestine. In 1933 he fled Nazi-dominated Germany and accepted a lifetime professorship at Princeton's Institute for Advanced Study.

Although a pacifist in his early years, Einstein abandoned this position following the rise of fascism in Germany and Japan. In 1939 he wrote a letter to Franklin D. Roosevelt urging the U.S. to develop the atomic bomb before the Germans did. His action led to the establishment of the Manhattan Project in 1942. However, the 1945 bombings of Hiroshima and Nagasaki horrified the physicist, and during the postwar period he became a leading spokesman for social responsibility on the part of scientists. As chairman of the Emergency Committee of Atomic Scientists, founded in 1946, Einstein sought to inform Americans of the realities of atomic warfare and the dangers of a nuclear arms race. He called on scientists to refrain from cooperation with the military and opposed the development of the hydrogen bomb. [See TRUMAN Volume]

Einstein scored the anti-Communist crusade of the late-1940s and early-1950s. In 1953 he urged clemency for Julius and Ethel Rosenberg [q.v.], convicted of espionage and later executed. Einstein also spoke out against the abuses of congressional investigating committees. In a letter made public in June 1953, he told a New York City high school teacher who had refused to testify before the Senate Internal Security Subcommittee that "every intellectual who is called before one of the committees ought to refuse to testify." Advocating "the revolutionary way of non-cooperation in the sense of Gandhi's," Einstein asserted that "it is shameful for a blameless citizen to submit to such an inquisition." His letter was cited by several witnesses who refused to testify before congressional committees later that year. In April 1954, when physicist J. Robert Oppenheimer's [q.v.] government security clearance was suspended, Einstein affirmed his confidence in his Princeton colleague.

Einstein continued to advocate disarmament until the end of his life. Early in 1955 he and Nobel Prize winner Lord Bertrand Russell, the British mathematician and philosopher, drafted an international appeal against the further development or use of atomic weapons. Warning that "a war with hydrogen bombs might quite possibly put an end to the race," they asked, "Shall we . . . choose death, because we cannot forget our quarrels?"

Einstein died of a ruptured aorta in April 1955. The Einstein-Russell statement, signed by six other Nobel Prize winners, was sent to various heads of state in July. It led to the first of the Pugwash Conferences, held in 1957, where scientists from all over the world met to further the cause of disarmament.

[MDB]

For further information:
Banesh Hoffman, *Albert Einstein, Creator and Rebel* (New York, 1972).
Robert Jungk, *Brighter Than a Thousand Suns* (New York, 1958).

EISENHOWER, DWIGHT D(AVID)
b. Oct. 14, 1890; Denison, Texas
d. March 28, 1969; Washington, D.C.
President of the United States, 1953-61.

Born into a family of Swiss descent, David Eisenhower was raised in Abilene, Kan., where his father worked at a local creamery. While a child he earned the nickname "Ike," which remained with him throughout his life. Despite his mother's pacificism and his father's lack of political influence, Eisenhower won appointment to West Point in 1911. He enrolled under the name Dwight D., which he used thereafter. He graduated in 1915 near the bottom of his class.

Eisenhower served as a tank instructor during World War I and remained in the Army after the armistice. He graduated from the Command and General Staff School in 1926, the Army War College in 1929 and the Army Industrial College in 1932. During the 1930s he worked under Gen. Douglas A. MacArthur, both as his personal assistant and as assistant military adviser to the Philpphine Commonwealth.

After the American entry into World War II Eisenhower served as Gen. George C. Marshall's chief of operations. In 1942 he assumed command of the U.S. forces in Europe and oversaw the Allied invasion of North Africa in 1942 and Sicily and Italy in 1943. The following year, as supreme commander of all Allied forces, he took charge of planning the Normandy invasion. Eisenhower's strength as a commander lay in his political ability to unite and utilize Allied leaders, maintain good public relations and administer a vast bureaucracy. He was also a noted strategist.

In 1945 President Harry S. Truman appointed Eisenhower Army Chief of Staff. He remained at that post until 1948, when he accepted the presidency of Columbia University. Uncomfortable in the academic world, he resigned his appointment in 1951 to assume command of forces being organized under the North Atlantic Treaty Organization (NATO).

During the late-1940s and early-1950s representatives of the liberal Eastern wing of the Republican Party—politicians such as Sen. Henry Cabot Lodge (R, Mass.) [q.v.] and financiers like Paul Hoffman [q.v.] attempted to persuade Eisenhower to run for President. These men, anxious to win control of the Party from Midwestern nationalists led by Sen. Robert Taft (R, Ohio) [q.v.], felt the General would be their ideal candidate. He supported their stand for a strong American economy unencumbered by government. More importantly he was anxious to continue a bipartisan foreign policy with full U.S. participation in European affairs. Too, they thought that Eisenhower, with his lack of political background and high moral purpose, could lead a crusade that would return the U.S. to its traditional values. "The people want another George Washington," wrote Harry A. Bullis to Eisenhower, "to them you are the man who can best help them keep their liberty and their freedom." However, Eisenhower, anxious to develop a collective security system in Europe and opposed to military men in politics, refused.

By 1951 he had begun to change his mind. Private discussions with Taft left him convinced that a Taft presidency would jeopardize American interests in Europe. Lodge had also convinced Eisenhower that he was the only man to unite the Republican Party and prevent it from becoming a splinter group outside the mainstream of American politics.

Toward the end of 1951 Eisenhower assumed he would run. However, he decided to remain publicly uncommitted as long as possible to continue his work in Europe and maintain his image of a man above partisan politics. The initial moves in his campaign were left to such men as Hoffman and Lodge, who entered his name in the March New Hampshire primary. That election proved a dramatic display of the General's appeal. Without campaigning, he received approximately 50% of the total Republican vote to Taft's almost 37%. The result was similar in Minnesota, where Eisenhower's name was not even on the ballot. He received 108,692 write-in votes to Harold Stassen's [q.v.] 129,976.

Following these victories Eisenhower decided to return home and actively participate in the race. His campaign focused on his position as a leader above politics. It extolled him as a common, no-nonsense man representing traditional values synonymous with Americanism. His major weapon was his candor and personality. "He is direct," wrote James Reston [q.v.], "he speaks in sentences and avoids intellectual detours, a political rarity not practiced since the days of Woodrow Wilson."

By the time of the Chicago Convention in July, the struggle for the nomination centered around the seating of rival delegations from Georgia, Florida, Louisiana and Texas. The pro-Taft regulars on the Republican National Committee seated Taft's delegates in most cases. However, Eisenhower took the struggle to the floor, where he won a crucial vote on the issue. The General then easily won the nomination. On the advice of his senior staff members, Eisenhower chose conservative California Sen. Richard Nixon [q.v.] as his running mate.

Eisenhower campaigned on a pledge to "lead a great crusade for freedom in America and freedom in the world." Attempting to gain the support of Republican conservatives, he moved to the right on domestic issues but continued to press for American involvement in European affairs. Eisenhower concentrated on three issues, abbreviated as K_1C_2. He attempted to link his Democratic opponent, Adlai Stevenson [q.v.], to the Truman Administration ·and that Administration to the nation's frustrations. He charged that the Democrats had continued an unpopular war in Korea and permitted corruption and Communists in government. In September the campaign was briefly stalled by revelations that Nixon had benefited from a special political fund. But following Nixon's successful defense in his "Checkers speech," Eisenhower used his running mate extensively. During the last months of the race, public opinion polls showed that Eisenhower was ahead. His announcement in October, "I shall go to Korea," although not accompanied by any specific plan to end the war, clinched the election.

The turnout in November was nearly 61.5 million—the highest to date. Eisenhower won easily, taking 41 states and receiving 442 electoral votes. He showed remarkable strength in the South, carrying Texas, Virginia, Tennessee and Oklahoma. Yet Eisenhower's landslide did not extend to the congressional races. Republicans gained a majority of only eight seats in the House and tied with the Democrats in the Senate.

Eisenhower assumed the presidency with a narrow constitutionalist view of his role. He saw himself as a man above partisan politics whose major duty was to give direction to American foreign and domestic policy. The formation of specific proposals and the task of getting plans accepted was left to his subordinates, his cabinet and his staff. The new President believed it was his duty to propose legislation on the advice of his counselors, but to go further and push its passage would have been an infringement on the prerogatives of Congress. It also would have impaired the dignity of his office. "I don't feel like I should nag them," he said, and at times he carried this belief to the point of refusing to comment on bills. Because Eisenhower wished to maintain the image of a man above politics, partisan tasks were left to subordinates working under his direction.

Seeing himself in many ways as "a chairman of the board," Eisenhower restored the cabinet to its place as the highest advisory panel of the executive branch. He appointed men to cabinet posts who shared his belief in the need to limit government action and who supported his emphasis on maintaining a free, healthy economy to form the basis for a socially, politically and militarily strong America. With the exception of John Foster Dulles [q.v.] and Martin Durkin [q.v.], he chose his advisers from the upper ranks of business management. Three cabinet members, Charles Wilson, [q.v.], Arthur Summerfield [q.v.] and Douglas McKay [q.v.] had ties to General Motors. The New Republic quipped, "The New Dealers have all left Washington to make way for the car dealers."

Although a conservative, Eisenhower was essentially a pragmatist: in the words of historian Herbert Parmet, "a practitioner of the art of the possible." He often reacted on an *ad hoc* basis to the human aspect of a problem rather than on the basis of political philosophy. He, like his advisers, had come to terms with the New Deal and realized they could not turn back the clock to the 1920s. Yet he believed the American people needed a period of rest and consolidation after the dramatic changes of the previous 30 years. He came to office not with an activist philosophy but with the intention of healing the nation's wounds and unifying the country.

During his first term Eisenhower focused his attention on achieving two goals: restoring and strengthening the free economy by holding down government expenses, balancing the budget, and reducing taxes, and restricting the role of the federal government wherever possible. Shortly after taking office, Eisenhower removed wage and price controls established by the Truman Administration. With the goal of eventually balancing the budget, he cut Truman's fiscal 1953 appropriations. However, he refused conservative calls for a tax cut that year because revenues were needed to support the continuing war in Korea. Although he hoped to eventually cut taxes, Eisenhower believed that a reduction would have to wait until he achieved a balanced budget. As it turned out, Eisenhower cut taxes in 1954. Despite Democratic pleas for an across-the-board reduction, he approved a cut aiding the wealthy and businesses on the grounds that it would stimulate investment and thus ultimately benefit all Americans. Eisenhower finally achieved a balanced budget in 1956, when records showed a surplus of $1.75 billion.

The President was intent on reducing the government's size and restricting its role as much as possible. He dramatically curbed federal government's size and restricting its role. He dramatically curbed hiring and cut the number of federal contracts. Agencies such as the Reconstruction Finance Corp., which he thought unnecessary, were eliminated. Eisenhower took the White House out of labor relations, leaving the settlement of most strikes to the National Labor Relations Board rather than to executive intervention. During the recession of 1954 he refused pleas for a massive government program of housing construction, slum clearance, and improved unemployment compensation to create jobs and put money back into the economy. Instead, he instituted a modest tax cut and relied on American confidence that he would act if the situation worsened to pull the country to pull the country out of the slump.

Eisenhower also supported Secretary of Agriculture Ezra Taft Benson's [*q.v.*] agricultural policies despite opposition from small farmers. The plans called for the removal of rigid price supports and their replacement with a sliding scale which would have gradually moved agriculture toward an open market. In the spring of 1956, Eisenhower vetoed a Democratic bill restoring rigid parity supports. However, he accepted a compromise measure establishing a "soil bank" that payed farmers for keeping land out of production.

Natural resource and power development was one of the major areas in which Eisenhower attempted decentralization. He quickly redeemed a campaign pledge to return oil-bearing tidelands to the states by signing the submerged lands bill in 1953. He also approved New York State's development of power sites on the U.S. side of the proposed St. Lawrence Seaway and backed private construction of generating facilities at Hell's Canyon on the Snake River.

However, Eisenhower was defeated when he attempted to limit the government operated Tennessee Valley Authority (TVA). Pointing to it as an example of "creeping socialism" and maintaining that he would sell it if there was any way possible, in 1954 he took steps to prevent its further expansion. In January he ordered the Atomic Energy Commission (AEC) to sign a contract with a private utility, headed by Edgar Dixon [*q.v.*] and Eugene Yates, to build a generating plant near West Memphis, Ark. The utility would then sell power to the AEC facilities in the area, obviating further TVA expansion. But because of Democratic pressure and revelations of scandals in the awarding of the contract, Eisenhower canceled it in July 1955.

Unlike traditional conservatives, Eisenhower was not adverse to all federal development projects. He managed to push the St. Lawrence Seaway project through Congress in 1954, where it had been stalled for more than three decades. However, he preferred to handle development in conjunction with states whenever possible. His most ambitious project was the construction of a federal highway system, authorized in 1956. The project called for the building of some 42,000 miles of controlled-access roads linking major cities. Under the proposal both state and federal governments took part in the effort, but the federal government paid 90% of the cost.

While Eisenhower attempted to limit government intervention in many areas, he did not believe large cuts should be made in social services. He described himself as a "conservative when it comes to money and liberal when it comes to human beings." During his first term services were expanded in several areas. In 1954 Congress passed the single biggest expansion of Social Security to date, extending coverage to the self-employed. Two years later Eisenhower sought an increase in the minimum wage from 75 to 90 cents. Congress passed a bill raising the wage to $1. The President also supported limited expansion in housing, medical care and education. In 1954 he signed a measure to finance the construction of 45,000 units over four years. He also proposed a plan for subsiding private health insurance programs. However, it died in Congress as a result of opposition from the American Medical Association, which thought the plan would lead to socialized medicine, and liberal Democrats, who maintained it was inadequate. In 1956 Eisenhower called for federal grants to states for school construction. The bill died after Rep. Clayton Powell Jr. (D, N.Y.) [q.v.], inserted an amendment denying funds to racially segrated school districts.

Eisenhower was primarily interested in foreign and defense policy. During his eight years in office, he worked closely with Secretary of State Dulles to mold a policy that reflected his conception of a bipolarized world engaged in a struggle between freedom and Communism. Dulles was the conceptualizer and prime mover of foreign policy. Nevertheless, Eisenhower knew his own mind on foreign affairs, and in many crises, he exercised restraint on his more headstrong Secretary. Although often resorting to bellicose language, Eisenhower dismissed war as an option. His primary goal was to remain at peace while containing Communism and extending American influence throughout the world.

Shortly after he was elected President, Eisenhower began steps to end the Korean war. Fulfilling his campaign pledge to go to Korea, he staged a brief visit in November to inspect troops and to talk to South Korean President Syngman Rhee. The journey did not aid peace efforts, but it reassured the American people that the new President, with his vast military experience, was focusing his attention on the problem. After his inauguration Eisenhower began pressuring both Communist China and South Korea into accepting an armistice. He removed the Seventh Fleet from the Formosa Straits, thus "unleashing" Chiang Kai-shek for a possible attack on the mainland. He also increased U.S. air forces in Korea and announced that nuclear weapons were being moved to Okinawa. While developing a hard-line attitude toward Communist China, he firmly opposed South Korean demands for an agreement to resume fighting if Korea was not unified within 90 days of an armistice. The peace agreement was signed on July 27.

Eisenhower's primary focus was on Europe, which he considered the major front of the Cold War. There he continued Truman's containment policy of redeveloping and eventually unifying Western Europe economically and militarily to prevent further Communist expansion. The President quickly stopped his attacks on the Yalta and Potsdam agreements, which conservatives contended led to the division of Europe. He feared that repudiation might deny Western access rights to Berlin, affirmed at Yalta, and he disliked the prospect of renouncing agreements he had carried out while Army Chief of Staff. In a resolution to Congress during the early months of 1953, Eisenhower pointed to a Soviet perversion of the agreements rather than a Roosevelt betrayal as responsible for Communist expansion in Eastern Europe. He also dropped calls for the "liberation" of Eastern Europe, which the Republican Party had pledged during the 1952 campaign and which had become hollow in light of U.S. impotence during the 1953 East German uprising. The President's attempt to unify Western Europe met with only modest success. Despite his and Dulles's vigorous support, the French voted down the European Defense Community for fear of German rearmament. He did, however, succeed in integrating West Germany into NATO.

Despite his continuation of Cold War policies and often strident rhetoric, Eisenhower believed that a reduction in tensions between the two superpowers was possible. However, the conditions he imposed made accomodation unlikely. Over the objections of his Secretary of State, he responded to the Soviet peace overtures made shortly after the death of Stalin. In a speech before the American Association of Newspaper Editors in April, Eisenhower deplored the price of the continued arms race. "This is not a way of life at all," he said, "in any true sense. Under the cloud of threatening war, it is humanity hanging from a cross of iron." He expressed American hope of cooperation and announced that he would regard even a "few clear and specific acts of reciprocation," such as the beginning of Soviet withdrawal from Eastern Europe, as "impressive signs" that the Russians shared his desires. Because of domestic pressures on both sides, the peace overtures produced no results. Two years later Eisenhower, again over the objections of Dulles, attended a summit conference between Soviet leaders and those of the Western bloc. No agreement was reached on the issues dividing them— Germany and disarmament—but the fact that leaders had actually confronted problems led to a brief period of relaxed tensions.

Eisenhower faced two major threats to peace during 1954: in Vietnam and in the Formosa Straits. In the spring of 1954 the French requested American military aid to relieve their beleagured garrison at Dien Bien Phu in northern Vietnam. Eisenhower refused the Joint Chiefs of Staff's plans for using American air strikes and atomic weapons if necessary against the Communist Vietminh.

Several months later the President resisted further suggestions that the U.S. permit Nationalist China to bomb the mainland in retaliation for Communist shelling of the Nationalist held islands of Quemoy and Matsu. Instead, he sent Dulles to negotiate a mutual defense treaty to prevent China from undertaking offensive operations without American consent. Meanwhile, Eisenhower put pressure on the Communists. In January 1955 he asked Congress to pass the Formosa Resolution, giving the President full authority to take whatever action he deemed necessary to defend Formosa. Shortly after passage Eisenhower conceded that the U.S. would use atomic weapons in a general Asian war. The Chinese diminished shelling, and in 1955 they indicated they were ready to negotiate the issue.

Eisenhower's defense policy was determined by several factors but principally his belief that a large defense budget would weaken the U.S. economy. "This country could choke itself to death piling up military expenditures," he said, "just as surely as it can defeat itself by not spending for protection." He, therefore, worked to reduce and hold down the size and coast of the military establishment. Eisenhower also assumed that the U.S. would never start a war and should therefore focus its resources on deterrence rather than attack. Refusing to become involved in ground wars that drained the military and sapped the economy and believing that future wars would quickly turn into nuclear combat, Eisenhower relied on the delivery of nuclear weapons by strategic aircraft as America's major deterrent. This program was designed to provide an alternative to the costly Truman policy of funding both conventional and nuclear forces.

Eisenhower began implementing the new plans in fiscal 1955. In a policy paper approved in October 1954, the Administration called for a 25% reduction in the size of the American military in 1956. This was to be achieved primarily through cutbacks in Army and Navy manpower and budgets.

On the other hand, the Air Force was slightly enlarged and its funding increased. Despite opposition from the Army and some Navy personnel, Eisenhower, playing on the belief that as a military man he understood the situation, pushed the budget through Congress.

During his first term, Eisenhower was forced to devote a large amount of his time to assuaging the Republican Right. Throughout his presidency he was challenged by the China bloc, a group of conservative members of Congress led by such men as William Knowland (R, Calif.) [q.v.], who opposed any accommodation with Communist China. It was partly in response to this attitude that Eisenhower remained stridently opposed to the admission of Communist China to the U.N. and rejected suggestions of negotiating differences with the mainland.

Yet Eisenhower often successfully opposed the Right. Shortly after taking office he faced a difficult struggle over the nomination of Charles Bohlen [q.v.] to be ambassador to the Soviet Union. Conservatives linked the Foreign Service official with what they called the "Truman-Acheson policy of appeasement" and suggested that he was a security rick. Nevertheless, Eisenhower stood firm against requests from several high officials to withdraw the appointment. With the help of Taft, the nomination was confirmed in late March.

The following year Eisenhower faced a more serious challenge when Sen. John Bricker (R, Ohio) [q.v.] resubmitted a proposal which, among other things, limited the President's treaty-making powers. Fearing to anger the Republican Right and refusing to become personally involved in a vigorous partisan debate, Eisenhower directed the attack against the proposal from the background, letting the State Department play the principal role. He privately denounced the amendment as "senseless and plain damaging to the prestige of the U.S." After a lengthy battle, the proposal was defeated by one vote.

Eisenhower's biggest challenge came from Sen. Joseph McCarthy (R. Wisc.) [q.v.], then in the midst of his controversial anti-Communist crusade. The President personally detested the man and his methods. Nevertheless, despite requests from aides such as Emmet J. Hughes [q.v.], he refused to counter him directly. Eisenhower questioned whether a presidential attack would solve the problem. He feared that any attempt to discipline McCarthy would estrange conservatives and might prompt the Senate the defend its member. Preferring to remain above political strife, he refused to "get down into the gutter with that guy."

Just as important in explaining Eisenhower's lack of action was his perception of the prevailing mood of the nation. Like many of his countrymen, he questioned McCarthy's methods but was sympathetic to his goal, believing it necessary to destroy domestic Communism. In response to challenges from the Right and to his own anti-Communism, Eisenhower strengthened the executive branch's security program. Under Executive Order 10450, issued in April, 1953, federal employment was contingent on whether retention was "clearly consistent with the interests of the national security." Thus individuals could be fired not only because they were proved security risks but also because they had questionable associations or personal habits. In one of his most controversial actions, in December 1953 Eisenhower suspended J. Robert Oppenheimer's [q.v.] security clearance after receiving information that the scientist had been associated with Communists during World War II.

Eisenhower made two overt moves against Sen. McCarthy during 1953. At a speech at Dartmouth College during June, he denounced the "book burners," a reference to McCarthy aides Roy Cohn [q.v.] and G. David Schine [q.v.], who were conducting searches for subversive literature in State Department libraries overseas. The following month he replied to an article in which McCarthy aide J. B. Matthews [q.v.] maintained the Protestant clergy was heavily infiltrated by Communists. In a latter to the National Conference of Christians and Jews, Eisenhower castigated such "generalized and irresponsible attacks."

Anxious not to offend the Right but intent on preserving the privileges of the executive branch, Eisenhower moved against McCarthy in early 1954. The President supported Army Secretary Robert Stevens's [q.v.] refusal to continue testifying before McCarthy's Permanent Investigation Subcommittee after he had been vigorously attacked by McCarthy. Several times during March, Eisenhower, without mentioning McCarthy's name, publicly cautioned that "we can't defeat Communists by destroying the things in which we believe." On March 10 he defended Sen. Ralph Flanders (R. Vt.) [q.v.], then publically attacking McCarthy. Eisenhower, however, played little part in the events leading to the Senate's condemnation of McCarthy in December.

In September Eisenhower suffered a "moderately severe" heart attack from which he made a rapid recovery. His health, however, made him dubious about seeking a second term. Pressure from party regulars and friends as well as opinion polls showing that he could win easily forced him to consider a race. Upon receiving assurances from his doctors that he was in good health, Eisenhower announced his candidacy on Feb. 25. After several weeks of hesitation, he stated that Nixon would again be his running mate.

Eisenhower ran on a platform emphasizing the peace and prosperity he had brought the nation and promising more of the same. His Democratic opponent, Adlai Stevenson, had difficulty finding an issue on which to attack the popular President. At length he focused on Eisenhower's health. But the President's obvious physical well-being and Stevenson's own exhaustion after a grueling primary negated the issue.

Eisenhower's handling of two diplomatic crises during the campaign strengthened his position. In the fall the British, French and Israelis attacked Egypt in an effort to regain control of the Suez Canal, nationalized after American refusal to finance the Aswan Dam. Eisenhower refused to join the invasion and instead brought the matter before the U.N. There the U.S. joined the USSR in calling for a ceasefire and withdrawal. In late October, Hungarians rebelled against Russian occupation. Eisenhower personally appealed to Soviet leaders to let Hungary alone, but did nothing to aid the rebels.

On Nov. 6 the President won reelection by a landslide. Taking every state but seven, Eisenhower accumulated 457 electoral votes against Stevenson's 74. Nearly 58% of the voters supported Ike. Once again his popularity failed to carry the Party. Democrats maintained control of Congress.

During his second term the President became embroiled in the growing struggle for civil rights. Eisenhower, himself, took a moderate stand on the issue. Questioning the value of coercion and anxious not to overstep his constitutional authority, he refused to take a firm stand in support of the *Brown* decision of 1954, outlawing segregation in public schools. He told an assistant, "I am convinced that the Supreme Court decision set back progress in the South at least 15 years. No matter how much law we have, we have a job in education and getting people to understand what are the issues here involved." He also questioned the value of sweeping civil rights legislation and said he had no use for those who "believed that legislation alone could institute instant morality." Nevertheless, Eisenhower believed strongly that all citizens should have the right to vote.

Under growing pressure from the public and at the urging of his aides, particularly Attorney General Herbert Brownell [q.v.], he submitted a voting rights proposal to Congress in April 1956. The bill was stalled in committee, and 1957 Eisenhower submitted a stronger measure. It guaranteed voting rights, empowered the Justice Department to institute suits on behalf of blacks denied their rights and suspended jury trials for people held in contempt of court for interfering with the voting rights of others. Eisenhower signed a modified version of the bill without the enforcement provision and with a compromise on the jury trials issue in September. Privately he had worked for the passage of the measure. However, because of his formalistic view of the President's role, he refused to attempt to rally public support behind the measure. Three years later Eisenhower supported a second bill strengthening the existing law.

Eisenhower did act forcefully in September 1957, when Arkansas Gov. Orval Faubus raised a serious challenge to federal authority by refusing a court order to desegregate Little Rock's Central High School. Acting in defense of national supremacy over states rights, the President federalized the National Guard, which Faubus had used to prevent integration, and he sent a thousand paratroopers to enforce the court's decision. The troops remained there until December.

The first two years of his second administration proved a difficult time for Eisenhower. The popular President, once immune from personal attack, was increasingly criticized by the press and politicians. The conservative *U.S. News and World Report* said he had been "lucky" as President but that "things had changed." Other reporters questioned his golfing vacations and appointments while legislators complained of his failure to support important bills. A series of conflict-of-interest scandals rocked the Administration and eventually led to the resignation of Eisenhower's chief of staff, Sherman Adams [*q.v.*], in September 1958. The President, who in 1952 had promised to lead a moral crusade, was denounced for "self-righteous moralizing."

American interests abroad seemed increasingly threatened. The U.S. position in the Middle East had deteriorated as a result of the Administration's failure to come to grips with growing nationalism. Instead of a united front to resist Communist aggression, the section was divided into supporters of the Soviet and Western blocs. Fearing the loss of the area to Communists, Eisenhower moved to commit the U.S. more deeply to the Middle East. In January 1958 he received congressional approval for a resolution, known as the Eisenhower Doctrine, giving the President the power to use American forces to support nations facing "armed aggression from any country controlled by international Communism."

During 1958 tensions in the area mounted. Anti-Western elements gained power in Iraq and threatened to take over Jordan and Lebanon. In response to a request from Lebanese President Camille Chamoun, Eisenhower sent American troops in July to prevent a possible coup by Pan-Arab elements which the Lebanese leader thought might have Communist ties. The effect was successful, yet it did not strengthen the American position in the area. Nationalism remained a strong force which Eisenhower could not understand. Soviet influence in the area increased and Arab belief that the U.S. was pro-Israeli, despite Eisenhower's efforts to remain neutral, strained relations.

Just as Lebanon settled down the Communist Chinese resumed shelling Quemoy and Matsu. Eisenhower again attempted to use a hard-line posture to force the Chinese to back down. In September he announced that the U.S. was prepared to defend the islands. However, his stand won support neither in the nation nor among the U.S. allies, and he was forced to retreat. Dulles acknowledged that the U.S. was under no obligation to defend the islands and termed Chaing Kai-shek's stationing of large garrisons on Quemoy "rather foolish." Responding to Eisenhower's signal, Peking gradually reduced its shelling.

The U.S. position in Europe was also weakened. The crisis of 1956 had left the alliance severely strained. Although Eisenhower was able to restore relations with Great Britain, France, under Charles De Gaulle, decided to pursue an independent foreign policy. Eisenhower had difficulty in getting the allies to accept U.S. missiles and had to acquiesce to further talks with the Soviets before an agreement was reached. A severe crisis developed in November 1958, when Nikita Khrushchev announced that the West would have to make Berlin an autonomous, free city within six months or the USSR would transfer control of the transit routes into West Berlin to the East Germans. Because relations among the allies were strained, Eisenhower had difficulty in getting a united stand on the issue.

On the domestic front Eisenhower faced increasing problems with the Democratic controlled Congress. In 1957 the President and the legislature engaged in what was termed "the great budget battle." Eisenhower submitted a 1958 fiscal budget calling for a modest program of school construction grants, water resource development and expansion of social welfare programs. Only small increases were scheduled in defense and foreign aid. Fearing the pleas by various government departments, particularly the Pentagon, would increase the budget, Eisenhower asked Congress to carefully consider possible cuts. Congress reacted by slashing the budget, and the President was put in an incongruous position of asking the legislature to restore the funds. A recession compounded his problems. During 1957 and 1958 industrial production dropped by 14% and unemployment reached 7%, a high for the decade. Because of the recession tax revenues dropped, and the Administration faced a projected half-billion dollar deficit instead of a $1.8 billion surplus.

Eisenhower's greatest domestic problems in his second term came in the fall of 1957 following the Soviet Union's launching of the *Sputnik*, the first artificial earth satellite. The announcement, coming just after the USSR had successfully fired an intercontinental ballistic missile, destroyed the U.S. sense of security and opened debate on American defense policy. Eisenhower faced open criticism from the military, which objected to his limiting defense expenditures and to continuing reliance on the policy of massive retaliation in light of growing nuclear parity. Members of the Army and Navy, led by such men as Gen. Maxwell Taylor [*q.v.*] and Adm. Arleigh Burke [*q.v.*], maintained that future conflicts would be primarily limited wars and insisted that increased funds be given to conventional forces. The Air Force, in turn, stressed the need for an accelerated program of missile development to maintain U.S. superiority. It was joined by a number of influential individuals, including Sens. Stuart Symington (D, Mo.) [*q.v.*] and John F. Kennedy (D, Mass.) [*q.v.*], who suggested that Eisenhower had permitted a potentially fatal "missile gap" to grow between the U.S. and the USSR. Eisenhower, who had given up the concept of nuclear superiority in favor of one of sufficiency, vainly attempted to convince his critics that despite USSR superiority in missiles, American nuclear delivery capacity still far outweighed that of the Soviet Union.

Eisenhower was also criticized for not encouraging U.S. scientific and technological potential. Some individuals called upon him to develop a crash program in education to produce a greater number of scientists. Others wanted a firm commitment to a space race, with the U.S. pledged to achieve superiority over the USSR in astronautics. Reacting to criticism the President cautioned that despite a "high sense of urgency" the U.S. should not "mount our charger and trot to ride off in all directions at once." He announced the appointment of James Killian [*q.v.*] as special assistant to the President for science and technology and supported reorganization of government efforts to encourage individuals to enter scientific careers. Eisenhower submitted a budget in 1958 that called for increased spending on an accelerated missile program and on educational proposals designed to improve U.S. technical knowledge. He warned that "to amass military power without regard to our economic capacity would be to defend ourselves against one kind of disaster by inviting another." Therefore, while educational funds were increased, other domestic welfare projects were reduced to compensate for defense costs. Congress gave the President more than he asked. The result was a dramatic $12.5 billion deficit, the biggest of the Eisenhower period.

Never fully convinced that space flight was either practical or intrinsically valuable, Eisenhower only reluctantly developed a space program in 1958. He was anxious to use space only for peaceful scientific exploration and so refused recommendations that the missile and satellite programs be combined. Despite protests from the Air Force, he put the new space program under the auspices of the National Aeronautics and Space Administration (NASA), a civil agency created in July 1958.

By April 1958 Eisenhower's support was dramatically reduced from that at the beginning of his second term. Shortly after his election 72% of the people had backed the President, less than 2 years later, only 49% did. In November Eisenhower was faced with still another Democratic victory in the congressional elections. Democrats controlled the Senate 64 to 32 and the House 282 to 54. Only 14 Republican governors remained in office.

The last two years of his Administration marked an Eisenhower resurgence. He proved an effective champion of fiscal conservatism against efforts to add new domestic programs and fund existing ones. He accepted moderate increases in military funding but refused calls for continued increases in missile and space programs. In 1959 he vetoed public housing bills, public works appropriations and other domestic legislation he considered extravagant. The following year Eisenhower's threatened veto and the inability of liberal Democrats to overcome the opposition of Republicans and Southern Democrats limited domestic legislation. In contrast to previous years, when foreign aid bills were often slashed, Eisenhower's expanded program received gram received only limited cuts. By the beginning of 1960 polls showed that 71% of the nation approved his leadership.

America's position in foreign affairs also improved. The USSR retreated from its stand on Berlin, announcing that the West would be given an 18-month extension to consider its proposals. Khrushchev's visit to the U.S. in September 1959 produced a thaw in U.S.—USSR relations. The two superpowers took their first step toward nuclear weapons limitation in December 1959, when both countries joined 10 others in signing the Antarctic Treaty, establishing a nuclear free zone in the area.

After the death of Dulles in May 1959, Eisenhower concentrated foreign policy in his own hands. Increasingly he felt that his historic mission was to encourage a "just and lasting peace." He told the nation: "There is no place on this earth to which I would not travel, there is no chore I would not undertake, if I had any faintest hope that, by so doing, I would promote the general cause of world peace." Eisenhower undertook a series of goodwill visits to Latin America, Asia and Africa which, while doing little to settle outstanding issues, increased his personal standing.

Eisenhower gradually began reorienting U.S. policy towards Latin American. Still intent on preventing Communist expansion in the area, he initiated steps to bring down the government of Fidel Castro, the left-wing Cuban leader who had come to power in 1959. In response to the confiscation of American property in July, Eisenhower cut Cuba's sugar quota by 700,000 tons. Later that year he took steps to prohibit Cuban sugar from the U.S. market for the early part of 1961. In March 1960 he approved a Central Intelligence Agency plan to train Cuban exiles for an invasion of the island.

In other areas of Latin America, however, the President began efforts to prevent Communist expansion through the use of massive long-term economic aid. He warned that the choice was "social evolution or revolution." In September 1960 the Administration proposed a program, known as the Act of Bogata, to assist health services, expand housing and educational facilities and aid agriculture. It was supported by all Latin American nations with the exception of Cuba. Eisenhower's policies formed the basis for President Kennedy's Alliance for Progress.

Two events marred Eisenhower's last months in office. In May his summit meeting with Khrushchev was canceled following the Soviet downing of a U.S. spy plane over Russian territory. The President took personal responsibility for the incident. For the first time in history a head of state openly admitted that his nation engaged in espionage against another country. In June his trip to Japan was canceled because of anti-American riots generated by the Japanese Parliament's ratification of an unpopular military treaty with the U.S.

Eisenhower played only a small part in the 1960 presidential race. He accepted the nomination of Vice President Richard Nixon as inevitable. However, he waited until March 1960 to give the Vice President a less than enthusiastic endorsement. At Nixon's request Eisenhower did not campaign actively. The Vice President wished to establish his own identity without contradicting the Administration's policies. Anxious to defeat John F. Kennedy, the Democratic nominee, the President grew impatient with Nixon's delay in asking his participation. Only during the last week of the race did Eisenhower energentically campaign for his Vice President. On election night he made a television appeal to West Coast voters which helped Nixon carry California. However, the intervention came too late. Kennedy, who had not directly attacked Eisenhower during the campaign because of his immense popularity, narrowly defeated Nixon.

In his January farewell address to the nation, Eisenhower delivered one of his most famous speeches. He warned of the pervasiveness of a growing "military-industrial complex." He regretted the "conjunction of an immense military establishment and a large arms industry. . . . The total influence—economic, political, even spiritual —is felt in every city, every state house, every office of the federal government." He warned of the need to guard against its unwarranted influence and its potential "for the disastrous rise of misplaced power." The weight of this combination, he suggested, could "endanger our liberties or our democratic processes."

Eisenhower retired to his farm near Gettysburg, Pa. The General, as he wished to be called, consistently opposed increases in defense spending during the Kennedy Administration. He also called for reduced troop commitments to NATO. Eisenhower remained the most popular leader of the Republican Party, but his refusal to join in party infighting limited his political influence during the remainder of his life. He supported President Lyndon B. Johnson's Vietnam policies and frequently advised the President. Eisenhower endorsed Nixon for President in 1968 and denied that he had "never really liked or supported or really believed in Nixon." Three weeks before the election he suffered a severe heart attack from which he never recovered. Eisenhower died on March 28, 1969. [See KENNEDY, JOHNSON Volumes]

During the decades after Eisenhower left office, historians and political scientists' assessments at his presidency changed. In the late-1950s and early-1960s, Eisenhower was criticized for his formalist view of the presidency, his lack of an activist domestic program and his cold war rhetoric. William

Shannon viewed the Administration as a "time of great postponement" while others described it as "the bland leading the bland." Richard Rovere [q.v.] termed Eisenhower's leadership "mastery in the service of drift." In polls asking scholars to evaluate the presidency in terms of previous ones, Eisenhower was ranked near the bottom with James Buchanan and Chester Arthur.

By the end of the 1960s historians' assessment of the Eisenhower Administration had changed. Disillusioned with the "Imperial Presidency" and reacting to the domestic tensions of the period, scholars viewed Eisenhower as a man of peace. He had united a deeply divided society, prevented the development of political extremism and furthered the acceptance of the welfare state. More importantly, Eisenhower held down the arms race and gave the nation almost eight years without war.

[EWS]

For further information:
Sherman Adams, *Firsthand Report: The Story of the Eisenhower Administration* (New York, 1961).
Charles Alexander, *Holding the Line: The Eisenhower Era, 1952-1961* (Bloomington, 1975).
Dwight D. Eisenhower, *The White House Years*, 2 vols. (Garden City, 1963-65).
Emmet John Hughes, *The Ordeal of Power: A Political Memoir of the Eisenhower Years* (New York, 1963)
Arthur Larson, *Eisenhower: The President Nobody Knew* (New York, 1968).
Herbert S. Parmet, *Eisenhower and the American Crusade* (New York, 1972).

EISENHOWER, MILTON S(TOVER)
b. Sept. 15, 1899; Abilene, Kan.
Presidential adviser; President, Pennsylvania State University, 1950-56; President, Johns Hopkins University, 1956-67.

Milton Eisenhower, the younger brother of Dwight D. Eisenhower, earned a B.S. in industrial journalism from Kansas State University in 1924. That year he entered the Foreign Service as vice counsul in Edinburgh and continued his university studies there. Eisenhower was appointed an assistant to the Secretary of Agriculture in 1926 and became Department information director two years later.

In March 1942 President Franklin Roosevelt appointed Eisenhower head of the War Relocation Authority, which was responsible for evacuating Japanese-Americans from the West Coast to government relocation centers. Eisenhower became associate director of the Office of War Information that year but resigned in June 1943 to take over the presidency of Kansas State College of Agriculture and Applied Science. He remained at Kansas State until 1950, when he was named president of Pennsylvania State University.

During the postwar period Eisenhower remained a government consultant. In June 1945 he helped Secretary Clinton Anderson [q.v.] reorganize the Department of Agriculture, and, at the end of the year, he served on President Harry S. Truman's fact-finding board in the General Motors-United Auto Workers wage dispute. From 1946 to 1948 he was chairman of the U.S. National Commission for the United Nations Economic and Social Council.

Milton Eisenhower was initially no more enthusiastic about a 1952 presidential campaign than his brother. However, after Gen. Eisenhower met with Sen. Robert Taft (R, Ohio) [q.v.], the Republican front-runner, in February 1951, both Milton and Dwight Eisenhower felt that "Ike" ought to leave open the possibility of the Republican nomination in view of Taft's refusal to commit himself to the concept of mutual security in Europe. Early in 1952 Milton joined a personal advisory group counseling the General on the complexities of presidential politics. In June he became a member of an Eisenhower for President steering committee and was active at the Republican National Convention in July.

During his brother's Administration Dr. Eisenhower held no top-level, full-time position because both he and the President wished to avoid any charges of nepotism. He preferred to work intermittently as a consultant, without financial compensation for his services. Eisenhower was particularly valuable to the President for his expertise in education and agriculture. He also

helped write speeches, took on emergency assignments, served as the President's personal representative in U.S.-Latin American relations and was a member of the Permanent Advisory Committee on Government Organization (PACGO).

PACGO, which initially consisted of Nelson Rockefeller [q.v.], Arthur Flemming [q.v.] and Eisenhower, began operations in November 1952 and was formally established by executive order in January 1953. Meeting approximately 120 times in the course of the Administration, the Committee at first advised on Cabinet appointments and reorganization of the White House staff. However, its main assignment was to study the entire federal structure. The Eisenhowers felt that the New Deal and Fair Deal, although they had undertaken many necessary social tasks, had produced unnecessary duplication and inefficiency in administration. The President, therefore, intended to consolidate and streamline the Roosevelt-Truman bureaucracies.

Working from 1953 to 1955 in cooperation with the Second Hoover Commission, PACGO formulated 14 plans that became effective under the Reorganization Act (which allowed the President to make changes in the federal government structure if Congress did not disapprove), seven measures effected by executive order and two enacted by Congress. PACGO was also responsible for many changes in departments' working procedures and for giving the Cabinet a greater policymaking function than it enjoyed under preceding administrations. After the President's second heart attack, PACGO helped reorganize the White House staff to relieve the chief executive of many burdens. The work of PACGO and the Hoover Commission led to the creation of the Department of Health, Education and Welfare, the United States Information Agency, the International Cooperation Administration (later the Agency for International Development), the Federal Aviation Agency, the National Aeronautics and Space Administration and the Federal Council on Science and Technology. PACGO studies resulted in legislation unifying the Department of Defense and assuring its civilian control. Finally, PACGO, in accordance with Secretary of State John Foster Dulles's [*q.v.*] wishes, removed a number of agencies from the control of the State Department.

Latin America, where he already had many friends and acquaintances, became Dr. Eisenhower's special province, and his work in that area constituted probably his most notable contribution to the Administration. In June and July 1953 Eisenhower made his first tour of the hemisphere. He reported to the President in November, recommending expanded trade and private investment in the area, increased technical aid, strong U.S. support for international agencies aiding the hemisphere and a more extensive exchange of students, teachers and workers between the U.S. and Latin American nations. Eisenhower returned to Latin America on extended tours in July 1958 and in February and March 1960. He chaired a committee of representatives of heads of American states, which issued a May 1957 report recommending ways to improve inter-American relations. From November 1959 to November 1960, he was a member of the National Advisory Committee on Inter-American Affairs, a group whose creation he had proposed to the President.

Milton Eisenhower believed that the U.S. should cultivate the special relationship with other nations of the hemisphere that Roosevelt's Good Neighbor policy had developed. His work, in fact, laid the groundwork for President Kennedy's ambitious Alliance for Progress. It was clear to Eisenhower that, in view of Communist competition and the need to expand U.S. investments, the U.S. should help develop Latin America's economic infrastructure and encourage democratic governments in order to ensure stability. Although he was opposed to a non-recognition policy, Eisenhower, in January 1959, said that he agreed with Vice President Richard Nixon's [*q.v.*] suggestion of extending only "a formal handshake" to Latin American dictators while offering an "abrazo" to democratic leaders. He believed that bank loans, not grants, should be the predominant form of U.S. aid and that long-term development projects should be emphasized. Eisenhower also stressed the need for improved educa-tional opportunities in Latin America, better sanitation and better health care. He helped initiate plans for a concerted attack on malaria and smallpox. Summing up his achievements in his book *The President Is Calling* (1974), Eisenhower claimed that his brother's Administration "doubled the flow of private and public capital"; strengthened the role of the Organization of American States in economic and social affairs; instituted the Development Loan Fund to provide 'soft' loans"; promoted common markets, "created for the first time commodity study groups" to minimize the price fluctuations of Latin America's raw commodity exports; "established the Inter-American Bank as an instrument that could make loans with conditions requiring social reform"; "tripled cultural exchanges; tripled the shipment of food to needy countries . . . and in Public Law 86-735 of September 1960 and the Act of Bogota one week later laid the legal basis, domestically and intergovernmentally, for the social reform and economic development program we came to call the Alliance for Progress."

Despite his efforts to maintain a low profile in the Administration, Milton Eisenhower, as brother of the President, could not avoid consistent attention from the press and other public figures. After the President's heart attack in 1955, Milton's name was mentioned as a possible Republican presidential candidate, and in 1960 he was considered for the second spot on the Nixon ticket. In both cases he and the President firmly declared their unwillingness to set up an Eisenhower dynasty. Milton also served as a convenient target for critics who feared to attack directly a figure as popular as Dwight D. Eisenhower. Although as conservative in fiscal and domestic affairs as his brother, Dr. Eisenhower's intellectual reputation and relatively liberal views on foreign policy made him an ideal target for Sen. Joseph R. McCarthy (R, Wisc.) [*q.v.*]. Suggesting that Milton was responsible for leading the President astray on foreign policy, McCarthy, in a November 1955 interview, opposed him as too "left-wing" to be a suitable substitute for the General in the 1956 presidential race. In January 1957 McCarthy characterized Dr. Eisenhower as an "extreme radical" who "tops the list" of the "motley crowd" that influenced the President. Milton tried to get his brother to vigorously attack McCarthy but later claimed that the President's cautious and distant attitude towards the Senator had ultimately proven to be the best strategy.

While Eisenhower served the Administration he remained president of Pennsylvania State University until June 1956. He then became president of Johns Hopkins University, where he was officially installed in February 1957. He was made president emeritus of the school in 1967, returning to active leadership temporarily in 1971-72.

Eisenhower also offered his services to the Kennedy and Johnson Administrations. He undertook missions abroad for Johnson, and in 1968 he headed the President's Commission on the Causes and Prevention of Violence. Remaining active in the Republican Party, Eisenhower strongly opposed the conservative trend which began with the 1964 presidential campaign. [See KENNEDY, JOHNSON Volumes]

[JCH]

For further information:
Milton S. Eisenhower, *The President Is Calling* (Garden City, 1974).

ELLENDER, ALLEN J(OSEPH)
b. Sept. 24, 1890; Montegut, La.
d. July 27, 1972; Bethesda, Md.
Democratic Senator, La., 1937-72;
Chairman, Agriculture and Forestry Committee, 1951-53, 1955-71.

Born in the bayous of southern Louisiana, Allen Ellender graduated from St. Aloysius College in New Orleans and earned a law degree from Tulane University in 1913. While in his twenties he served as district attorney of Terrebonne Parish and established himself as the area's leading potato farmer. In 1924 Ellender was elected to the state House of Representatives as an opponent of Huey P. Long, but he soon allied himself with the Governor's populist administration. Emerging as a key figure in the Long machine, Ellender was speaker of

the House when Long, then a U.S. senator, was assassinated in 1935. He won election to the Senate vacancy the following year. In office he was appointed to the Agriculture Committee and coauthored the Agricultural Adjustment Act of 1937.

Abandoning Long-style populism early in his Senate career, Ellender became known chiefly as a spokesman for his states wealthy sugar, rice and cotton growers, whose interests he protected on the Agriculture Committee. As Committee chairman during all but two years of the Eisenhower Administration, he was particularly energetic in attempting to revise U.S. sugar marketing quotas to make them more favorable to domestic producers. In 1955 Ellender introduced legislation restricting the importation of lower-cost sugar from the Caribbean and thus guaranteed American growers a larger share of the domestic market. Five years later, in response to the confiscation of American-owned property by the Castro regime in Cuba, he helped secure the suspension of Cuban sugar quotas. Ellender also used his control of the Agriculture Committee to block the Eisenhower Administration's attempt to lower price supports on basic farm commodities to bring them closer to world prices. Although most of the Administration's program of flexible supports was enacted in 1954, Ellender helped push through a bill two years later restoring high, rigid supports on basic crops. However, the measure was vetoed by the President.

Although a staunch Southern conservative on most domestic issues, Ellender was an advocate of closer relations with the USSR and a critic of defense spending. In 1957, after a 28-nation trip abroad, he issued a controversial report praising Soviet society and attacking the whole concept of foreign aid as an "abysmal failure."

During the 1960s Ellender continued to play a major role in the shaping of farm policy, while leading Southern opposition to civil rights legislation. His long tenure increased his Senate power, and in 1971 he resigned the chairmanship of the Agriculture Committee to become chairman of the key Appropriations Committee. At the time of his death in 1972, Ellender was President Pro Tempore of the Senate and third in the line of presidential succession. [See KENNEDY, JOHNSON, NIXON/FORD Volumes]

[TLH]

ENGLE, CLAIR
b. Sept. 21, 1911; Bakersfield, Calif.
d. July 30, 1964; Washington, D.C.
Democratic Representative, Calif.,
1943-58; Chairman, Interior and Insular Affairs Committee, 1955-58; Democratic Senator, Calif., 1959-64.

Engle received an LL.B. degree from the University of California in 1933. The following year he won election as a county district attorney, the youngest in California's history. Reelected in 1938 and cited by state Attorney General Earl Warren [q.v.] for his aggressiveness, Engle spent one term in the state Senate before successfully running as a Democrat for U.S. Representative in a 1943 special election. His district was the nation's largest, covering one-third of California from the Mojave Desert to Oregon. Engle specialized in water resources legislation and sponsored every expansion of the California Central Valley Reclamation Project between 1943 and 1957. In 1952 he wrote a pioneer authorization for research into conversion of salt water to fresh. Engle was assigned to the Interior and Insular Affairs Committee in 1951. The following year he chaired an Interior Affairs Subcommittee examining proposals to build a federal hydroelectric dam in Hell's Canyon, Ida. His astute questioning of witnesses on water rights resulted in the Committee's unanimous vote against the power project. In 1953 he became ranking Democrat on the Interior and Insular Affairs panel.

Engle supported statehood for Hawaii against Southern opposition on racial grounds in March 1953 and testified in its favor at Senate hearings. A strong opponent of racial discrimination, he supported the Administration's 1957 civil rights bill. When President Eisenhower threatened to veto Congress's version of the measure in August after it had been weakened in the Senate, Engle charged that the chief executive was trying to maximize political mileage by appealing to both supporters and opponents of civil rights.

In 1955 Engle became chairman of the Interior and Insular Affairs Committee and assistant Democratic whip. As chairman, he was a backer of public power development. In June 1956 Engle said that, according to legal views cited by the Library of Congress, the federal government could build power projects in Hell's Canyon even though the Federal Power Commission had given the right to a private company. His Committee then passed a Hell's Canyon bill, but it was killed in the Senate by opponents of public power. During the same year Engle backed a bill authorizing $760 million for Upper Colorado River reclamation and a power project backed by the Administration. The bill was signed into law in April 1956.

Engle entered the race for Knowland's Senate seat in 1958. In an election complicated by California's cross-filing system which permitted candidates to run as both Democrats and Republicans, Engle defeated Republican Gov. Goodwin Knight [q.v.] for the Democratic senatorial nomination and in the November election. Sen. Engle was assigned to committees on Armed Services, Small Business and Interstate Commerce. The liberal freshman participated in a January 1959 move to limit anti-civil rights filibustering. This effort failed when the Senate leadership succeeded in substituting a much weaker measure that did not offend Southerners. According to Congressional Quarterly, Engle opposed the conservative coalition on 85% of key role call votes.

In 1960 Engle led opposition to Senate ratification of the U.S.-Soviet Antarctica Treaty which pledged that "peaceful use" of the frozen continent. Testifying in June before the Senate Foreign Relations Committee, Engle charged the pact did not insure against secret Soviet military operations and gave the USSR equal rights in an area where the U.S. had been predominant. Two months later the Senate ratified the treaty.

Engle generally supported President John F. Kennedy's legislative program. He was accorded a 100% rating by the liberal Americans for Democratic Action in 1961. In 1963 Engle fell ill and required repeated brain surgery. He voted from a wheelchair for the Johnson Administration's landmark civil rights bill in June 1964 and died the following month. [See KENNEDY Volume]

[MJS]

ERVIN, SAM(UEL) J(AMES), JR.
b. Sept. 27, 1896; Morgantown, N.C.
Democratic Senator, N.C., 1954-75.

Ervin received an A.B. degree from the University of North Carolina at Chapel Hill in 1917. Following service in World War I, he was admitted to the North Carolina bar. Ervin then enrolled at Harvard and obtained his LL.B. degree there in 1922.

Ervin was elected to the North Carolina General Assembly three times during the mid-1920s and early-1930s. After sitting on the Burke Co. Criminal Court, he was appointed to the North Carolina Superior Court in 1937, where he served for six years. In January 1946 Ervin won a special election to fill a vacancy in the U.S. House of Representatives created by the death of his brother, but he did not run for reelection the following fall. In February 1948 he was appointed an associate justice of the North Carolina Supreme Court.

The governor of North Carolina appointed Ervin to fill a vacant Senate seat in June 1954. Because of Ervin's judicial experience, Minority Leader Lyndon B. Johnson (D, Tex.) [q.v.] tapped him to serve on a special six-man committee created to investigate censure charges against Sen. Joseph R. McCarthy (R, Wisc.) [q.v.]. Ervin did not participate extensively in the questioning of witnesses during the panel's hearings. In September he concurred with the committee's recommendation to censure McCarthy. On Nov. 10, as the Senate began its deliberations on the committee's recommendation, McCarthy inserted in the *Congressional Record* a statement asserting that the panel "had done the work of the Communist Party" and had

"imitated Communist methods." Eight days later Ervin made an unusually sharp attack on his Wisconsin colleague, declaring that if McCarthy believed these charges he had "mental delusions," and if he did not he was suffering from "moral incapacity."

A strict constructionist, Ervin regarded himself as a defender of the rights of individuals and of the states under the Constitution against the encroachments of the federal government. He opposed government attacks upon Southern racial discrimination as threats to these rights. In 1956 Ervin asserted that segregation was "not the offspring of racial bigotry or racial prejudice" but the result of the exercise of "a fundamental American freedom—the freedom of selecting one's associates." He opposed the Administration's 1957 civil rights bill, designed to protect black voting rights, claiming that it infringed upon the constitutional right of the states to determine voter qualifications. Ervin succeeded in weakening the measure by amending it to guarantee a jury trial in some cases to those accused of intimidating or coercing voters. Three years later he participated in a Southern filibuster against another Administration civil rights bill, which he denounced as giving special privileges to racially defined groups. At the Democratic National Convention in July 1960, Ervin unsuccessfully fought against the inclusion of a civil rights plank in the party platform.

Some observers regarded Ervin's constitutional arguments as mere rationalizations for racial discrimination, but he voted with liberals on a number of civil liberties issues. In its June 1957 *Jencks* decision, the Supreme Court ruled that defendants were entitled to see statements of prosecution witnesses. Many members of Congress criticized the Court, but Ervin defended the ruling, and in August he voted against Sen. Everett M. Dirksen's (R, Ill.) [q.v.] proposals aimed at limiting the effects of the decision. In April 1958 Ervin joined a nine-to-five Judiciary Committee majority that rejected an amendment applying the federal security program to non-sensitive as well as sensitive jobs.

Ervin opposed the reversal of criminal convictions based on procedural technicalities. In June 1957 the Supreme Court established the so-called Mallory rule when it overturned a rape conviction on the ground that there had been unnecessary delay before arraignment. Fourteen months later Ervin unsuccessfully proposed that trial judges be empowered to determine whether delays were reasonable and to make their decisions binding on appellate courts if founded upon substantial evidence.

In 1957 Ervin was appointed to the Senate Select Committee on Improper Activities in the Labor or Management Field, which investigated corruption in the Teamsters and other unions for the next three years. In 1959 he and Sen. John F. Kennedy (D, Mass.) [q.v.] introduced a labor reform bill aimed at cleaning up the kind of labor racketeering and labor-management collusion exposed by the investigation. The proposal contained anti-corruption, fair election and trusteeship guarantees. Fearing that it would weaken support for the bill, the two men deliberately did not deal with major Taft-Hartley Act issues affecting rights in collective bargaining. The Senate passed the measure with little modification in April. However, the House changed it dramatically. Finally enacted in September as the Labor Management Reporting and Disclosure Act, the bill also extended the Taft-Hartley Act's prohibitions against secondary boycotts.

During the early 1960s Ervin opposed federal aid to parochial schools on the ground that it violated the constitutional separation of church and state. Although continuing to oppose most social welfare and civil rights legislation, Ervin earned the admiration of liberals in the late-1960s and early-1970s for his opposition to "no-knock" crime legislation, his probe of Army surveillance of civilians and his role in 1973 as chairman of the Watergate Committee. He declined to run for reelection in 1974. [See KENNEDY, JOHNSON, NIXON/FORD Volumes]

[MLL]

For further information:
Paul R. Clancy, *Just a Country Lawyer: A Biography of Senator Sam Ervin* (Bloomington, 1974).

FAIRLESS, BENJAMIN F(RANKLIN)
b. May 3, 1890; Pigeon Run, Ohio.
d. Jan. 1, 1962; Ligonier, Pa.
Chairman of the Board, United States Steel Corporation, 1952-55; President, American Iron and Steel Institute, 1955-62.

The son of poor Welsh immigrants, Benjamin Williams was sent to live with his aunt and uncle, Sarah and Jacob Fairless, at the age of five to provide access to better schooling. They later adopted him, legally changing his name to Fairless. He worked his way through Ohio Northern University and, following his graduation in 1913, went to work as a surveyor for the Wheeling and Lake Erie Railroad. Soon after, however, he joined the Central Steel Co. as a civil engineer. Fairless was promoted rapidly, becoming president and general manager in 1928. When his company and several others merged to form the Republic Steel Corp. in 1930, he was appointed its executive vice president. Fairless became president of the Carnegie-Illinois Steel Corp. in 1935. In January 1938 he was elected president and chairman of the executive committee of its parent company, U.S. Steel.

During World War II Fairless served on various advisory boards, including the Iron and Steel Industry Advisory Committee and the War Production Board. In the postwar years he defended U.S. Steel against government investigations of monopolistic trends. He criticized those who thought there was "something inherently vicious in bigness and growth and success" and described detractors of big business as people who "think small." During 1952 Fairless helped negotiate the settlement of a 55-day strike which crippled the industry. [See TRUMAN Volume]

In May 1952 Fairless was elected chairman of the board and chief executive officer of U.S. Steel. He held these positions until May 1955, when he retired at the age of 65. He was subsequently named chairman of the executive advisory committee and continued as a member of the board. That same year he became president of the American Iron and Steel Institute (AISI).

Fairless often represented the industry before government committees and served on various presidential committees. Early in 1955 he appeared before the Senate Banking and Currency Committee, during a "friendly" study of the stock market, to detail financial problems faced by U.S. Steel. He stressed restoration of "investor confidence" as a major concern. In late 1955 he served on a task force, established by presidential disarmament adviser Harold E. Stassen [q.v.], to study the role of the steel industry in determining disarmament policies. The steel industry executive also became a member of the presidential board of consultants to monitor and evaluate U.S. intelligence operations.

In 1954 Eisenhower named Fairless to head the Citizens Advisers on the Mutual Security Program. The panel was to study U.S. foreign aid problems, especially those posed by a Soviet shift from direct intervention to the use of economic aid to extend its influence. During 1956-57 the committee made a 52-day tour of 21 countries. Its report, issued in March 1957, urged the continuation of the program. While acknowledging that military assistance was vital to prevent Communist expansion, the panel maintained that economic development was as important for future security. It recommended that economic aid be focused on long-term development and urged the formation of regional markets such as the European Economic Community. The advisers said that "foreign investment of private capital is far more desirable than investment by government" and urged increasing incentives for such investment "by providing more equitable taxation of foreign business income." The report also urged that foreign aid programs be presented to each Congress, rather than to each session, to permit more efficient planning and utilization of funds.

Fairless continued to represent big steel through the remainder of the decade and conferred with Vice President Richard M. Nixon [q.v.] in 1959 in an unsuccessful effort to avert a steel strike. He remained AISI president until his death in 1962.

[RB]

FARLAND, JOSEPH S(IMPSON)
b. Aug. 11, 1914; Clarksburg, W. Va.
Ambassador to the Dominican Republic, May 1957-June 1960; Ambassador to Panama, June 1960-August 1963.

Farland graduated from West Virginia University in 1936 and received his law degree there two years later. He practiced law in West Virginia and from 1942 to 1944 was an FBI agent. After service in the Naval Reserve during World War II, Farland resumed his law career. In 1956 he became a State Department consultant for the mutual security program in Latin America. The following year President Dwight D. Eisenhower nominated Farland to be ambassador to the Dominican Republic. He was confirmed in May 1957.

Farland failed to establish good relations with dictator Rafael Trujillo; he made little secret of his distaste for the totalitarian regime. Because of his inability to deal with Trujillo, whom the Administration supported, Farland was shifted to Panama. The Senate confirmed his appointment as ambassador to that nation in June 1960.

Farland was a warm sympathizer of the Panamanian peasants and an opponent of American foreign aid programs. The Ambassador objected to granting foreign aid to governments rather than to private groups, believing the policy prevented money from reaching the local level. He as particularly troubled by Washington bureaucracy, which insisted on surveys and other procedures that delayed aid. During his tenure Farland, on his own initiative, built roads so that small farmers could get their produce to market. With only minimum foreign aid funds, he helped Panamanians build vocational schools, low-income housing and medical facilities.

As ambassador Farland supported increased Panamanian control of the Canal Zone, but the Kennedy Administration refused his suggestions. In July 1963 he resigned his post. Shortly after his departure the liberal *New Republic* praised him as "a figure from the romance of what we would like the American abroad to be." In 1964 Farland headed an advisory panel on Latin

American affairs for presidential candidate Barry Goldwater [q.v.]. After the campaign he returned to his law practice. President Richard Nixon appointed him ambassador to Pakistan in 1969. He became ambassador to Iran in 1972. The following year Farland retired from diplomatic service.

[AES]

FAST, HOWARD M(ELVIN)
b. Nov. 11, 1914; New York, N.Y.
Writer.

Born to Jewish parents in New York City, Fast spent his youth in self-described "utter poverty." He applied for service in the Navy while still in his mid-teens but was rejected because of his age. Subsequently he spent years drifting from job to job, mixing with multitudes of people, "fighting" and, most of all, reading. In his autobiography, *The Naked God*, Fast marked 1932, a year when he worked in a Harlem branch of the New York Public Library, as the point when his career as a writer truly opened up. Between the years 1932 and 1944 he wrote 13 books, including novels, biographies, stories and juvenile publications. He showed particular interest in writing historical novels that probed the American past for new perspectives. They included *Two Valleys* (1932), *Conceived in Liberty* (1939), *The Unvanquished* (1942) and *Citizen Tom Paine* (1943). By the early 1940's Fast's books were accumulating both weighty praise and a substantial readership. During World War II he worked for the Office of War Information.

In 1943 Fast became a member of the U.S. Communist Party, a commitment that was to alter drastically his entire career. Long before 1943 he had attended meetings of Communist and radical groups, and in that year he firmly "came to accept the proposition that the truest and most consistent fighters in the anti-fascist struggle were the Communists." His full commitment to the Party came at a time when the majority of American writers on the Left had long since abandoned the organization.

Fast's presence in 1949 at the Peekskill, N.Y., riots that marred the performance of suspected Communist Paul Robeson [q.v.] was highly publicized. After that time Fast's name was regularly invoked as "the public face" of American Communists. In 1950 he was called before the House Un-American Activities Committee (HUAC) as a member of the Anti-Fascist Refugee Committee. He was charged with contempt for refusing to answer the Committee's questions and served a short time in prison in 1950. He ran a symbolic and futile campaign for Congress in 1952 on the American Labor Party ticket.

In 1953 Fast was called before Sen. Joseph McCarthy's (R, Wisc.) [q.v.] Permanent Investigations Subcommittee of the Committee on Government Operations to testify on such subjects as alleged subversive books in the U.S. State Department libraries and alleged sabotage of Voice of America (VOA) broadcasts in Europe. As a result of the hearings, his books were removed from the libraries. McCarthy admonished VOA officials for suggesting that a few of his works might be suitable for overseas readers.

Although in America his name was most often mentioned in the early-1950s for purposes of vilification, Fast was a literary hero in the USSR. He was credited there with creating true "proletarian heroes" in his books and with portraying American history in a light favorable to a Communist perspective. By his own account millions of his books had been printed in the USSR, two plays performed, one book transformed into an opera and two book-length critical studies of his work published. In 1953 he was awarded a Stalin prize by the Russian government. Meanwhile, Fast found himself blacklisted in the U.S. His books generally went out of print, and he could not find publishers for his new works. Only certain of his earlier works, which had been called "patriotic" at the time of their publication, were still deemed suitable reading according to reviewers and publishers.

A dedicated Communist, Fast wrote for Party publications, attended meetings and conventions and contributed considerable sums to party coffers until 1956. At that time he broke from the organization after the publicity over what he subsequently termed the "revelations" in Nikita Khrushchev's report to the Russian Twentieth Congress detailing the atrocities of Stalin's dictatorship. He made no public pronouncement of his renunciation of Communism until 1957. Later that year he published *The Naked God*, a loosely constructed autobiography that attempted to explain his journey from "fellow traveler" to "deserter." Historian Daniel Aaron criticized the book as a "white paper" rather than a "self-exploration," while others called it an effective anti-Communist book. He was called again to testify before HUAC in 1957 to serve as a public example of a "reformed" American Communist.

During the late-1950s and the 1960s Fast again found a market for his writing. He continued to publish novels, stories and plays, worked in Hollywood and contributed to mainstream American publications such as *Saturday Evening Post* and *Ladies Home Journal*.

[TGD]

FAUBUS, ORVAL E(UGENE)
b. Jan. 7, 1910; Combs, Ark.
Governor, Ark., 1955-67.

The son of a socialist and liberal Democrat, Faubus was born in the Ozark mountains of northwestern Arkansas. He worked as a school teacher and itinerant fruit picker while attending State Vocational High School at Huntsville. Following graduation Faubus was employed in the lumber industry in Washington. In 1936 he ran unsuccessfully for the Democratic nomination for representative to the state Assembly. He was elected Madison Co. circuit clerk in 1938 and reelected in 1940. Faubus served in the Army during World War II. He returned home in 1947 and bought the local Madison Co. *Record*. His liberal editorials caught the attention of Gov. Sidney McMath, who brought the young Faubus to Little Rock as state highway director. He served at that post from 1949 to 1952.

Denouncing incumbent Gov. Francis Cherry [*q.v.*] as the tool of special inter-

ests, Faubus won the August 1954 Democratic gubernatorial primary and went on to win a two-year term in November. As governor he instituted a populist program of social and economic development. Under his direction the legislature reformed welfare laws, established a conservation commission, increased mental health facilities and formed the Arkansas Industrial Development Commission, under the chairmanship of Winthrop Rockefeller, to encourage the industrialization of the state. Faubus also began complying with the 1954 Supreme Court decision banning segregation in public schools. Six out of seven state colleges were desegregated as were schools in Fayetteville, Hoxi and Charleston.

Seeking a second term in 1956 against segregationist Jim Johnson, Faubus began to modify his stand on racial integration. Following a statewide survey indicating the 85% of the people opposed desegregation, he announced that he "could not be a party to any attempt to force acceptance of a change to which the people were so overwhelmingly opposed." During the fall the Governor campaigned for a law giving the state power to assign pupils to school by race and a resolution interposing state law against federal acts deemed illegal. Both measures passed, and Faubus won reelection. Faubus openly opposed forced integration and favored local option in the desegregation controversy. Yet none of his proposals would have penalized communities that integrated their schools, and he consistently rejected calls to nullify the Supreme Court decision.

Following the Little Rock School Board's decision to integrate Central High School in the fall of 1957, the Capital Citizens' Council launched an intensive propaganda campaign demanding the Governor intervene to prevent bloodshed and preserve segregation. On the other hand, Little Rock school superintendent Virgil Blossom [*q.v.*] asked the Governor for a public commitment to law, order and peaceful desegregation. Faubus steadfastly refused to take a stand on the issue. His last-minute call for help to the Justice Department was answered by a statement that the Administration did not wish to get involved. The Administration compounded Faubus's problems by leaking his conversation to the press.

Fearing the revelation would injure his chance for reelection, Faubus was forced into a more extreme position. After attempts to delay desegregation through court action had failed, he ordered the National Guard to prevent desegregation at Central High School on Sept. 2. Four days later President Eisenhower announced he opposed using federal troops to enforce court orders and would not exercise his option of federalizing the National Guard. Moderate Democratic Rep. Brooks Hays (D, Ark.) [q.v.] arranged a meeting between Faubus and Eisenhower in an attempt to reach a compromise, but the Sept. 14 conference ended inconclusively.

Responding to a federal injunction on Sept. 20, Faubus abruptly removed the Guard. The city appealed to the federal court and the Justice Department for marshals to escort black students, but its request was turned down. Desegregation began on Sept. 23, but the limited number of city police and state troopers could not control the hostile mob. Eisenhower issued a proclamation ordering obstruction of justice to cease. The following day Little Rock Mayor Woodrow Mann officially asked Eisenhower for federal intervention. The President issued a second proclamation federalizing the Arkansas National Guard and ordering the 101st Army Airborne Division to Little Rock. On Sept. 25 federal troops escorted black students through white mobs to class. The troops remained in Little Rock through November.

Faubus continued to oppose integration throughout 1958. In August he called on Little Rock's School Board to avoid desegregating the remaining high schools or resign. This time Eisenhower indicated he would enforce court decisions. When the Supreme Court reaffirmed its desegregation ruling in September, Faubus signed 14 segregation bills and closed all Little Rock high schools. Later that month Little Rock citizens backed the Governor by voting more than 70% against reopening their schools on an integrated basis. That year Faubus also disbanded the NAACP by

executive fiat on the grounds that it was delinquent in tax payments.

By early 1959 a reaction began to set in against Faubus's actions. In March the city's Chamber of Commerce called for reopening Little Rock schools on a desegregated basis. That May three moderates were elected to the school board over segregationists backed by Faubus. The city peacefully desegregated its high schools in August.

Faubus ran a moderate campaign the following year and won reelection against a strong segregationist. He went on to win two more terms and retired in 1967. Opposing school busing in 1970, he again ran for governor but lost the Democratic primary. In 1977 Faubus was reportedly employed as a bank teller.

[MJS]

For further information:
Numan V. Bartley, The Rise of Massive Resistance (Baton Rouge, 1969).
Virgil T. Blossom, It Has Happened Here (New York, 1959).
Corinne Silverman, The Little Rock Story (University, Ala., 1959).

FERGUSON, HOMER
b. Feb. 25, 1889; Harrison City, Pa.
Republican Senator, Mich., 1943-55.

After earning a law degree from the University of Michigan in 1913, Ferguson became a practicing lawyer in Detroit and, in 1929, a circuit judge. In 1939 he was appointed to sit as a one-man grand jury to investigate corruption in the Detroit police department. As a result of a three-year probe, the county prosecutor, an ex-mayor and many high police officials and underworld figures were sent to jail, Ferguson became a local hero. In 1942 he ran against and narrowly defeated Democratic incumbent Sen. Prentiss M. Brown.

A conservative on domestic questions and an isolationist on foreign policy, Ferguson voted against the Roosevelt and Truman Administrations on most issues, opposing foreign aid and supporting protectionist trade barriers and immigration restrictions.

In the late 1940s he was one of the first senators to raise the specter of Communist subversion in government. He was an early supporter of Sen. Joseph McCarthy's (R, Wisc) [*q.v.*] anti-Communist crusade. [See TRUMAN Volume]

In June 1953 Ferguson became chairman of the Senate Republican Policy Committee when William Knowland (R, Calif) [*q.v.*] replaced the deceased Robert Taft (R, Ohio) [*q.v.*] as majority leader. As part of the Republican congressional leadership, which planned its legislative program in close cooperation with the White House, Ferguson was gradually won over to an "internationalist" position, backing the Eisenhower Administration on foreign aid, refugee immigration, trade policy and other issues. At first, for example, Ferguson led the Republican opposition to the confirmation of Charles Bohlen [*q.v.*] as ambassador to the USSR. Bohlen, a career diplomat, had served as an adviser at the 1945 Yalta conference, and the GOP right wing regarded him as a symbol of what it termed the "Truman-Acheson crowd" in the State Department. When it became clear that the Administration would not withdraw the nomination, however, Ferguson joined other Republicans on the Foreign Relations Committee in voting for confirmation.

In another foreign policy debate in 1953, Ferguson reversed his position on the Bricker amendment. The proposal had been offered by Sen. John W. Bricker (R, Ohio) [*q.v.*], who feared that American domestic affairs could become subject to an international authority such as the United Nations. It would have limited the power of the executive to enter into treaties and other international agreements. Ferguson had supported the amendment since it was first introduced in 1951. The President opposed the resolution, and Ferguson worked with Knowland to draft a series of new amendments ostensibly aimed at satisfying both the Administration and the Bricker forces. In fact, they merely affirmed that treaties must not violate the Constitution and did not propose any real modification of the President's treaty-making powers. The Bricker amendment fell one vote short of the two-thirds majority needed for passage.

The Senate subsequently rejected the Knowland-Ferguson amendments as well.

In 1954 Ferguson was narrowly defeated for reelection by Patrick V. McNamara [*q.v.*], a union official vigorously supported by Michigan labor organizations. In 1955 Ferguson was appointed ambassador to the Philippines. After a year he returned to Washington to become an associate judge on the U.S. Court of Military Appeals. In 1971 he became a senior judge on the court.

[TLH]

FIEDLER, LESLIE A(RON)
b. March 8, 1917; Newark, N.J.
Writer, educator.

The son of a Jewish pharmacist, Fiedler began his interest in politics as a child. At 12 he read Thoreau and the following year Marx. As a student Fiedler took part in pacifist and labor demonstrations, but he described his involvement as "tourism," entailing no risks. Fiedler attended New York University, graduating magna cum laude with a B.A. in English in 1938. He did his graduate work at the University of Wisconsin, receiving his Ph.D. in English in 1941. That year he joined the faculty of Montana State University. During World War II he served as a Japanese translator in various Pacific areas.

At Montana State Fiedler immediately established a reputation for iconoclasm, offering a unique perspective on the American literary past that was both roundly scorned and accepted with admiration. In three collections of essays—*An End to Innocence* (1955), *Love and Death in the American Novel* (1959) and *No! In Thunder; Essays on Myth and Literature* (1960)—he traced patterns in American literature and developed a thesis illuminating American writers' peculiar modes of dealing with sexual and racial themes.

Fiedler contended that the bulk of American novelists clearly had been unable to write convincingly of mature, heterosexual love because they, like most Americans, were crippled by adolescent views of sexuality. American readers were often presented with an "innocent, homoerotic relationship between a white and a non-white male." American writers—mostly white males—clung to this "last believed-in stronghold of life without passion" in order to justify their hatred of the "Fallen Woman" (one who feels and demonstrates passion); and concurrently assuage the burning guilt they felt for America's destruction of its non-whites. If such a relationship did not appear in a novel, readers were likely to find themes of pathological obsessions—rape, murder, betrayal—but rarely fully realized, honest, loving relationships.

Fiedler's view of the hypocrisy in American literary claims to innocence also extended to his perspectives on American political events. Always politically minded as an author and educator, he wrote numerous articles in the 1950s that helped shape the general intellectual climate. Perhaps the best-known of these articles were three collected in *An End to Innocence:* "Hiss, Chambers and the Age of Innocence" (1950), "Afterthoughts on the Rosenbergs" (1953) and "McCarthy and the Intellectuals" (1954). Fiedler's examinations of the Hiss and Rosenberg cases moved on the presupposition of their guilt. He accused Hiss of "opportunism or perverted idealism, moral obtuseness or the habit of Machiavellianism"; the Rosenbergs were "palpable liars." His central belief was that all three were Communists, radicals or ex-Communists deluded by a "dream of innocence," a dream shared by most liberals, that "the man of good will is identical with the righteous man, and . . . the liberal is *per se* the hero." Recognition of moral guilt and repentance for having indirectly supported crimes of Stalinist totalitarianism was all-important to Fiedler, and he criticized Hiss and the Rosenbergs for not confessing their actions in the courtroom, either with the defiance of true radicals or the wisdom of failed innocents. He did, however, deplore the execution of the Rosenbergs for its violation of the basic principles of human mercy.

Fiedler viewed Sen. Joseph R. McCarthy (R, Wisc.) [*q.v.*] in much the same light. Although he was disgusted by the Senator himself, he declared that "to assess McCar-

thyism justly means to admit that good and evil are divided." Sharing a view held by other intellectuals, particularly some conservative thinkers, he called McCarthyism "an extension of the ambiguous American impulse toward [direct democracy] with its distrust of authority, institutions and expert knowledge," a logical progression of the wrecked Progressive movement.

Increasingly unhappy at Montana State University, Fiedler left in 1963 to become a professor at the State University of New York at Buffalo. There he continued to write voluminous literary and cultural criticism, novels and short stories. In 1967 he was arrested and convicted of "maintaining a premise" where marijuana was used. He denied the charge and appealed the case. During the 1970s Fiedler continued to teach at Buffalo and act as a distinguished visiting professor at major universities around the world.

[TGD]

FINLETTER, THOMAS K(NIGHT)
b. Nov. 11, 1893; Philadelphia, Pa.
Attorney.

A member of a prominent Philadelphia family, Finletter graduated from the University of Pennsylvania in 1915. After serving in the Army during World War I, he attended the University of Pennsylvania law school and was admitted to the New York bar in 1921. That year he entered law practice in New York City. Finletter joined the State Department as a special assistant to the Secretary of State in 1941. Two years later he was appointed executive director of the Office of Foreign Economic Coordination, which supervised economic planning in Allied-controlled areas. During World War II Finletter was also a consultant to the committee laying the foundation for the U.N. He attended the 1945 San Francisco Conference, at which the U.N. was founded, as an aide to Adlai Stevenson [*q.v.*]

In July 1947 President Truman appointed Finletter chairman of the Air Policy Commission (later known as the Finletter Commission), formed to study all phases of aviation and develop a national air policy. The committee report, issued in 1948 as "Survival in the Air Age," emphasized the need to strengthen U.S. air power to meet the threat posed by the Soviet Union. Finletter served as Secretary of the Air Force from 1950 to 1952. [See TRUMAN Volume]

Finletter supported Stevenson for President in 1952. In the years following Stevenson's defeat, he headed an informal advisory panel, known as the "Finletter Group," which met regularly to discuss issues and suggest positions Stevenson should take as "leader of the loyal opposition." The group, which included Arthur Schlesinger, Jr. [q.v.], John Kenneth Galbraith [q.v.] and Chester Bowles [q.v.], provided Stevenson with material on such issues as civil rights, foreign affairs and civil liberties. Although Stevenson did not want this group considered his personal brain trust, as the 1956 election drew closer the panel started preparing positions for the upcoming campaign and policies for a Stevenson administration. During the 1956 campaign Finletter headed the New York State Stevenson for President Committee.

In January 1957 Democratic National Chairman Paul Butler [q.v.] organized the Democratic Advisory Council with Finletter as one of its members. The group was created to limit the power of congressional leaders Rep. Sam Rayburn (D, Tex.) [q.v.] and Sen. Lyndon B. Johnson (D, Tex.) [q.v.] and give liberals a greater voice in shaping legislative policy. However, the congressional leaders refused to join the panel, and so the Council had little influence on legislation.

Finletter again pushed for a Stevenson presidency in 1960. He helped organize a draft-Stevenson movement and prepared speeches for the former Governor, hoping they would get him the publicity needed to capture the nomination. Despite massive demonstrations for Stevenson at the Convention, he never formally declared his candidacy, and his backers failed to win sufficient delegates to prevent Sen. John F. Kennedy's (D, Mass.) [q.v.] nomination on the first ballot.

Throughout the decade Finletter spoke and wrote on foreign policy and defense issues. In his book *Power and Policy* (1954),

he scored the failure of leadership which lost the U.S. its nuclear supremacy. Predicting that by 1956 the Soviet Union would have enough nuclear weapons to totally destroy the U.S., he urged the Eisenhower Administration to build up a massive nuclear deterrent to discourage attack. He argued against cuts in the defense budget and recommended increased spending, particularly for the Air Force, which would bear the main burden of defense.

In 1955 Finletter came out in opposition to the Administration's disarmament proposals, which called for a reduction, first in conventional forces and then in nuclear weapons, supervised by an elaborate inspection system. The former Air Force Secretary questioned whether such a system could ever be effective in dealing with a large country such as the Soviet Union which was also controlled by a secretive government. Instead, he advocated enforced disarmament backed by a U.N. military force strong enough to compel compliance. The U.S. would give up its major deterrent—nuclear weapons—only after the enforcement system was completely developed.

At the end of the decade, Finletter was still scoring the Administration, pointing out that the Russians were ahead of the U.S. in defense and space research. He was one of the Democrats who claimed that a "missile gap" existed between the U.S. and the Soviet Union, and he urged Americans to reorient their priorities to regain their superiority. According to Finletter, money had to be channeled from consumer goods to education, science, natural resource development and armaments. In his opinion this could best be accomplished if the U.S. were led by a liberal Democrat.

During the 1950s Finletter was extremely active in New York politics. In 1958 he sought the Democratic nomination for senator but was turned down by Tammany boss Carmine DeSapio [q.v.]. To fight what they considered a blatant exercise of machine power, Finletter, Herbert Lehman [q.v.] and Eleanor Roosevelt [q.v.] organized the New York Committee for Democratic Voters the following year. In 1961 the reform candidate for mayor,

Robert Wagner, Jr. [q.v.], defeated Arthur Levitt, DeSapio's handpicked nominee, effectively ending the boss's power in New York.

President Kennedy appointed Finletter ambassador to the North Atlantic Treaty Organization in 1961. He held that post until 1965, when he returned to law practice in New York.

[JB]

FLANDERS, RALPH E(DWARD)
b. Sept. 28, 1880; Barmet, Vt.
d. Feb. 19, 1970; Springfield, Vt.
Republican Senator, Vt., 1946-59.

Born into a poor family, Flanders was "bound out" to a farmer as a child. He never went to college and, instead, studied engineering by mail. Thereafter he became both a working engineer and a noted writer on machine designing. After World War I he lectured and wrote on the causes of economic dislocation. In 1933 Flanders succeeded his father-in-law as president of the Jones and Lamson Machine Co. He lost the Vermont Republican senatorial primary to George Aiken [q.v.] in 1940. During World War II Flanders served in a number of federal agencies, including the office of Price Administration and the Economic Stabilization Board.

In 1946 the governor appointed Flanders to fill the unexpired term of Sen. Warren Austin (R, Vt.); later that year he won a full term. A deeply religious man, Flanders toured the country, lecturing on the need for a moral approach to government. Identified with the Republican Party's liberal wing, in 1948 he declared that the correction of substandard housing was a responsibility of the national government. Following the presidential election of that year, he called upon the Republican Party to liberalize its policies. In 1950 Flanders joined four other Republican senators to save an Administration bill providing famine relief for Yugoslavia. A strong anti-Communist, in 1951 he expressed great doubt that the bombing of China in retaliation for its invasion of Korea would cause a world war. He opposed the Korean armi-

stice of 1953 because it required what he termed "a costly moral compromise."

Flanders had ambivalent feelings about Sen. Joseph R. McCarthy (R, Wisc.) [q.v.] and his anti-Communist crusade. He believed that many of Franklin D. Roosevelt's and Harry S. Truman's ideas paralleled the Communists', but he was skeptical of the charges of Communist infiltration in the Truman Administration. Flanders surmised that 90% of McCarthy's allegations were baseless, but he was not prepared to dismiss all the charges automatically. Until the spring of 1954 he believed that the best way to stop McCarthy's crusade lay in implementing alternatives to controversial Democratic programs. However, in a March 1954 radio address, he acknowledged that McCarthy was becoming an increasing problem for the GOP. Flanders mocked McCarthy's crusade: "He dons his war paint. He goes into his war dance. He emits his war-whoops. He goes forth to battle and proudly returns with a scalp of a pink Army dentist." The nationally televised Army-McCarthy hearings, held from April 22 to June 17, 1954, damaged the Wisconsin Senator's reputation further. On June 1 Flanders again scored McCarthy, comparing him to "Dennis the Menace." But on a more serious note, he implied that some of McCarthy's activities paralleled those of Hitler. Flanders said, "Established and responsible government is besmirched. Religion is set against religion, race against race. Churches and parties are split asunder. All is confusion and doubt."

Flanders realized that any Senate move to discipline McCarthy had to be initiated by a Republican to avoid the appearance of partisanship. After notifying McCarthy, on June 11 he introduced a resolution to strip the Wisconsin Senator of his committee and subcommittee chairmanships. However, many senators, including Republican leaders and Southern Democrats, opposed the measure on the grounds that it would tamper with the seniority system. Therefore, on July 16, he announced that in two weeks he would present a resolution calling for McCarthy's censure. With the support of several important Democrats, Sen. John McClellan (D, Ark.) [q.v.], Sen. J. William

Fulbright (D, Ark.) [q.v.] and Sen. Mike Monroney (D, Okla.) [q.v.], he submitted a resolution on July 30 charging McCarthy with, among other things, refusal in 1952 to answer questions about his finances before the Rules and Administration Committee's Subcommittee on Privileges and Election; responsibility for "frivolous and irresponsible conduct" of aides Roy Cohn [q.v.] and G. David Schine [q.v.]; and "habitual contempt for people" as illustrated by his denunciation of Gen. Ralph W. Zwicker [q.v.] during an Army investigation. On Aug. 2 Flanders added 33 specifics to his resolution. Other senators added charges, and on the same day the Senate voted to refer the resolution to a special bipartisan committee. In November the panel introduced a censure resolution. The Senate voted condemnation the following month. Flanders did not play a leading role in the Senate debate.

An early backer of Dwight D. Eisenhower for the 1952 Republican presidential nomination, Flanders was a supporter of the Administration and an advocate of liberal causes. He endorsed the 1955 Formosa Resolution, and in 1957 he opposed Democratic amendments to the Eisenhower Doctrine. But in 1956 Flanders opposed further aid to Yugoslavia. In the area of domestic policy, he cosponsored, with Sen. Irving Ives (R, N.Y.) [q.v.], a 1954 bill to improve private health plans through federal assistance. The measure was drafted along lines favored by the Administration. Two years later he supported an Administration-backed bill to provide aid for depressed areas. During the same year Flanders favored a bill to exempt natural gas users from federal rate control, a measure that President Eisenhower vetoed only because of revelations of improper activities by gas industry representatives.

In 1958 Flanders declined to seek reelection and became a pig farmer in his native state. He died at 89 in February 1970.

[MLL]

For further information:
Robert Griffith, *The Politics of Fear* (Lexington, Ky., 1970).

FLEMMING, ARTHUR S(HERWOOD)
b. June 12, 1905; Kingston, N.Y.
Director, Office of Defense Mobilization, January 1953-May 1958; Secretary, Department of Health, Education and Welfare, May 1958-December 1960.

Arthur Flemming graduated in 1927 from Ohio Wesleyan University. He then moved to Washington D.C., where he taught government at American University and earned an M.A. degree in political science from George Washington University. In 1933 Flemming obtained a law degree there. The following year he became director of the American University's School of Public Affairs. He remained at this position until 1938, when he became executive officer of the university.

In 1939 Franklin D. Roosevelt appointed Flemming the Republican member of the three-man Civil Service Commission. He held this position until 1948. During World War II Flemming was also chief of labor supply for the Office of Production Management and member of the War Manpower Commission. In 1947 President Harry S. Truman appointed Flemming to the Hoover Commission, charged with evaluating the structure of the executive branch. Flemming left government service in 1948 to accept the presidency of Ohio Wesleyan University. However, three years later he took a leave of absence to become assistant to the Director of Defense Mobilization, Charles Wilson [q.v.], and chairman of the manpower policy committee of the Office of Defense Mobilization (ODM). Both agencies supervised the organization of the nation's resources to fight the Korean war.

When President Eisenhower took office, he made ODM a permanent government agency and appointed Flemming its acting head. In June 1953 he reluctantly accepted the directorship on a permanent basis. At that post he prepared a comprehensive plan for national mobilization in the event of nuclear war. This included proposals for industrial mobilization, rationing, wage and price controls and personnel training. He also prepared contingency plans in case of an oil shortage during the Suez crisis of 1956. In February 1958 Flemming resigned his position to return to Ohio Wesleyan as president.

Three months later Eisenhower appointed Flemming Secretary of Health, Education and Welfare (HEW) to succeed retiring Marion Folsom [q.v.]. Eisenhower's selection drew the praise of many liberals and moderates who were impressed with Flemming's commitment to the social welfare programs of the past Administrations. Conservatives, who were generally skeptical of Flemming's liberalism, were nevertheless satisfied because of his administrative skills and his support for a balanced budget.

Flemming's background and attitudes differed from those of many of the men in the President's cabinet, which was drawn largely from business circles. A quiet, withdrawn man, he had risen through the government bureaucracy, Journalist William S. White described his profession as "the bland, fairly non-policital, and highly expert management of what are inherently political enterprises." He was described as an "endurable do-gooder" and "spender" in a cabinet dominated by conservative business thinking. Yet, Flemming was adept at political maneuvering and in dealing with Congress.

As Secretary of HEW, Flemming advocated increased federal aid to education to meet what was viewed as America's weakness in science and mathematics in light of the Soviet launching of *Sputnik* during the fall of 1957. The National Defense Education Act, passed one month after Flemming took office, was designed to remedy the situation. It offered loans to college students, particularly those interested in teaching, as well as matching grants to schools of all levels for laboratories, textbooks and other facilities. It also provided fellowships for graduate students. Flemming backed the measure but urged the repeal of the loyalty oath requirement for the loan program. Not satisfied with the scope of the bill, Flemming, in 1959, proposed a program to spur school construction through $5 billion in loans and matching grants over a

five-year period. Flemming's bill and several more ambitious Democratic-sponsored measures were debated in Congress in 1959 and 1960, but none were ever passed.

Soon after becoming Secretary, Flemming became embroiled in the school desegregation crisis. In September 1958 he warned areas practicing segregation that federal installations in the areas might be shut down if the schools were not integrated. In December he denounced the closings of schools in Virginia and Arkansas as "indefensible."

Flemming opposed liberal recommendations for medical care for the aged financed through Social Security. In May 1959 he offered the Administration's own proposal calling for state programs subsidized by the federal government to provide health care for persons over 65. The states would have collected fees from those who could afford payments while the aged on relief would have gained free coverage. Eligible persons would have been given the option of purchasing private insurance plans which the federal and state governments would have subsidized up to 50%. Congress never passed the Administration's proposal.

During his tenure as HEW Secretary, Flemming called for increased efforts to combat air and water pollution and the use of color additives in foods, drugs and chemicals. In November 1959 he precipitated a national scare when he warned that certain cranberries from the Pacific Northwest had been contaminated by weed-killers linked to cancer. Occuring right before Thanksgiving, Flemming's action did produce bans in numerous states. He defended his announcement by saying, "My position all along has been that when we in the government develop information of this nature, we have an obligation to make it available to the public."

During the 1960s Flemming served as president of the University of Oregon. He was also a consultant to President Kennedy, advising him on medicare and the Peace Corps. In the late-1960s he called for a step-up in the government's War on Poverty. Flemming joined the Nixon Administration as a special consultant to the President on aging. He then became commissioner on aging and was also a member of the Civil Rights Commission. In 1971 he chaired a special Administration conference on the elderly. [See NIXON/FORD Volume]

[JB]

FOLSOM, JAMES E(LISHA)
b. Oct. 9, 1908: Coffee County, Ala.
Governor, Ala., 1947-51, 1955-59.

Raised in impoverished northern Alabama, James E. Folsom quit college in 1929 when flood damage to the family farm wiped out his tuition money. Following two years in the merchant marine, he returned to Alabama to work as an administrator in the Works Progress Administration. In 1933 he went to Washington on assignment and studied political science and public speaking at George Washington University while working with the Alabama congressional delegation. A huge man—he was six feet, eight inches tall and weighed 245 pounds—with a showman's flare that earned him the nickname "Kissin' Jim," Folsom ran unsuccessfully for Congress in 1936 and 1938 and governor in 1942. Elected a delegate to the 1944 Democratic National Convention, he split from his delegation to support the vice presidential candidacy of Henry Wallace.

In 1946 Folsom again campaigned for the gubernatorial nomination on a classic populist platform that waged political war against the rich and city dwellers. He pledged legislative reapportionment, old age pensions, aid to schools, repeal of the poll tax and a highway construction program to link farms to markets. With the support of the rural population and labor, he won the Democratic gubernatorial primary and general election. Folsom was a moderate on racial questions and considered white supremacy a spurious issue that diverted attention from more important social problems. After his inauguration in January 1947, he pushed through a law prohibiting masks on state highways, thus undercutting the Ku Klux Klan. Except for his roads program, few of Folsom's proposals were enacted. His social programs were criticized by the urban press and blocked by the rural-dominated legislature. Unable to

succeed himself, Folsom left government service in 1951.

In 1954 Folsom was again elected governor on a reform platform similar to that of 1946. However, much of his attention during his second term was devoted to the issue of segregation. Although not an integrationist, Folsom insisted that the Supreme Court's 1954 decision outlawing segregation in public schools was the law. He called for racial cooperation and maintained that the problem of race relations could be solved through action on the local level. During 1955 Folsom succeeded in preventing the enactment of most segregationist bills introduced by the legislature. He refused to sign a pupil placement bill and vetoed three anti-NAACP measures. He also ignored a resolution calling for Congress to curtail the federal judiciary and threatened to veto any measure censuring the Supreme Court.

Folsom was unable to maintain racial moderation during 1956. White supremacist Citizens Councils grew in importance; the black boycott of Montgomery's buses strained tempers; and Folsom's failure to anticipate trouble when black student Autherine Lucy [q.v.] entered the University of Alabama led to riots. By far Folsom's gravest political error occurred when he invited Rep. Adam Clayton Power, Jr. (R, N.Y.) [q.v.], to the governor's mansion for a drink. Powell later addressed a black crowd, claiming the Governor had called integration "inevitable." It was a comment white Alabamans never forgot. In January Folsom convened a special session of the legislature to deal with reapportionment, but the lawmakers refused to adjourn without passage of segregationist measures, including an interposition resolution nullifying the Supreme Court's decision. The Governor called the measure "hogwash" and likened the resolution to "a hound dog baying at the moon and claiming it's got the moon treed." The legislature also enacted two constitutional amendments permitting the state to abandon its public school system.

Folsom unsuccessfully attempted to regain control of the political situation through a call for a commission to combat racial tensions and with a strong series of statements upholding law and order. Trying to broaden his support, he spoke in favor of segregation and in April 1956 signed a bill implementing the private school amendment. However, he continued to call for a sane approach to race relations. Folsom ran for Democratic national committeeman in the spring of 1956 against Charles McKay, chairman of a Citizens Council chapter and the legislator who had introduced Alabama's interposition resolution, which directed the use of state power to prevent desegregation. He suffered a crushing defeat in the April election, and in the balloting all other candidates associated with his Administration lost. The atmosphere killed Folsom's biracial commission plan.

By 1957 most Alabama politicians were endorsing "massive resistance" to the Supreme Court decision. Folsom offered only limited opposition to segregationist measures and signed a resolution once again nullifying the *Brown* decision. The May 1958 Democratic primaries confirmed his political demise. Attorney General John Patterson [q.v.] was nominated for governor as a staunch segregationist, and a large number of Folsom's legislative supporters were unseated.

James Folsom tried a political comeback in the 1960s but was defeated in the 1962 gubernatorial primary by George Wallace.

[MJS]

FOLSOM, MARION

b. Nov. 23, 1893; McRae, Ga.
d. Sept. 28, 1976; Rochester, N.Y.
Undersecretary of the Treasury, January 1953-July 1955; Secretary of Health, Education and Welfare, July 1955-May 1958.

Marion Folsom graduated from the University of Georgia in 1912 and received an M.B.A. from Harvard University two years later. He served in the Army during World War I. In 1921 he became assistant to George Eastman, president of Eastman Kodak, Co., and in 1935 was made treasurer. During the 1930s Folsom developed the old age pension plan for Kodak, which

was later expanded to include 13 other firms under the title "the Rochester Plan."

Because of the wide interest in this program, President Franklin D. Roosevelt appointed Folsom to the President's Advisory Council on Economic Security in 1934 and to the Federal Council on Social Security in 1937. During World War II Folsom served as a member of the War Manpower Commission and of the Committee for Economic Development (CED), headed by Paul Hoffman [q.v.]. As a member of the CED, Folsom developed plans for the reconversion of the wartime to a peacetime economy with the objective of ensuring maximum production and full employment.

Folsom was appointed undersecretary of the Treasury in January 1953. During his tenure he represented the Treasury on a cabinet committee to determine how federal employe benefits compared with private industry. As a result of the investigation, Folsom sponsored a life insurance program for Civil Service employes underwritten by private industry. The plan provided that federal employes pay the rate generally contributed by workers in the private sector with the federal government paying the difference. In August the President signed the bill making Civil Service life insurance mandatory unless an employe signed a statement saying he did not want to be covered. Between 1954 and 1961 the program covered almost 2.5 million employes.

Folsom also helped revise the federal corporate income tax. The Income Tax Revision Act of 1954 enabled industry to make larger provisions for depreciation during the early years of an asset. According to Folsom, it contributed to the generally high level of private investment after 1954.

In 1955 Folsom succeeded Oveta Culp Hobby [q.v.] as Secretary of Health, Education and Welfare. The new Secretary continued to support the Salk polio vaccine program instituted in 1955. He coordinated the effort to insure the country's vaccine needs were met, and in December 1956 he announced that there was no longer a shortage but a surplus of 17 million doses.

Along with Secretary of State John Foster Dulles [q.v.], Secretary of the Treasury

George Humphrey [*q.v.*] and Attorney General Herbert Brownell, Folsom served on the cabinet committee investigating narcotics traffic during 1956. In February the committee disclosed that there were 60,000 addicts in the U.S., 13% under the age of 21. The panel recommended that the states develop treatment programs and increase penalties for drug pushers and that the U.S. work with international agencies to control drug traffic.

From 1955 to 1958 Folsom lobbied for passage of the national defense education bill. The Secretary believed that the U.S. lagged behind other major nations in the teaching of sciences and languages, and he assumed there would be an inadequate supply of Ph.D.s over the next 10 years. He, therefore, called on Congress to pass a bill providing fellowships and loans to graduate students, grants to gifted high school students, and aid to states for teaching languages, mathametics and the sciences. The bill also gave assistance to colleges and universities to establish training programs for teachers of modern, especially rare, languages. The National Defense Education Act became law in September 1954. It authorized the expenditure of $1 billion over a four year period.

After resigning as Secretary in 1958, Folsom, along with Ford Foundation president Henry T. Heald and Carnegie Foundation president John W. Gardner, served on the New York State Committee on Higher Education. In December 1959 the panel recommended to Gov. Nelson A. Rockefeller [*q.v.*] that the state increase its funds for public undergraduate and graduate education, limit expenditures for private institutions and discontinue tuition-free higher education except for rebates to needy students. It also proposed making 11 state teachers colleges into liberal arts colleges and establishing a new state university which included two graduate schools.

From 1958 to 1968 Folsom was director of Kodak. He also served as chairman of the advisory committee for personnel for the U.S. Public Health Service in 1961 and 1962, and was chairman of the National Commission on Community Health Services from 1962 to 1967 and vice chairman of the White House Conference on Health in 1967.

[RSG]

For further information:
Marion B. Folsom, *Executive Decision Making* (New York, 1962).

FORD, GERALD R(UDOLPH)
b. July 14, 1913; Omaha, Neb.
Republican Representative, Mich., 1949-73.

Raised by his stepfather in Grand Rapids, Mich., Ford was a football star at the University of Michigan, where he received a B.A. degree in 1935. Subsequently Ford studied law at Yale University and received an LL.B. degree in 1941. He briefly practiced law with a Grand Rapids firm before joining the Navy in 1942. After his discharge four years later, Ford returned home to resume his legal career.

In 1948 Ford's stepfather, a Republican county chairman, and Sen. Arthur H. Vandenberg (R, Mich.) urged Ford to challenge incumbent isolationist Rep. Bartel J. Jonkman (R, Mich.) in the Republican congressional primary. Ford won easily and went on to defeat his Democratic opponent with 61% of the vote. In subsequent elections he never won less than 60% of the vote. Ford generally supported President Harry S. Truman's foreign policy while opposing most of his domestic social welfare programs.

Although Ford's views and voting record were conservative, he was a political pragmatist and a party loyalist. In 1952 he was an early backer of Dwight D. Eisenhower for the Republican presidential nomination, partly because he believed that Eisenhower would run better in Michigan than conservative Sen. Robert H. Taft (R, Ohio) [*q.v.*]. Although Ford was a strong anti-Communist, he did not join Sen. Joseph R. McCarthy (R, Wisc.) [*q.v.*] in criticizing the Eisenhower Administration for allegedly tolerating subversives in its midst. According to *Congressional Quarterly*, in the 83rd and 84th Congresses (1953-54, 1955-56) Ford was among the five House Republicans who most often supported President Eisenhower.

Ford served on the Appropriations Committee and, as a member of that panel's Department of Defense Subcommittee, became an expert on military spending. A backer of high defense appropriations, he unsuccessfully sought to add $80 million to the Army's budget in 1957. Ford was also a strong supporter of military assistance to friendly countries. In 1956 he deplored Congress's 33% cut of the President's foreign military aid requests. The following year Ford criticized similar reductions, asserting that "we have made [them] in the wrong areas. . . . We ought to increase the [foreign aid] funds related to our own security and reduce the funds in those other non-military areas." In 1960 Ford headed a task force of the House Republican Policy Committee that produced recommendations, based on papers written by academic, professional and legislative experts, for a comprehensive national security strategy.

During the 1950s Ford's reputation for candor and honesty earned him the respect of his fellow-Republicans. A congenial man, he was also on good terms with the Democratic House leadership. In 1959 he was chosen to serve on a select committee that examined the budget of the Central Intelligence Agency. Hoping someday to become House Speaker, Ford turned down opportunities to run for the Senate in 1952 and 1954 and for governor of Michigan in 1956. But the Republican Party's failure to win the congressional elections of 1954, 1956 and 1958 made him more receptive to other possibilities. In 1960 he allowed a group of Michigan Republicans to conduct a Ford vice presidential campaign, but Republican presidential nominee Richard M. Nixon [q.v.] chose Henry Cabot Lodge [q.v.] as his running mate. Ford, believing that many Midwestern Republicans would find Lodge too liberal, did not think the choice a good one. But as a party loyalist he acceded to Nixon's request that he second Lodge's nomination at the National Convention.

In January 1963 a group of young Republican representatives led a revolt against Minority Leader Charles A. Halleck (R, Ind.) [q.v.] and chose Ford to replace Rep. Charles B. Hoeven (R, Iowa) as chairman of the Republican Conference Committee. Two years later Ford defeated Halleck in a contest for minority leader. In December 1973 President Nixon nominated Ford for vice president following the resignation of Spiro Agnew. Ford became President when Nixon resigned his office. Jimmy Carter defeated him in the 1976 presidential election. [See KENNEDY, JOHNSON, NIXON/FORD, CARTER Volumes]

[MLL]

For further information:
Jerald F. terHorst, *Gerald Ford and the Future of the Presidency* (New York, 1974).

FORD, HENRY II
b. Sept. 4, 1917; Detroit, Mich.
President, Ford Motor Company, 1954- .

The grandson of pioneer auto manufacturer and industrialist Henry Ford and the son of Ford Motor Co. president Edsel Ford, Henry Ford II was groomed at an early age for leadership in the family's enterprises. At the time of his father's death in May 1943, Ford was serving in the Navy, having left Yale University before completing his studies. He was released in August and began an apprenticeship in Ford's top management under the tutelage of his 80-year-old grandfather, who had resumed control of the company. In September 1945 the elder Ford reluctantly stepped aside to let his grandson assume the presidency at the age of 28.

Unlike his conservative grandfather, an autocratic manager and a bitter foe of unionism, the younger Ford determined to delegate responsibility in running the company and adopted a more flexible policy toward the demands of the United Auto Workers (UAW). In the immediate postwar period Ford promoted a sweeping reorganization of the company's administrative structure, hiring a specially-recruited "Whiz Kid" management team, which included Robert S. McNamara, later Secretary of Defense under the Kennedy and Johnson Administrations, to modernize the firm's production facilities and marketing techniques. To a large extent Ford adopted the more decentralized structure of its giant rival, the General Motors Corp. (GM). [See TRUMAN Volume]

After government restrictions on auto production were lifted following the Korean war, Ford embarked on a campaign to overtake GM in production and sales. Ford and his "team" sought to move the company, hitherto essentially a producer of one popular car, the Ford, plus the less successful Lincoln and Mercury, into more diversified production. With the unprecedented demand for passenger cars in the early 1950s and with profits reaching an all-time high as a result, Ford thought the time ripe to break GM's domination of the middle-priced car market. In 1957 Ford introduced the Edsel, which proved to be one of the biggest marketing failures in corporate history, losing the company about $350 million. Ford was more successful in offering other new models during the 1950s, but the company failed to achieve first place among the Big Three auto makers.

Prior to the 1955 auto industry contract talks, UAW president Walter Reuther [q.v.], selecting Ford as the target company, launched a campaign for a "guaranteed annual wage" to protect auto workers against interruptions in employment. Ford refused to pay the guaranteed annual wage but, after first offering to sell workers stock on liberal terms and then advance them interest-free loans on the stock during layoffs, it devised a system of unemployment compensation to supplement government insurance. Ford's Supplemental Unemployment Benefit plan (SUB) was accepted by the union and later adopted by other auto makers.

During the early-1950s Henry Ford II was a leading advocate of "free trade" in the auto industry, calling for the abandonment of high tariffs on foreign car imports. With increasing competition from foreign-made small cars in the latter part of the decade, however, he began to reverse his position. A strong supporter of the Eisenhower Administration, Ford was named by the President in 1953 to serve as an alternate delegate to the United Nations. In the fall

of 1960, however, he came into conflict with the White House over the issue of trade policy. Despite Administration pleas to cut down overseas spending, Ford proceeded with its plans to pay out $360 million to European stockholders for the public shares in its British affiliate. Secretary of the Treasury Robert Anderson [q.v.] personally urged Ford to hold up the stock purchase, but the company leadership refused to cooperate. The week the purchase went through, U.S. gold reserves dropped $204 million.

Ford was a prominent critic of the Kennedy Administration's intervention in the 1962 steel crisis. In 1964, however, he abandoned lifelong Republicanism to support Lyndon B. Johnson's presidential candidacy. Ford was also a backer of civil rights organizations and anti-poverty programs during the 1960s. [See KENNEDY, JOHNSON, NIXON/FORD Volumes]

[TLH]

FOSTER, WILLIAM C(HAPMAN)
b. April 27, 1897; Westfield, N.J.
Chief Delegate, Geneva Conference on the Prevention of Suprise Attacks, November 1958-December 1958.

Foster left the Massachusetts Institute of Technology at the end of his junior year to serve as a lieutenant and military aviator in World War I. In 1922 he joined Pressed and Welded Steel Products Co., Inc., where he was an officer and then a director until 1946. Impressed by Foster's knowledge of the problems of small business. Secretary of Commerce W. Averell Harriman [q.v.] convinced President Harry S. Truman to appoint the Republican undersecretary of commerce in 1946. Two years later, when Harriman was named ambassador at large to Western Europe to oversee the first operations of the Marshall Plan, Foster went along as general deputy in charge of the Paris headquarters. In June 1949 Foster became deputy administrator of the Economic Cooperation Administration (ECA). The following year he became administrator. As undersecretary of defense from 1951 to 1953, Foster headed a panel that prepared a secret report on the comparative military strengths of the U.S. and USSR. Foster resigned in 1953 to become president of the Manufacturing Chemists Association. He joined Olin Mathieson Chemical Corp. in 1955 as executive vice president. Concurrently, he was chairman of the board of Reaction Motors, Inc., and a director of Detroit Edison. [See TRUMAN Volume]

Foster returned to government service in 1958 to head the U.S. delegation to the Geneva Conference on the Prevention of Surprise Attacks. With only two months notice, Foster familiarized himself with the U.S. position which focused on technical matters: the definition of the "instruments of surprise attack" and the application of inspection and observation techniques to the problem.

Throughout the conference, convened in November, the Western and Eastern blocs differed significantly on what should be discussed. Foster working on the premise that the major threat to security arose from long-range missiles and manned aircraft carrying thermonuclear weapons, stressed the need for technical weapons control. He, therefore, outlined a proposal for the development of a comprehensive inspection system to deal with existing weapons. He noted the danger of inadequate partial inspection, believing it could give one nation a temporary advantage and cautioned that any step-by-step implementation of inspection systems would require careful negotiations to circumvent that problem.

The Soviets, on the other hand, emphasized disarmament rather than control, maintaining the two could not be separated. Assuming that the chief danger of surprise attack came from concentrations of conventional forces, they demanded the liquidation of military bases on foreign soil, the reduction of conventional arms and troops and the abolition of nuclear weapons. They were particularly anxious to create a nuclear-free zone in Central Europe to prevent the rearming of West Germany. The USSR rejected the call for a comprehensive inspection system because it might compromise its security and instead offered a ￢tem of self-inspection.

The conference ended in December with no agreement. Yet it did have long-range benefits. The technical papers the U.S. prepared for the meeting provided valuable data on weapons and inspection technology for future negotiations. More importantly, it marked the first time the U.S. had developed concrete proposals rather than vague principles for weapons control. It also was a major turning point in U.S. thought on the issue of disarmament and arms control. Instead of focusing on control of fissionable materials, the U.S. stressed the elimination of nuclear warfare through the control of the means of delivery of nuclear arms. Foster, testifying before the Senate Subcommittee on Disarmament in January 1959, said the conference had shown him the need to define the issues involved in control and disarmament more clearly. It had also given him valuable experience in dealing with the Soviets and in understanding the importance they placed on defending their security.

In September 1961 Foster was appointed director of the Arms Control and Disarmament Agency. At that post he was involved in the negotiation of a partial nuclear test ban treaty, which received Senate ratification in September 1963. During the Johnson Administration Foster helped negotiate the 1968 nuclear non-proliferation treaty. Foster left office in January 1968 and became president of Porter International Co., in 1970. [See KENNEDY, Volume]

[ACD]

For further information:
Bernard G. Bechhoeffer, *Postwar Negotiations for Arms Control* (Washington, D.C., 1961).

FRANKFURTER, FELIX
b. Nov. 15, 1882; Vienna, Austria
d. Feb. 22, 1965; Washington, D.C.
Associate Justice, U.S. Supreme Court, 1939-62.

Felix Frankfurter emigrated to the United States with his family at the age of 12. He graduated from the City College of

New York in 1902 and from Harvard law school in 1906. During the next eight years he was an assistant U.S. attorney in New York and an aide to Secretary of War Henry Stimson. A faculty member at Harvard law school from 1914 to 1939, Frankfurter became a noted scholar on the Supreme Court, the Constitution and administrative law. He also maintained a wide range of extracurricular activities that won him a liberal reputation. He served as an adviser to the NAACP and the American Civil Liberties Union, supported labor unions and fought to have the convictions of Italian anarchists Nicola Sacco and Bartolomeo Vanzetti overturned. During the New Deal Frankfurter acted as a counselor to President Franklin Roosevelt, advising him on legislation, appointments and speeches. Roosevelt named him to the Supreme Court in January 1939.

On the Court Justice Frankfurter became the leading advocate of judicial restraint. Legislatures, he contended, were the policymaking bodies in a democratic society, and the Court must defer to their judgments and sustain laws with a constitutional basis, however unwise the justices might think them to be. Frankfurter used this approach not only in the economic arena to uphold New Deal legislation but also in the realm of civil liberties to sustain laws curtailing freedom of belief and expression. Although it meant voting against causes he had earlier championed, Frankfurter insisted that judges must be disinterested and detached and must not read into the Constitution their own notions of good policy. Unlike Justice Hugo Black [q.v.], Frankfurter did not give First Amendment rights any preferred position over other constitutional guarantees nor did he consider any provisions in the Bill of Rights absolutes. He insisted that the Court must balance the conflicting interests in each case, making its judgments without any doctrinaire presuppositions. [See TRUMAN Volume]

Although often labeled a conservative, Frankfurter was not insensitive to individual liberties. In February 1957 he spoke for a unanimous Court to hold unconstitutional a Michigan obscenity law banning all

sale of books deemed inappropriate for children. He joined in a June 1957 decision reversing the contempt conviction of an economics professor who had refused to answer a state official's questions about the content of his lectures and his association with the Progressive Party. In a concurring opinion he delivered a strong defense of the rights to academic and political freedom. Frankfurter also voted against the government in a number of other loyalty-security cases of the 1950s, though generally for narrow procedural or statutory reasons rather than on broad and inflexible constitutional grounds. In April 1956 he was part of a six-man majority that overturned a state sedition law because Congress had superseded it in the Smith Act, and he concurred in a June 1957 decision placing limits on congressional investigations of subversion. But Frankfurter often upheld government security interests against claims of individual freedom and, therefore, occupied a center position on the Court on such issues during this period. He joined the majority in two June 1959 cases that sustained the contempt convictions of individuals who refused to answer questions or supply information during congressional and state investigations of Communism. Frankfurter also voted in several cases to uphold the dismissal of municipal and county government employes who had refused to answer questions concerning their political views and associations.

The Justice was far more willing to have the Court take an active role in overseeing federal criminal procedure and was especially exacting regarding search and seizure and confessions. Building on an opinion he had written in 1943, Frankfurter ruled in the June 1957 Mallory case that when there was any unnecessary delay between the arrest and arraignment of a defendant, a confession obtained during that period was inadmissible in federal courts. However, Frankfurter contended that the Constitution placed fewer limits on state criminal procedures, and so he applied less rigid standards to the states. He delivered the majority opinion in a March 1959 decision holding that a state did not deny due process of law when it tried a person for a crime for which he had already been tried and acquitted in a federal court.

Throughout his judicial career Frankfurter voted in support of black Americans' claims for equality under the law. There is considerable evidence that he had a significant part in bringing about the Court's unanimous May 1954 decision in *Brown* v. *Board of Education,* which held public school segregation unconstitutional. Frankfurter believed a unanimous opinion would be best for the Court and the country, and so he sought to delay a final decision until the Court had reached a consensus. He had one of his clerks research the relevant constitutional history in detail and circulated several memos among the justices on the question of how to implement the decision. The Court's final decree, issued in May 1955, followed the gradualist approach Frankfurter favored and called for school desegregation "with all deliberate speed," a phrase the Justice had used in several other cases and had suggested in one of his memos. When state officials later attempted to forestall school integration in Little Rock, Ark., Frankfurter joined in the Court's September 1958 order mandating the resumption of school desegregation in that city. He also wrote a special concurring opinion affirming the supremacy of the law and condemning defiance and obstruction of its enforcement.

Frankfurter was by all accounts personally vivacious and ebullient, a man of considerable wit and charm with a charismatic, captivating personality. An avid and lively conversationalist and correspondent, he numbered among his friends leading figures in law, government, journalism and scholarship. When he retired from the Court in August 1962, no commentator doubted that Frankfurter's nearly 50 years at Harvard and on the Court had made a deep impact on American law. His critics felt that he had, nonetheless, missed greatness by taking too narrow a view of the judicial function and that his adherence to a philosophy of judicial restraint in the field of civil liberties "uncoupled him," as Joseph Lash put it, "from the locomotive of history." Frankfurter's defenders, however, argued that he had been an important and necessary stabilizing force on the Court. They agreed with Philip Kurland that the Justice "was the latest of the great keepers of the legend: a legend of a nonpartisan Supreme Court dedicated to the maintenance of a government of laws founded on reason and based on a faith in democracy." [See KENNEDY Volume]

[CAB]

For further information:
Liva Baker, *Felix Frankfurter* (New York, 1969).
Joseph P Lash, "A Brahmin of the Law: A Biographical Essay," in *From the Diaries of Felix Frankfurter* (New York, 1975).
Wallace Mendelson, ed., *Felix Frankfurter: The Judge* (New York, 1964).
Albert M. Sacks, "Felix Frankfurter," in Leon Friedman and Fred L. Israel, eds., *The Justices of the United States Supreme Court, 1789-1969* (New York, 1969), Vol. 3.

FREEMAN, ORVILLE L(ORTHROP)
b. March 9, 1918: Minneapolis, Minn.
Governor, Minn., 1955-61.

The son of a Minneapolis storekeeper, Freeman graduated *magna cum laude* from the University of Minnesota in 1940. Following service with the Marines during World War II, he returned to the University to obtain his law degree in 1946. While practicing law he joined Hubert Humphrey [*q.v.*] and other liberals in reviving the Democratic-Farmer-Labor Party. Freeman became the state chairman in 1948 and managed Humphrey's successful Senate campaign that year.

Freeman made two unsuccessful races for governor in 1950 and 1952 but won the 1954 gubernatorial contest. A fine administrator, he was responsible for major improvements in education and welfare: building schools, increasing space in state mental hospitals and expanding state aid to local school districts. But to finance this program he had to raise property taxes to an all-time high and attempt to install pay-as-you-go income taxes. Freeman's tax policies and his decision to send state militia to close a strikebound meat-packing company contributed to his reelection defeat in 1960.

As governor, Freeman opposed Secretary

of Agriculture Ezra Taft Benson's [q.v.] policy of reducing price supports on agricultural commodities which, the Secretary maintained, aided only the larger farmers who could control production. In 1959 Freeman created the Minnesota Farm Policy Committee, composed of agricultural economists, to evaluate the Benson program. Its report called for the establishment of a national food policy with production goals set for domestic and foreign use. Once the production goal was determined, marketing allotments would be distributed to farmers on a graduated basis with the largest farms receiving the proportionately largest reductions. The report also advocated the reduction of agricultural surpluses through overseas sales, the establishment of school lunch programs and the granting of aid to depressed areas.

Freeman and Humphrey were early supporters of Adlai Stevenson [q.v.] for the 1956 Democratic presidential nomination and assured their candidate of Farmer-Labor support in the Minnesota primary. Therefore, Stevenson campaigned very little in the state. Sen. Estes Kefauver (D, Tenn.) [q.v.], running on the proposition that Freeman and Humphrey were political bosses, won an upset victory that slowed down Stevenson's drive for the nomination and damaged the Governor's prestige. Following Stevenson's defeat in the November election, Freeman joined the Democratic Advisory Council, a panel of leading Democrats who prepared position papers for the Party on important issues. He was considered one of the most liberal members of the panel, especially on agriculture, civil rights and foreign policy issues.

Freeman supported Humphrey for President in 1960, and after the Senator's withdrawal from the primary race, he endorsed Sen. John F. Kennedy (D, Mass.) [q.v.]. At the Democratic National Convention the Minnesota delegation split between supporters of Kennedy and Stevenson. Freeman and Humphrey led the pro-Kennedy forces against the group, headed by Sen. Eugene McCarthy (D, Minn.) [q.v.], fighting for Stevenson. Gov. Freeman placed Kennedy's name in nomination, calling him a "proven liberal" and a demonstrated leader. In the

early part of the primary race, Kennedy considered Freeman a leading contender for vice president. However, he was reluctant to choose a northern liberal and selected Sen. Lyndon Johnson (D, Tex.) [q.v.] as his running mate.

Freeman served as Secretary of Agriculture during the Kennedy and Johnson administrations and put into practice many of the recommendations of his 1959 Farm Policy Committee. In 1970 he became president of the Business International Corp. [See KENNEDY, JOHNSON Volumes]

[JB]

FRITCHEY, CLAYTON
b. 1905 (?); Bellefontaine, Ore.
Deputy Chairman, Democratic National Committee, 1953-57.

Fritchey began his long career in journalism as a reporter for the *Baltimore American* in 1924. Promoted to editorial positions on Cleveland, Pittsburgh and other Baltimore newspapers, he won an honorable mention for the Pulitzer Prize in 1936 and became editor of the *New Orleans Item* in 1944. Fritchey served as director of the Department of Defense's public relations bureau from 1950 to 1952. In that post newmen rated him as "competent, but not outstanding." An outspoken liberal Democrat, he was appointed an assistant to President Harry S. Truman in 1952.

After the National Democratic Convention in July, Fritchey served as liaison between Truman and presidential nominee Adlai E. Stevenson [q.v.]. Fritchey was appointed Democratic deputy chairman by National Chairman Stephen Mitchell [q.v.] in December. He served in that post until 1957, principally concerning himself with editing the National Committee's official magazine, *Democratic Digest*. In November 1953 Fritchey charged Republican Attorney General Herbert Brownell [q.v.] with using allegations of Communists in government under Truman to "divert attention" from corruption charges leveled against himself. Fritchey's "no-holds-barred" attitude toward Republicans was appreciated by Democrats.

The January 1956 trial of private investigator Paul Hughes for perjury revealed that Hughes had sold Fritchey false information on "illegal activities" of Sen. Joseph McCarthy (R, Wisc.) [q.v.] and the Senate Government Operations Committee's Permanent Investigations Subcommittee in 1954. Fritchey testified that he had lent Hughes $2300 but had become disillusioned with him and had dropped the project.

The deputy chairman's aggressiveness was rewarded in August 1956 when he was chosen press secretary for Democratic nominee Stevenson, who was making his second presidential race. Fritchey was picked specifically to counter the aggressive salesmanship of President Eisenhower's press secretary, James C. Hagerty [q.v.]. As the campaign progressed, Fritchey was accused of spending too much time with Democratic officials and not enough with reporters. Fritchey found difficulty reaching Stevenson through the candidate's aides and opportunities for press conferences were missed. When Stevenson lost in November, Fritchey resigned his party post.

In 1957 Fritchey purchased the *Northern Virginia Sun* and continued publishing it until 1961. From 1961 to 1965, Fritchey served as special assistant to the ambassador to U.N. and during that time he began writing a syndicated political column.

[MJS]

FULBRIGHT, J(AMES) WILLIAM
b. April 9, 1905; Sumner, Mo.
Democratic Senator, Ark., 1945-75.

The son of a wealthy banker and prominent businessman, Fulbright grew up in Fayetteville, Ark., in the northwestern part of the state. He graduated from the University of Arkansas in 1925 and spent the next three years at Oxford on a Rhodes scholarship. Upon his return to the U.S. in 1928, Fulbright entered George Washington University law school. Following his graduation he worked for the Justice Department's antitrust division, where he helped prosecute the Schechter chicken case. Fulbright left government service after a year to accept a

position as law instructor at George Washington University.

In 1936 Fulbright returned to Fayetteville, where he combined teaching at the University of Arkansas with managing the family's businesses. Three years later Fulbright, then 34, was appointed president of the University. He was the youngest university president in the U.S. As president, he first gained national attention by raising university standards. He also spoke out in opposition to isolationists, an effort that earned him the enmity of Homer Adkins. When Adkins was elected governor in 1940, he pushed Fulbright from his post.

In 1942 Fulbright won a seat in the House of Representatives, where he was assigned to the Foreign Affairs Committee. Several months after his entry into Congress, he defended Franklin D. Roosevelt's war policies and postwar plans against an attack by Rep. Claire Boothe Luce (R, Conn.) [q.v.]. He also offered specific plans for the establishment of an international organization to prevent future wars. These proposals became the basis for the Fulbright resolution, passed in 1943, which gave House support to U.S. participation in international agencies to promote peace.

Two years later Fulbright, in a campaign that emphasized his conservative domestic program, won a Senate seat. In the upper house he continued his bold stand on foreign affairs while maintaining a politically safe position on domestic issues, particularly segregation. In September 1945 Fulbright offered a bill for the educational exchange program that would bear his name. The bill passed in 1946. During the Truman Administration Fulbright became one of the President's foremost domestic critics. In 1950 he chaired an investigation of influence peddling in the Reconstruction Finance Corp. that reached to the White House. [See TRUMAN Volume]

During the Eisenhower Administration Fulbright maintained his bold stand on foreign policy and conservative position on domestic affairs. He was a spokesman for the economic interests of the South, supporting the Dixon-Yates power combine and opposing an increase in the minimum wage. Yet Fulbright was not a conservative who feared and wished to restrict government action. He instead wanted to reorient government from a concentration on defense and highway spending to an emphasis on housing, education and antitrust programs.

Fulbright was an early critic of Sen. Joseph McCarthy (R, Wisc.) [q.v.]. In 1953 he was called on to defend the Fulbright Fellowship program, which McCarthy changed with supporting pro-Communists. The Arkansas Senator, whom McCarthy called "Halfbright," not only countered McCarthy's criticism but also volunteered to gain proof that the fellows were loyal Americans. Several officials connected with the program termed Fulbright's defense the first successful resistance to McCarthy within government since the Senator's attacks began. Early in 1954, when McCarthy was at the height of his power, the Senate voted on further appropriations for McCarthy's Permanent Investigations Subcommittee. The vast majority of Senators, fearing McCarthy, voted the funds. Only Fulbright opposed the bill.

Fulbright played a leading role in the Senate's condemnation of McCarthy in 1954. Because McCarthy's conduct in the Army-McCarthy hearings of the spring had alienated many important senators, Fulbright thought it would be an appropriate time to act against him. Believing that it would be best if the lead were taken by a Republican, Fulbright approached Sen. Ralph Flanders (R, Vt.) [q.v.], who agreed to sponsor a censure resolution. Fulbright helped Flanders prepare the measure, which simply stated that McCarthy had brought discredit to the Senate. He also did the bulk of the research on the legal and historical precedents for the censure action and handled negotiations with the Democratic leadership. When the original measure proved too vague to attract support, Fulbright amended it with a bill of particulars. In early November a select committee, headed by Sen. Arthur Watkins (R, Utah) [q.v.], recommended McCarthy's censure. When the final debate began at the end of the month, Fulbright took the Senate floor to denounce the hatred and fears engendered by McCarthy. On Dec. 2 the Senate

voted to condemn the Wisconsin Senator.

Fulbright remained an opponent of integration throughout the 1950s. In March 1956 he joined 18 other senators and 82 representatives in signing the "Southern Manifesto," which denounced the Supreme Court's 1954 decision outlawing segregated schools. The congressmen maintained that the Court had "substituted naked power for established law" and laid the basis for interracial strife. They, therefore, pledged to resist integration by "any lawful means." Although considered inflamatory by many liberals, the statement was a moderate version of one originally proposed by Sen. Strom Thurmond, (D, S.C.) [q.v.]. That proposal had endorsed the theory of interposition (the use of state power to nullify the Court's decision) and had branded the Court's action illegal and unconstitutional. Fulbright had opposed that extreme language, and the Manifesto was modified to gain his support. He voted against the Civil Rights Acts of 1957 and 1960.

During the 1950s Fulbright frequently clashed with President Eisenhower and Secretary of State John Foster Dulles [q.v.] over U.S. foreign affairs. He urged a reorientation of U.S. policy from one based on an ideological confrontation with the Soviet Union to one resting on big power interests. He stressed the need to supply economic and technical rather than military aid to U.S. allies and questioned the Administration's dependence on nuclear weapons for defense.

Fulbright also opposed the President's emphasis on the formation of defense pacts with underdeveloped nations. He disapproved of the Southeast Asian Treaty of 1954, which established the Southeast Asia Treaty Organization (SEATO), and the formosa Resolution of 1955, giving the President the right to use force to defend Formosa and the Pescadores. In 1957 the Senator opposed the Eisenhower Doctrine, which authorized the President to use the Armed Forces to aid a Middle Eastern nation resisting "armed attack from any country controled by international Communism." Fulbright used the hearings on the resolution to denounce Eisenhower's foreign policy, which he claimed would weaken Western influence in the Middle East, was disastrous to the North Atlantic Treaty Organization and damaging to U.S. friendship with Great Britain and France. The resolution passed the Senate in March 1957. Fulbright was one of 19 senators who voted against it.

Fulbright continued to urge an end to foreign policy based on cold war ideology throughout the 1960s. He opposed the Johnson Administration's conduct of the Vietnam war and, by the end of the decade, had become the preeminent symbol of growing congressional discontent with the conflict. In 1974 he lost the Arkansas Democratic primary. His defeat was attributed to his preoccupation with foreign affairs at the expense of his constituents' interests. [See KENNEDY, JOHNSON, NIXON/FORD Volumes]

[EWS]

For further information:
Haynes Johnson and Bernard M. Gwertzman, *Fulbright: the Dissenter* (New York, 1968).

FUNSTON, G(EORGE) KEITH
b. Oct. 12, 1910; Waterloo, Iowa
President, New York Stock Exchange, 1951-67.

G. Keith Funston grew up in Sioux Falls, S.D., where his father owned the International Savings Bank. He won a scholarship to Trinity College in Connecticut and graduated as class valedictorian in 1932. After earning an M.B.A. from the Harvard Graduate School of Business Administration, he worked from 1935 to 1940 for the American Radiator Co., where he set up a sales incentive plan. In 1940 he joined the Sylvania Electric Products Co. as sales planning director. Funston left Sylvania to become a dollar-a-year man during World War II, serving at the War Production Board as special assistant, first to former investment banker Sidney Weinberg and then to chairman Donald Nelson. Toward the end of the War, he was chosen president of Trinity College, where he launched a vigorous public relations campaign, rais-

ing $5 million in six years for the small institution. Funston also served on the boards of directors of seven corporations until 1951, when upon Weinberg's recommendation he was selected as president of the New York Stock Exchange (NYSE).

The NYSE provided the physical environment for the buying and selling of stocks, but it also was responsible for "self-regulation," policing its members' ethical behavior in areas outside the purview of the Securities and Exchange Commission (SEC). The 40-year-old Funston had no background in the securities business when he took the $100,000-a-year post of NYSE president, but his wholesome image and success in selling and public relations equipped him for the task of representing the Stock Exchange before Washington and the public.

Funston undertook a crusade to improve the public image of the stock market. He promoted the virtues of stock ownership by an ambitious advertising campaign that included pamphlets and movies. His major vehicle for disseminating stock ownership among a wider public was the Monthly Investment Plan (MIP) for small investors. Begun in January 1954, after an Exchange survey indicated that less than seven million Americans owned shares of stock, the MIP enabled people to buy stocks on an installment basis. Funston touted the plan across the country, but its high commission costs and the competing appeal of mutual funds kept participation low.

As the official spokesman of the NYSE's 1,300 members, Funston was quick to defend a free market in securities whenever the government attempted to tighten regulation. On Jan. 4, 1954 the Federal Reserve Board raised the margin requirement from 50% of a stock's price to 60%. The next day Funston criticized the Board's action as "hard to understand" because "it comes at a time when industry is seeking new funds to build new plants and equipment." He added that "an active and liquid stock market is essential to the vitality of our economy" and that the increased margin requirement would "inhibit the proper functioning of the market and the free interplay of the basic law of supply and demand."

During a speculative boom in 1955 the Senate Banking and Currency Committee conducted a study of the stock market. In March Funston testified that, despite the recent sharp rise in speculation, the market was healthy, for the high price level was "not the product of undue extension of credit or of unsound market activity but reflects the confident appraisal of the general public." Funston dismissed alarms that the current market conditions were similar to those that had caused the 1929 crash, and he opposed proposals to raise margin requirements.

Funston's tenure coincided with the biggest bull market in history. During the 1960s he found it increasingly necessary to defend the Exchange against criticisms of its "private club" exclusiveness, abuses in stock trading and the laxity of its performance as self-regulator. He left the NYSE in April 1967 to become chairman of the Olin Mathieson Chemical Corp. [See KENNEDY Volume]

[TO]

GAITHER, H(ORACE) ROWAN, JR.
b. Nov. 23, 1909; Natchez, Miss.
d. April 7, 1961; Boston, Mass.
President, Ford Foundation, 1953-56;
Presidential adviser, 1957.

H. Rowan Gaither obtained his B.A. from the University of California at Berkeley in 1929 and a law degree there four years later. He then moved to Washington, D.C., to serve as a special assistant to the Farm Credit Administration. In 1936 Gaither returned to California to practice law and teach at Berkeley's law school. During World War II Gaither served as assistant director of the Radiation Laboratory of the Massachusetts Institute of Technology. Following the War he returned to private law practice. In 1948 he became president of the Rand Corp., the prestigious think tank that conducted research for government agencies, particularly the Pentagon. At Rand Gaither worked closely with the Ford Foundation, which funded many of the corporation's projects. In 1951 the Foundation

appointed Gaither associate director in charge of the investigation of human behavior and conduct. Two years later he was elected president. He held that post until 1956, when he was named board chairman.

In 1954 the House Special Committee to Investigate Tax-Exempt Foundations heard testimony on charges that the Ford, Rockefeller, Carnegie and other foundations supported subversive activities. On July 24 Gaither charged that the Committee "maligned" the foundation with irresponsible testimony and called its accusations "erroneous and baseless . . . sheerest nonsense." Gaither asked for an opportunity to appear before the Committee to avert a damaging effect on the "morale, initiative and freedom of scientific, educational and charitable organizations." However, public hearings ended before representatives of the foundations were heard.

In December the Republican majority on the Committee issued a report maintaining that, while the foundations did not support Communist organizations, they "have directly supported 'subversion' in the true meaning of that term, namely, the process of undermining some of our vital protective concepts and principles." Gaither joined Dean Rusk [q.v.], president of the Rockefeller Foundation, in calling the report biased and unfounded.

In the spring of 1957 President Eisenhower secretly commissioned Gaither to head a blue ribbon panel charged with studying Soviet offensive capabilities and U.S. defense needs. Gaither became ill before completing the project, but the panel's secret report bore his name. Although the Administration refused to make it public, the report's major findings were leaked to the press in November 1957. The group found that because of increased Soviet spending, the USSR would achieve missile superiority over the U.S. by 1959, primarily as a result of its concentration on the development of intercontinental ballistic missiles. It predicted that the Soviet Union might be able to launch as many as 100 missiles with nuclear warheads delivering a massive single knockout blow to the U.S. The group recommended increased military spending and the development of a fallout shelter program to meet the challenge. It also predicted that future conflicts were likely to be limited wars rather than all-out nuclear ones. The panel recommended the U.S. build up its capacity to handle small conflicts rather than concentrate on the massive retaliatory capability required for general nuclear war.

Despite demands from the press and leading Democrats to release the full report, Eisenhower refused, claiming he had the right to keep secret a project he initiated for his own personal use. White House Press Secretary James G. Hagerty [q.v.] denied the report found the U.S. weaker than the Soviet Union. He told the press on Dec. 28, 1957 that the report stated the opposite. Gaither himself refused to volunteer any information on the report. "A secret is a secret," he said, "I must be a clam. There is no other course." President John F. Kennedy also refused to release the report. Gaither died of cancer in April 1961.

[JB]

GALBRAITH, JOHN KENNETH
b. Oct. 15, 1908; Iona Station, Canada.
Economist.

Born on a farm in Canada, John Kenneth Galbraith received a B.S. from the University of Toronto in 1931 and his Ph.D. in economics from the University of California at Berkeley in 1934. He then taught at Harvard from 1934 to 1939. After a year at Princeton he went to Washington, D.C., to serve as economic adviser to Chester Davis, agricultural member of the National Defense Advisory Committee. In 1941 Galbraith moved to the Office of Price Administration as director of price controls. He resigned in 1943 under fire from a host of business and congressional critics who objected to his support of a comprehensive control system.

In 1945 Galbraith directed the United States Strategic Bombing Survey to assess the effects of the air war against Germany and Japan. After the War he served as director of the State Department's Office of

Economic Security Policy, which took control of the economic affairs of the Axis powers. From 1943 to 1948 Galbraith also was a member of the board of editors of Fortune magazine. [See TRUMAN Volume]

In 1949 Galbraith returned to Harvard as professor of economics. During the 1950s he published a number of highly influential analyses of the American economy. Through trenchant expression, deft use of statistical evidence and witty debunking of the "conventional wisdom" of liberal as well as conservative dogma, Galbraith reached a wide audience for his iconoclastic brand of Keynesian economics and liberal politics.

In American Capitalism: The Concept of Countervailing Power (1951), Galbraith argued that the classical model of small competing units did not apply to the modern American economy, which was dominated by large power combinations. This state of affairs should cause no alarm, he maintained, because these powers were "countervailing." Big business was offset by big labor, both of which were counterbalanced by big government, the protector of societal units too weak or unorganized to maintain a fair equilibrium. Galbraith's essentially sanguine picture of the structure of the American economy and his advice to liberals that bigness per se was not harmful were of seminal importance in shaping attitudes on these questions during the decade.

In 1955 Galbraith published The Great Crash: 1929, a colorful account of the stock market debacle. He made clear that the cause of the market collapse was the "speculative orgy" that preceded it. The crash did not "cause" the Great Depression, Galbraith acknowledged, but helped trigger it. Had the economy not had grave underlying weaknesses, such as a severe maldistribution of income and a bad banking structure, the crash probably would not have precipitated such a deep depression.

In March 1955 Galbraith appeared before the Senate Banking and Currency Committee investigating the current stock market boom. He testified that the speculative hysteria was unhealthy and was one of several disturbing resemblances to conditions preceding the 1929 crash. He urged raising margin requirements on stock purchases to

100%, a proposal sharply at variance from the recommendations of the stock exchange officials who testified.

Galbraith's testimony piqued the Committee's senior Republican, Sen. Homer Capehart (R, Ind.) [q.v.], who later accused the Harvard economist of disparaging the American economy and "praising Communism." In a public telegram Galbraith answered Capehart's charge by pointing out that the Senator had lifted some sentences out of context from a pamphlet Galbraith had written and had omitted other sentences critical of Communism. The dispute flared briefly on the front pages and then died.

Galbraith's most important work of the decade was *The Affluent Society* (1958), a major critique of national priorities. The title was semi-ironic: the American economy was producing an ever-growing abundance of goods for a satisfied majority, while pockets of poverty continued to fester and social problems were ignored. Galbraith questioned the national consensus that greater production was the answer to America's needs. In his acerbic style he derided the American preoccupation with the variety and quantity of consumer goods, a craving that owed more to advertising than real need. In contrast Galbraith held up the deterioration of American cities, juvenile delinquency and substandard housing as examples of grave social problems neglected in the pursuit of abundance. His prescription was a rearrangement of national priorities: an increase in spending in the public sector to meet social needs outside the scope of private affluence.

Galbraith treated the question of inflation in an essay in the *The Liberal Hour* (1960). In his analysis much of inflation resulted from price rises in a few highly concentrated industries, like steel, automobiles, rubber and machinery. Because of the power of the "largest and strongest firms" and the "largest and strongest unions," prices rose in an inflationary spiral, a condition insensitive to market fluctuations. "Modern inflation is not neutral," he declared. "Because of its inevitable identification with economic strength, it is inequitable, regressive and reactionary." Galbraith rejected as solutions monetary or fiscal ad-

justments: the former was ineffective and the latter, by severely cutting demand, output and employment, was "worse than the disease." His solution was wage and price restraints applied to unwarranted increases in the highly concentrated industries.

Galbraith worked on Adlai Stevenson's presidential campaign staff in 1952 and 1956. From 1956 to 1960 he was chairman of the Democratic Advisory Council's economic panel. An early supporter of Sen. John F. Kennedy's (D, Mass.) [q.v.] presidential nomination, Galbraith served President Kennedy as an unofficial economic adviser and as ambassador to India from 1961 to 1963. Returning to Harvard in 1963, he spent four years producing *The New Industrial State* (1967), his most thorough analysis of the U.S. political economy. During the Johnson and Nixon years, Galbraith continued to reach a broad readership via his important monographs as well as by his polemical essays and popular works like *Money* and *The Age of Uncertainty*. He was a sharp critic of the Vietnam war and a prominent figure in the left wing of the Democratic Party. Galbraith retired from the Harvard faculty in 1975. [See KENNEDY, JOHNSON, NIXON/FORD Volumes]

[TO]

For further information:
John Kenneth Galbraith, *American Capitalism: The Concept of Countervailing Power* (Boston, 1951).
—————, *The Great Crash* (Boston, 1955).
—————, *The Affluent Society* (Boston, 1958).
—————, *The Liberal Hour* (Boston, 1960).
Charles H. Hession, *John Kenneth Galbraith and his Critics* (New York, 1972).

GARDNER, TREVOR
b. Aug. 24, 1915; Cardiff, Wales.
d. Sept. 28, 1963; Washington, D.C.
Assistant Secretary of the Air Force for Research and Development, February 1955-February 1956.

Gardner became an American citizen in 1937 and received a B.S. degree in engineering from the University of Southern

California during the same year. In 1939 he earned his M.B.A. Gardner became general manager and executive vice president of the General Tire and Rubber Co. of California in 1945. Three years later he was named president of the Hycon Co., a manufacturer of electrical parts.

In the spring of 1953 Air Force Secretary Harold Talbott [q.v.] appointed Gardner special assistant to look into Air Force research and development. He quickly found an area of particular interest in the long-range missile porgram. Through both official and unofficial efforts, Gardner enormously speeded development of the nation's first intercontinental ballistic missiles (ICBMs) over the next few years.

While the budget-minded Republican Administration was interested in reducing defense spending, Gardner questioned whether enough money was being allocated to develop a workable ICBM ahead of the Soviet Union. In June 1953 Secretary of Defense Charles Wilson [q.v.] joined Talbott in asking Gardner to widen his probe of the long-range missile program. But while the Defense Secretary had economy in mind, Gardner was contemplating a crash development program for the Atlas missile estimated at $2.75 billion. By the fall of 1953 Gardner had created the Strategic Missiles Evaluation Committee (SMEC), a missile review committee chaired by Dr. John von Neumann of Princeton University. In February 1954 SMEC reported that insufficient attention was being given missile development at the highest Air Force levels. This coincided with Gardner's conclusions. He urged Secretary Talbott to create a new missile agency headed by a high-level officer within the Air Force. Although certain military elements felt their authority threatened, the Air Force Council decided to promote the establishment of the new agency. As a result the Western Development Division under Gen. Bernard A. Schriever was created in the spring of 1954 and charged with overseeing the ICBM program.

President Eisenhower nominated Trevor Gardner for assistant Air Force Secretary in August 1954. But Sen. Bourke Hickenlooper (R, Iowa) [q.v.] blocked confirma-tion because of allegations that Gardner had supported nuclear scientist Dr. J. Robert Oppenheimer [q.v.] in a dispute with the loyalty review board the same year. Talbott announced he would retain Gardner as his special assistant. In February 1955 President Eisenhower resubmitted the nomination; Hickenlooper withdrew his objection and Gardner was quickly confirmed.

Seven months later President Eisenhower publicly stated that development of an atomic-armed ICBM had the highest national priority. Assistant Secretary Gardner had been hoping for such support. He and Gen. Schriever sought to bypass obstructive Air Force review procedures by asking that a new ballistic missiles committee be created within the office of the Secretary of Defense. This request was approved by Secretary Wilson in November 1955. The same month President Eisenhower assigned development of intermediate-range ballistic missiles (IRBMs) equal status with the ICBM. Gardner opposed this, believing that all effort should be concentrated on building the Atlas ICBM.

Gardner also believed the ICBM program should be more generously funded. In January 1956 he requested an additional $120 million in research funds for fiscal year 1956 and an additional $250 million for 1957. Air Force Secretary Donald A. Quarles [q.v.] rejected Gardner's proposal twice, and in February Trevor Gardner resigned. President Eisenhower accepted his resignation within a few days. Gardner then publicly stated he did not believe the U.S. could maintain military superiority over the Soviet Union at current spending levels. In a post-resignation appearance on television's *Meet the Press*, Gardner asserted that the Soviet Union led the U.S. in ICBM development and warned that the 1957 military budget "guaranteed this nation the second best Air Force in the world." He repeated these charges in June, testifying before the Senate Armed Services Committee's Air Force Subcommittee, chaired by Sen. Stuart Symington (D, Mo.) [q.v.].

Following his resignation Gardner returned to the presidency and chairmanship of the Hycon Co. From 1960 to 1961 he was chairman of the Air Force Space Task Force. Gardner died in Washington, D.C., on Sept. 28, 1963.

[MJS]

GATES, THOMAS S(OVEREIGN) JR.

Secretary of the Navy, March 1957-February 1959; Deputy Secretary of Defense. June 1959-December 1959; Secretary of Defense, December 1959-January 1961.

Thomas S. Gates, Jr. received his B.A. from the University of Pennsylvania in 1928. He joined his father's investment banking firm of Drexel and Co. the same year. He became a partner in 1940. During World War II Gates graduated from the Quonset Point Air Intelligence School in Rhode Island and helped organize naval air intelligence in Europe. After the War he returned to Drexel.

Nominated by President Dwight Eisenhower to be undersecretary of the Navy Nominated by President Dwight Eisenhower for undersecretary of the Navy in October 1953, Gates removed himself from an active role in banking and was confirmed without difficulty. Naval division heads reported directly to the Undersecretary, and in 1955 Gates settled a dispute over the exact relationship between the Navy and Marine Corps commands. Gates actively promoted a naval nuclear strike force as part of Eisenhower's "New Look" defense policy. In November 1956 he defended aircraft carriers under construction as more mobile and thus safer for launching aircraft than land-based runways.

Gates's basic agreement with Administration policies led Eisenhower to propose him for Secretary of the Navy in March 1957. Days after his confirmation he stated that aircraft carriers would be the Navy's principal strike force. He accurately forecast the future importance of missile armed atomic submarines. To begin building the nation's first atomic carrier in July 1957, he sacrificed funds for conventional vessels.

After the Soviet Union launched the first earth satellite on Oct. 4, 1957, the missile programs of the U.S. Armed Services faced mounting criticism. In response Gates revealed plans for the submarine-based Polaris missile system. Following his own previous example, the Secretary sacrificed projects on which the Navy had spent over $680 million for the success of Polaris over the next two years.

Unhappy with the 1958 reorganization of the Defense Department that increased the power of the Secretary of Defense at the expense of the service secretaries, Gates resigned from the Navy in February 1959. In a resignation-eve speech he pointed to the increased Communist capacity to wage limited war and called for building the Navy and Marine Corps capacity to counter limited aggression.

Gates was confirmed deputy defense secretary the following June. The next month he testified before the House Armed Services Committee investigating charges that a "munitions lobby" heavily staffed by retired Pentagon officials sought to influence the awarding of defense contracts. Gates upheld the right of former officers to work in defense industries, denied feeling lobbying pressure and said he closely watched for conflict of interest among ex-officers.

When Neil McElroy [q.v.] resigned as Defense Secretary in December, President Eisenhower appointed Gates to his post. Although expected to exercise a caretaker's role during the final year of the Eisenhower Administration, Gates plunged into promoting greater cooperation between the Joint Chiefs of Staff and their civilian superiors. Much of Gates's year as Defense Secretary was devoted to defending the Administration's $41 billion defense budget against Democratic charges of inadequacy and a "missile gap." In January 1960 Sen. Stuart Symington (D, Mo.) [q.v.] led the attack, claiming the Soviets would soon boast a three-to-one missile lead over the U.S. He called for a step-up in all missile programs and for an around-the-clock airborne bomber alert. Symington was supported by Strategic Air Command commander-in-chief Gen. Thomas Power. In hearings before the

House Defense Appropriations Subcommittee and the Senate Armed Services Committee, the Defense Secretary countered by revealing new intelligence estimates of a much smaller gap and asserting that an adequate defense did not hinge on a missile-to-missile ratio. Although the Democratic Congress approved a $39 billion defense budget roughly in line with Administration requests in April, missile gap charges continued throughout the election year.

The Department of Defense was embarrassed in May when a U-2 spy plane was shot down over Soviet airspace. The incident came on the eve of summit talks between the U.S. and the USSR and led Soviet Premier Nikita S. Khrushchev to break off the meeting. Called before the Senate Foreign Relations Committee the following month, Gates defended the flights as producing a wide range of vital information. He termed a military alert he had ordered during the summit as "absolutely essential" and non-provocative.

After the November 1960 elections President-elect John F. Kennedy [q.v.] seriously contemplated retaining Gates as Defense Secretary but eventually nominated Ford Motor Co. president Robert S. McNamara. Not wishing to commit McNamara to a last-minute Eisenhower decision, the outgoing Secretary suspended Navy and Air Force projects for new supersonic aircraft and eliminated the proposed Skybolt missile system from the January 1961 defense budget.

Upon retiring Gates became president of New York's Morgan Guaranty Trust Co. President Gerald R. Ford [q.v.] chose the former Secretary to lead the United States liaison mission to China in March 1976.

[MJS]

GAVIN, JAMES M(AURICE)
b. March 22, 1907; New York, N.Y.
Chief of Research and Development, Army General Staff, October 1955-March 1958.

Orphaned at the age of two, Gavin was raised by Irish-Catholic foster parents in a Pennsylvania coal-mining town. After serving briefly in the Army as a private in 1924, he entered the U.S. Military Academy at West Point and graduated in 1929. Gavin began his military career in the infantry but became an expert in air operations while teaching tactics at West Point in 1940. In April 1942 he was appointed chief of military operations of the Airborne Command at Fort Bragg, N.C. The following year Gavin led the 505th Parachute Infantry Regiment in the invasion of Sicily. Promoted to brigadier general at age 36, he led the 82nd Airborne in the Normandy landing and the Battle of the Bulge. Gavin briefly served in Berlin, administering the American occupation zone, and returned to Fort Bragg in December 1945. In 1949 he was assigned to the Defense Department's Weapons System Evaluation Group; he returned to Germany in 1952 to command the Seventh Corps. In 1954 Gavin was appointed assistant chief of staff for plans and operations and was given the temporary rank of lieutenant general. He became chief of Research and Development for the Army general staff, with the rank of deputy chief of staff, in 1955.

Gavin soon emerged as a prominent advocate of increased missile development and an opponent of the Eisenhower Administration's "New Look" policies. These downgraded the use of conventional military weaponry, tactical nuclear weapons, and missile and satellite development in favor of a primary reliance on the use of Strategic Air Command (SAC) bombers to deliver high-megaton nuclear bombs. Testifying before the House Appropriations Committee in April 1956, Gavin asked additional funds for the development of an anti-missile missile (AMM) to counter increased Soviet development of intercontinental ballistic missiles (ICBM). The following year he joined Army Chief of Staff Maxwell Taylor [q.v.] in urging the Army's Nike-Zeus missile be armed with nuclear warheads and developed to track down and destroy attacking ICBMs. He defended the plan against Air Force opposition, cautioning that the SAC was losing its effectiveness. He asserted that missiles rather than strategic air power would be the greatest deterrent in the future because "the man who controls the land will control the space above it.

Gavin stirred a political controversy in January 1958 by announcing that he would retire on the grounds that he "could do more on the outside for national defense than on the inside." The move came after Taylor told him he would no longer be considered for promotion. Gavin denied that his quitting was a result of difficulties over promotion and said that his real reason was his inability "to get something done about the deteriorating position of the Army." In final testimony before the Senate Preparedness Subcommittee, chaired by Majority Leader Lyndon B. Johnson (D, Tex.) [q.v.], Gavin denounced Administration policy, maintaining that Army leaders "were asked to lead men into battle but denied necessary weapons." He also said that Eisenhower's $1.26 billion supplemental defense appropriation request contained "not one red penny" for the Army. Gavin again warned that U.S. retaliatory power was declining in the face of Soviet missile production. Despite requests from Johnson and other powerful members of Congress that he remain, Gavin resigned effective March 1958.

Following his resignation Gavin joined the industrial research and management consulting firm of Arthur Little, Inc., but continued as a prominent critic of Eisenhower's defense policy. In 1958 he published *War and Peace in the Space Age*, which warned that the U.S. would need to develop more flexible military policies to fight future wars. Gavin cautioned that America's reliance on strategic nuclear weapons had left it incapable of fighting limited wars. This, in turn, would lead to a series of political and military defeats and "invite general war." He predicted "such a war is one that no one will win."

Sen. John F. Kennedy (D, Mass.) [q.v.], reviewing the book, praised it as "sensitive to the imperatives of a space and missile age." In 1958 Gavin joined a group of academic leaders advising the presidential aspirant. The following year he supported the contention that a "missile gap" existed between the U.S. and the USSR. Kennedy later used the allegation in his presidential campaign.

In 1961 Kennedy appointed Gavin ambassador to France. He resigned the post in 1962 because of the high personal expenses of running the embassy. During the mid-1960s Gavin gained prominence as an exponent of the "enclave theory" in Vietnam. This plan would have limited American ground forces to defensive operations and brought a halt to the bombing of North Vietnam. [See KENNEDY, JOHNSON Volumes]

[AES]

For further information:
James M. Gavin, *War and Peace in the Space Age* (New York, 1958).

GENOVESE, VITO
b. Nov. 27, 1897; Rosiglino, Italy
d. Feb. 14, 1969; Springfield, Mo.
Organized crime figure.

Vito Genovese immigrated to New York in 1919. He was arrested for the first time when he was 19, and he served a short prison term for carrying a pistol. The ambitious gangster preferred to maintain a low profile, hiding his illicit income behind a legitimate front. In 1925 he set up the Genovese Trading Co. Throughout his life he portrayed himself as an honest junk dealer.

During the 1930s Genovese rose in the hierarchy of the underworld and became involved in narcotics trafficking. In 1936 he fled to Italy after being named "king of the rackets" by New York Special Prosecutor Thomas E. Dewey. He donated $250,000 to the fascist government and received Italy's highest civilian award from Benito Mussolini. After the dictator's fall Genovese became a black marketeer, dealing in gasoline and drugs until he was recognized by a member of the Army's Criminal Investigation Division (CID). He was jailed in 1944 and returned to Brooklyn for trial. However, the state's chief witness was found poisoned in jail, and Genovese went free.

During the 1950s Genovese tried to consolidate his power in the underworld, allegedly through the attempted assassination of Frank Costello [q.v.] and the murder of Albert Anastasia [q.v.]. In November 1957 he convened an underworld conference in

Apalachin, N.Y., to declare himself head of New York's organized crime. On the agenda was a directive from the Mafia's 12-man national commission, of which Genovese was a member, ordering the mob out of narcotics because of the high arrest risk. Police broke up the Apalachin meeting, focusing attention on Genovese that he wished to avoid.

Genovese was summoned before the Senate Committee on Improper Activities in the Labor or Management Field to answer questions on his narcotics activities in July 1958. He invoked the Fifth Amendment 150 times. Genovese was arrested five days later for conspiracy to transport and deal in narcotics. In 1959 he received a 15-year sentence. Genovese continued directing his criminal operations from Atlanta's federal prison and so was transferred to Leavenworth.

During the 1960s Joseph Valachi, convicted mobster and member of Genovese's gang, went to the authorities claiming Genovese was trying to have him killed. In retaliation Valachi testified before the Senate Permanent Investigations Subcommittee for 10 weeks starting in September 1963. He sketched a nation-wide crime syndicate in what Attorney General Robert F. Kennedy [q.v.] called the biggest intelligence breakthrough of the century. Held responsible for Valachi's testimony, Genovese fell in mob esteen. Increasingly ill, he was transferred to the medical facility at Springfield, where he died in 1969.

[MJS]

GEORGE, WALTER F(RANKLIN)
b. Jan. 29, 1878; Preston, Ga.
d. Aug. 4, 1957; Vienna, Ga.
Democratic Senator, Ga., 1922-57;
Chairman, Foreign Relations Committee, 1955-57; Ambassador to the North Atlantic Treaty Organization, January 1957-August 1957.

The son of a tenant farmer, Walter George distinguished himself in intercollegiate oratorical contests while attending Mercer University, a Baptist institution from which he graduated in 1900. He received his law degree a year later and for the next two decades pursued successive careers as a lawyer, solicitor general for the Cordele judiciary circuit and state judge. He retired as a judge of the Georgia Supreme Court in 1922 and ran for the Senate seat left vacant by the death of the fiery populist Tom Watson. Supported by Atlanta business interests as well as South Georgia Watsonites, George was elected by a landslide vote and reelected in each of five subsequent contests.

In the Senate George gradually rose to power through diligence, seniority and quiet promotion of conservative policies. Although a supporter of some early New Deal measures, including the Tennessee Valley Authority, the Social Security Act and the Wagner Labor Relations Act, by Roosevelt's second term he had emerged as a leading foe of reform legislation, mobilizing opposition to housing and wage-hour bills and managing the defeat of Roosevelt's "court-packing" plan. In the election of 1938 Roosevelt campaigned against George as part of the so-called purge of key congressional conservatives obstructing his program, but the strategy backfired. George won reelection over New Deal supporter Lawrence Camp and rural demagogue Eugene Talmadge.

Assuming the chairmanship of the Foreign Relations Committee in November 1940, George helped win passage of the President's Lend-Lease program. In August 1941 he resigned the Foreign Relations chairmanship to take over that of the Finance Committee. Except for the 1947-48 session, he held that position until 1953. As head of the tax panel, George generally opposed progressive tax reforms and favored lower tax rates and preferences for corporate income. During the Truman years he was a powerful foe of the Fair Deal. George provided crucial support for Truman's foreign policy initiatives, however, backing Greek-Turkish aid, the Marshall Plan and the North Atlantic Treaty. [See TRUMAN Volume]

When the 83rd Congress convened in January 1953 with Republican majorities, George had to give up his chairmanship of the Finance Committee to Sen. Eugene Millikin (R, Colo.) [q.v.]. He remained the ranking Democrat on the Finance and Foreign Relations Committees, and his 30 years of service made him the Senate's most senior member. During the first term of the Eisenhower Administration, George was a pillar of the Senate "establishment" whose pronouncements on public policy always won respectful attention from his colleagues and the Administration.

George played an important role in the Senate controversy over the Bricker amendment, designed to limit the power of the President in making foreign policy. In response to criticism that a clause in the amendment would necessitate approval by every state for all foreign agreements, George proposed a substitute removing that requirement while mandating that all executive agreements win Senate ratification. In February 1954 George's bill achieved a 60-31 majority in the Senate, a margin one vote short of the required two-thirds.

For the most part George served as an influential ally of the Eisenhower Administration on foreign policy questions. When Sen. William Knowland (R, Calif.) [q.v.] called for a blockade of mainland China in November 1954 in order to secure the release of 13 captured Americans, George endorsed the Administration's refusal to take such action. George assumed the chairmanship of the Foreign Relations Committee in January 1955 and later that month sponsored a resolution giving the President unlimited authority to use U.S. Armed Forces to protect Formosa and the Pescadores Islands off China. The Senate passed the measure overwhelmingly.

Increasingly concerned about the peaceful settlement of international disputes, George spurred preparations for a four-power summit conference with his call for such a conclave on "Meet the Press" on March 20, 1955. The White House and the State Department responded favorably to his suggestion that the summit meeting need not be put off until the Soviets made peaceful gestures in "deeds, not words," as the Administration had previously demanded. The conference took place in July

1955 with the United States, the Soviet Union, Great Britain and France participating.

In April 1955 George declared that "we ought to be willing to talk" with the Communist Chinese "because we certainly owe a high obligation to all mankind everywhere." Two months later he proposed resumption of trade between Japan and China. Referring to complaints he had received from Southern textile manufacturers about trading concessions made by the U.S. to Japan, he maintained that resumption of Japan-China trade would relax "cut-throat competition" against American companies.

George provided valuable service to the Eisenhower Administration in the 1956 congressional battle over foreign aid. In June he led the effort in the Foreign Relations Committee to restore a $1 billion cut by the House from the Administration's $4.8 billion foreign aid request. The Committee refused to restore the total sum but did agree to put back $600 million. George then successfully steered the measure past efforts to reduce it on the Senate floor. The absence of any U.S. financial support for Egypt's Aswan Dam project was due partly to George's opposition. He based his stand on his objection to long-term aid commitments and to the possibility that the Aswan Dam would make two million acres available for cotton-growing, thereby cutting into U.S. cotton exports.

Owing to Republican control of the Senate in 1953-54 and his growing preoccupation with foreign affairs, George had less influence on economic policy than he had enjoyed as Finance Committee chairman. However, he continued to exert considerable sway on behalf of fiscal conservatism. In January 1953 he responded to the $78.5 billion budget submitted by the outgoing Truman Administration with the statement, "The principal duty of this Congress and the new Administration is to see to it that the budget is cut." Throughout Eisenhower's first term he unsuccessfully pushed a bill to cut taxes by increasing the personal exemption from $600 to $1,000. In March 1955, however, he voted against a temporary tax cut of $20 offered by his fellow Democrats. He was among the half-dozen

Southern Democrats providing the Republicans with the 50-44 margin by which the cut was rejected.

A lifelong segregationist, George was one of the leaders of the movement behind the 1956 "Southern Manifesto." The strategists met in George's office to draft the statement, and George acted as the group's spokesman in reading the declaration in the Senate on March 12. The Manifesto, signed by 19 senators and 77 representatives, denounced the Supreme Court's decision on public school desegregation and "the explosive and dangerous condition created by outside meddlers" and pledged resistance by "all lawful means."

Faced with a stiff primary challenge by white-supremacist Herman Talmadge, George announced in May 1956 that he would not seek reelection. In July, in an unexpected move, he sponsored an amendment to a Social Security bill to qualify totally disabled workers for full Social Security benefits at age 50. The measure, which never would have passed without the Southern conservative's surprise blessing, carried by a 47-45 vote.

In January 1957 President Eisenhower appointed the Georgian ambassador to the North Atlantic Treaty Organization. Seven months later George died of heart disease on Aug. 4, 1957.

[TO]

GINSBERG, ALLEN
b. June 3, 1926; Newark, N.J.
Poet.

Ginsberg's childhood was scarred by the harrowing experience of watching his mother's psychological deterioration, first at home, then in a mental hospital. His anguish and love for her were articulatly expressed in the elegy, "Kaddish for Naomi Ginsberg" (1961). His father, Louis, was a teacher and poet of a more traditional style who was critical of Ginsberg's first attempts at poetry. He entered Columbia College in 1943. While there Ginsberg became good friends with writers William S. Burroughs and Jack Kerouac [q.v.]. He graduated in 1948, dropping his plan to study law be-

cause of a temporary school suspension. Ginsberg worked as a market research consultant between 1951 and 1953 while writing in his spare time.

In 1953 Ginsberg decided to devote himself completely to his poetry. While doing graduate work at the University of California at Berkeley, Ginsberg acquainted himself with such writers as Kenneth Rexroth, Michael McClure and Gary Snyder, who shared his need to divorce himself from traditional styles and develop a new type of poetry.

The result of Ginsberg's search for a poetic voice was the long epic poem Howl, one of the major literary and social documents of the 1950s. With the opening lines, "I saw the best minds of my generation destroyed by madness,/starving histerically naked. . . ." Howl both attacked American spiritual stagnation and affirmed personal joy in all things holy—"Everything is holy!"

The poem, with Kerouac's On the Road, signified the beginning of the San Francisco Renaissance and the Beat Generation, cultural and literary movements which powerfully influenced the "counter-culture" of the 1960s. They seemed to galvanize the feelings of those who deplored American materialism and sought to restore a deep sense of community to their lives. Most literary reviewers scorned Howl, rejecting its exhuberant use of sexual and scatological language, while a few applauded what they termed the important, "messianic" voice of the poem. Meanwhile, Ginsberg won a wide American audience. As the author of Howl he was charged with obscenity and brought before a San Francisco court in 1957; but witnesses testified to its unquestionable literary merit, and the book continued to be printed.

Ginsberg wrote prolifically, and his poems appeared in both smaller and established publications during the late-1950s. He fully emerged as a cultural spokesman for a segment of American youth and left-oriented individuals in the 1960s. During those years he advocated the liberalization of laws against non-addictive drugs and proselytized for unrestricted sexual freedom. He also organized anti-war demonstrations and initiated efforts to halt ecological destruction and the spread of nuclear weapons. In 1974 Ginsberg's achievements as a poet were recognized with a National Book Award for his collection of poetry, *The Fall of America*. [See JOHNSON Volume]

[TGD]

For further information:
John Tytell, *Naked Angels: the Lives and Literature of the Beat Generation* (New York, 1976).

GOLD, BEN
b. Sept. 8, 1898; Bessarabia, Russia.
President, International Fur and Leather Workers Union of the United States and Canada, 1939-54.

Gold immigrated to the U.S. in 1910, at the age of 12, and joined the International Fur Workers Union of the U.S. and Canada (IFWU) two years later. He became a member of the Socialist Party in 1916. In 1919 Gold joined the Communist faction of the New York Furriers' Joint Board and became its manager in 1925. He served at the post until 1929, although he was expelled from the IFWU as a Communist after an unsuccessful general strike in 1926. Gold also served as secretary of the Communist-dominated Needle Trades Workers Industrial Union in 1928. He was reinstated in the IFWU in 1935 and elected president of the group two years later. When the IFWU merged with the National Leather Workers Association in 1939, he became president of International Fur and Leather Workers Union of the U.S. and Canada (IFLWU). Gold was elected president of the American Jewish Labor Council in 1946.

In 1948 Gold testified before a House Labor subcommittee investigating Communist leadership of labor unions that he was a long-time Communist Party member, but he denied that the Party dominated his union or that he advocated the violent overthrow of the U.S. government. He was removed from the Congress of Industrial Organizations' executive board for his Communist sympathies the following year.

In 1950, when the IFLWU convention

instructed its officers to sign non-Communist affidavits in accordance with the provisions of the Taft-Hartley Act, Gold publicly quit the Communist Party and signed the statement. However, two years later Gold refused to tell the National Labor Relations Board (NLRB) or a federal grand jury whether his affidavit was truthful or deny he had supported the Communist Party since he signed it. He was indicted by a federal grand jury for perjury in August 1953 on the grounds that he had lied when he signed the affidavit.

Following a six-week trial Gold was convicted of perjury in April 1954 and received a one-to-three-year jail sentence. He was reelected IFLWU president in May. As a result of the election, the NLRB prohibited the union from making use of its services in collective bargaining. Concerned with the effect this ruling would have on the union, Gold resigned the presidency in October.

In 1956 the U.S. Court of Appeals unanimously upheld Gold's conviction, but the Supreme Court ruled that the union could not be deprived of NLRB services because of it. The following year the Supreme Court ordered that Gold be given a new trial because the FBI had interrogated members of the jury before the trial in what the Court regarded as a violation of their privacy. Gold was freed in May 1957, when the Justice Department moved that his indictment be dismissed because "certain material evidence . . . [was] not available."

[AES]

GOLDBERG, ARTHUR J(OSEPH)
b. Aug. 8, 1908: Chicago, Ill.
General Counsel, Congress of Industrial Organizations, 1948-55: General Counsel, United Steelworkers of America, 1948-61.

Goldberg was born the youngest of 11 children of Russian-Jewish parents on Chicago's West Side. After working his way through Northwestern University, he took a law degree in 1930 and set up his own practice shortly afterwards. Through his activity on behalf of Franklin D. Roosevelt's 1936 presidential campaign, Goldberg came into contact with labor leaders, and he soon represented several important Chicago-based unions. Following service with the Office of Strategic Services during World War II, he was appointed general counsel in 1948 for both the Congress of Industrial Organizations (CIO) and the United Steelworkers of America (USW). Goldberg replaced Lee Pressman, an alleged pro-Communist, in these positions, and in 1949 and 1950 he devised the legal procedures under which such Communist-dominated unions as the United Electrical Workers were expelled from the CIO.

In February 1955 Goldberg sat down with J. Albert Woll, counsel for the American Federation of Labor (AFL), to draft a merger agreement between the ALF and CIO. Both organizations agreed to retain previous organizing jurisdictions for each member union and to recognize the equal legitimacy of both craft and industrial unions. Unity was formally proclaimed at a joint convention in December.

Although he asked for the job of AFL-CIO general counsel, Goldberg did not enjoy the full confidence of the dominant federation leadership and was made special counsel instead. He also served as general counsel for the organization's Industrial Union Department. During the McClellan Committee investigations of 1957 and 1958, spotlighting corruption in the labor movement, Goldberg helped formulate the AFL-CIO's ethical practices code, which led to the expulsion of the Teamsters and several other scandal-ridden member unions. At the same time he worked closely with Sen. John F. Kennedy (D, Mass.) [q.v.] in drawing up moderate labor reform legislation providing for full public disclosure of union finances. He also attempted to forestall the more punitive measures that were ultimately embodied in the Landrum-Griffin Act—measures such as bans on "hot cargo" contracts, under which union members were allowed to refuse to work with non-union materials.

During the Eisenhower Administration Goldberg continued to represent the USW and acted as ex officio adviser to several other industrial unions as well. Within the USW President David McDonald's [q.v.] interest in extra-union activities increasingly left important decisions in Goldberg's hands. In 1959 and 1960 he conducted USW negotiations during the 116-day steel strike, winning important concessions from the industry on matters of wages and working conditions. Included in the new contract, signed in January 1960, was Goldberg's proposal for a "Human Relations Committee," composed of representatives of the union, the industry and the public, which was aimed at preventing future strikes.

Goldberg played a leading role in mobilizing labor behind Kennedy's presidential primary campaign, and in December 1960 the new President chose Goldberg as his Secretary of Labor over five elected union officials nominated by AFL-CIO President George Meany [q.v.]. According to labor historian Thomas R. Brooks, Kennedy picked Goldberg because he was "from the unions but not of them" and thus could be relied upon to enforce the reform provisions of the Landrum-Griffin Act.

An activist Secretary of Labor, Goldberg intervened frequently in labor-management disputes to secure non-inflationary wage settlements as a means of ending the nation's balance of payments deficit and enabling the Administration to conduct a vigorous foreign policy. By 1962 Goldberg's relations with organized labor had begun to deteriorate as a result of his wage restraint policies. Partly for this reason Kennedy nominated him to a seat on the Supreme Court. Goldberg spent 34 months on the bench, during which time he continued to advise Presidents Kennedy and Johnson on national labor problems. In July 1965 Johnson appointed him ambassador to the United Nations. He resigned in 1968 to aid Hubert Humphrey's [q.v.] campaign for the presidency and later spoke in opposition to American policy in Vietnam. In 1970 Goldberg ran an unsuccessful race for governor of New York. [See KENNEDY, JOHNSON, NIXON/FORD Volumes]

[TLH]

GOLDFINE, BERNARD
b. Kovno, Russia.
d. Sept. 21, 1967; Boston, Mass.
Businessman.

Born in Russia, Goldfine immigrated to the U.S. at the age of eight. He had one year of high school and started his own textile business when he was 19. At first buying and selling woolen remnants, he owned several textile mills and real estate holdings by the Depression. During the 1930s and 1940s he bought businesses and land at bargain prices, increasing his wealth. In June 1958 the House Special Subcommittee on Legislative Oversight opened hearings with documentary evidence that Sherman Adams [q.v.], President Eisenhower's chief aide, had accepted favors from Goldfine between 1953 and 1958. Subcommittee investigators displayed copies of hotel bills, totaling over $3,000, incurred by Adams during Boston visits but paid by Goldfine.

Goldfine, in statements made through his lawyers, admitted paying the bills and added that he had given Adams a vicuna coat and loaned him a $2,400 oriental rug. Adams acknowledged the gifts; but both men described them as personal exchanges between friends and denied that they had influenced Adams in intervening on Goldfine's behalf with the Federal Trade Commission (FTC) and the Securities and Exchange Commission (SEC). In 1954 and 1955 the FTC had charged Goldfine's textile companies with the deliberately inaccurate labeling of products. FTC officials, testifying before the subcommittee, stated that Adams had twice inquired on specific agency charges against Goldfine; Adams then passed on the information to the industrialist, in possible violation of law. In 1955, at Goldfine's request, Adams had arranged a meeting between Commission officials and the businessman. Though some FTC lawyers had recommended a civil suit against Goldfine, a cease-and-desist order in 1957 was the final settlement. Meanwhile, the SEC considered action against Goldfine for his refusal to file required reports on his real estate operations. Adams initiated an

inquiry into the SEC charges in 1956; no further actions against Goldfine were taken.

Later in June 1958 Adams testified before the subcommittee, admitting the accuracy of factual evidence but denying any intentions of impropriety. In early July Goldfine, a gregarious and friendly man, testified before the subcommittee and said that he had declared the hotel bills and gifts to Adams as business expenses on his tax returns, but he maintained that he never expected favors in return for his generosity. The subcommittee revealed that Goldfine had also paid hotel bills for Sens. Norris Cotton (R, N.H.) [q.v.], Styles Bridges (R, N.H.) [q.v.] and Frederick Payne (R, Me.) and had given cash gifts to many lower-echelon government workers. Committee investigators also uncovered $776,879 in uncashed treasurer's checks—lacking the purchaser's name—which Goldfine dispersed in his generous moments. For refusing to answer 22 subcommittee questions about his financial affairs, Goldfine was cited for contempt of Congress. In September 1958 Adams was forced to resign.

In December 1958 Goldfine was cited for contempt of court because of his refusal to submit records for a tax investigation. He was convicted and served his three-month sentence in 1960. For his contempt of Congress Goldfine was fined and given a suspended one-year sentence in 1959. While in prison in 1960 he was charged with evading over $790,000 in federal income taxes between 1953 and 1957. Lawyers questioned his mental competency to stand trial, and he was placed under psychiatric observation until he was determined fit. Goldfine pleaded guilty in 1961 to the tax evasion charges and received a sentence of one-year and-a-day in prison and a $110,000 fine. He suffered a slight stroke in confinement and was released in 1962 after serving seven-and-one half months of his sentence. Subsequently he was judged insolvent, and his assets were sold to settle government tax claims against him. He died in 1967.

[TGD]

For further information:
David Frier, *Conflict of Interest in the Eisenhower Administration* (Ames, Iowa, 1969).

GOLDWATER, BARRY M(ORRIS)
b. Jan. 1, 1909; Phoenix, Ariz.
Republican Senator, Ariz., 1953-65;
1969-

The son of a Jewish businessman, Goldwater was educated at Virginia's Staunton Military Academy, where he graduated in 1928. After a year at the University of Arizona, he returned home in 1929 to take over his father's department store. During World War II Goldwater served as an instructor in the Air Transport Command. A member of the Arizona National Guard since 1930, he was its chief of staff from 1945 to 1952 and eventually rose to major general in the Air Force Reserve in 1962. Goldwater's political career began in 1949, when he was elected to the Phoenix City Council. In 1952 he defeated the incumbent, Ernest W. McFarland (D, Ariz.) for a seat in the U.S. Senate.

In the upper house Goldwater was a vigorous anti-Communist and conservative who supported limiting the federal government and maintaining the unbridled freedom of the individual. During his first term he urged reduction of foreign aid and retaliation against nations trading with Communist China. On the domestic scene he opposed farm price supports, federal aid to education, minimum wage laws and tax reductions for low-income families, while he urged increasing rights for women and giving offshore oil reserves to the states.

Goldwater explained his conservative philosophy in his book *The Conscience of a Conservative* (1960), in which he assailed the growth of government and pointed to its deleterious effects on American society. He criticized the graduated income tax as an effort by radicals to "redistribute the nation's wealth" and achieve "an egalitarian society—an objective that does violence both to the charter of the Republic and the Laws of Nature." He opposed compulsory social security payments because they deprived the worker of the opportunity to dispose of income as he wished. Goldwater also advocated abolishing government responsibility for welfare, reasoning that private charities would take over the burden once taxes were reduced. He opposed federal aid to education and price supports for farmers as dangerous government interference with states rights and individual liberties. Although he believed segregation was morally wrong and favored withholding federal funds from public works projects in states that practiced discrimination, Goldwater opposed civil rights legislation as violations of states rights and the individual's freedom to discriminate.

Goldwater supported Sen. Joseph R. McCarthy's (R, Wisc.) [q.v.] anti-Communist crusade and was one of 22 senators who voted against his condemnation in December 1954. He told a Wisconsin Republican convention that "because Joe McCarthy lived, we are a safer, freer, more vigilant nation today," but he believed McCarthy's accusations that Eisenhower was a Communist appeaser were improper.

During the 1950s a large portion of Goldwater's attention was devoted to work on the Labor and Public Welfare Committee. He was an ardent foe of labor unions and supported tightened federal and state control of their activities. With Vice President Richard Nixon [q.v.] he succeeded in defeating a measure aimed at liberalizing the Taft-Hartley Act in March 1953. That same month he proposed stricter legislation to eliminate Communists from labor unions. The following year Goldwater suggested amending the Taft-Hartley Act to grant states greater authority over labor-management disputes and weaken the power of unions in collective bargaining.

Goldwater was a member of the Select Committee on Improper Activities in the Labor or Management Field created in 1957 to investigate charges of corrupt union leadership. Over the objections of Goldwater and the Republican minority, the probe focused primarily on the Teamsters Union. They condemned committee counsel Robert F. Kennedy's [q.v.] refusal to thoroughly investigate the United Automobile Workers (UAW) and its president, Walter Reuter [q.v.], a staunch Democratic supporter. When the Arizona Senator attacked Reuter in a 1957 Detroit speech as "more dangerous to America than anything Russia might do," Reuter labeled him as "this country's number one political fanatic, its number one anti-labor baiter, its number one peddler of class hatred." Their feud continued through Goldwater's election campaign in 1958. Despite labor's efforts to defeat him, Goldwater won 56.1% of the vote in a campaign that stressed illicit union support of his opponent.

Goldwater's opposition to organized labor continued after his reelection. He opposed the Kennedy-Ervin labor reform bill in April 1959 as being too lenient toward labor unions and was the sole senator to vote against it. Instead, he supported the stricter Landrum-Griffin Act, adopted after Kennedy's bill failed in the House.

At the Republican National Convention in 1960, Goldwater was recognized as the leader of the Party's conservative wing. He led the attack on the preconvention platform compromise reached by Vice President Richard M. Nixon [q.v.] and New York's Gov. Nelson A. Rockefeller [q.v.]. Enraged conservative delegates nominated Goldwater for President as a protest against Nixon's accommodation with Rockefeller. However, Goldwater asked that his name be withdrawn in a speech calling for party unity. He received 10 votes from the Louisiana delegation on the first ballot.

During the 1960s Goldwater dominated the conservative wing of the Republican Party. After a bitter struggle in which the conservatives gained control of the Republican National Convention, Goldwater won the Party's presidential nomination in 1964. However, he lost the election to President Lyndon B. Johnson in an historic landslide. After semi-retirement from politics between Goldwater again won election to the Senate in November 1968. [See KENNEDY, JOHNSON, NIXON/FORD Volumes]

[AES]

GOODPASTER, ANDREW J(ACKSON)
b. Feb. 12, 1915; Granite City, Ill.
White House Staff Secretary, September 1954-January 1961.

After attending McKendree College in Lebanon, Ill., for two years, Goodpaster transferred to the U.S. Military Academy at West Point, from which he graduated second in his class in 1939. He served in various engineering assignments before World War II and then saw combat in North Africa and Italy as commander of the 48th Engineer Batallion.

Goodpaster was attached to the general staff of the War Department from 1944 to 1947 and then went to Princeton Unnversity, where he earned an M.A. in engineering in 1948 and a Ph.D. in international relations in 1950. He was the Army's representative on the Joint Advanced Study Committee of the Joint Chiefs of Staff in 1950. Six months later Goodpaster went to Europe as an aide to Gen. Dwight D. Eisenhower in organizing the military forces of the North Atlantic Treaty Organization (NATO). He also worked with W. Averell Harriman [q.v.] in developing a statement of political aims for NATO. In 1954 he took over the post of U.S. district engineer in San Francisco.

In September 1954 President Eisenhower appointed Col. Goodpaster White House staff secretary. His duties consisted of clearing all communications to the President and coordinating cabinet operations. He also served as liaison between the White House and the various departments and agencies concerned with defense and national security matters. Goodpaster's most important duty was handling all correspondence dealing with national security and supervising day-to-day operations of the National Security Council. Characterized as a man of "calmness and efficiency," he enjoyed Eisenhower's strong faith in his "exceptional ability."

As staff secretary, Goodpaster had little influence on policymaking and served primarily as an aide and factfinder for the President. During the Quemoy and Matsu crisis of 1954-55, he participated in meetings to evaluate the Nationalist Chinese ability to defend Formosa and, at the President's request, he also conferred with military leaders on the subject. In July 1955 he attended the East-West summit at Geneva as President Eisenhower's personal assistant. The following year Goodpaster was liaison between the Pentagon, the Central Intelligence Agency and the White House during the Suez Crisis. He also kept a close record of intelligence reports during the U.S. military action in Lebanon in 1958.

Because of his military background, Goodpaster fit easily into the White House staff, which was organized on the model of a military chain of command. In addition, his empathy enabled him to anticipate Eisenhower's needs. After the President was stricken with a heart attack in September 1955, his secretary reduced the amount of Eisenhower's work by delaying action on some measures and proceeding with others "by direction of the President." When the President suffered a mild stroke in 1957, Goodpaster kept the White House running smoothly while the chief executive recovered.

Following the resignation of Sherman Adams [q.v.] in September 1958, Goodpaster's authority increased as the President instructed him to bring all Defense and State Department problems directly to him without first going through formal channels. Thus, in May 1960, it was Goodpaster who first brought Eisenhower the news of the downing of the U-2 spy plane over the Soviet Union.

Goodpaster remained in the White House during the early part of 1961 to aid John F. Kennedy in his transition to office. He then served with the Army in Europe and in 1962 returned to Washington as special assistant to Gen. Maxwell Taylor [q.v.]. In 1967 he became senior U.S. Army member of the U.N. Military Staff Committee and directed special studies in the office of the Army Chief of Staff. From July 1967 to June 1968 he served as commandant of the National War College. Goodpaster was promoted to general in 1968. He served as deputy commander of U.S. forces in Vietnam from 1968 to 1969 and then became Supreme Allied Commander in Europe and Commander-in-chief of U.S. military forces in Europe. Goodpaster retired in 1974 and became a senior fellow in security and strategic studies at the Woodrow Wilson International Center for Scholars. In 1977 President Carter appointed him commandant of the U.S. Military Academy at West Point.

[RJB]

GORDON, THOMAS S(YLVY)
b. Dec. 17, 1893: Chicago, Ill.
d. Jan. 22, 1959: Chicago, Ill.
Democratic Representative, Ill., 1943-59: Chairman, Foreign Affairs Committee, 1957-58.

The son of Polish immigrants, Gordon succeeded to his father's position as office manager of *Dziennik Chicagoski*, a Polish language newspaper, in 1922. His post on the newspaper helped him enter Democratic politics, and in 1939 he became Chicago city controller. Gordon was elected to Congress in 1942 from Chicago's predominately Polish eighth district and was immediately assigned to the Foreign Affairs Committee. He supported President Harry S. Truman's foreign policies and domestic welfare programs.

Gordon generally voted with the liberal Democrats in the House during the Eisenhower Administration. In 1955 he supported a bill to restore rigid farm price supports and opposed a measure exempting producers of natural gas from federal public utility regulation under the Natural Gas Act. Two years later Gordon was among 80 Democratic liberals backing a comprehensive legislative program that called, among other things, for civil rights measures, repeal of the Taft-Hartley Act, aid to depressed areas and revision of immigration and naturalization standards to eliminate the national origins system.

In 1957 Gordon became chairman of the Foreign Affairs Committee. During his first month in that post, he backed the Administration's draft of the Eisenhower Doctrine for the Middle East. On Jan. 5, 1957 President Eisenhower addressed a joint session of Congress to ask for authority to use U.S. Armed Forces to protect the Middle East from Communist aggression. Minutes after the address Gordon introduced a joint resolution authorizing the President to use U.S. forces "as he deems necessary to secure and protect the territorial integrity and political independence" of Middle East nations against countries "controlled by international Communism." The House passed this Administration-initiated version of the Doctrine, but the Senate eliminated the clause permitting the President to use troops "as he deems necessary" and stated only that the U.S. was "prepared to use Armed Forces" if the President "determines the necessity." Gordon opposed the Senate alteration but preferred accepting its version to further debate. The upper chamber's resolution was adopted by the House.

Gordon backed the Mutual Security Act of 1957, which authorized over $3.3 billion in military and economic foreign aid for fiscal 1958. It introduced a new approach to foreign economic assistance, eliminating the grants-in-aid program and authorizing a new $500 million Development Loan Fund. Gordon defended the change against charges that the loans would really be grants because they could be repaid in foreign currencies. He criticized those who opposed foreign aid in all forms, stating that a fortress America could not survive economically.

Gordon stepped down as chairman of the Foreign Affairs Committee in February 1958 because of ill health. He died in Chicago of heart disease on Jan. 22, 1959.

[MLL]

GORE, ALBERT A(RNOLD)
b. Dec. 27, 1907; Granville, Tenn.
Democratic Senator, Tenn., 1953-71.

A country school teacher who received a law degree from the Nashville YMCA night law school, Albert Gore was elected to Congress in 1938 as a New Deal supporter. The liberal Gore combined populist oratory with diligent study of economic issues in his 14-year House career. In 1952 Gore ran for the Senate against the aged Sen. Kenneth McKellar (D, Tenn.), representative of the state's once-powerful Crump machine and chairman of the Senate Appropriations Committee. Vigorously affirming his support for liberal economic policies and the Tennessee Valley Authority (TVA), Gore defeated McKellar in the primary and won election over his Republican challenger in November. [See TRUMAN Volume]

In the Senate Gore matched the outspoken liberalism of his fellow Tennessean, Sen. Estes Kefauver (D, Tenn.) [q.v.],

although each concentrated on different issues. Where Kefauver won national attention with his investigations of crime, price-fixing and the drug industry, Gore worked energetically on behalf of public power, highway construction and tax reform. During the Eisenhower Administration his Senate votes paralleled the position of the liberal Americans for Democratic Action 70% of the time.

Gore played an important role in the controversial Dixon-Yates affair of 1954-55. Edgar Dixon [q.v.] and Eugene Yates were presidents of Southern utilities seeking a government contract to build a steam plant near West Memphis, Ark. to supply power to the Tennessee Valley Authority which, in turn, would sell it in the Memphis area. The Eisenhower Administration, guided by a philosophy favoring private development of power sources, instructed the Atomic Energy Commission (AEC) to negotiate a contract with the Dixon-Yates combine.

Gore spearheaded the vocal Democratic efforts to cancel the contract. In November 1954 he charged that it "reeks of government subsidy," that there "is no private enterprise in it" and that Dixon-Yates's profits were "practically guaranteed" at an unreasonably high level. He also highlighted a conflict of interest on the part of a Budget Bureau consultant who recommended the contract. In January 1955 Gore and the other nine Democrats on the Joint Atomic Energy Committee urged that the contract be rejected as "not in the public interest." The AEC went ahead with Dixon-Yates, but as a result of adverse publicity, President Eisenhower ordered the agency to cancel the contract in July 1955.

Gore was the chief Senate architect of the Federal Highway Aid Act of 1956 and the Highway Revenue Act of 1956. The measures authorized the biggest road-building program in American history, the expenditure of $31.5 billion in federal-state funds over a 13-year period to construct 42,500 miles of interstate highways. Gore managed the defeat of the Eisenhower Administration's plan to finance the program by bond sales and then won passage of his substitute "pay-as-you-go" arrangement by which the highways were to be paid for by increased taxes on gasoline, fuel, tires, trucks and buses.

Gore's record on civil rights issues was moderate compared to those of most of his Southern colleagues. Lyndon Johnson (D, Tex.) [q.v.], Kefauver and he were the only senators from the states of the Old Confederacy who refused to sign the 1956 "Southern Manifesto" advocating resistance to desegregation. Gore voted in favor of the Civil Rights Act of 1957, although he supported amendments diluting its enforcement powers and ensuring jury trials for accused violators. He also voted against attempts to amend the Senate's Rule 22 by which Southerners and conservatives blocked civil rights initiatives with filibusters.

Along with Sen. Paul Douglas (D, Ill.) [q.v.], Gore was the most persistent Senate advocate of tax reform. In 1957 he moved from the Public Works Committee to the tax-writing Finance Committee, where he and Douglas waged a usually futile struggle to close loopholes favoring the rich and corporations. Among the tax preferences they fought unsuccessfully to reduce or eliminate were the 27½% oil depletion allowance, the dividend credit, the foreign tax credit and stock option abuses. In addition, they sought to institute withholding taxes at the source of interest and dividend income. Gore also frequently denounced the "tight money" policies of the Federal Reserve Board and strenuously opposed the Eisenhower Administration's effort in 1959-60 to remove the 4½% interest rate ceiling on government bonds. He contended that higher interest rates only hurt consumers and enriched bankers.

A member of the Foreign Relations Committee, Gore expounded the liberal internationalism of his hero, Cordell Hull. Like Hull, he was a strong advocate of reciprocal trade agreements. He supported foreign aid and generally backed the foreign policy of the Eisenhower Administration. Gore's November 1958 proposal that the U.S. suspend all nuclear tests for three years won widespread attention. As a delegate to the disarmament conferences of the late Eisenhower and early Kennedy years, he helped negotiate the limited nuclear test ban treaty, finally signed and ratified in 1963.

Gore's maverick bent and crusading fervor, particularly his attacks on the tax system, often brought him into conflict with Majority Leader Lyndon Johnson. At the January 1960 Democratic caucus, he led an abortive revolt against Johnson's autocratic powers. Charging that party identity had been blurred by the leadership's willingness to compromise with the Eisenhower Administration, he proposed that the Democratic caucus instead of the majority leader choose Democratic Policy Committee members and that the Committee actually make policy instead of merely scheduling legislation. The caucus rejected Gore's motion by a 51-12 vote. Johnson did agree, however, to Sen. William Proxmire's (D, Wisc.) [q.v.] demand to hold periodic caucuses to discuss policy positions before bills came up on the floor.

Gore was a candidate for the vice presidential nomination in 1956 and 1960. In 1956 he finished third in convention balloting behind Kefauver and Sen. John F. Kennedy (D, Mass.) [q.v.] before throwing his support to Kefauver. He was again hopeful in 1960, but Kennedy chose Johnson instead as his running mate. Gore won reelection in 1958 against a white supremacist challenge. He won a third term in 1964 but was unseated in 1970 by conservative Rep. William E. Brock III (R, Tenn.) [See KENNEDY, JOHNSON, NIXON/FORD Volumes]

[TO]

For further information:
Albert Gore, *Let the Glory Out: My South and Its Politics* (New York, 1972).

GRAHAM, BILLY (WILLIAM) (FRANKLIN)
b. Nov. 7, 1918: Charlotte, N.C.
Evangelist.

A descendant of pre-Revolutionary Scotch-Irish pioneers, Graham was raised on a farm near Charlotte, N.C. At 16 he experienced a conversion and "made a decision for Christ." Graham was ordained a Baptist minister in 1939. He graduated from the Florida Bible Institute in 1940 and fundamentalist Wheaton College with a B.A. in anthropology in 1943. Following service as a minister in Western Springs, Ill., from 1943 to 1945, Graham traveled around the U.S. and Great Britain staging "Youth for Christ" rallies. From 1947 to 1951 he was president of Minneapolis Northwestern College, a job which he subordinated to the task of touring the country seeking converts. At huge rallies he pleaded with sinners to stand up and come forward to demonstrate their acceptance of Christ. The young evangelist attained national prominence in the fall of 1949, when the Hearst papers publicized his successful proselytizing efforts in Los Angeles.

Graham was a strong opponent of President Harry S. Truman's domestic and foreign policies and warned that "Communists [were] doing their deadly work in government, education and in religion." A critic of the Korean war, he compared Truman's decision to send troops there to Adam's original sin. Graham aimed at making evangelicalism, organized through the National Association of Evangelicals (NAE), a political power bloc. In a 1952 speech to the NAE convention, he urged Protestants to compete with other organized groups such as the Irish, Jews, Roman Catholics and labor.

Although he professed political neutrality during the 1952 presidential campaign, Graham became a firm supporter of the President Eisenhower. When the evangelist made his world tours in the summer of 1954 and again in the spring of 1956, Secretary of State John Foster Dulles [q.v.] endorsed the trips. Graham visited Eisenhower after the 1956 tour to India to inform him of the results and urge him to visit to that country.

Graham often focused on Communism and the possibility of a nuclear holocaust in his sermons. He emphasized Soviet determination to conquer the world for atheism and Communism and stressed its opposition to the American mission of extending capitalism and democracy. Because of Russia's "deviousness," only evangelical Christianity could, in his view, ensure America's victory. Although he preached that the millenium was near, he believed it would come only after a devastating nuclear struggle with the USSR. Americans would emerge relatively unscathed from World War III if they adopted Christianity and were "born again." The millenium would bring laissez-faire capitalism and "rugged individualism" to the world, he suggested, informing an audience at Greensboro, N.C. in 1953 that "in the Garden of Eden there would no union dues, no labor leaders, no snakes, no disease."

After 1952 Graham's style of preaching became more subdued. He called himself a Christian rather than a fundamentalist and was less extreme in his literal interpretation of the Bible. Although some former critics commented favorably on his new manner, extreme fundamentalists and liberal theologians still distrusted him. Reinhold Niebuhr [q.v.] condemned Graham's failure to promote social reform, terming his preaching a form of "Christian pietism quite irrelevant to the political life of man." His use of mass media and gigantic rallies also angered some theologians who felt it created a show business-like atmosphere. The *Christian Century* complained in 1957 that "at this strange new junction of Madison Avenue and the Bible Belt, the Holy Spirit is not overworked, he is overlooked."

During the 1960s Graham continued his mass crusades. He supported integration efforts but urged civil rights leaders to proceed slowly. In his sermons he minimized the effects of the Vietnam war, favorably comparing its casualties to those from automobile accidents. His popularity with Presidents increased during the late-1960s, when he was a frequent visitor to the White House, and reached its peak under Richard Nixon, who had been his acquaintance for 20 years. [See KENNEDY, JOHNSON, NIXON/FORD Volumes]

[AES]

For further information:
William G. McLoughlin, Jr., *Modern Revivalism* (New York, 1956), pp. 482-530.

GREEN, EDITH S(TARRETT)
b. Jan. 17, 1910, Trent, S.D.
Democratic Representative, Ore.,
1954-74.

An English teacher and radio commentator before she entered politics, Green narrowly won a congressional seat in 1954 from a district including Portland and part of its suburbs. In the House she served on the Education and Labor Committee and quickly established a liberal reputation.

Green supported a full range of liberal programs, including civil rights, tax reform, repeal of the Taft-Hartley Act, a higher minimum wage, equal pay for equal work performed by women, campaign finance disclosure and public rather than private resource development. However, her main efforts focused on education. In her first month in office, she introduced a bill to provide emergency federal assistance to states and territories for construction of urgently needed school facilities, but no action was taken on the proposal.

Green's interest in education was sometimes linked to her commitment to civil rights. In 1956 Green and seven other Democratic representatives asked President Eisenhower to declare that he would refuse to allocate federal funds to school systems defying the Supreme Court's 1954 decision outlawing school segregation. The President, however, refused.

The successful launching of the Soviet satellite, *Sputnik*, in 1957 aroused American fears that the U.S. lagged behind the Soviet Union in educational programs, and in 1958 Congress approved an unprecedented educational appropriation, the National Defense Education Act (NDEA). Green helped shape and win passage of the measure, which provided more than $1 billion over a seven-year period for loans and grants to schools and students. In April 1959 she joined two college presidents in urging Congress to remove the loyalty oath required of NDEA fund recipients. No action was taken on the request.

Although she supported the large defense expenditures she believed were mandated by the Cold War, Green was among seven Democratic representatives who drafted a resolution in 1959 against atomic exchange agreements between the United States and seven NATO countries. The group feared that such pacts would heighten the risk of war. In May 1960 she joined 27 other House Democrats who wrote the President urging him to oppose "any unwise cuts" in the mutual security appropriations bill.
tions bill.

Although Green had only narrowly won her first House race, her subsequent majorities never fell below 63%. Her strong base encouraged her to play a role in national Democratic politics. At the 1956 convention she seconded the nomination of Adlai Stevenson [q.v.] for President and in 1960 managed John F. Kennedy's (D, Mass.) [q.v.] successful Oregon primary campaign. She seconded the Massachusetts Senator's nomination at the 1960 Los Angeles convention. Green maintained a record of solid support for the Kennedy and Johnson Administrations and continued to play an active role in education legislation. However, she grew increasingly conservative in the late-1960s and early-1970s. She did not seek reelection in 1974. In the 1976 presidential election she supported Gerald Ford [q.v.]. [See KENNEDY, JOHNSON Volumes]

[MDB]

For further information:
Hope Chamberlin, *A Minority of Members: Women in the U.S. Congress* (New York, 1973).

GREEN, THEODORE FRANCIS
b. Oct. 2, 1867: Providence, R.I.
d. May 19, 1966: Providence, R.I.
Democratic Senator, R.I., 1937-61;
Chairman, Foreign Relations Committee, 1957-59.

After receiving a B.A. degree from Brown University in 1887, Green studied law at Harvard and the Universities of Bonn and Berlin from 1888 to 1892. In the latter year he entered the Rhode Island bar and two years later joined his father's law firm. His legal career was interrupted briefly by service in the Spanish-American War. Green was elected to the state House of Representatives for the 1907-08 term. He unsuccessfully ran for the U.S. House of Representatives in 1920 and for governor in 1912, 1928 and 1930. He was finally elected Rhode Island governor in 1932.

In 1936 Gov. Green won a seat in the U.S. Senate. He was a supporter of New and Fair Deal legislation and was an internationalist in foreign affairs both before and after World War II. In 1944 and 1945, as chairman of the Committee on Campaign Expenditures, Green led an investigation of violations of limitations on campaign spending prescribed by the Hatch Act. In 1945 the panel recommended repeal of the law as "unrealistic."

A member of the Foreign Relations Committee, Green compiled a liberal, internationalist record in foreign policy during the 1950s. He joined the panel's other Democrats in 1953 in opposing a resolution, inspired by Secretary of State John Foster Dulles [q.v.], annulling secret foreign agreements used to justify the "enslavement" of other peoples. The resolution represented an implicit attack on Democratic Presidents Franklin D. Roosevelt and Harry S. Truman for allegedly making agreements with the Soviet Union at Yalta and Potsdam that were inimical to American interests. The resolution died in committee in March because many Republicans believed it was not sufficiently forthright in denouncing those agreements. Two years later Green strongly supported a resolution, adopted by both houses, opposing all forms of colonialism. Urging passage of the resolution on the Senate floor, he declared that "we have been tarred with a kind of colonial guilt-by-association in many parts of the world."

In 1957 Green gave up the chairmanship of the Rules and Administration Committee to become head of the Foreign Relations panel. During that year he defended his Committee's $250 million cut in the Administration's foreign aid request on the grounds that the reduction would not impair the national interest and would compel tighter administration of the program. But when Congress, following action by the Sen-

ate and House Appropriations Committees, reduced the request by another $750 million, Green asserted that his colleagues were "acting emotionally, rather than intelligently, on the question. . . ." The following year he and seven other Foreign Relations Committee members signed a letter to President Eisenhower asking for greater emphasis on economic aid and less on military assistance.

According to Tristam Coffin, in *Senator Fulbright: Portrait of a Public Philosopher*, Green, over 90 years old, "dozed at the [Foreign Relations Committee] hearings and presented an ineffectual image. The Democrats, getting ready for the 1960 elections with the theme they would get things moving, were unhappy with Green." Senate Majority Leader Lyndon B. Johnson (D, Tex.) [q.v.] helped induce him to voluntarily relinquish his chairmanship to second-ranking Democrat Sen. J. William Fulbright (D, Ark.) [q.v.].

As a member of the Rules and Administration Committee, Green in 1959 and 1960 criticized proposed "clean elections" bills for not including primaries in their financial disclosure provisions. He did not seek reelection in 1960. Green died on May 19, 1966 at the age of 98.

[MLL]

GREENEWALT, CRAWFORD H(ALLOCK)
b. Aug. 16; 1902; Cummington, Mass.
President and Chairman of the Executive Committee, E.I. du Pont de Nemours & Co., 1948-62.

The son of a physician and symphony pianist, Greenewalt graduated from the Massachusetts Institute of Technology in 1922. He became a control chemist at E.I. du Pont de Nemours & Co. that year. In June 1926 he married Margaretta du Pont, daughter of company president Irenee du Pont. During the 1920s and 1930s he was involved in developing commercial methods to produce nylon.

Greenewalt was elected to the board of directors in 1941 and was named chemical directors in 1941 and was named director of the Grasselli Chemical Department of du Pont in 1942. He witnessed the first self-sustaining atomic chain reaction engineered by Enrico Fermi at the University of Chicago in 1942. Thereafter, he helped maintain a close contact between du Pont and the atomic project. Du Pont was involved in the design, construction and operation of the plutonium plant near Hanford, Wash. During World War II he was frequently consulted by the government's ment and served as adviser to the Chemical Warfare Service and the Manhattan Project.

After the War Greenewalt was promoted, first to vice president in 1946, then to president, chairman of the executive committee and member of the finance committee in 1948. Soon after his appointment the board voted $30 million to expand the company's research program, a move attributed to Greenewalt's influence.

During Greenewalt's tenure the Justice Department antitrust division conducted several investigations of du Pont. A suit, begun in 1947, charging monopolistic practices in the manufacture and sale of cellophane, was thrown out in December 1953. A separate suit, filed in 1949, charged that du Pont's $560 million investment in General Motors, giving it a controlling share of the stock, violated the Clayton Antitrust Act. In 1951 the Supreme Court reversed the ruling of a federal district court that the government had failed to prove conspiracy. The court said that du Pont's control made it possible for the company to monopolize a substantial part of the market for auto fabrics and finishes. The case was then sent back to the lower court to determine equity. In 1959 that court ruled that the company could keep its 23% interest but would have to give up voting rights in the stock. The Supreme Court rejected this decree in 1961 and ordered du Pont to divest itself of its 63 million shares (valued by that date at almost $3 billion) within 10 years.

During the 1950s Greenewalt served on several government commissions. His most important assignment was as a member of the Commission on National Goals, formed in 1959. The panel report, released in November 1960, called for "extraordinary

personal responsibility, sustained effort and sacrifice" from every American in the 1960s to help the U.S. achieve "high and difficult goals" in a period of "grave danger" ahead.

Greenewalt, while approving the report, added his own statement cautioning that the goals would call for unprecedented expenditures which would create an unsupportable tax burden given the present economy. He, therefore, recommended improving the atmosphere for vigorous growth through, among other things, cutting income tax rates in the higher brackets. Although supporting the report's recommendation for free trade, he cautioned that it could lead to higher unemployment and the move to reduce tariffs should be taken cautiously.

Greenewalt resigned the presidency of du Pont in 1962, but he remained on as chairman of the board until 1967.

[RB]

GRIFFIN, (SAMUEL) MARVIN
b. Sept. 4, 1907; Bainbridge, Ga.
Governor, Ga., 1955-59.

The son of a state legislator and founder of the Bainbridge *Post-Searchlight*, Griffin grew up in an atmosphere of small-town politics and journalism. He worked as a page in the Georgia legislature at the age of 10. After receiving a B.A. from The Citadel in 1929, Griffin taught military science and served in the state legislature from 1935 to 1936. Following an unsuccessful bid for a U.S. House seat in 1940, Griffin served in the Army, rising to lieutenant colonel before his appointment as adjutant general of Georgia in 1944. Griffin lost a 1946 race for lieutenant governor but was elected two years later. In 1950 he won reelection for a four-year term under segregationist Gov. Herman Talmadge.

In January 1954, anticipating a desegregation ruling by the Supreme Court, Talmadge and Griffin created the Georgia Commission on Education to develop a plan to maintain segregation. Talmadge promoted a state constitutional amendment giving the state power to convert its public schools into a private system. State funds would then be used for tuition grants for private school students. Griffin championed this plan and gained Talmadge's last-minute support against eight other contenders in the 1954 gubernatorial race. Running as an extreme segregationist, he won the September primary and was elected in November.

Assuming office without a social, economic or political program, Griffin focused his attention on preserving segregation. In April he opposed integration in a debate with New York State Attorney General Jacob K. Javits [q.v.] at the Harvard law school. Five months later he held a top-level segregation strategy conference in Atlanta which resulted in the formation of the States Rights Council to enlist 100,000 dues-paying members to promote white supremacy. In December 1955 Griffin declared, "The South stands at Armageddon. The battle is joined. We cannot make the slightest concession to the enemy in this dark and lamentable hour of struggle." During January Griffin and other state officials traveled through Georgia promoting the Council and enlisting members. State employes were virtually compelled to contribute.

That month Virginia Gov. Thomas Stanley [q.v.] called a Southern governors conference to urge interposition, the use of state power to prevent desegregation. Griffin alone held an even more extreme position, urging outright nullification of the Supreme Court decision. In February 1956 he had the Georgia legislature invoke interposition and approve nullification.

Griffin refused to join the Dixiecrat call for a new political party but accepted nomination as Georgia's favorite son candidate for President at the August 1956 Democratic National Convention. The Governor took advantage of the national coverage to denounce the Supreme Court in his acceptance speech. The following August Griffin avowed Georgia's resistance anew at a white supremacist Citizens' Council dinner in Little Rock, Ark., where school desegregation was planned for that fall. When President Eisenhower ordered federal troops to enforce integration in Little Rock the following month, Gov. Griffin

joined other southern leaders in urging the South to take unified political action to prevent desegregation.

By 1958 Griffin was occupied defending his administration against charges of corruption, including one that the Georgia Commission on Education had borrowed $45,000 for an alleged subversive activities investigation. One Atlanta journalist described what he termed the "if-you-ain't-for-stealing-you-ain't-for-segregation" *modus operandi* of Griffin's administration. Prevented by law from succeeding himself, he retired from government service in 1959. Griffin attempted a political comeback in 1962 but was overwhelmingly defeated in the Democratic primary.

[MJS]

For further information:
Numan V. Bartley, *The Rise of Massive Resistance* (Baton Rouge, 1969).

GRIFFIN, ROBERT P.
b. Nov. 6, 1923: Detroit, Mich.
Republican Representative, Mich., 1957-66.

The son of a factory worker, Griffin studied to be a teacher at the Central Michigan College of Education at Mount Pleasant. After service in the Army during World War II, he returned to the College and received B.A. and B.S. degrees in 1947. By that time, however, Griffin had decided to become a lawyer. He attended the University of Michigan law school, where he was an associate editor of the *Michigan Law Review*, and received a law degree in 1951. Admitted to the Michigan bar in 1950, he cofounded a law firm in Traverse City and specialized in labor law.

In 1956 Griffin entered the Republican congressional primary in the ninth district against conservative incumbent Rep. Ruth Thompson. He won that contest and went on to defeat his Democratic opponent by 14,000 votes. Because of his expertise in labor matters, he asked for and was given an assignment on the Education and Labor Committee. Griffin was less conservative than Thompson. Disagreeing with six conservative Republican members of the Education and Labor panel who contended that states and localities did not need federal school construction aid, Griffin backed a 1957 bill providing such assistance. The following year he supported a measure establishing a seven-year program of federal loans and grants to schools and individual students. On the House floor he succeeded in adding an amendment to include junior colleges among the institutions eligible for aid to improve instructional facilities in science, mathematics and modern languages.

In 1959 Griffin earned the enmity of organized labor by his cosponsorhip of a labor reform measure. The bill stemmed largely from investigations begun in 1957 by Sen. John McClellan's (D, Ark.) [q.v.] Select Committee on Improper Activities in the Labor or Management Field. That probe revealed extensive corruption, embezzlement and collusion between management and labor leaders. In April 1959 the Senate passed a bill designed to curb racketeering. The measure, sponsored by Sen. John F. Kennedy (D, Mass.) [q.v.], required labor unions to file annual reports containing financial and other information; required secret ballot union elections at regular intervals; and provided criminal penalties for bribery, extortion, misappropriation of union funds, failure to maintain proper union financial records and other practices.

President Eisenhower, Republican congressional leaders and Southern Democrats favored a more restrictive bill including amendments strengthening the Taft-Hartley Act. When the House Education and Labor Committee in July 1959 reported a measure that did not go much beyond the Kennedy proposal, Griffin and Rep. Phil M. Landrum (D, Ga.) [q.v.] introduced their own bill, adding the desired amendments to the Senate legislation. The most significant provisions of the original Landrum-Griffin bill were adopted by both houses in September. The amendments to the Taft-Hartley Act defined as an unfair labor practice a labor-management contract under which the employer agreed not to do business with another firm; restricted organizational and recognition picketing and secondary boycotts; brought several additional categories of workers within the scope of

the Taft-Hartley Act's restrictions on picketing and secondary boycotts; and barred unions from picketing a retail store to protest that the store was handling the goods of a firm that the union was striking.

In 1960 Griffin opposed a bill to legalize common-site picketing in the construction industry. He also opposed liberal efforts to increase the minimum wage by more than 15 cents above the existing $1 minimum, asserting that a larger increment would be harmful to marginal and physically handicapped workers and would cause serious economic dislocation.

In 1963 Griffin and several other younger Republican representatives led a revolt against the Party's House leadership, which elevated Rep. Gerald R. Ford (R, Mich.) [q.v.] to the chairmanship of the House Republican Conference Committee. Two years later they unseated Minority Leader Charles A. Halleck (R, Ind.) [q.v.] and replaced him with Ford. In 1966 Griffin was appointed to a Senate vacancy and won election in the fall of that year. Two years later he organized successful opposition to President Lyndon B. Johnson's nomination of Supreme Court Associate Justice Abe Fortas to be Chief Justice. In 1969 he became minority whip. Eight years later Griffin lost that post when he ran unsuccessfully for the position of minority leader. [See KENNEDY, JOHNSON, NIXON/FORD Volumes]

[MLL]

GROSS, H(AROLD) R(OYCE)
b. June 30, 1899; Arispe, Iowa.
Republican Representative, Iowa,
1949-75.

Gross was raised on a southern Iowa farm, and after serving in World War I he attended the University of Missouri School of Journalism for about two years. From 1921 to 1935 he worked on several newspapers as a reporter or editor and for the next 13 years was a news commentator for Iowa radio stations.

In the June 1948 Republican primary Gross defeated the incumbent U.S. representative in Iowa's predominantly agricultural third congressional district and went on to win the election. Gross quickly established himself as a persistent advocate of reductions in federal spending, and in May 1950 he voted for a $600 million cut in the national budget. However, in 1949 and 1950 Gross backed Administration bills for high farm price supports.

An isolationist, Gross in 1953 unsuccessfully offered an appropriations bill amendment that would have cut America's contribution to the U.N. by 90%. Two years later he opposed an extension of reciprocal trade legislation, contending "it has been a program of give, give and give some more to appease our so-called free world friends. . . ." In 1957 Gross voted against U.S. appropriations for the U.N. Emergency Force in the Middle East. During the same year he opposed the Eisenhower Doctrine which stated that the U.S. was prepared, if the President believed it was necessary, to use force to help Middle Eastern nations repel Communist aggression. In 1959 he offered a mutual security bill amendment declaring that the U.S. should have as little political connection with other nations as possible. It was rejected by voice vote.

Continuing to advocate fiscal frugality during the 1950s, Gross opposed an increase in the national debt limit in 1955, asserting that "the answer to financial stability on the part of the federal government is reduced spending, not steadily increasing debt." During the same year he denounced congressional junkets and opposed increased salaries for District of Columbia judges and cabinet officers. His economy-mindedness led him to oppose many social welfare expenditures. In 1956 he criticized a 37% increase in funds for the National Institutes of Health. Two years later Gross asserted that the funds allotted by the Appropriations Committee for the Labor and Health, Education and Welfare Departments were excessive.

Gross persisted in backing high farm price supports during the Eisenhower presidency and in 1954 voted against the Administration's omnibus farm bill, which lowered support levels. He opposed the 1957 Civil Rights Act but voted for the Civil Rights Act of 1960. According to *Congressional Quarterly*, Gross voted contrary to Eisenhower positions on key bills more often than he backed the Administration.

Gross consistently opposed New Frontier programs in the early 1960s and continued his efforts to reduce U.S. financial support of the U.N. During the 1960s and early-1970s, Gross retained his reputation as a leading opponent of what he regarded as excessive government spending. He did not run for reelection in 1974. [See KENNEDY, JOHNSON Volumes]

[MLL]

GRUENING, ERNEST H(ENRY)
b. Feb. 6, 1887, New York, N.Y.
d. Aug. 26, 1974, Washington, D.C.
Democratic Senator, Alaska, 1959-69.

Ernest Gruening graduated from Harvard medical school in 1912 but then chose a career in journalism. He served as editor of several liberal journals during the 1920s and 1930s, including *The Nation* and *The New York Herald Tribune*, and espoused such controversial causes as racial integration and birth control. An opponent of American military intervention in Latin America, Gruening wrote a much-acclaimed account of the Mexican Revolution, *Mexico and Its Heritage*, published in 1928.

Although he directed public relations for Robert LaFollette's 1924 presidential campaign and supported Herbert Hoover in 1928, Gruening became a loyal Democrat during the New Deal years. In 1934 President Roosevelt appointed him director of the division of territories and island possessions in the Department of the Interior. Gruening simultaneously administered relief and reconstruction programs in Puerto Rico. In 1939 Roosevelt appointed him territorial governor of Alaska, a position he held until 1952.

Gruening later wrote that when he assumed the governorship, "Alaska was in the grip of absentee interests and had been for a quarter of a century." As governor, he proposed a tax system that weakened the influence of non-resident businessmen, and he worked for improved transportation, particularly the construction of the Alcan Highway. Gruening also won anti-discrimination legislation designed to protect Alaska's Eskimos.

Convinced that "Alaska's territorial status burdened it with insuperable handicaps," Gruening became a leading advocate of statehood. After leaving office he wrote *The State of Alaska*, a history of the area published in 1954. Gruening also appeared on numerous occasions before congressional committees charged with weighing Alaska's possible admission to the union. Anticipating statehood, the Alaska territorial legislature called a constitutional convention, which assembled in September 1955 with Gruening as its keynote speaker. His address, entitled "Let Us End American Colonialism," was widely circulated in pamphlet form by pro-statehood groups.

In his campaign Gruening had to answer objections to statehood stemming from Alaska's remoteness, small population and strategic military value. Its opponents included President Eisenhower who did, however, endorse statehood for Hawaii. In *The Battle for Alaska Statehood* (1967), Gruening attributed Eisenhower's opposition to "the assumption that Hawaii would elect Republicans and Alaska Democrats."

To promote its cause, the Alaska legislature adopted the "Tennessee Plan," a device first used by Tennessee in 1796 to achieve statehood. Under the plan the territory in November 1956 elected two senators, including Gruening, and one representative to the U.S. Congress to lobby for statehood. Their efforts met with success. In June 1958 Congress approved statehood for Alaska and Hawaii. Alaska Democrats won all state-wide offices that November, and Gruening won a four-year Senate term.

In the Senate Gruening soon established a liberal record. Early in his Senate career he called for a more vigorous congressional role in foreign policy, particularly in the area of foreign aid. In May 1960 the Senate accepted his amendment to a foreign aid bill that required detailed explanations and cost projections for military assistance projects. However his amendment requiring officials to give Congress detailed country-by-country budgets for all foreign aid programs was defeated. Gruening was a co-sponsor of Sen. Patrick McNamara's [q.v.] program to provide medical care to the aged through Social Security, and he supported most civil rights legislation.

Gruening was a staunch supporter of Kennedy and Johnson Administration domestic programs, but he won national prominence as one of the earliest congressional opponents of the Vietnam war. Gruening lost the 1968 Democratic Senate primary. He continued his anti-war activities and campaigned for Sen. George McGovern (D, S.D.) in the 1972 presidential election. Gruening died in Washington in August 1974 at the age of 83. [See KENNEDY, JOHNSON Volumes]

[MDB]

HAGERTY, JAMES C.
b. May 9, 1909; Plattsburgh, N.Y.
White House Press Secretary, January 1953-December 1960.

The son of James Hagerty, senior political writer for the *New York Times*, James Hagerty, Jr., graduated from Columbia College in 1934, where he had been the campus reporter for his father's paper. Hagerty then joined the paper and was legislative correspondent in Albany from 1938 to 1942. During that period he covered Thomas Dewey's gubernatorial campaign and Wendell Willkie's presidential race. In 1943 Hagerty became press secretary to Gov. Dewey. He supported Dwight D. Eisenhower for the 1952 Republican presidential nomination and worked closely with the candidates chief advisers during the presidential campaign.

Eisenhower appointed Hagerty his press secretary in November 1952. Hagerty was responsible for maintaining good relations with the press, issuing reports on presidential activities, defending presidential policies and planning Eisenhower's diplomatic visits. He was the aide who kept the press informed of the President's condition following his heart attack in September 1955 and stroke in November 1957. Hagerty transmitted Eisenhower's "full confidence" in Sherman Adams [q.v.] when the

President's chief aide was under congressional investigation for conflict of interest in 1958. He also reported events resulting in the cancellation of the 1960 summit conference following the downing of a U-2 spy plane over the Soviet Union. While arranging the President's trip to Japan in 1960, Hagerty bore the brunt of leftist Japanese anger over the American-Japanese Security Treaty. His car was stoned for about an hour-and-a-half before a U:S. Marine Corps helicopter rescued him. A few days later Eisenhower canceled his upcoming visit.

Hagerty was not simply a passive reporter of information. The seemingly unflappable press secretary was a close adviser to Eisenhower, working well with a President known for his temper. Hagerty offered advice on many domestic matters involving the press. In 1953 he urged Eisenhower to denounce McCarthy aide J.B. Matthews's [q.v.] attack on the Protestant clergy as a major source of Communist sympathizers in the U.S. and drafted the President's reply. Hagerty was among the 13 presidential confidants who played a large role in persuading Eisenhower to run for reelection in 1956.

The press secretary was one of the White House staff members sympathetic to the cause of civil rights. During the 1956 debate over the President's possible stand on the so-called Powell amendment. Hagerty urged Eisenhower to support it. The proposals, attached to several pieces of legislation, barred federal funds to areas practicing discrimination. Several advisers, including Gerald Morgan [q.v.], cautioned against backing it because such action would jeopardize passage of the legislation. The press secretary, however, questioned how the "party of Lincoln" could ignore a call for integration. Eisenhower ignored Hagerty's advice and, though not opposing the amendment, refused to take a strong stand in favor of it. During the 1957 school segregation crisis in Little Rock, Ark., Hagerty took part in the inconclusive meetings between Eisenhower and Arkansas Gov. Orval Faubus [q.v.], called to find a compromise plan for integrating the schools.

With the election of John F. Kennedy,

Hagerty became a vice president of American Broadcasting Systems, Inc. He served at that post from 1961 through 1975.

[RSG]

HALL, LEONARD W(OOD)
b. Oct. 2, 1900: Oyster Bay, N.Y.
Chairman, Republican National Committee, 1953-57.

The son of a White House librarian, Hall earned his LL.B. at Georgetown University law school in 1920. He was admitted to the New York bar the following year and began a lucrative law career. Hall entered politics as a GOP campaign worker in 1926. He served as state assemblyman in 1927-28 and again from 1934 to 1938. In 1939 he won election to the U.S. House of Representatives, where he voted primarily with the internationalist Eastern wing of the Republican Party. Hall managed Thomas Dewey's unsuccessful presidential campaign in 1948. He supported Gen. Eisenhower for the Republican presidential nomination four years later and established a personal relationship with the General during the fall campaign.

Hall became Eisenhower's choice for Republican National Chairman following C. Wesley Roberts's [q.v.] resignation in March 1953. The decision was based not only on Hall's relationship with the President but on his high standing with Party leaders on Capitol Hill. He had also organized the Republican Campaign Congressional Committee to unify the Party and increase its influence in Washington, and so he was known by Republican leaders throughout the country. Just as importantly, Hall had experience in organizing campaigns, a significant factor for a party facing difficult midterm elections in 1954.

Hall's candidacy was opposed by both Sen. Robert Taft (R, Ohio) [q.v.] and Thomas Dewey. Taft's objections were based on Hall's alliance with Eastern Republicans, while Dewey's could be traced back to the disappointing loss in the 1948 election. However, as a result of pressure from the Administration and House Speaker

Joe Martin (R, Mass.) [*q.v.*], both men eventually agreed to subordinate their own feelings and support Hall. He was officially installed as chairman in April 1953.

Hall's first challenge was to maintain Republican control of Congress in the 1954 elections. The outstanding problem was whether to endorse or reject Sen. Joseph R. McCarthy's (R, Wisc.) [*q.v.*] anti-Communist crusade. With McCarthy at the peak of his popularity in November 1953, the National Chairman declared that Communism in government would be a major campaign issue. However, four months later, after the President had stepped back from the Senator and a Gallup Poll had indicated a decline in McCarthy's popularity, Hall said that McCarthy had been hurting the Party. The election was a defeat for the Republicans. When the votes were counted the Democrats controlled the Senate by one vote and the House by 29. The Republicans also lost heavily in the gubernatorial races.

During late-1955 and early-1956, Hall led the drive to preserve an Eisenhower-Nixon ticket in light of the President's reluctance to commit himself to the Vice President. Hall discussed the need to keep Richard Nixon [*q.v.*] on the ticket to satisfy conservatives and convinced Nixon to directly confront the President with his desire for renomination. Eisenhower expressed his approval at an April 26, 1956 meeting. The Republican ticket went on to win the election. However, the victory was a personal one for Eisenhower. For the first time in over 100 years, a victorious presidential candidate failed to give his party control of either house of Congress.

In 1955 and 1956 Hall became enmeshed in scandals involving the General Services Administration (GSA). During 1955 GSA Administrator Edmund Mansure [*q.v.*] was charged with awarding contracts to upgrade a U.S. government-owned nickel plant in Nicaro, Cuba on a political basis. Before the House Special Government Activities Subcommittee, Mansure testified that early in the Nicaro negotiations he had submitted a list of contractors to Hall for approval. A confidential memo obtained by the panel indicated that Hall had Mansure make the award to the Snare Co. only after he was personally assured that it had no Democrats in executive positions and would contribute to the 1954 Republican election effort. Invited to refute these charges in late 1956, Hall promised to appear after the election but never did. Despite the fact that Hall may have been in violation of the law in the Nicaro incident, he was never subpoenaed by the subcommittee or directed to testify by the President.

Hall resigned as GOP chairman in January 1957 and returned to his private law practice. The following year he unsuccessfully sought the Republican nomination for governor of New York. In 1964 and 1968 he backed the unsuccessful presidential candidacies of New York Gov. Nelson Rockefeller [*q.v.*].

[MJS]

HALLECK, CHARLES A(BRAHAM)
b. Aug. 22, 1900; Demotte, Ind.
Republican Representative, Ind., 1935-69; House Majority Leader, 1947-49, 1953-55; House Minority Leader, 1959-65.

The son of two lawyers, Halleck received an LL.B. degree from Indiana University in 1924, graduating first in his class. During the same year he entered his parents' law firm and won election as prosecuting attorney for Indiana's 13th judicial district. He served for 10 years before winning a special congressional election in 1935. A conservative Republican, Halleck consistently opposed New Deal measures. He was an isolationist until the Japanese attack on Pearl Harbor.

In 1940 Halleck became Minority Leader Joseph W. Martin's (R, Mass.) [*q.v.*] informal assistant. When Martin became House Speaker in 1947, Halleck took the post of majority leader. The Indiana Representative endorsed New York Gov. Thomas E. Dewey for the Republican presidential nomination in 1948, although Dewey represented the Eastern, moderate wing of the Party. Halleck hoped to be the New York Governor's choice as the Party's vice presidential candidate, but his expectations were disappointed. [See TRUMAN Volume]

When the Republicans regained control of the House in 1953, Halleck again became majority leader. Although more conservative than President Dwight D. Eisenhower, he was first and foremost a party loyalist. Halleck sympathized with the efforts of conservative Republicans to secure an income tax cut in 1953 but supported the Administration's opposition to a reduction. While a critic of Truman's foreign aid and reciprocal trade programs, he backed similar measures under Eisenhower.

When the Republicans lost their majorities in both houses of Congress in 1954, Halleck considered a race against Martin for minority leader. Two years later he again considered a bid. Both times the White House, fearing the consequences of a bitter Republican fight, dissuaded Halleck.

After the Democratic sweep of the 1958 congressional elections, however, the President indicated that he would not stand in Halleck's way. Eisenhower blamed the Republican defeat to a large extent upon weak congressional leadership rather than the recession. His hands-off policy was, in effect, an endorsement of Halleck. In addition, many GOP representatives believed that Martin was guilty of bipartisan cronyism with the Democratic leadership headed by Speaker Sam Rayburn (D, Tex.) [q.v.]. On Jan. 6, 1959 the House Republican caucus voted, 74-70, to unseat Martin and make Halleck minority leader. Some representatives ostensibly exacted from Halleck the promise of an enlarged role for the Republican Policy Committee as a condition of their support.

Halleck was a more aggressive and partisan minority leader than his predecessor. Shortly after assuming his post he demonstrated his disinclination for compromise by replacing on the Rules Committee two moderate Republicans defeated for reelection with conservatives. The Rules panel could block the flow of legislation to the House floor, and Halleck's action made it more difficult for Rayburn to bring liberal measures to a vote.

Later in the year Halleck was given considerable credit for the passage of the Landrum-Griffin labor reform bill in the House. The measure added to a Senate-passed labor corruption proposal prohibitions against secondary boycotts and curbs on union organizational and recognition picketing. In 1959 he was a leader in the successful effort to place a limit on the area served by the Tennessee Valley Authority.

Aligned with conservative Southern Democrates, Halleck helped defeat a number of President John F. Kennedy's bills, including school aid and omnibus housing measures in 1961 and a farm bill in 1962. In January 1963 his candidate for Republican Policy Committee chairman was defeated by Rep. Gerald R. Ford (R, Mich.) [q.v.], who was backed by the younger House Republicans. Two years later Ford unseated Halleck as minority leader. Halleck announced his retirement in 1968. [See KENNEDY, JOHNSON Volumes]

[MLL]

For further information:
Henry Z. Scheele, *Charlie Halleck* (New York, 1966).

HANNAH, JOHN A(LFRED)
b. Oct. 1, 1902; Grand Rapids, Mich.
President, Michigan State University, 1941-53, 1954-69; Assistant Secretary of Defense for Manpower, February 1953-September 1954; Chairman, Civil Rights Commission, January 1958-February 1969.

The son of a poultry breeder, Hannah graduated from Michigan State University (MSU) in 1923. He then entered the poultry business, eventually becoming president of the International Baby Chick Association and supervising egg production for the National Recovery Administration during the 1930s. In 1935 Hannah returned to his alma mater as business manager. He became president of the University in 1941. Hannah was at MSU for 26 years, during which time he transformed a small land-grant campus with 6,000 students into a modern "megaversity," with an enrollment of over 40,000. Although not a scholar, the president became well known for his "academic pitchmanship," as his critics called it, which garnered large amounts of state and federal aid for increased enrollment and construction. By 1951 MSU's building budget had reached $31 million, two-thirds from the state and federal governments. Funds also came from federally financed foreign aid projects that the University directed in Asia, Africa and Latin America. Under Hannah's leadership the University emphasized popular and practical courses to attract students. His critics claimed that he was sacrificing academic quality for expansion, but Hannah replied that his purpose was "not to de-emphasize scholarship but to emphasize its application."

In 1953 President Eisenhower appointed Hannah assistant secretary of defense for manpower. During his short term in office, he was instrumental in ending segregation in civilian schools attended by children of members of the Armed Forces. He also attempted to raise the caliber of the Armed Forces by increasing intelligence requirements and extending training periods. Hannah returned to MSU in September 1954.

Three years later Hannah was appointed chairman of the newly formed Civil Rights Commission. He took office in February 1958. That year he announced that the panel would investigate violations of black voting rights in Alabama, Florida and Mississippi. The Commission's first report, released in September 1959, emphasized that many blacks were denied voting rights and recommended a series of legislative proposals to solve the problem. The panel suggested measures authorizing the temporary use of federal officials to register qualified voters in federal, general, special or primary elections. It also recommended a census survey of voting statistics by race and the preservation of voting records. The Commission urged that it be empowered to apply directly to federal courts for orders enforcing directives that witnesses appear and produce records.

Hannah and two other liberal members of the group, Rev. Theodore M. Hesburgh and George M. Johnson, also proposed a constitutional amendment to abolish literacy tests in voting. They further recommended

that federal aid be withheld from segregated colleges and universities. However, the Commission's three Southern members opposed the suggestions.

Hannah continued as chairman of the Civil Rights Commission during the Kennedy and Johnson years. In 1966 an article in *Ramparts* charged that a federally financed MSU project in South Vietnam had provided a cover for Central Intelligence Agency (CIA) operations. Hannah admitted the possibility of CIA infiltration but denied that Michigan State University had knowingly tolerated or encouraged this. [See JOHNSON Volume]

In 1969 President Richard M. Nixon appointed Hannah director of the Agency for International Development. He served in that post until 1973. [See NIXON/FORD Volume]

[SY]

HARLAN, JOHN MARSHALL
b. May 20, 1899; Chicago, Ill.
d. Dec. 29, 1971; Washington, D.C.
Judge, U.S. Court of Appeals for the Second Circuit, 1954-55; Associate Justice, U.S. Supreme Court, 1955-71.

Named after his grandfather, who had also been a U.S. Supreme Court justice, Harlan received a B.A. from Princeton in 1920 and then was a Rhodes Scholar at Oxford for three years. He joined a major Wall Street law firm in 1923, obtained his law degree from New York law school in 1924 and was admitted to the New York bar in 1925. Harlan undertook several public service jobs over the years, acting, for example, as an assistant to the U.S. attorney in New York from 1925 to 1927 and as chief counsel to the New York State Crime Commission from 1951 to 1953. However, the bulk of his career was spent in private practice. During his 25 years with a prestigious Wall Street law firm he became the principal litigation partner, a specialist in corporate and antitrust cases. Harlan gradually emerged as a recognized leader of the New York bar.

A life-long Republican of proven legal ability, Harlan became a judge on the U.S. Second Circuit Court of Appeals in March

1954. Eight months later President Eisenhower named Harlan to the U.S. Supreme Court. The Senate Judiciary Committee held up action on the appointment, reportedly because some Southern senators hoped the delay would lead the Supreme Court to postpone implementation of its 1954 school desegregation decision. Finally, in March 1955, the Senate confirmed Harlan's nomination by a vote of 71-11. He took his seat that month.

As his Southern opponents feared, Justice Harlan supported his colleagues' view that school segregation was unconstitutional. He joined in the Court's May 1955 ruling that called for school desegregation with "all deliberate speed" and voted in later cases against segregation in public facilities. In June 1958 Harlan spoke for a unanimous Court to reverse a $100,000 fine imposed by the state of Alabama on the NAACP when the organization refused to turn over its membership lists. His opinion explicitly held that the right of free association was protected by the Constitution.

In his earliest years on the Court, Harlan took a center position in loyalty-security cases. With the Court's liberal members he often opposed the government's position, but usually on narrow, technical grounds rather than on a broader, constitutional basis. He frequently spoke for the Court in important cases. In June 1956, for example, Harlan's majority opinion reversed the dismissal of a federal food and drug inspector on the ground that federal law authorized the summary dismissal of a government employe as a security risk only if he held a sensitive job.

The Justice also spoke for a six-man majority in the June 1957 *Yates* case, which reversed the conviction of 14 California Communist Party leaders under the Smith Act. Harlan's opinion ruled that the Smith Act did not outlaw advocacy of the forcible overthrow of the government as an abstract doctrine, but only such advocacy when directed at promoting concrete, unlawful action. This interpretation made further convictions of Communists under the law's conspiracy clause virtually impossible. In the same month Harlan joined the majority in the *Watkins* case to reverse the contempt conviction of a witness who had refused to answer questions about former Communist associates before the House Un-American Activities Committee (HUAC).

After this, however, Harlan began taking a more conservative stance in most loyalty-security cases. In June 1959, for example, he wrote for a five-man majority to sustain the contempt conviction of a professor who had refused to answer the questions of a HUAC subcommittee about his Communist Party membership and activities. Balancing government interests against individual rights, Harlan ruled that the Committee had not violated the right to academic freedom and had met the necessary legal requirements in its questioning of the witness.

The Justice's position in these later cases was more representative of his overall record on the bench and clarified the main principles in his judicial philosophy. Like Justice Felix Frankfurter [*q.v.*], with whom he developed a close personal and intellectual relationship, Harlan believed the Court had only a limited role to play in a federal system of government. He argued that the justices should exercise restraint and avoid claiming excessive authority for themselves at the expense of the other branches of the federal government and the states. He espoused an analytical, dispassionate approach to cases and contended that political and social ills should be remedied through political processes and not by the Court. Himself a "judge of cases and not of causes," as one commentator put it, Justice Harlan believed in following precedent unless there was a clear and strong demonstration that a past decision had been made in error.

In federal criminal cases Harlan was often willing to reverse lower court convictions if the defendant had not been afforded the proper procedural guarantees. He gave greater leeway to the states, however, and argued that so long as state criminal procedures were "fundamentally fair," they were constitutional. Harlan opposed the notion that the states, under the Fourteenth Amendment, had to give defendants all the guarantees designated in the Bill of Rights. He usually rejected constitutional claims based on the allegedly unequal treatment received by the poor. Thus in April 1956 he dissented when the majority held that states must supply an indigent convicted person with a free trial transcript when the right of appeal was conditioned on having such a transcript. Harlan also insisted that the Constitution placed different limits on state and federal power to regulate obscenity. In a separate opinion in a June 1957 case, he maintained that the states had greater authority to regulate pornography than the federal government.

Following Frankfurter's retirement in 1962, Harlan became the Court's leading spokesman for a philosophy of judicial restraint. Once a liberal activist majority emerged on the Warren Court in the 1960s, the Justice was frequently cast as a dissenter to major judicial trends. He opposed the Court's decisions on reapportionment and many of the liberal majority's criminal rights rulings. He also voted to uphold state laws on obscenity. [See KENNEDY, JOHNSON, NIXON/FORD Volumes]

Throughout his years on the Court, Harlan took great care to write opinions that would fully elucidate the questions in the case and the reasons for his judgement. His scholarly opinions with their clear, orderly style were widely praised, and Harlan was considered a diligent and thorough worker on the Court. When he retired in September 1971 because of ill health, Harlan was highly regarded even by critics for his learning and craftsmanship, his penetrating analysis of the issues in cases and his unquestioned intellectual integrity. Harlan died in Washington on Dec. 29, 1971.

[CAB]

For further information:
Norman Dorsen, "John Marshall Harlan," in Leon Friedman and Fred L. Israel, eds., The Justices of the United States Supreme Court, 1789-1969 (New York, 1969), Vol. 4.
David L. Shapiro, ed., The Evolution of a Judicial Philosophy: Selected Opinions and Papers of Justice John Marshall Harlan (Cambridge, Mass., 1969).
J. Harvie Wilkinson III, "Justice John M. Harlan and the Values of Federalism," Virginia Law Review, 57 (October, 1971), pp. 1185-1221.

HARLOW, BRYCE N(ATHANIEL)

b. Aug. 11, 1916; Oklahoma City, Okla.
Special Assistant to the President, January 1953-September 1958; Deputy Assistant to the President, September 1958-January 1961.

After graduating from the University of Oklahoma in 1936 and attending graduate school at the University of Texas, Harlow went to Washington in 1938 as assistant librarian of the House of Representatives. He returned to the University of Oklahoma in 1940 and earned a masters degree two years later. Following service in the Army during World War II, Harlow worked for the House Armed Services Committee, as a staff assistant and later as its chief clerk. In 1951 he became vice president of Harlow Publishing Corp.

In 1953 Harlow was appointed special assistant to President Eisenhower, serving as a speechwriter. Because of his previous legislative experience, Harlow was also chosen as an assistant to the chief of congressional liaison, Gen. Wilton B. Persons [q.v.]. As a member of the Administration's legislative team, Harlow lobbied for Eisenhower proposals on Capitol Hill. Both personally popular and politically knowledgeable, he drew praise as the man who knew more about the legislative apparatus and the behavior of members of Congress than any other individual in the Administration. He particularly excelled at communicating with the powerful Democratic leaders, Speaker of the House Sam. Rayburn (D, Tex.) [q.v.] and Senate Majority Leader Lyndon Johnson (D, Tex.) [q.v.]. Harlow also sat in on White House defense, science and foreign policy discussions, advising on probable congressional reactions.

Harlow was one of the liberal members of the White House staff. When Sen. Joseph R. McCarthy (R, Wisc.) [q.v.] attacked Eisenhower in 1953, Harlow sided with the small group of White House staffers urging the President to take the offensive against the Wisconsin Republican. As a consequence McCarthy pilloried Harlow and the others as the White House's "dangerous liberals."

Harlow's main focus was on civil rights. His actions on the issue often appeared to be motivated by political considerations. For example, to improve Republican chances of garnering black votes in 1956, he urged other White House congressional liaison officers to maneuver Southern Democrats into filibustering a proposed 1956 civil rights bill. Yet in the school integration crises of 1957 and 1958, Harlow supported a stronger position on civil rights. After a tour of the South and Southwest in the summer of 1958, Harlow urged Eisenhower to exert strong leadership to defuse the school desegregation controversy immediately.

In 1958 Eisenhower assigned Harlow to congressional liaison work on a full-time basis. When Persons succeeded Sherman Adams [q.v.] as assistant to the President that September, Harlow took over Persons's post. As criticism of Eisenhower grew Harlow had an increasingly difficult time in dealing with Congress. He frequently pointed to the inefficiency of a government in which one party controlled the executive branch and the other the legislative.

After leaving the White House in January 1961, Harlow became a lobbyist for Procter and Gamble Co. When Richard M. Nixon won election as President in 1968, Harlow was again appointed White House congressional liaison. However, he did not prove to be as effective as in the 1950s; one congressman commented, "He seems to have lost the touch he had during the Eisenhower years." In 1969 Nixon appointed Harlow counselor to the President with cabinet rank. He left the White House in 1971 to become a vice president of Procter and Gamble. Harlow returned briefly in 1974 to serve as counselor to President Gerald Ford. [See NIXON/FORD Volume]

[RJB]

HARRIMAN, W(ILLIAM) AVERELL
b. Nov. 15, 1891: New York, N.Y.
Governor, N.Y., 1955-59.

A son of financier and railroad magnate Edward Henry Harriman, Averell and his brother inherited a fortune estimated at be-

tween 70 and 100 million dollars when their father died in 1909. After attending Groton Harriman entered Yale and received a B.A. in 1913. Within two years of his graduation, he became a vice president of the Union Pacific Railroad, founded by his father. Shortly afterwards he started a shipping company. In 1920 he established W.A. Harriman and Co., a private bank.

Harriman was initially a Republican but became a Democrat in 1928 as a result of personal contact with New York Gov. Al Smith. He entered government service in 1934, when President Franklin D. Roosevelt appointed him administrator of Division II of the National Recovery Administration (NRA). The following year he became the NRA administrative officer. From 1937 to 1940 Harriman was chairman of the Business Advisory Council of the Department of Commerce. In 1941 he became chief of the raw materials branch of the Office of Production Management and worked to accelerate arms production. Subsequently Harriman facilitated the disbursement of Lend-Lease aid to Britain and the Soviet Union. From 1943 to 1946 he was ambassador to the USSR. He was ambassador to Britain from March to September 1946 and then served as Secretary of Commerce from 1946 to 1948. Harriman was director of economic aid to Europe under the Marshall Plan from 1948 to 1950, special assistant to the President from 1950 to 1951 and director of the Mutual Security Agency from 1951 to 1953. [See TRUMAN Volume]

In April 1952, shortly after Illinois Gov. Adlai E. Stevenson [q.v.] professed to be uninterested in the Democratic presidential nomination, Harriman entered the primary race. He declared himself a supporter of the New and Fair Deals and stated that no one else in the country had his qualifications for the presidency in both domestic and foreign affairs. He had strong support from many liberals, but after finishing fourth on the first two ballots at the Democratic Convention, Harriman withdrew from the contest.

Two years later Harriman entered the race for the New York Democratic gubernatorial nomination. With the crucial assistance of New York City Tammany Hall boss Carmine DeSapio [q.v.], Harriman defeated Rep. Franklin D. Roosevelt, Jr., at the Democratic State Convention. Harriman's opponent in the general election was liberal Republican Sen. Irving M. Ives [q.v.]. Few substantive political issues separated the candidates. Therefore, when polls showed Harriman in the lead, Ives attacked his Democratic opponent for allegedly corrupt business practices in previous decades. Harriman defeated Ives by 11,000 votes out of 5 million cast.

Harriman received substantial praise for placing the State Commission Against Discrimination under the direction of a vigorous opponent of racial bias in housing. He also gained plaudits for appointing an effective director for New York's mental health hospital system and for establishing the nation's first office of consumer affairs. To Republican charges that he was a spendthrift for increasing the state budget by 50% during his gubernatorial tenure, Harriman replied that most of the increased expenditures represented necessary additions to the education budget. Hoping to expand his political base in the Republican-dominated upstate region, he promoted the building of roads and schools in that area and developed Adirondack resort facilities.

However, even many of Harriman's political sympathizers regarded his administration's accomplishments as scanty. One reason for his limited achievements was the obstacle posed by a Republican-controlled legislature. Another important reason was the Governor's preoccupation with pursuing the Democratic presidential nomination. Maintaining his status as a national figure in 1955 and early 1956 by continually attacking the Eisenhower Administration's domestic and foreign policies, he officially declared his candidacy in June 1956. Harriman, hoping to capture northern liberal, labor and big-city support, staked out a position on the Party's left wing, taking, for example, a strong position in favor of civil rights. But opposition from Democratic conservatives; the failure of Sen. Estes Kefauver's (D, Tenn.) [q.v.] campaign to stop Stevenson's bid; and Harriman's lack of rhetorical flair combined to block the New York Governor. Stevenson easily won the nomination on the first ballot.

After this defeat Harriman, despite his advancing age, still had hopes of receiving the Democratic presidential nomination. He regarded a successful 1958 gubernatorial reelection bid as a step towards a 1960 nomination. However, his campaign ran into serious difficulties. He and Party liberals hoped to nominate either former Air Force Secretary Thomas Finletter [q.v.] or Atomic Energy Commissioner Thomas Murray for U.S. senator, but DeSapio dominated the state convention in August and chose Manhattan District Attorney Frank Hogan [q.v.]. Therefore, during the campaign Harriman was vulnerable to the charge that the Democratic Party was boss-dominated. Furthermore, he had a formidable foe in Nelson A. Rockefeller [q.v.], the grandson of John D. Rockefeller. A liberal Republican and an outstanding campaigner with great wealth and talent at his disposal, Rockefeller won what was billed as a battle of millionaires.

In June 1959 Harriman visited the USSR and spoke at length with Soviet Premier Nikita S. Khrushchev. Harriman warned that the Soviets posed a serious threat to West Berlin. The following year he toured West Africa on behalf of Democratic presidential candidate Sen. John F. Kennedy (D, Mass.) [q.v.].

Harriman was assistant secretary of state for Far Eastern affairs from 1961 to 1963 and undersecretary of state for political affairs from 1963 to 1965. He negotiated the agreement neutralizing Laos in 1962 and the nuclear test ban treaty in 1963. Harriman served as ambassador at large from 1965 to 1968. In 1968 he headed the U.S. delegation at the Paris peace talks on Vietnam. During the Nixon Administration Harriman pressed for a complete withdrawal of Americans from Vietnam on a fixed schedule and in 1970 scored the Cambodian invasion as an unwarranted expansion of the war. In 1971 he urged Congress to use its power of the purse to end the conflict. [See KENNEDY, JOHNSON Volumes]

[MLL]

HARRIS, OREN
b. Dec. 20, 1903; Belton, Ark.
Democratic Representative, Ark.,
1941-66; Chairman, Interstate and
Foreign Commerce Committee, 1956-
66.

Oren Harris grew up in southern Arkansas. He graduated from Henderson State Teachers College in 1929, and, after a one-year law course at Cumberland University, he set up practice in El Dorado, Ark., a town whose economy was closely tied to the region's vast oil and natural gas industries. In 1940 Harris won election to the U.S. House of Representatives. He chaired a special 1952 House Commerce Committee investigation of television programs. Four years later Harris acquired a 25% interest in an El Dorado TV station.

Like most of his Dixie colleagues, Harris usually voted as a Democrat but always supported his sectional interests. He opposed the St. Lawrence Seaway project in May 1954 and the minimum wage increase in July 1955. He favored the Administration's foreign aid appropriations. According to *Congressional Quarterly*, Harris, who enjoyed close links to House Speaker Sam Rayburn (D, Tex.) [q.v.], tended to vote with the majority of his fellow Democrats through the 1950s. However, he generally opposed consumer legislation and civil rights measures. In 1956 Harris joined 100 other Southern members of Congress in signing the "Southern Manifesto," scoring the Supreme Court's decision in *Brown v. Board of Education*.

Through much of his House career, Harris closely identified himself with efforts to deregulate the oil and natural gas industry. Early in 1955 he and Sen. J. William Fulbright (D, Ark.) [q.v.] proposed a measure that would have exempted independent producers and gatherers of natural gas from the regulatory authority of the Federal Power Commission. Its waiver of price controls aroused determined opposition from Northern urban and consumer groups. Yet the legislation enjoyed White House and Southern Democratic support and passed both houses. In February 1956, however,

Eisenhower reluctantly vetoed the bill following the attempted bribery of Sen. Frances Case (R, S.D.) by a gas producer. Harris unsuccessfully resubmitted his natural gas bill in the 85th Congress.

Assuming the chairmanship of the House Commerce Committee in January 1957, Harris became embroiled in an investigation of the federal regulatory agencies. At the urging of Speaker Rayburn, the House agreed in 1957 to establish a Special Subcommittee on Legislative Oversight to examine the actions of the independent commissions. According to historian David Frier, Harris initially showed little interest in a detailed, critical inquiry because of his connections with the gas and TV industries. Instead, he selected the chairman, Rep. Morgan Moulder (D, Mo.), and chief counsel, Bernard Schwartz [q.v.], because he considered them "safe," cautious inquisitors. Just in case they proved otherwise, Harris attended the subcommittee sessions as an *ex-officio* member.

Schwartz, however, quickly upset Harris's well-laid plans. In leaks and official statements to the press in early 1958, Schwartz made detailed charges implicating high Administration figures in conflicts of interest. Harris first tried to discredit Schwartz. He suggested to reporters that the counsel had, like some of those he accused, overbilled the government on expenses. When that tactic failed, Harris persuaded the subcommittee to dismiss Schwartz and had his papers seized. Moulder thereupon resigned in protest, and Harris made himself chairman.

Schwartz's charges, however, appeared too serious to be dismissed outright. Subpoenaed as a witness, he elaborated on cases he had made against two members of the Federal Communications Commission (FCC), Richard Mack [q.v.] and John Doerfer [q.v.], and the President's chief aide, Sherman Adams [q.v.]. Aware of the extensive news coverage Schwartz's testimony had received, Rayburn demanded that Harris pursue the allegations. Harris dutifully pledged "the most thorough investigation Capitol Hill has ever seen." Following hearings in March 1958, Harris demanded and secured Mack's dismissal. (As a result of the probe, Doerfer resigned in 1960.)

In the summer of 1958 Harris's panel pursued rumors that Sherman Adams had interceded with the Federal Trade Commission and the Securities and Exchange Commission on behalf of Bernard Goldfine, [q.v.] who had given him gifts. At first Adams stymied the Goldfine investigation by invoking "executive privilege" and refusing to honor House subpoenas. But he soon relented and testified in June. To his detractors' surprise, Harris asked the key, incriminating questions. Adams acknowledged that he might have acted "more prudently" in inquiring of federal agencies about matters involving Goldfine. However, he said that it was "unwarranted and unfair" to charge that he had secured favored treatment for Goldfine from the agencies. Adams was forced to resign in September.

Another sensational offshoot of the Legislative Oversight panel's labors was its probe of the TV industry. Under its authority to investigate the FCC, the Harris subcommittee took testimony in the fall of 1959 from quiz show participants which revealed that the programs had been rigged. The extension of the inquiry into 1960 added to the mounting pressure on broadcasters for greater self-regulation.

Overall, the Legislative Oversight Subcommittee accomplished little. Although Adams and others fell from power, the panel failed to follow all of Schwartz's leads. Furthermore, administrative procedure code revisions enacted in 1959 and 1960 did not resolve the fundamental problems in regulating business.

During the 1960s Harris favored less government regulation by independent commissions and occasionally clashed with the Kennedy and Johnson Administrations over the issue. In July 1965 President Lyndon B. Johnson named Harris U.S. judge of the Eastern and Western Arkansas District, a post he had long coveted. He assumed office in February 1966. [See KENNEDY, JOHNSON Volumes]

[JLB]

For further information:
David A. Frier, *Conflict of Interest in the Eisenhower Administration* (Ames, Iowa, 1969).

HARRIS, REED
b. Nov. 5, 1909; New York, N.Y.
Deputy Administrator, International Information Administration, 1950-53.

After attending a military academy in Virginia, Harris entered Columbia University in 1928. He became editor of the school newspaper, *The Spectator*, which, under his direction, made a radical departure from its former conservative tradition. The paper attacked the "semi-professionalism" of the University's football team and supported a group of Columbia sociology students on a fact-finding mission in the Kentucky coal-mining region. His criticism of the University's food services prompted the college dean to expel him for a "long series of discourtesies, innuendos and misrepresentations." Harris's case because a *cause celebre* for liberals and journalists across America. The uproar over his expulsion compelled the University authorities to reinstate him, but he afterward dropped out of Columbia. Harris summarized his views on college sports in his book *King Football* (1932). In it he attacked such American institutions as the Daughters of the American Revolution and the American Legion. In 1931 Harris turned to freelance journalism, working for the *New York Times* and the *New York Evening Journal*. In 1934 he became assistant director of the Federal Writer's Projects and executive editor for the Federal Emergency Relief Administration.

From 1950 to 1953 Harris served as Deputy Administrator of the International Information Administration. While at that post he became embroiled in a dispute over the decision of the Voice of America (VOA) to discontinue Hebrew broadcasts to Israel. The move had been made for budgetary reasons. Nevertheless, before the order was issued, staff members asked Harris if the decision had been considered in the light of growing Communist anti-Semitism, a theme they hoped to exploit in the broadcasts. The decision was confirmed and the order issued in December 1952. However, as a result of opposition from Sidney Glazer, chief of the Hebrew Service of the VOA, Gerald Dooher, acting chief of the South Asian and

African Near East Service, and various members of Congress, the State Department reversed the move.

In February 1953 the Senate Internal Security Subcommittee, chaired by Sen. Joseph R. McCarthy (R, Wisc.) [q.v.], held hearings on Harris's decision. Using Dooher's testimony, McCarthy implied that Harris had aided the Communists through his action. The Chairman asked Dooher if he felt that "if Harris's order had been followed, [he] would have been performing a great service to the Communist cause?" McCarthy later asked Dooher if he felt this action would have been the same "if [Harris] had been representing Joe Stalin." In both cases Dooher answered yes. In another session, McCarthy queried Harris on his college record and his book, *King Football*, implying that the official had once had left-wing ties.

Harris contended that his plea for economy was backed by two other officials in the VOA who felt there were more effective ways of communicating with the Israeli people. He charged McCarthy with using "unfair tactics" in questioning him about his activities in college and swore he had never been a Communist. After the hearings he told the Senator, "It is my public neck you are skillfully trying to wring."

Harris resigned his post on April 1953. McCarthy called his departure "the best thing that has happened there in a very long time." Harris then founded Publications Services Inc., a firm used by agencies for processing information materials. Edward R. Murrow [q.v.] made Harris his executive assistant at the United States Information Agency in 1961. In 1966 Harris received the Edward R. Murrow Award for public diplomacy.

[ACD]

HARRIS, SEYMOUR E(DWIN)
b. Sept. 8, 1897; New York, N.Y.
Economist.

Following his graduation from Harvard University in 1920, Harris taught economics at Princeton. He returned to Harvard in 1922 as an instructor and obtained a doctorate there in 1926. Harris rose through the academic ranks, becoming a professor in 1945. During World War II he was a member of the Economic Welfare Policy Committee and served in the Office of Price Administration and on the War Production Board. Harris also advised several Latin American governments on fiscal matters.

During the postwar period Harris served on the advisory boards of several government commissions and wrote two books, *National Debt and the New Economic Policy* and *The New Economics* expounding Keynesian economic theory, both published in 1947. The economist also became interested in the problems of financing higher education. He recommended that college costs be borne primarily by tuition payments rather than tax dollars. In the 1950s Harris showed great concern about New England's declining textile industry. He denounced reduced tariffs on Japanese textile imports in 1954 and urged greater government-labor cooperation to solve the problems of the region.

In 1952 Harris served as an adviser to Democratic candidate Adlai Stevenson [q.v.], who had been his student at Princeton. Following his defeat Stevenson made Harris his fiscal policy adviser in preparation for a political comeback. From 1953 to 1956 Harris was a member of an informal advisory panel, known as the "Finletter Group," which met regularly to discuss issues and suggest positions the Democrats should take as members of "the loyal opposition."

During the Eisenhower Administration Harris was often called to testify on fiscal policy before congressional committees. He opposed the Republicans' emphasis on a balanced budget at the expense of full employment and social welfare. Harris also maintained that the President's policies put "excessive burdens on state and local governments." He did, however, support reductions in the defense budget. At hearings before the Senate Disarmament Subcommittee in March 1957, he agreed with Federal Reserve Board Chairman William McChesney Martin [q.v.] that a 50% cut in

U.S. military spending would not seriously damage the U.S. economy if business and government cooperated in a well planned readjustment program.

After Stevenson was defeated for the Democratic presidential nomination in 1960, Harris became John F. Kennedy's [q.v.] adviser. From 1961 to 1968 he was senior consultant to the Secretary of the Treasury. In 1964 Harris left Harvard to become chairman of the economics department of the University of California, San Diego.

[AES]

HARRISON, WILLIAM K(ELLY), JR.

b. Sept. 7, 1895; Washington, D.C.
Senior United Nations Delegate at the Panmunjom, Korea, Truce Meeting, May 1952-July 1953.

Harrison graduated from West Point in 1917 and served in France during World War I. He remained in Europe after the War, learning French and Spanish and returned to the U.S. in 1920 to teach at West Point. Over the next 20 years Harrison served in various assignments in the U.S. and the Philippines, rising steadily in rank; by 1942 he held the temporary rank of brigadier general. During World War II he commanded infantry in Europe and later served under Gen. Douglas MacArthur with the occupation troops in Japan. Harrison worked in the office of the Chief of Staff during 1949 and 1950. In January 1952 Gen. Matthew B. Ridgway [q.v.] placed Harrison, then deputy commander of the Eighth Army in Korea, on the Korean armistice delegation under the U.N. command. Harrison became chief U.N. delegate to the Korean truce negotiations in May of 1952.

By the time Harrison took command of the delegation, only the issue of the repatriation of prisoners of war (POWs) blocked the signing of an agreement. The U.N. forces refused to release prisoners who didn't want to return to North Korea or Communist China. The Communists, in turn, demanded the return of all prisoners and

claimed they would use force if necessary to secure them.

Throughout 1952 the talks remained deadlocked on the issue. In July 1952 Harrison attempted to circumvent the problem by suggesting that U.N. prisoners who refused repatriation simply be classified out of POW status. However, the Communists rejected the plan and countered with an offer to accept any 116,000 U.N.-held prisoners. Harrison rejected the proposal.

During the late summer and early fall, the negotiations were clouded further by uprisings at the U.N.'s Koje Island POW camp. When U.N. forces wounded and killed some Communist POW's in suppressing these riots, the Communists accused the U.N. of "persecuting and butchering" prisoners and of conducting a "bloody yet cowardly massacre." During that period they rejected three new POW-exchange plans advanced by Harrison, two of which suggested that a neutral commission decide the fate of prisoners who resisted repatriation. The talks were recessed indefinitely in October.

Finally, in March 1953, the Communists agreed to a U.N. proposal to exchange sick and wounded prisoners immediately, asked for a resumption of truce meetings and offered their own repatriation proposal. The exchange took place in mid-April. At that time Harrison began preparation for full-scale talks. In a letter to North Korean negotiator Gen. Nam Il, he expressed approval of the Communist proposal that POWs unwilling to return home be placed in the custody of a neutral nation. Harrison suggested that a traditionally neutral country like Switzerland assume charge of the prisoners in Korea so that they would not have to be sent out of the area. Finally, he recommended a 60-day period for questioning POWs after which the neutral custodian would determine the fate of those still unwilling to return.

The Communists initially rejected Harrison's three-stage proposal outright, but the threat of new recesses caused them to modify their stand. Nam dismissed the idea of Switzerland as a neutral custodian and proposed a five-nation commission composed of Czechoslovakia, Poland, Switzerland, Sweden and India. The eventual POW exchange agreement, signed on June 8, 1953, embodied the Communists' idea of a five-nation neutral commission and allowed 90 days for unwilling prisoners to be interviewed by the panel and by "persuasion delegates" from their respective nations. If any prisoners still would not return home after 90 days, a "major political conference" would decide their fate.

The Eisenhower Administration initially expressed unwillingness to comply with the agreement and sought to have the U.N. command release prisoners before the POW exchange began. However, adverse reaction from such world leaders as Indian Prime Minister Jawaharlal Nehru and British Prime Minister Winston Churchill forced Eisenhower to abandon this objective. South Korea also opposed the prisoner repatriation agreement and the armistice itself. On June 18 it released 25,000 Communist prisoners in defiance of the U.N. command. However, U.S. government pressure forced South Korea to accept the armistice.

After signing the agreement in July 27, Harrison returned to military duty. In April 1954 he was named commander of the new Army Caribbean Forces. He retired in February 1957. Harrison again emerged in the public eye during the 1960 presidential campaign. A fundamentalist Protestant lay preacher, he attended a September meeting that questioned whether a Catholic such as Democratic presidential candidate John F. Kennedy, [q.v.] should be President because he might be the target of pressure from the Pope.

[RJB]

HART, PHILIP A(LOYSIUS)
b. Dec. 10, 1912; Bryn Mawr, Pa.
d. Dec. 26, 1976; Washington D.C.
Democratic Senator, Mich., 1959-76.

Born into an Irish-Catholic family, Philip Hart was the son of a former landscape gardener who had worked his way up to the presidency of a small bank in suburban Philadelphia. Hart attended Georgetown University, where he roomed with the son of Walter O. Briggs, the Detroit auto-parts

millionaire and owner of the Detroit Tigers baseball team. He subsequently married his roommate's sister, who inherited a portion of the family's $100 million fortune. Hart received his law degree from the University of Michigan in 1937, and after military service in World War II, he established a legal practice in Detroit.

While in law school Hart had befriended G. Mennen ("Soapy") Williams [q.v.], the heir to the Mennen soap fortune and an enthusiastic supporter of the New Deal. In 1948 Williams fashioned an alliance of Democratic liberals and organized labor, which carried him to the governorship and inaugurated a period of social reform that lasted through the 1950s. During this period Williams steadily promoted Hart's political career, appointing him state corporation and securities commisioner in 1948. In 1952 Hart was named U.S. district attorney for the Eastern District of Michigan. In the latter post he secured the conviction of six Michigan Communist leaders for conspiracy to teach or advocate the violent overthrow of the government. In 1953 Hart became Williams's legal adviser and the following year made a successful bid for lieutenant governor with Williams's support. His reelection in 1956 made him the first Democrat to serve two terms in this office. In 1958 Hart was Williams's choice for the Senate nomination. Campaigning in favor of civil rights and tax reform, and with the strong backing of the state's labor unions, he beat the Republican incumbent with 53% of the vote.

As a freshman senator, Hart quickly earned a reputation as one of the most liberal members of the upper house. During the opening days of the 1959 session he joined a group of liberal insurgents in an unsuccessful attempt to ease Senate Rule 22—the so-called filibuster rule requiring the vote of two-thirds of the entire Senate membership to shut off debate—as a prelude to the enactment of civil rights legislation. Hart also took a firm stand against political censorship of the arts. When the American National Exhibition in Moscow was criticized because it included the works of artists who had been associated with alleged Communist-front organizations, Hart declared that "it is the Soviet Union which has lost face by attempting political censorship of its artists. We do not want to get ourselves into that situation."

In January 1960 Hart was one of about a dozen liberal insurgents who organized a challenge to Majority Leader Lyndon B. Johnson [q.v.] in the Senate Democratic Conference. Hart supported a motion aimed at stripping Johnson of his power to appoint members of the Democratic Policy Committee, which scheduled legislation for floor action, by making it an elective body. He also voted against a motion confirming Johnson's power to fill vacancies on the Democratic Steering Committee, which made Democratic committee assignments. The reformers were defeated on both issues.

In the 1960s Hart became a highly effective leader of the Democratic liberal bloc in the Senate, particularly on civil rights and consumer issues. During the Nixon Administration Hart's firm stands in favor of busing and handgun control aroused some of his constituents to mount unsuccessful recall campaigns in 1971 and 1972. Hart did not seek reelection in 1976 because he was suffering from cancer. He succumbed to the disease near the end of his third term in the Senate. [See KENNEDY, JOHNSON, NIXON/FORD Volumes]

[TLH]

HAUGE, GABRIEL
b. March 7, 1914; Hawley, Minn.
Administrative Assistant to the President for Domestic and Economic Affairs, 1953-56; Special Assistant to the President for Economic Affairs, 1956-58.

Gabriel Hauge graduated from Concordia College in 1935. Between 1935 and 1948 he taught economics at Harvard and Princeton, served in the Navy and worked for the Federal Reserve Bank. In 1948 he earned a Ph.D. in economics from Harvard. Through his Harvard professors Hauge came in contact with New York Gov. Thomas E. Dewey and became his economic adviser during the 1948 presidential campaign.

Hauge was research and statistics chief for the New York Banking Commission between 1947 and 1950 and an editor with *Business Week* from 1950 to 1952.

Early in 1952 Hauge joined Dwight D. Eisenhower's presidential campaign, emerging as one of its principal speech writers and editors. He proved to be among the more liberal members of the Eisenhower entourage. Historian Walter Johnson later called Hauge "the chief theoretician of Modern Republicanism." Especially critical of Sen. Joseph R. McCarthy (R, Wisc.) [q.v.], Hauge was among those staff members urging Eisenhower to separate himself from McCarthy and his anti-Communist crusade during the campaign.

With Eisenhower's election Hauge joined the White House staff as the President's personal economic adviser. With Arthur Flemming [q.v.] and investment banker James Brownlee, Hauge developed a plan for dismantling all government price controls within weeks of the inaugural. The plan would have ended controls gradually and on a commodity-by-commodity basis. Once he decided for deregulation, however, Eisenhower moved more swiftly. By the end of February 1953, he had lifted all controls. Hauge also defended and explained Administration policies before business and economic forums and sometimes drafted speeches for the President. In their respective memoirs Eisenhower looked to Hauge as a future leader of the GOP while presidential chief aide Sherman Adams [q.v.] declared Hauge to be a "much more important and valuable figure" within the Administration "than most people in Washington realized."

As a member of the Eisenhower team, Hauge joined fellow economist Arthur Burns [q.v.] in an ongoing Administration debate over fiscal policy. Burns, chairman of the Council of Economic Advisers, had been introduced to Eisenhower by Hauge (who judged his part in bringing Burns into the government to be "one of my most significant accomplishments"). Together they fought for a more flexible response to budget deficits than the policy approved by Secretary of the Treasury George Humphrey [q.v.]. Despite much rhetoric extolling a balanced budget, the Administration accepted Hauge's recommendation for limited deficit spending.

Hauge and Burns failed to convince Eisenhower to endorse an aid-to-depressed areas program which they had worked out in 1955. Three years later Secretary of the Treasury Robert B. Anderson [q.v.] opposed a tax cut offered by Hauge as an emergency anti-recession measure. Although Hauge enlisted Vice President Richard M. Nixon's [q.v.] support, Eisenhower sided with Anderson and blocked action.

Hauge left government in July 1958 to become finance chairman of the Manufacturers Trust Co. of New York. In an attempt to keep him in the capital, Eisenhower offered Hauge a cabinet secretaryship (unnamed, but probably Commerce). He refused the honor but did continue to consult with Eisenhower on the budget and Republican politics. In 1961 Hauge became vice chairman of the board of Manufacturers Hanover Trust Co. He became president in 1963 and board chairman in 1971.

[JLB]

HAYDEN, CARL T(RUMBULL)

b. Oct. 2, 1877: Hayden's Ferry, Ariz.
d. Jan. 25, 1972; Mesa, Ariz.
Democratic Senator, Ariz., 1927-69;
Chairman, Appropriations Committee, 1955-69.

Hayden was born in Hayden's Ferry, (now Tempe), Ariz., a town originally named in honor of his English immigrant family. After attending Stanford University from 1896 to 1900, he returned to Arizona to serve as a county treasurer and sheriff from 1904 to 1912. In 1912 he won election to the U.S. House of Representatives, where he led the fight to establish the Grand Canyon National Park and supported women's suffrage. Upon his election to the Senate in 1926, he began to win himself a reputation as a man who was "never . . . affected by the arrogance of power," in the words of the New York Times.

Hayden made few speeches during his 42 years in the Senate, but he wielded considerable power because of his seniority and his effectiveness in backstage legislative maneuvering. The people of Arizona regularly returned him to Congress because he continually proved himself a champion of water and land reclamation legislation vital to his arid state. During 1951 and 1952 Hayden, as chairman of the Rules Committee, led an investigation of Sen. Joseph R. McCarthy's (R, Wisc.) [q.v.] role in the 1950 Maryland elections. He supervised the drafting of its final report, a vague but critical examination of the Wisconsin Senator's conduct. [See TRUMAN Volume]

Throughout his career Hayden was a proponent of federal highway construction. Beginning with his sponsorship of the Hayden-Cartwright Act of 1934, he supported a coordinated national road network. Twenty-two years later Hayden coauthored the Federal Highway Aid Act of 1956. The measure called for the creation of over 42,000 miles of four-to-eight lane, controlled-access roads linking major urban areas. The system, scheduled to be completed by 1970, was 90% financed by the government. The project, only partially completed by its target date, had a profound effect on American life, increasing geographic mobility and facilitating communication.

One of Hayden's most important legislative achievements was his sponsorship of the Central Arizona Project (CAP), a plan to provide Colorado River water to Arizona. Through the years Hayden battled California representatives over rights to water, and in the early-1950s a CAP bill was passed in the Senate but rejected in the House. Hayden continued to lead the Arizona cause until 1968, when Congress passed the $1.3 billion Colorado River Project, from which $892 million was authorized for CAP.

Hayden was named dean of the Senate and served as its President Pro Tempore from 1957 to 1969. He was chairman of the powerful Appropriations Committee from 1955 to 1969 and in 1962 was involved in a feud with Rep. Clarence Cannon (D, Mo.)

that slowed government appropriations for months. He retired in 1969 and died in his home state in 1972. [See KENNEDY, JOHNSON Volumes]

[TGD]

HAYS, (LAWRENCE) BROOKS
b. Aug. 9, 1898; London, Ark.
Democratic Representative, Ark.,
1943-59.

After graduating from the University of Arkansas in 1919 and George Washington University law school three years later, Brooks Hays opened a law practice in Russellville, Ark. Hays served as assistant state attorney general from 1925 to 1927 and ran unsuccessfully for governor in 1928 and 1930. From 1936 to 1942 he held various posts in the Farm Security Administration. Hays won election to the House of Representatives from Arkansas's fifth district, which included Little Rock, in 1942.

On Capitol Hill Hays was one of a small group of Southern moderates who often joined Northern Democrats in supporting social welfare legislation. In 1949 and 1950 he unsuccessfully urged the adoption of a compromise civil rights plan in place of Truman's proposal. The plan called for the abolition of poll taxes by constitutional amendment, federal action against segregation in interstate travel and against lynching when a state failed to act and encouragement of fair employment practices.

Assigned to the Foreign Affairs Committee in 1951, Hays was an internationalist on most policy issues. He voted for Eisenhower's foreign aid bills in 1953 and 1954, and in 1957 he convinced the Committee to support an extension of the Administration's foreign aid authorization from one to three years. He also approved the 1957 Eisenhower Doctrine giving the President the power to use force to assist Middle Eastern nations threatened by Communist aggression. Hays was an outspoken champion of the U.N., describing it as the world's best hope for peace. In 1955 he served as a member of the U.S. delegation to the General Assembly.

During the 1950s Hays became em-broiled in the controversy stemming from the Supreme Court's 1954 decision outlawing segregation in public schools. A moderate on civil rights, he reluctantly signed the 1956 "Southern Manifesto" challenging the legal basis of forced school desegregation and pledging legal resistance to the "clear abuse of judicial power."

In September 1957, when Gov. Orval Faubus [q.v.] used the Arkansas National Guard to prevent court-ordered desegregation of Little Rock's Central High School, Hays attempted to arbitrate the deadlock. He arranged a meeting on Sept. 14 between President Eisenhower and Faubus in hopes of arriving at a compromise solution, but the conference ended inconclusively. Ten days later Eisenhower took command of the National Guard and dispatched 1,000 armed paratroopers to ensure that desegregation would be carried out peacefully.

In the months that followed the Little Rock crisis, Hays's moderate position, calling for compliance with all laws, no matter how unpopular, became increasingly untenable. Race relations deteriorated and segregationist sentiment hardened. In 1958 Hays was challenged for reelection by arch-segregationist Dale Alford, whom Faubus had persuaded to mount a write-in campaign against the Congressman. After campaigning only one week, Alford defeated Hays.

After losing his seat Hays was appointed a director of the Tennessee Valley Authority. He served there until February 1961, when he was appointed assistant secretary of state for congressional affairs. From December 1961 to February 1964, Hays was a special assistant to the President. During the last part of the decade, he taught at various universities.

[MJS]

HAYS, WAYNE L(EVERE)
b. May 13, 1911; Bannock, Ohio.
Democratic Representative, Ohio,
1949-76.

The son of a farmer, Hays graduated from Ohio State University in 1933. After studying in the pre-law program at Duke

University for two years, he became a high school teacher in Flushing, Ohio. In 1939 Hays was elected to the first of three consecutive two-year terms as mayor of Flushing. While mayor he also began serving a term in the state Senate in 1941. Two days after Pearl Harbor Hays enlisted in the Army and was honorably discharged the following year. In 1945 he left his mayoral post to operate a dairy farm. Three years later Hays was elected to the U.S. House of Representatives from a poor agricultural and industrial district in southeastern Ohio. He was a supporter of President Harry S. Truman's foreign policies and voted for the Internal Security Act of 1950. Hays also consistently backed the Administration's social welfare programs.

In 1953 Hays was appointed to the newly created Select Committee to Investigate Tax-Exempt Foundations. The panel, established to determine whether tax-exempt educational and philanthropic foundations had financed subversive activities and propaganda, held hearings during May and June 1954. They were marked by frequent clashes between chairman B. Carroll Reece (R, Tenn.) and Hays, who believed that witnesses and Committee staff members were unfairly charging individuals and institutions with Communist views and affiliations. Attempting to demonstrate that out-of-context quotations could be used to suggest Communist sympathies, he read excerpts from encyclicals by Popes Leo XIII and Pius XI without attribution and induced a staff member to assert that they were "closely comparable to Communist literature." He demanded that the investigation be extended to include Facts Forum, a tax-exempt, right-wing radio and television production company funded by Texas oil millionaire H. L. Hunt. Hays charged that programs produced by Facts Forum engaged in "discrediting liberals in general . . . and lumping them with Socialists, Communists and totalitarians."

The Committee's majority report said there was little evidence that the foundations directly supported Communism. However, it asserted that they encouraged attacks on the American social and governmental system and promoted collectivist ideas. Hays and Rep. Gracie Pfost (D, Ida.), the other Democrat on the panel, filed a minority report charging that the "theme of prejudgment . . . characterized the entire course of this Committee's activities" and that with few exceptions only anti-foundation witnesses had been called.

Generally a liberal on domestic policy issues, Hays unsuccessfully tried to double the authorization for urban and public-works planning in the 1954 omnibus housing bill. Two years later he attacked a modest Administration program to create a $50 million revolving loan fund for depressed rural areas. Hays stated that the plan showed "no understanding of the social devastation which is wreaked by these chronic unemployment areas. . . ." In 1957 he was among 80 House Democrats who offered a list of liberal domestic and foreign policy programs for congressional action. He favored economic rather than military assistance to underdeveloped areas, "where the people do not want guns, where the guns will not maintain the regime in power."

In the 1960s Hays broke with many of his liberal colleagues over the Vietnam war, which he supported, and school busing for integration, which he opposed. As Hays accumulated seniority on the House Administration Committee, he was increasingly resented as an arrogant and abrasive representative who used his power over the budgets of other committees to retaliate against congressmen he disliked or disagreed with. The resentment grew after he became chairman of the Committee in 1971. Five years later he became involved in a sex-payroll scandal and resigned first his chairmanship and then his House seat. [See JOHNSON, NIXON/FORD Volumes]

[MLL]

HEBERT, F(ELIX) EDWARD
b. Oct. 12, 1901: New Orleans, La.
Democratic Representative, La., 1941-77.

In 1919 Hebert began a 21-year journalistic career in New Orleans. He attended Tulane University from 1920 to 1924 but did not complete the required work for his law degree. In 1937 he became city editor of the *New Orleans States,* and two years later he wrote a series of articles exposing corruption in Louisiana state politics that resulted in the imprisonment of businessmen and high-ranking government officials. In 1940 Hebert won a U.S. House seat from the state's first district, consisting of eight wards in New Orleans plus Plaquemines and St. Bernard's Parishes.

In 1943 Hebert was assigned to the Naval Affairs Committee, which in 1947 was merged with the other service panels to form the Armed Services Committee. A staunch defender of segregation and opponent of what he regarded as federal encroachment upon the rights of the states, he supported South Carolina Gov. Strom Thurmond's [*q.v.*] third party presidential candidacy in 1948. That year Hebert was assigned to the Un-American Activities Committee, but he lost his seat the following year as a result of his support of Thurmond. As chairman of the Armed Services Committee's Subcommittee for Special Investigations, in 1949, 1951 and 1952, he led probes of wasteful procurement procedures in the military. [See TRUMAN Volume]

Hebert continued to oppose what he regarded as unnecessary defense expenditures during the Eisenhower Administration. In 1956 he opposed an Administration-sponsored reorganization of the Defense Department that would have created the office of assistant secretary for research and development for each of the three services.

Despite his crusades against waste, Hebert was a leading advocate of a strong military establishment. A critic of Eisenhower Administration efforts to reduce the manpower of the Armed Services, in 1959 he attacked Secretary of Defense Neil McElroy [*q.v.*] for imposing a "gag" on military officers who were against the cutbacks. That year he opposed the Administration's wishes in voting to provide an additional $99 million to maintain the Army's strength at 900,000 men.

In 1959 Hebert's Subcommittee on Special Investigations probed the hiring of retired military officers by the defense industry. Critics of the practice charged that

such officers exerted influence upon their former colleagues still in the military. In January 1960 the subcommittee released a report supporting legislation to check this syndrome. Hebert offered a bill barring military and civilian Defense Department personnel from accepting compensation for helping a private company secure a government defense contract within two years after their departure from the Department. The measure imposed a $10,000 fine, two years imprisonment and denial of retirement pay during the period of violation for those found guilty. In the full Armed Services Committee, however, chairman Carl Vinson (D, Ga.) [*q.v.*] succeeded in eliminating the fine and imprisonment provisions. Hebert unsuccessfully attempted to restore them on the House floor. The measure died in the Senate.

Hebert was a consistent opponent of civil rights and social welfare legislation. According to *Congressional Quarterly,* in the 1959-61 sessions he voted with the Southern Democrat-Republican conservative coalition on 53% of key roll-call votes while opposing it on only 3% of such votes.

During the Kennedy and Johnson Administrations Hebert maintained his conservative stance on domestic issues and backed American participation in the Vietnam war. In 1971 he became chairman of the Armed Services Committee, but five years later the House Democratic caucus voted to oust him from the chairmanship. Hebert declined to seek reelection in 1976. [See KENNEDY, JOHNSON, NIXON/FORD Volumes]

[MLL]

HENNINGS, THOMAS C(AREY), JR.

b. June 25, 1903; St. Louis, Mo.
d. Sept. 13, 1960; Washington, D.C.
Democratic Senator, Mo., 1951-60; Chairman, Rules and Administration Committee, 1957-60.

Hennings received a B.A. degree from Cornell University in 1924 and an LL.B. degree from Washington University law school in 1926. He entered a St. Louis law firm the same year, and from 1929 to 1934, he served as assistant circuit attorney in that city. Elected to the U.S. House of Representatives in 1934, he supported Franklin D. Roosevelt's domestic and foreign policies. In 1940 Hennings successfully ran for circuit attorney in St. Louis, but the following year he was called from the U.S. Naval Reserve to active duty. After his discharge in 1944 he resumed his post as circuit attorney.

In 1950 Hennings ran for the Senate against incumbent Republican Sen. Forrest C. Donnell. During the campaign he warned that Sen. Joseph R. McCarthy's (R, Wisc.) [q.v.] activities posed a threat to freedom. Hennings defeated the incumbent by 90,000 votes.

During his early years in the Senate, Hennings continued his campaign against the Wisconsin Republican. He served on the Rules and Administration Committee's Subcommittee on Privileges and Elections which considered a resolution to expel McCarthy from the Senate in 1951. In the course of the investigation, Hennings clashed with McCarthy, accusing him of using distortion and deceit to divert attention from the probe. [See TRUMAN Volume]

In July 1953 Hennings denounced the removal of books from United States Information Agency libraries under pressure from McCarthy. Expressing gratitude that the works of Missouri's Mark Twain had not been taken off the shelves, Hennings described the matter as a "literary comedy." He also criticized Secretary of State John Foster Dulles [q.v.] for his Department's indecisiveness in establishing standards of suitability for books in overseas libraries.

In July 1954 Hennings backed Sen. Ralph E. Flanders's (R, Vt.) [q.v.] resolution calling for McCarthy's censure. Wanting an immediate showdown and fearing that the resolution might be buried, Hennings was one of 12 senators who in August voted against referring it to a special panel.

After McCarthy's censure in December 1954, Hennings continued to oppose what he regarded as threats to civil liberties. Late in 1955 the Judiciary Committee's Constitutional Rights Subcommittee,

chaired by Hennings, began an investigation of the possible erosion of freedom in the United States, which included a critical examination of the federal government's loyalty program. The following year, as a member of the Internal Security Subcommittee of the Judiciary Committee, he was critical of the security panel's investigation of Communist influence in the press. Hennings expressed doubts about the propriety of calling individuals whose Communist activities had ended many years before. In 1958 he moved to table a House-passed bill that would have barred federal courts from applying the federal preemption doctrine unless a federal and state statute were irreconcilably in conflict or unless Congress had specifically stated its intention to preempt a particular field of legislation. The immediate purpose of the bill was to enable states to pass anti-sedition laws. Hennings's motion failed, but a recommital motion succeeded shortly thereafter.

Hennings was a persistent but unsuccessful proponent of election reform. As a member of the Rules and Administration Committee, in 1953 and 1955 he led efforts to pass legislation raising spending limits for national campaigns and tightening disclosure requirements. Neither attempt got beyond the Committee. Hennings became chairman of the Rules and Administration Committee in 1957, and two years later the panel reported another reform measure. In an individual view filed with the Committee's report, he criticized the bill for failing to bring primary elections within the scope of the reporting requirement. On the Senate floor the following year, Hennings successfully amended the bill to include primaries.

Consistently liberal in his voting, Hennings opposed a 1956 natural gas bill to exempt independent producers from federal utility regulation, declaring that consumers could not be protected "by regulating one or two parts of a monopolistic system and leaving the other parts unregulated." On the Judiciary Committee he sought to expedite Senate consideration of the Eisenhower Administration's civil rights bill in 1957 and opposed Southern efforts to weaken the measure. In 1960 Hennings cosponsored Sen. Pat McNamara's (D, Mich.) [q.v.] bill to provide medical care for the aged within the Social Security system. Hennings died in Washington, D.C., on Sept. 13, 1960.

[MLL]

HENSEL, H(ERMAN) STRUVE
b. Aug. 22, 1901; Tenafly, N.J.
Assistant Secretary of Defense for International Security Affairs, February 1954-May 1955.

The son of a stockbroker, Hensel graduated from Princeton in 1922 and received an LL.B. from Columbia three years later. During the 1930s he established a reputation as a leading corporate lawyer in New York. With the outbreak of World War II, he went to Washington as a legal adviser to the Navy. Hensel was appointed an assistant secretary of the Navy in 1945 with the responsibility for procurement of naval material. After a brief return to private law practice, he joined the Economic Cooperation Administration in 1948 and was sent to South America to enlist the cooperation of Argentina in the Marshall Plan.

In 1952 Hensel went to work for the Defense Department as general counsel. In 1954 he was made assistant secretary of defense for international security affairs. Shortly after the appointment he was drawn into the dispute between the Army and Sen. Joseph R. McCarthy (R, Wisc.) [q.v.]. Early in the year high officials in the Department of the Army began drawing up a "chronology" of McCarthy's efforts to gain preferential treatment for a recently inducted member of his staff, G. David Schine [q.v.]. According to historian Robert Griffith, Hensel's only role in the preparation of the Army's case was to sign a letter of transmittal forwarding the chronology to a member of McCarthy's Permanent Investigations Subcommittee. However, McCarthy charged that Hensel had helped write it in an attempt to "blackmail" him into calling off his investigations of alleged

subversion in the military. In formal charges to this effect, filed with the subcommittee in April, McCarthy named Hensel as a co-principal along with Secretary of the Army Robert T. Stevens [q.v.] and Army counsel John G. Adams [q.v.]. At the same time McCarthy added the charge that Hensel had a personal motive for discrediting him: to block an investigation of alleged conflict of interest involving Hensel's partnership in a ship supply firm while he was in charge of procurement for the Navy during the War. Hensel labeled these charges "barefaced lies" and challenged McCarthy to drop his congressional immunity and repeat them in court.

Hensel was never called to testify at the subcommittee hearings. On May 17 McCarthy admitted that he had no evidence to show that Hensel had been involved in the Schine affair. Shortly afterwards the subcommittee dismissed the charges against him. In 1955 Hensel left the Defense Department and returned to private law.

[TLH]

HERBERG, WILL
b. Aug. 4, 1909; New York, N.Y.
d. March 27, 1977; Chatham, N.J.
Philosopher, theologian.

The son of Russian-Jewish parents, Herberg was a brilliant and disciplined student. He knew six languages while still a teenager. Herberg earned a B.A. from Columbia in 1928, an M.A. in 1930 and a Ph.D. two years later. During the 1920s he was a prominent American Communist, but when the American Communist Party split in 1929 over the issue of autonomy from the Soviet Party, Herberg joined the Lovestoneites who advocated an independent course. He then wrote for the Lovestoneite publication *Workers Age*. A versatile scholar, he could also engage in protracted debate with other intellectuals over Marxist interpretations of literature, art and religion. In 1935 he became the educational director of the International Ladies Garment Workers

Union, a post he held until 1948. Unlike many other Marxists he had kind words for some New Deal programs, particularly those that advanced social welfare. His early experience with labor led him to believe that the American working class was not prepared to assert itself in a revolutionary movement.

By 1940 Herberg had become disenchanted with Marxism and horrified by the evolution of Stalinism in the USSR. Throughout the 1940's he considered himself a political liberal. His initial response to U.S. involvement in World War II was vigorously pacifist, but he later withdrew into silence. The philosopher who once embraced Communism as his only religion now repudiated it as a relativistic doctrine lacking true spiritual values. Previously an atheist, Herberg became a prophet of universal irony and existentialism who, in 1947, announced his commitment to Judaism. He joined other existential theologians like Martin Buber in his belief that humankind, after confronting its crisis of identity in a depersonalized contemporary world, must ultimately turn to faith in God. Herberg elaborated his beliefs in his first book, *Judaism and Modern Man*, published in 1951. No more, he said, could humankind look to science for explanations of its existence. He believed that humankind could "transcend" its spiritual crisis only by making the great "leap of faith" toward a God not understandable through science or cognitive experience.

Herberg continued to be a prominent philosopher with a loyal readership, but his spiritual and intellectual journeys were troubled. In 1955 he published *Protestant, Catholic, Jew: An Essay on American Religious Sociology*. At that time the U.S. was experiencing an apparent revival in organized religion, as evidenced by substantially increased church attendance and the prominence of such religious popularizers as Fulton Sheen [q.v.], Norman Vincent Peale [q.v.] and Billy Graham [q.v.]. But Herberg analyzed the religious trend as one toward a secularized, "pop" spiritualism based on "faith in faith itself" rather than as a movement founded upon deeply held values. He particularly questioned the tendency of individual Americans and their

leaders—including President Eisenhower —to amalgamate their religion with a faith in America's political destiny. Herberg held that such a superficial religion was sure to dissipate in fast-paced, socially mobile America. Contemporary humans, he was coming to believe, were not able to overcome their existential crisis with faith in transcendent, timeless values alone; they needed the support of a system of beliefs tested by history and human experience.

During the active years of the Cold War, however, Herberg found his theological pronouncements at odds with some of his political rhetoric. Like ex-Communist Whittaker Chambers [q.v.], he saw the battle of the free world versus Communism as the "struggle for the soul of modern man." Like religious leaders he had criticized, he was willing to advance theological arguments in a political cause.

Herberg, though obviously anti-Communist, strongly disliked Sen. Joseph R. McCarthy (R, Wisc.) [q.v.], but not for the conventional reason of the Senator's abuse of civil liberties. To Herberg, McCarthy was an outgrowth of left-wing populism, of a "government by rabble-rousing" that had made great strides during the tenure of President Franklin Roosevelt. McCarthy's popularity demonstrated the evils of "irresponsible mass democracy," he felt. Herberg's criticism represented, in the words of historian George Nash, American conservatives' "aloofness from the masses."

By the early-1960s Herberg was clearly identified as a political and philosophical conservative. Since 1955 he had served as a graduate professor at Drew University, a Methodist-oriented school in New Jersey. In 1961 he became a contributing editor to William F. Buckley's [q.v.] *National Review*, which served as his primary journalistic forum for the next 15 years. Herberg, strongly committed to social order, opposed the civil rights movement led by Martin Luther King, Jr. [q.v.], though he softened his views in the 1970's. He criticized the liberalizing tendencies of Pope John XXIII as damaging to spiritual fiber and beneficial to the Communist movement. While others saw the 1960s counterculture "hippie" movement as a new spiritual force, he believed it to be basically empty of lasting values and self-indulgent. Herberg continued to be a spokesman for conservative causes until his illness and death in 1977.

[TGD]

For further information:
John P. Diggins, *Up from Communism* (New York, 1975).

HERTER, CHRISTIAN A(RCHIBALD)
b. March 28, 1895; Paris, France.
d. Dec. 30, 1966; Washington, D.C.
Governor, Mass., 1953-57; Undersecretary of State, February, 1957-April 1959; Secretary of State, April 1959-January 1961.

The son of expatriate American artists, Adele and Albert Herter, Christian Herter was born in Paris. After receiving his primary education there, he went to the Browning School in New York and in 1915 graduated from Harvard. Herter entered Columbia University's School of Architecture but left in 1916 to join the Foreign Service. He was assigned to the American embassy in Berlin. In 1918 Herter was a member of the U.S. delegation to Versailles and served on the special commission that negotiated a prisoner of war agreement with the Germans. The following year he helped Herbert Hoover [q.v.] supervise the American Relief Administration. When Hoover became Secretary of Commerce in 1921, he asked Herter to be his assistant. Herter held this post until 1924, when he left government service to become editor of *The Independent* and *The Sportsman*. He also lectured on international relations at Harvard.

A Republican, Herter sat in the Massachusetts House of Representatives from 1930 to 1942; for the last four of those years, he was Speaker of the House. In 1942 he won a U.S. House seat, which he held for 10 years. A member of the internationalist wing of the Republican Party, he supported the creation of the United Nations and the development of the Marshall Plan.

In 1952 Herter successfully ran for governor of Massachusetts. In the state house he presented a liberal program establishing a state department of commerce, introducing a public housing program and increasing aid to the elderly. Herter was reelected in 1954. However, the Republicans lost control of the lower house of the General Court, preventing the enactment of the Governor's proposed judicial reorganization.

In 1956 liberal Republicans, led by Harold Stassen [q.v.], proposed Gov. Herter replace Richard Nixon [q.v.] as the Party's vice presidential candidate. However, Herter headed off this campaign when he decided to deliver the speech nominating Nixon at the Convention. *The New York Times* maintained that Herter was promised the post of undersecretary of state for bowing out of the race. Secretary of State John Foster Dulles [q.v.] wanted to appoint another man to that post and attempted to convince Herter to accept the lower position of assistant secretary of state. However, Nixon persuaded Eisenhower to insist on the original appointment. Once in the State Department Herter quickly developed a close relationship with Dulles, often standing in for the statesman, who was dying of cancer. Dulles personally designated Herter his successor.

Herter assumed the office of Secretary of State in April 1959. Characterized as an impeccable patrician, Herter was known for his gentleness and inner toughness. Cruelly bent by arthritis, he was frequently seen stooped over crutches. Although initial relations between Eisenhower and Herter were cool and some suggested Herter's appointment had been made only to please Dulles, the Secretary soon gained Eisenhower's confidence. However, he never wielded the power Dulles had used. During his first year in office, many of his duties were of a ceremonial nature, accompanying the President on trips and standing by to advise.

Herter's first major problem as Secretary was to coordinate the Allied response to Soviet Premier Nikita S. Khrushchev's November 1958 demand that the Western Allies withdraw their troops from West Berlin in six months and make it a "free city." In April 1959 Herter attended a Paris conference at which he mediated conflicting policies on the issue. At the end of the meeting the Western foreign ministers announced they were in complete agreement on strategy to be presented at a May conference with the Soviet Union in Geneva. The plan called for a four-stage "permanent settlement in Europe": stage 1—the unification of East and West Berlin through free elections; stage 2—the establishment of a "mixed" German committee to expand technical contacts between the two Germanys; stage 3—the election of an all-German assembly to establish a "liberal, democratic and federative system" in Germany; stage 4—the recognition of a unified Germany. The conference, held in May and again in August, resulted in a deadlock on the issue.

Herter was also rebuffed in Administration attempts to negotiate a disarmament treaty with the Soviet Union. In a speech before the National Press Club in Washington in March 1960, he outlined the U.S. disarmament program. The plan called for disarmament under the supervision of an international controls panel and for the establishment of talks beginning on the technical level and leading to the eventual reduction of military forces. However, throughout the remainder of the Eisenhower Administration, the Soviet Union refused to accept the proposal because of its provision for on-site inspection of missile stations and atomic installations.

On May 5, 1960, just before the scheduled East-West Summit Conference, Khrushchev announced that the Soviet Union had downed an American U-2 plane on a reconnaisance mission over the USSR. The Administration initially denied the charge. However, Herter argued that Washington should accept responsibility for the flights with an explanation of why they were needed. On May 7 the State Department admitted that a flight over Soviet territory had been made by an "unarmed civilian U-2." Two days later Herter defended the missions and indicated that they would continue to prevent possible Communist aggression. With the U-2 incident still in the headlines, Herter left on May 12 for Geneva to prepare for the meeting between

Eisenhower, Khrushchev and British Prime Minister Harold Macmillan. The Summit collapsed five days later, when Khrushchev demanded that Eisenhower apologize for the U-2 flight.

Worsening relations with Cuba plagued Herter during his last year in office. In response to Cuban Premier Fidel Castro's virulent attacks against the U.S. and his decision to confiscate American property, Herter urged a policy of restraint. Eisenhower accepted the recommendation, promising in January 1960 that there would be no reprisals for Castro's actions. However, in August, after Castro began to accept Soviet weapons, Herter obtained a resolution from the Organization of American States censuring the dictator.

With the coming of the Kennedy Administration, Herter resigned his post and retired from public life. In November 1962 President John F. Kennedy named Herter chief planner and negotiator on foreign trade. His main duty was to head talks with the European Economic Community as a special representative of the President. He remained in this post until his death in December 1966.

[JB]

For further information:
Bernard Noble. *Christian A. Herter* (New York, 1970).

HICKENLOOPER, BOURKE B(LAKEMORE)

b. July 21, 1896; Blockton, Iowa
d. Sept. 4, 1971; Shelter Island, N.Y.
Republican Senator, Iowa, 1945-69.

A Cedar Rapids lawyer of Dutch ancestry, Hickenlooper began his political career in the Iowa state legislature. He was elected governor in 1942 and two years later defeated the Democratic incumbent to win a seat in the U.S. Senate. In Congress Hickenlooper stood with the right wing of the Republican Party, voting against social welfare legislation and supporting Sen. Joseph McCarthy's (R, Wisc.) [*q.v.*] anti-Communist crusade. In December 1954 he voted against the Senate's censure of

McCarthy. Reflecting the two major concerns of conservative cornbelt constituents in the postwar period—international Communism and farm prices—Hickenlooper served on the Foreign Relations and the Agriculture and Forestry Committees.

Like many Republicans, Hickenlooper interpreted the Eisenhower victory in 1952 as a mandate to repudiate the 1945 Yalta and Potsdam agreements, which had recognized the primacy of Soviet interests in areas bordering the USSR. When Eisenhower submitted a foreign policy resolution to the Senate in February 1953 condemning the wartime agreements but stopping short of actually disavowing them, Hickenlooper and other Republican members of the Foreign Relations Committee expressed their disappointment. They offered an amendment to the resolution stipulating that the U.S. could regard agreements violated by the Soviets as strictly temporary. However, with the news of Stalin's death in March, Secretary of State John Foster Dulles [q.v.] persuaded the senators to postpone further action in view of the uncertain course of Soviet policy. In another clash with the Administration in 1953, Hickenlooper joined 10 other Republican senators in voting against the confirmation of Charles E. Bohlen [q.v.] as ambassador to the USSR. Hickenlooper branded him a "Yalta man" and a typical representative of the Roosevelt-Truman regime in the State Department.

Hickenlooper became chairman of the Joint Congressional Committee on Atomic Energy in 1949. In 1954 he cosponsored a major bill that amended the Atomic Energy Act of 1946 to provide for exchange of information on military uses of atomic energy with international regional defense organizations. It also authorized private industry to initiate a program of peaceful atomic energy use, primarily in the generation of electric power from nuclear materials.

Despite his earlier reservations about Eisenhower's foreign policy, Hickenlooper emerged as one of the Administration's most consistent supporters in the Senate. As representative of a heavily agricultural state dependent on corn and hay prices, he favored high price supports on these commodities, but he backed the Administration's policy of flexible rather than rigid supports. Hickenlooper voted for most of the civil rights legislation of the late-1950s and opposed domestic welfare programs.

During the 1960s Hickenlooper rejected such liberal programs as aid to education, medicare and the War on Poverty. He added a controversial amendment to the 1962 foreign aid bill, providing for the automatic denial of American aid to a foreign country that expropriated the property of U.S. citizens without adequate compensation. In 1967 he helped pass a heatedly debated consular treaty with the USSR. Hickenlooper retired from the Senate in 1969 and died two years later. [See KENNEDY, JOHNSON Volumes]

[TLH]

HILL, LISTER
b. Dec. 29, 1894; Montgomery, Ala.
Democratic Senator, Ala., 1938-69;
Chairman, Labor and Welfare
Committee, 1955-69.

The son of a nationally prominent surgeon, Hill was born into a family that dominated Montgomery, Ala., politics. After serving as president of the Montgomery Board of Education from 1917 to 1922, he won a special election in 1923 for a vacant seat in the U.S. House of Representatives. There he became a staunch supporter of New Deal programs, especially the Tennessee Valley Authority (TVA), which played a significant role in the economic development of northern Alabama. Hill ran for the Senate as an ally of President Roosevelt in 1937, a low point in the New Deal's popularity. Gaining urban and labor support, he defeated his right-wing opponent. In the Senate he worked for medical and mental health legislation. His most important accomplishment was the Hill-Burton Act of 1946, which provided federal grants for hospital construction. [See TRUMAN Volume]

Health and medical legislation remained Hill's dominant concern during the Eisenhower Administration. His ability to influence health programs was enhanced when he became chairman of the Senate Labor and Welfare Committee in 1955. He also served as chairman of the Appropriations Committee's Subcommittee for Health and Welfare Agencies. In May 1955 Hill introduced a bill to provide free distribution of the newly discovered Salk polio vaccine to all children in the U.S. The American Medical Association (AMA) opposed the measure, which Health, Education and Welfare Secretary Oveta Culp Hobby [q.v.] said would lead to "socialized medicine by the back door." Instead, the AMA supported an Administration proposal to give free vaccine to needy children. The Senate Labor and Public Welfare Committee killed the Administration bill and reported Hill's version instead. Eisenhower signed the measure in August. Hill also sponsored successful amendments to the 1956 Health, Education and Welfare appropriation for additional money for the National Institute of Health and for nurses training. In 1959 he introduced a "health for peace" bill, passed the following year, that provided funds for international cooperation in medical research.

During the 1950s Hill remained an advocate of public rather than private resource and power development. In 1953 he opposed the Administration's proposal to grant oil-rich submerged coastal lands to the states because he believed that private oil companies would be the main beneficiaries. In January he participated in a 28-day liberal filibuster against the Administration's bill. Hill supported a measure, introduced by Sen. Clinton Anderson (D, N.M.) [q.v.], calling for federal control of submerged lands beyond the three-mile limit. He also introduced an amendment to Anderson's proposal to set aside all federal revenue from offshore oil for national defense and education. Anderson's bill, however, was defeated in April 1953.

Hill also opposed the 1954 Dixon-Yates contract. Edgar Dixon [q.v.] and Eugene Yates, presidents of Southern utilities, had been given a government contract by the Atomic Energy Commission (AEC) to build a steam plant near Memphis, Tenn. The plant would have supplied power to the TVA for use in the Memphis area. Hill

charged that Dixon and Yates were being hired by the government "as hatchet men to destroy TVA." In February 1955 he was appointed head of an Appropriations Committee subcommittee to handle AEC-TVA funds. During hearings that month Hill disclosed that Adolphe Wenzell, a Bureau of the Budget consultant, was a vice president and director of the First Boston Corporation, the company which was to finance the Dixon-Yates combine. Hill accused Wenzell of conflict of interest and denounced Budget Director Rowland Hughes [q.v.] for concealing the connection. Hughes acknowledged that Wenzell had participated in contract talks but denied any concealment. That same month Memphis officials announced they intended to build a power plant, obviating the necessity for the private plant. Eisenhower canceled the Dixon-Yates contract in July.

Hill supported most liberal domestic legislation but joined his Southern colleagues in opposing civil rights measures. Along with 100 other Southern members of Congress he signed the "Southern Manifesto," presented to Congress in March 1956. The document criticized the Supreme Court's 1954 school integration decision as "a clear abuse of judicial power" that substituted "personal political and social ideas for the established law of the land." Hill voted against the Civil Rights Acts of 1957 and 1960.

Hill's voting record grew increasingly conservative after 1962, when he nearly lost his seat to a conservative Republican. Although he continued to work for health legislation and maintained his support for social welfare programs designed to aid rural areas, he voted against most urban social programs and continued to oppose civil rights legislation. In 1968, at the age of 73, Hill declined to run for reelection. [See KENNEDY, JOHNSON Volumes]

[MBD]

For further information:
Numan V. Bartley and Hugh D. Graham, *Southern Politics and the Second Reconstruction* (Baltimore, 1975).
William S. White, "Medicine Man from Alabama," *Harpers Magazine*, 219 (November, 1959), 90-94.

HILL, ROBERT C(HARLES)
b. Sept. 17, 1917; Littleton, N.H.
Ambassador to Costa Rica, October
1953-December 1954; Ambassador to El
Salvador, December 1954-September
1955; Special Assistant to the Undersecretary of State for Mutual Security
Affairs, September 1955-March 1956;
Assistant Secretary of State for Congressional Relations, March 1956-May
1957; Ambassador to Mexico, May
1957-January 1961.

The son of a physician, Hill graduated
from Dartmouth College in 1942. He then
worked as a junior executive for the Todd
Shipbuilding Corp. and went to Washington, D.C., as the company's representative. In 1943 Hill joined the State Department as an officer of the Foreign Service
Auxiliary and served as a vice-consul in various posts in the China, Burma, India theater. After the World War II Hill briefly
studied law at Boston University but left in
1947 to become a law clerk to the Senate
Banking and Currency Committee. Returning to the private sector in 1949, he joined
W.R. Grace and Co., which operated sea
and air transportation in Latin America.

In October 1953 Eisenhower appointed
Hill ambassador to Costa Rica. While in
that country he was an official "observer" in
the negotiation of a contract between Costa
Rica and the powerful, American based
United Fruit Company. The youngest ambassador in American history, Hill served
there for only about a year before being
transferred to El Salvador. During his stay
in Latin America he traveled extensively to
familiarize himself with the problems of the
population. In September 1955 Hill was
named special assistant to Herbert Hoover,
Jr. [q.v.], the undersecretary of state for
mutual security affairs. Confirmed in October, he spent the next five months coordinating foreign aid programs and developing and presenting to Congress legislative
proposals for the mutual security program.
The young diplomat specialized in aid to
Third World nations. As a result of his successful dealings with Congress, Hill was
promoted to assistant secretary of state for

congressional relations in February 1956.

As a legislative liaison officer, Hill's diplomatic skills helped smooth the passage of
the Administration's foreign aid requests.
During 1956 and 1957 observers credited
Hill with playing an important part in getting Congress to approve aid to Yugoslavia
over conservative objections that it would
help Communism. In May 1957 Hill confronted the issue of a Saudi Arabian ban on
the assignment of Jewish servicemen to that
country. Though some New York members
of Congress had charged the U.S. government with tacit compliance with the ban,
Hill assured the representatives that the
U.S. "does not condone" any foreign
government's discrimination against U.S.
citizens. However, he expressed doubt that
the ban would soon be lifted.

In May 1957 Hill was confirmed as ambassador to Mexico. As in Costa Rica and
El Salvador, Hill proved adept at winning
the good will of the populace despite tensions between the two nations over aid,
tariffs and oil development. Aware of the
value of the press, he visited Mexico's most
important newspapers and its major television network to promote American-Mexican
friendship. In October 1958 he scored a
diplomatic triumph for the U.S. when he
presented an interracial and international
group of baseball stars at a Mexican movie
festival. The ballplayers' appearance followed
the showing of the movie *The Defiant
Ones*, a film which stressed interracial har-
mony and which helped dampen the anti-
American feeling.

Elected to the New Hampshire State
Legislature in November 1960, Hill resigned as ambassador to Mexico effective
January 1961. After one term Hill returned
to private business, becoming director of a
number of corporations, including United
Fruit Co. During the mid-1960s he served
on the Republican National Committee's
Foreign Policy Task Force. Hill returned to
diplomatic service in 1967 when he was appointed ambassador to Spain, serving until
1972. From 1973 to 1974 he was assistant
secretary of defense for international security Affairs. Hill became ambassador to
Argentina in 1974.

[RJB]

HOBBY, OVETA CULP
b. Jan. 19, 1905: Killeen, Tex.
Administrator, Federal Security
Agency, January 1953-April 1953;
Secretary of Health, Education and
Welfare, April 1953-July 1955.

The daughter of a prominent Texas lawyer, Oveta Culp studied law at Mary Hardin-Baylor College and the University of Texas. At 20 she became assistant city attorney in Houston. After running unsuccessfully in 1931 for the Texas state legislature, she married Texas Gov. William Pettus Hobby, publisher of the *Houston Post*. In 1937 she published *Mr. Chairman*, a text on parliamentary procedure widely used in Texas and Louisiana public schools. While a mother of two young children, Oveta Culp Hobby served as associate editor and executive vice president of the *Houston Post*.

Beginning in July 1941 Hobby worked in Washington, D.C., as a $1-a-year public relations executive with the War Department In September 1941 Gen. George C. Marshall asked Hobby to plan a women's army. The following May Congress passed a law officially establishing the Women's Auxiliary Army Corps (WAACS). The unit received full status in the Army in late 1943, losing the term "Auxiliary." By the end of the War, at least 100,000 women had served.

Oveta Culp Hobby helped organize Democrats for Eisenhower in Texas, and following Eisenhower's victory in the 1952 election, she was appointed head of the Federal Security Agency. When the agency became the nucleus of the new Department of Health, Education and Welfare (HEW) in April, Hobby was appointed Secretary. Except for Frances Perkins, Secretary of Labor under Franklin D. Roosevelt, Hobby was the only woman to that date to serve in the Cabinet.

Opposed to socialized medicine as being "undemocratic and economically unsound," Hobby nevertheless supported a "health reinsurance program." Under Hobby's plan the federal government would assume 76% of the cost of "abnormal losses" incurred by private insurance companies for health insurance. In exchange, the companies would pay the government reinsurance fees totaling $25 million. But neither the companies, the American Medical Association (AMA) nor the public supported this program. The AMA opposed it as an attempt at socialized medicine, while advocates of federal health insurance believed it would leave the needs of lower income groups unsatisfied.

In June 1953 Rep. Adam Clayton Powell, Jr. (D, N.Y.) [*q.v.*], charged that Hobby had "countermanded" President Eisenhower's program for desegregating schools on Army bases by sending Secretary of Defense Charles Wilson [*q.v.*] a memorandum telling him not to follow the President's directive.

A strong anti-Communist, Hobby supported the President's loyalty-security program. In 1954 she reported that the Department had dismissed 238 employes as "security risks," 114 of whom were "suspected subversives." According to HEW, security risks were defined as persons who "drank or gossiped too much or were found to be unstable mentally."

Hobby's most important contribution during her tenure in office was federal support for the polio vaccine developed by Dr. Jonas Salk [*q.v.*]. In April 1955 Hobby licensed six drug companies to manufacture and distribute the Salk vaccine. During the following months the program met sharp criticism. By May 1955 the Public Health Service announced a temporary halt in free distribution of the vaccine by the National Foundation for Infantile Paralysis after 77 children were reported to have contracted polio despite earlier vaccination. Several weeks later, after Public Health Service scientists had reviewed testing procedures at the laboratory facilities of the drug companies, the program began again, only to be stopped once more in some areas after an additional 20 vaccinees were reported to have contracted polio in late June 1955.

While grade school inoculation proceeded at a leisurely pace, Congress debated whether the federal government should finance the free distribution of the vaccine. At a meeting of the Senate Labor and Public Welfare Committee in June 1955, Hobby advocated a means test before distributing free vaccine to children up to the age of 19 because otherwise the program would amount to "socialized medicine by the back door." Sen. Lister Hill (D, Ala.) [q.v.], however, urged that all children be given free inoculations. While the debate raged Adlai Stevenson [q.v.] charged that the Republicans were not making adequate plans for producing and distributing the Salk vaccine, and Sen. Wayne Morse (D, Ore.) [q.v.] demanded that Hobby be fired for "gross incompetence" in the vaccine program. Hobby resigned as Secretary of Health, Education and Welfare in July ostensibly because of the illness of her husband. In August Congress passed Hill's bill establishing a free vaccine program.

Hobby succeeded her husband as president of the Houston Post Publishing Co. in 1955. During the 1960s and 1970s she served on numerous boards of major institutions. She became a director of the General Foods Corp. and of the Corporation of Public Broadcasting in 1968.

[RSG]

HODGES, LUTHER H(ARTWELL)
b. March 9, 1898; Pittsylvania
County, Va.
d. Oct. 6, 1974; Chapel Hill, N.C.
Governor, N.C., 1954-61.

One of nine children, Luther Hodges worked as an office boy while attending public school. He financed his studies at the University of North Carolina by selling books, firing furnaces and waiting on tables. After serving in the Army during World War I, Hodges returned to the University, graduating in 1919. That year he became secretary to the general manager of Marshall Field & Co.'s eight textile mills in the Leaksville, Ky., area and rose through the company to become general manager of all Field textile mills in 1939. Three years later he was elected a vice president.

In 1944 Hodges took charge of the textile division of the Office of Price Administration and in 1945 became a consultant to the Secretary of Agriculture. Retiring from the textile business in 1950, Hodges headed the industry division of the Economic Cooperation Administration and served as State Department consultant at the International Management Conference in 1951. With little previous political experience, Hodges was elected lieutenant governor of North Carolina in 1952. When Gov. William B. Ulmstead died in November 1954, Hodges succeeded him and was elected in his own right in 1956.

Disturbed that North Carolina ranked 44th out of the 48 states in per capita income, Hodges embarked on a course of industrial development. Through a program of courting out-of-state industries by tax incentives and creating the North Carolina Business Development Corp. in 1955 to make long-term credit more accessible, Hodges stimulated the state economy. Over a billion dollars of capital was invested in the state and 140,000 new jobs created during his tenure.

The Supreme Court's *Brown* decision in May 1954 outlawing segregation in public schools was of intense concern to Hodges because North Carolina had the largest percentage of blacks in the population of any state outside the Deep South. While personally a segregationist, the Governor opposed extreme demands for nullification of the ruling and called for moderation and the concept of voluntary compliance.

Hodges's final approach to the problem involved a three-part plan. First, a pupil assignment law, passed in 1955, gave county and city boards the power to assign pupils to schools. By the fall of 1957 three North Carolina cities became integrated under this system. Second, a voluntary segregation plan, advocated in August 1955, stated that those who wished to remain segregated could do so. A public school law was enacted that struck from the law any reference to race, transferred ownership and operation of state school buses to local administrative units and substituted yearly contracts for teachers in place of the continuing contract. Third, the Pearsall Plan (named after Thomas J. Pearsall, who headed an advisory committee) provided for two "safety valves," one allowing for local elections to close schools in "intolerable situations" and another providing tuition grants for children wishing to attend segregated schools. This recommendation passed as an amendment to the state's constitution in September 1956.

Because of North Carolina's success at curtailing racial violence while achieving a degree of integration, Hodges played a key role in the Little Rock, Ark., dispute. During the Southern Governors Conference of September 1957, President Eisenhower sent paratroopers to Little Rock to enforce court-ordered integration of the public schools. Concerned about the action, the Conference authorized a committee of five, chaired by Hodges, to speak with the President and ask him to withdraw the troops. At the meeting, held in late September, Hodges questioned the desirability rather than the legality of sending the troops, while Eisenhower replied that if Arkansas Gov. Orval Faubus [q.v.] would agree to maintain order during the integration process, the paratroopers would be withdrawn. The committee persuaded the President to leave out critical comments about Faubus in a written statement read to the Governor over the telephone. Faubus agreed to Eisenhower's conditions and indicated a confirmation would be wired. The wire was never sent, but he instead contacted the President, indicating that he as an individual would do nothing to interfere with the court order. The statement was unsatisfactory to Eisenhower. Hodges reported the failure of the negotiations on a nationwide broadcast and terminated his personal involvement in the incident. The troops remained in Little Rock until the end of November.

During the latter part of the decade, Hodges continued to build up North Carolina's industry, developed the state's "research triangle" (consisting of the University of North Carolina, North Carolina State College and Duke University), supported the minimum wage and furthered highway safety.

During the 1960 presidential campaign Hodges actively supported Sen. John F. Kennedy's (D, Mass.) [q.v.] candidacy. He served as Secretary of Commerce from 1961 to 1965. After leaving government service he returned to business, assuming the directorships of several major corporations. He died of a heart attack in Chapel Hill, N.C., in 1974, at the age of 76. [See KENNEDY Volume]

[GAD]

For further information:
Numan V. Bartley, *The Rise of Massive Resistance* (Baton Rouge, 1969).
Luther H. Hodges, *Businessman in the Statehouse* (Chapel Hill, 1962).

HOFFA, JAMES R(IDDLE)
b. Feb. 14, 1913; Brazil, Ind.
d. presumed July, 1975.
Vice President, International Brotherhood of Teamsters, Chauffeurs, and Warehousemen and Helpers of America, 1952-57; President, 1957-67.

Hoffa's father, an itinerant coal driller, died when the boy was seven. Hoffa was forced to quit school in the seventh grade to help support the family. At the age of 17 he helped organize a union of loading dock workers in Detroit. Two years later he became president of Joint Teamster Local 299, the largest local in the city. The young Hoffa soon emerged as the indisputable boss of the Detroit Teamsters.

In 1937 he helped Farrell Dobbs set up the Central States Drivers Council, formed to organize long-haul drivers, and in 1940 he became its chairman. He became president of the Michigan Conference of Teamsters in 1942 and president of Teamsters Joint Local 43 in Detroit in 1946. During the 1940s Hoffa organized new locals and represented the Central State Drivers Council in collective bargaining. Although Hoffa obtained good settlements for his workers, he had no reservations about using strong-armed tactics to win contracts or to defeat rivals both inside and outside the union. By employing former racketeers as business agents and allying himself with the notorious Purple Gang of Detroit, Hoffa intimidated employes and employers into cooperating with him. He also established contacts with members of organized crime in other Midwestern cities, enabling him to expand his power. For example, in 1949 Hoffa and Paul "Red" Dorfman [q.v.] worked out an agreement that allowed Hoffa to expand his operations in Chicago. Dorfman, a former member of the Al Capone mob, represented Hoffa in the Chicago underworld in exchange for Dorfman's son, Allan, being appointed insurance broker for the huge Central States health and welfare fund.

Hoffa became one of nine vice presidents of the International Brotherhood of Teamsters (IBT) in 1952. Because of his power in the central states, he could have challenged Dave Beck [q.v.] for the presidency. However, he decided to back Beck, realizing that he would succeed to the presidency when the older man retired. In gratitude for Hoffa's loyalty Beck gave him a free hand to consolidate his hold on the Teamsters in the Midwest. According to Hoffa's biographer, Walter Sheridan, this blank check included Beck's endorsement of his continuing collusion with organized crime figures in such cities as Chicago, St. Louis, Minneapolis, Cleveland and Cincinnati. By the middle of the decade, Hoffa had become the undisputed Teamster boss of the Midwest. His order could tie up all trucking there, and he personally approved all strikes. He also controlled the finances of Central States Council. Through a sophisticated web of political contacts and the use of violence and intimidation, Hoffa forestalled any attempts by local authorities to interfere with his operations. He once bragged that "every man had a price" and demonstrated this by bribing judges, juries, prosecutors and local elected officials. When dissident locals refused to follow Hoffa's orders, they found they had no support for their position. Dave Beck refused to help them. The local political officials, either bribed by Hoffa or afraid of him, refused to prosecute those charged with intimidating the locals. Hoffa even conspired with the dissident locals' employers to break the power of rebellious groups.

During the mid-1950s Hoffa moved to extend his power to the East Coast and eventually throughout the nation. He first gained control of the Teamsters in the New York metropolitan area. Through the help of two reputed organized crime figures, Tony "Ducks" Corallo and Johnny Dio, Hoffa set up a number of paper locals to obtain the majority vote on the Teamsters Joint Council, the local's representative body. Hoffa also secured control of the Philadelphia locals. Through an alliance with Tony Provenzano, New Jersey Teamsters official and reputed organized crime figure, Hoffa exercised his power in that state. Hoffa even had connections with the International Longshoremen's Association, expelled from the AFL, because of corruption. With this network of connections Hoffa could tie up trucking and the East Coast docks. Hoffa then proceeded to consolidate his power nationwide. When Dave Beck was forced to resign in 1957 because of corruption charges, Hoffa became the IBT's president. It is believed that Hoffa leaked the evidence that discredited Beck.

From 1957 to 1961 the Senate Committee on Improper Activities in the Labor or Management Field, chaired by Sen. John L. McClellan (D, Ark.) [q.v.], led an investigation of Hoffa's leadership of the IBT. Robert F. Kennedy [q.v.], the panel's majority counsel, supervised the investigation into Hoffa's past and led the questioning of witnesses. The Committee elaborately documentsd Hoffa's connections with organized crime. Kennedy, on numerous occasions, listed names of racketeers on Hoffa's payroll as business agents. In questioning before the panel, Kennedy asked Hoffa if he were aware of their past and if he would remove them from their positions. Hoffa promised he would, but as Kennedy frequently showed, the Teamster leader failed to expel them. The panel also revealed how underworld figures enriched themselves as union officials. Often they would extort money from companies the Teamsters worked for to guarantee labor peace. The employers payed them off by having them on their payroll, although they never worked.

The Committee also found that Hoffa personally profited from his connections with the Teamsters Union. Under his wife's name he was part-owner of a trucking business. This type of relationship was prohibited by the Taft-Hartley Act, which barred a union official from owning a business in which his union was represented. Hoffa also indirectly borrowed union money for personal investments. This was done by having a friendly union member take out a loan and transfer it to Hoffa. Often the investments were made in Hoffa's wife's maiden name. Hoffa arranged for the transfer of $300,000 in union funds to a Florida bank to invest in a proposed retirement community for Teamsters. The Committee charged that Hoffa never consulted the union membership in making this transaction and that he and his friends personally profited from the investment. Hoffa annually listed $10,000 on his income tax form as "collections." Although he told Kennedy that he won this money at the racetrack, many believed that the funds came from employers who received favorable treatment by Hoffa.

During the two year probe Hoffa rarely took the Fifth Amencment when testifying. Instead, he developed artful techniques to evade questioning. He often engaged in what Sen. Irving Ives (R, N.Y.) [q.v.] termed convenient "forgetery." The Teamster leader frequently expounded his philosophy of labor relations to avoid a question. Often he repeated the same answer countless times or asked that a question be repeated to stall the committee. Sometimes he scheduled plane flights for just after the hearing so testimony could not be drawn out. Hoffa's conduct proved frustrating for the Committee. However enough evidence of his wrongdoing emerged to convince Congress that there was a need for legislation to prevent union corruption. In 1959 it passed the Landrum-Griffin Act, which among other things, prevented individuals with criminal records from holding union leadership posts. It also stiffened fine and prison penalties for union officials charged with misusing funds.

In 1957 the AFL-CIO expelled Hoffa and his union for unethical practices. This action did not trouble Hoffa. He believed that, because the IBT was the largest union in the federation, it would hurt the AFL-CIO more than the Teamsters, primarily because the IBT would no longer be paying dues. In addition, Hoffa had already cultivated contacts with leading AFL-CIO

officials, and inspite of George Meany's [q.v.] order to isolate the union, the leaders did cooperate with him.

During the last half of the decade, the federal government tried to bring criminal action against Hoffa. In 1957 he was indicted for attempting to bribe the Senate committee staff lawyer, John Cye Cheasty, in an attempt to receive advanced information on the investigation. The case seemed to be foolproof, but Hoffa was acquitted by a Washington jury consisting of eight blacks and four whites. Halfway through the trial a black newspaper, featuring a pro-Hoffa cover article, was delivered to the homes of black jurors. Later the black fighter, Joe Louis, came to court for a picture with his friend, Jimmy Hoffa. The move was arranged by Hoffa's underworld contacts. It was later learned that four of the jury members had criminal records. In 1958 Hoffa was indicted twice for wire-tapping fellow Teamsters. The first case ended in a hung jury; the second in acquittal.

When Robert F. Kennedy became Attorney General in 1961, the Justice Department pursued a relentless campaign against Hoffa; a special team was organized to obtain evidence on his activities. Hoffa was found guilty in 1963 and 1964 of jury tampering and fraud. In 1967 he began his eight-year prison sentence for jury tampering; this was followed by another five years for fraud.

When Hoffa reported to jail in 1967, control of the IBT passed to Frank Fitzsimmons, Hoffa's loyal assistant who had been chosen general vice president of the IBT in 1966. Hoffa did not immediately resign the union presidency; there was speculation that he continued to influence the union from jail. In June 1971 Hoffa retired. The following December Richard Nixon pardoned him on condition that he not engage in union business for the duration of the sentence. In 1975 Hoffa disappeared, evidently murdered at the time he planned to reenter Teamsters politics. [See KENNEDY, JOHNSON, NIXON/FORD Volumes]

[JB]

For further information:
Walter Sheridan, *The Rise and Fall of Jimmy Hoffa* (New York, 1972).

HOFFMAN, CLARE E.
b. Sept. 10, 1875: Vicksburg, Pa.
d. Nov. 3, 1967: Allegan, Mich.
Republican Representative, Mich.,
1935-63; Chairman, Committee on Expenditures in the Executive Departments, 1947-49; Chairman, Government Operations Committee, 1953-55.

Hoffman received an LL.B. degree from Northwestern University law school in 1895 and was admitted to the Michigan bar the following year. He became district attorney of Allegan, Mich., in 1906 and subsequently served as municipal attorney. For several decades Hoffman was Republican chairman for Allegan Co. before winning election to the U.S. House of Representatives in 1934. A conservative isolationist, he voted against most New Deal measures and before Pearl Harbor opposed U.S. involvement in World War II. Hoffman was a vehement critic of organized labor; in January 1947 he introduced a measure to outlaw the closed shop, work slowdowns, picketing, dues checkoffs and certain types of strikes. Later in the year he voted for the Taft-Hartley Act.

Hoffman became chairman of the Committee on Expenditures in the Executive Departments in 1947. In that capacity he led investigations of surplus war property disposal, federal enforcement of anti-racketeering legislation and a Midwestern meatpacking strike. He also unsuccessfully pressed for legislation to penalize reporters who divulged confidential information given to congressional committees. [See TRUMAN Volume]

In 1953 Hoffman resumed his chairmanship of the Committee on Expenditures, whose name had been changed in the interim to the Government Operations Committee. In that post his major concern was gangsterism in labor unions, which he described as "twice as dangerous to the country" as Communism. During the first half of 1952, Hoffman appointed a special Government Operations subcommittee, which included himself, to cooperate with an Education and Labor Committee panel in investigating labor corruption in Kansas City. In September he signed the joint subcommittee's report recommending that a federal grand jury investigate the subject.

Hoffman came into conflict with the other members of the Committee when he asked subcommittee chairmen to cut down their staffs and expenditures after July 31, 1953. In retaliation the Committee voted 23-1 to limit Hoffman's power to appoint ad hoc panels for special investigations (while permitting him to continue his subcommittee's participation in the Kansas City probe). On July 29 the full House voted 171-6 to allow the Government Operations subcommittees to spend all the funds allotted to them.

Consistently conservative, Hoffman criticized a 1955-56 Government Operations subcommittee investigation of the Eisenhower Administration's policy of cutting back federal power development. In 1955 he denounced the probe as an attempt "to sabotage President Eisenhower's program of getting government out of business." Hoffman was one of the few Republican representatives to vote against the Eisenhower Administration's 1957 and 1960 civil rights bills. In 1957 he opposed a school construction aid bill. With five other Education and Labor Committee Republicans, he asserted that the classroom shortage was "nowhere near as serious" as the majority contended and that the states and localities were taking care of whatever need existed. Three years later Hoffman denounced a minimum wage bill and a measure to permit common-site picketing by construction unions.

Hoffman was one of the few isolationist congressmen of the 1930s who continued to take an isolationist position during the 1950s. In 1955 he abstained in the vote on the Administration's Formosa resolution, stating, "I think it is a declaration of war, and I don't think the cost in lives will justify it." Two years later Hoffman voted against the Eisenhower Doctrine for the Middle East, declaring that a "foreshortened" world made "the minding of our own business" more essential than ever.

As a member of the Republican Right, Hoffman criticized the 1957 appointment of Meade Alcorn [q.v.], an exponent of what

President Eisenhower called "modern Republicanism," as Republican National Chairman. Hoffman said that Alcorn's appointment meant the "conservative wing of the Republican Party . . . was being liquidated." Early in 1958, after the Administration submitted a record $71.8 billion budget, he contended that President Eisenhower and "his left-wing, free-spending, international one-world advisers propose to disinfect, fumigate, purify, renovate, unify and remake the Republican Party."

In 1962 Hoffman did not run for reelection. He died in Allegan, Mich., on Nov. 3, 1967 at the age of 92.

[MLL]

HOFFMAN PAUL G(RAY)
b. April 26, 1898; Chicago, Ill.
U.S. Delegate to the United Nations, 1956-60.

Hoffman left the University of Chicago, where he had gone to study law, after two years and became an automobile salesman for Studebaker Co. He served in the Army during World War I and then resumed his sales work. By 1925 he was reportedly doing several million dollars worth of business annually. That year he was made vice president in charge of sales and a member of the board of directors. Ten years later Hoffman became president of Studebaker, a position he held until 1948. During World War II he coordinated the company's transition from car manufacturing to military truck and aircraft engine production.

In 1948 Hoffman was appointed administrator of the Marshall Plan, distributing approximately $10 billion for the economic development of Europe. In the early-1950s he also became an outspoken defender or civil liberties. In 1952 he denounced Sen. Joseph R. McCarthy's (R, Wisc.) [q.v.] charges that Secretary of Defense George C. Marshall was connected with a pro-Communist conspiracy. [See TRUMAN Volume]

In 1951 Hoffman became president of the Ford Foundation. During his two years at that agency, he expanded its operations considerably, particularly in the area of education. Starting in 1951 the Foundation's Fund for the Advancement of Education spent about $6 million a year on travel and study fellowships for high school and college teachers and on expanded liberal arts programs for education students. From 1951 to 1955 the Ford Foundation for Adult Education also spent over $25 million, a third for educational TV and radio. In addition to education the Foundation gave large sums to work with refugees, particularly from Eastern Europe.

Hoffman was an early, enthusiastic supporter of Dwight D. Eisenhower for President. As far back as 1949 he tried to persuade the General to run, believing that Eisenhower was the one man who could unite postwar America and lead a "moral crusade" to return the country to traditional values. Hoffman saw Eisenhower as a man able to reorient the Republican Party. "I think," he said, "[Eisenhower] is going to put 'new heart' in the Republican Party and recast it in the image of Abraham Lincoln. We can use a party which takes its orders neither from the NAM [National Association of Manufacturers] nor the CIO [Congress of Industrial Organizations]."

As chairman of the Advisory Committee of Citizens for Eisenhower in 1952, Hoffman, along with Henry Cabot Lodge [q.v.], led the efforts to persuade Eisenhower to run and then win for him the Republican presidential nomination. During March 1952 Hoffman campaigned for the General in New Hampshire, where his name had been entered on the primary ballot without his public consent. Hoffman told a large audience at the University of New Hampshire that a vote for Eisenhower was the only way to ensure the continuance of a vital two-party system. After Eisenhower's dramatic victory in the New Hampshire primary, Hoffman spent several days with the General in Europe, persuading him to return to the United States and openly campaign. During the primary and the general election race, Hoffman gave a considerable number of speeches and press conferences and coordinated primary activities. His major theme was that Eisenhower was the only man who could unify the Party, ensure peace by negotiating with the Kremlin, gain the votes of the South, independents and youths, and restore the domestic economy. Hoffman also thought that the General could lead an administration able to achieve disarmament, a cause he considered vital.

Hoffman returned to Studebaker as chairman of the board after the election, but he remained a close companion and adviser to the President. In 1954 the executive urged Eisenhower to directly attack Sen. McCarthy, then criticizing the Administration for what he considered its reluctance to rid itself of subversive elements. He was one of the business leaders who urged Eisenhower to run in 1956 despite the President's earlier heart attack.

Hoffman's campaign for Eisenhower in 1956 resulted in one embarrassing incident for the President. In an October article in *Collier's*, Hoffman described what he saw as Eisenhower's concern for transforming the Republican Party from a series of factions into a centralized national party. Hoffman maintained that Eisenhower could "achieve something unique in American politics, a party that is fundamentally pressure-proof; something profoundly superior to its rival, the Democratic Party, whose irreconcilable differences leave it permanently open to the pressures of contending narrow interest groups." Hoffman maintained that, although the President had unified the Party to a great degree, "senators claiming the label Republican who embrace none or very little of the Eisenhower program and philosophy," remain within the Party. He divided these individuals into "unappeasables," including McCarthy, Sen. William E. Jenner (R, Ind.) [*q.v.*] and Herman Welker (R, Ida.) [*q.v.*] and "faint hopes" including Sen. Barry Goldwater (R, Ariz.) [*q.v.*]. Goldwater, upset by the article, asked presidential aide Sherman Adams [*q.v.*] to clarify his standing with Eisenhower. Adams assured him that Eisenhower did not intend to avoid him. The President also assured Republicans that there was room for dissent within the Party.

In 1956 Hoffman was appointed a member of the U.S. delegation to the United Nations. His appointment was opposed by conservatives, led by McCarthy, who disapproved of Hoffman's defense of civil liberties. Nevertheless, he won confirmation in July. During his tenure he urged the U.N. to form a permanent military force. In March 1959 Hoffman called on the developed nations to increase their private and public foreign aid by 100-400% during the next 10 years to promote peace. He asked the United States in particular to raise aid from a current $1.4 billion per year to an aggregate of $30 to $40 billion over the next 10 years.

Hoffman remained active in U.N. affairs during the 1960s and early-1970s, serving as managing director of the U.N. Special Fund, administrator of the U.N. Development Program and of the U.N. Fund for Population Activities.

[RSG]

HOFFMAN, WALTER E(DWARD)
b. July 18, 1907; Jersey City, N.J.
U.S. District Judge, Eastern District, Va., 1954- .

Hoffman, a 1928 graduate of the University of Pennsylvania, received his law degree from Washington and Lee University in 1931 and then entered private practice in Norfolk, Va. A Republican who made unsuccessful races for Congress and for state attorney general, he was among the first party leaders in Virginia to support Dwight D. Eisenhower for the Republican presidential nomination in 1952. At the Republican National Convention in Chicago, Hoffman's firmness in backing the General within the divided Virginia delegation reportedly contributed to Eisenhower's nomination. Eisenhower appointed Hoffman the U.S. district judge for the eastern district of Virginia in 1954. He took his seat that September.

On the bench Judge Hoffman proved to be a stalwart and forthright jurist who insisted on state and local compliance with the U.S. Supreme Court's school desegregation decision of May 1954. In September 1956 the Virginia legislature passed a series of laws designed to thwart school integration, including a pupil placement act and a measure requiring the governor to close any public school faced with a final desegregation order. Hoffman held the pupil placement law unconstitutional in January 1957. The next month, after assailing the state Assembly for adopting "obstructionist" legislation, he ruled that Norfolk, Va., must begin desegregating its schools in the coming fall term. A higher court granted a delay of this judgment, but the U.S. Supreme Court upheld Hoffman's integration order in October 1957.

Hoffman ruled in June 1958 that his 15-month-old desegregation decree for Norfolk must take effect at the opening of the 1958-59 school year. Under this order 151 black pupils applied for admission to all-white schools in the city, but the local school board rejected all the applicants. On Aug. 21 Hoffman opened a hearing on the rejections, and on Aug. 25 he gave the school board four days to reconsider its action. The board agreed on Aug. 29 to admit 17 blacks to formerly all-white schools. Over the next few weeks Judge Hoffman denied a school board plea for a one-year delay of desegregation and enjoined a state court from interfering with his desegregation ruling. After the Fourth Circuit Court upheld Hoffman's order for immediate desegregation in Norfolk on Sept. 27, Gov. J. Lindsay Almond, Jr. [q.v.], closed the six senior and junior high schools involved in the case. By the end of September some 13,000 students had been locked out of nine public schools throughout the state. With the schools closed, the pressure from moderates to end Virginia's "massive resistance" policy grew.

On Jan. 19, 1959 both a three-judge federal court in Richmond, of which Hoffman was a member, and the state Supreme Court of Appeals handed down decisions declaring Virginia's school closing law unconstitutional. The Governor then called a special session of the state legislature, which repealed the massive resistance laws but passed other, less stringent acts to try to discourage school desegregation. In Norfolk, after final orders from Hoffman, 17 black students finally began attending the reopened white public schools on Feb. 2, 1959.

Hoffman was also active in race-related cases not involving the school system. In July 1955 he ordered the integration of Virginia's Seashore State Park. In January 1958 Hoffman was a member of a three-judge federal panel that ruled three of Virginia's six anti-NAACP laws unconstitutional.

According to J.W. Peltason in 58 *Lonely Men*, Hoffman's "bluntness and his open criticism of Virginia Democratic leaders" during the school desegregation controversy of the late-1950s "made him one of the major verbal targets of segregationists" in the state. Despite phone calls and letters criticizing his desegregation decisions, Hoffman refused to give way on his rulings.

In Norfolk, where only token school desegregation began in 1959, the NAACP continued to fight the city's school integration plans in court. The litigation finally ended in March 1966, when Hoffman approved an integration plan worked out in negotiations between the school board, the NAACP and the Justice Department. Hoffman served as chief judge for the Eastern District of Virginia from 1962 to 1973 and became a senior district judge in 1974.

[CAB]

HOFSTADTER, RICHARD
b. Aug. 6, 1916; Buffalo, N.Y.
d. Oct. 24, 1970; New York, N.Y.
Historian.

Richard Hofstadter grew up in Buffalo and graduated with honors from the University of Buffalo in 1937. He enrolled at New York Law School but quickly moved to the study of history at Columbia University, where he was awarded his Ph.D. in 1942. His doctoral dissertation, "Social Darwinism in American Thought, 1860-1915," won the American Historical Association's Albert J. Beveridge Memorial Prize in 1944. Hofstadter taught history at the City University of New York and the University of Maryland before joining the faculty at Columbia in 1946 as an assistant professor. He became a full professor in 1952.

In 1948 Hofstadter published his most popular work, *The American Political Tradition: And the Men Who Made It*. The book was received well by scholars and became assigned reading for a generation of American history students. It was a collection of incisive, iconoclastic profiles of the shapers of American political history from the Founding Fathers to Franklin D. Roosevelt. In Hofstadter's analysis American leaders, whatever their individual variations and policy differences, shared a central concern for the protection of property and the promotion of free enterprise.

Hofstadter's emphasis upon the common assumptions and values held continuously by Americans rather than the conflicts that divided them became a familiar theme in the works of postwar American historians and the heart of the "censensus" school of history ascendant in the 1950s. Although often grouped with the consensus school, Hofstadter did not join in the celebration of American entrepreneurial and "pragmatic" values; he was critical of the mainstream political tradition, "a democracy in cupidity rather than a democracy of fraternity."

In the 1950s Hofstadter emerged as a leading academic critic and analyst of America's extreme Right at a time when Sen. Joseph McCarthy's (R, Wisc.) [q.v.] anti-Communist crusade was at its peak. Hofstadter said of his 1954 essay, "The Pseudo-Conservative Revolt," "I have written nothing of comparable brevity that aroused more attention or drew more requests for quotation or reprinting." "Although they believe themselves to be conservatives," he said, "pseudoconservatives" have "little in common with the temperate and compromising spirit of true conservatism." With their "hyper-patriotism and hyper-conformism," their belief in an internal conspiracy permeating American life, their accusations that national leaders were guilty of betrayal and treason and their desire for sweeping authoritarian solutions, Hofstadter wrote, "pseudo-conservatives" threatened to destroy the values and institutions they professed to defend.

The most distinctive aspect of Hofstadter's argument was his analysis of the common social-psychological circumstances supposedly shared by pseudo-conservatives. Focusing on "status politics" as opposed to traditional "interest politics," he suggested that pseudo-conservatism was "a product of

the rootlessness and heterogeneity of American life." Intense status concerns, Hofstadter maintained, were shared by two disparate groups: old-stock Anglo-Saxons, feeling displaced in modern America, and certain ethnic groups, experiencing anxiety about their Americanism and the need to prove it genuine. Both groups found satisfaction in advertising their patriotism and challenging the loyalty of others—liberals, intellectuals, non-conformists. A decade later Hofstadter modified his case somewhat, acknowledging that he had "overstated the role of certain ethnic minorities in the right wing" and ignored the role of religious fundamentalism.

In *The Age of Reform: From Bryan to F.D.R.*, awarded the Pulitzer Prize for History in 1955, Hofstadter brought to bear on the history of Populism and Progressivism several of the critical concepts he had applied to the right wing of the 1950s. Populists and Progressives felt bewildered and threatened by rapid social change, he argued. The Populists sought solace in a sentimentalization of America's agrarian past, a conspiracy theory of history and agitation for such panaceas as "free silver." Hofstadter analyzed the Progressives' crusades for municipal reform, public morality and antitrust laws as unconscious efforts to relieve their "status anxiety" and their fears of being eclipsed by vulgar plutocrats from above and overwhelmed by urban immigrants from below. While praising Populism as "the first such movement to attack seriously the problems created by industrialism" and recognizing the well-meaning goals of Progressivism, Hofstadter highlighted the intellectual flaws of both movements: the provincialism, chauvinism and anti-Semitism of many Populists and the moralistic and nostalgic nature of Progressivism. These critical judgments implicitly paralleled his strictures against the contemporary right wing.

In the 1960s Hofstadter's scholarly output continued to reflect his concept of the interaction between history and current politics. He pointed out that his 1963 study *Anti-Intellectualism in American Life* "was conceived in response to the political and intellectual conditions of the 1950s." He produced an updating of his 1954 analysis of "pseudo-conservatism" and a critique of the Goldwater phenomenon around the middle of the decade before returning to more conventional historical works such as *The Progressive Historians* (1968). He was at work on a social history of America in the eighteenth century when he died of cancer in October 1970.

[TO]

For further information:
Richard Hofstadter, *The Paranoid Style in American Politics and Other Essays* (New York, 1965).

HOGAN, FRANK S(MITHWICK)
b. Jan. 17, 1902; Waterbury, Conn.
d. April 4, 1974; New York, N.Y.
District Attorney, New York County, 1941-73.

The son of Irish immigrants, Frank Hogan attended parochial school in Waterbury, Conn. He worked his way through college, graduating from Columbia college in 1924 and Columbia law school in 1928. During the next seven years he worked as an insurance investigator and then as an attorney with a struggling practice. In 1935 he joined the staff of Thomas E. Dewey [q.v.], who as special prosecutor and then as Manhattan district attorney waged a flamboyant crusade against racketeering and political corruption. Having played an important role in the convictions of gangster Lucky Luciano and Tammany Hall leader James Hines, Hogan, a Democrat, was chosen by the Republican Dewey to succeed him in 1941. Hogan was elected in November with the support of all the city's major parties, as he was every four years until 1973.

In his 32 years as Manhattan's district attorney, Hogan won national fame for the successful prosecutions his office conducted against scores of well-known underworld and political figures. In 1945 he won convictions against labor racketeers Joseph Fay and James Bove—the only case Hogan personally tried as district attorney. He also sent to prison "King of the Bookmakers"

Frank Erichson and Mayor William O'Dwyer's deputy fire commissioner, James J. Moran, who had organized an extortion racket that victimized city contractors. His office provided the Kefauver Committee with most of its information on gangster Frank Costello [q.v.], which was of sensational value during the Committee's televised hearings concerning organized crime in 1951.

Hogan's office uncovered and prosecuted some of the most highly publicized scandals of the 1950s and 1960s. Among these were fixed college basketball games, rigged television quiz shows and the "payola" bribery of radio disk jockeys. During the 1960s his office handled the payoff scandal concerning New York's State Liquor Authority, unearthed most of the evidence used to convict New York City Water Commissioner James Marcus by federal prosecutors and frustrated writer Clifford Irving's scheme to profit from a fraudulent biography of Howard Hughes [q.v.].

Hogan made two abortive attempts to win higher office. In 1949, amid rumors that Mayor O'Dwyer would not run for reelection, Hogan was Tammany Hall's candidate for mayor. When O'Dwyer did not withdraw, however, Hogan pulled out of the race.

In 1958 Hogan was a candidate for the U.S. Senate. Again he was sponsored by a Tammany Hall boss, Carmine DeSapio [q.v.], who had influenced the other county Democratic leaders of New York City to support his man. Hogan took little part in the bitter struggle to win the nomination for him over his two rivals, former Secretary of the Air Force Thomas K. Finletter [q.v.] and former head of the Atomic Energy Commission Thomas Murray, who was favored by Gov. Averell Harriman [q.v.]. Hogan won the Democratic nomination, but his campaign against Rep. Kenneth B. Keating (R, N.Y.) [q.v.] was crippled by his connection with DeSapio and machine politicians and the hostility of Democratic Party reformers. He also proved to be a lackluster campaigner. In November Hogan lost to Keating by 110,000 votes.

His political association with the controversial DeSapio did little to dim Hogan's luminous reputation as district attorney. For most of his tenure he was America's most famous prosecutor. This was due in part to media interest in the colorful style of criminality in Manhattan. However, most of Hogan's prestige was built on his personal honesty and the unquestioned integrity and competence of his office, which set the standard for district attorneys around the country. His office had a high conviction rate, and his former assistants populated the higher reaches of the bar and bench in the New York area.

By the late-1960s Hogan's reputation was on the decline. Along with that of other law enforcement officials, his status was undermined by the growing irreverence toward authority figures. Hogan came under increasing criticism for allegedly pursuing personal vendettas as district attorney. His most controversial prosecution was that of comedian Lenny Bruce in the mid-1960s. An appeals court later overturned Bruce's conviction for obscenity. Hogan's determined prosecutions of Columbia students and black radicals a few years later intensified the controversy around him and fueled the criticism that he was outdated. He won his ninth term as district attorney in 1973, although he faced primary opposition for the first time in his career. However, he had suffered a disabling stroke that summer and resigned only a month after his final victory. Semi-comatose for the next three months, Hogan died on April 4, 1974.

[TO]

For further information:
Barry Cunningham with Mike Pearl, *Mr. District Attorney: The Story of Frank S. Hogan and the Manhattan D.A.'s Office* (New York, 1977).

HOLIFIELD, CHET (CHESTER) (EARL)
b. Dec. 3, 1903; Mayfield, Ky.
Democratic Representative, Calif., 1943-75.

Holifield left high school before graduation, and after working in a tailor shop, he established his own men's clothing business. He entered Democratic politics during the 1930s as a party leader in the Los Angeles area. In 1942 he was elected to the U.S. House of Representatives from California's 19th district, a predominantly blue-collar area with a substantial Mexican-American population. On Capitol Hill Holifield focused his attention upon the problems of atomic energy development. A proponent of civilian control of the atom, he was placed on the newly created Joint Committee on Atmoic Energy, which supervised the Atomic Energy Commission (AEC) in 1947. During the mid and late 1940s Holifield was an outspoken opponent of the House Un-American Activities Committee and defended AEC chairman David Lilienthal and Edward U. Condon, nuclear physicist and director of the National Bureau of Standards, against charges of "being soft on Communism."

During the Eisenhower Administration Holifield emerged as a leading champion of public atomic energy development. In 1954 he opposed an Administration-backed bill permitting the AEC to license private construction of atomic power plants. Holifield charged that the bill, which proposed a five-year period of compulsory patent sharing, "would set a pattern of monopoly" in the atomic energy industrial field and contended that the period should be extended to at least 10 years. He also objected to its limitations on the AEC's authority to produce power, to its allegedly insufficient safeguards for protecting the public interest, and to a "built-in subsidy" for industry in the provision for government purchase of privately produced nuclear materials. However, the legislation passed Congress in essentially the form requested by the Administration.

In 1956 Holifield supported a bill authorizing $400 million for expanded reactor construction by the AEC. He asserted that the building of reactors during the experimental stage should be undertaken by government rather than by private enterprise. The bill was opposed by the Administration, and in July the House, by a vote of 203 to 191, recommitted the bill to the Joint Committee on Atomic Energy.

Holifield was a leading critic of the controversial Dixon-Yates contract. The dispute began in 1954 when President Eisenhower ordered the AEC to buy power for one of its plants from the Mississippi Valley Generating Co. owned by Edgar Dixon [q.v.] and Eugene Yates. Power had previously been supplied by the Tennessee Valley Authority (TVA). Holifield was prominent among a group of liberals who argued that the private power would be more expensive than that provided by TVA, and he charged that Eisenhower was using the AEC to subsidize a private utility and undermine the government owned agency. When the Democrats gained control of Congress in 1955, the Joint Committee on Atomic Energy recommended cancellation of the contract. In July 1955 the Administration ordered it dropped.

In 1953 Holifield served as a member of the Commission on Organization of the Executive Branch of Government, chaired by former President Herbert Hoover [q.v.]. The Commission's 1955 report urged drastic cutbacks in many government activities. Holifield was the leading dissident on the panel, charging the Commission with exceeding its jurisdiction and distorting facts. He denounced its opposition to public power and its call for reductions in federal legal and lending services.

During 1957 Holifield, as chairman of the Joint Committee on Atomic Energy's Special Subcommittee on Radiation, held hearings on the consequences of radioactive fallout from nuclear weapons. At the conclusion of the probe, he denounced the AEC for "playing down" fallout hazards. Meanwhile, in 1957 and 1958, the Government Operations Committee's Subcommittee on Military Operations, also chaired by Holified, investigated civil defense policy. During the course of the hearings, Holifield became a strong proponent of compulsory fallout shelter construction, and his subcommittee was instrumental in persuading the Office of Civil Defense to request $32 billion for shelter funds.

In 1957 Holifield was one of the founders of a liberal House Democratic caucus. Among the measures the group endorsed were federal aid for housing, school construction and medical education; assistance to depressed areas; repeal of the Taft-Hartley Act; and the elimination of the national origins system from immigration and naturalization laws. In 1959 the caucus was formally organized as the Democratic Study Group, and the following year Holifield was chosen its chairman.

During the 1960s Holifield rotated with Sen. John O. Pastore (D, R.I.) [q.v.] as chairman of the Joint Committee on Atomic Energy. In the early-1960s Holifield was a strong backer of President Kennedy's fallout shelter and public power proposals. After 1965 he came under increasing fire from liberals for his support of the Vietnam war and of Pentagon appropriations requests. He became chairman of the Government Operations Committee in 1971. Three years later Holifield announced that he would not seek reelection. [See KENNEDY, JOHNSON, NIXON/FORD Volumes]

[MLL]

HOLLISTER, JOHN B(AKER)
b. Nov. 7, 1890; Cincinnati, Ohio.
Executive Director, Commission on the Organization of the Executive Branch, October 1953-July 1955; Director, International Cooperation Administration, State Department, July 1955-September 1957.

Hollister graduated from Yale in 1911 and, after studying at the University of Munich, attended Harvard law school, where he received his degree in 1915. Following service in the artillery during World War I, he helped administer U.S. relief in Poland and Lithuania. He returned to Ohio to practice law and in 1924 became a member of the firm of Taft, Stettinius and Hollister, beginning a lifelong friendship with Robert A. Taft [q.v.].

Hollister was elected to the U.S. House of Representatives from Ohio's first district in 1931. A conservative Republican, he opposed the New Deal effectively as a member of the House Banking and Currency Committee. He returned to his law practice in 1937 but remained active in Republican politics throughout the 1930s and 1940s.

In 1953 Herbert Hoover [q.v.] appointed Hollister executive director of the Commission on the Organization of the Executive Branch. During the next two years Hollister investigated the allocation of foreign aid by the State Department's Foreign Operations Administration (FOA). His report recommended cutting $360 million annually from foreign aid appropriations and increasing efficiency in the allotment of technical aid.

In April 1955 President Eisenhower, seeking to appease conservative Republicans, appointed Hollister head of the newly created International Cooperation Administration (ICA), a semi-autonomous agency within the State Department that replaced the FOA. As director of the ICA Hollister coordinated economic and military aid "except for matters which . . . requir[ed] final decision by the President."

As director Hollister supported increased exports by Western nations to Soviet satellites in an effort to lessen their dependence on the USSR. This policy drew the wrath of Sen. Joseph McCarthy (R, Wisc.) [q.v.], who, in 1956, demanded an investigation of secret agreements, made in 1954, between the U.S. and 14 other Western nations to liberalize trade with Communist countries. Hollister refused to appear in open hearings before the Senate Permanent Investigations Subcommittee on the issue but agreed to testify behind closed doors.

That month Hollister testified before the House Foreign Affairs Committee on the whereabouts of surplus foreign military aid appropriations from the Truman Administration, which Democrats charged Eisenhower had used to balance the budget. Hollister disclaimed responsibility for Eisenhower's actions and agreed that the funds had to be restored, particularly in the area of military aid. At the same hearing, he reported reductions in economic aid and the closing of most ICA offices in Europe.

Hollister spend a large portion of his time defending the Eisenhower Administration's emphasis on military aid before skeptical congressional committees. In May 1956 he defended Eisenhower's request for $4.9 billion in foreign aid, of which $3 billion was allocated for military purposes—triple the fiscal 1956 sum. He contended that the arms aid was needed to update NATO weaponry and warned that despite the USSR's stress on economic aid to nonaligned nations, "the constantly changing situation in the Middle East and Asia" made it "essential" for Congress to increase the military portion of foreign aid to prevent Communist expansion in these areas. His proposals were bitterly attacked by Senate Democrats who described the Administration's emphasis on military aid as poorly conceived.

Hollister submitted his resignation as ICA director in July 1957 following the passage of a foreign aid bill that greatly reduced his power. It converted economic aid from a grant system to a revolving loan fund. Aid was administered by an advisory committee headed by the deputy undersecretary of state for economic affairs. Although Secretary of State John Foster Dulles [q.v.] opposed the bill, Eisenhower gave it his endorsement.

Despite Hollister's public defense of the Administration's foreign aid program, irreconcilable differences existed between the conservative Republican and the President. These became public as Hollister was about to leave his post. In a directive issued on Sept. 12, 1957, the day before his departure, Hollister scored U.S. assistance to government-owned enterprises, maintaining that the ICA's basic policy was to administer American aid "in such a way as will encourage the development of the private sectors" of foreign economies.

After his resignation, Hollister returned to his old law firm.

[AES]

HOOK, SIDNEY
b. Dec. 20, 1902; New York, N.Y.
Philosopher.

Sidney Hook grew up in Brooklyn. After graduating from the College of the City of New York in 1923, he went to Columbia University on a scholarship, where he studied philosophy under John Dewey. In 1927 Hook was awarded his Ph.D. and appointed to the faculty of New York University. During the 1930s Hook was prominently associated with various radical causes. In 1932 he helped organize a group of leading American intellectuals to endorse the Communist candidate for President, William Z. Foster. Shortly afterwards, however, he moved towards the independent socialism of A. J. Muste's [q.v.] American Workers Party, which merged with the Trotskyists in 1934. At the same time Hook emerged as the foremost American interpreter of Marxist theory. His *Towards the Understanding of Karl Marx* (1933) argued that revolutionary action brought with it the truest form of social knowledge; *From Hegel to Marx* (1936) was a widely acclaimed exploration of Marxism's intellectual genesis. Beginning in the late-1930s, however, Hook's anti-Communism began to overshadow his radicalism, and by the early-1940s he became a critic of Marxism.

During the postwar period Hook won broad support from American liberals for his anti-Communist views, which he vigorously expounded in his books and in the *New York Times, Commentary*, the *New Leader* and other periodicals. In 1949, following the controversial firing of several alleged Communist professors at the University of Washington, Hook called for the ouster of all Communist teachers from American classrooms, arguing that Communist Party membership in itself constituted proof of professional incompetence and commitment to a subversive conspiracy. The following year he attended the founding meeting of the Congress for Cultural Freedom in West Berlin, an international association of intellectuals that aimed at encouraging collaboration between socialists, liberals and conservatives in uniting Western nations against the threat of Communist aggression. Shortly afterwards Hook joined with James Burnham [q.v.], Arthur Schlesinger, Jr. [q.v.] and novelist James T. Farrell in organizing the American Committee for Cultural Freedom (ACCF). Initially a coalition of conservative and moderate liberal scholars and cultural leaders, many of them ex-Communists, the ACCF looked forward to an era when, in Hook's words, "references to 'right', 'left' and 'center' will vanish from common usage

as meaningless." [See TRUMAN Volume]

As a leading spokesman for the ACCF, Hook called on liberalism to "toughen its fiber," to break from a tradition of uncritical tolerance and recognize Communism as a powerful conspiracy requiring a new political approach. He set forth this view in "Heresy, Yes—Conspiracy, No!," originally published in the *New York Times* and issued by the ACCF as a pamphlet in 1953. Arguing that Communism, as "a secret or underground movement which seeks to attain its ends not by normal political or educational processes, but by playing outside the rules of the game," must be distinguished from a dissenting opinion, or "heresy," Hook insisted that Communist Party members were not entitled to the protection of civil liberties. Hook defended the Smith Act, which made it illegal for any individual to advocate the overthrow of the government by force and violence, as consistent with democratic legal and political processes, although he opposed its application to speech instead of organizations. He argued further that Communists did not have the right to teach on the grounds that Communist teachers "indoctrinated" students.

As a member of the ACCF's committee on academic freedom, Hook supported the firing of Communist teachers but warned that academic tenure should be left in the hands of colleges and boards of education and not turned over to congressional bodies such as the House Un-American Activities Committee. Hook condemned what he called the "cultural vigilantism" of Sen. Joseph McCarthy (R, Wisc.) [q.v.] and the Right but sought to minimize what many liberals termed a "witch hunt" that threatened civil liberties and democracy. Hook and the ACCF protested the government's refusal to permit Charlie Chaplin's reentry into the U.S. and its probe of playwright Arthur Miller [q.v.]. They also criticized McCarthy's investigations of the Voice of America, but in general they concentrated their fire on those writers who they believed were exploiting the civil liberties issue to the advantage of Communism.

During the 1960s Hook continued to

write extensively on civil liberties, Marxism and American politics as well as progressive education, philosophical theory and other subjects. In 1968 he published *Academic Freedom and Academic Anarchy*, an attack on the New Left.

[TLH]

HOOVER, HERBERT (CLARK)
b. Aug. 10, 1874; West Branch, Iowa
d. Oct. 20, 1964; New York, N.Y.
President of the United States, 1929-33; Chairman, Commission on Organization of the Executive Branch, 1947-49, 1953-55.

Orphaned at the age of nine, Herbert Hoover migrated to California to live with relatives. He graduated from Stanford University in 1894. In the next 20 years Hoover made a fortune as a mining engineer and executive. He directed various Allied relief efforts during World War I and in 1917-18 headed the U.S. Food Administration; his personal assistants included Robert A. Taft [q.v.] and Lewis L. Strauss [q.v.]. Between 1921 and 1928 Hoover served with distinction as Secretary of Commerce. With a large national following originating from his World War I humanitarianism, and representing the Republican Party during an economic boom, Hoover was easily elected President in 1928.

Hoover had the ill-fortune to be President at the onset of the Great Depression. Although he took unprecedented actions to reverse the world economic breakdown, forces beyond his control proved insurmountable. He also lacked the skilled, charismatic leadership necessary at a time of great national crisis. Hoover could manipulate neither the Congress nor public opinion. The voters rejected him for reelection in 1932 by wide margin. For the rest of Hoover's long life, Democratic orators and large numbers of people identified him and his party with the Depression.

Hoover remained out of government

through the Roosevelt Administration. More conservative with age, he criticized the New Deal severely. He viewed the emerging American welfare state with its budding bureaucracy as a menace not only to free enterprise but to individual initiative and dignity. He opposed U.S. involvement in World War II and the retention of U.S. ground forces in Europe thereafter.

Hoover returned to government service after Roosevelt's death. As after World War I, he directed relief efforts for a devastated Europe. Between 1947 and 1949 Hoover chaired the first "Hoover Commission," a special panel that recommended a more efficient, vertical organization of the executive branch. [See TRUMAN Volume]

The election of Dwight D. Eisenhower, the first Republican President since Hoover, further improved the ex-President's national stature. Although Hoover had not supported Eisenhower for the presidential nomination and disagreed with him on some policy matters, he and Eisenhower became good friends. Hoover attended White House functions and Western fishing outings and barbecues. The President named Hoover's eldest son, Herbert Hoover, Jr. [q.v.], undersecretary of state in August 1954.

During the Eisenhower Administration Hoover chaired the Second Hoover Commission on the Organization of the Executive Branch. As before, Hoover strove to make the executive branch less wasteful. But he also determined that a reformed administration would be one more accountable to the people through a better, more systematic presentation of official "facts and records" for public discussion. In addition, the second Commission, unlike its predecessor, enjoyed the broader mandate of surveying policy as well as functional coordination.

The Commission covered much ground in issuing its reports through the first half of 1955. Its 11 members, from both parties and several special study groups, studied such diverse problems as intelligence gathering, foreign aid, budget and accounting, military supply, administrative procedure and water power. In all, the Commission investigated 95% of all executive departments and agencies. Many of its findings related gross examples of mismanagement and poor planning. In April 1955, for example, the Commission reported that the Navy's supply of hamburger would last 60 years. Hoover promised that, if adopted, his panel's recommendations would save the government untold billions of dollars.

The Hoover Commission's reports proved to be conservative in domestic policy. The panel uncovered about 3,000 examples of governmental competition with the private sector and requested that one-third of the programs be dismantled. Others, it declared, should be denied certain exclusive privileges. The Rural Electrification Administration, it proposed, should be forced to operate on a self-supporting basis. (Hoover himself privately wished to sell the popular Tennessee Valley Authority [TVA], a product of the New Deal era. "I would sell the TVA if I could only get a dollar for it," he reportedly told one GOP senator.) The Commission called for the dissolution of such federal lending programs as the Agricultural Marketing Act Revolving Fund and the Federal Farm Mortgage Act.

Eisenhower had mixed reactions to the Commission's findings. He approved of certain structural reforms, in budgeting for example, but he refused to endorse the Commission's more conservative recommendations. He politely ignored Hoover's idea (and own draft) of a message to Congress promoting them. Of the Second Hoover Commission's 314 suggestions, the Administration adopted 64% (compared to Truman's 72% rate of implementation).

Hoover, for his part, played the role of elder statesman practically to the very end of his life. He addressed and was well received by the 1956 and 1960 Republican National Conventions while remaining an object of derision at Democratic ones. His public image from that of the 1930s did improve; in December 1959 a Gallup survey listed him ninth on a list of Most Admired Americans. Democratic President Kennedy, whose father, Joseph P. Kennedy, served on the Second Hoover Commission, consulted with Hoover. "You will discover," Hoover wrote Richard M. Nixon [q.v.] in 1961,

"that elder statesmen are little regarded . . . until they are over 80 years of age and thus harmless."

[JLB]

HOOVER, HERBERT, JR.
b. Aug. 4, 1903; London, England
d. July 9, 1969; Pasadena, Calif.
Special Consultant to the Secretary of State, 1953-54; Undersecretary of State, October 1954-December 1956.

The son of the 31st President of the United States, Herbert Hoover, Jr., graduated from Stanford University in 1925. He received his M.B.A. from Harvard Business School in 1928 and remained there as an instructor during the next two years. Hoover worked as a communications engineer from 1929 to 1934 for Transcontinental and Western Air, Inc. In 1935 he was a teaching fellow at the California Institute of Technology. Like his father, Herbert Hoover, Jr. was a mining engineer. After inventing a number of radio and electronic devices to detect oil, Hoover founded the United Geophysical Co. at Pasadena, Calif., in 1935, which employed over 1,000 persons prospecting all over the world. During World War II Hoover invented several instruments to measure the vibration and strain in aircraft.

As a result of his dealings with the oil producing nations, Hoover was asked to negotiate the settlement of the Iranian-British dispute over the Abadan oil fields in 1953-54. In May 1951 the Premier of Iran, Mohammed Mossadegh, nationalized all oil fields under the operation of the British-controlled Anglo-Iranian Oil Co. Over the next two months the company shut down its refinery and ordered its British technicians to leave Iran. Great Britain, in turn, withdrew permission for Iran to exchange sterling credits for dollars and placed an embargo on the sale of essential goods to that country. Iran ordered the British to close all their consulates in January 1952 and severed all diplomatic relations with Great Britain by October. From 1951 to 1953, as relations became more embittered, the Anglo-Iranian Oil Co., the International Court of Justice, the U.S., Great Britain and Iran tried to negotiate a settlement but without success. It was only after the Shah of Iran, supported by major segments of the population and with possible aid from the Central Intelligence Agency, overthrew Mossadegh at the end of 1953 that the tide of negotiations turned. Iran was also eager to negotiate because over the two year period England and the U.S. had shifted much of their oil trade to other Middle Eastern countries. Thus, when President Eisenhower sent Hoover to arrange a settlement, he met a warm reception. As a result of Hoover's efforts, Secretary of State John Foster Dulles [q.v.] and British Foreign Secretary Anthony Eden agreed in August 1954 to the marketing of Iran's oil by a consortium of five American companies and British, Dutch and French interests. The British also agreed to turn over their oil industry to Iran for $70 million. The consortium agreed to pay the Anglo-Iranian Oil Co. $600 million for over half of the future oil market during the next 25 years.

Eisenhower appointed Hoover undersecretary of state in August 1954. During the Suez Canal crisis of 1956, Hoover was acting Secretary of State while John Foster Dulles recovered from a stomach operation. That December Hoover resigned from the State Department to that resume his career as a mining engineer. He was replaced by Christian Herter [q.v.]. Hoover then returned to private business. He died of cancer at the age of 65.

[RSG]

HOOVER, J(OHN) EDGAR
b. Jan. 1, 1895; Washington, D.C.
d. May 2, 1972; Washington, D.C.
Director, Federal Bureau of Investigation, 1924-72.

J. Edgar Hoover grew up in Washington, D.C., where his father worked for the Coast and Geodetic Survey. After graduating from high school in 1913, Hoover worked as an indexer for the Library of Congress while attending George Washington University law school at night. He received his degree in

1916 and then served as a clerk in the Justice Department. Three years later he was assistant to Attorney General A. Mitchell Palmer, then conducting a roundup of thousands of alleged Communists and anarchists for deportation. In 1921 he was appointed assistant director of the Bureau of Investigation (the name was changed to Federal Bureau of Investigation in 1935).

Three years later Hoover became director. He was given the task of reforming the Bureau, then implicated in the scandals of the Harding Administration. At his insistance the agency was depoliticized and a merit system introduced for recruiting agents. The new director immediately improved morale by recruiting an honest and well-disciplined staff. Hoover also built the Bureau into a major police resource and educational center. He established a national fingerprint file in 1925, a major crime laboratory in 1932 and a training school for local police officers in 1935. Gradually the Bureau increased its powers. During the 1930s the agency, which initially was only a federal investigatory body, was given the authority to deal with certain intrastate crimes, and its agents were permitted to make arrests and carry firearms. Hoover and the "G-men," as agents were known, became heroes during the decade for their efforts to arrest such "public enemies" as John Dillinger and "Baby Face" Nelson.

In 1936 President Franklin D. Roosevelt gave Hoover the authority to investigate espionage and sabotage. Following Pearl Harbor Hoover expanded his operation to include the surveillance of right-wing individuals and organizations, labor unions, and civil rights groups, all of which, he believed could undermine the war effort. The FBI also kept a list of American Communists for possible arrest and detention.

After World War II the FBI became increasingly involved in investigating Communist subversion. The fear of espionage, as well as the belief that American Communists, directed by Moscow, were in sensitive government positions was used to justify the institutionalization of the covert operations deemed temporary during the War. President Harry S. Truman permitted Hoover to continue FBI surveillance of ex-

tremist movements. The Bureau also conducted security checks of federal employes
and continued to compile lists of "disloyal"
Americans for possible detention in case of
a national emergency. In 1952 Truman
liberalized the FBI's wiretapping authority.
Hoover stretched the delegation of power
to justify opening Americans' mail and conducting illegal burglaries to obtain damaging evidence. Information gathered by the
FBI played an important role in the prosecution of Alger Hiss and Julius and Ethel
Rosenberg [q.v.]. [See TRUMAN Volume]

When Eisenhower became President, he
made it clear that Hoover had a free hand to
continue his investigations. Attorney General Herbert Brownell [q.v.] liberalized
even further the Bureau's authority to conduct wiretaps and investigate government
employes. Bureau agents crossed the country
asking people for information about their
relatives, friends, fellow workers and
neighbors. Some of the key questions were:
whether the subject in question voted for
Henry Wallace in 1948, read The New Republic, supported civil rights and favored
socialized medicine. In an article in the 1954
Northwestern University Law Review,
Hoover said the FBI processed five million
loyalty forms. He claimed that 560 people
were removed from federal jobs or denied
employment as a result of FBI investigations. Over 6,000 other Americans left their
jobs in the private sector or withdrew their
applications because of the probes.

In November 1953 Hoover testified before the Senate Internal Security Subcommittee. The panel was then investigating
Brownell's charges that Truman had appointed Harry Dexter White to be director
of the International Monetary Fund while
knowing he was a Communist. Hoover cor-
roborated Brownell's accusation. However,
the issue quickly died.

During the decade Hoover embarked on
a crusade to educate the American public
on the evils of Communism. Although he
was a secretive man who never held press
conferences, he did consent to be interviewed when he was able to discuss "the
Communist menace" in American life. He
also had his staff ghost-write magazine articles for him on the subject.

Hoover's widely sold book, Masters of
Deceit: The Story of Communism in
America and How to Fight It (1958), written by his FBI staff, was designed to serve
as a primer on the history, aims, and successes of Communist infiltration. He asked
Americans to guard against subversives and
report any evidence of it to the FBI. He
warned his readers to be wary of slogans
used by Communists and their liberal supporters to camouflage their real intentions.
According to Hoover, Communists used such
words as "peace," "disarmament," "academic freedom" and "trade with the East"
to gain support and strengthen their position at home and abroad.

The FBI made a series of spectacular arrests during the decade. In 1957 the agency
arrested Soviet Col. Rudolf Abel, head of a
large espionage ring. The following year,
using a Soviet agent turned informer, the
Bureau closed another spy operation.
Hoover's fears of espionage led him to oppose increasing economic and cultural contacts with the Soviet bloc. The FBI considered every Soviet visitor a potential spy.

In 1975 the Senate Select Committee to
Study Government Operations, known as
the Church Committee, investigated FBI
activities during the Eisenhower era. Its
report documented illegal wiretaps, mail
openings and burglaries. The panel revealed the existence of COINTELPRO, an
operation designed to disrupt and neu-
tralize the Communist Party in the U.S.
Hoover began this project in 1956 because
the federal judiciary had made it increasingly difficult to prosecute Communists for
subversive activities under existing legislation. COINTELPRO involved the use of
"dirty tricks" to undermine the Party.
Under the plan the Bureau leaked information to the press on Party activities, sent
anonymous letters to employers of Communists demanding they be fired and
harassed Party members and disrupted
Party operations. The Church Committee
reported that Hoover had informed the
President, the White House staff, the
cabinet and the Attorney General of the operation, but no objection had been raised.

Hoover also provided intelligence information of a personal nature for the White

House. He informed Eisenhower of the activities of such individuals as Eleanor Roosevelt [*q.v.*], Norman Thomas [*q.v.*], Bernard Baruch and Justice William O. Douglas [*q.v.*]. Hoover also reported on the activities of civil rights organizations, labor unions and far right groups.

Despite congressional investigations of the underworld during the decade, Hoover refused to acknowledge the existence of organized crime. According to some critics, he devoted little attention to the problem because convictions were difficult to obtain. Rather, the FBI investigated the more spectacular types of crimes, such as kidnappings, that obtained media coverage and impressed Congress and the President.

J. Edgar Hoover's career lasted well into Richard Nixon's first term as President. During the 1960s he continued his domestic surveillance programs. Hoover died in May 1972, just before revelations of some of the Bureau's more questionable practices.

[JB]

For further information:
Sanford J. Ungar, *The FBI* (Boston, 1975).

HOPE, CLIFFORD R(AGSDALE)
b. June 9, 1893; Birmingham, Iowa.
d. May 16, 1970; Garden City, Kan.
Republican Representative, Kan.,
1927-57; Chairman, Agriculture Committee, 1947-49, 1953-55.

Hope received an LL.B. degree in 1917 from the Washburn law school in Topeka, Kan. After serving as a second lieutenant in World War I, he opened a law office in Garden City, Kan., in 1919. He entered the Kansas state legislature in 1921.

Five years later Hope was elected to the U.S. House of Representatives. From his freshman term in the House, he was a member of the Agriculture Committee. In 1936 Hope was appointed chairman of the Republican National Committee's farm division, and many observers anticipated that he would become Secretary of Agriculture in the event of Republican candidate Alf Landon's victory in the presidential elec-

tion. Hope became chairman of the House Agriculture Committee after the Republicans won the 1946 elections. A backer of the Democratic program of high price supports, he favored a 1948 measure establishing 90% parity for basic commodities. However, the following year Hope opposed an Administration plan to give Secretary of Agriculture Charles Brannan increased authority to limit farm production. [See TRUMAN Volume]

A moderate Republican, Hope was one of 19 representatives who sent a letter to Dwight D. Eisenhower in February 1952 urging him to seek the Republican presidential nomination. Following the Republican landslide of that year, Hope again became chairman of the Agriculture Committee. In 1953 he supported an Eisenhower Administration bill increasing the authority of the Secretary of Agriculture within his Department. He also backed the Administration's proposal authorizing the President to use farm products stored under the price support program to relieve famine conditions abroad, warning that the program would fall into disrepute if the stored crops rotted while people starved.

In 1953 Hope introduced a bill enabling farmers, ranchers and stockmen in a drought area that included parts of Kansas to obtain government loans and other assistance. The same year he also introduced a measure reorganizing the Farm Credit Administration, divorcing it from the Agriculture Department and increasing "farmer participation and control of the farm credit system." In 1954 Hope and Sen. George D. Aiken (R, Vt.) [*q.v.*] introduced a watershed protection bill authorizing the Secretary of Agriculture to cooperate with state and local agencies to improve soil conservation in the upriver watershed or "subwatershed" areas of streams and rivers.

Hope opposed the major feature of the Administration's 1954 omnibus farm program, which was the establishment of flexible price supports between 75% and 90% of parity for the six basic farm commodities. The bill that emerged from his Committee retained 90% parity through 1955. The final measure provided flexibility but limited it to between 82.5% and 90% of parity. In

1955, as ranking minority member of the agriculture panel, Hope favored a Democratic-inspired proposal to reestablish 90% parity. However, he declined to join other Midwestern Republicans in publicly criticizing Secretary of Agriculture Ezra Taft Benson [q.v.].

Hope did not run for reelection in 1956. He died of a stroke on May 16, 1970 in Garden City, Kan.

[MLL]

HUGHES, EMMET J(OHN)
b. Dec. 26, 1920; Newark, N.J.
Administrative Assistant to the President, January 1953-September 1953; July 1956-January 1957.

The son of Irish Catholic parents, Hughes graduated summa cum laude from Princeton in 1941. He pursued graduate study there until 1942, when his adviser was appointed ambassador to Spain; Hughes accompanied him as press attache and remained there until 1946. During World War II he also served with the Office of Strategic Services. In 1946 Hughes accepted a job as head of the Time-Life bureau in Rome; two years later he became head of its Berlin bureau. In 1949 he was made articles editor of *Life* magazine. Hughes left the Luce organization in 1952, when he volunteered as a speechwriter for Republican presidential candidate Dwight D. Eisenhower.

An independent liberal who maintained he would have voted Democratic had he been in the U.S. during the 1940s, Hughes nevertheless believed a Republican victory in 1952 was vital to the survival of the two-party system. As a result he threw himself into the campaign with vigor. In consultation with Eisenhower's strategy board of Herbert Brownell [q.v.], Harold Stassen [q.v.] and C. D. Jackson [q.v.], Hughes drafted the major speeches of the 1952 Eisenhower campaign. He also contributed ideas of his own, principally that leading to Eisenhower's promise to go to Korea if elected. According to some historians, Hughes's finest effort, the "I will go to Korea" speech, delivered in October, helped clinch the presidential victory

for the Republican candidate in November.

During the transition period following the November election, Eisenhower enlisted Hughes as an administrative assistant to draft statements and speeches. Hughes's principal duty was to collaborate with the President-elect on his inaugural address. Once in the White House Eisenhower continued to use Hughes as a speechwriter. The President frankly admired his phrase-making abilities and relied upon him to turn raw ideas into flowing prose. According to Eisenhower's special assistant, Sherman Adams [q.v.], one of Hughes's more notable contributions was the President's April 1953 speech signaling an American desire for peaceful coexistence with the Communist world.

During his eight months at the White House, Hughes became increasingly disillusioned with the Administration's irresolution, particularly in dealing with Sen. Joseph R. McCarthy (R, Wisc.) [q.v.]. Following McCarthy's denunciation of the State Department and his aides' European trip to investigate subversive literature in U.S. overseas libraries, Hughes urged Eisenhower to take the offensive against the Senator. However, the President, attempting to remain above politics, refused, as he said "to get in the gutter with that guy." In July 1953 Hughes seized a request for a presidential message to the American Library Association as a chance to draft a warning against McCarthy's excesses. Eisenhower signed the letter, but the President generally ignored Hughes's other reqeusts for action.

Disillusioned with Eisenhower, Hughes resigned in September 1953 to take a post as foreign correspondent in Europe for *Life*. Away from the White House he continued to score the Administration. In November 1953 he sent a long letter to the President explaining that the Administration appeared indecisive because of bickering within the cabinet. Despite his criticisms, Hughes readily accepted an invitation to speak on Eisenhower's behalf at the 1956 Republican National Convention. Soon after, he rejoined the President's staff as a special assistant on speeches and campaign strategy. He drafted Eisenhower's Nov. 1 policy speech on the Suez crisis in which the President scored British, French and Israeli action and urged U.N. intervention on the matter.

The day after Eisenhower's second inaugural, Hughes ended his White House career. While he helped draft a presidential speech on foreign aid in May 1957, Hughes otherwise resumed his work with Time-Life. In the 1960s he served as an adviser to the Rockefeller family and as a special assistant to Gov. Nelson Rockefeller [*q.v.*] in his unsuccessful 1968 presidential bid. In between his work with the Rockefellers, Hughes wrote a column for *Newsweek*, and published a critical study of the Eisenhower years. In 1970 he joined the political science department of Rutgers University.

[RB]

For further information:
Emmet John Hughes, *The Ordeal of Power* (New York, 1963).

HUGHES, HOWARD R(OBARD)
b. Dec. 24, 1905; Houston, Tex.
d. April 5, 1976; Aboard an Acapulco-Houston flight.
Industrialist.

At the age of 18 Howard Hughes inherited his father's tool company. The elder Hughes held exclusive patent rights to oil-well drilling equipment, and this monopoly enabled his son to earn close to $2 million a year. With an independent income Hughes turned his attention to film making in the late-1920s and early-1930s, quickly establishing himself as one of Hollywood's leading independent producers.

In 1935 Hughes founded the Hughes Aircraft Co. He also earned a distinguished record as an aviator who, between 1935 and 1938, broke three major speed records, including one for flying around the world. In 1937 Hughes purchased Trans World Airlines (TWA) and developed it into the first intercontinental air carrier. Hughes's enterprises prospered during the 1940s, and the relatively young playboy, known for his eccentric and reclusive lifestyle, gained national attention.

Hughes purchased the controlling interest in the RKO Motion Picture Co. for $8 million in 1948. He became managing director of production and arranged to have his associates placed in top management positions. During Hughes's six years of control, the company lost close to $20 million. In September 1952 he sold his shares to offset criticism of his leadership, but he loaned the company $8 million. Hughes also faced law suits from many irate RKO shareholders who charged him with incompetence in running the studio. In 1954 Hughes surprised Hollywood by purchasing all RKO stock for close to $25 million, thereby becoming the first sole owner of a major studio. Optimists predicted that Hughes would lead RKO out of debt, but the following year he divested himself of all his RKO holdings. It is believed he made $10 million dollars profit on this transaction.

During the late-1940s and 1950s, Hughes was a vigorous anti-Communist who often used his position as producer and movie company owner to blacklist presumed Communist sympathizers. In 1951 Hughes fired Paul Jarrico, one of RKO's leading writers, for refusing to cooperate with the House Un-American Activities Committee. Hughes also ordered that Jarrico's name not be included in the credits of a film he had recently written. Jarrico sued Hughes in a case that came to court in 1957. Hughes's lawyer argued that at the time of the firing the American public felt animosity toward Communist sympathizers. He claimed that anyone who refused to cooperate with a government committee would be viewed as a Communist, and thus it would have hurt RKO to have use Jarrico's name. The court ruled in Hughes's favor.

On Jan. 27, 1953 Hughes made a rare public appearance before the American Legion's Hollywood post. In his speech he agreed that Communists had infiltrated the motion picture industry. Hughes maintained that an individual's refusal to disclose whether or not he was a Communist was enough to incriminate him and claimed that those who defended the civil liberties of suspected Communists did not have the best interests of the nation at heart. He also supported the Legion's efforts to bar Charlie Chaplin's film *Limelight* from American theaters because of Chaplin's left-wing sympathies. Hughes promised to use his influence to convince RKO Theaters Corp., one of the largest national movie chains, not to present the film. The drive was successful.

In the late-1950s TWA began to lose money because of stiff competition as well as poor management. Hughes procrastinated in making the decision to order Boeing 707s. The company therefore lagged behind its competition in converting to an all-jet fleet. During the 1960s Hughes fought a grueling court battle with his creditors for control of the airline. He sold off his stock in 1966 for $546.5 million, the second largest stock transaction in U.S. history. [See JOHNSON Volume]

After the TWA fiasco Hughes began investing in large amounts of land in Nevada, including hotels in Las Vegas. During the late-1960s and early-1970s, Hughes lead a reclusive, rumor-filled existence, traveling frequently throughout the world to avoid court battles and government probes of his business dealings. He died in April 1976 on a flight from Acapulco, Mex., to Houston, Tex. [See NIXON/FORD Volume]

[JB]

For further information:
Albert B. Gerber, *Bashful Billionaire* (New York, 1967).
John Keats, *Howard Hughes* (New York, 1966).

HUGHES, ROWLAND R(OBERTS)
b. March 28, 1896; Oakhurst, N.J.
d. April 2, 1957; San Francisco, Calif.
Director, Bureau of the Budget, April 1954-March 1956.

Rowland Hughes worked for the National City Bank of New York from his senior year in college until he joined the Eisenhower Administration in 1953. In the 10 years following his graduation from Brown University in 1917, he was employed at the bank's branches in Shanghai, Bombay, Osaka and Tokyo. Recalled to New York in 1927, Hughes was made assistant controller in 1929 and controller in 1934. Beginning in the 1940s he became an active member of the tax committees of the Controllers Institute of America, the American Bankers Association and the Council of State Chambers of Commerce.

Hughes entered the Eisenhower Administration in April 1953 as assistant director of the budget. He became deputy director in August and in April 1954 succeeded Joseph M. Dodge [*q.v.*] as director. Hughes's background and beliefs placed him in full accord with the Administration's objective of reducing the size of the federal budget. Seeking to promote economy and efficiency by example, he reduced his own agency's appropriation request by $33,500 in May 1955. In July it was revealed that the federal deficit for fiscal year 1955 had been $300 million less than expected.

Hughes also vigorously sought to end government competition with private business wherever possible. On Jan. 25, 1955 he directed all government agencies to complete by April 15 an inventory of their commercial activities and report by July 15 which of their manufacturing facilities could be shifted to the private sector.

Hughes was a key figure in the Dixon-Yates affair, the Eisenhower Administration's most controversial attempt to replace government activity with private enterprise. The plan was to have a Southern utilities combine construct a steam power plant near West Memphis, Ark., to supply power to Atomic Energy Commission installations in the area and to surrounding municipalities previously served by the Tennessee Valley Authority. The project had originated in the Budget Bureau when Hughes was second in command. Hughes took part in drawing up the contract with utility executives Edgar Dixon [*q.v.*] and Eugene Yates, promoted it within the government and defended it before congressional committees. His testimony, however, was ambiguous and contradictory. His appearance before the Joint Committee on Atomic Energy in November 1954 prompted *The New Republic* to remark that Hughes "proved to be as inept a witness as reporters could remember. He appeared to know so little about the major provisions of the Dixon-Yates contract, which he had approved, that with some justification Sen. Clinton

Anderson (D, N.M.) [q.v.] asked him if he had ever read it."

Early in 1955 critics of the contract charged that one of the officials responsible for drawing it up was guilty of conflict of interest. It was revealed that a Budget Bureau consultant, Adolphe Wenzell, was an employe of the First Boston Corp., which was acting as a financial agent for the Dixon-Yates combine. Testifying before the Senate Antitrust and Monopoly Subcommittee, which investigated the affair in June, Hughes stated that Wenzell's role had been insignificant, that he had "never had anything to do with the policy of Dixon-Yates." Hughes also professed ignorance of the fact that First Boston was acting as a financial agent of Dixon-Yates. A few days later Wenzell himself contradicted Hughes's statements, asserting that he had been called to Washington in January 1954 by Hughes to serve as an expert in the financing of the project, had attended some 20 meetings on the subject and had made First Boston's interest in the contract "abundantly clear" to Hughes. The subcommittee report, issued in August 1955, concluded "the testimony that Hughes gave . . . defies understanding." By that date President Eisenhower had ordered the contract canceled.

Within the Eisenhower Administration Hughes was the focal point of conflicting pressures to spend more in individual cases while balancing the total budget. On March 30, 1956, the day before his retirement, Hughes submitted a memo to the President criticizing special interests and department heads, "special pleaders for particular expenditures," for lobbying for increased allocations "regardless of the impact on the budget as a whole." The chief offender, in Hughes's view, was Secretary of Defense Charles Wilson [q.v.], who persistently sought larger appropriations for new projects. Such pressures were undermining the Administration's initial zeal for reducing expenditures, Hughes maintained. As it happened, the government enjoyed a $1.75-billion budget surplus for fiscal year 1956, the first surplus since 1951.

Hughes died of arteriosclerosis in 1957.

[TO]

HUMPHREY, GEORGE M(AGOFFIN)

b. March 8, 1890; Cheboygan, Mich.
d. Jan. 20, 1970; Cleveland, Ohio.
Secretary of the Treasury, January 1953-July 1957.

George Humphrey grew up in Saginaw, Mich., and attended the University of Michigan, from which he received a law degree in 1912. He worked for his father's law firm in Saginaw until 1918, when he became general counsel for the M. A. Hanna Co. of Cleveland. Humphrey rose rapidly in the firm, becoming vice president by 1922 and president in 1929. When Humphrey joined M. A. Hanna, it was a money-losing shipper of iron ore and coal in the Great Lakes region. Under his leadership it became a prosperous, expanding industrial enterprise, branching out into mining and becoming involved in steel, rayon, plastics, oil and copper production and even banking. Through mergers Humphrey placed the National Steel Co. and the Pittsburgh Consolidated Coal Co. under M. A. Hanna's corporate umbrella. By 1952 M. A. Hanna had assets totaling more than $120 million.

In 1946 Humphrey was named chairman of the Department of Commerce's Business Advisory Council. In 1948 Paul Hoffman, [q.v.], head of the Economic Cooperation Administration, chose him to head the five-man Reparations Survey Committee to advise the Allied powers on the issue of dismantling German industrial plants, a task Humphrey carried out delicately and successfully. He was a strong supporter of Sen. Robert Taft (R, Ohio) [q.v.] in his pre-convention campaign of 1948 but played no prominent role in the 1952 election. In November 1952, on the recommendation of Hoffman and Gen. Lucius Clay [q.v.], President-elect Dwight D. Eisenhower designated Humphrey his Secretary of the Treasury.

Although previously unacquainted, Eisenhower and Humphrey quickly established a warm personal rapport that was both lasting and politically significant. The President frequently hunted quail and played golf with Humphrey at the latter's plantation in Thomasville, Ga. The two men were in essential agreement on political issues. "In cabinet meetings," Eisenhower said, "I always wait for George Humphrey to speak. I sit back and listen to the others talk while he doesn't say anything. But I know that when he speaks he will say just what I am thinking." Armed with this unique presidential trust in addition to his own forceful personality, Humphrey was the dominant figure in the domestic area during the first term of the Eisenhower Administration.

Humphrey's views were staunchly conservative and pro-business. He believed that the federal government was too large and meddlesome, hindering economic growth and eroding self-reliance and individual initiative. Chronic budgetary deficits were especially dangerous, Humphrey held. He was the Administration's strongest advocate of paring the size of government and balancing the budget in order to cut inflation and invigorate private enterprise. To this end he also favored cutting taxes, which he believed were too high and a hinderance to investment.

Humphrey's opinions reflected conventional Republican doctrine and were generally shared by President Eisenhower. Nevertheless, Eisenhower's top assistant, Sherman Adams [q.v.], recalled that "while [Eisenhower] had great respect for Humphrey's judgment, it seemed to him that Humphrey was sometimes too quick to think of government economic problems in the terms of private industry and occasionally too impatient for fast action."

Humphrey first asserted his influence in the debate that took place among President-elect Eisenhower's top advisers in the winter of 1952-53 over the continuation of the Korean war wage and price controls. Humphrey was the most vocal advocate of the elimination of all controls, on the ground that they brought only economic stagnation. He contended, against the arguments of some of Eisenhower's moderate advisers, that the resulting increased production would absorb any wage increases, while a policy of "tight money" would forestall price inflation. In his January 1953

State of the Union message, Eisenhower announced that all controls on prices and wages would be removed shortly. The ensuing decontrol was not followed by any deleterious rise in prices.

In line with his belief in the efficacy of monetary policy in controlling inflation and his preference for long-term over short-term borrowing by the government, Humphrey in April 1953 brought out an issue of 30-year bonds with the attractive interest rate of 3.25%, the highest in 20 years. A group of Democratic senators denounced the interest boost as "drastically deflationary," the same hard-money tactics that led to the Great Depression. Humphrey retorted that the high interest was necessary for "economic stability." The move did dampen the possibility of inflation but precipitated a credit squeeze that contributed to an economic slump in the summer and fall of 1953 as the bond issue soaked up money that otherwise would have been invested in stocks and mortgages. The Federal Reserve moved to ease the crisis by lowering member banks' reserve requirements, thus widening the pool of lending money. Humphrey, himself, later admitted that he had tightened credit too much. Throughout his tenure, nevertheless, he pressed for high interest rates to ward off the threat of inflation, although his Treasury increased the heavy concentration of short-term government debt he had condemned in the Truman Administration and had pledged to reduce. In this regard "we did not accomplish what we wanted to," he acknowledged in June 1957, adding that "my successor is going to find no improvement in this mess."

The Eisenhower cabinet's strongest voice of fiscal conservatism, Humphrey spearheaded the Administration's campaign to cut the federal budget. His rhetorical prodding helped reduce the $9.9 billion deficit projected by the outgoing Truman Administration for fiscal 1954 to $3.1 billion. The end of the Korean war in 1953 was also a factor in the reduction. Humphrey persistently sought to reduce foreign aid and military outlays as well as expenditures on social programs and the daily operations of government. He frequently drew analogies between government finance and that of a business or a household to illustrate his conviction that the government had to live within its income or face ultimate ruin. The budget for fiscal 1955, however, again showed a sizeable deficit (of $1.2 billion). It was not until 1956 that the Eisenhower Administration balanced its budget, showing a surplus of $1.75 billion, the first since 1951.

For the most part, Humphrey's primary objective of balancing the budget superseded his desire to cut taxes. In 1953 he opposed a Republican movement in the House, led by Rep. Danial Reed (R, N.Y.) [q.v.], chairman of the Ways and Means Committee, to reduce income taxes and eliminate the wartime excess profits tax. Humphrey argued that having the higher wartime rates expire on July 1, 1953, as the congressmen wanted, instead of on Dec. 31, as the Administration requested, would cost the government revenue, exacerbate the deficit and fuel the threat of inflation. In alliance with congressional leaders, the Administration defeated the tax-cut forces.

Humphrey supported the expiration of the excess profits tax and the wartime income tax increases on Dec. 31, 1953, as well as the ending of various excise levies on luxury products on April 1, 1954. He also endorsed a special tax revision enacted in 1954 that exempted from taxation a portion of income derived from stock dividends. Against the objections of liberal Democrats that such loopholes favored the well-to-do, Humphrey defended this principle of taxation with the argument that it would stimulate equity financing and capital spending and thus ultimately benefit low-income families by creating jobs and bringing over-all prosperity.

Despite his oft-repeated sermons about the desirability of tax reduction, Humphrey usually used his influence to block tax cuts, particularly broad-based tax reductions initiated by Democrats in Congress. In March 1955 he attacked a Democratic plan to stimulate the economy by giving each taxpayer a $20 tax cut as "silly" and "irresponsible," a "political quickie gimmick." The $20 cut was approved by the House but rejected by the Senate. At the same time Congress approved the Administra-

tion's request to defer scheduled excise and corporate tax cuts for a year and thus add $2.8 billion to government income. In 1956 and 1957 Humphrey's concern over the budget continued to override his discomfort over high taxes. He declared in a speech on Feb. 1, 1956 that taxes should be cut as soon as possible because they were so high that they were curtailing the "very basis of our freedom—incentive." However, he testified two days later before the Joint Economic Committee that the anticipated budget surplus for fiscal 1956 was too small to permit a tax cut.

Owing to the President's confidence in his judgement, Humphrey exercised a strong influence in policy areas outside the normal authority of Treasury Secretaries. He sat on the National Security Council at the President's invitation. His powerful fiscal conservatism was often a formidable barrier to advocates of ambitious new weapons systems. He was unpersuaded by the arguments of some generals in favor of an increased, highly mobile force of ground troops equipped with sophisticated arms and materials. His cautionary counsel about the fiscal impact of such an expensive undertaking helped persuade Eisenhower that high troop levels were not worth the expense. Humphrey was also the most vigorous proponent within the Eisenhower Administration of the St. Lawrence Seaway, which he had supported for years as M.A. Hanna's president. The project, to convert the St. Lawrence River into an inland waterway connecting the Great Lakes with the Atlantic Ocean by building a deepwater navigation channel, was completed in 1959.

In the first half of 1957, his last months as Treasury Secretary, Humphrey played a controversial and unconventional role in the battle over the budget for fiscal 1958. In January he declared to reporters that the $71.8 billion spending figure submitted by the Administration was too high and invited Congress to make cuts in the Administration's own requests, although he did not specify where. He said that the government must reduce "the terrific tax take we are taking out of this country," because "if we don't over a long period of time, I predict that you will have a depression that will curl your hair." In response to the stir caused by Humphrey's dire prophecy, Eisenhower, a week later, said that Humphrey was not talking about the near future but about a long-term possibility. He affirmed his "complete agreement" with his Treasury Secretary's view that Congress should make cuts in the budget. As it turned out, congressional conservatives enthusiastically slashed appropriations for several departments and programs more deeply than the Administration found acceptable. The Eisenhower Administration ended up pleading, with mixed success, for the restoration of money, particularly for foreign aid and defense. The appropriations bill passed in August totaled $4 billion less than the President's January request, a serious setback for Eisenhower.

In June 1957 Humphrey defended the Eisenhower Administration's fiscal performance, asserting that it had cut government spending, balanced the budget, arrested inflation, achieved a "record-breaking tax reduction" of $7.4 billion in 1954, and "encouraged an expansion of enterprise to new high levels." He conceded that the Administration had not cut non-defense spending below Truman Administration levels nor achieved "some of our debt management objectives."

Humphrey left the Treasury in July and returned to M.A. Hanna as honorary chairman. During the Kennedy years Hanna and Humphrey were the targets of a Senate subcommittee investigating charges that the company and its subsidiaries made "excessive and unconscionable profits" selling nickel ore to the government for its stockpile. Humphrey denied any wrongdoing. He died on Jan. 20, 1970. [See KENNEDY Volume]

[TO]

HUMPHREY, HUBERT H(ORATIO)
b. May 27, 1911; Wallace, S.D.
Democratic Senator, Minn., 1949-65; 1971-

The son of a South Dakota druggist, Hubert Humphrey was profoundly influenced by his father's reverence for William Jennings Bryan and Woodrow Wilson. He was a star debater and class valedictorian in high school, but he had to leave the University of Minnesota early in the Depression to work in his father's drugstore. He became a registered pharmacist and managed the store, while his father participated actively in South Dakota Democratic Party politics. Humphrey returned to the University of Minnesota in 1937, earning his B.A. in 1939 and an M.A. in political science from Louisiana State University a year later. His master's thesis, entitled "The Political Philosophy of the New Deal," was a glowing tribute to Franklin D. Roosevelt's response to the Depression.

After a brief teaching career, Humphrey plunged into Minnesota politics. He played a key role in the 1944 merger of the Farmer-Labor and Democratic Parties and won election as mayor of Minneapolis the next year. As mayor he waged an anti-vice war, created the first municipal fair employment practices commission in the United States, expanded the city's housing program and took an active part in settling strikes. Reelected in 1947 Humphrey helped organize the liberal, anti-Communist Americans for Democratic Action (ADA) and fought a successful battle to purge the Communist faction from the Democratic-Farmer-Labor Party. He gained national attention at the 1948 Democratic National Convention with a stirring oration in favor of a strong civil rights plank, regarded by political observers as one of the most memorable convention speeches of modern times. In November Minnesota voters elected Humphrey to the Senate over the conservative Republican incumbent.

Humphrey quickly moved into the vanguard of the Senate's liberal minority, promoting a wide variety of social welfare, civil rights, tax reform, aid to education and pro-labor legislation. The first bill he introduced was a proposal to establish medical care for the aged financed through the social security system, a principle finally enacted into law as medicare in 1965. In Humphrey's early career powerful Senate conservatives were alienated by his sharp debating style and effusive liberalism, and their hostility reduced his effectiveness. [See TRUMAN Volume]

"I was one of those eager-beaver young liberal Democratic progressives who didn't quite understand that the way to get legislation through is not merely to have a good idea," Humphrey later said. "You have to nourish and nurse it through the Congress. You have to know the system . . . " In the early-1950s Humphrey gradually eased his way into the Senate "establishment," toning down his combative ideological approach and working closely with Democratic leader Sen. Lyndon Johnson (D, Tex.) [q.v.], who used Humphrey as his liaison with liberals and intellectuals. Their partnership resulted in some small liberal advances, such as the Civil Rights Act of 1957, but for the most part Humphrey's persistent liberal advocacy did not bear fruit until the 1960s.

The same was equally true of Humphrey's efforts in the area of foreign affairs. Moving to the Foreign Relations Committee under Johnson's sponsorship in 1953, he promoted several projects reflecting the spirit of Wilsonian idealism that softened his staunch anti-Communism. As chairman of the Committee's Disarmament Subcommittee, created at his urging in 1955, Humphrey kept the issue of nuclear arms control alive through the 1950s. The culmination of his agitation to halt the arms race was the nuclear test ban treaty of 1963.

Humphrey was also a principal advocate of the distribution of American foodstuffs to needy nations abroad. Proposing "an international program for making . . . food available to avert famine and combat Communism" in 1954, he was instrumental in the passage that year of Public Law 480, which authorized both the sale and the distribution of U.S. agricultural surpluses abroad. Humphrey helped expand the law into the more ambitious Food for Peace program in 1961. The program was popular with farmers, whose cause Humphrey championed by lobbying for higher domestic price supports and tariffs on foreign agricultural imports and by relentlessly attacking the Administration's agricultural policies.

Humphrey outdid many anti-Communist conservatives in 1954 by introducing the communist controll bill which, in its original form would have outlawed the Communist Party and provided criminal penalties for membership. "I am tired of reading headlines about being 'soft' toward Communism," he said. "I want to come to grips with the Communist issue." He also maintained that his proposal would make it easier for persons wrongly accused of being Communists to sue their accusers. The bill passed the Senate easily but was altered so drastically in the House-Senate conference that its vague wording rendered it a mullity. Civil Libertarians sharply criticized Humphrey for his stand. In 1959 Humphrey told biographer Michael Amrine that "the purpose of the bill—to take Communist-hunting out of headlines and committee circuses, and put it in the courts—was sound," but by 1965 another biographer reported Humphrey's admission that the Communist Control Act was "not one of the things I'm proudest of."

Humphrey's first try for national office was his abortive run for the Democratic vice presidential nomination in the summer of 1956. Believing that he would be presidential nominee Adlai Stevenson's [q.v.] choice for a running mate, Humphrey was shocked when Stevenson announced he would let the Convention pick the vice presidential candidate. Unprepared for the necessary floor fight, he ran a poor fifth on the first ballot and withdrew, throwing his support to Sen. Estes Kefauver (D, Tenn.) [q.v.].

Humphrey began his campaign for the presidency on Dec. 30, 1959, the first candidate to declare in the 1960 campaign. He was the most liberal of the Democratic hopefuls—the symbol of welfare state liberalism in Congress—and had recently gained visibility as a foreign policy spokesman with a highly publicized eight-and-a-half-hour talk with Soviet Premier Nikita S. Khrushchev on Dec. 1, 1958. Only Humphrey and Sen. John F. Kennedy (D, Mass.) [q.v.] campaigned actively in the 18 months prior to the nominating convention in July.

The West Virginia primary in May was Humphrey's crucial test. The state's depressed economic condition and Kennedy's

Catholicism were important issues, but the campaign soon devolved into bitter personal attacks. Humphrey highlighted Kennedy's wealth and contrasted it with his own campaign's impoverishment. Kennedy partisans, particularly Franklin D. Roosevelt, Jr., accused Humphrey of being a draft-dodger during World War II. (Humphrey had been deferred because of a double hernia and color blindness.) Kennedy won a smashing victory with 60.8% of the vote compared to Humphrey's 39.2%. Humphrey supported Kennedy after the latter's nomination in July and was himself reelected to his third Senate term in November.

During the Kennedy years Humphrey tirelessly promoted the Administration's legislative program as Senate majority whip. He worked with equal fervor for President Johnson's Great Society programs after his election as vice president in 1964. His own race for the presidency in 1968 was crippled by his association with the unpopular Vietnam war and Democratic Party divisions, and he lost by a narrow margin to Republican Richard M. Nixon [q.v.]. Humphrey returned to the Senate in 1971. [See KENNEDY, JOHNSON, NIXON/FORD Volumes]

[TO]

For further information:
Albert Eisele, *Almost to the Presidency: A Biography of Two American Politicians* (Blue Earth, Minn., 1972).
Winthrop Griffith, *Humphrey: A Candid Biography* (New York, 1965).
Hubert Humphrey, *The Education of a Public Man: My Life and Politics* (New York, 1976).

HUTCHESON, MAURICE A(LBERT)
b. May 7, 1897; Saginaw County, Mich.
President, United Brotherhood of Carpenters and Joiners of America, 1952-72.

Maurice Hutcheson was the son of William Hutcheson, president of the United Brotherhood of Carpenters and Joiners (UBC) and one of the most powerful union leaders in the twentieth century. In 1914 Maurice became a carpenter's apprentice

and worked as a journeyman from 1918 to 1928, when he became a UBC auditor. In 1938 he was elected first vice president of the UBC; he became president upon his father's retirement in 1952.

Shortly after assuming that office Hutcheson took the union out of the American Federation of Labor (AFL) in a dispute over a no-raiding agreement the AFL had negotiated with the Congress of Industrial Organizations (CIO). He reaffiliated with the AFL a few weeks later and became a Federation vice president and member of the Executive Council in 1953. When the AFL merged with the CIO in 1955, Hutcheson retained these positions.

In 1957 Hutcheson was charged with bribing an Indiana state highway official to obtain advanced information on the location of a planned highway. Hutcheson, it was maintained, then bought up the land and sold it to the state at a huge profit. A Lake Co. Ind., grand jury failed to indict the union leader on the charges. However a Marion Co., grand jury did so on similar charges the following year.

While his case was pending, the Senate Committee on Improper Relations in the Labor or Management Field, chaired by Sen. John McClellan (D, Ark.) [q.v.], ordered Hutcheson to testify on that case and on other questionable activities. These included charges that William Hutcheson had embezzled money from the UBC and that Maurice Hutcheson had conspired with Jimmy Hoffa [q.v.] to fix a jury. The Committee also contended that he had paid Max Raddock, whom it termed a "shrewd confidence man," $519,000 in union funds "with noticeably little return." According to a Committee investigator, Hutcheson had used Raddock as a "fixer in a successful move to block the Lake Co., Ind., indictment." Hutcheson refused to testify on the grounds that it could prejudice the pending Indiana case. The Senate cited him for contempt of Congress, and he was eventually sentenced to six months in jail and fined $500.

In November 1959 two members of Baltimore Local 107 of the UBC asked the Marion Co. Circuit Court to appoint monitors to halt alleged corruption in their union. They accused Hutcheson and 13 other union officers of bribery, threatening opponents with injury or death, destroying possibly incriminating union records, withholding pensions of retired members who opposed them and of not letting rivals speak at union conventions. The members also reported that the officials had accepted over $100,000 in "gratuities" from employes and maintained that they had paid back income taxes for individuals who knew what they had done.

Hutcheson's legal difficulties jeopardized his position in the AFL-CIO. In 1958 the Executive Council asked him to explain his Indiana indictment and his refusal to answer questions before the McClellan Committee. Hutcheson absented himself from Council meetings, but he sent AFL-CIO President George Meany [q.v.] a letter denying any violation of the AFL-CIO ethical code. James B. Carey [q.v.], president of the International Union of Electrical Workers, proposed suspending Hutcheson until he appeared before the Council, but the panel deferred action until Hutcheson appeared. No union discipline was taken against the UBC leader.

Hutcheson was convicted in the Indiana highway case in 1960 and sentenced to 2-to-14 years imprisonment. This verdict was overturned in October 1963 by the Indiana Supreme Court. The panel ruled that the conviction was based on insufficient evidence.

During the 1960s Hutcheson and other union leaders resisted efforts to eliminate racial discrimination in the construction trades. However, they eventually approved a compromise plan on the issue making entrance into trade unions based on merit. Hutcheson was appointed to a panel established by the labor and management Construction Industry Joint Conference to administer the compromise plan. Meany and other labor leaders petitioned the federal court to reduce Hutcheson's contempt of Congress sentence from jail to probation. The court complied in 1964. That year Hutcheson was pardoned by President Lyndon B. Johnson. He retired as UBC president in 1972. [See KENNEDY Volume]

[JB]

HUTCHINS, ROBERT M(AYNARD)
b. Jan. 17, 1899; New York, N.Y.
d. May 14, 1977; Santa Barbara, Calif.
Associate Director, Ford Foundation, 1951-54; Chief Executive Officer, Fund for the Republic, 1954-   ; President, Center for the Study of Democratic Institutions, 1959-74, 1975-   .

The son of a Presbyterian minister who became president of Berea College, Hutchins interrupted his studies at Oberlin College in 1917 to serve in the ambulance corps in World War I. He received Italy's *Croce di Guerra* for his work and returned to earn A.B. and LL.B. degrees at Yale University in 1921 and 1925 respectively. Appointed dean of Yale law school in 1927, Hutchins introduced a new curriculum for law students emphasizing judicial and legal philosophy and the social sciences rather than detailed case studies.

In 1929 Hutchins became president of the University of Chicago and in 1945 was named chancellor, a post he held until 1951. At Chicago Hutchins instituted drastic reforms directed at moving the University away from overspecialization and toward a strong liberal arts orientation. He abolished intercollegiate football, pioneered the "Great Books" program, introduced college-level study for high school students and reorganized the graduate school. An outspoken defender of freedom of speech and particularly academic freedom, Hutchins led the Commission for Freedom of the Press in 1947. He opposed faculty loyalty oaths, and as a result, he was investigated by a subcommittee of the Illinois State legislature in 1949.

In 1951 Hutchins became an associate director of the Ford Foundation, where he concentrated on education. Three years later the Foundation gave a $15 million grant for the creation of the Fund for the Republic. Hutchins became its first president. The Fund was an independent organization designed to further "activities directed toward the elimination of restrictions on freedom of thought, inquiry and expression . . . and the development of policies and procedures best adapted to protect these rights." Anticipating that the Fund would be highly criticized by conservatives, the Ford Foundation stipulated that the original grant was terminal; it would not be renewed. Hutchins described the Fund as a "wholly disowned subsidiary of the Ford Foundation."

Hutchins soon became the focus of rightist criticism. During the summer of 1954 Francis E. Walter (D, Pa.) [q.v.], chairman of the House Un-American Activities Committee, wrote Hutchins asking whether the Fund was "friend or foe in the fight against Communism." Hutchins replied that the letter had cast "unjust and unwarranted" doubt on the integrity of Fund officers.

That September American Legion National Commander Seaborn P. Collins, Jr., urged Legionnaires to "have no truck with" the Fund. He charged that the Fund "is threatening and may succeed in crippling the national security" by "constant, loaded criticism" of congressional and Administration efforts to resist Communist infiltration. Collins said Hutchins was "particularly unsuited" to head the organization because of his alleged doubt that Communist subversion threatened the U.S.

Despite this criticism Hutchins continued to support freedom of speech. In Nov. 7 he told reporters that he considered the Communist Party a danger to the nation but "wouldn't hesitate to hire a Communist for a job he was qualified to do, provided I was in a position to see he did it." Hutchins defended the Fund's action in giving a temporary press relations job to a newsman who had invoked the Fifth Amendment when a Senate Internal Security subcommittee questioned him about Communism. Yet that month he announced that the Fund would revise its "Bibliography on the Communist Program in the United States," an index of pro- and anti-Communist literature. The bibliography had been attacked by conservatives for omitting some anti-Communist material.

In 1957, with more than two-thirds of the Ford money gone, the Fund announced that it was reorganizing and moving to California. Two years later it formed the Center for the Study of Democratic Institutions, a residential center where full-time participants would discuss a Basic Issues Program. Hutchins then set about defining the issues facing contemporary America. Six were chosen for concentrated study: the corporation, the trade union, the common defense, the political process, religious institutions and the mass media. The Center's scholars conducted no basic research there but rather attempted to promote provocative discussion that cut across academic disciplines. It frequently involved practicing politicians in its activities, distributed thousands of topical pamphlets reporting Center discussions and published a journal, *The Center*. During the 1960s individuals such as Michael Harrington, Adolph Berle, Jr., Henry Luce [q.v.] and Reinhold Niebuhr [q.v.] participated in Center discussions.

In 1962 Hutchins became the chairman of the board of the Center while continuing as president. He became a life senior fellow in 1974 but returned as president in 1975.

[SY]

IVES, IRVING M(cNEIL)

b. Jan. 24, 1896; Bainbridge, N.Y.
d. Feb. 24, 1962; Norwich, N.Y.
Republican Senator, N.Y., 1947-59.

Born of old New York stock, Ives served in the Army during World War I and then completed his B.A. degree at Hamilton College. Following his graduation in 1920 Ives entered the banking business. He established his own insurance firm in 1930. The same year he was elected to the state Assembly. Ives served 17 years in Albany, the last 10 as majority leader. In 1945 he cosponsored the nation's first state law against racial and religious discrimination in employment, thus gaining wide popularity among New York's large ethnic minorities. Ives's liberal reputation was so strong that, when he ran for the U.S. Senate in 1946, the state American Federation of Labor (AFL) refused to give its traditional endorsement to the Democratic candidate, popular former Gov. Herbert H. Lehman [q.v.]. His anti-discrimination record earned Ives thousands of black and Jewish votes, giving him a narrow edge over Lehman at the polls.

During the Truman Administration, Ives was a leading member of the Senate's liberal Republican bloc. However, his support of the Taft-Hartley Act in 1947 temporarily ended his "honeymoon" with labor. AFL President William Green promised to defeat him in the next election. Nevertheless, in 1952 Ives beat his Democratic opponent by 1,330,000 votes—the largest plurality obtained by a candidate in New York to that date. [See TRUMAN Volume]

In 1954 the Republicans chose Ives as their candidate to succeed Gov. Thomas E. Dewey. He lost to W. Averell Harriman [q.v.] by only 11,000 votes, in what was the closest election in New York in a century and the only electoral defeat of Ives's career.

In the Senate Ives was associated with several important pieces of labor and social legislation. As chairman of the Labor and Public Welfare Committee's Subcommittee on Welfare and Pension Plans, he began a Senate study of such plans in 1954. An outgrowth of these investigations was the Welfare and Pension Plans Disclosure Act of 1958, which aimed at safeguarding the plans by compelling their registration with the Labor Department and requiring annual reports on their fundings and operations.

In 1957 and 1958 Ives served as vice chairman, under Sen. John L. McClellan (D, Ark.) [q.v.], of the Select Committee on Improper Activities in the Labor or Management Field. The Committee's investigations drew attention to widespread racketeering in certain labor unions and forced the resignation of Dave Beck [q.v.] as head of the International Brotherhood of Teamsters. In the wake of these disclosures, Ives cosponsored, with Sen. John F. Kennedy (D, Mass.) [q.v.], a labor reform bill containing both stiff anti-corruption provisions and several changes in the Taft-Hartley Act favored by the AFL-CIO. The bill passed the Senate by 88 to 1. However, after meeting vigorous opposition from Secretary of Labor James P. Mitchell [q.v.] and organized business, it was defeated in the House by a coalition of Republicans and Southern Democrats.

The question of labor reform became a major issue in the 1958 elections, encouraging Republicans to campaign for so-called right-to-work laws in several states. Ives, however, opposed such legislation as antiunion extremism, and he viewed his bill as the only means of forestalling it. In the same year he announced that he would not seek reelection due to ill health. Ives died in February 1962.

[TLH]

JACKSON, C(HARLES) D(OUGLAS)
b. March 16, 1902; New York, N.Y.
d. Sept. 19, 1964: New York, N.Y.
Special Assistant to the President for Cold War Planning, January 1953- March 1954.

Following his graduation from Princeton in 1924, Jackson took over his late father's marble and stone importing business. He was forced to sell the firm during the early days of the Depression, and in 1931 he joined Time, Inc. Moving up through the ranks, Jackson became a vice president by 1940, when he took a leave of absence to organize the Council for Democracy to educate the American public about the dangers of isolationism. During World War II Jackson helped Gen. Dwight D. Eisenhower organize a psychological warfare squad to generate support in occupied Europe for the Normandy invasion. He returned to Time, Inc., after the War and, except for a brief stint to help set up Radio Free Europe, remained with the Luce organization until joining the Eisenhower presidential campaign in 1952.

A man who enjoyed both Eisenhower's respect and friendship, Jackson played an important role in the 1952 Republican campaign as a member of Eisenhower's unofficial strategy team, which included Harold Stassen [q.v.] and Herbert Brownell [q.v.] He formulated themes for addresses, researched and drafted speeches and advised Eisenhower on local political conditions.

Eisenhower appointed Jackson his special assistant for cold war planning shortly after the November election. The newly created position was designed to permit the President take the psychological offensive in dealing with the Soviet Union. During his early days at the post, Jackson helped prepare the Inaugural and State of the Union Addresses. More importantly, he advised the President of the effect domestic policy decisions on world opinion.

Jackson objected to Eisenhower's failure to consider allied opinions in refusing the clemency appeal of convicted spies Julius and Ethel Rosenberg [q.v.] in February 1953. He complained that it had been handled as though it were exclusively an American legal problem, whereas in fact the decision "was political warfare raised to the nth power." In his opinion, problems with allies were exacerbated when Eisenhower announced that at a later date he would ask Congress for a resolution condemning the Yalta agreements. Jackson pointed out that here, too, action had been taken without regard to European reaction.

In March 1953 Jackson helped write Eisenhower's first major foreign policy declaration. The address, delivered in April in response to the so-called Soviet peace offensive that followed the death of Stalin, was designed to seize the psychological initiative on the issue of peace. It expressed the American desire for cooperation and appealed to the new Soviet leaders for a few "clear and specific acts" as signs that they shared this goal.

During 1953 Jackson became embroiled in a debate over U.S. response to the growing demand for an end to the arms race. He joined J. Robert Oppenheimer [q.v.] in urging a full disclosure of the realities of atomic warfare to promote awareness of the danger and problems. Eisenhower, however, felt the plan would only alarm the American people and trigger panicky demands for large, ineffectual defense appropriations. Instead, he proposed establishing an international agency to increase the supply of fissionable materials available to other nations for peaceful purposes. Soviet willingness to accept the plan might, Eisenhower believed, reverse the arms race. The proposal became the basis for the Atoms-for-Peace program established in 1955.

Jackson was one of the few White House aides who urged Eisenhower to use his prestige and popularity to stop Sen. Joseph

R. McCarthy's (R, Wisc.) [q.v.] vitriolic anti-Communist crusade. Eisenhower, however, rejected Jackson's advice, stating that he "would not be drawn into the gutter" with McCarthy.

As a result of Jackson's stand, McCarthy described him as a man "unsympathetic toward 'strong patriotism' and Americanism who would coddle Communists and left wingers in government and listen to their advice." McCarthy's assistant, Roy Cohn [q.v.], listed Jackson as one of a group, along with Emmet Hughes [q.v.] and Bryce Harlow [q.v.], of "dangerous liberals" threatening to subvert the White House.

Jackson resigned his White House post in March 1954 to return to Time, Inc. In his later years he also became involved in a number of service and philanthropic projects, including the International Executive Service Corps, a private organization similar to the Peace Corps. He died of cancer in 1964.

[RJB]

JACKSON, HENRY M(ARTIN)
b. May 31, 1912: Everett, Wash.
Democratic Senator, Wash., 1953- .

Born and raised in Everett, a mill town and minor seaport north of Seattle, Henry Jackson was nicknamed "Scoop" after an enterprising comic strip character of the time. His mother and his father, a small building contractor and an official in the local plasterers and cement masons union, were Norwegian immigrants. Jackson attended the University of Washington, where he received a law degree in 1935. Returning to his hometown, he won election in 1938 as prosecuting attorney for Snohomish Co. A sober, moralistic individual, he was dubbed "Soda Pop Jackson" by hard-drinking local politicians whose enmity he earned by his raids on illegal, but officially tolerated, gambling houses and bootleg liquor establishments.

On the strength of his crusading reputation and pro-New Deal politics, Jackson was elected to the House of Representatives in 1940. During his 12 years in the lower house, Jackson compiled one of the most liberal records in Congress. He was an effective advocate for his district's maritime interests and earned strong support among his constituents. Nevertheless, as a member of a congressional delegation that included alleged pro-Communists, Jackson had to fight hard for reelection in 1946. He was the only Democrat in the Northwest to retain his House seat in the Republican landslide of that year.

Jackson opposed the anti-Communist investigations of the Truman Administration. He voted against funding the House Un-American Activities Committee and against overriding the President's veto of the 1950 Internal Security Act. However, he was a strong supporter of Truman's anti-Communist policies abroad. As a member of the Interior Subcommittee of the Appropriations Committee and the Joint Congressional Committee on Atomic Energy, he was instrumental in gaining public works projects for his state and in promoting the Pacific Northwest as a center for the defense industry.

In 1952 Jackson ran for the Senate against the Republican incumbent, Harry P. Cain. A charismatic war hero and one of the most vocal conservatives in the upper house, Cain had lost popularity among the state's voters for his opposition to federal funds for Washington's Grand Coulee Dam, the world's largest irrigation and hydroelectric project. Campaigning as a champion of public power and atomic energy development, Jackson stressed the state's strategic role in nuclear fission, created by its vast hydroelectric reserves. With the backing of the Grange, farm co-ops and organized labor, he won election in one of the only two Senate contests in which a Democrat unseated a Republican in the Eisenhower landslide.

Arriving in the Republican-dominated upper house in 1953, Jackson was assigned to the Government Operations Committee and its Permanent Investigations Subcommittee, both chaired by Sen. Joseph McCarthy (R, Wisc.) [q.v.]. Although he initially raised no objections to the subcommittee's wide-ranging and sensational investigations of alleged Communist sub-

version in the State Department and Armed Services, Jackson began to express cautious criticism of McCarthy's methods in June 1953. In July Jackson and Sens. John McClellan (D, Ark.) [q.v.] and Stuart Symington (D, Mo.) [q.v.] made headlines by demanding the firing of committee staff director, J.B. Matthews [q.v.], who had written a magazine article accusing the Protestant clergy of pro-Communism. When McCarthy refused to permit a vote on the issue, the three Democrats resigned from the subcommittee. They returned in January 1954 after McCarthy permitted them to hire their own staff assistant, Robert F. Kennedy [q.v.], as minority counsel.

Jackson again came before the public eye during the nationally televised Army-McCarthy hearings of 1954. In March the Army charged McCarthy and his aide, Roy Cohn [q.v.], with threatening to use the investigations subcommittee to "wreck the Army" unless special privileges were given their recently drafted associate, G. David Schine [q.v.]. McCarthy retaliated by accusing the Army of trying to blackmail him into discontinuing his investigation of security leaks at Fort Monmouth, N.J. During the subcommittee's hearings in April, May and June, Jackson pursued a methodically legalistic line of questioning aimed at uncovering clear-cut perjury on either side. No decisive conclusion emerged from the tumultuous proceedings, but Jackson did succeed in putting McCarthy on the defensive at several points.

For his role in the hearings, Jackson was rewarded by the Democratic leadership with a seat on the Interior and Insular Affairs and the Armed Forces Committees. In January 1955, when the Democrats had regained control of the Senate, he was given a place on the Joint Committee on Atomic Energy, making him the only freshman senator with four committee assignments. On the Interior Committee Jackson helped lead the fight for a federally financed Hell's Canyon Dam. He was also involved throughout the 1950s in problems of power development, reclamation, national parks and mining—issues of deep concern to his constituents.

During the Eisenhower Administration Jackson compiled a strong liberal, pro-labor record in the Senate. He was given the highest ratings among his colleagues by the liberal Americans for Democratic Action (ADA), and he never voted against legislation favored by the AFL-CIO's Committee on Political Education (COPE). Although a consistent advocate of increased welfare spending, federal aid to education, national health insurance and civil rights, Jackson did not take the lead on these issues. Instead, he focused on military affairs and defense policy, interests that arose from his conviction that "the Cold War was going to be the greatest challenge of [our] time. Just as the challenge of the 1930s was the Depression, now the predominant issue was the survival of the Western world."

As a member of the Armed Forces and Atomic Energy Committees, Jackson became a strong critic of the Administration's defense policies and a leading exponent of the thesis that a "missile gap" existed between the U.S. and the USSR. In January 1956 Jackson made a major Senate speech warning that the Russians were ahead of the U.S. in the development of an intermediate-range ballistic missile that would enable them to engage in what he called "nuclear blackmail." Coming at the beginning of an election year, the speech stirred up a raging controversy. From then on Jackson relentlessly attacked the President and Defense Secretary Charles E. Wilson [q.v.], insisting that the Administration's defense policy was causing the U.S. to "lose our lead" in weapons technology. Stressing the urgent need to develop an intercontinental ballistic missile (ICBM), he advocated a crash program similar to the Manhattan Project that had produced the atomic bomb during World War II. Jackson also worked closely with Adm. Hyman G. Rickover [q.v.] in promoting the nuclear submarine program, and he repeatedly came to Rickover's assistance when the Navy attempted to force him into retirement.

In 1959 Jackson chaired the newly created Government Operations Committee's National Policy Subcommittee, which conducted a two-year investigation of the government's methods in making and

executing foreign policy. As a result of these investigations, he became intimately acquainted with the inner workings of the Defense and State Departments and acquired an expertise that made him the foremost Democratic spokesman on defense matters. Jackson's ominous warnings of a missile gap were taken up by Sen. John F. Kennedy (D, Mass.) [q.v.] in the 1960 presidential campaign. They were later proven to have been based on erroneous intelligence information.

During his first term in the Senate, Jackson began to develop a strongly personal, almost non-partisan, appeal among Washington voters and the state's private interests. His popularity was due, in large part, to his ability to bring federal money and jobs to his constituents in the form of reclamation, defense and aerospace projects. But it was also the result of his assiduous courting of businessmen and Republican voters. (Washington's blanket-primary system allowed Republicans to cross over and vote for Democrats.) In his 1958 reelection campaign, in which he won 68% of the vote, Jackson received contributions from important corporations that generally supported Republican candidates. He began a particularly close association with the Boeing Co., one of the country's largest defense contractors and the state's biggest private employer.

Although Jackson had been mentioned as a vice presidential possibility in 1956, it was in 1960 that he emerged as a serious contender for the second spot on the Democratic ticket. Endorsed in the opening days of the Democratic National Convention by New York Mayor Robert Wagner [q.v.], California Gov. Pat Brown [q.v.] and Sen. Mike Mansfield (D, Mont.) [q.v.], he was also Robert F. Kennedy's personal choice. Jackson was passed over at the last minute, however, when John Kennedy chose Sen. Lyndon B. Johnson (D, Tex.) [q.v.] in the belief that the ticket could not win without carrying Texas and a few Southern states. Instead, Jackson was asked to run the presidential campaign as chairman of the Democratic National Committee. He reluctantly accepted the post, but found that Robert Kennedy was the real director of the Kennedy election effort. Jackson was even unable to prevent Richard M. Nixon [*q.v.*] from carrying Washington, and he resigned from the Committee as soon as the election was over.

Jackson's relations with the Kennedy Administration were distant, and he was particularly critical of its efforts to control the arms race with the Soviet Union. In 1963 he succeeded to the chairmanship of the Interior and Insular Affairs Committee, where he spearheaded congressional passage of major conservation measures. He was one of the Senate's most enthusiastic supporters of the Johnson Administration's Southeast Asia policies. Initially confident of America's ability to win the Vietnam war, he subsequently placed much of the blame for military reverses on the domestic peace movement. In the fall of 1968 Jackson declined President-elect Richard Nixon's offer to appoint him Secretary of Defense. He became widely known as a leading supporter of Israel and of the rights of Soviet Jews during the early-1970s. In 1972 he was an aspirant for the Democratic presidential nomination. Four years later Jackson again waged an unsuccessful contest for his party's nomination. [See KENNEDY, JOHNSON, NIXON/FORD Volumes]

[TLH]

For further information:
William W. Prochnau and Richard W. Larsen, *A Certain Democrat* (Englewood Cliffs, 1972).

JACKSON, ROBERT H(OUGHWOUT)

b. Feb. 13, 1892; Spring Creek, Pa.
d. Oct. 9, 1954; Washington, D.C.
Associate Justice, U.S. Supreme Court, 1941-54.

Raised in the small town of Frewsburg, N.Y., Jackson learned his law by the apprentice method, clerking in the legal offices of a cousin. Following his admission to the bar in 1913, he built a thriving practice in Jamestown, N.Y. Jackson entered government service in February 1934 as general counsel of the Bureau of Internal Revenue. He then held posts as assistant attorney general from 1936 to 1938, Solicitor General from 1938 to 1940 and Attorney General from 1940 to 1941. Jackson was nominated to the Supreme Court in June 1941 and confirmed by the Senate the following month. From May 1945 to October 1946, he took a leave from the Court to act as chief U.S. prosecutor at the Nuremberg Trials, a role in which he reportedly felt he had performed the most important and enduring work of his life.

On the bench Jackson's views placed him somewhat right of center. He often eloquently defended the individual's freedom of thought, but the Justice also contended that government could regulate the way in which individual views were expressed and could limit the right of free speech when the speech involved was intrusive, aggressive or a threat to public order. Jackson generally was willing to give the government all the power reasonably needed to maintain national security, particularly against what he thought was the threat of the Communist Party.

In criminal cases the Justice gave more emphasis to the interests of society than to the rights of the defendant, and he opposed requiring the states to conform to the procedural guarantees of the Bill of Rights. However, Jackson strongly favored giving full effect to the Fourth Amendment's prohibition on unreasonable searches and seizures by federal officials, for he believed unrestrained searches a prime tool of arbitrary and tyrannical governments. Jackson gave wide sway to the federal government in economic matters, and more than any other justice of his day, he also wanted the Court to promote the development of a unified national economy by severely restraining the states' power to infringe on interstate trade and commerce. In all fields of law Jackson encouraged the Court to lay down clear, workable standards that the everyday lawyer and his client could understand and apply with assurance. [See TRUMAN Volume]

In his final two years on the Court, Jackson largely adhered to his early views. His majority opinion in a March 1953 case ruled that the Army could refuse a commission to an inducted psychiatrist who invoked the Fifth Amendment when asked whether he was a Communist. However, later the same month Jackson showed that he would object, even in a national security case, if the government resorted to unfair methods of procedure. When the majority held that the government could deny an alien reentry to the U.S. without any hearing and for unspecified reasons of security, Jackson dessented, arguing that the man was entitled to a fair hearing with notice of the charges against him. Jackson gave the opinion of the Court in a February 1954 case upholding a state conviction for gambling that was based on illegally obtained evidence. He strongly condemned police conduct in the case but said that the Constitution did not require the states to follow the federal court rule that illegally seized evidence be excluded at trial.

Although he suffered a heart attack on April 1, 1954, Jackson returned to the bench on May 17 when the Court handed down the decision in *Brown* v. *Board of Education*, holding racial segregation in public schools unconstitutional. Jackson had largely supported the Court's expansion of the rights of blacks, and his presence when *Brown* was announced vividly demonstrated the Court's unanimity in the case and Jackson's personal support for the decision. The Justice died of a heart attack in Washington on Oct. 9, 1954, just after the opening of a new Court term.

Jackson's service on the Court was marred by his disappointment at not being named Chief Justice and by a personal and doctrinal feud with Justice Hugo Black [*q.v.*] that became public in 1945 and 1946. However, Jackson has been ranked highly by constitutional scholars. He had a strong, disciplined intellect and was a superb writer with what Louis Jaffe has called "a 'big' virtuoso style, magnificent and athletic in exposition, powerful and ingenious in argument, racy, sardonic, alive with the passion and wit of his personality." A proponent of judicial self-restraint, Jackson generally took a conservative stance while on the Court. His views resulted from a thoughtful search for a practical, workable balance between the individual

and society and from his belief that progress and liberty were achieved only with public order, not apart from it.

[CAB]

For further information:
Philip B. Kurland, "Robert H. Jackson," in Leon Friedman and Fred L. Israel, eds., *The Justices of the United States Supreme Court, 1789-1969* (New York, 1969), Vol. 4.
Eugene C. Gerhart, *America's Advocate: Robert H. Jackson* (Indianapolis, 1958).
"Mr. Justice Jackson," *Harvard Law Review*, 68 (April, 1955), pp. 937-998.
"Mr. Justice Jackson," *Columbia Law Review*, 55 (April, 1955), pp. 438-525.
"Mr. Justice Jackson," *Stanford Law Review*, 8 (December, 1955), pp. 1-76.

JAVITS, JACOB K(OPPEL)
b. May 18, 1904; New York, N.Y.
Republican Senator, N.Y., 1957-   .

Javits's father, a rabbinical student in Austria, emigrated to New York City and worked as a tenement janitor and Tammany Hall ward heeler on the Lower East Side. Javits studied law at New York University while supporting himself with part-time jobs. He was admitted to the bar in 1927 and then, with his older brother, established a law firm specializing in bankruptcy and corporate reorganization. During World War II he worked in the Chemical War Service in Washington, D.C.

An opponent of Tammany Hall and a supporter of New York Mayor Fiorello La Guardia, Javits joined the Republican Party in the 1930s. In 1945 he was the chief of research for the New York City Republican mayoral candidate. The following year Javits, running on a liberal platform, was elected to the U.S. House of Representatives from the city's Upper West Side. He was the first Republican to carry the district since 1920. One of the most liberal Republicans in Congress, Javits often backed the Truman Administration on controversial issues. In 1947 he voted to uphold President Harry S. Truman's veto of the Taft-Hartley bill, and he endorsed the anti-poll tax bill in 1947 and 1949.

After 1952 Javits, defending his Republican credentials against party colleagues who regarded him as too liberal. He described himself as a mainstream Eisenhower Republican in contrast to the Party's conservatives. In fact, Javits's record was more liberal than the Administration's. A strong opponent of discrimination against minorities, Javits in April 1954 unsuccessfully proposed an amendment to an Administration's omnibus open housing bill that would have banned segregation in housing financed through federal mortgage insurance. In August he criticized a bill, requested by Attorney General Herbert Brownell [q.v.], to give the Justice Department authority to grant immunity to congressional and court witnesses. Critics of the bill claimed that it would have the effect of compelling witnesses to testify or go to jail. Javits stated that the right of protection against self-incrimination "is hundreds of years old and cannot be impaired without the most profound consideration." He voted against the bill, which passed Congress and was signed by President Eisenhower later in the month.

In 1954 Javits combined Jewish support and a large share of New York City's liberal vote with the traditional upstate Republican majority to win an upset victory over the popular Franklin D. Roosevelt, Jr., in the race for attorney general of New York. As the state's chief law enforcement officer, he maintained his liberal reputation by supporting such measures as anti-bias employment legislation and a health insurance program for state employes. He also continued to speak out on national issues, backing aid to Israel, expanded federal public housing and a higher federal minimum wage.

Javits sought the Republican senatorial nomination in 1956. His bid was endangered when, shortly before the Republican State Committee Convention met in September to make its choice, former Senate Internal Security Subcommittee counsel Julian G. Sourwine accused Javits of having been "mixed up" with a staff member of the Communist *Daily Worker*. Javits responded aggressively to the charge, appearing at his own request before the subcommittee on Sept. 5 to deny vehemently any past Communist affiliations or sympathies. Five days later the Convention unanimously chose him as its senatorial nominee. In November he defeated his Democratic opponent, New York City Mayor Robert F. Wagner, Jr. [q.v.], by about 450,000 votes.

In the Senate Javits resumed his role as a leading Republican congressional liberal. He endorsed the Administration's 1957 civil rights bill as "the minimum which should be enacted at this time." Three years later Javits unsuccessfully sought to strengthen the Administration's 1960 civil rights bill by expanding its voting rights provisions and establishing a permanent Commission on Equal Job Opportunity. In August 1959 Javits and Sen. Hugh Scott (R, Pa.) [q.v.] were the only two Republicans in the upper chamber who voted to override a veto of a public housing bill, which President Eisenhower had criticized as "extravagant." In May 1960 he was among five Republican senators supporting an effort to override a presidential veto of an area redevelopment bill. The Senate sustained both vetoes.

Occasionally Javits broke with liberal Democratic colleagues by attempting to link social welfare programs to private enterprise. In 1960 liberal Democrats supported the Forand bill, which provided for the establishment of a medical care plan for the aged within the social security system. Javits and seven other Republicans offered a voluntary plan involving federal and state grants to subsidize the purchase of private health insurance.

In the area of foreign policy, Javits was a staunch supporter of the Administration. He backed the Eisenhower Doctrine for the Middle East in 1957. Two years later Javits endorsed the Administration's program of foreign military and economic assistance and criticized Sen. Mike Mansfield's (D, Mont.) [q.v.] proposal for tapering off economic aid.

During the 1960s Javits, despite his position as part of the liberal minority within the minority party, became one of the most prominent figures in Congress by serving on as many committees and subcommittees as possible and by speaking out on a wide range of issues. In 1962 he was reelected by almost one million votes, and in 1968 he won by over a million ballots. Six years later he received a reduced margin of 300,-000 votes. [See KENNEDY, JOHNSON, NIXON/FORD Volumes]

[MLL]

JENNER, WILLIAM E(ZRA)
b. July 21, 1908; Marengo, Ind.
Republican Senator, Ind., 1944-45,
1947-59.

Jenner graduated from Indiana University in 1930 and then earned his law degree from George Washington University in 1932. Two years later he won election to the Indiana State Senate. He became minority leader in 1937 and was president pro tempore and majority leader from 1939 to 1941. Following service in the Army Air Corps during World War II, Jenner was appointed to fill the unexpired term of the late Sen. Samuel D. Jackson (D, Ind.). He served during 1944 and 1945 and then returned to Indiana to become chairman of the Republican State Committee. Jenner won a full Senate term in 1946.

Jenner immediately joined the "Class of 1946," a group of new Republican legislators whose domestic conservatism and orientation toward Asia created problems for the Truman Administration. He voted against most of Truman's Fair Deal legislation. He also opposed the Marshall Plan and the establishment of the North Atlantic Treaty Organization, which he thought would bankrupt the United States. However, he vigorously supported increased American aid to Nationalist China. As one of the most vocal members of the China bloc in the Senate, Jenner charged that the Administration's refusal to help Chiang Kai-shek doomed China to Communism. He also supported Sen. Joseph R. McCarthy's (R, Wisc.) [q.v.] contention that the Communist conspiracy in the State Department was responsible for the loss of China. In August 1950 he described Secretary of Defense George C. Marshall as "either an unsuspecting stooge or an actual co-conspirator with the most treasonable array of political cut-throats ever turned

loose in the executive branch of government." Jenner opposed Truman's dismissal of Gen. Douglas MacArthur in 1951 and called for the President's impeachment. The Senator charged "that this country is in the hands of a secret coterie which is directed by the Soviet Union." [See TRUMAN Volume]

Jenner campaigned hard for Eisenhower in 1952. The Senator proclaimed, "If Adlai [Stevenson] [q.v.] gets into the White House, Alger [Hiss] gets out of jail." He further charged that a Stevenson victory would provide safety for the "Red Network" to operate for the destruction of the U.S. "Bodies of thousands of American boys," he said, "would be tossed onto Truman's funeral pyre in Asia."

Despite Jenner's support for Eisenhower, the General tried to dissociate himself from the Senator. On Sept. 9 Eisenhower sat on the same podium with Jenner at a Republican rally in Indianapolis. In his speech Eisenhower endorsed the entire Republican ticket but refused to mention the Senator's name. Following the address Jenner quickly moved toward Eisenhower to force photographers to take a picture of him embracing the General. Embarrassed, Eisenhower quickly left the rally. He later told his speech writer, Emmet J. Hughes [q.v.] that "he felt dirty from the touch of the man." Moderates in both parties deplored Eisenhower's unwillingness to publicly repudiate Jenner.

In an effort to block McCarthy's excesses in investigating subversion, Majority Leader Robert Taft (R, Ohio) [q.v.], appointed Jenner chairman of the Internal Security Subcommittee in 1953. Although he disliked Jenner, Taft felt the Indiana Senator was more reliable than McCarthy because Jenner would submit to party discipline. Taft hoped that Jenner would continue his attacks on the past Democratic Administration without embarrassing his own party. Taft's early hopes were well founded. During the opening years of the Eisenhower Administration, Jenner repeatedly denounced the previous Administration. In July 1953 the Internal Security Subcommittee issued a report entitled "Interlocking Subversion in Government." Reprinted and circulated by the Republican National Committee, it attempted to document what Attorney General Herbert Brownell [q.v.] called "the very successful Communist espionage penetration in our government during World War II and thereafter." The noted civil libertarian, Norman Redlich, examined the charges in the Feb. 6, 1954 edition of *The Nation*. He wrote that the report was a rehash of old charges and questioned the accuracy of the findings. He suggested that Jenner skillfully "pile[d] one inference on another until the unwary reader [was] convinced that the original charge was true."

The Senate Internal Security Subcommittee also resumed the inquiry into the Harry Dexter White affair. Through documents and testimony provided by former Secretary of State James Byrnes [q.v.], Attorney General Herbert Brownell [q.v.] and FBI Director J. Edgar Hoover [q.v.], the panel concluded that President Truman had known that White was a Communist when he had appointed him to head the International Monetary Fund. Truman defended his actions on national television and little action was taken on the report.

In early 1954 Jenner claimed that the Republican Administration had found "heaps of evidence of the stupidity, the corruption, even the treason of its predecessors." Jenner said the Democrats had "permitted traitors to bring us close to military defeat." In a speech in Indiana he said, "The Fair Dealers and their Communist brain trusts . . . put every possible handicap on our Armed Forces" and sent them to Korea where they "were supposed to be defeated."

From 1953 to 1955 Jenner's subcommittee investigated a wide range of alleged Communist activities: subversion in the clergy, Army, United Nations and, most particularly, the schools. Jenner proudly claimed that as a result of his probes many teachers had been dismissed. He complimented school systems, such as those in California and New York, for cooperating with his subcommittee in the task of rooting out Communists.

Reacting to the Supreme Court's increased restrictions on the investigation of subversion, Jenner introduced a bill to curb its power in 1957. The measure called for Congress to deprive the Court of the right to review cases dealing with congressional investigations, security dismissal of federal employes and state and local laws designed to check subversion. Attorney General William Rogers [q.v.] and the American Bar Association condemned the Jenner bill. Joseph Rauh [q.v.], a leading civil liberties lawyer, called the measure not unconstitutional but "anti-constitutional."

Jenner continued to be a loyal supporter of Sen. McCarthy during the Eisenhower Administration. In November 1954 he charged the Watkins Committee, which had recommended censure of the Wisconsin Republican, with having failed to consider "the most important evidence"—that McCarthy "was fighting a conspiracy." Jenner maintained that the censure movement "was initiated by a Communist conspiracy" and that the Watkins Committee was aiding it. He interrupted the final debate on condemnation and personally attacked Sen. Ralph Flanders (R, Vt.) [q.v.], whose actions during the spring of 1954 had helped spur the censure movement. He asked the Vermont Republican why he had referred to "Soviet tyrants and murderers as 'my friends, my brothers.' " The words Jenner cited came from a Voice of American broadcast, which Flanders had made to the Soviet-bloc countries. Flanders retorted that Jenner had "taken leave of his intelligence." He explained that the broadcast was directed to the Soviet people and not the government. Despite Jenner's efforts the Senate voted to condemn McCarthy in December.

During the Eisenhower Administration Jenner continued to be one of the leading members of the China bloc in the Senate. In May 1954 he called on the U.S. to arm 20 million Nationalist Chinese, Korean, Japanese and other anti-Communists in Asia to support Taiwan's attacks on the mainland and divert Communist forces from Indochina. Jenner expressed outrage that the U.S. prevented Chiang Kai-shek from raiding the mainland and opposed any further attempts by the U.S. government to resume normal relations with Communist China. He also asked the President to issue a "final statement" that the U.S. would not recognize Communist China or sanction its admission to the U.N. During the Quemoy-Matsu dispute of late 1954, Jenner supported a blockade of the mainland. On April 28, 1955, Jenner introduced a resolution that would have repudiated in advance any concessions that the U.S. might make to Peking.

In December 1957 Jenner announced he would not run for reelection. He resumed his law practice in his home state.

[JB]

JOHNSON, FRANK M(INIS), JR.

b. Oct. 30, 1918; Haleyville, Ala.
U.S. District Judge, Middle District, Ala., 1955-   .

Born in the Republican hill country of northern Alabama, Frank Johnson worked his way through the University of Alabama, receiving his law degree in 1943. He engaged in private law practice from 1946 to 1953 and in 1952 was one of the Dwight D. Eisenhower's presidential campaign managers in Alabama. Johnson was appointed U.S. attorney for the northern district of Alabama in 1953; two years later Eisenhower named him U.S. district judge for the middle district of the state. Johnson began his judicial service on Nov. 7, 1955.

In his Montgomery courtroom Judge Johnson decided several important civil rights cases and in the process won a reputation among most observers as a fair and principled jurist. On June 6, 1956, during the Montgomery bus boycott led by Martin Luther King, Jr. [q.v.], Johnson was in the majority on a three-judge federal court that ruled Alabama's bus segregation law unconstitutional. Three years later he held racial segregation in Montgomery's public parks illegal.

In December 1958 Judge Johnson had the first of many run-ins with George C. Wallace, a former law school classmate who was then a state circuit court judge. On Dec. 8 Wallace defied a subpoena from the U.S. Civil Rights Commission and refused to turn over voter registration records in two counties under his jurisdiction. In three separate decrees issued between Dec.

11 and Jan. 9, Johnson ordered Wallace to let Commission agents examine the records. Wallace kept up his resistance but finally, on Jan. 12 and 13, gave the records to county grand juries which then let Commission employes see the data. On Jan. 26 Johnson dismissed contempt charges against Wallace, explaining that Wallace had complied with court orders, though indirectly, and that punishing him would only promote his political fortunes. Johnson also overturned a state court injunction blocking federal investigators from examining voter registration records in Montgomery in August 1960. At the same time he upheld the constitutionality of the 1960 Civil Rights Act against a challenge from the state.

With his even-handed, considered approach, Johnson did not always decide civil rights cases in favor of blacks or the federal government if he thought law or precedent was against them. In one of the first major tests of the 1957 Civil Rights Act, Johnson ruled in March 1959 against the Justice Department. He held that the law did not allow the federal government to bring a voting discrimination suit directly against the state of Alabama. The Fifth Circuit Court upheld his interpretation, and as a result of the adverse ruling Congress included a provision to authorize voting rights suits against the states in the 1960 Civil Rights Act. In a 1960 decision Johnson upheld the expulsion without a hearing of six black students from Alabama State College for having led sit-ins in Montgomery and Tuskegee. A higher court later reversed Johnson, who frequently seemed to disapprove of civil rights demonstrations.

Throughout the 1960s Judge Johnson's rulings pushed reluctant white Alabamans toward desegregation. In March 1961 he entered a sweeping decree, which served as a model for other federal courts, outlawing voting discrimination in Macon Co. Johnson enjoined a planned civil rights march from Selma to Montgomery in March 1965, but later in the month he authorized the march and ordered the state to supply police protection to the demonstrators. Johnson ordered officials in various counties under his jurisdiction to prepare school desegregation plans and in March 1967 was a member of a three-judge court that placed all of Alabama under a school desegregation order. During the 1960s Johnson was a frequent target of criticism from Alabama Gov. George C. Wallace. In the next decade he was further censured by Wallace for rulings requiring the state to upgrade its institutions for the mentally ill and retarded and its prison system. In 1977 President Jimmy Carter nominated him as FBI director.

[CAB]

JOHNSON, LYNDON B(AINES)
b. Aug. 27, 1908; Stonewall, Tex.
d. Jan. 22, 1973; Stonewall, Tex.
Democratic Senator, Tex., 1949-61; Senate Minority Leader, 1953-55; Senate Majority Leader, 1955-61.

Lyndon Johnson was the eldest son of Sam Johnson, a small farmer and cattle speculator, and Rebecca Baines, the daughter of a prosperous lawyer. At the age of five Lyndon moved from Stonewall, Tex., to nearby Johnson City, founded by his grandfather, a populist politician. He worked his way through Southwest Texas State Teachers College and graduated with a B.S. degree in 1930. For the next two years he taught in the Houston public school system.

In 1932 Johnson went to Washington, D.C., as secretary to Rep. Richard Kleberg (D, Tex.) of the 14th district. There he assiduously gathered information about the operation of Congress and took advantage of every opportunity to meet influential people, including Reps. Sam Rayburn (D, Tex.) [q.v.] and Wright Patman (D, Tex.) [q.v.], who had both served in the Texas state legislature with his father. Three years later he was appointed Texas Director of the National Youth Administration (NYA), becoming the youngest state NYA director. In that post Johnson built up a political constituency through the gratitude he received from those who obtained NYA jobs.

In 1937 Johnson entered a special election for the congressional seat from Texas's 10th district, a relatively liberal area in a conservative state. He distinguished himself from his seven opponents by proclaiming total support for President Franklin D. Roosevelt's programs, including his plan to enlarge the Supreme Court. Johnson received twice the votes of his closest opponent. By making a favorable impression on Roosevelt, Johnson was able to obtain a seat on the powerful Naval Affairs Committee and to procure public works projects for his district.

Power in the House was based on seniority, and the impatient Johnson did not want to travel the long road to preeminence. In 1941 he ran for a Senate seat in a special election but lost by 1,300 votes to Texas Gov. Wilbert L. "Pappy" O'Daniel. Immediately after Pearl Harbor Johnson asked to be called up for active duty. He served as the President's special emissary in Australia and New Zealand for seven months and returned to Congress in July 1942. Six years later Johnson ran for the Senate again and defeated former Gov. Coke Stevenson in the Democratic primary by 87 votes, out of one million cast, despite the loser's charge of fraud. (In 1977 a Texas voting official, Luis Salas, stated that he had certified enough fictitious ballots to steal the election for Johnson.)

In the Senate Johnson shifted significantly to the right. His new, statewide constituency was much more conservative than the 10th district. Furthermore, Johnson wanted to associate himself with conservative Sen. Richard Russell (D, Ga.) [q.v.], the most powerful figure in the Senate. To get closer to Russell he requested an appointment to the Georgia Senator's Armed Services Committee, which he received. With Russell's assistance he became party whip in 1951. [See TRUMAN Volume]

After Democratic Senate Majority Leader Ernest McFarland (D, Ariz.) was defeated in the 1952 elections, Johnson devoted all of his energies to behind-the-scenes efforts to win the post while publicly feigning disinterest. He succeeded with the help of key public endorsements from Russell and Sen. Earle Clements (D, Ky.), who had ties to the liberal wing of the Party. Because the Republicans had gained control of both houses of Congress in 1952, Johnson became the Senate minority leader.

The Senate party leadership post was not

highly coveted. It had historically been a largely titular office, a front for an informal inner club of powerful senators. McFarland, for example, had merely been the spokesman for Russell, the real leader of the upper chamber's Democrats. But shortly after assuming the post, Johnson subtly expanded his powers to become the center of his party's Senate power structure. He reformed the seniority system so that every Democratic senator, including freshmen, was guaranteed a good committee assignment. In the name of a fairer distribution of committee seats, he gained a discretionary power in making assignments that previous leaders had not possessed. By party rule the leader was also chairman of the Democratic Policy Committee. Johnson broke its ties and accountability to the Party as a whole, making it a purely senatorial institution fully under his control. He eliminated its function of determining legislative programs, limiting its responsibility largely to that of determining the flow of legislation to the floor. This gave him considerable influence over senators seeking the passage of particular bills. Johnson virtually eliminated the Democratic Caucus, thereby ending group discussions of issues and depriving Democratic senators of a collective decision-making apparatus beyond the leader's control. Johnson channeled the funds of the Senate Democratic Campaign Committee into the smaller states, where they were more likely to have a visible impact. This gave him a clear claim to the gratitude of senators elected with the help of the Committee. He used his responsibility for assigning office space to reward cooperative senators with the better offices and punish rebellious colleagues with cramped quarters.

Johnson supplemented these powers with an elaborate intelligence network that enabled him to learn the desires and needs of all senators. He used this information to dangle before his party colleagues those rewards or (usually by implication) punishments most likely to influence their votes. Johnson also was extremely skilled in the art of persuasion on a one-to-one basis. Few Democratic senators were completely immune to what became known as the "Johnson Treatment."

Although Johnson was extremely assiduous and successful in making himself a powerful party leader, his legislative goals were modest. In February 1953 he declared that Senate Democrats would engage in the "politics of responsibility" rather than the "politics of partisanship," which meant that despite the wishes of Party liberals, he would not offer a comprehensive alternative to the Administration's program. Johnson believed that only the President could initiate major legislation. In addition, his Texas political base was conservative. Also, his style of behind-the-scenes manipulation was conducive to the politics of concession and compromise, not the formulation of ideological programs. Finally, Johnson felt that because of President Eisenhower's great popularity, it would be politically suicidal to attack him frontally.

Therefore, Johnson proceeded cautiously, challenging the Administration on a selective basis and only when he believed that his party's conservatives and liberals could unite on the issue involved. He took strong stands in favor of strengthening the social security system and extending rural electrification while refusing to move to Eisenhower's left on such controversial issues as public power and civil rights. Often he presented the Democrats as the best ally of the President, supporting him against right-wing Republicans. In 1953 Sen. Robert A. Taft (R, Ohio) [q.v.] demanded that a proposed Eisenhower resolution denouncing Soviet "enslavement" of Eastern Europe be amended to include condemnation of the Yalta and Potsdam agreements, an implied attack on the Democrats. Johnson denounced Taft for trying to "divide us in the face of the enemy" and praised Eisenhower for having issued "a clear call for America to speak with a united voice against the Soviet enslavement of free peoples."

Johnson's approach to Sen. Joseph R. McCarthy (R, Wisc.) [q.v.] typified his cautiousness. He feared that a Democratic attack on the Wisconsin Senator would unite Republicans and make it appear that the Democrats were trying to cover up the alleged subversive influences in the Truman Administration. Johnson did not move against McCarthy until he believed that immediate success was possible. The time came after the Senate, in August 1954, voted to establish a select committee to investigate censure charges. The unanimous Democratic opposition to McCarthy in the December 1954 censure vote was in large measure due to Johnson's efforts. To avoid charges by McCarthy's supporters that Democrats were soft on Communism, Johnson in 1954 suggested that the U.S. might withdraw from the United Nations if Communist China were admitted and that the nation should act against the left-wing government in Guatemala.

When Johnson became majority leader in 1955, he continued his policy of cautious compromise. During that year he added protectionist provisions to a reciprocal trade bill to secure its passage. In 1955 he also opposed liberal Sen. Paul Douglas's (D, Ill.) [q.v.] effort to raise the minimum wage level in an Administration bill from 90 cents to $1.25. Johnson agreed to increase the figure to $1. At the same time, however, he eliminated a provision extending minimum wage coverage to additional workers because he feared that it would split the Party along North-South lines. In July of that year Johnson suffered a heart attack but recovered by the end of September.

In 1956 Johnson, with Rayburn's backing, headed an attempt to wrest control of the Texas Democratic Party from conservative Gov. Allan Shivers [q.v.], who had led most of the organization in a 1952 pro-Eisenhower bolt from the national Party. To bolster this effort he offered himself as Texas's favorite-son candidate for President. With the aid of Texas liberals he won control of the May 1956 state convention and was elected chairman of the delegation to the National Democratic Convention. Some of his advisers urged him to turn his favorite-son candidacy into an active, full-scale bid for the presidential nomination. But Johnson, because he was a Southerner with a conservative political base, decided to forego the primary popularity contests and rest his hopes on the possibility of a deadlocked Convention. However, Adlai E. Stevenson [q.v.] won the nomination on the first ballot.

In September 1956 the Majority Leader split with his Texas liberal allies of the previous spring, leaving the Johnson-Rayburn moderates with exclusive control of the state Party. Under their leadership the organization rejected both state interposition against the Supreme Court's 1954 school desegregation decision, the strategy favored by Shivers, and active implementation of the Court's ruling, the policy backed by the liberals.

Johnson also took a middle-of-the-road position on civil rights at the national level. In 1957 the Democratic Party faced a North-South division over President Eisenhower's civil rights legislation. He was widely credited with exhibiting great legislative skill in passing a bill without a Southern filibuster. Johnson subsequently informed biographer Doris Kearns that he told Southern senators that because blacks were getting "uppity" and Northerners were becoming hysterical in their advocacy of a "nigger bill," some kind of diluted civil rights measure had to be passed to avoid a second Reconstruction. He told Northern senators that a "long-overdue" civil rights bill for "Negro-Americans" could pass only if concessions were made to Southerners. To gain Southern support he had to remove from the bill Part III, which authorized the Attorney General to institute civil action for preventive relief in a wide range of civil rights cases. Its elimination essentially restricted the bill to the area of voting rights. Knowing that this would alienate the more extreme liberals, he first approached moderate liberals from the mountain states and won their backing by informing them that in exchange for the elimination of the section he could get Southern votes for the Hell's Canyon dam project in Idaho. Building on his moderate liberal-Southern base, he was ultimately able to gain overwhelming support for the bill.

Johnson was also widely credited for his handling of the furor over the American space program following the launching of the Sputnik space satellite by the Soviet Union in October 1957. The Armed Services Committee's Defense Preparedness Subcommittee, of which Johnson was chairman, conducted an investigation of U.S. space efforts from October 1957 to January 1958. Eschewing direct partisan attacks on the Administration, he made the hearings into a forum for educating the American public on the need for accelerating the space program. The creation of the National Aeronautics and Space Administration in 1958 was one of the results of the probe.

The Democratic sweep of the 1958 congressional elections weakened Johnson's hold over his Democratic Senate colleagues. A number of liberal freshmen Democrats entered the upper house, strengthening the ranks of senators favoring a clear-cut alternative program. Meanwhile the Administration turned towards the right, and President Eisenhower became more aggressive in his determination to minimize spending. Sen. Everett Dirksen (R, Ill.) [q.v.], the new Republican leader, was much more inclined than his predecessor, Sen. William Knowland (R, Calif.) [q.v.] to exert pressure in order to secure Republican unity. The approaching 1960 presidential election intensified political polarization. Under these circumstances Johnson, whose system of operation was founded on compromise, could not function at his best. Early in 1959, in an effort to please liberals, he introduced extensive airport construction and housing bills. However, on the floor he angered liberals by cutting funds from both measures to secure veto-proof bills. Nevertheless, he still failed to get enough votes to override subsequent Eisenhower vetoes of these measures.

In 1960 Johnson made a hesitant bid for the Democratic presidential nomination. Johnson was indecisive about running because, as in 1956, he knew the disadvantages faced by Southerners in Democratic presidential politics and feared that a bid for the presidency might destroy his conservative Texas political base. Johnson decided to wait for front-runners Sens. John F. Kennedy (D, Mass.) [q.v.] and Hubert H. Humphrey (D, Minn.) [q.v.] to eliminate each other in the primaries before announcing his candidacy. The strategy fell apart in May 1960 when Kennedy eliminated Humphrey in the West Virginia primary. Johnson's second-line strategy was to encourage all candidates to remain in the race in the hope of blocking a first-ballot Kennedy victory at the July Democratic National Convention. In a late-June last-minute act of desperation, he and House Speaker Rayburn announced that Congress would recess July 2 and reconvene between the Democratic Convention and the election. This was an act of political blackmail intended to convey the impression that if anyone but Johnson were nominated, the Majority Leader would stall liberal legislation to the detriment of the candidate. He did not announce his candidacy until July 5.

Johnson's bid failed in part because of his delay in announcing. Another reason was his lack of ties to the urban machines, labor unions and minority groups that formed the heart of the Democratic Party. Johnson concentrated excessively on influencing the senators whom he knew so well but whose influence in the delegate-selection process was far less important than he realized.

Kennedy won the nomination on the first ballot with 806 votes to 409 for Johnson. Kennedy surprised many observers (and disappointed many liberals) by selecting Johnson as his vice presidential running mate. Having received only 9½ delegate votes from the South, the Massachusetts Senator selected the Majority Leader to strengthen the ticket in that region, where it was feared there was considerable anti-Catholic sentiment. Johnson decided to accept the candidacy for an almost powerless office because he saw it as a chance to escape the restrictions imposed on him by his Texas constituency and thereby become a national political figure. His presence on the ticket was widely regarded as crucial in Kennedy's narrow victory over Vice President Richard M. Nixon [q.v.].

While vice president, Johnson served as chairman of the National Aeronautics and Space Council and of the President's Committee on Equal Opportunity. But most of his activity involved good-will foreign travels and ceremonies. Accustomed to wielding power, he intensely disliked the vice presidency.

Immediately after the assassination of

President Kennedy on Nov. 21, 1963, Johnson was sworn in as his successor. Early in 1964 he secured the passage of Kennedy's civil rights bill. In November 1964, with Humphrey as his running mate, Johnson easily defeated conservative Republican candidate Sen. Barry M. Goldwater (R, Ariz.) [q.v.] to win a full presidential term. With an extensive knowledge of Congress and a large electoral mandate, he was able to enact additional civil rights bills, antipoverty programs, medicare and other major domestic social welfare programs.

The Vietnam war proved to be Johnson's political undoing. Each year more American soldiers were sent to South Vietnam to combat what the President claimed was North Vietnamese aggression. But in the U.S. disillusionment with the war intensified. In March 1968 Sen. Eugene McCarthy (D, Minn.) [q.v.], a peace candidate for the Democratic presidential nomination, nearly defeated Johnson in the New Hampshire primary. On March 31, 1968 Johnson announced, in a national television broadcast, that he would not seek reelection.

In January 1969 Johnson retired from public life to write his memoirs and supervise the establishment of the Johnson Library at the University of Texas in Austin. He died of a heart attack in Stonewall, Tex., on Jan. 22, 1973. [See KENNEDY, JOHNSON, NIXON/FORD Volumes]

[MLL]

For further information:
Rowland Evans and Robert Novak, *Lyndon B. Johnson: The Exercise of Power* (New York, 1966).
Doris Kearns, *Lyndon Johnson and the American Dream* (New York, 1976).

JONES, HOWARD P(ALFREY)
b. Jan. 2, 1899; Chicago, Ill.
d. Sept. 18, 1973; Stanford, Calif.
Ambassador to Indonesia, January 1958-January 1965.

After attending the University of Wisconsin for three years, Jones transferred to Columbia University, where he received an Litt.B. in 1921. He then began a career in journalism with the New York branch of the United Press. He became the managing editor of the Evansville, Ind., *Press* at the age of 24. A few years later he was editor-in-chief of a chain of nine newspapers in Michigan. He did graduate work in public affairs at the University of Michigan from 1925 to 1927 and at Columbia from 1929 to 1930.

From 1933 to 1939 Jones served as executive director of the National Municipal League and editor of its publication. In 1938, after an unsuccessful bid for a seat in the New York State Assembly, he was appointed to the state's civil service commission. Following service in the Army during World War II, Jones played a key role in helping reestablish German financial institutions. He joined the Foreign Service in 1948. From 1949 to 1951 he was deputy director and then director of the Berlin office of the U.S. High Commissioner for Germany. In 1952 he was assigned to the Far East as counselor of embassy in Tapei, Formosa. Two years later Jones became director of the U.S. operations mission to the Republic of Indonesia. As deputy assistant secretary of state for Far Eastern economic affairs from 1955 to 1958, he urged more technical assistance and private investment in Southeast Asia to prevent Communist expansion.

Jones was named ambassador to Indonesia in January 1958, replacing John M. Allison [q.v.]. The former Ambassador had been removed because he supported Indonesian President Sukarno's attempt to force a U.N. resolution of the question of whether to keep West Irian under Dutch rule or to incorporate it into Indonesia. Largely because of Sukarno's increasing ties to the Soviet Union, the Administration had refused to follow Allison's advice. Yet as ambassador, Jones also recommended that Washington seek Sukarno's friendship by offering him support on the issue.

Jones became ambassador during a critical period in Indonesian history, when an anti-Communist rebel group in Central Sumatra challenged the central government. In light of the situation he began a reappraisal of U.S. policy. He recommended that the U.S. not view this as an ideological struggle between Communists and anti-Communists, and he suggested that the nation follow a policy of strict non-intervention in Indonesia's internal conflicts. His even-handed policies proved conducive to good relations. After Sukarno finally brought the rebel forces under control, he ended anti-American demonstrations. The U.S. then reciprocated by beginning an economic and military assistance program to Indonesia to counter aid from the USSR.

Jones continued as ambassador during the first half of the 1960s. In 1961 he helped avert war between the Netherlands and Indonesia over West Irian by persuading both parties to negotiate the issue. In 1962 the dispute was resolved when the two nations agreed to a U.S. proposal to cede the territory to Indonesia pending a U.N. supervised plebscite.

During the mid-1960s relations between the U.S. and Indonesia became strained as Sukarno made more dramatic moves toward Communism. Jones failed to convince President Lyndon B. Johnson that Sukarno's actions were motivated by nationalism. After Indonesia's withdrawal from the U.N. in January 1965, he gave up all hope and resigned. He accepted the chancellorship of the East-West Center, a cooperative organization with the University of Hawaii for the furtherance of understanding between the U.S. and the Far East. In 1971 Jones published *Indonesia: The Possible Dream*, in which he recounted his diplomatic career.

[JPL]

For further information:
Howard P. Jones, *Indonesia: The Possible Dream* (New York, 1971).

JUDD, WALTER H(ENRY)
b. Sept. 25, 1898; Rising City, Neb.
Republican Representative, Minn., 1943-63.

Born and raised in a small Nebraska town, Walter Judd earned B.A. and M.D. degrees from the University of Nebraska. In 1925 he went to China as a medical missionary and, with the exception of a four-year leave of absence, worked there for the next 13 years. Judd returned to the U.S. after the Japanese takeover of his hospital in 1938. For the next two years he toured the Midwest warning of Japanese aggression and calling for U.S. support of China. Discouraged by the widespread isolationist mood in this period, however, he settled down to a medical practice in Minneapolis. After Pearl Harbor Judd's views became popular, and in 1942 he won a U.S. House seat, replacing the isolationist incumbent.

During the postwar period Judd emerged as a leader of the China bloc in Congress. He was an outspoken critic of the Truman Administration's hands-off policy in the Chinese civil war and continually pressed for support of Chiang Kai-shek. Judd blamed the State Department for Chiang's defeat in 1949; after 1950 he began to suggest that the loss was due to Communist influence in the government.

Judd was a leading spokesman for the "China Lobby," a powerful pressure group composed of officials from the Nationalist embassy in Washington, paid propaganda agents and a large number of American anti-Communist businessmen, journalists, union leaders and policy groups, who zealously promoted Chiang's cause in the U.S. He also served as an adviser to the lobby's two main policy groups, the American China Policy Association and the China Emergency Committee, both of which worked closely with the congressional China bloc in the closing years of the Truman Administration. [See TRUMAN Volume]

During the Eisenhower Administration the Congressman continued to press for a hard-line policy on Communist China. In the summer of 1953 Judd, who was chairman of the Foreign Relations Committee's Subcommittee on Far Eastern Affairs, introduced a resolution opposing the admission of Communist China to the United Nations. The Congressman believed that it would be "plain hypocrisy" to admit a regime "which brazenly went to war with the U.N. itself." More importantly, he argued, admission would have increased the prestige of the enemies of the U.S. and the U.N. The House unanimously adopted the resolution in July.

In the fall of 1953 Judd and other leaders

of the China Lobby formed the Committee for One Million Against the Admission of Communist China to the U.N. With the blessings of Eisenhower and the backing of the American Legion, the American Federation of Labor and the General Federation of Women's Clubs, the Committee collected the million signatures in just nine months.

Judd reacted vigorously to the Communist Chinese capture of two American flyers in 1954 and the resumption of hostilities between Nationalist and Communists in 1955. He objected to Eisenhower's call for a cease-fire between the two belligerents. In his opinion such a move would have neutralized the Nationalist Chinese instead of permitting them to remain a threat to the mainland's flank and prevent Communist expansion into Southeast Asia. He also urged Eisenhower not to permit relatives to visit the downed flyers and thus draw attention away from the conflict.

Shortly thereafter Judd helped reconstitute the Committee for One Million as the Committee of One Million Against the Admission of Communist China to the U.N. The organization then launched a broad campaign to rally public opinion against not only admission of China to the U.N. but also diplomatic recognition or trade relations with the Communist Chinese. In 1957 the Committee organized a nationwide postcard mailing that helped kill proposed Senate hearings on trade with mainland China. In 1959 it issued a rebuttal to the Colon Report, a widely publicized private study urging closer U.S.-China relations.

Judd delivered the keynote address at the Republican National Convention in 1960. During the campaign The Committee of One Million supported the Congressman for Secretary of State, but the effort died with John F. Kennedy's election.

During the Kennedy Administration Judd supported the President on several important foreign policy measures, including the Trade Expansion Act of 1962, but he opposed such programs as medicare. Although he described himself as a "progressive conservative," Judd became associated with the burgeoning Far Right during the early-1960s. He participated in the Christian Anti-

Communist Crusade but was critical of the John Birch Society. In 1962 Judd lost reelection by a small margin. However, he remained prominent in the Republican Party and continued to speak for the still-active China Lobby. [See KENNEDY, JOHNSON Volumes]

[TLH]

For further information:
Stanley D. Bachrack, *The Committee of One Million* (New York, 1976).
Foster Rhea Dulles, *American Policy Toward Communist China 1949-1969* (New York, 1972).

KEATING, KENNETH B(ARNARD)
b. May 18, 1900; Lima, N.Y.
d. May 5, 1975; New York, N.Y.
Republican Representative, N.Y., 1947-59; Republican Senator, N.Y., 1959-65

Keating earned an A.B. degree from the University of Rochester at the age of 19, and, after teaching high school Latin for a year, he entered Harvard law school. He received his degree in 1923 and established a lucrative legal practice in Rochester. During World War II he served as an Army officer in the China-Burma-India theater. Keating was elected to the U.S. House in 1946 as a moderate Republican from New York's 40th district, a conservative upstate area which included Rochester and several surrounding cities.

Keating was a strong anti-Communist as well as a supporter of many liberal social welfare measures and civil rights proposals. In 1956 he sponsored a bill to limit judicial appeals by aliens sentenced to deportation. Two years later he introduced a bill, written by Secretary of State John Foster Dulles [q.v.], that would have given the President the authority to deny passports to Communists and others deemed dangerous to U.S. security.

On domestic measures Keating introduced bills during 1955 that would have allowed 18-year-olds to vote and given the President power to veto individual items in appropriations bills. He also led efforts in the House to reform the immigration quota system. The following year he cosponsored a successful bill limiting bank mergers and consequent asset acquisition.

Keating was a vigorous supporter of civil rights. He strongly defended the Supreme Court's desegregation decisions at a time when many of his colleagues refused to take a stand. As a member of the Judiciary Committee, he helped draft the Civil Rights Act of 1957, granting the federal government the power to seek injunctions against obstruction or deprivation of voting rights.

The Congressman strongly favored American support for the state of Israel. He opposed the Eisenhower Administration's decision not to sell U.S. arms to Israel in 1956. That year he headed a special five-man committee, representing 50 GOP members of Congress, formed in an unsuccessful attempt to pressure the Administration to reverse its decision.

In November 1958 Keating won the New York Senate race, defeating Manhattan District Attorney Frank Hogan [q.v.]. The following month he joined other liberal Senate Republicans in an unsuccessful effort to dump conservative leaders Styles Bridges (R, N.H.) [q.v.] and Everett Dirksen (R, Ill.) [q.v.]. In the Senate he consistently voted against massive public housing and large-scale public works projects. However, in 1960 he and four other Republican senators joined the Democratic majority in an unsuccessful attempt to override Eisenhower's veto of a bill to provide aid to depressed areas.

As a senator, Keating remained a strong supporter of civil rights. In 1959 he opposed the seating of segregationist Dale Alford, contending that his election had been accomplished by means of fraudulent write-in ballots and unregistered voters. The following year he waged an unsuccessful fight to strengthen that year's civil rights bill by adding an amendment that would have provided technical assistance to areas desegregating their schools and endorsed the Supreme Court's 1954 *Brown v. Board of Education* decision. Keating also proposed the 23rd Amendment to the Constitution, permitting the largely black population of the District of Columbia to vote in presidential elections. Congress approved the bill that session.

In 1960 Keating and seven other Republican senators proposed a voluntary federal-state health insurance program for all Americans over 65. Under the plan the states would have contracted with private firms for the coverage and subscribers would have made payments based on income, with the federal and state governments sharing the remaining costs. Keating's proposal was more liberal than the Administration's plan, which limited aid to single elderly persons with adjusted gross incomes of up to $2,500 a year and married couples with annual incomes of up to $3,800. The plan finally adopted in August contained most of the basic features of Keating's proposal but required a means test and permitted each state to determine the type and extent of medical assistance that would be provided.

Keating became the center of controversy in 1962, when he announced that Soviet missiles existed in Cuba but refused to reveal his sources. It took almost a week before the Administration could ascertain that he was in fact correct. Keating was defeated for reelection in 1964 by Robert Kennedy [q.v.]. He was elected associate justice of the New York Court of Appeals in 1965 and served there until 1969, when President Richard Nixon appointed him ambassador to Israel; he held that post until his death in May 1975. [See KENNEDY, NIXON/FORD Volumes]

[AES]

KEFAUVER, C(AREY) ESTES
b. July 26, 1903; Madisonville, Tenn.
d. Aug. 10, 1963; Bethesda, Md.
Democratic Senator, Tenn., 1949-63;
Chairman, Judiciary Committee, Subcommittee on Antitrust and Monopoly, 1957-63.

The scion of a socially prominent Tennessee family, Estes Kefauver attended the University of Tennessee, where he excelled in athletics, edited the campus newspaper and served as president of the student body. After graduating in 1924 he earned a law degree from Yale University. He returned to Tennessee and for the next 12 years conducted a prosperous corporate law practice in Chattanooga. He served as president of the Chattanooga Jaycees and helped organize the Volunteers, a political reform group. Defeated in his first run for office in 1938 by the local Democratic machine, Kefauver was appointed state commissioner of finance and taxation the following year. In a special election for a vacant House seat in the summer of 1939, he won the primary with organization backing and defeated his isolationist Republican opponent in the general election.

In his nine-year House career, Kefauver established a generally liberal, pro-labor voting record unusual for a Southern congressman. He stood out as a strong proponent of public power and a defender of the Tennessee Valley Authority (TVA), an advocate of internal congressional reform and a critic of monopoly power. He chaired a small business subcommittee that produced a 1947 report calling attention to the acceleration of corporate concentration since 1940. By 1948 Kefauver had won the enmity of the powerful Crump machine centered in Memphis. That year he outpolled two conservative opponents, incumbent Sen. Tom Steward (D, Tenn.) and Crump-backed Judge John Mitchell, in the Democratic primary. He was elected to the Senate in November over Republican B. Carroll Reece.

In the Senate Kefauver's outspoken civil libertarian, views, moderation on civil rights questions and liberal voting behavior continued to mark him as a maverick Southerner. As in the House, he consistently backed the Truman Administration's foreign policy initiatives. His most important legislative accomplishment of this period was the 1950 Kefauver-Celler Act, an amendment to the Clayton Antitrust Act closing a loophole allowing companies to purchase the assets of competing firms.

Kefauver catapulted to national attention in 1950-51 with his sensational investigation of organized crime. The Kefauver Committee conducted hearings in cities around the country amid extensive press coverage. The climax of the hearings was the New York City session, carried over nationwide television to record audiences. Although the Committee's investigation uncovered little that was genuinely new, it dramatized the crime problem for the nation and, according to the Internal Revenue Service, resulted by 1957 in 874 convictions and the recovery of $336 million in taxes and penalties.

Capitalizing on his new national prominence and the widespread dissatisfaction with the Truman Administration, Kefauver became a candidate for the Democratic presidential nomination. In his first test in the March New Hampshire primary, he was given little chance of coming close to President Truman. However, Kefauver won a stunning upset by 3,873 votes. Two weeks later Truman announced that he would not run for reelection, and suddenly Kefauver was cast in the role of front-runner.

Kefauver's campaign was distinctive for its homespun style. Voters identified him by his coonskin cap, his trademark since his 1948 Senate race. Kefauver's basic technique was to establish personal contact with as many voters as possible through energetic handshaking tours. Although he refrained from direct criticism of the Truman Administration, his most effective talking point was his special ability to clean up corruption in government.

Kefauver followed his New Hampshire triumph with a string of primary victories, the impact of which was diluted by the fact that he faced little opposition. Only in Nebraska did he overcome an organized, well-financed opponent, Sen. Robert Kerr (D, Okla.) [q.v.]. Kefauver lost the Florida primary to Sen. Richard Russell (D, Ga.) [q.v.] and the District of Columbia contest to Averell Harriman [q.v.]. Nevertheless, he went to the July Convention with an overwhelming majority of the popular primary votes and a plurality of primary-selected delegates.

At the Chicago Convention Kefauver's proven appeal to a sizeable portion of the electorate was offset by the weakness of his candidacy within the Democratic Party itself. Party professionals and urban leaders were alienated by his independence and his crime investigation, which had caused problems for some Democratic machines. The Truman Administration remained hostile to him, a vital Convention factor, and all Southern delegations except Tennessee's rejected him for his liberalism and civil rights moderation. Kefauver led on the first two ballots, but Illinois Gov. Adlai Stevenson [q.v.] was victorious on the third. Stevenson was also popular among the Party's rank and file. However, the circumstances of Kefauver's defeat convinced him and his followers that the will of the people had been thwarted and the nomination taken from him by the party bosses. [See TRUMAN Volume]

During the Eisenhower Administration Kefauver was a frequent adversary of the President. In April 1953 he participated in an unsuccessful liberal filibuster to block an Administration bill to return offshore oil deposits to the states. Kefauver led Democratic criticism of the Administration's controversial Dixon-Yates contract which enabled a private power group to replace the TVA as a power supplier in the Tennessee Valley area. He repeatedly denounced the secrecy and conflict of interest surrounding the plan's inception, the alleged windfall for its private beneficiaries and the damage to public power that would result if the contract went through. He headed a special panel of the Judiciary Committee's Antitrust and Monopoly Subcommittee investigating the affair. On July 11, 1955, while Kefauver was holding hearings, the Administration announced the cancellation of the Dixon-Yates contract. The panel's report, issued at the end of August, accused the Eisenhower Administration of "contempt of Congress and its constitutional powers" and condemned its use of "devious, indirect and improper administrative practices."

Kefauver provided crucial support for the Administration in its battle against the Bricker amendment, a measure intended to restrict the President's power in the conduct of foreign affairs. He warned that the amendment would upset the "constitutional division of powers between the legislative and executive branches of government, which has worked so well for 164 years." The anti-Bricker forces were victorious, by one vote, in denying the amendment the required two-thirds vote of the Senate.

Kefauver was an outspoken critic of Sen. Joseph McCarthy (R, Wisc.) [q.v.] and resisted pressure to join in Democratic efforts to outdo Republican anti-Communism. When the Communist Control Act was passed in August 1954 by an 81-1 vote, Kefauver cast the sole dissenting vote against the measure outlawing the Communist Party. Pleading with Democrats not to be intimidated by "soft-on-Communism" charges, he said: "Our Democratic Party is the traditional defender of civil liberties . . . . A grievous wrong inflicted upon us by the Republicans does not justify our inflicting an even greater wrong upon the protections given our people by the Bill of Rights."

Kefauver's maverick stands gave rise to a general belief that his reelection was in jeopardy in 1954. His conservative Democratic challenger, Rep. Pat Sutton (D, Tenn.), called him a "coddler" of Communists, a left "winger" and an integrationist, and scorned Kefauver's support of foreign aid and opposition to the House Un-American Activities Committee. Despite forecasts of a close race, Kefauver overwhelmed Sutton in the August primary, by a vote of 440,497 to 186,363, and easily defeated his Republican opponent in November.

In 1956 Kefauver made his second run for the presidency. As in 1952 he was initially given little chance: it was widely assumed that Adlai Stevenson would again be the Democratic nominee. Following a win in New Hampshire, Kefauver's upset victory over Stevenson in the Minnesota primary again exploded conventional expectations and cast the Tennessean into the serious contention. Stevenson edged Kefauver in the Florida primary, however, and his smashing triumph in the climactic California primary extinguished the Senator's hopes. On July 31 Kefauver withdrew from the race and endorsed Stevenson.

At the Convention in August presidential nominee Stevenson unexpectedly threw the choice of a vice presidential running mate to the Convention at large. Kefauver's supporters organized hastily on his behalf, and he won a dramatic victory over Sen. John Kennedy (D, Mass.) [q.v.]. During the fall race Kefauver campaigned vigorously in the regions of his greatest popularity: the Middle West and the West. In his characteristic populist rhetoric he attacked the Eisenhower Administration as being dominated by special interests and "readers of the *Wall Street Journal.*" He repeatedly denounced the farm policies of Secretary of Agriculture Ezra Taft Benson [*q.v.*], whose department, he believed, injured the family farmer to favor "the food processors and meat packers and grain traders and big bankers and miscellaneous other millionaires." However, the Stevenson-Kefauver ticket could not overcome the great popularity of President Eisenhower and the widespread satisfaction with the conditions of peace and prosperity. The Republicans won a landslide victory.

His 1956 defeat effectively ended Kefauver's career in presidential politics. Thereafter he devoted himself to his Senate duties and made his mark as Congress's most dedicated foe of monopoly in a generation. In the six years following his ascendancy to the chairmanship of the Antitrust and Monopoly Subcommittee in 1957, he conducted a series of well-publicized investigations into economic concentration. Kefauver focused on the problem of "administered prices," that is, prices of major products set artificially high, insensitive to market fluctuations. The Subcommittee's hearings concerning administered prices in the steel, automobile, bread, drug and electrical equipment industries, among others, filled 26 volumes and kept the issue before the public for six years. Kefauver frequently criticized the role of administered prices in inflation. He warned that growing corporate concentration hurt consumers and small businessmen and that the loss of economic freedom on their part ultimately could lead to the loss of political freedom.

Kefauver's voting record on civil rights questions was generally moderate. He supported liberal attempts to modify the Senate filibuster rule. He was one of only three Southern senators who refused to sign the 1956 "Southern Manifesto" denouncing the Supreme Court's desegregation decision. He voted for the Civil Rights Act of 1957. Yet in the legislative struggle over the measure, Kefauver helped win Senate

passage of the controversial jury trial amendment, mandating that individuals accused of violating a federal court injunction not to interfere with the voting rights of blacks would be given a trial by jury. Opponents of the amendment charged it was intended to weaken federal protection of blacks voting rights, but he maintained that "any miscarriage of justice will not be remedied by eliminating the right to trial by jury." The final version of the bill permitted judges to try minor violations of the law but assured defendants another trial, by jury, if severe penalties were imposed. Kefauver's civil rights record grew more conservative as his 1960 reelection contest approached. In 1959 he criticized the Civil Rights Commission's recommendations for specific legislation to ensure equal voting, education and housing rights. The following year he voted with the Southern bloc on a variety of amendments to weaken the Civil Rights Act of 1960, but he backed the final bill.

As in 1954 Kefauver entered his reelection battle amid pessimistic speculation and again surprised observers with an overwhelming primary victory. According to his biographer, Joseph B. Gorman, by the end of the decade Kefauver was considered by some colleagues to be a "walking legend" who "could deliver at least 10 votes on any issue by the sheer force of his reputation as champion of the public interest." His most significant achievement during the Kennedy Administration was the passage of the Kefauver-Harris Act, which greatly strengthened federal regulations to ensure that drugs be proven safe and effective before being marketed. Another milestone was the passage of the 24th Amendment outlawing the poll tax. Kefauver, a career-long opponent of the poll tax, initiated the measure and guided it through the Senate. The final state ratified the amendment after his death. Kefauver died of a burst aorta on Aug. 10, 1963. [See KENNEDY Volume]

[TO]

For further information:
Joseph B. Gorman, Kefauver; *A Political Biography* (New York, 1971).

KENNAN, GEORGE F(ROST)
b. Feb. 16, 1904; Milwaukee, Wisc.
Foreign policy critic.

George Kennan, the descendant of a pre-Revolutionary Scotch-Irish family, graduated from Princeton University in 1925 and entered the Foreign Service the following year. From 1927 to 1931 he served in Central and Eastern Europe. Kennan was a member of the first American embassy to the USSR in 1933 and served there as third secretary until 1936. The young diplomat was then stationed in Prague and Berlin, where he remained until the War began. From December 1941 to May 1942, he was interned by the Nazis. During the early War years Kennan served at the American embassy in Portugal and in 1943 joined the European Advisory Commission in London, where he worked on plans for postwar Germany.

In 1944 Kennan was again posted to the USSR. While serving in Moscow he sent Washington dispatches predicting that the Russians would seek military, economic and ideological expansion in Western Europe and urged the U.S. to develop a firm policy to counteract it. As a result of Kennan's work, Secretary of State George C. Marshall appointed him head of the State Department's policy planning staff in 1947. That year he wrote an article for *Foreign Affairs* magazine, under the name of Mr. X, which served as an outline for the Truman Administration's Soviet policy. In his writing Kennan urged a policy of containment toward Soviet expansion through the use of counterforce wherever there was a possibility of aggression. When Dean Acheson [*q.v.*] became Secretary of State in 1949, he appointed Kennan counselor of the Department. However, the two quickly broke over the implementation of containment, and in 1955, Kennan took a leave of absence to carry on research at the Institute of Advanced Study in Princeton. [See TRUMAN Volume]

Kennan was appointed ambassador to the Soviet Union in the fall of 1951. His stay in Moscow was short; the Soviets declared him *persona non grata* for his statements criticizing the Russian treatment of Western

diplomats. Kennan returned to the U.S. in October 1952 during the presidential campaign in which the Republican Party condemned containment as "negative, futile and immoral." Instead, the Republicans, directed by John Foster Dulles [*q.v.*], promised to extend the hope of liberation to Eastern Europe. In January 1953, while awaiting reassignment, Kennan delivered a speech warning against any "government action that was designed to interfere with the internal affairs of another country" and spoke out in favor of containment rather than liberation. Fearful of having the author of the containment policy in the Republican Administration, Dulles took advantage of a rule requiring the reassignment of chiefs of missions within 90 days to force Kennan's retirement. Kennan then returned to the Institute at Princeton to write Russian history.

During the 1950s Kennan was one of the Eisenhower Administration's foremost critics. Pointing out that Communist expansion was ideological and economic, not military, he opposed reliance on military alliances such as the North Atlantic Treaty Organization. He also objected to Dulles's defining the struggle against the USSR in terms of a moral crusade.

At the end of 1957 Kennan delivered a series of lectures over the British Broadcasting Corp. that called for a reassessment of American policy toward the USSR. He suggested that since Stalin's death in 1953 a liberalizing trend had appeared in Russia which made the Kremlin leaders more inclined to diplomatic negotiation than military conquest. Kennan dismissed the Administration's idea of giving Germany nuclear arms to prevent Russian expansion. Instead, he recommended that the U.S. use the threat of that possibility to negotiate with the Russians on the neutralization of Central and Eastern Europe. The Soviet Union and the U.S. could then withdraw or "disengage" their forces from the area.

Kennan's disengagement policy generated a debate among foreign policy officials. Dean Acheson [*q.v.*] and Henry Kissinger [*q.v.*] were among his most forceful critics. Acheson wrote that Kennan "has never in my judgment grasped the realities of power relationships, but takes a rather mystical attitude toward them." Disengagement, the former Secretary of State claimed, would be the "new isolationism." Professor Kissinger argued that the Russians should still be considered a military threat to Western Europe and American troops should remain there as a major deterrant. Sen. John Kennedy (D, Mass.) [q.v.], on the other hand, wrote Kennan complimenting his lectures for their "brilliance and stimulation." Walter Lippmann [q.v.], who had advocated disengagement in the late-1940s, praised Kennan's change of position.

In 1959 Kennan questioned the Eisenhower Administration's reliance on nuclear weapons of indiscriminate mass destruction for America's defense. He proposed, instead, that the U.S. and Russia abolish them and that this country rely on conventional forces to defend itself.

Kennan was a leading expert on Russian history as well as a foreign policy commentator. His book, *Russia Leaves the War* (1956), won the Pulitzer Prize of 1957. Its sequel, *The Decision to Intervene* (1957), was equally well received. Kennan's short book, *American Diplomacy: 1900-1951* (1952), based on lectures he gave at the University of Chicago in 1951, was one of the most popular appraisals of twentieth century American foreign policy.

During the Kennedy Administration Kennan served as ambassador to Yugoslavia. In the latter part of the decade, he was a forceful critic of U.S. policy in Indochina. [See KENNEDY, JOHNSON Volumes]

[JB]

KENNEDY, JOHN F(ITZGERALD)
b. May 29, 1917; Brookline, Mass.
d. Nov. 22, 1963; Dallas, Tex.
Democratic Senator, Mass., 1953-61.

The son of millionaire stock market speculator and investment banker Joseph P. Kennedy, John Kennedy was brought up in a political family. Kennedy's maternal grandfather had been mayor of Boston and his paternal grandfather had served in the Massachusetts State Senate. Kennedy graduated from Choate School and in 1935 began attending Princeton. He switched to Harvard one year later and graduated in 1940 with a degree in political science. While a student, Kennedy spent several summers in England, where his father was ambassador. Out of this experience he conceived the topic for his senior thesis, "While England Slept," which warned against Great Britain's policy of appeasement. In 1940 he published the work, which became a best-seller.

After a brief stint at Stanford business school, Kennedy joined the Navy in 1940. In one highly publicized incident, he narrowly escaped death when the PT-boat he commanded was rammed by a Japanese ship. Following the War he briefly pursued a career as a reporter for International News Services but decided to pursue a political career. In 1946 he won the Democratic primary in Boston's 11th district against the machine candidate. Labeling himself as "fighting conservative," an anti-Communist who supported the New Deal, he easily won the general election.

In the House Kennedy usually voted with other Northern liberals in support of Fair Deal legislation. However, he maintained a more conservative position on foreign policy and the issue of domestic Communism. Kennedy created a minor incident in 1949, when he attacked President Harry S. Truman for what he considered the unnecessary loss of mainland China to the Communists. In 1950 he contributed to conservative Rep. Richard M. Nixon's (R, Calif.) [q.v.] reelection campaign against Helen Gahagan Douglas. That November he made a speech praising Sen. Joseph R. McCarthy (R. Wisc.) [q.v.] and supporting the McCarran Internal Security Act.

In 1952 Kennedy ran for the U.S. Senate seat held by Henry Cabot Lodge [q.v.]. Very little distinguished the two men on the issues, and the race became a conflict of personalities and campaign styles. Kennedy's campaign exhibited many of the characteristics of his later races. The well planned effort was conducted by a staff of dedicated workers headed by the candidate's family. His father used his influence to obtain the support of Taft Republicans, convincing Joe Fox, publisher of the isolationist *Boston Post*, that John Kennedy was a strict anti-Communist and a supporter of McCarthy. When liberal Democrats urged young Kennedy to sign an anti-McCarthy manifesto during the campaign, his father opposed the move, declaring that it was the surest way to lose the election. Kennedy never signed the document. His mother, Rose Kennedy, held large tea parties to introduce her son to women representing various interest groups. It was hoped that these gatherings would not only win their vote but, through word of mouth, spread the Kennedy name. Kennedy's biographer, James McGregor Burns, pointed to these parties as decisive in winning the election. In November Kennedy defeated Lodge, then engaged in Dwight D. Eisenhower's election effort, by 70,000 votes.

During his early years in the Senate, Kennedy focused primarily on the needs of his section, then in the midst of economic depression. Kennedy introduced several bills to aid Massachusetts's fishing, textile, building and watch industries through tariff protection and increased federal aid. He also supported higher minimum wage laws to force Southern textile industries to maintain comparable labor costs with their New England competitors. In May 1953 he made several speeches in the Senate on New England's plight and helped form a bloc of New England senators. Despite his support for his section, he backed construction of the St. Lawrence Seaway, opposed by many in New England who feared it would reduce the role of the port of Boston. The only New England senator to vote for the measure, he justified his stand by insisting that Canada was prepared to go on with the project alone. At the same time, he maintained that national economic and security interests should take precedence over sectionalism.

By 1954 Kennedy had become disillusioned with McCarthy's investigations, although he muted his criticism. A member of the Senate Government Operations Committee, chaired by the Wisconsin Senator, Kennedy voted against the witness immunity bill of August 1954. The bill would have given the Justice Department authority to grant immunity to congres-

sional and court witnesses. Critics of the measure claimed that it would have the effect of compelling witnesses to testify or go to jail. Plagued by a continual back problem, Kennedy was in the hospital in December 1954, when the Senate voted to condemn McCarthy. He had earlier revealed his support of the vote, contending that McCarthy's tactics had impinged the "honor and dignity of the Senate."

During 1954 Kennedy opposed any attempt to aid the French, then under siege at Dien Bien Phu. He told the Senate in April that a French victory was impossible and that, the American people should be "told the truth" that "no amount of military assistance" could prevent Communist takeover. He warned that the U.S. could prevent Communist expansion in Asia only by supporting independence.

Kennedy was absent from the Senate from November 1954 until May 1955 while recuperating from several severe spinal operations. During that period he wrote his Pulitzer Prize winning book, *Profiles In Courage*, a study in fidelity to political principle by seven American politicians over a 150-year period. The book, published in early 1956, was a best-seller and gave Kennedy important national exposure.

During 1956 Kennedy waged a vigorous battle against Rep. John McCormack (D, Mass.) [q.v.] for the leadership of the Massachusetts Democratic Party. McCormack hoping to control the state delegation to the Democratic National Convention and thus influence the Convention's choice for President, won the state's non-binding presidential primary in 1956. Kennedy, on the other hand, supported Adlai Stevenson's [q.v.] nomination. When Massachusetts state chairman William H. Burke, Jr., a McCormack supporter, made a speech hinting that Stevenson backers were Communists, Kennedy campaigned against Burke's reelection. His candidate, John M. Lynch, won the office by a large margin, solidifying Kennedy's leadership of the state Party.

Kennedy nominated Stevenson for President at the Democratic National Convention in 1956. When Stevenson threw the vice presidential nomination open to the Convention, Kennedy and a few aides organized a spirited campaign for the second place on the ticket. He lost to Sen. Estes Kefauver (D, Tenn.) [q.v.] on the third ballot.

Over the next three years, Kennedy layed the groundwork for a 1960 presidential campaign. He made some 1,000 speeches in all parts of the nation, demonstrated his popularity by winning reelection to the Senate by almost a million votes in 1958 and carefully built a national legislative record that would appeal to Democratic Party liberals and moderates.

Kennedy supported the Administration's 1957 civil rights bill, including its most liberal provision, Part III, giving the Attorney General power to issue injunctions for a variety of civil rights violations. The section was later defeated. He also voted for a conservative amendment giving violaters of the statute the right to jury trials.

Kennedy established a mixed record on labor issues. The AFL-CIO's Committee on Political Education announced that he had voted "right" on 15 out of 16 important labor issues during the period. From 1957 to 1959 he played an active role in the McClellan Committee's investigations of improper activities in labor unions. These activities earned him the opposition of a number of labor leaders. In 1959 Kennedy sponsored a labor reform bill designed to clean up the kind of labor racketeering and labor management collusion exposed by the McClellan Committee. The measure called for unions and officers along with management to file annual financial reports with the Secretary of Labor. The bill provided criminal penalities for bribery, extortion and misappropriation of union funds. It passed the Senate in April 1959 but was replaced in conference by the much stricter House version, known as the Landrum-Griffin bill.

Kennedy took an increasing interest in foreign affairs. In 1957 he edged out Kefauver to win a seat on the coveted Foreign Relations Committee. He was particularly prominent in urging a reorientation of U.S. policies toward underdeveloped nations. Keenly aware of the force of anti-colonialism in emerging nations, he

pointed out in a 1957 article in *Foreign Affairs* that American leaders underrated the strength of nationalism in Asia and Africa and that the Administration lacked a definable Middle Eastern policy.

Kennedy caused a controversy in July 1957, when he brought the Algerian question to the Senate floor and urged that the civil war there be ended with Algerian independence. He offered a resolution proposing that the U.S. negotiate the conflict. Maintaining that nationalism was a prime ingredient in most rebellions, he warned that mere "economic and social reform" would not prevent the demise of colonialism. He was severely criticized by the Eisenhower Administration and members of both parties for antagonizing France. Kennedy also urged the U.S. give priority to economic over military foreign aid and proposed economic aid to some Soviet satellites.

Kennedy was a cold warrior who saw Communist expansion as a major threat to the U.S. In 1957 he supported the Eisenhower Doctrine which gave the President authority to use U.S. troops to protect Middle Eastern nations threatened by Communist take over. In August 1957, he introduced legislation providing funds for "educational materials" to inform the public of the nature of the Communist threat. He urged Americans to support increased military expenditures for defense against the Soviet Union, fearing that a "Maginot Line" mentality had developed in the U.S. which might prove fatal and "would not only have the effect of tempting the Soviet Union to initiate an all out attack, but would also affect the position of our diplomacy, the security of our basis. . . ." Beginning in 1958 he suggested a "missile gap" existed between the U.S. and the USSR, and predicted it would grow more serious in the 1960s. He claimed that *Sputnik* and other technological advances gave the USSR the advantage in the world balance of power and warned of a Russian attack that would destroy the world. Kennedy questioned the value of trying to appease the Soviet Union and urged a strong military stand to prevent a "second Munich."

Kennedy announced his candidacy for the

Democratic Presidential nomination in January 1960. After a series of spectacular wins in the West Virginia and Wisconsin primaries, proving that his Roman Catholicism was not a handicap to his candidacy, he won the Democratic nomination on the first ballot in Chicago. He selected as his runningmate Sen. Lyndon B. Johnson (D, Tex.) [q.v.].

As President, Kennedy took a strong anti-Communist stand, approving the disastrous Bay of Pigs invasion to topple Cuban Premier Fidel Castro in 1961 and forcing the Soviet Union to remove offensive weapons from that island the following year. He urged the rethinking of American policy toward underdeveloped nations and revamped of foreign aid to emphasize long-term economic development. Kennedy's domestic program called for federal aid to education, new civil rights laws, medicare and tax cuts to stimulate economic growth. Many of these proposals were blocked by Congress at the time of his assassination. [See KENNEDY Volume]

[AES]

For further information:
James McGregor Burns, *John F. Kennedy: A Political Profile* (New York, 1959)

KENNEDY, ROBERT F(RANCIS)
b. Nov. 20, 1925; Brookline, Mass.
d. June 6, 1968; Los Angeles, Calif.
Assistant Counsel, Senate Permanent Subcommittee on Investigations of the Government Operations Committee, January 1953-July 1953, Minority Counsel, February 1954-September 1956; Chief Counsel, Senate Select Committee on Improper Activities in the Labor or Management Field, January 1957-September 1959.

The seventh of nine children of Joseph P. and Rose Fitzgerald Kennedy, Robert F. Kennedy was born into one of the wealthiest families in the United States. While his father was busy with financial dealings and his diplomatic service, Robert was raised in part by his brother Joseph, Jr., who instilled a fiercely competitive spirit into his younger

brother. When Joseph was killed in the crash of a Navy plane in 1944, Robert left Harvard to enlist in the Navy and was assigned to seaman's duty aboard a destroyer newly named for his brother. Kennedy returned to Harvard after the War and graduated in 1948. He then went on to the University of Virginia law school. He received his law degree in 1951 and then worked for the Department of Justice prosecuting graft and income tax evasion cases. He resigned in mid-1952 to manage his brother John F. Kennedy's [q.v.] successful senatorial campaign.

In 1953 Kennedy secured, through his father's friendship with Sen. Joseph R. McCarthy (R, Wisc.) [q.v.], an appointment as assistant counsel to the Senate Permanent Investigations Subcommittee of which McCarthy was chairman. Kennedy's badgering tone with witnesses, mild compared to that of McCarthy or chief committee counsel Roy Cohn [q.v.], nevertheless earned him the enmity of many liberals, intellectuals and civil libertarians. Cohn and Kennedy soon clashed over the chief counsel's methods of examination, which Kennedy considered "inefficient, inaccurate and untrustworthy." Kennedy suggested that McCarthy control his aide's excesses. McCarthy promised to do so, but when no such disciplinary effort was forthcoming, Kennedy left the Committee staff.

After working briefly for the Hoover Commission, of which his father was a member, Robert Kennedy rejoined the Permanent Investigations Subcommittee, this time as minority counsel, at the request of Democratic committee members John McClellan (D, Ark.) [q.v.], Henry Jackson (D, Wash.) [q.v.], and Stuart Symington (D, Mo.) [q.v.]. In 1954 Kennedy became involved in the dispute between the Army and McCarthy, which began when Cohn allegedly asked for preferential treatment for Pvt. G. David Schine [q.v.], an aide of McCarthy. The Army revealed what it thought to be pressure on behalf of Schine, and McCarthy retorted that the branch of the service was heavily infiltrated by Communists.

The subcommittee investigated the controversy in televised hearings during April,

May and June. During the hearings Cohn's viscious verbal attack on Army Signal Corps clerk Annie Moss prompted Kennedy to challenge Cohn's knowledge of the facts. This incident began a feud between the two men which nearly led to physical violence at the later stage of the hearings. Later that year Kennedy compiled evidence used in the debate over McCarthy's possible censure. Despite their conflicts, Kennedy's personal liking for McCarthy never waivered; in 1957 he even attended the Senator's funeral.

Kennedy's tenure with the investigations subcommittee continued until late 1956. During that period he worked chiefly on conflict-of-interest cases involving prominent Eisenhower Administration figures. His probes led to the resignations of such officials as Air Force Secretary Harold Talbott [q.v.] and Assistant Defense Secretary Robert Tripp Ross [q.v.].

During this period reporter Clark Mollenhoff brought Kennedy evidence of corruption in the Teamsters Union. Kennedy then began his own investigation, accumulating evidence of Teamsters President Dave Beck's [q.v.] blatant misuse of funds, findings which led the Senate to create the Select Committee on Improper Relations in the Labor or Management Field in January 1957. Kennedy immediately became the Committee's chief counsel.

The investigations of the Senate Rackets Committee, as the Select Committee soon came to be called, uncovered glaring evidence of dishonesty and extortion in the Teamsters Union. It also brought chief counsel Robert Kennedy and Committee member John F. Kennedy national attention. Though Kennedy's initial target was Teamsters President Dave Beck [q.v.], the hearings soon focused upon James Hoffa [q.v.], the Teamsters vice president who succeeded Beck as president in 1957, when the latter refused to run for reelection because of charges of misuse of union funds. Kennedy's investigation revealed a complicated story of conflict of interest and collusion with underworld figures to further Hoffa's interests in the union. Hoffa's many appearances before the Committee were highlighted by clashes between the union

leader and the counsel. Kennedy's animosity toward Hoffa continued until the 1960s when, as Attorney General, he created a special branch within the Justice Department to continue the investigation of the Teamsters. Robert F. Kennedy resigned from the Rackets Committee in 1959 to manage his brother's presidential race.

Following the November victory, John Kennedy chose his brother to be his Attorney General. During the Kennedy presidency the Justice Department dealt with such sensitive areas as civil rights, crime, labor legislation, economic monopoly and juvenile delinquency, and earned the respect of minorities and the poor.

After John Kennedy's assassination Robert resigned as Attorney General. In 1964 he ran successfully for a Senate seat from New York. Continuing to plead the cause of the poor and minorities, Kennedy gradually became an outspoken critic of the Vietnam war. He ran for the Democratic presidential nomination in 1968, but he was assassinated in June, after his triumph in the California primary.

[RJB]

For further information:
Lawrence J. Quirk, *Robert Francis Kennedy: The Man and the Politician* (Los Angeles, 1968). Nick Thimnesch, *Robert Kennedy at Forty* (New York, 1965).

KENNON, ROBERT F(LOYD)
b. Aug. 21, 1902; Minden, La.
Governor, La., 1952-56.

Robert F. Kennon received a B.A. and LL.B. from Louisiana State University. In 1925 he was admitted to the Louisiana bar and elected mayor of Minden, La. From 1930 to 1936 Kennon served as state district attorney. He continued his private law practice and became an appeals judge in 1940. Following service in the Army during World War II, Kennon returned to Louisiana and was appointed state supreme court justice for a term ending in 1947. In 1948 he ran as an anti-Long candidate in the Democratic gubernatorial primary and lost to Earl K. Long [q.v.], brother of the late Huey Long. The anti-Long faction was primarily composed of oil and gas businessmen opposed to the pension plans and other share-the-wealth measures of the Long brothers. A few months after losing to Earl, Kennon lost the Democratic nomination for senator to Huey's 27-year-old son, Russell Long [q.v.].

Kennon's third try for governor succeeded. He defeated Long-candidate Carlos G. Spaht in the January 1952 Democratic primary and subsequent runoff. Campaigning on a platform that called for lowering the gasoline tax, economizing in government and reducing the governor's power, Kennon was elected over Republican Harrison Bagwell in April. He supported Sen. Richard B. Russell (D, Ga.) [q.v.] for the 1952 Democratic presidential nomination. At the July National Democratic Convention Gov. Kennon led his delegation in refusing to sign a loyalty oath pledging to support the Party's presidential and vice presidential nominees. Following the Convention he said there was "considerable uncertainty" in the South regarding presidential nominee Adlai E. Stevenson [q.v.]

Louisiana was second only to Texas in oil lands claimed on the continental shelf. The Democratic platform supported federal ownership of these lands. When Republican presidential candidate Dwight D. Eisenhower promised to back state claims to the offshore oil in September, Kennon endorsed him. Later that month the Governor organized Louisiana "Democrats for Eisenhower" but refused to work with the state GOP. Eisenhower narrowly lost Louisiana in November.

Following the Republican President's January 1953 inauguration, Kennon testified for state claims to submerged oil lands before the Senate Interior and Insular Affairs Committee. When in February the panel pondered whether maritime or state law should apply to the tidelands oil areas, Kennon spoke up for the latter. The long-disputed bill turning offshore oil over to the states was signed into law by President Eisenhower in May 1953. Kennon continued to dissociate himself from the national Democratic Party. He joined fellow Southern Democratic Govs. Allan Shivers [q.v.] of Texas and James F. Byrnes [q.v.]

of South Carolina, who had also supported Eisenhower, in refusing to attend a national Democratic conference in September 1953.

When the U.S. Supreme Court declared public school segregation unconstitutional in May 1954, Kennon avoided rabble-rousing demagoguery and did not ask for new segregation laws. However, he promised that segregation would be maintained within existing statutes and that the legislature would provide a school system "which will include segregation in fact." In 1956 Kennon defied an Interstate Commerce Commission order requiring integration of railroad and bus waiting rooms. The Governor instructed all state and municipal officials to enforce state segregation laws.

In July 1954 Kennon was elected chairman of the U.S. Governors Conference. He conferred with his fellow executives on the President's proposed $50 billion interstate highway program. In December Kennon presented Eisenhower with the governors' report calling for highway expenditures of $101 billion over the next 10 years. As the 1956 national elections approached, it became evident that Govs. Kennon and Shivers would again support Eisenhower. Prohibited by law from succeeding himself, Kennon endorsed anti-Long candidate Fred Preaus, who lost to Earl K. Long in the 1956 Democratic gubernatorial primary. Kennon joined Shivers in endorsing and campaigning for Eisenhower during his last year in office. He returned to his law practice in Baton Rouge following his term.

[MJS]

KEROUAC, JACK
b. March 12, 1922; Lowell, Mass.
d. Oct. 21, 1969; St. Petersburg, Fla.
Writer.

Kerouac was born Jean Lours Lebris de Kerouac in the small town of Lowell, Mass. He briefly attended Columbia College in 1940 but left in 1941 for a stint in the Navy. Discharged for unspecified psychiatric reasons, he served in the Merchant Marine before returning to Columbia in 1942. There he met future writers William Borroughs and Allen Ginsberg [*q.v.*] and began his own writing career.

Kerouac's first book, *The Town and the City*, written between 1946 and 1948, was a thinly disguised autobiography recounting his boyhood in Lowell. It was in this work that the word "beat" first appeared in his writings. The term came to be used to describe the movement, developing in the mid-1950s, to oppose contemporary values. Kerouac, however, protested that the use had destroyed his meaning. At times he claimed that "beat" came from "beatific or beatitute." On other occasions he maintained it meant the despair arising from being poor and sad.

Kerouac broke with traditional literary styles in his next work, *On the Road* (1957). Originally typed on a long roll of teletype paper, it was written in speech rhythms shaped by the spontaneity of American jazz. The book was a thinly veiled narrative of Kerouac's travels throughout the U.S. during which he met Ginsberg and Burroughs. Kerouac briefly considered calling the book *The Beat Generation*. For some it provided a blueprint for the joy-riding, drug-taking and outright rebellion against the values of the 1950s. Kerouac's next book furthered his reputation as an influence on alienated youth. *The Dharma Bums* (1958) was an account of his mountain climbing with poet Gary Snyder and of his experiences with Buddhism. Critics later saw it as a prelude to the San Francisco youth renaissance of the 1960s.

Kerouac continued writing autobiographical novels throughout the 1960s. Composed at top-speed because he believed that when he worked "without consciousness" he produced more valid work, the novels were often of uneven literary quality. "At his best," said critic Bruce Cook, "there was a beauty, urgency and energy to his style that was altogether new in American writing."

Kerouac had an important impact on his own generation of the 1950s, but he was an even greater inspiration to the "Beat Generation" of the 1960s. Although he was pointed to as one of the founders of the Beat Generation, his political ideas were often quite different from the young people influenced by his writings. He was a liber-

tarian, not a radical. In 1954 he said in a letter to Ginsberg that Communist dissent was treason. Four years later he wrote a denunciation of the New Left. Throughout the Vietnam war he insisted he was "still a Marine" and ready to serve. Kerouac grew increasingly bitter at what he saw as the deliberate distortion of his views and gradually withdrew from society. He died of an abdominal hemorrhage in October 1969.

[MJS]

KERR, CLARK
b. May 17, 1911; Reading, Pa.
President, University of California, 1958-67.

Clark Kerr, the son of an apple farmer, received a B.A. from Swarthmore College in 1932. The following year he earned an M.A. from Stanford University. Kerr attended the London School of Economics during the latter part of the decade and in 1939 won his Ph.D. in economics at the University of California, Berkeley.

From 1939 to 1940 Kerr taught labor economics at Stanford University. In 1942 he undertook his first labor assignment, arbitrating between unions and management in a wage dispute. He became the most highly paid labor-management negotiator on the West Coast over the next 20 years. After five years of teaching at the University of Washington, Kerr returned to the University of California in 1945. He established the Institute of Industrial Relations at Berkeley while teaching a full schedule. In 1949 the University's state-appointed regents demanded that faculty members sign a special loyalty oath in addition to their legally required constitutional affirmation. Kerr signed the oath but opposed the regents' demand so spiritedly that in 1952 he was named first chancellor of the Berkeley campus upon the recommendation of a faculty committee. Over the next six years he spurred the physical expansion of Berkeley and, as cold war tensions increased, encouraged scientific research. Kerr also continued to serve as a labor mediator. In April 1958 United Auto Workers president Walter Reuther [*q.v.*] chose Kerr to sit on an independent ethics panel to which union members could appeal disputes with their leaders.

Kerr became president of the University of California, the largest university in the U.S., in September 1958. Charged with regulating affairs on seven campuses and competing for state funding, he brought all his mediating skills into play. A crisis occurred in 1958 when other state colleges demanded equal fiscal status with the University and the right to confer doctorates. As though entering a labor dispute, Kerr recommended Arthur G. Coons as mediator. Coon's plan for strengthening the state colleges, coordinating the recruitment and building programs of the colleges and the University and expanding the entire state system of higher education was accepted. It was then used by President Kerr as a basis for reorganizing the University and building new campuses at Irvine and Santa Cruz.

The model of a modern educator, Kerr was appointed an economist to President Eisenhower's Commission on National Goals in February 1960. The Commission's report, issued the following November, stressed the need for Americans to make great sacrifices in the 1960s to defend freedom against anticipated Communist expansion. In an individual report Kerr said the nation should seek to eliminate racial discrimination by 1970.

Kerr made the University of California into the largest research and doctorate-awarding institution in the country. Much of its work was vital to the economics of large corporations and state government that dominated boards of regents under both Republican and Democratic governors. Kerr's University, according to some, grew impersonal, oblivious to students' needs and obsessed with funding and growth. Student unrest began at Berkeley in 1964 with the Free Speech Movement, which criticized restrictions on campus political activity. In 1967 newly-elected Gov. Ronald Reagan convinced the Board of Regents to fire Kerr for his alleged softness in dealing with student protest. [See KENNEDY, JOHNSON Volumes]

[MJS]

KERR, ROBERT S(AMUEL)
b. Sept. 11, 1896; Ada,
Indian Territory (Okla.)
d. Jan. 1, 1963; Washington, D.C.
Democratic Senator, Okla., 1949-63.

The son of an ardent Progressive Democrat, Robert Kerr was born in a log cabin in Indian Territory, later the state of Oklahoma. He attended three Oklahoma colleges, taught school and clerked in a law office until the U.S. entered World War I in 1917. Kerr served overseas as a second lieutenant in the field artillery. Returning to Oklahoma after the War, he passed the state bar examinations in 1922 and joined his brother-in-law's oil-drilling business a few years later. They struck it rich in 1932, drilling within Oklahoma City, where other oil firms feared possible property damage. The success of Kerr's 1936 campaign to persuade the city's voters to extend the drilling area even further and his lucrative contracts with the Continental Oil Co. and the Phillips Petroleum Co. made him a millionaire by the end of the Depression. He formed Kerr-McGee Industries, Inc. out of a partnership with geologist Dean McGee; the company expanded into all phases of the oil business, except distribution, and obtained substantial interests in other natural resources as well, including gas, helium, potash and beryllium. By the 1950s Kerr-McGee controlled 25% of known uranium reserves in the U.S. Throughout his Senate career Kerr remained chairman of the board of Kerr-McGee.

Kerr became well-known in Oklahoma in the 1930s as a spokesman for the oil and gas industry, and he was also active in American Legion affairs. Elected Democratic governor of Oklahoma in 1942, he was the keynote speaker at the Democratic National Convention in 1944. In 1948 Kerr was elected to the Senate, where he generally endorsed Truman Administration policies and tried unsuccessfully to exempt natural gas from federal regulation. He won assignment to the Public Works and Finance Committees. [See TRUMAN Volume]

Kerr rose to power quickly in the Senate.

During the 1950s he consolidated his position; his close relationship with Majority Leader Lyndon Johnson (D, Tex.) [q.v.] placed him at the center of the directorate that dominated the upper house. Equipped with an agile mind and a forceful personality, Kerr used both reason and intimidation with extraordinary effectiveness to get his way. His colleague and frequent antagonist, Sen. Paul Douglas (D, Ill.) [q.v.], described his impact: "He was a keen and remorseless bargainer, who usually won the lion's share of any spoils that were divided. He was formidable in counsel and terrified many of his colleagues in debate. When deeply stirred he discarded reason to pour out a stream of cutting and witty ridicule or fiery denunciation. He was more feared than liked, and the vast majority, not caring to tangle with him, preferred to go along, lest they excite his anger." For some years, said Douglas, Kerr was the "uncrowned king of the Senate."

Kerr was blunt about his purpose in politics: "I represent myself first, the state of Oklahoma second, and the people of the United States third—and don't you forget it." He was the wealthiest man in the Senate. His personal fortune, estimated at $10 million when he entered the Senate in 1949, swelled to an estimated $40 million by the time of his death 14 years later.

Kerr's chief activity in behalf of his constituents was the promotion of federal projects to develop Oklahoma's natural resources. His chairmanship of the Rivers and Harbors Subcommittee of the Public Works Committee enabled him to push through a vast program of regional development projects. They included hydroelectric plants, irrigation projects, an improved inland waterway system and pollution control and recreational facilities. In the years before Kerr went to the Senate, Army engineers spent roughly $63 million on Oklahoma water development projects; during his tenure they spent approximately $312 million. In 1962 Oklahoma received about 10% of all federal works projects. Kerr was instrumental in the transformation of his state from the dust bowl of the Depression era to a prosperous agricultural area.

Kerr's chairmanship of the Rivers and Harbors Subcommittee was also the cornerstone of his Senate power, enabling him to control the fate of other senators' water projects. With political debts thus accumulated, he was able to wield enhanced power in other matters that concerned him, such as taxes and trade. Kerr was the Senate's leading champion of the oil and gas industry and managed easily to rebuff any attempts to eliminate or reduce the 27½% oil depletion allowance.

Kerr was also able to win enactment of special tax benefits for favored individuals. In 1955 the U.S. tax court ruled that an Oklahoma City contractor, Leo Sanders, owed the government $955,000 in taxes he had neglected to pay. Two months after the Supreme Court rejected Sanders' appeal in February 1956, Kerr inserted in a tax measure an extraneous section that applied to Sanders and no one else. The special provision, which won passage, specified that in Sanders' unique situation the maximum tax rate was 33%, instead of 91%, and excused him from the large penalties he would have had to pay for his failure to file proper returns. The measure saved Sanders most of the $955,000 he had owed.

Kerr was a spirited adversary of the Eisenhower Administration on a number of issues involving the interests of his state. A strong protectionist, he fought hard to restrict foreign imports that injured Oklahoma's lead, zinc and oil industries. The stance placed him in opposition to the Administration's espousal of free trade. He voted against a three-year extension of the Administration's reciprocal trade bill in 1955, and in 1958 he unsuccessfully sought to limit the President's authority to override Tariff Commission decisions.

A proponent of high farm price supports, Kerr was a constant critic of Secretary of Agriculture Ezra Taft Benson's [q.v.] policy of flexible price supports. In October 1953 he charged that Benson's failure to support cattle prices at 90% of parity had cut farmers' share of the national income to the lowest percentage in 15 years. He said that Eisenhower "knew far too little about farm problems." In September 1955 Kerr called Benson "directly responsible" for the decline in farm prices and urged his ouster.

Kerr's desire for higher federal spending in such areas as public works and agriculture clashed with the Administration's budget-cutting propensity. In 1957 he launched a broad attack on the economic performance of the Eisenhower Administration. In June, armed with a battery of statistics, he subjected Secretary of the Treasury George Humphrey [q.v.] and chairman of the Federal Reserve Board William McChesney Martin [q.v.] to intensive critical interrogation during Senate hearings. Kerr assailed the Eisenhower Administration for allowing "big business to reinforce its position and its share of the economy; while the farm industry has been almost bankrupted, small business had been penalized and jeopardized and those in the lending business have increased their share by 40%." Kerr's invective reached its peak during a Senate debate on July 15, when he said that if the country's fiscal experts were "marched . . . by Eisenhower for months" he would remain "uninformed" on fiscal matters because it took "brains" to understand them and "he doesn't have them."

Kerr played a key role in the struggle to enact legislation providing medical care for the aged in 1960. He won passage on the Finance Committee for a measure allowing the federal government to make matching grants to the states to pay for medical care for the elderly indigent. Kerr's plan was actually a conservative substitute for a more sweeping medicare plan. The proposal, sponsored by Sen. John F. Kennedy (D, Mass.) [q.v.] and favored by most Senate Democrats, was vehemently opposed by the American Medical Association. After the defeat of medicare, 51-44 in August, the Kerr bill passed, 91-2. Known as the Kerr-Mills Act, it financed medical care out of general revenues only for the aged needy and only in those states which chose to set up matching programs. Medicare would have extended medical care to all people over 65 and financed the aid from social security taxes. Kerr later complained that doctors gave him only 22% of their votes in his 1960 reelection campaign, despite his labors against medicare. When medicare again came up for a Senate vote in 1962, he managed its defeat.

For the most part, Kerr worked on behalf of the Administration's domestic program during the Kennedy years. As chairman of the Aeronautical and Space Sciences Committee and ranking Democrat on the Finance and Public Works Committees, he reached the peak of his power in the Senate. He was able to gain such concessions as the appointment of a Kerr-McGee employe, James Webb, to head the National Aeronautics and Space Administration. In return Kerr became the Administration's most powerful Senate ally and guided many Administration-backed bills through the Senate. He died of a heart attack on Jan. 1, 1963. [See KENNEDY Volume]

[TO]

KEYSERLING, LEON H(YMAN)
b. Jan. 22, 1908; Charleston, S.C.
Economist

A graduate of Harvard law school, Leon Keyserling left the economics faculty of Columbia University in 1933 to join the Roosevelt Administration. Later that year he became secretary to Sen. Robert F. Wagner (D, N.Y.) and helped draft much of the New Deal's social legislation. President Harry S. Truman named Keyserling to the original Council of Economic Advisers in 1946. There Keyserling built on an already liberal reputation; he called for both full employment and a better distribution of income through governmental initiative. [See TRUMAN Volume]

Following the Democrats' loss of the executive branch in 1952, Keyserling emerged as a leading party economist critical of the Republican Administration. Like many Democratic economists, he freely warned of another Depression under Eisenhower. (Eisenhower, in turn, repeatedly railed against the Democratic "prophets of doom.") In July 1954 a study group led by Keyserling predicted seven million unemployed by the year's end.

Keyserling was one of the earliest Democratic liberals to point to the persistence of widespread poverty in America and advocate federal government action to eradicate it. He opposed the Administration's emphasis on preventing inflation. Unemployment, not inflation, warranted the higher priority. His 1954 study called for a $5.4 billion tax cut, mostly for low income groups, increased government spending and lower interest rates. Following Eisenhower's reelection in 1956, Keyserling joined the economic policy committee of the Democratic Advisory Council. The group, created in late November, was formed to enable liberals to circumvent the House and Senate Democratic leadership in the formulation of the Party's legislative programs.

Keyserling remained outside of power after the Democrats regained the White House in 1961. President John F. Kennedy did not make him a member of his official family and did not immediately implement most of Keyserling's views. Keyserling responded by criticizing the Kennedy Administration for its relative fiscal and domestic policy conservatism. [See KENNEDY Volume]

[JLB]

KILLIAN, JAMES R(HYNE)
b. July 24, 1904; Blacksburg, S.C.
President, Massachusetts Institute of Technology, 1948-58; Member, Office for Defense Mobilization Science Advisory Committee, 1951-57; President's Special Assistant for Science and Technology, 1957-59; Chairman, President's Science Advisory Committee, 1957-59; Member, President's Science Advisory Committee, 1957-61.

Killian graduated from the Massachusetts Institute of Technology (MIT) in 1926 with a degree in engineering and business administration. He then worked for the Institute's scientific journal, *Technology Review*, and became its editor in 1930. Killian served as executive assistant to MIT's president from 1939 to 1943 and as an executive vice president for the next five years. In 1948 he was named president of the Institute.

As president, Killian promoted its ties with private business and its research in weapons technology. However, he also stressed broader training for scientists. During his presidency MIT established a School of Humanities and Social Sciences and a Center of International Studies. In the postwar period Killian also served on a number of government panels formed to study management, defense and education problems.

Killian continued his government work under Eisenhower. In 1954-55 he was chairman of a study group that compared U.S. and USSR scientific programs for the National Security Council, and in 1955 he headed a top secret committee to study America's technical military capabilities. The latter committee's report had a significant impact on defense planning. It stressed the need for better delivery of nuclear warheads and for better continental defense in an age of nuclear parity, and it urged the rapid development of the intercontinental ballistic missile. In January 1956 Eisenhower appointed Killian chairman of the eight-member Board of Consultants to act as a watchdog committee for the Central Intelligence Agency.

The launching of the Soviet satellite *Sputnik* in October 1957 generated a demand for increased emphasis on science in education and defense. To coordinate an accelerated science program, the President appointed Killian his special assistant for science and technology, authorizing him to work for improvements in scientific education at all levels, more basic research programs, coordination of scientific activities with allied nations, a greater missile development effort and an end to interservice competition.

Simultaneously Eisenhower ordered the creation of the President's Science Advisory Committee (PSAC) and named Killian its chairman. Killian was soon involved in a wide range of studies and decisions concerning national science and defense issues. In November 1957 he participated in the decision to order the Army to produce the Thor and Jupiter intermediate range ballistic missiles, and in February 1958 he undertook a study of the feasibility of civilian control of the U.S. space program. The study led Congress to authorize the formation of the National Aeronautics and Space Administration in July 1958. Killian also headed a committee that, in March 1958, reported the possibility of a manned moon flight within two decades.

Killian played an important role in the Eisenhower Administration's decision to pursue a nuclear test ban agreement with the Soviet Union, and he was credited with helping convince Secretary of State John Foster Dulles [q.v.] of the advantages of such a policy. In March 1958 Killian appointed a committee of scientists, headed by Hans Bethe [q.v.], to study the possible effects of such a ban and the adequacy of methods for detecting nuclear tests. The committee reported that the U.S. could benefit from a test ban monitored by a good detection system, a finding that helped allay the fears and refute the objections of many who had earlier opposed a ban.

In July 1959 Killian resigned as Eisenhower's special assistant and as PSAC chairman to become chairman of the MIT Corporation. He did, however, remain a member of the PSAC until 1961. In February 1960 Eisenhower appointed him to the Commission on National Goals. The Commission report, issued in November, advocated "extraordinary personal responsibility, sustained effort and sacrifice" from "every American" in the face of the "grave danger" posed by "the Sino-Soviet threat and modern weapons." It also recommended an expanded government role in insuring all Americans, regardless of color, the right to vote.

Killian continued to serve as an presidential adviser under the Kennedy and Johnson Administrations. When the Corporation for Public Broadcasting was established in 1967, Johnson appointed him to its board of trustees. He retired as chairman of the MIT Corporation in 1970.

[MDB]

For further information:
Robert Gilpin, *American Scientists and Nuclear Weapons Policy* (Princeton, 1962).
"James Killian" *Current Biography Yearbook, 1959* (New York, 1960) pp. 229-231.

KING, MARTIN LUTHER, JR.

b. Jan. 15, 1929; Atlanta, Ga.
d. April 4, 1968; Memphis, Tenn.
President, Montgomery Improvement Association, 1956-59; President, Southern Christian Leadership Conference 1957-68.

Born into a middle class family in Atlanta, Ga., Martin Luther King, Jr., followed his father into the ministry and was ordained at his father's Ebenezer Baptist Church in 1947. He graduated from Morehouse College the next year at the age of 19 and then studied at Crozer Theological Seminary in Chester, Pa., receiving his divinity degree in 1951 with highest honors. King next enrolled at Boston University and was awarded a Ph.D. in systematic theology in June 1955.

In September 1954 King undertook his first pastorate at the Dexter Avenue Baptist Church in Montgomery, Ala. He was still relatively unknown in Montgomery's black community when, on Dec. 1, 1955, Rosa Parks [q.v.], a black seamstress, was arrested for refusing to give up her seat on a city bus to a white man. Her arrest sparked an almost total boycott of the city's segregated buses by the black community on Dec. 5. That same day the Montgomery Improvement Association (MIA) was formed to organize the protest and demand the hiring of black drivers and a fairer seating system. King, who had not been a major figure in the protest thus far, was chosen to head the organization. King was made president of the MIA because he was an educated, intelligent man and dynamic speaker who could effectively represent the protesters. He could also play a unifying role since he was not identified with any one faction in the black community and was young enough to relocate should the boycott fail and there be retaliation against its leaders.

Under King's leadership the MIA established a highly efficient car pool of some 300 vehicles to transport the city's black population. It began holding twice-weekly mass meetings to communicate the latest developments, raise funds and sustain morale as the protest lengthened and white opposition intensified. Negotiations between the MIA leadership, city officials and representatives of the financially strapped bus company broke down in December 1955. Late the next month the city inaugurated a "get tough" policy against the protesters, and on Jan. 26, 1956 King was arrested on a charge of speeding. His home was bombed on Jan. 30 and two other MIA officials' houses were bombed on Feb. 1. King and nearly 100 other blacks were indicted on Feb. 21 on a charge of conspiring to organize an illegal boycott. He was found guilty on March 22, but his $500 fine was suspended pending appeal.

The violence and arrests only heightened the resolve of Montgomery's blacks, who by this time were demanding a complete end to segregation on city buses. With the aid of NAACP lawyers, five Montgomery black women filed a suit in federal court on Feb. 1, 1956 challenging the constitutionality of the city and state laws which required segregation on local buses. On June 19 a three-judge federal court in Alabama voted two-to-one that the laws violated the Fourteenth Amendment. Segregation continued, however, while the city appealed this judgment to the U.S. Supreme Court. While the appeal was pending, city officials moved to enjoin operation of the MIA car pool. During a hearing on the issue on Nov. 13, 1956, word arrived that the Supreme Court had decided the Montgomery case and ruled bus segregation unconstitutional. Nonetheless, a local judge issued an injunction against the car pool, and the MIA disbanded it. Blacks remained off the buses for another month, walking or sharing rides, until the Supreme Court's desegregation order arrived in Montgomery on Dec. 20. The next day, at 5:55 a.m., King and several associates boarded a bus and began the integration of Montgomery's public transit. Over a month of white retaliation and violence followed. On Jan. 10, 1957 the homes of two ministers and four black churches were bombed. More bombings followed at the end of the month, including an unsuccessful attempt to dynamite King's home. The terrorism subsided soon after this, once city officials and white community leaders took action against the violence.

The 382-day Montgomery protest was a momentous event for King and for the civil rights movement. The boycott attracted national and international attention and thrust King into prominence as a major black leader and spokesman. It also helped establish nonviolent resistance as King's basic philosophy. The young minister had been interested in Gandhian techniques of passive resistance since his student days, and from its start the Montgomery boycott was nonviolent, with King preaching the doctrine of Christian love and forgiveness to his followers. Only gradually, however, did King see a connection between this doctrine and Gandhian precepts and begin articulating a philosophy of nonviolent resistance to segregation and discrimination. By the end of the boycott, King had made nonviolent direct action the explicit ideological framework of the protest. Montgomery's blacks had proved that passive resistance could work on a mass scale. The boycott popularized nonviolent resistance, making it a major tactic of the civil rights movement. Many observers also asserted that the protest helped give blacks a new sense of dignity and self-respect. Montgomery marked the beginning of a new era of aggressive nonviolent direct action by Southern blacks.

On Jan. 10-11, 1957 King and some 60 other black leaders from 10 Southern states met in Atlanta and formed the organization that later became the Southern Christian Leadership Conference (SCLC). At a meeting in New Orleans the next month, King was chosen president of the SCLC, which was established to help coordinate direct action protests in the South. In March King traveled to Ghana at the invitation of Prime Minister Kwame Nkrumah to attend the country's independence ceremonies.

On his return King joined other civil rights leaders in organizing a Prayer Pilgrimage to Washington, D.C., to demand federal action on school desegregation and voting rights for blacks. Held on May 17, 1957, the pilgrimage was the largest civil rights gathering to that time and was the forum for King's first truly national address. Speaking to the crowd of 15-25,000 demonstrators, King urged the federal government, Northern white liberals and Southern white moderates to take stronger action on behalf of civil rights, and he stressed the importance of the vote for Southern blacks. He met with Vice President Richard Nixon [q.v.] on June 13, 1957 and with President Eisenhower on June 23, 1958, both times encouraging stronger federal protection of civil rights. In September 1958 King's account of the Montgomery protest, *Stride Toward Freedom*, was published. On Sept. 20, while autographing copies of the book at a Harlem department store, King was stabbed in the chest by a woman later judged insane. He recovered from the injury and was released from the hospital on Oct. 3.

Following the Prayer Pilgrimage King and the SCLC undertook a voter registration campaign, but the minister's most significant activity between 1957 and 1960 was his further development of the philosophy of nonviolent resistance. After the Montgomery boycott King deepened his study of nonviolence, and in February 1959 he traveled to India at the invitation of the Gandhian National Memorial Fund. King and his wife Coretta were warmly received, and they met with leading students and followers of Gandhian passive resistance. The trip solidified King's commitment to nonviolence, which for him was not simply a tactic but the one valid method of social change. Beginning with the Montgomery boycott King traveled extensively throughout the U.S. speaking on nonviolence, and by 1960 he was the primary exponent of nonviolent direct action within the civil rights movement.

In January 1960 King moved from Montgomery to Atlanta, where the SCLC had established its headquarters, and became co-pastor at his father's church. He supported the sit-in movement that began the next month and was often hailed as the "spiritual father" of the protesters because they used nonviolent direct action techniques. The SCLC sponsored a meeting of sit-in leaders in Raleigh, N.C., in April 1960, which led to the formation of the Student Nonviolent Coordinating Committee (SNCC).

In October 1960 King was arrested by officials of DeKalb County, Ga., near Atlanta, for allegedly having violated the one year's probation he was serving on a charge of driving without a Georgia license, and he was sentenced to four months in a rural penal camp. On Oct. 26 Democratic presidential candidate Sen. John F. Kennedy (D, Mass.) [q.v.] and his brother Robert [q.v.] intervened to help get King released on bail the next day. The incident was widely publicized in the black community and was credited with increasing the black vote for Kennedy in the November election.

By 1960 Martin Luther King, Jr., was a national symbol of a new black leadership in the South, a leadership that was young, indigenous to the region, fearless and determined to seek full equality for blacks. King had also articulated a philosophy of nonviolent direct action that became the primary mode of black protest in the early 1960s. With the sit-ins King began playing the roles of a mediator between the militant and conservative wings of the civil rights movement and a channel of communication between black and white Americans. He would eventually lose both roles, but for more Americans King was the leader of the direct action movement and perhaps the preeminent civil rights leader during the 1960s. Although historical developments external to himself helped make King the leader he was, he was still, as his biographer David Lewis has said, a rare individual, possessed of ample intelligence, great courage and convictions, and an arresting, charismatic presence.

King led a momentous desegregation campaign in Birmingham, Ala., in the spring of 1963 that helped secure passage of the 1964 Civil Rights Act. He participated in the August 1963 March on Washington, where he delivered his famed "I Have a Dream" speech and was awarded the Nobel Peace Prize in December 1964. He led a voting rights campaign in Selma, Ala., early in 1965 that spurred enactment of the 1965 Voting Rights Act. In the mid-1960s King began turning his attention to the problems of the black poor in Northern ghettos. He was preparing to lead a Poor People's Campaign in Washington when he was assassinated in Memphis, Tenn. on April 4, 1968. [See KENNEDY, JOHNSON Volumes]

[CAB]

For further information:
Lerone Bennett, Jr., *What Manner of Man: A Biography of Martin Luther King, Jr.* (Chicago, 1968).
Martin Luther King, Jr., *Stride Toward Freedom: The Montgomery Story* (New York, 1958).
David Lewis, *King: A Critical Biography* (New York, 1970).
C. Eric Lincoln, ed., *Martin Luther King, Jr.: A Profile* (New York, 1970).

KINSEY, ALFRED C(HARLES)
b. June 23, 1894; Hoboken, N.J.
d. Aug. 25, 1956; Bloomington, Ind.
Scientist.

After taking a B.S. from Bowdoin College in 1916, Kinsey spent the next four years as an instructor in biology and zoology at Harvard while he worked for his Sc.D. in entomology. In 1920 he was awarded his degree and appointed to the faculty of Indiana University at Bloomington. Over the next 18 years the zoology professor earned the reputation as a leading authority on the gall wasp and an author whose biology texts were widely used in high school classrooms.

At first financing his research project solely with his own funds, Kinsey in 1938 began his ground-breaking studies of human sexual behavior. He was motivated, he said, "by the fact that a large area of living had not been studied on a broad, objective basis." Kinsey received the approval of Indiana University officials for his highly controversial sex research, and in 1940 he was awarded a grant from the National Research Council and, soon afterward, from the Rockefeller Foundation. His Institute for Sex Research proceeded in its investigations by taking interviews from volunteer subjects and compiling data into a variety of statistical categories; all work was recorded in a highly secret code. The original project called for a nine or 10 volume study. In Kinsey's lifetime the Institute published *Sexual Behavior in the Human Male* (1948) and *Sexual Behavior in the Human Female*

(1953). Taken together the books constituted an original and highly debated examination of a subject previously considered taboo for scientific inquiry and public discussion.

The findings of the first volume, *Sexual Behavior in the Human Male*, were based on interviews with 5,300 white males of different cultural, occupational, educational and economic groups. Kinsey deemed the histories taken of non-whites to be too few for statistical reliability. Interview questions were divided into nine major categories: social and economic data, marital histories, sex education, physical and psychological data, nocturnal dreams, masturbation, animal contacts and both heterosexual and homosexual histories. Many of the report's conclusions contradicted popularly believed, or at least tacitly accepted, dictums on human sexuality. Social class differences were found to affect individuals' attitudes, with the "lower" classes preferring a more direct, genital sexuality. Masturbation, frequently decried as "immoral," was practiced at some time by 92%-97% of the male population. Kinsey's statistics indicated that 37% of males experienced homosexual contact to the point of orgasm at some time. Premarital and extramarital intercourse occurred at high levels, varying according to age group and social class differences. The fundamental conclusion of the study was that American males' sexual practices conflicted with predominant repressive moral codes. Kinsey pointed to his findings to plead for a greater public understanding and tolerance for the varieties of sexual experience.

Kinsey began his studies of the human female in 1938 with those of males but published his report of female sexuality in 1953. His categories of interview questions were the same as those in the male survey; his informants included 5,940 volunteer white females, with a higher urban, college-background distribution. The study's findings indicated that women's sexual behavior was not as conditioned by social mores was was men's. Kinsey and his fellow scientists found no basic differences in the physiological nature of male-female orgasms, but they did perceive differences in responsiveness to psychosexual stimuli. Kinsey declared that "frigidity" occurred in females at a level much lower than previously supposed, and generally for reasons of partner insensitivity rather than physical malfunctioning. Though he found slightly fewer instances of masturbation, homosexuality and extramarital intercourse in females than in males, he emphasized that such activities should be viewed as common and normal in a biological sense, irrespective of prevailing social dogmas.

Though Kinsey in his private life was often described as being "normal" to the point of dullness, he was attacked by critics of his studies as degenerate, a purveyor of secrets so intimate as to be unfit for publication, regardless of their truth. Such notable leaders as anthropologist Margaret Mead, theologian Reinhold Neibuhr [q.v.] and literary critic Lionel Trilling said the Kinsey reports undermined the moral fabric of interpersonal relationships by ignoring the spiritual implications of sex. Some criticized his interviewing and statistical methods. Others in the scientific and intellectual community and in the general public praised Kinsey for promoting "increasing candor and knowledge of human relationships." The male report sold well, the female report less briskly; all royalties from publications were funneled into continued sex research at the Institute.

Public clamor over the Kinsey reports grew after the publication of *Sexual Behavior in the Human Female*. A weekly Catholic newspaper in Indianapolis even suggested that Kinsey's books "pave the way for people to believe in Communism and to act like Communists." The House Select Committee to Investigate Tax-Exempt Foundations in May 1954 opened hearings on alleged improper awarding of funds by American foundations. The Committee eventually concluded that certain tax-exempt foundations gave money to studies that supported "subversion," and it considered the Kinsey reports "an example . . . of the extremely limited positive value—combined with extremely grave possibilities of averse social effect—of much of the empirical research in the social sciences." Under congressional and public

pressure, the Rockefeller Foundation in late 1954 ceased funds for the Institute, and the National Research Council was able to supply only meager funds for sex research.

With the vigorous support of Indiana University, Kinsey attempted to continue his Institute's research with funds from book royalties and fees from his own lectures. Against the advice of his doctors, he engaged in rigorous speaking tours of the country. On Aug. 25, 1956 he died in Bloomington of a heart ailment and pneumonia. At the time of his death, the Institute was planning a volume on the vagaries of sex laws in the U.S. In a *New York Times* editorial in 1956, the late Dr. Kinsey was praised as a "conscientious, valuable and controversial scientist."

[TGD]

For further information:
Cornelia V. Christenson, *Kinsey: a Biography* (Bloomington, 1971).
Paul Robinson, *The Modernization of Sex* (New York, 1976).

KIRK, RUSSELL (AMOS)
b. Oct. 19, 1918; Plymouth, Mich.
Political writer.

The son of a railroad engineer, Kirk grew up in a small town in Michigan's "stump country"—a depressed agricultural area that had been cut away by timber companies at the turn of the century. As a youth he embraced his parents' fear that the "assembly-line civilization" represented by Henry Ford would destroy the tradition-bound, family-oriented life of the region. His conservative tendencies were further confirmed when he entered Michigan State College on scholarship in 1936 only to find "an institution where humane learning was barely tolerated." Brought up to savor the old literary disciplines, Kirk was horrified by the university's emphasis on technical skills and worldly advancement. In his later writings he was fond of recalling the way he refused to get a job during his college years and thus was forced to subsist on peanut butter and crackers—all so he could have time to read the classics that were not a part of the regular curriculum.

During World War II Kirk was drafted into the Army and stationed in the deserts of Utah as a sergeant in the Chemical Warfare Service. He had much free time to pursue his readings and to discover the solitude of the desert. While in Utah Kirk had a religious experience that added the final element to his conservative outlook.

In 1946, while still serving in the Army, Kirk wrote an article attacking peactime conscription. He feared that the New Dealers would seek to perpetuate a wartime economy by stirring up conflict with the Soviet Union. He also wrote numerous articles on education, the humanities and the conservative tradition. After leaving the Army in 1946, he accepted a position teaching the history of civilization at Michigan State College. During the same period he also pursued his doctorate on a part-time basis at Saint Andrews College in Scotland. Between 1948 and 1955 much of Kirk's time was spent in Europe, where he was impressed by the deep traditions still evident in the European village and profoundly concerned at the leveling operations initiated by liberal governments. His writings abounded in descriptions of beautiful medieval buildings destroyed in order to make way for uniform, concrete housing projects.

In 1953 his dissertation was published as *The Conservative Mind*. The book traced a tradition of conservative Anglo-American thinkers stemming from Edmund Burke. It defended the values of tradition, authority and community against the liberal faith in reason, equality and individualism. The impact of the book was enormous. By providing conservatism with a tradition of distinguished thinkers, Kirk made it intellectually respectable. Even liberal reviewers praised the book. As a result Kirk suddenly found himself the founder of a movement, the so-called new conservatives. Mostly academics, these people distinguished themselves from other conservatives by their emphasis on tradition and community rather than the rights of big business and the virtues of free enterprise.

In 1954 Kirk seized upon his newly won fame and published *A Program for Conservatives*, which dealt with the role of the conservative in the contemporary world. But because the book maintained that conservatism was an affair of family, church and community rather than of individualistic capitalism, it had the effect of splitting the conservative movement. The book stirred a debate between the traditionalists and the libertarians, which received perhaps its most striking expression in the confrontations between Kirk and Ayn Rand [q.v.]. Kirk totally rejected Rand's philosophy of "objectivism," which held that altruism was an illusion and that people should consciously exalt only their self-interest. He countered that "we human beings were made for brotherhood, and if we live only for our own petty little selves, our souls shrivel." The disagreement with the libertarians also lay behind Kirk's 1955 request that his name be removed from the masthead of the *National Review*, although he continued to contribute his monthly column, "From the Academy."

Kirk consolidated his stand against the noise, pollution and spiritual vacuity of a mechanized age in a number of books and articles written throughout the 1950s. In these writings he idealized small family businesses over corporate enterprises, dismissed the proposal to develop a project for landing on the moon as both useless and impossible to carry out and insisted that poverty was not a bad thing unless combined with the ugliness of modern urban slums and the degradation of social welfare programs. In 1956 Kirk accepted a part-time position as research professor of politics at Long Island University. Limited to two months a year, the job effectively released him from those duties in the university which, considering the general state of modern education, he had always found distasteful. Thereafter he spent most of his time carrying out his functions as justice of the peace in Mecosta, Mich. (pop. 200), delivering lectures throughout the country and pursuing his writing. His work was summed up in *Confessions of a Bohemian Tory*, published in 1963. He was a friend and consultant of such politicians as Barry Goldwater [q.v.] and Richard Nixon [q.v.].

[JPL]

KISSINGER, HENRY A(LFRED)
b. May 27, 1923; Furth, Germany.
Foreign and military policy adviser

The son of middle-class Jews, Kissinger and his family left Germany in 1938 to avoid Nazi persecution. He settled in New York City and took evening courses in accounting at the City College of New York. Kissinger served in the U.S. Army from 1943 to 1946 as an infantryman, intelligence specialist and military administrator in occupied Germany. After earning a B.A. summa cum laude from Harvard in 1950, he continued his graduate studies there while working as the executive director of the Harvard International Seminar and editing its publication, *Confluence: An International Forum.*

Kissinger received his Ph.D. in government in 1954. His dissertation, a study of European diplomacy after Napoleon, was published in 1957 as *A World Restored: Castereagh, Metternich and the Restoration of Peace 1812-1822.* The work focused on the structure of peace created by Castlereagh and Metternich, in a historical period when forces of revolution were constantly in conflict with the forces of conservatism. Kissinger had intended to portray Metternich as a villain, but he came to respect the statesman's ability to establish a viable "stability," if not peace. He found the two European diplomats' policies of secret diplomacy, calculated use of force, complicated alliances and manipulation of national parliamentary bodies to be most effective for the needs of their era. Their diplomacy "may not have fulfilled all the hopes of an idealistic generation," wrote Kissinger, "but it gave this generation something perhaps more precious: a period of stability which permitted their hopes to be realized without a major war or a permanent revolution."

In 1955 Kissinger was named the director of a Council on Foreign Relations project examining U.S. policy alternatives for dealing with the Soviet military threat. The Council commissioned Kissinger to record the panel's conclusions; the result was his book, *Nuclear Weapons and Foreign Policy,* published in 1957. A dark, pessimistic work, it viewed the Soviet Union as an expansionist power dedicated to worldwide revolution and to undercutting American stability. It criticized the U.S. response to the threat, the reliance on "massive retaliation." This plan called for the use of strategic nuclear weapons as America's first deterrent against Soviet attack and expansion. Kissinger, instead, proposed a strategy of graduated deterrence with an emphasis on tactical nuclear weapons in limited warfare. The concept of massive retaliation, he said, grew from outmoded notions of unconditional surrender. But with the U.S. and USSR in a nuclear stalemate, the only plausible wars were those for limited, essentially political, objectives. To fight these the U.S. needed a "spectrum of capabilities" from conventional to total nuclear war to pose the maximum credible threat to aggression. U.S. willingness to fight a limited nuclear war would lessen chances of a holocaust, because the USSR could see clearly that threats of force were not meaningless. The book caused a major uproar in Washington, where defense theorists had discounted the concept of limited nuclear war, and prompted many leading Administration figures to modify their views. Vice President Richard M. Nixon [q.v.] congratulated Kissinger while Secretary of State John Foster Dulles [q.v.], who had helped mold the policy of massive retaliation, accepted the possibility of a limited nuclear war.

After completion of his work with the Council in 1956, Kissinger was appointed by Nelson A. Rockefeller [q.v.] to direct the Special Studies Project of the Rockefeller Brothers Fund, a gathering of prominent Americans who examined America's future foreign and domestic problems. Kissinger participated in all the panels and directed the writing of the project's final report, issued in 1958 as "International Security: The Military Aspect." The report warned of massive Soviet success in improving technology and approaching military weapons parity with the U.S. and repeated Kissinger's assertion that allied nuclear powers must be willing to use tactical nuclear weapons in limited warfare. In a relentless, pessimistic tone, the panel members urged a committed national effort to develop a vast civil defense system and a $3 billion short-term increase in defense spending. They also advocated American capability for a peculiarly 20th century, covert style of war: "the disguised or obscure war concealed as internal subversion or takeover by coup d'état or civil war." Copies of the report were requested by many thousands of Americans already tormented by the threat of nuclear war. Rockefeller, in his 1960 campaign for the presidency, used the study as a more sophisticated policy statement to complement his popular slogan, "a bomb shelter in every house."

Kissinger returned to Harvard in 1957 and became a professor of government in 1962. As associate director of Harvard's Center for International Affairs from 1958 to 1960 and as director of the Defense Studies Program from 1958 to 1959, he established a wide range of contacts with influential government policymakers, academicians, military officials and businessmen. He also strengthened his connections with the government as a consultant to the Weapons Systems Evaluation Group of the Joint Chiefs of Staff from 1955 to 1960.

In January 1961 Kissinger published *The Necessity for Choice: Prospects of American Foreign Policy*. The book marked a distinct shift in his strategy for defense policies: he amended his advocacy of a tactical nuclear strategy to support a new emphasis on conventional forces. While challenging the optimists' hope for U.S.-Soviet detente, he recommended increased aid to important non-Communist nations "on the comparative scale of the Marshall Plan."

Kissinger was an adviser to the Kennedy Administration's National Security Council in 1961 and 1962. He served as a consultant to the Arms Control and Disarmament Agency from 1961 to 1967 and to the State Department from 1965 to 1969, in which capacity he toured South Vietnam and recommended policies supporting U.S. intervention in Southeast Asia. Kissinger became assistant to President Richard Nixon for National Security Affairs in 1969 and

Secretary of State in 1973. During the Nixon Administration he helped shape U.S. Vietnam policy, open contacts with Communist China, establish detente with Russia and initiate peace talks in the Middle East. [See JOHNSON, NIXON/FORD Volumes]

[TGD]

For further information:
Marvin Kalb and Bernard Kalb, *Kissinger* (New York, 1974).

KISTIAKOWSKY, GEORGE B(OGDAN)

b. Nov. 18, 1900: Kiev, Russia
President's Special Assistant for Science and Technology, May 1959-June 1961.

Kistiakowsky grew up in the Ukraine, where his father was a professor of international law at the University of Kiev. In the fall of 1918 he joined the White Army in its futile struggle against the Bolsheviks. After two years of fighting, Kistiakowsky fled to Yugoslavia and from there made his way to Germany, where he entered the University of Berlin in 1921. In 1925 he received his Ph.D. in chemistry and then came to the United States to pursue postgraduate research at Princeton. In 1930 he became a professor of chemistry at Harvard, where he remained throughout his career. He actively pursued scientific research, publishing over 150 articles in addition to his book, *Photochemical Processes*, which appeared in 1928. His work was concentrated in physical chemistry, particularly chemical kinetics.

During World War II Kistiakowsky was responsible for all work in explosives done under the National Defense Research Committee. In 1943 he became a consultant for the Manhattan Project. In this capacity he prepared the conventional explosives used to detonate the first atomic bomb. After the War he returned to Harvard and served as chairman of the chemistry department from 1947 to 1950.

In 1953 Kistiakowsky became a member of the ballistic missiles advisory committee of the Department of Defense, a post he held until 1958. He also served as chairman of the President's Science Advisory

Committee (PSAC), formed in 1957 in response to the launching of the Soviet *Sputnik*. During these years Kistiakowsky played a particularly important role in the decision to develop an intercontinental ballistic missile. In the spring of 1959 he was chosen to replace James R. Killian [*q.v.*] as special assistant to the President for science and technology. In this capacity he chaired meetings of the PSAC, participated in the National Aeronautics and Space Council (NASC) and the National Security Council, and coordinated scientific matters of general interest to the government.

Kistiakowsky was a fiscal and political conservative who opposed high-cost budgets submitted by the Defense Department and NASC but urged spending for basic research. He echoed the Eisenhower Administration's general insistence that space exploration was less a matter of national prestige than of scientific progress. Consequently he played down the importance of the spectacular manned space endeavors and emphasized instead the development of instrumental satellites. This position was sharply reversed by the Kennedy Administration's exploitation of the political possibilities inherent in space exploration.

Kistiakowsky supported Eisenhower's emphasis on nuclear deterrence as America's first line of defense but also backed the Administration's efforts to achieve a limited test ban treaty with the USSR. While he maintained that the U.S. needed to continue a limited degree of testing in order to develop a "clean bomb" free from fallout, he did not believe it necessary to create a more destructive nuclear arsenal. Kistiakowsky mitigated the fear that the Soviet Union would violate a treaty by pointing out that scientific research was close to yielding seismic indicators sensitive enough to guard against the possibility.

Although the physical sciences received predominant attention throughout the 1950s, under Kistiakowsky's directorship the PSAC organized a life sciences panel in January 1960. Its primary concern stemmed from the disclosure that the 1959 cranberry crop had been contaminated by a herbicide which had probable carcinogenic effects. As a result of the crisis, the powers of the Food and Drug Administration were substantially strengthened. Kistiakowsky's own reaction, however, was to attempt to reassure the public by playing down the idea that chemicals used in the food industry might have harmful effects on the nation's health.

After John F. Kennedy's inauguration in 1961, Kistiakowsky handed over his duties as science adviser to Jerome Wiesner. He continued to serve on the PSAC through 1963 and in 1962 was appointed to the General Advisory Committee of the newly created Arms Control and Disarmament Agency. After 1960 he devoted himself principally to his work at Harvard. He retired in 1972 and in 1976 published an edition of his private diary covering the period he spent as presidential adviser.

[JPL]

For further information:
George B. Kistiakowsky, *A Scientist at the White House* (Cambridge, Mass., 1976).

KNIGHT, GOODWIN (JESS)
b. May 9, 1896; Provo, Utah
d. May 22, 1970; Inglewood, Calif.
Governor, Calif., October 1953-January 1959.

The descendent of early Western settlers, Knight moved with his family to Los Angeles at the age of eight. During his youth he wrote a collection of boys stories published in 1910. Knight worked as a miner and reporter before entering Stanford University. After an interruption for service in the Navy during World War I, he returned to the University and graduated in 1919. He then practiced law in Los Angeles and took part in Hiram Johnson's presidential primary campaign in 1920 and 1924. Knight was appointed a judge of the superior court of Los Angeles Co. in 1935 and was elected to bench in 1936. He served there until 1946.

As a result of the publicity he received as judge and from a weekend job as public affairs analyst for a San Francisco radio show, he gained a statewide reputation, which he used to further his political career. Knight, who possessed an affable personality, became one of the first politicians to exploit radio and television. In 1946 he won election as lieutenant governor with the backing of Gov. Earl Warren [q.v.].

Four years later Knight again ran on the Warren ticket, although he had often made clear his disagreements with Warren's progressivism and his own ties to the state Party's right wing. He opposed the Governor's advocacy of pre-paid health insurance and a fair-employment practices bill. Unlike Warren he wanted University of California teachers to sign a loyalty oath. In September 1953, when Warren announced that he would not seek a fourth term, Knight immediately declared his gubernatorial candidacy. However, he succeeded to the governorship without an election in early October, when Warren was appointed Chief Justice of the U.S.

Knight's accession was viewed as a triumph for conservative Republicans. The Governor promised to "conduct a business-like administration with emphasis on reducing spending." However, he proved a more liberal governor than observers had predicted and conservatives had hoped. To cope with California's rapidly growing population, Knight pledged his support of highway programs, metropolitan rapid transit systems and development of water resources. In October 1954 he announced the allocation of $100,000 to study health problems caused by smog. Most importantly for Knight's future, he raised unemployment insurance payments and informed labor that he would veto any "right-to-work" legislation. The Governor's new friendship with organized labor paid off. With the strong support of the American Federation of Labor, he won the 1954 gubernatorial contest by 500,000 votes over Democrat Richard Graves in a state where Democrats held a three-to-two edge in voter registration.

Although Knight was titular head of the California Republican Party, he had to share control with Vice President Richard Nixon [q.v.] and Sen. William Knowland (R, Calif.) [q.v.]. Relations among the three were not always amicable. In August 1954 Knight and Knowland combined to de-

feat Nixon's candidate for vice-chairman of the California State Republican Central Committee. In October 1955 the Governor said that he would enter the 1956 Republican National Convention as a "favorite son" candidate should President Eisenhower decide not to run, thereby implicitly rejecting Nixon's claims to the presidential succession. Throughout early 1956 he withheld his endorsement of Nixon for a second vice presidential term, and at the August National Convention he was one of the principal opponents of Nixon's renomination.

In 1957 Knight's political relations with Knowland worsened. The Senator announced that he planned to give up his Senate seat to opposed Knight for the 1958 gubernatorial nomination. He reportedly enjoyed Vice President Nixon's backing for the governorship. Knight and Knowland engaged in a bitter campaign, sharply disagreeing in their views towards labor, with Knowland voicing his support for right-to-work legislation. Finally, in November 1957, following consultations with Nixon and Eisenhower, Knight—who was short of money and press support—announced that he was quitting the gubernatorial race and would instead seek Knowland's Senate seat.

The Governor's Senate primary contest with San Francisco Mayor George Christopher produced another severe intraparty conflict. After both Knight and Knowland won their primaries in June, the Governor refused to endorse Knowland, while the Senator's wife attacked Knight as a "macaroni spine" under whose administration California was fast becoming "another satellite of Walter Reuther's [q.v.] labor political empire." Although some labor leaders supported Knight, the lack of party unity, the cynicism of the Knowland-Knight office switch and Knowland's extreme right-wing views damaged Republican chances. November 1958 brought big Democratic victories in California, including Knight's loss to Rep. Clair Engle (D, Calif.) [q.v.] by a margin of 723,356 votes.

Knight planned to undertake another gubernatorial primary campaign in 1962 but withdrew in January because of a case of hepatitis. He died of pneumonia in 1970.

[JCH]

KNOWLAND, WILLIAM F(IFE)
b. June 26, 1908; Alameda, Calif.
d. Feb. 23, 1974; Oakland, Calif.
Republican Senator, Calif., 1945-59;
Senate Majority Leader, 1953-55; Senate Minority Leader, 1955-59.

The son of a six-term member of the House of Representatives, Knowland became involved in politics while still a child, making speeches for the Harding ticket at the age of 12. He graduated from the University of California in 1929 and then joined the staff of his father's paper, the Oakland *Tribune*. Knowland entered politics in 1933, successfully running as a Republican for a seat in the state Assembly. Two years later he won a seat in the state Senate. In 1938 Knowland was elected to the Republican National Committee and in 1941 became chairman of its executive committee.

While serving in the Army in 1945, Knowland was notified that Gov. Earl Warren [q.v.] had appointed him to finish the term of the late Sen. Hiram Johnson (R, Calif.). In the upper house Knowland quickly emerged as a leader of the Republican Right, gaining prominence for his ardent anti-Communism and support for Nationalist China.

During the Truman Administration Knowland became a leader of the so-called China Lobby. This was an informal group of men and women inside and outside government who decried the "loss" of China to the Communists in 1949 and supported the return of Chiang Kai-shek from Formosa. His preoccupation with China prompted critics to term him "the Senator from Formosa." Knowland was a longtime supporter of Sen. Joseph R. McCarthy (R, Wisc.)[q.v.] and his anti-Communist probes. During the first years of the decade he backed McCarthy's contention that such China experts as John Paton Davies [q.v.] and Owen Lattimore were pro-Communist. [See TRUMAN Volumes]

The ambitious Senator rose quickly through the Senate hierarchy. In 1953 Knowland became chairman of the GOP's Policy Committee, frequently standing in for ailing Sen. Robert A. Taft (R, Ohio)

[q.v.] as Majority Leader. When Taft died in July 1953 Knowland assumed his post; following the Republican loss of Congress in 1955, Knowland served as minority leader.

According to the *New York Times*, Knowland was known for his hard work, courage and candor. In the Senate his methods were described as "subtle as a Sherman tank—a little unseeing and rough, but he gets there." He took liberal positions on many issues, including civil rights, but during the Eisenhower Administration he was still primarily known as a defender of Nationalist China.

Knowland was never able to develop a close relationship with Eisenhower because of this strident stand. He vigorously opposed the admission of Communist China to the U.N. and supported the efforts of the Committee for One Million Against the Admission of Communist China to the United Nations to pressure the Administration to take a firm stand on the issue. On numerous occasions he attempted to get Senate passage of a resolution supporting U.S. withdrawal from the U.N. if Communist China were admitted. In April 1954 Chinese Premier Chou En-lai announced that his country desired peaceful relations with the U.S. and asked for negotiations on outstanding issues. Knowland maintained that acceptance of the Chinese peace initiative would be "another Munich." Pressure from Knowland and from other Nationalist supporters prompted Secretary of State John Foster Dulles [q.v.] to announce that the Administration opposed Communist China's admission to the world body. Still unsatisfied, in July Knowland threatened to resign his majority leadership in the Senate if the Communists were admitted and to campaign for the U.S. withdrawal from the U.N.

Knowland was particularly concerned over the Geneva Conference on Indochina and Korea, scheduled for the spring of 1954. He believed that any negotiation with the Chinese would be tantamount to recognition of the Communist regime. With Dulles preparing to attend the conference in April, he warned against any "steps that could be interpreted as recognition." Knowland's pressure had an important effect on the Administration, which felt it had to placate the China Lobby. Dulles flew to Geneva for a brief time and at one session refused to shake hands with Chou En-lai. He then downgraded the U.S. delegation to the status of observer and instructed Undersecretary of State Walter Bedell Smith [q.v.] to take no part in the negotiations and ignore the Chinese.

When the Communist Chinese began shelling the offshore islands of Quemoy and Matsu during the fall of 1954, Knowland called for a vigorous response by the U.S. and advocated blockading the Chinese coast. The Joint Chiefs of Staff recommended bombing the mainland, while Dulles considered threatening the Chinese with a nuclear attack. Eisenhower resisted the pressure and took no military action.

During 1954 Knowland defended McCarthy against Senate attempts to curb his activities. When Sen. Ralph Flanders (R, Vt.) [q.v.] introduced a resolution in March to deprive McCarthy of his committee and subcommittee chairmanships, Knowland labeled it a mistake, "contrary to established procedures" and an obstruction to the Administration's legislative program. Four months later Flanders introduced a resolution to censure the Wisconsin Republican. Knowland then successfully moved to have a special committee examine the charges in hope, according to some historians, of preventing a vote on the issue. The committee, headed by Sen. Arthur Watkins (R, Utah) [q.v.], unanimously issued a report urging censure. The resolution passed the Senate in December; Knowland voted against the action.

On numerous occasions Knowland expressed interest in running for the presidency. In 1956 he announced that he would be a candidate for the Republican nomination if Eisenhower decided to retire. Two years later he sought the Republican nomination for governor of California as a springboard to a 1960 presidential campaign. Knowland forced the incumbent, Gov. Goodwin J. Knight [q.v.], out of his renomination effort, but the former Senator lost the general election to the popular Democratic attorney general, Edmund (Pat)

Brown [q.v.]. Following the defeat, Knowland returned to his newspaper business. In 1964 he served on Sen. Barry Goldwater's (R, Ariz.) [q.v.] campaign staff, and backed Ronald Reagan for President four years later. In February 1974 Knowland died, an apparent suicide.

[JB]

KOHLBERG, ALFRED
b. 1887: San Francisco, Calif.
d. April 7, 1960: New York, N.Y.
China policy lobbyist

Born in San Francisco, Kohlberg graduated from the University of California in 1908. During the years from 1916 to 1955, he spent a great deal of time traveling between the U.S. and China in connection with his textile business. He provided Chinese children with materials which they embroidered for him at what critics later charged were extremely low wages.

As a result of his travels, Kohlberg became deeply concerned with the fate of China during the civil war of the 1940s. He belonged to the Institute of Pacific Relations (IPR), the United China Relief and the American Bureau for Medical Aid to China. Under the latter's auspices Kohlberg visited China to determine whether the reports of graft and corruption among Chiang Kai-shek's Nationalists were accurate. He determined to his own satisfaction that they were not and quickly set out to discover the source of such false charges. Kohlberg focused his attention on the IPR, a prominent scholarly organization dealing with research on Asia. After comparing its reports of Nationalist abuses to those in the Communist paper the *Daily Worker*, he concluded in an 88-page report to the IPR that "your employes have been putting over on you a not too well camouflaged Communist line." After failing to convince the organization of this, he resigned.

During the postwar era Kohlberg was often called the "head of the China Lobby," an informal group of diverse organizations and individuals who urged all-out military and economic aid to the Chiang government. In 1946 Kohlberg helped organize the America China Policy Organization in support of Nationalist China; he became its first vice president and later chairman of the board. He also wrote articles for the *China Monthly*, considered by many to be the nation's most vocal pro-Nationalist journal, in which he maintained that Chiang was being "sold out by pro-Communist U.S. Foreign Service officers." His targets were John Paton Davies [q.v.], John Carter Vincent [q.v.] and John S. Service [q.v.], all of whom were dismissed or asked to resign during the early-1950s as a result of charges of disloyalty.

In 1950 Kohlberg began working with Sen. Joseph R. McCarthy (R, Wisc.) [q.v.] in delving into what he considered subversive or anti-American activities in the State Department. Over the next seven years he debated liberals, published articles, delivered speeches and wrote countless letters to newspapers and politicians in defense not only of McCarthy's goals but also of his methods. Kohlberg was one of the founding members of the American Jewish League Against Communism and was also active in the special committee on radio and television of the Joint Committee Against Communism in New York. This Committee played an important role in blacklisting many individuals in the entertainment industry.

In 1952 Kohlberg endorsed conservative Sen. Robert Taft (R, Ohio) [q.v.] during the Republican primary campaign but backed Eisenhower after the General won the nomination. However, during the 1950s Kohlberg became increasingly dissatisfied with Eisenhower's cold war policies. He questioned what he believed to be the President's lack of aggressiveness toward Communism, pointing out that Eisenhower had succumbed to the same defeatist policies as the Truman Administration. Two years later he wrote to the President that "in spite of the anti-Communist, anti-containment and pro-liberation planks of the 1952 platform, you have joined the neutralists. . . ." In 1955 Kohlberg set up a Committee of Endorsers, which took newspaper advertisements demanding a new, aggressive foreign policy. Its program, which Kohlberg presented at congressional hearings, called on the U.S. to use economic, political, psychological and military means to defeat the Communists. However, Kohlberg never outlined a specific program to achieve this goal.

Although Kohlberg suffered a heart attack in 1954 and had to restrict his activities, he continued his crusade until the end of the decade. With possible help from the Central Intelligence Agency, he developed a successful plan to disrupt the Communist Seventh World Youth Congress, held in Vienna in 1959. Kohlberg died of a heart attack in New York City on April 7, 1960.

[JB]

KOHLER, HERBERT (VOLLRATH)
b. Oct. 21, 1891; Sheboygan, Wisc.
d. July 29, 1968; Sheboygan, Wisc.
President, Kohler Company, 1937-62;
Chairman of the Board, 1940-68.

Kohler's father founded the Kohler Co., a manufacturer of plumbing ware, in 1873. As a boy Kohler worked in the plant during his vacations. In 1914 he received a Ph.B. from Yale University's Sheffield Scientific School and entered the family-owned business on a full-time basis. In 1937 Kohler became president of the firm. Three years later he succeeded his half-brother, Walter J. Kohler, former governor of Wisconsin (1929-30), as the company's chairman of the board. Under his leadership the Kohler Co. became the nation's largest manufacturer of plumbing fixtures.

In 1953 Local 833 of the United Auto Workers (UAW) won an election to represent Kohler employes at the enterprise's Sheboygan, Wisc., plant, replacing a company union. On April 5, 1954 the employes went on strike, demanding a closed shop, dues check-offs, a grievance arbitration procedure and a 10-cent-an-hour wage increase. The company rejected the first three demands and offered a three-cent increase. For two months the factory was closed by sometimes-violent mass picketing by the approximately 3,600 striking workers (out of 4,000 company employes). However, the plant was reopened in June after the company obtained a state circuit court injunction halting the mass picketing and hired replacements for the employes who did not return to work. In 1955 a near-riot developed when a group of strikers prevented a shipment of clay from reaching the factory.

Although Kohler delegated responsibility for strike negotiations to others, the company's position reflected his views. As the strike wore on year after year, he gained a reputation among businessmen and conservatives as an heroic, beleaguered, old-fashioned individualist. He denounced UAW President Walter Reuther [q.v.] as "a Moscow-trained socialist" and charged that the union was trying to tell him how to run his company. He also accused the union of resorting to violence against non-strikers. After mass picketing ended and the strikers were fired and replaced, Kohler said the union no longer represented his company's employes. The Wisconsin judge who issued the anti-mass picketing injunction subsequently stated that after the company won the injunction Kohler was not interested in negotiating because he felt he had won the strike. The union offered to send the strike issues to arbitration, but the company refused, despite the pleas of Walter J. Kohler, Jr., governor of Wisconsin and nephew of the company president. In 1958 the National Association of Manufacturers awarded Herbert Kohler its "Man of the Year" award.

To liberals and labor union spokesmen, Kohler's position on the strike represented a throwback to the aggressive anti-union attitudes of nineteenth-century businessmen. Reuther denounced him as "the most reactionary, anti-labor, immoral employer in America." The UAW charged the Kohler Co. with, among other things, stockpiling weapons in anticipation of the strike, instigating violence and attempting to intimidate the strikers by hiring detectives to spy on them and on union officials. The union ultimately spent $12 million on strike benefits alone during the walkout.

In February and March 1958 the strike received national attention when the Senate Select Committee on Improper Activities in the Labor or Management Field, chaired by Sen. John McClellan (D, Ark.) [q.v.], investigated the strife in Sheboygan. Kohler, appearing as a witness, accused the union of "mob rule" and "night-riding vandalism" and asserted that his company was performing a public service by resisting such tactics. Reuther testified that the Kohler Co. was not negotiating in good faith. Conservative Sen. Barry M. Goldwater (R, Ariz.) [q.v.], a member of the panel, denounced the UAW's methods, particularly its efforts to organize a boycott of Kohler products. Sen. Pat McNamara (D, Mich.) [q.v.] resigned from the Committee, charging that some of its Republican members were using the probe to attack the UAW.

In August 1960 the five-man National Labor Relations Board (NLRB) ruled that the Kohler Co. had used unfair labor practices during the strike. The Board stressed particularly the granting of a wage increase to non-striking employes in 1954, describing it as an attempt to undermine the union's bargaining effectiveness. The NLRB ordered the reinstatement of most of the strikers who had been fired. The strike officially ended when the Board filed its ruling on Sept. 2, 1960.

In January 1962 the U.S. Court of Appeals in Washington, D.C., upheld the NLRB ruling. Six months later the Supreme Court refused to hear the company's appeal. The following month Kohler, who in 1961 had received the Freedom Award in business from the Young Americans for Freedom, resigned his post as chairman of the board. In December 1962 the Kohler Co. and the UAW agreed on a contract. The pact provided for expanded fringe benefits, a major medical plan, an improved pension plan and an additional paid holiday but not for a closed shop or a wage increase. Three years later all issues relating to the strike were settled when the company and the union agreed on the amount of back pay and pensions to be granted to employes who had been fired during the walkout.

Kohler died in Sheboygan, Wisc., on July 28, 1968 of cerebral thrombosis and pneumonia.

[MLL]

KROCK, ARTHUR

b. Nov. 16, 1886; Glasgow, Ky.
d. April 13, 1974; Washington, D.C.
Journalist.

Krock was born in a small market town in Kentucky. The son of a bookkeeper, he attended Princeton in 1904 but was forced to leave after one semester because of financial problems. He then studied at the Lewis Institute in Chicago, where he was awarded an A.A. degree in 1906. The following year he began his career in journalism as a cub reporter for the *Louisville Herald*. He lost his job in 1908 when the paper was forced to retrench. Krock became the Washington reporter for the *Louisville Times* in 1910 and gradually rose to become its editorial manager and editor in chief. In 1919 he covered the Versailles Conference; his reporting earned him the French Legion of Honor.

After a dispute with his paper's owner, Krock accepted a position in New York as assistant to Will Hays, head of the Motion Picture Producers and Distributers of America. Krock's separation from journalism was shortlived. He soon joined the editorial staff of the *New York World* and in 1923 became assistant to its publisher, Ralph Pulitzer. Krock joined the *New York Times* in 1927 as an editorial writer. Five years later he took over its Washington bureau. Besides his administrative duties he remained a correspondent and also wrote his famous column, "In the Nation." He gave up his post as head of the bureau in 1953, but continued writing his column.

A conservative on a liberal paper, Krock's writings revealed, in the words of James Reston [*q.v.*], "his longings for the comfortable past." Although he occasionally wrote about foreign affairs, he concentrated primarily on domestic problems. He regarded the New Deal as a menace to states rights and free economics. Quickly realizing the importance of fiscal and monetary policy, Krock soon emerged as an expert on New Deal economic theories. During the Roosevelt Administration the journalist won two Pulitzer prizes: for general excellence

in reporting and for an interview with the President in which Roosevelt revealed his future plans, including his determination to add new members to the Supreme Court.

In 1951 Krock created a stir when he revealed that President Harry S. Truman had suggested that Gen. Dwight D. Eisenhower run for the Democratic presidential nomination. Eisenhower, however, would not accept the Democratic Party's pro-labor attitude and the discussion ended. Although the President denied the conversation, Krock stated that his source was a Democrat in "an eminent position." (Years later he revealed it had been Supreme Court Justice William O. Douglas [*q.v.*].)

Krock supported Eisenhower for the presidency and looked optimistically to the future with the nation guided by the steady conservative hand of the new President. During the early years of the Eisenhower Administration, he vacillated between charges that the President was acting tentatively and, in the words of historian Herbert Parmet, "suspecting that strong Eisenhower leadership was just around the corner." A few weeks after the inaugural, he wrote that the Administration lacked direction and that Eisenhower was acting in a "timorous manner." Yet after the State of the Union message in February, during which the President pledged to take charge of loyalty-security investigations, Krock hailed the address as the advent of vigorous presidential leadership.

By 1956 Krock was criticizing Eisenhower for his inability to lead the nation. Krock praised Democratic presidential candidate Adlai Stevenson [*q.v.*] for bringing this to the attention of the American people. In his column he outlined the Democrats charges, including Eisenhower's inability to get Congress to pass his legislative program and his failure to restrain the Republican Right. Yet by 1958 he was again supporting the President against charges that he was "merely serving out his term." In January he wrote that the White House was making a concerted effort to restore the image of Eisenhower as a national leader.

The Southern-born Krock responded cautiously to the Supreme Court's 1954 desegregation decision. He termed it a "milestone in more ways than one" because political and ideological differences had been submerged by agreement on the basic proposition that segregation in educational facilities was unconstitutional. Krock supported the Court's refusal to give a specific date by which desegregation had to be accomplished. Gradualism was necessary, he maintained, because the ruling struck deeply at the social, political and economic systems of the South. He predicted that the "problem will not instantly disappear" and asked that those who had pressed for the decision "be foremost in cooperating with those who are confronted with its incalculable consequences at first-hand." Following the desegregation crisis in Little Rock, Ark., in 1957, Krock wrote that the South had left a period in which it would try to oppose the Court ruling by legal or "positive" means. He predicted that "the negative period of state and local resistance will now begin," during which school systems in some states might be shut down entirely.

Krock continued writing his column until 1968, when he retired. Throughout the decade he remained skeptical of presidential power and liberal economics. In 1968 he published his *Memoirs*. Although Krock personally liked President Richard M. Nixon, he was shocked by the Watergate scandal. Krock died in April 1974.

[JB]

For further information:
Arthur Krock, *In the Nation* (New York, 1966).

KUCHEL, THOMAS H(ENRY)
b. Aug. 15, 1910; Anaheim, Calif.
Republican Senator, Calif., 1953-69.

Kuchel was born into a pioneer family which helped found the southern California town of Anaheim and owned and edited the Anaheim *Gazette*. In 1936, shortly after receiving his law degree from the University of Southern California, he won election to the state Assembly from Orange Co. Following several terms in the Assembly and, after 1940, in the state Senate, Kuchel was appointed state controller by Republican Gov. Earl Warren [q.v.] in February 1946. In November he was elected to a full term. In 1950 Kuchel won the Democratic nomination for controller as well as that of his own party (then a common practice under California's cross-filing primary system) and ran unopposed in the general election. After Richard M. Nixon [q.v.] was elected vice president in 1952, Warren named Kuchel to fill Nixon's U.S. Senate seat until the 1954 elections. The following year he defeated his opponent, Rep. Samuel Yorty (D. Calif.), for a Senate term ending in 1957.

Although he described himself as a "middle-of-the-road Eisenhower Republican," Kuchel took conservative, anti-Administration stands on some issues during his first years in the Senate. He was one of 64 senators who sponsored the Bricker amendment, which sought to curb the President's treaty-making power and impose greater congressional regulation over the conduct of foreign affairs. In 1954 the measure fell one vote short of the two-thirds vote needed for passage of a constitutional amendment. Kuchel was also one of a minority of senators to oppose the censure of Sen. Joseph R. McCarthy (R, Wisc.) [q.v.] in 1954.

Kuchel soon began to moderate his positions, and by the late-1950s he was identified with the liberal Republican minority in the Senate. His political moderation was, in part, a recognition of the fact that in California, with its majority of registered Democrats and its large proportion of independent voters, a Republican candidate had to appeal to the liberal urban vote as well as to conservative elements in the state. As a result, Kuchel pursued a course that earned him the support, not only of the business community, but also of some labor unions. In his 1956 reelection bid Kuchel followed the Warren tradition of personal, almost non-partisan campaigning, emphasizing his individuality and independence from other Republican office-seekers, forming his own campaign committee and tapping independent sources of funds.

Although Kuchel's independence won him broad electoral support, it cost him his potential influence within the state Republican Party. Warren's retirement from

California politics in 1953 to become Chief Justice left the Party without any generally accepted leader. For several years a struggle for control ensued between Sen. William F. Knowland [q.v.], Gov. Goodwin J. Knight [q.v.] and Vice President Nixon. Kuchel stood aloof from the contending factions, and he did not even intervene after the 1958 elections, when Knowland's and Knight's defeat in a Democratic landslide left him the only Republican holder of a major statewide office. As a result, his position in the state Party deteriorated after 1958 as conservatives gradually took over its organizational apparatus. In addition, the repeal of California's cross-filing system in 1958 meant that he could no longer count on Democratic votes to secure the Republican nomination in a future primary election.

Following heavy nation-wide Republican losses in the 1958 elections, Kuchel joined a group of Republican liberals in challenging the conservative leadership of the Party's Senate caucus. Although Sen. Everett Dirksen (R, Ill.) [q.v.], the conservative candidate for minority leader, offered the post of whip to Kuchel in order to avoid a fight, liberals, led by Sen. George Aiken (R, Vt.) [q.v.], refused this compromise and prepared to block Dirksen's election. During the crucial weeks before the opening of the 1959 session, Eisenhower unexpectedly threw his support to the "old guard," and by the time the Party caucus met in January 1959, the conservatives had enough votes to win all the leadership posts. Dirksen, however, in an effort to construct a coalition leadership, backed Kuchel instead of the conservative candidate for whip, Karl Mundt (R, S.D.) [q.v.]. He followed this gesture by arranging Kuchel's assignment to the important Senate Appropriations Committee.

As Republican whip, Kuchel helped promote legislation on which the Party position had been determined by the Republican Policy Committee. Occasionally this meant supporting legislation favored by the Republicans' Southern Democratic partners in the Senate conservative coalition. In 1959, for example, Kuchel introduced an amendment to a labor anti-corruption bill

that weakened a provision permitting the Secretary of Labor to seek federal court injunctions blocking unions from depriving their members of voting and other rights. Southern Democrats feared this provision as a possible precedent for civil rights action on behalf of black members of Southern unions. However, Kuchel often voted against the majority of his Party.

Kuchel joined liberals in an unsuccessful attempt to strengthen the Civil Rights Act of 1960 by empowering the Attorney General to enter private suits for school desegregation. In the same year he voted to override the President's veto of salary increases for federal employes, a measure opposed by most Republicans as fiscally irresponsible. As a result of these liberal stands, he had little influence over most of his Republican colleagues in the Senate.

During the Kennedy and Johnson Administrations, Kuchel continued to side with Senate liberals on many domestic issues. In 1964, for example, he was one of only five Republicans to vote for medicare, and he played a significant role in the passage of conservation measures. Kuchel's refusal to support Sen. Barry Goldwater's (R, Ariz.) [q.v.] 1964 presidential campaign led to an unsuccessful attempt to oust him as whip the following year. In 1968 California conservatives defeated him for the Republican Senate nomination. Kuchel returned to legal practice with a Beverly Hills firm, and he subsequently became a lobbyist for Columbian sugar interests. [See KENNEDY, JOHNSON Volumes]

[TLH]

LADEJINSKY, WOLF I(SAAC)
b. March 15, 1899; Ukraine
d. July 3, 1975; Washington, D.C.
Agricultural expert.

Ladejinsky, the son of a well-to-do Jewish miller, was born in the Ukraine. At the age of 21 he fled Russia to escape the Bolshevik Revolution. He arrived in the U.S. in 1922. Penniless and knowing no English, he supported himself as a window washer, translator and newspaper seller while attending Columbia. He earned a masters degree in agricultural economics from that institution in 1934. The following year Ladejinsky joined the Department of Agriculture as a specialist on Asian problems. He also published frequent articles denouncing Soviet agricultural policies under Stalin.

During the postwar period Ladejinsky emerged as a major force behind land reform in Asia. In 1945 Gen. Douglas MacArthur called him to Japan to supervise reform in that country. Under his direction the old Japanese feudal system was abolished and millions of acres redistributed to peasants. He also went to China to implement reform there, but he was eventually forced out when the Communist Chinese took power. As an adviser to Chiang Kai-shek, Ladejinsky also aided land redistribution in Formosa. In 1950 he became an agricultural attache with the State Department. By 1954 he was in charge of the American agricultural program in the Far East.

As a result of bureaucratic reorganization, agricultural attaches were transferred to the Department of Agriculture in 1954. Ladejinsky, therefore, had to undergo a security check despite the fact that State Department had declared him loyal seven months earlier. Under the Eisenhower security plan, department heads were responsible for final decisions on clearance. They did not have to be guided by previous decisions.

In December 1954 the Department of Agriculture informed Ladejinsky that he would not be reassigned because he did not meet "technical standards and security requirements." The Department based its decision on the fact that Ladejinsky had connections with two Communist-front organizations and had made a visit to the USSR in 1939. Secretary of Agriculture Ezra Taft Benson [q.v.] also maintained that because Ladejinsky had family in the Soviet Union he could not conduct effective anti-Communist activities. Many officials, including Sen. Hubert Humphrey (D, Minn.) [q.v.] and Rep. Walter Judd (R, Minn.) [q.v.] came to his defense. They pointed out that Ladejinsky's trip was at the request of the Agriculture Department and that his connection with Communist-front activities

meant that he was on their mailing list. Prominent Japanese officials also denounced the action as destroying U.S. prestige in the Far East. Sen. Olin D. Johnston (D, S.C.) [q.v.], head of the Senate Post Office and Civil Service Committee, began an investigation of the Administration's security program. One of the primary focuses of the study was the examination of the program's decentralized procedure making each department and agency head directly responsible for security in their area. The Committee's report, released in July 1956, recommended that security procedures be clarified and that security requirements pertain only to sensitive jobs.

On Jan. 5, 1955 Ladejinsky was given full security clearance by the Foreign Operations Administration (FOA) and hired to supervise land-reform projects in South Vietnam. When FOA functions were transferred to the International Cooperation Administration (ICA) in May 1955, Ladejinsky was assigned to that agency.

In a July 1955 letter to Sen. Frank Carlson (R, Kan.) [q.v.], Benson reversed his decision. He attributed his original action to confusion caused by the reorganization of security procedures in his department, and he said he would defer to the expertise of other departments in determining Ladejinsky's security status.

Ladejinsky was forced to resign his post in February 1956, when he inadvertently violated an ICA rule forbidding its employes from investing in companies receiving U.S. aid. He remained in South Vietnam until 1961 as an adviser to President Ngo Dinh Diem. During the 1960s and 1970s he served as a consultant in numerous countries and spent a great deal of time working for the World Bank. He died in July 1975.

[RB]

LANDRUM, PHIL(LIP) M(ITCHELL)
b. Sept. 10, 1907; Martin, Ga.
Democratic Representative, Ga.,
1953-76.

Landrum was born in a small village in northeast Georgia. During the early and mid-1930s he worked as a coach in local high schools; in 1937 he was appointed superintendent of public schools in Nelson, Ga. While teaching Landrum attending college and was awarded his B.A. from Piedmont College in 1939. In 1941 he received his LL.B. degree from Atlanta Law School.

The following year Landrum ran unsuccessfully for the Democratic nomination for the U.S. House of Representatives. After service in the Army Air Force during World War II, he returned to Georgia, where he was appointed assistant attorney of the state. Between 1947 and 1949 he served as executive secretary to Gov. M. E. Thompson. He then set up a law practice in Jasper, Ga. In 1952 Landrum defeated five other Democrats to win the Party's nomination for a U.S. House seat. In November he was unopposed for election. He represented a poor agricultural area of the state with an economy based on poultry raising and low-wage textile manufacturing.

Landrum accumulated a conservative record in Congress, opposing public power development and large-scale government projects such as the St. Lawrence Seaway. During the 1955 debates in the Education and Labor Committee on raising the minimum wage from 75 cents to $1 an hour, he was the only Democrat to oppose the measure. However, he voted for the bill when it went to the floor.

Landrum was a strong opponent of civil rights legislation. In March 1956 he joined 100 other Southern members of Congress in signing the "Southern Manifesto," denouncing the Supreme Court's desegregation decisions and pledging to use "all lawful means" to reverse them. In July he voted against the school construction aid bill which contained the Powell amendment, prohibiting the extension of funds to areas practicing segregation. He voted against the Civil Rights Acts of 1957 and 1960, and he opposed extending the life of the Civil Rights Commission. Landrum also voted against granting statehood to Alaska in 1958 and Hawaii the following year on the grounds that it would reduce the South's influence in Congress.

As a member of the Education and Labor Committee, Landrum became deeply involved in developing measures to eradicate corruption in labor unions. The efforts were promoted largely by investigations, begun in 1957, by Sen. John McClellan's (D, Ark.) [q.v.] Select Committee on Improper Activities in the Labor or Management Field. The panel revealed extensive corruption, embezzlement and collusion between management and labor leaders. During 1958 and 1959 Congress debated whether reform legislation should be combined with efforts to change the rules of collective bargaining under the Taft-Hartley Act. In July 1959 the Education and Labor Committee reported out a moderate measure, sponsored by Karl Elliot (D, Ala.), focusing on the prevention of financial and electoral misconduct by union leaders. Landrum, however, believed the bill "too weak" and joined the President and Republican members of Congress in demanding that it be strengthened. Together with Rep. Robert P. Griffin (R, Mich.) [q.v.], he developed an alternative measure designed to strengthen the Taft-Hartley Act. In early August President Dwight D. Eisenhower made a special radio-television speech supporting the Landrum-Griffin bill as "a good start toward a real labor reform law." The bill was adopted by both houses of Congress in September despite opposition from liberals and organized labor.

The measure contained a labor "bill of rights," setting criminal penalties to prevent abuse of union offices and guarantee union members free elections. Its most controversial provisions were amendments to the Taft-Hartley Act expanding the ban on secondary boycotts to prohibit unions from coercing employers to stop doing business with other firms, extending secondary boycott provisions to additional workers, and permitting state agencies and courts to take jurisdiction under state law of cases the National Labor Relations Board refused to accept. In December Landrum urged further amendment of the Taft-Hartley Act to deal with "national emergencies" such as the steel strike of that year. He declared the Landrum-Griffin Act "only the beginning of real reform."

Landrum was a spokesman for the Southern textile industry during the 1960s. He remained a conservative on civil rights but played a leading role in the passage of Lyndon Johnson's domestic legislation, particularly the War of Poverty. [See KENNEDY, JOHNSON, NIXON/FORD Volumes]

[EWS]

LANGER, WILLIAM
b. Sept. 30, 1886; Everest, N.D.
d. Nov. 8, 1959; Washington, D.C.
Republican Senator N.D., 1941-59;
Chairman Judiciary Committee, 1953-55.

William Langer was born and raised on his family's Dakota territory farm. After studying law at the University of North Dakota and joining the state bar, Langer enrolled as an undergraduate at Columbia University; he earned his B.A. there with honors in 1910. Langer then returned to North Dakota, where he allied himself with the state's Non-Partisan League (NPL). The NPL, a populist farmers' alliance fostering state cooperatives, slowly took over the Republican Party. An unorthodox politician, he won the 1932 gubernatorial race while endorsing Franklin D. Roosevelt for President. In 1934 the state Supreme Court removed him from office on the charge that he unlawfully sought campaign contributions from state employes. The action, later overturned by a federal court, would always affect Langer's reputation. North Dakota voters, however, ignored the allegations and elected Langer governor again in 1936 and a U.S. senator in 1940, 1946 and 1952.

In the Senate Langer proved a rigid isolationist both before and after World War II. Unlike many Republican isolationists, he took generally liberal positions on social and economic issues, voting for example, against the Taft-Hartley Act of 1947. He was also a vigorous defender of the interests of Indians and civil service employes. During the 1952 presidential campaign Langer endorsed neither candidate, but he appeared in North Dakota with President Harry S. Truman, who was campaigning for Adlai Stevenson [q.v.]. [See TRUMAN Volume]

Langer failed to support most of the Eisenhower Administration's legislative programs, and he earned the poorest overall record of Republican support for the President in the Senate. During the 83rd (1953-54) Congress, Congressional Quarterly reported that he backed the President 29% of the time on legislation endorsed by the White House. In 1955, 1956, 1958 and 1959, Langer was the Republican senator who most frequently voted against Administration positions.

Langer's support of public power development conflicted sharply with the Administration's emphasis on private development and operation of utilities. In 1954 the Administration approved the Dixon-Yates contract, granting the private combine permission to construct a power plant in the Tennessee Valley area. The plant was designed to replace the Tennessee Valley Authority as the power supplier for the Atomic Energy Commission (AEC) in the area. Public power forces, concentrated in the Democratic Party but joined by Langer, challenged the move. In August 1954 Langer insisted on investigating charges that Edgar Dixon [q.v.] had been involved in questionable business practices. When the Republican Senate leadership blocked Langer, the North Dakota Republican paid for hearings himself. "As long as I pay the bills," he declared, "who's going to stop me?" Senators defending the Administration—Everett M. Dirksen (R, Ill.) [q.v.] and John Marshall Butler (R, Md.)—argued that Langer's funding of the proceedings was improper. Langer ignored them. As chairman of the Judiciary Committee's Antitrust Subcommittee, Langer took testimony in August and issued a report on Dixon's Mississippi Power and Light Co. The subcommittee's analysis, which Dirksen, a member, refused to sign, cited "monopolistic trends and abuses" in Dixon's operations and attacked the Administration's support of private power development. A year later, in July 1955, Langer accused Dixon of committing perjury when testifying on his role in the negotiation of the contract.

Langer's opposition to Dixon-Yates resulted in his refusal to back Lewis L.

Strauss's [*q.v.*] appointment as Secretary of Commerce in 1959. Strauss had been chairman of the AEC and had played a pivotal advisory role in forming the Administration's public power policy. Of the Senate's Republicans, only Langer and Sen. Margaret Chase Smith (R, Me.) [*q.v.*] voted against Strauss's nomination. The appointment was defeated in the full Senate.

Langer also split with the Administration over foreign policy. In February 1954 he voted for the Bricker amendment to limit the President's treaty-making powers. Langer, who had opposed mutual security treaties in voting against the North Atlantic Treaty Organization agreement in 1949, was the only senator to vote against ratification of the Manila Pact in February 1955. That month he also opposed the China Mutual Defense Treaty, which the Senate ratified 65-6. He later supported initiatives which would have restricted America's defense commitments to Taiwan.

In December 1954 Langer opposed the condemnation of Sen. Joseph R. McCarthy (R, Wisc.) [*q.v.*]. The North Dakotan usually disagreed with McCarthy on the rights of accused Communist sympathizers, yet he felt a personal obligation to McCarthy for his help during his 1952 reelection campaign.

Langer chaired the Judiciary Committee during the Republican-controlled 83rd Congress. In 1953-54 he headed the panel's special investigation of juvenile delinquency, which made a broad study of the mass media's effects on child deviancy. In January 1954, Langer briefly delayed the confirmation of California Gov. Earl Warren [*q.v.*] as Chief Justice of the U.S. The President's tendency to appoint figures from the largest states angered him Although he eventually supported Warren, Langer voted against the nomination of John M. Harlan [*q.v.*] of New York as associate justice of the Supreme Court a year later. Harlan, Langer complained, came from a large state.

With Sen. Hubert Humphrey (D, Minn.) [*q.v.*], Langer sponsored a constitutional amendment that would have abolished the electoral college. Both Langer's and Humphrey's plans would have called for the direct, popular election of the President. Langer's measure also included provisions for a national primary for party presidential nominations. However, in 1955 and 1956 the Senate refused to act on Langer's proposal.

Despite failing health, Langer would not relinquish his Senate seat. Angry over his crusty independence, the state Republican Party officially opposed his renomination in 1958 and endorsed a regular Republican candidate for the primary nomination. However Langer won the primary by a vote of two-to-one, carrying every county. He easily won in the general election without making a single campaign appearance. Contrary to his normal practice Dirksen had endorsed Langer's renomination. Langer returned the favor in January 1959 by supporting the conservative Dirksen for senate minority leader.

Langer's health declined during his last years in the Senate. By 1959 he was both diabetic and blind. He died in November 1959 of a heart attack. Sen. Wayne Morse (D, Ore.) [*q.v.*], who had often fought with Langer against the Senate consensus, termed Langer the last of the American Populists.

[JLB]

LANSDALE, EDWARD G(EARY)
b. Feb. 6, 1908; Detroit, Mich.
Air Force officer, 1947-63.

Following his graduation from the University of California at Los Angeles, Lansdale worked for a San Francisco advertising agency. He left the firm in 1941 to serve first in the Office of Strategic Services (OSS) and then in the Army as an intelligence officer on the Pacific front. He joined the newly formed Air Force in 1947.

During the early-1950s Lansdale served as an adviser to Ramon Magsaysay, Philippine defense minister and later president, in his campaign against the Communist Huk rebels. Believing that the guerrilla war could not be won through the use of conventional military force, Lansdale counseled Magsaysay on counter-insurgency techniques and the use of what he called psychwar, the technique of preying on Huk weaknesses and fears while developing social, economic and political programs to win the allegiance of the rural population. Lansdale's psychwar, financed by the U.S. Central Intelligence Agency, proved successful. By the time he left the Philippines, the Huks had been defeated, and Magsaysay had assumed the presidency in the 1953 election.

Lansdale's success in the Philippines prompted President Eisenhower and Secretary of State John Foster Dulles [q.v.] to send him to Vietnam in 1954 to prevent a Communist takeover of the entire country. His assignment, according to David Wise and Thomas Ross, was "to find a popular leader in Vietnam and throw the support of the Invisible Government [U.S. intelligence services] behind him." Lansdale quickly determined that the newly designated premier, Ngo Dinh Diem, was the only individual with a popular base broad enough to unite the country, and in the weeks after Diem took office he became the Premier's close personal adviser.

During the two years he was in Vietnam, Col. Lansdale developed a number of programs designed to broaden Diem's base of support while preventing the expansion of the Communist Vietminh and destroying the power of local warlords, known as sect leaders. Following the partition of Vietnam under the Geneva Accords in 1954, Lansdale helped the Diem government set up plans for the quick integration of northern refugees into southern life and aided in the development of programs to train governmental administrators for provinces vacated by the Vietminh. This later program was designed to win the loyalty of the rural population through plans for economic development, self-defense and self-government. It formed the basis for the rural pacification programs of the 1960s. In addition, Lansdale trained the Vietnamese Army in intelligence operations and psychological warfare and developed the Village Self-Defense Corps.

Lansdale became embroiled in many of the government's political problems during this period. In the autumn of 1954 he

helped prevent a coup against Diem by disgruntled army officers and during the spring of 1955 defended the Premier against attempts by the French and Eisenhower's personal representative, Gen. J. Lawton Collins [q.v.], to have him removed. Both the French, who hated Diem because of his anti-French attitude, and Collins felt that Diem could not win the necessary backing of the army or make the governmental reforms required to establish a broad political base. When Diem launched an attack against the sects in the spring of 1955, Lansdale, although unable to officially advise him, informally offered suggestions on the conduct of the successful campaign.

Backed by the French, Vietnamese Chief of State Bao Dai ordered Diem to leave office in April 1955. Diem, however, refused and contemplated a coup against Bao Dai. Lansdale dissuaded him, convincing him instead to hold a plebiscite in which the voters could choose between Bao Dai and Diem, who promised constitutional reform. The American colonel acted as Diem's adviser in the October election, in which the Premier won 98% of the vote.

After the plebiscite Lansdale's influence declined. He insisted that Diem permit a loyal opposition and warned the new President that, because of the need for a nonpartisan national leader, he should not form his own political party. Diem did not follow his advice. In early 1956 Lansdale went to Washington to try to persuade Secretary of State John Foster Dulles [q.v.] and Director of Central Intelligence Allen Dulles [q.v.] to push Diem on reform. Both men indicated that the U.S. would back Diem without qualification. Shortly thereafter Lansdale requested and received a transfer from Vietnam.

In 1961 Lansdale returned to Vietnam on an inspection mission. His report criticized the Diem regime for not instituting needed political, economic and social reform but particularly scored the U.S. for not supporting the President with a full range of programs to solidify support behind the regime. President Kennedy, impressed with the report, used Lansdale as an adviser throughout his Administration. From 1965 to 1968 he served as a special assistant to the U.S. ambassador in Vietnam but personally had little influence on policymaking decisions. [See KENNEDY Volume]

Throughout his career Lansdale remained a controversial figure. To some he exemplified the best kind of American military adviser, interested not only in warfare but also in helping the nation for which he fought. He was represented as such in *The Ugly American* by William J. Lederer and Eugene Burdick. To others he was a naive foreigner who did not understand the complexities of a foreign culture and whose well-intended efforts often led to chaos and strife. Graham Green described him this way in *The Quiet American*.

[EWS]

For further information:
Edward G. Lansdale, *In the Midst of Wars* (New York, 1972).
David Wise and Thomas B. Ross, *The Invisible Government* (New York, 1974).

LARSON, ARTHUR L(EWIS)
b. July 4, 1910; Sioux Falls, S.D.
Undersecretary of Labor, March 1954-February 1957; Director, United States Information Agency, February 1957-October 1957; Special Assistant to the President, February 1957-August 1958.

The son of a judge, Arthur Larson graduated magna cum laude from Augustana College in 1931. The following year he received a Rhodes scholarship to Oxford, where he earned a B.A. and M.A. in jurisprudence. Larson began practicing law in Milwaukee in 1935. In 1937 he accepted an appointment as assistant professor at the University of Tennessee law school, where he specialized in labor law. During World War II he worked as a counsel for the Office of Price Administration and the Foreign Economic Administration. Larson joined the law faculty of Cornell University in 1948. Over the next four years he served as a consultant on corporation law to the New York Law Revision Commission and published *The Law of Workmen's Compensation* (1952), which became the standard

work in that field. In 1953 Larson became dean of the University of Pittsburgh law school.

Eisenhower appointed Larson undersecretary of labor in March 1954. Larson emerged as one of the Administration's leading liberals. Over the next two years he lobbied for an extension of unemployment insurance benefits, an increase in disability payments under workmen's compensation and meaningful attempts to employ the elderly.

In 1956 the publishing company of Harper & Row, Inc., asked the Eisenhower Administration to write a book analyzing the Republican Party. Larson responded with *A Republican Looks at His Party* (1956). In it he defined Eisenhower Republicanism as the true center of American politics. According to Larson, "New Republicanism" combined the two most positive features in American politics: a commitment to free enterprise and an endorsement of social welfare legislation. The book so impressed Eisenhower that he asked Larson to aid him in writing his acceptance speech at the 1956 Republican National Convention.

In February 1957 Larson became head of the U.S. Information Agency. He served at that post until October, when Eisenhower appointed him his special aide on overseas information activities. Larson resigned from government in 1958 to become director of the Rule of Law Center at Duke University.

During the 1960s and 1970s Larson served on a number of economic and foreign policy advisory commissions. He also published several books on foreign and economic policy. Larson refused to support Barry Goldwater [q.v.] for President in 1964. In 1968 he wrote *Eisenhower: The President Nobody Knew*, in which he described Eisenhower's record as a good one. Larson praised the General's foreign policy and repeated his earlier view that Eisenhower's record on domestic affairs was a liberal one.

[JB]

For further information:
Arthur L. Larson, *Eisenhower: The President Nobody Knew* (New York, 1968).

LAUSCHE, FRANK J(OHN)
b. Nov. 14, 1895; Cleveland, Ohio
Governor, Ohio, 1949-57; Democratic
Senator, Ohio, 1957-69.

The son of Slovenian immigrants, Frank J. Lausche grew up in Cleveland. Upon his father's death Lausche helped support his family by lighting street lamps, acting as a court interpreter and playing semi-professional baseball. He served in the Army during World War I. In 1920 Lausche earned a law degree at Cleveland's John Marshall University. After several unsuccessful runs as a Democrat for the state legislature, Lausche won election in 1933 as municipal court judge. In 1941 Cleveland voters elected him mayor. Honest, popular and conservative, Lausche easily won election as Ohio governor in 1944. Narrowly defeated in 1946, he regained the governorship in 1948 and won reelection in 1950, 1952 and 1954. [See TRUMAN Volume]

Lausche's popularity was strongly related to his political independence. In a traditionally Republican state, he undercut potential criticism from the fiscally conservative GOP by limiting state expenses while favoring popular projects like the state turnpike. Lausche avoided tax hikes by having the state borrow heavily, a course which caused large budget deficits after his departure. During his gubernatorial campaigns he ignored the regular Democratic city organizations and organized labor and campaigned heavily in normally Republican areas. Owing the party machines and unions nothing for his political success, Lausche ignored them. Although a proponent of civil rights and fair employment legislation, for example, he also favored "right-to-work" legislation, anathema to union leaders.

Lausche's positioning himself as a political independent netted him a hard-fought political victory in 1956. That year he ran for the Senate against the incumbent Sen. George H. Bender (R, Ohio), whose prospects appeared good, sharing the GOP ticket with strong national and gubernatorial candidates. Yet Lausche completely outmaneuvered Bender by telling Republican audiences, among other things, that if elected he might vote with the Republicans in the organization of the Senate in 1957. An indignant Bender accused Lausche of "trying to grab Ike's coattails." Lausche succeeded. He won 52.9% of the vote against Bender, while Eisenhower swept the state. In January 1957 Lausche voted with the Senate Democrats, an act which denied the GOP control of the upper chamber.

In the upper house Lausche was a strong supporter of Eisenhower. According to *Congressional Quarterly*, Lausche ranked first of all Senate Democrats during the 85th Congress in his support of Administration legislation. Indeed, his 65% support for Eisenhower surpassed by 2% that of Ohio's "Old Guard" Republican Sen. John W. Bricker [q.v.]. During the 1958 session Lausche was the senator who voted most often (69%) against a majority of his fellow Democrats. That year he refused to endorse Bricker's liberal Democratic opponent.

Sen. Paul H. Douglas (D, Ill.) [q.v.] dubbed Lausche "the northern Harry Byrd [q.v.]." The Ohio Democrat often imitated Byrd in his attention to minor budgeting detail. As a member of the Senate Commerce Committee, Lausche proved a leading and lonely critic of appropriations for airline capital gains benefits in February 1958 and shipping "superliners" in June 1958. Yet Lausche occasionally sided with Senate Democrats. He voted for major civil rights legislation proposed between 1957 and 1960. On close terms with Senate Majority Leader Lyndon B. Johnson (D, Tex.) [q.v.], Lausche sometimes switched positions to save a key piece of Democratic legislation.

Lausche easily won reelection in 1962. He retained his skepticism of Democratic domestic spending programs and continued to offend powerful elements within the Ohio Democratic Party. Lausche lost the May 1968 senatorial primary to a young liberal, John J. Gilligan. Estranged from his party, he endorsed Republican presidential nominees in 1972 and 1976. [See KENNEDY, JOHNSON Volumes]

[JLB]

LEADER, GEORGE M(ICHAEL)
b. Jan. 17, 1918; York, Pa.
Governor, Pa., 1955-59.

Leader was born into a prominent farming family active in Democratic politics. He received a B.S. degree in education from the University of Pennsylvania in 1939. When his father fell ill he became secretary-treasurer of Guy A. Leader & Sons, the family farming business. At the same time he followed his father into politics, joining the York Co. Democratic Committee in 1940. He rose to Committee secretary two years later.

After service in the Navy during World War II, Leader returned to the family farm. In 1946 he became a county justice of the peace and succeeded his father as county Democratic committee chairman. Leader won election to a four-year term in the Pennsylvania Senate in 1950. Generally liberal, he healed splits in the state's minority Democratic Party and displayed a good grasp of state finances. In 1952 he ran for state treasurer. Although defeated by his Republican opponent, Leader gained statewide recognition.

With the backing of the Pittsburgh and the Philadelphia Democratic organizations, Leader ran for governor in 1954. Campaigning against veteran Republican Lt. Gov. Lloyd H. Wood, Leader appeared a youthful and articulate crusader. He concentrated his attack on an unpopular 1% sales tax enacted by incumbent Republican Gov. John S. Fine and courted farmers in traditionally Republican areas. In November Leader staged a dramatic upset, defeating Wood by over 200,000 votes and becoming the third Democrat and youngest governor ever elected in Pennsylvania.

Leader focused on the problem of eliminating the state's $86 million deficit and compensating for a revenue shortfall of $500 million resulting from his 1955 record $1.8 billion budget. In April he called for a 1% state income tax and a tax on investments. These levies were opposed by both parties. Reaching a legislative impasse, he reluctantly sought to increase the sales tax to 3%. Since he had campaigned against Fine's 1% tax, voters felt betrayed and his popularity diminished.

In September Leader began speaking out on national issues. He became one of the first Democrats to publicly urge his Party to criticize President Dwight D. Eisenhower. In October Leader announced he would support Adlai E. Stevenson [q.v.] for the 1956 Democratic presidential nomination. Mentioned himself as a dark-horse possibility, the Governor declined to run because of his lack of national experience. Campaigning energetically for Stevenson, he supported the candidate's plan to end atmospheric H-bomb testing and criticized Vice President Richard M. Nixon [q.v.]. Despite the Governor's activities Stevenson failed to carry Pennsylvania. In addition Republicans won control of both houses of the state's legislature in November.

Leader did not handle patronage demands to the satisfaction of the Democratic machine and progressively alienated himself from its leadership. A strong civil rights advocate, he probably further eroded his political base in August 1957, when he ordered state police to protect the home of a harassed black family in Levittown, Pa.

Anxious to run for the U.S. Senate in 1958, the Governor abandoned the city machines that had elected him and tried to identify himself with the Party's reformers, whose power was declining. He fired Philadelphia ward leaders and announced he would support Philadelphia reform Mayor Richardson Dilworth [q.v.] for governor. However Dilworth declined to run.

Leader won the senatorial primary, but in his race against Republican Rep. Hugh Scott [q.v.], organization workers deserted Leader in large numbers. In Democratic Philadelphia, Lawrence ran 40,000 votes ahead of Leader. He even failed to rally his own Pennsylvania Dutch county. Scott bucked a national Democratic trend election as senator by 113,000 votes while Lawrence won the governorship by an 80,000-vote margin. Following his defeat, Leader returned to run Willow Brook Farm.

[MJS]

For further information:
Neal Peirce, *The Megastates* (New York, 1972).

LEE, J(OSEPH) BRACKEN
b. Jan. 7, 1899: Price, Utah.
Governor, Utah, 1949-57.

The descendant of Utah pioneers, Lee graduated from Carbon Co. High School and entered the Army in 1917. Following his discharge he went into the insurance business, eventually becoming president of the Equitable Insurance Agency and the Equitable Finance Co. Lee, who entered politics at age 21, served 12 years as Republican mayor of Price, Utah. Defeated in primaries for governor in 1939 and U.S. representative in 1942, he won the Republican gubernatorial primary in 1944 but lost the general election. The Party again nominated Lee in 1948. Campaigning with the support of the Mormon church, Lee promised to run the state on a conservative, businesslike basis. He correctly predicted that liberal Republican presidential nominee Thomas E. Dewey would not carry Utah and dissociated himself from Dewey's candidacy. When the votes were in, Lee was elected governor, while Democrats swept every other office in the state.

During 1952 Lee became embroiled in the maneuvering over seating rival Taft and Eisenhower delegations at the Republican National Convention. The Governor, whose support was vital to a Republican victory in the West, backed conservative Sen. Robert A. Taft's (R, Ohio) [q.v.] bid for the presidential nomination. However, during May 1952, Eisenhower backers manipulated Lee to give the impression that he supported the General. Eisenhower's forces put together a two-page "unity" statement proposing that contested delegates he kept from voting on the right of others to be seated, a position that would strengthen the General's candidacy. They planned to have the statement signed jointly by Eisenhower and Taft supporters. Induced to read the statement by the assurance of national press coverage, Lee left the press conference after reading the first page, which contained platitudes about Party aspirations to fairness. Only after boarding a plane did he discover the delegate reference on the second page. Too embarrassed to retract, Lee won the September gubernatorial primary

as an Eisenhower supporter. In November he and the General carried Utah. The "endorsement" left Lee with a lasting distaste for the new President. Throughout Eisenhower's Administration he was one of his sharpest critics on the Republican Right.

During the first half of the decade, Lee was an outspoken supporter of Sen. Joseph R. McCarthy (R, Wisc.) [q.v.]. He opposed the Senate's decision in December 1954 to censure McCarthy, and in 1955 he met with other conservatives on the matter. Lee charged Eisenhower with steering America leftward and recommended formation of a third, conservative party in 1956. McCarthy returned the Governor's support in a November 1955 radio interview by recommending Lee for President.

The Governor continued to attack Eisenhower throughout 1956. He refused to pay federal income tax in January, challenging the constitutionality of foreign aid, and was sued in court by Secretary of the Treasury George Humphrey [q.v.]. In June Lee charged that Eisenhower had allegedly lied in declaring his presidential candidacy following a heart attack. Lee lost the 1956 Republican gubernatorial primary to an Eisenhower ally and, running as an independent, also lost the general election. During the same period the Supreme Court rejected his income tax plea.

Lee challenged Sen. Arthur V. Watkins (R, Utah) [q.v.], who had chaired the committee investigating the possible censure of McCarthy, for the Republican senatorial nomination in 1958. Losing the primary, Lee then entered the general election as an independent. He deeply split the Republican vote, and Watkins lost to Democrat Frank Moss. From 1960 to 1971 Lee served as mayor of Salt Lake City.

[MJS]

LEE, RICHARD C(HARLES)
b. March 12, 1916; New Haven, Conn.
Mayor, New Haven, Conn., 1954-70.

Lee was born and raised in a working-class section of New Haven. Following his graduation from high school in 1935, he worked as a city hall reporter for the New Haven *Journal-Courier*. Running as a

Democrat, Lee was elected to the Board of Alderman in 1939. He served for a short time in the Army during World War II before receiving a medical discharge. He then returned to New Haven to resume his position as alderman. In 1943 Lee went to work for the *Yale News Digest* and the following year was appointed director of the University's public relations service. During the 1940s he became prominent in Democratic politics. In 1949 and 1951 he campaigned for mayor, losing by narrow margins.

Lee ran for mayor again in 1953. Realizing he would need a dramatic issue to galvanize support for his race, he focused his attention on urban renewal. He assembled a campaign staff of highly motivated young urban planners who drew up his proposal for "the rebirth of New Haven." Campaigning on that issue, Lee won the November general election by a narrow margin.

Lee began his program by enlisting the aid of noted French urban designer Maurice Rovital to help him draw up a master redevelopment plan. Rovital based his plans on the belief that the city would have to attract well-to-do suburbanites to its stores and recreational facilities to develop a viable economic base. Revitalization was, therefore, linked to the growing interstate highway system that spanned southern Connecticut. Lee quickly won authorization for the construction of a superhighway linking the Connecticut Turnpike to the heart of the downtown area. Working closely with Edward J. Logue, the young attorney he named as supervisor of the program, he then initiated massive slum clearance projects to permit the widening of local streets and the construction of new offices, department stores, middle-income apartments and parking garages. He also began a program for developing low-income housing. To finance these projects, the Mayor applied for federal assistance under the Federal Housing Act of 1954, which provided grants and loans for cities to purchase rundown property. After upgrading, the city could sell the property to private developers.

In order to achieve his goal, Lee worked to gain control of the city bureaucracy. He had inherited a government made up of numerous independent departments. These agencies were often more responsive to the desires of powerful advisory committees, led by businessmen indifferent to Lee's goals, than to the mayor's office. Lee gradually appointed individuals loyal to him to head and staff the city departments. The Mayor then arranged for his supporters to sit on the advisory committees. Realizing that a large portion of his political strength lay in the Democratic organization, Lee maintained good relations with the local machine. He often appointed political regulars to city jobs, mingling them with the urban specialists he had brought in to reconstruct the city. By 1956 Lee controlled the city bureaucracy.

During the last half of the decade, Lee won massive electoral victories over his Republican rivals. His dependence on the Democratic machine thus ended, though he always had cordial relations with the party regulars. Lee endeavored to keep politics out of urban renewal. He also tried to gather further support for his plan. The Mayor enlisted the help of Yale and attempted to gain the support of the business community. When the city's chamber of commerce proved skeptical of his dream, Lee created an alternate business group to advise him.

By the end of the decade, Lee had gained a reputation as one of the most imaginative mayors in the nation; his city was one of the most promising examples of urban renewal. During the 1960 presidential campaign Lee served as an adviser to Democratic candidate John F. Kennedy [*q.v.*]. Lee remained mayor until 1970. The city continued to draw nationwide praise for its urban renewal projects and job training programs for the poor. New Haven received money from private corporations and foundations for its reconstruction. It was the first city to receive a grant from the Johnson Administration's Office of Economic Opportunity. However, in the summer of 1967 a riot broke out in the black section of the city, tarnishing the Mayor's reputation. After Lee retired in 1970 he taught political science at Yale and the University of Connecticut. [See KENNEDY, JOHNSON Volumes]

[JB]

LEHMAN, HERBERT H(ENRY)
b. March 28, 1878; New York, N.Y.
d. Dec. 5, 1963; New York, N.Y.
Democratic Senator, N.Y., 1949-57.

The son of wealthy German-Jewish immigrants, Lehman joined the family's investment banking firm in 1908. He became active in philanthropic activities and directed war relief programs in 1916. Following service in World War I, he returned to Lehman Brothers and also acted as a labor mediator in the heavily Jewish garment industry. Lehman forged close ties with labor groups, particularly the International Ladies Garment Workers Union (ILGWU) and the Amalgamated Clothing Workers, which supported him enthusiastically throughout his political career.

During the late-1920s and the 1930s, Lehman's political fortunes rose with those of the New York State Democratic Party. He was finance director of New York Gov. Alfred E. Smith's unsuccessful presidential campaign in 1928, the year that Franklin D. Roosevelt was elected governor and Lehman lieutenant governor. When Roosevelt went on to the White House four years later, Lehman won the governorship. During his years as governor he maintained his close political association with Roosevelt and brought a "Little New Deal" of broad social legislation to New York.

In 1942 Roosevelt appointed Lehman chief of the newly established Office of Foreign Relief and Rehabilitation Operations; the following year he became director general of the United Nations Relief and Rehabilitation Administration (UNRRA). Lehman left his post in 1946 to run for the Senate, but despite the backing of New York's Liberal Party and the American Labor Party as well as his own party's designation, he suffered his first electoral defeat. Three years later he routed John Foster Dulles [q.v.] in a special election to fill the Senate seat vacated by Sen. Robert F. Wagner (D, N.Y.). Lehman won a full Senate term in 1950.

On Capitol Hill Lehman became known as "the conscience of the Senate." He was a strong supporter of President's Harry S.

Truman's [q.v.] Fair Deal and was a staunch defender of civil liberties, alien rights and liberal immigration regulations. Lehman also served as the upper chamber's leading spokesman on civil rights. [See TRUMAN Volume]

Lehman consistently opposed the Eisenhower Administration's policy of encouraging private rather than public power and resource development. In April 1953 he participated in a 28-day liberal filibuster against a Republican proposal to grant oil-rich submerged coastal lands to the states. The senators opposing the bill called it a "big steal" because it gave three states valuable property they believed should be controlled by the federal government. In 1954 Lehman participated in a filibuster against the proposed Dixon-Yates contract which would have required the Atomic Energy Commission to buy its electrical power from private developers instead of the Tennessee Valley Authority. Lehman termed the scheme "one of the greatest giveaways in history" and charged that the measure would encourage the private development of atomic energy by "a few very large monopolistic companies." The Senator won a victory for public power development in 1956, when he sponsored a successful measure authorizing the New York State Power Authority to build and operate a $405 million Niagara Falls power project.

Lehman was among Sen. Joseph McCarthy's (R, Wisc.) [q.v.] earliest and most ardent critics. In 1952 he told the Senate that it was "protecting" McCarthy by allowing him to create a repressive political atmosphere. The two traded accusations in July 1953, when McCarthy alleged that criticism of his aides, Roy M. Cohn [q.v.] and G. David Schine [q.v.], was motivated by anti-Semitism. Soon afterward McCarthy read a 1948 letter to the Senate in which Lehman had expressed "complete confidence" in the loyalty of Alger Hiss. Lehman replied that the letter had been written months before any "real evidence" against Hiss was disclosed and before his indictment and conviction for perjury. McCarthy also accused Lehman of hiring Communists and Communist sympathizers while UNRRA director.

In June 1954 Lehman endorsed Sen. Ralph Flanders's (R, Vt.) [q.v.] resolution to censure McCarthy. He was sole cosponsor of a bill, introduced in August 1954 by Sen. Wayne Morse (Ind, Ore.) [q.v.], aimed at curbing McCarthy by requiring a code of procedure for all congressional committees. The two joined other senators as cosponsors of Sen. Estes Kefauver's (D, Tenn) [q.v.] proposal for a "Code of Conduct for Congressional Committees." No action resulted in either case. In September of that year he supported the Watkins Committee's recommendation that McCarthy be censured. That December Lehman received the Four Freedoms Foundation's annual award for his work against McCarthyism.

During his last year in Congress, Lehman focused his attention on civil rights. He protested in March 1956 when the Senate awarded segregationist Sen. James O. Eastland (D, Miss.) [q.v.] the chairmanship of the Judiciary Committee on the traditional basis of seniority. In June Lehman announced that he would sponsor an anti-segregation amendment to a proposed $1.6 billion school construction appropriation. However, the bill was defeated in the House in July.

That month the House passed an Administration civil rights bill which established a Civil Rights Commission and created a new division in the Justice Department for civil rights cases. When the bill came to the Senate, Lehman and others attempted to remove it from Eastland's Judiciary Committee, an effort that was defeated, 76-6. The Committee failed to report the bill, and Lehman blamed the Administration for submitting its recommendations late in the congressional session. "The Administration wants to get the credit for making these recommendations," Lehman declared, "without running the danger of having the legislation enacted."

Lehman also attacked civil rights opponents in his own party, and at the August 1956 Democratic Convention, he called for a floor fight on civil rights. However, the Convention accepted a subcommittee platform draft that attempted to reconcile Southern segregations and Northern liberals within the Party by supporting the Supreme Court's rulings against segregation without pledging specifically to apply the Court's decisions.

Lehman declined to run for reelection in 1956. Out of office he returned to some of the concerns of his earlier career. In March 1958 he mediated a general strike by the ILGWU. Later that year Eleanor Roosevelt [q.v.] and Lehman formed the National Council for Industrial Peace to promote harmonious labor-management relations and to oppose state "right-to-work" laws.

In January 1959 Mrs. Roosevelt and Lehman, with the support of New York Mayor Robert F. Wagner, Jr. [q.v.], formed the New York Committee for Democratic Voters. The group aimed to win control of the state Party from the "hands of the old-style party professionals," specifically Tammany leader Carmine DeSapio [q.v.]. They achieved their goal in 1961, when the reform candidates won several municipal offices, forcing DeSapio out of his post as Manhattan Co. leader. Lehman remained the "patriarch of the reform movement," as the *New York Times* described him, until his death in 1963.

[MDB]

For further information:
Richard M. Fried, *Men Against McCarthy* (New York, 1976).
Robert Griffith, *The Politics of Fear: Joseph R. McCarthy and the Senate* (Lexington, Ky, 1970).
Warren Moscow, *Last of the Big-Time Bosses: The Life and times of Carmine DeSapio and the Rise and Fall of Tammany Hall* (New York, 1971).
Allan Nevins, *Herbert H. Lehman and His Era* (New York, 1963).

LeMAY, CURTIS E(MERSON)

b. Nov. 15, 1906; Columbus, Ohio
Air Force Vice Chief of Staff, April 1957-May 1961.

Unable to secure an appointment to West Point, LeMay attended Ohio State University school of engineering but did not graduate with his class because of insufficient credits. (He later obtained his degree while stationed in Columbus with the Army.) As a member of the Reserve Officers' Training Corps, he was accepted into the Army's flying cadet program and successfully completed both its primary and advanced courses. He was commissioned a second lieutenant in 1930.

LeMay rose through the ranks and at the age of 37 became a major general in the Army Air Corps. An innovator in the use of strategic bombers, he played a major role in formulating tactics used in the European theater and planned the devastating B-29 raids on Tokyo in the last months of World War II. After the War he commanded the U.S. Air Force in Europe and helped direct the Berlin airlift of 1948-49. He returned to the United States to head the Strategic Air Command (SAC) in October 1948. He retained that post even after his appointment as Air Force vice chief of staff in April 1957.

LeMay was a major proponent of increased bomber production, defending the SAC against Administration attempts to limit its budget. He constantly warned that the Soviet Union was steadily narrowing the American lead in strategic air power and that any war with the Russians would become increasingly costly with each passing year unless the U.S. bolstered its nuclear-delivery arsenal. Sherman Adams [q.v.] credited LeMay's 1955 testimony before a Senate armed forces subcommittee with inducing Congress to provide an additional $900 million for B-52 bombers that the U.S. "did not need."

In 1956 LeMay supported Gen. Nathan Twining's [q.v.] contention that a "bomber gap" existed between the U.S. and the USSR. In a speech given at Georgetown University in December, he warned that the USSR was "steadily narrowing" the U.S.'s "presently favorable margin" in long-range nuclear attack capability and continental air-defense. He stated that the U.S. could win a war with Russia under current conditions but would suffer "serious damage." LeMay predicted that "we will be still more vulnerable to still greater damage . . . five years hence" unless "we continue to improve the combat capacity, readiness and security of our air power." The

SAC must be freed, he believed, "from dependence on refueling and on overseas bases." He also urged the development of reliable intercontinental ballistic missiles.

After the successful launching of the Soviet satellite *Sputnik* in the fall of 1957, the military pressured the Administration increase defense spending. Once again LeMay was in the forefront of the struggle. In testimony before the Senate Preparedness Subcommittee in December 1957, he reiterated his demand for rapid expansion of the manned bomber fleet. He noted that his previous requests for larger appropriations had "fallen on deaf ears" at the White House and that even when Congress had appropriated such funds the Administration had impounded them. Once again, LeMay warned that failure to provide planes, bases and intercontinental ballistic missiles would cause the U.S. to drop behind the Soviet Union in striking power. This time he targeted mid-1959 as the date when the U.S. would lose its lead in air power. He predicted that the U.S. would thus "invite a cataclysmic pre-emptive strike by the superior Communist intercontinental ballistic missile force at some future date." In response to earlier testimony by Army Chief of Staff Maxwell D. Taylor [q.v.], LeMay cautioned that funds should not be diverted from the Air Force to increased conventional forces and attacked the Army's overriding concern with its "conventional war cause." He believed air power provided the nation with a wide variety of military capabilities. To those who questioned the effectiveness of bombers in a guerrilla war, he said, "I do not understand why a force that will deter a big war will not deter a small war too, if we want it to and say it will."

In 1961 President John F. Kennedy promoted LeMay to Air Force Chief of Staff. He continued to champion the production of manned bombers in opposition to Secretary of Defense Robert S. McNamara's demand for missile development. High officials in both the Kennedy and Johnson Administrations feared that LeMay might become a formidable political threat upon his retirement; therefore, his tour of duty at the Pentagon was repeatedly extended.

After his retirement in 1965 LeMay became an outspoken critic of the Johnson Administration's restrictions on bombing raids in both North and South Vietnam. In 1968 George C. Wallace chose LeMay to be his vice presidential running mate on the American Independent Party ticket. During the campaign LeMay denounced President Lyndon B. Johnson's decision to halt the bombing of North Vietnam and promised that if elected he would resume the air war, using nuclear weapons if necessary to defeat the North. The ticket won 13.4 % of the popular vote. [See KENNEDY, JOHNSON]

[RJB]

For further information:

Richard A. Aliano, *American Defense Policy from Eisenhower to Kennedy: The Politics of Changing Military Requirements, 1957-1961* (Athens, Ohio, 1975).

Curtis LeMay with McKinley Kantor, *Mission with LeMay: My Story* (New York, 1965).

LEWIS, JOHN L(LEWELLYN)
b. Feb. 12, 1880; Lucas, Iowa
d. June 11, 1969; Washington, D.C.
President, United Mine Workers of America, 1920-60.

Lewis quit school after completing the seventh grade and entered the mines at the age of 15. In 1909 he moved to the coal fields of southern Illinois, where he quickly took over a local of the United Mine Workers of America (UMW). From this base Lewis launched a successful campaign for state mine safety and workmen's compensation laws. A dramatic and persuasive orator and a skillful organizer, he soon came to the attention of Samuel Gompers, the head of the American Federation of Labor (AFL). In 1911 he was made an AFL field representative, a job that enabled him to travel widely through the mining areas and to build up a strong personal machine within the miners' union. As a result Lewis became UMW vice president in 1917, acting president in 1919 and president in 1920. At that time the UMW was the largest union within the AFL.

A Republican, Lewis backed Warren Harding, Calvin Coolidge and Herbert Hoover during the 1920s. Despite his insistence that the economic aims of labor and capital were identical, the coal industry fought the UMW fiercely throughout the decade. The employers offensive, combined with Lewis's ruthless expulsion of left-wing internal opposition, nearly destroyed the union by 1930. With the advent of the New Deal, however, Lewis took advantage of the 1933 National Industrial Recovery Act to launch a massive organizing drive in the coal fields, recruiting 300,000 miners to the UMW in two months.

Convinced that the mass production industries should be organized on an industry-wide rather than a craft basis, in 1935 Lewis joined the leaders of 10 other unions in forming the Committee for Industrial Organizations (CIO). It proceeded at once to initiate a sweeping organizing campaign in auto, rubber, steel and other basic industries. Jurisdictional conflicts with AFL craft unions led to the expulsion of the Committee from the Federation in 1938. That year the CIO became the Congress of Industrial Organizations. As CIO president, Lewis emerged as the very symbol of a new, dynamic labor movement to millions of Americans.

Lewis vigorously backed President Franklin D. Roosevelt's reelection campaign in 1936 but was increasingly at odds with the White House during the late-1930s. When World War II began, he opposed American intervention and endorsed Wendell Wilkie for the presidency in 1940. That year he kept his promise to step down from the CIO presidency if Roosevelt won a third term.

After an unsuccessful bid to regain control of the CIO, Lewis pulled his miners out of the organization in 1942 (the UMW rejoined the AFL in 1946 but stayed less than two years). Repudiating the no-strike pledge made by the AFL and CIO during World War II, he led several wartime strikes in defiance of federal court injunctions and in the face of increasingly hostile public opinion. By the War's end the miners had won a 35-hour work week, pay for underground travel time and improved mine safety. In 1946 Lewis introduced an innovative collective bargaining demand for a royalty on each ton of coal mined to finance union health and welfare benefits. After strikes that led to government seizure of the mines, Lewis reached a settlement with federal administrators that became the basis for a permanent royalty agreement with the coal industry. [See TRUMAN Volume]

Increasingly isolated from the rest of the labor movement during the 1940s and 1950s, Lewis nevertheless continued to cherish hopes of regaining some of his former national power by reuniting the AFL and CIO under his own leadership, or failing that, creating a new labor center outside the two federations. With the accession of George Meany [q.v.] and Walter Reuther [q.v.] to the presidencies of the AFL and CIO, respectively, Lewis sought to bring together those union heads who felt excluded by the new leaderships. In 1954 he initiated talks with Dave Beck [q.v.], president of the million-member International Brotherhood of Teamsters, and David MacDonald [q.v.], head of the Unites Steel Workers of America, with the aim of either forming a new federation or forcing the AFL and CIO leaders to include him in their unity negotiations. Beck and MacDonald soon lost interest in the plan. Afterwards Lewis concentrated almost exclusively on the affairs of his own union. But the coal miners no longer commanded the public attention they had once had, and as a result Lewis gradually faded from national prominence.

During the 1950s, as intense competition from oil, natural gas and hydroelectricity steadily reduced the importance of coal as an energy source, coal operators sought to protect profits by cutting labor costs. Large operators were able to do this by increasing productivity through mechanization. Moreover, the emergence of the Tennessee Valley Authority as a major coal consumer fostered hundreds of small, nonunion mines in Kentucky and Tennessee which remained competitive by escaping royalty payments to the UMW's welfare and retirement fund. These developments weakened Lewis's union by reducing both the size of the workforce under its potential jurisdiction and its employed membership.

Believing that strikes would hurt the union by forcing coal consumers to seek alternative fuels, Lewis turned from conflict to cooperation with the industry. In order to insure the operators against work stoppages, he tightened his personal control over the UMW, replacing public negotiations with secret contract talks, making most union district leaders appointive rather than elected and dealing harshly with wildcat strikes. In addition, Lewis acted as an industry spokesman in Washington, where he argued for government promotion of coal exports and stricter mine safety laws, which had the covert aim of forcing small companies out of business by imposing on them the same expensive safety standards required of larger producers. The big coal companies also urged Lewis to organize the rising number of nonunion mines, since the larger mechanized enterprises could benefit from lower labor costs only if other producers could not achieve the same advantage by simply operating on a nonunion basis. With Lewis's tacit approval, his aide W.A. "Tony" Boyle initiated virtual guerrilla war in the unorganized areas. Bands of UMW agents converged on ·nonunion operations. They marched the miners out of the pits at gunpoint and in many cases coerced them into joining the union.

In return for Lewis's assistance, the industry accorded major wage and fringe concessions to the UMW. Although the number of working miners fell by three-fifths between 1947 and 1960, creating extensive and chronic unemployment in the coal producing regions, UMW members who remained employed earned the highest hourly wage in American industry by 1959. During the same period, moreover, the union's income actually grew despite declining membership, since it was based on a per ton royalty rather than a payroll tax. As a result, the UMW became a wealthy institution, claiming assets in 1960 of $110 million—almost as much as the Teamsters, auto, steel and machinists unions combined. With Cleveland industrialist Cyrus Eaton [q.v.] serving as his informal adviser, Lewis used the health and welfare fund to build a partially-concealed financial empire for the union, acquiring major stock holdings in several coal companies and a controlling interest in the National Bank of Washington, the capital's second largest bank. In 1960 Lewis resigned as UMW president and became president emeritus. Nine years later the union leader died at the age of 89.

[TLH]

For further information:
Melvyn Dubovsky and Warren Van Tine. *John L. Lewis: A Biography* (New York. 1977).

LIEBMAN, MARVIN
b. July 21, 1923
Secretary, Committee For One Million Against the Admission of Communist China to the United Nations, 1953-55: Secretary, Committee of One Million Against the Admission of Communist China to the United Nations, 1955-69.

Originally a member of the Young Communist League and the American Communist Party during the 1930s and 1940s, Liebman resigned in protest against the purging of Earl Browder. He then became involved in the right-wing terrorist Israeli organization, the Irgun Zvai Leumi. While working for the International Rescue Committee, which aided Iron Curtain refugees, Liebman came to view the USSR as a threat to world peace. In 1952 he helped start Aid to Refugee Chinese Intellectuals. During the 1950s Liebman became a public relations specialist, first working for Harold L. Oram, Inc., and in 1958 founding his own firm, Marvin Liebman Associates Inc., which represented conservative organizations, Journalist Richard Dudman called him "the best single-action group organizer on the Far Right."

Liebman was one of the principal organizers of the Committee For One Million Against the Admission of Communist China to the United Nations, created in 1953. On Oct. 22, 1953 Liebman and other supporters of Nationalist China presented President Eisenhower with a petition signed by 210 prominent Americans calling for the U.S. to oppose Communist China's admit-

tance into the U.N. The event was the first step in a massive drive to get one million American signatures on the document and thus throw the weight of public opinion against possible Administration support of Communist China's entry. Liebman handled the publicity and fund raising for the Committee. On July 6, 1954 the one millionth American signed the petition. The Committee planned the conclusion of the campaign to coincide with the Geneva Conference on Indochina and Vietnam as an indication to the Administration of public displeasure with possible negotiations with the Communists at the high-level Conference.

Liebman then set out to turn the Committee into a permanent lobbying organization designed to be a watchdog over the Administration's China policy. In 1955 the Committee For One Million became the Committee of One Million with Marvin Liebman as its secretary. Although the group contained individuals from both political parties, most members were conservative Republicans. The Committee had three goals: creation of a bipartisan foreign policy; opposition to "appeasement" of Communists by the West, especially the U.S.; and, resistance to "indirect" Communist aggression in Southeast Asia. Liebman kept the Committee members informed of the progress of Americans and neutralist nations who lobbied for China's entry into the U.N. In addition, he publicly opposed any trade with mainland China and lobbied extensively against the relaxation of the American economic boycott of the Communist regime. The Committee had a powerful impact on U.S. China policy. Both Administration officials and Democratic leaders reiterated their support for the organization's positions.

During the Kennedy and Johnson Administrations, the Committee of One Million continued to function as an effective lobby influencing China policy. In 1969 Liebman closed his office and moved to London to be a theatrical producer. The Committee disbanded in the 1970s following President Richard Nixon's overtures to mainland China.

[JB]

LIPPMANN, WALTER
b. Sept. 23, 1889; New York, N.Y.
d. Dec. 14, 1974; New York, N.Y.
Journalist

The son of well-to-do Jews, Lippmann studied at Harvard, where he was deeply influenced by William James's pragmatism and George Santayana's belief in an "aesthetic aristocracy." Lippmann worked briefly for Lincoln Steffens's *Everybody's Magazine* and then became secretary to the socialist mayor of Schenectady, N.Y. Although flirting briefly with socialism, Lippmann had become openly hostile to the doctrine by 1914, when he wrote *Drift and Mastery*. That same year he joined Herbert Croly in founding *The New Republic*, a journal supporting the ideas of the Progressive movement. During World War I Lippmann served as an assistant secretary of war and contributed to the formulation of Woodrow Wilson's Fourteen Points and the development of the League of Nations.

During the 1920s Lippman edited the liberal *New York World* and published several books which reflected his growing pessimism with popular democracy. Lippmann's influence grew after 1931, when he began writing "Today and Tomorrow" for the Republican *New York Hearld Tribune*. He gained popularity for his ability to analyze current issues and relate them to general problems and the historical roots of U.S. democracy. In the words of the *New York Times*, "he was also a public school master who obliged his readers to think of the transient in terms of the everlasting."

Lippmann initially supported Franklin D. Roosevelt's New Deal, but after 1935 he became increasingly hostile to what he believed was the President's drift toward socialism. He did, however, support Roosevelt's foreign policies, urging the U.S. to prepare for war as early as 1937.

By the end of World War II, Lippmann was one of the nation's most eminent political critics, particularly in foreign affairs. Although once a proponent of the Wilsonian ideas of internationalism and world peace, during the postwar period he viewed world affairs in terms of a balance of power. The Cold War deeply troubled him. In his 1947 book by that title, Lippmann proposed that the U.S. and USSR each recognize the other's sphere of influence to prevent the further deterioration of relations. Focusing on the importance of Germany, he believed that there would be no peace until all troops were withdrawn from the area. Lippmann opposed Truman's policy of "containing" the Soviet Union, maintaining it was doomed to failure. He rejected the argument that the Russians sought expansion for ideological reasons, stressing that Soviet interest in Eastern Europe was determined more by history than Communist doctrine. Lippmann supported the Marshall Plan and the Truman Doctrine but was disturbed by the fact that they were presented to the American people in terms of an anti-Communist crusade. He distrusted crusades and warned that the U.S. might be forced to defend anti-Communist but undemocratic forces. [See TRUMAN Volume]

Lippmann supported Dwight D. Eisenhower for President in 1952, hoping that a Republican President could check what he considered the irresponsible and demagogic actions of Sen. Joseph R. McCarthy (R, Wisc.) [*q.v.*]. However, during the decade he frequently criticized Eisenhower. In 1953 he wrote that Eisenhower had brought about a crisis by his "abdication" of the presidency. Lippmann held Eisenhower responsible for McCarthy's continuing power. Four years later he maintained that, rather than have leadership, the nation drifted "with no one to state our purposes."

Lippmann was a particularly strong opponent of Secretary of State John Foster Dulles's [*q.v.*] foreign policy. He denounced Dulles's failure to define clearly the Administration's "New Look" policy or elaborate on the consequences of "massive retaliation" (the use of nuclear weapons as America's first deterrent against Soviet expansion and attack). When Dulles attempted to qualify the conditions under which he would use nuclear force, Lippmann commented that it would take a career itself to keep up with the Administration's "New Look" policy or elaborate on the consequences of "massive retaliation" (the use of nuclear weapons as America's first deterrent against Soviet expansion and attack). When Dulles attempted to qualify the conditions under which he would use nuclear force, Lippmann commented that it would take a career itself to keep up with the Administration's official explanation of the New Look.

Lippmann also opposed unilateral intervention to protect Quemoy and Matsu, shelled by Communist China in the fall of 1954. He rejected the Administration's contention that they had strategic importance for Formosa and proposed that the Nationalist Chinese withdraw from the islands. Lippmann found the American military alliance with Chiang Kai-shek a liability that could entangle the U.S. in an unnecessary war.

The journalist also focused his attention on Europe, particularly the problem of a divided Germany. He proposed a gradual movement toward unification with Big Power guarantees that Germany would be neutral and demilitarized. This, he hoped, would dispel both French and Russian fears of a resurgent Germany. When this proved unfeasible, Lippmann advocated a mutual reduction of foreign troops from Germany and encouraged attempts towards normalization of relations between the East and West German governments.

Lippmann expounded his views on U.S.-USSR relations in *The Communist World and Ours*, published in 1957, shortly after he returned from a visit to the Soviet Union. The journalist opposed American reliance on military pacts to prevent the expansion of Communism, maintaining that it would leave the U.S. open to Soviet charges of warmongering. Communist success in the world, Lippmann wrote, "lies in the force of [its] example, in the visible demonstration of what the Soviet Union has achieved in 40 years, of what Red China has achieved in about 10 years." The only way to prevent Communism's continued expansion was for the U.S. to demonstrate to developing countries how effectively, and in a more humane way, the American system could match its achievements. India, he thought, would be the ideal nation to prove the success of democracy. Lippmann also understood the Soviet dilemma in Eastern Europe. Without its troops there, he thought, the Communist regime would find it difficult to survive. He thus wrote, "we are missing the bus as long as we fail to identify ourselves with the idea of bringing to an end . . . the military occupation of the European continent."

Disillusioned with Eisenhower, in 1960 Lippmann hailed John F. Kennedy [q.v.] as the first presidential candidate since Roosevelt who could stir and unite the American people. However, in the early 1960s he became increasingly critical of Kennedy's foreign and domestic policies. Although at first an enthusiastic supporter of Lyndon B. Johnson, he eventually broke with the Administration over Vietnam. From 1963 to 1968 Lippmann wrote a column for *Newsweek*. He died in December 1974. [See KENNEDY Volume]

[JB]

LIPSET, SEYMOUR MARTIN
b. March 18, 1922; New York, N.Y.
Sociologist

Lipset was the son of a Russian-Jewish immigrant who worked as a printer in New York City. Through his father he was introduced to the politics of the printer's union, later a subject of one of his major studies. He became involved in the Young People's Socialist League during his high school years, at a time when the main concern of American socialists was the ineffectiveness of the European labor movement against the fascist threat. Lipset was particularly impressed by the degeneration of socialism in Russia into a totalitarian form of government. He was a Social Democrat when he graduated from the City College of New York in 1943. He then enrolled in the Ph.D. program in sociology at Columbia University, where he studied under Robert K. Merton. He taught at the University of Toronto from 1946 to 1948 and from 1948 to 1950 was an assistant professor at the University of California at Berkeley. He received his Ph.D. in 1949.

In 1950 Lipset published his first book, *Agrarian Socialism*, which was a revised version of his doctoral dissertation on the Cooperative Commonwealth Federation, a mass socialist party which had arisen in Canada during World War II. The purpose of the study was to force a revision of conventional explanations for the weakness of socialist movements in North America.

Lipset left Berkeley in 1950 to teach at Columbia, where he remained until 1956. In 1955 he published an important article on the social and economic origins of what he branded as "the radical right." The article purported to show how the right persistently recruited its members from marginal groups that either aspired to higher status or feared that they were about to lose what status they had. In particular he singled out the uneducated lower-middle class as the seedbed of right-wing attitudes. The book that Lipset acknowledged as his model was T.W. Adorno's *The Authoritarian Personality* (1950). Both Adorno and Lipset regarded the right as politically deviant. Their writings drew a sharp protest from the *National Review* and other conservative publications, which insisted that the right be recognized as a responsible voice of dissent.

In 1956, in collaboration with other members of the Bureau of Applied Social Research, Lipset published *Union Democracy*. The book accorded him a reputation as one of the nation's leading sociologists. In it he and his associates countered the widespread notion in sociology that organizations necessarily developed an elite governing body. The scholars did this by describing the democratic practices maintained within the International Typographical Union (ITU), one of America's oldest and most powerful labor organizations. They showed how a healthy level of disagreement was generated most easily among people who regard themselves as social equals. Equality and conflict then combined to provide the framework for two-party democracy. The book conceded that the ITU was unique and that most labor unions were in fact dominated by only a very small minority. But Lipset implied that under conditions of equality and conflict, democracy would work.

Lipset generalized his views in *Political Man* (1960), considered one of the classic works of contemporary sociology. The book attempted to determine the social and economic conditions that made a democratic system possible. Its conclusions were largely pessimistic. Lipset first attempted to undercut the myth that the working classes represented a liberal force in history by presenting the phenomenon of working-class authoritarianism. He contended that it was the educated middle classes, rather than the traditional conservative forces in Germany, which brought Hitler to power. Lipset believed democracy needed a delicate balance to endure, and he was clearly pessimistic about the chances that the balance could be maintained. Above all he warned that what he believed was the approaching "end of ideology" would mean the end of that kind of healthy dissent and spirited debate which lay at the heart of democracy.

In 1956 Lipset returned to Berkeley, he taught there until 1966. From 1962 to 1966 he also headed the Institute of International Studies at the University of California. After the disturbances at Berkeley in 1964, Lipset devoted much of his attention to an analysis of student unrest. His views became discernibly more conservative, although in 1970 he published *The Politics of Unreason*, in which he again characterized the extreme right as a social aberration. In 1966 Lipset accepted a position at Harvard University. Despite attacks by members of the New Left, Lipset was still widely regarded as a spokesman for the liberal academic community.

[JPL]

LODGE, HENRY CABOT
b. July 5, 1902; Nahant, Mass.
Ambassador to the United Nations,
January 1953-August 1960.

Born into a distinguished New England family that dated back to the colonial period, Henry Cabot Lodge was raised by his grandfather, Sen. Henry Cabot Lodge, Sr., (R, Mass.) after the death of his father in 1909. Following his graduation from Harvard in 1921, Lodge began a career in journalism as a reporter and then editorial writer for the *New York Herald Tribune*. In

1933 he was elected to the Massachusetts House of Representatives. Three years later he defeated veteran Democratic politician James M. Curley for a seat in the U.S. Senate. With the exception of periods of service in the Army from 1941 to 1942 and 1944 to 1945, he remained in the upper house over the next 15 years. [See TRUMAN Volume]

The liberal Lodge was a long-time opponent of conservative Republican leader Sen. Robert A. Taft (R, Ohio) [q.v.] because of his opposition to U.S. involvement in European affairs. Lodge also believed that Taft's failure to accommodate the more liberal Eastern wing of the Party would eventually take the GOP out of the mainstream of American politics. By 1950 he was convinced that the Republican Party could maintain its viability only if it could find a presidential candidate who could unify it and hold the political center. He thought Gen. Dwight D. Eisenhower would be the most suitable choice.

During the early-1950s Lodge persistently attempted to persuade the reluctant General to run. First meeting Eisenhower in June 1950, Lodge was unable to get the General to commit himself to a campaign because the NATO commander feared his entry into partisan politics would jeopardize the formation of a European defense system. Eisenhower did agree, however, that if he thought the two party system would be threatened by his refusal, he would accept "the public duty." Taking this oblique statement as a mandate, by the end of 1951 Lodge had organized a committee to push Eisenhower's candidacy. Lodge then became the General's campaign manager.

Lodge initially found it difficult to raise funds for the campaign. Eisenhower, who was still in Europe, refused to make any political statements. The public was also uncertain about the General's political affiliation. During the opening months of 1952, Lodge worked to push Eisenhower into the Republican fold and convince him of his popular support. In January the Senator, attempting to enter Eisenhower's name in the New Hampshire primary, wrote Gov. Sherman Adams [q.v.] affirming that Eisenhower was a Republican. A few days later Lodge held a press conference to announce his candidate's political affiliation. Asked how he knew of Eisenhower's GOP leanings, he gambled and told reporters to ask the General. Several days later Eisenhower issued a statement that "Lodge's announcement . . . gives an accurate account of the general tenor of my political convictions and of my Republican voting record." In February Lodge staged a rally at Madison Square Garden for the General. The boisterous, disorganized affair attended by 30,000 supporters helped convince Eisenhower of his popularity.

Despite his absence, Eisenhower won the New Hampshire primary. Encouraged by the showing, Lodge visited the General once more in April and solicited his promise that he would return to the U.S. in June to campaign. During the ensuing months Lodge made numerous speeches for his candidate in Utah, Texas, Colorado, Kansas, California and Washington.

During the late spring and early summer, the campaign seemed threatened by Taft's high standing among regular party officials in the Midwest and South. By late June the contest appeared very close. But Taft's Texas supporters had arbitrarily ignored substantial Eisenhower support expressed at local party precinct meetings in choosing the state's delegation. With the cry "Thou Shalt Not Steal," Lodge, his staff and liberal journalists, turned the Texas situation into a moral issue. Taft's lieutenants proved powerless in response. The full Convention voted to seat a rival, pro-Eisenhower delegation and displace the Texas Taft slate. It acted similarly regarding the credentials of the Georgia and Louisiana delegations, even though the issues there appeared less clear. The successful credentials challenge provided Eisenhower with the votes necessary for a first ballot victory.

Because of his preoccupation with Eisenhower's nomination, Lodge neglected his own senatorial race against 35-year-old Rep. John F. Kennedy (D, Mass.) [q.v.]. As a result of this the ardent opposition of Taft Republicans in Massachusetts and Kennedy's superior campaign, he lost his bid for reelection by 70,000 votes out of 2.3 million cast.

Following his election, Eisenhower made Lodge his personal liaison to arrange the transfer of power. He also appointed the Senator chief delegate to the U.N., a position which, he assured Lodge, was second in the State Department to that of Secretary of State. The President-elect also made him a member of the cabinet and of the National Security Council.

Lodge viewed himself not as the head of an embassy who was obliged to take directions from the State Department but as one of Eisenhower's senior policy advisers. According to Assistant Secretary of State for U.N. Affairs Robert Murphy [q.v.], "The political influence and exceptional ability of Ambassador Lodge gradually transformed the American delegation at the U.N. until, as the years passed, [the] mission behaved less like an embassy than a second foreign office of the United States government." Lodge was permitted to speak in U.N. debates without prior clearance from Washington. President Eisenhower often remarked that his ambassador had articulated the position he would have taken had he been consulted.

At the U.N. Lodge played the role of a cold, unbending foe of Communism, while keeping the lines of communication open to the Soviets through his staff, particularly his assistant, James Wadsworth [q.v.]. He represented the U.S. at important debates during the Suez crisis and Hungarian revolt of 1956 and explained U.S. action in sending troops to Lebanon two years later. As Eisenhower's official representative, Lodge accompanied Soviet Premier Nikita Khrushchev on his 12 day tour through the U.S. in 1959. Ambassador Lodge was also with the two leaders during their talks at Camp David.

In 1960 Lodge resigned his post to campaign as the Republican Party's vice presidential candidate on a ticket headed by Richard M. Nixon [q.v.]. As ambassador to Vietnam during the Kennedy and Johnson Administrations, Lodge played a leading role in the formulation of policy toward Southeast Asia. From 1968 to 1969 he served as ambassador to West Germany. The following year he was chief U.S. negotiator at the Paris peace talks and was

then named presidential envoy to the Vatican. [See KENNEDY, JOHNSON, NIXON/ FORD Volumes]

[RSG]

For further information:
Alden Hatch, *The Lodges of Massachusetts* (New York, 1973).
Henry Cabot Lodge, *The Storm Has Many Eyes* (New York, 1973).
William J. Miller, *Henry Cabot Lodge* (New York, 1967).

LONG, EARL K(EMP)

b. Aug. 25, 1895; Winnfield, La.
d. Sept. 5, 1960; Alexandria, La.
Governor, La., 1939-40; 1948-52, 1956-60.

Born in a poor agricultural section of Louisiana, Earl Long grew up in the shadow of his older brother Huey. He followed Huey through law school at Tulane and Loyola Universities and was admitted to the Louisiana bar in 1926. Two years later Earl helped Huey win the governorship. He was then named inheritance tax collector, his first political post. Volatile tempers and a belief in share-the-wealth populism characterized both brothers. When Huey, then a senator, refused Earl a place on the 1932 gubernatorial ticket because his younger brother was headstrong, Earl ran against the designated candidate. Badly beaten, Earl testified against his brother at a 1933 Senate investigation of Louisiana voting fraud. The brothers reconciled before Huey's assassination in September 1935.

Elected lieutenant governor in 1936, Long served as governor in 1939-40, following the resignation of his corrupt predecessor. He was elected governor in 1948 with the support of organized labor. Pledging to "share-the-wealth" without raising taxes, he promised to increase welfare benefits, provide hot lunches for school children and raise teachers' salaries. Once in office he raised taxes for rich and poor alike. As governor, he viewed society in populist terms of producers and non-producers, and he directed his appeals toward common men of all colors. Earl Long followed Huey in politically evading the race issue.

After the Supreme Court's May 1954 decision outlawing public school segregation, Long publicly proclaimed himself for segregation "1,000 percent" while privately saying "a lot of other fellows would be killed for doing [for blacks] what I tried to do for them." During 1956 he ran for reelection as a racial moderate concentrating on economic issues. In May he denounced politicians using race to confuse the issues. In the general election blacks provided his margin of victory.

Facing growing racial hysteria during his second term, Long attempted to avoid taking a firm stand on integration. He recommended no white supremacy legislation and cautioned against unconstitutional segregation bills while signing the anti-integration legislation lawmakers passed. Both Earl Long and Alabama Gov. James E. Folsom [q.v.] refused to join state segregationists and other Southern governors in publicly denouncing the Supreme Court ruling. However, Long, unlike Folsom, did not oppose massive resistance. He was willing to accept segregationist measures focused on maintaining racial separation in schools.

When white Citizens' Councils attempted to block black voter registration, the Governor, whose power base rested in part on blacks, openly attacked the move. In June 1958 he scored segregationist State Sen. William Rainach for too zealously defending white supremacy. In September, when Rainach attempted to purge black voters from the registration rolls in Long's home parish, the Governor denounced the action as partisan. Their battle came to a head before the 1959 legislature. Rainach introduced legislation restricting voter registration still further, while Long countered with a measure to protect registrants from future purges. The two sides stalemated. During the struggle Long suffered a nervous breakdown.

In May 1959 Long demanded the state legislature accept his scheme for retaining power despite a law forbidding a governor two consecutive terms. He proposed to resign and let the lieutenant governor take over while he ran for reelection. The legislature might have accepted this plan had he not introduced a bill making registration easier for his poor white and black supporters. When the state Senate turned down the measure as "integrationist-inspired," Long publicly upbraided the legislature in language so abusive as to suggest mental imbalance. Shortly after this he entered the hospital for treatment as a paranoid schizophrenic. He emerged from a series of commitments in September 1959 to bow out of the gubernatorial race. Instead, he ran for lieutenant governor on a moderate ticket headed by former Gov. James A. Noe. Both were beaten in the December primary, but at the same time, Long narrowly defeated the incumbent for the Democratic nomination for a seat in the U.S. House of Representatives. His erratic behavior continued, notably when he walked out of an April 1960 New Orleans luncheon given for visiting French President Charles DeGaulle. Winning the August congressional runoff while in the hospital, Gov. Long emerged wan and emaciated to campaign. He candidly told an interviewer he thought "Lincoln was right" on race relations. He died of a heart attack the following month.

[MJS]

For further information:
Numan Bartley, *The Rise of Massive Resistance* (Baton Rouge, 1969).

LONG, RUSSELL B(ILLIU)
b. Nov. 3, 1918; Shreveport, La.
Democratic Senator, La., 1949-   .

Russell Long was the eldest son of Huey Long, the Louisiana governor and U.S. senator whose political machine dominated the state in the 1920s and 1930s. Russell Long received a B.A. degree from Louisiana State University in 1941 and an LL.B. degree from the University's law school the following year. After serving in the Navy during World War II, he opened a law practice in Baton Rouge. In 1948 Long helped his uncle, Earl Long, win the Democratic gubernatorial nomination. Later in the year he narrowly defeated anti-Long candidate Robert Kennon [*q.v.*] in Louisiana's Democratic senatorial primary on the basis of a strong showing in rural constituencies. Elected in November to complete two years of an unexpired term, Long was reelected to a full term in 1950.

Long was a moderate Southerner who, as a member of the Finance Committee, consistently sought to expand social security coverage. In 1954 he unsuccessfully proposed, against Administration wishes, a social security amendment increasing Old Age and Survivors Insurance (OASI) benefits without cutting beneficiaries' public assistance checks. Two years later Long joined Sens. Walter F. George (D, Ga.) [*q.v.*] and Paul H. Douglas (D, Ill.) [*q.v.*] in criticizing the Finance Committee for eliminating social security provisions for disability payments to workers who became disabled after age 50. In 1958 Long failed in an effort to increase public assistance payments to the aged, blind and disabled by about five dollars a month.

Long criticized Administration tax policies as favoring the wealthy. In 1954 he unsuccessfully opposed President Eisenhower's proposed cut in dividend income taxes in favor of Sen. George's amendment to replace it with an increased personal exemption. The following year Long supported a narrowly defeated Democratic effort to grant a $20 tax credit to all persons. He declared that people "in the middle and lower-income brackets are entitled to tax reduction as a matter of simple justice."

Long, however, was a staunch defender of the natural gas, oil, sulphur and sugar interests that formed the backbone of Louisiana's economy. In 1955 he fought, without success, for Senate approval of a bill giving domestic sugar producers a larger share of the expanding U.S. market at the expense of Cuban growers. However, a similar measure was passed in 1956.

In 1956 Long supported a controversial measure to exempt independent producers of natural gas from federal utility rate control. He asserted that opponents of the bill failed to realize that if it were defeated, the producers would withhold their new reserves from interstate commerce and sell their gas within their states at higher prices than they could get under federal utility regulation. President Eisenhower vetoed the bill after improper lobbying activities by natural gas representatives were uncovered. Two years later Long, lamenting that the measure had no immediate chance of passage, cosponsored a compromise proposal exempting only the smaller independent producers from federal rate regulation, but it did not reach the Senate floor.

In 1957 Long spoke on the Senate floor against attempts to reduce the 27.5% oil depletion allowance for large oil companies while retaining the rate for smaller operators. He contended that the proposal would spare the relatively small but personally wealthy independent producer while hurting the small, low-income investor in the companies.

A strong critic of foreign aid, Long annually attempted to cut funds for foreign assistance programs. In 1955 he asked, "Why do we insist on treating foreigners better than we treat Americans?" Long opposed treaties and other foreign commitments that did not exact equal obligations from the other concerned parties. He voted against the Korean Mutual Defense Treaty of 1954 and the renegotiated Japanese Mutual Defense Treaty of 1960 for that reason.

In 1965 Long was chosen majority whip, and the following year he became chairman of the Finance Committee. He annoyed many of his colleagues by his unreliability and his willingness to delay Senate business. In 1969 he lost his post as whip. Hawkish in foreign affairs during the 1960s, he strongly backed the landing of U.S. troops in Santo Domingo in 1965 and American involvement in Vietnam. [See KENNEDY, JOHNSON, NIXON/FORD, CARTER Volumes]

[MLL]

LOVESTONE, JAY
b. 1898; Lithuania
Director, Free Trade Union Committee, 1944-63.

Born to poverty-stricken Russian-Jewish parents, Jacob Liebstein came to the U.S. at the age of nine and later changed his name to Jay Lovestone. A socialist from youth, he was a delegate to the founding convention of the American Communist Party, which split from the Socialist Party in 1919. Lovestone quickly became a major Communist leader, editing the Party's theoretical journal and working in its underground apparatus during the early-1920s. In the bitter intraparty disputes of these years, which reflected the post-Lenin struggle for power in the USSR, Lovestone's faction was aligned with the Soviet leaders around Nikolai Bukharin, the president of the Comintern. As General Secretary of the American Party in 1928, Lovestone carried out the Moscow-ordered expulsion of the U.S. supporters of Leon Trotsky. In the following year, however, he was deposed as head of the U.S. Party and roughly ejected from its ranks when Bukharin, in turn, fell from power. He then led a small Communist group of his own, popularly known as the "Lovestoneites," which sought readmission to the parent organization for several years before becoming anti-Soviet and finally disbanding in 1940.

A self-proclaimed expert on Communism, Lovestone offered his services in the late-1930s to labor leaders seeking to curb Communists and other radicals within their unions. After briefly acting as a behind-the-scenes adviser to United Auto Workers President Homer Martin, he and his factional entourage found a more durable base in the New York needle trades, where International Ladies Garment Workers Union (ILGWU) president David Dubinsky [q.v.] used their talent to combat his Communist opponents. During World War II Lovestone directed the ILGWU's International Relations Department, organizing aid to the Allies and helping European labor leaders escape Axis countries. He also became a confidant of American Federation of Labor (AFL) secretary-treasurer George Meany [q.v.]. In 1944 Lovestone was named by the AFL to head the Free Trade Union Committee (FTUC), which was created to help rebuild the labor movements of Europe and Japan and to counter the influence of the World Federation of Trade Unions (WFTU), in which both Communist and non-Communist unions, including the American Congress of Industrial Organiza-

tions (CIO), cooperated. Using a network of personal friends and political associates as overseas operatives, Lovestone worked with the Central Intelligence Agency (CIA) to weaken Communist unions in France and Italy. In 1949 he helped pro-Western unions from the WFTU form the International Confederation of Free Trade Unions (ICFTU). According to CIA official Thomas Braden, the FTUC received more than $2 million annually from the Agency to finance its activities during the postwar years. [See TRUMAN Volume]

During the 1950s Lovestone shifted his attention increasingly from Western Europe to Latin America. With continued CIA assistance the FTUC worked through the Inter-American Regional Organization of Workers (ORIT) to train pro-U.S. labor leaders in Central and South American countries, many of whom, Lovestone admitted to the *Chicago Tribune* in 1954, were later engaged in intelligence work for Washington. In 1954 FTUC agent Serafino Romualdi helped organize the CIA-backed coup that toppled the government of Guatemalan President Jacobo Arbenz, which the Eisenhower Administration charged was permitting Communists to gain a political base in the region. ORIT-trained unionists took part in the "liberation army" of Col. Carlos Catillo Armas which overthrew Arbenz in June. Shortly afterward, however, the new regime effectively outlawed all trade unions, including non-Communist organizations, and instituted what AFL leaders themselves described as a brutal dictatorship of employers and landlords over Guatemalan workers.

During the 1950s Lovestone also dispatched Romualdi to British Guiana, where he attempted to undermine popular support for radical Prime Minister Cheddi Jagan with the aid of the conservative Man-Power Citizens Association, a union ostensibly representing sugar workers but sponsored by the sugar companies themselves. These efforts culminated in 1963 with a CIA-financed general strike which led to Jagan's ouster in the following year.

Lovestone's policy toward Cuba, which he regarded as another potential trouble spot, was more ambivalent. He protested

Fulgencio Batista's 1952 coup d'etat but refrained from criticizing the regime too sharply so long as the Cuban Confederation of Labor (CTC) was permitted to function legally. When Batista's fall appeared inevitable in the late-1950s, Romualdi was sent to Cuba to propose CTC support to Fidel Castro in exchange for a guarantee of the Confederation's freedom to operate in the event he took power. Castro rejected the offer, and after seizing control of the island in 1959, he was denounced by the AFL-CIO for turning Cuba into an "advanced outpost" of Soviet Communism.

Lovestone's intransigent anti-Communism and government-related foreign operations aroused increasing controversy in the American labor movement. Although the FTUC supported North African unionists fighting French colonialism and denounced fascism and apartheid, Lovestone generally subordinated questions of democracy and national independence to what he regarded as the overriding issue of Communist expansion. A member of the Committee of One Million Against the Admission of Communist China to the U.N. and the Council Against Communist Aggression, which supported Chiang Kai-shek, he opposed any steps toward detente with the Communist world. As a result, AFL representatives in the ICFTU quarreled increasingly during the 1950s with Western European socialist labor leaders, who favored a relaxation of cold war tensions. Lovestone's tactics and political posture came under fire from Walter Reuther [q.v.] and other CIO leaders. At their insistence the FTUC was disaffiliated from the merged AFL-CIO in 1955. With Meany's strong support, however, Lovestone maintained firm, if unofficial, control of foreign labor operations and kept most of his personnel on the Federation's payroll.

Lovestone's continued role as Meany's chief adviser on foreign affairs was given official recognition in 1963, when he was appointed AFL-CIO Director of International Affairs. In 1961 he helped organize the American Institute for Free Labor Development (AIFLD), which sponsored an extensive program to train Latin American labor leaders and to plan union housing projects, banks and other projects in Latin American countries. The bulk of the AIFLD's income was supplied by the U.S. government and American corporations. [See KENNEDY Volume]

[TLH]

For further information:
Sidney Lens, "Lovestone Diplomacy," *The Nation* (July 5, 1965).
Ronald Radosh, *American Labor and United States Foreign Policy* (New York, 1969).

LUCE, CLARE BOOTHE
b. April 10, 1903; New York, N.Y.
Ambassador to Italy, March 1953-November 1956.

The daughter of a violinist and a dancer, Clare Boothe was raised in Nashville and Chicago. At the age of 16 she left home to work in New York City and enroll in a drama school. In 1923, at the age of 20, she married George T. Brokaw, a millionaire son of a clothing manufacturer. The marriage ended in divorce six years later. Boothe joined the staff of *Vogue* in 1930 and became associate editor of *Vanity Fair* the following year. In 1933 she was promoted to executive editor. She resigned her post in 1934 to write a newspaper column and begin work on her first play. In November 1935 Boothe married Henry R. Luce [q.v.], president of Time, Inc. After her marriage she continued writing plays, including the successful *The Women* (1936), which ran for 657 performances on Broadway.

Luce won a seat from Connecticut in the U.S. House of Representatives in 1942. During her two terms in Congress, the sharp-tongued Representative became a prominent critic of Franklin D. Roosevelt's foreign policy. A strident anti-Communist, Luce scored the postwar division of Europe and warned that U.S. failure to be "firm, precise and clear in our foreign policy . . . will result in an increasing drift toward world catastrophe." She declined to run for public office in 1946 and withdrew from public life to resume her writing career. However, Luce remained a prominent critic of the Truman Administration's foreign policy and, like her husband, a strong supporter of Nationalist China. [See TRUMAN Volume]

Luce campaigned extensively for Gen. Dwight D. Eisenhower during the 1952 presidential race. Shortly after his inauguration she was appointed ambassador to Italy. She arrived in Italy during a period of strained relations between the two nations. In the postwar years the U.S. had exerted financial and political pressure to prevent Italy's Communist Party from gaining control of the government. In 1953 the U.S.-backed government of Premier Alcide de Gaspari faced an election in which it was feared his Christian Democratic Party would lose its majority. Believing that the only way to save Italy from a Communist takeover was to maintain de Gaspari, Luce used all her power to ensure his victory. Just before the election she saw to it that de Gaspari was on *Time's* cover. The accompanying article extolled him as a bulwark of Italian religion and morality and denounced Italian Communists as wolves slashing at "the shaky legged colt of Italian democracy." Luce also made a speech suggesting that a de Gaspari defeat would have grave consequences for Italian-American relations. Despite her efforts, which some Italian politicians decried as open meddling, the de Gaspari government fell two months after the election.

During 1954 Luce's concern over Communist influence in the Italian labor movement prompted her to protest the U.S. policy of purchasing material for the North Atlantic Treaty Organization's defense needs from foreign suppliers. This act was designed to restore the industrial capacity of U.S. allies, but Luce felt it aided Communist unions. Luce threatened to resign unless contracts were canceled with plants where Communist unions were in control. Eisenhower and Secretary of State John Foster Dulles [q.v.] agreed to give her a free hand in attacking the problem with the understanding that she would be held accountable if her plans failed. Back in Italy Luce threatened to cut off U.S. government contracts with Fiat, the nation's largest manufacturer. As a result of her pressure, the Communists lost control of the company's union in the spring of 1955.

During her tenure Luce helped resolve the Italian-Yugoslav dispute over Trieste, which had been smoldering since World War II. Luce succeeded in convincing the Administration to promote a secret conference between the two nations in a neutral country. Negotiations began in London in the spring of 1954 but bogged down in August when Marshall Tito insisted on more concessions than the Italians, British and U.S. representatives were prepared to grant. Prompted by a Central Intelligence Agency operative's report that Tito's tough stand was designed to draw domestic attention from his country's poor harvest, Luce suggested that the U.S. offer wheat to Yugoslavia in return for concessions. She also convinced Robert Murphy [q.v.] to undertake the sensitive diplomatic negotiations necessary to get Tito to accept the proposals. The Trieste dispute was formally settled in October 1954.

Citing ill health Luce resigned her post in November 1956. In a much publicized incident it was revealed that Luce was being accidently poisoned by lead-based paint falling from the ceiling of her residence.

Eisenhower nominated Luce to be ambassador to Brazil in February 1959. Her appointment was challenged by Sen. Wayne Morse (D, Ore.) [q.v.], who questioned her views on Roosevelt's war policies and her role in Italian politics. Despite confirmation by both the Foreign Relations Committee and the Senate, Morse continued to criticize the Ambassador. Luce countered by issuing a statement that her troubles with Morse began "when [he] was kicked in the head by a horse." At her husband's request, she resigned the office, maintaining that as a result of the conflict she would no longer be able to fulfill her mission.

During the 1960s Luce resumed her writing career, contributing articles to a number of magazines. She remained active in Republican politics and in 1964 supported Sen. Barry Goldwater [q.v.] for President.

[EWS]

For further information:
Stephen Shadegg, *Clare Boothe Luce* (New York, 1970).

LUCE, HENRY R(OBINSON)
b. April 3, 1898; Tengchow, China
d. Feb. 28, 1967; Phoenix, Ariz.
Editor-in-chief, *Time* and *Time*, Inc.,
1923-64.

The son of a Presbyterian missionary, Luce was born and raised in China, where he learned to speak Chinese before he spoke English. He was educated in Chefoo, a strict British public school, the Hotchkiss School and Yale University. Following his graduation in 1920 Luce studied briefly at Oxford and then began a career as a reporter for the *Chicago Daily News*. In 1923 he joined Briton Hadden in forming *Time*, a weekly news magazine. Initially, Luce handled the business affairs of the corporation while Hadden ran the editorial side. With Hadden's death in 1929, Luce assumed editorial duties as well. During the 1930s his publishing empire grew with the addition of *Fortune* in 1930 and *Life* in 1936. The latter, a largely photographic magazine, was a wedding gift to Luce's second wife, Clare Boothe Luce [*q.v.*]. Luce also developed "The March of Time," a radio series later adapted to movies.

During the 1930s Luce used his publications to score New Deal spending and curbs on free enterprise. Like some conservatives he so feared Communism that he initially found encouragement in the rise of fascism. Only after the 1939 invasion of Czechoslovakia did he demand that the Allies stop Hitler.

Luce viewed the twentieth century as the "American Century" in which the U.S., because of its political and moral superiority, would extend its dominance throughout the world. He believed the results of World War II would accomplish this. Describing the USSR as the anti-Christ who was the only force likely to compete with the U.S. in the postwar period, Luce urged the U.S. not to let Russia win too much from the War. The publisher was a strong supporter of Chiang Kai-shek and used his publications to promote the Chinese leader as a full-fledged member of the grand alliance.

During the postwar period Luce publications continued to support Chiang and urge the containment of Communism in both Europe and Asia. Although only a lukewarm supporter of Sen. Joseph R. McCarthy (R, Wisc.) [*q.v.*], Luce championed the domestic fight against Communism, which he saw in terms of a religious crusade. [See TRUMAN Volume]

Luce was a major supporter of Dwight D. Eisenhower's 1952 presidential campaign and used his magazines' great influence to press first for the General's nomination and then for his election. *Time* extolled Eisenhower and presented him as a smiling, earnest candidate while showing Adlai Stevenson [*q.v.*] as unappealing. Its cover story on the Democratic candidate carried the words "Does he make sense to the American people?" John Sparkman [*q.v.*], the Democratic vice presidential candidate, was also ridiculed, while Richard Nixon [*q.v.*], who shared Luce's views on foreign policy, was praised even after the revelation that he had access to a private political fund. One of Luce's critics called *Time*'s election stand "more partisan than had ever been seen even in that forum of bias."

Luce was a strong supporter of Secretary of State John Foster Dulles's [*q.v.*] foreign policy and shared his belief in America's moral mission to unilaterally defend the world from Communist expansion, even if it meant military intervention. He was particularly concerned that the U.S. take a strong stand on Vietnam to prevent Communist expansion in Indochina. During the 1954 siege of Dien Bien Phu, Luce supported Dulles's recommendation for direct American intervention. Following the decision against action, he chided the Western allies for being disorganized, confused and divided. Luce later supported Dulles's attempts to vitiate the 1954 Geneva agreements, prevent Vietnamese elections, which might bring the Communists to power, and take over France's role.

The publisher supported the Administration's policy of "Massive Retaliation" with its reliance on nuclear weapons to contain Communism. Viewing the Soviet Union and China as an eternal monolithic enemy of the U.S., he opposed any thaw in the Cold War. During Soviet Premier Nikita Khrushchev's visit to the U.S. in 1959, the Luce press continually used Khrushchev's phrase "we will bury you" out of context, distorting its meaning.

In 1959 rioting broke out in Bolivia over a *Time* story quoting a U.S. embassy official as saying that the U.S. spent $129 million in that country without effect. According to the magazine, the official maintained the only solution was to "abolish Bolivia and let its neighbors divide the country and its problems among themselves." The incident was protested not only by Bolivia but also by other journalists who wondered whether Luce had made up the story. The article also contributed to Clare Booth Luce's resignation as ambassador to Argentina.

During the 1960 presidential campaign Luce initially refused to back either Richard Nixon or John F. Kennedy [*q.v.*]. He announced that he would view each candidate's stand on anti-Communism as a prime factor in a future endorsement. Luce's concern helped make anti-Communism a prime issue in the campaign. In October *Life* finally came out for Nixon. However, Kennedy viewed Luce's refusal to give Nixon early support with pleasure.

During the 1960s Luce praised the handling of the 1962 Cuban missile crisis and promoted American intervention in Vietnam. He supported Lyndon B. Johnson's domestic programs and backed him for President in 1964. Luce retired as editor-in-chief of *Time* in April 1964 but maintained his authority over the direction of his magazines as editorial chairman until his death in 1967. [See KENNEDY, JOHNSON Volumes]

[EWS]

For further information:
W. A. Swanberg, *Luce and His Empire* (New York, 1972).

LUCY, AUTHERINE J(UANITA)
b. (?) 1929; Shiloh, Ala.
School desegregation figure

The youngest of nine children, Lucy was born on her parents' farm near Shiloh in southwestern Alabama. She graduated from

Miles College, a church-supported black school in Birmingham, Ala., in 1952. Soon afterwards Lucy decided to try to enter the all-white University of Alabama at Tuscaloosa to get a degree in library science. When she was refused admission, NAACP attorneys sued the University. In October 1955 the U.S. Supreme Court ordered the school to end segregation and admit Lucy. The University acquiesced and let Lucy enroll for the spring term in 1956, but it continued to bar her from the dormitories and dining halls on campus.

By the fall of 1955 blacks had entered the state universities in all but five Southern states. Desegregation at the college level had been peaceful, but after the Supreme Court's May 1954 decision holding segregation in public elementary and secondary schools unconstitutional, white resistance to integration at even the university level stiffened in the deep South, including Alabama. The first black ever admitted to any white public school in the state, Lucy attended her first class on the Tuscaloosa campus on Friday, Feb. 3, 1956. That evening a cross was burned on campus and a crowd of about 1,200 students exploded firecrackers, sang "Dixie," and marched on the school grounds. The next night a group of students again massed for demonstrations. On Monday Feb. 6 a mob of over 1,000, including many people not connected with the University, roamed the campus shouting their opposition to Lucy's enrollment. They threw rocks and eggs at Lucy when she arrived for classes and yelled threats at her through classroom windows. Lucy was finally removed from the campus under heavy police guard, and the University's board of trustees suspended her indefinitely on the ground that this was necessary to ensure her safety.

Three days later NAACP attorneys asked a federal court in Birmingham to order that Lucy be allowed to attend her classes. They also filed a contempt action against the University trustees and in their petition alleged that University officials had conspired with the mob on Feb. 6 to bar Lucy. The University's president denounced this charge as "untrue, unwarranted and outrageous," and at a court hearing later in the month, Thurgood Marshall [q.v.], head of the NAACP Legal Defense Fund, withdrew the conspiracy charge, saying that a careful investigation had failed to substantiate it. On Feb. 29, after the hearing, Judge H. Hobart Grooms dismissed the contempt action but ruled that the University had to reinstate Lucy. That evening the University's board of trustees permanently expelled Lucy on disciplinary grounds for having made the "false and baseless" conspiracy accusation against school officials in her court pleadings.

Throughout the crisis Lucy stayed with relatives in Birmingham, where she received numerous threatening phone calls. On March 1 she flew to New York City for rest and medical attention. Eight days later her attorneys began a court challenge to the University's expulsion order. On Jan. 18, 1957 Judge Grooms upheld the trustees' action in ousting Lucy. Lucy, who had married in April 1956 and was then living in Texas, officially ended her fight to enter the University soon afterwards. She dropped from public view and was reported in 1968 to be living with her husband and two children in Shreveport, La., where she taught English part-time in local public schools.

The crisis caused by Lucy's enrollment at the University of Alabama received nationwide publicity and resulted in what was generally regarded as a victory for pro-segregation forces. Neither state nor local officials made a strong effort to prevent mob action or to disperse the rioters, and the federal government refused to intervene even though University officials reportedly appealed to Attorney General Herbert Brownell [q.v.] for aid. President Eisenhower publicly deplored the rioters' "defiance of law" but added he would not interfere in the situation so long as the state was doing "its best to straighten it out." Many observers felt that the federal government's inaction during the Lucy crisis invited the official resistance to school desegregation that led to another crisis in Little Rock, Ark., in 1957. After Autherine Lucy, no blacks were admitted to the University of Alabama until June 1963, when state officials finally gave in to court-ordered desegregation.

[CAB]

MacARTHUR, DOUGLAS, II
b. July 5, 1909; Bryn Mawr, Pa.
Counselor of the State Department, March 1953-December 1956; Ambassador to Japan, January 1957-February 1961.

The nephew of Gen. Douglas MacArthur, Douglas MacArthur II graduated from Yale University in 1932, where he had majored in history and economics. After spending a few months in the merchant marine and over two years as a first lieutenant in the Officers Reserve Corps, he joined the Foreign Service and became vice consul first in Vancouver and then in Naples. When World War II began he was serving as a diplomatic secretary in Vichy, France. After the Vichy Government handed him over to the Nazi authorities in November 1942, MacArthur spent over 16 months in confinement. Returning to the U.S. in March 1944, he was soon reassigned to the French Provisional Government in Paris. In 1951 MacArthur became Gen. Dwight D. Eisenhower's chief adviser on international affairs while Eisenhower was Supreme Allied Commander in Europe.

When Eisenhower became President in January 1953, he appointed MacArthur counselor of the State Department. Along with John Foster Dulles [q.v.] and Sens. H. Alexander Smith (R, N.J.) [q.v.] and Mike Mansfield (D, Mont.) [q.v.], MacArthur attended a three-day conference in Manila that led to the signing in September 1954 of the Southeast Asia Collective Defense Treaty by the U.S., Great Britain, France, Australia, the Phillipines, New Zealand, Pakistan and Thailand. In the treaty the eight countries agreed to develop their military capabilities both for their own defense and for collective security, to expand trade and technical programs with each other and to extend the treaty's military and economic benefits to Cambodia, Laos and South Vietnam. The treaty also included a Pacific Charter in which the countries pledged peacefully to promote the self-government and independence of all countries that were able and willing to undertake it.

In 1957 MacArthur became ambassador to Japan, where he helped renegotiate a Japanese-American security pact. In September 1951 the U.S. and Japan had signed a mutual security pact that proved unsatisfactory to both parties. For many Japanese the pact's provision for the maintenance of American troops in Japan signified virtual American occupation. For John Foster Dulles and other Americans, the pact seemed to slight the need for Japanese rearmament, mentioning it in only the most general terms. In the aftermath of the Korean war, Dulles found the need to rearm Japan against the threat of future Asian Communist expansion ever more urgent.

Representing the U.S., MacArthur negotiated a second security pact, signed in January 1960. It committed both the U.S. and Japan to resist "the armed attack against either party in territories under the administration of Japan." It also removed the condescending tone towards Japan and the specific limitations on Japanese sovereignty of the earlier treaty and provided that the U.S. consult Japan before making major changes in the use of American troops or American bases in that country.

The political maneuvers necessary to get the treaty passed by the Japanese Diet discredited the Japanese government of Prime Minister Nobusuke Kishi and MacArthur. Because of mounting Socialist opposition to the treaty, the Japanese government ordered the police to bodily remove leftist members from the Diet, and in their absence the government called for a vote. Upset by this undemocratic tactic, Socialists staged protests against Eisenhower's forthcoming visit, scheduled for the day the treaty would take effect. Assuming the opposition reflected dissatisfaction with his own conduct of foreign affairs, Prime Minister Kishi refused to ask Eisenhower to cancel his trip. MacArthur, backing Kishi and believing that Eisenhower's withdrawal would jeopardize the final ratification of the security treaty, instructed the President to adhere to his plans unless Kishi asked him to withdraw. Only after a major battle between police and demonstrators in June, in which a girl was crushed to death, did Kishi ask Eisenhower to cancel his trip to Japan. A week after the cancellation Kishi resigned as prime minister.

When John F. Kennedy became President in 1961, he appointed Edwin O. Reischauer, a leading critic of the Eisenhower-MacArthur Japanese policy, as ambassador. MacArthur became ambassador to Belgium, a post he held until 1965, when he became secretary of state for congressional relations. He served as ambassador to Austria from 1967 to 1969 and ambassador to Iran from 1969 to 1972. Following his retirement he became a business consultant.

[RSG]

For further information:
I. M. Destler, *Managing an Alliance: the Politics of U.S.-Japanese Relations* (Washington, 1976).

McCARRAN, PATRICK A(NTHONY)
b. Aug. 8, 1876: Reno, Nev.
d. Sept. 28, 1954: Hawthorne, Nev.
Democratic Senator, Nev., 1933-54.

The son of Irish immigrants, McCarran was educated at the University of Nevada. Following his graduation in 1901 he engaged in farming and stock raising while studying law in his spare time. McCarran began his career as a lawyer in the boom mining towns of Nevada, rising eventually to the state supreme court and, in 1932, winning election to the U.S. Senate. Although he arrived in Washington on the Roosevelt landslide of that year, McCarran emerged almost immediately as an opponent of the New Deal. His quarrels with President Roosevelt and his Catholic sympathies drove him to extreme right-wing positions on many issues, including support for the Franco dictatorship in Spain.

During the latter years of the Truman Administration, McCarran played a leading role in the resurgence of conservatism in Congress, shaping strategy on issues of internal security and immigration. In 1950 he sponsored the Internal Security Act, later known as the McCarran Act, which required the registration of the Communist Party. The Senator was one of the few Democrats who publicly endorsed Sen. Joseph McCarthy's (R, Wisc.) [q.v.] attack on Truman's foreign policy and supported his investigations of Communist influence in the Sate Department. In 1952 McCarran collaborated with Rep. Francis E. Walter (D, Pa.) [q.v.] in writing an immigration and naturalization bill, known as the McCarran-Walter Act, that continued the discriminatory national-origins quota system. [See TRUMAN Volume]

The McCarran-Walter Act became an issue in the 1952 presidential campaign when Democrats implied that its restrictions were based on anti-Semitism and anti-Catholicism. Eisenhower himself repudiated the Act as a "blasphemy against democracy," and in his 1953 State of the Union message asked Congress to write a new bill. In April 1953 the President asked for emergency legislation to admit 240,000 non-quota immigrants, consisting mainly of refugees from Eastern Europe. McCarran convinced the Senate to drastically reduce that number and to provide elaborate screening procedures for those admitted to ensure against "Communist infiltration."

McCarran supported the conservative drive to bring foreign policy under congressional control. In 1953 he joined several Republican senators, led by McCarthy, in trying to block the nomination of Charles E. Bohlen [q.v.] as ambassador to the USSR. Although Secretary of State John Foster Dulles vouched for Bohlen's loyalty, McCarran and his allies persisted in linking the career diplomat to what they termed the Truman policy of appeasement of Soviet aggression. In what some State Department officials viewed as a test of Eisenhower's willingness to support the Foreign Service, the Administration stood firm on the nomination. Despite continued opposition from the conservatives, it was approved. In 1953 and 1954 McCarran was a leading backer of the Bricker amendment, a proposed constitutional revision aimed at restricting the President's treaty-making powlers. Eisenhower opposed the measure, and in February 1954 it narrowly failed to obtain the necessary two-thirds vote in the Senate.

As chairman of the Internal Security Subcommittee, McCarran remained a strong supporter of McCarthy's anti-Communist crusade, but he began to resent what he viewed as the Republican's trespass on the subcommittee's mandate to probe subversion. Nevertheless, on Sept. 27, 1954, he delivered a speech on the Senate floor assailing the Watkins Committee for recommending McCarthy's censure. The next day McCarran died of a heart attack while addressing a rally in Nevada.

[TLH]

McCARTHY, EUGENE J(OSEPH)
b. March 29, 1916: Watkins, Minn.
Democratic Representative, Minn., 1949-59; Democratic Senator, Minn., 1959-71.

McCarthy graduated from St. John's University in Minnesota in 1935 and for the next 13 years taught economics and sociology at Catholic high schools and colleges. He also spent nine months in a monastery as a Benedictine novice in 1942-43. While teaching sociology at St. Thomas College in St. Paul in 1947, he entered politics in support of Hubert Humphrey [q.v.], then fighting the Communist-led wing of Minnesota's Democratic Farmer-Labor Party (DFL). After leading a successful drive to take control of the DFL in St. Paul and Ramsey Co., McCarthy won election to the House of Representatives in 1948.

In the House McCarthy compiled a liberal, pro-labor voting record and generally supported the Eisenhower Administration on foreign policy. In 1955 he began to voice his concern about the unsupervised activities of the Central Intelligence Agency and introduced legislation to create a congressional watchdog committee. McCarthy's pragmatism and intelligence won the approval of Speaker of the House Sam Rayburn (D, Tex.) [q.v.], who secured him a seat on the prestigious Ways and Means Committee in 1955.

Beginning in 1956 McCarthy organized an informal caucus of liberal House Democrats to draw up a more dynamic legislative program and to counter the recently issued "Southern Manifesto," a call for resistance to desegregation signed by most Southern members of Congress. This liberal bloc, sometimes known as "McCarthy's

Mavericks," scored few successes during the Eisenhower years. Institutionalized as the Democratic Study Group in 1959, however, it played an important role in the 1961 battle to reform the House Rules Committee and paved the way for the enactment of the liberal laws of the 1960s.

In 1958 McCarthy won election to the Senate in an upset victory over the two-term Republican incumbent, Sen. Edward Thye (R, Minn.) [q.v.]. Aided by Thye's association with the unpopular farm policies of the Eisenhower Administration, McCarthy's success was interpreted as an indication of the willingness of a Protestant electorate to elect a Catholic.

Assigned to the Public Works Committee and the important Finance Committee, McCarthy continued his liberal voting habits without alienating such powerful conservatives as Sen. Harry Byrd (D, Va.) [q.v.] and Sen. Robert Kerr (D, Okla.) [q.v.] or the moderate Senate Majority Leader Lyndon B. Johnson (D, Tex.) [q.v.]. His first accomplishment was the Senate's rejection of President Eisenhower's nominee for Secretary of Commerce, Lewis Strauss [q.v.], in June 1959. McCarthy was one of the first to oppose Strauss's confirmation on the grounds that, as chairman of the Atomic Energy Commission, Strauss had gone "beyond reasonable limits" in refusing to cooperate with Congress. Over the next two decades McCarthy often called attention to the deterioration of the separation of powers principle, particularly the expansion of executive power and the atrophy of the congressional role in the making of foreign policy.

In September 1959 Johnson named McCarthy chairman of the newly created Special Senate Committee on Unemployment Problems, an unusual honor for a freshman senator. Over the next six months the Committee held hearings in 12 states and heard 538 witnesses. Its findings were contained in a 4,000-page report published in March 1960. Warning that the postwar baby boom would swell a work force already afflicted with growing unemployment, the report proposed a 12-point plan to combat joblessness, including aid to distressed areas, stimulative economic policies,

ambitious job retraining programs, higher unemployment benefits over longer payment periods and expanded public works. While not original, the conclusions of the McCarthy Committee helped publicize the unemployment situation and outlined the solutions enacted later in the New Frontier and Great Society programs.

With his dry wit and aloof demeanor, McCarthy stood apart from his Senate colleagues. He never gained commanding influence within the Senate and grew increasingly bored with his duties. McCarthy made a great impact upon the course of American politics, however, when he took his opposition to the Vietnam war into the national arena and ran an underdog campaign for the Democratic presidential nomination in 1967-68. Although he ultimately lost the nomination by a large margin, McCarthy's surprisingly strong showing in the March 1968 New Hampshire primary revealed a vigorous undercurrent of anti-war feeling and contributed to President Johnson's decision later in the month not to seek reelection. McCarthy's candidacy drew much of the anti-war movement into electoral politics and was distinctive for its reliance on legions of idealistic young volunteers instead of party professionals.

McCarthy retired from the Senate in 1971. He made two more unsuccessful runs for the presidency in 1972 and 1976 but never kindled the enthusiasm he had ignited in 1968. [See KENNEDY, JOHNSON, NIXON/FORD Volumes]

[TO]

McCARTHY, JOSEPH R(AYMOND)
b. Nov. 14, 1909; Grand Chute, Wisc.
d. May 2, 1957; Bethesda, Md.
Republican Senator, Wisc., 1947-57; Chairman, Government Operations Committee, 1953-55; Chairman, Permanent Investigations Subcommittee of the Government Operations Committee, 1953-55.

McCarthy, the fifth of seven children, was born on his father's 142-acre farm in northeastern Wisconsin. He was an intelligent, shy and sensitive boy who avoided strangers and looked to his mother rather than his stern father for protection. Upon completing eighth grade McCarthy left school and raised chickens on land rented from his father. At age 19 he moved to Manawa, Wisc., where he managed a general store, hiding his shyness behind a facade of humor. In an impressive burst of energy, McCarthy returned to high school in 1929 and completed four years of work in one year while holding a job as an usher in a movie theater.

In 1930 McCarthy entered the school of engineering at Marquette University in Milwaukee but shifted to law after two years. At Marquette McCarthy was known as an intensely competitive and talkative young man. He received his LL.B. degree in 1935 and was admitted to the Wisconsin bar the same year. He opened a private legal practice but attracted little business. McCarthy supplemented his income at poker, which he played ruthlessly. He began joining civic and fraternal organizations in preparation for a political career. In 1936 he ran unsuccessfully as the Democratic candidate for district attorney of Shawano Co., Wisc. Three years later he ran as a Republican for judge of the 10th circuit court and upset the incumbent of 35 years after conducting a 20-hour-a-day campaign. On the bench McCarthy became known for the rapid-fire decisions by which he disposed of a large backlog of cases.

McCarthy volunteered for service in the Marine Corps in 1942 and was assigned as an intelligence officer to the South Pacific, where he briefed and debriefed flying personnel. Although in subsequent political campaigns he called himself "Tail-Gunner Joe," he did not fly in combat. McCarthy had not resigned his judgeship, and judges were barred by Wisconsin law from running for any other public office. In addition, military regulations forbade servicemen from speaking on political issues. Despite these prohibitions he entered the Wisconsin Republican senatorial primary in 1944 while stationed in the U.S. Although running ahead of two other challengers, he was handily defeated by incumbent Sen. Alexander Wiley (R, Wisc.) [q.v.].

In 1946 McCarthy entered the senatorial primary for the state's other Senate seat, held by Wisconsin Progressive Party leader Robert M. La Follette, Jr. In that year La Follette decided to dissolve the Party and enter the Republican primary. McCarthy profited from the Wisconsin Republican leadership's dislike of La Follette and the Senator's record of ignoring state interests for national issues. In addition many trade unionists refused to follow La Follette into the Republican Party and cast their votes in the Democratic contest. McCarthy campaigned indefatigibly and defeated the incumbent by a slim 5,000-vote margin. He went on to easily beat his Democratic opponent by 620,000 votes to 279,000.

During his first three years in the Senate, McCarthy did not consistently identify himself with any one issue. He was known for a time as "the Pepsi-Cola Kid" because of his close ties to lobbyists for that company. In 1947 he led a Senate campaign to end sugar rationing. In 1947 and 1948 McCarthy played a major role in blocking public housing legislation sponsored by Sen. Robert A. Taft (R, Ohio) [q.v.] while receiving favors from the Lustron Corp., a manufacturer of prefabricated housing. In 1949 McCarthy, whose district had a large German constitutency, gained attention for questioning whether 73 Nazi SS soldiers had been fairly convicted by an American war-crimes tribunal for the "Malmedy Massacre" during the Battle of the Bulge. Overall, McCarthy had a conservative voting record on domestic issues while taking an internationalist stand in foreign affairs.

During the latter part of the 1940s, internal subversion became a major national issue. Many Republicans, including Sen. Richard M. Nixon (R, Calif.) [q.v.], made frequent and effective use of the charge that the Truman Administration was infiltrated by pro-Communist elements. President Harry S. Truman, while rejecting the accusation, in 1947 created a loyalty-security program for screening government employes and workers for private firms doing certain kinds of work for the government.

In 1949 the Communist victory in China, the explosion of a Soviet nuclear bomb and the conviction of U.S. Communist Party leaders for conspiring to advocate the violent overthrow of the American government heightened public consciousness of the alleged Communist threat to the nation. The January 1950 perjury conviction of Alger Hiss, who had purportedly been a Soviet spy while serving as a State Department official under President Franklin D. Roosevelt, further aroused public concern.

McCarthy initially gave the question of internal Communism little attention, but early in 1950 he was looking for an issue with which to associate himself. Taking advantage of the political climate, from February 1950 he staked his career entirely on the issue of domestic subversion. At a Lincoln Day rally in Wheeling, W. Va., on Feb. 9, McCarthy stated, according to a local reporter, that he had in his hand a list of 205 Communist Party members presently holding major posts in the State Department. At his next speaking engagement he said that there were 205 "bad risks" and 57 "card-carrying Communists" in the Department. On the Senate floor later in the month he claimed to have 108 documented cases.

Amid the sensation and confusion caused by his charges, a special subcommittee of the Senate Foreign Relations Committee, headed by Sen. Millard Tydings (D, Md.), was established in late February to investigate McCarthy's claims. After examining the Senator's charges against such men as Ambassador-at-Large Philip C. Jessup and Professor Owen J. Lattimore, allegedly the head of a pro-Communist clique in the State Department, the Democratic majority on the panel issued a report in July denouncing the charges as false and condemning McCarthy for unethical tactics. The Republican minority defended the Wisconsin Senator and called the report a whitewash of the State Department.

In June 1950 Sen. Margaret Chase Smith (R, Me.) [q.v.] and six other Republican senators issued a "Declaration of Conscience" criticizing McCarthy for making irresponsible charges. However, because Republicans had found the issue of internal subversion an effective political weapon against Truman, even those who believed

McCarthy's accusations to be reckless were reluctant to criticize him for fear of undermining the future usefulness of that issue and creating a reaction that would discredit the entire Party.

Many Democrats, on the other hand, felt that if they attacked McCarthy, they might appear to be confirming Republican charges that they were soft on Communism. The 1950 congressional elections, by seeming to demonstrate McCarthy's popularity, reinforced their disinclination to challenge the Senator. In Maryland John Marshall Butler, an obscure Republican, defeated Tyding with McCarthy's help. Illinois Sen. Scott Lucas, the Democratic majority leader, lost to Republican. Everett M. Dirksen [q.v.] in a campaign in which McCarthy had become involved. Republican victories in Idaho and Utah also appeared related to McCarthy's electoral efforts.

While McCarthy's success was greatly facilitated by postwar American fears of internal Communist subversion and by the political considerations that caused other politicians to refrain from attacking him, his own demagogic abilities were also a crucial factor in his meteoric ascendancy. McCarthy's intensely aggressive style overwhelmed and intimidated his opponents. He had a flair for attracting publicity by making sensational charges and for obscuring setbacks by immediately launching into still more sensational accusations. McCarthy's incessant flow of allegations led large numbers of people to believe that even if many were untrue or exaggerated, some must be accurate. When criticized he charged his accuser of being pro-Communist or at least soft on Communism.

The impunity with which McCarthy was able to make his charges after 1950 was best illustrated by his denunciation of Secretary of Defense George C. Marshall from the Senate floor on June 14, 1951. Army Chief of Staff during World War II and subsequently Secretary of State, Marshall had been involved in many key postwar foreign policy decisions. Although he was one of the most respected men in America, no one in the Senate objected when McCarthy charged that Marshall was part of a "great conspiracy" that had produced a long series of American setbacks at the hands of the Communists since World War II.

In August 1951 Sen. William Benton (D, Conn.) [q.v.] introduced a resolution calling for an examination of McCarthy's conduct by the Rules Committee to determine if he should be expelled from the Senate. The resolution was referred to the Committee's Subcommittee on Privileges and Elections, which had just issued a report denouncing McCarthy for unethical activities in the Tydings-Butler campaign. The subcommittee's investigation dragged on for over a year. Its January 1953 report, written largely by Sen. Thomas Hennings (D, Mo.), raised questions about McCarthy's finances, but no action was taken. [See TRUMAN Volume]

The 1952 presidential and congressional campaigns provided further evidence of McCarthy's great political strength. Republican presidential candidate Dwight D. Eisenhower was a personal friend of Marshall's and owed his rapid advancement during World War II to the General. Eisenhower appeared to be repudiating McCarthy at an August press conference in Denver when he said he had "no patience with anyone who can find in his [Marshall's] record of service for this country anything to criticize." In an October campaign appearance in McCarthy's home state, he planned to denounce accusations of disloyalty against Marshall as well as endorse the struggle against internal subversion. However, under pressure from the Wisconsin Senator, Wisconsin Gov. Walter Kohler, who said that an attack on McCarthy would split the state organization, and others, the statement on Marshall was omitted from the candidate's speech. Without this section the address appeared to be an endorsement of McCarthy and his methods. The deletion was widely publicized and interpreted as a surrender to pressure from McCarthy and his supporters.

Campaigning for Eisenhower, McCarthy climaxed his efforts to link Democratic presidential candidate Adlai E. Stevenson [q.v.] with the allegedly Communist-influenced Roosevelt and Truman Administrations in an Oct. 27 television address. He referred to Stevenson as "Alger-I mean Adlai" to suggest a tie between him and convicted perjurer Alger Hiss. McCarthy also stated that if he had a club he might be able to make Stevenson a patriotic American.

Meanwhile, the Republican National Committee used McCarthy as much as possible in campaigns throughout the country. The defeat of Benton, Democratic Majority Leader Ernest W. McFarland (D, Ariz.) and other Democrats against whom McCarthy campaigned enhanced his political status. Largely ignored was the fact that while Eisenhower carried Wisconsin by over 350,000 votes, McCarthy won reelection by less than 140,000 votes and ran behind all other statewide candidates.

Shortly after the 1952 elections McCarthy indicated that he would cooperate with the Administration and concentrate on investigations of graft and corruption rather than Communist influence in government. He chose the chairmanship of the Government Operations Committee, a panel that traditionally did not investigate subversive activities, in the Republican-controlled 83rd Congress. After McCarthy made this decision Majority Leader Robert Taft (R, Ohio) [q.v.] stated, "We've got McCarthy where he can't do any harm."

McCarthy soon made it clear that he would not be shunted aside and would continue his sensational investigations. His choice of committee chairmanship proved no obstacle. He made himself chairman of the Government Operations panel's Permanent Investigations Subcommittee and used it as a forum for his accusations.

McCarthy's first sallies against the Eisenhower Administration, however, were not launched from the subcommittee. In January 1953 McCarthy joined Republican conservatives who criticized President Eisenhower's nominations of Gen. Walter Bedell Smith [q.v.] as undersecretary of state and James B. Conant [q.v.] as U.S. high commissioner to Germany. In March he backed Sen. Styles Bridges (R, N.H.) [q.v.] and Pat McCarran (D, Nev.) [q.v.], who were leading the more serious opposition to the nomination of Charles E. Bohlen [q.v.] as ambassador to the Soviet Union.

Bohlen had served in the State Department under Roosevelt and Truman, and McCarthy questioned his loyalty. When Secretary of State John Foster Dulles [*q.v.*] said there was "no substantial evidence" for doubting Bohlen's patriotism, McCarthy called Dulles a liar.

After a protracted dispute Bohlen's nomination was confirmed. However the Administration did not want further confrontations with the Wisconsin Senator for fear they would cause a Republican split that would make it impossible for the President to pass his legislative program. Some of the President's advisers urged him to repudiate McCarthy, but Vice President Nixon and others who advocated a conciliatory approach prevailed. Eisenhower heartily disliked McCarthy but reportedly said on several occasions that he would not "get in the gutter" with him. The appointment of Scott McLeod [*q.v.*], a close friend of McCarthy's, as chief security officer for the State Department demonstrated the White House's disposition to work with the Senator.

In late March 1953 McCarthy announced that he had negotiated an agreement with a group of Greek shipowners in which they had promised to halt trade with Communist China and North Korea. On March 31 Mutual Security Director Harold Stassen [*q.v.*] denounced McCarthy for "undermining" the Administration's conduct of foreign affairs. The next day at a press conference, Eisenhower indicated that Stassen might have meant "infringed" rather than "undermined," and Stassen accepted this interpretation of his meaning.

The Administration's retreat from confrontation with McCarthy on this and many other matters made other Republicans unwilling to challenge the Senator. Democrats still feared that attacks on McCarthy would simply provide more ammunition for those trying to link them to Communism and subversion. They preferred to regard McCarthy as, in the words of Senate Minority Leader Lyndon B. Johnson (D, Tex.) [*q.v.*] "a Republican problem."

In February McCarthy began to use his subcommittee for a full-scale attack on alleged subversives in the executive branch.

He suggested that Voice of America (VOA) broadcasts had been canceled and that transmitters had been improperly located in order to aid the Communist cause. He also charged that the VOA's director of religious programming was an atheist.

In April the panel investigated the State Department's overseas libraries to determine whether they had any books by subversives on their shelves. McCarthy sent the subcommittee's chief counsel, Roy M. Cohn [*q.v.*], and the panel's chief consultant, G. David Schine [*q.v.*], on a tour of the Department's European libraries. Meanwhile, he called before the subcommittee allegedly leftist writers whose works were in the libraries. When *New York Post* editor James Wechsler quoted articles from Communist publications denouncing him to prove he was not a Communist, McCarthy asked him if he had written the articles.

The State Department panicked, and it ordered the libraries to remove material written by "Communists, fellow-travelers, et cetera. . . ." Since no one knew what "et cetera" meant, books well beyond any reasonable definition of Communist propaganda were discarded. Some books were burned.

In a June address at Dartmouth College, President Eisenhower admonished students, "Don't join the book burners," and he urged them not to be afraid to read any book. But at a press conference two days later, he backed down, refusing to attack McCarthy by name, expressing his opposition to the use of government funds to promote Communist propaganda and stating that he could approve the burning of books trying to convert people to Communism.

McCarthy suffered an embarrassment after he hired J.B. Matthews [*q.v.*], an ex-radical who had moved to the far right, as executive director of the Investigations Subcommittee's staff on June 22, 1953. At about the same time an article by Matthews appeared in the July issue of the *American Mercury*. It charged that "the largest single group supporting the Communist apparatus in the United States today is composed of Protestant clergymen." Sen. John McClellan (D, Ark.) [*q.v.*], the ranking minority member on the subcommittee, and the other Democratic members on the panel demanded that Matthews be fired. McCarthy refused, but a storm of protest resulted in Matthew's removal. The White House gained credit for the dismissal by releasing a presidential statement on July 9 denouncing Matthews before McCarthy announced the executive director's resignation later in the day. As a result of the affair, the Democratic subcommittee members began a boycott of the panel to protest the refusal of the chairman and the Republican majority to give the minority a voice in the hiring and firing of staff.

After the Matthews episode McCarthy demonstrated his ability to rebound from adversity. On the day after Matthews's resignation, he announced plans to investigate the Central Intelligence Agency and subpoena its director, Allen Dulles [q.v.]. McCarthy never conducted such an investigation, but the announcement made headlines and diverted attention from his setback.

In September McCarthy began an investigation of the Army and Defense Department. In the search for continuous publicity, he became increasingly frenetic. For a few days in early September, he investigated civilian Army personnel and then quickly moved into a probe of an allegedly pro-Communist Army intelligence document. In October McCarthy turned to an examination of civilian scientists working at the Army Signal Corps Engineering Laboratories at Fort Monmouth, N.J. The following month he briefly dealt with alleged subversion and espionage in defense plants and in December returned to the Fort Monmouth probe.

McCarthy's investigations generally produced sensational revelations based on either slim or questionable evidence or upon information uncovered years before and known to the FBI or other investigative agencies. The probes were often held in executive session, with McCarthy frequently dashing out of the hearing room to inform assembled reporters that he was uncovering spy rings or other subversive activities that were never heard of again. In that way he maintained his association with the issue of domestic subversion.

The mere mention of a government employe's name in the subcommittee's hearings could lead to his firing or forced resignation. If the individual did not work for the government, he still might lose his job and suffer social ostracism. The fear of domestic Communism and the attendant assault upon suspected left-wing dissidents had preceded McCarthy. But his ability to keep the issue of the internal Communist menace before the public helped perpetuate and proliferate such practices as the firing and blacklisting of suspected subversives in the private sector, the passage of anti-subversive legislation on the national and state levels and the establishment of state loyalty boards. McCarthy created a political climate in which even those who opposed his methods accepted (or at least did not challenge) his assumption of a Communist threat from within. They tried to outdo each other in proving their opposition to subversion by supporting the suppression of alleged leftists.

Towards the end of 1953 it seemed increasingly apparent that McCarthy was on a collision course with the Administration. In November Attorney General Herbert Brownell [q.v.] charged that former President Truman had appointed Harry Dexter White executive director of the International Monetary Fund knowing that White had been a Soviet espionage agent. Truman replied that Brownell had "embraced McCarthyism" (an already-popular term that would eventually enter the dictionary meaning the public leveling of unsubstantiated charges). On Nov. 24 McCarthy appeared on television ostensibly to rebut Truman, but he used the occasion to attack the Eisenhower Administration. McCarthy stated that the President had not acted decisively to eliminate subversives from government employment and that America had been "reduced to a state of whining, whimpering appeasement." Responding to a recent statement by Eisenhower that the issue of Communism would not be a factor in the 1954 elections, the Senator said, "The raw, harsh, unpleasant fact is that Communism is an issue and will be an issue in 1954."

In December 1953 McCarthy, perhaps concerned over a possible battle at the beginning of the second session of the 83rd Congress over his subcommittee's appropriations, again indicated that his investigatory activities might veer away from the Communist controversy. The following month, after he agreed to give up his exclusive authority to hire and fire the subcommittee staff and to allow the Democratic minority to hire a staff counsel and clerical help, the Democrats ended their boycott of the panel.

Later in the month McCarthy uncovered a new case of alleged subversion that ultimately caused a major confrontation with the Army and led to his downfall. Irving Peress [q.v.], a member of the left-wing American Labor Party, was an Army dentist at Camp Kilmer, N.J. In November 1953 he had been automatically promoted to major under the Doctor Draft Law, although he had claimed the Fifth Amendment in refusing to answer questions on loyalty certification forms. During the same month, however, the Pentagon bureaucracy, discovering his background, ordered him discharged as soon as possible.

McCarthy learned of the matter in December 1953, and Peress was subpoenaed to testify before the Investigations Subcommittee. He appeared at an executive session on Jan. 30, 1954, before his discharge, and took the Fifth Amendment in refusing to answer questions about his politics. On Feb. 1 McCarthy demanded that Peress be court-martialed, but immediately afterward the Army gave him an honorable discharge.

On Feb. 18 McCarthy called the commanding officer of Camp Kilmer, Gen. Ralph W. Zwicker [q.v.], before the subcommittee. After Zwicker refused to give the panel the names of all officers involved in granting Peress his discharge, McCarthy treated the General with withering contempt, describing him as "not fit to wear that uniform" and as not having "the brains of a five-year old." Secretary of the Army Robert T. Stevens [q.v.] quickly announced that he would not permit Zwicker, to appear before the subcommittee again because "I cannot permit loyal officers of our Armed Forces to be subjected to such unwarranted treatment."

On Feb. 24 Stevens met with McCarthy and the other Republicans on the subcommittee in a peacemaking effort. A "memorandum of understanding" read by panel member Sen. Karl Mundt (R, S.D.) [q.v.] after the conference made it clear that Stevens had given in to almost all of McCarthy's demands. The next day McCarthy allegedly told a reporter that Stevens could not have surrendered "more abjectly if he had got down on his knees."

In humiliating Stevens McCarthy reached the apex of his career. But the Senator's very success in dealing with the Secretary led to his downfall. By demonstrating his power to discredit even an established and respected institution such as the Army, he convinced influential people both within and without the Administration, conservatives as well as liberals, that a counterattack was necessary. On March 9 Edward R. Murrow [q.v.] used his "See It Now" television program as a vehicle for denouncing the Senator's methods. On the same day Sen. Ralph Flanders (R, Vt.) [q.v.] attacked McCarthy in a radio broadcast, ridiculing the discrepancy between his shrill statements and his meager achievements. Later in the day President Eisenhower wrote Flanders a letter of praise for his remarks. On March 13 Vice President Nixon, speaking on behalf of the Administration, stated that "men who have in the past done effective work exposing Communism in this country have, by reckless talk and questionable methods, made themselves the issue, rather than the cause they believe in so deeply."

On March 11 the Army itself responded to McCarthy by making charges of its own. It alleged that McCarthy and Roy Cohn were seeking preferential treatment for G. David Schine, who had been drafted into the Army the previous year. The next day McCarthy answered, accusing the Army of holding the former aide as a hostage to blackmail him into ending his investigation of Communism in the Armed Forces.

Additional charges and countercharges followed until even McCarthy's staunchest supporters agreed that an investigation was necessary. McCarthy's own subcommittee, over the opposition of its Democratic members, voted to probe the matter. McCarthy temporarily gave up his seat on the panel. Subcommittee member Karl Mundt acted as chairman, and Sen. Henry Dworshak (R, Ida.) [*q.v.*] filled McCarthy's seat. Since charges had been leveled at Cohn, Ray Jenkins replaced him as subcommittee counsel. The Army chose Joseph Welch [*q.v.*] as its attorney.

The Senate's Democrats, taking their cue from Minority Leader Johnson, successfully insisted upon having the hearings televised, while McCarthy won the right to cross-examine witnesses (with the Army receiving the same right). These conditions proved crucial because they enabled an estimated 50 million American families to evaluate McCarthy's conduct.

The investigation, popularly known as the Army-McCarthy hearings, opened on April 22, 1954. It was widely agreed that McCarthy's public image suffered in the course of the probe. Dominating the proceedings through his cross-examinations and his persistent interventions on points of order, he often appeared to be bullying witnesses. He asked the Army's first witness, Gen. Miles Reber, if he knew that his brother, Samuel Reber, former deputy high commissioner in Germany, had been forced to resign as a security risk. Then McCarthy tried to prevent the General from denying the false accusation against his brother. Later in the hearings he directed abusive comments towards Sen. Stuart Symington (D, Mo.) [*q.v.*], one of the subcommittee Democrats.

The credibility of McCarthy and his staff was damaged by Jenkins's introduction in late April of a photo of Schine and Stevens together. It apparently was intended to suggest that Stevens was being friendly towards Shine in the hope that the Investigations Subcommittee would drop its Army probe. However, Welch produced an enlargement of the same photo to show that the one presented to the subcommittee had been cropped to exclude other individuals. The Army's counsel traced the cropping to McCarthy's staff.

The emotional climax of the hearings oc-

curred on June 9, when McCarthy interrupted Welch's cross-examination of Cohn to charge that Frederick Fisher, a member of Welch's firm, had been a member of the National Lawyer's Guild, an allegedly pro-Communist organization. Welch, who seemed close to tears, explained that Fisher had left the Guild many years before and had become a Republican. He declared, "Until this moment I think I never really gauged your cruelty or your recklessness." When McCarthy attempted to continue discussing the matter, Welch said, "Have you no sense of decency, sir, at long last?" He then left the room to loud applause from the spectators at the hearing. Some observers felt that this dramatic episode damaged McCarthy more than anything he had done previously and that it represented a turning point in the Senator's career.

When the hearings ended on June 17, McCarthy had lost little of his hard-core support. However, many moderates who had previously supported or at least not objected to the Senator's methods now turned against him. An increasing number of newspapers openly assailed him, and in Wisconsin a recall movement against McCarthy garnered 400,000 petition signatures between March and June.

Roy Cohn, under intense pressure from Republicans, resigned as subcommittee counsel on July 19. At the end of August both Republicans and Democrats on the Army-McCarthy panel issued reports criticizing Cohn for his efforts to help Schine, although only the Democrats charged that McCarthy was implicated in Cohn's activities. By that time, however, the Senate was preoccupied with a move to censure McCarthy.

Despite the damage inflicted upon the Wisconsin Senator by the Army-McCarthy hearings, most members of the upper house wanted to avoid a confrontation with a politician whose skills had enabled him to recover from adversity in the past. However, to those wishing to act, the time seemed favorable. Flanders, who had decided not to seek reelection, forced the issue. On June 11 he introduced a resolution to remove McCarthy from his committee chairmanships unless he answered questions raised about his finances in the January 1953 Hennings report.

With a Republican taking the initiative, most Democrats were willing to follow, but Southern Democrats opposed the form of the resolution as threatening the seniority system. On July 30 Flanders introduced a new resolution calling for McCarthy's censure for conduct unbecoming a member of the Senate. Shortly afterwards Flanders, Sen. J. William Fulbright (D, Ark.) [q.v.] and Sen. Wayne Morse (I, Ore.) [q.v.] introduced specific charges in the form of amendments to the resolution. On Aug. 2 the resolution was referred to a six-member Select Committee. Carefully chosen by the leaders of both parties (no senator volunteered for the assignment), all the members were moderate conservatives from the South and the West (where the McCarthy issue had aroused less emotion than elsewhere) who had not taken strong stands either for or against McCarthy.

They adopted a set of rules designed to minimize disruption by McCarthy. Only firsthand testimony was accepted, eliminating Flanders, Fulbright and Morse as witnesses and reducing the chances of dramatic personal confrontations. Either McCarthy or his lawyer, but not both, were allowed to conduct cross-examinations. Since much of the evidence to be introduced was technical and legal and McCarthy was not a particularly good lawyer, his opportunity to make himself the center of attention was reduced. Furthermore, no television cameras were allowed in the hearing room. "In short," wrote Robert Griffith, "the Committee denied McCarthy all the familiar props for his earlier performances." The Committee chairman, Sen. Arthur Watkins (R, Utah) [q.v.], was a stern Mormon determined to carry on orderly proceedings. From the beginning of the hearings on Aug. 31 until their conclusion on Sept. 13, Watkins maintained firm control over McCarthy, gaveling him to order when he attempted to interject himself into the proceedings in defiance of the panel's rules of procedure.

The Committee faced two problems: defining specific censurable acts and censuring McCarthy without weakening the prerogatives of the Senate. On Sept. 27 the Com-

mittee released a unanimous report recommending censure on two counts. The first was for his refusal to appear before the Subcommittee on Privileges and Elections in 1952. The second was for his conduct towards Gen. Zwicker while chairman of the Investigations Subcommittee in February 1954.

Neither Republicans nor Democrats wanted to deal with the matter until after the November elections, and debate was postponed. In contrast to the 1950 and 1952 campaigns, McCarthy was not a sought-after Republican speaker. The reelection of almost all liberal Democratic incumbents reinforced the growing impression that the Senator was in decline.

The Watkins Committee's report was officially filed with the Senate on Nov. 8. Two days later, as debate on the report began, McCarthy inserted in the Congressional Record a speech in which he said the Communist Party had "extended its tentacles to . . . the United States Senate [and] has made a Committee of the Senate its unwitting handmaiden." In the changing political climate, strident attacks merely solidified the opposition to him. On Nov. 11 Sen. Francis Case (R, S.D.), a member of the Watkins panel, proposed that McCarthy avoid censure by apologizing for his conduct; the Wisconsin Senator rejected this and subsequent compromise plans. After Case announced two days later that he would not vote for censure on the count involving McCarthy's abuse of Zwicker, it was replaced by a count charging contempt and abuse of the Watkins Committee itself.

On Dec. 2 the Senate voted to condemn on both counts by a vote of 67 to 22. All Democrats present supported censure, while Republicans divided evenly. McCarthy reacted on Dec. 7 with a stinging denunciation of Eisenhower in which he said he had been wrong in believing the President would vigorously fight Communism and apologized for having supported the General in 1952. Even his staunchest supporters were appalled by the attack, and thenceforth McCarthy was beyond the political pale.

During his remaining two-and-a-half years in the Senate, McCarthy continued to seek public attention as a fighter against internal subversion. In March 1955, for example, he charged that Secretary of State Dulles had hired 150 men to censor the records of the 1945 Yalta Conference. The following year he urged Republicans to choose FBI Director J. Edgar Hoover [q.v.] as their presidential candidate. However, McCarthy no longer carried any political weight, and his accusations and suggestions were ignored.

After his censure McCarthy realized that his power and ability to attract the attention he craved were gone. The effect on his public behavior was substantial. On the Senate floor the intensity and forcefulness of his personality gave way to listlessness. Appointed a member of the Select Committee on Investigations of Improper Activities in Labor or Management Field in January 1957, McCarthy wandered in and out of hearings and asked unfocused repetitive questions. His fellow-Committee members watched his performance with barely concealed contempt.

McCarthy's health deteriorated as his career collapsed. Always a heavy drinker, he reportedly became an alcoholic after his condemnation. He entered the Bethesda Naval Hospital with increasing frequency. By the autumn of 1956 he had lost 40 pounds. In April 1957 McCarthy entered the hospital for the last time. He died on May 2, 1957 of an acute hepatic infection, according to Bethesda officials. Persons claiming to have inside information said the cause of death was cirrhosis of the liver.

The investigation of internal Communist subversion did not end with McCarthy's downfall. The Wisconsin Senator was condemned for exceeding the bounds of decency and violating the Senate's code of ethics. The fundamental assumptions behind his activity—that, in the words of Robert Griffith, "the Communist Party constituted a real and immediate threat to the nation's security and that the way to meet this threat was through repression"—went unchallenged. The Senate Internal Security Subcommittee and the House Un-American Acitivities Committee continued to investigate not only public agencies but private institutions such as the news media. Loy-

alty-security programs and blacklisting continued.

However, the easing of cold war tensions beginning in the late 1950s gradually altered the climate of fear that prevailed during the decade after World War II. By the end of the 1960s, McCarthy had few defenders aside from extreme right-wing ideologues. When in 1973 supporters of President Nixon, a former sympathizer of the Wisconsin Senator, attacked the Senate Watergate Committee for using tactics similar to McCarthy's, it was clear that McCarthyism had come to mean the leveling of any kind of unfair political charges and that the repudiation of McCarthy cut across almost the entire political spectrum.

[MLL]

For further information:
William F. Buckley, Jr., and L. Brent Bozell, *McCarthy and His Enemies: The Record and Its Meaning* (Chicago, 1954).
Roberta Feuerlicht, *Joe McCarthy and McCarthyism: The Hate That Haunts America* (New York, 1972).
Robert Goldston, *The American Nightmare: Senator Joseph R. McCarthy and the Politics of Hate* (Indianapolis, 1973).
Robert Griffith, *The Politics of Fear: Joseph R. McCarthy and the Senate* (Lexington, Ky., 1970).
Richard Rovere, *Senator Joe McCarthy* (New York, 1959).

McCLELLAN, JOHN L(ITTLE)
b. Feb. 25, 1896; Sheridan, Ark.
Democratic Senator, Ark., 1943- .
Chairman, Government Operations Committee, 1949-53, 1955-72;
Chairman, Select Committee on Improper Activities in the Labor or Management Field, 1957-60.

The son of a country lawyer, John McClellan was born on a farm in southern Arkansas. Although he never attended college, McClellan studied law in his father's office and was admitted to the bar in 1913 at the age of 17. He served as city attorney of Malvern, Ark., from 1920 to 1926 and as prosecuting attorney for the state's seventh judicial district from 1927 to 1930. In 1934 McClellan won election to the U.S. House of Representatives, where he supported most New Deal policies. Four years later he lost the Democratic senatorial primary but won election to the upper house in 1942.

During the postwar years McClellan voted as a conservative, opposing civil rights legislation and most Fair Deal programs, while supporting the Republican-sponsored Taft-Hartley Act in 1947. However he backed some liberal conservation and social welfare measures. In 1949 he was appointed to the powerful Appropriations Committee and assumed the chairmanship of the Expenditures in the Executive Departments Committee, which became the Government Operations Committee in 1952. [See TRUMAN Volume]

When the Republicans took control of the Senate in January 1953, McClellan was replaced as Government Operations Committee chairman by Sen. Joseph McCarthy (R, Wisc.) [q.v.]. During the next two years he came to national attention as the ranking minority member of the Committee's Permanent Investigations Subcommittee, also chaired by McCarthy. While not opposed to the panel's numerous investigations of alleged Communist infiltration of government agencies, Sen. McClellan occasionally took vigorous exception to what he charged were the Wisconsin Republican's undemocratic methods.

In July 1953 a controversy arose on the panel over a magazine article by subcommittee staff director J.B. Matthews [q.v.] who alleged there were widespread pro-Communist sympathies among the American Protestant clergy. McClellan demanded that Matthews be fired. McCarthy refused at first, then agreed. After subcommittee Republicans adopted a face-saving motion giving the chairman sole power to hire and fire staff personnel, however, McClellan first led the panel's Democrats in an unprecedented walkout and then threatened to help block renewal of the unit's Senate authorization for the following year. In January 1954, after McCarthy agreed to relinquish exclusive authority over staff appointments and to allow the minority to

hire its own counsel the Democrats returned to the panel. In March McClellan helped overcome Republican resistance to television coverage of the Army-McCarthy hearings, but he took little part in the proceedings themselves.

With renewed Democratic control of the Senate in January 1955, McClellan regained the chairmanship of the Government Operations Committee and named Robert F. Kennedy [q.v.] chief counsel of the Investigations Subcommittee. Under McClellan's direction the panel launched a series of probes into charges of graft and corruption in the handling of government contracts for military supplies. Hearings on the business connections of Air Force Secretary Harold E. Talbott [q.v.] and other Defense Department officials, conducted in July 1955, revealed that Talbott had continued as a partner in a New York industrial engineering firm after taking his Pentagon post. As a result of this revelation, Talbott resigned in August.

In March 1956 McClellan was appointed chairman of the Special Committee to Investigate Political Activities, Lobbying and Campaign Contributions. The Senate established the special panel in the wake of disclosures by Sen. Francis Case (R, S.D.) that he had rejected a $2,500 campaign contribution from a lobbyist interested in the natural gas bill. After hearings in May, in which lobbyists for various businesses and labor unions testified on their efforts to influence senators, the Committee recommended new legislation to regulate lobbying and campaign financing by requiring all political committtees to report expenditures and limit individual campaign contributions to $15,000 a year. McClellan sponsored a bill containing these proposals. However, strong opposition from the U.S. Chamber of Commerce, the National Association of Manufacturers and other business groups prevented the measure from ever reaching the Senate floor.

The subcommittee's continued probing of Defense Department procurement policies in 1956 revealed the involvement of leading East Coast gangsters in the manufacturing and trucking of military uniforms. Early in January 1957 the panel released its findings on collusion between the garment industry and racketeers in the International Brotherhood of Teamsters. The report prompted demands for a major investigation of corruption in labor-management relations. Jurisdiction over the probe was disputed, however, between the Investigations Subcommittee and the Labor and Public Welfare Committee's Labor Subcommittee. Management groups exerted pressure against placing the liberal-dominated labor panel in charge of the inquiry. Unions, on the other hand, feared turning it over to McClellan's unit, whose membership had changed little since the days of McCarthy's domination. Finally, on Jan. 30 the Senate set up a compromise Select Committee on Improper Activities in the Labor or Management Field, composed of four members from each Party and from each of the two subcommittees, with McClellan as chairman and Robert Kennedy as chief counsel.

Holding hearings in several cities over the next two-and-a-half years, the McClellan Committee, as it was known, investigated charges of theft, embezzlement and misuse of union funds; rigging of union elections; "sweetheart" contracts unfavorable to workers for which union officials were rewarded by management; and, violence and threats by union officials to enforce demands against employers and their own rank-and-file. Although elaborate steps were taken initially to maintain impartiality between labor and management, the Committee's spotlight soon focused on alleged corruption in unions alone and especially in the Teamsters union.

Hearings in early 1957 featured Teamster President Dave Beck [q.v.], who repeatedly pleaded the Fifth Amendment in response to charges that he had taken more than $30,000 in union funds to pay for personal gifts and real estate. Indicted for tax fraud and other crimes and suspended from the AFL-CIO Executive Council, Beck resigned his Teamster post. He was succeeded in October by James Hoffa [q.v.], who was in turn brought before the McClellan Committee and confronted with allegations that he was deeply involved with underworld figures. Late in 1957 the Committee also probed the United Textile Workers,

Bakers and Confectioners and some smaller unions. As a result of the panel's findings the Teamsters, the bakery and confectioners union and the laundry workers union were expelled from the AFL-CIO in December.

While hearings continued the Committee issued its first interim report on March 24, 1958. Describing Hoffa as a national menace running a "hoodlum empire," the panel recommended legislation to regulate pension, health and welfare funds, ensure union democracy, and curb the activities of middlemen in labor-management disputes. It also suggested clarifying the so-called no man's land in labor relations (disputes which were not included in the jurisdiction of the National Labor Relations Board, but which were nevertheless preempted by federal jurisdiction from being handled by state courts). As a result, in April the Labor Subcommittee, under the chairmanship of Sen. John F. Kennedy (D, Mass) [q.v.], favorably reported a bill to provide for the public disclosure of pension and welfare funds financial data, which had been introduced in the previous session by Sen. Paul Douglas (D, Ill.) [q.v.]. In August the measure was passed by the Senate without a dissenting vote.

In June McClellan endorsed a second, broader labor reform measure which was put together by the Senate Democratic leadership in response to Republican demands for more comprehensive legislation. The measure, known as the Kennedy-Ives bill, included restrictions on the authority of national and international unions to place locals under trusteeship, conditions and standards for election of union officers, a code of ethical practices, and amendments to the Taft-Hartley Act favored by building trades unions. Endorsed by the AFL-CIO and passed by the Senate in June, the measure subsequently died in the House.

Early in 1959 Sens. John F. Kennedy and Sam Ervin (D, N.C.) [q.v.], with the backing of the Democratic leadership, introduced a new measure containing the same relatively moderate reform proposals as the previous year's Kennedy-Ives legislation. Heavily out-numbered in the upper house, Republicans abandoned plans to introduce a bill of their own and instead cast themselves in the role of a group interested in "strengthening" the Kennedy-Ervin measure to meet the abuses highlighted by the McClellan probe. Sen. McClellan's personal prestige, plus his command of a large block of Southern Democratic votes, made him the key to the success of this strategy for establishing broader regulation of union activities.

When debate began in April, McClellan first demanded the elimination from the bill of the Taft-Hartley changes desired by the AFL-CIO. Kennedy refused, thereby prompting Ervin to withdraw his sponsorship and releasing a number of Southerners from their obligation to support the measure. Then on April 22, after an emotional two-hour speech on the necessity of labor reform, McClellan introduced a "bill of rights" amendment aimed at guaranteeing voting, speaking, litigation and other rights for union members. Kennedy and other liberals opposed the measure as too great an interference in the internal affairs of the labor movement. Later that same day the amendment was unexpectedly passed by one vote.

With the addition of McClellan's amendment the bill was no longer acceptable to Kennedy. The AFL-CIO also withdrew its support of the legislation, arguing that the bill of rights would cripple unions with procedural snares. With McClellan's approval the amendment was subsequently modified to qualify the language in the equal rights section and to eliminate a provision permitting the Secretary of Labor to seek federal court injunctions against union officers, which Southerners feared as a possible precedent for future civil rights legislation. On April 25 the final bill was passed by the Senate and sent to the House.

The initial vote on the bill of rights proved a turning point in the legislative battle. Only when the House began to write its own bill in the summer of 1959 did it become clear that the liberals on the Senate Labor Subcommittee had lost control of labor reform legislation to McClellan and the conservative coalition that he now led. On August 15 the House passed a con-

servative measure sponsored by Reps. Philip Landrum (D, Ga.) [q.v.] and Robert Griffin (R, Mich.) [q.v.]. Signed into law in September, the Landrum-Griffin Act featured several of McClellan's recommendations that the Senate had earlier rejected as amendments to the Kennedy bill. These included stronger prohibitions against secondary boycotts by unions, curbs on picketing rights and provisions for state takeover of "no-man's-land" labor disputes.

During the 1960s McClellan continued to lead Senate investigations. In 1963 he headed probes of organized crime, the awarding of Defense Department contracts and the relationship between the Agriculture Department and Texas financier Billie Sol Estes. McClellan presided over several subsequent inquiries into areas such as missile procurement policies and race-related riots. In 1972, after the death of Sen. Allen J. Ellender (D, La.) [q.v.], chairman of the Appropriations Committee, McClellan gave up his Government Operations post to become head of the appropriations panel. [See KENNEDY, JOHNSON, NIXON/FORD Volumes]

[TLH]

For further information:
David A. Frier, *Conflict of Interest in the Eisenhower Administration* (Ames, Iowa, 1969).
Alan K. McAdams, *Power and Politics in Labor Legislation* (New York, 1964).
Walter Sheridan, *The Fall and Rise of Jimmy Hoffa* (New York, 1972).
Charles Morrow Wilson, "Corruption, The Committee— and Senator McClellan," *Reader's Digest* (June, 1959), pp. 85-90.

McCLOY, JOHN J(AY)
b. March 31, 1895; Philadelphia, Pa.
Chairman of the Board, Chase National Bank, 1953-55; Chairman, Chase Manhattan Bank, 1955-60.

John McCloy was raised by his mother in Philadelphia. He attended a Quaker boarding school and Amherst College, entering Harvard law school in 1916. Following service in the Army during World War I, he received his law degree in 1921. For the next two decades McCloy practiced law with prestigious New York law firms. He spent 10 years on the famous Black Tom case, involving a 1916 explosion at a munitions plant in Hoboken, N.J. By establishing that the blast was the work of German saboteurs. McCloy helped win a $50 million award for his side in 1939.

Having become an expert on German espionage, McCloy joined the War Department in 1940 at the request of Secretary of War Henry Stimson. From 1941 to 1945 he served as assistant secretary of war, playing a key role in the enactment of the Lend-Lease Act, the internment of Japanese-Americans in the West and, in the War's later stages, the administration of occupied areas. After World War II McCloy practiced law again until 1947, when he returned to government service as president of the World Bank. In 1949 President Truman appointed him U.S. high commissioner for Germany, a position in which he worked to restore the German economy to orderly operation and supervised the transition of West Germany from an occupied zone to a sovereign state. [See TRUMAN Volume]

In January 1953 McCloy became chairman of the Chase National Bank in New York. His main task was to bring about the proposed merger between Chase and the Bank of Manhattan, a union stymied by a requirement in the latter's charter that such a change have the approval of every stockholder. McCloy sidestepped this legal impediment by having Chase technically absorbed by the smaller Bank of Manhattan, rather than the reverse as his predecessors had desired. The merger took place in March 1955. The new Chase Manhattan Bank, with McCloy as chairman, was the second largest commercial bank in the United States.

In February 1954 McCloy became a target of Sen. Joseph R. McCarthy's (R, Wisc.) [q.v.] crusade against domestic subversion. As assistant secretary of war McCloy had helped draft a memorandum directing commanders to disregard the political views of soldiers under their command "unless there is a specific finding that the individual involved has a loyalty to the Communist Party as an organization that overrides his loyalty to the United States." McCarthy charged that McCloy had ordered the destruction of all Army intelligence files on Communists. McCloy denounced the accusation as "absolutely false," and McCarthy retracted it two days later. The Wisconsin Senator still maintained that McCloy had been a "moving force" for commissioning Communists because of his directive not to discriminate against them.

Besides his position with Chase Manhattan, McCloy exerted a strong if inestimable influence on private and public policy through membership in a host of elite institutions. During the 1950s he served as chairman of the Ford Foundation and chairman of the Council of Foreign Relations. He was also a director of several major corporations, including the United Fruit Co., the American Telephone & Telegraph Co., the Dreyfus Corp. and the Westinghouse Electric Corp. The journalist Richard Rovere [q.v.] wryly referred to McCloy as the "chairman of the Establishment."

McCloy continued to undertake high-level diplomatic tasks on an *ad hoc* basis for Presidents Eisenhower, Kennedy and Johnson and other world leaders. In 1956-57 he went to Egypt as United Nations Secretary General Dag Hammarskjold's special financial adviser for the Suez crisis. He served Presidents Eisenhower and Kennedy as a special adviser on disarmament and helped draft the legislation creating the U.S. Arms Control and Disarmament Agency in 1961. He served as President Johnson's special envoy to the 1966 mutual defense talks between the U.S., Great Britain and West Germany.

In 1968 McCloy became a member of the Senior Advisory Group on Vietnam, convened to consider the military's request that over 200,000 additional troops be sent to Vietnam. McCloy was among those men who were dissatisfied with the existing policy but were reluctant to declare for a dramatic change.

In 1974 a Senate investigation of the petroleum industry revealed that since 1961 McCloy had been in the forefront of attempts to unite U.S. oil companies in their negotiations with the producing nations. After retiring from Chase Manhattan in December 1960, McCloy had returned to the law firm of Milbank, Tweed, Hope & Hadley. [See KENNEDY, JOHNSON Volumes]

[TO]

McCONE, JOHN A(LEX)
b. Jan. 4, 1902: San Francisco, Calif.
Director, Atomic Energy Commission, July 1958-January 1961.

McCone graduated from the University of California College of Engineering at Berkeley in 1922. Thereafter, he worked as a riveter and boilermaker for the Llewellyn Iron Works; he became construction manager in the late-1920s and in 1933 was appointed executive vice president and director. As head of the California Shipbuilding Corp. during World War II, he directed the construction of almost 500 ships. After the War McCone served as a special deputy to Secretary of Defense James V. Forrestal and as undersecretary of the Air Force, in which capacity he pressed for a major expansion of American air power. McCone returned to private business in 1953.

In June 1958 President Dwight D. Eisenhower chose McCone to head the Atomic Energy Commission (AEC); he was confirmed the following month. McCone led the agency during a period in which there was a growing demand to end nuclear testing because of the danger of fallout. Although the Director initially opposed a nuclear test ban treaty with the Soviet Union because he believed the U.S. needed more time for research, by 1959 he supported Eisenhower's one-year moratorium on testing. The same year McCone attended talks with the Soviets in Geneva on controlling nuclear energy. This discussion produced no agreement because of Soviet-American differences over on-site inspection and a ban on underground testing.

McCone supported the Administration's efforts to expand international research on the peaceful uses of atomic energy. He backed Eisenhower's plan to disseminate information on nuclear reactors to North Atlantic Treaty Organization powers. In 1958 he signed a treaty between the U.S. and West Germany, France, Italy, Belgium, Luxembourg and the Netherlands providing an $135 million American loan and a 20 year supply of uranium to fuel allied reactors. The agreement also called for an $100 million American-European research effort on nuclear power. A year later McCone helped formulate a pact with the Soviet Union establishing a joint U.S.-USSR nuclear research program. This included the exchange of scientists and research data on high energy physics, nuclear power reactors and radioisotopes for medicine and industry.

During the last half of the decade, the AEC was criticized for suppressing information on the growth of radioactive fallout. In March 1959 Sen. Hubert H. Humphrey (D, Minn.) [q.v.] charged that the agency had been "playing down the dangers of radioactive fallout as it pursued its weapons program." He asserted that the data had been held back because it cast doubt on government statements on the danger of atomic weapons tests. The Senator said that it was "becoming apparent that the [AEC], . . . with its important and primary interest in the field of atomic weapons and power [was] not the best agency to conduct research on fallout and its effects on human health and heredity." McCone defended the Commission, denying that it had suppressed fallout information. He did, however, call on the National Academy of Sciences to arrange a government-wide review of the problem. In October 1960 the AEC reduced the maximum permissible radioactive dosage for workers in nuclear plants.

McCone resigned his AEC post in January 1961. Eleven months later President John F. Kennedy appointed him to head the Central Intelligence Agency (CIA). He resigned from the CIA in April 1965. During the latter part of the decade, he served on the government panel investigating the Watts riots and testified on urban violence before congressional committees. In 1968 he became chairman of the Hendry International Co. [See KENNEDY, JOHNSON Volumes]

[RSG]

McCORMACK, JOHN W(ILLIAM)
b. Dec. 21, 1891; Boston, Mass.
Democratic Representative, Mass.,
1928-71; House Majority Leader,
1940-47, 1949-53, 1955-62; House
Minority Whip, 1947-49, 1953-55.

McCormack, the son of a bricklayer,
grew up in South Boston. His father died
when he was 13, and John had to leave
school to support his family. He was a
newsboy, then an errand boy for a brokerage house and later an office boy in a law
firm. McCormack's income was supplemented by a "pauper's basket" from the welfare department.

While working for the law firm, McCormack studied for the state bar examinations,
which he passed when he was 21. He
began practicing law and in 1917-18 was a
member of the Massachusetts Constitutional Convention. McCormack served in
the state House of Representatives from
1920 to 1922 and in the state Senate from
1923 to 1926. In the latter year he lost a
Democratic congressional primary but was
elected to the U.S. House of Representatives the following year after his victorious
opponent died.

In the House McCormack impressed the
Democratic leadership, headed by Minority
Leader John Nance Garner (D, Tex.) and
his close ally, Rep. Sam Rayburn (D, Tex.)
[q.v.], with his undeviating obedience to
their wishes, his hard work and his poker-
playing ability. When the Democrats
gained control of Congress in 1933,
McCormack was placed on the powerful
Ways and Means Committee. In 1936 he
helped round up votes for Rayburn as
majority leader and succeeded to that post
when the Texas Representative became
Speaker of the House four years later.
McCormack was an ardent supporter of
both New Deal and Fair Deal domestic
programs. He was an internationalist before
World War II and a strong supporter of resistance to Communist expansion after the
War. [See TRUMAN Volume]

McCormack was a flamboyant speaker
who often antagonized colleagues by his
sarcasm. When the House formed itself into
a committee of the whole, Rayburn saw to
it that McCormack was chosen chairman. In
that post the Majority Leader excelled in
embarrassing Republican representatives,
but in person-to-person contact his manner
was far more engaging. His major functions
entailed behind-the-scenes work. As Rayburn's assistant he kept track of House Democrats to make sure they were available
for key votes, scheduled the order of debate and watched for concealed opposition strategy.

Although an ardent liberal, McCormack
believed that reasonable compromise was
essential for preserving party unity and did
not question Rayburn's moderate opposition
to Eisenhower Administration policies during the 1950s. Democratic representatives
of a more intellectual bent, such as Frank
Thompson (D, N.J.) [q.v.] and Richard
Bolling (D, Mo.), regarded McCormack as a
machine politician with little concern for
principles. McCormack returned their
scorn, viewing them as representatives
who, having derived their knowledge from
books rather than experience, had little
sense of political reality.

As minority whip from 1953 to 1955 and
majority leader during the remainder of the
Eisenhower Administration, McCormack
was a partisan spokesman for the Democratic opposition. In 1953 the Republican
controlled Congress voted to set a 20,000-
unit limit on new public housing construction
instead of the 75,000-unit limit recommended by former President Harry S.
Truman. McCormack charged that public
low cost housing was being destroyed by
the Republican Party. In 1955 he backed an
unsuccessful Democratic effort to provide
the individual taxpayer with a $20 income
tax credit. McCormack charged that the
Administration's omnibus tax revision bill of
the previous year had given considerable
reductions to large corporations but little
relief to most individual taxpayers. In 1959
he and Rayburn successfully introduced a
bill to extend by three months the period of
eligibility for unemployment compensation.
The following year McCormack circumvented the Rules Committee and brought
to the floor an area redevelopment bill by
invoking the rarely used Calendar Wednes-

day procedure, which permitted any chairman to call up a bill under a two-hour debate limit. However, the bill was vetoed by the President.

As a devout Catholic with close ties to the Church hierarchy, McCormack was fiercely anti-Communist. Declaring that Communism had the "mind of a world killer," in 1954 he backed the Communist Control Act, which denied the Communist Party legal standing. During the same year McCormack questioned the adequacy of the Administration's defense budget. In 1955 he urged an "overwhelming" vote for the Administration-proposed Formosa Resolution as a display of unity. Some Democrats objected that the Resolution gave the President excessively broad authority to defend Nationalist China against attacks from the Chinese mainland. However, McCormack stated that the "calculated risks" entailed in passage would be less than those that would stem from inaction. In 1960 he again backed increased defense spending.

Despite previous political conflicts with Sen. John F. Kennedy (D, Mass.) [q.v.], McCormack chaired the pro-Kennedy Massachusetts delegation to the 1960 Democratic National Convention. On the convention floor he helped overcome liberal opposition to Kennedy's selection of Senate Majority Leader Lyndon B. Johnson (D, Tex.) [q.v.] as his running mate by calling for voice-vote approval of Johnson as the Party's vice presidential nominee. This enabled the convention chairman to use his discretion in judging the vote.

McCormack almost always backed President Kennedy's programs, but in 1961 he broke with the President in supporting federal aid to parochial schools. In January 1962, after Rayburn died, McCormack was elected Speaker. After the assassination of President Kennedy, McCormack was first in line to succeed to the presidency. Some officeholders and observers believed he should have resigned the speakership because of his age and alleged lack of creative ideas and leadership ability.

During the mid and late 1960s McCormack found himself under increasing attack as being an ineffective leader. Liberals criticized him for his support of the Viet-

nam war. In 1969 his administrative assistant and a friend were connected to influence-peddling activities. In May 1970, four months after they were indicted. McCormack announced that he would not seek reelection. [See KENNEDY, JOHNSON, NIXON/FORD Volumes]

[MLL]

McDONALD, DAVID J(OHN)
b. Nov. 22, 1902: Pittsburgh, Pa.
President, United Steelworkers of America, 1952-65.

The son of a skilled Irish-Catholic steelworker, McDonald had intended to be an actor. He entered the labor movement in 1922 with a job as personal secretary to Murray, then vice president of the United Mine Workers Union. During the next 13 years McDonald worked as Murray's aide in the bitter strikes in the Appalachian coal fields and in the formation of the Congress of Industrial Organizations (CIO). In 1936 CIO President John L. Lewis [q.v.] named Murray to head the organizing drive in the steel industry. Murray, in turn, appointed McDonald secretary-treasurer of the newly formed United Steel Workers of America (USW). McDonald's career continued to rise with that of his mentor, and after Murray became president of the CIO in 1940 and the USW two years later, McDonald was increasingly regarded as the older man's heir apparent. With Murray's death in 1952 McDonald immediately assumed control of the million-member USW. However his chosen candidate to replace Murray as CIO president was defeated by Walter Reuther [q.v.] of the United Auto Workers. McDonald then launched an acrimonious feud with Reuther, threatening to withdraw the USW from the CIO and either affiliate with the American Federation of Labor (AFL) or set up a rival third federation with Lewis of the United Mineworkers and Dave Beck [q.v.] of the Teamsters. Although nothing came of these maneuvers, McDonald's hostility to the new CIO leadership undermined its bargaining position in the negotiations that preceded merger with the AFL in 1955 and subsequently helped isolate Reuther within the AFL-CIO.

Known as a leading conservative within the labor movement, McDonald proposed a labor-management "mutual trusteeship" for the steel industry, and in 1953 he conducted a two-week tour of the steel plants with Benjamin Fairless [q.v.], chairman of the board of the U.S. Steel Corp. Increasing employer resistance to USW wage demands, however, precipitated two major strikes during the Eisenhower Administration. A 1956 work stoppage was settled behind the scenes by Secretary of the Treasury George Humphrey [q.v.], who convinced the industry to give the steelworkers a generous economic package, which was immediately passed on to steel buyers in the form of higher prices. When negotiations for a new contract opened in 1959, McDonald insisted that high profits and productivity in steel justified a substantial wage boost without price increases, but the most important issue on this occasion was automation. The USW sought to maintain control over work rules in the plants in order to safeguard jobs (employment in steel had dropped from 540,000 to 461,000 during the preceding decade), while the industry wanted a free hand to introduce new production methods. The strike began in July, shutting down 85% of the country's basic steel capacity. After 116 days the President invoked the emergency provisions of the Taft-Hartley Act, ordering the Justice Department to seek an 80-day injunction against the union. Industry leaders expected this "cooling-off" period to induce the workers to approve their last offer. When polls indicated that they would reject it and resume the strike, Vice President Richard Nixon [q.v.] personally intervened to obtain a settlement favoring the union's position.

McDonald's tenure as USW president was plagued by growing internal opposition. In 1955 his candidate for union vice president was unsuccessfully opposed by a coalition of district directors. The next year a two-dollar-a-month dues increase inspired a rank and file "Dues Protest Movement." That faction's candidate against McDonald, Donald Rarick, garnered 35% of the vote in the first contested presidential election in the USW's history. The surprisingly strong showing by the relatively unknown Rarick was seen by many as a serious blow to McDonald, who had the international's treasury and thousand-man staff at his disposal.

Although Sen. John F. Kennedy (D, Mass.) [q.v.] refused to back USW proposals for a 32-hour week to fight unemployment, McDonald strongly endorsed him for the Democratic presidential nomination in 1960. Unlike others in the AFL-CIO leadership, moreover, he supported Sen. Lyndon B. Johnson (D, Tex.) [q.v.] for the vice presidential nomination. At the Democratic National Convention he worked to overcome labor's opposition to Johnson after Kennedy had publicly announced his choice.

During the early part of the Kennedy Administration, McDonald cooperated with Secretary of Labor Arthur Goldberg [q.v.], the former counsel for the USW, to mesh USW bargaining strategy with the government's overall economic policy. McDonald's limiting of wage demands to conform with Administration "guidelines" and his tendency to negotiation in secret through a labor-management "Human Relations Committee," however, alienated a section of the union's top leadership and caused discontent in the USW ranks. In 1965 USW secretary-treasurer I.W. Abel defeated him in a close race for the union presidency. [See KENNEDY, JOHNSON Volumes]

[TLH]

For further information:
David J. McDonald, *Union Man* (New York, 1969).

McELROY, NEIL H(OSLER)
b. Oct. 30, 1904; Berea, Ohio
d. Nov. 30, 1972; Cincinnati, Ohio
Secretary of Defense, August 1957-December 1959.

After graduating from Harvard College in 1925, Neil McElroy began a long career with Procter & Gamble. Starting as a door-to-door salesman, he became manager of the promotions department in 1929, vice president and general manager in 1946 and president in 1948. By that time Procter & Gamble, the maker of cleansers, had the largest advertising budget of any company in the world. In 1947 it spent an estimated $33 million a year in advertising. Under McElroy's directorship company profits expanded from $28.6 million in 1949 to $59.3 million in 1956.

In 1957 President Dwight D. Eisenhower appointed McElroy Secretary of Defense to replace Charles Wilson [q.v.] who was retiring to return to private business. He accepted on condition that if Procter & Gamble dropped its small number of defense contracts so that he could avoid conflict of interest, he would take a leave of absence rather than quit the company. He also stipulated that he would serve only two years. The President agreed to both conditions.

McElroy entered the Pentagon in the midst of controversy. In August 1957 the Soviet Union had launched the world's first intercontinental ballistic (ICMB) missile. Two months later it orbited *Sputnik*, the world's first artificial satellite. These events destroyed U.S. confidence in its defenses and initiated a debate on military organization and weapons development programs. A number of powerful senators, among them Stuart Symington (D, Mo.) [q.v.], Henry Jackson (D, Wash.) [q.v.] and Lyndon B. Johnson (D, Tex.) [q.v.], called for a speed-up in missile production. In response McElroy defended Eisenhower's plan for doing everything possible to increase production within the guidelines of the current defense budget.

Shortly after the *Sputnik* launching, McElroy announced that he was assuming personal direction of the missile program. He also outlined a proposed program for defense. It included accelerating operational development of intermediate range ballistic missiles (IRBM), protecting the strategic bomber force, improving detection devices, speeding up development of an anti-missile missile, and continuing development of the ICBM. He also began a public relations counter-offensive designed to show U.S.

advances in missiles and strategic weapons. Under McElroy's guidance, the Air Force fired its Thor IRBM, the Army its Jupiter IRBM and the Navy its Vanguard within two weeks of *Sputnik*. The Army also orbited its own satellite, Explorer I in January 1958.

In November 1957 McElroy testified before the Senate Preparedness Subcommittee. He admitted that the USSR was "obviously" ahead of the U.S. in missiles that could put a satellite into orbit, but he refused to agree that the Soviets led in long-range missiles. Several months later McElroy argued against a crash program for missile development. He maintained that "a rather frantic . . . program would be of dubious effectiveness" and stated that there was "little we can do to make a significant change in the date by which we can achieve the first operational intercontinental ballistic missile."

McElroy defended the U.S.'s overall military capacity in view of the Symington allegation that the Soviet Union had surpassed the nation in "total military strength." He dismissed the contention and argued that the U.S. did not need a total reorganization of its defense plans. At an American Legion Convention in September, he said "the spending of more tax dollars would, at this time, be an unwarranted risk of your money." "There is a point," he declared, "beyond which granting huge sums on untried weapons would be foolhardy—would, in fact, endanger [U.S.] economic and even . . . military security."

During 1958 McElroy defended Eisenhower's plan for the reorganization for the Defense Department. The proposal, submitted in the spring, was designed to consolidate operational U.S. Armed Forces units under unified commands reporting directly to the Secretary of Defense. The Secretary's authority would be strengthened. He would have control over strategic planning and operations and increased power over the budget, since most funds would be appropriated to the Defense Department rather than the services.

McElroy made it clear that the military and service secretaries were free to criticize the program without fear of reprisal. However, when Adm. Arleigh Burke [q.v.] did this in June, the Secretary was questioned about retaliation. McElroy said he "had no plans to have [Burke's] position changed" but that "I am not the only one that is responsible for his future." Later McElroy insisted in a clarifying statement that his words did not constitute "a rebuke" of Burke. However, Richard B. Russell (D, Ga.) [q.v.], chairman of the Senate Armed Services Committee, charged that "the clear implications" of McElroy's remarks were that military officers "must conform or be purged." The dispute ended when the plan was defeated in Congress.

Returning to Procter & Gamble in 1959, McElroy also served as Director of the General Electric Co., the Chrysler Corp. and the Equitable Life Insurance during the next decade. He died in 1972.

[RFG]

For further information:
Richard A. Aliano, *American Defense Policy from Eisenhower to Kennedy, 1957-1961* (Athens, Ohio, 1975).
Carl W. Borklund *Men of the Pentagon* (New York, 1956).

McKAY, DOUGLAS
b. June 24, 1893; Portland, Ore.
d. July 22, 1959; Salem, Ore.
Secretary of the Interior, January 1953-April 1956.

Douglas McKay, the son of a carpenter, drove a butcher wagon, worked as a meatcutter and delivered papers while still in high school. After working as an office boy for two years, he entered Oregon State College, where he graduated in 1917. He served in the Army during World War I, worked as an insurance salesmen in 1923, and then sold cars until 1927, when he opened his own auto agency. A Republican, McKay became mayor of Salem in 1932 and was elected to the state Senate in 1935. With time out for Army service from 1942 to 1943, McKay remained in the legislature until 1948, when he won the three-way race for governor.

McKay first came to Eisenhower's atten-

tion when, during the Republican National Convention of 1952, he sent a telegram to the National Committee urging the seating of a pro-Eisenhower delegation from Texas. In January 1953 he was appointed Secretary of the Interior. Eisenhower wanted a Westerner at that post because of the importance of conservation and water power development to that area. He also wanted an individual who shared his desire to balance the budget, and more importantly, who was committed to . limiting the federal government's role in the development of natural resources.

The conservative McKay fit the criteria well. In July 1953 he presented a draft of an Administration power policy statement. The paper reversed the Truman Administration's emphasis on federal power development and placed responsibility on local communities for supplying power needs. Only if "economically justified and feasible" would the Interior Department build plants, and then only if they were too large to be financed by other organizations. He emphasized that he did not approve of federal development of steam plants to generate electricity.

The Administration gradually moved to implement this program. Even before the draft proposal, McKay had announced that the Truman Administration's refusal to license the Idaho Power Co. to build the Oxbow Dam would be reversed, ending plans for a large federally built facility at Hell's Canyon in Idaho. After two years of hearings the Federal Power Commission granted the Idaho Power Co. the license in August 1955. McKay also supported the Submerged Lands Act of 1953, which redeemed Eisenhower's campaign pledge to give control of oil-rich tidelands to the states. As a result of McKay's conduct critics called the Secretary "give-away McKay."

McKay soon became one of the most controversial cabinet figures. Some observers believed his combative personality (many compared him to Truman) evoked strong reactions. The Secretary gained a reputation of favoring business interests and Republicans over Democrats within the Department. In April 1953 McKay announced that Albert M. Day, director of the Wildlife

Service since 1946, would be replaced by John L. Farley, former head of the California Fish and Game Commission and currently with a paper-manufacturing firm. The Secretary's critics accused McKay of favoring Farley because of his ties to Alaska salmon packers and commercial hunters. That same month McKay announced the resignation of career civil servant Marion Clawson as director of the Bureau of Land Management. He said he would appoint Clawson's successor and reinstate the former director in a lower-paying job. Clawson denied he had resigned and asked McKay to explain his dismissal. The Secretary then charged him with insubordination and denied him the other position. Soon afterward McKay nominated Tom Lyon to replace John J. Forbes as director of the Bureau of Mines. United Mine Workers President John L. Lewis [q.v.] protested the nomination on the grounds that Lyon favored the administration of the Mine Safety Act by the states rather than by the federal government. Subsequent hearings revealed that Lyon held a pension from the Anaconda Copper Co. that could be revoked at their displeasure. The nomination was withdrawn in June 1953. By the summer Eisenhower insisted that all high-ranking appointments in the Interior Department be given his personal scrutiny.

McKay's most important achievement was his improvements in the national park system. Early in 1954 Eisenhower sent a memo to the Secretary voicing his concern about the deterioration of the parks. McKay thereafter developed a program of improvements known as "Mission 66," a 10-year development plan designed to equip parks to accommodate an expected 80-million visitors in 1966. The Secretary succeeded in protecting park lands, notably blocking a possible transfer of lands in the Wichita Wildlife Refuge for use by the Army. The Department instituted exacting guidelines for oil and gas leasing in wildlife areas and added nine new wildlife reserves. McKay supervised the addition of 400,000 acres to the parks from 1953 to 1956.

McKay also furthered the integration of Indians into American society by curtailing federal supervision of their lives and facilitating voluntary relocation from marginal economic areas. The Department improved schooling opportunities for 10,000 Navajo children and developed programs of economic improvement in reservation areas. Indian health services were transferred to the Department of Health, Education and Welfare. While McKay was Secretary, the Department provided for an orderly termination of federal supervision over six Indian groups.

In the spring of 1956 McKay resigned to challenge to Sen. Wayne Morse's (D, Ore.) [q.v.] bid for reelection. He stated that the race would symbolize his opposition to "socialists and leftwingers." Although waging a vigorous campaign, McKay was defeated for the first time in his political career. McKay became chairman of the International Joint Commission, which dealt with boundary water problems between Canada and the United States, in 1957.

[GAD]

McLEOD, R(OBERT) W(ALTER) SCOTT
b. June 17, 1914; Davenport, Iowa.
d. Nov. 7, 1961; Concord, N.H.
Administrator, Bureau of Security, Consular Affairs and Inspection, 1953-57; Ambassador to Ireland, 1957-61.

After graduating from Grinnell College in 1937, McLeod became a want-ad salesman for the Des Moines Register and Tribune. In 1938 he took a job as police reporter for the Cedar Rapids (Iowa) Gazette and four years later became an FBI agent. From 1949 to 1953 he served as administrative assistant to conservative Sen. Styles Bridges (R, N.H.) [q.v.]. In that post McLeod caught the attention of Sen. Joseph R. McCarthy (R, Wisc.) [q.v.], who considered him an "excellent man." He also helped write the Republican report protesting President Harry S. Truman's dismissal of Gen. Douglas MacArthur.

Reacting to the scandels within the State Department during the Truman Administration, President Eisenhower and Secretary of State John Foster Dulles [*q.v.*] attempted to purge the Department of possible security risks. To quiet congressional conservatives, McLeod was given the job. As the administrator of the bureau of security, consular affairs and inspection, McLeod was the Department's security contact with the FBI, the Central Intelligence Agency and congressional officials. He administered Eisenhower's controversial Executive Order 10450, signed in April 1953, under which all Department officials were subject to investigation not only into their political beliefs but also into their private lives. At McLeod's insistence the office of personnel was also put under his control to facilitate the probe, but his post was taken from him in March 1954. In April 1954 Dulles also put him in charge of investigating Foreign Service officers.

Under McLeod's direction and with the aid of a staff of 1,000, every State Department worker, including janitors, was investigated on the premise that every post was "sensitive." His motto to investigators was, "Be completely ruthless." McLeod often admitted that his aims were partisan. He told an American Legion Convention in Topeka, Kan., in August 1953 that his job was essentially "political"—to ferret out traitors, homosexuals, security risks and Democrats—and lamented that civil service legislation made it difficult to replace all of the latter with Republicans. Charging that State Department officials like Undersecretary of State W. Bedell Smith [*q.v.*], with Dulles's connivance, were not removing enough Democrats, McLeod wrote articles for the *U.S. News and World Report* that contained false information on party affiliations of Department employes. During his first year in office, 300 agency workers were dismissed or forced to resign, including Charles W. Thayer, a respected Foreign Service officer and brother-in-law of Ambassador Charles E. Bohlen [*q.v.*].

McLeod sought to replace professional Foreign Service officers with political appointees responsible to him. He asked the Civil Service Commission to change 300 posts from career to political classifications; it reclassified 100 of them. McLeod also supervised the Foreign Service Institute, which trained diplomatic officers, clearing all lecturers and even course contents.

McLeod's methods soon upset Dulles, who was particularly disturbed by the securely chief's agreement to give Sen. McCarthy limited access to classified State Department personnel files. Dulles was especially aroused by McLeod's efforts to prevent Senate confirmation of Bohlen as ambassador to the Soviet Union in March 1953. Not only did McLeod condemn Bohlen as a "security risk" on the basis of FBI reports he had received, but he also supplied information to conservative Sen. Pat McCarran (D, Nev) [*q.v.*] and McCarthy to use against him in the Senate. In addition McLeod went to Eisenhower's liaison with Congress, Gen. Wilton Persons [*q.v.*], to seek his support. Although Dulles considered firing him after this incident, the Secretary feared McCarthy's reaction and retained McLeod.

As supervisor of the passport and visa divisions and the office of special consular services, McLeod was responsible for the enforcement of the Refugee Act of 1953. This measure was designed to allow more than 200,000 over-quota refugees from Communist countries to enter the U.S. over a three-year period. McLeod conducted a careful screening of each immigrant, and under his administration only nine refugees were admitted in 1953-54. His conduct drew the anger of Edward Corsi [*q.v.*], a special adviser for immigration affairs. Corsi was eventually phased out of the Department for his objections to McLeod's actions and refusal to work under him. After leaving, Corsi told a Senate Judiciary subcommittee that the administration of the act was a national scandal. "The police job is the thing," he maintained, "not the admission of the refugees—that is just incidental."

In 1957 McLeod was appointed ambassador to Ireland. His nomination was opposed by Democratic senators and Irish liberals. Sen. Joseph Clark (D, Pa.) [*q.v.*] attacked him during the confirmation debate" as the "symbol of the witch hunter" McCarthy's worst attributes. Nevertheless his appointment was approved, 60 to 20.

McLeod resigned his post at the end of the Eisenhower Administration. In 1961 he was appointed general counsel to Republican members of the Senate Appropriations Committee. He died of a heart attack in November 1961.

[AES]

McNAMARA, PATRICK V(INCENT)
b. Oct. 4, 1894; Washington, D.C.
d. April 30, 1966; Washington, D.C.
Democratic Senator, Mich. 1955-56.

The son of Irish immigrants, McNamara studied at Fore River Apprentice School to be a pipe fitter. After playing professional football, he went to Detroit in 1920 to become foreman of a construction gang. He held a succession of unpaid minor offices in Pipe Fitters Local 636 before becoming its president. He held that post for 20 years prior to his election to the U.S. Senate in 1954. McNamara was also employed by a Michigan mechanical contracting firm as a customer contact man, head of labor relations and vice president in charge of sales. During World War II, he served as rent director for the Office of Price Administration in Detroit. He was elected to the Detroit Common Council in 1946 and to the Detroit Board of Education three years later.

McNamara was given little chance of winning when he sought the Democrat senatorial nomination against former Sen. Blair Moody in 1954. Moody had the backing of Gov. G. Mennen Williams [q.v.] and of powerful labor organizations in the area. However, after Moody's sudden death in July, the regular Democratic machine reluctantly supported McNamara. He opposed powerful incumbent Homer Ferguson [q.v.], who had the support of President Eisenhower, in the November election. McNamara campaigned on a platform calling for the repeal of the Taft-Hartley Act, denouncing the Eisenhower Administration's foreign policies and advocating federal aid to education. He narrowly won the general election.

McNamara earned a liberal record in the upper chamber. He opposed a 1956 bill exempting independent natural gas producers from rate regulations of the Federal Power Commission and voted for federal construction of power facilities at Hell's Canyon in 1957. He backed federal housing, public works and education measures, and he supported the continuation of the Truman Administration's rigid price supports for agriculture. In 1957 the liberal Americans for Democratic Action gave him a 100% rating.

McNamara was a strong supporter of civil rights. In November 1956 he was one of six liberal senators who issued a 16 point "Democratic Declaration of 1957." Among its proposals were a call for a "reasonable" substitute for Senate Rule 22, which permitted filibusters, and a demand for a guarantee of equal voting and educational rights for blacks. The following year he backed the controversial Part III of the Administration's 1957 civil rights bill. The section gave the Attorney General broad powers to seek injunctions in any type of civil rights case with or without the consent of the alleged victim. In the final act the section was amended to limit the Attorney General's enforcement powers to voting rights cases alone. McNamara also opposed a conservative amendment requiring jury trials for all accused of violating the statute. This provision was modified in the final measure to limit jury trials to certain cases. Three years later he supported the Civil Rights Act of 1960, designed to strengthen the original statute.

McNamara was also a strong supporter of labor. He backed efforts to increase the minimum wage, and in February 1959 he introduced a bill to establish a 75-cents-per hour wage for farm workers. The Senator was a member of the Select Committee on Improper Activities in the Labor or Management Field, established in 1957 to investigate corruption in unions and industry. He opposed the investigation of the United Auto Workers (UAW) proposed by conservative Sens. Karl Mundt (R, S.D.) [q.v.] and Barry Goldwater (R, Ariz) [q.v.]. In December 1957 he wrote a letter to UAW president Walter Reuther [q.v.] charging that "certain members of the Committee" were out to "get" the union and Reuther. McNamara opposed the Committee report, issued on March 24, 1958, which found extensive instances of corruption and collusion between management and labor leaders. He charged that despite an effort to "give a semblance of balance," the overall effect of the report was "to frame a blanket indictment against the labor movement." McNamara resigned from the Committee on March 31. That year the AFL-CIO Committee on Political Education gave him a 100% rating.

During the 1960s McNamara was a strong supporter of medicare, wage and hours legislation and aid to education. He died of a stroke on April 30, 1966.

[EWS]

MACK, RICHARD A(LFRED)
b Oct. 2, 1909: Miami, Fla.
d. Nov. 22(?), 1963: Miami, Fla.
Commissioner, Federal Communications Commission, June 1955-March 1958.

Richard Mack graduated from the University of Florida in 1932 and for the next nine years worked as an insurance salesman, credit manager and farm supply company executive. He was an infantry officer during World War II. In 1947 he returned to Florida to become a member of the State Railroad and Public Utilities Commission. There Mack assumed a leading role in forcing utilities to undergo a detailed financial examination when requesting rate increases. His work led many state observers to predict Mack's eventual election as Florida's governor or U.S. senator. In May 1955 President Eisenhower appointed Mack to a seven-year term on the Federal Communications Commission (FCC).

During the early months of 1958, the House Special Subcommittee on Legislative Oversight carried out an investigation of six regulatory agencies, including the FCC. As a result of the probe, Subcommittee Chief Counsel Bernard Schwartz [q.v.] charged Mack with plotting to fix the granting of a license to Miami's Television Channel 10. In February 1957 Mack had joined three other FCC members in voting to allocate the lucrative Miami channel to Public Service, Inc., a National Airlines subsidiary. In doing so they had overruled the opinion of a hearing examiner who had recommended the petition of A. Frank Katzentine, a local civic leader with experience as a radio station owner-operator. National Airlines had no record in broadcast management, nor did its participation in Miami community affairs compare to that of Katzentine and his major investors.

In well-publicized hearings during February 1958, the subcommittee found that Mack had agreed to support National following the lobbying efforts of Thurman Whiteside, a Miami attorney regarded by some opponents as something of a "fixer" in Florida political circles. A close friend of Mack's, Whiteside had lent him $7,830 interest-free, since 1950. Over $2,500 of this had been received by Mack since joining the FCC. In addition, Whiteside had secured Mack an interest in two Florida companies worth $6,416. Given to understand that National Airlines would reward him for his efforts, Whiteside used his financial leverage with Mack to compel him to vote for Public Service, Inc. Schwartz also produced an affidavit in which Katzentine also admitted having tried to approach Mack. Mack countered that he had done nothing wrong and that money he had received from Whiteside was based on long personal friendship.

As a result of publicity and pressure from Commerce Committee Chairman Oren Harris (D, Ark.) [q.v.], the White House asked for Mack's resignation in March 1958. Mack immediately quit, saying that his "character and good name had been sacrificed to political expediency."

A grand jury indicted both Mack and Whiteside for conspiracy in September 1958. The trial jury deadlocked in July 1959. Slowly Mack became an alcoholic. He spent time in and out of psychiatric institutions, and his wife later divorced him for desertion. The prosecution dropped plans for a second trial in 1961. On Nov. 26, 1963 Miami police found Mack's body in a rooming house. He had been dead for four or five days.

[JLB]

For further information:
Victor G. Rosenblum, "How to Get into TV: The Federal Communications Commission and Miami's Channel 10," in Allen F. Westin, ed., *The Uses of Power* (New York, 1962), pp. 173-228.

MAGNUSON, WARREN G(RANT)
b. April 12, 1905; Moorehead, Minn.
Democratic Senator, Wash., 1944- .

Orphaned at the age of three weeks, Magnuson was adopted by a Swedish immigrant family and moved with them to North Dakota. At 19 he rode the freight trains west to Seattle, where he studied law at the University of Washington. He received his degree in 1929. Elected to the state legislature in 1932, Magnuson sponsored a bill that became the nation's first unemployment compensation law. After serving as county prosecutor in Seattle for two years, he won election in 1936 to a seat in the U.S. House of Representatives, which had been vacated by the suicide of Rep. Marion Zioncheck (D, Wash.), a former law school classmate of Magnuson's. A staunch supporter of the New Deal, Magnuson strove to generate public works projects to revive his state's economy, which had been particularly hard-hit by the Depression. In 1944 he was elected to the Senate, where he succeeded in channeling large amounts of federal aid to Washington for dams, timber development and the maritime industry. Strongly supported by organized labor, Magnuson fought against the Taft-Hartley Act in 1947 and introduced a bill in 1950 which restored the maritime union hiring hall. [See TRUMAN Volume]

During the Eisenhower Administration Magnuson's seniority on key committees further enhanced his ability to deliver the federal defense contracts and resource development projects on which his state's economy depended. In 1952 he became chairman of the powerful Interstate and Foreign Commerce Committee (later renamed the Commerce Committee). He also served on the Appropriations and the Aeronautics and Space Sciences Committees. Washington's economic boom in the 1950s, which was based on large expenditures on aircraft industry, atomic installations and naval yards located in the state, owed much to Magnuson's efforts. As a result, despite his strongly liberal, pro-labor voting record in the Senate, Magnuson earned the support of Washington business interests, as well as labor unions and liberal groups.

Magnuson opposed the Republican "partnership" policy for water and power projects, which encouraged private business, rather than the federal government, to develop natural resources. He denounced it as a "giveaway" to "favored corporations." In 1954, when the Administration endorsed a bill to permit a local public utility to build and operate a $360 million hydroelectric dam at Priest Rapids, Wash., on the Columbia River, he condemned the measure as a first step in the ceding of public water sites to private interests. Magnuson eventually dropped his opposition, however, declaring that even a non-federal project was better than none at all.

Beginning in the late-1950s Magnuson became a leading advocate of government-sponsored oceanography research as an aid to national defense. Citing the nuclear submarine program's need for information about ocean tides, currents and weather, he urged the creation of a federal office, funded on a long-range rather than an annual budgetary basis, to coordinate the oceanographic activities of different government agencies. In 1960 Magnuson sponsored legislation to set up a new division of marine sciences in the National Science Foundation, but the bill died in the House.

During the Kennedy Administration Magnuson's activity on the Commerce Committee began to shift from local interest advocacy to issues of broader national significance. In 1964 he figured prominently in the passage of the controversial public accommodations section of that year's Civil Rights Act. During the Johnson and Nixon years Magnuson played a leading role in consumer and environmental legislation. [See KENNEDY, JOHNSON, NIXON/FORD Volumes]

[TLH]

MAHON, GEORGE H(ERMAN)
b. Sept. 22, 1900; Mahon, La.
Democratic Representative, Tex.
1935- ; Chairman, Department of Defense Subcommittee of the Appropriations Committee, 1949-53, 1955- .

Born on a cotton farm near Haynesville, La., Mahon migrated with his family to rural west Texas in 1908. After receiving his LL.B. from the University of Texas in 1925, he entered politics, winning election as attorney general for Mitchell Co. in 1926, district attorney for the 32nd judicial district in 1927 and representative from the newly created 19th congressional district in 1934. Five years later Mahon was named to the House Appropriations Committee's War Department Subcommittee, which later became the Defense Department Subcommittee. A strong supporter of Roosevelt and Truman Administration foreign policy and defense programs, Mahon nevertheless delivered few speeches and received little publicity during the course of his steady rise on House seniority lists. In 1949 he became chairman of the defense subcommittee, the same year all Defense Department appropriations were consolidated into a single bill.

Although a fiscal conservative, Mahon generally opposed Eisenhower Administration efforts to trim the military budget. As the ranking subcommittee Democrat in 1953, he led the panel's minority members in a fight against a proposed $5 billion cut in Air Force appropriations. Mahon insisted that 143 Air Force wings would be needed by 1955, rather than the 120 wings requested by the President. However, the Republican controlled House and Senate eventually reduced Air Force funds even more than the Administration had wished.

After regaining the defense subcommittee chairmanship in 1955, Mahon warned that the Soviet Union was developing the same nuclear capability as the U.S. and urged slow yearly increases in the rate of military spending in order to maintain American defense superiority. Confronted in 1957 with Administration estimates of total spending that were $3 billion higher than the previous year's, however, Mahon called for economy and cut the President's defense requests by almost $2.6 billion. The Senate subsequently restored $972 million to the appropriations measure. In July, as conferees sought to bridge the gap between the two versions of the bill, the President announced that he was reducing the Armed Services by 100,000 men, thus weakening Senate arguments for increased spending. As a result, the conference report in July added only $199 million to the original House bill.

Mahon brought his budget-cutting campaign to an abrupt halt in October 1957 following the Soviet Union's successful launching of Sputnik, the world's first artificial space satellite. The launch revealed a higher level of Soviet space and missile technology than U.S. intelligence sources had assumed. As a result, Mahon's panel began urging larger defense appropriations in order to immediately strengthen U.S. strategic offensive and defensive weapons systems.

With the death of Rep. Clarence Cannon (D, Mo.) [q.v.] in 1964, Mahon assumed the chairmanship of the full Appropriations Committee and thus became one of the most influential House leaders. Although a key supporter of the Johnson Administration's early Vietnam policy, he joined Southern Democratic colleagues in opposing the President's civil rights, medicare and poverty programs. Mahon endorsed increased defense expenditures during the 1960s and in the latter part of the decade backed the development of a "China-oriented" anti-ballistic missile defense system. During his years of service in the House, Mahon earned a reputation for personal integrity and hard work and for a refusal to practice "pork barrel" politics for his West Texas constituency. [See KENNEDY, JOHNSON, NIXON/FORD Volumes]

[TLH]

MANN, THOMAS (CLIFTON)
b. Nov. 11, 1912; Laredo, Tex.
Ambassador to El Salvador, October
1955-September 1957; Assistant Secretary of State for Economic Affairs, September 1957-July 1960; Assistant Secretary of State for Inter-American Affairs,
July 1960-March 1961.

Thomas Clifton Mann grew up in Laredo,
Tex., a town on the Mexican border. After
earning an LL.B. from Baylor University
and practicing law in his home town, Mann
joined the State Department in 1942,
specializing in Latin American affairs and
international economics. He became a
Foreign Service officer in 1947 at the request of Assistant Secretary of State for
American Republic Affairs Spruille Braden
[q.v.]. Mann worked as Braden's special
assistant for a few months, and in August
1947 he left for Caracas, Venezuela, to take
charge of the embassy's political and petroleum affairs. He directed the State Department's office of Middle American affairs
from January 1950 to the end of the year,
when he was named deputy assistant secretary in the bureau of inter-American affairs.
In August 1953 Mann became embassy
counselor in Athens and assumed similar
duties in Guatemala City in September
1954. From October 1955 to September
1957, he was ambassador to El Salvador.

In September 1957 Mann was appointed
assistant secretary of state for economic affairs. At his new post he represented the
U.S. at many international trade conferences. In his dealings with foreign nations,
he preferred to concentrate on immediate
problems and to avoid long-term economic
planning. In December 1958, for example,
he criticized Brazilian President Juscelino
Kubitschek's call for an "Operation Pan
America," which urged a development program to increase Latin American per capita
income by 1980. The U.S. was expected to
shoulder a large part of the economic burden in the development effort. Mann argued that the U.S. was already doing its
share to help Latin America and suggested
that Latin Americans realistically focus on
short-term plans.

Mann was particularly concerned about
stabilizing prices of raw materials and increasing Latin American markets. In 1958
he induced Latin American coffee-producing nations, perennially plagued by
large surpluses and low prices, to institute
controls to stabilize quotas and prices. A
year later he brought African nations into
the agreement. When he spoke before the
U.S. Commission on International Commodity Trade in March 1959, Mann advised
other nations not to follow the U.S. practice
of using price supports and stockpiling as
means of stabilizing markets and prices of
agricultural goods. In December 1958
Mann pledged U.S. cooperation with the
Organization of American States' plan to
develop common market areas in Latin
America.

Vice President Richard Nixon's [q.v.]
troubled tour of Latin America in the
spring of 1958 and Fidel Castro's takeover
in Cuba prompted the Administration to
review its Latin American policy. It was
apparent that the U.S., in imposing high
tariffs and import restrictions on Latin
American metals and in refusing to approve
a Marshall Plan for the Hemisphere, had
severely damaged its political influence.
Mann was one of the first to argue that, in
view of the Communist threat, economic
policy had to be designed with attention
to its political ramifications. Despite his
reservations Mann agreed to the creation of
a $1 billion Inter-American Development
Bank with the U.S. subscribing to 45% of
the stock. At the same conference Castro
suggested that the U.S. undertake a $30
billion aid program in Latin America. Although he never publicly responded to Castro's challenge, Mann argued that the U.S.
was already supporting all feasible projects,
mainly through international bank loans.

After his appointment as assistant secretary of state for inter-American affairs in
July 1960, Mann and C. Douglas Dillon
[q.v.], undersecretary of state for economic
affairs, attended the September meeting of
the Inter-American Economic Conference
in Bogota. With the notable exception of
Cuba, the U.S. and all other Latin American nations agreed to the Act of Bogota, a
common policy for a "new and vigorous" at-

tack on the sources of political unrest and economic underdevelopment. Emphasizing action on housing, agrarian reform, health and education, the measure was an expanded version of President Eisenhower's social development plan, which pledged an initial fund of $500 million. In view of the increasingly leftist stance of the Castro regime, the program was criticized in the U.S. as an ill-timed attempt to ensure Latin American support for U.S. policies. Nonetheless, the Act of Bogota was the forerunner of President Kennedy's Alliance for Progress.

From March 1961 to December 1963, Mann served as ambassador to Mexico. Under President Johnson he took complete charge of Latin American policy. Observers credited Mann with the creation of a distinctive Johnson Latin American policy, which some believed to be a regression from the idealism of the Kennedy years. A self-styled pragmatist, Mann stressed economic development over social and political reform and did not believe that the U.S. should favor democratic governments over dictatorships. In February 1965 Mann was named undersecretary of state for economic affairs, but he left government service in April 1966 for private life. In 1967 he became president of the Automobile Manufactures Association. [See KENNEDY, JOHNSON Volumes]

[JCH]

MANSFIELD, MIKE (MICHAEL) (JOSEPH)
b. March 16, 1903; New York, N.Y.
Democratic Senator, Mont., 1953-77;
Senate Majority Whip, 1957-61.

Born in New York City's Greenwich Village, Mansfield was sent to Montana at the age of three to live with relatives after his mother died. He left school in the eighth grade and served successively in the Navy, Army and Marine Corps between 1918 and 1922. He worked as a miner and mining engineer in Montana's copper mines for the next eight years. In 1933 Mansfield received a B.A. degree from Montana State University and earned an M.A. from that

institution the following year. He remained there to teach Latin American and Far Eastern history.

Mansfield failed to win a Democratic congressional nomination in 1940 but two years later captured a House seat. Because of his academic interest in foreign affairs, he was placed on the Foreign Relations Committee. In 1944 President Roosevelt sent him on a tour of inspection in China. Four years later Mansfield was a delegate to the ninth Inter-American Conference in Colombia, and in 1951-52 he sat on the American delegation to the U.N. General Assembly. During the Truman Administration he compiled a generally liberal record, supporting anti-poll tax bills while opposing creation of the House Un-American Activities Committee and the Taft-Hartley Act.

In 1952 Mansfield, despite the Republican tide of that year, defeated incumbent Sen. Zales N. Ecton (R, Mont.) Since foreign affairs continued to be Mansfield's primary concern, he was seated on the upper chamber's foreign relations panel. Mansfield was a leading critic of the Eisenhower Administration's foreign aid program, contending that it was too extensive and indiscriminate and was poorly administered. In June 1953 he attacked the President's mutual security bill as preparing for "never-ending foreign aid on a large scale." In July 1954 he called for an end to foreign economic aid except for technical assistance and a few other programs. Five years later he unsuccessfully proposed that the Administration be required to reduce all non-military grant aid (as opposed to technical assistance and loans) to zero within three years. He also suggested, as efficiency measures, the transfer of the functions of the semi-autonomous International Cooperation Administration to the State Department and the shifting of responsibility for military aid from the State Department to the Defense Department. The former proposal was rejected by the Senate, while the latter was incorporated into the Mutual Security Act of 1959.

Mansfield played a key role in formulating the Democratic congressional response to Eisenhower Administration foreign policy. The usual bipartisanship of cold war foreign policy was reflected in President Eisenhower's appointment of Mansfield as a delegate to the 1954 Southeast Asia Conference, which drafted the SEATO pact (to which Mansfield was a signatory), and as a member of the U.S. delegation to the U.N. General Assembly in 1958. However, at joint hearings of the Foreign Affairs and Armed Services Committees in February 1957, Mansfield and Sen. Hubert H. Humphrey (D, Minn.) [q.v.] amended the Administration's version of the Eisenhower Doctrine, which would have permitted the President to use American armed forces at his discretion to block Communist expansion in the Middle East. The Humphrey-Mansfield amendment, which was incorporated into the final version of the Doctrine, stated that the U.S. was prepared, if the President believed it necessary, to provide such assistance when requested by the nation attacked.

In 1957 Majority Leader Lyndon B. Johnson (D, Tex.) [q.v.] selected Mansfield to replace Sen. Earle Clements (D, Ky.), as majority whip. It was generally believed that Johnson had chosen the Montana Senator because of the latter's unassertiveness, which made him an unlikely challenger of the majority leader's authority. As whip, Mansfield's tasks included helping persuade Senate Democrats to vote as the leadership wished and making sure that his Party colleagues were on the floor for roll calls. He preferred a low-key, conciliatory approach to arm twisting and threats.

Mansfield compiled a generally liberal record on domestic legislation. In August 1959 he voted to override a presidential housing bill veto, and the following May he backed an attempt to override a veto of an area redevelopment bill. Mansfield supported the civil rights bills of 1957 and 1960, but as majority whip he opposed liberal amendments to the 1960 bill.

Mansfield succeeded Johnson as majority leader in 1961. Some of his Democratic colleagues, particularly liberals, criticized him for not being a strong leader. He became increasingly opposed to the Vietnam war during the Johnson Administration, and during President Nixon's tenure he sought

to increase Senate influence over the conduct of foreign policy. In March 1976 Mansfield announced he would not seek reelection. [See KENNEDY, JOHNSON, NIXON/FORD Volumes]

[MLL]

MANSURE, EDMUND F(ORSMAN)
b. March 14, 1901; Chicago, Ill.
Administrator, General Services Administration, April 1953-February 1956.

While earning his law degree at Kent College, Edmund F. Mansure worked for the E.L. Mansure Co. He was promoted to vice president two years before his admission to the Illinois bar in 1927. He became president of E.L. Mansure in 1935 and chairman of the board in 1952. After serving on numerous state commissions, Mansure was chosen by President Eisenhower to head the General Services Administration (GSA) in April 1953. The appointment was made at the request of a Chicago insurance broker and Republican leader, William J. Balmer. Not subject to congressional confirmation, Mansure entered the government as a political appointee heading one of Washington's largest agencies.

According to political scientist David Frier, during his 36 months in office, Mansure showed himself an inept administrator, immersed in trivia, incapable of overseeing his subordinates and unable to withstand pressure from top officials to use the GSA to reward the party faithful. One of his neighbors described him as a man who "could easily get over his head in very shallow water."

In October 1955 Mansure became implicated in a scandal involving building commissioner Peter Strobel [q.v.], charged with using his post to further his private interests. Mansure acknowledged that he had allowed Strobel to retain a 90% interest in the engineering firm of Strobel and Salzman, although he reportedly told the Commissioner that he must give up "active management" of the firm. He did not check the legality of this action with the Attorney General or question Strobel when the Commissioner failed to sign the government's code of ethics and provide the GSA with a list of his firm's clients. Strobel resigned his post in November 1955.

In a 1955 article in *Fortune*, journalist Herbert Solow charged that the GSA was "Washington's most durable mess" and was guilty of "favoritism, factionalism, sloppiness and waste." He further implied that outside political interests, and that Balmer in particular, exercised an unhealthy influence over the Administrator. He pointed particularly to the awarding of contracts for the expansion of the government-owned nickel plant in Nicaro, Cuba. Instead of contracting builders directly, Mansure took the unprecedented step of choosing the National Lead Co., which ran the refinery for the government, to supervise and subcontract. He did this despite staff advice that National Lead would cost more than comparable supervision by the Public Building Service.

Rather than give the major contract to the Frederick Snare Corp., which had built the plant and had the work permits necessary to begin construction immediately, National Lead insisted that Snare share the contract with Merritt-Chapman and Scott Corp., which had no experience in building in Cuba. Solow suggested a number of reasons for this unprecedented move, among them the fact that Air Force Secretary Harold Talbott [*q.v.*] had contacted Mansure on Merritt's behalf and that Balmer was a friend of the company's executive vice president. The insurance brokerage fee for the project was, in fact, obtained by the small company of Balmer and More, which did not have a brokerage license at the time.

As a result of the article, the House Special Government Activities Subcommittee began in inquiry into the Nicaro expansion in January 1956. Its probe, although unable to ascertain what forces were responsible for granting the contract to National Lead, established a strong inference that Mansure had been under heavy pressure from members of Congress, executive departments and the Republican Party to reward Republicans. At the hearings, Randall Cremer, executive vice president of Snare, testified that he had awarded the insurance to Balmer because Mansure had told him to do so. At a news conference Mansure denied that he had instructed Cremer to give the contract to a "specific firm" but acknowledged that he wanted to place the contract with a "firm friendly to the Republican Party." (Snare had few Republicans in high positions within the corporation.) In testimony before the panel, Mansure said he had been under political pressure in awarding the contract from Postmaster General Arthur Summerfield [*q.v.*], Secretary of Commerce Sinclair Weeks [*q.v.*], Air Force Secretary Harold Talbott, and particularly from Republican National Chairman Leonard Hall [*q.v.*]. Despite these revelations neither the Justice Department nor the subcommittee took action against Mansure.

In February 1956 Mansure resigned citing "personal obligations" and returned to head E. L. Mansure Co.

[MJS]

MARSHALL, THURGOOD
b. July 2, 1908: Baltimore, Md.
Director-Counsel, NAACP Legal Defense and Educational Fund, 1940-61.

Born and raised in Baltimore, Marshall graduated from Lincoln University in 1930 and from Howard University law school, where he was first in his class, in 1933. He then practiced in Baltimore until 1936, when he was named assistant special counsel to the NAACP. Two years later Marshall became special counsel; when the NAACP Legal Defense and Educational Fund was separately established in 1940, he was appointed its director-counsel. As head of the NAACP's legal program, Marshall became the nation's foremost civil rights attorney, coordinating attacks on racial discrimination in various fields. His Supreme Court victories included a 1944 decision prohibiting the exclusion of blacks from Democratic primaries because of their race and a 1946 case outlawing segregation in interstate transportation. A convivial and seemingly tireless individual, Marshall traveled thousands of miles throughout the South each year to represent black litigants in court and to encourage local NAACP chapters in their efforts to secure equal rights for blacks. [See TRUMAN Volume.]

In perhaps the most significant court battle of his career, Marshall supervised the preparation of five cases challenging the validity of racial segregation in public schools. He personally represented the black plaintiffs from Clarendon Co., S.C., in one of the suits, and during oral arguments before the Supreme Court in December 1952 and December 1953, Marshall contended that state-enforced segregation violated the 14th Amendment. On May 17, 1954 the Supreme Court ruled unanimously in *Brown v. Board of Education* that segregation in public education was unconstitutional. During argument in April 1955 on how the decision should be carried out, Marshall urged the Court to order complete desegregation of public schools no later than the fall term of 1956. The Court, however, announced a far more flexible standard in May 1955 and ordered school desegregation "with all deliberate speed." Over the next several years Marshall and the NAACP led a massive program of litigation to enforce the *Brown* decision.

Along with several other NAACP lawyers, Marshall also represented Autherine Lucy [*q.v.*] in her suit to enter the University of Alabama and won a Supreme Court decision in October 1955 ordering her enrollment. Marshall was with Lucy on Feb. 6, 1956, when she was attacked by a mob on the University's campus. After the University's trustees suspended Lucy the next day, Marshall secured a federal court order for her reinstatement. The trustees then expelled Lucy, and she withdrew from the case shortly afterwards.

Marshall was also counsel for the black students who desegregated Central High School in Little Rock, Ark., in the fall of 1957. When Gov. Orval Faubus [*q.v.*] tried to thwart integration of the high school in September 1957, Marshall got an injunction barring the Governor from further interference with the school's desegregation plan. Later in the school year the local school board sought to postpone its desegregation program for two-and-a-half

years. In a special Supreme Court term in September 1958, Marshall argued against this delay and won a unanimous decision from the Court ordering continuance of school integration plans.

Marshall also handled cases extending the *Brown* principle to such areas as public recreation and public transit. He participated in the suit growing out of the Montgomery, Ala., bus boycott, which resulted in a November 1956 Supreme Court ruling that segregation in local transportation was unconstitutional. In his last oral argument before the Supreme Court in October 1960, Marshall successfully contended that segregation in restaurants at interstate bus terminals violated federal law.

In his final years with the NAACP, Marshall aided the defense of hundreds of students arrested during the sit-ins, the Freedom Rides and similar nonviolent protests. He helped prepare the December 1961 case in which the Court reversed the convictions of blacks arrested for peaceful lunch counter sit-ins.

In September 1961 Marshall was named a judge on the U.S. Second Circuit Court of Appeals in New York. President Johnson appointed him Solicitor General in July 1965 and nominated him to the Supreme Court in June 1967. Marshall was the first black to serve in either of these two jobs. Even before these appointments, however, many commentators asserted that Marshall had won a place in history because of his legal work for the NAACP. He spearheaded efforts which brought major changes in civil rights law, and his activities made him "a symbol of decades of struggle for social change through the orderly processes of the law." [See KENNEDY, JOHNSON, NIXON/FORD Volumes]

[CAB]

For further information:
Randall W. Bland, *Private Pressure on Public Law: The Legal Career of Justice Thurgood Marshall* (Port Washington, 1973).
John P. MacKenzie, "Thurgood Marshall," in Leon Friedman and Fred L. Israel, eds., *The Justices of the United States Supreme Court, 1789-1969* (New York, 1969), Vol. 4.
Richard Kluger, *Simple Justice* (New York, 1976).

MARTIN, JOSEPH W(ILLIAM), JR.
b. Nov. 3, 1884; North Attleboro, Mass.
d. March 6, 1968; Hollywood, Fla.
Republican Representative, Mass.,
1925-67; Speaker of the House, 1947-
49, 1953-55; House Minority Leader,
1939-47, 1949-53, 1955-59.

After graduating from high school in 1902, Martin turned down a scholarship to Dartmouth College and became a reporter. In 1908 he and several associates purchased a newspaper in North Attleboro, Mass., his home town. His newspaper work brought him into politics, and in 1911 he made a successful race for a seat in the Massachusetts House of Representatives. He served there until 1914. In that year Martin was elected to the state Senate. He retired from politics in 1917 but returned in 1922 to become executive secretary of the Massachusetts Republican Party. Two years later he won election to the U.S. House of Representatives.

Martin opposed most New Deal programs and was a moderate isolationist during the 1930s. In 1939 he was elected minority leader. Seven years later, after the Republicans had gained control of Congress, he became Speaker of the House. As Speaker he helped President Harry S. Truman pass the Greek-Turkish aid program and the Marshall Plan while opposing most of the Administration's Fair Deal legislation, including its national health insurance and public housing programs.

In April 1951 Martin became involved in the dispute between President Truman and Gen. Douglas MacArthur over the conduct of the Korean war. On April 5 Martin, a MacArthur supporter, revealed the contents of a letter he had received from the General criticizing the failure to use Nationalist Chinese troops in the war. The letter was a contributing factor in Truman's recall of MacArthur on April 11. [See TRUMAN Volume]

In 1953 Martin again became House Speaker. He was disappointed in President Dwight D. Eisenhower's legislative programs, believing that they were too similar to those of Presidents Roosevelt and Truman. He also thought they did not accurately reflect the conservatism of most House Republicans. However, as the leader of his party in the lower chamber, he felt obliged to back the President. Martin personally favored Rep. Daniel Reed's (R, N.Y.) [q.v.] 1953 tax cut measure, but he bottled the bill up in the Rules Committee at the request of the White House. President Eisenhower's reciprocal trade bill of 1953 was similar to measures that Martin had opposed since the 1930s, but again the Speaker backed the Administration.

One of the few issues on which Martin broke with the President was the 1954 St. Lawrence Seaway bill. The measure was widely opposed in his home district because of fear that the Seaway would reduce traffic in the port of Boston. Despite pressure from the President, Martin declined to abandon his opposition.

In the 1954 elections the Democrats regained control of both houses of Congress, and Martin reverted to the status of minority leader. He blamed the Party's electoral failures in part on President Eisenhower. Martin felt that the President was not sufficiently partisan and did not help build up local and state Republican organizations. He was particulary critical of Eisenhower for not consulting either members of Congress or party officials on patronage matters. Martin contended that the Party could not be built up if those working hardest for it were not rewarded with jobs. He also felt that the President did not have politically astute advisers and did not have enough personal contact with Congress.

Martin was a conservative by temperament rather than ideology. He had worked his way up through party ranks by pragmatically bending to the exigencies of politics instead of attempting to alter fundamentally the political system. Therefore, Martin was acutely aware, for example, of constituent pressures on his colleagues and generally did not press Republican representatives to vote for Administration bills unpopular in their home districts. His credo, "You've got to follow in order to lead," reflected his belief that there were some political givens that no leadership could overcome.

Martin's partisan efforts on behalf of the Administration were also eroded by his close friendship with House Democratic leader Rep. Sam Rayburn (D, Tex.) [q.v.], which dated back to the 1930s. He sometimes helped Rayburn pass bills as a personal favor. During the 85th Congress (1957-58), for example, he used his influence with Republicans on the Rules Committee to aid Rayburn in bringing to the floor several bills favored by the liberal Democratic Study Group.

Therefore, just as Martin criticized President Eisenhower for insufficient partisanship, so Martin himself met similar criticism from Republicans both in and out of Congress. Many observers believed that he was too easygoing and did not sufficiently stress the need for party discipline and unity.

In February 1958 Martin attended a fund-raising dinner for the Republican National Committee held in Houston, Tex. Shortly afterwards it was revealed that a letter from the state's national committeeman to Texas oilmen had linked contributions for the dinner to the fate of a bill exempting independent natural gas producers from Federal Power Commission regulation. As a result the bill died. Martin, who would have had the task of helping muster votes for the Administration-backed bill, denied any knowledge of an attempt to connect contributions with the measure's passage.

After the Republicans' 1954 and 1956 electoral defeats, Rep. Charles Halleck (R, Ind.) [q.v.], Martin's assistant, expressed a desire to replace Martin as minority leader. However, both times he decided not to run after President Eisenhower indicated he wished to avoid intraparty warfare. Eisenhower blamed the 1958 Democratic landslide in part on ineffective leadership by Martin. When Halleck, a more aggressive and partisan Republican than Martin, again showed interest in the minority leadership, the President let it be known that he would not discourage the effort. This stance was interpreted as an indication of support for Halleck. A number of the President's aides were reported to have worked on behalf of the Indiana Representative. On

Jan. 6, 1959 he defeated Martin in the House Republican caucus by a vote of 74 to 70. In *My First Fifty Years in Politics* (1960), Martin expressed bitterness against President Eisenhower and Vice President Richard M. Nixon [q.v.]. He wrote, "I knew that if either of them merely spoke a word for me any revolt would be quelled. This was little enough to expect in view of what I had done for them, sometimes to my own distinct political disadvantage."

Following his defeat Martin lost significant influence in Congress and the Republican Party. In 1966 he was defeated in his district's Republican congressional primary. On March 6, 1968 he died in Hollywood, Fla., of peritonitis.

[MLL]

For further information:
Joe Martin, *My First Fifty Years in Politics* (New York, 1960).

MARTIN, WILLIAM McCHESNEY
b. Dec. 17, 1906; St. Louis, Mo.
Chairman, Board of Governors of the Federal Reserve System, 1951-70.

Martin was the son of a banker who at one time served as president of the Federal Reserve Bank of St. Louis. Following graduation from Yale University in 1928, he spent a year as a clerk at the St. Louis Federal Reserve Bank. Martin then became head of the statistical department of A. G. Edwards & Sons, a St. Louis brokerage firm, and in 1931 acquired a seat on the New York Stock Exchange.

In 1938 Martin became president of the Exchange, at 31 the youngest man ever to hold the post. Inducted into the Army as a private in 1941, he was promoted rapidly, served with the Munitions Allocation Board and eventually supervised much of the Lend-Lease program to the Soviet Union. In February 1946 President Harry S. Truman appointed him president and chairman of the board of the Export-Import Bank, formed to grant loans to foreign countries. Three years later Martin became assistant secretary of the Treasury for international finance. In that post he engineered the famous "accord" between the Treasury and the Federal Reserve Board freeing the Federal Reserve from "pegging" the bond market to permit the Administration to borrow at low interest rates. In 1951 Truman named Martin chairman of the Board of Governors of the Federal Reserve System. [See TRUMAN Volume]

Although Martin had functioned mainly as a conciliator in the resolution of the Treasury-Federal Reserve conflict, the "accord" was a reflection of his belief in the independence of the Federal Reserve and a free market in the buying and selling of domestic securities. Martin sternly defended these principles in his two decades as chairman of the Federal Reserve.

During the Eisenhower years Martin aroused controversy because of his conservative attitude toward credit. As the chief steward of the country's money supply, he was the most influential exponent of "tight money," that is, restriction of credit to banks in order to temper the pace of economic expansion and curtail inflation. This could be accomplished chiefly by raising reserve requirements of banks belonging to the Federal Reserve System and by increasing the rediscount rate, the rate of interest charged by the Federal Reserve on loans to member banks.

In the spring of 1953 Martin reinforced the Eisenhower Administration's anti-inflation effort by tightening credit restrictions. At about the same time Martin made major speeches in which he asserted that the Federal Reserve's action must be held to a minimum. His statement that "use of the discount window is a privilege not a right" led many dealers in government securities to conclude that the Federal Reserve would be cutting off credit to member banks. According to *Fortune*, "The 'bond panic' of May 1953 followed. The Federal Reserve had to jump in with heavy openmarket purchases before apprehension subsided."

Over the decade, gradually but adamantly, Martin enforced a policy of tighter money. The rediscount rate rose from 1½% in early 1954 to 3% by 1960. Democratic politicians and many economists denounced Martin's policy, charging that tight money was a major cause of the recessions of the 1950s. Martin persistently defended his actions, arguing in December 1956, for example, that a proposed drop in interest rates would only swell the money supply and accelerate inflation. He insisted, moreover, that the current monetary tightness was due more to an over-demand for credit than to any Federal Reserve action. "Creating more money will not create more goods," he maintained. "It can only intensify demands for the current supply of labor and materials. That is outright inflation."

In addition to the direct impact he exerted on financial policy, Martin often added his prestigious counsel to public debates on other economic issues. Throughout the 1950s he argued against Democratic proposals to stimulate the economy by cutting taxes. Opposing a congressional plan to lower personal income taxes, he said in February 1954: "If you increase the money consumers have . . . there is no guarantee that the consumer will spend the money. . . . Emphasis needs to be on the production side at this juncture." In June 1957 Martin argued that a proposed tax cut would make the Federal Reserve's effort to curb inflation "well-nigh impossible." During the 1958 recession as well, he opposed an anti-recession tax cut.

Martin espoused his free market principles during the Senate Banking and Currency Committee's 1955 probe into recent price fluctuations on the stock market. Criticizing proposals to ban buying stocks on credit, he said: "The stock market should not be denied access to credit unless you want to promote a lower standard of living." He insisted that higher margin requirements could not be "cure-alls for all stock market excesses" and defended risk-taking and speculation as the "proper function" of a securities market.

In 1956 President Eisenhower appointed Martin to a full 14-year term on the Federal Reserve's Board of Governors. During the 1960 campaign the presidential candidates disputed Martin's policies, with Sen. John F. Kennedy (D, Mass.) [*q.v.*] attacking tight money and Republican Richard Nixon [*q.v.*] promising to uphold the "independence" of the Federal Reserve. After his defeat, however, Nixon blamed his loss in part on the Federal Reserve's slowness in responding to the 1960 recession.

During the 1960s Martin remained to many conservatives the symbol of the sound dollar, while to populists like Rep. Wright Patman (D, Tex.) [q.v.] he represented a high-interest finance that enriched big banks and Wall Street and choked small businessmen. Martin got along well with Presidents Kennedy and Johnson and eased monetary policy for a time in an accommodation to their stimulative fiscal policies. During the Vietnam war interest rates rose to their highest levels since the 1920s, and Martin was again at the center of a storm of controversy. Martin retired from the Federal Reserve in 1970. [See KENNEDY, JOHNSON, NIXON/FORD Volumes]

[TO]

MATTHEWS, J(OSEPH) B(ROWN)
b. June 28, 1894; Hopkinsville, Ky.
d. July 16, 1966; New York, N.Y.
Staff Director, Permanent Investigations Subcommittee of the Senate Government Operations Committee, 1953.

As a young man J. B. Matthews served as a Methodist missionary in the Dutch East Indies (now Indonesia), where he wrote a hymnal in the Malay language. Returning to the U.S. in 1921, he pursued divinity and linguistic studies at Union Theological Seminary in New York and embraced the ideas of the Social Gospel movement. In 1924 he was appointed an instructor at Scarritt College, a Methodist institution in Nashville, Tenn. However, his activities on behalf of Robert LaFollette's Progressive presidential campaign that year resulted in his forced resignation shortly afterwards. In 1929 Matthews took the post of executive secretary of the pacifist Fellowship of Reconciliation. Although a member of the Socialist Party, he became a sponsor of numerous pro-Soviet organizations. In 1935 he was suspended by the Party as a result of these activities.

In the mid-1930s Matthews turned sharply to the right, and in 1938 he appeared as a star witness before the Special House Committee on Un-American Activities, naming 94 Communist front groups" with which he had been associated. He was hired as chief investigator by chairman Martin Dies (D, Tex.) and supervised the collection and indexing of vast amounts of information on Communist-inspired activity. Matthews left the Committee in 1945, taking with him voluminous files based on the Committee's investigations—including a private list of 22,000 alleged "fellow travelers." He continued to maintain a network of connections with disillusioned ex-Communists and such powerful conservative publishers as William Randolph Hearst, Jr.

In 1950 Matthews came to the aid of Sen. Joseph R. McCarthy's (R, Wisc.) [q.v.] anti-Communist crusade, convincing Hearst to support the Senator in his newspapers and providing much of the documentation for McCarthy's charges of subversion in the State Department. In 1953 he was named staff director for the Senate Government Operations Committee's Permanent Investigations Subcommittee, headed by McCarthy. Shortly after his appointment an article by Matthews, entitled "Reds in Our Churches," appeared in the *American Mercury*. Its allegation that "the largest single group supporting the Communist apparatus in the United States is composed of Protestant clergymen" provoked a storm of protest from churchmen of all denominations and a demand from Democratic subcommittee members that Matthews be fired. McCarthy at first refused but gave in after the White House released a press statement branding the article "irresponsible." Although the Matthews affair produced President Eisenhower's first public rebuke of McCarthy, the Republican majority on the subcommittee responded with a face-saving motion giving the chairman exclusive power to hire and fire staff personnel. This led the Democratic minority to take the unprecedented step of resigning in protest from the subcommittee.

Matthews privately continued to pursue research on Communism. In the 1960s his name appeared on the masthead of *American Opinion*, the periodical of the ultraright John Birch Society.

[TLH]

For further information:
Robert Griffith, *The Politics of Fear* (New York, 1970).

MEANY, GEORGE
b. Aug. 16, 1894; New York, N.Y.
President, AFL, 1952–55, AFL-CIO, 1955- .

Meany grew up in the Bronx, the son of an Irish Catholic plumber and union official. At age 16 he became a plumber's apprentice and later joined the union when he became eligible as a journeyman. Meany was elected to his first full-time union office in 1922 as business agent of the Plumbers Union Local 463, which included the Bronx and Manhattan. Twelve years later he won election as president of the New York Federation of Labor, a post that made him the chief labor spokesman in Albany and put him in close contact with the Roosevelt Administration and the national leadership of the American Federation of Labor (AFL). Meany proved a skillful lobbyist, and in 1940 AFL President William Green chose him to be secretary-treasurer of the Federation.

During World War II Meany served on the National Defense Mediation Board and the War Labor Board. In the postwar years he assumed increasing responsibility from the often-ailing Green for the AFL's day-to-day activity. Meany helped lead the Federation's fight against passage of the Taft-Hartley Act in 1947, but he supported the non-Communist affidavits required of union officials under the law. He also worked closely with the American government in building anti-Communist trade unions abroad and was instrumental in the formation of the pro-Western International Confederation of Free Trade Unions (ICFTU) in 1949. [See TRUMAN Volume]

In November 1952 Green died, and Meany was named AFL president by the Federation's executive council. Although a firm business unionist with great loyalty to the craft traditions of the AFL, Meany was less hostile to the rival Congress of Industrial Organizations (CIO) than others in the Federation hierarchy. One of his first acts as president was to revive merger negotiations (which had been suspended since 1950) with the CIO. CIO President Walter Reuther [q.v.] also favored unity but insisted on several preconditions, including the setting up of machinery to resolve jurisdictional disputes between industrial and craft unions in the same industries and the elimination of racketeering elements from AFL affiliates. In 1953 Meany moved against the East Coast's International Longshoremen's Association (ILA), which had long been dominated by gangsters, a situation spotlighted in 1952 and 1953 by a New York state crime commission. After ILA President Joseph Ryan refused to reform the union's hiring system and fire officers with criminal records, the AFL voted, at Meany's initiative, to expel the longshoremen at its convention in September. The Federation chartered a new union, the International Brotherhood of Longshoremen, but subsequently lost a representation election on the New York docks.

In June 1954 Meany reached agreement with Reuther on a no-raiding pact, which essentially froze the existing respective jurisdictions of AFL and CIO unions. Although several large AFL affiliates, including the Carpenters and Teamsters, disliked the pact, the Federation's executive council endorsed a final merger plan in February of the following year. Since the AFL was nearly twice as large as the CIO, Meany assumed the presidency of the new AFL-CIO in December 1955, while Reuther became a vice-president and head of the Industrial Union Department. CIO leaders also agreed to retain the loose structure of the AFL, which gave wide autonomy to member unions.

Among the more politically aggressive labor leaders in the postwar period, Meany helped found Labor's League for Political Education, the AFL political arm, which worked closely with the Democratic Party. He also persuaded the Federation to break officially with its nonpartisan tradition for the first time by endorsing Illinois Gov. Adlai Stevenson's [q.v.] 1952 presidential candidacy. From 1947 on, however, the AFL's primary political objective was to secure the repeal, or at least the substantial modification, of the Taft-Hartley Act. Although disappointed by Dwight D. Eisenhower's victory in 1952, Federation leaders applauded the new President's pledge to back certain revisions in the Act, including provisions for striking workers to vote in representation elections and a requirement that employers as well as union officers sign non-Communist affidavits. The appointment of Martin Durkin [q.v.], head of Meany's own plumbers' union, as Secretary of Labor raised hopes for an early revision in labor legislation. With the approval of the White House, Meany and Durkin drew up a set of amendments to Taft-Hartley early in 1953, including repeal of section 14b, which permitted states to pass so-called right-to-work laws barring the union shop. Before the proposals could be submitted to Congress, however, opponents within the Administration mobilized strong counter-pressures from business groups and finally persuaded the President to withdraw his support.

After Durkin's resignation in August 1953, the AFL found itself on the defensive in Congress. During most of the Eisenhower years, labor lobbyists devoted their efforts to defeating conservative moves to strengthen Taft-Hartley, including proposals to put unions under antitrust laws. Even after merger the AFL-CIO was no more successful in realizing its legislative goals. In 1957 Meany threw the Federation's resources behind an effort to win health insurance for the aged. Congressional labor lobbyists succeeded in blocking a weaker White House-sponsored bill for underwriting health insurance through private companies, rather than the social security system, but were unable to secure passage of the AFL-CIO measure. Meany blamed the conservative coalition in Congress as much as the White House for labor's legislative defeats. He grew increasingly skeptical of electoral activity, particularly because many powerful Southern Democrats were beyond the political reach of unions. In 1956 Meany unsuccessfully sought to withhold AFL-CIO endorsement from Stevenson, declaring that even if the Democrats won the presidency, the same anti-labor forces would continue to control congressional committees.

Despite his opposition on domestic issues, Meany supported the Eisenhower Administration's defense and foreign policies. Under his presidency the AFL cooperated with the Foreign Operations Administration, the State and Defense Departments and other government agencies in the conduct of overseas labor programs and in the realization of broader Administration policy objectives as well. In 1953 and 1954 Meany and his staff worked with the Central Intelligence Agency in an effort to topple the Guatemalan government of President Jacobo Arbenz. The AFL attempted to undermine the Communist-dominated Guatemalan labor federation by creating a rival union group, the leaders of which joined a CIA-sponsored "liberation army" led by Gen. Carlos Armas. After the overthrow of Arbenz in June 1954, however, the Armas government proceeded to suppress all trade unions in Guatemala, including the AFL-backed organizations.

In his staunch commitment to fighting Communist influence in the international labor movement and to defending what he perceived as being U.S. national interests, Meany was strongly influenced by Jay Lovestone [q.v.], head of the AFL Foreign Affairs Department and himself a former Communist Party leader. Under Meany's aegis Lovestone set up a network of associates, most of whom had been part of his former Communist entourage, stationed in various parts of the world with large, often untraceable funds at their disposal. (In the 1960s a series of articles in American newspapers and magazines revealed that most of these funds came from government sources, including the CIA.) After the merger Lovestone's operations became a source of continual conflict between Meany and Walter Reuther, who objected to Lovestone's clandestine methods and wanted the AFL-CIO to work through the International Confederation of Free Trade Unions. Meany and Lovestone regarded the ICFTU as insufficiently anti-Communist, however, and preferred instead to channel financial aid and political direction independently to trade unions abroad.

In 1957 sensational public exposures of union corruption forced Meany to again take action against Federation affiliates. When the Senate Select Committee on Improper Activities in the Labor or Management Field, headed by Sen. John L. McClellan (D, Ark.) [q.v.], began its investigation of the International Brotherhood of Teamsters in January, Meany instructed AFL-CIO officials to cooperate in answering all questions about their unions' affairs. The McClellan Committee quickly compiled a compelling case against Teamster President Dave Beck [q.v.], including allegations that he had taken more than $30,000 in union funds to pay for personal gifts and real estate. After Beck refused to answer more than 90 questions before the Committee in March, Meany had him suspended from his seat on the AFL-CIO executive council for "conduct detrimental to the trade union movement." Shortly afterwards the McClellan panel turned its attention to James Hoffa [q.v.], Beck's successor as Teamster president.

In October Meany recommended that the Teamsters be suspended from the Federation pending removal of Beck, Hoffa and other officials by a special committee appointed by the executive council. Teamster leaders refused to initiate internal reforms, however, and in December the AFL-CIO voted to expel the International. At the same time Meany moved against several smaller unions that had been subjects of the McClellan probe, expelling the Bakers and Confectioners and the Laundry Workers and placing the United Textile Workers on probation under a Federation monitor. While seeking to purge the Federation of racketeers, however, Meany also complained that the Senate investigations ignored business's role in corruption. The union leader denounced the McClellan Committee as "little more than a vehicle of reactionary elements seeking to discredit the American labor movement."

In 1958 demands for sweeping government regulation of union finances, internal governance and strike activities came to the forefront in Congress. Partly in order to forestall more stringent legislation, the AFL-CIO endorsed a bill sponsored by Sens. John F. Kennedy (D, Mass.) [q.v.] and Irving Ives (R, N.Y.) [q.v.], which included as "sweeteners" several amendments to the Taft-Hartley Act desired by building trades unions. Business groups and congressional conservatives sought to eliminate the labor-backed amendments. As result of their efforts the Kennedy-Ives bill, after passing the Senate in June, died when it reached the House.

Reacting vigorously to the threat of what it viewed as anti-labor legislation, the AFL-CIO threw its manpower and resources into the 1958 elections in an effort to defeat right-to-work proposals, which had been placed on several state ballots, and elect its "friends" to office. The results, which included the victory of 70% of the congressional candidates backed by the AFL-CIO's Committee on Political Education, were hailed by Meany as a vindication of organized labor after the unfavorable publicity generated by the McClellan investigations.

With the Senate almost two-thirds Democratic and Republicans warning of a "labor-bossed Congress," it came as a surprise to Meany when the AFL-CIO's efforts to block conservative reform proposals collapsed the following year. On April 22, 1959 a bill prepared by the liberal-dominated Senate Subcommittee on Labor in close consultation with Federation represenatives was amended by Sen. McClellan to include a "bill of rights" aimed at guaranteeing democratic procedures in union governance. Meany and other labor leaders strongly opposed the amendment as too great an interference in union affairs. He claimed that its equal rights provisions would, among other things, lead to the legally enforced membership of Communists, criminals or management agents in their organizations. The bill of rights was later modified to meet some of labor's objections before being passed by the Senate. In the House, however, a coalition of Southern Democrats and Republicans, supported by the Administration, introduced a substitute reform measure, the Landrum-Griffin bill. That bill contained the McClellan proposals as well as additional amendments strengthening prohibitions against secondary boycotts and curbing picketing rights. Despite strong opposition from the AFL-CIO, the bill was passed in August. President Eisenhower signed it into law on Sept. 14 as the Labor-Management Reporting and Disclosure Act.

During the late-1950s Meany came under increasing criticism from Reuther and other former CIO leaders for what they regarded as his insufficiently dynamic leadership at home and his hard-line, cold war posture on foreign policy questions. Reuther urged Meany to throw the Federation's resources into organizing the estimated 26 million non-union workers in the U.S. But Meany was unwilling to ask individual unions to abandon their jurisdictional claims in joint organizing drives. In his public remarks on foreign policy, Meany consistently opposed detente with the USSR and denounced neutral nations such as India as "in effect" allies of Communism. In 1959 he refused visiting Soviet leaders Anastas Mikoyan and Nikita Khrushchev permission to tour the AFL-CIO headquarters in Washington, D.C., or address the Federation's convention in San Francisco. He criticized Reuther for meeting with them.

Although the AFL-CIO pledged itself in 1955 to the rapid elimination of racial discrimination within its ranks, Meany soon came under fire from black unionists and civil rights leaders, particularly after the Federation in 1956 admitted two railroad unions which barred non-whites from membership. In 1958 the NAACP filed complaints with the AFL-CIO Civil Rights Department against the locals of 12 unions for discriminatory seniority provisions, systematic exclusion of blacks from leadership positions and other forms of bias. In the following year A. Philip Randolph [q.v.], head of the black Brotherhood of Sleeping Car Porters, brought these and other complaints to the floor of the AFL-CIO convention. After an angry exchange, during which Meany roared at Randolph, "Who in the hell appointed you as guardian of the Negro members in America?," the Federation refused to expel the accused locals.

Meany strongly backed John F. Kennedy at the July 1960 Democratic National Convention. He favored Sen. Henry Jackson (D, Wash.) [q.v.] for the second spot on the ticket and was deeply shocked when Kennedy chose Sen. Lyndon B. Johnson (D, Tex.) [q.v.] as his running-mate. Meany held Johnson responsible as Senate majority leader for allowing the Landrum-Griffin Act to pass, dubbing him "Lying Down Lyndon." Only Reuther's strenuous efforts on Kennedy's behalf prevented the AFL-CIO caucus at the Convention from publicly condemning the Johnson selection. The Federation's executive council finally endorsed the ticket in August, with Meany's consent.

Meany applauded the social welfare legislation of the Kennedy Administration but criticized the President for failing to reduce unemployment. At the same time he threw the Federation's support behind anti-Communist initiatives in foreign policy, helping to create the largely government-funded American Institute for Free Labor Development, which trained Latin American union leaders to oppose anti-U.S. regimes. After 1964 Meany enthusiastically backed the Johnson Administration's Great Society programs, as a result of which his earlier hostility to Johnson turned into a close friendship. In 1968 Meany mobilized AFL-CIO efforts on behalf of Sen. Hubert Humphrey's (D, Minn.) [q.v.] presidential candidacy. A strong supporter of the Vietnam war, he withheld AFL-CIO endorsement and resources from liberal anti-war Sen. George McGovern (D, S.D.) [q.v.] in his 1972 campaign. [See KENNEDY, JOHNSON, NIXON/FORD, CARTER Volumes]

[TLH]

For further information:
Joseph C. Goulden, *Meany* (New York, 1972).
Alan K. McAdams, *Power and Politics in Labor Legislation* (New York, 1964).
Ronald Radosh, *American Labor and United States Foreign Policy* (New York, 1969).

MERCHANT, LIVINGSTON T(ALLMADGE)

b. Nov. 23, 1903: New York, N.Y.
d. May 15, 1976: Washington, D.C.
Assistant Secretary of State for European Affairs, March 1953-April 1956, October 1958-August 1959: Ambassador to Canada, April 1956-October 1958: Deputy Undersecretary of State for Political Affairs, August 1959-January 1960; Undersecretary of State for Political Affairs, January 1960-February 1961.

Livingston Merchant, a descendant of Oliver Wolcott, George Washington's Secretary of the Treasury, and Gen. William Floyd, a signer of the Declaration of Independence, graduated from Princeton in 1926. He then joined the New York and Boston firm of Scudder, Stevens and Clark and during the 1920s and 1930s had a successful career as an investment counsellor. Several months after the Japanese attack on Pearl Harbor, Merchant joined the State Department, where he held various positions in the economic division. In 1947 he entered the career Foreign Service and was posted as counsellor in Nanking, China. Two years later he became assistant secretary of state for Far Eastern affairs.

In March 1953 John Foster Dulles [q.v.] named Merchant his assistant secretary of state for European affairs. During his three years at that post he undertook many top-level diplomatic assignments. He accompanied President Eisenhower on important missions to Berlin in 1954 and London and Paris the following year. In 1955 Merchant served as one of the major planners of the July "Big Four" Conference called to discuss the unification of Germany and the status of Berlin. At the conference he served as a close aide to Eisenhower; the *New York Times* characterized him as the man upon whom the President "leans most heavily." Later that year Merchant carried on a series of conferences in London, Paris and Bonn in preparation for an October foreign ministers meeting which focused on Germany and the relaxation of East-West tensions.

Eisenhower nominated Merchant as am-

bassador to Canada in April 1956. He assumed his post at a time when relations were strained by the Canadian Conservative Party's charges that the Liberal Government was "selling out to foreign capital"—the United States—through its policy of encouraging foreign investment. The appointment of a high-ranking diplomat as ambassador was designed to show U.S. recognition of Canada's importance and concern for its problems. However, relations between the two countries remained cool throughout Merchant's tour.

In 1959 Secretary of State Christian Herter [q.v.] sent Merchant to Panama in an attempt to ease tensions following anti-American riots over control of the Canal Zone. Despite his assurances that Panama maintained titular sovereignty over the area under the 1903 treaty and his suggestions that the U.S. would increase economic aid to the country, Merchant failed to stop the violence.

President Kennedy appointed Merchant to a second tour as ambassador to Canada in 1961. He served there until his retirement from the Foreign Service in 1962. During 1963 he became the President's special representative for Multilateral Force Negotiations. From 1965 to 1968 Merchant was U.S. executive director of the International Bank for Reconstruction and Development. He died in 1976. [See KENNEDY Volume]

[EWS]

METCALF, LEE

b. Jan. 28, 1911; Stevensville, Mont.
Democratic Representative, Mont., 1953-61; Democratic Senator, Mont., 1961-   .

Metcalf, the son of a bank cashier, grew up on his family's 300-acre farm outside Stevensville, Mont. In 1936 he obtained an LL.B. degree from Montana State University and was elected to the Montana House of Representatives the same year. The following year Metcalf was appointed an assistant state attorney general. In 1941 he resigned the post and entered private law practice. Following service in the Army during World War II, Metcalf was elected to a six-year term as an associate justice of the Montana Supreme Court. In 1952 he ran successfully for a U.S. House seat from Montana's first district, comprising the western third of the state and including the heavily Democratic Blackfeet Indian Reservation.

From his first term in Congress, the liberal Metcalf was outspoken on such issues as conservation. In 1953 he played a major role in defeating a grazing lands bill, opposed by conservationists and wildlife groups because it would have made grazing permits on federal lands tantamount to ownership. The following year Metcalf led successful floor opposition to a timberlands exchange bill requiring the federal government to give private interests timber rights on federal lands in payment for land requisitioned by the government. Metcalf first added several amendments to the measure, including one providing that timber rights, but not title, would be transferred to private interests. He then moved successfully to recommit the bill to the Interior Committee.

Three years later Metcalf was one of the founders of a caucus of young liberal Democratic representatives known as the Democratic Study Group (DSG). In January 1957 he joined 27 representatives in issuing the caucus's policy statement, which included recommendations for federal aid for school construction, medical education and housing; repeal of the Taft-Hartley Act and extension of the coverage of the Fair Labor Standards Act; protection of civil rights; and revision of immigration and naturalization laws to eliminate the national origins rule.

Later in 1957 Metcalf was one of the members of the Education and Labor Committee who voted unsuccessfully to deny the panel's chairman, Rep. Graham D. Barden (D, N.C.) [q.v.], the right to appoint subcommittee chairmen and staff members. In 1958 Metcalf and Sen. James E. Murray (D, Mont.), a member of the Labor and Public Welfare Committee, co-sponsored a bill to provide federal aid for school construction and scholarships. The measure was shunted aside, however, for an Administration bill that included only a scholarship plan. In 1959 the Murray-

Metcalf bill was stalled by the conservative-dominated Rules Committee.

Metcalf was elected to the Senate in 1960, where he continued to focus his attention on education, the regulation of power companies and conservation. In his 1967 book *Overcharge*, Metcalf maintained that state regulation of utility companies was a failure because state governments did not have the resources to discipline the industry. [See KENNEDY, JOHNSON Volumes]

[MLL]

MEYNER, ROBERT B(AUMLE)
b. July 3, 1908; Easton, Pa.
Governor, N.J., 1954-61.

The son of a silk-loom repairer, Robert B. Meyner attended Lafayette College and Columbia University law school. He received an LL.B. in 1933 and opened a private law practice in Phillipsburg, N.J., three years later. In 1941 Meyner ran unsuccessfully for the state Senate, losing by 50 votes. Following service in the Navy during World War II, he made an unsuccessful run for the U.S. House in 1946; he was elected to the state Senate in 1947 as a Democrat. Meyner became minority leader in 1950 and chairman of the state party convention in 1951. He was, nevertheless, defeated for reelection that year.

In 1953 Meyner won the Democratic gubernatorial primary against the candidate of the powerful Hudson Co. machine. Running on a platform that stressed the need to combat organized crime, revise taxes and increase aid to public schools, he went on to win the general election by 153,000 votes.

As governor, Meyner attempted to maintain a middle-of-the-road position, relying on his personal popularity to generate support for his programs. Meyner often promoted legislation with a bipartisan appeal. In 1954 he began the 164-mile Garden State Parkway and the following year established the Delaware Basin Authority. He opened the state's first medical college at Seton Hall in 1956.

Most of Meyner's proposals were not enacted into law, in part, because he lacked a political base. The Hudson Co. machine that provided Democrats astonishing pluralities for decades was in decline, and Republican Bergen Co. was growing. His removal of former Gov. Harold G. Hoffman as employment security director in March 1954 on charges of corruption did little to endear him to Hudson Co. boss John V. Kenny.

Warm and gregarious, at ease when talking affairs of state, Meyner dominated the 1954 Governors Conference and found himself a possible vice presidential candidate in 1956. He announced that he would not seek national office but would run for another term as governor. His slate of uncommitted delegates easily won the May New Jersey presidential primary against those pledged to Sen. Estes Kefauver (D, Tenn.) [q.v.]. He supported Adlai Stevenson [q.v.] at the August Democratic National Convention.

In November 1957 Meyner won reelection by a huge plurality, becoming the first New Jersey governor to serve two four-year terms. His second term saw passage of the 1958 Water Supply Act, providing $40 million to build reservoirs along the Raritan River and develop New Jersey's ground water resources. He got approval for the 1961 "green acres" bond issue, providing $60 million to buy land for public use. This made New Jersey one of the first states to approve large-scale recreational land purchases.

Much of Meyner's second term was spent traveling abroad and visiting national Democratic leaders in an attempt to build a viable candidacy for the 1960 Democratic presidential nomination. However, he was able to garner no real support and could not prevent Joseph P. Kennedy from making overtures to North Jersey political leaders on behalf of his son, Sen. John F. Kennedy (D, Mass.) [q.v.]. Angered by the elder Kennedy's presumption and with a Stevenson-Meyner ticket in mind, the Governor bound his delegation to his candidacy through the first ballot. At the July 1960 Democratic National Convention, Meyner did not release his delegates in time to put Kennedy over the top, and consequently, he was ignored by the new Ad-

ministration. After leaving public office Meyner returned to the practice of law. He attempted a political comeback in 1969, winning the Democratic gubernatorial primary. However he lost badly in the November election.

For further information:
David van Praagh, "New Jersey's Man-in-the-Middle," *Nation* (Sept. 7, 1957), pp. 105-08.

MILLER, ARTHUR
b. Oct. 17, 1915; N.Y., N.Y.
Playwright.

Born in New York City to an Austro-Hungarian immigrant father and native American mother, Miller was granted probationary acceptance to the University of Michigan in 1934, after an early adolescence of poor academic achievement and little interest in literature or drama. Vigorously pursuing his ambition to write plays, Miller wrote while attending school and received his B.A. in 1938. After a short time writing for the Federal Theater Project, he spent the war years—draft exempt for health reasons—writing radio dramas and working part time as a steam fitter and truck driver.

Miller's first critically and commercially well-received play was *All My Sons*, presented in 1947, for which he won the New York Drama Critic's Circle Award. In 1949 he wrote *Death of A Salesman*, which again won the Circle Award as well as the Pulitzer Prize. The work portrayed the disintegration of Willie Loman, a traveling salesman forced to confront his failures in business and in his home. The play was viewed as a drama of one man's destruction by his own flawed dreams and as an attack on the materialistic society that abetted the manufacture of those goals. During the 1940s Miller associated with a number of Communist writers and signed appeals and protests by groups the U.S. government classified as "Red-fronts" in the late-1940s.

Miller's next important play, *The Crucible*, produced in 1953, brought him to the forefront of the political controversy over Sen. Joseph R. McCarthy's (R, Wisc.) [q.v.] loyalty-security investigations.

Many people saw *The Crucible* as a direct challenge to the hysteria of McCarthyism. The play told the story of individuals' struggles to maintain both their integrity and their lives in confrontations with the Salem witch hunters of the 17th century. Playgoers readily drew parallels between extreme McCarthyites and the irrational Puritans whose violent fear of subversion caused the deaths of innocent people. Other viewers, including the Communist writer Howard Fast [*q.v.*], proclaimed the play to be a statement on the case of Julius and Ethel Rosenberg [*q.v.*]. (Miller himself was not entirely pleased that the artistic qualities of his play were often forgotten in arguments over its political implications.) In 1954 Miller published an ironic, unmistakably anti-McCarthy article entitled "Every American Should Go To Jail: A Modest Proposal for Pacifying the Public Temper."

Miller's work attracted the attention of the House Un-American Activities Committee (HUAC), which called him to testify during the hearings on the unauthorized use of U.S. passports. Ostensibly at issue was Miller's eligibility to travel abroad, given his suspected Communist leanings. Because Miller was an internationally respected figure, the Committee carried on a low-keyed investigation designed not to inflame public opinion. The hearings lacked the vitriol of other HUAC meetings. Miller was described by historian Walter Goodman as "responsive, collected and only moderately sententious." Miller was accused of having signed numerous statements connected with allegedly pro-Communist organizations and of having made a formal application to join the Communist Party. He calmly conceded his activities with Communists in the 1940s, but he denied the application charge, and stated, "I would not now support a cause or movement dominated by Communists." The Committee mildly praised him for his example of "repentence," but he angered the panel by his refusal to offer the names of those he believed to be Communists. Miller was cited for contempt of Congress and received a $500 fine and a 30-day suspended jail sentence. He appealed and won a reversal of the contempt citation in 1958.

Throughout the 1950s and 1960s Miller continued to write plays in a style sometimes described as "social realism." These included *A Memory of Two Mondays* (1955) and *A View from the Bridge* (1955). *After the Fall* (1964) was a personal work that fictitiously examined his married life with actress Marilyn Monroe and his relationships with artist-informers involved in anti-Communist investigations. He was elected president of P.E.N., the International Association of Writers, in 1965, and he wrote the well-received *The Prize* in 1967. Miller's political activity in 1960s included the rejection of an invitation to the White House in protest against the Vietnam war.

[TGD]

For further information:
Eric Bentley, ed., *Thirty Years of Treason, 1938-1968* (New York, 1971).

MILLIKIN, EUGENE D(ONALD)
b. Feb. 12, 1891; Hamilton, Ohio.
d. July 26, 1958; Denver, Colo.
Republican Senator, Colo., 1941-57;
Chairman, Senate Finance Committee, 1953-55.

Eugene Millikin grew up in Ohio, leaving at age 19 to enroll in the University of Colorado law school. Upon graduation in 1913 he became executive secretary to George Carlson, who was soon elected governor of Colorado. During World War I Millikin served with the Army in France and Germany. After the War he formed a law partnership in Colorado with Karl Schuyler. When Schuyler was elected to the U.S. Senate in 1932, Millikin accompanied him to Washington as his secretary but returned to Colorado the next year after Schuyler's death. He resumed his corporate law practice and served as president of the Kinney-Coastal Oil Co.

In 1941 Millikin was appointed to the Senate to fill the vacancy created by the death of Sen. Alva Adams (D, Colo.). He was elected to serve the remainder of Adams's term in 1942 and won reelection in 1944 and 1950. A close ally of Sen. Robert Taft (R, Ohio) [*q.v.*], Millikin shared the Ohioan's fiscal conservatism but was more inclined toward a bipartisan approach to foreign affairs. He became expert in the intricacies of trade and taxation, serving as chairman of the Senate Finance Committee during the 1947-48 session of Congress and as ranking Republican thereafter. Consistently friendly to business, Millikin often devoted his technical expertise and formidable debating skill to the creation and preservation of corporate tax preferences and the obstruction of Democratic social programs. [See TRUMAN Volume]

At the outset of the Eisenhower Administration, Millikin was the chairman of the Senate Republican Conference and, as a result of Republican majorities in the 83rd Congress, once again chairman of the important Finance Committee. He also sat on the Joint Committee on Atomic Energy and was second-ranking Republican on the Interior and Insular Affairs Committee. Millikin was one of a handful of congressional Republicans who met once a week to discuss policy with President Eisenhower. In January 1954 *Business Week* characterized him as "probably the most influential Republican in the Senate."

For the most part Millikin exercised his influence on behalf of the Administration's programs. His voting record placed him among the five most faithful supporters of the Administration in the Senate, according to *Congressional Quarterly*. More important from the Administration's point of view was his reliability as Finance Committee chairman, particularly since his House counterpart, chairman of the Ways and Means Committee Rep. Daniel Reed (R, N.Y.) [*q.v.*], pursued an independent course in defiance of the Administration.

For example, a six-month extension of the excess profits tax requested by the Administration passed the House in July 1953 only after experiencing great difficulty in Reed's committee. In the Senate, however, Millikin rushed the measure through the Finance Committee without holding hearings; it passed the Senate by a voice vote. He opposed Sen. John Williams's (R, Del.) [*q.v.*] amendment to raise the business tax credit from $25,000 to $100,000; the amendment was defeated. On the Administration's behalf Millikin pleaded suc-

cessfully against passage of any amendments because that would have necessitated having the revised bill passed in the House, a process which he compared to "passing a kidney stone."

In 1954 Millikin fought for a provision exempting from taxation a portion of income derived from stock dividends. The Senate passed the amendment but then reversed itself and rejected it. However, the dividend relief provision was partially restored in conference. Millikin also successfully led Republican opposition to a Democratic proposal to raise the personal tax exemption from $600 to $700. The combination of the dividend credit with rejection of a tax cut for wage earners prompted tax reformer Sen. Paul Douglas (D, Ill.) [*q.v.*] to brand the bill "an economic, social and moral monstrosity." Millikin gave a vigorous rebuttal to the charge and was still defending the bill a year later. In reply to a Democratic attack on the 1954 bill for treating "with brutality those in the lower-income brackets," Millikin cited 22 provisions that he said benefited individuals.

In trade policy Millikin steered a moderate course between his protectionist leanings and the Administration's desire to renew reciprocal trade agreements. In June 1954 he engineered Senate passage of a one-year extension of the agreements. In April 1955 he tried to limit extension to two years instead of three, but he lost in the Finance Committee, eight to seven. He did win passage, nine to six, of an "escape clause" amendment to limit certain imports if they "contributed materially" to a "threat of serious injury" to a domestic industry. Free trade advocates charged that Millikin's amendment "watered down" the bill, but the Senate passed it in that form.

From his senior position on the Interior Committee, Millikin was an influential supporter of the Colorado River Storage Project, a billion-dollar program to construct water storage facilities along the Upper Colorado River Basin. Millikin's vote for the St. Lawrence Seaway project in 1954 was interpreted as a trade-off for Administration backing for the Colorado enterprise. The Senate approved the Colorado Project in 1955, the House in 1956.

Despite his influence and ability, Millikin never betrayed any ambitions for the presidency and spurned opportunities to be Senate Republican leader. "He was valuable to the interests he represented," said his frequent adversary, Paul Douglas, "but he failed to become a national figure because of his natural indolence and the narrowness of his concerns." Ailing from arthritis, Millikin did not seek reelection in 1956. He died of pneumonia on July 26, 1958.

[TO]

MILLS, C(HARLES) WRIGHT
b. Aug. 28, 1916; Waco, Tex.
d. March 20, 1962; Nyack, N.Y.
Sociologist.

Mills grew up in a middle-class Texas family of Irish and English descent. He was educated in Catholic schools, and in 1939 he received his B.A. and M.A. degrees in philosophy and sociology from the University of Texas. He then went to the University of Wisconsin, where two years later, he received his Ph.D. in sociology. After teaching at the University of Maryland during World War II, he moved to Columbia University, where he soon emerged as one of the most controversial and widely read critics of postwar American society.

Using the methodologies of Karl Marx and Max Weber, Mills sought to identify the changing relationships of social and political power in the U.S. and, at the same time, offer recommendations for radical change. While fundamentally opposed to liberal social scientists' ideas of objective scholarship, Mills's work increasingly diverged from the traditional Marxist dialectic as well. His *New Men of Power* (1948) argued that the power which labor union leaders had achieved since World War II enabled them to form the basis of a radical coalition with intellectuals and white collar workers capable of "stopping the main drift towards war and slump." In *White Collar* (1951) Mills described the emergence of a new American middle class made up not of strong and independent entrepreneurs but of "the small creature who

is acted upon but who does not act, who works alone unnoticed in somebody's office or store, never talking loud, never talking back, never taking a stand." Miils viewed the rise of white collar workers as a tragic phenomenon. In particular, he regretted their political passivity and their indifference to processes and decisions that enormously affected their lives.

With *The Power Elite* (1956), his most controversial book, Mills completed his critical model of the American social structure. The growth of large-scale bureaucracies, the development of new techniques for the manipulation of people and the emergence of a vast military apparatus armed with weapons of mass destruction gave rise, according to Mills, to an interconnected military-governmental-corporate elite wielding unprecedented power through its control of great organizations. He attacked the popular theory of "countervailing power," propounded by economist John Kenneth Galbraith [q.v.], which maintained that the power of corporations was checked by government, and the "end of ideology" theories of sociologists Daniel Bell [q.v.] and Seymour Martin Lipset [q.v.], which celebrated the "pluralistic" character of American politics. Mills argued that "mass society" was easily manipulated by education, religion, television and movies because it lacked any truly independent organization and ideology to counter the power of the elite. Workers, Mills concluded, had come to accept the values sponsored by the power elite, and they yearned only for white collar jobs and suburban homes. The study was highly criticized by some sociologists, including Bell, who believed that the theory of a "power elite" implied a "unity of purpose and community of interest" among the elite that was asserted rather than proved.

Mills continued to focus on the elite in *The Causes of World War Three* (1958). The book was a highly polemic interpretation of the Cold War as a series of blunders on the part of Soviet and American leaders. Mills saw a new and devastating war as almost unavoidable, for the contemporary power structure left the fate of the world in the hands of an isolated few who, he thought, were both unscrupulous and incompetent. The only solution, he claimed in *The Sociological Imagination* (1959), lay in an exertion of leadership by a new generation of intellectuals. But before this would be possible, intellectuals would have to direct their research away from abstract issues to "urgent public issues and insistant human trouble."

In a 1960 "Letter to the New Left," Mills linked the student rebellions in Turkey and South Korea with the Cuban revolution and the civil rights movement in the American South. He attributed these movements to the "young intelligentsia."

Until the late-1950s Mills was a staunch anti-Communist, but visits to Poland and the USSR in 1956 and 1960 left him ambivalent about Communist societies. *Listen Yankee* (1960), published after a trip to Cuba in the summer of 1960, was a vigorous defense of the Cuban revolution which did much to generate enthusiasm for the Castro government among the American student Left. Arguing that the new regime was building the preconditions for a good society, while at the same time criticizing its lack of democracy, Mills warned that the U.S. would attempt to destroy the revolution by force.

Mills died of a heart attack in 1962. Despite his death, Mills greatly influenced the development of the New Left during that decade. [see KEENEDY Volume]

[TLH]

For further information:
Peter Clecak, *Radical Paradoxes: Dilemmas of the American Left, 1945-1970* (New York, 1973).
G. William Domhoff and Hoyt B. Ballard, eds., *C. Wright Mills and the Power Elite* (Boston, 1968).

MILLS, WILBUR D(AIGH)
b. May 24, 1909; Kensett, Ark.
Democratic Representative, Ark., 1939-77; Chairman, Ways and Means Committee, 1957-74.

The son of a country banker, Wilbur Mills attended Arkansas public schools and Methodist-affiliated Hendrix College before entering Harvard law school in 1930. He returned to Arkansas without receiving a degree in 1933 and took a job as a cashier in his father's bank. In 1934 he was elected county and probate judge for White Co. on a pledge to balance the budget. He fulfilled the campaign promise and was reelected. In 1938 the 29-year-old Mills ran successfully for a seat in the U.S. House of Representatives. He won reelection in every subsequent election with little or no opposition.

A protege of Speaker of the House Sam Rayburn (D, Tex.) [*q.v.*], Mills gained appointment under Rayburn's sponsorship to the Ways and Means Committee in 1943, an uncommonly swift ascension to the presitigious tax-writing committee. Mills industriously applied himself to the details of government finance and trade legislation, becoming by the 1950s the House's foremost tax expert. [See TRUMAN Volume]

Mills's voting record was generally that of a moderate; from 1953 to 1960 he voted for positions favored by the liberal Americans for Democratic Action an average of 45% of the time on major issues. He voted against statehood for Alaska and Hawaii and against the Saint Lawrence Seaway project. He voted in favor of public housing, the federal highway program and federal aid for prevention of water pollution, but against federal aid for school construction. He regularly opposed civil rights proposals and signed the 1956 "Southern Manifesto" which denounced the Supreme Court's 1954 decision declaring school segregation unconstitutional.

In 1953 Mills, as second-ranking Democrat on the Ways and Means Committee, supported the extension of the Korean war excess profits tax to the end of the year. The next year he voted in favor of an unsuccessful amendment to substitute general tax relief for the Eisenhower administration-backed provision to give preferential treatment to dividend income. Early in 1955 Mills introduced the Democratic plan to give a $20 tax credit to every taxpayer and his dependents. The measure passed the House by a 234-201 majority but was defeated in the Senate. A proponent of reciprocal trade treaties and lowered tariff walls, Mills worked on the Ways and Means Committee to block protectionist amendments to trade bills.

With the death of Rep. Jere Cooper (D, Tenn.) [q.v.] in December 1957, Mills rose to the chairmanship of the Ways and Means Committee, one of the most powerful positions in the House. Besides deliberating on legislative matters of such crucial importance as taxes, trade and social security, the Committee functioned as the House Democratic Committee on Committees, giving out committee assignments to Democratic representatives. Mills's power was augmented by the general respect he enjoyed, owing to his mastery of the complexities of the tax code.

Mills suffered a defeat in his first major test as chairman. In response to the economic recession and the growing number of workers whose unemployment benefits were being exhausted, the Ways and Means Committee, under Mills's leadership, passed a controversial unemployment relief bill by a 16-9 vote. The measure would have provided 16 additional weeks of federally financed emergency unemployment payments to roughly three million persons whose benefits had run out and would have made an additional two million uninsured workers eligible for benefits. The bill was opposed by the Eisenhower Administration and a House coalition of conservative Republicans and Southern Democrats. When Mills introduced his measure in the House on May 1, 1958, it was rejected by a 223-165 vote. This surprising rebuff had a far-reaching effect on Mills, accentuating his native caution and sharpening his sensitivity to the climate of opinion in the House as a whole. His famous role in the delay and obstruction of controversial social and economic legislation during the 1960s had its roots in his 1958 defeat; ever afterwards he held bills within his Committee until he had formed a broad consensus behind them and was certain of approval on the House floor.

Mills had greater success in his management of the Administration's trade program in 1958. With the support of most of his Democratic colleagues on the Committee, he won approval of a five-year extension of the Reciprocal Trade Agreements Act together with a liberal provision granting the President the authority to cut tariffs by 25% at a top rate of 5% a year. Mills's first hurdle on the House floor was a protectionist substitute offered by Rep. Richard Simpson (R, Pa.), which Mills called "far worse than no extension at all." The House rejected it by a 234-147 vote; the Committee's bill passed by a 317-98 vote. The Senate reduced the extension to three years and the President's tariff-cutting power to 15%. The compromise version emerging from the House-Senate conference placed the two figures at four years and 20%.

Beginning in 1960 Mills played a crucial role in the struggle over providing medical care for the aged. He blocked a liberal proposal, known as medicare, that would have provided free medical care for the aged financed through the social security system. The American Medical Association was a vehement opponent of this plan, and Mills was afraid of alienating the officials of his state medical society, which was influential in Arkansas politics. A fiscal conservative, he also questioned the feasibility of financing an ambitious program out of the social security system. In response to pressure from the party leadership, Mills agreed to consider the plan, promoted on his Committee by Rep. Thomas Forand (D, R.I.). He remained opposed to it, however, and the Forand bill lost on the Ways and Means Committee by a vote of 17-8 on June 3, 1960.

Mills then arranged passage of his own bill which permitted the federal government to make matching grants to the states to provide medical care for the aged poor. Unlike medicare, the Mills bill applied only to the elderly indigent and only in those states which chose to extend medical aid. The plan was financed out of general revenues, not the social security system. It passed the House, 380-83. With some modifications, inspired by Sen. Robert Kerr (D, Okla.) [q.v.], the Senate enacted the measure in August; it was thereafter known as the Kerr-Mills Act. Mills bottled up the medicare proposal in the Ways and Means Committee until 1965, when it became apparent that a majority of the House favored the program. He then supported the measure and became the chief House architect of the medicare bill which passed Congress that year.

Mills played a similar role in the great tax battles of the 1960s, when he reached the peak of his power in the House. When President John F. Kennedy proposed his sweeping tax cut in 1963 and President Lyndon B. Johnson requested a 10% income tax surcharge in 1967, Mills initially opposed each measure, both out of fiscal conservatism and doubt about the receptivity of the House. After he had extracted sufficient concessions and shaped each plan to his satisfaction, he steered the bills to passage in the Committee and the House floor.

Despite his oft-repeated aim of making a thorough revision of the complicated and inequitable tax code, Mills never attempted major tax reform during his tenure as Ways and Means Committee chairman. In fact he generally smothered reform possibilities within the Committee by means of extended study and relentless consensus-seeking. In December 1974 Mills stepped down as Committee chairman following a scandal involving his relationship with an Argentine stripper and public displays of drunkenness. He confessed to being an alcoholic and entered a hospital for treatment. Mills retired from Congress in January 1977 and devoted himself to speaking tours on behalf of Alcoholics Anonymous. [See KENNEDY, JOHNSON, NIXON/FORD Volumes]

[TO]

For further information:
John F. Manley, *The Politics of Finance: The House Ways and Means Committee* (Boston, 1970).

MINTON, SHERMAN
b. Oct. 20, 1890: Georgetown, Ind.
d. April 9, 1965: New Albany, Ind.
Associate Justice, U.S. Supreme Court, 1949-56.

Minton was class valedictorian at Indiana University, where he earned an LL.B. in 1915. He received an LL.M. from Yale the following year and then practiced law in Indiana and Florida. In 1933 Minton was named counselor of the Indiana Public Service Commission. He was elected to the U.S. Senate from Indiana in 1934. A Democrat, Minton was a firm and outspoken supporter of the New Deal. A critic of the Supreme Court's anti-New Deal decisions in 1935-36, he backed Franklin D. Roosevelt's Court reorganization plan in 1937. Defeated for reelection in 1940, Minton was named a judge on the U.S. Court of Appeals for the Seventh Circuit in May 1941. Harry S. Truman, who had known Minton since their days together in the Senate, appointed him to the U.S. Supreme Court in September 1949.

When nominated to the Court, Minton's Senate record led most observers to believe that he would be a liberal jurist. In fact, his accession to the bench helped create a five-man conservative bloc which held sway for four years. The basis of Minton's conservatism lay in his commitment to a policy of judicial restraint. The Court fight of the 1930s had convinced him that the judiciary should allow the other branches of the federal government and the states to take any actions that were constitutionally permissible, however unwise the Court might think them to be. As a result, Minton voted to uphold the government's position in most civil liberties and criminal rights cases, and he thus became known as one of the most conservative members of the bench. [See TRUMAN Volume]

Under Chief Justice Earl Warren [*q.v.*], Minton maintained this stance but found himself more frequently in the minority. A supporter of almost all government anti-subversive programs, he dissented in April 1956 when the Court overturned a state sedition law on the ground that federal statutes had pre-empted this field. In another case the same month, Minton objected to a majority ruling that a local government could not discharge without notice or hearing a teacher who invoked the Fifth Amendment during a federal investigation. He again dissented in June 1956 when the Court held that federal employes could be summarily suspended as security risks only if they held sensitive jobs. Minton joined the majority, however, in June 1955 to rule that the Civil Service Commission's Loyalty Review Board had exceeded its authority when it dismissed a consultant to the Public Health Service who had already been cleared twice by the Health Service's own loyalty board.

In criminal cases Minton was extremely reluctant to upset a conviction when a defendant made no claim of innocence but only charged that the government had made procedural errors in the course of arrest and prosecution. He also disliked interfering with the states' criminal justice systems. For that reason he dissented in April 1956 when the Court ruled that the states must furnish a trial transcript to an indigent defendant if the transcript was necessary to appeal a conviction.

In civil rights cases Minton generally followed a liberal course, voting to outlaw racial and religious discrimination. He believed that government had no constitutional power to discriminate, and so in this field he felt that the Court could legitimately intervene to protect minority rights against government infringement. Minton spoke for the Court in a June 1953 case holding that a homeowner could not be sued by his neighbors for violating a racial restrictive covenant by selling his property to blacks. He also joined in the May 1954 decision in *Brown* v. *Board of Education*, which ruled that racial segregation in public schools was unconstitutional. However, Minton was the lone dissenter in a May 1953 case in which the majority decided that the pre-primary elections of the Jaybird Democratic Association in one Texas county were in effect state actions and therefore blacks could not be excluded from them. Minton asserted that the Association was purely private, and however undesirable its policy of barring blacks, the Constitution did not prohibit such discrimination by private organizations.

Justice Minton retired from the Court on Oct. 15, 1956 because of declining health. A warm, gregarious and unpretentious man who often used earthy language, "Shay" Minton was well liked by all his colleagues throughout his years on the bench. He was not, however, a leading figure on the

Court, nor did he write many significant opinions. He did not have an outstanding intellect, and his strong regard for precedent and judicial restraint hampered the development of his legal creativity. Minton's career on the Court has generally been ranked as undistinguished. Following his retirement, Minton was active in the Indiana Bar Association. He died on April 9, 1965.

[CAB]

For further information:
David N. Atkinson, "Justice Sherman Minton and the Balance of Liberty," *Indiana Law Journal*, 50 (Fall, 1974), pp. 34-59.
Richard Kirkendall, "Sherman Minton," in Leon Friedman and Fred L. Israel, eds., *The Justices of the United States Supreme Court, 1789-1969* (New York, 1969), Vol. 4.
Henry L. Wallace, "Mr. Justice Minton: Hoosier Justice on the Supreme Court," *Indiana Law Journal*, 34 (Winter-Spring, 1959), pp. 145-205, 377-424.

MITCHELL, CLARENCE, M., JR.
b. March 8, 1911; Baltimore, Md.
Director, Washington Bureau, NAACP, 1950- .

An attorney educated at Lincoln University and the University of Maryland, Mitchell served on the Fair Employment Practices Commission and the War Manpower Commission during World War II. He headed the NAACP labor department after the War and became director of the Washington bureau of the NAACP in 1950. In this post Mitchell served as a lobbyist, brought the NAACP point of view to the public in the *Crisis*, the NAACP magazine, and worked with the executive branch to promote enforcement of civil rights.

Mitchell was an important force in shaping and articulating NAACP ideas and goals during the 1950s. His basic philosophy was that change would be brought about through legislation, sympathetic moves by whites, and public relations rather than by organized efforts and protests by blacks. In the early-1950s the main thrust of the NAACP was for peaceful desegregation through executive and legislative action.

The military was one of the prime targets because by 1953 the Supreme Court had made segregation illegal in government jobs and because an executive order could force immediate desegregation of the Armed Services. In 1953 Mitchell maintained that under Eisenhower desegregation of military bases was lagging and urged it be carried out quickly. He also charged that local opposition was blocking school desegregation on military posts.

Mitchell opposed the congressional seniority system because it often placed Southern Democrats at the head of important committees, where they could block civil rights bills. He singled out Sen. James O. Eastland (D, Miss.) [q.v.], chairman of the Senate Judiciary Committee, for particular criticism, calling him a "stinking albatross" around the neck of the Democratic Party. He threatened that blacks would vote Republican if Democrats did not support civil rights demands.

One means Mitchell advocated for pushing desegregation was withholding federal funds from segregated areas. In 1955 he supported Rep. Adam Clayton Powell's (D, N.Y.) [q.v.] amendments to Administration school construction and military reserve bills providing that no aid be given to areas practicing segregation. Mitchell believed that such action would result in compliance with the Supreme Court's 1954 decision outlawing segregated schools without provoking violence. That same year he demanded that the government refuse to pay the expenses of the South Carolina delegation to the first White House Conference on Education because of the state's resistance to school desegregation.

Mitchell focused his attention on the protection and extension of voting rights, believing that increased black suffrage would result in civil rights gains in other fields. In 1956 he urged the NAACP to give top priority to a bill that would "protect the right to vote and . . . protect individuals against violence." Mitchell was dissatisfied with the Civil Rights Act of 1957, maintaining that it contained ineffective provisions for enforcement. He also denounced the violence that followed its passage.

The NAACP official continued to press

for civil rights legislation during the 1960s and 1970s. He was disturbed by what he considered President John F. Kennedy's foot-dragging attitude on black rights. In contrast, he praised President Lyndon B. Johnson's strong civil rights stand and lobbied extensively for the 1964 Civil Rights Act. Mitchell scored the Nixon Administration as "anti-Negro" and not "up to the principles of the Republican Party." He continued in his post through the Ford Administration and into the Carter presidency.

[SY]

MITCHELL, JAMES P(AUL)
b. Nov. 12, 1899; Elizabeth, N.J.
d. Oct. 19, 1964; New York, N.Y.
Assistant Secretary of the Army, May 1953-October 1953; Secretary of Labor, October 1953-January 1961.

The son of a trade journal editor, James Mitchell graduated from high school in 1917. He worked for several years in a grocery store before establishing two stores of his own in 1921. When they failed in 1923, Mitchell worked as a truck driver and then as a salesman. In 1926 he became an expediter for the Wester Electric Co. By an agreement with Western Electric, he went to work for the New Jersey Relief Administration in 1931, directing activities for five years. In 1936 Mitchell joined the Work Projects Administration, where he was put in charge of labor relations in New York City.

Beginning in 1941 Mitchell became director of industrial personnel for the War Department, assuming responsibility for administration of nearly one million employes. Returning to private business in 1945, he directed personnel and industrial relations for R. H. Macy & Co. until 1947, when he became vice president in charge of labor relations at Bloomingdale Brothers. Concurrently, Mitchell conducted employment studies for the U.S. Army in Germany and served on the personnel advisory board of the First Hoover Commission. In April 1953 Eisenhower appointed him assistant secretary of the Army in charge of manpower and reserve board affairs. He remained there until October, when he was appointed Secretary of Labor. Mitchell replaced Martin Durkin [*q.v.*], who had resigned when Eisenhower failed to back his attempts to amend the Taft-Hartley Act.

Mitchell was highly respected by Eisenhower, who admired what he saw as the Secretary's moderation and realistic approach to labor problems. Mitchell did not wish to be considered the voice of organized labor in government. Yet he was particularly anxious not to be influenced by conservative members of the Administration, particularly Sinclair Weeks [*q.v.*]. Sherman Adams [*q.v.*], writing of Mitchell said, "He was blessed with a rare intuition that enabled him to sense exactly how far he could go in holding to an independent opinion on a public labor-management issue without materially disassociating himself from the Administration's policy. When he did leave the Eisenhower policy line, he did so openly after consultation with the White House, but always was careful to avoid positions that were associated with union extremists."

Mitchell believed that the White House should adopt a hands-off policy in regard to labor disputes. During 1955 the Secretary urged the President not to intervene in the strike against the Louisville and National Railroad in spite of pressure from several State governors and members of Congress. The following year Mitchell announced that he would not act to prevent a steel strike. However, the Secretary played a major role in the settlement of the 1959 steel strike. The strike, which began on July 15, 1959, continued for 116 days before it was halted by a 80-day injunction invoked under the provisions of the Taft-Hartley Act. At that point it was the longest major steel strike in U.S. history. During the last weeks of 1959, Mitchell and Vice President Richard M. Nixon [*q.v.*] worked behind the scenes to reach an agreement. A settlement was announced on Jan. 5. The unions and the major steel companies agreed wages and benefits costing 41 cents over two-and-one-half years.

Shortly after assuming office Mitchell backed an increase in the 75 cent-an hour

minimum wage. However, he wished to hold off the increase until there was an upswing in the economy. When the issue came before Congress in 1955, labor pushed for $1.25, while Eisenhower submitted an increase to 90 cents. When Congress passed a bill raising the figure to $1, Mitchell convinced Eisenhower not to veto the measure. Mitchell opposed a further raise in 1957 on the grounds that it would be inflationary. The Secretary also sought to increase the number of workers covered under the federal minimum wage. He extended coverage to industries dealing in office machinery, electric lamps, structural steel, pulp and paper. He liberally interpreted the Walsh-Healey Act, determining prevailing minimum wages in various industries. Consequently, workers on government contracts in the soft coal industry, woollen and worsted industries received raises.

In January 1958 Mitchell drew up an Administration program intended to end labor racketeering and "provide greater protection for the rights of individual workers, the public, and management and unions." The legislative plans were designed to deal with union corruption uncovered by the Senate Committee on Improper Relations in the Labor or Management Field. The program required unions to file annual financial reports, certify they operated under democratic procedures and obliged employers and unions to report financial dealings with each other. It prohibited labor-management collusion and set criminal penalties for bribes, embezzlement and misappropriation of union funds. In addition it called for efforts to tighten laws against secondary boycotts and certain types of organizational picketing. These proposals were designed to shift the balance in contract bargaining to management and abolish labor extortion practices through boycotts and picketing.

Congress took only limited action on the proposals during 1957. In August Eisenhower signed a welfare and pension plans bill designed to safeguard pension funds by requiring disclosure of the financial operations. A second measure, sponsored by Sens. John F. Kennedy (D, Mass.) [*q.v.*]

and Sam Ervin (D, N.C.) [*q.v.*], dealt with labor corruption. The proposal contained many general anti-corruption procedures favored by the White House, but it also included three changes in the Taft-Hartley Act strongly supported by labor. These dealt with union certification, voting rights of strikers and increases in the numbers of workers covered by Taft-Hartley. Mitchell opposed the measure saying that "the imperfections, omissions or loopholes" would make it "almost impossible to administer" and would give union members "illusory protection." He also objected to the fact that the bill did not tighten the ban on secondary boycotts or bar organizational picketing. The bill was killed in the House.

Eisenhower reintroduced Mitchell's program the following year. The Administration was particularly interested in strengthening procedures dealing with secondary boycotts and "blackmail picketing." After vigorous struggles in both the House and the Senate, these were eventually included in the Landrum-Griffin bill, signed into law in September 1959.

Mitchell was a strong supporter of civil rights. In one of his first acts as Secretary, he told the National Council of Negro Women that beginning Nov. 16, 1953 all contracts with the District of Columbia government would ban discrimination. During the Administration's internal debate over a civil rights proposal in 1956 and 1957, Mitchell advocated a strong bill to guarantee blacks equal rights. He disliked the Civil Rights Act of 1957, calling it "weak, watered-down and, in my opinion, ineffectual."

Mitchell greatly extended the power of his office. He established the new career position of deputy undersecretary of labor and three positions of deputy assistant secretary of labor. He added the office of research and development to the Department. Mitchell established the practice of meeting regularly with heads of independent agencies, such as the National Labor Relations Board, the Federation Mediation and Reconciliation Service, and the National Retirement Board. This action allowed him to influence these commissions

both in their policy and their personnel. The budget of the Department of Labor rose from $28 million in fiscal 1954 to $53 million dollars by fiscal 1960. Such an extension of power was possible because of Eisenhower's lack of interest in labor affairs and his desire to have someone else take the responsibility for the area.

Mitchell retired at the end of the Eisenhower Administration and made an unsuccessful run for governor of New Jersey in 1961. He joined the Crown Zellerbach Corp. as a consultant and a director and worked for the West Coast Pulp and Paper Co. as a senior vice president of industrial relations. Mitchell died of a heart attack in 1964 at the age of 63.

[GAD]

MITCHELL, STEPHEN A(RNOLD)
b. March 3, 1903; Rock Valley, Iowa
Chairman, Democratic National Committee, 1952-54.

After graduating from Creighton University preparatory school in 1921, Stephen Mitchell ran the family farm and then worked as an assistant credit manager in a dry goods company and as credit and sales manager for General Motors Acceptance Corp. Following completion of a pre-law course at Creighton University in 1926, he moved to Washington, D.C., and attended Georgetown University law school at night. Mitchell received his LL.B. in 1928. He continued as a General Motors executive in New York until 1932, when he joined a Chicago law firm. Mitchell served as head of the French division of the Lend-Lease Administration from 1942 to 1944 and then worked for the State Department as adviser on French economic affairs. In 1945 he returned to private law practice.

Mitchell became one of the postwar generation of politicians known as "Stevenson Democrats." Urbane in manner, upper-middle class in origin, these reformers had not set foot in a political clubhouse before 1945. Between 1945 and 1947 Mitchell helped reform the Illinois Democratic Party and in the latter year induced his old friend Adlai E. Stevenson [*q.v.*] to run for governor. In March 1952 he was appointed chief counsel to a House subcommittee investigating corruption in the Justice Department. He worked with Democratic Attorney General James P. McGranery in reorganizing the Department and in conducting a quiet, thorough investigation without seeking publicity.

Stevenson received the Democratic nomination for President in July 1952. Hoping to counter Republican charges of Democratic corruption, he appointed Mitchell as Democratic national chairman. The choice was based on Mitchell's connection with the investigation of the Justice Department and the fact that the lawyer was not associated with the Truman Administration. Among Mitchell's responsibilities during the campaign were scheduling radio and TV time, fund raising and administering the party treasury.

Mitchell's most important task was maintaining Democratic Party unity while disassociating Stevenson from the Truman Administration. He announced that Stevenson would hold a series of meetings with state politicians and candidates and assured party regulars that the candidate subscribed to the doctrine that the fruits of victory should go to those "laboring in the vineyards." In September Mitchell attempted to use the issue of corruption against the Republicans after it had been revealed that vice presidential candidate Richard Nixon [*q.v.*] had amassed a secret political fund. However, Nixon successfully countered the charges in the "Checkers" speech that same month. Although Mitchell tried to separate the Democratic campaign from Truman and countercharges of Democratic corruption, his efforts failed. The American electorate, seeking an end to the divisions of the postwar period, gave Dwight D. Eisenhower a large margin of victory in November.

In the years following the election, Mitchell attempted to maintain Democratic unity, counter charges of left-wing drift within the Party and mount an effective opposition against Eisenhower. Reacting to criticism from conservatives that the Party was too closely linked to the liberal Ameri-

cans for Democratic Action (ADA), Mitchell attempted to minimize the ADA's significance. He mentioned that he had never seen a "live" member and maintained that Democratic candidates could "get along without" ADA endorsement. In an interview with the *Chicago Sun Times*, Mitchell charged that the organization was injuring the Democratic Party because it was competing for the same money from wealthy liberals.

Mitchell was continually bedeviled by the problem of promoting an effective opposition to an Administration led by a President both Democrats and Republicans perceived as a popular father figure. While most prominent Democrats were content to attack Eisenhower programs, he attacked Eisenhower personally. In March 1954 he announced that the President should be held responsible for the actions of all Republicans and charged that Eisenhower was promoting McCarthyism as the Republicans' best formula for success. Five months later Mitchell charged Eisenhower with cronyism in promoting the Dixon-Yates contract. This agreement provided for a private utility to replace the Tennessee Valley Authority as the Atomic Energy Commission's chief power supplier in that region. Mitchell charged that professional golfer Bobby Jones, a friend of Eisenhower's and director of one of the companies involved in the proposal, had influenced the President's decision. Both Eisenhower and Jones denied the charge. The attack rebounded against Mitchell and the Democrats, and the *New York Times* charged the chairman with unfairness. Improper relations between Eisenhower and Jones were never proved, but following a congressional investigation, the President canceled the Dixon-Yates contract in 1955.

In December 1954 Mitchell announced that he wished to return to private law practice. Before leaving the post he saw to it that his successor would be a liberal able to hold the center of the Party. The Party endorsed Mitchell's personal choice, Paul Butler [*q.v.*], that month.

Mitchell remained active in Democratic politics throughout the decade. While chairman and after his retirement, he strengthened Stevenson's connection with Southern leaders, particularly Rep. Sam Rayburn (D, Tex.) [q.v.] and Sen. Richard Russell (D, Ga.) [q.v.], and helped stave off efforts by conservative segregationists to splinter the Party. He helped prevent a loyalty oath dispute at the 1956 Democratic National Convention similar to one which had disrupted the 1952 meeting. Mitchell set up a special advisory committee on rules composed of men who could blend ideology with expediency to solve the problem. The panel came up with a resolution, acceptable to most party members, stating that it was understood that a state Democratic Party would put the names of convention nominees on the ballot. Mitchell also negotiated a moderate civil rights plank in the 1956 platform and helped prevent a possible conservative bolt over that issue. He again served in Stevenson's campaign, helping him win the Democratic presidential nomination in August 1956 and guiding his race. Following the election he returned to his private law practice.

In April 1960 Mitchell lost the Illinois Democratic gubernatorial nomination. Eight years later he worked for the unsuccessful presidential candidacy of Sen. Eugene McCarthy (D, Minn.) [q.v.].

[MJS]

MONRONEY, A(LMER) S(TILLWELL) MIKE

b. March 2, 1902; Oklahoma City, Okla.

Democratic Senator, Okla., 1951-69.

Born into a pioneer Oklahoma family, Mike Monroney became a political reporter for the *Oklahoma News* following his graduation from the University of Oklahoma in 1924. His newspaper career was cut short four years later, however, when his father's illness forced him to take over the family furniture business. In 1938 he was elected to the House of Representatives, where he supported most New Deal and Fair Deal programs. He gained public attention during the 1940s as a champion of congressional reform, sponsoring legislation to reduce the number of committees, modify

seniority rules and limit the power of the Rules Committee. Elected to the upper house in 1950, Monroney was one of the few senators who challenged Sen. Joseph McCarthy (R, Wisc.) [q.v.] during the latter years of the Truman Administration. [See TRUMAN Volume]

Monroney continued to oppose McCarthy during the Eisenhower Administration. In July 1953 he charged the Senator with making a "shambles" of the State Department's Foreign Service and endangering the Central Intelligence Agency. He also ridiculed a tour of Europe made by McCarthy aides Roy Cohn [q.v.] and G. David Schine [q.v.] in search of subversive literature in U.S. overseas libraries as a "keystone cops" chase. As a member of the Interstate and Foreign Commerce Committee, Monroney unsuccessfully opposed the nomination of McCarthy's friend, Robert E. Lee, to the Federal Communications Commission. He interpreted the appointment as a bid by McCarthy to gain control of the broadcast industry. A year later Monroney was one of the few senators who supported Sen. Ralph Flanders's (R, Vt.) [q.v.] resolution calling for McCarthy's removal from his committee chairmanships.

During the Eisenhower Administration Monroney supported most liberal domestic legislation. Despite his reputation as a congressional reformer, however, he was not always in sympathy with proposals aimed at easing the rules of the upper house. In 1953 and 1957 he opposed liberal attempts to ease cloture rules in order to bring civil rights legislation to the floor. Nevertheless, Monroney voted for the Civil Rights Acts of 1957 and 1960. A strong backer of foreign aid programs, he sponsored a resolution in 1958 that led to the eventual establishment of the International Development Association (IDA) to provide long-term, low-interest loans to foreign countries.

In 1955 Monroney was appointed chairman of the Interstate and Foreign Commerce Committee's Aviation Subcommittee, where he became an effective advocate of aviation interests. A year later he sponsored a bill removing the Civil Aeronautics Administration from the Commerce Department, which he charged was dominated by a "ground-minded transportation clique."

In conjunction with Sen. Joseph S. Clark (D, Pa.) [q.v.], Monroney proposed an amendment that shaped the school aid bill of 1960. The proposal authorized federal funds in the amount of $20 per school-age child for classroom construction and teachers' salaries. The bill passed the Senate but died in the House Rules Committee. It subsequently became an issue in the 1960 presidential election.

During the 1960s Monroney supported most of the programs of the Kennedy and Johnson Administrations and backed American policy in Vietnam. He also continued his efforts to aid the aviation industry and promote congressional reform. Although an effective politician, Monroney lost touch with his constituents and was defeated for reelection in 1968. [See KENNEDY, JOHNSON Volumes]

[TLH]

For further information:
Richard Fried, *Men Against McCarthy* (New York, 1976).

MORGAN, GERALD D(EMUTH)
b. Dec. 19, 1908; New York, N.Y.
d. June 15, 1976; St. Vincent Island, West Indies Associated States.
Special Presidential Assistant for Congressional Liaison, February 1953-September 1953; White House Administrative Assistant, September 1953-February 1955; Special Counsel to the President, February 1955-September 1958; Deputy Assistant to the President, September 1958-January 1961.

The son of a lawyer, Morgan graduated from Princeton in 1930 and Harvard law school three years later. He worked in the solicitor's office of U.S. Steel Corp. for one year and then moved to Washington, D.C., to become assistant legislative counsel for the House of Representatives. For a brief period beginning in 1938, Morgan entered private law practice in Louisville, Ky., but returned in 1939 to his former position with

the House. He resumed private practice in 1945 in Washington. During the postwar period he also undertook numerous assignments for House panels, including the Foreign Affairs and Un-American Activities Committees. Most notably, Morgan served as counsel to the Republican majority of the House Labor Committee between 1947 and 1949, when the Taft-Hartley Act was under consideration, and played a major role in drafting that legislation.

Morgan took no part in the 1952 presidential campaign and never met Dwight D. Eisenhower before the General became President. Nevertheless, in February 1953 Eisenhower appointed him a special presidential assistant and placed him under a mutual friend, Gen. Wilton B. Persons [q.v.], in the congressional liaison sector of the White House staff.

Morgan's appointment rested mainly on the strength of his work on the Taft-Hartley Act, and his early duties were, therefore, concentrated in the field of labor. During the opening months of the Administration, he attempted to formulate a labor policy that would woo labor support from the Democrats while retaining the loyalty of the conservative wing of the Republican Party and traditional Republican groups, such as the National Association of Manufacturers. One of Morgan's proposals was a series of pro-labor amendments to the Taft-Hartley Act, but these never stirred interest in the White House.

Like all early White House staff members, Morgan became embroiled in the controversy over how to deal with Sen. Joseph R. McCarthy's (R, Wisc.) [q.v.] vitriolic attacks on the Administration. One group urged the President to repudiate McCarthy; the other, including Morgan, favored "getting along" with the Wisconsin Republican. However, by early 1954, Eisenhower felt McCarthy's attacks were too blatant to ignore, and Morgan helped devise a moderate retaliatory policy calling for exposing McCarthy's more irresponsible charges to public scrutiny and attempting to limit the interrogation of White House personnel by congressional committees.

In February 1955 Morgan was promoted to special counsel to the President and helped develop Eisenhower's legislative policy. Morgan handled all bills the Administration planned to introduce to Congress and advised the President on legislation not initiated by the Administration. Thus he was in a position to influence the fate of all key bills.

Morgan's most noteworthy action came in the field of civil rights. During 1956 he was called on to give his advice on whether the Administration should support the Powell amendment to a White House-sponsored school construction bill. The rider, sponsored by Rep. Adam Clayton Powell, Jr. (D, N.Y.) [q.v.], called for the withholding of funds from school districts practicing racial discrimination. It was, therefore, opposed by Southerners and many Northern members of Congress who felt it would jeopardize the passage of the construction bill. Because Powell had frequently supported the Administration in the past, Eisenhower considered backing the amendment. However, the President was also on record as deeply concerned over the national classroom shortage. Morgan cautioned against wholehearted support of the amendment on the grounds that it would leave Eisenhower open to charges of insincerity on the shortage issue. The President adopted Morgan's suggestion, and the amendment later died without Administration backing.

As special counsel, Morgan also advised and often accompanied White House employes called to testify before congressional committees. When Sherman Adams [q.v.] refused to testify on possible conflict-of-interest activities before the House Government Operations Committee in 1955 and 1956, Morgan was believed to have counseled him to plead "executive privilege" to justify his action. In 1958, Morgan counseled Adams in testimony before the House Committee on Legislative Oversight. Adams had been called to answer questions concerning alleged influence-peddling for Boston financier Bernard Goldfine [q.v.]. His inability to explain his actions fully led to his resignation in September 1958.

Following Adams's departure Wilton Persons assumed command of the White House staff, and Morgan took over the number two staff post. He became the conduit to the President for any staff comments or suggestions concerning civil rights because Persons, an Alabamian, felt emotionally incapable of handling the issue objectively. Morgan was intensely dedicated to his work; he reportedly had no outside interests during his years at the White House.

When Eisenhower left office Morgan resumed private law practice. He returned to public service in 1971 as vice president for public and government affairs for the National Railroad Passenger Corp. (Amtrack) but resumed private practice in 1973. In June 1976 Morgan died while vacationing in the West Indies.

[RJB]

MORRISON, deLESSEPS S(TORY)
b. Jan. 18, 1912: New Roads, La.
d. May 22, 1964; Cuidad Victoria, Mexico.
Mayor, New Orleans, La., 1946-61.

The son of a Louisiana parish district attorney and a descendant of Suez Canal builder Ferdinand deLesseps, Morrison worked his way through Louisiana State University. Following his graduation from Louisiana State law school in 1934, he joined the National Recovery Administration and then formed his own law firm with his brother and a family friend, Hale Boggs [q.v.]. In 1936 Morrison became involved in New Orleans reform politics; three years later he helped form the People's League of Independent Voters, which opposed the Louisiana Democratic machine dominated by the Long family. Morrison won a seat in the state legislature in 1940 and was reelected in 1944 while still formally in the Army.

In 1946 Morrison ran as the reform candidate for New Orleans mayor against the Long-backed incumbent, Robert S. Maestri. Supported by veterans organizations, blacks and reform groups, he defeated Maestri in the Democratic primary. In predominantly Democratic New Orleans this was tantamount to winning the general election. Morrison took office in May 1946.

As mayor, Morrison gained a national reputation as a reformer and as a public relations-oriented executive who used personal popularity to create a new image for New Orleans. During the late-1940s he defeated Earl Long's attempts to control New Orleans politics and end the city's home rule. Under his guidance direction returned to the city's government. Morrison reformed municipal government, revamped the municipal purchasing system and reorganized the police department. In a successful effort to increase trade and industry, the Mayor established the first municipal international relations office in the U.S. He also toured the Caribbean and South America as a goodwill ambassador for the city. The Mayor instituted an extensive construction program to rebuild the decaying downtown area, provide housing for veterans and expand recreational facilities. Morrison was careful to maintain contacts with New Orleans blacks and improve municipal services and facilities in black areas. [See TRUMAN Volume]

Despite Morrison's reputation as a reformer, critics often charged that his efforts were more illusion than reality. The Mayor, whom reporters called "the consummate political animal," developed his own political machine and placed many of his backers in key posts vacated by other Democrats. When revelations of police corruption rocked the city in the early-1950s, Morrison urged his assistants to use every means available to "hamper, hinder and obstruct [an] investigation." Throughout his administration there were rumors that Morrison had contacts with the New Orleans underworld. His popular construction program imposed a financial burden on the city which, like many U.S. urban centers, was gradually losing its tax base as middle class citizens fled to suburbs. Investigations also revealed that the city had used poor materials and shoddy construction methods in an effort to speed development. Morrison's program for blacks proved to be tokenism in many cases; few had positions of responsibility in the local Party or in municipal government.

During the 1950s Morrison faced the problem of black demands for integration. Because of his need to maintain both black and white support, the Mayor attempted to maintain a moderate stand on the issue. He urged civil rights groups to accept gradual integration rather than stage dramatic protests to achieve their goals. Morrison's most serious problem involved the integration of the city's public schools, ordered desegregated by Judge J. Skelley Wright [q.v.] in 1960. After a survey indicated that white parents preferred integration to closing the schools, the Mayor opposed Gov. Jimmie Davis's [q.v.] attempts to take over the system and shut it down. Nevertheless, he refused to come out strongly for integration. New Orleans schools were integrated in November by court order. The openings were accompanied by demonstrations and student harassment, which some critics claimed could have been avoided had Morrison taken a more positive stand in the crisis.

While mayor, Morrison made two unsuccessful bids for the governorship in 1956 and 1960. However, his urban, Roman Catholic background proved a liability in rural, Protestant northern Louisiana. In addition, he was opposed by the Long machine and by segregationists who disliked his stand on integration. In 1961 Morrison unsuccessfully attempted to amend the city charter so that he could run for a fifth term.

In June 1961 Morrison accepted the post of ambassador to the Organization of American States, where his primary assignment was to sell the Alliance for Progress to Latin American countries. He resigned his appointment in 1963 to make another unsuccessful bid for the Louisiana governorship. After the election Morrison accepted a job with a New Orleans bank. He died in a plane crash in the Mexican mountains in May 1964. [See KENNEDY Volume]

[EWS]

For further information:
Edward Haas, *DeLesseps S. Morrison and the Image of Reform* (Baton Rouge, 1974).

MORROW, E. FREDERIC
b. April 20, 1909; Hackensack, N.J.
White House Administrative Assistant,
July 1955-September 1958; Administrative Officer for Special Projects, September 1958-January 1961.

Morrow studied at Bowdoin College from
1926 to 1930 but left without receiving a
degree. From 1937 to 1945 he served as
field secretary for the NAACP before becoming a writer for public affairs for CBS-TV. He remained with CBS until 1952,
when he took a leave of absence to work as
a consultant for Dwight D. Eisenhower's
presidential campaign.

Reacting enthusiastically to Morrow's
campaign efforts, Eisenhower's chief of
staff, Sherman Adams [q.v.], promised
him a White House staff position and urged
him to resign his CBS post while awaiting
appointment. However, six months after
leaving CBS, Morrow was told by one of
Adams's assistants that there were no positions available. Reluctantly Morrow concluded that prejudice prevented his becoming the first black appointed to a President's
staff. After living on his savings for several
months, Morrow found a position as an adviser on business to the Commerce Department. In July 1955 Morrow joined the
White House staff as an administrative assistant.

Morrow's tenure at the White House was
marked by frustration and embarrassment.
Colleagues on the staff generally were cold
but correct toward him, and at official functions he was usually mistaken for a servant.
Morrow found his duties often too vaguely
defined. Sometimes called upon to represent the President before black organizations or to attend state functions as an
example of black progress in the U.S.,
Morrow spent more time at ceremonial activities than in decision making.

Although Morrow hoped to avoid becoming a specialist on racial issues, he gradually
found himself holding that informal position. In his journal he stated that the White
House handled civil rights "like a bad
dream." Neither the President nor key
members of his staff took a strong stand for

black rights. As early as the summer of
1955 Morrow, distressed about racial violence in the South, urged Sherman Adams
and Maxwell Rabb to convince the President to speak out against white-racist tactics. Adams and Rabb, in turn, worried
about Eisenhower's continuing inability to
generate black support in public opinion
polls. However, they told Morrow that the
President could not afford to alienate the
white South by taking a stand for civil
rights. Time and again such conservative
advisers as Wilton B. Person [q.v.] and
Gerald Morgan [q.v.] argued for a cautious policy that avoided strong commitments
on the issue.

As a result the Administration appeared
indecisive on the question. When President
Eisenhower proposed a moderate civil
rights bill in 1957, his actions, described by
one historian as "confusing, erratic and
equivocal" and viewed by Morrow as
"shocking," contributed to its dilution
by Congress. That year the White House
refused to take action on the racial violence
exploding across the South. Morrow, in
turn, faced intense criticism from blacks,
many of whom saw him as an "Uncle Tom"
aiding an indifferent Administration. In
September 1957, when Eisenhower sent
troops to Little Rock, Ark., to carry out
court-ordered integration, Morrow concluded that the President's actions were
prompted mostly by Arkansas Gov. Orval
Faubus's [q.v.] personal defiance of executive authority and not concern for blacks.

In September 1958 Morrow was named
White House officer for special projects to
deal almost exclusively with civil rights. But
at the same time other White House staff
changes, resulting from the departure of
Sherman Adams, left Morrow with virtually
no access to the President. Persons, a
Southerner reluctant to discuss racial issues, replaced Adams as the man closest to
the President. Morrow now took his complaints and suggestions to Gerald Morgan,
but without any assurance that they would
receive a presidential hearing.

In January 1959, more than three years
after he began work at the White House,
Morrow was administered his oath of office.
President Eisenhower, who usually at-

tended such ceremonies, did not come. Later Morrow wrote in his journal, "The White House is a little embarrassed about me."

After leaving the White House in 1961, Morrow vainly attempted to find a job in business. Bitterly, he scored corporations that refused to hire blacks, even those with administrative ability. He finally became a vice president with the Bank of America in 1964. During these years Morrow shaped his White House journal into a book, *Black Man in the White House* (1963), labeled a "political bombshell" by the *New York Times*. In 1975 he became a member of the Presidential Clemency Board set up by President Gerald Ford.

[RJB]

For further information
E. Frederic Morrow, *Black Man in the White House* (New York, 1963).

MORSE, WAYNE (LYMAN)
b. Oct. 20, 1900; Madison, Wisc.
d. July 22, 1974; Portland, Ore.
Republican Senator, Ore., 1945-52, Independent, 1952-55, Democratic, 1955-69.

Raised on a Wisconsin farm, Wayne Morse graduated from the University of Wisconsin in 1923. He was an assistant professor of argumentation at the University of Minnesota from 1924 to 1928 and earned a law degree from that institution. In 1929 Morse accepted an assistant professorship of law at the University of Oregon. Two years later he became the dean of the law school. Morse, a specialist in labor law, also served as a leading arbitrator in West Coast labor disputes. By 1940 he was one of the nation's most prominent labor relations experts. He joined the War Labor Board in 1942 but resigned two years later in protest against what he considered excessive concessions to John L. Lewis's [q.v.] United Mine Workers.

In 1944 Morse, then a Republican, won a Senate seat from Oregon. He quickly established a reputation as a liberal maverick who often voted against his Party and supported most of President Harry S. Truman's domestic and foreign policies. Morse alienated many Senate members because of his refusal to compromise and his mocking self-righteous attitude toward those who disagreed with him. His abrasive personality prevented him from playing a leadership role in the upper chamber but won him the admiration of many who saw him as a man who placed principle over expediency.

Morse was one of the first Republicans to suggest that Gen. Dwight D. Eisenhower seek the Party's presidential nomination. However, after the 1952 Republican National Convention he abandoned the General, citing the choice of Richard Nixon [q.v.] as vice presidential candidate and the conservative party platform as evidence that the General had "sold out" to the Republican Right. On Oct. 18 Morse endorsed Adlai Stevenson [q.v.] for the presidency, stating that the Eisenhower he had supported for the nomination was not the same man who was seeking office. One week later he resigned from the Republican Party.

Morse continued to maintain his liberal stance throughout the Eisenhower Administration. He was a vocal supporter of federal power and resource development. In April 1953 he joined a small group of liberals opposing the submerged lands bill, which granted ownership of offshore oil deposits to the states. Morse delivered a 22 hour and 26 minute speech outlining the consequences of the proposal and charging that the measure was making a "raid on the public domain." (His filibuster broke the Senate record.) The Morse group lost the struggle; the measure was signed into law in May. From 1951 to 1955 Morse annually introduced a bill to have the government build a power plant at Hell's Canyon on the Snake River in Idaho. The measure failed each time, and in 1955 the Federal Power Commission turned the project over to a private utility.

Morse also opposed the use of evidence gained from wiretaps in federal courts. He called wiretapping "a cover-up for lazy, inefficient, unimaginative, ruthless law enforcement administration." Interested in congressional reform, the Senator annually introduced a bill requiring members of Congress to disclose their outside sources of income.

Morse was a staunch supporter of civil rights. As a member of the District of Columbia Committee, he was the chief Senate proponent of home rule for the nation's capital, whose population during the decade was approximately 50% black. He voted against the Civil Rights Act of 1957 because he believed it too weak.

The Senator was cautious in his criticism of Sen. Joseph R. McCarthy (R, Wisc.) [q.v.]. He joined other liberals in attempting to debate specific charges that McCarthy had made, but he also maintained that there was a need to investigate subversives. After McCarthy assumed the chairmanship of the Senate Government Operations Committee, Morse muted his criticism of the Wisconsin Republican. Morse's biographer, A. Robert Smith, maintained that this was because McCarthy was investigating the conduct of an Oregon lobbyist who was close to Morse. When the movement to censure the Wisconsin Senator grew during 1954, Morse again resumed his criticism of McCarthy.

Morse had a reputation for vicious personal attacks on any who opposed him. During a debate on the construction of federal power facilities, he claimed that President Eisenhower was as corrupt as Teamster president Dave Beck [q.v.], who was under investigation for using his position for personal profit. In 1958 Morse, campaigning on behalf of Oregon Gov. Robert D. Holmes, repeatedly raised the point that the Republican challenger, Mark Hatfield, had killed a young girl in an auto accident. Observers believed that Morse's conduct was one of the factors leading to Holmes defeat. That same year he broke with his protege, liberal Democratic Sen. Richard Neuberger (D, Ore.) [q.v.], because the younger man had supported some of the Administration's moderate proposals, including the Civil Rights Act of 1957.

Characterizing Sens. John F. Kennedy (D, Mass.) [q.v.] and Hubert H. Humphrey (D, Minn.) [q.v.] as "phony liberals," Morse entered the 1960 race for the Democratic presidential nomination. However, his defeats in the District of Columbia, Maryland and Oregon primaries ended his campaign. Morse supported most of the Kennedy and Johnson Administrations' domestic legislation. He was an early opponent of the Vietnam war. In August 1965 he and Ernest Gruening (D, Alaska) [q.v.] were the only two senators to vote against the Gulf of Tonkin Resolution. In 1966 he introduced an amendment to repeal it; his proposal was defeated by a vote of 95 to 5.

Republican Robert Packwood defeated Morse in the 1968 race for the U.S. Senate. Four years later Morse tried to make a comeback but lost to Mark Hatfield. In 1974 he won the Democratic senatorial primary, but he died that July of kidney failure. [See KENNEDY, JOHNSON Volumes]

[JB]

For further information:
A. Robert Smith, *The Tiger in the Senate: The Biography of Wayne Morse* (Garden City, 1962).

MORTON, THRUSTON B(ALLARD)

b. Aug. 19, 1907: Louisville, Ky.
Assistant Secretary of State for Congressional Relations, January 1953-February 1956; Republican Senator, Ky., 1957-68; Republican National Chairman, 1959-61.

Born into an old and established Kentucky family, Morton graduated from Yale University in 1929 and then entered Ballard and Ballard, a family grain and milling firm. After spending World War II in the Navy, he returned to Kentucky in 1946 to become president of Ballard and Ballard. That November he was elected, as a Republican in a traditionally Democratic state, to the U.S. House of Representatives, where he aligned himself with the liberal and internationalist wing of his party. Reelected in 1948 and 1950, Morton supported the Tennessee Valley Authority, was an early advocate of federal aid to education and stood behind the Truman foreign aid programs. In 1952 he was the lone Eisenhower supporter in Kentucky's 20-man Republican National Convention delegation. He managed John Sherman Cooper's [*q.v.*] Senate race in the same year.

Following his inauguration in January 1953, Eisenhower appointed Morton assistant secretary of state for congressional relations. In this post Morton fought the highly controversial Bricker amendment, which was designed to limit the President's treaty-making powers. In 1953 he also fought to save the reciprocal trade bill from defeat by the Republican Congress. Addressing himself to Sen. Joseph R. McCarthy's (R, Wisc.) [*q.v.*] anti-Communist crusade, Morton declared that while the threat posed by Communism was a severe one, it did not warrant the destruction of American liberties. He maintained that "you cannot chip away part of the structure of liberty without beginning to destroy the entire structure."

In 1956 Morton resigned his post to run for the Senate. He won by a narrow margin, aided by the President's position at the head of the Republican ticket and by the fact that Kentucky Gov. A.B. Chandler [*q.v.*] withheld his support from Earle Clements, the Democratic candidate. Morton was a loyal backer of Administration programs in the upper house. In both 1957 and 1958 he was Eisenhower's most consistent supporter in the Senate. A long-time proponent of racial integration, in 1957 he backed the Administration's civil rights bill, aimed primarily at establishing voting rights for blacks. Morton joined Senate liberals in an unsuccessful attempt to prevent the addition of a conservative-sponsored amendment requiring a jury trial for those accused of violating the statute. The provision effectively weakened the law. He also fought for the 1957 Eisenhower Doctrine, which granted the President authority to use troops to protect the Middle East in case of Communist aggression. With Sen. Cooper he presented a bill to Congress for a four-year, $1.6 billion aid-to-education program.

In 1959 Morton replaced the retiring Meade Alcorn [*q.v.*] as Republican National Chairman. He defended the Administration against criticism following the Soviet downing of a U-2 spy plane, asserting that "the American people should feel more secure now that they understand the

scope of the intelligence activities being carried out by the United States." During the Party's 1960 presidential convention, Morton had strong delegate backing, particularly from the Midwest, for the Republican vice presidential nomination, but Richard Nixon [*q.v.*] chose Henry Cabot Lodge [*q.v.*] instead. Morton served in the Senate until 1968, when he returned to Louisville and worked for the Liberty National Bank and Trust Co. [See KENNEDY, JOHNSON Volumes]

[JPL]

MUNDT, KARL E(RNST)
b. June 3, 1900; Humboldt, S.D.
d. Aug. 16, 1974; Washington, D.C.
Republican Senator, S.D., 1949-73.

The son of a pioneer small businessman, Karl Mundt was educated at Carleton College in Minnesota. After receiving his B.A. in 1923, he returned to South Dakota and subsequently became a speech instructor at Beadle State Teachers College in Madison. While teaching, Mundt also worked in his family's insurance, real estate and investment businesses and attained prominence as a civic leader in the largely German, conservative South Dakota corn belt. In 1938 he was elected to Congress on an isolationist, anti-British foreign policy platform. After Pearl Harbor, however, Mundt firmly backed the American war effort.

In the closing years of World War II, Mundt became one of the most outspoken congressional advocates of a hard-line anti-Communist foreign and domestic policy. As a member of the House Un-American Activities Committee (HUAC), he led the Republican attack on the Truman Administration's loyalty-security programs during the late-1940s. Presiding over the 1948 HUAC investigations of alleged Communist infiltration of government departments, Mundt helped secure the information that led to the grand jury indictment of Alger Hiss for perjury in the following year. In 1948 he also cosponsored, with Rep. Richard M. Nixon (R, Calif.) [*q.v.*], a bill that required the American Communist Party to register its membership with the Department of Justice, denied Communists passports and barred them from federal employment. Elected to the Senate that same year, Mundt introduced a similar measure in the upper house. Truman strongly opposed the Mundt bills as "police state tactics," but in 1950 Congress passed the omnibus McCarran Act, which incorporated the Mundt-sponsored legislation. [See TRUMAN Volume]

When the Senate convened in January 1953, Mundt was assigned to the Government Operations Committee and to its Permanent Investigations Subcommittee, both chaired by Sen. Joseph McCarthy (R, Wisc.) [q.v.]. A strong supporter of McCarthy's anti-Communist crusade ever since the Wisconsin Senator rose to prominence in 1950, Mundt worked closely with him in 1953 on the subcommittee's wide-ranging probes of alleged Communist subversion. In January and February 1954, however, after McCarthy began his investigations of Army security, he joined other Republicans on the panel in an effort to forestall a public rupture between the subcommittee and Army and White House officials. Acting as a mediator at a luncheon on Feb. 24, Mundt drew up a "memorandum of understanding" in which Army Secretary Robert Stevens [q.v.] conceded the subcommittee chairman's right to question Army officers. News reports terming the agreement a "capitulation" by Stevens, prompted the Army to proceed with its plans to expose the activities of McCarthy and subcommittee counsel Roy Cohn [q.v.] on behalf of their aide G. David Schine [q.v.]. In March the subcommittee voted to investigate the dispute. McCarthy temporarily resigned from the panel in order to testify, and Mundt reluctantly accepted the job of acting chairman for the duration of the Army-McCarthy hearings. After unsuccessfully attempting to bar the press from the committee room, he took almost no active part in the nationally televised proceedings. Despite the Wisconsin Senator's declining popularity in the aftermath of the hearings, Mundt remained one of his strongest partisans, working to block Senate condemnation of McCarthy's conduct and finally voting against censure in December.

As the issue of Communism in government began to wane after 1954, Mundt's name faded from public prominence. He remained a powerful force for conservatism in the Senate, however, opposing social welfare programs and domestic spending and advocating government curbs on labor unions. Although he voted with the conservative coalition of Southern Democrats and Republicans on most issues, Mundt backed civil rights and conservation measures.

As a member of the Permanent Investigations Subcommittee, Mundt was appointed in January 1957 to the Select Committee on Improper Activities in the Labor or Management Field, chaired by Sen. John McClellan (D, Ark.) [q.v.]. Following investigations of corruption in the International Brotherhood of Teamsters and other unions, the panel conducted hearings in February and March 1958 on a violent four-year old strike by the United Auto Workers (UAW) against the Kohler Co. of Kohler, Wisc. The probe was initiated at the insistence of Mundt and fellow Committee Republicans Barry Goldwater (Ariz.) [q.v.] and Carl Curtis (Neb.) [q.v.], partly in an effort to embarrass Committee counsel Robert F. Kennedy [q.v.] and the panel's liberal Democrats, who had close political ties with UAW president Walter Reuther [q.v.]. The investigation was marked by angry charges of partisanship and "whitewashing" that nearly resulted in the breakup of the panel. Little evidence was uncovered to support allegations of corruption against UAW officials. Mundt, Goldwater and Curtis later pressed for a separate inquiry into UAW political activities, but the Committee did not pursue this.

During the Kennedy years Mundt was again involved in several prominent investigations, including the 1962 Investigations Subcommittee probe of the relationship between the Agriculture Department and Texas financier Billie Sol Estes and hearings in 1963 on the Defense Department's conduct in the awarding of TFX fighter bomber contracts. In 1969 Mundt suffered a debilitating stroke that prevented him from carrying on his Senate duties. Three years later the Senate relieved him of his posts as ranking Republican on the Government Operations Committee and second-ranking minority member of the Foreign Relations and Appropriations Committees. Mundt died in the capital in August 1974. [See KENNEDY, JOHNSON, NIXON/FORD Volumes]

[TLH]

MUNOZ MARIN, LUIS
b. Feb. 18, 1998; San Juan, Puerto Rico.
Governor, Puerto Rico, 1949-65.

The son of Luis Munoz Rivera, "the George Washington of Puerto Rico," Munoz was raised in New York and Washington, D.C. and attended Georgetown University. After his father's death Munoz left law school to work in New York City as a writer, editor and translator. Although initially a Socialist and a strong proponent of Puerto Rican independence, Munoz entered island politics in 1926 as a Liberal. In 1932 he was elected to the Puerto Rico Senate. His stateside contacts helped him bring New Deal money to Puerto Rico, adding to his growing political popularity. In 1938 he left the Liberals to found the Popular Democratic Party (PPD), which mobilized the support of the rural masses to become the dominant political force in the territory. In the early-1940s Munoz and the appointed governor, Rexford G. Tugwell, worked together to initiate land reform, farm cooperatives and industrial and farm development corporations. Meanwhile, Munoz's influence grew, and he acquired a fanatically loyal mass following.

After World War II Munoz, recognizing Puerto Rico's inability to support a growing population on an agricultural base, helped create "Operation Bootstrap," an economic development program that offered a 12-year tax exemption and general assistance on labor problems and plant construction to new industries. He also sought to increase the island's autonomy from the U.S. In 1948 Puerto Ricans chose Munoz as their first elected governor. In July 1952 they ratified a constitution that established Puerto Rico as a commonwealth in free as-

sociation with the United States and in November elected Munoz to a second term as governor. [See TRUMAN Volume]

Commonwealth status constituted the dominant issue in Puerto Rican politics after 1952. Because of his popularity and the power of the PPD, Munoz was able to convince the majority of Puerto Ricans of the advantages of the commonwealth over independence or statehood. He argued that the commonwealth ensured Puerto Rico's fiscal and cultural autonomy, while giving its residents the benefits of U.S. citizenship, access to the mainland market and federal aid. However, the small *independentista*, or Nationalist Party, considered Munoz a traitor, and a terrorist wing marked him for assassination. The Nationalists' views came to mainland attention in March 1954, when several members sprayed bullets into the U.S. House of Representatives, wounding five congressmen. Munoz immediately flew to Washington to condemn the shootings and assure the mainlanders that the vast majority of Puerto Ricans wished to continue their close ties with the United States. However, the Nationalist position continued to receive international attention as Communist states asserted that commonwealth status was a shield for U.S. colonial domination of Puerto Rico.

Munoz faced greater immediate political difficulties from the pro-statehood Republican Party of Puerto Rico. In the 1956 gubernatorial election Munoz won a third term, but the Republicans received 25% of the total vote, double their 1952 share. Recruited mainly from the ranks of the island's growing middle class, the Republicans asserted that the commonwealth could only be a transitional solution to Puerto Rico's status problem. They argued that the U.S. Congress could rescind the law upon which the commonwealth was based at any time. Statehood, on the other hand, was irrevocable and ensured Puerto Ricans U.S. citizenship. Although the state of Puerto Rico would be subject to federal taxation, the Republicans stressed the dignity and equality that statehood would confer and suggested that statehood would provide the stability necessary to continued economic development. Munoz did not respond to their challenge until 1959, when the PPD-controlled Legislative Assembly called upon the U.S. Congress to clarify aspects of the U.S.-Puerto Rican relationship laid down in the Federal Relations Act. The modifications, embodied in the Fernos-Murray bill, would have slightly augmented Puerto Rican autonomy, but the bill was never reported out of committee.

During the 1950s Operation Bootstrap registered impressive economic gains. Industrial production and per capita income increased as industry became the dominant mode of economic activity on the island. Although a large migration to the mainland facilitated the economic performance, the new prosperity greatly enhanced Munoz's image at home and abroad. Having achieved a fair measure of economic success, Munoz decided to move in new directions. In 1955 he proposed "Operation Serenity," an effort to transcend economic values in setting Puerto Rico's goals. Vaguely formulated with references to freedom and knowledge, Operation Serenity was effectively translated into an ambitious government effort to upgrade education in the late-1950s. However, it also implied a strong desire to preserve the island's Hispanic traditions and rural values.

Munoz also sought to play a larger role in U.S.-Latin American relations. Speaking in May 1958, he asserted that Puerto Ricans, because of their Hispanic heritage, relationship with the U.S., democratic government and prosperity, could best translate U.S. political and economic ideals to Latin Americans and, at the same time, best explain Latin aspirations to the North Americans. In March 1958, for example, he told a Senate committee that Latin America had not received its fair share of U.S. foreign aid and urged more ambitious U.S. efforts to develop the Hemisphere economy and support democratic movements. Throughout 1959 Munoz defended Fidel Castro's new regime in Cuba, recommending that the U.S. try to understand that incidents of political violence stemmed from the brutality of the Batista years. Later Munoz became a severe critic of Castro.

Munoz won a fourth term as governor in

1960, but he stepped down in 1964 to enter the island's Senate. Meanwhile, the commonwealth controversy continued. Munoz's vigorous campaign in support of the commonwealth contributed to the voters' rejection of statehood or independence in a 1967 plebiscite. However, in 1968 the PPD lost the governorship to the pro-statehood New Progressive Party. Between 1968 and 1972 Munoz was in semi-retirement, but he campaigned actively in 1972 for the PPD. [See KENNEDY Volume]

[JCH]

For further information:
Henry Wells, *The Modernization of Puerto Rico: A Political Study of Changing Values and Institutions* (Cambridge, Mass., 1969).

MURPHY, ROBERT D(ANIEL)
b. Oct. 28, 1894; Milwaukee, Wisc.
Ambassador to Japan, April 1952-March 1953; Assistant Secretary of State for United Nations Affairs, March 1953-December 1953; Deputy Undersecretary of State for Political Affairs, December 1953-August 1959; Undersecretary of State, August 1959-October 1959.

Robert Murphy, the son of a steamfitter and railroad worker, was born and raised in Milwaukee, Wisc. He worked his way through Marquette University and George Washington University, where he received his law degree in 1920. Attracted by the opportunity to work abroad, he joined the Foreign Service and was posted as vice-consul to Zurich in 1921. During the 1920s Murphy served in a variety of positions in Washington and Europe and in 1930 began a decade of service in Paris. Murphy served as chief civil affairs officer on Gen. Dwight D. Eisenhower's staff during World War II. From 1944 to 1949 he was U.S. political adviser for occupied Germany and became acting director of the Office of German and Austrian Affairs in 1949. A year later the diplomat was appointed ambassador to Belgium. From 1952 to 1953 Murphy served as ambassador to Japan and adviser to Gen. Mark Clark [q.v.] on Korean armistice discussions. [See TRUMAN Volume]

In March 1953 Eisenhower appointed Murphy assistant undersecretary of state for U.N. affairs in order to help the delegation prepare for the scheduled debate on Korea. Although theoretically in charge of the U.S. mission, his effectiveness was limited by U.N. Ambassador Henry Cabot Lodge's [q.v.] demand for virtual autonomy from State Department direction, a position approved by both Eisenhower and Secretary of State John Foster Dulles [q.v.].

During the Eisenhower Administration Murphy acted as the State Department's chief "trouble-shooter." A man of remarkable charm and humor, he consulted allies on potentially dangerous situations and transmitted U.S. policy decisions to those affected by them. In 1954 Murphy handled the sensitive negotiations that resulted in an Italian-Yugoslavian agreement over the territorial division of Trieste.

Two years later Murphy became deeply involved in U.S. efforts to prevent British and French military action against Egypt following Premier Gamal Nasser's nationalization of the Suez Canal. He helped the British explore the legal grounds for opposition to the seizure and later suggested that a special U.N. agency be entrusted with control of the Canal. His negotiations proved unsuccessful. In November 1956 a joint French-British expedition seized the Canal.

Murphy next mediated the 1958 dispute between France and Tunisia, which resulted from the French bombing of a Tunisian village used to harbor Algerian rebels. Under an agreement he worked out, the French withdrew all troops in Tunisia to a base at Bizerte, while Tunisia granted France the right of indefinite occupation of the base in return for recognition of the Tunisian sovereignty over it. In July of that year Eisenhower sent Murphy to Lebanon following the landing of American troops there. The forces had been sent at the request of pro-Western President Camille Chamoun to prevent a possible takeover by pan-Arab rebels who opposed Chamoun's decision to retain office beyond his stipulated term. Through Murphy's skillful efforts an agreement was reached that provided for the President's dignified departure and the

election of Gen. Fuad Chehab, a candidate acceptable to both sides.

Murphy retired from the Foreign Service in 1959 and became director of the Corning Glass Works. During the 1960s he was a member of several presidential commissions on foreign intelligence activities. In 1964 Murphy published *Diplomat Among Warriors*, a personal account of his years in the Foreign Service.

[EWS]

For further information:
Robert D. Murphy, *Diplomat Among Warriors* (Garden City, 1964).

MURROW, EDWARD R(OSCOE)
b. April 25, 1908; Greensboro, N.C.
d. April 27, 1965; Pauling, N.Y.
Television journalist.

Edward R. Murrow grew up in rural northwest Washington State and graduated Phi Beta Kappa from Washington State College in 1930. Immediately thereafter he traveled throughout Europe as president of the National Student Federation. In 1935 he began a long and notable career with the Columbia Broadcasting System (CBS). Assigned to England during the Battle of Britain in 1940, Murrow achieved national recognition for his "This is London" radio accounts of the blitz. Creating sympathy for Britain, the broadcast identified Murrow with liberal internationalism. Murrow returned to America after World War II and made regular evening newscasts over CBS radio beginning in 1947. Many critics felt that Murrow raised radio journalism, and particularly that of CBS News, to a high art.

Murrow entered the then infant television field in 1951. Together with Fred W. Friendly, he produced "See It Now," a 30-minute weekly presentation on a usually provocative topic. Murrow anchored the program. In October 1953 "Person-to-Person," a weekly informal interview program, premiered with Murrow hosting. The show involved interviews with such diverse individuals as Cuban revolutionary

Fidel Castro, Secretary of State John Foster Dulles [q.v.], stripteaser Gypsy Rose Lee and movie star Marilyn Monroe.

"See It Now," however, proved the more newsworthy of the two shows, occasionally running programs that countered the anti-Communist hysteria of the period. In October 1953 Murrow presented the case of the young Lt. Milo Radulovich. The Air Force planned to muster out Radulovich as a security risk because of anonymous reports about his father and sister's left-wing sympathies. The Murrow-Friendly investigators found no evidence supporting the allegations, and the October telecast exonerated Radulovich. Friendley recounted that Radulovich program received "overwhelming viewer and critical acclaim," and caused Radulovich's full reinstatement. It also revealed how much popular outcry could be raised against an unjustified anti-Communist persecution.

In March 1954 Murrow devoted his program to Sen. Joseph R. McCarthy, Jr. (R, Wisc.) [q.v.], the powerful investigator of domestic Communism. Friendly and the "See It Now" staff put together film clips of the Wisconsin Senator's career, and Murrow wrote a carefully worded denunciation of McCarthy's methods. Murrow called for public discussion of McCarthy's ethics. "We must not confuse dissent with disloyalty," he declared at the program's end. "This is no time for men who oppose Sen. McCarthy's methods to be silent."

McCarthy attempted to counterattack. As proposed by Murrow and CBS President Frank Stanton [q.v.], he appeared the following week for a 30-minute defense. He accused Murrow of past involvement with subversive groups and of being "the symbol, the leader and the cleverest of the jackal pact" at odds with "anyone who dares to expose individual Communists." The Senator's charges did little to damage Murrow's reputation.

As after the Radulovich telecast, the McCarthy programs evoked widespread acclaim and showed that McCarthy could be successfully countered. One observer deemed it TV's "finest hour," and another determined that Murrow "had permitted McCarthy to hang himself." CBS management stood behind Murrow without reservation. Only *Saturday Review* critic Gilbert Seldes challenged the pro-Murrow consensus. Seldes argued that the "See it Now" editors had slanted the film segments in a McCarthy-like fashion and that, in his televised response, McCarthy had demonstrated Murrow's enormous telegenic advantages.

Some *See It Now* programs only created problems for CBS management. In January 1954, a broadcast focused on an amendment, sponsored by Sen. John W. Bricker (R, Ohio) [q.v.], to restrict the President's treaty-making powers. Afterwards, Bricker accused Murrow of slanting the program to discredit the proposal. Already critical of national news systems, Bricker emerged from the experience the most powerful congressional foe of national networks. Stanton deeply regretted the Bricker telecast, but he did little to stop Murrow.

After the McCarthy programs "See It Now" enjoyed one more regular season run. During 1954–55 the chain-smoking Murrow narrated a two-part series on the relationship between cigarettes and cancer. In January 1955 Murrow interviewed Dr. J. Robert Oppenheimer [q.v.], the renowned physicist who had been denied federal security clearance.

Murrow grew increasingly disenchanted with CBS, although he continued to host "Person-to-Person" and "Small World." When management removed "See It Now" from its regular schedule after 1955, Murrow's never cordial relations with Stanton declined further. In October 1959 Stanton publicly criticized "Person-to-Person," and Murrow bitterly denounced the CBS president.

Murrow possessed a liberal idealist's vision of news journalism and TV's educational function. In October 1958 he argued that TV "can teach, can illuminate, it can even inspire. But it can do these things," he said, "only to the extent that [people determine] to use this to those ends. Otherwise it is merely wires and lights in a box." Respected for his integrity and courage, his brand of moral, investigative broadcast journalism nevertheless came to be displaced by the semi-cynical detachment of

NBC's David Brinkley and the paternal neutrality of CBS's Walter Cronkite.

Early in 1958 a coalition of New York liberal Democrats, led by Eleanor Roosevelt [q.v.], nearly persuaded Murrow to run for the U.S. Senate from their state. After discussions with former President Harry S. Truman [q.v.] and others, Murrow rejected the offer on the grounds that he would be more effective as a newsman and that he was not a native New Yorker. He left CBS in 1961 to serve as director of the United States Information Agency in the Kennedy Administration. After a prolonged illness he died of cancer in April 1965. [See KENNEDY Volume]

[JLB]

For further information:
Edward Bliss, Jr., ed., *In Search of Light: The Broadcasts of Edward R. Murrow* (New York, 1967).
Alexander Kendrick, *Prime Time: The Life of Edward R. Murrow* (Boston, 1969).

MUSTE, A(BRAHAM) J(OHANNES)
b. Jan. 8, 1885; Zierikzee, Netherlands.
d. Feb. 11, 1967; New York, N.Y.
Clergyman, peace activist.

A. J. Muste was raised in Michigan in an atmosphere of religious and political conservatism. Ordained a Dutch Reformed minister in 1909, he joined the pacifist Fellowship of Reconciliation (FOR) during World War I and became active in the radical labor movement. During the Depression Muste played an important role in the creation of Unemployment Leagues to promote the cause of the jobless, but his campaign never reached the dimensions of a national mass movement.

Muste and his followers moved gradually to an independent Marxism with their formation of the American Workers Party (AWP) in 1933. A year later the AWP merged with the orthodox Trotskyist Communist League of America to form the Workers Party. However, after a meeting with Leon Trotsky in 1936, Muste became disillusioned with the factionalism of revolutionary politics and returned to an independent pacifist position.

As executive secretary of FOR from 1940 to 1953, Muste organized an intensive anti-war educational campaign and worked on behalf of conscientious objectors confined by the U.S. government during World War II. In 1948 he joined 300 ministers in calling on all young men to refuse to register or serve in the Armed Forces. Through his affiliation with FOR Muste had an important influence on civil rights activists James Farmer, Bayard Rustin [q.v.] and George Hauser, who organized the first Freedom Ride in 1947.

During the postwar years Muste opposed growing cold war sentiment and championed total disarmament. In 1954 he promoted the "Third Way International Movement," which tried to unify all groups opposing the policies of the U.S. and Soviet blocs. As chairman of the American Third Camp Committee, he helped found *Liberation* magazine in 1956 as a forum for these views. This attempt gained little support, and the following year Muste joined several peace groups in forming the Committee for Nonviolent Action to stage dramatic civil disobedience demonstrations. Taking the lead in organizing the first protests at nuclear testing sites, Muste was arrested for trespassing on the Mercury Project grounds in Nevada during 1957 and at the Mead, Neb., missile base two years later. He was also active in organizing the Polaris Action project in New London, Conn., in 1960 and participated in the annual civil defense protests held in New York's City Hall Park from 1955 to 1961. Muste received the War Resisters League Peace Award in 1958.

Although a committed anti-Communist, Muste carried on an open dialogue with Communists and defended their civil rights. In 1955 he joined Eleanor Roosevelt [q.v.] and Norman Thomas [q.v.] to appear before the Senate Internal Security Subcommittee. Although he offered to discuss his views with Hoover personally, Muste refused to comply with any governmental agency or official engaged in an investigation of religious or political opinions. During the same year he organized the American Forum for Socialist Education, an educational group sponsoring debates in which Communists were asked to participate.

Until his death in 1967 Muste traveled widely for the cause of peace. In 1963 he helped establish the International Confederation for Disarmament and Peace as a rival to the Communist-sponsored World Peace Council, which he criticized for endorsing the Chinese Communist position in the Vietnam struggle. A prominent opponent of U.S. involvement in Southeast Asia, Muste took an active part in organizing rallies, vigils and marches to protest the Vietnam war. [See KENNEDY, JOHNSON Volumes]

[FJD]

NATHAN, ROBERT (ROY)
b. Dec. 25, 1908: Dayton, Ohio.
Economist, National Chairman, Americans for Democratic Action, 1957-59.

Nathan earned an M.A. degree in economics from the University of Pennsylvania in 1933 and a law degree from Georgetown University in 1938. From 1940 to 1942 he was chairman of planning on the War Production Board, and he then became deputy director of the Office of War Mobilization and Reconversion (OWMR). Considered one of the most talented of the New Deal economists, he published *National Income in the U.S.* in 1939 and *Mobilizing for Abundance* five years later. In 1946 Nathan resigned from the OWMR in protest against the conservative policy of its director, Missouri banker John Snyder. Nathan then founded his own economic think tank, Robert Nathan Associates, to advise labor unions, businesses and foreign governments. An early member of the Americans for Democratic Action (ADA), Nathan was the organization's leading spokesman on economic policy during the Truman and Eisenhower years. In 1949 he joined other liberal economists in advocating a massive federal spending program to pull the U.S. out of the postwar recession.

Six months after Eisenhower's inauguration Nathan presented the first of many ADA critiques of the Administration's economic policies. He scored Eisenhower's failure to pursue economic planning and charged that farmers' incomes were shrinking, security prices were dropping and business was jittery. Speaking for the ADA, he called for a pledge of full employment, aid to farmers, a tax cut, expansion of public housing and an increase in the minimum wage from 75¢ to $1.25 an hour. During testimony before the Joint Committee on the Economic Report in 1956, Nathan advocated tax relief for lower income groups and repeal of loopholes favoring the rich taxpayer and corporations.

Nathan proposed a similar economic plan to counter the 1958 recession. Testifying before the House Ways and Means Committee in January 1958, he requested a tax cut and an increase in general welfare spending in such areas as education, mental health and housing. Even if this would unbalance the federal budget, it would, he said, "arrest the recession." On April 6 Nathan enlarged the scope of this program by suggesting federal grants to the needy, a federal food stamp program, extended and enlarged unemployment benefits, and a "vigorous program" to rebuild depressed areas.

Nathan stressed the importance of economic instead of military foreign aid. In his opinion, the Administration's "emphasis on military might and de-emphasis on economic and social considerations [was] playing havoc with America's role in world affairs." Nathan predicted that "hundreds of millions for economic development can save billions for defense and war." He was particularly impressed with the economic progress of South Vietnam. In 1959 Nathan predicted that it would outproduce the Communist North. The people, he said, "are hard working and capable and have demonstrated their determination to suffer and fight for high ideals and for freedom and independence."

In 1960 Nathan served as an adviser to Sen. Hubert Humphrey (D, Minn.) [q.v.] during his presidential campaign. Following John Kennedy's [q.v.] November victory, he served on the economic transition team. Kennedy often consulted Nathan on economic matters.

[JB]

NEUBERGER, RICHARD (LEWIS)
b. Dec. 26, 1912; Portland, Ore.
d. March 9, 1960: Portland, Ore.
Democratic Senator, Ore., 1955-60.

Neuberger graduated from the University of Oregon at Eugene in 1935 and later took law courses there. He joined the *New York Times* as its Pacific Northwest correspondent in 1939 and was elected to the Oregon Assembly the following year. Neuberger served in the Army during World War II. In 1945 he was military adviser to the U.S. delegation at the San Francisco Conference. That year Neuberger declined the Democratic gubernatorial nomination and ran unsuccessfully for the state Senate. He won the seat three years later.

In 1954 Neuberger ran for the U.S. Senate against incumbent Sen. Guy Cordon (R, Ore.) [*q.v.*], an advocate of the transfer of offshore oil reserves to the states. Aided by Adlai Stevenson [*q.v.*] and Sen. Wayne Morse (Ind, Ore.) [*q.v.*], Neuberger won a narrow victory after a campaign in which he stressed conservation of Oregon's natural resources.

In the Senate Neuberger established a liberal record as a vigorous backer of housing legislation, conservation measures, government financing of federal election campaigns and rigid price supports for farmers. In 1957 the liberal Americans for Democratic Action gave him a 100% rating as did the AFL-CIO's Committee on Political Education the following year. Along with Morse, he criticized Eisenhower's business-oriented policies, and in 1956 he suggested that the President not run for a second term.

Neuberger was a particularly strong supporter of civil rights. In 1956 he was one of six Democratic senators who announced that they would attempt to abolish Senate Rule 22, requiring two-thirds vote of the membership to cut off a filibuster, in order to facilitate the passage of civil rights legislation. This proposal was contained in a 16-point "Democratic Declaration of 1957," which also called on Congress to guarantee black voting and educational rights. Opposed by Senate Majority Leader Lyndon B. Johnson (D, Tex.) [*q.v.*], the motion to amend Rule 22 was tabled in January 1957. Neuberger supported another unsuccessful attempt to change the Rule in 1959.

The Senator backed the Civil Rights Act of 1957 and resisted attempts to weaken the proposal. In July he unsuccessfully opposed a motion to delete the measure's provision for federal government enforcement of school integration. The following month he again unsuccessfully fought a Southern attempt to weaken the bill by guaranteeing a jury trial to violators charged with criminal contempt. Neuberger chided Eisenhower for lukewarm support of the proposal, declaring that the President was responsible for its fate, and charging that his apathy had "made infinitely more difficult the task of those" who favored "meaningful and effective civil rights legislation."

Neuberger vigorously supported increased public housing, voting in August for the 1959 housing bill that would have promoted urban renewal and provided 37,000 new units of housing as well as loans and grants to aid home owners, the elderly, colleges and hospitals. That September he joined an unsuccessful attempt to overturn Eisenhower's veto of the proposal. Neuberger also voted to override the President's veto of a billion-dollar public works bill that month. In this case, the Senate's action was successful.

Neuberger died in March 1960, of a cerebral hemorrhage, at the age of 47. Although his term was completed by Oregon Supreme Court Justice H.S. Lusk, an appointee of the Governor, his wife Maurine Brown Neuberger won election to the Senate seat in November 1960.

[AES]

NEWSOM, HERSCHEL D(AVIS)
b. May 1, 1905; Bartholomew County, Ind.
d. July 2, 1970; Washington, D.C.
Master, The National Grange, 1950-68.

Herschel Newsom grew up on the family farm. He graduated from Indiana University in 1926 with a B.A. in chemistry and then became a farmer like his Quaker forebearers. A member of the Grange since his schoolboy days, Newsom became especially active in the organization in the 1930s. He was chosen master of the Columbus Subordinate Grange of Bartholomew Co. in 1933 and was elected master of the Indiana State Grange in 1937, an office which his father had once held and which Newsom retained for 13 years. In 1946 he joined the National Grange's executive committee. He became its chairman in 1949 and was elected master of the National Grange in November 1950.

The election of Newsom, a Republican, reflected increasingly conservative trends in the national farm organization. Newsom claimed that he was elected because he opposed "excessive governmental control of farm production in our daily lives." The Grange, which claimed to be the oldest farm organization in the world (founded in 1867), was, in fact, politically on the middle ground between the two other large U.S. farm groups, the conservative American Farm Bureau Federation (AFBF) and the liberal National Farmers Union (NFU). Especially strong in New England, Ohio and the Northwest, the Grange, or "Patrons of Husbandry," had over 850,000 dues-paying members, which made it larger than the NFU, but smaller than the AFBF.

Under Newsom the Grange tended to take a conservative position on farm issues during the first years of the Eisenhower Administration. Newsom applauded Secretary of Agriculture Ezra Taft Benson's [q.v.] farm program, including his plans to reduce acreage controls, price supports and direct subsidies to return American agriculture to the free market system and solve the problems of overproduction and declining farm income. Newsom, however, believed that immediate abolition of price supports would be ruinous for American farmers, who had long enjoyed 90% of parity price supports for basic crops. Speaking before the Senate Agriculture and Forestry Committee in March 1954, he recommended gradual cuts. Newsom also backed Benson's efforts to expand sales of U.S. farm products abroad, suggesting that they be integrated with a two-price system for wheat and cotton. Under a two-price system higher prices would be maintained for farm products in the U.S., while prices

would be lowered on the international market so that American farmers could successfully compete with foreign producers. In February 1955, as farm income continued the steady decline begun at the end of the Korean war, Newsom spoke out strongly against a measure to restore 90% of parity price supports.

Gradually, however, Newsom and the Grange, representing many small farmers, became dissatisfied with the Administration, which favored the interests of large growers. By 1956 Newsom's disenchantment seemed complete. In November he rejected the choice between 100% of parity price supports advocated by the NFU and most Democrats and the flexible support price program of Secretary Benson. Rather, Newsom wanted an individual commodity-by-commodity approach to price supports and dual parity, guaranteeing farmers high prices on food for domestic consumption but unsupported market prices on exports. In addition, Newsom and the Grange called for the creation of a bipartisan commission to study and recommend equitable revisions in the federal tax structure. Newsom opposed tax cuts that would require deficit financing. He said that if tax cuts were possible, they should be given to the lower income brackets. He also advocated the repeal of excise taxes on farm equipment not used on highways and suggested that the government use farm surpluses, not dollars, in foreign economic aid programs. In March 1958, in opposition to the Administration, Newsom supported congressional efforts to prevent the reduction in price support levels for a number of commodities. In June 1959 Newsom said that Congress had the responsibility to develop a workable farm program, whether or not the President would sign it. Referring to a compromise farm bill, he attacked Eisenhower, saying that "we may eventually have a President who will sign it."

Finally, in a November 1959 speech before the annual national meeting of the Grange, Newsom reversed his position on price supports by asserting that to attempt to remove the government from agriculture or any other area of the economy "is worst than sheer folly . . . it is tantamount to economic disaster." He said that "the nation can afford neither a continuation of the present system of price supports and subsidies nor a return to full free competition for agriculture." He was opposed to price fixing but argued that government measures should ensure a certain level of farm income, just as they helped determine industrial prices and the wages of labor.

During the Kennedy and Johnson years, Newsom worked closely with Secretary of Agriculture Orville Freeman [q.v.] to win adoption of the two-price wheat support plan the Grange had advocated for many years. In 1968 Newsom left the Grange to become U.S. tariff commissioner. He died in July 1970 after a heart attack.

[JCH]

NIEBUHR REINHOLD
b. June 21, 1892; Wright City, Mo.
d. June 1, 1971; Stockbridge, Mass.
Theologian

Niebuhr was the son of a German immigrant minister. He was educated at Eden Theological Seminary in Missouri and Yale Divinity School. In 1915 he became a minister of the Bethel Evangelical Church in Detroit, where he was active in labor, pacifist and socialist movements. A supporter of the Social Gospel during the early years of his career, Niebuhr became increasingly critical of liberal Protestantism and the secular society whose values it justified. He grew more insistent in his demands for social change, but with a theology emphasizing original sin, he was also increasingly pessimistic about achieving a just society.

His dark view of human nature was reflected in *Moral Man and Immoral Society*, published in 1932. While he conceded that individuals may sometimes interact in a moral and altruistic manner, he nonetheless insisted that social groups, especially those as large as nations, could operate only according to their particular interests. He abandoned pacifism as historically irrelevant to contemporary problems. The theologian broke with the Socialist Party in 1940 because of the failure of European Socialists to oppose Nazism. He then formed *Christianity and Crisis*, a biweekly paper designed to generate opposition to Hitler. The following year he played a leading role in the creation of the Union for Democratic Action, a group founded to mobilize former pacifists to support American entry into World War II.

After the War Niebuhr joined other liberals in forming the Americans for Democratic Action, an organization designed to be the "vital center" between the totalitarianism of both the left and right. He was a vigorous anti-Communist who warned of the need to remain vigilant to prevent Soviet expansion. Using his belief in original sin and the complete separation of heaven and earth, he criticized the Communist attempt to create a perfect society on earth [See TRUMAN Volume]

During the 1950s Niebuhr emerged as one of the major intellectual spokesmen for anti-Communist liberalism. Such prominent liberals as George F. Kennan [q.v.], Arthur Schlesinger, Jr., [q.v.] and Sen. Hubert Humphrey (D, Minn.) [q.v.] claimed him as the father of "realistic liberalism."

In foreign policy Niebuhr's realism resulted in an emphasis on America's need to live up to its responsibilities as leader of the free world. He maintained that nations were fundamentally immoral entities that could not be expected to cooperate with one another but, instead, were constantly involved in conflict. Niebuhr, therefore, insisted that foreign policy be based on maintaining a balance of power, with the U.S. as the primary counterweight to the totalitarian Communist nations. International organizations such as the U.N. played little role in his thought because they were not based on the realities of power politics. Thus, when the U.S. turned to the U.N. for a resolution of the 1956 Suez crisis, he complained that President Dwight D. Eisenhower was guilty both of collaborating with the USSR against the interest of American allies and of compounding the error by his pretense that the U.N. constituted a legitimate international authority. Niebuhr consistently advocated a strong American position in foreign affairs, particularly in Europe, which he considered the most important arena of international conflict.

By 1959, when he published *The Structure of Nations and Empires*, Niebuhr had somewhat softened his position on the Cold War. He conceded a Soviet trend away from the despotism of the Stalin era and hoped it would ultimately serve to ease international tensions. He even discerned a ray of hope in the "ultimate irony" of the contemporary situation: security could be established "under the umbrella of an atomic stalemate."

While his primary attention was devoted to foreign affairs, Niebuhr continued to campaign for social welfare programs during the Eisenhower Administration. He was an outspoken supporter of the Supreme Court's 1954 school desegregation decision. But, consistent with his pessimistic view of human nature, he expressed little hope for an easy resolution of U.S. racial problems and directed his personal attention almost exclusively to combating segregation within the church. In a July 1957 article in *Life* magazine, Niebuhr directed a controversial attack against Billy Graham [*q.v.*] and the wave of revivalism then sweeping the country. Niebuhr believed that Graham's emphasis on personal conversion and spiritual rebirth evaded the problem of social injustice that the U.S. had to face as a society.

Niebuhr continued his role as social, religious and political commentator until his death in 1971. [See KENNEDY Volume]

[JPL]

For further information:
Paul Merkley, *Reinhold Niebuhr: A Political Account* (Montreal, 1975).
Ronald H. Stone, *Reinhold Neibuhr: Prophet to Politicians* (Nashville, 1972).

NIXON, RICHARD M(ILHOUS)
b. Jan. 9, 1913; Yorba Linda, Calif.
Vice President of the United States, 1953-61.

Richard was the second of Frank and Hannah Nixon's five sons. Frank, who had held a number of blue collar jobs while moving west from Ohio, owned a lemon grove in Yorba Linda, Calif. When the grove failed in 1922, he moved to nearby Whittier, Calif., and opened a gasoline station and general store. At 10 or 11 Richard began his first job, working as a part-time farm laborer. He also worked in his father's store.

An extremely diligent and studious young man, Richard Nixon was student body president and an outstanding debater at both Whittier High School and Whittier College. In 1934 he received his B.A., graduating second in his college class. Nixon received a scholarship to attend Duke University law school. Although he graduated third in his class in 1937, he was unable to achieve his goal of joining one of New York City's prestigious law firms. After an unsuccessful attempt to get a job with the FBI, he returned to Whittier to practice law.

A month after the Japanese attacked Pearl Harbor, Nixon went to Washington and began working for the tire-rationing section of the Office of Price Administration (OPA). He later stated that, although he had been a liberal in law school, his experience with the inefficient OPA bureaucracy had made him more conservative. In August 1942 Nixon entered the Navy and was assigned to the Combat Air Transport Command in the South Pacific as a lieutenant, junior grade.

Before Nixon was mustered out of the service in January 1946, a group of prominent citizens in Whittier and its vicinity asked him to run for Congress against liberal Democratic Rep. Jerry Voorhis. Nixon had not previously demonstrated any significant interest in politics. He had not registered to vote until 1938. When asked by one of his potential sponsors if he were a Republican, Nixon reportedly replied, "I guess I'm a Republican. I voted for Dewey in 1944." However, he won the Republican primary and then waged an aggressive campaign against Voorhis. In a series of five debates with his opponent, Nixon linked the incumbent to the Congress of Industrial Organizations' (CIO) Political Action Committee (PAC). He charged that PAC was Communist-dominated and that Voorhis had voted for almost all measures supported by the CIO and PAC. Nixon won the election by 66,000 votes to 50,000.

Nixon was assigned to the House Un-American Activities Committee (HUAC) and the Education and Labor Committee. On the former panel he played a key role in pressing the investigation of Alger Hiss, accused of having been a Soviet spy while serving in the State Department during the 1930s. He arranged for a meeting between Hiss and his accuser, Whittaker Chambers [q.v.], before HUAC in August 1948. The confrontation led to Hiss's conviction for perjury in 1950. In 1948 Nixon also cosponsored the Nixon-Mundt bill to require the registration of Communist political organizations and their members and Communist-front groups and their officers. The measure did not pass, but portions of it were incorporated into the Internal Security Act of 1950.

Although conservative on most domestic issues, Nixon was an internationalist in foreign affairs. In 1947 he supported President Harry S. Truman's program of aid to Greece and Turkey. During the same year he served on a 19-member select panel, popularly known as the Herter Committee, that went on a fact-finding mission to Europe. He joined his colleagues on the panel in strongly endorsing the Marshall Plan.

Under California's cross-filing system Nixon won both the Republican and Democratic congressional primaries in 1948. Two years later he ran against Rep. Helen Gahagan Douglas (D, Calif.) for a Senate seat from California. Repeating his 1946 strategy, Nixon charged that "my opponent is a member of a small clique which joins the notorious Communist party-liner [Rep.] Vito Marcantonio in voting time after time against measures that are for the security of this country." His campaign organization distributed a pink-colored flyer linking the voting records of the two representatives. Douglas responded by describing Nixon and his supporters as "a backwash of young men in dark shirts," a clear reference to fascism. Nixon won the election with 2.2 million votes to Douglas's 1.5 million. [See TRUMAN Volume]

Nixon's success in linking the Democrat-ic Party and the National Democratic Administration with subversive influences enraged liberal Democrats and most intellectuals. By the early-1950s they thought of him as a notorious smear-artist and opportunist who would employ any means to win elections. After the 1950 elections Republicans regarded Nixon as a rising star who had played a key role in popularizing one of their Party's major issues. The freshman Senator quickly became one of the most sought-after Republican speakers in the country.

During the spring of 1952 New York Gov. Thomas E. Dewey and Herbert Brownell [q.v.], political advisers to Dwight D. Eisenhower, began seriously to consider Nixon as a running mate for the General, who was a candidate for the Republican presidential nomination. Nixon himself favored Eisenhower over Sen. Robert A. Taft (R, Ohio) [q.v.] for the nomination largely because he believed Eisenhower had a better chance to win. As a California delegate to the Chicago National Republican Convention in July, Nixon was committed to his state's favorite son, Gov. Earl Warren [q.v.]. However, Nixon told his followers in the California delegation that he expected Eisenhower to win on the first ballot. Warren's supporters charged that he was surreptitiously aiding the Eisenhower candidacy to assure himself the second slot on an Eisenhower ticket. A few hours after Eisenhower won the nomination, Brownell informed Nixon that he would be the vice presidential nominee. Eisenhower's advisers believed that Nixon's identification with the issue of subversive influence in Washington would aid the ticket. They also felt that the selection of Nixon would help mollify conservative supporters of Taft.

On Sept. 18, just after Nixon had begun his all-out national campaign, the *New York Post* ran a story asserting that a group of wealthy businessmen had established a "secret fund" for the candidate's personal use. The article referred to a fund created after the 1950 elections by Dana Smith and other California Republicans. Smith and Nixon contended that that the money was used only to help the latter pay the expenses involved in his extensive speechmaking tours.

It was never demonstrated that Nixon had used any of the money for personal aggrandizement. However, a number of Republican newspapers immediately called for Nixon's withdrawal from the ticket. On Sept. 20 Eisenhower stated in an off-the-record conversation that Nixon would have to prove himself "clean as a hound's tooth." Most of Eisenhower's campaign aides believed Nixon should resign.

To clear his name and retain his place on the ticket, Nixon made a half-hour television speech on Sept. 23. He denied that he had used the fund for personal expenses or that any of the contributors had received special favors from him. Claiming that he was not a wealthy man, Nixon gave what he called an "unprecedented" and "complete" financial account of his hordings. He said that his wife Pat, who appeared on camera when references were made to her, did not own a mink coat but only a "respectable Republican cloth coat." Finally, Nixon said that to avoid future charges he would reveal that a political admirer had sent his daughter Tricia a cocker spaniel that she had named Checkers. And, he continued, "regardless of what they say about it, we're going to keep it. . . ." The address subsequently was dubbed the "Checkers speech." Nixon urged viewers to inform the Republican National Committee whether they felt he should stay on the ticket.

Although Nixon was a combative politician, he sometimes gave way to despair following an intense effort to overcome adversity. Immediately after the broadcast he believed that the speech had been a failure because he had gone over his allotted half-hour and had been cut off the air. When Eisenhower indicated that he needed more time to make up his mind concerning his running-mate's status, Nixon dictated a telegram of resignation to Republican National Chairman Arthur Summerfield [q.v.]. Murray Chotiner [q.v.], Nixon's campaign manager, destroyed the message. Public reaction to the speech was overwhelmingly favorable. On the evening of Sept. 24, Eisenhower met Nixon at the Wheeling, W. Va., airport. He told Nixon he was "completely vindicated" and said to him, "You're my boy."

Resuming his campaign, Nixon charged that the Democrats had been soft on Communism and had permitted subversive influences to penetrate the national government. To demonstrate his own skill in dealing with subversives, Nixon, in a nationally televised campaign address on Oct. 13, described his role in the Hiss affair. In the same address he created a political stir by criticizing Democratic presidential candidate Adlai E. Stevenson [q.v.] for having attested to Hiss's good character at the latter's trial.

Nixon was an unusually active and visible vice president. Eisenhower created a precedent by assigning him to preside over cabinet and National Security Council meetings in the President's absence. He traveled extensively, visiting the Far East in 1953, Central America in 1955, Africa and Rome in 1957, South America in 1958 and the Soviet Union in 1959.

Nixon's major role in the Administration, particularly in the early years of the Eisenhower presidency, was as a congressional liaison and political adviser. He played a significant part in convincing Eisenhower to avoid attacks on Sen. Joseph R. McCarthy (R, Wisc.) [q.v.], arguing that a break between the President and the Senator could split the Republican Party and open the Administration of charges of being soft on Communism. In March 1953, after McCarthy had made personal efforts to stop Greek ship operators from trading with Communist China, Harold Stassen [q.v.], chief of the Mutual Security Administration, denounced the Senator for "undermining" President Eisenhower's foreign policy. Nixon, believing that the public approved of McCarthy's efforts, arranged a conference between the Senator and Stassen's chief, Secretary of State John Foster Dulles [q.v.]. The Secretary issued a statement praising McCarthy for acting in the national interest, and McCarthy promised to coordinate his actions with the State Department. In May 1953 McCarthy wrote a letter to the President asking why the Administration was not attempting to end Western trade with Communist countries. Nixon persuaded him to recall the letter. However, when McCarthy's attacks on the

Army made reconciliation seem impossible, Nixon abandoned his role as mediator. Speaking on behalf of the Administration in a March 13, 1954 television broadcast, he asserted that "men who have in the past done effective work exposing Communism in this country have, by reckless talk and questionable methods, made themselves the issue, rather than the cause they believe in so deeply."

In the 1954 congressional elections Nixon bore the brunt of the Administration's campaign efforts on behalf of Republican candidates. He charged that "the candidates running on the Democratic ticket in the key states are almost without exception members of the Democratic Party's left-wing clique which has been so blind to the Communist conspiracy and has tolerated it in the United States." Nixon warned that if the Democrats regained control of Congress, President Eisenhower's stern policy towards Communism would be jeopardized. To demonstrate Eisenhower's effectiveness in dealing with subversives, he claimed that thousands of security risks had been dismissed or had resigned from the federal government under the President's loyalty-security program. Democrats replied that most had departed for reasons having nothing to do with subversive activities and that some of the others had been hired after Eisenhower's inauguration.

Nixon's Checkers speech, his position on McCarthy and his electoral activities in 1952 and 1954 convinced his opponents more strongly than ever that he was a dangerously unscrupulous politician. However, beginning in 1955 his image began to soften even in the eyes of some of his staunchest foes, and there was talk of a "New Nixon." The process began with President Eisenhower's heart attack on Sept. 24, 1955. During the subsequent weeks of Eisenhower's hospitalization, Nixon maintained a low profile, playing down the significance of his role and avoiding any appearance of attempting to use the circumstances for political gain. He presided over cabinet and National Security Council meetings from his own chair rather than the President's. In the White House he used a conference room rather than the President's office. His prestige both within the Administration and in the country-at-large increased during this period.

The New Nixon image was enhanced by his 1956 reelection bid. In 1954, bearing an extraordinarily heavy campaign burden and finding himself the focus of Democratic attacks, he decided not to accept renomination in 1956. However, Eisenhower's heart attack in 1955 placed a new light on the vice presidency, and in 1956 he decided to run. After a period of indecision, which proved embarrassing to Nixon, the President announced on April that he wanted his Vice President to run for reelection. Eisenhower's reluctance had been generated by a desire to win the center during the election. His advisers convinced him that Nixon would not only appeal to that group but win solid right-wing support for the ticket as well.

During the 1956 campaign Nixon largely abandoned his customary electoral strategy of attack and concentrated on defending the record of the Eisenhower Administration. He stated that the President had extricated the country from the Korean war without abandonment of principle. Nixon also pointed to the healthy state of the economy and predicted that workers could anticipate a four-day week in the "not distant future."

During Eisenhower's second term Nixon's political stock was greatly enhanced by his foreign travels. His South American tour in May 1958 was plagued by leftist violence. In Lima, Peru, Nixon faced down a stone-throwing crowd at San Marcos University. In Caracas, Venezuela, the windows of his automobile were smashed by a raging mob, and troops arrived just in time to prevent him from being dragged from the car and killed. His fortitude and calmness in the face of great physical danger earned him considerable admiration throughout the Western Hemisphere.

In July 1959 Nixon went to Moscow to open the American National Exhibition at Sokolniki Park. He was the highest-ranking American official to visit the Soviet Union since Premier Nikita S. Khrushchev's rise to power. On the day after his arrival, Nixon and Khrushchev engaged in a debate over the respective merits of capitalism and

Communism. Part of the discussion took place in the model kitchen of the exhibition, and it became known as the "kitchen debate." Many Americans believed that Nixon had effectively "stood up" to the Soviet Premier.

Nixon managed to disassociate himself from the Republican Right and establish himself as a moderate during Eisenhower's second term. He became known as one of the stronger advocates of civil rights programs within the Administration. In 1957 he argued that the Administration should not agree to a conservative-sponsored amendment to its civil rights bill granting jury trials in criminal contempt cases arising from the measure. He also favored retention of a provision granting the Attorney General the power to enforce desegregation through federal court action. Two years later Eisenhower considered sending Congress a measure that would have merely extended the life of the Civil Rights Commission. Nixon, Attorney General William Rogers [q.v.], Health, Education and Welfare Secretary Arthur S. Flemming [q.v.] and Labor Secretary James Mitchell [q.v.] convinced the President to present a more comprehensive civil rights bill. During the same year Nixon, as chairman of the President's Committee on Government Contracts, urged that federal contractors be pressed to hire specific numbers of blacks and to place blacks in skilled as well as menial jobs. In 1957 and 1959 he assisted senators wishing to modify the filibuster rule by making favorable procedural decisions as president of the Senate.

In 1958 Nixon led those within the cabinet who favored more assistance for the unemployed and for depressed areas to fight the recession. Early the following year he fought successfully in the cabinet to keep federal aid for school construction on the Administration's legislative agenda. In December 1959 and January 1960 Nixon also established a reputation as a conciliator by helping to settle the 116-day steel strike.

Nixon emerged in the late-1950s as the strongest Administration advocate of aid for economically backward countries, including neutralist nations. He argued that economic aid was even more important than

military assistance. In 1957 President Eisenhower assigned him to help draw up mutual assistance, technical and direct aid programs.

Throughout the Eisenhower presidency, however, Nixon advocated a hard-line policy towards Communist expansion. In 1954 he suggested, off-the-record, the possibility of sending American troops to Indochina if the French pulled out. (Some observers believed that this was an Administration trial balloon rather than Nixon's personal view.) Four years later he stated that regardless of American public opinion, the Administration should stand by its commitment to defend the tiny Chinese Nationalist islands of Quemoy and Matsu against Chinese Communist attack. In 1959 Nixon met Cuban Premier Fidel Castro and reported to the Central Intelligence Agency that "he is either incredibly naive about Communism or under Communist discipline. . . ." In his book, Six Crises, Nixon claimed that after this meeting he urged the arming and training of Cuban exiles in the U.S. and Latin American countries.

While suspicion of Nixon among Democrats and intellectuals become somewhat muted during the late-1950s, it did not disappear. Their long-held distrust surfaced in January 1958, two months after President Eisenhower's third illness, a stroke that incapacitated him for two weeks. At that time Eisenhower drew up an agreement with Nixon making the latter acting President with the full powers of the presidency in the event of the former's incapacitation. Questions over the constitutionality of this arrangement in part reflected anxiety over the possibility of Nixon's becoming chief executive. The Vice President's characterization of Democrats as "radicals" in the 1958 congressional elections revived the suspicion among his traditional opponents that the New Nixon image was a facade.

Immediately after the 1958 elections Nixon gave his political backers permission to begin organizing his campaign for the 1960 Republican presidential nomination. The only significant obstacle was Nelson Rockefeller [q.v.], who had been elected governor of New York that year. However, Nixon, having assiduously campaigned for

Republican candidates across the country since the early-1950s, was the solid favorite of state and local party leaders. After discovering this through preliminary political feelers, Rockefeller announced in December 1959 that he would not seek the nomination.

Nixon needed the full support of Rockefeller, the leader of the Republican Party's Eastern liberal wing, to win the election. In July 1960 Rockefeller and Nixon met at the former's Fifth Avenue apartment in New York City. The Governor used his influence to secure changes in the Republican platform stressing stronger efforts in the areas of military preparedness and economic growth. Although the "Treaty of Fifth Avenue" upset many Republicans and was denounced by Sen. Barry Goldwater (R, Ariz.) [q.v.] as a "Munich," Nixon won the nomination almost unanimously on July 27. He chose Henry Cabot Lodge [q.v.] as his running mate. Lodge was ambassador to the United Nations and had gained national popularity through televised U.N. debates.

Since Nixon was the candidate of the minority party, he had to win the support of considerable numbers of voters who did not identify themselves as Republicans. To motivate independents and Democrats to vote for him, he tried to establish definitive differences between himself and his opponent, Sen. John F. Kennedy (D, Mass.) [q.v.]. He stressed his belief in the free enterprise system and criticized Kennedy for allegedly promising to solve all problems through federal intervention. However, since Nixon wanted to present himself as a middle-of-the-road figure, he could not take a clear-cut position against social welfare programs. Therefore, he and Kennedy appeared to have few differences on domestic issues.

In the field of foreign policy, Nixon criticized Kennedy for stating that Quemoy and Matsu were strategically worthless and indefensible. But this issue aroused little interest. Meanwhile, Kennedy took the offensive on the issue of policy towards Cuba. Although the Democratic candidate knew that the Eisenhower Administration was training Cuban exiles for an invasion of Cuba, he denounced the President for not

supporting the exiles and advocated an intervention similar to the one being planned. Nixon, who knew and strongly approved of the invasion plans but could not acknowledge them, denounced Kennedy for urging the violation of another country's sovereignty.

One of Nixon's advantages was the endorsement he received from President Eisenhower. But the usefulness of this backing was somewhat vitiated at an Aug. 24 presidential press conference. When asked to give an example of an important idea of Nixon's that he had adopted, Eisenhower replied, "If you give me a week, I might think of one." Despite the subsequent explanation that Eisenhower merely wanted to end the press conference and indicate that he would answer the following week, the remark raised questions about the enthusiasm of Eisenhower's support. The President's electoral inactivity during September and October further eroded the significance of Eisenhower's endorsement.

Nixon was better known to the public than Kennedy and, unlike his opponent, could claim executive experience. But both of these advantages were minimized by the four nationally televised debates between Nixon and Kennedy in September and October. Nixon agreed in July to the debates in part because of his success in debate against Voorhis in 1946, the effectiveness of his 1952 Checkers speech and the favorable reaction to his debate with Khrushchev in 1959. However, the mere exposure of Kennedy to audiences of up to about 70 million people did much to equalize the recognition factor. Furthermore, Kennedy's success in more or less holding his own in the debates weakened the argument that he was too inexperienced to be President.

Nixon was particularly damaged by the first debate, held on Sept. 26. He had lost weight during a recent period of hospitalization. As a result the candidate appeared gaunt and his clothes seemed oversized. He refused to wear makeup and his five o'clock shadow was clearly visible. One reporter described Nixon as looking "like a picture on a post office bulletin board." Television viewers gave Kennedy a clear edge in the debate, while radio listeners believed Nixon had done better. The debate became a classic example for those who argued that the visual media projected form more prominently than substance. Unfortunately for Nixon, many more people watched the debate on television than listened on radio. Many people believed that Nixon won the final three debates, but they had smaller audiences than the first one.

Kennedy won the election with an electoral vote margin of 303 to 219. His popular vote edge was only 113,000 votes out of 69 million, the smallest percentage difference in history. There was considerable evidence of vote fraud in Illinois and Texas, where Kennedy had won by narrow margins. Reversals of the results in these states would have given the election to Nixon, but recounts would have been time-consuming and probably would not have changed the outcome. Despite considerable pressure from Republicans to demand another tally, Nixon refused to ask for recounts.

In mid-November 1960 President-elect Kennedy offered Nixon a temporary foreign assignment, but the Vice President declined. He retired to private life, joining a Los Angeles law firm. In March 1962 his book, *Six Crises*, was published. Later in the year Nixon lost the California gubernatorial election to incumbent Gov. Edmund "Pat" Brown [*q.v.*]. At a press conference on the morning after the election, he contended that reporters had been biased against him throughout his career. He told them that "You won't have Nixon to kick around anymore because, gentlemen, this is my last press conference." The following year Nixon joined a New York City law firm.

Nixon actively worked for Sen. Barry Goldwater (R, Ariz.) [*q.v.*], the GOP's 1964 presidential candidate. In succeeding years he campaigned vigorously for many Republican candidates, as he had done in the 1950s. Nixon won the 1968 Republican presidential nomination and narrowly defeated Vice President Hubert Humphrey [*q.v.*] in the general election, with Alabama Gov. George Wallace running as a third party candidate. During his first term Nixon gradually withdrew American ground

forces from South Vietnam while resuming the bombing of North Vietnam and ordering an incursion into neutral Cambodia. In February 1972 he visited Communist China.

Nixon won a landslide reelection victory over Sen. George McGovern (D, S.D.) in 1972. However, during his second term suspicion mounted that he was covering up high-level complicity in a June 1972 break-in at Democratic National Headquarters by employes of his reelection committee. The House Judiciary Committee voted articles of impeachment in July 1974. Nixon resigned the following month after releasing tape recordings of White House conversations indicating his involvement in a cover-up. His successor, Gerald R. Ford [*q.v.*], granted him a full pardon in September 1974. In television interviews recorded and broadcast during the first half of 1977, Nixon admitted having made mistakes regarding the break-in but denied committing any illegal acts. [See KENNEDY, JOHNSON, NIXON/FORD Volumes]

[MLL]

For further information:
Earl Mazo and Stephen Hess, *Nixon: A Political Portrait* (New York, 1967).
Richard M. Nixon, *Six Crises* (New York, 1962).
Eric Sevareid, ed., *Candidates 1960* (New York, 1959).

NORSTAD, LAURIS
b. March 24, 1907; Minneapolis, Minn.
Supreme Commander, Allied Forces, Europe, April 1956-January 1963.

The son of a Lutheran minister, Norstad graduated from the U.S. Military Academy at West Point in 1930 and was commissioned a second lieutenant in the cavalry. In 1939 he joined the Army Air Corps; when the U.S. entered World War II, he was the assistant chief of staff for intelligence of the Air Force. Norstad directed Allied landings in North Africa in 1942 and in Sicily and Italy in 1943. He also planned the B-29 raids on Japan in August 1944 culminating in the atomic bombing of Hiroshima and Nagasaki a year later.

In 1946 Gen. Dwight D. Eisenhower secured Norstad's appointment to the War

Department General Staff to make plans for the postwar management of the Armed Forces. He was instrumental in establishing the Air Force as an independent branch of the Armed Services in 1947. That October he was promoted to lieutenant general and vice chief of staff for air operations and put in charge of planning for air defense. In 1950 Norstad assumed command of the U.S. Air Force in Europe and the following year became commander of Allied air forces in Central Europe. Norstad was made a full general in 1952, the youngest American to date to achieve that rank. In 1953 he was named air deputy to the Supreme Allied Commander, Europe (NATO), where he helped formulate atomic strategy and modernize the military communications system.

Norstad became Supreme Commander of Allied Forces, Europe, in November 1956. Reflecting the growing European belief that the alliance was too dependent on U.S. military power, he advocated the strengthening of NATO forces to respond to both conventional and nuclear warfare. He warned against British troop reductions in 1957 and the following year chided NATO foreign ministers for dilatoriness in meeting troop commitments. In April 1958 he asked for a buildup of active batallions in Europe over a five-year period.

While defending the maintenance of conventional troops in Europe as a first deterrent against Russian attack, Norstad felt the possession of land-based ballistic missiles was a necessary and important symbol of power. In November 1958 he announced a plan for increasing the number of NATO batalions equipped with short-range missiles from 30 to 100 over a five-year period. Norstad opposed a total reliance on strategic nuclear arms but advocated arming NATO forces with tactical atomic weapons. He initially defended U.S. control of the arms, but by 1959 he proposed that the alliance build its own nuclear force.

The General believed that a militarily strong Germany was vital for the security of Western Europe. In 1958 he rejected a Polish plan to make central Europe a demilitarized zone free of nuclear weapons, believing them "absolutely indispensable" to NATO's effectiveness. As a result of his ef-

forts, the Western European Union Council granted West Germany permission to build surface-to-air and air-to-air missiles in 1959. During the Berlin crisis of 1958-59, West Germany was equipped with rockets capable of carrying atomic warheads. They were placed under Norstad's control.

In the 1960s Norstad worked to develop closer working ties with alliance governments. Often operating in opposition to American policy, he continued to call for a NATO nuclear force. President John F. Kennedy's refusal to accept this position led to Norstad's resignation in 1963. [See KENNEDY Volume]

[AES]

OPPENHEIMER, J. ROBERT
b. April 22, 1904, New York, N.Y.
d. Feb. 18, 1967, Princeton, N.J.
Physicist; Atomic Energy Commisssion consultant, 1952-53.

The son of a German-born textile importer, J. Robert Oppenheimer graduated from Harvard, summa cum laude, in 1925. He began graduate study in physics at Cambridge University and received his doctorate from the University of Goettingen in 1927. Oppenheimer began teaching concurrently at the California Institute of Technology and the University of California at Berkeley in 1929. His comprehensive mastery of atomic physics won him virtual preeminence among American physicists, and he attracted a large, devoted following among students. During the early-1930s Oppenheimer explored aspects of the newly discovered positron and developed a new theory of cosmic ray showers. Prior to the outbreak of World War II, he helped develop the theory of "gravitational collapse," later used to explain quasars.

Oppenheimer had little interest in politics before 1936. However, his exposure to the left-wing ideology shared by many intellectuals of the period and his awareness of the harsh treatment of Jews in Nazi Germany rapidly aroused strong political commitments. Although Oppenheimer never belonged to the Communist Party, he joined and contributed funds to many organizations later characterized as Communist Party fronts by the House Un-American Activities Committee. In 1940 he married Katherine Puening, a former Communist. He began to disengage himself from political activity in 1940 and apparently completed this withdrawal within two years. However, his left-wing involvement led government officials to consider him a security risk when he undertook the direction of the Manhattan Project, formed to develop the atomic bomb, in 1942.

Late in 1942 George Eltenton, a British engineer with Communist sympathies, approached Haakon Chevalier, a close friend of Oppenheimer, and asked him to tell Oppenheimer that "he had means . . . of getting technical information to Soviet scientists." Chevalier told Oppenheimer of Eltenton's overture, but both men later claimed that they gave the matter no further consideration. Oppenheimer did, however, report it to Army officials during a general interrogation in August 1943. He finally received security clearance in 1943, but his failure to immediately report the Eltenton incident concerned intelligence officials, who monitored his activities closely throughout the War.

The U.S. atomic attack against Japan in August 1945 won Oppenheimer international acclaim as "the father of the atomic bomb." At the time, Oppenheimer stated that "it was necessary and right for us to make bombs," but by 1947 he questioned the scientists' social responsibility in developing the weapons. Despite his reservations he played a leading role in molding atomic policy after the war. He was the main author of the Acheson-Lilienthal report, which called for international control of nuclear energy, and of the Baruch Plan for U.N. supervision of atomic power. These proposals were rejected by the Soviet Union in 1946. Oppenheimer was named chairman of the Atomic Energy Commission's (AEC) General Advisory Committee (GAC) in 1947. That same year he became director of Princeton University's Institute for Advanced Study.

During the Truman Administration Oppenheimer became embroiled in the controversy over the development of the hydrogen (fusion) bomb. The possibility of creating such a device had been discovered in 1942, but the project had been stopped by seemingly insuperable technical obstacles in 1944. However, Edward Teller [q.v.] and others working on the fusion weapon advocated continuing the project. The Soviet Union's first atomic explosion in August 1949 increased demands for crash development. Oppenheimer and the majority of GAC members recommended only further theoretical study of the hydrogen bomb. They questioned the weapon's military usefulness and the morality of escalating the nuclear arms race. In 1950 President Truman authorized a crash program. During the Korean war Oppenheimer participated in Project Vista, which proposed the development of small tactical nuclear weapons for conventional ground warfare as alternatives to the massive strategic bombing favored by the Air Force. [See TRUMAN Volume]

In 1952 Truman named Oppenheimer chairman of a special State Department Advisory Committee on Disarmament. The Committee's report, published in July 1953, urged the Administration to speak more openly about the realities of nuclear warfare. It recommended a larger role in defense policymaking for the Western European nations and called for the accelerated development of continental air defense. Oppenheimer also reiterated his warning against total reliance on strategic nuclear weapons and again urged the development of tactical ones. However, Oppenheimer's proposals fell victim to the Eisenhower Administration's "New Look" in military policy. Overall arms spending was reduced and defense policy centered on air delivery of nuclear weapons to strategic targets.

In November 1953 William L. Borden, former executive director of the Joint Committee on Atomic Energy, sent FBI Director J. Edgar Hoover [q.v.] a letter in which he charged Oppenheimer with disloyalty. The letter outlined Oppenheimer's earlier ties to the Left, charged that he had brought Communists to work on the Manhattan Project and maintained that he had retarded the development of the hydrogen bomb. Borden stated that "more probably than not he has since been functioning as an espionage agent."

As a result of Borden's letter and pressure from Sen. Joseph R. McCarthy (R, Wisc.) [q.v.], who was in the midst of his anti-Communist crusade, President Eisenhower ordered Oppenheimer's security clearance suspended pending a review. AEC Chairman Lewis Strauss [q.v.] offered Oppenheimer the option of either resigning as an AEC consultant or requesting a hearing. He chose the hearing.

Oppenheimer's hearing before a special three-member board began on April 12. His eligibility for reinstatement was to be determined in accordance with the AEC's personnel security clearance criteria. Concrete actions, such as sabotage or espionage, were considered grounds for denial of clearance as were political attitudes and associations. The board was also bound by Eisenhower's 1953 Executive Order 10450 which required that employment be "clearly consistent with the interests of national security." In its review the board was required to consider the FBI's file on Oppenheimer, although the scientist and his lawyers lacked the clearance necessary for access to the material.

Numerous scientists, including Hans Bethe [q.v.], Linus Pauling [q.v.] and Albert Einstein [q.v.] expressed shock at the charges against Oppenheimer and affirmed their confidence in him. Of the several scientists who testified during the hearings, only Teller spoke against reinstating him on the grounds that he had delayed the development of the H-bomb.

Oppenheimer denied that he had opposed the development of the bomb after Truman had ordered it and asserted that he had worked for the project's success. He acknowledged his past involvement with left-wing groups but stated that he had "never accepted Communist dogma or theory" and that he had become completely disillusioned with the Communist movement. Referring to the charge that he had hired Communists to work on the Manhattan Project, Oppenheimer said that "past associations did not necessarily disqualify a man from employment, if we had confidence in his integrity and dependability."

In May the Board unanimously declared Oppenheimer a "loyal citizen" who "seems to have had a high degree of discretion reflecting an unusual ability to keep to himself vital secrets." It also found that despite moral, political, strategic and technical opposition to the hydrogen bomb, Oppenheimer had done nothing to frustrate its production after Truman's 1950 decision. However, two of the three board members, ex-Army Secretary Gordon Gray and Thomas Morgan of the Sperry Rand Corp., voted that clearance should remain suspended on the ground that his "continuing conduct and associations . . . reflected a serious disregard for the requirements of the security system."

In June Oppenheimer filed an appeal with the AEC, but on June 29 the Commission announced its four-to-one decision against reinstatement. The majority, including Lewis Strauss, said that its decision was based on "proof of fundamental defects in his character" and the finding that "his association with persons known to him to be Communists have extended far beyond the tolerable limits of prudence and self-restraint. . . ." They cited examples of what were termed "falsehoods, evasions and misrepresentations" in his dealings with the FBI, the Counter Intelligence Corps and the AEC, especially in his account of the Eltenton incident.

Although they saw Oppenheimer as a victim of the virulent anti-Communism of the postwar period, his defenders also considered him the target of a personal vendetta executed by the group of scientists around Teller. They believed that Oppenheimer, already vulnerable because of his unpopular associations and views, had exacerbated these tensions because of what Joseph and Stewart Alsop [q.v.] called his "regrettable tendency to be contemptuous of government flatfeet" and because "Oppenheimer did not willing suffer people whom he considered wrong." In a *Harper's* article entitled "We Accuse!," the Alsops denounced the security hearing as a "miscarriage of justice." However, most of the nation's newspapers endorsed the AEC's conduct.

Oppenheimer remained at Princeton, and in October 1954 he was unanimously reelected director of the Institute for Advanced Study by the University's trustees. However, according to Oppenheimer's attorney Lloyd K. Garrison, "the blow [of the AEC's ruling] was a lasting one which he took with him to his grave." In 1957, when the launching of the Soviet satellite *Sputnik* generated fresh interest in government-sponsored scientific projects, the possibility was raised of a new hearing which might clear Oppenheimer. However, Strauss announced in January 1958 that the case would not be reopened unless Oppenheimer could present "substantial new evidence." When John McCone [*q.v.*] succeeded Strauss as AEC chairman later that year, he ordered a legal review of the case. AEC lawyers found "a messy record" and "a primitive abuse of the judicial system," but took no further action.

The Federation of American Scientists petitioned the AEC to reopen the case after John F. Kennedy became President. The Commission again declined to do so. Kennedy, however, invited Oppenheimer to a White House dinner for Nobel Prize winners where Glenn Seaborg, the AEC's new chairman, offered him a new hearing. Oppenheimer refused. In 1962 Kennedy decided to vindicate Oppenheimer by presenting him with the AEC's Enrico Fermi Award but postponed the controversial award until after the 1962 elections. He was assassinated before Oppenheimer received the honor. President Lyndon B. Johnson made the award in December 1963. Oppenheimer died of throat cancer in 1967.

[MDB]

For further information:
Robert Gilpin, *American Scientists and Nuclear Weapons Policy* (Princeton, 1962).
John Major, *The Oppenheimer Hearing* (New York, 1971).

PACE, FRANK, JR.
b. July 5, 1912; Little Rock, Ark.
Chief Executive Officer, General
Dynamics Corporation, 1957-62.

After obtaining a bachelors degree from Princeton in 1933 and a law degree from Harvard three years later, Pace joined the

Arkansas district attorney's office. He served as the assistant district attorney for the 12th judicial district until 1938, when he joined the Arkansas Revenue Department. He worked as his father's legal partner in 1941 but left the following year for service in the Air Transport Command.

In 1946 Pace went to work as the Attorney General's special assistant on tax matters; he was transferred several months later to the postal service as executive assistant to the Postmaster General. Pace remained there from 1946 to 1948, when President Harry S. Truman appointed him assistant director of the Bureau of the Budget. In January 1949 he succeeded James Webb as Budget Director. The following year he was named Secretary of the Army. Pace resigned his post at the end of the Truman Administration and returned to private business. Nevertheless, he remained active in the Democratic Party and in 1954 turned down the post of chairman of the Democratic National Committee. [See TRUMAN Volume]

In May 1953 Pace was called before the Senate Armed Services Committee's Preparedness Subcommittee during an investigation of ammunition shortages in Korea. He testified that until January 1953 fighting in Korea was done solely with World War II surplus, leaving reserves severely depleted. The subcommittee's final report determined that these shortages had resulted in the "needless loss of American lives," but that "revised procedures had replenished stocks."

In 1953 Pace was elected executive vice president and director of the General Dynamics Corp. (GD). He became vice chairman and senior vice president of operations and fiscal affairs in 1955. Two years later he moved up to chief executive officer. During his tenure GD became one of the nation's prime defense contractors. In the period from 1950 to 1956 the company had a contract volume of $4.07 billion. From 1956 to 1957 it was second only to North American Aviation, with defense contracts totaling $1.33 billion. GD's electric boat division built the first atomic-powered submarine, the *Nautilus*, as well as two subsequent models. The company also received contracts to built the *Atlas* intercontinental ballistic missile and experimental atomic powered aircraft. Pace joined a group of American businessmen who, at a 1959 meeting with Soviet leader Nikita Khrushchev, expressed their hopes for disarmament. The industrialists said that under capitalism, "production for consumption" would be more profitable than military manufacture.

During the Eisenhower Administration Pace served on several government committees, including the President's Commission on National Goals, formed in 1959 to set general domestic and foreign policy goals for the 1960s. The panel's report, issued in November 1960, called for "extraordinary personal responsibility, sustained effort and sacrifice" to achieve "high and difficult goals" in the period of "grave danger" ahead. It assumed that the Cold War would continue and that bigger military outlays would be necessary. It stressed the need to increase domestic economic growth and aid the economic development of underdeveloped nations, which would be the focus of East-West struggle during the 1960s. In addition to an expanding economy, the major domestic goals included improved secondary and college level education open to all, aid to the arts and reformation of the federal bureaucracy. The panel emphasized that the federal government should insure every citizen the right to vote.

Pace resigned as chief executive officer of GD in 1962 to join the International Executive Service Corp. Two years later he became its president.

[RB]

PACKARD, VANCE (OAKLEY)
b. May 22, 1914; Granville Summit, Pa.
Author.

Vance Packard grew up in State College, Pa., where his father worked as college farm superintendent. Majoring in English, he received his B.A. degree from Pennsylvania State College in 1936. He received an M.A. from Columbia University school of journalism the following year. Between 1938 and 1956 he worked as newspaper reporter, magazine writer and editor. Packard's first book *Animal I.Q.*, dealing with animal intelligence and instinct, was published in 1950. Research for this project led him to investigate work being done by the Institute for Motivational Research in New York, a private corporation used by advertising agencies.

In 1957 Packard published *The Hidden Persuaders*, which discussed the manipulative techniques used by the advertising industry to sell products. Many of the new techniques were developed through "motivational research," using basic psychological testing and in-depth interviewing of sample consumers to determine human desires and motivations that could be met in the advertising campaign. Packard showed how Madison Avenue sought to stimulate "impulse buying" by indirectly appealing to deep human fears, urges and motivations. He described the newest technique, "subliminal projection," in which words or images were flashed before the senses too rapidly to be recognized by the conscious mind. The unconscious picked up the advertising message, however, and directed the consumer to satisfy the subliminal suggestion. Packard condemned this as an unfair assault on the human psyche. He maintained that before the 1950s advertising had been largely a matter of proclaiming the virtues of one product over another through appeals to the conscious mind. He advocated a return to this method and urged the industry to adopt a code of ethics. At a time when the nation was concerned with propaganda, brainwashing and the effects of television, *The Hidden Persuaders* became a best-seller.

Packard criticized American industry in his second and third books, *The Status Seekers* (1959) and *The Waste Makers* (1960). He accused large corporations of selling the status associated with their name rather than a quality product. He also suggested that advertising's emphasis on impulse buying encouraged shoddy production and planned product obsolescence. Packard urged consumers to protest these tendencies and look within for standards of quality, craftsmanship and emotional satisfaction rather than imagine they could buy it.

Packard's books laid the groundwork for the fiercely fought consumer issues of the 1960s. He continued to write during that decade, producing books about the ruthless competition for advancement in modern corporations and sexual confusion accompanying the decline of traditional values.

[MJS]

PARKS, ROSA (McCAULEY)
b. Feb. 4, 1913: Tuskegee, Ala.
Civil rights activist.

Rosa McCauley attended local black schools in Tuskegee and Montgomery, Ala. She married Raymond Parks when she was 19 and held several different jobs in Montgomery. Rosa Parks was active in black community affairs and worked for her church, for the Montgomery Voters League and for the NAACP, serving for a time as secretary of the local branch.

On Dec. 1, 1955 Parks boarded a city bus in downtown Montgomery to return home from her job as a seamstress at the Montgomery Fair department store. Shortly after she sat down, the driver ordered Parks to give up her seat on the racially segregated bus to a white person. Since the bus was already full, that meant she would have to stand. Parks quietly refused to move, and the driver called the police who arrested and jailed her. She was soon released on bail but ordered to stand trial on Dec. 5.

By the time of this incident, Montgomery's bus system had become a particularly sore spot within the black community. The bus drivers, all of whom were white, were often abusive toward black passengers and on occasion, assaulted them. Blacks had to pay their fare at the front door but then get off the bus and board through the rear door. Drivers would sometimes drive off after a black had paid but before he had reached the rear entry. The first four rows of seats on each bus were reserved exclusively for whites, and even when no white passenger was present a black could not sit there. Blacks also had to give up their seats in the unreserved section if more seats

were needed for whites. In the year before Parks's arrest, three other black women had refused to give up their seats and had been arrested, and there had been talk of a protest. Following one of these incidents, blacks did organize a citizens' committee to negotiate with the bus company management for improved treatment for blacks, but no results came from their meeting.

The arrest of Rosa Parks, a gentle and dignified woman who was highly respected in the black community, proved to be the catalyst for a boycott of the bus system by Montgomery's 50,000 blacks. The protest began on Dec. 5, the day of Parks's trial, in which she was found guilty of violating the bus segregation law and fined $10. The boycott continued for 381 days and resulted in a Supreme Court decision holding segregation in local transit facilities unconstitutional. The Montgomery boycott catapulted its leader, Martin Luther King, Jr. [q.v.], to national prominence and inaugurated an era of nonviolent protest against racial segregation and discrimination.

Parks's refusal to give up her bus seat in December 1955 was wholly unprompted and unplanned. She had no idea, she later declared, that it would cause the reaction it did. Parks explained that she had been tired after a long day of work and considered it an imposition to have to move. Her refusal to move back, as Martin Luther King, Jr., later asserted, was also an "intrepid affirmation that she had had enough." Parks had long believed that segregation was unjust. She decided that day, she later said, that she would be pushed no further.

During the boycott, Parks served on the program committee and the executive board of the Montgomery Improvement Association (MIA), the organization set up to supervise the protest. She occasionally traveled to other parts of the country to help raise funds for the MIA. In January 1956 she was fired from her job at the Montgomery Fair and had to take in sewing at home. She also received many threatening and harassing phone calls, and her husband encountered some pressures at his job as a barber.

In August 1957, eight months after the

boycott ended, the Parks moved to Detroit where Rosa's brother lived. She worked as a dressmaker for several years and then as a receptionist and staff assistant in the office of Detroit Rep. John Conyers, Jr. (D, Mich.). Although she did not have a major role in the civil rights movement of the 1960s, Parks joined King's Southern Christian Leadership Conference, remained a member of the NAACP, and participated in several protests such as the 1965 march from Selma to Montgomery. For the part she played in touching off the Montgomery bus boycott, Parks has been called "the mother of the civil rights movement." She was frequently honored by civil rights organizations in later years for her act of civil disobedience.

[CAB]

PARSONS, J(AMES) GRAHAM

b. Oct. 28, 1907; New York, N.Y.
Ambassador to Laos, May 1956-June 1958; Deputy Assistant Secretary of State for Far Eastern Affairs, June 1958-June 1959; Assistant Secretary of State for Far Eastern Affairs, June 1959-February 1961.

After receiving his B.A. from Yale in 1929 and doing graduate work at New York University, Parsons began a diplomatic career. He was private secretary to the U.S. ambassador to Japan from 1932 to 1936 and served as vice consul in Havana, Ottawa, and Mukden (Manchuria) from 1936 to 1943. Parsons then became the State Department's representative on the Permanent Joint Board of Defense of the U.S. and Canada. From 1945 to 1947 he was assistant chief of the division of British Commonwealth Affairs. After service as the assistant to the President's representative to the Pope from 1947 to 1948 and at the New Delhi and Nepal consulates from 1948 to 1950, Parsons returned to the State Department as deputy director of the Office of European Regional Affairs from 1951 to 1953. He then served as deputy chief of mission and minister at the American embassy in Tokyo. Parsons became ambassador

to Laos in 1956 and remained there until 1957, when he became deputy assistant secretary of state for Far Eastern Affairs. He was promoted to assistant secretary of state in 1959.

Shortly thereafter the House Government Operations Committee charged that during his tenure in Laos Parsons had "abetted" bribery and inefficiency in the disbursement of American aid. The panel maintained that he had removed a government auditor who was investigating charges of bribery in the program. The State Department, however, defended Parsons, praising his "superb job" in overseeing aid distribution.

During 1960 Parsons became involved in the Administration's internal dispute over U.S. policy toward Laos. In August the American supported government of Phoumi Nosavan was overthrown by Laotian Air Force Capt. Kong Le, who turned administrative power over to neutralist Prince Souvanna Phouma. Souvanna then attempted to form a coalition government composed of Phoumi supporters, neutralists and members of the Communist Pathet Lao. Phoumi refused to accept Souvanna's offer of a position in the new government. Instead he decided to use his control of the Royal Laotian Army to regain domination of the country through a military campaign.

Parsons supported a neutralist government, as did Ambassador Winthrop Brown [q.v.]. Both men believed it would be impossible to form a pro-Western government in the area because of the corruption of the Phoumi regime and the growing nationalist feelings among the Laotians. However, Parsons distrusted Souvanna because of what he thought was the Prince's naive attitude about Communism. He recommended that the coalition government exclude the Pathet Lao. Higher State Department officials, fearing that Souvanna would be another Fidel Castro, demanded his replacement. During August Parsons worked to keep U.S. policy options open while giving Brown a chance to persuade Souvanna to form a coalition government acceptable to the U.S.

In the beginning of October the U.S. cut off military aid until the situation was clarified. On Oct. 12 Parsons led a mission to Laos to outline the conditions under which the U.S. would support Souvanna. He demanded that the Prince end discussions with the Communists about entry into a coalition government; resume talks with Phoumi and agree to give him a major role in the cabinet; move his government away from Vientiene to Luang Prabang, where pro-Western influences were strongest; and, restrain Kong Le, who had been distributing U.S. military aid to the Communists. Souvanna refused.

Fearing that Souvanna would turn to the Soviet Union for military aid, Parsons and Brown worked for the resumption of assistance. On Oct. 17 Brown got Souvanna to agree to a continuation of aid to both camps. The neutralist did, however, ask that all cash assistance be funneled through his government. Parsons supported the agreement, but he was overruled by Washington. Souvanna, then under attack by Phoumi, turned to the USSR for help.

After the Prince's action Parsons joined his superiors in working for Souvanna's ouster. By November Phoumi had driven the Prince into exile and Kong Le into an alliance with the Communists. In an interview with the *New York Times* in January 1961, Souvanna denounced Parsons as "the most nefarious and reprehensible of men."

Parsons was appointed ambassador to Sweden in February 1961. He resigned that post in 1967 to become senior foreign service inspector. In 1969 Parsons was appointed deputy chairman of the U.S. delegation to the Strategic Arms Limitation Talks.

[AES]

PARSONS, TALCOTT

b. Dec. 13, 1902; Colorado Springs, Colo.
Sociologist

Parsons, the son of a Congregationalist minister, was born and raised in Colorado. He attended the Horace Mann school and graduated in 1920. In 1924 he received his B.A. in philosophy and biology from Amherst College. His interest in social science

developed at the London School of Economics during 1924-25, when he studied under the anthropologist Bronislaw Malinowski. Parsons then attended Heidelberg University, where he was introduced to the sociological writings of Max Weber, about whom little was known in the United States. He received his Ph.D. in 1927. Three years later his translated Weber's *The Protestant Ethic and the Spirit of Capitalism.*

Parson's first major work, *The Structure of Social Action,* was published in 1937, while he was teaching at Harvard University. In it he pointed to the common theme of "voluntarism" in the writings of Alfred Marshall, Vilfredo Pareto, Emile Durkheim and Max Weber. He used this theme to develop a system situated between the individualism of classical liberal theory and the organicism of theories such as Marxism. For Parsons the basic unit of social order was neither the individual nor large structures such as the class. Instead, it was action or behavior which was directed outward to other people. Society grew out of the actions of individuals as they were constrained and motivated by a complex set of norms and values.

During the next 20 years Parsons developed his theory in a number of articles and applied it in studies of fascism and Japanese militarism. In 1951 he published *The Social System.* Its extreme formalism and almost total lack of reference to empirical data caused much criticism, but the work nonetheless had a significant impact on both American and European sociology. In it Parsons attempted a comprehensive theory of social behavior which linked his earlier action frame of reference to the analysis of social systems. He insisted that empirical studies could proceed only after the system was conceptualized in its entirety. *The Social System* did, however, contain an illuminating case study on the Soviet Union. Writing about two years before Stalin's death, Parsons argued that Stalinism distinguished itself from Nazism by proving to be more adaptive to outside conditions. This process of adaptation, however, would ultimately mean that the USSR must give up any serious hope of realizing the Communist society its founders had envisioned. As an industrial nation it would find itself moving closer and closer to the kinds of values espoused in the United States. In sharp contrast to such theorists as Hanna Arendt [q.v.], who saw the whole world as moving towards totalitarianism, Parsons maintained that the totalitarian nations, once industrialized, would become increasingly democratic—or face complete collapse.

In 1955 he published *Family, Socialization and Interaction Process.* By attempting to integrate psychoanalysis and social theory, Parsons revealed his continuing effort to construct a comprehensive theory. *Economy and Society* (1956) was an attempt to establish the beginnings of a synthesis of economics and sociology. Parsons felt that the artificial separation of these disciplines in the university did not reflect a lack of common interests and concerns, but the disintegration of present institutional arrangements. His overriding goal, the comprehensive explanatory model of social behavior, was reflected in his belief that the various academic disciplines dealt with aspects of social life and could be integrated for the analysis of the entire social world.

In *Structure and Process in Modern Societies* (1960), Parsons attempted to discover the defining principles of formal organizations. But once again he provided an important case study. He dealt with McCarthyism as "a relatively acute symptom of the strains which accompany a major change in the situation and structure of American society." These strains were the results of increased social mobility and the international conflicts embodied in the Cold War. Parsons analysis differed little from that of sociologists such as Seymour Martin Lipset [q.v.] and Daniel Bell [q.v.], except that he was more confident that right-wing movements posed no real threat to American society.

Parsons later contributions never departed from his central organizing principles and his concern with integrating the various academic disciplines. He continued to write primarily on a theoretical level, although he also contributed more sub-

stantive studies such as *The American University* (1973). Summing up Parsons's importance, Alvin Gouldner stated "it is Parsons who has provided the focus of theoretical discussions for three decades now, for those opposing him no less than for his adherents." Parsons retired from Harvard in 1975 after more than 40 years.

[JPL]

William C. Mitchell, *Sociological Analysis and Politics: The Theories of Talcott Parsons* (Englewood Cliffs, 1967).
Talcott Parsons, *The Social System* (New York, 1951).
———, *Economy and Society* (New York, 1956).
———, *Structure and Process in Modern Societies* (New York, 1960).

PASSMAN, OTTO E(RNEST)
b. June 27, 1900; Washington Parish, La.
Democratic Representative, La., 1947-77; Chairman, Foreign Operations Subcommittee of the House Appropriations Committee, 1955-77.

Born on a farm near Franklinton, La., Otto Passman was the son of poor sharecroppers. After leaving school at 13, he worked at various jobs, finally settling in Monroe, La., where he established a successful business in wholesale restaurant equipment. While serving in World War II, Passman decided to enter politics. In 1946 he was elected to Congress from Louisiana's largely rural fifth district and was subsequently reelected every two years, usually without opposition.

During the Eisenhower years Passman opposed civil rights measures, advocated high price supports for farmers and curbs on labor unions and usually voted with the conservative coalition of Southern Democrats and Republicans. Since his assignment to the House Approprations Committee in 1949, moreover, Passman had developed a special expertise in budgetary matters, and he soon emerged as the lower chamber's leading opponent of foreign aid. In 1955 Rep. Clarence Cannon (D, Mo.) [q.v.], conservative chairman of the Appropriations

Committee, appointed Passman to head that panel's Foreign Operations Subcommittee, which initiated congressional consideration of foreign aid appropriations bills. With Cannon's support he led an annual and usually successful effort to severely cut the Administration's requests for foreign assistance funds. The subcommittee's recommendations were always quickly ratified by the full 50-member Committee and, with this powerful backing, easily passed the House.

Immediately upon assuming the chairmanship Passman slashed $627 million from the 1955 mutual security appropriations bill, most of which was subsequently restored by the Senate. The following year the subcommittee approved a $4 billion ceiling on foreign aid, with Passman warning that "the best way to destroy friends [overseas] . . . is to start supporting them with gifts and favors." The appropriations bill, as enacted in July 1956, assigned $3.7 billion for operations abroad, some $1 billion less than the sum requested by the Administration.

The Administration could bring little effective pressure to bear on Passman to modify his stand because his district contained no military bases or defense plants that it could threaten to remove or close. In 1957 Eisenhower, in desperation, invited him to the White House for a private conference, along with Secretary of State John Foster Dulles [q.v.] and the Joint Chiefs of Staff. Passman proved so recalcitrant, however, that the angry President afterward asked an aide to remind him "never to invite that fellow down here again." Later that year Passman cut the Administration's foreign aid request by 25%, despite a threat by the President to call a special session of Congress to force the House to vote the full amount.

Although the Senate usually restored some of the House-initiated foreign aid cuts, Passman was such an intransigent negotiator at House-Senate conferences that the final appropriations bill was always far below the Administration's original request. In 1958, after Speaker Sam Rayburn (D, Tex) [q.v.] personally pleaded with Passman to add more than the $220 million

he had offered as a compromise to Senate conferees, the adamant Chairman replied: "If they get $220 million, they'll be damn lucky. They can have [the money] in a half hour, or they can get it in 10 days." The Senate finally yielded to Passman's terms.

During the Kennedy and Johnson years, Passman continued to be the most powerful foe of foreign assistance programs on Capitol Hill. Rep. Cannon died in 1964, however, and the new Appropriations Committe chairman, George H. Mahon (D, Tex.) [q.v.], who did not share Passman's views on foreign aid, curtailed the subcommittee chairman's power both on his own panel and in the House as a whole. [See KENNEDY, JOHNSON, NIXON/FORD Volumes]

[TLH]

PASTORE, JOHN O(RLANDO)
b. March 17, 1907; Providence, R.I.
Democratic Senator, R.I., 1950–77.

The son of an Italian immigrant tailor, John Pastore attended Northeastern University law school at night while working as a claims adjuster for Narragansett Electric Co. After graduating in 1931, he opened a private legal practice in Providence. Pastore turned his attention to politics in 1933, when he asked the local political boss, Tommy Testa, to back him for the Democratic nomination for state representative. With Testa's support, Pastore won the election in a strongly Republican district in 1934 and was reelected two years later. During the late-1930s he served as state attorney general. He was elected lieutenant governor in 1944 and succeeded to the governorship in 1945.

Five years later Pastore won a Senate seat vacated by the incumbent, J. Howard McGrath (D, R.I.), who had become U.S. Attorney General. He was the first U.S. senator of Italian descent. During his first years in the Senate, Pastore established a liberal record on domestic affairs, supporting federal funds for public housing, hospitals and medical care and research. He also favored raising corporate and personal income taxes in the higher brackets. The

Senator supported President Harry S. Truman's foreign aid requests and opposed efforts to limit the number of troops the President might sent to Europe. In 1952 Pastore actively campaigned against the McCarran immigration bill. The same year he directed Adlai Stevenson's [*q.v.*] presidential campaign among Italian-Americans.

Pastore continued to back federal housing, school construction and public works bills throughout the Eisenhower Administration. In 1954 he led Senate opponents of a measure exempting independent natural gas producers from rate regulation by the Federal Power Commission. He supported Eisenhower's foreign aid requests and backed efforts to end the national origins quota system in immigration statutes.

Pastore supported the Civil Rights Act of 1957. However, he, like many other liberals, voted to delete Part III of the Administration's proposal. This section gave the Attorney General wide powers to seek injunctions in any type of civil rights case with or without the consent of the alleged victim. They held that it would give the Attorney General excessively-broad and insufficiently-defined powers, and by overly antagonizing the South, jeopardize the bill and make rights progress more difficult. Pastore also voted for a revised jury-trial amendment to the measure, guaranteeing jury trials not only in criminal contempt cases arising from the right-to-vote law but also in cases stemming from more than 40 other laws.

As a member of the Joint Committee on Atomic Energy, Pastore focused much of his attention on the questions of nuclear power development. In late 1954 he spearheaded Democratic efforts to delay the signing of the Dixon-Yates contract until the Democratic controlled 84th Congress had an opportunity to study it. The contract would have permitted a private utility to construct generating facilities near West Memphis, Ark., to supply the Atomic Energy Commission (AEC) with power. It would have replaced the Tennessee Valley Authority as the power producer for the agency. The Administration signed the agreement but was forced to cancel it in July 1955 after revelations of possible conflict of interest in awarding the contract.

During the decade Pastore supported efforts to stimulate private research and development of the peaceful uses of atomic energy. In 1954 he backed measures designed to limit the patent rights on inventions used in producing fissionable materials in order to encourage private initiative. Two years later he urged the production of demonstration reactors to spread nuclear technology. In 1957 the Senator stated that he backed government research in the use of atomic energy for peaceful purposes. However, he said that "the minute it becomes competitive . . . [and] no longer research, the government ought to get out of the operation, because that would be socialism."

Pastore supported the Administration's desire to share atomic energy information with friendly nations. In 1954 he offered an amendment to the atomic energy bill of that year giving the President the right to deal with groups of nations as well as with individual countries in sharing atomic energy for peaceful uses. The amendment, however, failed. Four years later Pastore chaired the Joint Atomic Energy Subcommittee on Agreements for Cooperation, which formulated a measure to permit free exchange of atomic information and materials between the U.S. and its allies. He guided the bill through Congress; the President signed it on July 2.

Pastore was a strong supporter of both the Kennedy and Johnson Administrations' domestic programs. He retired from the Senate at the beginning of 1977. [See KENNEDY, JOHNSON, NIXON/FORD Volumes]

[RSG]

PATMAN, (JOHN) (WILLIAM) WRIGHT

b. Aug. 6, 1893; Patman's Switch, Tex.
d. March 7, 1976; Bethesda, Md.
Democratic Representative, Tex., 1929-76; Chairman, Select Small Business Committee, 1955-1963.

Patman was the son of a tenant cotton farmer. After graduating from high school in 1912, he studied law on his own and raised cotton as a sharecropper so that he could complete his legal studies at Cumberland University in Tennessee. He received his LL.B. degree there in 1916. In 1920 Patman won election to the Texas House of Representatives and gained reelection in 1922. Two years later he moved to Texarkana, where he was elected district attorney. In 1928 Patman won a seat in the U.S. House of Representatives as an anti-Ku Klux Klan candidate.

Patman represented the poor northeastern corner of Texas and quickly gained a reputation as a controversial populist enemy of concentrated wealth. In 1932 he called for the impeachment of Secretary of the Treasury Andrew Mellon on the grounds of conflict of interest. Beginning in the same year he pressed for a veterans' bonus bill, which he felt would stimulate the economy by increasing consumer demand. In 1936 Congress overrode a veto by President Franklin D. Roosevelt to enact a bonus bill. Patman blamed its failure to stem the Depression on what he believed was the nullifying effect of a Federal Reserve Board decision to double bank reserve requirements.

In 1936 Patman coauthored the Robinson-Patman Act, also known s the Anti-Chain Store Act. It sought to protect small retailers by prohibiting wholesale price discrimination in favor of large-volume dealers and by banning the chain-store practice of cutting prices in areas served by small competitors while raising them elsewhere. During World War II he helped small businesses win an enlarged share of defense contracts. Patman played a key role in the enactment of the landmark Employment Act of 1946. It established the Council of Economic Advisers and Congress's Joint Economic Committee and stated that the President had the responsibility "to promote maximum employment, production and purchasing power." [See TRUMAN Volume]

The creation of the Small Business Administration (SBA) in 1953 was in large measure due to the efforts of Patman, who since 1940 had worked for the establishment of regional credit banks for small businesses. Patman unsuccessfully at-

tempted to amend the 1953 bill creating the SBA to increase the revolving fund from $250 million to $500 million and strike the limit of $100,000 in loans for any single firm. When the Select Small Business Committee was created in 1955, Patman became its chairman. Two years later he failed in an effort to boost the maximum loan for individual firms, by then set at $250,000 to $1 million.

In 1958 Patman introduced a bill to replace the SBA with a federal system of small business capital banks, to be located in each of the 12 Federal Reserve districts. Under Administration pressure the proposal was modified to create the Small Business Investment Division (SBID) within the SBA. As enacted into law, the SBID was authorized to loan money to state and federally chartered small business investment companies, which would provide credit to small businesses.

Patman believed that the welfare of small businessmen, farmers and individuals of little or modest means was jeopardized by the concentrated power large commercial banks wielded through the Federal Reserve System. He charged that the Federal Reserve's tight money policy and high interest rates benefited the commercial banks but restricted economic growth and caused unemployment. He denied the contention that low interest rates would cause inflation. He asserted that inflation could be checked if the Federal Reserve would increase its member banks' reserve requirements. Since the 1930s Patman had continually introduced legislation to restructure the Federal Reserve to end its independence of the federal government and thereby reduce the influence of the financial community upon it. These efforts had always failed, and they continued to fail during the 1950s.

Patman also charged that the Federal Reserve's Open Market Committee, which controlled the nation's money supply by buying and selling government securities, was dominated by the commercial banks. In 1955 he stated that the Committee "has the greatest financial power of any single group in all history" and unsuccessfully introduced a resolution authorizing the Banking and

Currency Committee, of which he was a member, to investigate it.

Patman persistently tried to check the power of large corporations. In 1953 he vainly opposed the sale of federal rubber plants. He argued that only "the big rubber companies" would have the resources to bid for them. In 1955 he failed in an effort to strengthen penalties against corporations and their responsible executives for violations of the Sherman Antitrust Act. Patman favored fines up to 5% of a corporation's total assets and jail sentences from 30 days to one year. The following year he was the sponsor of a bill requiring corporations worth more than a million dollars to notify the Justice Department and the Federal Trade Commission about merger intentions and giving the government more power to prohibit mergers. The House passed a bill incorporating Patman's proposals, but the Senate did not act on it. In 1959 Patman spoke out against a measure prohibiting states from taxing certain types of income earned by interstate businesses. He contended that the bill would give "a great advantage to the interstate chains" in their competition with small retailers. However, the bill was signed into law in September.

Although Patman generally favored liberal domestic legislation, he opposed measures aimed against racial discrimination. In 1956 he signed the "Southern Manifesto" protesting the Supreme Court's 1954 school desegregation decision. He also voted against the civil rights bills of 1957 and 1960.

In 1961 Patman, through the Select Small Business Committee, began a probe of private, tax-exempt foundations. The following year the panel, in the first of a series of reports, charged that many of these foundations were tax havens for wealthy people. In 1963 the Committee issued a report charging that there was an extensive network of interlocking connections between banks. That year Patman became chairman of the Banking and Currency Committee. Patman used the panel as a forum to present his views on Federal Reserve reform and to sharply interrogate banking and Federal Reserve officials.

In 1975 the House Democratic caucus ousted Patman as chairman of the Banking and Currency Committee. He died of pneumonia at the Bethesda Naval Medical Center in Maryland on March 7, 1976. [See KENNEDY, JOHNSON, NIXON/FORD Volumes]

[MLL]

PATTERSON, JOHN (MALCOLM)
b. Sept. 27, 1921: Goldville, Ala.
Attorney General, Ala., 1955-59;
Governor, Ala., 1959-63.

After his discharge from the Army at the end of World War II, Patterson studied law at the University of Alabama and received his LL.B. degree in 1949. He then practiced law with his father, Albert Patterson, in Phenix City, Ala. Albert Patterson led the opposition to the racketeers who controlled the town, and in 1954 he ran for state attorney general with a pledge to rid Phenix City of gangsters. The elder Patterson won the nomination but was assassinated shortly afterward. John Patterson ran in his father's place and was elected attorney general in 1955.

During Patterson's four-year term he devoted most of his efforts to combating organized crime. Patterson was also a strenuous opponent of integration and achieved prominence for his efforts to stop the operations of the NAACP in Alabama. In 1956 he brought suit against the Association for failing to register as a foreign corporation and for supporting the Montgomery bus boycott, which he termed illegal. As a result a state circuit judge issued a restraining order prohibiting the group from operating in the state. At the end of the decade, litigation was still being carried on over the issue, and the NAACP was unable to conduct business in Alabama.

Patterson ran for governor of Alabama in 1958. During the campaign he solicited the backing of individuals associated with the Ku Klux Klan. Several Klan officers also campaigned for him. He defeated George C. Wallace in the June runoff Democratic primary by 315,000 to 250,000 and easily defeated his Republican opponent in November.

In his inaugural address Patterson reiterated his adamant opposition to integration. He warned that if pressure for desegregation continued, Alabama's schools might be closed and "not be reopened in your lifetime or mine." In October 1959 Patterson urged state officials to refuse cooperation with the Federal Civil Rights Commission, which was investigating black voter registration complaints. The following month he signed legislation permitting voter registration boards to limit their registration activities to predominantly white precincts.

Despite his opposition to integration, Patterson opposed a break with the national Democratic Party. At the Southern Governors Conference in October 1959, he joined Govs. Leroy Collins [q.v.] of Florida and Luther Hodges [q.v.] of North Carolina in opposing a Southern bolt from the Party in 1960 over the issue. The following month he endorsed Sen. John F. Kennedy (D, Mass.) [q.v.] for President.

In March 1960 Patterson, as chairman of the state's Board of Education, expelled a number of students from all-black Alabama State College following their protest against lunch counter segregation. Later in the month the *New York Times* published an advertisement charging that Patterson had locked the school's dining room "to starve" the students. The Governor charged that the *Times* had published "false and defamatory matter," and the newspaper responded by retracting two paragraphs of the advertisement. But Patterson asserted that this did not represent a "full and fair retraction," and on May 30, 1960 he filed a $1 million libel suit against the *Times*.

After freedom riders were beaten in Montgomery on May 20, 1961, Patterson denounced those who would "take the law into their own hands." On the following day, after a Montgomery civil rights meeting was menaced by a white mob, Patterson declared martial law in the city. However, he remained an unyielding foe of integration and in September 1962 backed Mississippi Gov. Ross Barnett's [q.v.] defiance of federal authority in attempting to block the desegregation of the University of Mississippi.

In 1964 the Governor's suit against the *Times* was pending in state court when the Supreme Court ruled in a related suit. The Court stated that public officials could not recover damages for criticism of their official performance unless they could prove deliberate malice. Following this decision Patterson dropped his suit.

After retiring from the governorship in January 1963 under the provision of the state constitution barring consecutive terms, Patterson practiced law in Montgomery. He entered the 1966 Democratic gubernatorial primary but polled only about 4% of the vote. [See KENNEDY Volume]

[MLL]

For further information:
Numan V. Bartley, *The Rise of Massive Resistance* (Baton Rouge, 1969).

PATTON, JAMES G(EORGE)
b. Nov. 8, 1902; Bazar, Kan.
President, National Farmers Union, 1940-66.

James Patton grew up in Colorado in a family committed to the politics of rural populism. He earned a business administration degree from Western State College in 1929 and was working for a life insurance company in 1931, when he proposed a cooperative insurance program to the Colorado Farmers Union. He then worked for the farmers' organization, became its president in 1938 and in 1940 was elected president of the National Farmers Union (NFU). The NFU, based mainly in the Great Plains and Rocky Mountain states, represented the interests of small family farms. Patton revitalized the NFU, expanded its membership and brought it into a close alliance with the Roosevelt Administration and organized labor. The NFU became the most liberal of the nation's three major farm organizations.

Patton was a major figure in American liberalism with interests that extended far beyond the area of farm policy. After World War II he advocated federal aid to education and a national health plan. Influential in both the Roosevelt and Truman Administrations, Patton contributed to the creation of the United Nations Food and Agricultural Organization in 1945 and served on the public advisory board that helped administer the Marshall Plan. His proposals for maintaining full employment and full production in the postwar economy constituted the basis for the Employment Act of 1946. Patton was also said to be the author of the 1949 Brannan Plan, which sought to introduce direct government income payments to farmers with limits on the amount of government assistance available to big farms. [See TRUMAN Volume]

Under President Eisenhower Patton was appointed to the public advisory board of the Foreign Operations Administration in 1953. The following year he served as chairman of the Commission on School Support in Rural Areas, which presented a report to the White House Conference on Education in December 1955. Patton's influence in agriculture was generally diminished during the Eisenhower years because of the conservative stance of Secretary of Agriculture Ezra Taft Benson [*q.v.*], but as the leader of an organization representing 250,000 farm families, he still wielded considerable lobbying power. An NFU-sponsored "trading post" law, inspired by Patton, was passed by Congress in June 1954, making possible the shipment of surplus food to needy countries. In 1955 Patton proposed the "soil bank," a plan designed to alleviate the nation's chronic overproduction of basic crops by paying farmers to take portions of their land out of cultivation. Secretary Benson adopted the idea in 1956 as part of an Administration attempt to regain the confidence of farmers disturbed by their declining income. The soil bank became law the same year.

Patton spent much of the Eisenhower years fighting Benson's farm policies. The Secretary sought to cut the overproduction of basic crops by reducing the price at which the government would take the surplus of a given crop off the market. Thus, Benson reasoned, prices for farm products would decline, encouraging greater efficiency and discouraging overproduction. Eventually, American agri-culture would operate under the classical supply and demand market and the government could conclude its role as the buyer of crops. Patton believed that a sharp reduction of the level of price support payments, as advocated by Benson, would mean the collapse of farm prices, the economic ruin of thousands of farmers, the destruction of the family farm and vast social dislocation nationally. Patton favored continued federal management of farm prices at high levels with the use of production controls to deal with the surplus problem. Speaking before the House Agriculture Committee in March 1954, he backed maintaining price supports at 90% of parity and recommended extending price supports to a variety of grains at a level related to the support level for corn. After Benson succeeded in getting Congress to approve the elimination of price supports for basic commodities at 90% of parity in favor of flexible supports, Patton in June 1955 called for 100% of parity price supports. Although Patton was unsuccessful, Benson was unable to achieve his ultimate goal—the total elimination of price supports. The resulting compromise was a system of flexible price supports that pleased neither man and led to a consistent decline in farm income and the abandon ment of farming by many families.

Patton and the NFU took positions on a number of public issues, not all of them farm related, during the Eisenhower years. Patton supported proposals for a food stamp program that would enable the poor to purchase nutritious foods. In 1954 he favored the extension of social security benefits to farmers and the following year spoke in favor of an increase in the minimum wage. In May 1956 Patton, in opposition to the Administration, advocated government construction of nuclear energy reactors.

Patton played an important role in drawing up the farm policy of the Democratic administrations of the 1960s. He retired from the NFU presidency in 1966. Between 1967 and 1969 he was president of the United World Federalists and from 1971 and 1973 served as a special consultant to the Pennsylvania Department of Agriculture. [See KENNEDY Volume]

[JCH]

PAULING, LINUS C(ARL)
b. Feb. 28, 1901; Portland, Ore.
Chemist; disarmament activist

The son of a pharmacist, Pauling graduated from Oregon State College in 1922 and received his doctorate in physical chemistry from the California Institute of Technology three years later. As a Guggenheim Fellow in 1926-27, he worked with the Danish physicist Niels Bohr, a pioneer in the field of quantum mechanics. Pauling returned to Caltech where, during the 1930s, he applied quantum theory to the investigation of inorganic and simple organic molecules. This research led Pauling to explain these molecular structures as "resonating" between several bond structures, a theory that later led to the development of various plastics, drugs and synthetic fibers. In the late-1930s Pauling began to study the molecular structures of proteins, for which he later received the Nobel Prize.

During World War II Pauling served in the explosives division of the National Defense Research Commission and on the consultative committee on medical research of the Office of Scientific Research and Development. He helped produce the first synthetic antibodies from blood globulins in 1942 and supervised a project that developed a substitute for plasma from gelatin in 1945.

In the postwar years Pauling became the leader of the small group of scientists who opposed nuclear testing and supported multinational disarmament. He felt that America's short-range military interest in maintaining nuclear supremacy to prevent Soviet expansion would only increase conflict between the two countries. Instead of an arms race, he argued that nations should focus on developing an atmosphere of mutual confidence in which all would work together to control atomic energy. Because of cold war tensions Pauling's ideas carried little weight. [See TRUMAN Volume]

As a result of his unpopular position, Pauling was accused of being a Communist by Sen. Joseph R. McCarthy (R, Wisc.) [q.v.]. Pauling denied the charges, replying, "I am not even a theoretical Marxist." Nevertheless, his name appeared on a 1955 Senate Internal Security Subcommittee list of "most active and typical sponsors of Communist fronts in the past." In 1952 and 1954 the State Department denied him a passport. However, he was issued one following his receipt of the 1954 Nobel Prize for chemistry.

Pauling's ideas became increasingly influential after 1955. By that time fears that the Cold War might turn hot had begun to moderate, and both the U.S. and USSR had developed massive nuclear deterrents capable of destroying their enemies. Most importantly, scientists were beginning to discover the genetic and pathological effects of radioactive fallout from atomic blasts. In response to these dangers, scientists, particularly those in biological sciences, joined Pauling in demanding an end to nuclear testing. In 1955 Pauling was a leading participant at the first Pugwash Conference, composed of scientists who supported disarmament. Two years later he presented the U.N. with a petition, signed by over 9,000 scientists, urging immediate cessation of nuclear tests. The Pauling petition won increased support when Albert Schweitzer broadcast an appeal for a test ban.

Pauling continued his plea for disarmament in a book entitled *No More War*, published in 1958. In that work he warned that the U.S. and USSR had enough nuclear weapons to destroy each other completely and that atomic tests produced radioactive strontium 90 and carbon 14, which could cause cancer, leukemia and birth defects. He maintained that the arms race was due to misunderstanding and ignorance. Once men were informed of all the dangers of fallout, nuclear war would be impossible for a rational people. "I believe that the development of these terrible weapons forces us to move into a new period of peace and reason, when world problems are not solved by war or by force," Pauling wrote, "but are solved by the application of man's power of reason, in a way that does justice to all nations and that benefits all people."

In February 1958 Pauling debated the effects of radioactive fallout with Edward

Teller [*q.v.*], the developer of the H-bomb and major scientific proponent of continued testing. That year he also participated in an unsuccessful suit against the Defense Department and the Atomic Energy Commission, hoping to prevent them from conducting further atomic weapons tests.

Pauling continued his vigorous efforts on behalf of nuclear disarmament through the 1960s. On Oct. 10, 1963, the same day that a partial nuclear test ban treaty went into effect, it was announced that he had won the Nobel Peace Prize. Pauling later participated in the movement against American military involvement in Vietnam while continuing his scientific research. [See KENNEDY Volume]

[MDB]

For further information:
Robert Gilpin, *American Scientists and Nuclear Weapons Policy* (Princeton, 1962).

PEALE, NORMAN VINCENT
b. May 31, 1898; Bowersville, Ohio.
Clergyman.

Peale grew up in a family of ministers; his father was a Methodist pastor, and one of his brothers was later to become a clergyman. Peale himself could not decide between a career in journalism, politics or the ministry. He graduated from Ohio Wesleyan University in 1920 with a B.A. in liberal arts. Immediately afterwards he held several reporting jobs for newspapers in Ohio and Michigan, but within a year he began theological studies at Boston University. After his ordination in 1922 as a minister in the Methodist Episcopal Church, Peale took a pastorship in Rhode Island. He continued his studies at Boston University and received M.A. and Bachelor of Sacred Theology degrees in 1924. He served congregations in Brooklyn and Syracuse, N.Y., before beginning his long tenure at New York City's Marble Collegiate Church in 1932. In order to accept the pastorship there he had to change his religious affiliation to the Reformed Church in America. In 1937 he helped establish the American Foundation of Religion and Psychiatry.

Dubbed a high priest of the "cult of reassurance," Peale enlisted the aid of rabbis, priests, psychologists and social workers in his clinic with the aim of helping its patients sort out their mental problems and lead happier, "Christian" lives.

From his post in New York City, Peale became highly popular throughout America. He preached a brand of Christianity that exhorted believers to live positively, with full faith in their own ability to achieve inner peace and love of God. Peale delivered this message over the radio, beginning in 1935, in a long-running program called "The Art of Living." He published his first book, also called *The Art of Living*, in 1937; over the next 15 years he wrote five more books, including *You Can Win* (1938) and *A Guide to Confident Living* (1948), and countless inspirational articles. Beginning in 1946 Peale edited his own magazine, *Guideposts*. His written works' commercial success culminated in 1952 with publication of the very successful *The Power of Positive Thinking*. The book lacked any theological or philosophical analysis. Instead it gave advice on how to break "the worry habit," maintain constant energy, make people like you and release your "creative mind." Praised by many for its advice but scorned by others for "answers a little too pat," *Positive Thinking* remained at the top of the best-seller lists for three years. It was surpassed in all-time sales of inspirational books only by the Bible and a nineteenth century novel, *In His Steps*. In 1952 Peale also began a highly rated national television program called "What's Your Trouble?" that continued until 1968. His newspaper column was syndicated nationally, and he wrote a regular advice page for *Look* magazine.

Peale's huge popularity, along with that of fellow television personality Bishop Fulton J. Sheen [*q.v.*], came at the peak of a strong religious revival in America. During the Eisenhower Administration polls showed that fully 97% of Americans said they believed in God. Many admired preachers of the time were those who, like Dr. Peale, promised a path to a happier earthly existence through Christian faith.

"God and the doctor, that's what I give them. Anxiety is the great American disease," he said. Although Peale won millions of converts, he also attracted many critics, particularly among more scholarly religious thinkers. Rebuking Peale's religion as an insipid, secularized faith, neo-orthodox Christian theologians like Reinhold Niebuhr [q.v.] stressed original sin and the paltry ability of humankind to redeem itself through its own works. Reformers chastised Peale for being complacent about urgent social problems.

Peale also faced criticism for his public political pronouncements. In the 1952 and 1956 elections he openly urged the election of Dwight D. Eisenhower. During the 1960 elections he allowed his signature to be added to a statement that supported the continued separation of church and state and questioned whether such a division could be maintained if Catholic Sen. John F. Kennedy (D, Mass) [q.v.] were elected. Charged with propagating anti-Catholic sentiments, Peale submitted his resignation to Marble Collegiate Church officials, but his congregation refused to accept it. He refrained from further political activity in the election.

The ever-active Dr. Peale continued throughout the late-1950s and 1960s to publish books, articles and columns, speak on television and radio, and travel extensively to preach before devoted audiences. In 1963 his life story was portrayed in the film, One Man's Way. Peale was often requested by President Richard Nixon [q.v.] to preach at White House services; in 1969, at Nixon's request, he made a tour of war-torn South Vietnam, offering U.S. troops good wishes from fellow Americans. In the 1970s he retained his pastorship at Marble Collegiate Church, contributed to Guideposts publications and headed the Foundation for Christian Living, an organization which distributed pamphlets, books and recordings of his sermons.

[TGD]

For further information:
Arthur Gordon, One Man's Way: the Story and Message of Norman Vincent Peale (New Jersey, 1972).

PEARSON, DREW (ANDREW) (RUSSELL)
b. Dec. 13, 1897; Evanston, Ill.
d. Sept. 1, 1969; Washington, D.C.
Syndicated columnist.

After graduating from Swarthmore College in 1919, Pearson went to Europe to study diplomacy but, instead, became director of relief in the Balkans for the British Red Cross. He returned briefly to the U.S. in 1921 and then traveled throughout the Far East, where he lectured and wrote dispatches for Australian newspapers. Pearson worked as a free-lance journalist until 1929, when he joined the Baltimore Sun. As head of the paper's Washington bureau, he met journalist Robert S. Allen, with whom he published Washington Merry-Go-Round in 1931 and a sequel More Merry-Go-Round in 1932. Both books were muckraking exposes of the Hoover Administration. Because the books bucked the conservative media trends of the time, both Pearson and Allen lost their jobs. The two journalists then started writing a syndicated column, "Washington Merry-Go-Round," which began in December 1932 with 12 newspapers, rose by 1941 to 350 and in 1969 to about 600. In addition, Pearson and Allen articulated their special brand of liberal reformism on a popular radio program. During World War II Allen severed the partnership to join the Army; Pearson carried on alone. In the late-1950s Pearson began to share his writing chores and byline with Jack Anderson.

As a liberal activist, Pearson was a target of Sen. Joseph R. McCarthy's (R, Wisc.) [q.v.] anti-Communist campaign. Pearson often supported groups under investigation by the House Un-American Activities Committee and used alleged Communists Alger Hiss, Owen Lattimore and Harry Dexter White as sources for his column. Furthermore, Pearson vigorously denounced McCarthy himself and exposed the Senator's phony war record, his income tax evasion, the connections with the real estate lobby and his lack of substantiating evidence in his investigations. In December 1950 the animosity between the two came to physical blows at Washington's swank Sulgrave Club. McCarthy sought to destroy Pearson's radio program by organizing a sponsors' boycott that almost succeeded in removing the liberal journalist from the airwaves. [See TRUMAN Volume]

During the Eisenhower Administration Pearson shifted his crusade from McCarthy to conflict of interest within the executive branch. Pearson's "Washington Merry-Go-Round" column revealed in September 1955 that Peter Strobel [q.v.], commissioner of public buildings and second-in-command at the General Services Administration (GSA), had retained his ties with the consulting engineering firm of Strobel and Salzman after accepting the government position. Pearson also accused Strobel of refusing to provide his superior with a list of the firm's clients, an omission that prevented the government from discerning whether it was doing business with any Strobel and Salzman customers. A second Pearson column disclosed that Strobel had pressed his firm's claim against the Army Corps of Engineers and that the Commissioner had refused to sign a conflict-of-interest form until his GSA superior "practically ordered" him to do so. Subsequently Pearson granted Strobel two opportunities to reply to the varied charges, but Strobel ignored Pearson's offers.

Pearson's charges led to an investigation of the GSA by the House Antitrust Subcommittee. While the subcommittee turned up numerous irregularities, it was unable to decide whether any outright violations had been committed. Strobel resigned in November 1955, reportedly under pressure from the White House, although the Administration denied the report.

In January 1958 Pearson, who had received information leaked from the House Special Subcommittee on Legislative Oversight, revealed in his column that the panel had voted to table its inquiry into the Federal Communications Commission (FCC) because, in Pearson's words, "the facts were too hot to handle." Pearson accused subcommittee Republicans in particular of trying to bury the investigation and noted that the Republicans' view of corruption in

government had substantially altered since their out-of-office accusations against the Truman Administration.

Pearson's column dealt with suspicious circumstances surrounding the FCC's awarding of a Miami television license to National Airlines. He asserted that one of the FCC commissioners, Richard Mack [q.v.], had promised a Miami lawyer "close" to National Airlines that he would support National's application. Furthermore, Pearson noted that President Eisenhower's brother-in-law was a close friend of the president of National Airlines. A few days later the columnist charged that FCC Chairman John Doerfer [q.v.] had been reimbursed for a 1954 Western excursion by both the television industry and the government. Prompted by Pearson's allegations and by his own crusading zeal, the subcommittee's chief counsel, Bernard Schwartz [q.v.], pressed the case. He was fired for the manner in which he conducted the investigation, but eventually Schwartz's probe resulted in the ouster of both Doerfer and Mack.

Toward the end of the decade, Pearson began to attack Eisenhower himself. In June 1958, at a time when Congress was investigating the connection between top presidential adviser Sherman Adams [q.v.] and Boston financier Bernard Goldfine [q.v.], Pearson accused the President of accepting a vicuna coat from Goldfine. Though admitting that Goldfine had offered the present, the White House hotly denied that the President had accepted the coat. It insisted that the President had given the coat to a friend, whose name he could not recall. About a month later Pearson's associate, Jack Anderson, was caught in the process of bugging Goldfine's hotel room. Pearson's response, mimicking Eisenhower's defense of Adams, was that he would not dismiss Anderson, that his assistant was "imprudent, but I need him." In May 1960 Pearson alleged that various business tycoons had given Eisenhower gifts which the President used to buy machinery, livestock and agricultural tools for his Gettysburg farm. However, press corps apathy, or possibly the fact that Eisenhower was about to leave office, prevented Pearson's charges from stirring any real national interest.

During the 1960s Pearson continued his investigation of government officials, including Rep. Adam Clayton Powell (D, N.Y.) [q.v.] and Sen. Thomas J. Dodd (D, Conn.) [q.v.]. *The Senator*, his first novel, published in 1968, was met with critical reviews. Nevertheless, Pearson's reputation was at its height and his column at a peak of popularity when he died in September 1969.

[RJB]

For further information:
David A. Frier, *Conflict of Interest in the Eisenhower Administration* (Ames, Iowa, 1969).
Olivar Pilat, *Drew Pearson: An Unauthorized Biography* (New, 1973).

PERCY, CHARLES H(ARTING)
b. Sept. 27, 1919; Pensacola, Fla.
President, Bell and Howell Corporation, 1949-61; Chairman, Republican Platform Committee, 1960.

Charles Percy grew up in Chicago, Ill., where his father worked as an office manager for Bell and Howell Corp. At the age of five he sold magazines and while attending high school held four jobs simultaneously. In 1936 Percy joined a student training program at Bell and Howell with the help of his Sunday school teacher, company president Joseph H. McNabb. He entered the University of Chicago on scholarship the following year and started a service business supplying students. When Percy graduated in 1941, his campus cooperative agency was grossing $150,000 a year. He immediately joined Bell and Howell on a full-time basis and was named manager of the newly formed war contracts department. Recognizing Percy's efficiency, McNabb promoted him to director. In 1943 he enlisted as a Navy seaman and was promoted to lieutenant before his discharge in 1945. Returning to Bell and Howell, Percy became corporate secretary in 1946. He

was responsible for industrial relations and foreign manufacturing programs. When McNabb died in January 1949, Percy was elected company president. He was the youngest man ever to head a major U.S. corporation.

As president, Percy instituted a profit-sharing plan. He maintained close relations with employes, delegated responsibility to managers and established joint employee-executive boards concerned with research, merchandising and plant safety. Percy earmarked a large percentage of working capital for product research. At a time when most camera manufacturers feared imports and favored high tariffs, Percy favored low reciprocal tariffs and aggressively sought to penetrate foreign markets. His desire for overseas markets led Percy to make trips abroad that sparked an interest in politics. Percy doubled Bell and Howell's sales to $22 million within the first two years of his presidency. By 1961 sales of products Percy had introduced accounted for 82% of Bell and Howell's $100 million annual gross.

Charles Percy began his political career as a protege of President Dwight Eisenhower. He visited the White House as part of a business delegation in 1954 and supported the President's program for reducing tariffs. In May Eisenhower wrote Percy announcing he would be satisfied with a one-year congressional extension of reciprocal trade agreements and authority for moderate tariff reductions. In August 1955 he became state party finance chairman with Eisenhower's backing. Percy was chosen Eisenhower's special ambassador to attend presidential inauguration ceremonies in Peru and Bolivia in 1956. Two years later the President cited him for his fundraising efforts on behalf of Illinois Republican candidates. After the Republican defeat in the 1958 congressional elections, Eisenhower invited Percy to meet with him and others to discuss the Party's future.

Speaking with Vice President Richard Nixon [q.v.] and national chairman Meade Alcorn [q.v.], Percy proposed a committee to enunciate Republican programs and goals. This suggestion was endorsed unanimously by the Party. In February 1959 Percy was named chairman of a Committee on Program and Progress. He released the group's four-part report entitled *Decisions for a Better American* in October 1959. The panel backed most Adminstration policies but recommended matching grants to states for public school construction, a plan opposed by the President.

Eisenhower and Nixon chose Percy to head the 1960 Republican platform committee. Percy supported Nixon for President and tailored a platform that incorporated much of *Decisions* to suit the Vice President's wishes. But Nixon, meeting with New York Gov. Nelson Rockefeller [*q.v.*] without the Committee's knowledge four days before the Party's July National Convention, agreed to changes in the platform. Percy, having had little political experience, turned over to Nixon the job of pushing the alterations through the Committee. After the Convention Nixon declined most of Percy's offers of assistance and lost Illinois by 8,800 votes.

Percy returned to Bell and Howell and was named chairman of the board in 1961. He lost a race for governor in 1964 but was elected U.S. senator in 1966. [See JOHNSON, NIXON/FORD Volumes]

[MJS]

For further information:
Robert Hartley, *Charles H. Percy: A Political Perspective* (New York, 1975).

PERESS, IRVING
b. July 31, 1917: New York, N.Y.
U.S. Army officer.

A dentist with a private practice in Queens, N.Y., Irving Peress's brief career as an Army draftee became a major issue in the 1954 confrontation between Sen. Joseph R. McCarthy (R, Wisc.) [*q.v.*] and high military and Administration officials. Peress was inducted in 1953 with a captain's commission into the Dental Corps and assigned to Camp Kilmer, N.J.. Shortly after he entered the service, Army Intelligence was notified that he had claimed the Fifth Amendment privilege in refusing to answer questions on loyalty certification forms concerning membership in subversive organizations. An investigation concluded that suffi-

cient evidence of Communist tendencies existed to warrant the dentist's discharge as a security risk. In September 1953, while the investigation was in progress, Peress requested a promotion to the rank of major, to which he was automatically entitled by his age and by previous experience in the Army Reserve. His request was approved, but at the same time the commanding officer of Camp Kilmer, Gen. Ralph W. wrote a letter to his superiors recommending Peress's discharge. In November the Pentagon ordered him released at the earliest possible date.

In December 1954 McCarthy, who had been investigating alleged Communists in the Army, subpoenaed Peress to appear before the Senate Government Operations Committee's Permanent Investigations Subcommittee. At the Jan. 30 hearing the dentist declined to answer all questions about his political activities. McCarthy, therefore, demanded his court martial. Almost simultaneously the Army gave the Major an honorable discharge.

On Feb. 18 the subcommittee heard testimony from an undercover New York policewoman who claimed that Peress had acted as a liaison between a Communist cell and the American Labor Party. Gen. Zwicker testified the same day but refused to disclose the names of those who had promoted and then honorably discharged Peress while the dentist's loyalty was in question. Thereupon, McCarthy denounced the General as unfit for office. McCathy's harsh response to Zwicker's noncooperation brought hostility between the Army and the Senator to a peak, setting off the chain of events that led to the Army-McCarthy hearings in the spring of 1954 and the Senate's condemnation of McCarthy in the winter of that year.

In March 1955 the Permanent Investigations Subcommittee, with Sen. John McClellan (D, Ark.) [*q.v.*] replacing McCarthy as chairman, reopened hearings on the Peress case. Four months later the subcommittee filed a report criticizing the Army's handling of the case and recommending changes in military security procedures.

[TLH]

PERSONS, WILTON B(URTON)

b. Jan. 19, 1896; Montgomery, Ala.
d. Sept. 5, 1977, Ft. Lauderdale, Fla.
Special Assistant to the President,
January 1953-September 1953; Deputy
Assistant to the President, September
1953-September 1958; White House
Chief of Staff, September 1958-January
1961.

A 1916 graduate of Albany Polytechnic
Institute, Persons joined the Army and saw
service in France during World War I. He
then spent the following decade on engineering assignments for the service. In
order to prepare himself for an administrative career, he entered Harvard business
school in 1929 and graduated two years
later with an M.B.A degree. In 1933 the
Army transfered him to the office of the assistant secretary of war, where he served as
liaison with Congress. During World War
II Persons continued at his post. His work
was so valuable that Army Chief of Staff
Gen. George C. Marshall refused to allow
Gen. Dwight D. Eisenhower to transfer Persons (who was already a close friend) to his
staff.

During the postwar period Persons became director of legislative liaison for the
Army and later for the Department of Defense. Forced to retire from the Army in
1949 because of poor health, Persons had
sufficiently recovered by early 1951 to be
recalled to active duty as special adviser to
Eisenhower, then commander of North
Atlantic Treaty Organization (NATO) forces.
Persons again retired from the Army in August 1951. Once at home he joined the
Republican National Committee. In the
1952 presidential campaign Persons served
as liaison between Eisenhower and congressional Republicans.

A few weeks after his election victory,
Eisenhower placed Persons in charge of
congressional liaison, where he used his experience and warm personality to gain passage of Administration legislation. Persons
became extremely popular on Capitol Hill.
His ability to arrange a White House audience for members of Congress to discuss
their constituents' problems with the President accounted in part for this appeal. He
bolstered his standing with Congress by
virtue of his great respect (bordering on
deferences, according to Emmet J. Hughes
[q.v.]) for congressional prerogatives and
sensibilities.

Persons was one of President Eisenhower's more conservative advisers, in
part, because of his realization that the
Administration needed the support of the
Republican Right for passage of Administration legislation. He opposed any move by
Eisenhower to denounce Sen. Joseph R.
McCarthy (R, Wisc.) [q.v.] for his vitriolic
brand of anti-Communism even after
McCarthy began to directly attack the Administration for being "soft" on Communists
in government. When McCarthy attempted
to prevent the appointment of Charles
Bohlen [q.v.] as ambassador to the Soviet
Union and denounced him as a traitor, Persons counseled Eisenhower to act with caution. After McCarthy excoriated the Army
for lax loyalty procedures, Persons again
pleaded for presidential restraint. The adviser's recommendations greatly influenced
Eisenhower, who never publically repudiated
McCarthy and rarely refuted his charges.

Persons was deeply troubled by the issue
of civil rights. As a white Southerner, he
was uncomfortable about pushing desegregation. Furthermore, his political instincts
told him that a hard stand on the issue
would lose Eisenhower the vital support of
the South. For White House staffers who
urged a more aggressive pro-black civil
rights posture, Person's attitude was a
roadblock to achieving their goal. Frederic
Morrow [q.v.] the black presidential assistant, remembered that White House staff
meetings on civil rights proved "hard going" because the staff contained so many
conservatives. He especially pointed to Persons, who "while a 'liberal Southerner' [was]
obviously deeply affected by and emotional
about" civil rights issues, particularly school
desegregation. Persons was so close to the
President that his deep disquietude over
civil rights noticeably affected the Eisenhower civil rights policy, which for the
most part reflected a cautious approach to
the issue. Persons successfully strove, with
Eisenhower's blessing, to soften the civil

rights bill of 1957 by eliminating Part III, granting the Attorney General extensive powers to prosecute violators of the law.

Eisenhower admired Persons both personally and professionally; the President later remembered coming "to respect his ability, particularly as a coordinator among individuals holding vigorous and differing views." In September 1958 he was promoted to White House chief of staff to replace the departing Sherman Adams [q.v.]. His effectiveness in that post was a matter of dispute. Some saw him as a liberator of information flowing to the President, while others believed that he created "an atmosphere of indecision and fear" that paralyzed the inner workings of the White House.

After leaving the White House Persons became headmaster of Staunton Military Academy, where he had taught during his brief retirement from the Army from 1949 to 1951. He also accepted a position as a director of Univis Corp. Persons died in 1977 at the age of 81.

[RJB]

POTTER, CHARLES E(DWARD)
b. Oct. 30, 1916; Lapeer, Mich.
Republican Senator, Mich., 1953-59.

Charles E. Potter grew up in rural Michigan and did social work while earning his B.A. at Michigan State Normal College. During World War II Potter served with distinction as an Army infantry officer in France; he lost both legs. A Republican, he was elected to the House of Representatives in a special 1947 election. He won reelection in 1948 and 1950. Potter belonged to the House Un-American Activities Committee, a tie that he used greatly during his 1952 senatorial election race. He made anti-Communism the major focus of his campaign against incumbent Democrat Blair Moody. Potter told Michigan voters that they could choose between himself, "a man who believes in fighting Communism," and Moody. Potter's strategy, however, mattered less than the presidential candidacy of Dwight D. Eisenhower. Potter bested Moody by 45,000

votes, riding Eisenhower's coattails in the election.

During the 83rd (1953-54) Congress, Potter served on the Permanent Investigations Subcommittee, chaired by Sen. Joseph R. McCarthy (R, Wisc.) [q.v.]. Like other Republican members of the panel, Potter tried to prevent an open break between McCarthy and the Republican Administration. In 1954, when McCarthy intensified his investigation of subversion in the Army (allegedly in retaliation for Army charges that he had sought special treatment for his former aide, Pvt. G. David Schine [q.v.]), Potter joined Sens. Everett Dirksen (R, Ill.) [q.v.] and Karl E. Mundt (R, S.D.) [q.v.] in attempting to forestall the probe. After this failed Potter attempted to expedite the ensuing Army-McCarthy hearings. On the last day of the investigation, June 17, he issued a dramatic statement saying he was convinced "that the principle accusation of each side in this controversy was born out by testimony." He noted that the testimony was "saturated with statements which were untruthful and which might constitute perjury in the legal sense." He then demanded the ouster of those who "played top roles on both sides," including Roy Cohn [q.v.], McCarthy's chief aide, Army counselor John G. Adams [q.v.] and Army Secretary Robert T. Stevens [q.v.]. (In his memoir of the hearings, Potter termed Stevens's conduct "degrading." He faulted Stevens for failing to defend himself vociferously against Cohn's charges.) He also called for the revamping of the subcommittee staff. Potter asked the Attorney General to investigate the possibility of perjury by both McCarthy and Army witnesses. While issuing a statement severely critical of the principals involved, the Michigan Republican also signed the subcommittee's majority report of September 1954, which criticized McCarthy only mildly. Potter voted for McCarthy's condemnation in December.

Although marginally an Eisenhower Republican, Potter often voted against White House-favored legislation. He supported the Bricker amendment, which would have limited the President's treaty-making powers, in February 1954. During the 1956 congressional session, Potter opposed the natural gas bill, the Administration's farm bill and the sale of Air Force jets to Yugoslavia.

Potter actively supported strong civil rights legislation during the 1957 session. With other civil rights proponents he opposed granting jury trials to violators of the proposed statute. "The jury trial question is a strawman," he declared in July. The justification for the "denial of jury trials is obvious: in many instances Southern juries do not convict white men of offenses against Negroes." He voted for the final version of the civil rights bill in August.

Although first elected with Eisenhower's help, Potter, in seeking reelection in 1958, strove to separate himself from an increasingly unpopular Administration. As the 1957-58 recession worsened, he joined a group of Republican senators who unsuccessfully proposed a tax cut as an economic stimulant. To critics who thought the move inflationary, Potter responded in March 1958 that "it is rather hard to get [his constitutents] concerned about inflation when 350,000 people [in Michigan] are unemployed." Potter was also among the first GOP Senators to advocate (in June 1958) the dismissal of the President's chief aide, Sherman Adams [q.v.] for abuse of office.

Potter's political maneuvers failed. In a Democratic year he lost his Senate seat to Lt. Governor Philip A. Hart [q.v.] by a 170,000 vote margin. The Michigan Republican quit active politics and remained in Washington. In March 1974 he became one of three trustees charged with overseeing disbursements of the $3.57 million surplus left over from the 1972 reelection campaign of President Richard M. Nixon.

[JLB]

For further information:
Charles E. Potter. *Days of Shame* (New York, 1965).

POULSON, NORRIS
b. July 23, 1895; Baker County, Ore.
Mayor, Los Angeles, Calif., 1953-61.

The son of Danish immigrants, Poulson was born on a ranch near Haines, Ore. He attended Oregon Agricultural College from 1914 to 1915 and then became a farmer. He returned to school in 1923 and graduated two years later. Poulson worked as a certified public accountant before entering Republican politics. He served in the California Assembly from 1938 to 1942 and then won election to the U.S. House. He lost his bid for reelection in 1944 but won a seat two years later.

In 1953 Poulson ran for mayor of Los Angeles against the incumbent Fletcher Bowron, who had held the office for 15 years. Poulson campaigned on the issue of pollution. He aroused interest with his proposal that Congress grant tax rebates to industrial firms that installed antipollution equipment. He also promised to ask the Public Health Service, the Department of Agriculture and the Bureau of Mines for assistance in clearing up Los Angeles's smog problem, which he charged the Democratic administration had ignored. Poulson outpolled the mayor in the primary and won the general election in May.

As mayor, Poulson took an interest in the development of a civil defense program. Speaking on the NBC television program "American Forum of the Air" in February 1956, he insisted that the federal government had a duty to lay down guidelines for civil defense and arouse the public from its lethargy in the matter. Stunned by city health department reports that radioactive fallout in Los Angeles had increased 20% above the acceptable level following U.S. nuclear test in Nevada in October 1958, he called President Eisenhower to demand that the testing be discontinued immediately.

Poulson was a vigorous supporter of federal aid for housing and urban redevelopment. As vice president of the U.S. Conference of Mayors in 1958, ne joined New York Mayor Robert Wagner, Jr. [q.v.], in urging Eisenhower to release $450 million already granted by Congress for that purpose and allocate $350 million annually over the next 10 years for redevelopment. He also backed demands for increased mortgage credit for residential home construction. In a statement at the Conference, he opposed an emphasis on defense spending in light of the recent Soviet missile and satellite launchings. He said, "I fail to see what we could gain if we concentrate on a defense program that would make it necessary to neglect important local programs that mean so much for morale, loyalty and the prosperity necessary to support the federal government, especially in times of crisis." Chosen president of the Conference in September, Poulson pleaded with the Eisenhower Administration to reconsider threats to cut off aid to housing development and recommended that the proposed federal contribution to slum clearance projects be raised from two-thirds to 80% of costs.

In September 1959 Poulson caused a minor diplomatic incident when Soviet Premier Nikita Khrushchev visited his city. The mayor argued with the Soviet leader on the merits of capitalism and angered Khrushchev by chiding him for his prediction of capitalism's "burial." Poulson said, "We tell you in the friendliest terms possible we are planning no funerals—yours or ours." Khrushchev at first threatened to return home, but four days later he extended Poulson an invitation to visit Russia and made him a gift of bottles of vodka and caviar.

Poulson lost his bid for reelection in 1961 to Samuel Yorty, who charged that he was a tool of the "downtown machine" and was "apathetic, lethargic and indecisive." His narrow defeat (he lost by only 17,000 votes) was attributed to the disaffection of blacks and Mexican-Americans, who believed he had ignored their problems. Poulson served as California's water commissioner from 1963 to 1969. He then retired to his farm in Oregon.

[AES]

POWELL, ADAM CLAYTON, JR.
b. Nov. 29, 1908; New Haven, Conn.
d. April 4, 1972, Miami, Fla.
Democratic Representative, N.Y.
1945-66, 1969.

Adam Clayton Powell's father was pastor of the Abyssinian Baptist Church, whose 12,000 members constituted the largest Protestant congregation in the country at that time. His mother was the illegitimate heiress to the Shaefer brewing fortune. Born into comfortable surroundings, Powell graduated from Colgate University in 1930 and then obtained an M.A. from Columbia in 1932. In his last year at Colgate, Powell decided to become a minister; at the age of 29 he succeeded his ailing father as pastor of Abyssinian Baptist. Powell used his pulpit to plead for civil rights and social advances for blacks. The church opened a soup kitchen for the needy and organized boycotts of unions and companies practicing discrimination. In 1941 Powell became the first black to be elected to the New York City Council. Four years later, in a special election, he won a Democratic House seat representing Harlem.

During the 1950s Powell emerged as a leading spokesman for civil rights in the House. In the early months of the Eisenhower Administration, he accused Secretary of the Navy Robert Anderson [q.v.] of undermining the President's orders to desegregate military facilities. The bases were quietly integrated during the year.

Powell attempted to further integration by attaching a number of controversial anti-discrimination amendments to various appropriations bills: public housing, school construction and national reserve measures. These amendments stipulated that federal funds would be denied areas practicing segregation. His most controversial move came in 1956, when he attempted to attach the rider to a school construction bill. Although a coalition of northern Democrats and Republicans passed the amendment, they criticized the proposal. Such liberals as Eleanor Roosevelt [q.v.] and Adlai Stevenson [q.v.] felt that Powell's action would stall school funds needed during the critical classroom shortage of the period. When the House voted on the whole construction bill, Republicans joined Southern Democrats to kill the measure.

During the early years of the Eisenhower Administration, Powell publicly praised the President for aiding the cause of desegregation, but as the 1956 election approached, he condemned Eisenhower for not doing enough on civil rights. On Oct. 11 Powell again reversed himself by endorsing Eisenhower for reelection. In explaining his stand, he said that Eisenhower had a laudible civil rights record and a good image abroad. He also said that Democratic candidate Adlai Stevenson had snubbed him. Local Democrats condemned him, insinuating that Powell had come out for Eisenhower to obtain Administration help with his legal problems.

Powell's endorsement of the President angered New York City Democratic boss Carmine DeSapio [q.v.] who, with Harlem district leaders, decided to challenge Powell in the 1958 Democratic primary. Powell campaigned hard. In one speech he told DeSapio and Hulan Jack, the black borough president of Manhattan, to avoid walking the streets of Harlem. He warned, "We won't do what the Communists did to the Nixons in South America [Communists had stoned Nixon's car] but we will make it mighty uncomfortable." The NAACP and other leading civil rights groups deplored this statement. Powell retracted it, won the primary, and then went on to make peace with De Sapio.

Powell's flamboyant personality, his poor attendance record and his questionable financial and personal activities compromised his effectiveness as a civil rights leader. During the 1950s he and several staff members were involved in a number of legal problems. Several people in his office, as well as leading officials of the Abyssinian Baptist Church, were found guilty of financial irregularities. Powell fought a 1951 charge of preparing fraudulent income tax returns for his wife. He was finally acquitted in 1960. That year he was sued for libel by a Harlem woman whom he had accused of being a "bag-woman," or graft collector for the New York City police.

In 1961 Powell became chairman of the House Education and Labor Committee. Although he worked closely with Presidents John F. Kennedy and Lyndon B. Johnson to pass their domestic legislative programs, his reputation was tarnished by questions concerning his conduct as Committee chairman. In 1967 the House began an in-vestigation of his alleged misuse of committee funds. The House expelled him in March 1967, but he won reelection to his seat by a margin of seven-to-one. For two years his seat remained vacant. In 1969 the Supreme Court ordered the House to readmit him. Powell lost the Democratic primary in 1970. He died of cancer two years later. [See KENNEDY, JOHNSON Volumes]

[JB]

For further information:
Adam Clayton Powell, Jr., *Adam by Adam* (New York, 1971).

POWERS, FRANCIS GARY
b. Aug. 17, 1929; Burdine, Ky.
d. Aug. 2, 1977, Los Angeles, Calif.
U-2 pilot.

In January 1956 the Central Intelligence Agency (CIA) recruited Powers, then an Air Force officer, to serve as a pilot in the new U-2 over-flight program. The program, planned and supervised by Richard M. Bissell, Jr. [q.v.], special assistant to Director of Central Intelligence Allen W. Dulles [q.v.], had been conceived in 1955, after the Soviet Union had rejected President Dwight D. Eisenhower's "Open Skies Plan" for mutual aerial surveillance. The U-2 airplane, designed and built by Lockheed Aircraft, was capable of taking detailed aerial photographs and monitoring radar and communications systems while flying for extended periods at very high altitudes.

Following a training period in the U.S., Powers was assigned to a U-2 squadron stationed at Incirclik Air Force Base in Turkey. In November 1956 the squadron, publicly identified as a weather observation group, began flights over the Soviet Union and the Middle East. These missions were extremely successful in supplying the U.S. with intelligence data. The Soviet military soon became aware of the flights but was unable to stop them because its fighter planes could not reach the altitude at which the U-2s flew. By 1958 the Soviet Union was firing missiles at the planes but failed to stop them. Throughout this period neither the USSR nor the U.S. publicly disclosed the existence of the over-flights.

On May 1, 1960 Powers, on a over-flight from Pesawar, Turkey, to Bodo, Norway, was shot down by a Soviet surface-to-air missile near the city of Sverdlovsk. He successfully bailed out of the plane and was captured alive. Although the plane had been equipped with self-destruction devices and Powers supplied with a curare-soaked pin that could be used for suicide, he had been given no specific instructions about what to do if his plane were downed.

U.S. officials announced on May 2 that a weather observation plane had been lost over Turkey, but on May 5 Soviet Premier Nikita S. Khrushchev disclosed that a U.S. reconnaisance plane had been shot down over the Soviet Union. He charged that the flight was "an aggressive provocation" aimed at wrecking the forthcoming summit conference scheduled for Paris later that month. Khrushchev asked whether the flight had been authorized by Eisenhower or was an independent act of the U.S. military.

The State Department, not knowing that Powers was still alive, denied the Russian charges and continued to claim that the craft was a weather plane gone off course. On May 7 Khrushchev closed the trap he had set. He announced that Powers was still alive and had confessed to having been on a CIA-sponsored intelligence mission. Khrushchev also displayed five photos that had been developed from film found in the wreckage.

Following the Russian disclosures the State Department admitted that Powers had been on a spy mission. Secretary of State Christian Herter [q.v.] and Vice President Richard M. Nixon [q.v.] defended the flights as necessary to prevent surprise attacks by the USSR and implied that flights would continue. Finally, at a May 11 press conference, Eisenhower took personal responsibility for the U-2 flights.

On May 16, the eve of the scheduled summit, Khrushchev, already in Paris, demanded that Eisenhower apologize for the U-2 if the conference were to proceed. Eisenhower announced that the flights had been ended but accused Khrushchev of

using the issue to destroy the meeting and refused to discuss the subject further. As a result of this disagreement, the summit conference broke up before even getting under way. Shortly thereafter the Soviet Union withdrew its invitation to Eisenhower to visit the country. The U-2 incident and the collapse of the Paris summit marked the end of a period of improved U.S.-USSR relations following Khrushchev's September 1959 visit to the United States.

Powers pleaded guilty to a Soviet charge of espionage at the start of his three-day public trial in Moscow on Aug. 17. In testimony he gave details of the U-2 program and said that he was "deeply repentant" and "profoundly sorry" for his role in the spy efforts. He was sentenced to 10 years confinement on the charges, which could have resulted in a death sentence. As a result of his behavior at the trial and his failure to kill himself, Powers came under some criticism in the U.S., particularly from the American Legion Commander Martin McKneally.

Powers was released by the Soviet Union on Feb. 10, 1962 in exchange for U.S.-held Soviet spy Rudolf Abel. After his release criticism of Powers revived, but both a special CIA inquiry and a Senate Armed Services Committee cleared Powers of any wrongdoing. Powers left the CIA in October 1962 to join Lockheed Aircraft as a test pilot. In 1970 he published an account of his experiences. During the 1970s he became a traffic helicopter reporter. He was killed in a helicopter crash in August 1977. [See KENNEDY Volume]

[JBF]

For further information:
Francis Gary Powers, with Curt Gentry, *Operation Over-flight: The U-2 Spy Pilot Tells His Story for the First Time* (New York, 1970).

PRETTYMAN, E(LIJAH) BARRETT
b. Aug. 23, 1891: Lexington, Va.
d. Aug. 4, 1971: Washington, D.C.
U.S. Court of Appeals Judge, 1945-71.

Prettyman graduated from Randolph-Macon College in 1910 and a year later received an A.M. degree from the same institution. Following his graduation from Georgetown University law school in 1915, he practiced law in Hopewell, Va. He served in the Army during World War I and after his discharge became a special attorney for the Internal Revenue Department. In 1920 Prettyman returned to private law practice in Washington, D.C. For the next 25 years he alternated between this practice and government service as general counsel of the Bureau of Internal Revenue and as corporation counsel of the District of Columbia. In 1945 Prettyman was appointed judge of the U.S. Court of Appeals for Washington.

During the Eisenhower Administration Prettyman wrote several important opinions involving the conduct of congressional investigations of Communist subversion and the rights of the Communist Party. In July 1954 the Judge, speaking for the Appeals Court majority, dismissed the key count in the perjury indictment of Professor Owen Lattimore, a State Department adviser who had urged the U.S. to abandon its policy of confrontation with the Soviet Union in the Far East. Lattimore had been charged with lying before Sen. Joseph McCarthy's (R, Wisc.) [q.v.] Senate Internal Security Subcommittee in 1952, when he told the members he had never been a sympathizer with Communism or Communist interests. Prettyman's ruling held the charge "void for vagueness" because neither the indictment nor the statute defined "sympathizer."

In December 1954 Prettyman wrote the Appeals Court opinion upholding the constitutionality of the Internal Security Act of 1950. The ruling affirmed a Subversive Activities Control Board order that the Communist Party register with the Justice Department as an agency of the Soviet Union. Describing the American Communist Party as part of a world Communist movement whose purpose was the "destruction of all presently existing national governments" and "the establishment of a world dictatorship under Communist auspices," the Court held the Act did not violate First and Fifth Amendment rights or the right of due process. According to the ruling, the law did not unconstitutionally impinge on freedom of speech because "the right to unimped-

ed expression of views does not apply to unimpeded conduct." "A purpose to establish a totalitarian dictatorship is a program of action rather than of mere discussion. It can be met with action by the government." The statute was not a violation of the right against self-incrimination, Prettyman declared, since revealed membership in the Communist Party was not of itself a violation of any criminal statute. The court did not consider the penalties of the law a violation of due process. They were, instead, reasonable exercises by Congress of its power to protect the nation against a world-wide Communist conspiracy. Five years later in July 1959, the Court, with Prettyman again in the majority, again affirmed the Subversive Activities Control Board ruling.

During the Kennedy Administration Prettyman served on several presidential panels including the President's Advisory Commission on Narcotics and Drug Abuse, the Administrative Conference, formed to recommend improvement in the administration of federal agencies, and the board of inquiry that investigated Francis Gary Powers's [q.v.] conduct while a Russian prisoner. In 1967 Prettyman sided with the majority when the Appeals Court reversed the conviction of the Communist Party for failing to register under the provisions of the Internal Security Act. The Court declared the provisions of the statute "hopelessly at odds" with the Fifth Amendment because it singled out the Party for subjection to the "combined sanction of compelled disclosure and criminal punishment." Prettyman died in August 1971. [See KENNEDY Volume]

[EWS]

PROXMIRE, (EDWARD) WILLIAM
b. Nov. 11, 1915; Lake Forest, Ill.
Democratic Senator, Wisc., 1957-   .

The son of a prominent Chicago surgeon, William Proxmire received his B.A. degree from Yale in 1938 and an M.A. from Harvard in 1940. Proxmire served in the Army Counterintelligence Corps during World War II. Discharged as a lieutenant in 1946, he resumed graduate study and received a second M.A. degree in public administration from Harvard in 1948. The following year Proxmire moved to Wisconsin. He worked as a reporter and political analyst for the Madison *Capital Times* from 1949 to 1950. In 1950 Proxmire entered politics as a Democrat, beating a six-term incumbent and overcoming Republican opposition to win a seat in the state Assembly. As assemblyman, Proxmire distinguished himself by criticizing the tactics that Wisconsin's junior senator, Joseph R. McCarthy (R, Wisc.) [*q.v.*], used in investigating domestic subversion. He reiterated this theme in a 1952 race for governor against incumbent Republican Walter Kohler. Proxmire lost this election, a second run against Kohler in 1954 and a third try for governor in 1956.

When McCarthy died in May 1957, Proxmire won the Democratic nomination for his Senate seat. Kohler was again his opponent in the special August election. Most observers forecast an easy Kohler victory against the thrice-defeated Proxmire. The Democrat conducted an intense person-to-person campaign across the state. His platform called for closing corporate tax loopholes while raising personal exemptions. He also promised to increase farm incomes by raising price supports and lowering bank lending rates. He attacked President Eisenhower rather than Kohler and won a dramatic upset victory by more than 100,000 votes. Proxmire was the first Democratic senator from Wisconsin in 25 years.

In the Senate Proxmire won a reputation as a liberal. He backed increased farm price supports, medical care for the aged financed through social security and reforms designed to tax corporate interest and dividends at their source. During his first year in Congress, the freshman Senator received a 100% rating from the AFL-CIO's Committee on Political Action. Proxmire became known as a vocal opponent of government waste and favored a balanced budget. At the close of the Eisenhower years, he scored second-highest among Democratic senators in opposition to the President. He voted against Eisenhower 57% of the time on important Administration backed issues.

The Senator was a strong supporter of civil rights legislation, voting for the Civil Rights Act of 1957. The following year he joined a bipartisan effort for a 1958 civil rights bill giving the government greater powers to end school segregation. The bill died in the Senate.

Proxmire also favored housing and urban renewal measures. In March 1958 he and three other Democrats proposed lending $2 billion in construction funds to states and cities to fight the recession. He opposed Eisenhower's call for a partial federal withdrawal from urban renewal in early 1959. When the Banking and Currency Committee authorized $1 billion for more housing than Eisenhower had requested, the Senator dissented and insisted on an even larger appropriation.

Proxmire was passed over for a seat on Banking and Currency in February 1958. The individualistic Senator then denounced Senate Majority Leader Lyndon B. Johnson (D, Tex.) [*q.v.*] for his "unwholesome and arbitrary power" and demanded more frequent Democratic Party caucuses.

In the 1960s Proxmire continued to distinguish himself as a loner among liberals by criticizing presidential appointments when he detected conflict of interest and by calling for a balanced budget. During the 1970s he carried on a widely publicized campaign against waste in federal government. [See KENNEDY, JOHNSON, NIXON/FORD Volumes]

[MJS]

PUSEY, NATHAN M(ARSH)
b. April 4, 1907; Council Bluffs, Iowa.
President, Harvard University, 1953-71.

After attending public schools, Pusey earned a scholarship to Harvard, where he received his A.B. in 1928 and Ph.D. in 1937. Pusey taught Greek and ancient history at Harvard and several other colleges and universities. In 1944 he became president of Lawrence College, Appleton, Wisc. While at Lawrence, Pusey cosponsored a book attacking the reelection of Sen. Joseph R. McCarthy (R, Wisc.) [*q.v.*] in 1952. Pusey did so despite his nominal Republican Party membership and normally apolitical posture. In June 1953 the Harvard Board of Overseers named Pusey president of Harvard. Successor to physicist James B. Conant [*q.v.*], Pusey was expected to reemphasize Harvard's undergraduate education and humanities curriculum.

Soon after Pusey assumed office McCarthy attacked both Harvard and Pusey. In November 1953 he charged that a "smelly mess" existed at Pusey's university. "Communist professors" there threatened the students with Marxist "indoctrination," he declared. Telegramming Pusey, McCarthy asked about his "attitude" toward Associate Professor Wendell H. Fury, who had invoked the Fifth Amendment when asked if he had given Army secrets to Communists. Five weeks later McCarthy described Harvard as "a privileged sanctuary for Fifth Amendment Communists." His criticisms reenforced right-wing and anti-intellectual stereotypes of Harvard and other prominent private colleges. *Boston Post* publisher John Fox, himself a Harvard graduate, termed his alma mater "Kremlin on the Charles."

Pusey responded to McCarthy's accusations with moderation. In November 1953 he said that he was "not aware" of Communists on the faculty and stated his opposition to their employment. Indeed, both he and the dean of the faculty, McGeorge Bundy, refused to hire for administrative positions present or former members of the Communist Party. However, Pusey did not regard pleading the Fifth Amendment "as [a] confession of guilt." To a December regional education gathering, Pusey declared that "much of the outside criticism" directed against Harvard "is misguided, uninformed, unproductive, unwarranted and unnecessary." McCarthy dropped his campaign against Harvard.

Pusey served as Harvard's president for 18 years. Unlike many of his predecessors, he did not prove to be a great national educational reformer. Rather, Pusey allowed other university presidents to dominate opinion-making. A devout Episcopalian, he made no startling recommendations except to advocate a greater religiosity among students. The University expanded its physical plant, increased its already huge endow-

ment and, along with other major universities, received more and more direct support for pure and applied research. U.S. government monies accounted for one-fourth of Harvard's 1960 operating income.

Harvard's prestige rose with the election of Sen. John F. Kennedy (D, Mass.) [*q.v.*], class of 1940 and a Harvard overseer, as President in 1960. In staffing his Administration Kennedy borrowed heavily from the faculty. Pusey wryly remarked that "we can only admire the taste which our colleague, the President-elect, has shown" in making appointments.

Pusey's last years as president proved troubled ones. Angry students, protesting the Vietnam conflict, twice forced Pusey to shut down the campus prior to the spring semester's scheduled conclusion. In 1969 Pusey ordered the Cambridge police to end a student sit-in at an administration hall. The resulting bloodshed shattered Pusey's already tenuous hold on University opinion. Pusey retired as president in 1971 and became president of the Mellon Foundation.

[JLB]

For further information:
Nathan Marsh Pusey, *The Age of the Scholar* (Cambridge, Mass., 1964).

QUARLES, DONALD A(UBREY)

b. July 30, 1894; Van Buren, Ark.
d. May 8, 1959; Washington, D.C.
Assistant Secretary of Defense for Research and Development, September 1953-August 1955; Secretary of the Air Force, February 1956-April 1957; Deputy Secretary of Defense, April 1957-May 1959.

Quarles graduated from high school at the age of 15. Already known for his enormous appetite for work, he taught school in his hometown while taking summer courses at the University of Missouri before entering Yale at the age of 18. After receiving his B.A. degree in math and physics in 1917, he entered the Army and saw action in

France and Germany. Following World War I he joined the division of Western Electric Co. that later became Bell Telephone Laboratories; by 1940 he headed the radar program there. During World War II he directed the Bell Laboratories radar installation and was responsible for developments in telephone equipment for both military and commercial purposes. Quarles was one of the initial members and later chairman of the Joint Research and Development Board's Committee on Electronics, founded in 1946. By 1952 he was vice president of Western Electric and president of Sandia Corp., a subsidiary operating atomic research laboratories at White Sands, N.M.

In 1953 Quarles was appointed assistant secretary of defense for research and development, an assignment giving him the responsibility for billions of dollars worth of missile and satellite programs. He focused his attention on the development of the intercontinental ballistic missile (ICBM) and the earth orbiting satellite.

Eisenhower chose Quarles as Secretary of the Air Force in August 1955. Although the appointment was only confirmed in February 1956 because Congress was in recess when the nomination was made, he was sworn in and began to serve during the month of his nomination. Quarles's major problem was maintaining U.S. military superiority and proceeding with new programs despite cutbacks in defense spending. Secretary Quarles had to press the development of new missiles without sacrificing American superiority in such traditional weaponry as B-52 bombers. During testimony in 1956 he assured a House Appropriations Subcommittee that manned planes rather than missiles would be the Air Force's essential weapon for at least five more years. Heatedly defending the need for more bombers, he denied that the powerful new ICBM was some sort of ultimate weapon that ended the arms race and precluded the need for development of better conventional weapons.

Quarles gained a reputation as a "hardliner" who supported the Administration's emphasis on massive nuclear retaliation. Quarles forcefully defended the policy, insisting that even "mutual deterrence" would not preclude American usage of nuclear weapons. He warned that no aggressor should again presume that the U.S. would fight a war with conventional weaponry as it had in Korea. Instead, the U.S. would respond with "modern quality weapons needed to do the job on hand."

Although Quarles personally sought more money for the Air Force than President Eisenhower requested, he not only defended the Administration's pared-down military appropriations requests, but also assured members of Congress that the United States's retaliatory capability was more secure than ever. He continued to emphasize, as he had through his tenure as Air Force Secretary, that the United States's edge in quality more than made up for any Russian numerical superiority in planes or missiles. Nevertheless, Quarles and Air Force Chief of Staff Nathan W. Twining [q.v.] justified the Air Force's expenditure of nearly $1 billion which Congress had appended to the previous year's Air Force allocation. They maintained that although Russian bomber production was proceeding at a slower rate than previously predicted the Soviets were catching up and that therefore further funds were needed.

In April 1957 Quarles was confirmed as deputy secretary of defense, the second-ranking civilian position in the Pentagon. At that post he continued to assert U.S. ICBM superiority over the Soviet Union. He downplayed the Soviet Union's successful satellite launching in the fall of 1957. At a series of closed-door White House meetings in late October 1957, Quarles emphasized that the United States was on firm ground in not mixing its science and defense establishments as the Soviet Union had done. Furthermore, he indicated that while the Soviet achievement should not be minimized, there was no reason to regard it as ahead of the U.S. either technologically or militarily or to panic and attempt to accelerate the schedule of the U.S. satellite program. Quarles took the same stance during a House Appropriations subcommittee's brief two-day investigation of the U.S. missile and space program in November 1957.

However, his pleas fell on deaf ears. In reaction to *Sputnik* Congress increased funds for defense and space exploration.

In May 1959 Quarles suddenly died in his sleep of an apparent heart attack.

[RJB]

RADFORD, ARTHUR W(ILLIAM)
b. Feb. 27, 1896; Chicago, Ill.
d. Aug. 18, 1973; Bethesda, Md.
Chairman, Joint Chiefs of Staff, May 1953-August 1957.

At the age of 16 Radford entered the U.S. Naval Academy at Annapolis after having been refused admission to West Point. He graduated in 1916 and then saw action as an ensign on the battleship *South Carolina* during World War I. Following the War Radford moved up in rank as a naval aviator, eventually becoming a fighter squadron commander aboard the aircraft carrier, *Saratoga*. In 1941 he was selected to expand and centralize the Navy's pilot training program. During World War II Radford was promoted to rear admiral and commanded a carrier attack group in the South Pacific. After the War he became deputy chief and then vice chief of naval operations. In 1949 Radford took command of the Pacific fleet. A vigorous anti-Communist who declared that the U.S. would not be secure as long as Communists controlled mainland China, the Admiral gained the support of powerful congressional Republicans such as Sen. Robert Taft (R, Ohio) [*q.v.*]. At their urging Eisenhower selected Radford to be chairman of the Joint Chiefs of Staff in May 1953.

Radford was one of the chief architects of the Eisenhower Administration's "New Look" plan, hailed as a major departure in American defense policy. The failure of the U.S. Army to win the Korean war revealed what he believed was the futility of engaging in conventional ground warfare. He also questioned the need to have American troops in Western Europe when the U.S. had nuclear superiority over the Soviet Union. With these two facts in mind, Radford, his fellow Chiefs of Staff and Secretary of State John Foster Dulles [*q.v.*] formulated a policy stressing reliance on strategic nuclear weapons as America's first line of defense. Radford believed his New Look had many advantages. In the first place, American troops would not be called upon to fight unpopular wars such as that in Korea. In the second place, Radford argued, having supersonic bombers armed with nuclear weapons ready to attack at any moment would deter Soviet and Chinese aggression. The New Look also appealed to Administration budget cutters who believed it would reduce the cost of maintaining expensive conventional forces around the world. Critics such as Dean Acheson [*q.v.*], however, argued that the policy meant a return to unilateralism at the expense of American allies. They also believed that the threat of nuclear attack would prove irrelevant in the face of guerrilla warfare. Finally, they pointed out that the New Look was meaningless because the U.S. would never be the first nation to unleash a nuclear holocaust.

Radford took a hardline military stand toward Asian Communism that was often at odds with Eisenhower's own policies. In March 1954 French Chief of Staff Gen. Paul Henry Ely requested immediate U.S. aid to lift the Communist siege of Dien Bien Phu in northern Vietnam. At Eisenhower's request Radford outlined a proposal that included the use of American B-29 bombers to help relieve the embattled garrison. Ely hoped to use only enough air strikes to pressure the Communists to negotiate a face-saving withdrawal for the French from Southeast Asia. Radford, however, viewed American intervention as an open-ended commitment to stem the spread of Communism in Asia.

On April 3, 1954 Dulles called a secret meeting at the State Department between Radford and eight senior senators. Radford outlined his intervention plan but admitted he did not have the unanimous support of the other Chiefs and that the bombings could bring China into the war. Army Chief of Staff Gen. Matthew Ridgway [*q.v.*] issued a strong dissent to the Radford plan in which he maintained the bombings would be inconclusive and could lead to the introduction of American troops. The senators shared Ridgway's skepticism toward the operation. The following day Dulles and Radford met with Eisenhower, who overrruled the Admiral's proposal. Until the fall of Dien Bien Phu on May 7, Radford persisted in calling for U.S. entry into the war.

On Sept. 3, 1954 Communist Chinese shore batteries began shelling the Nationalist-held islands of Quemoy and Matsu. Three days later the Joint Chiefs, headed by Radford, voted three-to-one (with Ridgway again dissenting) that Eisenhower authorize Chiang Kai-shek to bomb the mainland. If the Communists retaliated, the group suggested that the U.S. join the attack. Radford believed that war between the U.S. and Communist China was inevitable and that it would be better to fight China when it was weak than wait until it had grown in strength. However, Eisenhower, believing that the islands had little strategic value and fearing a general war with China, gave the plan no support. In January 1955, when the Chinese shelled the Tachen Islands 200 miles north of Taiwan, Radford once again urged the U.S. bomb the mainland. Eisenhower rejected this suggestion and convinced Chiang to withdraw from the islands. In the spring of 1955 Eisenhower tried to defuse the crisis further by suggesting that Chiang reduce his troops on Quemoy and Matsu in hopes of a reciprocal gesture from Peking. He sent Admiral Radford and Assistant Secretary of State Walter Robertson to present the plan to the Nationalist leader. Chiang rejected their proposal. The Communists continued shelling the islands, although with less frequency.

Radford publicly opposed any attempt at disarmament with the Soviet Union. In May 1957, shortly before Radford retired, Eisenhower publicly rebuked the Admiral for declaring that "we cannot trust the Russians on this or anything." A man with a tough no-nonsense manner, Radford remained a controversial figure throughout his career. Although praised as a brilliant naval officer, he was often criticized for his tendency to dominate those around him and to portray his views as those shared by

the other Chiefs of Staff. His critics charged that he "abrogated more authority than he had."

Following his retirement in 1957, Radford continued to advise the Administration on military matters. He was Vice President Richard Nixon's [q.v.] military adviser during the 1960 presidential campaign and continued to recommend the defense of Quemoy and Matsu. In 1964 Radford served as an adviser to Republican presidential candidate Sen. Barry Goldwater (R, Ariz.) [q.v.].

[JB]

RAND, AYN
b. Feb. 2, 1905; St. Petersburg, Russia
Writer

Born in Russia, Rand came to New York in 1926 on a temporary visa to visit relatives. She then moved to Chicago and Hollywood; Rand never returned to Russia. In Hollywood Rand pursued a career as a motion picture scenarist, playwright and novelist. Between 1933 and 1942 she produced two novels, three plays and numerous movie scripts. Her first major novel, a nationwide best-seller, was *The Fountainhead*, published in 1943. The book was a dramatization of her own philosophy, which came to be known as Objectivism. Rand identified the novel's theme as "individualism versus collectivism, not in politics, but in man's soul," and its purpose as "a defense of egoism in its real meaning."

Rand assisted in writing the screenplay for the film, *The Fountainhead*, but left the project to devote full time to writing her next novel, *Atlas Shrugged*. Published in 1957, the book told the story of a railroad magnate and her few virtuous associates who fought social "parasites" and malingerers threatening to dominate society. Rand asserted "that man exists for his own sake, that the pursuit of his own happiness is his highest moral purpose. . ." and advocated laissez-faire capitalism, which would guarantee free trade and, implicitly, the protective economic dominance of the creative elite. She championed total faith in reason and scorned all religions as destructive of individual impulses and capacities.

Rand won a wide, devout following for her ideas and some praise for her merits as a novelist. However, Granville Hicks, reviewing *Atlas Shrugged*, said that "this gargantuan," overblown book "howls in the reader's ear and beats him about the head in order to secure his attention."

Because of her wide popularity Rand became both a spokesperson for her own ideology and a commentator on current political issues. She was usually identified as a conservative, although she often differed from other theorists of the Right. A fervent anti-Communist, she appeared before the House Un-American Activities Committee (HUAC) in 1947 to testify against an allegedly pro-Communist film. She also produced a pamphlet called *Screen Guide for Americans* for distribution to writers in Hollywood. The booklet sternly advised them not to smear industrialists or denigrate the free enterprise system in their scripts.

Rand and her followers often clashed with other conservatives, particularly the group led by William F. Buckley, Jr. [*q.v.*], and the writers of the *National Review*. She called the *Review* the "worst and most dangerous magazine in America." Whittaker Chambers [*q.v.*], speaking for the religious conservatives, termed *Atlas Shrugged* "the antireligious gospel of philosophic materialism." Classical scholar Garry Wills claimed that Rand was not a conservative at all: her characters work from "the first principle of historical Liberalism . . . the immediate perfectability of man." The feud became permanent, and Objectivism was not absorbed into the general conservative mainstream.

Rand continued to write in the 1960s and 1970s and served as a visiting lecturer at such universities as Yale, Princeton and Columbia. She joined other conservatives in supporting Republican Barry Goldwater [*q.v.*] for the presidency in 1964. Between 1962 and 1971 she edited *The Objectivist*. Since that time she has edited *The Ayn Rand Letter*.

[TGD]

For further information:
Nathaniel and Barbara Branden, *Who is Ayn Rand?* (New York, 1962).

RANDALL, CLARENCE B(ELDEN)

b. March 5, 1891; Newark Valley, N.Y.
d. Aug. 4, 1967; Ishpeming, Mich.
Chairman, Commission on Foreign Economic Policy, August 1953-January 1954; Special Consultant to the President on Foreign Economic Policy, January 1954-July 1956; Special Assistant to the President on Foreign Economic Policy, July 1956-January 1961.

After studying at the Methodist-affiliated Wyoming Seminary from 1906 to 1908. Randall attended Harvard, where he graduated in 1912. He received an LL.B. there three years later and then began practicing law in Ishpeming, Mich. His career was interrupted by service in the Army during World War I. Randall returned to his practice after the War and in 1925 joined Inland Steel Co. He became a vice president in 1930 and president in 1949. In 1953 he became chairman of the board.

During the postwar period Randall advised President Harry S. Truman on the Marshall Plan and served as a consultant to the Economic Cooperation Administration. When Truman seized the steel mills in 1952, he was chosen spokesman of the nation's 92 steel companies to protest the action. [See TRUMAN Volume]

In August 1953 President Eisenhower appointed Randall chairman of the 17-member Commission on Foreign Economic Policy, formed to study U.S. overseas economic policies. The Commission report, issued in January 1954, recommended that Eisenhower extend the reciprocal trade program for three years; cut tariffs "on products which are not being imported or which are being imported in negligible volume" to 50% of the Jan. 1, 1945 rates, even without reciprocal concessions; and reduce to 50% *ad valorem* any tariff rate in excess of that figure.

The Randall Commission also proposed a revision in foreign aid policy. It suggested giving grants to countries unable to maintain their own security while making loans to nations in need of economic aid. Although supporting the ban on exports to Communist China and North Korea and efforts to block trade in military materials with Eastern Europe, the panel recommended increased trade with the Soviet Union to "serve to penetrate the Iron Curtain and advance the day when normal relationships with . . . Eastern Europe may be resumed."

Randall's report was greeted favorably by both domestic and foreign officials. Impressed with the executive's work, Eisenhower appointed Randall a special White House consultant to help formulate trade legislation. Nevertheless, the panel's recommendations were attacked by 17 economic experts at a Princeton University conference on U.S. foreign economic policy in March 1954. They charged that the report failed to consider long-term questions in American foreign economic policy and they attacked it for ignoring the domestic recession and the particular problems involved in U.S. trade with Western Europe, Japan and the underdeveloped nations. Congress, too, proved reluctant to accept the Randall program. Eisenhower failed to push the program through Capitol Hill in 1954. After a bitter struggle he succeeded in getting approval for the extension of reciprocal trade agreements and implementation of tariff cuts over a three-year period in 1955.

Randall continued to serve as a government consultant after retiring as chairman of the board of directors of Inland Steel in April 1956. In July he was appointed special assistant on foreign economic policy and chairman of the President's Council on Foreign Economic Policy. At that post he criticized the failure of U.S. businessmen to prevent Soviet economic penetration of underdeveloped nations, deriding them as "stone deaf and sight blind" to the USSR's advances. In May 1958 Randall proposed a liberalization of travel restrictions between Communist and Western nations to ease East-West tensions. Eisenhower applauded the recommendation as a "powerful influence on behalf of peace."

Randall continued to serve as a presidential consultant during the Kennedy Administration. From 1961 to 1963 he headed a presidential panel reviewing federal pay schedules, and in 1963 he became chairman of the State Department's advisory committee on international business problems. He died in August 1967.

[AES]

RANDOLPH, A(SA) PHILIP
b. April 15, 1889; Crescent City, Fla.
President, Brotherhood of Sleeping Car Porters, 1929-68.

The son of a Protestant minister, A. Philip Randolph graduated from the Cookman Institute of Jackson, Fla., in 1911 and joined the prewar migration of Southern blacks to Harlem. A brilliant student, he held numerous jobs while studying political science, economics and philosophy at the City College of New York. Randolph joined the Socialist Party soon after his arrival and in 1917 cofounded *The Messenger*, a magazine designed to urge blacks to demand better wages and working conditions in wartime industries. He also began his lifelong association with the trade union movement. During World War I Randolph attempted to unionize black shipyard workers in Virginia and organized a small elevator operators local in New York City. In 1925 he began a campaign to unionize the Pullman sleeping car employes. After an epoch 12 year struggle Randolph's union, The Brotherhood of Sleeping Car Porters, obtained recognition from the company in 1937. By that time the cool, dignified Randolph had emerged as one of the nation's most prominent black leaders. In 1941 his threat of a march on Washington by over 50,000 blacks convinced President Franklin D. Roosevelt to issue his historic executive order banning racial discrimination in federal employment and in the new defense industries. Randolph's postwar campaign against segregation in the Armed Services helped prompt the President Harry S. Truman to outlaw segregation in the military.

When Randolph brought the Brotherhood into the American Federation of Labor (AFL) in 1935, many unions in the federation excluded blacks. Beginning that year Randolph annually introduced a resolution at the AFL convention calling on the group to devote more energy to organizing black workers and asking them to expel member locals who continued to practice discrimination. Randolph's familiar, booming voice failed to sway the convention delegates. His yearly podium appearance was a signal for many delegates to abandon the convention hall. William Green and George Meany [q.v.], who became president in 1952, defended Samuel Gomper's policy that racial politics were purely a matter for the locals.

When the AFL merged with the Congress of Industrial Organizations (CIO) in 1955 to become the AFL-CIO, the group adopted a constitution containing a strong anti-discrimination provision. Randolph, elected a member of its executive council, demanded immediate enforcement of its pledge. At the executive council meeting in 1956, he moved that the Federation bar the Brotherhood of Locomotive Firemen and Engineers, widely known for discriminating against blacks, from the AFL-CIO until it ended its racist policies. Meany opposed the motion, preferring to work behind the scenes to end discrimination. His position was supported by the executive council, which voted to admit the Brotherhood.

At the 1959 national convention Randolph introduced a resolution to deny the International Longshoremen's Association entry. Meany indignantly asked Randolph why he had never discussed the proposal with the executive council. The president then reprimanded Randolph for not "playing on the team," implying that the issue should never have been presented to the convention floor. Meany advised Randolph to sit "a little closer to the trade union movement and pay a little less attention to outside organizations . . . ."

A few moments later Randolph introduced another resolution calling for the expulsion of two railroad brotherhoods if they did not cease discriminating within six months. Meany, who supported gradual desegregation, opposed the time limit. He warned Randolph that integration might not be achieved in their lifetime. Randolph then introduced his third resolution calling

for the expulsion for member unions charged with racism. The resolution would have covered exclusively black unions as well white groups. Meany then exploded, "Who the hell appointed you the guardian of all Negroes!" The astonished Randolph replied, "Brother President, let's not get emotional."

Meany's outburst, embarrassing to him and the AFL-CIO, publicized the problem of racism in unions. Although the two men sought to downplay the incident, their rift continued. In 1960 Randolph and other black unionists formed the Negro American Labor Council to fight for change within the Federation. Randolph became its first president. In October 1961 the AFL-CIO censured him for his continuing struggle to reform the Federation. Meany told the press, "We can only get moving on civil rights if he comes to our side and stops throwing bricks at us."

Randolph worked closely with the other civil rights leaders during the 1950s and 1960s. While Martin Luther King, Jr. [q.v.] and Roy Wilkins [q.v.] agitated for civil rights, Randolph fought for the breaking down of economic barriers facing blacks. In 1958 he organized the youth march on Washington in support of the 1954 *Brown* decision, outlawing segregated public schools. Five years later, in August 1963, he organized the March On Washington at which King spoke of his dream of future equality.

Randolph enthusiastically supported Lyndon B. Johnson's War on Poverty and opposed U.S. intervention in Vietnam because it diverted needed funds from poverty programs. By the end of the decade, Randolph was eclipsed by younger, more militant members of the civil rights movement. In September 1968 Randolph, aged and ailing, retired as president of the Brotherhood of Sleeping Car Porters. [See [See KENNEDY, JOHNSON NIXON/FORD Volumes]

[JB]

For further information:
Jurvis Anderson, A. *Philip Randolph* (New York, 1973).

RANKIN, J(AMES) LEE
b. July 8, 1907; Hartington, Neb.
Solicitor General, 1957-61.

J. Lee Rankin earned his LL.B. degree at the University of Nebraska in 1930 and started law practice in Lincoln, Neb., that same year. He developed an interest in Republican politics in the late-1930s. Rankin managed New York Gov. Thomas E. Dewey's 1948 presidential campaign in Nebraska and chaired Dwight D. Eisenhower's Nebraska election committee. Eisenhower appointed Rankin assistant attorney general in charge of legal counseling under Rankin's friend and fellow Nebraskan, Attorney General Herbert Brownell [q.v.].

Rankin was chief adviser to Brownell in the formation of legal policy from 1953 to 1956. In December 1953 he testified as an amicus curiae before the Supreme Court in Brown v. Board of Education. Rankin supported the demands of black plaintiffs that public school segregation be declared unconstitutional on the grounds it violated the equal protection clause of the 14th Amendment. School segregation was outlawed the following year. Rankin also helped draft legal opinions on the questions of U.S. agricultural trade with the Soviet Union and on presidential succession. Eisenhower announced Rankin's appointment as Solicitor General in August 1956. Because of his role in the Administration's court fight for school desegregation and close identification with civil rights, it was thought Southern senators might block confirmation, but Rankin's nomination was approved in May 1957.

As Solicitor General, Rankin had charge of all government briefs and arguments in cases brought before the Supreme Court. It was he who decided which cases the government would appeal; only the Attorney General could overrule his decisions. During the 1956-57 Supreme Court term, Rankin argued for the government in cases arising from congressional investigations of alleged Communist activities. He argued unsuccessfully that the Court should sustain the conviction of United Automobile Workers organizer John T. Watkins for contempt of Congress in refusing to divulge the names of persons linked with Communist activities. Later that year he argued, again unsuccessfully, to uphold the conviction of Julius Shields under the 1940 Smith Act.

During 1957 and 1958 Rankin became embroiled in the dispute over state vs. federal ownership of tidelands oil. In December 1957 President Eisenhower reaffirmed his support of the 1953 Submerged Lands Act, which gave states jurisdiction to the three-mile offshore limit, and said he hoped the Court would rule Texas's ownership of claims beyond that point. Rankin supported the opposing view, maintaining that the federal government was entitled to oil revenues from drilling beyond the three-mile limit. Two days after Eisenhower's statement, Attorney General William P. Rogers [q.v.] silenced Rankin and gave assurances that the final Justice Department brief would not conflict with the President's position.

Rankin pressed for immediate implementation of court-ordered integration of Little Rock, Ark., high schools in 1957 and 1958. In August 1957 he said delaying desegregation on the basis of segregationist community sentiment would breed disrespect for law and lead to violence. The Supreme Court upheld this view and ordered the immediate integration of Little Rock's Central High School. The following year Rankin joined NAACP attorney Thurgood Marshall [q.v.] in urging immediate integration of Little Rock's remaining high schools. The Court again upheld the Solicitor General. In March 1960 he challenged a 1957 Alabama law that had redrawn the boundaries of Tuskegee, Ala., to exclude black voters. The Supreme Court voided the Alabama law in 1961.

When the Democratic administration took over in 1961, Rankin entered private law practice in New York City. In 1963 and 1964 he served as general counsel to the President's Commission to Investigate the Assassination of President Kennedy. Rankin served as New York City corporation counsel from 1966 to 1972 and then returned to private law practice. [See JOHNSON Volume]

[MJS]

RANKIN, KARL L(OTT)
b. Sept. 4, 1898; Manitowoc, Wisc.
Ambassador to the Republic of China,
February 1953-January 1958; Ambassador to Yugoslavia, January 1958-
February 1961.

Rankin, the son of a clergyman, graduated from Mercerburg Academy in Pennsylvania in 1916. After serving in the Navy during World War I, he attended the California Institute of Technology, graduating in 1919. He went on to study engineering at Zurich's Federal Polytechnic Institute in 1920 and 1921 and received a degree in civil engineering from Princeton University in 1922. He worked as an engineer and manager of a real estate development company for the next five years.

In 1927 Rankin began a long career in government as assistant trade commissioner in Prague. During the 1930s and 1940s he served as commercial attache and counselor for economic affairs in various European capitals. Rankin was transferred to the Far East in 1949, holding the post of consul general in Canton, Hong Kong and Macao. From 1950 to 1953 he was minister and charge d'affaires at Taipei. In February 1953 Rankin became ambassador to Nationalist China.

As ambassador, Rankin supported the U.S. defense of Taiwan against Communist Chinese invasion, but he opposed American aid to the Nationalist effort to maintain possession of the offshore islands of Quemoy and Matsu. He encouraged Chiang's government to formulate a mutual security pact with the U.S. as early as October 1953, and during July 1954 he conducted negotiations for such an agreement. The pact was finally signed in Washington in December 1954.

After Communist China began shelling Quemoy and Matsu in September 1954, Rankin attempted to minimize the islands' importance. When the Joint Chiefs of Staff recommended military action against Communist China over the incident, Eisenhower demurred and speeded up negotiations on the mutual defense pact with the Nationalists. Rankin supported the President's caution, warning Nationalist foreign Minister George Yeh against precipitating war with the mainland over the islands. He reported to Washington that the Nationalist strategy was to "exaggerate the military danger" of a Communist conquest of Quemoy and Matsu as a means of gaining more plentiful American aid. When Secretary of State John Foster Dulles [q.v.] made a trip to Taipei in February 1955 and was informed by Nationalist officials how vital the islands were to Formosa's defense, Rankin cabled the State Department that Yeh "may have exaggerated their importance." He maintained that their loss to the Communists would be "very serious but not necessarily disastrous." Significantly, Dulles, who advocated strong action against the mainland, failed to consult Rankin during his visit.

Rankin was not successful in cultivating the good will of the Formosan population. On May 24, 1957 he was mobbed during anti-American riots at the American Embassy following the murder of a Peeping Tom by an American soldier. Thirty-three thousand Nationalist troops restored order the following day.

Rankin was confirmed as ambassador to Yugoslavia in January 1958. He served at that post until 1961, when he resigned from the diplomatic corps. In 1964 he published his autobiography, *China Assignment*.

[AES]

For further information:
Karl L. Rankin, *China Assignment* (Seattle, 1964).

RAUH, JOSEPH L(OUIS)
b. Jan. 3, 1911: Cincinnati, Ohio.
Lawyer; National Vice Chairman,
Americans for Democratic Action,
1952-55, 1957-   ; National Chairman,
1955-57.

The son of a German immigrant businessman, Rauh graduated from Harvard law school in 1935 and served as law secretary to Supreme Court Justices Benjamin Cardozo and Felix Frankfurter [q.v.]

from 1936-39. He then worked for various New Deal agencies. During the War Rauh served on the staff of the Army's Pacific Command. From 1936 to 1947 he was deputy to Wilson Wyatt, head of the Veterans Emergency Housing Program. In 1947 Rauh joined Wyatt and other liberals in leaving the Truman Administration to protest the growing conservative influence in Washington.

Rauh was one of a group of liberals who, in 1947, formed the Americans for Democratic Action (ADA) to prevent the Communist-influenced Progressive Party from dominating left-of-center politics. He was selected chairman of its executive committee that year. Rauh served as its national vice chairman from 1952 to 1955 and chairman from 1955 to 1957. He resumed the post of vice chairman after 1957. During the Truman and Eisenhower Administrations, Rauh was also a leading civil liberties lawyer, representing such individuals as Lillian Hellman, Arthur Miller [q.v.], John T. Watkins and William Remington when they testified before the House Un-American Activities Committee. [See TRUMAN Volume]

As chief spokesman for the ADA during the Eisenhower Administration, Rauh scored both parties for their failure to pursue liberal goals. In 1954 he stated, "Eisenhower has produced the saddest excuse for a legislative program since McKinley. We have drift, confusion, bluff, blunder and a sunburnt Coolidge in the White House." The following year he held the President personally responsible for the "most corrupt administration since Harding." In early 1956 Rauh warned the Democratic Party that "compromise and timidity" never won elections. He also accused Sen. Lyndon B. Johnson (D, Tex.) [q.v.] of bringing the Democratic Party "to the lowest point in 25 years" by imitating rather than opposing Eisenhower.

Rauh even questioned Adlai Stevenson's credibility as leader of the liberal wing of the Democratic Party. Stevenson's 1956 statement that moderation "is the spirit of our times" particularly troubled Rauh, because some interpreted it as a call for caution on civil rights. In writing Stevenson, Rauh urged him to make a strong statement supporting school desegregation and condemning discrimination in voting rights. Stevenson answered, claiming his position on civil rights was clear. Rauh replied, "Ike has the squatter's rights on the middle road. Let him have it."

At the 1956 Democratic Convention Rauh and the ADA lobbied for a platform plank calling for support of the Supreme Court's *Brown* vs. *Board of Education* school desegregation ruling. One month before the Convention Sen. Hubert Humphrey (D, Minn.) [q.v.] promised to back Rauh, but when the Senator's name emerged as a possible vice presidential candidate, he withdrew this pledge. Stevenson and Eleanor Roosevelt [q.v.], the ADA's honorary chairman, also opposed Rauh's measure, and the proposal was not reported to the floor.

In 1960 the ADA's national board warned the Democratic Party that to win the election it had to nominate a liberal who would offer "a clear alternative to the reactionary Republican candidate." To accomplish this, Rauh's strategy was to stop Johnson. Observing that Humphrey's and Sen. John F. Kennedy's (D, Mass.) [q.v.] candidacies had already divided Party liberals, Rauh believed that if Stevenson entered the race a three-way split would deadlock the Convention and throw the nomination to the Texan. He, therefore, publicly called on liberals to end their sentimental loyalty to the former Illinois Governor. Rauh then endorsed Humphrey and became his unofficial campaign manager. When Humphrey withdrew from the race, Rauh endorsed Kennedy.

As in 1956 Rauh demanded a strong civil rights plank in the 1960 Democratic Platform. In July 1960 Rauh appeared before the Platform Committee to present the ADA's call for strong federal action to end all forms of racial discrimination. To his surprise, the Committee and delegates approved the measure. Rauh believed that Kennedy, hoping to gain support from Northern blacks, was responsible for its adoption.

Kennedy's selection of Johnson as vice presidential candidate was personally embarrassing to Rauh, who had promised many Stevenson supporters that he would not be chosen. He denounced the selection as a "double cross" of the liberals and predicted that Johnson would be a disaster for the ticket. Rauh joined other liberals in an abortive stop-Johnson movement, but when the campaign began, he enthusiastically spoke for the ticket.

During the 1960s Rauh continued as spokesman for the ADA. He repeated his demands for civil rights measures and labored to open the Democratic Party to blacks. Rauh opposed the Vietnam war and supported Sen. Eugene McCarthy (D, Minn.) [q.v.] for the presidency in 1968. [See KENNEDY, JOHNSON NIXON/FORD Volumes]   [JB]

RAYBURN, SAM(UEL T(ALIAFERRO)
b. Jan. 6, 1882; Roane County, Tenn.
d. Nov. 16, 1961; Bonham, Tex.
Democratic Representative, Tex.,
1913-61; Speaker of the House, 1940-47, 1949-53, 1955-61; Minority Leader, 1947-49, 1953-55.

Rayburn, the son of a Confederate veteran and poor corn farmer, was born in eastern Tennessee. When he was five the family moved to Fannin Co. in Northeastern Texas, where his father bought a 40-acre cotton farm. Rayburn left home at 17 to attend East Texas Normal School, earning his tuition by performing various chores at the college. After graduating Rayburn taught at local schools. With the parents of his pupils working on his behalf, Rayburn won election to the State House of Representatives in 1906. In 1912 he was elected Speaker of the House; he was the youngest man in Texas history to hold that post.

Rayburn ran for the U.S. House of Representatives in 1912 on a populist platform advocating income and inheritance taxes, low tariffs, direct election of U.S. senators and the right of recall on the state and local levels. He won the Democratic primary by a narrow margin and easily carried the general election. Rayburn backed most of President Woodrow Wilson's domestic programs but offended organized labor, which had lit-

tle influence in his predominantly rural district, by voting against child labor bills and opposing the nationalization of railroads.

Rayburn supported New Deal programs and played a major role in the passage of Franklin D. Roosevelt's regulatory legislation. After becoming majority leader in 1937, he mapped out legislative strategy with the President. In 1939 he began an unsuccessful effort to win a place on the 1940 Democratic presidential ticket. When Speaker William Bankhead died in September 1940, Rayburn was unanimously chosen to succeed him. He firmly supported all of Roosevelt's war measures except gasoline rationing, which was opposed by Texas's powerful oil interests.

Rayburn was President Harry S. Truman's chief supporter in Congress and one of his closest advisers. Except for civil rights measures, the Representative backed much of Truman's domestic program, which included national health insurance, housing, education and minimum wage proposals. As minority leader from 1947 to 1949, Rayburn opposed the Taft-Hartley Act, tried to limit Republican cuts in Truman programs and attempted to block tax reductions favoring upper income brackets. In 1947 he declined Truman's offer of the vice presidential nomination.

Rayburn became Speaker again after the 1948 election. In January 1949 he succeeded in securing the adoption of the 21-day rule, a device for reducing the power of the conservative, Southern Democrat-Republican dominated Rules Committee to block the flow of legislation to the House floor. Two years later, however, the next Congress refused to adopt the 21-day proviso. Rayburn often tried to forge compromises between the Truman Administration and congressional Dixiecrats. In 1951, for example, he proposed a middle-ground solution to the controversy over whether the federal or state governments should control tidelands oil, thereby offending the oil interests which favored state jurisdiction. Although inclined to search all possible avenues of cooperation with the Soviet Union, Rayburn reluctantly came to support Truman's cold war policy of containment. In January 1951 he broke the record of Henry Clay for length of service as Speaker. [See TRUMAN Volume]

When President Truman announced in March 1952 that he would not seek reelection, Sen. Monroney (D, Okla.) [q.v.] attempted to mount a campaign for Rayburn's nomination as a compromise presidential candidate acceptable to both the North and South. However, Allan Shivers [q.v.] the Dixiecrat governor of Texas and Rayburn's political enemy, dominated the state Democratic convention and chose its delegation to the Democratic National Convention. Without support from his own state, Rayburn lost his chance to win the Party's nomination.

As the permanent chairman of the National Convention, Rayburn used his power to gain the presidential nomination for Truman's candidate, Adlai Stevenson [q.v.]. Sen. Estes Kefauver (D, Tenn.) [q.v.] had won impressive primary victories and led on the first two ballots at the Chicago convention. The Kefauver forces, sensing imminent victory, wanted a third roll call immediately. However, Rayburn called a recess to enable Truman, who was en route to Chicago, to meet with key Convention figures. Stevenson was nominated on the third ballot.

During the 1950s Rayburn worked with the Eisenhower Administration to defeat Republican isolationist measures. As minority leader in the 83rd Congress, Rayburn backed the extension of the Reciprocal Trade Agreements Act and fought efforts to cut $2 billion from the Administration's foreign aid package. The following year he opposed the Bricker amendment, which would have limited the President's treaty-making power. Rayburn worked against a number of Administration proposals that he regarded as socially regressive, including a 1953 measure to strip the Southwest Power Administration of authority to transmit electricity to the Rural Electrification Administration cooperatives; a 1954 bill to free the stock issues of middle-size companies from the jurisdiction of the Securities and Exchange Commission; and a 1954 tax cut that, Democrats charged, primarily benefited corporations.

In the 1954 elections the Democrats re-gained control of Congress, and Rayburn once again became Speaker. During his previous tenure in that post, Rayburn had gained a reputation as one of the strongest Speakers in U.S. history. Nineteenth century Speakers had maintained their strength through their right to make committee assignments and sit on the Rules Committee, which controlled the flow of legislation from the committees of original jurisdiction to the floor. In the "Revolution of 1910" the Speaker lost these powers. But Rayburn, through informal influence, had been able to dominate the chamber. This influence was founded in large measure upon respect for his character. Highly regarded for his integrity and lack of pretension, he was extremely successful in exercising indirect control of the legislative process and of committee assignments through his relationship with committee and subcommittee chairmen. Rayburn used his powers to promote party regularity. Although he claimed that he never asked a man to vote against his principles, he generally expected Democratic representatives to back legislation supported by their leaders. His famous advice to freshmen representatives was "To get along, go along." Rayburn was also known as a conciliator of factional disputes.

With the Democrats in a majority in the House, Rayburn and Eisenhower worked more closely together than before. In 1955 and 1956 respectively, the Speaker again supported Administration reciprocal trade and foreign aid bills. During the latter year Rayburn pushed through the House Eisenhower's modest civil and voting rights bill, which was opposed by the great majority of Southern Democrats. However, the measure was blocked in the Senate.

Rayburn came into conflict with some Democratic liberals in 1955 when he backed the Formosa Resolution, giving the President authority to use U.S. troops in defense of Formosa and the Pescadores Islands against Communist Chinese attacks. A number of representatives believed that congressional authorization was superfluous and that the Resolution represented an effort by the Administration to procure blanket approval for any actions it might take. However, the Speaker contended that presenting a united front to the world should be the foremost consideration of Congress. The Resolution passed the House 410 to 3.

In 1956 Rayburn again served as permanent chairman of the Democratic National Convention, where he promoted his protege, Senate Majority Leader Lyndon B. Johnson (D, Tex.) [q.v.], as the Party's vice presidential nominee. Towards this end he had helped Johnson wrest control of the Texas party organization from Shivers. But Stevenson, after being nominated for President, decided, over Rayburn's vehement objections, to leave the choice of a running mate to the Convention. The leading contenders included Sens. Kefauver and John F. Kennedy (D, Mass.) [q.v.]. During the second ballot Kennedy was just 40 votes short of a majority when the Kentucky delegation asked for recognition to transfer its 30 votes from Sen. Albert Gore (D, Tenn.) [q.v.] to Kennedy. However, Rayburn recognized the Tennessee delegation, which switched its votes from Gore to Kefauver, thereby reversing the Kennedy tide and enabling Kefauver to win the nomination. Rayburn did not have a high opinion of Kennedy at the time, but it was not clear whether the Speaker's actions were calculated.

After the 1956 election Rayburn and Johnson came under increasing fire from Democratic liberals for being too conciliatory towards Eisenhower and for not promoting comprehensive social welfare legislation. In late November 1956 Paul Butler [q.v.], the national party chairman, formed the Democratic Advisory Council (DAC). It was intended as a vehicle to enable liberals to circumvent the House and Senate Democratic leadership in the formulation of the Party's legislative programs. Rayburn and Johnson refused to join the group, and so the panel had little influence.

The following year, after Rayburn's acceptance of the Senate's watered-down version of the Administration's civil rights bill and in response to the Rules Committee's obstructionism, House liberals formed the Democratic Study Group (DSG) to increase their influence. With the assistance of Minority Leader Joseph Martin (R, Mass.) [q.v.], Rayburn was able to pry some DSG-backed bills from the Rules Committee, chaired by conservative Rep. Howard W. Smith (D, Va.) [q.v.]. But major legislation, such as a multi-billion dollar housing bill, was pigeonholed by the panel, and DSG members became increasingly impatient.

Shortly after the Democratic sweep of the 1958 congressional elections, Rep. Chet Holifield (D, Calif.) [q.v.], speaking for the DSG, demanded Rayburn's assistance in the reestablishment of the 21-day rule. The Speaker refused on the grounds that the inevitably bitter struggle over the rule would polarize the Democratic Party just one year before the 1960 presidential election. However, he promised to induce the Committee to report out all major bills sent to it during the 1959-60 congressional term. Rayburn secured release of the housing bill in 1959 (although it was vetoed by President Eisenhower) but failed to keep his promise on a number of other bills, including area redevelopment and school aid legislation.

Liberal publications began to refer to Rayburn as an "Eisenhowercrat" in 1959. But Alfred Steinberg, Rayburn's biographer, contended that Rayburn's inability to force the passage of liberal legislation was in part the result of the selection of Rep. Charles Halleck (R, Ind.) [q.v.] to replace Martin as minority leader in January 1959. Rayburn and Martin had maintained a cooperative relationship, but Halleck was more partisan and combatative than his predecessor. He replaced two Republican moderates on the Rules Committee with more conservative men and was not disposed to use his influence on Rayburn's behalf.

Beginning in 1959 Rayburn backed Johnson's presidential bid. He urged Johnson to enter the primaries, but the Senator believed that the House and Senate leaders would provide him with the votes he needed from their states' delegations. Rayburn, who declined to serve again as National Convention chairman, nominated Johnson at the Democratic gathering. When Kennedy offered Johnson the vice presidential nomination, Rayburn at first urged his fellow-Texan to reject it as a political dead end but changed his mind after speaking with the presidential nominee. Rayburn campaigned heavily for the Democratic candidates in Texas, realizing that his prestige would suffer if a ticket including Johnson lost in their home state. Kennedy carried Texas by a narrow 46,000-vote margin.

In January 1961 Rayburn aided the Kennedy Administration in reforming the Rules Committee to facilitate passage of New Frontier legislation. On Jan. 31 Rayburn won a 217-212 vote for enlarging the panel from 12 to 15 members. Two pro-Administration Democrats and a Republican were added to the Committee, creating an eight to seven liberal majority. Rayburn's modified version of the President's minimum wage bill, tailored to meet Republican and Southern Democratic objections, became the basis of legislation adopted in May 1961. Suffering from cancer, Rayburn flew home to Bonham, Tex., in August 1961 and died in November. [See KENNEDY Volume]

[MLL]

For further information:
Alfred Steinberg, *Sam Rayburn* (New York, 1975).

REED, DANIEL A(LDEN)
b. Sept. 15, 1875: Sheridan, N.Y.
d. Feb. 19, 1959; Washington, D.C.
Republican Representative, N.Y., 1919-1959: Chairman, Ways and Means Committee, 1953-55.

Reed received an LL.B. degree from Cornell University in 1898 and, after practicing law in Chautauqua Co., was the Cornell football coach for nine years. In 1918 he was elected to the U.S. House of Representatives from New York's 43rd district, consisting of Allegany, Cattaraugus and Chautauqua Counties. During his first decade his major concerns were education measures and bills of particular interest to New York State. In 1932 Reed obtained a seat on the powerful Ways and Means Committee, where he became a supporter of sound money and strict limits on federal spending. An advocate of reduced taxes, he wrote a 1950 bill to raise exemptions to $700 and reduce most excise levies by 10% to 20%.

During the first year of the Eisenhower Administration, Reed served as the chairman of the Ways and Means Committee in the Republican-controlled Congress. There he clashed with the Administration over two tax bills. On Jan. 3 he introduced a bill to advance a scheduled tax reduction from Jan. 1, 1954 to July 1, 1953. The Ways and Means panel reported the bill favorably on Feb. 16. However, the President opposed a tax cut before the budget was reduced and, with the help of House Speaker Joe Martin (R, Mass.) [*q.v.*], succeeded in bottling up Reed's measure in the Rules Committee.

During the same period Reed attempted to block an Administration-backed bill to extend the excess profits tax on corporations from June 30, 1953 to Dec. 31, 1953. The Ways and Means Committee began hearings on the measure in June. Reed remained adamantly opposed to extension and rejected President Eisenhower's personal appeals for a Committee vote. The President and congressional leaders decided to circumvent Reed if necessary, and on June 25, the Rules Committee, at the behest of Speaker Martin, took the extraordinary step of reporting the bill to the House without a report from Ways and Means. Reed hinted at resigning from Congress in protest and stated that he was "fighting to preserve our system of government . . . [and] the integrity of my Committee." A confrontation was avoided when a scheduled June 29 House vote on the Rules panel's decision was postponed by the House Republican leadership. On July 8 the Ways and Means Committee overrode Reed's objections and voted to report the excess profits bill. Reed then offered two compromise versions of the measure, but both were rejected by the panel. The Administration's proposal was passed by Congress and signed into law in July.

Reed also opposed the Administration's reciprocal trade policy. In 1953 the President supported a bill for a modest one-year extension of the existing legislation. Although Reed voted for the measure, he condemned the principle of reciprocal trade. He stated that "the insatiable desire to promote exports at any cost has made it possible for our enemies to obtain from our own shores the war materials which they needed in order to wage aggressive war." In 1955 and 1958, when longer extensions and presidential tariff-cutting authority were included in reciprocal trade bills, Reed voted against the measures.

After the Democrats regained control of Congress in the 1954 elections, the New York Representative adopted a more partisan role as a defender of the Administration. In 1955 he attacked a Democratic personal income tax cut proposal, asserting that current defense and other budget needs made a reduction unwise. The following year Congress voted a temporary increase in the statutory limit on the public debt for fiscal 1957. Reed, noting that the limit was less than those for fiscal 1955 and 1956, praised "the magnificent accomplishments of this Administration in putting the fiscal affairs of the nation in order." In 1958 he introduced a bill incorporating President Eisenhower's suggestion that the states assume responsibility for federally financed programs in the areas of vocational education, waste-treatment facilities, slum-clearance planning and repair of public facilities damaged in natural disasters.

Reed died in Washington, D.C. on Feb. 19, 1959.

[MLL]

REED, STANLEY F(ORMAN)
b. Dec. 31, 1884: Minerva, Ky.
Associate Justice, U.S. Supreme Court, 1938-57.

After receiving B.A. degrees from Kentucky Wesleyan College in 1902 and Yale University in 1906, Reed studied law at the University of Virginia, Columbia University and the Sorbonne. From 1910 to 1929 he practiced law in Kentucky. He then served as counsel of the Federal Farm Board from 1929 to 1932 and as general counsel of the Reconstruction Finance Corp. from 1932 to 1935. A Democrat, Reed was named U.S. Solicitor General in March 1935, and over the next three years he defended before the Supreme Court such

major New Deal legislation as the National Industrial Recovery Act, the Agricultural Adjustment Act and the Tennessee Valley Authority. He was appointed to the U.S. Supreme Court in January 1938.

Two major themes underlaid Reed's judicial decisions. First, Reed believed in the importance of government and organization in society and saw the expansion of government as a positive development. He also favored a policy of judicial restraint in which the judiciary would defer to the legislature and the executive unless their actions were clearly unconstitutional. In Reed's earliest years on the bench, these views led him to sustain the federal economic and social welfare laws then at issue. He was cast as a liberal who helped secure Court approval of New Deal legislation.

By the Truman era, however, the Court frequently faced cases in which the rights of the individual conflicted with government interests. Reed's regard for the needs of government and society made him largely insensitive to individual claims. He was increasingly labeled a conservative, especially in civil liberties and criminal rights cases. [See TRUMAN Volume]

Throughout his years on the Court, Reed was a consistent supporter of government antisubversive efforts, and during the 1950s he objected when the Court in any way undermined loyalty-security programs. He dissented in June 1955 when the majority ruled that the Civil Service Commission's Loyalty Review Board had exceeded its authority in auditing a favorable loyalty judgment and had wrongfully commanded the dismissal of a Public Health Service employe. In April 1956 Reed wrote the minority opinion in a case where the Court overturned Pennsylvania's antisubversive law. Reed again dissented when the majority, in June 1956, held that government employes could be dismissed as security risks only if they held sensitive jobs.

Reed was more willing to restrain government action infringing on free expression. In two 1951 cases, for example, he had voted to hold unconstitutional state licensing laws requiring persons to secure permits before speaking or meeting in public parks or streets because the laws gave too much discretion to the officials granting the licenses. However, Reed believed some government regulation of expression was permissible. In April 1953 he wrote the majority opinion sustaining a similar New Hampshire licensing law because its standards were precise enough to make it constitutional.

Reed, a traditionalist in criminal cases, opposed extending to the states the guarantees given federal defendants in the Bill of Rights. He was also extremely reluctant to upset a conviction on the grounds that a defendant's confession had been coerced. Reed would do so only when there was strong and clear evidence that a confession had been given involuntarily.

From the time he joined the Court, Justice Reed regularly voted to support black demands for civil rights. However, Reed balked at holding racial segregation in and of itself unconstitutional. The issue was squarely presented to the Court during the 1952-53 session in five companion suits involving segregated schools. Reed evidently believed that segregation was allowable so long as blacks received equal treatment with whites. When the justices voted on the cases in conference early in 1954, Reed was alone in this view. After considering what would be best for the country and the Court, Reed yielded. He decided not to dissent and thus made unanimous the May 1954 decision in *Brown* v. *Board of Education*, which ruled that segregation in public schools violated the Constitution.

A soft-spoken man of unfailing courtesy and kindliness, Reed retired from the Court in February 1957, at the age of 72. Assessing Reed's 19 years on the high bench, C. Herman Pritchett called the Justice "a 'center judge,' occupying generally a middle position between the Court's conservative and liberal wings" but with a definite rightward bent in civil liberties cases. He was "a legal craftsman" who believed that the political branches of government, not the Court, had "the power and the responsibility for governing."

Following his retirement Reed spent time both in Washington and on his farm near Maysville, Ky. President Eisenhower named him chairman of the new six-member U.S. Civil Rights Commission in November 1957. However, Reed withdrew from the job in December because he feared his service in an investigatory and advisory post might lower public respect for the impartiality of the judiciary. In the years after this, he accepted many assignments to hear cases in the U.S. Court of Claims and the U.S. Court of Appeals for the District of Columbia.

[CAB]

For further information:
C. Herman Pritchett, "Stanley Reed," in Leon Friedman and Fred L. Israel, eds., *The Justices of the United States Supreme Court, 1789-1969* (New York, 1969), Vol. 3.
F. William O'Brien, *Justice Reed and the First Amendment* (Washington, 1958).

RESTON, JAMES
b. Nov. 3, 1909; Clyde-Bank, Scotland
Journalist

Born in Scotland, Reston emigrated with his parents to Ohio at the age of 11. He graduated from the University of Illinois in 1932 and began his newspaper career with the *Springfield (Ohio) Daily News*. Two years later he joined the Associated Press, first working in New York and then in London. Reston joined the *New York Times* London bureau in 1939. He remained there until 1941, when he was assigned to the Washington bureau. By that time Reston had earned a national reputation. His coverage of the London blitz and his book, *Prelude to Victory*, an appeal to Americans to shun materialist goals in World War II, made him one of the *Times's* most promising reporters. He worked for the Office of War Information for a short period but returned to the *Times* in 1944 to become publisher Arthur Hayes Sulzberger's administrative assistant.

In 1953 Reston succeeded Arthur Krock [*q.v.*] as head of the Washington bureau. Reston revitalized the bureau by bringing in new faces and introducing a sense of informality absent under his predecessor. His liberalism also contrasted with Krock's conservatism. In addition to his managerial responsibilities, Reston published his own column. It became so popular that President Dwight D. Eisenhower once remarked, "Who the hell does Reston think he is telling me how to run the country?" Reston earned his national reputation through his observations on foreign affairs. In his articles he combined realism with a strong sense of morality that came from his strict Presbyterian upbringing.

Reston was often critical of the Administration's foreign policy and particularly of Secretary of State John Foster Dulles's [*q.v.*] reliance on "brinksmanship." In a *Life* magazine interview in January 1956, the Secretary of State had told the American people that on a number of occasions he had brought the U.S. to the brink of nuclear war to force the Soviets to retreat. Reston wrote that Dulles had "added something new to the art of diplomatic blundering . . . the planned mistake." Dulles, the columnist stated, "Doesn't stumble into booby traps; he digs them to size, studies them carefully, and then jumps . . . ."

A liberal on domestic affairs, Reston frequently attacked Sen. Joseph R. McCarthy (R, Wisc.) [*q.v.*]. In March 1954 he condemned McCarthyism and the Administration's tacit endorsement of it. The White House, he lamented, is playing a waiting game, hoping the American people will get bored with the Senator. Reston warned that McCarthyism was not likely to disappear. So long as uncertainties existed as the United States adjusted to its responsibilities as a world leader, new McCarthys would emerge to exploit the fears and frustrations of the people. McCarthy, Reston claimed, had won a victory: "He has demonstrated, in this atmosphere of fear, that violence and defeat can be made to pay in American political life." The journalist claimed that McCarthy had already silenced many honorable men in Congress and elsewhere and seized control of a large part of the Republican Party. He had become a model for rising young politicians on Capitol Hill. Reston concluded by suggesting that only the President could silence him. Quoting Woodrow Wilson the columnist wrote, "The President may be both the leader of his party and the leader of his nation, or he may be one or the other. If he leads the nation, his party can hardly resist him . . . ."

When Eisenhower left office in 1961, Reston delivered an evenhanded assessment of the President's eight years. He acknowledged Eisenhower's accomplishments. The President had successfully avoided what he feared most—war and depression. Eisenhower broke the isolationist tradition of his party. Swift action on his part blocked Communist advances in Lebanon and Guatemala. The U.S. helped end the Suez crisis and avoided intervention in Hungary. The Administration accepted truces, no matter how temporary in Indochina, Korea, the Formosa Straits and Berlin. Reston wrote, "Nothing has been settled but nothing vital to the free world has been lost." On domestic affairs Reston praised Eisenhower for consolidating the gains of the New Deal and Fair Deal, both of which his party had originally opposed. Concluding, Reston wrote, "President Eisenhower at least maintained enough power to deter the big war and the big depression, that was his objective from the start."

Reston continued writing his column into the 1960s and 1970s. He became associate editor of the *New York Times* in 1964 and executive editor in 1968. In 1969 the *New York Times* appointed him a vice president.

[JB]

For further information:
James Reston, *Sketches in Sand* (New York, 1967).

REUTHER, WALTER P.
b. Sept. 1, 1907; Wheeling, W. Va.
d. May 10, 1970; Pellston, Mich.
President, United Automobile Workers, 1947-70.

The son of an immigrant German brewery worker and union leader in the Ohio Valley, Walter Reuther was raised in a closely knit socialist family. After completing high school in Wheeling, W. Va., he moved to Detroit in 1926 and became a skilled tool and die worker at the Ford Motor Co. Discharged for his union activity in 1931, Reuther joined the Socialist Party, attended Wayne State University for two years and campaigned vigorously for Norman Thomas's 1932 presidential candidacy. With his brother Victor he then set out on a world tour, which included a 16-month sojourn as skilled workers in a Soviet auto factory. Returning to Detroit in 1935, the two Reuthers joined another brother, Roy, in organizing the new United Automobile Workers (UAW). Walter Reuther played a secondary role in the turbulent sitdown strikes begun in 1936, that marked the UAW's birth, but in 1937 he created a power base in the union after helping organize 30,000 auto workers on Detroit's West Side.

Like many other radical unionists, Reuther resigned from the Socialist Party in the late-1930s and endorsed the Congress of Industrial Organizations (CIO) alliance with Franklin D. Roosevelt and the Democratic Party. With the approach of World War in 1940, the Reuther brothers formed a caucus that fought for control of the UAW against a leadership coalition that included a small but influential Communist grouping. During the War Reuther backed the labor movement's no-strike pledge but gradually shifted to the left to accommodate an increasingly restive UAW rank and file. In 1945 he led a dramatic 113-day postwar strike against General Motors (GM) despite continued CIO adherence to a no-strike policy. Reuther's unprecedented demand for wage increases without price increases and for union access to company books in order to prove that GM could afford such a concession earned him the allegiance of most non-Communist auto militants, a wide following among left-liberals outside union ranks and the presidency of the million-member UAW in March 1946. Emerging as a leading spokesman for an aggressive, politically oriented unionism, Reuther denounced the Truman Administration and called for the formation of a labor party.

During the late-1940s, however, Reuther shifted away from radicalism towards acceptance of the existing structure of American politics and industrial relations. He became a power within the national Democratic Party and at the same time sought incremental social and economic advances for UAW members through an innovative collective bargaining program. The 1948 auto

contracts included a pace-setting "escalator clause," providing for a cost-of-living allowance to be adjusted quarterly and an annual "improvement factor" based on long-range productivity gains. In 1950 Reuther signed a five-year contract with GM, hailed by *Fortune* magazine as the "treaty of Detroit," under which the union accepted the principle that advances in real wages would be gained only through advances in productivity. [See Truman Volume]

In 1952 Reuther won election as president of the CIO. Early in the following year he reached agreement with American Federation of Labor (AFL) president George Meany [q.v.] to revive the dormant Joint AFL-CIO Unity Committee as a first step towards merger of the two labor federations. Reuther demanded, as a precondition for unity, a strong no-raiding agreement that would prevent smaller unions from being swallowed up by larger ones and serious action against racketeering in AFL unions. Although the AFL partially fulfilled these conditions by expelling the gangster-dominated International Longshoremen's Association in 1953 and agreeing to curb competition for bargaining rights where CIO unions had already won contracts, Reuther's ability to win further concessions on these issues was undermined by the willingness of many CIO leaders to unify on the AFL's terms.

In February 1955 Reuther attended a meeting of the AFL Executive Council in Miami Beach, where CIO counsel Arthur Goldberg [q.v.] drew up a merger plan that was accepted by both sides. Under the Goldberg proposal the AFL retained both the presidency and the secretary-treasurership of the new organization, while Reuther became one of 27 vice presidents and head of the Industrial Union Department. The merger became final in December at the founding convention of the AFL-CIO.

When the UAW faced the Big Three auto corporations—GM, Ford and Chrysler—in the 1955 round of contract talks, production was at record-breaking levels, while workers continued to suffer from the hardships caused by annual layoffs during model changeovers. Reuther proposed a guaranteed annual wage for auto workers and selected Ford as the target company for the union's campaign. Rather than risk a strike while its major competitor, GM, continued to operate, Ford presented a "supplemental unemployment benefit" plan (SUB), which paralleled the UAW proposal. Under its provisions the company put five cents an hour into a fund that would be used to provide payments to idled workers. In combination with federal unemployment compensation, UAW members were guaranteed between 60% and 65% of their normal take-home pay for up to 26 weeks of a layoff. With GM and Chrysler accepting the SUB plan, the contracts were hailed as a stunning collective bargaining success for the UAW. Reuther's willingness to forgo a substantial wage boost antagonized skilled tool, die and maintenance workers, however, who complained that their wage rates were falling behind the scales of AFL craft unions. A rival organization, the Society of Skilled Trades, was formed, and it petitioned the National Labor Relations Board for recognition in several plants. However, both the UAW and the auto industry joined forces to block its efforts to win bargaining rights.

In 1957 Reuther proposed a shorter work week without reduction in pay as the major demand in the next round of negotiations. The recession in the following year hit the auto industry hard, reducing the UAW from 1.5 to 1.1 million members. Believing that the companies, with nearly one million new cars in inventory, could afford to postpone production for an extended period, Reuther decided to avoid a strike. He therefore backed down on the demand for a shorter work week, calling for a profit-sharing plan instead. When this was brusquely rejected by the Big Three, Reuther further scaled down UAW demands to a minimum package including improvements in the SUB, pension increases and other fringe benefits. After four months of negotiations, during which union members continued working without a contract, the UAW settled for what was little more than a three-year renewal of the old contracts. The 1958 accords were the first in the UAW's history which did not include any major contract gains.

Under Reuther's leadership the UAW won a dominant influence in the Michigan Democratic Party in the late-1940s, transforming a weak, relatively conservative state party into one of the most liberal and politically effective Democratic organizations in the country. The union mobilized Detroit's large population of auto workers to reelect Gov. G. Mennen Williams [q.v.] for seven consecutive terms between 1948 and 1960 and to oust two conservative Republican senators. Within the national Democratic Party Reuther was a principal spokesman for the labor-liberal coalition during the 1950s. In alliance with the NAACP and the Americans for Democratic Action (ADA), he led the effort at the 1956 Democratic National Convention to win a strong civil rights plank. But despite his earlier warning to party leaders that "you can't have Mr. Eastland (conservative Mississippi Sen. James O. Eastland [q.v.]) and have us at the same time," Reuther drew back from a floor fight over platform policy. As a strong supporter of Adlai Stevenson [q.v.], he also used his influence to prevent the Michigan delegation from backing Averell Harriman [q.v.] and to win AFL-CIO endorsement for the Party's nominee after the Convention.

Reuther was an early and outspoken critic of corruption and gangsterism in the labor movement and an advocate of greater internal union democracy. Unlike many union leaders he applauded the Senate Select Committee on Improper Activities in the Labor or Management Field (known as the McClellan Committee after its chairman, Sen. John McClellan (D, Ark.) [q.v.]) in its drive against racketeering. After the Committee's initial investigation of the International Brotherhood of Teamsters, Reuther called for the expulsion of that union from the AFL-CIO and played a major role in the formulation of codes of ethical practices for the Federation. In 1957 the UAW established a Public Review Board, consisting of seven prominent clergymen, lawyers and professors with authority to hear and make binding decisions on the appeals of union members against the UAW executive board.

At the urging of Sens. Barry Goldwater

(R, Ariz.) [q.v.], Karl Mundt (R, S.D.) [q.v.] and Carl Curtis (R, Neb.) [q.v.] and over the objection of chief counsel Robert Kennedy [q.v.], the McClellan Committee held hearings on the UAW intermittently between February 1958 and September 1959. Through an investigation of a prolonged UAW strike against the Kohler Co., a manufacturer of bathroom fixtures, Republican committee members tried to uncover criminal activity and large-scale violence in the union. But they failed to discover corruption on a scale significant enough to equate the UAW with the Teamsters and other gangster-ridden unions spotlighted by the Committee.

During the late-1950s Reuther was involved in a growing dispute with AFL-CIO President Meany over what Reuther considered the Federation's stagnation at home and rigid anti-Communism abroad. Reuther criticized Meany for failing to curb craft union jurisdictional raids on industrial unions and for refusing to throw Federation resources into large-scale organizing drives. He also attacked Meany for holding executive council meetings at Florida luxury hotels rather than in cities of the industrial North. Within the Federation the two labor leaders were frequently at odds over foreign policy issues. Reuther particularly objected to the government-supported, often clandestine overseas operations of Meany's aide, Jay Lovestone [q.v.], head of the Free Trade Union Committee. In 1959 disagreements surfaced on the occasion of a visit by top Soviet leaders to the U.S. Meany pointedly boycotted two Reuther-led union delegations which met with Soviet Deputy Premier Anastas Mikoyan and Premier Nikita Khrushchev.

Generally regarded as the most influential labor leader at the 1960 Democratic National Convention, Reuther helped deliver the first ballot nomination to Sen. John F. Kennedy (D, Mass.) [q.v.]. Although Kennedy's selection of Sen. Lyndon B. Johnson (D, Tex.) [q.v.] as his running mate shocked Reuther at first, he quickly fell into line behind the ticket, dissuading the Michigan delegation from initiating a floor fight over the nomination. Reuther also succeeded in blocking a public condemna-tion of Johnson by the AFL-CIO executive council.

As local UAW leaders and rank-and-file members became more concerned with non-economic grievances involving production standards and working conditions during the 1960s, Reuther encountered important and widespread internal union opposition to his policies and recurrent wildcat strikes following negotiation of each company-wide contract. At the same time, his disagreements with George Meany grew more intense, and in 1968 Reuther formally withdrew the UAW from the AFL-CIO. On May 9, 1970 Reuther and his wife were killed near Pellston, Mich., when their chartered jet crashed on landing. [See KENNEDY, JOHNSON, NIXON/FORD Volumes]

[TLH]

For further information:
Frank Cormier and William Eaton, *Reuther* (Englewood Cliffs, 1970).
Victor Reuther, *The Brothers Reuther* (Boston, 1976).
B.J. Widick, *Labor Today* (New York, 1964).

RIBICOFF, ABRAHAM A(LEXANDER)

b. April 9, 1910: New Britain, Conn.
Governor, Conn., 1955-1961.

The son of an immigrant Jewish factory worker, Ribicoff grew up in a poor section of New Britain, Conn. He worked his way through New York University and attended the University of Chicago law school while serving as Midwestern sales representative of a buckle and zipper manufacturer. After receiving his degree in 1933, he returned to Connecticut and established a private practice in Hartford. In 1938 Ribicoff was elected as a Democrat to the state General Assembly, where he served two terms and won acclaim from journalists as the state's "most able representative." From 1941 to 1943 and again from 1945 to 1947, Ribicoff served as a police court judge in Hartford.

In 1948 Ribicoff won election to the U.S. House of Representatives. Assigned to the House Foreign Affairs Committee, he helped formulate the Australia-New

Zealand-U.S. defense pact and the Philippine Security Treaty. Though generally known as a moderate and a supporter of the Truman Administration, Ribicoff backed the Internal Security (McCarran) Act of 1950. Near the end of his second term in the House, he ran against Republican Prescott Bush for the unexpired Senate term of Brien McMahon (D, Conn.), who had died in July 1952. Ribicoff lost narrowly and returned to private practice in his brother's Hartford law firm.

In 1954 Ribicoff resumed his career in Connecticut politics, running for governor against Republican incumbent John Davis Lodge. After a campaign stressing reform of state government and increasing state revenues, Ribicoff defeated his opponent by 3,115 votes. His narrow victory and Republican domination of the state legislature caused Ribicoff to adopt a cautious, "non-partisan" approach as governor. Avoiding new programs and reforms, he stressed administrative efficiency by eliminating or consolidating 20 state agencies. Officials were kept alert by the Governor's habit of holding daily press conferences and calling department heads for information on questions he could not answer.

Ribicoff gained national attention in early 1956 with a highway safety campaign that faced convicted speeders with automatic suspension of their licenses for 30 days or more. As a result of the campaign and increased state spending for highway safety measures, traffic fatalities in Connecticut fell 11% from their 1955 level. When state Republicans complained that traffic penalties were too severe, Ribicoff derisively dubbed them the "pro-speeding" party.

Ribicoff's open administration won such popularity that it temporarily upset Connecticut's normally close Democratic-Republican balance. Not only was Ribicoff reelected by nearly 247,000 votes in 1958, but Democrats riding his coattails took control of the state legislature for the first time since 1876. Although Ribicoff pronounced himself "overwhelmed" by the Democratic victory, his second term brought little change in his customary caution. One reform that he did introduce to the new legislature was a bill to eliminate Connecticut's outmoded system of county government, which had responsibility only for placing foster children and managing county jails. Ribicoff's bill, passed by the legislature in May 1959, transferred county functions to the state and abolished the county tax on cities and towns.

Already known for his record as governor, Ribicoff began to gain national importance in the Democratic Party as an early supporter of Sen. John F. Kennedy's (D, Mass.) [q.v.] presidential aspirations. A friend of Kennedy's since their days together in the House, Ribicoff backed his unsuccessful vice presidential bid in 1956 and joined with Connecticut Democratic chairman John Bailey in mapping Kennedy's New England strategy for the 1960 presidential race. In June 1960 Ribicoff served as Kennedy's chief spokesman at the annual Governors Conference, and the Governor later helped direct Kennedy forces at the Democratic National Convention in Los Angeles.

In return for his campaign help, Kennedy offered Ribicoff his choice of cabinet posts in the new Administration. According to Kennedy biographers Arthur Schlesinger, Jr. [q.v.] and Theodore Sorensen, Ribicoff would have liked to serve as Attorney General but felt it would be unwise for a Jewish official to prosecute controversial civil rights cases in the South. He chose instead to be Secretary of Health, Education and Welfare (HEW), resigning his governorship at the end of 1960 to assume the post. Ribicoff spent much of his time as head of HEW, pushing the Administration's medicare and aid-to-education bills, both of which were unsuccessful. Frustrated by a hostile Congress and a federal bureaucracy he considered cumbersome and unresponsive, he resigned his cabinet post in July 1962 to return to Connecticut politics. Ribicoff was elected to the Senate in 1962 and won reelection in 1968 and 1974 by wide margins. Serving as chairman of the Government Operations Subcommittee on Executive Reorganization, he gained wide attention for his work on issues of motor vehicle safety and urban problems. [See KENNEDY, JOHNSON, NIXON/FORD Volumes]

[SLG]

RICKOVER, HYMAN G(EORGE)
b. Jan. 27, 1900; Makow, Russia
Director of Naval Research, Atomic Energy Commission; Director of Nuclear Propulsion, Navy Bureau of Ships, 1953-

Hyman Rickover, the "father" of the nuclear submarine, was the son of Russian immigrants. He grew up in Chicago, graduated from Annapolis in 1922 and then served in a variety of naval assignments, including submarine duty. In 1939 he became head of the electrical section of the Bureau of Ships, a position he held throughout World War II. Following the War he was assigned to the Atomic Energy Commission's (AEC) Manhattan Project, where he first became convinced that a nuclear-powered submarine was feasible. Despite consistent Navy objections Rickover obtained approval for the project and was assigned to the AEC's naval reactors branch while retaining his naval post as head of the Nuclear Power Division.

With a personal style that one observer called "quasi-Prussian and autocratic," Rickover assembled a crack staff for his nuclear projects during the 1950s and committed military heresy by prizing ability over rank. His outspoken views and abrasive manner made him unpopular with his superiors, and Rickover was twice overlooked for promotion until an act of Congress promoted him from captain to rear admiral in 1953.

Under Rickover's guidance construction of the nuclear-powered submarine *Nautilus*, begun in June 1952, was completed in January 1954. Between 1954 and 1959 the Navy constructed three nuclear surface warships: the destroyer *Bainbridge*, the cruiser *Long Beach* and the aircraft carrier *Enterprise*.

Rickover's experiences in the personnel field as well as his efforts to cope with consistently shoddy workmanship by civilian contractors led him to frequently attack American education. He declared that U.S. students were ill-prepared to meet the demands of an increasingly technological society. In February 1958 Rickover stated that

he favored transferring money from the Defense Department if necessary to raise teachers' pay and improve education. He asserted that education was more important than defense expenditures and urged federal standards for teachers. He assailed "professional educators" as principally to blame for the inadequate educational system and warned Congress not to "make the mistake of strengthening the position of state boards of education." His book on the subject, *Education and Freedom*, was published in 1959.

During the Kennedy Administration Rickover clashed with Secretary of Defense Robert S. McNamara over construction of a second nuclear-powered aircraft carrier, which Rickover strongly and unsuccessfully advocated. In the early-1960s Rickover also continued to speak out on the flaws of the American educational system. President Lyndon B. Johnson waived Rickover's mandatory retirement in 1964, allowing the Admiral to continue in the service. During the Johnson years Rickover deplored the Navy's acceptance of inferior materials, which he asserted stemmed from the close connection between business and the military. [See KENNEDY and JOHNSON Volumes]

[FHM]

RIDGWAY, MATTHEW B(UNKER)
b. March 3, 1895; Fort Monroe, Va.
Army Chief of Staff, August 1953-June 1955.

Matthew B. Ridgway, the son of an Army colonel, was raised on various Army posts. Following his graduation from West Point in 1917, he taught languages there and then served on numerous assignments in Central America, the Far East and the United States. From 1939 to 1942 Ridgway was assigned to the War Department general staff, war plans division. During World War II Ridgway played an important role in the creation of Army airborne units and, as commanding general of the 82nd Airborne Division, participated in the invasion of Sicily, the Italian campaign and the invasion of Normandy. From 1945 to 1948 he had extended assignments with the Military Staff

Committee of the United Nations and the Inter-American Defense Board. After the dismissal of Gen. Douglas MacArthur as leader of the U.N. forces in Korea, Ridgway took his place. In 1952 he replaced Gen. Dwight D. Eisenhower as supreme commander of Allied forces in Europe. [See TRUMAN Volume]

President Eisenhower appointed Ridgway Army Chief of Staff in August 1953. Ridgway soon clashed with the Administration over its decision to implement the "New Look" defense policy. This plan, prompted in part by a desire to reduce expenditures, called for primary reliance on strategic nuclear weapons, or "massive retaliation," for defense. In 1954 he joined Gen. James M. Gavin [q.v.] in protesting the cutbacks in the defense budget and the reductions in Army personnel which the policy entailed. He objected to a defense policy based on what he thought were principally political decisions and called for one based on the ability to fight small-scale, guerrilla-type wars as well as all-out nuclear attacks.

In debates over a military policy, Ridgway often served as a voice of moderation, countering the more bellicose policies of Chairman of the Joint Chiefs of Staff Adm. Arthur Radford [q.v.]. During the spring of 1954, when the Administration was considering a French request for U.S. military intervention in Vietnam, Ridgway opposed Radford's plan to use air strikes. The General feared that if bombing failed to achieve its objective, there would be a strong temptation to send U.S. ground troops to maintain U.S. prestige. Ridgway ordered a team of experts to evaluate the situation in Vietnam. A subsequent report concluded that the U.S. was not ready to fight a guerrilla-type war similar to the ones in that area. Eisenhower eventually accepted Ridgway's advice and refused direct American aid.

Ridgway again opposed Radford's recommendations following the shelling of the Nationalist Chinese islands of Quemoy and Matsu by the Communist Chinese during the fall of 1954. Radford and the majority of the Joint Chiefs argued that, although the islands had no strategic value to Taiwan, their loss would bring on a collapse of Nationalist morale, which, in turn, was im-

portant for the defense of Asia. Therefore, they recommended that Eisenhower permit Chiang Kai-shek to bomb the mainland. If Quemoy were attacked, they urged direct U.S. military intervention. Ridgway, the only dissenter among the Joint Chiefs, argued that it was not the military's responsibility to judge the psychological value of the island and urged restraint. Eisenhower, determined not to exacerbate the crisis further, ruled out American military intervention.

Ridgway retired as Army Chief of Staff in June 1955 and became director of Colt Industries. A few days before his departure, he elaborated his views on the need for a "viable strategy for Cold War situations" to meet aggression in the "mountains of Greece and Korea or the jungles of Indochina."

After leaving the military Ridgway continued to oppose the Administration's emphasis on nuclear air power and criticized the placing of politics above the national interest. As a member of the Association of the U.S. Army, he worked for acceptance of his "limited strategy" views, which gained wider support among congressional, academic and public leaders, especially after 1957, when the launching of the Soviet satellite *Sputnik* convinced many that the USSR was gaining superiority in missiles. In a committee report for the Association in 1960, Ridgway outlined a proposal for the reorganization of the Army into a "mobile ready force" capable of fighting small wars. The plan was eventually implemented as the "flexible response" policy of the Kennedy Administration.

During the 1960s Ridgway was one of the military men, along with Gavin, who attempted to persuade the Johnson Administration to limit U.S. involvement in the Vietnam war. In 1966 he argued that the government must maintain a middle course between unilateral withdrawal and all-out war. A member of the Senior Advisory Group on Vietnam, which met with President Lyndon B. Johnson during March 1968, Ridgway continued to stress non-military options in the conflict. By 1970 he supported a total planned withdrawal. [See JOHNSON Volume]

[FDA]

RIVERS, L(UCIUS) MENDEL
b. Sept. 28, 1905; Gumville, S.C.
d. Dec. 29, 1970; Bethesda, Md.
Democratic Representative, S.C.,
1941-70.

Rivers, whose father owned a small farm and a turpentine still, was born in Gumville, S.C., in the Hell Hole Swamp area of Berkeley Co. When Mendel was eight he and his widowed mother moved to North Charleston, a drab industrial suburb of Charleston. Rivers received a law degree from the University of South Carolina in 1931. The following year he was elected to the state legislature, where he served until 1936. From 1936 to 1940 he was a special attorney with the Justice Department.

Rivers ran against Alfred Von Kolnitz in the 1940 Democratic congressional primary for Charleston and vicinity. According to a friend, when Rivers pronounced his opponent's name, "you could almost hear the Nazi troopers goose-stepping." Rivers lost the Charleston vote but won the primary on the basis of his appeal in rural areas. The general election was a formality in the overwhelmingly Democratic state. Rivers was immediately assigned to the Naval Affairs Committee, which in 1947 was merged into a new Armed Services Committee. In 1948 Rivers backed the States' Rights (Dixiecrat) presidential candidacy of South Carolina Gov. Strom Thurmond [q.v.]. As a member of the Armed Services Committee, he was an enthusiastic defender of large defense expenditures and of an aggressive military stance. In 1950 Rivers publicly urged President Harry S. Truman to threaten North Korea with the atomic bomb.

Believing that military strength was the only real guarantee of American security, Rivers continued to support increased military spending during the 1950s. In 1955 he unsuccessfully offered an amendment to a supplemental appropriations bill that would have nearly doubled funds for Navy public works. The following year Rivers backed a military pay raise bill, warning that it would endanger the U.S. if American soldiers were forgotten in peacetime. In 1960 Rivers

headed a special Armed Services subcommittee on military airlifts. The panel recommended an extensive program for the modernization of the Military Air Transport Service (MATS). As a result, the MATS fleet was expanded and updated through the purchase of more powerful airplanes.

Rivers used his position on the Armed Services Committee to secure a vast array of military installations for his district. In 1955 he was vice chairman of a special subcommittee examining military land transfers, and shortly afterwards he headed a special subcommittee investigating Pentagon property acquisitions. Between 1955 and 1960 the Navy established a Marine Corps air station at Beaufort; the Air Force built a recreation center at Berkely and an unmanned radar site at Parris Island. The Army located a National Guard office in Hampton and an Army Reserve installation in Charleston.

Rivers continued to favor an aggressive use of military power in the Eisenhower years. In 1960 he supported a bill to cut the Cuban sugar quota in retaliation for the policies of Cuba's Premier Fidel Castro. During floor debate on the bill, he urged further action, stating, "Let us revise our sugar quota and take the next step tomorrow, and probably the ultimate step will be to occupy that island to save those people. Let us take that step. Our stature is dwindling. Let us built it up while time remains."

Rivers was a staunch opponent of civil rights legislation and generally took conservative positions on other domestic as well as on military and foreign policy issues. He backed Eisenhower for President in 1952 and 1956. However, he sometimes supported social welfare measures opposed by the Administration. In 1958 he voted for social security increases criticized by the President for being too costly. The following year Rivers backed two housing bills vetoed by Eisenhower for their alleged extravagance.

In 1965 Rivers succeeded Rep. Carl Vinson (D, Ga.) [q.v.] as chairman of the Armed Services Committee. During that year he clashed with President Lyndon B. Johnson and Secretary of Defense Robert S.

McNamara over the closing of military bases. Rivers failed in an attempt to secure congressional veto power over base-closings. In 1965 Rivers succeeded in doubling the military pay raise requested by the Administration.

One of the strongest congressional backers of the Vietnam war, Rivers favored the use of nuclear weapons against Communist China. He was also a vitriolic critic of the antiwar movement. Rivers continued to obtain military installations for his district, and by the late-1960s defense-related facilities accounted for 35% of the payroll in the Charleston area. Becoming more liberal on domestic issues during the mid and late 1960s, he backed a number of Great Society programs.

On Dec. 29, 1970 Rivers died after undergoing open heart surgery. [See JOHNSON, NIXON/FORD Volumes]

[MLL]

For further information:
Don Oberdorfer, "Rivers Delivers," *The New York Times Magazine* (Aug. 29, 1965), pp. 31 +.

ROBERTS, C(HARLES) WESLEY
b. Dec. 14, 1903; Oskaloosa, Kan.
Chairman, Republican National Committee, January 1953–March 1953.

Roberts attended public schools and Kansas State College before becoming part-owner and coeditor of three small-town Kansas newspapers. Campaign manager for the 1936 Republican gubernatorial nominee, he became the Kansas Republican State Committee's assistant chairman in 1938 and chairman in 1947. He resigned three years later to manage the successful senatorial campaign of Frank Carlson [q.v.]. Although out of state party office after 1950, Roberts remained a singularly powerful figure in Kansas's overwhelmingly majority party. Together with Carlson and Gov. Edward Arn, Roberts led the conservative "palace guard" wing of the state GOP, which engaged in bitter intraparty fighting with a more reform-minded "Young Turks" faction.

Carlson was an early supporter of Eisenhower's presidential candidacy, and in 1952 he managed the General's preconvention Washington headquarters. In January 1953 outgoing Republican National Committee Chairman Arthur E. Summerfield [q.v.] designated Roberts his successor. The National Committee immediately ratified the selection, and President Eisenhower expressed his "hearty approval."

Less than one month after assuming office, Roberts stood accused of past conflict of interest. On Feb. 19 the *Kansas City Star* reported that Roberts had unlawfully used his connections as a state party leader to influence a 1951 state legislative appropriation. State investigators soon found that Roberts had received an $11,000 commission for helping a fraternal order sell the state a hospital building. (To add to the scandal, there was some question as to whether the state already owned the facility.) Though he acted as a lobbyist for the building's owners, Roberts had failed to register as one. Nor had he informed many state and legislative officials with whom he dealt that he represented private parties seeking their aid. To Roberts' surprise, a special, predominately Republican, state legislative committee charged him with having "deliberately and intentionally" violated the "spirit" if not the "letter" of the state's lobbying law.

Roberts resigned as Republican National Committee chairman upon release of the state committee's report. He had filled the post for nine weeks. Eisenhower, who had campaigned vigorously against corruption in the Truman Administration, termed Roberts's move "a wise one." He named Leonard Hall [q.v.] as Roberts's successor. Roberts returned to his newspapers and his insurance agency. In August 1953 the Kansas attorney general announced that he would not press criminal charges against Roberts because of the vague wording of the state's lobbying statute.

[JLB]

For further information:
David Frier, *Conflict of Interest in the Eisenhower Administration* (Ames, Iowa, 1969).

ROBERTSON, A(BSALOM) WILLIS
b. May 27, 1887; Martinsburgh, W. Va.
d. Nov. 1, 1971; Lexington, Va.
Democratic Senator, Va., 1946-67;
Chairman, Senate Banking and Currency Committee, 1959-67.

Robertson received his LL.B. from the University of Richmond in 1908 and began private law practice that same year. He served as a Democratic member of the Virginia Senate from 1916 to 1922. For the next six years he was attorney for Rockbridge Co. In 1932 he won election to the U.S. House of Representatives.

Roberston soon emerged as a conservative who, according to historian J. Harvie Wilkinson, "personified Spartan discipline, pioneer individualism [and] Calvinist morality." Like Harry Byrd [q.v.], whose Democratic machine dominated Virginia politics from the late-1920s to the mid-1960s, Robertson opposed government expansion and social welfare programs as well as integration. Yet Robertson was not on close terms with Byrd. It was his own extensive, informal network of supporters and friends who forced the machine to back him in his 1946 race for the Senate seat left vacant by the death of Carter Glass. Robertson was reelected to full terms in 1948, 1954 and 1960.

Robertson was an early supporter of Gen. Dwight D. Eisenhower for President. In 1948 he told Douglas Southall Freeman, a Virginia newspaper editor, that the General was the only man who could unite the nation and deal with the Soviet Union. He urged his Southern colleagues to draft Eisenhower at the Democratic National Convention, but they did not act on his advice. When it became evident that Eisenhower was a Republican, Robertson confidentially contacted financier Bernard Baruch in October 1951 and asked him to promote Eisenhower as the 1952 Republican candidate. [See TRUMAN Volume]

During the Eisenhower Administration, Robertson focused his attention on preventing the expansion of federal power. He also supported conservative fiscal policies, particularly those designed to balance the budget. He opposed the continuation of rent controls and the creation of a permanent Small Business Administration in 1953. He favored the bill establishing the St. Lawrence Seaway Development Corp. in 1954 but wanted toll money collected on the waterway applied toward the national debt. In 1957 Robertson successfully opposed federal construction of a hydroelectric dam at Hell's Canyon, Ida., maintaining that the project could be more justifiably left to private concerns. In 1958 he opposed accelerating the Administration's interstate highway program as inflationary. Despite his fiscal conservatism, Robertson consistently supported high defense spending. In 1956 he was one of 13 members of the Appropriations Committee who supported a $1.16 billion increase in the amount the House voted for the Air Force.

In 1956 Robertson headed a subcommittee which attempted to develop a legislative program for revising the U.S. banking code. At the request of the panel, the agencies involved in regulating banking submitted more than 175 proposed amendments. In December a 27-member advisory committee appointed by the subcommittee filed a report urging increased federal authority over interstate bank mergers and embodying more than 200 legislative recommendations. Action was finally taken in 1960, when Congress passed the Bank Merger Act, prohibiting mergers or consolidations on federally insured banks "without the prior written consent" of the appropriate supervisory agency.

Robertson became chairman of the Banking and Currency Committee in 1958. There he served as the leading spokesman for the conservative coalition of Southern Democrats and Republicans on fiscal matters. He cautioned that if government's $12.9 billion deficit continued to rise, foreign and domestic capital would flee the dollar. Robertson also warned against galloping inflation but discouraged wage and price controls as ineffective. In 1959 he was the only member of his committee to support the Administration and vote against an additional $1 billion in housing appropriations intended, in part, for classroom construction. President Eisenhower vetoed this bill as too costly, and Robertson led the Committee in rewriting it to meet most of the President's objections.

The Virginia Senator was a segregationist. He opposed the Supreme Court's May 1954 decision outlawing public school desegregation and signed the 1956 "Southern Manifesto," denouncing the decision as a "clear abuse of judicial power." When President Eisenhower proposed Solicitor General Simon E. Soboloff [q.v.] as a federal judge in 1956, Robertson spoke against the confirmation, accusing Soboloff of "prejudice" against the South on the segregation issue. He and Sen. J. Strom Thurmond (D, S.C.) [q.v.] led an unsuccessful 1958 fight to keep Alaska out of the Union. They feared its admission would dilute Southern congressional strength.

During the Kennedy and Johnson Administrations, Robertson continued to oppose civil rights and social welfare legislation. In 1966 he lost his Senate seat in the Virginia Democratic primary by a narrow margin. After Robertson retired from the Senate, he became a consultant to the National Bank for Reconstruction and Development. He died in 1971.

[MJS]

ROBESON, PAUL B(USTILL)
b. April 9, 1898; Princeton, N.J.
d. Jan. 23, 1976; Philadelphia, Pa.
Entertainer, political activist

Paul Robeson's father was a minister who had been a slave until he escaped at the age of 15. His mother was a Philadelphia school teacher of African, Indian and English heritage. After graduating from Rutgers in 1919, Robeson entered Columbia University law school, supporting himself by playing professional football on weekends. During his law years, Robeson first became involved in the theater, largely through the influence of his wife, Eslanda. He performed in Harlem and on Broadway and interrupted his school schedule to appear in England. After taking his LL.B. in 1923, he attempted a law career but decided to continue his stage work. Over the ensuing decades he became not only a stage and motion picture actor, but also a singer, recording folk songs and spirituals in over 20 languages.

Robeson was a prominent spokesman for black aspirations and causes of the Left. His advocacy of black demands for equality was militant for his time and alienated many. When he and his family toured the Soviet Union, they experienced a warmth and affection they had not found in America. Robeson became sympathetic to the Soviet government, thereby earning additional enmity from many Americans. In 1946 he appeared before a committee of the California legislature and denied any prior membership in the Communist Party. After that incident he refused to answer other questions on his political affiliations before investigating committees.

In 1949 Robeson declared to a world peace conference his belief that U.S. blacks "could not go to war on behalf of those who have oppressed us for generations against a country [the USSR] which in one generation had raised our people to the dignity of mankind." He was immediately attacked in the press. Later in the year the House Un-American Activities Committee (HUAC) called in black witnesses—including baseball star Jackie Robinson, whom Robeson had helped win entrance to the major leagues—to refute his contention. A scheduled Robeson concert in Peekskill, N.Y., precipitated a full-scale riot. In 1950 the State Department denied him a new passport, a decision which he fought in the courts for eight years. His winning of the Stalin Peace Prize in the USSR in 1952 further angered his opponents. [See TRUMAN Volume]

Robeson's stage career came to a halt after 1952. Eric Bentley stated, "In American history it would be hard to parallel the blackout of Robeson imposed by the government and the press during the early and mid 1950s." In 1956 Robeson was called before HUAC during hearings concerning the revocation of U.S. passports. In an appearance described by some as "all hollering and thumping and gaveling and speechifying," and by others as courageous and dignified, he refused to answer most questions on constitutional grounds. He denounced U.S. government racism and reiterated his affection for the Soviet people. HUAC threatened Robeson with a contempt citation but took no final action against him.

A 1958 Supreme Court decision in a related case won Robeson his passport renewal. Before he and his family left the country, he gave a warmly received, sold-out concert in Carnegie Hall. After living in Russia and Europe from 1958 to 1963, he returned to the U.S. where he continued to support the civil rights movement. In 1975 an unsuccessful attempt was made to induct him into the National Football Hall of Fame. He died in 1976.

[TGD]

For further information:
Eric Bentley, *Thirty Years of Treason, 1938-68* (New York, 1971).

ROCKEFELLER, NELSON A(LDRICH)

b. July 8, 1908; Bar Harbor, Me.
Undersecretary of Health, Education and Welfare, 1953-54; Special Assistant to the President, 1954-55; Governor, N.Y., 1959-73.

A grandson of Standard Oil millionaire John D. Rockefeller, Nelson Rockefeller graduated from Dartmouth College in 1930. During the early-1930s he worked in the family's Chase Bank and leased space in the new Rockefeller Center in New York City. From 1935 to 1940 Rockefeller was a director of the Creole Petroleum Co., an affiliate of Standard Oil. While in that post he developed an interest in Latin American affairs and advocated massive economic assistance to that region for both humanitarian and commercial reasons.

In 1940 President Franklin D. Roosevelt appointed Rockefeller to head the Office of the Coordinator of Inter-American Affairs, where he supervised an economic and cultural program for Latin America. From 1944 to 1945 he was assistant secretary of state for Latin American affairs. After World War II Rockefeller founded private organizations to advance world peace by improv-

ing living standards in underdeveloped regions of the world. From 1950 to 1951 he was an adviser to President Harry S. Truman on the Point Four program.

A liberal Republican, Rockefeller backed Gen. Dwight D. Eisenhower in the 1952 presidential election. Three weeks after Eisenhower's victory, the President-elect appointed Rockefeller to a three-man commission assigned to plan government reorganization. One of its recommendations was the formation of a Cabinet-rank Department of Health, Education and Welfare to replace the Federal Security Agency. When the Department was created the following year, Rockefeller became its undersecretary. In that post he originated the Eisenhower Administration proposal to create a federal health reinsurance fund to encourage private companies to write broader health and medical insurance plans.

Rockefeller left the Health, Education and Welfare Department in 1954 to become a special assistant to the President on foreign policy. He criticized what he regarded as the stopgap policies of the Eisenhower Administration and attempted to promote long-range expanded economic and military aid programs. He met strong opposition from budget-minded conservatives such as Secretary of the Treasury George M. Humphrey [*q.v.*] and Undersecretary of State Herbert Hoover, Jr. [*q.v.*]. At the end of 1955 Rockefeller left Washington and returned home to New York.

To promote the kind of comprehensive programs that he favored, Rockefeller in 1956 initiated the Special Studies Project of the Rockefeller Brothers Fund. The Project brought together some of the best minds in the country to make policy recommendations in the areas of defense, education and economics. The best-known of the reports was written under the direction of Henry A. Kissinger [*q.v.*], director of Harvard's Center for International Affairs. It was published in 1958 as "International Security: The Military Aspect." The report warned that the Soviet Union was advancing more rapidly than the United States in many crucial areas of military technology and that "if not reversed, this trend

. . . will place the free world in dire jeopardy." It criticized the Eisenhower Administration's reliance upon the strategy of massive retaliation and asserted the need for a more flexible defense policy. It urged, among other things, a major increase in the defense budget, a willingness to engage in limited nuclear warfare and the construction of fallout shelters. The report received a great deal of publicity in 1958, and Rockefeller used its recommendations and those of other Project reports in his subsequent political campaigns.

After his experiences in appointive federal positions, Rockefeller concluded that he had to win elective office to implement his ideas. In 1956 he began preparing to run for governor of New York. That year he became chairman of the Committee on the Preparation of the State Constitutional Convention and used the position to make contact with state and local party leaders. He won the Republican gubernatorial nomination without great difficulty in 1958. Some prominent Republicans felt that Rockefeller's name and wealth might damage his electoral prospects. But this problem was minimized by the fact that his opponent, incumbent Gov. W. Averell Harriman [q.v.], was also a millionaire. Few issues separated the candidates. Rockefeller's major charge was similar to his complaint against the Eisenhower Administration. He asserted that Harriman dealt with problems on a piecemeal basis rather than developing long-term goals. An enthusiastic, exuberant campaigner aided by expert political technicians, Rockefeller, who outspent Harriman by $1.8 to $1.1 million, defeated the incumbent by over half-a-million votes.

During the first two years of his governorship, Rockefeller laid the foundation for extensive social welfare programs. Early in 1959 he successfully procured from the legislature an increase in the state income tax to finance the programs on a pay-as-you-go basis, as mandated by the state constitution. Later in the year he appointed a three-member committee on higher education. In 1960 it recommended the establishment of a new state university with two new graduate schools and the transforma-

tion of the eleven state teachers colleges into liberal arts schools. In 1960 Rockefeller succeeded in establishing a State Housing Finance Authority, with a two billion dollar borrowing capacity, to encourage investment of private capital in middle-income housing.

During the same year Rockefeller signed New York State's first minimum wage bill, establishing a $1 hourly floor. In 1960 he also announced plans to build a four million dollar fallout shelter in Albany to accommodate 2,200 state employes. However, Rockefeller failed to gain legislative endorsement for his plan for mandatory shelters in public and private buildings.

Rockefeller saw the New York governorship as a steppingstone to the presidency. Immediately after his election as governor, he set up a large campaign organization to seek his Party's nomination. He endorsed liberal domestic programs such as civil rights, expanded aid to education and federal reinsurance of private health insurance plans. In defense and foreign policy he took a hard line, urging a resumption of underground nuclear tests and calling for caution in the expansion of East-West trade.

After concluding that he could not wrest the nomination from Vice President Richard M. Nixon [q.v.], Rockefeller withdrew from the race in December 1959. Hoping to influence the Republican platform, he declined to unqualifiedly endorse Nixon and continued to express his views, particularly in the area of defense. Reflecting the conclusions of the Rockefeller Brothers Fund's Special Studies Project, he stated that America's military position relative to the Soviet Union's had been declining for 15 years and insisted upon the need for greater defense efforts. On July 25, 1960, shortly before the Republican Platform Committee adopted its final draft, Rockefeller and Nixon met at the latter's Fifth Avenue apartment in New York City. In what became known as the Treaty of Fifth Avenue, Nixon agreed to accept a platform more reflective than the early Platform Committee drafts of the New York Governor's views on defense, foreign and domestic policy.

During the early and mid 1960s, Rockefeller's vast social welfare programs enormously expanded New York State's budget. The Governor employed additional tax increases and voter-approved bond issues to procure funds. When the electorate began rejecting the bond issues, he turned to so-called moral obligation bonds that did not require the voters' sanction.

Rockefeller again sought the Republican presidential nomination in 1964 but was defeated by conservative Sen. Barry M. Goldwater (R, Ariz.) [q.v.]. During the course of the campaign, Rockefeller became the bete noire of the Republican Right. In 1968 he lost the nomination to Nixon for the second time.

Faced with increasing criticism over New York State expenditures and with the continuing hostility of Republican conservatives throughout the country, Rockefeller began moving to the right in the late-1960s. In 1973 he resigned the New York governorship and established a study group called the Commission for Critical Choices for Americans. Some political observers believed the Commission was intended as a springboard for a future presidential bid. President Gerald R. Ford nominated him for vice president in 1974, and Congress confirmed him the following December. In November 1975 Rockefeller announced he did not want to be renominated for the vice presidency. [See KENNEDY, JOHNSON, NIXON/FORD Volumes]

[MLL]

For further information:
Stewart Alsop. "The Rockefeller Nobody Knows," *The Saturday evening Post* (July 25, 1959), pp. 13-15.

ROGERS, WILLIAM P(IERCE)
b. June 23, 1913; Norfolk, N.Y.
Deputy Attorney General, January 1953-October 1957; Attorney General, November 1957-January 1961.

William Rogers, the only son of an insurance agent, grew up in a small mill town in northern New York. He studied at Colgate University, where he obtained his degree in 1934. Rogers then attended Cornell law school, graduating fifth in his class in 1937. After working with a Wall Street firm for a short period, the lawyer was appointed assistant attorney general by New York District Attorney Thomas E. Dewey in 1938. He was involved in over 1,000 trials over a four-year period.

Following service in the Navy during World War II, he became chief of the bureau of special sessions under New York District Attorney Frank Hogan [q.v.]. A Republican, he moved to Washington to serve as counsel to the Senate Special Committee to Investigate the National Defense Program in 1947. When that Committee was succeeded by the Senate Investigations Subcommittee of the Executive Expenditures Committee the following year, Rogers was asked to remain by the chairman, Sen. Clyde R. Hoey (D, N.C.), who was impressed by his nonpartisanship. During this period Rogers became a friend of Rep. Richard Nixon (R, Calif.) [q.v.] and urged the Congressman to pursue his investigation of Alger Hiss. He returned to New York to practice law in 1950.

Rogers became a key figure in the 1952 Republican National Convention, convincing the Credentials Committee that it should seat the Eisenhower rather than the Taft delegates from Louisiana. During the campaign he remained close to Nixon. Following the disclosure that the vice presidential candidate had access to a "secret" political fund, Rogers advised Nixon to state his case on nationwide television and helped to arrange the "Checkers speech." After Eisenhower's victory Rogers was appointed deputy attorney general on Nixon's recommendation.

Rogers served as chief liaison officer between the Justice Department and Congress, the press and various federal agencies. He also drafted legislative proposals and developed a recruitment program for the Department. He was instrumental in the passage of the 1957 Civil Rights Act, working with House and Senate leaders to strengthen the final measure. In 1957 Rogers started a campaign to "speed up justice" and suggested that the Chief Justice address each new session of Congress with a state of the judiciary message. The newly created Executive Office for United States Attorneys and the Executive Office for United States Marshals were placed under Rogers's supervision.

Rogers remained close to Nixon throughout the Eisenhower Administration. He accompanied the Vice President late in 1953 to talk with Sen. Joseph R. McCarthy (R, Wisc.) [q.v.] in an attempt to slow down his controversial anti-Communist investigation and prevent a politically harmful split between the Senator and the President. After Nixon heard of Eisenhower's heart attack in September 1955, he spent the evening with Rogers, discussing problems of temporarily assuming presidential powers as well as the possibility of permanent succession should Eisenhower's health fail. In 1956, after the Hungarian revolt, Rogers visited refugees in Europe with Nixon.

When Attorney General Herbert Brownell [q.v.] resigned in October 1957, Eisenhower appointed Rogers to replace him. As Attorney General, Rogers made the enforcement of civil rights measures his major concern. He set up the civil rights division of the Justice Department as required by the 1957 statute. As a result of the problems created by the attempt to integrate Little Rock, Ark., schools in 1957, he established a Justice Department committee to deal with the federal aspects of the integration problem in 1958. He also sent U.S. marshals to Little Rock to facilitate enforcement of the law. In 1960 Rogers recommended stronger measures to guarantee voting rights.

The question of presidential infirmity became a pressing issue after Eisenhower's 1955 heart attack. In 1958 the Attorney General advocated a constitutional amendment which would have allowed the President to issue a written statement initiating and terminating the Vice President's assumption of presidential powers. Rogers was the chief Administration leader attempting to induce Congress to send the proposal to the states, but Congress did not act.

In 1958 Rogers instituted a special unit to combat racketeering. This organization was eventually integrated into the prosecutory

arm of the Department and helped to improve the record of indictments and prosecutions under the Hobbs Act, Taft-Hartley Act, income tax laws, antitrust laws and conspiracy statutes. Rogers advised Eisenhower to ignore political pressures and to appoint only qualified individuals to federal judgeships. He also convinced the reluctant President of the necessity of instituting antitrust suits against corporations such as General Electric and Westinghouse. During the spring of 1960 Rogers represented the Administration on a good-will trip to West Africa.

In 1961 Rogers returned to private law practice in New York and Washington. Four years later he became a member of the U.S. delegation to the U.N. General Assembly, and in 1967 he served as a delegate to the United Nations Committee on Southwest Africa. When Richard Nixon became President in 1969, he appointed Rogers Secretary of State. Rogers resigned in 1973 after continued conflicts with Henry Kissinger [q.v.]. After leaving Washington he returned to private law practice. [See NIXON/FORD Volume]

[GAD]

For further information:
"William P. Rogers," Current Biography Yearbook, 1969 (New York, 1970), pp. 372-375.

ROMNEY, GEORGE W(ILCKEN)
b. July 8, 1907: Chihuahua, Mex.
Chairman of the Board and President, American Motors Corporation, 1954-62.

Born to a poor American Mormon family then living in Mexico, George W. Romney grew up in Texas and Idaho. He attended the University of Utah and George Washington University. An aide to Sen. David I. Walsh (D, Mass.) in 1929 and 1930, Romney remained in Washington to lobby for the aluminum industry. In 1939 he accepted a similar job with the Automobile Manufacturers Association (AMA). During his years with the AMA, Romney became close friends with George Mason, an officer and later president of Nash-

Kelvinator, Inc., an automobile and home appliance manufacturer. Under pressure to prepare a successor, Mason hired Romney as his assistant in April 1948 and made him vice president two years later. That same year Romney oversaw initial production of a small, low-priced car, the "Rambler," capable of 35 miles on a gallon of gasoline. Sales proved sluggish through the first half of the decade, and the Nash division operated in deficit. In January 1954 Nash-Kelvinator joined with Hudson Motor Car Co. to form the American Motors Corp. (AMC) with Mason as chief executive officer.

Upon Mason's death late in 1954, Romney became chairman, president and general manager. When continued losses pushed AMC to the brink of of financial ruin in 1956, Romney successfully negotiated a revolving bank credit of $45 million. In 1956-57 he headed off an attempted takeover of AMC by stock market manipulator Louis Wolfson [q.v.].

As head of AMC Romney risked the company's future on the production of small cars. He limited and finally ended production of AMC's full-sized Hudson and Nash while continuing to promote the Rambler. In contrast, the "Big Three"—General Motors Corp., Ford Motor Co. and Chrysler Corp.—marketed large models, which Romney assailed as the "dinosaur in our driveway" and "gas guzzlers."

The severe 1957-58 recession transformed the once disregarded Romney into an honored prophet. As aggregate U.S. auto sales declined, AMC's unit production rose from 100,000 in 1956 to 500,000 in both 1958 and 1959. "A truly dramatic bit of market penetration," commented economist Harold G. Vatter. For the next three years the Big Three had to follow Romney's lead. Presenting its own compact models in 1960, Chrysler abandoned its full-sized "DeSoto," while Ford lost unreported millions on its recently introduced "Edsel."

Romney frequently criticized the auto industry. Before the Senate Judiciary Subcommittee on Antitrust and Monopoly in February 1958, he attacked "excess concentration of power in any form." The size and accompanying advantages of the Big Three, he said, made the "barriers to en-try" for prospective producers all but prohibitive. "It has been 34 years since a new United States manufacturer has successfully entered the automotive industry," he pointed out. Romney favored the dismemberment of General Motors into several fully autonomous companies. Smaller producers like AMC and Studebaker, he claimed, "have contributed relatively more basic product pioneering than their bigger competitors," but the Big Three had been unnecessarily slow in adopting their innovations. He cited the Rambler as one important example.

Romney scored the United Automobile Workers (UAW) and its president Walter Reuther [q.v.] with equal fervor. "Big Labor," he told the antitrust panel, "represented just as great a threat to freedom in America as did the business monopoly." He denounced industry-wide bargaining as unfair to the smaller manufacturer and berated the UAW for wage increases that outpaced labor productivity gains. As a relatively inexperienced but independent-minded executive, Romney's own relations with the UAW were never cordial. Fearing a loss of managerial authority, he constantly fought with local leaders over productivity and once threatened a plant closing over the issue. Although AMC avoided costly, prolonged strikes in the 1950s, it also paid higher wages than the Big Three.

Beginning in 1959 Romney engaged in state politics. He led in the formation of a nonpartisan "Citzens for Michigan" committee in June 1959, which sought to revise the state constitution, and in 1961-62 participated in the constitutional convention. In 1962 Romney won the first of three successful campaigns for governor. A brief try for the 1968 Republican presidential nomination failed badly. Romney served as Secretary of Housing and Urban Development in the first Nixon Administration. [See KENNEDY, JOHNSON, NIXON/FORD Volumes]

[JLB]

For further information:
Clark R. Mollenhoff, *George Romney* (New York, 1968).

ROONEY, JOHN J(AMES)
b. Nov. 29, 1903; New York, N.Y.
d. Oct. 26, 1975; Washington, D.C.
Democratic Representaive, N.Y.,
1944-75.

The son of Irish immigrants, Rooney received his education in Catholic schools, taking his LL.B. degree from Fordham University in 1925. Thereafter he maintained a law practice in Brooklyn, until, in 1940, he was appointed assistant district attorney of Kings Co., N.Y., by District Attorney William O'Dwyer. Rooney's relentless and effective prosecutions of illegal gamblers attracted the Democratic machine in Brooklyn; in 1944 he was chosen as the Democratic candidate to fill a vacant U.S. House seat. His election by a constituency with mixed ethnic and economic backgrounds brought him a House seat that was not to be seriously challenged for almost 30 years.

Rooney built a reputation in the House as a liberal Democrat who usually voted with his party's majority on foreign and domestic policy legislation. While he remained a congressman obscure to the general public, behind the scenes he became one of the most powerful politicians in the U.S. His membership on the House Appropriations Committee gave him a seat—and eventually the chairmanship—of the Subcommittee on the State and Justice Departments, the Judiciary and Related Federal Agencies. During 1943-53 and 1955-75 the parsimonious Rooney exercised tight control over those departments whose budgets were subject to his committee's approval. Feared by agency petitioners for his intense scrutiny of the most minute budgetary details, he was described in the *Saturday Evening Post* as a master at "making an appropriations-hunting civil servant appear like a confidence man." Not only did he dominate witnesses and his own subcommittee, but his recommendations were rarely questioned by the parent Appropriations Committee or the House leadership.

Although Rooney unquestionably saved

taxpayers money by his budget slashing—in 1959 he claimed to have eliminated $1 billion in spending during the previous decade—he was frequently criticized for failing to perceive expenditures in terms of a larger, cohesive policy. In 1958 columnist James Reston [q.v.] described Rooney as "one of the most powerful men in Congress, in a negative way." Reston referred specifically to the fact that in 1958 a Foreign Service Institute (FSI) advisory group meeting with President Eisenhower revealed that 50% of the Foreign Service officer corps did not have a speaking knowledge of any foreign language. Many U.S. ambassadors could not speak the languages of the countries they served. A startled Eisenhower was told that Rep. Rooney's meager budget appropriations made adequate language training impossible. Rooney defended himself by citing examples of FSI extravagance and waste, and a group of State Department officials publicly supported him as a valuable inspiration for examining their own spending policies.

The State Department was often subject to Rooney's most vigorous interrogations. The plain-speaking Brooklynite could by disdainful of "striped-pants," elite State officials who "don't know what they're talking about." In 1955 he refused a State Department request for extra ambassadors' funds, calling the money "booze allowances for cookie pushers." Officials claimed Rooney's decisions kept people of moderate means out of ambassadorial service. After returning from an overseas tour in 1955, he aimed his criticism at the United States Information Agency. He called the organization "futile . . . more interested in propagandizing the American public than in combating Communism overseas." In 1957 Rooney sponsored a bill to pare down appropriations for the United States Information Agency, claiming that its efforts during the Hungarian uprising had been "almost a complete failure."

One agency subject to Rooney's budgetary control that did not suffer verbal harassment and appropriations cuts was the FBI. Director J. Edgar Hoover [q.v.] and Rooney shared a mutual admiration and political philosophy. Hoover's appearances before the subcommittee usually brought forth from the chairman praise for the FBI's fiscal efficiency and open-ended questions intended to provide Hoover the opportunity to expound his political views. Historian Sanford Unger claimed that Rooney was informed of some of the Bureau's more controversial counterintelligence activities. His tacit approval of them was assumed to constitute congressional approval. Likewise, a directive from Rooney to the FBI was taken as a congressional mandate. Critics charged Rooney with inadequate oversight of FBI operations and lax control over the money allocated to the agency.

Rooney's voting record in the House reflected the varied constituency he served: large groups of Irish, Jews, blacks, Hispanics and Near Eastern immigrants. He voted in 1953 for increased immigration quotas, particularly for countries subject to Communist oppression. A staunch defender of Israel, he also supported Eisenhower's Mideast Doctrine which permitted the President to use Armed Forces to aid Middle Eastern nations threatened by Communism. He voted for the Civil Rights Acts of 1957 and 1960, and for the expanded public works bill of 1959.

Rooney supported the domestic policy programs of Presidents Kennedy and Johnson and stood behind Johnson's Vietnam war policy. He survived challenges in the 1970 and 1972 primary elections by candidates who criticized his position on the war and his ties to city machine politicians. He retired from office in 1975 and died on October 26th of that year in Washington. [See KENNEDY, NIXON/FORD Volumes]

[TGD]

ROOSEVELT, (ANNA) ELEANOR
b. Oct. 11, 1884; New York, N.Y.
d. Nov. 7, 1962; New York, N.Y.
Political figure.

The niece of Theodore Roosevelt, Eleanor Roosevelt was raised by her grandmother following the death of her parents. She was first tutored at her New York City home and then sent to finishing school in London. In 1905 she married Franklin D. Roosevelt, her fifth cousin. During the early years of her marriage, she encouraged her husband's political career as state senator, assistant secretary of the Navy and Democratic vice presidential candidate in 1920.

When polio interrupted Franklin Roosevelt's rising career in the 1920s, Eleanor stood in for him at Democratic Party functions. From 1924 to 1928 she served as finance chairman of the women's division of New York's Democratic State Committee, and in 1928 and 1930 she helped her husband's successful gubernatorial campaigns. During the 1920s Roosevelt developed her own interests in world disarmament, the creation of an international organization to keep the peace and the rights of women and minorities.

After Franklin Roosevelt became President in 1933, Eleanor continued to champion social reform and served as an unofficial ombudsman with the government for many Americans. She traveled thousands of miles to win support for New Deal legislation, acting as her husband's "eyes and ears" in many new projects. In 1935 she began a syndicated newspaper column, "My Day," which she used first to discuss women's problems and, after 1939, to advance her own views on public affairs. Following U.S. entry into World War II in December 1941, she served as assistant director of the Office of Civilian Defense and visited American troops in the Pacific and Caribbean in 1943 and 1944.

After Franklin Roosevelt's death in 1945, Eleanor accepted an appointment as a U.S. delegate to the U.N. During 1946 she served as chairman of the Commission on Human Rights and played a central role in drafting the Universal Declaration of Human Rights, which the U.N. adopted in 1948. Roosevelt left her U.N. post in 1953. [See TRUMAN Volume]

During the 1950s Roosevelt traveled extensively, championing reform and promoting the U.N. Under the auspices of the American Association of the U.N., she delivered countless speeches defending the international organization and advocating U.S. adoption of the Universal Declaration of Human Rights. She also visited such countries as India, Yugoslavia and Poland. On each of these trips Roosevelt promoted increased cultural contacts to break down barriers between East and West.

During 1957 Roosevelt traveled to the Soviet Union, becoming the most prominent American to make the trip since the early Cold War. Premier Nikita S. Khrushchev invited her to meet with him at Yalta. The interview was a candid exchange of views on the Cold War at which Roosevelt raised the question of human rights, pointing particularly to the Soviet refusal to permit its Jews to emigrate to Israel.

Roosevelt was often a severe critic of Eisenhower's foreign policy. She questioned the Administration's decision to send arms to conservative Arab states as a threat to Israel's security. Roosevelt longed for peace in the area, hoping that in the future Israel could offer economic and political guidance to the developing Arab nations. In 1956 she denounced Secretary of State John Foster Dulles's [q.v.] decision not to grant Egyptian President Gamal Abdul Nasser a loan to build the Aswan dam, maintaining that if the money had been given, Nasser would not have been forced to turn to the Soviet Union.

Roosevelt objected to the Administration's tacit position that equated neutralism with pro-Communism, arguing that for a nation such an India to be non-aligned and a democracy would still be in the interest of the U.S. She advised the Administration that an emphasis on social and economic development rather than choosing sides in the Cold War was India's first priority. The former first lady deplored congressional efforts to cut back or deprive India of foreign aid in retaliation for its friendly relations with the Soviet Union. She joined such liberals as Robert Nathan [q.v.] and Chester Bowles [q.v.] in opposing the Eisenhower Administration's reliance on military aid to prevent the expansion of Communism and advocated an emphasis on economic aid.

Roosevelt was troubled by Dulles's unilateralism, and she often asked why he did not use the U.N. in international crises.

Finally, she believed that the Administration did not do enough to seek a nuclear test ban treaty. Joining such Americans as Adlai Stevenson [q.v.], she suggested that the U.S. reduce its testing as a gesture to encourage the Soviet Union to end its testing.

As a leading spokesman for liberal Democrats, Roosevelt advocated the extension of New and Fair Deal programs, the expansion of public housing and slum clearance, increased aid to the agricultural poor and meaningful job training programs for the unemployed. Roosevelt was a particularly vigorous proponent of civil rights and of desegregation.

Roosevelt supported Stevenson for President in 1952 and 1956. She respected his knowledge of foreign affairs; he consulted her often on important matters. In 1956 she enthusiastically worked for him in the primaries, defended him against liberal charges that he was ambivalent on civil rights and devoted many hours to speaking for him during the fall campaign. Following Stevenson's defeat Roosevelt turned her attention to New York State Democratic politics. In conjunction with Herbert Lehman [q.v.] and Thomas Finletter [q.v.], she helped organize a Democratic reform movement to unseat Tammany boss Carmine DeSapio [q.v.] as New York Co. leader. In 1961 they succeeded in destroying his power.

Roosevelt favored Stevenson for President in 1960 but reluctantly accepted John F. Kennedy [q.v.] as the Democratic candidate. After his election he appointed her to advisory commissions on the status of women and on the Peace Corps and reappointed her a delegate to the U.N. Still active until her death in November 1962, Roosevelt wrote her columns and traveled, always advocating peace abroad and liberalism at home. After her death Presidents John Kennedy, Dwight D. Eisenhower and Harry Truman attended her funeral at Hyde Park.

[JB]

For further information:
Joseph Lash, *Eleanor: The Years Alone* (New York, 1972).

ROOSEVELT, KERMIT
b. Feb. 16, 1916; Buenos Aires,
Argentina.
Central Intelligence Agency official

The grandson of Theodore Roosevelt,
Kermit Roosevelt graduated from Harvard
in 1938 and then taught history at Harvard
and the California Institute of Technology.
He served in the Office of Strategic Services during World War II and after the
War joined its successor, the Central Intelligence Agency (CIA), where he became
an expert on Middle Eastern affairs.

According to journalists David Wise and
Thomas Ross, Roosevelt played a leading
role in the 1953 coup that overthrew Iranian Premier Mohammed Mossadegh. In
1951 Mossadegh undercut the power of the
conservative Shah, established contacts with
the country's Communist Party and
nationalized the giant Anglo-Iranian Oil
Co. Fearing that Iran's oil reserves would
flow to the Soviet Union, London and
Washington decided to overthrow Mossadegh and reinstall a pro-Western
government. Working under cover in Iran,
Roosevelt directed the operation. On Aug.
13 the Shah attempted to dismiss Mossadegh. The Premier refused the order and
anti-royalist rioting forced the Shah to flee
the country. During the next few days
Roosevelt organized pro-Shah demonstrations and directed the Shah's forces, which
deposed Mossadegh on Aug. 19.

Roosevelt was deeply involved in the
Suez crisis of 1956. In mid-August he was
sent to Egypt in a vain attempt to persuade
President Gamal Abdul Nasser not to accept
Soviet arms aid. Still hoping to dissuade
Nasser, Secretary of State John Foster Dulles [q.v.] sent Undersecretary of State
George Allen [q.v.] to Egypt with a stern
letter warning that the arms deal could
hand Egypt over to the Communists. Just
before Allen spoke to Nasser, Roosevelt
went to the Egyptian President to discuss
the message. Roosevelt's supporters maintained that he attempted to ease the way
for Allen. Critics, however, said that he
told Nasser to ignore the letter. Nasser
himself confirmed the latter report. Although Roosevelt's role remained unclear,
it prompted charges that the CIA had
undercut official U.S. policy.

Roosevelt resigned from the CIA during
the latter part of the Eisenhower Administration and became government relations director for the Gulf Oil Corp. Gulf named
him a vice president in 1960. Four years
later he formed his own corporation,
Roosevelt and Associates. In 1975 a Senate
Foreign Relations subcommittee reported
that Roosevelt had used his CIA contacts in
Saudi Arabia and Iran in an effort to win
government contracts for Northrop Corp., a
large aircraft manufacturer.

[EWS]

ROSE, ALEX
b. Oct. 15, 1898; Warsaw, Russian Poland
d. Dec. 28, 1976; New York, N.Y.
President, United Hatters, Cap and
Millinery Workers International Union,
1950-76; Vice Chairman, Liberal Party,
1944-76.

Rose left Poland intending to study
medicine in the U.S., but he became a millinery operator after World War I cut him
off from his parents' support. In 1918 Rose,
who had been active in the Labor Zionist
Organization, joined the "Jewish Legion" of
the British Army, serving for two years in
the Middle East. After his return to the
U.S., he defeated a Communist-backed
candidate for secretary-treasurer of his local
in the Cloth, Hat, Cap and Millinery
Workers Union (CHCMW). He became a
union vice president in 1927 and retained
that post when the CHCMW merged with
the United Hatters of North America to
form the United Hatters, Cap and Millinery
Workers International Union (UHCMW) in
1934.

Rose was appointed union president by
the UHCMW executive board in March
1950; later that year he was elected to the
position. As president, he led a successful
45-week strike in 1953-54 against the Hat
Corporation of America in Norwalk, Conn.
Usually, however, Rose strove to work
with manufacturers to bolster the industry's
declining fortunes in the Northeast, the

union's power base. The settlement of an eight-day cap industry strike in July 1958 included an agreement by manufacturers to join the union in sales promotion and in campaigns against cheaper imported and non-union caps.

Under Rose, who wrote in 1949 that "the class struggle is a thing of the past in my union," the UHCMW loaned $250,000 to the Kartiganer Hat Corp. in 1954. A smaller loan to a Baltimore hat firm in 1955 enabled it to resume production. In 1958 the union began to invest in real estate in New York City's garment district to prevent millinery companies from being dispossessed or from sustaining large rent increases. The following year it began what grew to be a $435,000 investment in the Merrimac Hat Corp. of Massachusetts, which began operating under union control in February 1959.

With International Ladies Garment Workers Union President David Dubinsky [q.v.] and others, Rose helped establish the American Labor Party (ALP) in 1936, but they withdrew in 1944 because of Communist influence in the organization. They formed the Liberal Party, and Rose became a vice chairman and key leader of the group. The Party occasionally ran congressional candidates, but the major goal of the organization was to influence the policies of the New York Democratic Party by endorsing those of its nominees who met the Liberals' political standards.

During the 1950s the Party's program included reform of New York State labor legislation, repeal of the Taft-Hartley Act, a higher minimum wage, tax reform at both the state and national level, anti-discrimination legislation, more federal aid for housing programs and increased consumer protection through new and existing state and federal agencies. The Party offered strong support to the U.N., which state Party Chairman A.A. Berle called "the only agency capable of restoring stability" internationally, while it endorsed the basic objectives of American foreign policy in the Cold War.

Rose also played an active role in national labor affairs. In 1957 he chaired the AFL-CIO appeals committee that expelled the International Brotherhood of Teamsters because of corruption within its leadership. Rose advocated the establishment of a "labor FBI" by the Federation to combat the kind of corruption found in the Teamsters union. With other garment union leaders he frequently petitioned the Eisenhower Administration to raise federal minimum wage standards.

Rose eschewed the AFL-CIO's official position of neutrality during the 1960 campaign for the Democratic presidential nomination and endorsed Sen. John F. Kennedy (D, Mass.) [q.v.] soon after the Senator's April victory in the Wisconsin primary. He and special AFL-CIO counsel Arthur Goldberg [q.v.] were the first important labor leaders to do so. Rose called the Kennedy campaign "a public referendum" on Jimmy Hoffa [q.v.], a reference to the role that Robert [q.v.] and John Kennedy played in the downfall of the Teamster leader. United Auto Workers President Walter Reuther [q.v.], also a Kennedy supporter, joined Goldberg and Rose as AFL-CIO liaison representatives at the Los Angeles Democratic Convention in July. The group objected vehemently to Kennedy's choice of Sen. Lyndon B. Johnson (D, Tex.) [q.v.] as his running mate but later helped rally other liberals to the Democratic national ticket.

Rose continued to play a dominant role in the Liberal Party through the 1960s and well into the 1970s. The Party's chief accomplishment during this period was to endorse and help elect John V. Lindsay mayor of New York. [See KENNEDY, JOHNSON, NIXON/FORD Volumes]

[MDB]

ROSENBERG, ETHEL G(REENGLASS)
b. 1915; New York, N.Y.
d. June 19, 1953; Ossining, N.Y.
Convicted espionage agent

Ethel Rosenberg was raised in poverty in Manhattan's East Side. Her youthful interests were in the arts; she performed in the Yiddish theater and sang at small neighborhood gatherings. To contribute to the family income, she held a job at a packing company, where she helped lead a successful strike of women workers. For her organizing efforts she was fired, but she found another job as a stenographer. Ethel became involved in union activities and various radical causes. At a union gathering she first met her husband, Julius.

In 1950 Ethel and her husband were arrested on charges of helping transmit atomic bomb secrets to the Soviet Union during 1944 and 1945. At the trial, beginning in March 1951, the U.S. government accused both Rosenbergs of being primary operatives in an espionage ring that included British physicist Klaus Fuchs, a Russian diplomat and Americans Harry Gold and Morton Sobell [q.v.]. Also accused was David Greenglass, Ethel's brother, who had worked as a machinist in the top-secret Los Alamos, N.M., atomic bomb project during World War II. The prosecution alleged that the Rosenbergs persuaded Greenglass to spirit to them, via Harry Gold, sketches and information on the bomb, which the Rosenbergs then gave to a Soviet diplomat in New York City. Because the USSR was an American ally at the time of the alleged acts, Julius and Ethel were charged with espionage rather than treason. Gold and Greenglass pleaded guilty to the espionage charges, while the Rosenbergs and Sobell maintained their complete innocence. After an unexpectedly short three-week trial, the defendants were convicted as charged and sentenced—Julius and Ethel to the electric chair, Sobell to 30 years in prison. Greenglass and Gold received lesser prison terms. [See TRUMAN Volume]

The trial and its aftermath provoked impassioned responses. Many believed existing government evidence against the Rosenbergs proved their guilt beyond a shadow of a doubt; others were certain Julius and Ethel had been "framed" victims of a political trial in an America swept by anti-Communist hysteria. All over the world people of various political backgrounds formed committees either to protest the Rosenbergs' death sentences or insist on their innocence. In the U.S. a Committee to Secure Justice in the Rosen-

berg Case was formed. These groups gained momentum for their cause when the Rosenbergs' first appeal was rejected in the Court of Appeals in February 1952. Over the next few months the Rosenberg Committee collected over one million dollars, while international protests grew with each newly decreed date of execution.

By early 1953 a number a distinguished scientists were pleading for the Rosenbergs. Dr. Harold Urey, a distinguished nuclear chemist who had been involved in the development of the A-bomb, scored Greenglass's testimony, declaring a man of Greenglass's abilities was "wholly incapable" of transmitting the complex mechanics of atomic weapons. Albert Einstein [q.v.] joined Urey in a plea for clemency.

President Eisenhower was faced with the Rosenbergs' formal clemency plea in February 1953, just weeks after President Harry S. Truman had refused to respond to the plea. Eisenhower described his decision as a difficult one, but he turned down the plea. He believed the evidence pointed clearly to their guilt. Their crime, he said in his formal reply of rejection, "involved the deliberate betrayal of the entire nation and could very well result in the death of many, many thousands of innocent citizens." In his memoirs Eisenhower also expressed the belief that a commutation of the couple's sentences—particularly that of Ethel—would have been an encouragement to current and future spies.

After Eisenhower refused clemency the Rosenbergs' lawyers, led by Emmanuel Bloch, worked feverishly in state and appellate courts and the U.S. Supreme Court to win trial reviews and stays of execution. Public appeals reached a crescendo in June 1953 as the Rosenbergs' third execution date approached. The government of Poland offered the couple asylum. French President Vincent Auriol made a quiet plea for clemency to Eisenhower, as did Nobel Prize-winners Francois Mauriac and Leon Jouhaux. Leftists in Italy were joined in the protests by the right-wing press and Pope Pius XII. Forty members of the British Parliament urged Eisenhower to stop the executions and crowds in Israel accused the U.S. government of anti-Semitism. In

Communist countries pleas for the Rosenbergs were incorporated into vitriolic anti-American statements.

On June 15 the Supreme Court once again refused, by a five-to-four vote, to review the case; marshals set June 18 as the execution date. On June 16 two lawyers who had had no previous connection with the defense appeared before Supreme Court Justice William O. Douglas [q.v.], arguing that the Rosenbergs had been sentenced illegally, in violation of the 1946 Atomic Energy Act. Justice Douglas saw merit in their appeal and granted a stay of execution on June 17. Attorney General Herbert Brownell [q.v.] vigorously protested the stay, and on June 18 Chief Justice Fred M. Vinson [q.v.] took the highly unusual step of calling together the recessed Court to consider Douglas's action. After hearing hours of intense argument, the Court, on June 19, nullified Douglas's order. President Eisenhower refused a second Rosenberg plea for clemency. At 8:00 P.M. that evening Julius and Ethel Rosenberg went to the electric chair, aware as they died of a Justice Department offer to spare their lives if they confessed to crimes of espionage.

Immediately after their deaths there were emotional demonstrations—some of grief, some of satisfaction—scattered over the world. Eight protest strikes were reported in Italy, while 400 demonstrators were arrested in Paris. In New York City 5,000 people gathered to denounce the action and pray.

Public interest in the Rosenberg case continued during the next two decades. Numerous writers and researchers reopened the case in books, and in 1969 the play, *The United States v. Julius and Ethel Rosenberg*, by Donald Freed, portrayed the couple as victims of blind injustice. With the passage of the amended Freedom of Information Act in 1974, defenders of the Rosenbergs were able to obtain many documents from FBI files. While they raised questions about the fairness and legality of the original trial and subsequent court proceedings, the new information revealed as of 1977 did little to settle the question of the Rosenbergs' guilt or inno-

cence. In 1975 FBI Director Clarence Kelley acknowledged that records relating to David Greenglass had been destroyed. In 1977 the Committee to Reopen the Rosenberg Case, led by the Rosenbergs' sons, Michael and Robert Meerpol, sued six government agencies for the release of all files relevent to the espionage case.

[TGD]

For further information:
Louis Nizer, *The Implosion Conspiracy* (New York, 1973).
Walter and Miriam Schneir, *Invitation to an Inquest* (Baltimore, 1973).

ROSENBERG, JULIUS
b. May 12, 1918; New York, N.Y.
d. June 19, 1953; Ossining, N.Y.
Convicted espionage agent

The son of poor Jews, Rosenberg was brought up on New York's Lower East Side. He initially wanted to become a rabbinical student, but in his late teens he committed himself to radical politics. With the encouragement of Ethel Greenglass, whom he first met at a union meeting, he completed his B.S. degree in electrical engineering at the City College of New York in 1939. Soon afterward they married. In 1943 Julius took a civilian job as an engineer with the Army Signal Corps, only to lose the position in 1945 when he was fired for alleged Communist activities. Thereafter he worked in a small machinist's business until he and his wife were arrested in 1950 on charges of helping transmit atomic bomb secrets to the Soviet Union during World War II. [See ROSENBERG, ETHEL Profile]

ROSS, ROBERT TRIPP
b. June 4, 1903; Washington, N.C.
Deputy Assistant Secretary of Defense for Legislative Affairs, March 1954-March 1955; Assistant Secretary of Defense for Legislative and Public Affairs, March 1955-February 1957.

Ross, described as a "pleasant, gregarious, outgoing man," spent much of his early life working in chain drug stores. Marrying shortly after his high school graduation, he left a drug store clerk's job to try to sell Florida real estate. A series of other sales jobs followed until finally Ross moved to New York City and found work as a clerk in a pharmacy of a large hotel. By 1940 he was managing a drugstore in the Jackson Heights section of Queens.

In 1946 Ross ran successfully as a Republican for a seat in the U.S. House. He lost 1948 and 1950 reelection efforts but won a February 1952 special election to fill an unexpired term by emphasizing the issues of "crime, corruption and Communism" in the Truman Administration. Defeated in the November 1952 general election, he accepted the post of Washington, D.C., representative for the New York State Republican Committee in 1953.

Ross was appointed deputy assistant secretary of defense for legislative affairs in March 1954. Nearly one year later he received a promotion to assistant secretary of defense for legislative and public affairs. In late March 1955 Secretary of Defense Charles Wilson [q.v.] issued a memorandum directing that information released by the Defense Department make a "constructive contribution" to the U.S. defense effort. Ross's rigid interpretation of Wilson's order elicited charges of censorship not only from congressional committees and reporters, but also from the Secretaries of the Armed Services and even members of the Joint Chiefs of Staff. The military officials protested that Ross was censoring their speeches to stifle all difference of opinion with the Administration's defense policy.

In November 1955 Rep. John E. Moss (D, Calif.), the chairman of the House Government Operations Subcommittee on Information, announced that he was suspending hearings on government information policies until January 1956, largely because of Ross's refusal to cooperate. During the summer of 1956 the subcommittee charged that the Defense Department's policies were the "most restrictive" of any government agency's. For his part, Ross consistently maintained that "security" was the only grounds on which he withheld information.

Ross again clashed with Congress in Oc-

tober 1956, when he accused three powerful senators of bilking the public for free air transportation from Europe to the U.S. On Oct. 20 he announced that the Air Force was sending two 66-passenger planes to Europe at a round-trip cost of $20,000 merely to bring home Sens. John L. McClellan (D, Ark.) [q.v.], John Stennis (D, Miss.) [q.v.] and Dennis Chavez (D, N.M.) [q.v.]. All three heatedly denied Ross's charges. They claimed they had arranged to return on scheduled military flights and suggested that the Administration made the charges to embarrass the Democratic Party. When McClellan and Stennis subsequently arrived together from Madrid on a regularly scheduled military flight and demanded a retraction of the charges, Ross apologized and conceded that they had never requested special treatment.

Ross's most serious difficulties began in January 1957, when both the Senate Permanent Investigations Subcommittee, led by McClellan, and the House Government Operations Subcommittee, led by Rep. Chet Holifield (D, Calif.) [q.v.], began investigations of conflict-of-interest charges leveled against him. The accusations stemmed from an $834,000 Army contract for wind-resistant trousers awarded to Wynn Enterprises of Knoxville, Tenn., of which Ross's second wife was president. (Ross had been vice president, sales manager and public relations director for the Knoxville branch, although he claimed to have resigned before running for Congress in February 1952.) The more than $12 million in federal contracts awarded Wynn companies during 1951-56, despite allegedly repeated violations of federal labor laws, also increased congressional suspicions.

At congressional hearings Ross denied any conflict of interest or violation of legal or ethical codes but admitted that he had arranged a conference between his brother-in-law, Herman Wynn, and a Marine general. He maintained that this meeting only concerned the quality of some baseball uniforms produced for the Marines by a Wynn company. McClellan's subcommittee also discovered that Ross had remained on the Wynn payroll through at least 1955.

The Assistant Secretary shrugged off the discrepancy between his claimed 1952 resignation and the subcommittee's finding as an "auditor's error."

Faced with the growing pressure of two congressional investigations, Ross resigned on Feb. 14, 1957. Subsequently, McClellan asserted that while Ross had probably done nothing illegal, the question of "whether he did anything improper is a matter of opinion." By mid-March Ross had secured an appointment as assistant commissioner of borough works in Queens.

[RJB]

ROSSITER, CLINTON L(AWRENCE), III

b. Sept. 18, 1917; Philadelphia, Pa.
d. July 11, 1970; Ithaca, N.Y.
Professor of Government, Cornell University, 1954-59; John. L. Senior Professor of American Institutions, 1959-70.

Clinton Rossiter graduated from Cornell University in 1939 and received an M.A. and Ph.D. at Princeton in 1941 and 1942. After service in the Navy during World War II, he received an appointment as instructor in political science at the University of Michigan in 1946. Later in the year he returned to Cornell as assistant professor and remained there for the rest of his career.

Rossiter's early books included *Constitutional Dictatorship: Crisis Government in the Modern Democracies* (1948) and *The Supreme Court and the Commander in Chief* (1951). His *Seedtime of the Republic: The Origin of the American Tradition of Political Liberty*, published in 1953, described the American Revolution as an effort to conserve British liberties and offered a laudatory description of American political institutions and traditions of freedom.

Although Rossiter claimed to be a moderate conservative, in his *Conservatism in America* (1955) he expressed doubt that American conservatism could cohere into a clear form because the U.S. was "a progressive country with a Liberal tradition" and "a liberal [political] mind." He criticized

conservatives who rejected New Deal programs as engaged in a hopeless effort to return to the past. Rossiter suspected that the opposition of conservatives to social welfare measures was often motivated by the desire to subordinate the American ideal of equality to the interests of business.

Rossiter's own conservatism seemed to consist of a desire for gradual, contained progress; a distrust of majoritarianism, of which he saw McCarthyism as a deplorable example; and a wish for leadership by an aristocracy of talent. Many conservatives, particularly those associated with *National Review* magazine, denounced Rossiter's views as virtually indistinguishable from those of liberals. Through the 1950s Rossiter offended conservatives by backing civil rights measures, arguing for world peace and supporting the United Nations.

In *The American Presidency* (1956) Rossiter described in favorable terms the growing power of the national government. His *Parties and Politics* (1960) was a panegyric of the two-party system's effectiveness in providing for peaceful change and articulating the majority will. Rossiter advocated peaceful coexistence with the Soviet Union in *Marxism: The View from America* (1960), asserting that "We must not slide hopelessly into an apocalyptic view of the struggle between their system and ours, lest we slam the door forever on all hopes of an evolution in Communism that would make it possible for East and West to live together in a reasonably peaceful world."

From 1953 to 1960 Rossiter served as consultant to the Ford Foundation's Fund for the Republic. He was consultant to the Rockefeller Foundation from 1956 to 1958 and a contributor to the report of the President's Commission on National Goals, published in 1960.

In the early 1960s Rossiter toured extensively throughout the world as a visiting lecturer on behalf of the State Department. His *Alexander Hamilton and the Constitution* was published in 1964 and his *1787: The Grand Convention* appeared two years later. Rossiter died in Ithaca, N.Y., on July 11, 1970. His *The American Quest, 1790-1860* (1971) appeared posthumously.

[AES]

ROVERE, RICHARD H(ALWORTHY)

b. May 5, 1915; Jersey City, N.J.
Journalist.

The son of an electrical engineer, Richard Rovere grew up in New York City. He attended Bard College in upstate New York and was editor of the school newspaper. Rovere became a Communist in college. After graduation in 1937 he joined the staff of *New Masses*, a radical organ which, he said later, "consistently, indeed slavishly followed the Communist line." "Like many others at the time, I looked at brutal authoritarianism and saw discipline." Rovere quit *New Masses* after the signing of the Nazi-Soviet Pact in August 1939. In the next five years he wrote as an anti-Communist liberal for *The Nation* and *Common Sense*.

In 1944, on the strength of a widely read, critical article he had written in *Harper's* on New York Gov. Thomas E. Dewey, Rovere was hired as a staff writer for *The New Yorker*. In the more than 30 years he wrote for that publication, Rovere became one of the most respected, influential political journalists in America. Early in his association with the magazine, he was chiefly a writer of "Profiles" of colorful individuals, political and non-political. His subjects ranged from New York politicians Newbold Morris and Edward Flynn to journalist John Gunther, memory expert Bruno Furst and litterateur turned meat-packer Henry Blackman Sell. With the beginning of his "Letter From Washington" column in 1948, Rovere concentrated on politics and politicians. There was little evidence of his younger polemical attitude in these detached, analytical accounts of controversial topics. Rovere's reputation rested not on any investigative contributions but on the distinctive style and quality of his reflective analyses.

Rovere's most vivid journalism dealt with personalities: his language came closest to passionate when the subject was the anti-Communist crusader, Sen. Joseph R. McCarthy (R, Wisc.) [*q.v.*]. In his *New Yorker* pieces on McCarthy and his aides were mingled amusement, revulsion, and incredulity. Rovere described his first encounter with McCarthy, during which the Senator introduced him to a formidable stack of documents which was supposed to prove a contention he had been making. Gradually, Rovere said, he realized that the papers McCarthy was showing him were all either irrelevant, contradictory to his own case, or useless. Rovere later coined a phrase descriptive of McCarthy's technique: the "Multiple Untruth." Rovere described this as "a long series of loosely related untruths, or a single untruth with many facets. In either case, the whole is composed of so many parts that anyone wishing to set the record straight will discover that it is utterly impossible to keep all the elements of the falsehood in mind at the same time." By boldly scattering falsehoods and distortions, McCarthy was able to confuse his opponents and keep ahead of the slow-moving process of factual refutation, while enjoying a full measure of publicity from his accusations.

In 1959 Rovere published a popular, controversial character study of McCarthy, *Senator Joe McCarthy*. He characterized the late Wisconsin Senator as a "master of flimflammery" and "the champion liar." "His talents as a demagogue were great," Rovere said, "but he lacked the most necessary and awesome of demagogic gifts—a belief in the sacredness of his own mission." McCarthy was a rare case, "a true cynic and a true hypocrite." "Beyond mischief, he never accomplished anything." With its obsession with the issue of Communists in government, McCarthyism was "a headlong flight from reality. It elevated the ridiculous and ridiculed the important." Rovere concluded his work: "McCarthy offered a powerful challenge to freedom, and he showed us to be more vulnerable than many of us had guessed to a seditious demagogy—as well as less vulnerable than some of us feared."

Rovere wrote noteworthy assessments of the other major political figures of the time. He praised President Harry S. Truman for acting vigorously in the face of staggering crises, in which he showed "moral courage under pressure, even a kind of moral grace." Rovere supported Truman's intervention in Korea: "Aggression had at that moment to be resisted . . . had we failed to respond, the slave world would have been greatly emboldened, the free world greatly dispirited." In July 1953 he cited the U.S.'s action as "the turning point of the world struggle against Communism."

Rovere eulogized Sen. Robert Taft (R, Ohio) [q.v.] as a "man of character." About Vice President Richard Nixon's [q.v.] career Rovere in 1955 wrote that, although Nixon had taken many stands, "there is no discernible pattern to his commitments." He was struck by "the flexibility that suggests an almost total indifference to policy. Nixon appears to be a politician with an advertising man's approach to his work. Policies are products to be sold to the public—this one today, that one tomorrow, depending on the discounts and the state of the market."

Rovere's 1956 appraisal of Dwight D. Eisenhower's performance as President coupled praise for foreign policy with criticism of his domestic actions. Recognizing that "such challenges as he chose to meet he met well," he lauded Eisenhower for fulfilling the urgent tasks of holding together the Western alliance and saving Western civilization "in a spirit of decency and maturity." However Rovere criticized the President's attitude toward the rest of the government as "neglectful." "Once Eisenhower has found a first-class automobile dealer, cotton broker, or razor manufacturer to head a department, he has acted as if the public interest has been satisfied and his own responsibility discharged." The Eisenhower program was nothing more than "a pastiche of pieties," Rovere declared. The Eisenhower Administration "has left the country almost exactly as he found it."

In 1962 and 1971 Rovere wrote retrospective assessments of Eisenhower that took his second term into account. He found the second four years disappointing but reiterated his essential judgment: Eisenhower's "command decisions" in foreign affairs were "generally wise," while his responses to domestic problems were complacent and inadequate. "With hindsight, we can see that practically all of the problems that bedeviled us in the sixties had been worsening in the fifties," Rovere said in his 1971 piece. He took pains to refute an increasingly popular liberal characterization of Eisenhower as a "political genius." Rovere contended that this assessment arose from the simple fact that the U.S. did not go to war while he was President, a circumstance Rovere held owed as much to luck as good management.

In 1962 Rovere produced The American Establishment and Other Reports, Opinions and Speculations. The title essay contained a semi-satiric listing of those elite institutions and individuals most influential in American life. During the 1960s he also published The Goldwater Caper (1965) and Waist Deep in the Big Muddy: Personal Reflections on 1968 (1968). The latter reflected his growing disgust with the Vietnam war, an enterprise that "threatens all mankind, that can liberate no one," and that "becomes daily more unconscionable."

[TO]

For further information:
Richard Rovere, Affairs of State: The Eisenhower Years (New York, 1956).
———, Arrivals and Departures: A Journalist's Memoirs (New York, 1976).
———, "Eisenhower Revisited—A Political Genius? A Brilliant Man?" in The New York Times Magazine (Feb. 7, 1971).

ROWE, JAMES H(ENRY), JR.
b. June 1, 1909; Butte, Mont.
Attorney.

Rowe graduated from Harvard law school in 1934 and clerked for Supreme Court Justice Oliver Wendell Holmes the following year. From 1935 to 1938 he worked for various New Deal agencies. Rowe served as an assistant to President Roosevelt's son James during the 1936 presidential campaign. A year later he joined the White House staff first as a secretary to the President and from 1939 to 1941 as an administrative assistant to the President. Rowe served as an assistant attorney general from 1941 to 1945. In 1946 he left government to form a Washington law firm with Thomas Corcoran, another

Roosevelt aide. During the Truman Administration Rowe advised the President on how to deal with the Republican-dominated Congress and helped plan strategy for the 1948 presidential campaign.

During the Eisenhower Administration Rowe advised such Democratic leaders as Sen. Lyndon B. Johnson (D, Tex.) [q.v.], Adlai Stevenson [q.v.] and Sen. Hubert Humphrey (D, Minn.) [q.v.]. He was particularly close to Johnson, whom he urged to speak out in opposition to Administration programs. The Senator refused, preferring to cooperate with Eisenhower rather than become a vocal opposition leader. Rowe also served as an intermediary between Stevenson and Johnson. Beginning in 1954 he advised Stevenson to court Johnson because the Senator's help would be needed to win the 1956 Democratic presidential nomination. Rowe's advice paid off; after initial wavering, Johnson endorsed Stevenson.

Rowe initially supported Johnson for the 1960 presidential nomination. However, after Johnson assured him in 1959 that he would not be a candidate, Rowe supported Humphrey. The Minnesota Senator valued his advice despite warnings from supporters that Rowe backed the candidate only to divide Party liberals. They believed that he was trying to create a three-way deadlock between Stevenson, Sen. John F. Kennedy (D, Mass.) [q.v.] and Humphrey so that the Convention would draft Johnson.

In late 1959 Rowe worked out the strategy for Humphrey's upcoming campaign. Because Humphrey was relatively unknown outside the Midwest and had only limited funds, Rowe urged him to devote all his time to campaigning in selected primaries. With enough victories Humphrey could obtain a minimum of 150 to 200 delegate votes and thus enter the Convention as a strong candidate in a floor fight. Rowe's plan failed when Humphrey lost the Wisconsin and West Virginia primaries. Following the West Virginia defeat Rowe urged the Senator to continue his campaigning, but Humphrey withdrew from the race. Rowe then encouraged Johnson to seek the nomination. At the Convention he was Johnson's leading floor manager.

Rowe remained Johnson's confidant throughout the 1960s. In 1964 he was part of the inner circle that directed Johnson's presidential campaign, and he was instrumental in convincing Johnson not to offer the vice presidential nomination to Robert F. Kennedy [q.v.] but to Humphrey. In late 1967 Rowe began planning Johnson's 1968 presidential campaign. Following the Tet offensive of February 1968, Rowe was a member of the Senior Advisory Group on Vietnam that urged Johnson not to escalate the war further. Johnson followed Rowe's advice and announced at the end of March that he was limiting the bombing of North Vietnam. He surprised many people, including his close friend Rowe, by also announcing his withdrawal from the presidential race. During the 1970s Rowe continued to be active in Democratic politics.

[JB]

RUSK, DEAN
b. Feb. 9, 1909; Cherokee County, Ga.
President, Rockefeller Foundation,
1952-61.

The son of a country school teacher and Presbyterian minister, Dean Rusk started school in second grade, having taught himself to read from his brother's textbooks. Graduating from Davidson College in North Carolina in 1931, he attended St. John's College at Oxford University as a Rhodes Scholar. In 1934 Rusk became an associate professor of government at Mills College in California and in 1938 dean of the faculty. During the same period he studied law at the University of California at Berkeley. Enlisting as an infantry reserve captain in 1940, Rusk rose to the rank of colonel by the time of his discharge at the end of World War II. He participated in the first and third Burma campaigns and was deputy chief of staff to Col. Joseph Stilwell.

After the War Rusk began his career in the State Department. As director of the office of special political affairs from 1947 to 1950, he was directly involved in policy concerning the establishment of the state of Israel. Rusk was appointed assistant secretary of state for Far Eastern affairs in 1950.

He supported American military intervention in Korea although he opposed any invasion of China. Rusk left the State Department to become president of the Rockefeller Foundation in 1952.

As president of the Rockefeller Foundation during the 1950s, Rusk directed the distribution of about $250 million to developing nations in Asia, Africa and Latin America to help them improve their methods of agriculture and promote health and social welfare. Under Rusk's leadership Rockefeller Foundation scientists promoted the "green revolution," improving the yields of rice and producing new varieties of rust-resistant wheat. The Foundation also funded research by the National Academy of Sciences in 1955 and 1956 on the health hazards of nuclear fallout and later research by Cornell University, the University of Chicago and the Social Science Research Council to ensure the safety of the peaceful use of atomic energy. In 1956 Rusk traveled to Hungary and Austria, where he directed the distribution of aid to Hungarian scholars and scientists.

As head of the Rockefeller Foundation, Rusk also played an important role in safeguarding academic freedom. In 1954 the Republican majority on the House Special Committee to Investigate Tax-Exempt Foundations charged that the Rockefeller, Carnegie, Ford and other foundations "directly supported 'subversion' by supporting attacks upon our social and governmental system and financing the promotion of socialism and collectivist ideas." The three-member majority—Reps. B. Carroll Reece (R, Tenn.), Jesse P. Wolcott (R, Mich.) and Angier L. Goodwin (R, Mass.)—believed the foundations had "propagandized blindly for the United Nations"; had supported assignment of articles by the *Encyclopedia of the Social Sciences* to Communist and other leftist writers; and had promoted excessive moral relativism in research. To the Committee's majority, the most shocking example of this was the Rockefeller Foundation's support of the Alfred Kinsey [*q.v.*] studies on sex. Responding to these charges, Dean Rusk denied the Rockefeller Foundation was infiltrated by Communists. He emphasized that

the Foundation would never try to control the type of research it funded and would fight any attempt by the government to use taxation to infringe on freedom of thought.

As Secretary of State during the Kennedy Administration, Rusk generally played an advisory role, allowing the President to determine policy. Initially, Rusk favored keeping the United States out of Vietnam, but after 1963 he came to support U.S. involvement. During the Johnson Administration he played a leading role in formulating and defending American Vietnam policy. After leaving the government in January 1969, he became a professor of law at the University of Georgia. [See KENNEDY, JOHNSON Volumes]

[RSG]

For further information:
Robert Shaplen, *Toward the Well-Being of Mankind* (New York, 1964).

RUSSELL, RICHARD B(REVARD), JR.
b. Nov. 2, 1897; Winder, Ga.
d. Jan. 21, 1971; Washington, D.C.
Democratic Senator, Ga., 1933-71;
Chairman, Armed Services Committee, 1951-53, 1955-69.

Russell graduated from the Agricultural and Mechanical School in Powder Springs, Ga., in 1914 and four years later received an LL.B. degree from the University of Georgia. He was in the Naval Reserve during World War I. Subsequently Russell practiced law for a short time and then won election as a county attorney. In 1921 he was elected to the Georgia Assembly, and he served as its speaker from 1927 until 1930. That November Russell was elected governor. He was sworn in the following January by his father, the chief justice of Georgia. Having promised economy in government during his campaign, he reduced his salary, consolidated executive departments, bureaus and commissions and established a state purchasing department.

In November 1932 Russell won an election to fill a vacant Senate seat. He supported most New Deal legislation but opposed measures aimed at altering race relations in the South, leading filibusters against anti-lynching bills in 1935 and 1937. He backed President Franklin D. Roosevelt's foreign policy in the years preceding American entry into World War II, favoring an end to the mandatory arms embargo and the establishment of Selective Service in 1940 and voting for lend-lease aid in 1941.

Like many other Southerners on Capitol Hill, Russell became an opponent of social welfare programs after the War. He was a leader of Southern opposition to President Harry S. Truman's 1948 civil rights platform and was among the many Democrats of various political views who favored Gen. Dwight D. Eisenhower for the Democratic presidential nomination that year. But Eisenhower disavowed interest in the presidency, and Russell, as the leader of the Southern bloc in the Senate, was placed in nomination at the National Democratic Convention. As a regional candidate, however, he received only 263 votes to Truman's 947½. Russell did not join the Dixiecrats who bolted the Party and nominated South Carolina Gov. Strom Thurmond [q.v.] for the presidency. He gave a *pro forma* endorsement of Truman.

In 1951 Russell became chairman of the Armed Services Committee. During that year he headed a joint Armed Services and Foreign Relations Committee investigation of President Truman's dismissal of Gen. Douglas MacArthur. His impartial, low-keyed and expeditious handling of the probe was credited with helping to defuse an explosive issue. [See TRUMAN Volume]

In 1952 Russell actively sought the Democratic presidential nomination, presenting himself as a conservative advocate of "the spiritual life and the simple faith and fullness which sustained our forefathers." He declared that "I do not think this dangerous period is the time to strike out on new adventures that could lead this country down the road to socialism." Attempting to broaden the base of his appeal, Russell advocated repeal of the Taft-Hartley Act (although he had voted to pass the law over President Truman's veto). However, he remained a sectional

candidate, running third on all three National Convention ballots, receiving a high total of 294 votes on the second ballot. Russell endorsed Adlai E. Stevenson [q.v.], the Party's nominee, in October but took little part in the campaign.

An intelligent, unpretentious and courteous man entirely devoted to public life (he never married), Russell was one of the most respected members of the Senate and was widely regarded as embodying the best traditions of the upper chamber. Many observers believed that he would have become President had he not been a Southerner, and Russell himself was somewhat embittered by his unsuccessful presidential effort in 1952. Subsequently he decided to forego a national political role and devote his abilities, including his formidable parliamentary skill, to leading the powerful bloc of Southern committee and subcommittee chairmen in the Senate. In 1953 he passed over an opportunity to become minority leader and instead helped Sen. Lyndon B. Johnson (D, Tex.) [q.v.] obtain that post.

Russell's leadership of the Southern bloc was most apparent in his role in the fight against integration and civil rights measures. In his capacity as a defender of the Southern system of race relations, he fought vigorously against all federal efforts to intrude upon Southern society. Yet in the 1950s Russell was prepared to make strategic compromises rather than take hopeless, diehard stands.

In 1956 Sen. Strom Thurmond (D, S.C.) drafted a Declaration of Constitutional Principles, popularly known as the "Southern Manifesto," that endorsed the doctrine of state interposition and declared the Supreme Court's 1954 school desegregation decision unconstitutional and illegal. But when a number of moderate Southern congressmen refused to sign the Manifesto, a committee headed by Russell wrote a new draft that excluded those clauses.

The following year, before the Senate considered an Administration civil rights bill aimed particularly at enabling blacks to vote, Russell warned that the measure would be "vigorously resisted by a resolute group of senators." He and his allies succeeded in eliminating clauses giving the President power to use troops to enforce existing civil rights laws and permitting the Attorney General to institute civil action for preventive relief in civil rights cases. They also added a clause guaranteeing a jury trial in contempt cases against persons interfering with the exercise of the right to vote.

On August 24 Russell declared that Southern leaders were still "unalterably opposed" to the bill. Reflecting a recognition that the compromise was the best the Southerners could hope to obtain, he added, however, that "there was no collective agreement that we would undertake to talk the proposition to death." On Aug. 28 Thurmond conducted a record 24-hour filibuster against the bill. Russell said that this action could have created an "unparalleled disaster" by beginning a move to restore provisions that had been eliminated by the Southerners. He denounced Thurmond, asserting that "if I had undertaken a filibuster for personal political aggrandizement, I would have forever reproached myself for being guilty of a form of treason against the people of the South."

In 1960 Russell and 17 other members of the Southern bloc succeeded, with the aid of the filibuster, in weakening Administration proposals to strengthen the 1957 Civil Rights Act. A plan for court-appointed referees to help blacks register and vote was amended to reduce the power of the referees. A provision enabling the federal government to pay half the costs incurred by local schools for desegregation was killed, as was an amendment strengthening anti-job discrimination provisions applying to companies with federal contracts. As in 1957 Russell denounced the final version of the civil rights bill but did not attempt to block its passage.

As chairman of the Armed Services panel, Russell opposed Eisenhower Administration attempts to cut the military budget by stressing nuclear deterrence over conventional forces. During Senate debate over a defense appropriations bill in 1955, he stated that Gen. Matthew B. Ridgway [q.v.] had asserted that Army manpower cuts proposed by the Administration would "endanger national security." However, the

reduction was not restored by Congress.

Early in 1956, following indications that the Soviet Union had made significant advances in developing long-range bombers, Russell appointed Sen. Stuart Symington (D, Mo.) [q.v.] chairman of a special five-man panel to investigate air power. The Democratic majority was critical of Eisenhower Administration defense cuts and warned that the USSR might soon have superiority in the air. Later in the year Russell joined a 13-12 majority on the Appropriations Committee in voting for an increase in Air Force funds to $800 million above Administration requests. After Secretary of Defense Charles Wilson [q.v.] described the increase as "phony," Russell, who as a senior senator was jealous of congressional prerogatives, denounced the Secretary for having "treated the Congress with disdain . . . at times almost with contempt. . . ." He charged that Wilson "has sought to intimidate the officers of the Armed Services from fully expressing their opinions to, and advising with, the Congress. . . ." Most of the increase in Air Force funds was retained in the final bill signed by the President.

Russell was often a critic of what he regarded as excessive foreign aid expenditures, and he insisted on careful scrutiny of Administration requests for aid funds. In 1957 he presented the major Senate obstacle to passage of the Eisenhower Doctrine for the Middle East. Russell proposed that passage of a provision for $200 million in economic aid to Middle East nations should be postponed until Congress made its annual study of the entire foreign aid program. His amendment, however, was defeated on the floor, 28 to 58.

In 1956 Russell, who had a close political and personal relationship with Sen. Johnson, backed Johnson's bid for the Democratic presidential nomination. Four years later a rift developed between them over Johnson's efforts, as majority leader, to pass the 1960 civil rights bill. The rift widened when Johnson accepted the Democratic vice presidential nomination after the Party's National Convention had adopted a strong civil rights platform that included implied support for peaceful sit-in demonstrations against segregated lunch counters. Russell initially declined to back the national ticket but gave his endorsement after receiving a personal appeal from Johnson.

Russell was a formidable but declining figure during the 1960s. He refused to compromise on President Johnson's civil rights bills, probably because they were far stronger than the 1957 and 1960 Eisenhower Administration measures. As a result, he suffered stinging defeats. Russell had misgivings about American involvement in Vietnam, but he maintained that since a commitment had been made, all necessary military force should be used to win the war. He believed that similar conflicts should be avoided in the future. In 1969 he gave up his chairmanship of the armed Services panel to become head of the Appropriations Committee.

Russell died of respiratory insufficiency on Jan. 21, 1971. [See KENNEDY, JOHNSON, NIXON/FORD Volumes]

[MLL]

RUSTIN, BAYARD
b. March 17, 1910: West Chester, Pa.
Civil rights leader

An illegitimate child raised by his Quaker grandparents, Rustin studied at Wilberforce College, Cheney State Teachers College and the College of the City of New York. In 1936 he joined the Young Communist League because he believed it was committed to peace and racial equality. However, he broke with the party in 1941 when, after the Nazi invasion of the Soviet Union, it abandoned its opposition to World War II and subordinated social protest to the cause of defeating Germany.

Soon afterward Rustin became a socialist and joined the Fellowship of Reconciliation (FOR), a nondenominational, pacifist religious group that opposed the war and racial injustice. As Roosevelt's director of race relations, he helped plan a march on Washington in 1941 to demand fair employment practices in the nation's defense industries. The march was canceled when Roosevelt issued an executive order banning racial discrimination by defense con-

tractors. In the same year Rustin helped found the Congress of Racial Equality (CORE). From 1943 to 1945 he was jailed as a conscientious objector. Upon his release he became chairman of the Free India Committee, and three years later he went to India to study Gandhi's nonviolent protest. In 1947 Rustin participated in CORE's first Freedom Ride into the South. At about the same time he became director of the Committee Against Discrimination in the Armed Forces, which helped secure President Truman's 1948 executive order barring discrimination in the services. [See TRUMAN Volume]

Rustin resigned his post with FOR in 1953 to become executive director of the pacifist War Resisters League. Five years later he traveled to England to help the Campaign for Nuclear Disarmament organize its first Aldermaston to London "ban the bomb" peace march, which took place in 1959. In 1960 Rustin was arrested in France for protesting atomic tests in the Sahara.

From 1955 to 1964 Rustin served as chief tactician of the civil rights movement. In 1955 he helped Martin Luther King, Jr., [q.v.] organize the Montgomery, Ala., bus boycott, and he played a significant role in the formation of King's philosophy of nonviolence. Rustin stressed the political advantages of peaceful direct action. In October 1956 he wrote that "insofar as the Negro retains the nonviolent approach, he will be able to win white sympathy and frustrate the aims of the White Citizens Council [white supremacists]. . . ." If white racists succeeded in provoking blacks to violence, Rustin contended, "Negroes will lose their moral initiative, liberals will become even more frightened and inactive and a deeper wedge will be driven between white and black workers." He also asserted that ongoing nonviolent direct action would exert immediate economic and social pressure on the South and was more important than "a one-shot performance at the polls in November."

In 1957, at King's request, Rustin drew up plans for the organization of Southern Christian Leadership Conference, which advocated racial equality through nonviolent means. That year he also wrote a series of statements used by King and the Rev. Ralph Abernathy [q.v.] at a meeting with Vice President Richard M. Nixon [q.v.]. They included the assertions that federal action would be needed to end racial discrimination and that neither political party had been sufficiently active in promoting civil rights. They also demanded that President Eisenhower make an appeal to the nation on behalf of racial equality; and that Nixon make a trip to the South and "speak out in moral terms" for civil rights in general and voting rights in particular.

In June 1960 Rustin drafted a letter which King sent to both national parties proposing action on civil rights. It called for them to repudiate the segregationists within their ranks; to reduce, in accordance with the 14th Amendment, the congressional representation of areas denying blacks the right to vote; to explicitly endorse the Supreme Court's 1954 school desegregation decision as both morally correct and the law of the land; and to oppose colonialism in Africa. The letter also urged Congress to include in the civil rights bill then under consideration a section empowering the federal government to bring suits on behalf of blacks denied civil rights and to frame the bill so as to place responsibility for the protection of black voting rights in the hands of the President rather than the Southern courts.

Rustin organized the August 1963 March on Washington for Jobs and Freedom. He opposed the black nationalist tendencies of the mid-1960s, calling instead for an alliance of organized labor, blacks and liberals within the Democratic Party. In 1964 Rustin became executive director of the newly created A. Philip Randolph Institute and in that post attempted to strengthen ties between blacks and the trade union movement. [See KENNEDY, JOHNSON, NIXON/ FORD Volumes]

[MLL]

For further information:
David L. Lewis, *King: A Critical Biography* (New York, 1970).
Bayard Rustin, *Down the Line* (Chicago, 1971).

SALISBURY, HARRISON E(VANS)
b. Nov. 14, 1908; Minneapolis, Minn.
Journalist.

Harrison Salisbury began his career in journalism as editor of the University of Minnesota student newspaper and part-time reporter for the *Minneapolis Journal*. Following graduation in 1930 he began his 18 year association with the United Press International (UPI) during which time he served as its correspondent in Chicago, Washington and New York. During World War II he managed the UPI London bureau and then covered the Soviet Union and the War on the Eastern front. In 1944 Salisbury returned to the United States to become UPI's foreign news editor.

In 1949 Salisbury joined the *New York Times* as its Moscow bureau chief. For the next five years he wrote about the Soviet Union's internal changes caused by Stalin's policies and the pressures of the Cold War. In September 1954 he requested a transfer from Moscow. After returning to the United States, Salisbury published his most important articles in a 14-part series entitled "Russia Re-viewed." Salisbury won the 1955 Pulitzer Prize for this candid appraisal of the Soviet Union. The articles were published in a book entitled *American in Russia* (1954).

The book included a large amount of narrative material on the Soviet life few Americans saw. He carefully described the customs and attitudes of the diverse nationalities which made up the Soviet Union and gave testimony that ethnic nationalism had not died with the Revolution. One of Salisbury's most startling conclusions was that Stalin might have been murdered "by a group of his close associates who now run Russia." If he was, Salisbury claimed, this act saved the lives of thousands of Russians because the dictator contemplated another purge.

Salisbury took what he termed a "realistic position" on relations with post-Stalin Russia. He believed that coexistence with the Soviet Union was possible. However, he cautioned that the U.S. must remain militarily strong "for to be second best in a nuclear war was unthinkable folly." He saw a possible danger to improved relations when young Soviet army officers, with little contact with the West, came to power. Salisbury believed the leadership of the Soviet Union displayed a new flexibility that was not met by the U.S. In his view, patience, Yankee common sense and the application of a little "honey as well as vinegar to the critical joints" of the Communist regime might enable the two superpowers to survive in peace. He envisioned an era of coexistence that could materialize if courage and goodwill were practiced by both sides.

Following his return to the U.S., Salisbury worked as the *Times's* New York City correspondent. He remained one of the leading American experts on foreign affairs and lectured extensively on this topic. In 1957 he visited Bulgaria and Albania, nations virtually closed to most Americans. The following year he was the second American reporter to travel through Mongolia since World War II. In 1959 he returned to the Soviet Union.

In 1952 Salisbury joined the editorial staff of the *Times*. He held a number of top level positions with the paper until his retirement in 1973. Salisbury traveled to North Vietnam to inspect the consequences of American bombing campaigns there during 1966. His claims that American air attacks inflicted high casualties among civilians created a stir in Washington, because President Lyndon Johnson had denied any intention of bombing civilian targets. Salisbury described his experiences in Hanoi in his book, *Behind the Lines* (1967). [See JOHNSON Volume]

[JB]

SALK, JONAS E(DWARD)
b. Oct. 28, 1914, New York, N.Y.
Professor of Epidemiology and Preventive Medicine, University of Pittsburgh, 1947-63.

Salk received his B.S. from the City College of New York in 1934 and received his M.D. from New York University in 1939. Three years later he won a research fellow-

ship in epidemiology at the University of Michigan, where he helped develop anti-influenza vaccines. During and after World War II, Salk served as a consultant on epidemic diseases, first to the War Department and then to the Secretary of the Army. He was appointed professor at the University of Pittsburgh and director of its Virus Research Laboratory in 1947.

During the late-1940s Salk worked on the development of an effective vaccine against poliomyelitis. Following successful tests on 100 children and adults, he announced his results at a conference of the National Institute for Infantile Paralysis and in the *Journal of the American Medical Association* in March 1953.

Salk became a national hero in April 1955, when a University of Michigan report, released on the 10th anniversary of the death of polio victim Franklin Roosevelt, demonstrated that a massive test of the vaccine had been a success. Later that month six pharmaceutical companies received federal licenses to manufacture and destribute the vaccine.

The nationwide vaccination program became the focus of political controversy. In May the Eisenhower Administration proposed that Congress appropriate $28 million in grants to states to vaccinate needy children. A rival proposal, introduced in June by Senate Labor and Public Welfare Committeee Chairman Lister Hill (D, Ala.) [*q.v.*], called for $135 million to provide free vaccine for all children. The American Medical Association (AMA) supported the Administration bill, while a National Foundation for Infantile Paralysis official gave implied approval to the Hill proposal. Hill's measure won congressional endorsement and was signed by Eisenhower in August.

Although marred by defective vaccines, the program was overwhelmingly successful. In June 1956 Salk told an AMA meeting that 100% prevention of polio was possible through the administration of vaccine booster shots. Between 1955 and 1961 paralytic polio cases averaged 2,000 a year compared with 20,000 to 30,000 cases a year before the vaccine's widespread use.

During the late-1950s and early-1960s, Salk worked on a single vaccine to stimulate immunity to several virus diseases simultaneously. In June 1961 the AMA adopted a resolution recommending the massive use of an oral live-virus polio vaccine developed by Albert Sabin as "offering longer protection" than the dead-virus Salk vaccine. Salk challenged the recommendation, describing it as "questionable." He became director of the Salk Institute for Biological Studies in LaJolla, Calif., in 1963.

[MDB]

SALTONSTALL, LEVERETT
b. Sept. 1, 1892; Chestnut Hill, Mass.
Republican Senator, Mass., 1944-67.

The scion of one of Massachusett's oldest, wealthiest and most politically prominent families, Leverett Saltonstall was educated at private schools and at Harvard University. After graduation from Harvard law school in 1917 and service in World War I, he practiced with a family legal firm in Boston. Saltonstall first entered local politics as an alderman in Newton, Mass., then rose quickly in the Republican Party, attaining the governorship in 1938. In 1944 Saltonstall was elected to fill the unexpired Senate term of Henry Cabot Lodge, Jr. [q.v.], who had resigned to return to Army service.

Although he generally voted against President Harry S. Truman's Fair Deal legislation, Saltonstall's support of foreign aid and international cooperation earned him a reputation as a liberal. He was an early opponent of what he believed were the excesses of Sen. Joseph McCarthy's (R, Wisc.) [q.v.] anti-Communist campaign and strongly opposed McCarthy's attacks on Secretary of State Dean Acheson [q.v.] and Secretary of Defense George C. Marshall. As a member of the internationalist wing of the national GOP, he was an early supporter of Dwight D. Eisenhower's presidential candidacy before the 1952 Republican National Convention. [See TRUMAN Volume]

During the Eisenhower years Saltonstall held the post of Senate Republican whip. Considered the most liberal member of the Party's three-man leadership in the upper house, Saltonstall was more sympathetic to the Administration's program during the Republican-controlled 83rd Congress (1953-55) than conservative Majority Leader William Knowland (R, Calif.) [q.v.] and Policy Committee Chairman Homer Ferguson (R, Mich.) [q.v.]. He strongly opposed the Bricker amendment, designed to limit the President's treaty-making powers. As the ranking Republican on the Armed Services Committee and Committee chairman in 1953 and 1954, Saltonstall backed the White House's foreign aid requests.

Saltonstall continued to oppose McCarthy during the 1950s but was cautious in approving motions to censure the Wisconsin Republican. Running for reelection in 1954 he backed efforts to delay consideration of the Watkins Committee report, recommending McCarthy's censure, until after the campaign. However, when the censure vote was taken in December 1954, he voted for the motion. Despite his position in the Senate hierarchy, Saltonstall generally avoided controversy and exerted little influence in the upper house, earning instead a reputation as a cautious, moderate legislator and an effective promoter of his state's fishing, electronics and military interests.

During the Kennedy and Johnson Administrations, Saltonstall maintained a moderately liberal voting record and a relatively low public profile. Pressure from the Massachusetts Republican Party, which supported the burgeoning political aspirations of state Attorney General Edward Brooke, led Saltonstall to retire from the Senate in 1967 in order to allow Brooke to seek his seat. [See KENNEDY, JOHNSON Volumes]

[TLH]

SARNOFF, DAVID
b. Feb. 27, 1891; Uzlian, Russia.
d. Dec. 12, 1971; New York, N.Y.
Chairman of the Board, Radio Corporation of America, 1947-71.

David Sarnoff emigrated from Byelorussia at the age of nine. To help support his family, settled in a Brooklyn slum, Sarnoff hawked newspapers, delivered for a butcher and sang in a synagogue. Following his father's death in 1906, he quit high school to work as a messenger boy for a cablegram company.

During the next three decades Sarnoff rose from messenger boy to board chairman of one of America's largest corporations. Teaching himself Morse code, Sarnoff became a radio telegraph operator for the American Marconi Co. In his spare time he studied all aspects of radio electronics. Sarnoff gained national attention in April 1912, when his was the only radio receiver able to take signals from the sinking luxury liner *Titanic*. The episode awoke millions to radio's potential and resulted in promotions for Sarnoff. In 1915 he became general manager of American Marconi. Radio Corporation of America (RCA) acquired Marconi in 1919 and made Sarnoff vice president the following year. To increase the market for RCA radio receivers, Sarnoff persuaded RCA to organize what proved to be the country's first successful commercial radio network, the National Broadcasting Company (NBC). RCA profited greatly from Sarnoff's vision, both through the manufacture of radio sets and the sale of advertising time for NBC radio programs. Sarnoff became RCA president in 1930 and board chairman in 1947. That year RCA's income reached about $300 million. (RCA had earned $2 million in 1920, Sarnoff's first full year with the company.) *Forbes Magazine* listed Sarnoff as one of America's "Fifty Foremost Business Leaders" in 1947.

As in the case of radio, Sarnoff proved the leading promoter of commercial television and RCA the ultimate beneficiary. In 1923 he predicted the advent of television and, seven years later, of color TV. Beginning in the 1930s, long before TV became commercially feasible, RCA invested some $50 million in television. It inaugurated regular telecasts at the 1939 World's Fair. However, technical problems and World War II delayed commercial TV until the late-1940s. During the early years of the new medium, RCA-NBC led the trade in profits and station access. In 1955 the corporation reported netting $1 billion from the sales, royalties and services of television. Sarnoff's unquestioned faith in television's eventual significance reflected his lifelong belief in research and development. RCA led the communications field in the number of patents granted. Between 1950 and 1961 Sarnoff committed an estimated $130 million into color TV, while his rivals hesitated. In 1958 RCA introduced the first stereo records. The same year it entered electronic data processing, a field then effectively dominated by International Business Machines Corp. In four years RCA spent $100 million on the project. The investment illustrated Sarnoff's recognition of the technological links between communications research and fields unrelated to entertainment. It also marked the beginning of RCA's transformation into a conglomerate.

Like many corporation executives, Sarnoff enjoyed some influence at the Eisenhower White House. (During the 1944 Normandy invasion Sarnoff had served as Gen. Eisenhower's chief communications officer.) Beginning in 1953, Sarnoff advised Eisenhower on cold war strategy. Chairman of the Citizens Advisory Committee on Utilization of Manpower in the Armed Services, he recommended in February 1953 an "at least 10%" cut in the defense budget. He declared that a minimum of $5 billion could be saved annually. The panel's report anticipated the Administration's "New Look" defense posture. In a 1955 essay Sarnoff praised the intercontinental ballistic missile system. The same year, he recommended the creation of a cabinet-level propaganda chief, delegated to win the Cold War through mass communications. In that spirit RCA's Sarnoff Research Center created special Radio Free Europe receivers, unbreakable and incapable of being jammed.

Sarnoff retired as RCA's chief executive officer in 1966 in favor of his son Robert, whom he had made head of NBC in 1955. He remained board chairman, but his involvement in management declined. After a prolonged illness he died in December 1971.

[JLB]

For further information:
Carl Dreher, *Sarnoff, An American Success* (New York, 1977).
Eugene Lyons, *David Sarnoff* (New York, 1966).
David Sarnoff, *Looking Ahead* (New York, 1968).

SAULNIER, RAYMOND J(OSEPH)
b. Sept. 20, 1908; Hamilton, Mass.
Chairman, Council of Economic Advisers, December 1956-January 1961.

Raymond Saulnier received a B.S. in economics from Middlebury College in Vermont in 1929 and an M.A. from Tufts University in 1931. He earned his Ph.D. at Columbia University in 1938, having written his thesis on monetary theory. He had joined the Columbia economics faculty in 1934 and had served as an instructor at Columbia College until 1938, when he moved over to Barnard College as an assistant professor; he became a full professor in 1949. Saulnier was an authority on banking and mortgage finance: among his publications were *Industrial Banking Companies and their Credit Practices* (1940) and *Urban Mortgage Lending by Life Insurance Companies* (1956).

In 1946 Saulnier became director of the financial research division of the National Bureau of Economic Research, where his Columbia colleague, Dr. Arthur Burns [q.v.] was director of research. When Burns, went to Washington as chairman of the Council of Economic Advisers (CEA) in 1953, he named Saulnier a special consultant to the CEA. President Eisenhower made him a member of the Council in April 1955 and in November 1956 appointed him to succeed Burns as chairman.

According to *Fortune* magazine, Saulnier was "a trifle more conservative than Burns" but did not enjoy the "intimate kind of rapport" his predecessor had had with the President. Particularly at the outset of his tenure as CEA chairman, Saulnier's influence in the high economic policymaking councils of the Eisenhower Administration did not equal that of Secretary of the Treasury George Humphrey [q.v.] or Eisenhower's personal economic adviser Gabriel Hauge [q.v.]. *Newsweek* reported in March 1958 that Saulnier was considered by politicians on Capitol Hill to be less forceful than either Burns or the last Democratic CEA chairman, Leon Keyserling [q.v.].

Nevertheless, Eisenhower depended on Saulnier for advice of a technical and predictive nature, and gradually the economist's counsel acquired greater weight in the White House. Most concerned with the stability of the business cycle, Saulnier was less inclined to regard inflation as the paramount economic problem than Hauge, Secretaries of the Treasury George Humphrey and Robert Anderson [q.v.] and the chairman of the Federal Reserve Board, William McChesney Martin [q.v.]. For most of 1957 he argued unsuccessfully against the Federal Reserve's "tight money" policy. In Saulnier's view the economic indicators called for a stimulus, but the Federal Reserve raised the rediscount rate in August from 3% to 3.5%. In November, however, in the face of a deepening economic recession, the Federal Reserve lowered the rediscount rate. In the next few months it also lowered bank reserve requirements in an effort to shore up the sagging economy by making lending money more available.

For his part Saulnier battled within the Administration for a more stimulative fiscal policy against budget cutting pressures from the Treasury and the Budget Bureau. As the 1957-58 recession worsened, Saulnier's case against a budget surplus for fiscal 1959 appeared more cogent. The Soviet Union's launching of the *Sputnik* satellite in October 1957 spurred the movement behind stepped-up military spending, while Saulnier also succeeded in gaining more funds for school and highway construction. He also favored lengthening the duration of unemployment insurance and stimulating private housing investment by providing more liberal government mortgage insurance.

In an April 1959 interview in the *U.S. News and World Report*, Saulnier declared that the "cornerstone" of the Eisenhower economic program was a balanced budget for fiscal 1961. He maintained that tax reduction was desirable but was not possible without a balanced budget. He proposed a number of tax revisions: liberalized depreciation allowances for businesses, lower tax rates on high bracket incomes, elimination of various excise taxes and the institution of a manufacturer's sales tax. He also emphasized the need for keeping the money supply in check, holding down wage boosts so as not to cause a price rise and pushing ahead with automation if the U.S. was to achieve a higher rate of economic growth.

Despite the continuing threat of inflation, Saulnier rejected wage and price controls as a remedy. "It is in the absence of controls," he said, "that we have the freedom that gives our economy its dynamic quality. We don't want to lose that quality in the process of trying to avoid cost and price inflation." In August 1959 Saulnier stated that general price stability could be achieved only if, in industries "where productivity gains are especially rapid," management cut prices and labor accepted raises less than the full productivity gain. It was understood that he was referring to the steel industry in particular. However, Saulnier still did not advocate any system of mandatory wage and price restraint.

Saulnier remained in his post until January 1961. Later in the year he resumed teaching at Barnard.

[TO]

SCHINE, G(ERARD) DAVID
b. Sept. 11, 1927; Gloversville, N.Y.
Chief Consultant, Permanent Investigations Subcommittee of the Senate Government Operations Committee, 1953.

Schine, the son of a wealthy hotel magnate, attended Andover Academy and in 1945 entered Harvard University. At Harvard he lived in opulence and had a private secretary who often attended his classes and took lecture notes. He flunked out in 1946 but was readmitted the following year after a stint in the Army Transport Service. Shortly after graduating in 1949, Schine was installed as president of Schine Hotels, Inc., although his father retained operational control. The easygoing, handsome Schine was interested in a show business career and tried writing popular songs. He also wrote a six-page pamphlet called "Definitions of Communism" that was placed in Schine-owned hotel rooms. In 1952 he met Roy Cohn [q.v.], an assistant U.S. attorney specializing in cases involving subversion. The young men became close friends and traveled the Manhattan social circuit together.

When Cohn was appointed chief counsel for Sen. Joseph R. McCarthy's (R, Wisc.) [q.v.] Permanent Investigations Subcommittee in January 1953, he brought Schine along as the panel's unpaid chief consultant. Although Schine's qualifications for conducting investigative work were unclear, he worked closely with Cohn in directing McCarthy's probes of alleged subversives in the International Information Administration, the Voice of America and the State Department early in 1953.

In April 1953 Schine and Cohn went on a 17-day, seven-country tour of Europe on behalf of the subcommittee to determine if the State Department's overseas libraries contained pro-Communist literature. They received extensive press publicity both in America and Europe. Reporters maintained that in Munich Schine chased Cohn with a rolled-up magazine through a hotel lobby. Journalists also claimed to have overheard them making snide remarks in public about alleged homosexuality among State Department employes. Critics of the two men charged them with immature and farcical behavior damaging to America's prestige abroad. As a result of their activities and of pressure exerted by McCarthy at home, the State Department ordered its libraries to remove works by "Communist, fellow-travelers, et cetera. . . ." In a June 1953 commencement address, President Eisenhower denounced "book-burners" but subsequently backed down from his oblique criticism of the Senator and his aides.

In July 1953 Schine was notified of his impending induction into the Army. McCarthy and Cohn immediately interceded to prevent any interruption in his subcommittee staff duties, making several unsuccessful attempts to get him an officer's commission or a job at the U.S. Military Academy. After Schine was inducted as a private in November, Cohn continued to exert pressure on his behalf, including numerous telephone calls to Schine's commanding officers and to Army Counsel John G. Adams [q.v.]. In the meantime, the

Permanent Investigations Subcommittee had begun a probe of Communist infiltration in the Army.

In January 1954 presidential aide Sherman Adams [q.v.] urged the Army to draft a chronology of McCarthy's and Cohn's campaign to secure preferential treatment for the former consultant. In March, after McCarthy had stepped up his attacks against the Army, the chronology was released. The document revealed that Schine had received such privileges as exemptions from training exercises and numerous weekend passes. On March 16 the subcommittee voted to investigate the Army's accusations as well as a set of counter-charges by McCarthy and Cohn.

The probe, known as the Army-McCarthy hearings, began in April. Late in the month the panel was presented with a photo of Schine together with Army Secretary Robert Stevens [q.v.]. It was apparently intended to suggest that Stevens was being friendly towards Schine in the hope that the subcommittee would drop its investigation of the Army. But Army Counsel Joseph Welch [q.v.] produced an enlargement of the photo indicating that the one presented to the subcommittee had been cropped to exclude other individuals. Welch traced the cropping to McCarthy's staff.

During the investigation McCarthy admitted under cross-examination that Schine had no investigative experience to qualify him for a subcommittee position but said that Schine had worked on a plan for psychological warfare against Communism. Sen. Henry Jackson (D, Wash.) [q.v.] later ridiculed the plan, calling attention to its proposals for the use of pin-ups, billboards and bumper-stickers. Despite the fact that his case was a central theme in the hearings, Schine was not called to testify.

Schine was discharged from the Army in 1955. During the next two decades he established a show-business management firm, a movie-production company and a music-publishing concern.

[TLH]

Richard H. Rovere, "The Adventures of Cohn and Schine," The Reporter (July 21, 1953), pp. 9-16.

SCHLESINGER, ARTHUR M(EIER) JR.
b. Oct. 15, 1917; Columbus, Ohio.
Historian.

Schlesinger was the son of the distinguished American historian, Arthur Schlesinger, Sr. He attended Harvard, where he graduated summa cum laude in 1938. As a senior he wrote an honors thesis on the 19th century American thinker, Orestes Brownson. It was published in 1939 and earned wide praise. After spending a year at Cambridge University, Schlesinger returned to Harvard where, as a member of the prestigious Society of Fellows, he began work on The Age of Jackson. He completed the book while working in Washington for the Office for War Information and published it in 1945. In 1946 he was awarded the Pulitzer Prize for history.

Schlesinger joined his father on the Harvard faculty in 1947. He helped organize the Americans for Democratic Action (ADA) the same year. During the postwar period he wrote articles for numerous magazines and a book, The Vital Center (1949), calling for a strong and realistic liberalism to ward off the dual challenges of the fascist right and the Communist left. [See TRUMAN Volume]

In 1952 Schlesinger took a leave of absence from Harvard to join Adlai Stevenson's [q.v.] campaign staff as a speech writer. He was widely regarded as too liberal for the task, and he was even denounced as a Communist by several Republican leaders. However, Stevenson stood by him, and the two men developed a close friendship during the decade.

In 1956 Schlesinger headed the research and writing group in Stevenson's second campaign. He advocated emphasizing the idea that the Republican Party was the party of big business and special interests while the Democratic Party represented the people. Because Eisenhower had established a reputation as a President of peace, Schlesinger recommended that Stevenson emphasize domestic over foreign policy issues. In a May 1956 article in The New Republic, Schlesinger strongly implied that liberals should be wary of international affairs, at least until America itself became an example for the rest of the world to follow. While he insisted that this emphasis on domestic affairs was only a campaign tactic, he was accused of developing a new brand of isolationism.

Schlesinger was a leading liberal spokesman during the decade. He was a vigorous opponent of domestic loyalty-security investigations. Schlesinger opposed Sen. Joseph R. McCarthy's (R, Wisc.) [q.v.] anti-Communist crusade, and in 1954 he wrote a careful defense of J. Robert Oppenheimer [q.v.], the former director of the wartime Manhattan Project, who had been denied security clearance by the Eisenhower Administration. During the latter part of the decade, he asserted that cold war rhetoric had exaggerated the authoritarian aspects of Soviet life. He viewed the Soviet Union as becoming both freer and more prosperous after Stalin's death and generally less of a threat to the life and values of democratic nations.

Schlesinger was often pessimistic in his assessment of the social changes of the decade. He believed that the economic advances since World War II had been bought at the price of communal disintegration and the loss of cultural diversity. He wrote often of the oppressive standardization of life in the new suburbs and of the emptiness of white collar existence. Schlesinger attacked the so-called New Conservatives, led by Russell Kirk [q.v.], who were concerned with the same issues. He insisted that conservatives could not consistently rally around the issue of community, for in America conservativism meant a defense of business interests before all else. He asserted that the idea of a conservative intellectual was a self-contradiction and worked hard to create the image of the Democratic Party as the party of "creative liberalism," guided by intellectuals.

In 1956 Schlesinger backed John Kennedy's [q.v.] unsuccessful bid for the Democratic vice presidential nomination. Schlesinger was a key figure in winning the support of the ADA and the liberal intellectual community for Kennedy. In 1960 he shifted his support from Stevenson to Kennedy and thus played a role in securing Kennedy's Democratic presidential nomination. Although many ADA members accused him of being a traitor, Schlesinger himself did not regard his shift as a dramatic one. He wrote in 1960 that "in his eight years as titular leader Stevenson renewed the Democratic Party. . . . Kennedy today is the heir and the executor of the Stevenson revolution." Schlesinger joined the Kennedy campaign staff and published *Kennedy or Nixon?*, a short book which contrasted Kennedy's decisiveness with Nixon's uncertainty. After the election he was appointed as special adviser to the President. In that capacity he concentrated on Latin American affairs. [See KENNEDY Volume]

Throughout these years Schlesinger continued to pursue his work as a historian. From 1957 to 1960 he published *The Age of Roosevelt* in three volumes. The fruit of nearly 15 years of research, the work portrayed Roosevelt as a strong and innovative reformer, the enduring model of progressive leadership. Schlesinger was widely praised for both the subtlety of his analysis and the effectiveness of his narration. In 1965 he published *A Thousand Days: John F. Kennedy in the White House*, a work which earned him the Pulitzer Prize for biography. In 1966 Schlesinger became Schweitzer professor of the humanities at the City University of New York. He continued to be a leading liberal spokesman, opposing the war in Vietnam and attacking the Nixon Administration. [See JOHNSON Volume]

[JPL]

For further information:
Arthur M. Schlesinger, *The Politics of Hope* (Boston, 1963).

SCHWARTZ, BERNARD
b. Aug. 25, 1923, New York, N.Y.
Chief Counsel, Subcommittee on Legislative Oversight of the House Commerce Committee, 1957-58.

Bernard Schwartz completed seven years of university study in four by attending the City College of New York (B.S., 1944) and

New York University (LL.B., 1944) simultaneously. He obtained a M.Law degree at Harvard in 1945 and a Ph.D. at Cambridge University in 1947. Schwartz joined the faculty of New York University law school that year and over the next few years wrote numerous articles and books on the Supreme Court and administrative law. During the early years of the Eisenhower Administration he served as counsel to the Second Hoover Commission on Executive Branch Reorganization and the House Government Information Subcommittee. In March 1957 Schwartz became, at age 33, chief counsel to the House Interstate and Foreign Commerce Committee's Subcommittee on Legislative Oversight.

This panel, created in February 1957 at the urging of House Speaker Sam Rayburn (D, Tex.) [q.v.], was charged with investigating improper industry influence and political pressure on federal regulatory agencies. Commerce Committee Chairman Oren Harris (D, Ark.) [q.v.] appointed Rep. Morgan M. Moulder (D, Mo.)—considered a mild, unassertive figure—chairman of the special committee. Under Schwartz's direction the subcommittee's staff concentrated on six of 20 government agencies: the Civil Aeronautics Board (CAB), the Federal Power Commission (FPC), the Federal Trade Commission (FTC), the Interstate Commerce Commission (ICC), the Securities and Exchange Commission (SEC) and the Federal Communications Commission (FCC).

Schwartz quickly encountered agency and congressional obstructionism. For a month-long period ending on Oct. 17, 1957. CAB chairman James R. Durfee denied Schwartz's staff access to pertinent records. Schwartz also came under congressional criticism for sending the 38 commissioners a detailed questionnaire inquiring about personal gifts, loans and other favors presented by companies subject to the regulators' authority. "Never before," Rep. Joseph O'Hara (R, Minn.) complained, "has any congressional investigating group started out by assuming everyone was crooked."

Reacting to the Committee's refusal to push his FCC investigation, Schwartz

leaked a confidential report on the Commission to the *New York Times* in January 1958. The memo accused FCC Chairman John Doerfer [q.v.] and other members of official misconduct and improper fraternization with the industry. Specifically, Schwartz charged the men with billing the government for expenses paid for by broadcasting figures, accepting gifts and loans and discussing pending agency litigation with industry litigants. As a result of these relationships, the memo alleged, the agency exhibited "a most disturbing inconsistency" in its awards of station licenses. In testimony before the subcommittee on Feb. 3, Doerfer denounced what he considered Schwartz's irresponsible tactics in investigating the Commission and leaking the memo. Under Schwartz's cross-examination he admitted accepting gifts but declared his innocence of any wrongdoing.

Soon after Doerfer's testimony the subcommittee fired Schwartz. Southern Democratic and Republican members resented Schwartz's method of cross-examining the Commission chairman and disapproved of his *Times* leak. On Feb. 10 the panel voted seven-to-four to dismiss Schwartz. Chairman Moulder, two other Democratic members and one Republican voted against his removal. Moulder resigned as chairman in protest, and Harris assumed the post. Schwartz immediately accused Harris, most subcommittee members and later Speaker Rayburn of seeking "a bipartisan whitewash."

The day following his ouster, Schwartz made a series of sensational charges against leading Administration officials. He declared that FCC Commissioner Richard A. Mack [q.v.] was guilty of conflict of interest in granting a Miami TV station license. He also added the names of former New York Gov. Thomas E. Dewey and the President's chief aide, Sherman Adams [q.v.] (considered by many to be the second most powerful man in Washington), to his list of distinguished influence peddlers.

The subcommittee subpoenaed Schwartz to detail his accusations. It also demanded and received "working papers" Schwartz had left with Sen. Wayne Morse (D, Ore.) [q.v.] for safekeeping following his dismissal. Before the subcommittee in mid-February, Schwartz presented additional materials strongly suggesting unlawful action by FCC Commissioner Mack and improper ones by Sherman Adams in his dealings with regulatory agencies.

Schwartz also revealed that he had secretly wiretapped a 1957 interview with Mack. The wiretapping, together with Schwartz's headline-catching list of influence peddlers, caused some liberal journals and politicians—and a great many Republican ones—to criticize Schwartz's investigative methods. They freely compared them to those of Sen. Joseph R. McCarthy (R, Wisc.) [*q.v.*]. The liberal *New Republic* found Schwartz "unprincipled." Sen. Morse called for an end to all government wiretaps.

Schwartz's appearance before the subcommittee—well-covered by the national news media—forced further investigations. Once hopeful of restricting the subcommittee's activities, Chairman Harris pursued Schwartz's allegations. The FBI entered the Mack case. By September the once powerful Sherman Adams had quit his White House post. The cumulative effects of the subcommittee's hearings, which lasted well into 1958, seriously damaged the Republican Party's already bleak prospects for the November congressional elections. New legislation enacted in 1960 revised commission procedure. Advocating more comprehensive reform, Schwartz returned to New York University.

[JLB]

For further information:
Bernard Schwartz, *The Professor and the Commissions* (New York, 1959).

SCOTT, HUGH D(OGGETT)

b. Nov. 11, 1900; Fredericksburg, Va.
Republican Representative, Pa., 1941-45, 1947-59; Republican Senator, Pa., 1959-77.

Scott graduated from Randolph-Macon College in 1919 and received a law degree from the University of Virginia three years later. He practiced law in Philadelphia and

from 1926 to 1941 served as assistant district attorney in that city. In 1940 and 1942 Scott was elected to the U.S. House of Representatives. Following service in the Navy from 1944 to 1946, he again returned to the House. In 1948 Republican presidential nominee Thomas E. Dewey chose Scott to be chairman of the Republican National Committee, a post held by the Pennsylvania Representative into 1949.

A moderate Republican, Scott opposed the selection of Sen. Robert A. Taft (R, Ohio) [*q.v.*] as the Party's 1952 presidential nominee and was an early participant in the "draft Eisenhower" movement. At a Young Republican Convention during the fall of 1951, he asserted that Eisenhower was the "one candidate who would be certain to become President on the Republican ticket." In February 1952 Scott was among 19 representatives who wrote Eisenhower urging him to seek the GOP nomination. During the presidential campaign Scott served as chairman of Eisenhower's headquarters committee.

In the mid-1950s Scott and Reps. Kenneth Keating (R, N.Y.) [*q.v.*] and Jacob Javits (R, N.Y.) [*q.v.*], all moderate-to-liberal Northeastern congressmen with urban constituencies, favored civil rights legislation. Their views were held partly responsible for President Eisenhower's decision to modify his previous opposition to federal civil rights laws in January 1956. The next month Scott and Rep. Adam Clayton Powell, Jr. (D, N.Y.) [*q.v.*], announced that a group of House members was determined to bring "right to vote" legislation before the House. In May 1957 Scott joined a Rules Committee majority that favored reporting a voting rights bill. On the floor he opposed a Southern attempt to weaken the bill by guaranteeing a jury trial to persons accused of intimidating or harassing voters.

Over the opposition of the Party's Pennsylvania machine, Scott won the 1958 Republican Senate nomination and defeated Gov. George Leader [*q.v.*] in the election. As a senator, Scott continued to stand towards the left of his Party, voting to override the President's housing bill veto in 1959 and his area redevelopment veto in

1960. In March 1960 he was among 16 senators signing a cloture petition in an unsuccessful effort to end a Southern civil rights filibuster.

Although Scott's voting record was significantly more liberal than those of most Republicans on, Capitol Hill, he frequently served as a partisan spokesman in Congress. In 1955 Democrats criticized the Administration-backed tax cuts of the previous year as tailored to the interests of big business and called for a $20 personal income tax credit. Scott denounced the proposal as a "gimmick . . . [to] buy the votes of the American people at 20 bucks a head." Five years later he attacked Democratic senatorial opposition to the nomination of Lewis Strauss [q.v.] as Secretary of Commerce, describing it as "a well-planned attempt at legislative lynching. . . ."

In 1962 Scott attempted to make the Pennsylvania Party more attractive to liberal voters by successfully promoting Rep. William Scranton for governor. Two years later Scott led an effort to block the nomination of conservative Sen. Barry M. Goldwater (R, Ariz.) [q.v.] for the presidency, and he urged Gov. Scranton to enter the race against Goldwater. In September 1969 Scott became Senate minority leader. During the Nixon Administration his voting record became more conservative. Compromised by his persistent defense of President Nixon during the Watergate crisis of 1973-74 and by the 1975 revelation that he had been receiving an annual fee from the Gulf Oil Corp. Scott did not seek relection in 1976. [See KENNEDY, JOHNSON, NIXON/FORD Volumes]

[MLL]

SEABORG, GLENN T(HEODORE)
b. April 19, 1912: Ishpeming, Mich.
Associate Director, Lawrence Radiation Laboratory, 1954-61; Chancellor, University of California, Berkeley, 1958-61; Member, President's Science Advisory Committee, 1959-61.

Seaborg received his doctorate in nuclear chemistry from the University of California at Berkeley in 1937 and joined the faculty there that year. His studies of atomic structure led to the discovery of numerous new isotopes of common elements by 1940. However, Seaborg's major achievement was the discovery of plutonium, a new element with fissionable properties. During World War II he worked on the Manhattan Project as section chief of the metallurgical laboratory at the University of Chicago. The separation process for plutonium, developed by Seaborg and his staff, contributed to the development of the atomic bomb. Seaborg was among seven scientists working on the bomb who, in June 1945, sent a petition to the Secretary of War forecasting a dangerous atomic arms race. Known as the Franck Report, this statement urged international control of nuclear weapons in the postwar period and called for a demonstration of the atomic bomb in an uninhabited place before its use in warfare.

After the War Seaborg returned to Berkeley and directed nuclear chemical research at the University's Lawrence Radiation Laboratory. His research proved the existence of several transuranium elements, and in 1951 he won the Nobel Prize for chemistry. Seaborg was also a member of the Atomic Energy Commission's (AEC) General Advisory Committee (GAC) from 1946 to 1950. He was absent from a GAC meeting held in October 1949 where the Committee members, including Chairman J. Robert Oppenheimer [q.v.], declared their opposition to a crash program to develop the hydrogen bomb. Abroad at the time, he had indicated his support for the project in a letter sent to Oppenheimer earlier that month. In 1950 President Truman ordered the AEC to develop the weapon. [See TRUMAN Volume]

Seaborg's letter figured prominently in the 1954 Oppenheimer security hearings. In late 1953 President Eisenhower had ordered Oppenheimer's security clearance suspended as a result of charges that the scientist had been disloyal. The suspension was based on his prewar associations with pro-Communist groups and his postwar ambivalence toward the development of the hydrogen bomb. At the AEC's April security hearing, all the scientists who had served on the GAC with Oppenheimer in

1949 testified on Oppenheimer's behalf except Seaborg. The hearing revealed conflicting evidence concerning whether or not Oppenheimer had publicized Seaborg's letter supporting the project. Citing Oppenheimer's conduct and the testimony regarding the Seaborg letter as well as other incidents, the board ruled two to one to maintain the suspension.

Seaborg was appointed associate director of the Lawrence Radiation Laboratory in 1954, and in 1958 he became chancellor of the Berkeley campus. The following year Eisenhower appointed him to the President's Science Advisory Committee. He won the Enrico Fermi Award in 1959.

President Kennedy appointed Seaborg head of the AEC in 1961. In 1962 Seaborg offered Oppenheimer a new hearing, which the latter declined. As AEC chairman, Seaborg advocated resumption of U.S. nuclear tests after the Soviet Union resumed testing in 1961. Nevertheless, he supported the 1963 nulcear test ban treaty. While the AEC's role expanded greatly in the late-1960s, it drew frequent criticism from those who considered its safeguards against atomic accidents inadequate. In 1971 Seaborg resigned as its chairman and returned to the University of California. [See KENNEDY, JOHNSON, NIXON/FORD Volumes]

[MDB]

For further information:
Robert Jungk, *Brighter Than A Thousand Suns* (New York, 1958).
John Major, *The Oppenheimer Hearing* (New York, 1971).

SEATON, FREDERICK A(NDREW)

b. Dec. 11, 1909; Washington, D.C.
d. Jan. 17, 1974; Hastings, Neb.
Assistant Secretary of Defense for Legislative Affairs, September 1953-February 1955; Administrative Assistant for Congressional Liaison, February 1955-June 1955; Deputy Assistant to the President, 1955-June 1956; Secretary of the Interior, June 1956-January 1961.

Seaton attended Kansas State Agricultural College from 1927 to 1931. Upon graduation he worked for several newspapers owned by his father, a prominent Kansas publisher and former secretary to Sen. Joseph L. Bristow (R, Kan.). While continuing his career as a newspaperman, Seaton became active in the Young Republicans Club and eventually became a member of the Kansas Republican State Committee in 1934. In 1936 he became secretary to Alfred M. Landon, the Republican presidential nominee. Establishing residence in Nebraska in 1937, Seaton served in that state's legislature from 1945 to 1949. Seaton was appointed interim U.S. senator from Nebraska in December 1951. In 1952 he served on Dwight D. Eisenhower's campaign staff as Sherman Adams's [q.v.] deputy. He was credited with formulating the campaign strategy in the wake of Richard Nixon's [q.v.] "Checkers speech." After the campaign Seaton returned to Kansas to run his papers and radio and television stations.

In September 1953 Seaton became an assistant secretary of defense. At this post he persuaded Secretary of Defense Charles E. Wilson [q.v.] to hold weekly press conferences and improve relations between the Department and Congress. In 1955 Seaton joined the White House staff as the President's administrative assistant for congressional liaison. He was promoted to deputy assistant to the President in charge of patronage and liaison in June. At this post Seaton advanced the enactment of a military reserve law, recommended legislation for more school classrooms and better roads and encouraged the inclusion of the "soil bank" program in the 1956 farm bill.

After Douglas McKay [q.v.] resigned as Secretary of the Interior, Seaton was assigned the task of finding his successor. Eisenhower was anxious to mollify tensions within the Department generated by McKay's controversial personnel policies and abrasive personality. Therefore, he offered the even-tempered Seaton the position in May 1956. The appointment drew widespread approval, and Seaton's friendly "open door" policies soon established his popularity within the Department.

Seaton vigorously pursued McKay's policies in the area of park development and Indian programs. Park attendance reached record highs during his tenure; the

29th national park was developed in the Virgin Islands. Seaton continued to launch new Indian education programs, providing courses on the reservations as well as vocational training for those 18 to 35. He fostered the development of job opportunities near the reservations. The Secretary stressed that the program would continue only where approved by the Indians.

While Douglas McKay had supported the use of private enterprise to develop resources whenever possible, Seaton promoted joint federal/private cooperation. He endorsed teamwork projects in the Trinity River division and San Luis unit of the Central Valley Project in California, and he promoted the Fryingpan Arkansas Project in Colorado, construction of which began in the fall of 1956. Seaton continued the hydro-generating program in the Pacific Northwest. In 1959 facilities for 5.8 million kilowatts were already under construction or scheduled for completion in 1969. For fiscal 1960 the Bureau of Reclamation planned a nine million dollar program of construction involving 59 projects.

Under Seaton wildlife protection became a major goal of the Department. In 1958 the Secretary sponsored the Duck Stamp amendment, raising from two to three dollars the fee for duck stamps (used as hunting licenses). The proceeds were to go for the acquisition of additional national water fowl refuges. He also prohibited the leasing of oil and gas reserves on refuges except for the purposes of drainage. That same year Seaton promoted amendments to the Coordination Act of 1946 designed to further wildlife conservation. Under the existing act agencies and groups constructing water projects were required to include features to prevent harm to wildlife. The amendments went further and ordered agencies to consider ways of enhancing and developing new fish and wildlife resources. The measure was deemed one of the most important conservation bills of the postwar era.

Resource development remained another major priority. In 1958 Seaton detailed for a Senate Internal Affairs subcommittee a plan for federal subsidization of domestic protection of copper, lead, zinc and other minerals. He furthered the production of a

$12 million helium extraction plant completed in November 1959. The Secretary also administered the 1959 mandatory import controls on crude oil, which were designed to nourish domestic production and development.

Seaton was credited with leading the drive in the White House and Congress for the acceptance of statehood for Alaska and Hawaii in 1958 and 1959. Some Republicans singled out the Secretary as a possible vice presidential candidate in 1960.

Seaton left government in January 1961 and returned to the Seaton Publishing Co. In 1962 he ran for governor of Kansas, unsuccessfully challenging the Democratic incumbent, Frank B. Morrison. Seaton then returned to his publishing activities, where he remained until his death in 1974.

[GAD]

SERVICE, JOHN S(TEWART)
b. Aug. 3, 1909: Chengtu, China
Foreign Service officer.

The son of American missionaries, Service spent his early years in China. He graduated from Oberlin College in 1931 and two years later became a Foreign Service clerk at the U.S. consulate in Kumming, China. In 1935 he was named language attache at the embassy in Peking. Service remained in China until 1945, when he returned to Washington as State Department adviser to Gen. Douglas MacArthur.

In 1945 Service was arrested and charged with passing confidential material to Phillip Jaffee, editor of *Amerasia*, a scholarly magazine dealing with Asia. Service defended himself, claiming he had given "normal and proper background information" to the journalist. A grand jury cleared him, and he was reinstated in the State Department that same year.

During the next six years Service faced a series of investigations by the State Department and the Department's Loyalty Security Board, some prompted by Sen. Joseph R. McCarthy's (R, Wisc.) [q.v.] charges that the Department was harboring disloyal Americans. In each case Service was cleared. The undersecretary of state also reviewed the clearance findings and approved them. However, on Dec. 13, 1951 the Loyalty Review Board of the Civil Service Commission auditing Department proceedings, found "reasonable doubt" of his loyalty and recommended dismissal. Secretary of State Dean Acheson [q.v.] did so the following day. He based his action on the McCarran rider to the State Department appropriation bill of 1947 giving the Secretary of State absolute discretion to remove from office any employe when he deemed it in the national interest.

Service decided to challenge the constitutionality of Acheson's action. In 1956 a federal district court ruled that the Loyalty Review Board had no authority to audit favorable decisions by departments and ordered that doubts of Service's loyalty be stricken from his record. However, it held that under the McCarran rider Acheson had a right to discharge Service and refused to order his reinstatement.

On Jan. 17, 1957, by a vote of eight to zero, the Supreme Court ruled that Acheson was in error for discharging Service. It argued that under State Department regulations the Secretary had no right to overrule the final decision of the undersecretary of state and had violated Service's rights by doing so. The Court then returned the case to a lower court, which reinstated Service to the State Department with all back pay. The decision was seen as a significant shift from the Court's willingness to restrict liberties in the interests of national security to a concern for an individual's rights.

Service returned to work in September 1957 and was assigned to make a survey of how the Department could save money in shipping the household goods of Foreign Service officers sent to new posts. In 1959 he was transferred to Liverpool, England, as consul. Service retired three years later to become a resident China scholar at the University of California at Berkeley. In 1971 he visited Communist China.

[JB]

For further information:
E.J. Kahn, Jr., *The China Hands* (New York, 1976).

SHANLEY, BERNARD M(ICHAEL)
b. 1903; Newark, N.J.
Special Counsel to the President, January 1953-January 1955; Presidential Appointments Secretary, January 1955-November 1955, January 1956-November 1957.

Shanley studied briefly at Columbia University in 1925 and then attended law school at Fordham University, receiving his degree in 1928. From 1929 to 1952 he practiced law in Newark, N.J. He also held directorships in several insurance companies. He had a lifelong involvement in New Jersey Republican politics and served as chairman of the New Jersey Republican Committee for an Effective Assembly and of the executive committee of the Republican National Committee.

A longtime supporter of Harold Stassen [q.v.], Shanley became national chairman of the Stassen-for-President Volunteer Committee in late 1951. However, by the Republican National Convention of June 1952, Shanley had switched his support to Dwight D. Eisenhower and worked for him during the general election campaign.

On the recommendation of Sherman Adams [q.v.], who had worked closely with him during the campaign, Shanley was appointed White House special counsel in January 1953. The following month he became involved in the Administration's debate over possible revision of the Taft-Hartley Act. Along with congressional liaison assistant Gerald D. Morgan [q.v.], Shanley produced a position paper attempting to reconcile differences between Secretary of Labor Martin Durkin [q.v.] and the more conservative Secretary of Commerce Sinclair Weeks [q.v.]. It detailed what the Administration needed to attract labor votes without losing support from the National Association of Manufacturers, a powerful, traditionally Republican business organization. The Shanley-Morgan note, reflecting many of Durkin's proposals, called for substantial revisions of the Taft-Hartley Act and especially of its more anti-labor sections. However, their proposal bogged down in intra-Administration bickering and never advanced beyond the planning stage. When Durkin resigned in September 1953, he accused Shanley and Morgan of sabotaging their own reform proposals as well as his own efforts to revise the statute.

Shanley later performed public relations assignments for the Eisenhower Administration. In November 1953 Eisenhower handed Shanley the task of dealing with protests from the press about Administration policies and public utterances. Shortly thereafter Shanley embroiled himself in controversy when he implied that 1,456 government employes, separated from their jobs, were dismissed as "subversives." Publicly apologizing in February 1954, Shanley admitted that his statement had been an "unfortunate mistake." Nevertheless, Adlai Stevenson [q.v.] denounced the Republican Party and the Eisenhower Administration for McCarthyite tactics in the "deception." Although Shanley and others had declared them to be traitors and subversives, Stevenson said, the only concrete fact was that the government reluctantly admitted it found "only one alleged active Communist" in all its security investigations.

In January 1955 Shanley assumed the post of appointments secretary following the resignation of Thomas E. Stephens [q.v.]. He resigned that fall to resume his law practice but returned to the White House in January 1956. In November 1957 Shanley again resigned to seek the Republican senatorial nomination from New Jersey. The following April Winthrop Kean defeated him in the primary.

Shanley remained politically active in the 1960s. He won the New Jersey Republican senatorial nomination in 1964 but lost the general election to Democrat Harrison Williams [q.v.]. In 1968 he became vice chairman of the Republican National Committee for the northeastern region.

[RJB]

SHEEN, FULTON J(OHN)
b. May 8, 1895; El Paso, Ill.
Clergyman

Sheen began lengthy and distinguished university training at St. Viator College of Illinois, receiving his B.A. in 1917 and M.A. in 1919. He studied at St. Paul's Seminary in Minnesota in 1919 and was ordained a priest in 1920. Sheen was awarded Bachelor of Sacred Theology and Bachelor of Canon Law degrees from Catholic University in 1920, a Ph.D. from the University of Louvain in 1923 and a D.D. from the Collegio Angelico in Rome in 1924. The following year he made Agrege en Philosophie at Lovain. He served briefly in 1925 and 1926 as curate of St. Patrick's Church in a poor Peoria, Ill., parish. In 1926 Sheen accepted appointment to the philosophy department of Catholic University, a position he held until 1950.

Quickly Sheen became one of the most popular spokesmen for Catholicism in America. He lectured at Catholic universities and accepted invitations to speak at churches nationwide. He also wrote many books and articles during the 1930s and 1940s, a few of which sold heavily. His effectiveness as an orator was utilized in 1930 by Catholic officials when he was chosen to speak weekly on the radio program "Catholic Hour." He remained a popular radio personality until 1952, when his television program, "Life is Worth Living," began broadcasting.

Made a monsignor in 1934, Sheen was known during the 1930s and 1940s not only as an articulate preacher who brought many converts to the Catholic church—including prominent ex-Communists Elizabeth Bentley and Louis Budenz—but also as a firm anti-Communist who supported Generalissimo Francisco Franco in Spain, denounced America's alliance with Russia in World War II and opposed any postwar concessions to the USSR or relaxation of the Cold War. In 1950 Sheen was named the national director of the Society for the Propagation of the Faith, an international Catholic organization which distributed funds for missionary activities. He was consecrated an auxiliary bishop of New York in 1951. Many Catholics expected him to rise to greater prominence in the Church hierarchy, but while bringing converts to the Church he was making enemies among its officials. Described by his biographer, Rev. D.P. Noonan, as a "consumate egocentric," Sheen could, in his words, "captivate, inspire, persuade and stimulate," on the one hand and "belittle, antagonize and alienate" on the other.

Sheen's television program, "Life is Worth Living," won consistently high ratings, at one point surpassing those of the entertainment show of popular comedian Milton Berle, a prime-time competitor. Noonan described the program as "not a dogmatic one, but a mixture of common sense, logic and Christian ethics" which did not attempt to proselytize for Catholicism. Sheen's subjects ranged from war, motherhood, psychiatry and Communism to the Divine sense of humor. He frequently supplemented his scriptless discussions and his captivating oratorical style with jokes solicited from friends or humor books. In 1953 the program was honored with the Freedom Foundation Award, and in the same year Sheen received an Emmy Award as an "outstanding personality." The program went off the air in 1957 but resumed in 1959 to continue until 1965. Printed transcripts of the programs were compiled in books also named *Life is Worth Living*; volumes of the collection repeatedly appeared on the best-seller lists during the 1950s. Bishop Sheen returned all revenues connected with the program to the Society for the Propagation of the Faith.

Like many other Catholics in the U.S. during the 1950s, Bishop Sheen believed Communism to be the most ominous threat to freedom and Christianity and the church to be the most powerful force in doing battle against it. He was not timid about pointing to what he believed was Communist subversion, and in 1952 he accused U.S. Communists of having attempted to infiltrate the Catholic priesthood in 1936. However, he professed not to sympathize with the methods of Sen. Joseph R. McCarthy's (R, Wisc.) [*q.v.*] anti-Communist probes. Nevertheless, much of the public readily identified him as a conservative ideologue and anti-Communist at a time when Catholic leaders frequently were prominent in the anti-Communist crusade.

Sheen continued to write books and syndicated columns in the late-1950s and 1960s. In his lifetime he published over 70 books. His expected promotion in the church did not materialize because, it was believed, he had incurred the disfavor of the Archbishop of New York, Francis Spellman [*q.v.*]. After refusing Spellman's offer of a bishopric in New York City, he was appointed Bishop of Rochester, N.Y., in 1966. Sheen had had little previous experience as a parish leader, and he shocked his conservative congregation by advocating a variety of liberal causes. In 1967 he became the first major Catholic figure to urge a total and immediate withdrawal of American troops from Vietnam. He later modified his position, however, and supported President Richard Nixon's gradual "Vietnamization" plan. In 1969 Sheen resigned his bishopric in Rochester and retired from active church service. Thereafter he made occasional appearances on television and radio programs and contributed to national and religious magazines.

[TGD]

For further information:
D.P. Noonan, *The Passion of Fulton Sheen* (New York, 1972).

SHIVERS, ALLAN
b. Oct. 5, 1907; Lufkin, Tex.
Governor, Tex., 1949-57.

The son of a prominent judge, Allan Shivers was admitted to the Texas bar in 1931. Two years later he completed his LL.B. at the University of Texas. In 1934 Shivers won election to the state Senate, where he focused his attention on defending Texas ownership of tidelands oil and gas properties claimed by the federal government. From 1943 to 1945 he served in the Army in the European theater. Shivers returned to Texas and in 1946 won election as lieutenant governor on the Democratic ticket. Reelected with the incumbent in 1948, he became governor in July 1949 following the death of Gov. Beauford H. Jester. He easily won election in November 1950. A strong believer in states' rights, the new Governor continued to assert Texas's claim to tidelands oil.

When Dwight D. Eisenhower stated that he favored state control of offshore oil, Shivers endorsed him for President. Conservative Democrats, or "Shivercrats" as they came to be called, helped the General win 53% of the Texas vote in November. Shivers was reelected at the same time, running on both Republican and Democratic tickets.

Shivers was harshly critical of the Supreme Court's May 1954 decision, *Brown v. Board of Education*, outlawing segregation in public schools. However his remarks were followed by moderate action. In August 1955 he appointed a conservative advisory committee on segregation to recommend ways of preventing integration. Yet no legislation was passed impeding voluntary compliance, and the state offered assistance in implementing locally developed desegregation plans. By the end of 1955, with 84 districts integrated, Texas had made more progress toward desegregation than the rest of the Southern states combined.

During the mid-1950s Shivers found himself losing his political base. In 1954 the Governor was challenged for renomination by liberal Ralph Yarborough [*q.v.*] and forced into a bitter runoff. Two years later he faced serious opposition for control of the state delegation to the 1956 Democratic National Convention. Eisenhower's stand on offshore oil undercut Shivers's major issue of states' rights, while charges of corruption and malpractice in his administration further embarrassed the Governor.

Faced with declining popularity, Shivers seized the idea of interposition to unite his followers. This doctrine pledged the use of state power to oppose the *Brown* decision by consolidating public school authority in the state instead of local school boards, thus placing the "sovereignty of the state" between local school officials and federal courts. In February 1956 Shivers called on the state Democratic Party to conduct a referendum on interposition and, if endorsed, to place the doctrine in the party platform. The following month the Governor promoted an interposition plank for the Democratic national platform. In May a moderate coalition led by Rep. Sam Rayburn (D, Tex.) [*q.v.*] and Sen. Lyndon Johnson (D, Tex.) [*q.v.*] ousted Shivers as party leader and wrote a mild statement

scoring interposition but supporting states rights. The state convention named Johnson its favorite-son candidate for President.

The issue of interposition continued after Shivers's defeat. In July the white supremacist Citizens' Councils forced a statewide referendum on three segregation propositions. All three, including an interposition resolution, received heavy approval. The large vote for segregation reinforced Shivers's stand. In the fall of 1956 he successfully used Texas Rangers to block court-ordered desegregation in Mansfield and Texarkana. President Eisenhower took no action on the matter.

Shivers endorsed Eisenhower for President in 1956. The President carried Texas in November at the same time moderate conservative Democrat Price Daniel [*q.v.*] was elected governor. In late 1956 Shivers's advisory committee returned 21 proposals to maintain segregation. They were too late for his signature and awaited action by the new administration. Following Shivers's retirement from politics in January 1957, he was named chairman of Western Pipe Line, Inc.

[MJS]

For further information:
Numan Bartley, *The Rise of Massive Resistance* (Baton Rouge, 1969).

SHORT, DEWEY
b. April 7, 1898; Galena, Mo.
Republican Representative, Mo., 1929-31, 1935-56; Chairman, Armed Services Committee, 1953-55; Assistant Secretary of the Army for Civil-Military Affairs, March 1957- January 1961.

Born into a family that settled in Missouri after the Civil War, Short began campaigning for Republican candidates at age 18. After receiving a B.A. degree from Baker University in 1917, he attended Boston University, where he received an Bachelor of Sacred Theology degree in 1922. He spent a year studying theology and philosophy abroad and from 1921 to 1926 took law courses at Harvard University. Short was first elected as a U.S. representative from Missouri in 1928. He was defeated for reelection in 1930. Redistricting enabled him again to win election to the House in 1934.

In 1939 Short became the second-ranking Republican on the Military Affairs Committee. After a European trip he became a leading isolationist and was proposed as a vice presidential candidate at the 1940 Republican National Convention. Short maintained his distrust of foreign entanglements and opposed lend-lease in March 1941. Following World War II he urged the U.S. to build Pacific bases to counter Soviet aggression and predicted Korea would be a "hot spot." Short became ranking Republican on the Armed Services Committee in 1949 and supported creation of the Department of Defense during the 80th Congress (1947-48). In September 1952 he urged that U.N. forces in Korea go "all the way" to the Yalu River and end the division of that country.

Short became chairman of the Armed Services Committee when Republicans organized Congress in January 1953. The Korean war occupied most of the first six months of his term. In January Short dismissed charges brought by Rep. Clare E. Hoffman (R, Mich.) [q.v.] that the Army had staged a useless Korean raid to impress visitors. While President Eisenhower tried to set the stage for peace talks in April, Short urged that negotiations be delayed until the Communists permitted international inspection of prison camps. When a truce was signed in July, Short stated that military victory would have been possible if the Army had not been restricted.

Eisenhower conferred with Short over his proposed 1954 budget in May 1953. The President stressed the fact that it gave the Air Force $20 billion, "more than 40% of all defense funds," as part of an effort to build 120 combat wings by July 1955. After the conference Short announced that the Administration did not deserve "full credit" for the buildup. He and other members of Congress had originally proposed increasing the number of combat wings to 143 by July 1955. Nevertheless, Short supported the Eisenhower budget.

Short became involved in the defense debate over the defense reorganization bill drafted by the Administration and sent to Congress in April. The plan was intended to streamline and improve the Department of Defense by making the chairman of the Joint Chiefs of Staff responsible for the staff's work and giving him tenure power over personnel. The Representative initially opposed the plan as possibly leading to a "military dictatorship" but was persuaded to support it by presidential aide Bryce Harlow [q.v.]. Supported by Short and the ranking Democrat on the Committee, Rep. Carl Vinson (D, Ga.) [q.v.], the reorganization plan was approved by the House and went into effect in June 1953.

Chairman Short attempted to calm American fears of nuclear attack in April 1954 by announcing that U.S. A-bomb defenses were "in pretty good shape" and saying it was "silly" to talk of evacuating large cities. He counselled moderation in July when Senate Majority Leader William F. Knowland (R, Calif.) [q.v.] stated that the U.S. should quit the U.N. if Communist China were admitted. The Democratic leadership supported Knowland but other senators and Rep. Short announced they opposed withdrawal.

The Democrats organized the 84th Congress in January 1955, and Short lost his chairmanship. In June 1956 he opposed an $800 million supplemental increase in Air Force funds proposed against Administration wishes by a House-Senate conference committee. Short objected to the increase on the grounds that the Air Force lacked facilities and manpower to utilize the extra money and that it would lead to an unbalanced budget. The additional funding was nevertheless approved.

Short lost his House seat to Democrat Charles H. Brown in November 1956. The following February President Eisenhower nominated him to be assistant secretary of the Army for civil-military affairs. His selection was confirmed by the Senate in March. In August 1957 he declared that decreased purchases of weapons by the Armed Services due to inflation would not seriously impair American defenses. In 1959 Short told a subcommittee of the House Armed Services Committee that charges of enlisted men being used to perform menial chores for officers were exaggerated. He retained his post until the end of the Eisenhower Administration.

[MLL]

SHUMAN, CHARLES B(AKER)
b. April 27, 1907; Sullivan, Ill.
President, American Farm Bureau Federation, 1954-70.

Shuman grew up on a family farm, earned B.S. and M.S. degrees in agriculture at the University of Illinois and became active in farm organizations in the 1930s. He said that in those years he "learned about bureaucracy." Although a Democrat, he was an enemy of many of Franklin D. Roosevelt's agricultural policies. Shuman became a member of the Board of Directors of the Illinois Agricultural Association in 1941 and its president in 1945. In the latter year Shuman also became a director of the American Farm Bureau Federation (AFBF).

In 1954 Shuman was elected to the AFBF presidency, succeeding Albert B. Kline. The largest general farm organization in the U.S., the AFBF had a membership of over 1.6 million farm families, concentrated mainly in the Midwest. Under Shuman's influence it moved away from support of New Deal farm policies and in the 1950s was characterized as the representative of the large commercial farmers. In response to charges that he had made the AFBF an agent of big business, Shuman said that it was incorrect to claim that "we represent either big or little farmers. We're a cross section of the entire farm population." However, observers noted that the AFBF membership included many farmers whose wealth and large holdings inclined them to oppose government controls. In contrast, members of the next two largest farm organizations, the National Farmers Union and the National Grange, tended to own small and medium-sized farms.

As a spokesman for the free enterprise

system, Shuman generally favored the conservative policies of President Eisenhower's Secretary of Agriculture, Ezra Taft Benson [q.v.]. In Shuman's first year as AFBF president, he strongly backed Benson's proposal for flexible government price supports for basic farm products, viewing it as a feasible, gradual method of returning American agriculture to the free market. When Democrats and some farm organizations called for a return to rigid 90% of parity farm price supports in 1955, Shuman characterized the plan as a "backward step" that would "wreck this economy" and further depress declining agricultural income. Shuman applied his free enterprise philosophy and opposition to government interference even more consistently than Benson. In September 1955 he rejected Benson's plan for government support purchases of pork and proposed instead a program calling for promotion to increase pork and lard use and to develop export markets, including the Soviet bloc. Shuman and the AFBF consistently viewed the expansion of foreign markets as a superior strategy to government price supports as a means of increasing farm income. However, he overcame his aversion to government interference in agriculture in January 1956, when he told the Senate Agriculture and Forestry Committee that Secretary Benson's "soil bank" plan, a program in which the government would pay farmers to remove a specified acreage from cultivation, was a "step in the right direction" of reducing the overproduction of basic crops. In both 1956 and 1958 Shuman supported President Eisenhower's vetoes of farm bills that sought to restore high price supports.

Shuman was a severe critic of the agricultural policies of the Kennedy and Johnson Administrations. He especially opposed Democratic efforts to impose strict marketing controls. Shuman left the AFBF in 1970, but he remained active on the boards of a number of agencies and companies, including the Export-Import Bank, the Economic Development Administration, the Illinois Power Co. and the Chicago Mercantile Exchange. [See KENNEDY, JOHNSON Volumes]

[JCH]

SHUTTLESWORTH, FRED L(EE)
b. March 18, 1922; Mugler, Ala.
President, Alabama Christian Movement for Human Rights, 1956-70;
Secretary, Southern Christian Leadership Conference, 1957-70.

Shuttlesworth grew up near Birmingham, Ala., and received a B.A. from Selma College and a B.S. from Alabama State College. A Baptist minister, he began preaching in 1948 at two rural churches near Selma. In March 1953 he became pastor of Birmingham's Bethel Baptist Church. There Shuttlesworth began to involve himself in civil rights causes, participating, for example, in an unsuccessful attempt in 1955 to get blacks placed on the local police force. He joined the NAACP, and when the organization was outlawed in Alabama in 1956, he helped establish the Alabama Christian Movement for Human Rights (ACMHR) to continue the fight for black equality in Birmingham. Shuttlesworth was elected its first president.

Called the "Johannesburg of America" by some blacks, Birmingham was governed in the late-1950s by officials who firmly opposed any attempts at desegregation. As the leader of the integration movement in the city, Shuttlesworth headed many attempts to end segregation in local public facilities. On Dec. 20, 1956, shortly after the Supreme Court had declared segregation on local transportation illegal, Shuttlesworth called on the city commissioners to end segregated seating on Birmingham's buses. His home was destroyed by dynamite on Christmas night, but Shuttlesworth still led more than 20 blacks the next day onto local buses, where they sat in the seats reserved for whites. Following the arrest of 22 blacks, Shuttlesworth called off any more demonstrations until the segregation law could be tested in the courts. In October 1958, just before a federal court hearing on the law was to be held, the city commission repealed the statute and passed a new one authorizing the bus company to establish its own segregation rules. Shuttlesworth then helped organize a test of this new ordinance. Thirteen blacks were arrested on

Oct. 20 for sitting in seats reserved for whites, and Shuttlesworth himself was arrested the next day for having "incited" the protest. A legal challenge to the new law was started the next month, but not until November 1961 did a federal district court finally order an end to segregation on Birmingham's city buses.

Shuttlesworth also tried to desegregate the waiting rooms at Birmingham's railroad terminal in March 1957. That September he tried to enroll four black children, two of them his own, at a white high school. He was beaten by a mob outside the building, and the children were refused admittance. Shuttlesworth filed a court suit challenging the 1957 Alabama pupil placement law, which was intended to forestall school desegregation. However he lost the case in November 1958 when the U.S. Supreme Court ruled that the statute was not unconstitutional on its face. In June 1958 an attempt was made to dynamite Shuttlesworth's church. It failed only because a volunteer guarding the church removed the explosives before they went off. During the spring of 1960, Shuttlesworth aided student sit-ins in Birmingham and was arrested for his participation.

A believer in the philosophy of nonviolent direct action espoused by Martin Luther King, Jr. [q.v.], Shuttlesworth helped organize the Southern Christian Leadership Conference (SCLC) in 1957. He was elected its secretary and became one of King's top aides in the SCLC. He spoke at the May 1957 Prayer Pilgrimage in Washington, D.C. In April 1960 Shuttlesworth, three other black ministers and the *New York Times* were sued for libel by the city commissioners of Montgomery, Ala., because of an ad placed in the *Times* criticizing municipal officials. The Supreme Court overturned the $500,000 judgment against the defendants in March 1964.

Shuttlesworth became pastor of a Baptist church in Cincinnati, Ohio, in 1960, but he remained president of the ACMHR and a leader of Birmingham's integration movement. He suggested and then led a major anti-segregation campaign in Birmingham in the spring of 1963 which contributed to passage of the 1964 Civil Rights Act. He participated in other desegregation campaigns sponsored by the SCLC and remained a key aide to King during the 1960s. [See KENNEDY, JOHNSON Volumes]

[CAB]

SMATHERS, GEORGE A(RMISTEAD)
b. Nov. 14, 1913; Atlantic City, N.J.
Democratic Senator, Fla., 1951-69.

Son of a New Jersey judge and Democratic leader who moved to Florida for his health, George Smathers was raised in Miami. As a young lawyer in the late-1930s, he became a political protege of Sen. Claude Pepper (D, Fla.), a strong supporter of the New Deal. Pepper subsequently helped Smathers obtain the post of assistant U.S. district attorney for southern Florida and in 1946 backed his successful bid for a seat in the House of Representatives.

Although regarded as a "Pepper man" in the House, Smathers turned sharply to the right when he challenged his mentor for the senatorial nomination in 1950. The Florida primary attracted national attention in what was viewed as the first major test of the Communist issue in the 1950 elections. Smathers attacked his opponent, who had long been an advocate of friendlier relations with the USSR and had spoken before organizations later characterized as Communist-front groups, as a Communist sympathizer bent on entangling the state in "the spiraling spider web of the Red network." The most important issue in the campaign, however, was 'the New Deal-Fair Deal tradition itself, with which Pepper was closely identified. Backed by a coalition of powerful business interests who opposed Pepper's liberal stands on taxes and labor legislation, Smathers appealed to upper-income voters, including many Republicans, with a program of economic conservatism and opposition to what he called "creeping socialism" in Washington. Smathers defeated Pepper by 60,000 votes, and in November he won the general election. [See TRUMAN Volume]

As a senator during the 1950s, Smathers was a conservative on social and economic issues, an outspoken defender of racial segregation in the South and a foe of civil rights legislation. While in the upper house he became a close aide to Senate Majority Leader Lyndon B. Johnson (D, Tex.) [q.v.] and a powerful member of the small group of senators, known as the Senate "Establishment," who made committee appointments and could often decide the fate of legislation. Johnson placed him in charge of the Senate Democratic Elections Committee in 1956, where he used his position to disburse campaign money to conservatives and build important political connections among influential Southern senators. Smathers's power was enhanced still further when he was named acting majority leader in Johnson's absence.

During the Eisenhower Administration Smathers used his influence on Capitol Hill to promote bills that were in the interests of oil companies and railroads, some of which were clients of his Miami law firm. He was one of the leading backers of the successful drive in 1953 to get the oil-rich tidelands away from the federal government and into the hands of the states, which were regarded as more generous in granting concessions to private enterprise. As chairman of the Commerce Committee's Surface Transportation Subcommittee, Smathers introduced the Transportation Act of 1958. The measure aided financially pressed railroads by granting them loan guarantees for the purchase of new equipment and making it easier for them to discontinue unprofitable passenger services.

Under the Kennedy Administration Smathers maintained a conservative voting record, but after the 1964 enfranchisement of 300,000 Florida blacks, he became more liberal on many domestic issues. His attempts to satisfy his constituents and his continued efforts to aid the associations and businesses that supported his campaigns resulted in a contradictory voting pattern during the Johnson Administration. Smathers remained a powerful force in the Senate during the 1960s, but towards the latter part of the decade, as many of his business dealings became known, he became the target of frequent charges of influence peddling. Claiming poor health, he did not seek reelection in 1968. However, Smathers stayed in Washington as the chief lobbyist for a powerful alliance of rail, trucking and water transportation interests. [See KENNEDY, JOHNSON Volumes]

[TLH]

For further information:
Robert Sherrill, *Gothic Politics in the Deep South* (New York, 1968).

SMITH, EARL T.A.
b. July 8, 1903; Newport, R.I.
Ambassador to Cuba, June 1957-
January 1959.

Soon after graduating from Yale in 1926, Smith became a member of the New York Coffee and Sugar Exchange. From 1930 to 1937 he was a partner of Paige, Smith & Remick, an investment brokerage firm. Smith served in the U.S. Air Force during World War II and was a member of the War Production Board. During the 1950s he actively entered Republican politics, serving from 1954 to 1955 as chairman of the Florida State Finance Committee and from 1954 to 1956 as a member of the Republican National Finance Committee.

In June 1957 Eisenhower appointed Smith ambassador to Cuba. Having no experience in diplomacy, he owed his appointment to his fund raising activities for the Republican Party and his personal ties to Cuban political and business leaders. He had made frequent trips to Cuba in the previous 30 years. Justifying his appointment, Smith said he "knew Cuba well and . . . felt I could judge the thoughts and moods of the Cuban people."

Smith's appointment marked an official change in the attitude of the State Department toward the government of Gen. Fulgencio Batista. During the early years of the decade, the U.S. had supported the Cuban dictator, but by 1957 the Department, aware of growing opposition to the repressive regime among broad segments of the Cuban population and in the U.S., abandoned this policy. Smith was instructed to adopt a position of neutrality in the con-

flict between the government and the leftist rebels led by Fidel Castro.

Smith's initial activities as ambassador reflected the change in policy. Installing himself in office in mid-July, he quickly created an image that differed markedly from that of his predecessor, Arthur Gardner, who had been thoroughly pro-Batista. In a July 24 press conference he said, "We have nothing substantial to make us believe [that Castro's movement] is red-inspired." Visiting Santiago in the midst of an upsurge in terrorist activity, he labeled Batista's methods in combating the rebels "excessive police action."

As the revolt progressed the State Department remained divided over which faction to support. Smith, however, became increasingly anti-Castro, believing that the movement was infiltrated by Communists. In early 1958 the Batista government used U.S. military equipment to quell disturbances in Cienfuegos in violation of a 1951 military assistance agreement with the U.S. In reaction, an anti-Batista group in the State Department convinced the Administration to end arms shipments to the dictator. Smith vigorously opposed the action, declared by the U.S. government in March 1958. He maintained it only weakened the chances of eventual constitutional order in Cuba.

By the end of 1958 Castro's movement had gained broad support among the American public. In part, the sympathy was generated by a conscious reaction against the domestic anti-Communist crusade of the early-1950s. In part it was the result of the reactionary reputations of many of Castro's assailants in America. More importantly, Smith's attitudes were at odds with the State Department which, by 1959, had decided to take a conciliatory stand towards the rebel leader.

Castro's victory in the Cuban civil war resulted in Smith's replacement. The more conciliatory Phillip W. Bonsal took over the post as ambassador. President Eisenhower accepted Smith's resignation Jan. 10, 1959. During Senate Internal Security Subcommittee's hearings in 1960, Smith charged that Batista's downfall had been assisted by the Central Intelligence Agency, State Department officials, most U.S. officials connected with the U.S. embassy and "segments of the press." After his resignation from government service, Smith returned to his business dealings.

[ACD]

SMITH, GERALD L(YMAN) K(ENNETH)
b. Feb. 27, 1898; Pardeeville, Wisc.
d. April 15, 1976; Glendale, Ca.
National Director, Christian Nationalist Crusade, 1947-76.

The son of four generations of rural evangelical preachers, Gerald L.K. Smith began his oratorical career as a child. He attended Valparaiso and Butler Universities in Indiana. At the age of 19 Smith heard a spiritual call and ordained himself a minister in the Disciples of Christ Church. His popularity as a preacher grew so that in 1928 he was invited to lead a fashionable congregation in Shreveport, La. There he met Huey P. Long who was running for governor.

Smith worked in Shreveport as a social reformer and union organizer. His and Long's views on social injustice corresponded. When Long was elected governor, Smith became his right-hand man. In one instance he convinced Gov. Long to save Shreveport homes from foreclosure by real estate interests. In 1934, when Long founded the "Share Our Wealth" crusade, a populist movement to redistribute income and build public projects, Smith toured Louisiana setting up clubs. The Long-Smith brand of oratorical populism always teetered between reform and demagoguery—blaming certain groups or interests for the deprivations of their followers.

Following Long's assassination in September 1935, Smith scrambled to maintain control of the Share Our Wealth movement, but with no base in Louisiana he failed to rally the Long machine. His opponents had him arrested for inciting to riot and deported from Louisiana. At this point Smith became an extreme conservative.

Smith was an ardent opponent of President Franklin Roosevelt, whom he charac-

terized as "Franklin Delano Jewsvelt." He joined Rev. Charles Coughlin in founding the Union Party in 1936 and running William Lemke for President. Lemke received less than a million votes. Following American entry into World War II in 1942, Smith founded his racist, pro-fascist paper *The Cross and the Flag*, which soon found its way onto the Attorney General's list of seditious publications. He organized the America First Party which ran him for President in 1944. He failed to get on the ballot in most states. Using his list of America First supporters after the War, Smith founded the Christian Nationalist Crusade in 1947 to realize his dream of "a white, Christian America." The platform of the Crusade called for "deportation of Zionists," the breakup of "Jewish Gestapo organizations," shipment of blacks to Africa and dissolution of the United Nations.

In 1952 Gerald Smith denounced Republican presidential candidate Dwight Eisenhower as "a Swedish Jew" and hence unfit for office. He supported Gen. Douglas MacArthur for President. Vice President Richard Nixon's [q.v.] humble Protestant beginnings and anti-Communism appealed to Smith, who supported Sen. Joseph McCarthy's (R, Wisc.) [q.v.] crusade against alleged Communists in government. Running for reelection in 1956, Nixon received Smith's unsolicited supported, which he quickly disavowed.

Smith denounced the Supreme Court's decisions banning segregation in public schools and asserting constitutional protection for works deemed pornographic. On many occasions he demanded that "the pro-criminal, pro-Communist, pro-pornographic Supreme Court must be impeached." He castigated Congress as "impotent, insipid and cowardly" when it passed civil rights legislation in 1957 and called Sen. McCarthy's death "murder" the same year. Smith characterized himself as "the persecuted victim of a gang of international character assassins" that had destroyed McCarthy, dismissed MacArthur during the Korean conflict and campaigned to "destroy" the House Un-American Activities Committee.

Continually appealing for funds from his followers, Smith had amassed a fortune by the end of the 1950s. It has been speculated that the former preacher's switch from left to right was motivated purely in hopes of financial gain. "Religion and patriotism, keep going on that, it's the only way you can really get them het up," he said, "and then a fellow like myself . . . will have the people with him hook, line and sinker. I'll teach them how to hate."

Gerald L. K. Smith moved to Eureka Springs, Ark., in 1965. There his erection of a seven-story statue of Jesus and production of an anti-semitic passion play aroused considerable controversy. He died in 1976.

[MJS]

SMITH, H. ALEXANDER
b. Jan. 30, 1880; New York, N.Y.
d. Oct. 28, 1966; Princeton, N.J.
Republican Senator, N.J., 1944-58.

Smith graduated from Princeton University in 1901 and earned his law degree from Columbia a few years later. He was admitted to the New York bar but after an attack of tuberculosis moved to Colorado to regain his health. He opened a law practice there and also engaged in mining, public utilities, railroad and land speculation. Deeply influenced by his Princeton professor Woodrow Wilson's idea of an international organization to prevent wars, Smith joined the League to Enforce Peace. When the U.S. entered World War I Smith worked for the Federal Food Administration as Herbert Hoover's [q.v.] assistant. After the War, he participated in Hoover's European relief program. Smith then returned to Princeton in 1919 as the University's executive secretary, where he supervised the modernization of the curriculum. He held that post until 1927, when he became a lecturer in international affairs. In 1932 Smith resumed his law practice with a prestigious New York law firm.

A life-long Republican, Smith worked for the election of Hoover as President in 1928 and 1932. In 1934 he became the state party treasurer and seven years later was elected state party chairman. Campaigning on a platform stressing the acceptance of the country's increasing role in world affairs, Smith won a Senate seat from New Jersey in 1944.

In the upper house Smith continued to support U.S. involvement in world affairs. He backed U.S. entry into the U.N. and supported most Truman Administration foreign policy. However, he broke with the President on the question of policy toward Nationalist China. He joined such Nationalist supporters as Sen. William Knowland (R, Calif.) [q.v.] in advocating all-out aid to the Nationalists in the civil war against the Communists. When the Nationalist government fell in 1949, Smith joined the so-called China bloc in the Senate that pressured the government into refusing to recognize the Communist regime and opposing its entry into the U.N. [See TRUMAN Volume].

Smith maintained his militant stand on China throughout the Eisenhower Administration. He was a member of the steering panel of the Committee of One Million, founded in 1953 to prevent the admission of Communist China to the U.N. The following year he traveled to Formosa and returned to the U.S. reporting that Chiang Kai-shek urged the U.S. to give him the "green light" for an invasion of the mainland. In January 1955 Smith said he would favor a U.N. blockade of the mainland as a last-ditch action to free U.S. prisoners of war held by the Communists. During the Quemoy and Matsu crisis of 1958, when Communist China renewed shelling the Nationalist held offshore islands, the Senator said the U.S. would definitely fight to prevent Communist seizure of the islands.

A quiet, thoughtful, deeply religious man, Smith was troubled by the way Sen. Joseph R. McCarthy (R, Wisc.) [q.v.] conducted his anti-Communist crusade. Yet he never publicly expressed his displeasure with McCarthy. Known as a conciliator in the Senate, Smith sought to offset Senate attempts to censure McCarthy in 1954. On June 15, Sen. Ralph Flanders (R, Vt.) [q.v.] announced that within two weeks he would introduce a resolution to censure the Wisconsin Republican. The measure would state that McCarthy's conduct was "unbecoming a member of the United States Senate . . . contrary to senatorial tradition, and tended to bring the Senate into disrepute, and such conduct is thereby condemned." One week later, on July 31, Smith proposed the Senate discard the Flanders resolution in favor of one providing for a special committee of three Republicans and three Democrats, with Vice President Richard M. Nixon [q.v.] as ex-officio chairman, to study "problems created by the fact that there had been infiltration of Communists and others security risks into sensitive positions and the method and procedures employed in exposing and eliminating such security risks . . . ." No action was taken on his plan. The following week Smith, in a television interview, said that the move to censure "had embarrassed" his efforts to get McCarthy to go to Eisenhower with an "offer to work with the government and not against it." Smith, however, voted for the condemnation of the Senator in December 1954.

In 1958 Smith decided not to seek reelection to the Senate. He then served as a foreign policy adviser to the State Department. In 1959 he attended the Colombo Conference at which he proposed an ambitious American foreign aid program for Asia. Smith then retired from public life. He died in October 1966.

[JB]

SMITH, HOWARD W(ORTH)
b. Feb. 2, 1883; Broad Run, Va.
d. Oct. 3, 1976; Alexandria, Va.
Democratic Representative, Va.,
1931-67; Chairman, House Rules
Committee, 1955-67.

Smith attended the Bethel Military Academy and received his Bachelor of Laws degree from the University of Virginia in 1903. He practiced law in Alexandria for the next 20 years and then became judge of the Alexandria Corporation Court in 1922. He was appointed judge of the 16th Circuit Court of Virginia in 1928. Two years later he was elected to the House of Representatives.

Smith maintained a conservative record in the House, opposing civil rights legislation and excessive federal spending. During the 1940s the Representative became known principally as the author of the Smith Act, giving the government the right to prosecute anyone advocating the violent overthrow of the U.S. government, and of the Smith-Connally Labor Disputes Act, limiting the right to strike during national emergencies.

In 1955 Judge Smith became chairman of the Rules Committee. Often called the "third house" of Congress, this panel determined the length and manner of floor debate on a bill and whether the House should enter into conference with the Senate if different, but similar bills were passed. In polls taken by legislators and journalists, Judge Smith was ranked as one of the most powerful men on Capitol Hill—second only to House Speaker Sam Rayburn (D, Tex.) [q.v.]. Smith was often called "the traffic cop of the House" (a term he resented) because he controlled what bills his Committee should vote on and whether they should proceed to the floor.

From 1955 to 1960 Smith used all his legislative skill to block civil rights measures. In March 1956 he joined 100 other Southern members of Congress in signing the "Southern Manifesto." This declaration denounced the Supreme Court's 1954 public school desegregation decision and pledged to fight it through lawful means. Judge Smith introduced it into the House, where he presented a fiery defense of states rights against federal usurpation of local power. He said that he had "a sacred obligation" to warn his fellow Americans that the decision countervened the Constitution.

The following year Smith attempted to prevent passage of the 1957 civil rights bill. In August the House leadership called a meeting with Smith to clear the way for the full chamber to consider the measure. Smith, however, could not be found in Washington. His office finally informed the public that he had had to return to one of his dairy farms because a barn had burned down. Rayburn humorously stated he knew that Smith would have done anything to prevent a vote on the bill, "but I never suspected he would resort to arson." Smith delayed Committee consideration of a civil rights bill for over a month and was finally forced, as a result of a petition from his own Committee, to hold hearings. He then arranged for a large number of civil rights opponents to testify before his panel in a further attempt to stall the bill. However, because the Administration and House leaders favored the measure, Smith finally had to report it favorably to the House floor. The House passed the bill in June.

Smith almost succeeded in killing the central portion of the 1960 civil rights bill, which provided for voting referees to enroll black voters. He and his Southern cohorts supported an ultra-liberal amendment to that portion, hoping that Republicans would then join Southern Democrats in voting down the whole section. The amended segment of the bill was voted down. However, the Republicans offered a new referee plan similar to the one before the amendment and the central section was passed.

A fiscal conservative who opposed the expansion of federal government spending, Smith was more successful in blocking or slowing down housing and education legislation. During the last days of the 85th Congress (1957-58), Smith avoided holding hearings on a dozen major bills, including relief to depressed areas and mineral subsidies, by simply disappearing. He returned after a week saying "he had had some hay on his farm that needed tending." The conservative *Newsweek* columnist Raymond Moley wrote that Smith should be considered one of the "most valuable members" of Congress for his conduct.

In April 1956 the Supreme Court ruled that states had no power to punish persons advocating forceable overthrow of the federal government. Smith disagreed with the decision and introduced legislation giving the states the right to pass their own acts. However, the measure failed.

During the Kennedy Administration the House reduced the Rules Committee's and thus Smith's power. This made it easier to pass civil rights and liberal legislation, which the aged Congressman opposed. As a result of reapportionment, which placed many moderates in Smith's district, he lost the 1966 primary. Smith then returned to his dairy farms and died in 1976. [See KENNEDY, JOHNSON Volumes]

[JB]

SMITH, MARGARET CHASE
b. Dec. 14, 1897; Skowhegan, Me.
Republican Senator, Me., 1949-73.

After graduating from Skowhegan High School in 1916, Margaret Chase taught in a local primary school and then worked as a switchboard operator and later as an executive of the local telephone company. In 1919 she became circulation manager of the Skowhegan *Independent Reporter*. In May 1930 Chase married Clyde Harold Smith, who served in the U.S. House of Representatives from 1936 to 1940. When Rep. Smith died in 1940, Margaret Chase Smith was elected to fill his seat.

In the House Smith fought for passage of the Woman's Armed Services Integration Act of 1948, which improved the status of women in the military, and voted with the six other congresswomen to defeat the House proposal withdrawing half of the funds for day-care facilities for wartime factory workers. Although strongly supported by Maine's organized labor movement, she voted with other Republicans to override President Truman's veto of the Taft-Hartley bill in 1947. In 1949 Smith became the first woman elected to the Senate. [See TRUMAN Volume]

Smith emerged as an early critic of loyalty-security investigations. Although she had backed the Dies Committee's investigation of "un-American" activities in 1945, she did not support the establishment of a permanent House Un-American Activities Committee in 1950. She was also one of the first senators to condemn Sen. Joseph R. McCarthy's (R, Wisc.) [*q.v.*] anti-Communist crusade. In the 1954 Maine Republican primary, Smith defeated a McCarthy protege by a five to one margin. That December Smith voted in favor of censuring the Wisconsin Republican. Perhaps because of these efforts, Lee Mortimer and Jack Lait implied in their book, *U.S.A. Confidential*, that Smith was pro-Communist, an allegation which led Smith to successfully sue them for $1 million for libel in 1956.

An independent senator, Smith joined Republicans in supporting the reduction of funds for the Tennessee Valley Authority and voting for state ownership of offshore oil in 1952. She also backed the Civil Rights Act in 1957. However, Smith voted for the Democratic depressed areas bill in 1959, despite Eisenhower's opposition, and proposed a constitutional amendment in December 1960 for the direct nomination and election of the President and the vice president and the elimination of the electoral college.

As an active member of the Senate Armed Services Committee, Smith organized a five-member subcommittee in 1953 to investigate the reasons behind a shortage of ammunition in Korea. She voted with the Democrats, over Republican objections, for an additional half-million dollars for the Air Force beyond Eisenhower's request in 1956.

During the Kennedy and Johnson Administrations, Smith was one of only a few Republicans to generally vote for the Presidents' domestic policies. On the other hand, she accused the Kennedy Administration of lacking the will to use nuclear weapons when necessary and opposed the 1963 nuclear test ban treaty. The ranking Republican on the Armed Services Committee after 1967, Smith consistently voted for expenditures for the Vietnam war. During the Nixon Administration, she opposed the Safeguard antiballistic missile system and the supersonic transport. Smith was defeated for reelection in November 1972 after 32 years in Congress. [See KENNEDY, JOHNSON, NIXON/FORD Volumes]

[RSG]

SMITH, WALTER BEDELL
b. Oct. 5, 1895; Indianapolis, Ind.
d. Aug. 9, 1961; Washington, D.C.
Undersecretary of State, February 1953-September 1954.

A descendent of 18th century settlers, Smith became a private in the Indiana National Guard in 1911, while attending St. Peter and Paul's School. He later enrolled in Butler University but left before graduating to support his family. He saw action as a lieutenant in France during World War I. During the 1920s and 1930s Smith was as-

signed to a number of different stations in the U.S. and the Philippines. He rose gradually through the ranks and was a brigadier general (temporary) in 1942, when he became Gen. Dwight D. Eisenhower's chief of staff. Smith was responsible for planning and coordinating the invasions of North Africa, Italy and Normandy. He then negotiated the surrender of Italy and received the unconditional surrender of Nazi Germany. Immediately following World War II. Smith served as the chief of staff of the American occupation forces in Germany.

In February 1946 President Harry S. Truman appointed Smith ambassador to the Soviet Union, an experience he later described in his book *My Three Years in Moscow* (1950). Smith returned home in 1949 to resume his military career as commander of the First Army. In September 1950 Truman appointed him to head the Central Intelligence Agency (CIA). [See TRUMAN Volume]

Smith resigned from the CIA in 1953 to become undersecretary of state. Because John Foster Dulles [q.v.] spent most of his time formulating policy and traveling abroad, Smith held the major responsibility for administering the State Department. He expected to be a close adviser to Eisenhower and to have an influence on the Administration's foreign policy, but Dulles's centralization of decision making in his own hands prevented Smith from realizing these goals.

In the spring of 1954 Smith headed the National Security Council's Special Committee on the U.S. and Indochina, formed to study the American response to the deteriorating situation in Vietnam. By that time the French had concluded that without massive American aid the beleaguered fortress of Dien Bien Phu would fall. Desperate to maintain the post, French Chief of Staff Gen. Paul Henry Ely asked Eisenhower for direct American military intervention in March. The following month the Committee issued a report advocating collective action by the U.S. and her allies on the problem and recommending the creation of a mutual Asian defense treaty, underwritten by the major Western powers, to protect Southeast Asia from further

Communist aggression. The report was one of the factors leading to the establishment of the Southeast Asian Treaty Organization later that year.

In a CBS television interview on April 11, Smith explained the importance of Indochina for American strategy and economic interests in Asia. If this area fell to the Communists, he predicted, the other free states would fall like dominoes to the enemy. Smith, considered by many to be one of the leading hawks in the Administration, advocated direct American military intervention in the war. He supported Dulles's futile attempts to enlist the British in a united show of force against the Communists. After the British rebuffed Dulles, Smith, on his own initiative, proposed that the U.S., with the endorsement and help of Australia and New Zealand, enter the war. However, Eisenhower and the two nations rejected this suggestion.

With the opening of the Geneva Conference on Korea and Indochina on April 26 and the fall of Dien Bien Phu on May 7, Smith privately conceded that, as a result of U.S. refusal to aid the French, Vietnam would be partitioned into a Communist-controlled northern zone and a Western-dominated southern area. Smith, who led the U.S. delegation to the conference in the absence of Dulles, was instructed to play a passive role and not approve any settlement that would turn territory over to the Communists. He announced that the U.S. "took note" of the July 24 Geneva settlement that temporarily partitioned Vietnam until free elections could be held.

Smith retired from the State Department in October 1954. He continued to be an unofficial adviser to Eisenhower and Dulles on disarmament matters. He also wrote a second book, *Eisenhower's Six Great Decisions*, published in 1956.

[JB]

SMYLIE, ROBERT E.
b. Oct. 31, 1914: Marcus, Idaho
Governor, Ida., 1955-67.

Robert E. Smylie graduated from the College of Idaho and took his law degree at George Washington University in 1942.

Following service in the Coast Guard during World War II, he practiced law while becoming active in Idaho Republican politics. Smylie served as state attorney general from 1947 to 1954 and became deeply involved in the controversy over private versus federal development of a hydroelectric dam in Hell's Canyon on the Snake River.

During the early years of the Eisenhower Administration, Smylie was a prominent critic of government power development. He opposed the federal plan because he feared that the loss of state control of water rights would result in the diversion of water to neighboring states and because the giant dam would despoil the scenic Hell's Canyon area. Smylie favored the private development of three smaller dams spread along the Snake River. He was opposed by other Northwest governors, powerful Idaho congressmen and Oregon's Sen. Wayne Morse (Ind., Ore.) [q.v.], who argued that the dam was necessary for a cheap hydroelectric power system throughout the Northwest. In 1954 Smylie ran for governor of Idaho on a plank opposing the dam. In a state more concerned with water rights than cheap electrical power, Smylie won the election by 50,000 votes.

As governor, Smylie continued to oppose the dam. In hearings before the Senate Interior Committee in April 1955, he testified that federal development would be "tragic" and called for its "swift rejection," declaring that "75% of the people of Idaho" agreed with his stand. A year later, in July 1956, the Senate killed the bill authorizing a federal hydroelectric plant at Hell's Canyon.

Smylie went on to serve two more terms as governor. His last years, 1963 to 1965, were innovative, producing a landmark sales tax to aid local schools, extending the state's parks and recreation program and setting up a water resources board. Smylie's opposition to Sen. Barry Goldwater (R, Ariz.) [q.v.] as 1964 Republican presidential candidate earned him the ire of conservative state Republicans, and he lost the 1966 Republican nomination to a relative unknown. After leaving government he retired to his legal practice. [See KENNEDY, JOHNSON Volumes]

[MJS]

SOBELL, MORTON
b. April 11, 1917; New York, N.Y.
Convicted espionage agent

After receiving his B.S. degree from City College of New York in 1938, Sobell moved to Washington, D.C., to work for the Navy Bureau of Ordinance. He took an M.A. in electrical engineering from the University of Michigan in 1942 and then moved to Schenectady, N.Y., to work for the General Electric Co. Late he and his family returned to New York City, where he did research for a company working on classified government contracts.

Sobell was arrested in August 1950 on charges of conspiring to commit espionage for the Soviet Union. Although not accused of working directly with Ethel and Julius Rosenberg [q.v.] to transmit atomic secrets, he was tried with them. Trial evidence against him fell into two areas: testimony that he was involved in an espionage apparatus with the Rosenbergs and charges that he and his family took flight to Mexico after the Rosenbergs were taken into custody, in order to avoid his own arrest. Only one witness, his long-time friend Max Elitcher, testified without documentary proof of Sobell's involvement in espionage. Letters Sobell wrote from Mexico, in which he used different aliases, and reports of his activities there proved damaging to him. Later he maintained that he had been kidnapped in Mexico and delivered illegally to FBI agents at the border. Sobell was judged guilty with the Rosenbergs and given a maximum 30-year sentence. [See TRUMAN Volume]

From the moment of his arrest, Sobell steadfastly asserted his innocence. Many who believed the Rosenbergs had been unjustly convicted also felt that Sobell had suffered abuse by the law. In fact, many people who thought the Rosenbergs guilty still claimed that he had not received a fair hearing. After the Rosenberg executions, money and legal efforts that had been devoted to their defense was used to aid the Committee to Free Morton Sobell (an organization led by his wife, Helen). Support for Sobell became so vocal that, during a 1956 court

meeting to hear new trial motions, Judge Irving Kaufman—the original trial judge—denounced what he called "extralegal means resorted to in order to arouse emotions, public opinion or anything of that character."

On the advice of his lawyers, Sobell never testified on his own behalf during the original trial. In 1953 he regretted that action. He submitted to the Court of Appeals—which had previously upheld his conviction by a 2-1 vote—an affidavit detailing his activities before he left the U.S. and after he arrived in Mexico. Again he denied any involvement in espionage and challenged the government to verify his own account of events. The court rejected his appeal. Sobell heard of the rejection from a cell in Alcatraz Federal Penitentiary, where he had been transferred in late 1952. His supporters charged that the government placed him in one of the nation's most notorious prisons in order to make him confess to non-existent crimes.

In 1957, while the Supreme Court was considering once again whether to review his case, Sobell was connected in the press to another spy trial. A witness, testifying against accused Soviet spy Rudolph Abel, said he had been instructed by the USSR to give money to Helen Sobell and solicit her help in espionage work. He said he never contacted her but kept the money himself. Mrs. Sobell ridiculed the highly publicized testimony as a transparent attempt by government prosecutors to influence the Supreme Court. No legal actions were taken against her. Shortly afterwards the Supreme Court refused for the eighth time to review Sobell's case.

Sobell won a minor victory in 1958, when he was transferred from Alcatraz to the more relaxed Atlanta Penitentiary. In 1963 he moved to a Springfield, Mo., prison for medical treatment, and in 1965 he was changed to the Lewisburg, Pa., prison. Six years later President John F. Kennedy received an appeal for clemency for Sobell. The petition included the names and statements of such American leaders as Rev. Martin Luther King, Jr. [q.v.], Sen. Lee Metcalf (D, Mont.) [q.v.], Reinhold Niebuhr [q.v.], scientist Harold Urey and historian Maxwell Geismar. Clemency was denied.

In 1962 Sobell became eligible for parole; but it was refused. After serving 17 years and 9 months in prison, he was released in 1969 with time off for good behavior. He again faced court proceedings in 1971, when his parole board denied him permission to attend anti-Vietnam war demonstrations or speak before a Communist-sponsored group. Sobell filed suit, charging violation of his constitutional rights. Terming the parole board's reasons for denial "silly," a federal judge upheld Sobell's suit. In 1974 Sobell wrote *On Doing Time*, a book describing the background of his case and his experiences in federal prisons. He returned to school to update his education and training and then worked as an engineer in medical electronics. He and Helen Sobell also give their time to political causes and to efforts by a national committee to win vindication for the Rosenbergs and Morton Sobell.

[TGD]

For further information:
Louis Nizer, *The Implosion Conspiracy* (New York, 1973).
Walter and Miriam Schneir, *Invitation to an Inquest* (Baltimore, 1973).

SOBELOFF, SIMON E(RNEST)
b. Dec. 3, 1894; Baltimore, Md.
d. July 11, 1973; Baltimore, Md.
U.S. Solicitor General, 1954-56;
Court of Appeals Judge, 1956-73.

A 1915 graduate of the University of Maryland law school, Sobeloff interspersed a private legal practice with a variety of public positions. He served as assistant city solicitor in Baltimore from 1919-23, as deputy city solicitor from 1927-31 and as U.S. attorney for Maryland from 1931-34. He was an adviser and confidant of liberal Republican Theodore McKeldin, and when McKeldin became mayor of Baltimore in 1943, he chose Sobeloff as city solicitor. Elected governor of Maryland in 1950, McKeldin appointed Sobeloff head of a spe-

cial commission on the reorganization of state government and in 1952 named him chief judge on the Maryland Court of Appeals. Sobeloff was then nominated U.S. Solicitor General by President Eisenhower in January 1954. The Senate confirmed the nomination on Feb. 25.

As Solicitor General, Sobeloff represented the federal government before the Supreme Court and decided which government cases should be appealed from lower to higher federal courts. During his tenure Sobeloff received special publicity in March 1955 when he failed to sign the government's brief in the case of John Peters, a Yale University physician who had been a consultant to the U.S. Public Health Service until dismissed as a security risk on order of the Civil Service Commission's Loyalty Review Board. The board refused to reveal the source or nature of the information it had against Peters, and the doctor challenged the board's procedures in court. The Justice Department's brief argued that the government had unlimited power to conceal the names of informants in security cases and that a federal employe had no right to confront or cross-examine his accusers in a loyalty proceeding. Although Sobeloff defended the government's position in other loyalty-security cases, he refused to do so in this instance because he considered the board's methods a violation of due process. Ultimately the Supreme Court decided the case in Peters's favor in June 1955 but on narrow, technical grounds.

In April 1955 Sobeloff presented in the Supreme Court the government's views on how school desegregation should be achieved. The Court had decided in May 1954 in *Brown* v. *Board of Education* that public school segregation was unconstitutional and had called for further argument on how to implement this ruling. Sobeloff took a middle position between attorneys for the black plaintiffs who wanted the Court to set a fixed deadline for desegregation and attorneys for several Southern states who wanted the matter left entirely to the discretion of federal district court judges in the South. The Solicitor General proposed that local school boards be given the primary responsibility for developing desegregation plans which would then be reviewed by the district courts. Although they must be careful not to let local officials frustrate school desegregation, he contended, district judges should approve programs for gradual integration so long as the local authorities made a genuine start toward desegregation in their proposals. In its second *Brown* decision of May 31, 1955, the Supreme Court unanimously adopted a position very similar to that put forward by Sobeloff.

On July 14, 1955 Eisenhower nominated Sobeloff to a judgeship on the Fourth Circuit Court of Appeals, which included the states of Maryland, Virginia, West Virginia and North and South Carolina. Several Southern Democratic Senators opposed the appointment because of Sobeloff's position in the *Brown* case, and they managed to hold up Senate confirmation for a year. On July 16, 1956 the Senate finally approved Sobeloff's appointment by a 64-19 vote with the opposition coming from Southern Democrats. Sobeloff was sworn in as a circuit court judge on July 19 and became chief judge for the Fourth Circuit in March 1958.

In the many school desegregation cases heard by the Fourth Circuit in the late-1950s, Judge Sobeloff regularly voted to sustain district court orders mandating the admission of black pupils to previously all-white schools. In September 1958, when he refused to stay three such desegregation orders for Warren Co., Charlottesville and Norfolk, Va., Gov. J. Lindsay Almond, Jr. [*q.v.*], in accordance with the state's "massive resistance" laws, closed the schools in each locale. Sobeloff was on the three-judge federal court that held the Virginia school closing laws unconstitutional on Jan. 19, 1959; token school desegregation followed shortly thereafter in several Virginia communities. Sobeloff also voted, however, in a 1956 case to hold state pupil placement laws constitutional on their face, even though the statutes were intended to forestall school desegregation.

In other types of cases Sobeloff showed a concern for protecting individual rights, and he gained recognition as an advocate of civil libertarian principles. He was highly regarded by fellow jurists and lawyers and was active in several Jewish organizations.

During the 1960s Sobeloff showed greater impatience at the slow pace of school desegregation, and he became more willing to overturn evasive local laws and to insist on full and immediate rather than partial and gradual compliance with *Brown*. He resigned as chief judge in December 1964 when he reached the mandatory retirement age of 70, but he remained a fully active member of the court. He became a senior circuit judge in 1971 and died in Baltimore on July 11, 1973.

[CAB]

For further information:
"A Tribute to the Hon. Simon E. Sobeloff," *Maryland Law Review*, 34 (1974), pp. 483-540.

SPARKMAN, JOHN J(ACKSON)
b. Dec. 20, 1899; Morgan County, Ala.
Democratic Senator, Ala., 1949- ;
Chairman, Senate Select Small Business Committee, 1950-53, 1955-57;
Chairman, Housing Subcommittee of the Senate Banking and Currency Committee, 1955-

The son of a sharecropper, Sparkman worked his way through college and law school. Two years after receiving his law degree from the University of Alabama in 1923, he began private practice in Huntsville, Ala. In 1936 he was elected to the House of Representatives, where he supported most New Deal programs. He was particularly interested in the creation of the Tennesee Valley Authority, which played a major role in the development of the North Alabama region he represented.

In 1946 Sparkman won a special election to fill a Senate vacancy created by the death of Sen. John H. Bankhead (D, Ala.). Unlike most Southern Democrats, Sparkman supported President Harry S. Truman's Fair Deal. As a member of the Joint Committee on Housing and as chairman of the Banking and Currency Committee's Housing Subcommittee, he played a key role in the passage of almost all housing legislation during the late-1940s, the 1950s and the early-1960s. A strong segregationist, Sparkman refused to support Truman's civil rights program. He opposed the inclusion of the controversial civil rights plan in the 1948 Democratic platform and supported Strom Thurmond's [q.v.] states rights candidacy. Following the election he helped bring the Southern insurgents back into the Democratic Party. [See TRUMAN Volume]

Adlai Stevenson [q.v.] chose Sparkman to be the Democratic Party's vice presidential candidate in 1952. The choice was influenced by the desire to maintain the loyalty of the South and to satisfy liberals, many of whom were impressed by Sparkman's support for New and Fair Deal legislation. During the campaign Sparkman made 400 speeches and traveled 36,000 miles. He defended the Party's ambivalent civil rights plank, calling on the federal government to "exercise the powers vested in it by the Constitution" to end discrimination in employment and protect blacks from intimidation. Sparkman said that the plank, which he helped write, "represents as near a meeting of the minds as we can work out." He refused to commit himself to aid efforts to curb Senate filibusters or back a fair employment practices commission.

Sparkman spent a large portion of his campaign defending the Truman Administration against charges of corruption and of tolerating subversives in government. Attempting to counter accusations that Truman had been soft on Communism, Sparkman quoted a 1945 statement by Republican candidate Dwight D. Eisenhower that "nothing guides Russian policy so much as the desire for friendship with the U.S." Sparkman added that "there are more Communist infiltrators from Eisenhower's own Columbia University than from any other school in the U.S." He criticized the Republican for associating with Sens. William Jenner (R, Ind.) [q.v.] and Joseph R. McCarthy (R, Wisc.) [q.v.], the two major critics of Eisenhower's former commander Gen. George C. Marshall. He expressed confidence that America would not "stomach a crusade" that included such men. When Sparkman's opponent, Richard Nixon

[q.v.], attempted to counter charges that he had use of a secret political fund, he noted that Sparkman employed his wife on his Senate staff. The Alabama Senator angrily countered this charge by saying that his wife earned "every dollar she got."

Following the defeat of the Democratic ticket, John Sparkman returned to the Senate as one of the most respected leaders of the Democratic Party. He played a leading role in the controversy over the appointment of Charles Bohlen [q.v.] as ambassador to the Soviet Union in 1953. The Republican Right, led by McCarthy and Jenner, contended that the diplomat had been involved in the alleged "sell-out of Eastern Europe" during the Yalta Conference and implied that the State Department was covering up evidence of disloyalty found in his security record. Sparkman, along with Sen. Robert Taft (R, Ohio) [q.v.], was chosen to review the record. After examining the files the two men notified the Senate that Bohlen had no subversive ties. The appointment was then confirmed.

As one of the senior members of the Foreign Relations Committee, Sparkman frequently criticized the Administration's diplomacy. In the spring of 1954 he charged that the Geneva Conference on Indochina, which partitioned Vietnam, was a surrender of Southeast Asia to the Communists. During the Quemoy-Matsu crisis in the fall of the same year, Sparkman warned that a possible blockade of the mainland, contemplated by some members of the Administration, would invite war. He labeled Eisenhower's handling of the 1956 Suez Crisis the worst diplomatic disaster in memory. Although he supported the 1957 Eisenhower Doctrine giving the President the right to use troops to aid Middle Eastern nations threatened by Communists, Sparkman argued that economic help was more important in ensuring political stability in the area.

As chairman of the Senate Small Business Committee and the Housing Subcommittee of the Senate Banking and Currency Committee, Sparkman supported federal aid for small businesses and increased government spending on housing. He lobbied for corporate income tax relief and the establishment of a federally insured loan program to help small businessmen. During the recession of 1958 and 1959, Sparkman advocated a ambitious housing program to stimulate the economy and improve the housing of the poor. He charged that the Administration had abandoned the plan, set up during the Truman years, to provide decent housing for all. In March 1958 he introduced an emergency housing bill designed to stimulate residential construction. The legislation gave the Federal National Mortgage Association, $1 billion to buy Federal Housing Association and Veterans Administration-insured mortgages and extend Veterans Administration mortgages and loan programs. The President signed the bill, with some reluctance, in April. The following year Sparkman submitted an ambitious omnibus housing bill focusing on urban renewal and the stimulation of rental as well as private housing construction. However, major cuts were made on the Senate floor under the guidance of Sen. Lyndon B. Johnson (D, Tex.) [q.v.], who was anxious to avoid a presidential veto. Despite the cuts Eisenhower vetoed the bill as too costly.

During the Eisenhower Administration, Sparkman continued to oppose civil rights proposals. He joined 100 other Southern members of Congress in signing the "Southern Manifesto." This declaration denounced the Supreme Court's school desegregation ruling and pledged to reverse it by "all lawful means." In 1957 Sparkman supported attempts to amend the Administration's civil rights bill by including a conservative proposal giving violators of the statute the right to a jury trial. In 1959 he voted against modifying Rule 22, which dealt with the procedures for filibusters.

Sparkman remained active in national Democratic politics during the 1950s. In early 1956 he endorsed Stevenson's presidential candidacy. In March the Democratic National Committee requested that the Senator respond to Eisenhower's announcement that he would seek a second term in spite of his recent illness. Sparkman raised the possibility that Eisenhower would be a part-time President and that much power would be delegated to appointed officials. This, he said, would demote the office of President

and play havoc with the separation of powers under the Constitution. He urged his audience to "think carefully" before "allowing such a fundamental change."

During the late-1960s and early-1970s John Sparkman became one of the most important powerful Democratic senators. He assumed the chairmanship of the Banking Committee in 1967, and in 1975 he succeeded Sen. J. William Fulbright (D, Ark.) [q.v.] as head of the Senate Foreign Relations Committee. [See KENNEDY, JOHNSON, NIXON/FORD Volumes]

[JB]

SPELLMAN, FRANCIS J(OSEPH)
b. May 4, 1889; Whitman, Mass.
d. Dec. 2, 1967; New York, N.Y.
Roman Catholic Archbishop of New York, 1939-67.

The son of a grocery store proprietor, Spellman was ordained a Roman Catholic priest in 1916. He was named the archbishop of New York in 1939; in 1946 he became a cardinal. Spellman was one of the most powerful conservative clergymen in America. During the postwar period, as Catholics moved rapidly into the middle class and took a more prominent role in national politics, his influence increased. A successful fund raiser, he built churches and schools in New York and helped finance Catholic missionary work abroad. The Cardinal also distributed money for relief of refugees from Communist-controlled areas. As military vicar-general of the U.S. Armed Forces, a post he assumed in 1939, he visited American troops around the world and was often identified with the interests of the American military.

Spellman was a strong cold warrior who opposed Communist expansion in Eastern Europe and Asia. During the Eisenhower Administration he was particularly concerned about preventing a Communist takeover of Indochina. In a speech given before the American Legion National Convention in August 1954, Spellman condemned the Geneva Accords of July 1954, which partitioned Vietnam. He labeled the truce "taps for the buried hopes of freedom in Southeast Asia," and he warned that it was a further step toward the Communist goal of total world domination. On a visit to South Vietnam in January 1955, he brought with him a check for $100,000 to help the refugees who had fled from the North. In that same year, with the assistance of Joseph Kennedy, Spellman helped influence the Eisenhower Administration into giving full support to South Vietnam Premier Ngo Dinh Diem.

The Cardinal also supported the pro-American government of Syngman Rhee in South Korea. Beginning in 1951 Spellman flew to Korea each Christmas to offer encouragement to American soldiers stationed there. In January 1956 he described Korea as "the most difficult theater of defense against atheistic forces."

Spellman opposed any attempts toward peaceful coexistence with the Soviet Union, fearing that any lowering of the American guard would lead to a Communist takeover. In September 1959, one week before the Soviet Premier Nikita Khrushev arrived on a visit to the U.S., the Cardinal summoned the archdiocese to participate in an hour of prayer for America. Moscow did not take Spellman's attacks in silence; he was often a target for Soviet invective. The Soviet press once labeled him "the archangel of atomic war" because he likened Communism to a "wild beast in the forest."

Spellman supported Sen. Joseph R. McCarthy's (R, Wisc.) [q.v.] anti-Communist crusade and defended him whenever he was attacked. In an important address in Brussels delivered in October 1953, the Cardinal rebuked European critics of McCarthyism and said that Americans would not be dissuaded from their determination to root out Communist subversives. In April 1954, during a communion breakfast at which McCarthy was present, Spellman complimented him for his exposure of Communists. The Cardinal continued his support of the Senator even after he was condemned by the Senate in December 1954.

Spellman was a vigorous opponent of what he considered to be pornography. In December 1956 the Cardinal, in one of his rare addresses from the pulpit of St. Pat-

rick's Cathedral, denounced a film called *Baby Doll* and exhorted Catholics to refrain from viewing it.

During the 1960s the Cardinal became involved in the battle surrounding the federal school aid program and the Supreme Court decision banning prayer in the public schools. His strong support of the Vietnam war brought him in constant conflict with Pope Paul VI and Catholic anti-war activists in the U.S. Despite their disagreement Pope Paul refused Spellman's October 1966 offer to resign as archbishop because of his age. The Cardinal died of a stroke in December 1967. [See KENNEDY, JOHNSON Volumes]

[EF]

STANLEY, THOMAS B(AHNSON)
b. July 16, 1890; Spencer, Va.
d. July 11, 1970; Martinsville, Va.
Governor, Va., 1954-58.

Raised on a small tobacco farm, Thomas Stanley received a degree in accounting from Eastern Business College in Poughkeepsie, N.Y. He established a furniture manufacturing firm in conservative southern Virginia in 1924. The town that grew up around it bears his name. Stanley won election to the Virginia House of Delegates in 1930 and became its speaker in 1942. A member of the conservative Byrd organization which dominated Virginia politics, he won a seat in the U.S. House of Representatives in 1946. There he opposed a large part of President Harry S. Truman's Fair Deal legislation.

At the request of Sen. Harry Byrd (D, Va.) [q.v.], Stanley resigned from Congress to run for governor in 1953. Campaigning on a platform that pledged the continuation of the poll tax, a pay-as-you-go balanced budget and an adherence to the Byrd machine's conservative principles, he beat back the Republicans' strongest challenge of the century.

As governor, Stanley became embroiled in the controversy that followed the Supreme Court's *Brown* ruling outlawing segregation in public schools. In response to the decision Stanley counseled moderation and announced he would work toward a plan acceptable to Virginians while obeying the Court edict. He then asked black leaders to reject integration. They refused. By June 1954, at Byrd's urging, Stanley said he would use every legal means to oppose desegregation, and he promoted repeal of the state constitutional provision requiring a public school system.

With anti-integration sentiment hardening, in August he appointed the Commission on Public Education to study the problem. The panel, weighted with political regulars and conservatives, was headed by State Senator Garland Gray, a leading member of the Byrd organization. Fifteen months later the Gray Commission recommended local school autonomy, token integration and private school tuition grants for students refusing integration. The plan represented a compromise between the extreme white supremacist views of southern Virginia and the moderate attitude of the rest of the state. Stanley praised the plan and convened the state legislature to approve the tuition payments. When voters approved the legislative package in a December 1955 referendum, Byrd interpreted the results as total endorsement of segregation.

During the early months of 1956, rightist forces gained momentum within the state. Powerful organization leaders, including Stanley, demanded a showdown with the Supreme Court and a rejection of what they termed its illegal demand for desegregation. Stanley approved an interposition resolution at a Richmond, Va., conference of Southern governors he called in January 1956. The resolution asked the states to interpose their "sovereignty" between the federal government and local school boards to prevent desegregation. In July Stanley reversed himself, rejecting the local-option features of the Gray report as conducive to integration. Rent with internal dissension, the Commission also rejected its own report. During August and September Stanley recommended 13 anti-integration bills, including a controversial proposal for cutting off state funds to integrated schools. In December 1956 his anti-integration legislation became law.

By law Stanley could not succeed himself. He retired to his furniture business in 1958.

[MJS]

For further information:
Numan Bartley, *The Rise of Massive Resistance* (Baton Rouge, 1969).

STANTON, FRANK
b. March 20, 1908; Muskegon, Mich.
President, Columbia Broadcasting System, 1946-73.

Frank Stanton grew up in Dayton, Ohio, and received his B.A. from Ohio Wesleyan in 1930. Five years later he earned a Ph.D. in psychology at Ohio State University and went to work for the Columbia Broadcasting System (CBS), conducting research on radio listening habits. For CBS Stanton devised the first automatic recording instrument, placed in home radios to measure set operation. As CBS director of research between 1938 and 1945, he worked closely with and helped support the work of sociologist Paul Lazarsfeld, a pioneer in public opinion calculation and social statistics. Stanton became CBS president in 1946. Although CBS chairman and founder William F. Paley remained the ultimate arbiter of power, Stanton administered the network at a time of its expansion into television. Stanton himself cared little for show business and discounted RCA's huge investments in color TV.

Unlike Paley, Stanton maintained a high visibility. During the May 1954 Senate hearings on UHF-VHF stations, Stanton defended VHF (Channels 2-13) against charges made by the struggling UHF station operators. (CBS owned five VHF stations in five of the largest markets.) He attacked PAY-TV saying television could not long survive "half fee, half free." A literate and forceful speaker, he repeatedly defended the national networks whenever Congress proposed regulating them. To critics of TV program content, both in the Congress and elsewhere, Stanton countered that "a program in which a large portion of the audience is interested is by that very fact . . . in the public interest."

Like its competition, CBS had standardized its TV programming by the late 1950s. Predominantly live shows gave way to film. "I Love Lucy," a CBS program, set an industry pattern for situation comedy, as did "The Honeymooners," which CBS won away from the doomed DuMont network. CBS News, once the industry leader, lost valued ground to the National Broadcasting Co. "See It Now," coproduced by Edward R. Murrow [q.v.], lost its regular time spot after the 1954-55 season. Unlike Dumont and the American Broadcasting Co., CBS did not cover the Army-McCarthy hearings. Stanton later tried, unsuccessfully, to secure broadcast rights to the McCarthy censure hearings.

In 1959 revelations that producers had rigged quiz shows forced a change in CBS policy. The quiz show scandals greatly embarrassed the national networks, whose chief executives actually had exerted less control over the programs than had the shows' individual producers and advertisers. Interestingly, opinion surveys showed a general indifference to the affair, but Stanton and his fellow broadcasters feared greater government regulation as a result of the episode. In May 1959 he announced that, henceforth, CBS would exercise far greater authority in program operation. He also pledged to revise the news division by presenting regular prime time one-hour documentaries. "We are determined," he said, "to press the [television] medium to its fullest development as an informational force." In October he canceled all quiz programs and programming "conceits", such as canned applause and laughter.

Stanton played a leading role in the 1960 presidential debates. Long opposed to the "equal time" section of the Federal Communications Act, he continually argued that its literal interpretation compelled networks to offer equal access to candidates of every minor party. Congress suspended the equal time rule in August 1960, and Stanton personally devoted great attention to the 1960 debate production. After the television debates between Republican candidate Richard Nixon [q.v.] and Democratic aspirant John Kennedy [q.v.] in September,

Republicans criticized CBS for placing too much light on the pale face of their candidate. However, Stanton's arrangements greatly pleased Kennedy.

In December 1960 President-elect Kennedy offered Stanton the directorship of the United States Information Agency. When Stanton declined the post, Kennedy appointed Murrow. Stanton remained president of CBS until 1973. [See KENNEDY Volume]

[JLB]

STASSEN, HAROLD E(DWARD)
b. April 13, 1907; West St. Paul, Minn.
Director, Mutual Security Administration, January 1953-August 1953;
Director, Foreign Operations Administration, August 1953-March 1955;
Special Assistant to the President for Disarmament, March 1955-February 1958.

Stassen was born on a truck farm outside of Minneapolis. Hard driving and persistent, he finished elementary school in four years. He graduated from high school by the age of 15 and managed the family farm during his father's illness before entering the University of Minnesota in 1922. He worked as a Pullman car conductor to help finance his education. After receiving his B.A. in 1927, he entered the University of Minnesota law school, where he undermined his health with his intense regime. He received his law degree in 1929.

That same year Stassen entered politics, campaigning successfully for county attorney for Dakota Co., Minn., an office he occupied from 1930 to 1938. In 1938 Stassen overcame strong opposition from the incumbent, Elmer A. Benson, to win election as governor of Minnesota. He was reelected in 1940 and again in 1942. In 1943 Stassen resigned his office to go on active duty in the U.S. Naval Reserve.

After the War Stassen directed his efforts toward an eventual presidential bid. He was the first to enter the 1948 primary race. In his year-long campaign Stassen ran on a platform reflecting progressive Republicanism in domestic affairs and international cooperation in foreign policy. Stassen wanted a system of modern capitalism whose strength and stability would rule out any serious economic depression and which would also be responsive to human needs. He opposed the isolationist wing of the Republican Party and believed that the U.S. should be willing to face war if necessary to overcome totalitarianism. [See TRUMAN Volume]

Stassen's 1948 bid for the presidency was unsuccessful, but he tried again four years later. Gen. Dwight D. Eisenhower's election staff, of which Stassen himself was a central figure, saw his campaign as an integral element in its own plans for Eisenhower at the 1952 Republican National Convention. They believed that Stassen's candidacy would be a useful tool to draw delegates from Sen. Robert Taft (R, Ohio) [q.v.], Eisenhower's major opponent. They also assumed that Stassen would switch his delegates to Eisenhower during the Convention.

At the Republican National Convention Stassen remained hopeful of a presidential nomination through the first ballot. He resisted all pressures within his Minnesota delegation to declare for Eisenhower. After the first ballot, however, when his delegates gave him only 19 votes, Stassen, somewhat puzzled, withdrew his name for the nomination and advised his delegates to support Eisenhower. Minnesota's shift provided Eisenhower with a narrow majority. Stassen opposed the selection of Richard Nixon [q.v.] as Republican vice presidential candidate. After the revelation that Nixon had been able to draw from a "secret" political fund, Stassen wrote a letter to Eisenhower suggesting that he drop out of the race and that Earl Warren [q.v.] replace him.

As a reward for his support, Eisenhower appointed Stassen chairman of the Foreign Operations Administration (FOA), a post which he held from 1953 to 1955. As chairman Stassen headed the foreign aid program and pushed the Administration for increased emphasis on economic aid. In January 1955 Stassen supported agricultural expert Wolf Ladejinsky

[q.v.], dismissed from his job at the Agriculture Department by Secretary of Agriculture Ezra Taft Benson [q.v.] as a security risk. At the behest of Eisenhower, Stassen gave Ladejinsky a position in the FOA comparable to the one he had lost and released a detailed statement explaining why he had cleared Ladijinsky on the security charges.

In March 1955 Eisenhower, disturbed by the prospect of an arms race with the Soviet Union, created the position of special assistant to the President for disarmament, with cabinet rank, and named Stassen to fill the post. The former Governor was to develop and negotiate a plan for disarmament with the Soviet Union. In response to a Soviet offer, Eisenhower suggested a plan called "Open Skies" at the Geneva summit conference in July. He offered to swap military blueprints and suggested that the U.S. was willing, if the Soviets were, to allow complete aerial surveillance and photography to prevent surprise attack.

Over the next two years Stassen worked to develop this general statement into a specific proposal and attempted to get powerful forces within the Administration to accept disarmament. Secretary of State John Foster Dulles [q.v.], in particular, opposed any accomodation with the Soviet Union on the issue. He feared that because U.S. defense focused on "massive retaliation," the reliance on strategic nuclear weapons as America's first deterrent, any arms limitation agreement would jeopardize U.S. security. Stassen, on the other hand, believed that as the two superpowers reached nuclear parity the U.S. must begin serious arms control discussions with the Soviets. Stassen was particularly anxious to stop nuclear testing while the U.S. had the numerical and technological advantage.

The two nations outlined tentative proposals in 1957 at meetings held in London under the direction of a subcommittee of the U.N. Disarmament Commission. The U.S. proposed an end to nuclear testing with an elaborate system of on-site inspections to ensure compliance. The Soviet Union on the other hand opposed inspection, believing secrecy would help it compensate for U.S. superiority in nuclear weapons. In addition, it called for a halt to the use of hydrogen bombs long before a cutoff in fissionable material production, a step that would inhibit use of the superior U.S. Air Force. The USSR also asked for aerial inspection of Europe outside the Soviet Union.

The tacit intention to include West Germany under the provision for aerial inspection immediately provoked German Chancellor Konrad Adenauer, a friend of Dulles, who demanded reassurance that his nation's interests would not be endangered. The pledge was forthcoming and effectively blocked Stassen's further efforts to form a mutually acceptable accord with the Soviets.

During the London Conference Stassen made a diplomatic blunder that led to his fall from grace in the eyes of the Administration. Eisenhower had permitted him to use a so-called talking paper. Less firm than a proposal, this included an aerial inspection scheme and a plan to prohibit the use of nuclear weapons except in defense or retaliation in case of nuclear attack. Most important was a clause in the paper calling for the devotion of future production of fissionable material to peaceful purposes. Without any prior negotiations with the U.S. allies, Stassen had revealed the substance of the paper to the Russians. Thereupon British Prime Minister Harold Macmillan complained directly to Eisenhower that the clause on fissionable materials would prevent Britain "from developing the nuclear strength which she is beginning to acquire."

The President reprimanded Stassen for the "acute embarrassment" his action had caused. In his response to the Stassen incident, Sen. Hubert H. Humphrey (D, Minn.) [q.v.] announced on June 18 that he would open "a thorough investigation" of U.S. disarmament policies, including the "the present role of Harold Stassen." Stating publicly that the unanimous assent of the allies would be necessary for any agreement, Dulles himself went to the conference to present the Western position. His usefulness at an end, Stassen resigned his post in February 1958. That year he lost a Pennsylvania primary campaign for the Republican gubernatorial nomination.

During the 1950s Stassen remained active in Republican politics. In the 1956 presidential primary race, the liberal Stassen mounted a campaign to replace Nixon as the vice presidential nominee. On July 23 he suggested Massachusetts Gov. Christian A. Herter [q.v.] would make a stronger candidate. Stassen said "the negative side" of the Eisenhower-Nixon ticket was most apparent in polls of "the best informed and the younger voters." He maintained that Nixon would only decrease support for the Party. He pointed to the findings of private polls that showed an Eisenhower-Herter ticket would run six percent stronger than an Eisenhower-Nixon ticket. In these public pronouncements Stassen insisted that he was acting "as an individual and not as a representative of the President." Stassen also asked his supporters not to advance his own name for the vice presidential nomination.

Almost every major figure in the Republican Party rallied to Nixon's side. Former New York Gov. Thomas E. Dewey regarded Nixon's renomination as "all settled." Sen. Barry Goldwater (R, Ariz.) [q.v.] suggested that the GOP give Stassen a "transfer" to the Democratic Party for "trying to create dissent in an otherwise harmonious" party. On Aug. 22 Stassen had a private meeting with Eisenhower. Presidential Assistant Sherman Adams [q.v.] permitted Stassen to see the President with the proviso that he second Nixon's nomination. Immediately thereafter Stassen made a public statement of his decision to give Vice President Nixon his "full support" and called upon the GOP to "close ranks" for the campaign.

In 1960 Stassen opposed Richard Nixon's nomination for President at the Republican National Convention. Eight years later Stassen ran for the office on a peace platform calling for the deescalation of the war in Vietnam. After the unsuccessful bid, he returned to private law practice in Philadelphia.

[ACD]

STENNIS, JOHN C(ORNELIUS)
b. Aug. 3, 1901; Kemper County, Miss.
Democratic Senator, Miss., 1947-

Raised in rural Mississippi, Stennis received his B.A. in 1923 from Mississippi Agricultural and Mechanical College and his LL.B. in 1928 from the University of Virginia. He maintained a law practice while serving in the Mississippi House of Representatives from 1928 to 1932 and then filled the position of district prosecuting attorney from 1931 to 1935. In 1937 he was appointed a circuit court judge. He won a U.S. Senate seat in 1947 in a special election to replace the segregationist Sen. Theodore Bilbo (D, Miss.). Stennis, a calm, genteel Southerner, did not inject the race issue into his campaign, but his support of a "reasonable and proper segregation" was well-known. Once in the Senate he aligned himself with fellow conservative Southern Democrats in opposing civil rights and much social welfare legislation. He was strongly anti-Communist and supported most of President Truman's policies to contain the Soviet Union, including the Marshall Plan of 1947. [See TRUMAN Volume]

Stennis often opposed the Eisenhower Administration's foreign policy, voting to limit foreign aid and opposing American troop commitments abroad. Although he had originally supported the Marshall Plan, he voted to lower its budget, and in 1953 he backed reduced foreign aid to Western Europe. In 1956 he again voted for cuts in President Eisenhower's foreign aid and military assistance proposals. Stennis opposed the U.S. Mutual Defense Treaty with Korea in 1954, arguing that the U.S. was "stretching-out" its commitments so thinly that it might not be able "to deliver." Instead of a formal treaty he proposed a "firm declaration of assurances" that the U.S. would "stand by Korea under present conditions."

Stennis advocated a cautious policy toward American military involvement in Vietnam. In 1954 he warned against sending American technicians to Indochina, believing that such action might provoke renewed fighting in Korea. When French forces were besieged by the Communists at Dien

Bien Phu that spring and the French government pleaded for U.S. military assistance, Stennis worried that the Western allies would again be content to have the U.S. assume the burden of fighting. He stated that he could not think of any circumstances in which "our land troops should go into Indochina and be committed in this war area." When Sen. John F. Kennedy (D, Mass.) [q.v.] warned that a French or U.S. military victory there was impossible, Stennis called it "the finest statement I have heard on this subject."

Respected by his fellow senators for his personal integrity, Stennis was selected in 1954 to sit on the Senate Select Committee to Study Censure Charges, chaired by Sen. Arthur Watkins, (R, Utah) [q.v.]. The six so-called neutral senators assembled in the fall of 1954 to study the Flanders resolution censuring Sen. Joseph R. McCarthy (R, Wisc.) [q.v.] for his conduct in carrying out anti-Communist investigations. Although Stennis was a strong anti-Communist, he felt McCarthy had violated traditional Senate standards of prudence and fairness in his probes. For him the issue was "one purely of political morality in senatorial conduct," not partisan or ideological conflict. In joining the unanimous committee vote to recommend censure, Stennis rejected what he described as McCarthy's "slush and slime as a proper standard of senatorial conduct." He warned his colleagues that "something big and fine will have gone from this chamber" if the Wisconsin Senator's behavior were condoned. The Senate censured McCarthy, by a 67-22 vote, in December.

During the 1950s Stennis was one of the Senate's most prominent critics of civil rights proposals. An acknowledged authority on Senate procedures, he often used this knowledge to dilute or delay legislation through filibuster and manipulation of other parliamentary measures. In 1956 he joined 100 other Southern members of Congress in signing the "Southern Manifesto," which assailed the U.S. Supreme Court's decisions in favor of public school desegregation. While basing its attack on legal grounds, the group made it clear that its members would oppose any federal attempts to integrate schools. Stennis voted against the Civil Rights Acts of 1957 and 1960. In 1959 he supported a proposed constitutional amendment to grant states and localities the right to decide questions of school desegregation. Some observers believed Stennis to be trapped by a constituency that favored outright segregation. Others, like civil rights activist Aaron Henry, saw Stennis as "shrewd and sophisticated in promulgating segregation . . . Northern style"—and perhaps more dishonest for doing so.

Stennis generally opposed most social welfare legislation. He supported only limited federal aid to education despite the fact that Mississippi schools remained among the poorest in the nation. In 1960 he opposed raising the national minimum wage from $1 to $1.25 and the same year voted against a plan to provide medical benefits to the elderly through social security funds.

As a member of the Armed Services Committee, Stennis generally supported the military's budget requests. He joined other senators who accused the Administration of allowing a "missile gap" in U.S. defenses. Claiming the U.S. was behind the USSR in missile numbers, he urged more intense research and production in the missile program. During partisan wrangling over a supposed "deterrent gap" in 1960, Stennis championed the B-70 bomber as "essential" to U.S. security.

Stennis fluctuated in his views about the U.S. role in Vietnam in the 1960s. But when American dollars and troops poured into Indochina, he believed the U.S. had to uphold its commitment with a full military effort. His reputation for fairness and honesty brought him into the center of the Watergate scandal in 1973. As a compromise in his battle to withhold the "Watergate tapes" from public, court and congressional scrutiny, President Richard Nixon offered Sen. Stennis, as the representative of Congress, the opportunity to listen to the tapes and verify their content. The compromise plan was never initiated because congressional and judicial demands for the tapes themselves escalated. [See KENNEDY, JOHNSON, NIXON/FORD Volumes]

[TGD]

STEPHENS, THOMAS E(DWIN)
b. Oct. 18, 1903; Ireland.
Presidential Appointments Secretary, January 1953-January 1955, March 1958-January 1961.

Thomas Stephens began his career as a real estate title searcher and insurance fraud investigator. While working he studied law, receiving an LL.D. degree from St. Lawrence University in 1932. He then served as assistant corporate counsel for the City of New York, representing the city at the state legislature in Albany. In 1936 Stephens began private practice with the firm of Lord, Day and Lord. However, he left in 1938 to become administrative assistant to the president of the New York City Council. During the 1940s he became active in national Republican politics as director of the campaign division of the Republican National Committee in 1945 and 1946 and as assistant to the Republican national campaign manager in 1948. After working as administrative assistant to Sen. John Foster Dulles (R, N.Y.) [q.v.] in 1949, he served as secretary of the New York State Republican Committee from 1950 to 1952.

On the advice of Sherman Adams [q.v.], President Eisenhower appointed Stephens appointments secretary with the title of special counsel in January 1953. Stephens's new position involved little formal counseling. Instead, he dealt with many small but significant details of the White House routine, choosing speaking invitations for the President and coordinating security arrangements with the Secret Service. He also arranged and logged Eisenhower's appointments, but he had little authority because Adams actually controlled access to Eisenhower. More informally, Stephens was the staff's chief comedian and practical joker; Eisenhower relied on him to relieve tension during heated discussions with "exactly the right comment."

Stephens made solid and significant contributions to the Eisenhower Administration as a political adviser. He possessed shrewd political instincts and was a thoroughly perceptive judge of people. Eisenhower believed Stephens to be one of his most "politically astute" aides, and the President's reliance upon his appointments secretary as a "rock of good sense and sound judgment" gave Stephens more influence than most people in Washington realized. Just before leaving office Eisenhower, reflecting on his term, credited Stephens with educating him politically during the early days of his presidency. The President portrayed himself as a political neophyte whom Stephens "intuitively and skillfully" tutored in the practical aspects of political life.

Although ill-health and the need to resume private law practice forced Stephens to resign as appointments secretary in January 1955, he continued to advise Eisenhower and on occasion to perform some duties for the White House. He was, for example, an "advance man" at the 1956 Republican National Convention. With the resignation of Stephens's replacement, Bernard Shanley [q.v.], Stephens resumed his old appointments post in March 1958. When Eisenhower left office in January 1961, Stephens announced his intention to enter business. However, two years later he returned to politics, helping coordinate operations for the manager of New York Gov. Nelson A. Rockefeller's [q.v.] reelection campaign. In 1964 Stephens participated in Rockefeller's unsuccessful presidential bid and Kenneth B. Keating's [q.v.] losing battle to retain his U.S. Senate seat. Four years later Stephens again aided Rockefeller's unsuccessful presidential campaign and Jacob K. Javits's [q.v.] victorious Senate reelection effort.

[RJB]

STEVENS, ROBERT T(EN BROECK)
b. July 31, 1899; Fanwood, N.J.
Secretary of the Army, February 1953-July 1955.

Stevens served as a second lieutenant in the field artillery during World War I. After the War he studied at Yale, receiving his B.A. in 1921. He then entered the textile business founded in 1813 by a New England ancestor. Stevens continued with the firm, J.P. Stevens and Co., becoming president in 1929 and chairman of the board of directors in 1945. In 1933 he was an administrative representative in the industry section of the National Recovery Administration. From 1934 to 1953 he was the director of the Federal Reserve Bank of New York.

During World War II Stevens was assigned to the office of the Quartermaster General, where he was director of purchases. President-elect Eisenhower appointed him Secretary of the Army in December 1952. When the nomination was sent to the Senate Armed Services Committee, the majority of the Committee asked Stevens to dispose of his stock in companies doing business with the Defense Department. Stevens promised that he would sell all holdings except his stock in the J.P. Stevens Co., frankly citing sentimental reasons for the exception. The Committee refused to permit the exception, and Stevens agreed to sell the stock totaling $1.4 million.

While in office Stevens was called upon to answer charges that budget cutbacks were impairing Army effectiveness. In response to a special Senate inquiry into alleged shortages of ammunition in Korea, Stevens, in March 1953, assured the senators that production and supply were increasing rapidly. In July of that year he told a Senate Appropriations subcommittee that the proposed cut of about $1 million from the estimates presented by Harry S. Truman would not adversely affect the Army's current combat effectiveness.

In the summer of 1953 Stevens began a tense, year-long ordeal when Sen. Joseph R. McCarthy (R, Wisc.) [q.v.], chairman of the Permanent Investigations Subcommittee, launched probes into possible Communist infiltration of the Army. McCarthy's first attack was on the Army Signal Corps laboratories at Monmouth, N.J. On Nov. 16 he promised "evidence of actual stealing of classified materials" at Monmouth, a claim that contradicted an Army inquiry which had produced no evidence of "current" spying. The subcommittee met with opposition from Army officers who refused to reveal the names of officials who had given security clearances to persons suspected of Communist connections. In his first encounter with McCarthy, Stevens, whom the Senator termed "a fine, naive, not-too-brilliant Republican," appeared conciliatory. He promised to review the problem and indicated a desire to cooperate with the subcommittee. However, the matter was eventually dropped.

In January 1954 a new investigation brought Stevens and McCarthy to loggerheads. Dr. Irving Peress [q.v.], a dentist and a member of the left-wing American Labor Party, had been inducted into the Army in October 1952. In accordance with the automatic provisions of the Doctor Draft Act, Peress was promoted to the rank of major. When given a loyalty questionnaire, he refused to answer any questions regarding his political beliefs. The Army then gave him an honorable discharge. Infuriated, McCarthy insisted that Peress should have been courtmartialed. He also asked to know the identity of Pentagon officials who had promoted Peress and then ordered his discharge. In testimony before the subcommittee, Gen. Ralph W. Zwicker [q.v.] refused to reveal names. Thereupon, McCarthy asserted that Zwicker was "not fit to wear that uniform." Stevens directed Zwicker to refuse to appear for further questioning and denounced McCarthy's behavior as unwarranted. The Secretary of the Army announced that he would personally testify.

Stevens's order brought the Senator and the Administration into open conflict over what constituted the proper relation between the executive and legislative branches of government. In an effort to head off a major dispute, leading Republicans invited the principals to discuss the dispute over lunch. At the meeting on Feb. 24, Stevens agreed to cooperate with McCarthy if respect were accorded the Army's personnel. The press represented the conversation as a complete victory for McCarthy. To save face, President Eisenhower, Vice President Richard M. Nixon [q.v.], Stevens and several others worked out a statement claiming the Secretary had in no way departed from his principle that Army personnel were not to be "browbeaten or humiliated." After Sen. Everett M. Dirksen (R, Ill.) [q.v.] failed to conciliate Stevens and McCarthy, the Secretary read the statement at a press conference.

The Army then took the offensive against McCarthy. On March 11, 1954 Stevens released a report stating that McCarthy and Roy M. Cohn [q.v.], the subcommittee's counsel, had made direct threats to Army officials to assure favored treatment for G. David Schine [q.v.], a former consultant of McCarthy's who had been drafted into the Army in November of the previous year. Stevens issued the report to each Republican member of the panel and to the press. McCarthy, embarrassed and caught off guard, labeled the report "blackmail" and, in addition, accused Stevens of trying to divert his attention to an investigation of the Air Force and Navy. Cohn charged that it was a subterfuge to halt the probe of alleged subversives at the Monmouth laboratories.

McCarthy's Senate Permanent Investigations Subcommittee voted to hold hearings on the charges and countercharges. The nationally televised probe began on April 22 and continued until June 17. Most of the examination was devoted to petty haggling interrupted by McCarthy's calling, "point of order, Mr. Chairman!" In the words of historian Charles Alexander, "Even the closest followers could make little sense of the confused proceedings." Stevens himself had only a minor role in the hearings. Attention was focused on the dramatic clashes between McCarthy and the Army's chief counsel, Joseph Welch [q.v.]. The probe revealed McCarthy at his most boorish and ruthless and contributed to his downfall in December 1954. Assessing Stevens's role in the Senator's political demise, the New York Times said, "[Stevens's] courage and persistence . . . was the beginning of McCarthy's own downfall as a power in the Senate."

Stevens resigned from his post on July 20, 1955 for what he termed "only compelling personal consideration." He returned to the presidency of J. P. Stevens and Co. From 1963 to 1964 he was president of the American Textile Manufacturers.

[ACD]

STEVENSON, ADLAI E(WING)
b. Feb. 5, 1900; Los Angeles, Calif.
d. July 14, 1965; London, England.
Democratic presidential candidate,
1952, 1956.

Stevenson was the grandson of Adlai Stevenson, vice president in Grover Cleveland's second term, and the son of Lewis Stevenson, who was active in Illinois Democratic politics. The younger Adlai Stevenson attended the Choate School in Wallingford, Conn., and graduated from Princeton University in 1922. He worked for his family's newspaper in Bloomington, Ill., and studied law at Northwestern University, receiving a J.D. degree in 1926. The following year Stevenson entered a Chicago law firm.

In 1933 Stevenson became special counsel to the Agricultural Adjustment Administration and the following year transferred to the Federal Alcohol Control Administration as assistant general counsel. In 1935 he returned to private law practice in Chicago. Six years later Stevenson went back to Washington as special assistant to Secretary of the Navy Frank Knox. In 1945 he became special assistant to Secretary of State Edward Stettinius. Later in the year he was U.S. minister and representative to the Preparedness Commission for the United Nations. He was senior adviser to the American delegation to the first U.N. General Assembly session, which opened in London in January 1946. Stevenson was alternate delegate at subsequent sessions in 1946 and 1947.

In 1948 Stevenson won the Democratic nomination for governor of Illinois with the backing of Eleanor Roosevelt [q.v.] and Supreme Court Justice William O. Douglas [q.v.]. He then ran as a reform candidate against what he charged was the scandal-ridden administration of incumbent Republican Gov. Dwight H. Green. Stevenson defeated Green by 572,000 votes, the largest plurality in Illinois history.

Stevenson's accomplishments as governor included a reform of the state police force that substituted a merit system for political appointments; a doubling of state aid to schools; an increase in unemployment compensation and pensions for the aged and blind; and a 10-year road building program. The Illinois legislature declined to approve his proposals for establishing a fair employment practices commission, imposing greater restrictions on gambling, reforming the criminal justice system and revising the state's 1870 constitution. Stevenson vetoed an anti-subversive activities bill, claiming that it infringed upon the rights of free speech and the presumption of innocence. [See TRUMAN Volume]

From the time of his election as governor, Stevenson was mentioned as a possible 1952 Democratic presidential candidate. But the Governor first received major national attention after President Harry S. Truman, in an immediately publicized private meeting with Stevenson in January 1952, said he would not run for reelection and offered Stevenson his endorsement. Stevenson persistently said that he did not want to be a presidential candidate and would run for another term as governor. Some observers believed that he really did not want the nomination. Others claimed that he did not want to be associated with the unpopular Truman Administration and felt he could win the election only if nominated by popular draft.

Despite Stevenson's refusal to encourage a national movement on his behalf and his assertions that he would not even accept a draft, a Stevenson-for-President movement began to form in February 1952. Over the next few months Sen. Estes Kefauver (D, Tenn.) [q.v.], Mutual Security Director W. Averell Harriman [q.v.] and Sen. Richard B. Russell (D, Ga.) [q.v.] were the major announced candidates for the nomination. On the first ballot at the July Democratic National Convention in Chicago, Stevenson, with 273 votes, ran second to Kefauver, with 340. But no candidate came close to the 615½ votes needed for nomination. After Kefauver made only minor gains on the second ballot, Stevenson, who had decided before the first ballot to accept a draft, was selected on the third. His running mate was a moderate Southerner, Sen. John Sparkman (D, Ala.) [q.v.].

In his acceptance speech Stevenson appealed for an issue-oriented campaign based on thought rather than emotion. His comment, "Let's talk sense to the American people," became for many the trademark of his campaign. Liberal intellectuals in particular came to admire the thoughtful, analytical and urbanely witty character of his speeches, his general avoidance of personal attacks and innuendo and his minimization of traditional campaign ballyhoo.

To many others Stevenson's intellectual style smacked of uncertainty, indecisiveness and lack of a fighting spirit. President Truman, for one, complained that Stevenson's campaign was not aggressive. Stevenson was overheard early in the Convention saying to the Illinois delegation, "I do not dream myself fit for the job [of President] . . . ," and this comment reinforced the impression of uncertainty.

Furthermore, Stevenson's campaign was haunted by the record of the beleaguered Truman Administration. He supported the President's major domestic and foreign policies, including Truman's conduct of the indecisive war in Korea. Stevenson stated that the fight against Communism was a long and difficult one and that only persistence, not miracles, could end the conflict on favorable terms. On Oct. 24 his Republican opponent, Dwight D. Eisenhower, promised to go to Korea to seek peace. Stevenson contended that this promise was a grandstand play without meaningful content, but many observers believed that it clinched the election for Eisenhower.

Republicans attempted to link Stevenson to their charge that the Truman Administration was soft on Communism and had allowed subversive elements to penetrate the national government. On Oct. 10 Sen. Richard M. Nixon (R, Calif.) [q.v.], the Republican vice-presidential nominee, denounced Stevenson for having testified favorably regarding the character of Alger Hiss at the latter's 1949 perjury trial and called him a "graduate of Dean Acheson's [q.v.] spineless school of diplomacy. . . ." On Oct. 27 Sen. Joseph R. McCarthy (R, Wisc.) [q.v.] climaxed his campaign attacks impugning Stevenson's patriotism, stating that if he could board Stevenson's campaign train with a club, he might be able to make

a "good American out of him." The Republicans also capitalized on the numerous conflict-of-interest and other scandals that had developed during the Truman Administration.

Stevenson's greatest difficulty was Eisenhower's overwhelming, non-partisan popularity. Contrary to his stated hope, the campaign did not center around a clear-cut debate over issues. He took well-defined stands on most political subjects. Stevenson opposed McCarthyism, calling for "free enterprise for the mind," and took a moderate but firm position in favor of civil rights for blacks. However, Stevenson's supporters and many independent observers contended that Eisenhower won support across the political spectrum by blurring his views on these and other matters and presenting himself as a trustworthy father-figure who stood above not only parties but issues. Eisenhower swept the election by an electoral vote margin of 442 to 89, taking the Southern states of Virginia, Florida and Texas and the border states of Oklahoma and Tennessee. He received 33.9 million votes to Stevenson's 27.3 million.

In March 1953 Stevenson began a six-month tour of the Far East, Middle East and Europe. Upon his return he wrote a series of articles for *Look* magazine. He stated that in the Cold War "anti-Communist preaching wins few hearts." The United States, he said, had to promote economic development in backward countries and live up to its ideals by rejecting McCarthyism and opposing Western colonialism.

As its latest presidential candidate, Stevenson was the unofficial national spokesman of the Democratic Party, and in that capacity he remained in the public eye. At the Democratic National Committee's Southern Conference in March 1954, he denounced McCarthyism, stating that "it is wicked and it is subversive for public officials to try deliberately to replace reason with passion; to substitute hatred for honest difference. . . ." During the same speech he attacked the "massive retaliation" policy recently announced by Secretary of State John Foster Dulles [q.v.], which relied on the use of strategic nuclear weapons as the

U.S. primary defense against Soviet attack and expansion. Stevenson warned that the Soviet Union also had massive retaliatory power and that implementation of the plan "would certainly mean World War III and atomic counter-retaliation." In 1955 he opposed the Administration-sponsored Formosa Resolution on the grounds that it committed the Senate to support almost any action of the President to protect Nationalist China against Communist Chinese attack, including defense of what he believed were the strategically worthless islands of Quemoy and Matsu. In an April 11 radio address, Stevenson warned that the U.S. might lose allies if it went to war over those islands.

During the period between the 1952 and 1956 elections, Stevenson gained a reputation not only as a political critic of the Eisenhower Administration but also as a social critic of America. He outlined his views on the state of contemporary American society in a commencement address at Smith College in June 1955, in a speech at the University of Texas the following September and in a *Fortune* article the next month. Stevenson stated that while the American standard of living was high, the people had little sense of purpose beyond material acquisition. Complacency and conformity prevailed, Stevenson said. At Smith College he attacked the theory of education whose main purpose was the production of citizens "who can fit painlessly into the social pattern. . . ." Stevenson's admirers regarded such comments as an extension and deepening of his political criticism of President Eisenhower, whose alleged blandness and lack of creative ideas or strong commitments they blamed for the emphasis on conformity.

By the summer of 1955 Stevenson believed that he was the best available candidate for the 1956 Democratic presidential nomination; on Nov. 15, 1955 he formally announced his candidacy. Stevenson's emphasis in his campaign for the nomination was upon what he believed to be the excessive influence of business interests on Eisenhower Administration policy. On the race issue his strategy was geared toward reconciling the Northern and Southern

wings of the Party by taking a moderate stand on civil rights. He advocated gradualism in the enforcement of the Supreme Court's 1954 school desegregation decision and expressed the hope that Southern moderates would be able to implement the ruling without the use of federal force. His major opponents, Sen. Kefauver and Averell Harriman, by then governor of New York, wrote off the South and took a more liberal position on race matters.

After Stevenson received a surprisingly low write-in vote in the March 1956 New Hampshire primary and suffered a stunning defeat at Kefauver's hands later in the month in the Minnesota primary, he altered his customary campaign style. Kenneth S. Davis, his biographer, wrote: "Gone from his prepared talks were the witticisms that had sparkled from his speeches of '52; gone was the evident reluctance to campaign for the presidency as though it were a popularity prize. The new Stevenson was bussed by pretty girls in California, donned cowboy boots in Arizona, carried a stuffed alligator and thumped a bass fiddle in Florida and everywhere shook hands by the hundreds, the thousands." He went on to win successive primaries in Illinois, New Jersey, Pennsylvania, Alaska, Alabama, the District of Columbia, Oregon and the crucial polls in Florida on May 29 and California on June 5. Stevenson won the nomination on the first ballot at the August Democratic National Convention. He then surprised the Convention by allowing it to choose his running mate; the delegates selected Kefauver.

In the general election rematch with Eisenhower, Stevenson continued to deviate from his 1952 campaign style. He followed a brutally crowded schedule, concentrating on key states, counties and wards. Some of his speeches reflected the haste with which they were written.

Although disturbed by Stevenson's more traditional style of campaigning, his supporters felt that the candidate demonstrated his continuing commitment to creativity and thought by raising two provocative ideas. Addressing the American Legion Convention on Sept. 5, Stevenson stated that the draft could be ended in the "foreseeable future" because the modern Armed Forces needed technically skilled specialized personnel serving for long periods rather than partly trained men enlisted for brief terms. Eisenhower denounced the suggestion as "incredible folly" that led "down the road of surrender," and Republicans ridiculed Stevenson for claiming to know more about military matters than the President, a former military man.

On Oct. 15, during a nationwide television appearance, Stevenson suggested that the United States unilaterally halt further testing of H-bombs in the hope that the Soviet Union would reciprocate. (He had made a similar proposal the preceding April.) Stevenson argued that such a cessation could be a first step towards nuclear disarmament or at least towards a halt to the poisoning of the atmosphere with radioactive fallout. He contended that any subsequent Soviet H-bomb explosions could be detected and that the U.S. could then resume its tests. The Administration believed that testing could not be monitored without on-site inspection in the countries participating in a moratorium, and it therefore opposed any unilateral halt. Stevenson's suggestion became a political debacle when Soviet Premier Nikolai A. Bulganin, in an Oct. 21 letter to President Eisenhower, backed the Democratic candidate's proposal and called for a test suspension without inspection.

Eisenhower had not lost his nonpartisan popularity since 1952 and now spoke with the authority of an incumbent. Furthermore, Stevenson's controversial proposals probably cost him votes. In 1956 he was defeated even more soundly than in his first presidential bid, receiving only 73 electoral votes to Eisenhower's 457. Eisenhower extended his inroads into the South, capturing Oklahoma, Kentucky, Tennessee, Texas, Louisiana, Florida and Virginia. The incumbent received 35.6 million votes to Stevenson's 26.0 million.

In late November 1956 Stevenson joined with National Democratic Chairman Paul Butler [q.v.] in establishing the Democratic Advisory Council. It was created to serve as a national voice for the Party.

Stevenson played the leading role in drawing up the Council's statements and papers. In addition, he continued to speak throughout the country after his second defeat, and his speeches gained national attention.

In the fall of 1957 the Administration decided to invite Stevenson to help draw up an American program for the North Atlantic Treaty Organization (NATO) and participate in the forthcoming NATO conference in Paris. Stevenson decided not to attend the conference but agreed to work on the program. He stressed the importance of programs to improve living conditions in backward countries and stated in one of his memoranda that "if the Atlantic Community had multilateral economic and trade development plans it would mean a lot more to many people than its purely military anti-Communism does now." However, his views had little influence on the American position at the conference, which stressed military might in deterring the spread of Communism.

During the summer of 1958 Stevenson visited the Soviet Union and met with Soviet Premier Nikita S. Khrushchev. Stevenson concluded that the current leadership of the USSR was more sensitive to public opinion than Stalin and was more pragmatic than ideological. Therefore, he believed, the Kremlin would seriously weigh the desire of the people in the Soviet Union and throughout the world for peace.

Stevenson repeatedly declined to actively seek a third presidential nomination in 1960. However, early in that year Democratic Party liberals led by George Ball, Thomas Finletter [q.v.] and Sen. Mike Monroney (D, Okla.) [q.v.] formally organized a draft-Stevenson movement. Stevenson did not encourage the movement but did not attempt to stop it, either. The strategy of the movement was to try to prevent any of the active candidates from winning on the first ballot and then, according to Davis, "stampede the Convention in much the same way as the Wilkie amateurs had stampeded the Republican Convention of 1940."

The Stevenson-backers had little difficulty in attracting the amateurs, as many idealistic young people who admired the high level of Stevenson's rhetoric and his commitment to serious thought volunteered for the effort. But Sen. John F. Kennedy's (D, Mass.) [q.v.] victory over Sen. Hubert H. Humphrey (D, Minn.) [q.v.] in the May 1960 West Virginia primary severely damaged hopes for a deadlocked Convention. Despite demonstrations by thousands of enthusiastic Stevenson supporters outside the convention hall and a tumultuous 20-minute demonstration inside, Kennedy won the nomination on the first ballot at the July gathering. Stevenson received 79½ delgate votes.

Although many people regarded Kennedy as an idealistic young man who represented a continuation of the Stevensonian tradition in the Democratic Party, Stevenson and a number of other Democratic liberals regarded the Party's nominee as a cold, ambitious politician without a strong commitment to principles. (Kennedy, like many others, regarded Stevenson as indecisive and prissy.) But Stevenson disliked Vice President Nixon, the Republican nominee, far more, and his support of Kennedy induced many Democratic liberals such as Eleanor Roosevelt [q.v.] to back the Massachusetts Senator wholeheartedly.

During the primary campaign Kennedy had indicated that he would give Stevenson a high post in his Administration. Stevenson expected to be appointed Secretary of State, but instead he received the post of ambassador to the United Nations. In April 1961 Stevenson was not informed about the American role in the Cuban Bay of Pigs invasion, and he denied American involvement before the Security Council. He was enraged upon learning the truth. Subsequently, his influence in the Administration declined, and he was forced to defend policies that he had no role in formulating. Stevenson retained his post under President Lyndon B. Johnson. He died of a heart attack in London on July 14, 1965. [See KENNEDY, JOHNSON Volumes]

[MLL]

For further information:
Stuart Gerry Brown, *Conscience in Politics: Adlai E. Stevenson in the 1950s* (Syracuse, 1961).

STEWART, POTTER
b. Jan. 23, 1915; Jackson, Mich.
Associate Justice, U.S. Supreme Court, 1958- .

Born into a long-established Cincinnati family, Potter Stewart graduated from Yale in 1937 and Yale law school four years later. After working with a Wall Street law firm, he began a practice in Cincinnati in 1947 and served as a city council member from 1950 to 1953. President Eisenhower named Stewart to the Sixth Circuit Court of Appeals in April 1954. He soon emerged as a leading federal circuit judge, admired for his closely reasoned and well-written opinions. Stewart generally pursued a moderate course, especially in loyalty-security cases, and he showed a high regard for protecting the right to counsel.

Mentioned as a possible Supreme Court nominee as early as 1957, Stewart was appointed to the high court when Harold Burton [q.v.] retired in October 1958. Stewart began serving on the Court under a recess appointment that month. The Senate confirmed his nomination in May 1959, by a vote of 70-17, with the opposition coming from Southern Democrats who disliked Stewart's stance on civil rights.

In his early years on the Court, Stewart was often characterized as a "swing" justice who moved between the Court's liberal and conservative wings. During his first term, for example, he joined the majority in two June 1959 cases in which a closely divided Court upheld the contempt convictions of witnesses who had refused to answer questions or produce information for congressional and state anti-Communist investigations. However, later the same month Stewart voted to overturn a federal industrial security program because Congress had never authorized certain of the procedures used.

Such decisions showed that Stewart tended toward a policy of judicial self-restraint, but he was not insensitive to claims of individual rights. He would object if government encroached too greatly on individual liberties or violated principles of fair procedure. However, he generally preferred to overturn government action on narrow grounds, placing only limited restrictions on government power. In a February 1960 case Stewart spoke for the majority to void the convictions of two Arkansas NAACP officials who had refused to give their membership lists to local authorities because the forced disclosure would cause un unwarranted intrusion into the right of free association. The Justice's opinion for the Court in a December 1960 case ruled unconstitutional an Arkansas law requiring public school teachers to list all organizations to which they had belonged in the past five years. The Court held it was too extreme an infringement on free association. Stewart also showed his concern for First Amendment rights in his opinion in a June 1959 case overturning New York State's ban on the showing of the film *Lady Chatterley's Lover*.

Justice Stewart had a special concern for the right to counsel and wrote two opinions for the Court in February and June of 1959 overturning convictions where the defendant had been denied counsel. However, he was a moderate on other criminal rights issues. In March 1959 he voted to hold that persons tried for the same offense in federal and state courts had not been subjected to double jeopardy.

Usually labeled a moderate, Stewart found himself more often in dissent once a liberal majority emerged on the Court in the early-1960s. He voted with the liberals in many cases involving the right to counsel, civil rights and obscenity, but he opposed them on most criminal rights issues, on legislative reapportionment and in many loyalty-security cases. His opinions have been applauded for being concise, lucid and literate, and Stewart himself has been appraised as a "cautious, judicious, fairminded student of judicial power." [See KENNEDY, JOHNSON, NIXON/FORD Volumes]

[CAB]

For further information:
Jerold H. Israel, "Potter Stewart," in Leon Friedman and Fred L. Israel, eds., *The Justices of the U.S. Supreme Court, 1789-1969* (New York, 1969), Vol. 4.

STONE, I(SIDORE) F(EINSTEIN)
b. Dec. 24, 1907: Philadelphia, Pa.
Editor, Publisher, *I.F. Stone's Weekly*, 1953-67 (*Biweekly*, 1967-71).

Stone was reared in Haddonfield, N.J., and during his high school years he worked for the *Haddonfield Press* and the Camden (N.J.) *Courier-Post*. He was a philosophy student at the University of Pennsylvania but left in 1927 before the end of his junior year. A member of the Socialist Party's New Jersey State Committee, Stone did publicity work for Norman Thomas's [*q.v.*] 1928 presidential campaign. Soon afterwards he divorced himself from partisan political activity to pursue a journalistic career. From 1933 to 1952 Stone worked for such liberal and left-wing publications as the *New York Post*, *The Nation*, *PM*, *The New York Star* and *The New York Daily Compass*.

Stone was a critic of the Truman Administration's anti-Communist foreign policy from an independent leftist perspective. In November 1947 he denied that Soviet rule in Eastern Europe was maintained only by brutal terror and asserted that the planned economies of that region were bringing benefits to industrial and agricultural workers. The following year he supported the Progressive Party presidential candidacy of former Vice President Henry A. Wallace, who urged accommodation with the USSR. Stone refused to accept the American government's explanation of the causes of the Korean war, and in his *Hidden History of the Korean War* (1952), suggested that the U.S. and South Korea had provoked the North Korean invasion of the South. [See TRUMAN Volume]

After the *Daily Compass* folded in 1952, Stone could not find a job because of his views. Using that newspaper's subscription list he began publishing *I.F. Stone's Weekly*, an independent radical newsletter, in January 1953. Stone maintained the autonomy of the publication by rejecting advertising. He did all research, reportorial and editorial work, while his wife managed the newsletter's business affairs.

A staunch opponent of Sen. Joseph R.

McCarthy (R, Wisc.) [*q.v.*], Stone wrote in April 1953 that "no one is doing so much to damage the country's prestige abroad and its power to act effectively at home." However, he also criticized McCarthy's foes, stating in March 1954 that they accepted his underlying premise that Communism was an evil conspiracy against the peace and stability of the world. "To acquiesce in the delusions which create a panic," Stone commented, "is no way to stem it."

Stone believed that Eisenhower was a lackadaisical chief executive who was indifferent to the responsibilities of his office. In March 1959 he described the President as "a cardiac case whose chief interest is in getting away from his job as often as possible for golf and bridge." Stone was one of the few prominent journalists who attacked the Administration's foreign and domestic policies from a radical point of view. In January 1958 he charged that Secretary of State John Foster Dulles [*q.v.*] sought to promote the arms race to force the USSR to increase its arms budget and thus maintain poverty and increase domestic tension within the Soviet bloc. During March 1959 Stone wrote that the Berlin crisis demonstrated that U.S. and USSR leaders believed in "their sacred right to consign millions to death if they so choose."

Stone hailed the Supreme Court's 1954 school desegregation decision in *Brown v. Board of Education.* On a number of occasions, he attacked the Eisenhower Administration for not vigorously investigating the lynching of blacks in the South, and in May 1958 he chided the President for urging black leaders to be patient in the face of the slow pace of integration. In August 1958 Stone warned that if blacks were not assimilated into American society, they might become embittered and turn from integration to racist nationalism.

In addition to his dissident views, Stone was known for turning up facts that would otherwise have gone unnoticed. A critic of the U.S. insistence upon on-site inspection as a condition for the cessation of nuclear tests, Stone discovered in 1958 that the Atomic Energy Commission's first underground test had been detected 2,600 miles away.

In 1961 Stone regarded President John F. Kennedy as a promising liberal, but in December 1963 he wrote that Kennedy had been no more than an "enlightened conservative." He was an early and relentless critic of President Lyndon B. Johnson's Vietnam policies, and as a result, during the mid and late 1960s his newsletter became increasingly popular. He ceased publication of the newsletter in December 1971 and became a contributing editor to the *New York Review of Books.* [See KENNEDY, JOHNSON Volumes]

[MLL]

For further information:
Neil Middleton, ed., *The "I.F. Stone's Weekly" Reader* (New York, 1974).

STRAUSS, LEWIS L(ICHTENSTEIN)
b. Jan. 31, 1896; Charleston, W. Va.
Chairman, Atomic Energy Commission, June 1953-June 1958.

The son of a wholesale shoe manufacturer, Strauss wanted to become a physicist but could not afford a college education. Instead, he went to work in his father's business and soon became vice president. He served as Herbert Hoover's [*q.v.*] secretary in the U.S. Food Administration during World War I and helped arrange the final terms of the armistice. Strauss joined the leading Wall Street banking house of Kuhn, Loeb and Co. in 1919, becoming a partner nine years later. He also became active in philanthropic and cultural affairs, especially within the American Jewish community, and promoted scientific research. A member of the U.S. Naval Reserve since 1926, Strauss was ordered to active duty early in 1941. During World War II he coordinated ordnance production and procurement. President Truman made him a rear admiral in 1945, an honor rarely extended to reservists.

In 1947 Truman appointed Strauss to a three-year term on the newly-created Atomic Energy Commission (AEC), a civilian agency formed to oversee nuclear development. During the late-1940s Strauss joined Edward Teller [*q.v.*] in advocating the immediate development of the hydrogen bomb as a means of maintaining U.S. military supremacy over the Soviet Union. He was opposed by other members of the Commission and its General Advisory Committee, headed by J. Robert Oppenheimer [q.v.] who argued that work on the weapon should be restricted to the theoretical level for technical, strategic and moral reasons. Truman, siding with Strauss, ordered the Commission to proceed with the H-bomb's development in 1950. [See TRUMAN Volume]

In March 1953 President Eisenhower named Strauss chairman of the AEC. The following year he became involved in the Oppenheimer security hearings. In late 1953 Oppenheimer, then an AEC consultant, had his security clearance suspended following charges that he had been disloyal as a result of his prewar association with left-wing groups and his ambivalence about developing the H-bomb. A special AEC security board found Oppenheimer "loyal" but voted two to one to deny him clearance in April. Oppenheimer then appealed his case to the full AEC. The Commission ruled four to one in May to withhold clearance. Strauss was among the majority, which stated that the decision was based on "proof of fundamental defects in [Oppenheimer's] character."

Strauss was also embroiled in the Dixon-Yates contract, which became a major political controversy in 1954-55. In June 1954 Eisenhower ordered the AEC to end its contract with the Tennessee Valley Authority (TVA) and buy its power from a private combine headed by Edgar Dixon [q.v.] and Eugene Yates. Strauss enthusiastically endorsed this plan, describing it as "fair" and "a splendid example" of private enterprise serving public interests. However, congressional Democrats denounced it as an attempt to curb the TVA. The contract was signed in October. Four months later a Senate investigation revealed that Adolphe Wenzell, the Budget Bureau consultant who had recommended the plan, was a member of the bank that was to finance the Dixon-Yates plant. As a result of this disclosure, Eisenhower ordered the AEC to cancel the contract in July 1955.

During the decade Strauss continued to oppose a nuclear test ban despite the heated debate over the effects of radioactive fallout. In 1954 fallout from an H-bomb test caused radiation sickness among Japanese fishermen on a trawler hundreds of miles from the test site. Reports also circulated that radioactive fish had reached Japan. At a press conference following the incident, Strauss argued that radiation levels would decrease rapidly. Japanese scientific studies failed to substantiate the claim and convinced many scientists that Strauss was trying to cover up the effects of atomic testing. The official AEC report on the incident, issued 11 months later but minimized the effects and claimed no long-term problems, did little to allay their fears.

As the controversy over the effects of testing continued, the Administration, following Strauss's advice, continued to emphasize the importance of U.S. nuclear supremacy while stressing the peaceful uses of nuclear energy. As part of this policy, Eisenhower announced the Atoms-for-Peace program in 1955. Under the plan the International Atomic Energy Agency was established to increase the supply of fissionable materials available to other nations for non-military purposes.

The rancor and bitterness generated by the debate over the danger of radioactive fallout continued through the end of the decade with Strauss defending the increasingly unpopular tests. In 1956 Strauss announced that within four years the U.S. would develop methods for localizing fallout from atomic blasts. However, two years later he was forced to withdraw the claim.

Strauss further enraged proponents of a test ban in March 1958 when the AEC announced that the maximum distance for detection of an underground atomic blast was 250 miles. Critics charged that the announcement was designed to sabotage attempts to achieve an atmospheric nuclear test ban treaty, which was dependent on U.S. ability to detect Soviet underground explosions. Challenges to Strauss's statement forced the AEC to admit one week later that a blast could be detected 2,300 miles away.

Strauss's extreme opposition to a test ban

agreement conflicted with the Eisenhower Administration's growing commitment to such a treaty in the late-1950s. In 1958 Strauss declined Eisenhower's offer of reappointment to another five-year term as AEC chairman, saying that "circumstances beyond the control of either of us make a change in the chairmanship . . . advisable." The Administration announced in June that Strauss would become Eisenhower's special assistant for Atoms-for-Peace.

In October 1958 Eisenhower appointed Strauss to replace Sinclair Weeks [q.v.] as Secretary of Commerce. However, his role in the Dixon-Yates affair and the Oppenheimer hearings as well as his hostility to disarmament prompted strong opposition to his confirmation. Although Eisenhower defended Strauss as "a valuable public servant . . . of the utmost integrity and competence" and refused to withdraw the appointment, the Senate rejected the nomination 49 to 66 on June 19, 1959. He resigned June 30, the first cabinet appointee denied confirmation since 1925. Strauss retired from government and remained active in charitable activities during the 1960s.

[MDB]

STREIBERT, THEODORE C(UYLER)

b. Aug. 29, 1899; Albany, N.Y.
Director, United States Information Agency, August 1953-November 1956.

Streibert graduated from Wesleyan University in 1921 and received an M.B.A. from Harvard two years later. He remained at Harvard business school first as a research staff member and from 1929 to 1933 as assistant dean. Simultaneously Streibert began a long involvement with the communications industry.

In 1935 Streibert began a career in radio. Over the next 18 years he was vice president and then president of radio station WOR and treasurer, vice president and chairman of the board of the Mutual Broadcasting System. During the opening months of the Eisenhower Administration, Streibert served as an adviser to the International Information Administration and to the U.S. high commissioner to Germany.

Eisenhower appointed Streibert the first director of the proposed U.S. Information Agency (USIA) in July 1953. The Senate confirmed the appointment on Aug. 3, two days after Congress passed the law creating the agency. Streibert's task was to reorganize the department and restore morale in the wake of Sen. Joseph R. McCarthy's (R, Wisc.) [q.v.] attacks and severe budget cuts. The director created the Office of Policy and Programs to centralize administration and appointed assistant directors for the four geographical divisions comprising the USIA to coordinate policy. Streibert called these directors his "traveling vice presidents for sales and supervision." These assistants determined media content as well as policy. Because of budget cuts, the director was forced to close 26 overseas libraries, reduce Voice of America (VOA) broadcasts by 25% and reduce staff by over one third. However, he was able to increase allocations for the Office of Private Cooperation which was designed to get American business and labor involved in sponsorship of USIA activities. Although Streibert was regarded as somewhat tyrannical, he was able to improve staff morale, increase efficiency and upgrade the quality of his personnel.

Streibert was continually forced to defend his agency against McCarthy's charges that it was Communist infiltrated. At the end of 1953 his Office of Security conducted an investigation in which he reported that "there were no Communists discovered" in the USIA. Streibert told the Senate Foreign Relations Committee in January 1954 that he had combed his agency and that only about 20 out of 7,800 employes had been dismissed as security risks. After Eisenhower's Advisory Committee on Information suggested in February that McCarthy discontinue his probe of the Voice of America because he was hurting the agency's reputation, McCarthy threatened to call Streibert to testify before his Senate Permanent Investigations Subcommittee. Streibert responded in an address to Congress in which he defended the VOA. He told Congress that the agency tried to "forcefully" stress the facts and avoid "strident and propagandist material," and he proudly claimed that a poll of East European refugees rated the VOA as their favorite show. He assured Congress that he had dismissed security risks and banned works by Communist authors in USIA libraries.

Despite Streibert's announcement that the USIA would "concentrate on objective factual news reporting and appropriate commentaries," the Agency reflected the cold war thinking of the Eisenhower Administration. The USIA praised the United States sponsored overthrow of the leftist Arbenz regime in Guatemala, calling it a victory of free men over "red colonialism." It also tried to convince India and Egypt to renounce their neutralist policies, but it failed.

Streibert was particularly concerned about depicting the dark side of Soviet totalitarianism. He focused a large amount of the Agency's resources on publicizing Russian repression of the Hungarian revolt in 1956. The director also launched a "worldwide offensive to explore this spurious intellectual and ideological appeal of Communism." He ordered 54 selected books for USIA libraries, including such titles as *Forced Labor in Soviet Russia* and *Death of Science in Russia*.

In February 1955 Eisenhower appointed Streibert a member of the National Security Council's operations coordinating board. Beginning in 1956 he was invited to attend cabinet meetings. However, his influence on policymaking was slight because of Eisenhower's indifference and Secretary of State John F. Dulles's [q.v.] opposition to the agency. Streibert continued to be a cold warrior, questioning the easing of tension between the U.S. and the USSR which followed the 1955 summit conference and reminding the President that "the Cold War is still on."

Streibert resigned his post in November 1956 and joined the business staff of Nelson and Lawrence Rockefeller. In 1960 he became a vice president of the Time-Life Broadcasting Corp. and two years later president of the Radio Free Europe Fund. He served at that post until 1965.

[AES]

STROBEL, PETER A(NDREAS)
b. 1901: Denmark.
Commissioner, Public Buildings Service, General Services Administration, 1954-55.

Strobel graduated from Copenhagen's Technical University with a degree in civil engineering at the age of 24. He immediately emigrated to the U.S., accompanied by his wife and daughter. After a long apprenticeship in the building trades, Strobel worked as chief engineer at the 1939 New York World's Fair. During World War II he designed prefabricated Army barracks and portable airplane hangers. After the War his new firm, Strobel and Salzman, built shopping centers, railroad stations and the cosmotron building at Brookhaven National Laboratory.

Upon the recommendation of the Republican National Committee, Strobel was appointed Commissioner of the Public Buildings Service (PBS) of the General Services Administration (GSA) in 1954. As commissioner, Strobel operated 6,000 government buildings, supervised the construction of over 100 others and directed the 45 factories of the National Industrial Reserve. He willingly cut his income from $100,000 earned annually in the private sector to $14,800 in the government job.

In September 1955 columnist Drew Pearson [q.v.] charged that Strobel had not dissolved his connection with Strobel and Salzman after becoming commissioner. Strobel demanded an opportunity to refute the charges but refused to do so in Pearson's column.

When the House Judiciary Committee's Antitrust Subcommittee opened hearings on the matter in October, Strobel cooperated fully. He admitted maintaining a 90% interest in his engineering firm, but he insisted that he never used government time for private business. Strobel acknowledged that while commissioner he pressed his firm's claim for $7,500 against the Corps of Engineers, unaware that he was violating a law forbidding federal employes from acting as agents in claims against the government. He also negotiated a $71,050 contract with the Corps after being appointed commissioner but before taking office. The Commissioner's testimony revealed that he had recommended several of Strobel and Salzman's clients for PBS contracts, including one for work on the new $46 million Central Intelligence Agency headquarters. However, he maintained that the firm received no profits from the jobs. The subcommittee also learned that Strobel had not signed the required standard of conduct statement, stipulating that employes get written approval before engaging in outside business activity, and had not submitted a list of his firm's clients to the agency until August 1955.

In evaluating Strobel's testimony, Subcommittee Chairman Emanuel Celler (D, N.Y.) [q.v.] said that, although some of the Commissioner's actions might have been in violation of the criminal code, Strobel was not an intentionally dishonest man. Celler set Nov. 22 as the deadline to hear what action the GSA contemplated against him. Strobel resigned on Nov. 8 and returned to his firm amid rumors of White House pressure. The Justice Department decided not to initiate criminal charges against him.

[MJS]

SULZBERGER, C(YRUS) L(EO)
b. Oct. 27, 1912; New York, N.Y.
Journalist.

Following his graduation from Harvard in 1934, Sulzberger began a career in journalism, working for the *Pittsburgh Press*, the United Press and the *London Evening Standard*. He joined the *New York Times* in 1939 as the Balkan bureau manager. During his first three years with the paper, he traveled more than 100,000 miles through 30 countries reporting the progress of World War II.

Following the War Sulzberger became the *New York Times's* chief foreign correspondent and headed its foreign desk. Unimpressed with ideology, he argued that powerful leaders such as Truman, Stalin, DeGaulle and Churchill and not ideas that shaped history. He predicted continued clashes between the U.S. and the

USSR with the U.S. successfully containing Soviet aggression. He warned that two events might aggravate tension between the two superpowers: the rearming of West Germany and the intervention of the U.S. in Indochina.

In October 1954 Sulzberger, in his own words, "ceased being a reporter and became a journalist." Following the death of its distinguished columnist Anne O'Hare McCormick, the *Times* awarded Sulzberger his own column, "Foreign Affairs." Reflecting his belief that great men shape events, the column focused on interviews with foreign leaders. Through Sulzberger's writing these individuals, often no more than names to the American public, emerged as personalities. Sulzberger began by holding interviews with Secretary of State John Foster Dulles [q.v.] and former Secretary of State Dean Acheson [q.v.]. From these discussions the journalist was able to outline the differences in attitudes between the two cold warriors. Dulles emerged as a moralist anxious to carry on a crusade against Communism, while Acheson appeared as a realist maintaining that morality produced useless slogans. Churchill and DeGaulle were Sulzberger's favorite subjects. He thought of both as symbols of the most positive and negative expressions of their cultures. Sulzberger called them "the last of the giants of the past age."

Sulzberger wrote two major books on foreign policy during the Eisenhower Administration. Both synthesized views he had expressed in his columns. The first book, *The Big Thaw: A Personal Exploration of the "New" Russia and the Orbit Countries* (1956), discussed what he saw as the relaxation of Stalin's oppressive internal policies following the dictator's death. Sulzberger argued that the Soviets were extending this "thaw," in varying degrees, to its satellite nations. He believed the West would benefit from this because it could lead to a break up in monolithic Communism. He advised the U.S. to encourage more "Titoist heresies" in Eastern Europe. The publication of Sulzberger's book coincided with the Soviet supression of the Hungarian revolt. Although in the long run his analysis proved correct, one reviewer recommended that

Sulzberger revise his thesis in light of this event.

In 1959 Sulzberger published *What's Wrong With U.S. Foreign Policy*. Reiterating a theme he had first used in the 1940s, he wrote that the U.S. had failed to demonstrate a strong enough sense of realism and direction in its policies. Sulzberger urged America to stop using abstract ideology as a means of interpreting its rivals intentions. Russian imperialism, he stated, rather than Marxism, motivated Soviet leaders. Reflecting the importance he placed on men who molded policy, Sulzberger recommended greater care be used in the selection of diplomats.

Throughout the 1960s and 1970s Sulzberger continued to be one of the nation's leading foreign policy observers. Through his travels to distant lands, his meetings with foreign leaders and his own contacts with foreign policy experts at home and abroad, Sulzberger continued to document the changes in American diplomacy.

[JB]

For further information:
C. L. Sulzberger, *Long Row of Candles*. (New York, 1969).

SUMMERFIELD, ARTHUR E(LLSWORTH)
b. March 17, 1899; Pinconning, Mich.
d. April 26, 1972; West Palm Beach, Fla.
Postmaster General, January 1953-December 1960.

The son of a postmaster, Arthur Summerfield left school at the age of 13 and worked at Buick and Chevrolet plants. He soon entered his own business as a Pure Oil distributor in Flint, Mich., and during the decade developed it into one of the largest individual oil distributorships in the state. In 1929 he also launched the Summerfield Chevrolet Co., which eventually became one of the largest dealerships in the nation with branches throughout his home state of Michigan. In 1937 he gave up his Pure Oil business and the following year established a profitable real estate business.

Summerfield entered politics during the Wendell Wilkie campaign for the presidency in 1940. Seeing the failure of the local Republicans to mobilize support for Wilkie, Summerfield organized his own county committee. Wilkie carried the county, a factor crucial for the Republican's upset victory in Michigan. The automobile magnate thus earned a reputation as a top political organizer.

Summerfield unsuccessfully sought the Republican nomination for Michigan secretary of state. He then decided to devote his attention to political fund raising and organization. He expanded the Party's drives, which had been concentrated on the wealthy, to include Republicans of all means. The method proved so successful that it was adopted by several states. In 1946 he made an unsuccessful bid for the Republican senatorial nomination. The same year Summerfield was named to the Party's National Finance Committee. There his fame as a money raiser approached the "legendary," according to one newspaper.

During a postwar period Summerfield attempted to promote Sen. Arthur S. Vandenberg (R, Mich.) for President, but the Senator refused to run. In 1948 the Republican presidential candidate, Thomas Dewey, contemplated appointing Summerfield national chairman. However Summerfield removed his name from consideration. The following year he accepted the chairmanship of the National Republican Strategy Committee.

Arthur Summerfield headed the Michigan delegation to the Republican National Convention in 1952. Prior to the Convention he shrewdly announced his neutrality in the race between Dwight D. Eisenhower and Sen. Robert Taft (R, Ohio) [*q.v.*]. The morning of the nomination meeting, he then threw his support behind Eisenhower. His action helped create momentum for the General. Thirty-five of his 45 Michigan delegates voted for Eisenhower on the first ballot. Pennsylvania, the other large uncommitted state, then joined Michigan in coming out for Eisenhower. Summerfield became Republican National Chairman following the Convention. During the summer he successfully unified the Party, split by the primary fight between Taft and Eisenhower.

After the November victory President-elect Eisenhower announced that Summerfield would become Postmaster General, a position traditionally held by one of the top functionaries of the victorious party. He surprised many when he announced that he would resign as National Chairman to devote his attention to the postal service.

In taking over the postal department, Summerfield sought to introduce business techniques to improve service and reduce the deficit. He appointed businessmen to top administrative positions. Summerfield standardized equipment throughout the nation to introduce uniformity of machinery so that costs could be kept down. He also closed uneconomical post offices and ended uneconomical routes. Summerfield used a substantial amount of funds to invest in new machinery. In 1956 he claimed he had sharply reduced the deficit. His critics ridiculed his assertion, pointing out that the reduction resulted more from a rise in the parcel post rate and in clever bookkeeping tricks. They also questioned the success of his reforms, charging that improvements in the department tended to be cosmetic— newly painted mailboxes, new uniforms for mailmen, and the availability of chained pens on desks in front of postal windows.

During his tenure as Postmaster General, Summerfield experimented with several ways to speed the mails. In 1959 a guided missile carried 3,000 letters from a submarine in the Atlantic to a field near Jacksonville, Fla. He heralded the flight as the first known "official use of missiles by any Post Office Department in any nation." The following year he demonstrated an electronic facsimile system to deliver mails across the nation in seconds. However, this system proved to costly to operate.

Summerfield's attempts to modernize the Department were often hindered by Congress, which controlled the postal budget. The legislature refused rate increases Summerfield felt necessary for modernization. He also wanted to increase salaries of management personnel to attract better administrators, but Congress focused its attention on the average postal worker, rais-

ing his pay by 8% in 1955. The move was politically proper but added to Summerfield's operating costs without corresponding rate increases. The Postmaster General discovered that it was difficult to close uneconomic local post offices. Many members of Congress pressured him to reopen them, and he was forced to do so to maintain their support for his budget.

Summerfield waged a relentless campaign against obscene material sent through the mail, believing that he had the vague endorsement of the courts to bar pornography. He reported in 1959 that 315 arrests had been made that year on such charges. That same year he attempted to ban from the mails a new, unexpurgated edition of D. H. Lawrence's *Lady Chatterley's Lover*. He stated, "Any literary merit the book may have is far outweighed by the pornographic and smutty passages and words, so that the book taken as a whole, is an obscene and filthy work." A U.S. district court barred Summerfield's action, and on March 25, 1960 a U.S. Court of Appeals upheld the lower court's ruling.

Following his retirement from public service, Summerfield returned to his business ventures. He died in April 1962.

[JB]

SYMINGTON, (WILLIAM) STUART
b. June 26, 1901; Amherst, Mass.
Democratic Senator, Mo., 1953-77.

Symington was born into a well-to-do family in Amherst, Mass., where his father taught Romance languages at Amherst College. After serice in the Army during World War I, he attended Yale University, graduating in 1923. During the 1920s and 1930s he helped reorganize a variety of businesses. In many cases he was able to make foundering enterprises into major financial successes.

Symington's greatest business achievement came as president of the Emerson Electric Manufacturing Co. from 1938 to 1945. When he joined the firm it was suffering from serious labor and financial problems. Symington successfully negotiated with the unit of the United Electric and

Radio Machine Workers that represented Emerson and started a profit-sharing program. As a result, the employes rallied to the support of the company, profits rose and Emerson was the only large war plant in St. Louis not to have labor problems during World War II.

After the War President Harry S. Truman appointed Symington head of the Surplus Property Board, where he directed the disposal of $90 billion in surplus war property. As director, Symington helped alleviate the housing shortage for veterans by ordering federal agencies to turn over to states without charge surplus materials, equipment and land for emergency housing. In 1946 Truman appointed Symington the first Secretary of the Air Force. Believing that the U.S. had to act from a position of military superiority against the expansionist policies of the Soviet Union, Symington became a leading proponent of increased defense spending. He particularly advocated the development of a large nuclear equipped Air Force as the cornerstone of a modern defense system. In 1950, shortly before the Korean war, Symington resigned to protest a series of economy-minded armament reduction. [See TRUMAN Volume]

Symington was elected to the Senate from Missouri in 1952. While a liberal on domestic issues, he was primarily known as a "single issue man" devoted to protecting the interests of the Defense Department and particularly the Air Force. Shortly after taking his seat he scored the U.S. for lagging behind the Soviet Union in developing missiles and bombers. Several years later he joined such military men as Gen. Nathan Twining [q.v.] in suggesting that a "bomber gap" existed between the U.S. and USSR.

In April 1956 Symington headed a special subcommittee of the Senate Armed Forces Committee which held hearings on the state of American air power. In a Senate speech in May, he stated, "It is now clear that the U.S. . . . may have lost control of the air" and called for an accounting of U.S. air strength. During the three month hearings the panel heard testimony from a number of military leaders, including Air Force Gen. Curtis LeMay [q.v.], predicting that the U.S. would be behind the Soviets in air power within the decade unless spending was increased. Administration witnesses, however, defended the President's limited budget and maintained that U.S. defenses would continue to be superior to those of the USSR. Following testimony by Secretary of Defense Charles Wilson [q.v.], Symington charged that the Defense Department was considering going against the wishes of Congress by refusing to increase production. He also maintained that someone in the Department was misleading the American people in describing comparative U.S. and USSR defense strengths.

The subcommittee majority report, issued in January 1957, concluded that U.S. vulnerability to sudden attack had "increased greatly" and that the Soviet Union exceeded America in combat aircraft and would soon close the "quality gap." It stated that the Administration was vacillating on policies regarding preparation for limited and general war and had a "tendency to either ignore or underestimate Soviet military progress." It also said that the Eisenhower Administration had placed financial considerations ahead of defense requirements.

In 1959 Symington charged that a "missile gap" existed between the U.S. and the USSR. He predicted that the Soviet Union would soon have a three-to-one lead over the U.S. in operational intercontinental ballistic missiles. He maintained it would enable the Russians to "wipe out our entire manned and unmanned retaliatory force" with one blow.

Throughout the early 1950s Symington was a strong opponent of Sen. Joseph R. McCarthy (R, Wisc.) [q.v.]. In February 1953, as a member of McCarthy's Permanent Investigations Subcommittee, Symington defended Annie Lee Moss. McCarthy had charged the Pentagon clerk with having seen decoded messages while being a member of the Communist Party. Symington believed that the Annie Lee Moss under investigation was actually the wrong Annie Lee Moss since there were three listed in the Washington D.C. telephone directory. He offered to help her find another job if she was fired as a result of the McCarthy inquiry.

Symington also played a principle role in the Army-McCarthy hearings the following year. According to historian Robert Griffith, he was "McCarthy's most intransigent foe [and] remained doggedly in opposition throughout the hearings." When Republicans on the subcommittee tried to get the hearings adjourned, Symington, with the aid of the White House, pressed for their continuation. Accused by McCarthy of using the investigation to destroy the Republican Party and Eisenhower, Symington assured the nationwide television audience watching the hearings that he was "not afraid of anything about [McCarthy] or anything [McCarthy had] to say, at any time, any place, anywhere."

In 1959 Symington entered the campaign for the Democratic presidential nomination, running on a platform that attacked Eisenhower's defense policies. Although he had the backing of former President Harry S. Truman, his candidacy failed. Avoiding what proved to be the decisive primary campaigns, he had predicated his hopes on a deadlocked convention.

During the 1960s Symington continued his advocacy of increased military spending. By the end of the decade, the Senator was an opponent of the Vietnam war. Reversing his early belief that the U.S. must take a dominant role in world defense, in 1973 Symington called on President Richard Nixon to bring home many of the U.S. servicemen throughout the world because of the detrimental affect large-scale defense commitments had on the U.S. economy. Symington also fought for the reassertion of congressional authority in foreign policy. He did not run for reelection in 1976. [See KENNEDY, JOHNSON, NIXON/FORD Volumes]

[RSG]

For further information:
Richard A. Aliano. *American Defense Policy from Eisenhower to Kennedy* (Athens. Ohip. 1975).
Richard M. Fried. *Men Against McCarthy* (New York. 1976).
Robert Griffith. *The Politics of Fear* (Lexington. Ky.. 1970).

TABER, JOHN
b. May 5, 1880; Auburn, N.Y.
d. Nov. 22, 1965; Auburn, N.Y.
Republican Representative, N.Y..
1923-63; Chairman. Appropriations
Committee, 1947-49, 1953-55.

Taber received a B.A. degree from Yale University in 1902 and then attended the New York Law School for one year. Following his admission to the New York bar in 1904, he began practice in Auburn. Soon afterwards Taber became involved in Republican Party politics, and in 1922 he was elected to the U.S. House of Representatives from New York's Finger Lakes region.

In 1933 Taber became the ranking minority member of the Appropriations Committee. A conservative, economy-minded critic of government spending, he consistently opposed New Deal social welfare programs. Taber was an isolationist until 1941, when he declared his support for Lend-Lease aid. During the Truman Administration he continued to oppose social welfare measures. While often taking internationalist positions in foreign affairs, he was a critic of foreign economic aid programs. As chairman of the Appropriations Committee, a post he held from 1947 to 1949, Taber played a key role in cutting foreign relief funds in 1947. He unsuccessfully sought substantial reductions in Marshall Plan appropriations in 1948. [See TRUMAN Volume]

Taber again became Appropriations Committee chairman in 1953, following the Republicans' electoral victory of the preceding year. In July 1953 Taber's panel cut $700 million from President Eisenhower's $5.1 billion foreign aid request, despite a personal appeal by the President at a breakfast meeting with the New York Representative. Most of the cuts were in the area of economic assistance. However, in order to secure the expeditious enactment of a foreign military aid package, Taber was willing to accept a higher economic aid figure at a House-Senate conference two weeks later. He urged the House to approve the conference bill on the grounds that "the world is facing a very difficult situation" and "we have got . . . to develop military strength sufficient to combat the Communist threat." The following year, after the French defeat at Dien Bien Phu in northern Vietnam, Taber defended that year's foreign aid bill. He believed that recent international developments required the U.S. to "do whatever we can to build up support for the defense of the Far East, Southeast Asia and the Western Pacific."

An inveterate budget-cutter, Taber often defended his Committee's reductions on the House floor. In 1953 the House restored school aid funds eliminated by the panel for areas crowded by the Korean war defense effort. Taber took the floor in a futile effort to reinstate the cut, declaring that only the "wildest speculation" could justify approval of the school funds. During the same year he successfully fought off House efforts to increase the Committee's $60 million appropriation for the State Department's International Information Administration (IIA). Taber charged that there were "thousands and thousands of incompetents" on the IIA payroll. Followers of Sen. Joseph R. McCarthy (R, Wisc.) [q.v.] voted with Taber on the grounds that the IIA harbored leftwingers. The following year Taber successfully opposed an effort to restore Census Bureau funds for a business census. He contended that such censuses were of no help to business and "have just historic value."

After the Democrats regained control of Congress in the 1954 elections, Taber reverted to the status of ranking Republican on the Appropriations Committee. For the remainder of the decade he was particularly vehement in opposing public works projects. In 1956 Taber asserted that "we cannot go along continuing to pile up projects that are . . . to cost a tremendous amount of money and yet have the nation land right side up. . . ." A critic of the Tennessee Valley Authority (TVA), he attacked an appropriation for additional TVA power facilities in 1956 and the following year unsuccessfully attempted on the House floor to cut TVA funds from $13.3 million to $3.5 million. Continuing his budget-minded approach to foreign economic assistance, Taber unsuccessfully attempted in 1960 to eliminate appropriations for U.S. participation in the International Development Association (IDA). Taber denounced the IDA fund as a "giveaway."

The "watchdog of the Treasury," as Taber was sometimes known, made a trip to Bermuda in 1959 at government expense, ostensibly on behalf of the Appropriations Committee.

Taber opposed most New Frontier legislation. In 1962 he announced that he would not seek reelection. Taber died on Nov. 22, 1965 in Auburn, N.Y.

[MLL]

TAFT, ROBERT A(LPHONSO)
b. Sept. 8, 1889; Cincinnati, Ohio.
d. July 31, 1953; New York, N.Y.
Republican Senator, Ohip, 1939-53;
Senate Majority Leader, 1953.

The grandson of Ulysses Grant's Attorney General and son of the 27th President and 10th Chief Justice of the United States, Robert A. Taft graduated first in his class both at Yale in 1910 and Harvard law school in 1913. During World War I he was an assistant counsel to U.S. Food Administrator Herbert Hoover [q.v.]. In the 1920s and early-1930s, he served in the Ohio legislature as a state representative, house speaker and state senator. In 1938 he won the first of three campaigns for the U.S. Senate. A master of detail and an expert on parliamentary procedure, Taft all but led the Republican minority virtually from the beginning of his Senate career.

Taft quickly emerged as the most articulate champion of the GOP's Midwestern, conservative-isolationist wing. He repeatedly denounced most New and Fair Deal social programs as both needlessly wasteful and hazardous to individual liberties. He distrusted government bureaucracies as the harbingers of "creeping socialism." Occasionally, however, Taft veered sharply from the "Old Guard" orthodoxy. Beginning in 1945 and 1946 Taft sponsored decidedly liberal federal housing and aid-to-education measures. However, he angered organized labor by coauthoring the Taft-Hartley Labor Act of 1947, which set strict guidelines for union operations.

A prominent isolationist prior to Pearl Harbor, Taft rejected calls by some Republican leaders after the War for a cooperative "bipartisanship" in foreign policymaking. Skeptical of postwar Europe's military and economic weakness, Taft took exception to President Harry Truman's emphasis upon Western Europe in the struggle against Communist expansion. Although he favored the Truman Doctrine for Greece and Turkey, Taft originally criticized the Marshall Plan and voted against the North Atlantic Treaty, creating the North Atlantic Treaty Organization (NATO). Later he would accept American NATO membership, although he sought reductions in America's military commitment to the alliance. Taft determined, that Asia merited a greater U.S. role than Europe.

Popularly known as "Mr. Republican," Taft enjoyed the respect of his colleagues and conservatives nationally, yet he never achieved his greatest goal: the presidency. His campaigns for the GOP nomination tended to be badly managed, and he lacked broad voter appeal. Powerful liberal Republicans, aggravated by Taft's Western European policies, relentlessly opposed his presidential bids. Three times, in 1940, 1948 and 1952, Taft lost the Party's nomination to candidates of the Eastern "internationalist" wing. [See TRUMAN Volume]

Taft's last and narrowest defeat proved his greatest personal disappointment. Expecting to win, he labored mightily, only to see the nomination go to the self-avowed political amateur, Dwight D. Eisenhower. Taft's defeat embittered many loyal party workers and left deep wounds only temporarily healed by Eisenhower's singular popularity. Concerned over the Taftites' sentiments, Eisenhower agreed in September to a list of policy positions personally dictated by Taft and issued publicly in a famous "surrender at Morningside Heights." Their joint statement promised a drastic reduction in government spending and a tax cut. It minimized their differences over foreign policy.

In the weeks after his November election, Eisenhower displayed only the most formal regard for Taft's sensitivities. Several of his cabinet choices annoyed the Senator,

who felt the panel included too many big businessmen. None perturbed him more, however, than the nomination of Martin Durkin [q.v.], a Democrat and avowed foe of the Taft-Hartley Act, as Secretary of Labor. To the announcement of Durkin's selection, Taft could only respond "incredible."

In December 1952 Senate Republicans unanimously elected Taft majority leader. Ever the party loyalist, Taft tried to forget the frustrations of the previous year. Although his Party held only a narrow, 48-47, Senate majority, Taft achieved a workable consensus on most of Eisenhower's domestic program. "No President," reporter William S. White wrote of the period 1933-53, "had so effective a Senate leader as Eisenhower had in Taft." Some termed Taft Eisenhower's "Prime Minister."

Sen. Joseph R. McCarthy, Jr. (R, Wisc.) [q.v.] posed Taft's first major problem as majority leader. Supporting some of McCarthy's broader goals, Taft had defended the controversial anti-Communist investigator despite private misgivings over his methods and doubts over the extent of a domestic Communist menace. Nevertheless, he considered the popular McCarthy an asset needed by the Party for the 1954 elections. He therefore charged Sen. William Jenner (R, Ind.) [q.v.], chairman of the Internal Security Committee, with the responsibility for investigating domestic subversion and relegated McCarthy, who might embarrass the Administration, to the chairmanship of the heretofore insignificant Government Operations Committee. There, Taft reasoned, "We've got McCarthy where he can't do any harm." Events proved him incorrect.

Eisenhower's nomination of Charles Bohlen [q.v.] to be ambassador to the Soviet Union provided Taft with the greatest single challenge during his majority leadership. Largely because of Bohlen's participation in the controversial 1945 Yalta conference, McCarthy and other militantly anti-Communist GOP senators quickly denounced him as a security risk. Sensing a potentially disastrous rift within his own ranks and an early humiliation for the new President, Taft personally examined Bohlen's FBI file. He found nothing to validate charges made by the nominee's detractors. Taft refused to allow McCarthy to examine the confidential file. With impeccable anti-Communist credentials of his own, Taft ardently defended Bohlen, thus assuring his confirmation in March, 74 to 13. McCarthy dissented.

Defense policy continued to divide Eisenhower and Taft after the election. In a February 1953 speech Taft anticipated the President's own Farewell Address by declaring, "We could destroy our liberty by a military and foreign expenditure in time of peace so great that a free economic system cannot survive." Excessive military spending, he warned, might make America a "garrison state." However he failed to convert Eisenhower during an April budget meeting; Eisenhower refused to reduce Defense Department requests for fiscal 1954. The President did acquiesce to Taft's suggestion that, as part of an overall effort to distinguish his image from that of his predecessor, he should replace all members of the Joint Chiefs of Staff, including his old Army comrade Omar Bradley.

Though essentially loyal to Eisenhower, Taft publicly differed with the President on certain aspects of foreign policy. He criticized NATO's dependence on American military power and called upon European members to play a larger role. He remained more anxious over Communist expansion in Asia than in Europe. In a widely reported speech on Korea during May, Taft faulted the United Nations for impeding the war there. If truce negotiations failed, Taft suggested that the U.S. must "reserve to ourselves a completely free hand" and expand operations against China. America must insist on a united, free Korea. The White House quickly denied sharing Taft's opinions.

Taft became seriously ill with cancer in the late spring and died on July 31, 1953. In June he had selected as his successor William F. Knowland (R, Calif.) [q.v.], then viewed as a bridge between the Senate's Midwestern and Eastern factions. Robert Taft displayed rare intellectual acumen and integrity. Years later his various positions would be taken up by a wide

range of public figures. Democrats quoted his speeches in favor of public housing and "New Left" scholars of American diplomacy praised his skeptisicm over the need for a cold war leviathan state. Many Republican partisans sought revenge for his 1952 defeat into the 1960s. In 1959 the Senate designated Taft as one of the five greatest senators in history.

[JLB]

For further information:
James T. Patterson, *Mr. Republican* (Boston, 1972).
Robert A. Taft, *A Foreign Policy for Americans* (New York, 1951).
William S. White, *The Taft Story* (New York, 1954).

TALBOTT, HAROLD E(LSTNER)
b. March 31, 1888; Dayton, Ohio.
d. March 2, 1957; Palm Beach, Fla.
Air Force Secretary, February 1953-August 1955.

A 1910 graduate of Yale University, Harold Talbott joined his father's industrial firm in 1911. During World War I he helped found the Dayton Wright Airplane Co. and served as its president from 1916 to 1923. In 1918 a Justice Department investigation revealed that government contracts with the company resulted in profits of approximately $3.5 million, including $100,000 salaries for Talbott and his Dayton Wright partners. These salaries were charged to the government as part of the cost of production. The government attempted to prosecute the firm in 1922, but the case was dismissed.

After serving as aircraft production director of the War Production Board during 1942-43, Talbott joined the board of directors of Chrysler Corp. in 1944 and also served as a member of the finance committee of the Electric Auto-Lite Co. As chairman of the Republican National Finance Committee in 1948-49, he was responsible for financing Thomas Dewey's presidential campaign.

President-elect Eisenhower nominated Talbott Air Force Secretary in December 1952. Because of regulations requiring government personnel to divest themselves of stock held with firms that had government contracts, Talbott was forced to sell his stock in Chrysler and Electric Auto-Lite. However, he was allowed to continue his partnership with the Paul Mulligan Co., a general management engineering firm. Talbott was confirmed by a Senate vote of 76 to 6 in February 1953.

In 1955 the Senate Permanent Investigations Subcommittee held hearings on Talbott's continued connections with Mulligan. The probe revealed that Talbott had actively promoted Mulligan Co. business from his Pentagon office and successfully negotiated new contracts with Olin Industries, Owens-Illinois Glass Co. and Avco Co., all of which also had contracts with the Defense Department. Mulligan Co. profits had risen substantially since Talbott's appointment, and the Secretary's personal income from the firm had averaged over $50,000 per year after his appointment.

The most damaging testimony was the revelation that the Radio Corporation of America (RCA) had refused to renew a contract with Mulligan because it could not secure an advisory opinion from the Justice Department clearing it of impropriety under the conflict-of-interest laws. Talbott reportedly told an RCA attorney that his position was "foolish" and pointed out that a number of companies doing work for the Air Force were also under contract with Mulligan. The lawyer testified that Talbott had told him RCA should "come off [its] high horse and stop acting so high and mighty." Talbott admitted approaching many of Mulligan's new clients but contended that he had not used his official position to influence them. Claiming that his memory was hazy, he still maintained that he had never made the alleged statement about RCA.

As a result of the hearings and newspaper coverage, Talbott was forced to resign in August 1955. In a letter to the President, he asserted that his conduct had been "within the bounds of ethics" and blamed his predicament on "distorted publicity." Eisenhower praised Talbott's administrative ability but admitted that the Secretary's decision to resign had been the right one.

Talbott was given one of Washington's most spectacular farewells at Bolling Air Force Base and received the Medal of Freedom, the Defense Department's highest civilian award, from Secretary of Defense Charles Wilson [q.v.]. He returned to the business world "to make a little dough" and died of a stroke in 1957.

[FJD]

TAYLOR, MAXWELL D(AVENPORT)
b. Aug. 26, 1901; Keytesville, Mo.
Army Chief of Staff, June 1955-June 1959.

Stirred by his grandfather's tales of the Confederate Army, Taylor decided on a military career. He won appointment to West Point and graduated fourth in a class of 102 in 1922. During the 1920s and 1930s he served as a military engineer at various posts, attended a series of officers' schools and taught at West Point. Maj. Taylor served as artillery commander of the 82nd and 101st Airborne Divisions during World War II, winning high praise from Gen. Dwight D. Eisenhower for discharging his "weighty responsibilities . . . with unerring judgment."

After the War Taylor, who had risen to the rank of general, served as superintendent of West Point. In 1949 he became first commander of the American military government in Berlin. Taylor also led the Eighth Army during the final stages of the Korean war. In April 1955 he began a brief assignment as U.S. and U.N. commander in the Far East. That June President Eisenhower selected Taylor to replace Gen. Matthew B. Ridgway [q.v.] as Army Chief of Staff.

Taylor received his appointment because Eisenhower wanted someone sympathetic to his defense policies to head the Army. The Administration's "New Look" policies were prompted by a desire to hold down defense spending and a reluctance to commit American fighting men to unpopular wars. Funds were, therefore, diverted from conventional forces toward the strengthening of air power and nuclear capabilities.

The Administration announced that the U.S. would avoid debilitating ground wars such as the Korean conflict and instead would respond "swiftly and selectively" with nuclear air power to stop Communist aggression. "Massive retaliation," as this doctrine became known, was to be the center of U.S. defense.

In his initial years as Army Chief of Staff, Taylor avoided public criticism of Eisenhower's defense policy. When he testified in 1957 at the House Appropriations Committee's hearings on the proposed fiscal 1958 defense budget, he strongly endorsed the Defense Department's military funding request and outlined ways in which the Army was more efficiently spending funds.

Months later, before the Senate Appropriations Committee, Taylor reiterated his strong support for the Eisenhower budget. He casually admitted that he had originally urged greater funding for long-range modernization of conventional forces, but he did not complain about being turned down. He did, however, warn that as the U.S. and the USSR reached nuclear parity, the Soviet Union would grow increasingly reluctant to risk nuclear war. Consequently, the threat of subversion and limited wars would increase greatly. To meet such a danger the U.S. needed a well-equipped, highly-prepared Army ready to "intervene quickly with substantial forces." At this time, however, no one on the Committee regarded Taylor's comments as especially important, nor did the General himself consider them anything other than pleas for the restoration of the House cuts in the Administration's defense budget.

The Soviet launching of *Sputnik* in the fall of 1957 opened a debate within the various branches of the military on defense strategy. Taylor, with the backing of top Navy personnel, spoke for the "finite deterrence/limited war" group. He contended that the launchings portended the end of American nuclear superiority and that conventional forces (especially Army units) would be vitally important in the era of stalemate to follow. He opposed a primary reliance on missiles and nuclear weapons as limiting defense options. Countering Taylor was the "assured superiority/air power" faction

headed by the Air Force. This group proposed that the U.S. maintain its traditional nuclear superiority by increased funding for strategic aircraft and missiles.

Taylor also clashed with Eisenhower over his demands for increased defense spending. He drew angry criticism from the President for his failure to appreciate the broader, especially economic, considerations involved in making defense policy. As a result of his stand, Taylor was eased out of his position as Army Chief of Staff. He retired in June 1959 but continued to air his views both in print and on television.

Later that year he published *The Uncertain Trumpet*, a biting attack on the Administration's massive retaliation doctrine. Instead of a defense policy offering what he thought was general war or compromise and defeat, Taylor favored a "flexible response" which would enable the U.S. to cope with "anything from general war to infiltration, aggression" or subversion. He believed such a policy could only be achieved by willingness to build up both conventional and nuclear forces.

Taylor's book impressed John F. Kennedy [*q.v.*], who used the arguments to support his own attacks on the Eisenhower Administration's defense policy during his 1960 presidential campaign. Following his election Kennedy named Taylor as his military representative in July 1961. Taylor became chairman of the Joint Chiefs of Staff in October 1962. His theories shaped America's early military response to the Vietnam war. In June 1964 President Lyndon B. Johnson appointed him ambassador to Vietnam. He remained at that post until July 1965. [See KENNEDY, JOHNSON Volumes]

[RJB]

TELLER, EDWARD
b. Jan. 15, 1908; Budapest, Hungary
Associate Director, Lawrence Livermore Laboratory, Atomic Energy Commission, 1954-

The son of well-to-do Jewish parents, Teller completed his doctorate in physical chemistry at the University of Leipzig in

1930 and then studied with Niels Bohr. When the Nazis came to power in 1933, he fled Germany for England. He settled in the U.S. in 1935 and became an American citizen in 1941.

During World War II Teller worked on the Manhattan Project, which developed the atomic bomb. In 1942 he participated in a scientific conference that discovered the possibility of creating a hydrogen bomb through the thermonuclear fusion of isotopes of hydrogen, deuterium and tritium. Teller then went to Los Alamos, N.M., to work with government scientists on the weapon. However, in 1944 the project encountered a major obstacle when scientists found that such an explosion would require extremely high temperatures, then considered unattainable. Following the first successful atomic bomb test in 1945, the sense of urgency surrounding the H-bomb's development diminished.

During the postwar period Teller continued to champion the immediate development of the H-bomb, believing it necessary to maintain U.S. military superiority over the Soviet Union. The first Soviet atomic explosion in 1949 prompted military leaders to support Teller's demand. However, the majority of the Atomic Energy Commission's (AEC) General Advisory Committee (GAC), including chairman J. Robert Oppenheimer [q.v.], were hesitant about quick development. They questioned the project's military value, believing that it would escalate the arms race, and thought it too costly as well as fraught with technical problems. The scientists recommended gradual development. President Truman supported Teller's position and ordered a crash program in 1950. The first H-bomb was exploded in November 1952. [See TRUMAN Volume]

Teller was a key figure in the Oppenheimer security hearings of 1954. Oppenheimer's security clearance had been suspended in 1953 as a result of allegations that his prewar leftist associations and reluctance to develop the H-bomb raised significant doubts about his loyalty. Of the six scientists involved in the H-bomb controversy who testified at the AEC hearing, only Teller supported the charges. He

maintained that the thermonuclear weapon might have been produced "about four years earlier" if "at the end of the war people like Oppenheimer had lent . . . moral support" to the project, Teller said. He told the security board that, while he considered Oppenheimer a loyal American, it would be "wiser not to grant [him] clearance" to work on security projects. The board followed Teller's recommendation.

As the dangers of radioactive fallout became publicized in the late-1950s, demands for a nuclear test ban grew. Teller continued to support tests, believing they were necessary not only to maintain U.S. military superiority but also to improve nuclear weapons and solve the problem of fallout. In meetings with the President and congressional committees in 1957 and 1958, Teller assured government leaders that the U.S. would produce a "clean bomb," free of fallout, within four or five years. Although he conceded that "thousands of genetic mutations might result from test radioactivity," he warned that the U.S. "may be sacrificing millions of lives in a 'dirty' nuclear war later" if it agreed to a test ban.

Following successful orbiting of the Soviet satellite *Sputnik* in 1957, Teller advocated space research for both its scientific and military value. He also recommended that the government develop plans for quick industrial recovery from a nuclear missile attack and that it institute a massive fallout shelter program. Teller participated in a Rockefeller Brothers Fund panel that urged "substantially increased defense expenditures" in its January 1958 report.

Teller resigned as a member of the GAC in August 1954. He continued to oppose a nuclear test ban and helped develop a technique for carrying out underground nuclear tests free of detection. The technique was revealed in December 1959. Teller continued to press for further nuclear tests during the Kennedy Administration. [See KENNEDY Volume]

[MDB]

For further information:
Robert Gilpin, *American Scientists and Nuclear Weapons Policy* (Princeton, 1962).

THOMAS, CHARLES S(PARKS)

b. Sept. 28, 1897; Independence, Mo.
Undersecretary of the Navy, February
1953-July 1953; Assistant Secretary of
Defense for Supply and Logistics, July
1953-April 1954; Secretary of the Navy,
April 1954-March 1957.

Thomas moved with his parents from Independence, Mo., to Los Angeles, Calif., in 1911. He attended the University of California at Berkeley during 1915-16 before transferring to Cornell University. He left school during his junior year to serve as a naval aviator during World War I. In 1919 Thomas joined the Los Angeles investment house of George H. Burr Co., subsequently becoming a partner and vice president. Named vice president and general manager of Foreman and Clark, Inc., a retail clothing manufacturer, in 1932, he saved the company from bankruptcy during the Depression and advanced to become president and director by 1937.

During World War II Thomas became special assistant first to Artemus L. Gates, assistant secretary of the navy for air, and later to Secretary of the Navy James L. Forrestal. He returned to Foreman and Clark after the War. Thomas also served as airport commissioner of Los Angeles from 1945 to 1950 and assumed several corporate directorships, including one with Lockheed Aircraft Corp.

In February 1953 President Dwight D. Eisenhower appointed Thomas undersecretary of the navy and five months later promoted him to assistant secretary of defense for supply and logistics. Thomas's duties were similar in both capacities. His major project was to formulate a single catalogue of equipment used by the three Armed Services, thus preventing duplication and saving money.

In March 1954 Eisenhower nominated Thomas to be Secretary of the Navy. One of the Secretary's most pressing concerns was loyalty-security issues. In October, acting on the recommendation of Vice President Richard M. Nixon [q.v.], he suspended the security clearance of Edward U. Condon. The scientist, then working on a secret Navy project, had already obtained lower echelon clearance. Nevertheless, Condon was denied further access to secret projects because of suspicions of having knowingly or unknowingly associated with alleged Soviet espionage agents. In August of the following year, Thomas announced that he would personally review the case of Eugene W. Landy, a U.S. Merchant Marine Academy graduate who had been denied a Naval Reserve commission because his mother had been a member of the Communist Party from 1937 to 1947 and still subscribed to the *Daily Worker*, the party organ. Landy's mother protested that she had left the Party at her son's urging. Thomas appointed a special review board which, in late September, recommended against issuing Landy's commission. However, Thomas overruled the board and made Landy an ensign in the Naval Reserve. As in the Condon case, Thomas consulted Nixon before rendering the decision.

Thomas spent much of his time attempting to defend the Administration's desire to prevent the expansion of the military budget. In January 1958 he testified before the House Armed Services Committee that the Navy and the Marine Corps could maintain and even increase their striking power despite Administration budget cuts resulting in both manpower and vessel reductions. Two years later the Secretary returned to Capitol Hill to defend the threatened Administration "lean year" program, which eschewed large increases in the military budget and instead emphasized more efficient use of equipment on hand over the building of costly new weapons systems. "In essence," said the Navy Secretary, "the United States could not endure if it either permitted its military arsenal to rust," or if "in response to some transient danger," it undertook a "prolonged and full mobilization during peace time."

In March 1957, shortly after his testimony before the House, Thomas resigned as Secretary of the Navy. In June 1957 he became chairman of the Republican National Finance Committee. From 1958 to 1960 he was president and chief executive officer for Trans World Airlines. He became president of the Irvine Co. of Tostin, Calif., in 1960. In 1971 President Richard Nixon appointed Thomas chairman of the National Tourism Review Commission, a group composed of business leaders and government officials organized to encourage foreign travel in the United States.

[RJB]

THOMAS, NORMAN (MATTOON)
b. Nov. 20, 1884: Marion, Ohio.
d. Dec. 19, 1968: Huntington, N.Y.
Peace and reform advocate

Thomas, who came from a middle class, fundamentalist background, was trained for the ministry at the Union Theological Seminary. There he was influenced by the social gospel of Dr. Walter Rauschenbusch. In 1911 Thomas received a bachelor of divinity degree and became pastor of the East Harlem Presbyterian Church in New York City. Five years later Thomas joined the Fellowship of Reconciliation, a religious pacifist group. He opposed American participation in World War I and assisted in the founding of the National Civil Liberties Bureau (later known as the American Civil Liberties Union) during the War.

In 1918 Thomas joined the Socialist Party and abandoned his religious activity. During the 1920s he emerged as the Party's leader and headed its national ticket in every presidential election from 1928 through 1948. He won his greatest electoral support in 1932, polling about 3% of the total vote. Viewing war as a threat to American democracy, Thomas opposed U.S. entry into World War II. However, after Pearl Harbor he gave the war effort qualified support.

During the late-1940s Thomas was a severe critic of Soviet despotism and expansionism. He denounced Henry A. Wallace, the Progressive Party presidential candidate in 1948, as an apologist for Russian aggression and an advocate of peace by appeasement of Stalin. Nevertheless, Thomas favored international agreements to reduce arms and in 1950 urged President Harry S. Truman to propose disarmament in a forthcoming speech at the United Nations. During the same year Thomas urged the

Socialist Party to abandon its increasingly ineffectual electoral efforts, but its National Convention rejected this proposal. [See TRUMAN Volume]

Thomas was widely admired even by those who strongly disagreed with his views. His often impassioned rhetoric was tempered with wit, and he refrained from expressions of personal animosity. His integrity and genuine compassion for the weak were almost universally acknowledged. Furthermore, he rejected Leninism, advocating the peaceful establishment of a democratic form of socialism.

During the 1950s Thomas's prestige rose still further because he became increasingly identified as an individual advocate of reform rather than as a partisan leader of the Socialist Party. Although continuing to act as a spokesman for the group, Thomas gave up his posts in the dwindling organization during the decade. In 1952 and 1956 he backed Adlai E. Stevenson [q.v.], the Democratic presidential nominee, rather than the Socialist Party national tickets.

Thomas believed that Communists should be excluded from policymaking posts in government on the grounds that the history of the Communist movement clearly demonstrated its subversive nature. But he denounced McCarthyism as a threat to civil liberties and defended the right of Communists to engage in legal political activity. In an October 1953 meeting with Eisenhower, Thomas protested the exclusion of Socialists from policymaking positions and opposed the broad definition government officials had given to such posts.

Thomas condemned Communist tyranny but supported peaceful coexistence with the Soviet Union as necessary to avoiding a nuclear holocaust. He was a persistent advocate of disarmament and placed part of the blame for failures to achieve arms reductions upon the U.S. In 1955 Thomas criticized the Administration for rejecting a British-French proposal, accepted by the Soviet Union, to reduce conventional forces. In 1957 he condemned the U.S. for turning down a Soviet plan for a first-step, monitored moratorium on nuclear tests.

In 1957 Thomas and Norman Cousins

[*q.v.*] were key figures in organizing the Committee for a Sane Nuclear Policy (SANE). In 1960 the group held a rally in New York City, attended by over 17,000 persons, to urge an end to nuclear testing and a concerted attack upon poverty. During the same year Sen. Thomas Dodd (D, Conn.) [*q.v.*], vice chairman of the Internal Security Subcommittee, charged that SANE was heavily infiltrated by Communists and fellow-travelers. The organization's national board issued a policy statement, endorsed by Thomas, barring Communists from membership in the organization. Shortly afterwards 37 members of its New York City chapter, which openly opposed this policy, were subpoenaed by Senate investigators. The national board, at Thomas's insistence, refused to come to their defense. Subsequently the board revoked the local chapter's charter.

In 1960 Thomas favored Stevenson for the Democratic presidential nomination. He reluctantly backed Sen. John F. Kennedy (D, Mass.) [*q.v.*] in the general election. Thomas testified before a Senate committee in July 1963 as a supporter of the Administration's civil rights bill, which he regarded as a commendable but timid initial step towards ending racial injustice. During the Johnson Administration he was harshly critical of America's military involvement in Vietnam. Thomas died on Dec. 19, 1968 after suffering a stroke. [See KENNEDY, JOHNSON Volumes]

[MLL]

For further information:
Harry Fleischman, *Norman Thomas—A Biography: 1884-1968* (New York, 1969).
Bernard K. Johnpoll, *Pacifist's Progress: Norman Thomas and the Decline of American Socialism* (Chicago, 1970).

THOMPSON, FRANK, JR.
b. July 16, 1918: Trenton, N.J.
Democratic Representative, N.J., 1955- .

The son of a newspaperman and nephew of a New Jersey Democratic leader, Thompson studied law at Wake Forest College in Winston-Salem, N.C., and was admitted to the bar in 1948. The following year he ran successfully for the New Jersey State Assembly from Democratic, industrial Trenton. In 1954 Thompson was elected to Congress as a self-styled "New Deal-Fair Deal Democrat of the Adlai Stevenson School." During his campaign he called for a bipartisan foreign policy and drastic revision of the Taft-Hartley Law.

In the House Thompson compiled a consistently liberal record, voting in agreement with the AFL-CIO Committee on Political Education's (COPE) recommendations on most issues. As a member of the Education and Labor Committee, he quickly emerged as a leading advocate of federal aid to education as a means of alleviating the problem of rising student enrollment in the nation's schools and the increased cost of school construction since World War II. In January 1959 Thompson took over the sponsorship of a bill drafted by the National Education Association to provide $1.3 billion in federal grants to local school districts for school construction and teachers' salaries. He claimed that the bill would finance 25,000 new classrooms and, through provisions for federal-state matching funds, would encourage the states to provide for 15,000-16,000 more. In January 1960 the Senate passed a version of the proposal, but strong conservative opposition threatened its passage in the House. Responding to Administration pressure to water down the bill, Thompson removed the provisions for aid to teachers' salaries and amended it to require 50-50 matching of federal with state funds during every year of the proposed four-year program.

Passage of the bill was further threatened by an anti-segregation rider attached by Rep. Adam Clayton Powell, Jr. (D. N.Y.) [*q.v.*]. Thompson, recalling that a similar rider had led to the defeat of a 1956 school bill, accused the House conservative coalition of supporting the Powell amendment solely to prevent the bill's final passage. He declared that individual school districts defying court orders to desegregate could be denied funds under the bill "without the addition of any amendment" because the Constitution is "self-enacting." The bill was passed with the rider in May 1960. However, it was blocked by the House Rules Committee's refusal to authorize a House-Senate conference, which might have resolved the differences between the House and Senate versions of the proposal.

Despite his opposition to the Powell amendment, Thompson had a pro-civil rights voting record throughout his congressional career. In 1959 he helped bring a number of younger liberal members of Congress together in the Democratic Study Group, and he led an unsuccessful fight the same year to curb the power of the conservative-dominated Rules Committee to keep legislation from the floor.

Thompson actively supported John F. Kennedy in the 1960 presidential campaign, and he introduced the new Administration's school aid proposal in 1961. In 1966 he led the fight in the Education and Labor Committee to limit the power of its chairman, Adam Clayton Powell, Jr. [See KENNEDY, JOHNSON, NIXON/FORD Volumes]

[TLH]

THOMPSON, LLEWELLYN E., JR.
b. Aug. 24, 1904: Las Animas, Colo.
d. Feb. 2, 1972: Bethesda, Md.
High Commissioner for and Ambassador to Austria, July 1952-April 1957: Ambassador to the Soviet Union, April 1957-August 1962.

The son of a rancher, Thompson graduated from the University of Colorado in 1928 and then entered the Foreign Service School of Georgetown University. The following year he joined the Foreign Service as vice consul in Ceylon. In 1933 Thompson moved to Geneva, where he served as vice consul and consul over the next seven years. During the latter half of the decade, he also worked as adviser to the conferences of the International Labor Organization. In November 1940 Thompson was appointed second secretary and consul at the American embassy in Moscow. He remained there through the siege of Moscow and won the admiration of the Russian leaders for his willingness to share their hardship.

Following the war Thompson held a number of important administrative positions in the State Department: chief of the division of Eastern European affairs from 1946 to 1947: deputy director for European affairs from 1947 to 1949, and deputy assistant secretary of state for European affairs from 1949 to 1952. President Truman appointed Thompson high commissioner and ambassador to Austria in July 1952.

As commissioner, Thompson was primarily concerned with negotiating the Trieste settlement of 1954 and the Austrian State Treaty of 1955. Both Italy and Yugoslavia claimed the key port of Trieste, which had been placed under U.N. jurisdiction following World War II. In 1954, after eight months of quiet negotiations with both sides, Thompson worked out an agreement dividing the port. Under a memorandum of understanding issued in October, Italy took possession of the northern half of the territory, including the city of Trieste, and Yugoslavia occupied the southern area, including the Slovene town of Crevatini. Thompson later recalled that the agreement "was one of the few things we have done that even the Russians approved."

Simultaneously, Thompson worked on the Austrian State Treaty signed in May 1955. After World War II Austria had been placed under the joint occupation of France, Great Britain, the USSR and the U.S. Over the next 10 years the U.S. made repeated attempts to negotiate an independence treaty for that country, but Russia, fearing a revitalized, pro-Western Austria bordering on Eastern Europe, refused to normalize relations. In 1955, however, the USSR dramatically announced its willingness to negotiate the issue. In 11 days of arduous bargaining, Thompson worked out the final terms of the agreement. Under the State Treaty Austria regained her independence in return for her military neutrality.

In 1957 Eisenhower appointed Thompson ambassador to the Soviet Union. Because Secretary of State John Foster Dulles [q.v.] centralized policymaking in his own hands, Thompson had little role in molding the U.S. response to Soviet actions. He was used primarily as a reporter of events and a negotiator who arranged many of the top-level conferences of the period. At Thompson's urging, Eisenhower invited Soviet Premier Nikita Khrushchev to visit the U.S. in 1959. The Ambassador arranged the trip and accompanied the Soviet leader. He also took part in the Khrushchev-Eisenhower meetings at Camp David, Md. Following the visit Thompson was instrumental in laying the groundwork for the ill-fated 1960 Paris summit conference, which was cancelled after the downing of a U-2 intelligence plane over the Soviet Union. Despite the incident Thompson's relations with the Soviets remained good.

The Ambassador remained in Moscow for the first two years of the Kennedy Administration. During this period he helped arrange the 1961 Vienna summit conference and aided in the negotiations leading to the 1963 nuclear test ban treaty. In August 1962 Thompson was appointed ambassador at large and special adviser to the State Department on Soviet affairs. From 1967 to 1969 he again served as ambassador to Moscow. Thompson retired from the Foreign Service in 1969 and died three years later. [See KENNEDY, JOHNSON Volumes]

[JB]

THURMOND, STROM

b. Dec. 5, 1902; Edgefield, S.C.
Democratic Senator, S.C., 1955-56, 1956-64; Republican Senator, S.C., 1964-.

The son of a South Carolina politician, Thurmond received a B.S. degree from Clemson College in 1923 and for the next six years worked as a high school teacher. He was admitted to the South Carolina bar in 1930 and joined his father's law firm. In 1933 Thurmond was elected to the state Senate from Edgefield. While in the legislature he supported a number of social welfare programs, including the state's first bill providing aid to the aged, to the blind and to needy children. In 1938 Thurmond became a circuit judge. He enlisted in the Army shortly after American entry into World War II.

Thurmond resumed his judgeship after being discharged from the service in January 1946, but he stepped down from the post the following May to run for governor. His opponents in the Democratic primary charged him with being a New Dealer and hinted that he was receiving money from the Congress of Industrial Organizations. Nevertheless, he won his party's nomination, which was equivalent to election in South Carolina. As the state's chief executive, Thurmond increased appropriations for education and health care facilities, led a successful drive to repeal the poll tax and backed a minimum wage and maximum hour bill. He made a strong but unsuccessful effort to convict a white mob charged with lynching a black and appointed a black to the state board of medical examiners.

However, Thurmond entered the national political scene as a staunch conservative. In 1948, when portions of President Harry S. Truman's civil rights program were adopted at the National Democratic Convention, some of the Southern delegates bolted the meeting. They then organized the States' Rights Democrats, popularly known as the Dixiecrats, and nominated Thurmond for President. Opposing what he regarded as federal encroachment upon the constitutional powers of the states, Thurmond denounced Truman's civil rights and social welfare programs and the President's call for federal control of tidelands oil. Thurmond received nearly 1.2 million popular votes, almost all from the South. In subsequent national campaigns Thurmond did not endorse the Democratic national ticket. In 1950 he lost the Democratic senatorial primary to incumbent Sen. Olin D. Johnston (D, S.C.) [q.v.]. Thurmond then returned to private law practice. [See TRUMAN Volume]

In 1954 Thurmond reentered politics when incumbent Sen. Burnet R. Maybank (D, S.C.) died after winning renomination in the Democratic primary. The South Carolina Democratic Executive Committee, dominated by loyalist Democrats, chose State Sen. Edgar A. Brown to replace Maybank as the Party's nominee. Gov. James F. Byrnes [q.v.] and the Dixiecrat faction of the Party opposed the selection. Thurmond, taking advantage of this division, won the support of the Governor and the Dixiecrats as a write-in candidate in the general election. He defeated Brown by 59,000 votes, becoming the first person to win a U.S. Senate seat through a write-in campaign. In the Senate he joined the Democratic caucus. He resigned his seat in April 1956 and successfully ran as a Democrat for election to the remainder of his term.

Thurmond was one of Congress's most aggressive opponents of integration and civil rights legislation. In 1956 he initiated a movement among Southern members of Congress to issue a Declaration of Constitutional Principles as a challenge to the Supreme Court's 1954 opinion in *Brown v. Board of Education* outlawing segregation in public schools. Thurmond wrote the initial draft, which contained sections endorsing the doctrine of interposition and declaring the Court's decision to be unconstitutional and illegal. He and Sen. Harry F. Byrd (D, Va.) [*q.v.*] circulated the draft among Southern members, but moderates would not sign it until these clauses were removed. As modified by Sen. Richard B. Russell (D, Ga.) [*q.v.*] and others, the Declaration, popularly known as the "Southern Manifesto," was presented to Congress on March 12, 1956 with the signatures of 101 Southerners. It described the school desegregation opinion as "a clear abuse of judicial power" and urged the states "to resist forced integration by any lawful means."

In 1957 Thurmond conducted a record-breaking filibuster against a civil rights measure aimed primarily at protecting voting rights. The bill initially proposed by the Administration was weakened by the deletion of provisions authorizing the President to use troops to enforce existing civil rights laws and permitting the Attorney General to institute civil action for preventive relief in civil rights cases. It was further diluted by the addition of an amendment permitting jury trials in criminal contempt cases against those obstructing voters. Most Southern congressmen believed that the final version of the bill did not pose a serious threat to their region's racial practices and that it was the most favorable measure they could obtain. On Aug. 28,

Sen. Sam Ervin (D, N.C.) [*q.v.*], speaking on behalf of senior Southern senators, said there would be no filibuster against it. Later in the day, however, Thurmond began a one-man filibuster lasting 24 hours and 18 minutes, the longest in Senate history. Many of his fellow Southerners believed that Thurmond's action could have created a backlash leading to a strengthening of the bill. Agreeing with Sen. Herman Talmadge's (D, Ga.) description of the filibuster as a "grandstand" performance, they branded Thurmond an opportunist who would seek to advance his political career even at the expense of the Southern cause.

Thurmond was an arch-conservative opponent of expansion of the public sector of the economy and of national social welfare programs. In 1956 he joined three colleagues on the Public Works Committee in issuing the panel's minority report opposing public power development at Niagara Falls. They stated that private enterprise had pioneered the project and that public development would be "tantamount to saying that all public resources must be publicly developed." The Senate passed the bill, but it died in the House Rules Committee. In 1960 Thurmond successfully amended a minimum wage bill to reduce the number of workers covered by overtime pay provisions. The bill died in conference. According to *Congressional Quarterly*, Thurmond voted with the Southern Democrat-Republican conservative coalition on 94% of key roll-call votes in the 86th Congress (1959-60) while opposing it on only 3% of the votes.

Thurmond advocated a strong anti-Communist foreign policy and was skeptical of efforts to reduce East-West tensions. In 1955 he backed a bill authorizing the President to use U.S. forces in defense of Formosa and the Pescadores Islands, warning that "war might come as the result of any display of weakness, of disunity or of hesitation." Five years later Thurmond joined Sens. Russell, Clair Engle (D, Calif.) [*q.v.*] and Thomas Dodd (D, Conn.) [*q.v.*] in leading unsuccessful opposition to the Antarctic Treaty, signed by 12 nations including the U.S. and USSR. The senators contended that the pact did not fully ensure against secret Soviet military operations in Antarctica and that it gave Russia equal rights with the U.S. in an area in which the U.S. had previously predominated.

Concerned with the effects of tariff reductions on South Carolina's textile industry, Thurmond, in March 1955, expressed reservations about an Administration-sponsored reciprocal trade bill. The measure would have permitted the President to reduce tariffs up to 15% for three successive years beginning July 1, 1955. Thurmond feared that his state's textile enterprises might be severely injured because a treaty with Japan lowering textile tariffs was anticipated before July 1. But in April Sen. Walter George (D, Ga.) [q.v.] successfully proposed an amendment moving back the effective date of the President's new tariff-reduction power to Jan. 1, 1955. This eliminated the possibility of a double textile tariff reduction in 1955. Once the George amendment was adopted, Thurmond supported the bill.

During the early-1960s Thurmond associated himself with such ideological right-wing groups as the John Birch Society and the Young Americans for Freedom. In September 1964 he became a Republican so he could openly support conservative Sen. Barry M. Goldwater (R, Ariz.) [q.v.] for the presidency. He uniformly opposed President Lyndon Johnson's civil rights and Great Society programs while criticizing the Administration for using insufficient military force in Southeast Asia. In 1968 his endorsement of Richard M. Nixon's [q.v.] bid for the Republican presidential nomination kept most Southern delegates to the Republican National Convention out of the camp of California Gov. Ronald Reagan. Some observers believed that the endorsement followed Nixon's agreement to back Southern views on integration and other issues. Thurmond continued to compile a conservative voting record in the early and mid 1970s but began to actively seek federal social welfare funds to win the support of his state's growing black electorate. [See KENNEDY, JOHNSON, NIXON/FORD, CARTER Volumes]

[MLL]

THYE, EDWARD J(OHN)
b. April 26, 1896; Frederick, Minn.
d. Aug. 28, 1969; Northfield, Minn.
Republican Senator, Minn., 1947-59.

Thye attended the Minneapolis Tractor and Internal Combustion School and the American Business College prior to World War I. He volunteered as a private, and following his discharge as a second lieutenant, he worked as a tractor expert for a local manufacturing concern. Thye resigned in 1922 and became a successful dairy farmer. His political career began with his 1925 election to the local school board and continued through various local offices through 1939. In the early-1930s Thye met Harold Stassen [q.v.]. When Stassen decided to run for governor in 1938, Thye campaigned actively on his behalf. Stassen appointed him state dairy and food commissioner and deputy commissioner of agriculture in 1939. Thye was elected lieutenant governor in 1942, following Stassen's second successful reelection campaign. When the Governor resigned to go on active naval duty, Thye assumed his position; he was subsequently elected governor in 1944. As governor, Thye approved a low-cost, pre-paid medical care plan, launched extensive highway construction, and set up a state postwar planning commission. He also developed a wide reputation for his ability to settle labor disputes.

Thye ran for the U.S. Senate in 1946. In the primary campaign he attacked the isolationist record of his opponent, the incumbent Sen. Hendrick Shipstead (R, Minn.) and defeated him by a wide plurality. He then went on to win the general election. Thye became a prominent proponent of a bipartisan foreign policy during the Truman Administration. He sided with the President in the passage of the Greek and Turkish aid bills, the North Atlantic Security Pact and the foreign mutual aid bill.

During the 1950s Thye, a liberal Republican, championed aid to education and civil rights legislation. He also supported the Eisenhower Administration's foreign policy.

The Senator backed the Refugee Relief Act of 1953, the creation of the St. Lawrence Seaway Development Corp. in 1954, the Formosa Resolution of 1955 and the Eisenhower Doctrine of 1957.

Thye was particularly concerned about the problems of the small farmer. He consistently opposed Secretary of Agriculture Ezra Taft Benson's [q.v.] plans to phase out price supports for farm commodities. The Senator opposed the Secretary's 1954 farm program, which established a flexible scale of price supports, from 75% to 90% of parity, for basic farm commodities. Thye, a member of the Senate Agriculture and Forestry Committee, supported extension of the existing rigid price system at 90% of parity. He felt that lower prices, an inevitability with growing postwar surpluses, would result in greater production as farmers tried to maintain their existing income levels. Thye recommended that surpluses be reduced through production controls "before we start tampering with the price supports." In late April 1954 he introduced an amendment to the 1949 Agricultural Act limiting the downward adjustment of price supports on dairy products. It was defeated, and parity on dairy products was reduced to 75%.

Thye supported the Agricultural Act of 1956, which provided for the development of a "soil bank." Under this program the government paid farmers either to retire a specified amount of land from production or to devote the land to conservation purposes. The Congress had substantially reworked the Administration's proposal reintroducing high price supports. President Eisenhower vetoed it, citing the provision calling for a return to 90% of parity as "unacceptable." Two years later Thye again failed to prevent a reduction of price supports on dairy products.

Thye lost his Senate seat to Eugene J. McCarthy [q.v.] in the 1958 election. He resumed his agricultural interests and remained active in Republican Party affairs. In 1960 Thye represented Minnesota as a delegate at large at the Republican National Convention. He died in August 1969.

[ACD]

TILL, EMMETT L(OUIS)
b. July 25, 1941; Chicago, Ill.
d. Aug. 28, (?) 1955; Money, Miss.
Lynching victim.

In the summer of 1955 Emmett Till, a 14-year-old black from Chicago, went to visit his uncle in LeFlore Co., Miss., near the town of Money. Sometime around Aug. 28 Till was murdered; his body was pulled from the Tallahatchie River on Aug. 31. Till arrived in Mississippi when racial tension was at its peak. The White Citizens Council had publicly defended segregation and had called for armed resistance to the Supreme Court's school desegregation decision of 1954. Several blacks had been murdered throughout the South in reprisal for black voter registration. In LeFlore Co. threats and intimidation had stopped blacks from voting in the August 1955 primary.

Till's uncle named Roy Bryant and J. W. Milam as the men who had kidnapped Till. The two men were tried for murder. They admitted abducting the boy to question him about having whistled at and insulted Mrs. Bryant in a store in Money. An all-white jury acquitted Bryant and Milam on the grounds that the body was too decomposed to identified. A grand jury later refused to indict them for kidnapping. Despite requests from the NAACP and other organizations, the Administration refused to enter this sensitive case. Presidential advisers deliberated suggesting that Congress probe the matter, hoping that it could put the onus of delay on Southern Democrats. However, the plan was never accepted, and the Justice Department announced it did not have the authority to enter the case.

The verdict aroused a storm of protest throughout the world and increased efforts to win strong government support for civil rights. The NAACP, the Jewish Labor Committee, the Brotherhood of Sleeping Car Porters and other organizations held protest demonstrations in the North to demand that President Eisenhower call a special session of Congress to enact an anti-lynching law. Roy Wilkins [q.v.], urged black voters to boycott the 1956 presidential ticket. Sen. Estes Kefauver (D, Tenn.)

[*q.v.*], announcing in October 1955 his candidacy for the Democratic presidential nomination, made the Till case a cornerstone of his civil rights stand. He said that he would ask Congress for anti-lynching legislation.

As a result of the growing demand for federal action on civil rights and the Administration's fear of losing black votes during the 1956 election, Attorney General Herbert Brownell [*q.v.*] began to draft legislation designed to protect voting rights and create a civil rights commission to investigate rights problems. The bill made little progress on Capitol Hill during 1956 but became the basis for the Civil Rights Act of 1957.

[SY]

For further information:
Steven F. Lawson, *Black Ballot: Voting Rights in the South, 1944-1969* (New York, 1976).

TIMMERMAN, GEORGE B(ELL)
b. March 28, 1881; Edgefield
County, S.C.
d. April 22, 1966; Columbia, S.C.
U.S. District Judge, S.C., 1942-62.

After receiving his law degree from South Carolina College in 1902, Timmerman entered private practice and became involved in local Democratic politics. He was solicitor for his local judicial circuit from 1905 to 1920, a state representative in 1923-24 and a state highway commissioner from 1931 to 1939. A Democratic state committeeman from 1938 to 1942, Timmerman was named a federal district court judge for South Carolina by President Franklin Roosevelt in 1942.

In May 1951 Timmerman was part of a special three judge federal court that heard a case challenging public school segregation in Clarendon County, S.C. Brought by the NAACP, the suit was the first in the deep South to make an all-out legal attack on racial segregation in elementary and secondary schools. By a two-to-one vote, with Timmerman in the majority, the court ruled in June 1951 that segregation was constitutional but that the schools for blacks in Clarendon County had to be made equal

to those for whites. The court, again with Timmerman's approval, reaffirmed this judgment in March 1952 and decided that the school equalization program underway in the county was satisfactory. The NAACP appealed the case, and on May 17, 1954 the Supreme Court reversed the lower court and ruled in this and four other cases that segregated public schools were unconstitutional. In compliance with this decision, known as *Brown* v. *Board of Education,* Timmerman and his colleagues in July 1955 ordered officials in Clarendon Co. to stop requiring racial segregation in local public schools.

Judge Timmerman soon made it clear, however, that he was a confirmed segregationist who strongly disapproved of the Supreme Court's decision and who would issue a desegregation order only when he had no alternative. While his son, South Carolina Gov. George B. Timmerman, Jr. [*q.v.*], led state efforts to forestall desegregation in the late-1950s, the judge attempted to limit the scope of the *Brown* decree. In April 1955 he dismissed a case challenging South Carolina's bus segregation laws on the ground that *Brown* applied only to public education. The Fourth Circuit Court reversed Timmerman in July, holding that *Brown* had invalidated legally enforced segregation in other public facilities such as transit and remanded the case for trial. Timmerman dismissed the suit a second time for more technical reasons in June 1956, but the circuit court again reversed his decision in November.

In March 1956 South Carolina adopted a law forbidding the employment of NAACP members as teachers in the state, and Timmerman was on the three-judge federal panel that heard a challenge to the statute. The court dismissed the case by a two-to-one vote in January 1957. In a concurring opinion, Timmerman said the law was "designed to protect young minds from the poisonous effects of NAACP propaganda"; he believed it fully constitutional. The case was appealed to the Supreme Court, but the state legislature repealed the law before the Court could act.

In August 1959 Judge Timmerman also dismissed a suit challenging segregated facilities at the municipal airport terminal in Greeneville, S.C. In his opinion he declared that whites "still have the right to choose their own companions and associates and to preserve the integrity of the race with which God Almighty has endowed them." The Fourth Circuit Court reversed Timmerman's action in April 1960. After he again ruled against the black plaintiff in October, the Circuit Court in December ordered him to issue an injunction against the segregation of the airport. In February 1961 Timmerman prohibited segregated facilities at the air terminal but made it clear that he was doing so only because a higher court had commanded it.

Timmerman publicly criticized the Supreme Court in a speech to a Thomson, Ga., Rotary Club in July 1957. Aside from the desegregation decision Timmerman objected to Court judgments in loyalty-security and criminal rights cases. He attacked the Court as a "hierarchy of despotic judges that is bent on destroying the finest system of government ever designed."

In October 1962 at the age of 81, Timmerman retired from the federal bench. He then lived with his son in Batesburg, S.C., until his death on April 22, 1966.

[CAB]

TIMMERMAN, GEORGE BELL, JR.
b. Aug. 11, 1912; Anderson, S.C.
Governor, S.C., 1955-59.

The son of a conservative South Carolina judge, George Bell Timmerman received his LL.B. from the University of South Carolina in 1937. He was admitted to the bar that year and set up practice in Lexington, S.C. After serving in the U.S. Naval Reserve from 1942 to 1946, Timmerman returned home and won election as lieutenant governor. During his second term in office he served under Gov. James E. Byrnes [q.v.], one of the South's major states' rights advocates and opponents of desegregation.

Running on a platform supporting states' rights and opposing the Supreme Court's *Brown* decision, which outlawed school segregation, Timmerman was elected

governor in 1954. In his inaugural address he asserted that the Court had usurped powers the Constitution had never meant it to have and possessed "a power that endangers the future freedom of all citizens."

As governor, Timmerman concentrated his efforts on opposing desegregation. With three other Southern governors he endorsed the doctrine of interposition in 1956. This doctrine pledged to use the state's power to prevent desegregation by placing the "sovereignty" of the state between local school boards and federal courts. Timmerman supported a measure, passed in 1956, making members of the NAACP ineligible for state employment and declaring that the group exerted "constant pressure on its members contrary to the principles upon which the economic and social life of our state rests."

Timmerman also tried to suppress dissent in the state's black colleges. When a Hungarian refugee enrolled in previously all-black Allen University in September 1957, talk of Communist influence at the school spread. The Governor informally advised the school's board of trustees to dismiss faculty members who favored desegregation. When it refused, he cancelled the school's accreditation. The following January Timmerman devoted a large part of his annual address to alleged Communist influence in black colleges and added three members of the black Benedict University faculty to his growing list of subversives. Political pressure mounted against the black schools throughout the spring. They finally surrendered and dismissed the accused professors. Their accreditation was then restored.

During 1956 Timmerman devoted considerable energy to building a new Dixiecrat coalition, which would promote a united Southern front at the Democratic National Convention. He presented his plan at two conferences held in Atlanta in July and August, but received little support. Advocates of conciliation, led by Mississippi Gov. James Coleman [q.v.], dominated the discussion, and the Southern delegates went to the August National Convention intent on working for change within the Party. South Carolina Democrats, led by Timmerman and Sen. Strom Thurmond (D,

S.C.) [*q.v.*], continued to be critical of the national Party, but by November they had approved the presidential ticket. Adlai Stevenson [*q.v.*] carried the state.

Legally limited to one term, Timmerman retired to his law practice in 1959. He served as a Democratic elector in the 1964 presidential election.

[MJS]

For further information:
Numan Bartley, *The Rise of Massive Resistance* (Baton Rouge, 1969).

TRUMAN, HARRY S.
b. May 8, 1884; Lamar, Mo.
d. Dec. 26, 1972; Kansas City, Mo.
President of the United States, April 1945-January 1953.

Truman, the first of three children, moved with his family to Independence, Mo., at the age of seven. After graduating from high school he was rejected by West Point because of poor eyesight. He held a number of jobs, including that of bookkeeper, before becoming a farmer at 22. Truman served in World War I and then formed a partnership with a friend in a Kansas City haberdashery shop; the business failed in 1921.

That year Truman came to the attention of Tom Pendergast, boss of the powerful local Democratic machine. In 1922 Pendergast nominated him as one of the three judges of the Jackson Co. Court, an administrative body that supervised the construction of highways and public buildings. Truman won his contest for that post but lost his reelection bid two years later. He was elected president of the Court in 1926 and occupied that position for eight years.

Truman won a seat in the U.S. Senate in 1934. He was a consistent supporter of President Franklin D. Roosevelt's domestic and foreign policies. As chairman of subcommittees of the Interstate and Foreign Commerce Committee, he played a role in the drafting of the Civil Aeronautics Act of 1938 and the Railroad Transportation Act of 1940. He first gained national prominence

in 1941, when, as chairman of the Special Committee to Investigate Contracts under the National Defense Program, his panel uncovered misconduct and waste in the nation's defense administration and contracting system.

In 1944 the left wing of the Democratic Party favored the renomination of Henry A. Wallace for vice president while the Southern conservatives backed presidential assistant James F. Byrnes [*q.v.*]. Roosevelt settled upon Truman, who was not as close to organized labor as Wallace but who also was not a conservative, as a compromise candidate.

Truman's tenure as vice president was brief; Roosevelt died on April 12, 1945. Truman, who had not been closely briefed by Roosevelt on the progress of the war, was soon put in the position of guiding the American war effort during the last months of the conflict and formulating foreign policy during the postwar period. In August Truman decided to use the newly developed atomic bomb to compel a Japanese surrender. During the next few years Truman formulated the containment policy designed to prevent Communist expansion in Europe. The policy called for massive U.S. economic and military aid to the countries bordering the Soviet Union. It was implemented primarily through the Truman Doctrine and the Marshall Plan of 1947 and the North Atlantic Treaty Organization (NATO), established in 1949.

Although Truman secured a general consensus on these measures, his conduct of the Korean war aroused controversy. Truman favored a restoration of the status quo that had existed before the North Korean invasion of the South, and warning of a possible third world war, he opposed Gen. Douglas MacArthur's proposal to expand the conflict by bombing mainland China. In April 1951 the President relieved MacArthur of his command. Initially the General rallied considerable support, particularly among those who were already critical of the Truman Administration for having allegedly lost China to the Communists in 1949. The furor over the dismissal subsided after a few weeks, but as the conflict dragged on with no end in sight, the electorate became increasingly impatient with the Administration.

The heaviest criticism of Truman's policy on Communism centered around the charge that the Administration was infiltrated by subversives. The President initiated a loyalty program for federal employes in 1947. However, in 1949 the first Soviet nuclear test and the conviction of alleged Soviet spy Alger Hiss for perjury convinced many that a large number of Communists and Communist sympathizers still held posts in the national government. Beginning in 1950 Sen. Joseph R. McCarthy (R, Wisc.) [q.v.] denounced the Truman Administration for harboring subversives.

Truman attempted to extend New Deal social programs, calling for higher minimum wages, housing programs, national health insurance and civil rights for blacks. However, the Republican-dominated Congress blocked most of his measures. Truman, hitting hard at the "do-nothing Congress," won the 1948 election in an unexpected upset. The victory came despite the defection of Southern Democrats who opposed his civil rights program and left-wing Democrats who criticized his containment policy. Although the Democrats controlled both houses of Congress for the remainder of Truman's presidency, Southern members of the majority party and Republicans were able to block many of Truman's programs. [See TRUMAN Volume]

Attacked by McCarthy and others for not rooting Communists out of government and criticized for failing to end the Korean stalemate, Truman became increasingly unpopular. On March 29, 1952 he announced that he would not seek reelection. Truman offered to endorse Illinois Gov. Adlai E. Stevenson [q.v.] for the Democratic presidential nomination. Stevenson, however, believed that he could not win if he was associated with an unpopular Administration. Anticipating a draft, he insisted upon his noncandidacy. After he received the nomination Stevenson took care to maintain a distance from the Administration. Stevenson's strategy offended the President, and Truman, who was a hard-hitting campaigner, disliked the candidate's low-keyed, analytical style. In subsequent years Tru-

man asserted that Stevenson's defeat was the candidate's own fault.

In his final State of the Union message on Jan. 7, 1953, Truman warned Soviet Premier Joseph V. Stalin that war would mean ruin for the USSR, and he stressed the necessity of Western resistance to Communist expansion without plunging the world into atomic conflict. He also cautioned against legislation aimed at domestic Communism that would promote an "enforced conformity." Truman asserted that the economy had "grown tremendously" under his Administration, and while acknowledging increases in prices, he said that income had increased more.

Later in the year Truman became embroiled in a controversy that raised a fundamental issue involving the relationship between the executive and legislative branches of the federal government. On Nov. 6 Attorney General Herbert Brownell [q.v.] charged that Truman knew that the late Harry Dexter White was a Russian spy when he promoted White from assistant secretary of the treasury to U.S. executive director of the International Monetary Fund in 1946. South Carolina Gov. James F. Byrnes [q.v.], Truman's Secretary of State at the time, backed the charge, but Truman immediately denied it.

On Nov. 10 the House Un-American Activities Committee (HUAC) subpoenaed Truman, Byrnes and Supreme Court Justice Tom C. Clark [q.v.], Truman's former Attorney General. Such a summons to an ex-President was unprecedented. Two days later Truman rejected it. He offered to testify regarding any acts unrelated to his presidential role but said that the constitutional position of the presidency would be jeopardized if he accepted the congressional subpoena to testify on his conduct as President. HUAC chairman Rep. Harold H. Velde (R, Ill.) [q.v.] said he would not attempt to compel Truman to appear before the panel.

Truman remained in the public eye during the 1950s. He criticized the Eisenhower Administration for cutbacks in both social and defense spending. Truman, who thought of himself as an active and decisive chief executive, denounced Eisenhower as a "do-nothing" President in April 1956. The following August Truman issued a much-awaited presidential endorsement, announcing his support of New York Gov. Averell Harriman [q.v.]. He said that the Governor's "long experience in top government positions" made him the best candidate. Three days later the ex-President stated at a news conference that he did not think Stevenson could win the election. In 1960 he declined to attend the Democratic National Convention on the grounds that it had been rigged in advance to assure the nomination for Sen. John F. Kennedy (D, Mass.) [q.v.]. However, Truman campaigned strongly for Stevenson in 1956 and Kennedy in 1960.

After the 1956 election Truman became a member of the newly created Democratic Advisory Council (DAC) along with Stevenson, Eleanor Roosevelt [q.v.], Sen. Estes Kefauver (D, Tenn.) [q.v.] and other liberals. The purpose of the Committee, formed at the urging of National Party Chairman Paul Butler [q.v.], was to provide a means of developing Democratic legislative programs in a forum independent of House Speaker Sam Rayburn (D, Tex.) [q.v.] and Senate Majority Leader Lyndon B. Johnson (D, Tex.) [q.v.], whom Party liberals regarded as too conservative. In 1958 Truman joined other DAC members in proposing stronger civil rights legislation, curbs on Senate filibusters, higher minimum wages and other measures.

In 1957 the Harry S. Truman Library Institute for National and International Affairs, built by private subscription and given to the government, opened its doors in Independence. It housed the ex-President's papers, a large book collection and many museum-like exhibits depicting Truman's life. Truman subsequently spent much of his time working in an office there.

By the late-1950s many Americans regarded Truman as a beneficent elder statesman endowed with an earthy common sense that made his judgments superior to those of intellectuals. In 1958 a Gallup Poll listed him as the fifth most popular man in America.

During 1961 and 1962 Truman gave extensive recorded interviews to author Merle Miller. In 1973 a portion of the transcripts were published by Miller in *Plain Speaking: An Oral Biography of Harry S. Truman.* The book contained highly negative comments about many people, including the entire Kennedy family, which he regarded as power hungry; Stevenson, whom he considered a "sissy"; and Justice Clark, whom he described as a "dumb son of a bitch." Truman died on Dec. 26, 1972 at 88.

[MLL]

For further information:
Merle Miller, *Plain Speaking: An Oral Biography of Harry S. Truman* (New York, 1973).

TWINING, NATHAN F(ARRAGUT)
b. Oct. 11, 1897; Monroe, Wisc.
Air Force Chief of Staff, June 1953-April 1957; Chairman, Joint Chiefs of Staff, April 1957-September 1960.

The descendent of Plymouth Colony settlers, Twining began his military training as a member of the Oregon National Guard in 1916. He graduated from the U.S. Military Academy at West Point in 1918 and then served with the Allied occupation forces in Germany. During the 1920s and 1930s Twining served as an Army Air Force flight instructor. Twining entered World War II as a major but in 1942 was appointed commanding general of the 13th Air Force, fighting in the Solomon Islands. In 1943 he was transferred to the European front, where he saw action in the Mediterranean theater. After VE Day he returned to the Pacific and directed the incendiary raids on Japan that culminated in the dropping of atomic bombs on Hiroshima and Nagasaki. After the War he held a series of posts in the U.S. until his appointment as Air Force Chief of Staff in 1953.

Twining's selection as Air Force Chief of Staff reflected Eisenhower's desire to break with Truman's policy of dependence on both conventional and nuclear forces for U.S. defense. The General supported Eisenhower's belief that the major U.S. deterrent should be a mobile nuclear strike force capable of meeting any threat. However, Twining objected to the budget cuts that accompanied the Administration's "New Look" policy. In testimony before the Senate Armed Services Committee in 1953, he stated that proposed Air Force cuts would delay the creation of 143 wings he deemed necessary for U.S. security. He also warned that the U.S. could not maintain its superiority over the Soviet Union without enough trained men. He contended that the Air Force could not attract or keep them because of low pay.

In 1956 Twining joined a number of Air Force generals and congressmen in maintaining that a "bomber gap" was growing between the U.S. and the USSR. Appearing before the Senate Appropriations Committee's Subcommittee on Defense in May, Twining said "the people above" him had cut $272 million from his funds for Air Force bases and stated he would have to request more money if all installations and early warning systems were to be completed by the targeted 1958 date. He said that he had asked for six additional wings of B-52 type bombers to increase Strategic Air Command strength by 300 planes but that Eisenhower was still considering his request. Twining assured the congressmen that the U.S. could deter a Soviet attack "this year" but questioned how long the advantage would continue. After a trip to the Soviet Union in July, he again reported that the Russians were out-producing the U.S. in modern planes and were catching up in aircraft quality. As a result of continued pressure, nearly $1 billion dollars was added to the Administration's fiscal 1957 request for the Air Force.

Twining took a broader outlook on the Administration's defense policy after assuming the post of Chairman of the Joint Chiefs of Staff in 1957. He defended Eisenhower's plan for cutting back B-52 production and the development of the B-70 bomber and restraints on the development of missiles. Questioned by Sen. Dennis Chavez (D, N.M.) [q.v.], chairman of the Senate Subcommittee on Defense, Twining explained that less money would be needed in fiscal 1958 than in fiscal 1957 because intelligence showed a slower rate of Soviet bomber production than anticipated. He also assured

the subcommittee, "I know of nothing that could be done to give us operationally effective ballistic missiles appreciably sooner."

Twining advocated American intervention in the Middle East and Asia to contain Communism. In the spring of 1954 he proposed that the U.S. use tactical atomic weapons to relieve the besieged French garrison at Dien Bien Phu in northern Vietnam. When the Communist Chinese began shelling Quemoy and Matsu in September of the year, Twining joined Chairman of the Join Chiefs of Staff Adm. Arthur Radford [q.v.] in recommending that the Nationalist Chinese be permitted to bomb the mainland and suggesting that American aircraft enter the battle if the Communist retaliated. In 1958 he successfully argued for the landing of U.S. Marines in Lebanon at the request of President Camille Chamoun to quell a pro-Nasser rebellion.

Following his retirement in 1960 Twining became chairman of the board of Holt, Rinehart and Winston, Inc. He remained a strong anti-Communist, testifying against the limited nuclear test ban treaty of 1963 and supporting U.S. involvement in Vietnam. In 1964 Twining served as an adviser to Republican presidential nominee Sen. Barry Goldwater (R, Ariz.) [q.v.]. Two years later he ran unsuccessfully as the GOP candidate for the U.S. Senate from New Hampshire.

[JB]

VANDENBERG, HOYT S(ANFORD)

b. Jan. 24, 1899; Milwaukee, Wisc.
d. April 2, 1954; Washington, D.C.
Air Force Chief of Staff, April 1948-
June 1953.

A descendent of early Dutch settlers, Vandenberg was the nephew of influential Republican Sen. Arthur Vandenberg (R, Mich.). Following his graduation from West Point, he began a career in Army aviation. After filling a number of routine assignments, Vandenberg attended the Air Corps Technical School, the Command and General Staff School and the Army War College. In 1938 he became an instructor in fighter-plane tactics.

During the early part of World War II, Col. Vandenberg helped formulate the Allied invasion of North Africa and later participated in the operation. In 1944 Vandenberg, by then known as the "flying general," commanded the Ninth Air Force, one of the largest tactical air units in the War. He also attended diplomatic conferences at Quebec, Cairo and Teheran. In 1946 he became director of Central Intelligence. Vandenberg returned to the Army Air Corps in 1947 to be its chief of staff. When Vandenberg became a full general at the age of 49, he was the youngest member of the military to hold that rank. The following year, after the establishment of the Air Force as an independent branch of the Armed Services, Truman appointed him Air Force Chief of Staff.

During the postwar period Vandenberg lobbied for a strong Air Force, which he considered essential in light of Soviet advances in the production of jet fighters and bombers. He also was a leading figure in the drive for a unified Armed Services. In 1951 Vandenberg joined other members of the Joint Chiefs of Staff in defending President Harry S. Truman's dismissal of Gen. Douglas MacArthur from his Korean command. Vandenberg was scheduled to retire as Air Force Chief of Staff in 1952, but his term was extended 14 months so that he could retire after 30 years service at the highest rank he had attained in the Air Force. [See TRUMAN Volume]

During the last months of his tenure, Vandenberg was an outspoken critic of the Eisenhower Administration's proposed cuts in the defense budget. In May 1953 Secretary of Defense Charles Wilson [q.v.] announced a $5 billion reduction in appropriations to the Air Force. The cut precluded the service's anticipated addition of 143 wings. Quiet and easy-going in manner unless aroused, Vandenberg testified against the cuts before the Senate Appropriations Committee in June. He warned that the 143-wing increase was the absolute minimum needed for U.S. air defense and that anything short of that goal "would increase the risk to national security beyond the dictates of national prudence." He claimed

that the Air Force was being crippled by five types if restrictions: limitations on personnel, base construction, appropriations, force levels, and expenditures and research. Vandenberg claimed that he had heard no sound military reason for the cut "at a time when we face an enemy who has more modern jet fighters than we have and enough long-range bombers to attack this country in a sudden all-out atomic effort." He charged that Wilson's plan would provide the U.S. with a "second-best air force" to meet growing Soviet strength. It would be a "one-shot" service, which would not have any reserve strength if the Soviets launched an all-out atomic war against the U.S.

Secretary of Defense Wilson and Secretary of the Air Force Harold E. Talbott [q.v.] challenged Vandenberg's assertions, claiming the cuts would not impair American air power. They maintained that the decision had been made "by those competent"—i.e., Eisenhower—but would be reviewed by the incoming Joint Chiefs of Staff. The cuts went into effect in July 1953, immediately after Vandenberg retired.

The General retired on a 100% medical disability and died of cancer in April 1954.

[JB]

VAN DOREN, CHARLES
b. Feb. 12, 1926; New York, N.Y.
College instructor; television quiz show contestant.

Charles Van Doren's father, Mark, was a poet and university teacher; his mother, Dorothy, wrote fiction. Both parents had been editors of The Nation. Young Van Doren studied music and mathematics and earned his B.A. from St. John's College in Maryland in 1947. After receiving his M.A. in mathematics at Columbia University, Van Doren switched to English literature. While a lecturer at Columbia he wrote a dissertation on William Cowper, the pre-romantic poet, obtaining his doctorate and an assistant professorship from the University in 1959.

Van Doren gained national attention as a

quiz show contestant during the 1956-57 television season. Beginning in late 1955, evening TV game programs, awarding large cash prizes, quickly emerged as the most popular program format on TV. Van Doren appeared on "Twenty-One," a Barry and Enright production. Possessing good looks and an appealing, boyish charm, he proved an immediate hit as a contestant. He defeated the current "Twenty-One" champion, Herbert Stempel, in December 1956 and went on to win $129,000. When Van Doren made his 14 appearances, "Twenty-One" climbed to the first position in the TV ratings. A housewife, Mrs. Vivian Nearing, defeated Van Doren in March 1957. The National Broadcasting Co., which aired "Twenty-One," capitalized on Van Doren's continuous popularity by signing him to a contract and making him a host for the popular "Today Show."

While Van Doren co-hosted "Today" in August 1958, former contestant Stempel charged in a New York *World-Telegram* story that his and others' appearances on "Twenty-One" had been staged by Barry and Enright. On "Today" Van Doren denied Stempel's allegations; he persisted in defending the programs well into 1959. But Manhattan District Attorney Frank J. Hogan [q.v.] began a grand jury investigation of all TV quiz programs and took testimony from 150 contestants. Ratings for the programs plummeted; NBC canceled "Twenty-One" in October 1958. After Hogan's grand jury completed its work in June 1959, a Manhattan judge took the unusual step of keeping its report confidential. Prior to its release, House Commerce Committee Chairman Oren Harris (D, Ark.) [q.v.] launched his own inquiry and subpoenaed Van Doren and others in October.

On Nov. 2, Van Doren made a dramatic appearance before a House subcommittee chaired by Harris. Van Doren admitted that he had been given the answers to questions beforehand; that he had been coached in delivering his responses; and that he had agreed to lose to Nearing "in a dramatic manner." The "Twenty-One" producers had persuaded him, Van Doren recounted, that his cooperation would create goodwill for "the intellectual life." Van Doren also ad-

mitted to lying before the Hogan grand jury. NBC fired him Nov. 3; Van Doren had resigned from the Columbia faculty the previous day.

Van Doren's confession shocked the nation and altered network program policies. The Columbia scholar had been a much admired figure and his fall disillusioned many TV viewers. Yet a majority of Americans, surveys found, did not hold Van Doren and other participants either legally or morally culpable for their actions. Most of the condemnation of quiz show producers and panelists came from opinion leaders—editors, ministers and the like—not the public at large. On Nov. 8 President Eisenhower called the affair "a terrible thing to do to the American public." He blamed the advertisers ("the grey-flanneled hucksters from Madison Avenue") and compared the event to the "fix" of the 1919 World Series. However, because of the vague wording of communications law, the federal government took no action against the programs' producers or the networks. For their part the networks, led by Frank Stanton [q.v.], canceled the quiz shows and scheduled more "public service" news and cultural programs.

Van Doren avoided imprisonment and fell into obscurity. Hogan obtained perjury indictments against Van Doren and 13 other contestants in October 1960, but most pleaded guilty and all received suspended sentences in January 1962. Out of academic life, Van Doren edited several reference works and served as a consultant to the Center for the Study of Democratic Institutions. In 1973 he became vice president and editor of the Encyclopedia Britannica.

[JLB]

VELDE, HAROLD H(IMMEL)
b. April 1, 1910; Parkland, Ill.
Republican Representative, Ill., 1949-1957; Chairman, Un-American Activities Committee, 1953-54.

Born to parents of East Frisian and German ancestry, Harold Velde grew up in rural Illinois. He attended both Bradley and Northwestern Universities, graduating from the latter in 1931. He earned a law degree from the University of Illinois in 1937 and then practiced law in his home state until entering the Army Signal Corps in 1942. After a year of military service, Velde served as an agent in the FBI's sabotage and counterespionage division. He was elected an Illinois county judge in 1946.

Velde won a seat in the U.S. House of Representatives in 1948 after campaigning on the slogan, "Get the Reds out of Washington and Washington out of the Red." He gained a reputation in Congress as an ardent anti-Communist alarmed by what he saw as widespread subversion within the U.S. government. His background in the FBI brought him a post on the House Un-American Activities Committee (HUAC), and in 1953 he became chairman of the panel. [See TRUMAN Volume]

During 1953-54 HUAC held a record 178 days of hearings. Velde led HUAC investigations of the motion picture industry, education and labor—areas the Committee had investigated in previous years. However, he broke new ground in March 1954 by announcing that a probe of the nation's clergy was "entirely possible." His charges that the clergy spent more time in questionable politics than in the ministry ignited protests from church groups, citizens and fellow congressmen. One of HUAC's members, Rep. Franklin D. Roosevelt, Jr. (D, N.Y.), introduced a resolution calling for Velde's removal as chairman. The American Council of Christian Churches supported Velde's charges, and a Gallup poll showed 36% of the public in favor of a probe. General public disapproval, however, prevented him from vigorously pursuing the investigation, though several clergymen did testify before the panel. At one point Velde charged those church leaders who had criticized his allegations with the "sin" of subversion.

During Velde's term as chairman HUAC continued investigations of the entertainment industry, a long-favored target. In March 1953 Velde took HUAC to Los Angeles to hear testimony from various writers, performers and technicians who had been accused of having Communist ties. In May HUAC investigators in New York interrogated such celebrities as Artie Shaw, Carin K. Burrows, Robert Rossen and Lionel Stander. These and other investigations stirred intense public debate over constitutional rights of due process and protection against self-incrimination versus the alleged need to uncover American Communists at all costs. In March 1953 a group of 23 actors and motion picture workers sued Velde and other congressmen who had served on HUAC in 1951 because of their subsequent blacklisting in the industry after they had refused to testify before the Committee. The case was later dismissed in California courts.

HUAC's probe of Communist infiltration in education began embarrassingly when Velde inaccurately accused Mrs. Eugene Meyer, wife of the board chairman of the *Washington Post*, of having praised the USSR in a letter to a Soviet publication. After Mrs. Meyer warned educators that they were about to be "attacked," the fact that the letter had been sent by a "Mrs. G.S. Mayer" was discovered. Velde promptly fired the HUAC investigator on the case. He defended himself, however, by saying it was "better to wrongly accuse one person of being a Communist" than allow the true Party members to roam freely. Velde opened his probe in February 1953, eliciting from Dr. Robert Davis the names of 21 people whom he claimed were fellow Communists while he taught at Harvard University from 1937 to 1939. Among the names were those of eminent writers and educators Daniel Boorstin and Granville Hicks, both of whom had since become anti-Communists. The investigations moved to Philadelphia in November 1953, where admitted ex-Communists accused the Philadelphia Teachers Union of being a "Communist-led organization." The hearings resulted in the suspension of 26 Philadelphia teachers by the Board of Education. In 1954 HUAC cited for contempt of Congress nine witnesses who had refused to testify in the Committee's investigations of alleged Communist educators in Philadelphia and New York City.

Velde captured the attention of the nation in November 1953 when he issued, without prior approval of the Committee, subpoenas to former President Harry S. Truman [q.v.], former Secretary of State James Byrnes [q.v.] and former Attorney General Tom Clark [q.v.]. Velde made the move after Attorney General Herbert Brownell [q.v.] charged that Truman had appointed accused Communist Harry Dexter White to a government position while knowing that an FBI report accused White of spying for the USSR. Although the three men expressed a willingness to cooperate with HUAC, each rejected the subpoena after it was served: Truman, on grounds of executive privilege; Byrnes, then governor of South Carolina, on grounds of states rights; and Clark, then a justice of the Supreme Court, on grounds of judicial privilege. President Eisenhower declared he would not have subpoened Truman or Clark, and Truman made a nationally televised address primarily denouncing Brownell. No further actions were taken on the subpoenas.

Velde continued his HUAC investigations throughout the 1953-54 session, opening hearings on alleged subversives in the Navy Department and expanding probes of supposed Communist infiltration of labor unions. Although shouts and accusations continually flew through HUAC's hearing rooms, Velde himself never won the notoriety that his more famous colleague, Sen. Joseph R. McCarthy (R, Wisc. [q.v.], achieved. Velde retired from office in 1957.

[TGD]

For further information:
Walter Goodman, *The Committee: The Extraordinary Career of the House Committee on Un-American Activities* (New York, 1968).

VIERECK, PETER (ROBERT) (EDWIN)
b. Aug. 5, 1916; New York, N.Y.
Political scientist

Of German ancestry, Viereck studied in Germany and in Switzerland in his early youth. His academic career at Harvard University was marked by numerous awards, including Phi Beta Kappa and a fellowship to Oxford University. He graduated with B.S., M.A. and Ph.D. degrees at Harvard in literature and history and was also well versed in the German, French and Russian languages and in politics.

Viereck won admiration early in his career for his book *Metapolitics from the Romantics to Hitler,* published in 1941. The son of famous Nazi supporter George Sylvester Viereck, Peter Viereck took an entirely different view of German fascism, asserting that the American and Nazi ways of life were "irreconcilable." The work was praised for its harsh analysis of Nazi ideology and was used in many American universities. In 1949 he wrote *Conservatism Revisited: The Revolt Against Revolt,* which immediately established him as a forceful articulator of a conservative consciousness in America. Expanding on his earlier writings, in which he called for a "supremacy of law and of absolute standards of conduct," Viereck criticized the collectivism of both fascism and Stalinism as robbing the individual soul of dignity. Citing the merits of the Judaic, Hellenic, Roman and medieval intellectual traditions, he hoped to see a revival of spiritual humility, self-discipline and respect for order in both social and personal relations. He ridiculed the idea of the "common, natural man," stating that in contemporary terms such a person represented rootless, "impersonal man."

As the 1950s progressed it became clear that Viereck spoke for a conservativism different from that espoused by other philosophers of the right. In the words of historian John P. Diggins, Viereck sought a synthesis of "philosophical conservatism and political liberalism." Viereck eschewed nineteenth century laissez-faire capitalism and "rugged individualism." He supported many of the reforms of the New Deal and identified Adlai Stevenson [q.v.] as the foremost political exponent of his own brand of conservativism. Although he disdained ideologies of the far left, he was much less eager to attack liberals than were other conservatives. He admitted that he hoped to see a fusion of liberals and conservatives in a front against all forms of totalitarianism. Although strongly anti-Communist, he formulated a conservativism grounded primarily in philosophical and moral principles. Economic theories, he believed, were hollow unless set in an ethical context.

Unlike some other conservatives, Viereck repudiated Sen. Joseph R. McCarthy (R, Wisc.) [*q.v.*] and the popular movement the Senator helped create. Adopting an unusual stance similar to that of another conservative American philosopher, Will Herberg [*q.v.*], Viereck viewed McCarthyism as a kind of populist phenomenon, "the same old isolationist, Anglophobe, Germanophile revolt of radical Populist lunatic-fringers against the eastern, educated Anglicized elite." Vierick's position alienated him from many other anti-Communist conservatives.

However, Viereck also rebuked those of McCarthy's critics who in his view deliberately minimized the Communist threat. In addition he denounced the U.S. foreign policy of containment of Communism. Viereck believed it was "heartless" to consign Eastern European peoples to Communism without offering them hope of liberation in the future.

Viereck's views prevented him from becoming part of the ideological conservative group that was emerging in the late-1950s around the *National Review*, edited by William F. Buckley, Jr. [*q.v.*]. In a 1956 *National Review* article, Frank Meyer denounced Viereck for his "unexceptionably liberal sentiments" that he was "passing off" as conservative philosophy. Buckley later commented with satisfaction on this "expulsion" from "our movement."

Although noted primarily for his philosophical and political views and writings, Viereck considered literature as his first love and wrote numerous books of poetry and fiction. He won a Pulitzer Prize for poetry in 1949 and served as a distinguished visiting professor of poetry at several universities in the U.S. and abroad. From 1948 he was a professor of modern European and Russian history at Mount Holyoke College in Massachusetts. He was a speaker and commentator on events of the 1960s and 1970s.

[TGD]

VINCENT, JOHN C(ARTER)
b. Aug. 19, 1900: Seneca, Kan.
d. Dec. 3, 1972, Cambridge, Mass.
Foreign Service officer.

Vincent graduated from Mercer University in 1923 and two years later entered the Foreign Service. Learning to speak fluent Chinese, he served as a diplomatic officer in a number of major Chinese cities over the next decade. From 1935 to 1939 he was assigned to the State Department's division of Far Eastern affairs. During World War II he returned to China to resume his counselor duties. He developed close personal relationships with Chou En-lai, one of the Communist leaders, and Chiang Kai-shek, the Nationalist leader whom he thought could unify the nation following the War. In 1944 Vincent was recalled to Washington to be chief of the division of Chinese affairs. The following year he headed the office of Far Eastern affairs.

By 1945 Vincent was considered the Foreign Service's leading expert on China. As such, he was one of the architects of the Marshall mission to China in 1945-47. The delegation, headed by Gen. George C. Marshall, was instructed to urge Chiang to make necessary reforms and attempt reconciliation with the Communists. The failure of the mission convinced Vincent that Chiang would lose the war regardless of the amount of American support. He, therefore, recommended that the U.S. reduce military and economic aid.

Following the fall of the Nationalists in 1949, Sen. Joseph R. McCarthy (R, Wisc.) [*q.v.*] charged Vincent with sabotaging the Marshall mission by placing impossible demands on Chiang and asked that Vincent be fired. In 1950 the Tydings Committee upheld Vincent's conduct. However, the following year the Senate Internal Security Subcommittee, under the leadership of conservative Sen. Patrick McCarran (D, Nev.) [*q.v.*], accused Vincent of Communist affiliation. McCarthy then renewed his demand that Vincent be removed from the State Department. A Department loyalty board cleared Vincent, but the Civil Service Loyalty Review Board concluded that there was reasonable doubt about Vincent's loyalty. Not wishing to see Vincent dismissed from government service, President Truman and Secretary of State Dean Acheson [q.v.] formed a new panel, headed by Judge Learned Hand, to review the case. [See TRUMAN Volume]

The panel had not finished its investigation when the Eisenhower Administration took office. In March 1953 Secretary of State John Foster Dulles [q.v.], ignoring the board, ruled that, although there was no reasonable doubt about his loyalty, "Mr. Vincent's reporting of the facts, evaluation of the facts, and policy advice during the period under review show a failure to meet the standard which is demanded of a Foreign Service officer. . . ." Vincent was given the choice of resigning or being dismissed. Vincent chose to quit. The Secretary of State ordered him to hand deliver his letter of resignation to the Dulles home. During their last meeting, Dulles asked Vincent to discuss China. "After all," Dulles told the diplomat's lawyer, "he knows the situation there better than just about anybody."

Critics charged that Vincent's departure, one of several in the Department during the period, weakened the Foreign Service "beyond real hope of recovery." It revealed to many Foreign Service officers that Dulles would not protect them from right-wing attacks and prompted many to make policy recommendations on the basis of accepted ideology rather than on expert opinion. According to journalist David Halberstam, the effects could be seen more than a decade later in the inability of the State Department to deal with the war in Indochina.

At the age of 52 Vincent retired to Cambridge, Mass., with some advice for the Eisenhower Administration. He recommended that it study the charge that the U.S. had "lost China," which he called a "phony idea" peddled by the China Lobby. If Washington were to acknowledge this, Foreign Service officers would become free from loyalty to Chiang and develop "an objective and, we hope, effective policy regarding China." Vincent lectured on foreign affairs at Radcliffe College. The Foreign Policy Association's speakers bureau adver-

tised him as a lecturer on Asia and China, but he had few offers. In 1972 Chou En-lai invited Vincent to visit China, but he could not accept the invitation because he was suffering from terminal cancer.

[JB]

For further information:
E.J. Kahn, Jr., *The China Hands* (New York, 1976).

VINSON, CARL
b. Nov. 18, 1883; Baldwin Co., Ga.
Democratic Representative, Ga., 1914-65; Chairman, Armed Services Committee, 1949-53, 1955-65.

After graduating from the Georgia Military College, Vinson entered Mercer University in Macon, Ga., where he received his LL.B. degree in 1902. He served in the Georgia House of Representatives from 1909 to 1912, when he was elected judge of the Baldwin Co. Court. In 1914 Vinson was elected to the U.S. House of Representatives. He became chairman of the Naval Affairs Committee in 1932. For the remainder of the decade, Vinson pressed for a major enlargement of the Navy, pushing naval expansion bills through the House in 1938, 1939 and 1940.

At the end of World War II, Vinson unsuccessfully opposed President Harry S. Truman's call for a merging of the separate military service departments into a Defense Department. When the Defense Department was created in 1947, the House's military panels were combined to form the Armed Services Committee. Two years later, when the Democrats regained control of Congress, Vinson became chairman of the Committee. The following year he attacked reductions in military expenditures proposed by Defense Secretary Louis Johnson. [See TRUMAN Volume]

Vinson was not widely known outside of Congress, but he played a crucial role in the formulation and passage of military-related bills. He dominated his Committee by dividing the panel into subcommittees without specific jurisdictions (except for the Subcommittee on Special Investigations) and deciding himself which subcommittee would receive each bill. Vinson thereby determined who would introduce bills on the House floor. On the floor itself he was, according to Speaker Sam Rayburn (D, Tex.) [q.v.], the "best legislative technician in the House." The lower chamber approved almost all legislation adopted by his Committee.

A leading advocate of a strong military establishment, Vinson supported the Army officers, led by Army Chief of Staff Maxwell Taylor [q.v.], who criticized the Eisenhower Administration's "massive retaliation" doctrine. They felt that the strategy placed too much emphasis upon nuclear weapons and did not prepare the country for fighting limited wars.

Linked to this doctrine were attempts to economize on conventional forces, a policy Vinson opposed. In January 1955 he attacked an Administration proposal to reduce the strength of the Army from 1.1 to 1 million men. The following month Vinson ended his opposition, reportedly because of Administration promises that future troop strength would not be reduced below 900,000 men. Three years later the Appropriations Committee approved an Administration request to cut the Army's strength to 870,000 men. On the floor of the House, however, members of the Armed Services panel, backed by Vinson, led a successful drive to restore the troop level to 900,000.

Vinson jealously guarded what he considered to be the prerogatives of his Committee and of Congress in the military field. In 1956 the Administration proposed a reorganization of the Defense Department that would have established three new offices of assistant secretary for research and development, one for each of the services. Vinson declared that he had no objection to the plan but had not been informed of the proposal until it was sent to Capitol Hill. He therefore opposed Committee ratification of the measure. The panel voted unanimously to recommend disapproval.

In 1958 Vinson opposed an Administration reorganization plan to strengthen the authority of the Secretary of Defense. The Congressman particularly objected to a proviso that appropriated all funds to the Secretary rather than to the separate service departments and gave him flexibility in shifting funds between the departments to meet new military developments. Vinson denounced this proposal as an invitation to Congress to "surrender its constitutional responsibilities."

As a foe of the concentration of military authority in the hands of the Secretary of Defense, Vinson also raised objections to provisions of the plan removing restrictions on the Defense Secretary's power to reassign combat functions and personnel among the three service departments. He also opposed a proviso repealing the 1947 law that stipulated that the departments were to be separately administered by their respective secretaries. The Committee's version of the reorganization plan reflected Vinson's views. The bill passed by Congress and signed by the President did not appropriate funds to the Defense Secretary. However, it gave him increased authority to reassign combat functions and strengthened his administrative authority over the three departments while acknowledging that they were separately organized.

In 1960 Rep. F. Edward Hebert (D, La.) [q.v.], chairman of the Special Investigations Subcommittee, proposed a bill to limit the hiring of retired military officers by the defense industry on the grounds that they exerted influence upon their former colleagues still in the military. The bill would have barred retired officers from helping a private company secure a defense contract within two years after their retirement. It would have imposed a $10,000 fine, two years imprisonment and denial of retirement pay during the period of violation. In the full Armed Services Committee, however, Vinson successfully eliminated the fine and imprisonment penalties. The House voted for the Committee's version of the measure. No action was taken by the Senate.

During the early and mid 1960s Vinson opposed efforts by the Kennedy and Johnson Administrations to phase out manned bombers in favor of missiles. He attacked Secretary of Defense Robert S. McNamara's efforts to transfer powers from the services to the Defense Department. In

1964 Vinson announced that he would not seek reelection. By that time he had exceeded the late Speaker Sam Rayburn's record for length of service in the House. [See KENNEDY, JOHNSON Volumes]

[MLL]

VINSON, FRED(ERICK) M(OORE)

b. Jan. 22, 1890; Louisa, Ky.
d. Sept. 8, 1953; Washington, D.C.
Chief Justice of the United States, 1946-53.

After receiving his law degree in 1911 from Centre College in Kentucky, Vinson practiced privately in Louisa and later in Ashland, Ky., and entered local Democratic politics. He was elected to the first of six terms in Congress in 1924. By the 1930s he had become a key figure on the House Ways and Means Committee. A loyal supporter of President Franklin Roosevelt, Vinson helped develop New Deal tax and coal programs. In May 1938 he was appointed a judge of the U.S. Court of Appeals for the District of Columbia. Beginning in May 1943 he served successively as Director of Economic Stabilization, Federal Loan Administrator and Director of War Mobilization and Reconversion. A key adviser to President Harry Truman, Vinson was named Secretary of the Treasury in July 1945 and then Chief Justice of the U.S. in June 1946. Truman admired Vinson's record of government service and his political philosophy. He also hoped that the genial, patient Kentuckian, who was known as a skilled negotiator and compromiser, would be able to bring unity to the then faction-ridden Supreme Court.

Vinson failed in that task; the number of his dissenting opinions was high throughout his seven years as Chief Justice. Beginning in 1949, however, when Truman named two more members of the Court, Vinson was able to bring together a five-man bloc that dominated the Court until 1953. The group generally took a conservative position on civil liberties cases and upheld government interests against individual rights claims. Vinson himself wrote the Court's opinion in two significant cases. In May

1950 the Court upheld the provision of the Taft-Hartley Act requiring union leaders to swear they were not Communist Party members. In June 1951 it upheld the Smith Act provision outlawing conspiracy to teach and advocate forcible overthrow of the government. Vinson believed that the government needed broad powers to deal with the threat of Communism at home and abroad as well as other national and international problems. He favored a restrained, limited role for the Supreme Court and wanted the justices to give wide latitude to the executive and legislative branches, especially in loyalty-security cases. Thus, in civil liberties decisions, Vinson compiled a record that made him, according to C. Herman Pritchett, "very nearly the most negative member of the Court on libertarian claims." Vinson also voted in 1947 and 1952 to sustain the government's seizure of coal mines and steel mills in order to quell industrial disputes. In addition he took a conservative stance on most criminal rights issues, particularly on search and seizure questions.

On civil rights, however, the Vinson Court established a liberal and relatively unified record. The Chief Justice wrote some of his most important opinions in this area. He spoke for a unanimous Court in May 1948 to hold restrictive covenants barring the sale of residential property to blacks and other minorities legally unenforceable. In two June 1950 decisions Vinson ruled it a denial of equal protection to exclude a black student from the University of Texas law school and to segregate black graduate students in classes and other facilities at the University of Oklahoma. The Chief Justice, though, was among the more cautious members of the Court on the race question. His opinions expanded the rights of minorities but went only as far as was needed to decide the issue at hand. Vinson occasionally dissented from majority rulings favorable to blacks. [See TRUMAN Volume]

In his final term on the Court, Vinson again displayed his relative conservatism on racial issues. He was the lone dissenter in June 1953, when the majority extended the rule of his 1948 restrictive covenant decision and held that a white home owner could not be sued for damages by neighbors for having violated a covenant by selling to blacks. The previous December the Court had heard arguments in five cases challenging the legality of segregated public schools and raising the fundamental question of whether segregation was constitutional even when facilities for the two races were equal. Rather than decide the issue the Court, on June 8, 1953, ordered reargument of the cases in the next term. Vinson died before the suits were finally disposed of, but the available evidence suggests that had he lived he would most likely have voted to hold segregation *per se* constitutional. Ultimately, in May 1954 under Chief Justice Earl Warren [*q.v.*], the Court voted unanimously that public school segregation violated the Constitution.

In June 1953 Vinson and the Court were briefly caught up in the case of Julius and Ethel Rosenberg [*q.v.*], who had been sentenced to death for giving atomic secrets to the Soviet Union. The Supreme Court three times refused to review the Rosenbergs' conviction and on June 15, 1953 denied what seemed to be all final motions in their case. Two days later, however, Justice William O. Douglas [*q.v.*] granted a stay of execution because a new legal argument had been raised on behalf of the convicted couple. Vinson immediately called a special session of the Court which, on June 18, heard oral argument on whether to uphold Douglas's stay. On June 19 Vinson read the decision of a six-man majority that the legal question raised was "not substantial," that further proceedings to litigate it were "unwarranted" and that the stay of execution was therefore vacated. Later that day the Rosenbergs were executed.

On Sept. 8, 1953 Vinson died of a heart attack at his home in Washington, D.C. A man of action rather than reflection who had a pragmatic mind and a common sense approach to problems, Vinson was not a judicial philosopher or legal theorist while on the Court nor was he its intellectual leader. Under him the Court generally played a limited role permitting other branches of government the freedom he thought they should have. All commen-

tators have recognized that the Vinson Court helped improve the status of black Americans. However, their assessments of the Chief Justice apart from this have largely depended on whether they felt the needs of the time justified the judicial restraint and conservatism the Court normally displayed, especially in civil liberties cases. Vinson, legal scholar John P. Frank has observed, will be remembered as the Chief Justice who presided over the reversal of a trend toward judicially enforced civil liberty that had begun in the 1930s.

[CAB]

For further information:
John P. Frank. "Fred Vinson and the Chief Justiceship." *University of Chicago Law Review,* XXI (Winter, 1954), pp. 212-246.
Richard Kirkendall. "Fred M. Vinson." in Leon Friedman and Fred L. Israel, eds., *The Justices of the U.S. Supreme Court, 1789-1969* (New York, 1969), Vol. 4.
C. Herman Pritchett, *Civil Liberties and the Vinson Court.* (Chicago, 1954).

VON BRAUN, WERNHER
b. March 23, 1912; Wirsitz, Germany.
d. June 16, 1977; Alexandria, Va.
Director, Guided Missile Development Division, Redstone Arsenal, 1950-56; Director, Development Division, Army Ballistic Missile Agency, 1956-60.

A member of an aristocratic Prussian family, Von Braun became fascinated with the idea of space travel as a boy. He began experimenting with rockets in Berlin while studying engineering, and in 1932 he became chief of the German Army's rocket experiment station. By 1938 Von Braun had created the model for the V-2 missile employed against the Allies in World War II. He joined the Nazi Party in 1940.

In 1945 Von Braun surrendered to the advancing American forces. He later said he did this because the U.S. seemed more likely to support his research and because "the next time, I wanted to be on the winning side." Von Braun signed a contract with the U.S. Army and, together with 119 scientists and engineers who had worked with him in Germany, flew to the U.S. in September 1945.

Initially Von Braun worked as technical director at Fort Bliss, Tex., teaching Army personnel to handle captured V-2s. Soon, however, he was again developing new missiles. In 1950 he and his team moved with the expanding Army Ordnance Guided Missile Center to the Redstone Arsenal in Huntsville, Ala.

Von Braun later described the years 1952-54 as "critical" to the subsequent development of all U.S. missiles. During the Korean war his group was directed to conduct a feasibility study for a surface-to-surface ballistic missile with a 500-mile range. The rocket, named the Redstone, had a shorter range than expected, but it laid the technical base for future rocket development. Capable of carrying a nuclear warhead, it was successfully tested in August 1953. The missile became part of the U.S. Army's arsenal in 1958.

In 1955 the Von Braun team began elaborating on the Redstone to devise rockets capable of the higher speeds needed for intermediate range ballistic missiles (IRBMs). The result was called the Jupiter, consisting of a Redstone with two additional stages. To attain the carrier capabilities needed to place a satellite in orbit, Von Braun added a fourth stage, creating the Juno I.

In February 1956 the Army Ballistic Missile Agency (ABMA) was established, incorporating the Redstone Arsenal's Guided Missile Division. Von Braun became ABMA director under the military command of Gen. John B. Medaris With the Navy working on its own Polaris missile and the Vanguard rocket, and the Air Force authorized to develop the Intercontinental Ballistic Missile, the ABMA was restricted to work on IRBMs and limited feasibility studies of missiles with greater ranges.

Eager to advance the projects allotted to them, in April 1957 Von Braun and Medaris proposed to the Defense Department's Research and Development Council a schedule for ABMA Jupiter satellite launchings beginning that September. The Council initially rejected the proposal, but after the Soviet Union placed its Sputnik satellite into orbit in October 1957, the Army won approval for its plan. On Jan. 31, 1958 Von Braun's modified four-stage Jupiter-C rocket launched the first U.S. space satellite, Explorer I.

As in Germany, Von Braun's main efforts were focused on the development of rocket weaponry. However, he advocated the use of rockets for space exploration well before Soviet advances in the field convinced American officials of the importance of a space program. In 1951 Von Braun proposed that the U.S. develop a doughnut shaped space station, and in *Mars Project*, published in 1952, he envisioned the eventual construction of an interplanetary space fleet.

Although these suggestions were regarded as utterly fantastic in the early-1950s, even Von Braun's more ambitious ideas appeared less ridiculous after the Soviet Union placed its *Sputnik* satellite into orbit. During testimony before the Senate Preparedness Subcommittee in December 1957, he proposed that the U.S. establish a national space agency with a $1.5 billion annual budget. Such an agency, he told the subcommittee, could have "a man orbiting the earth on a returnable basis" within five years and could produce a manned space station in 10 years. President Eisenhower endorsed the plan in the following spring. In July 1958 the National Aeronautics and Space Administration (NASA) was formed independent of the Defense Department. Von Braun became director of the Huntsville NASA center, renamed the George C. Marshall Flight Center, in 1960.

In the early-1960s Von Braun continued to supervise the development of the Saturn rocket later used by Project Apollo. He was a leading advocate of manned moon flight as the focus for the American space program, and he participated in much of the decision making surrounding the Apollo missions. A frequent spokesman for NASA, his books and articles helped stimulate national interest in the space program. Von Braun was the director of the Marshall Center until 1970 and served as associate NASA director for two more years. He left the Agency in 1972 to become a vice president of Fairchild Industries.

[MDB]

For further information:
Werner Von Braun and Frederick I. Ordway III, *History of Rocketry and Space Travel* (New York, 1966).
Hugo Young, Bryan Silcock and Peter Dunn, *Journey to Tranquility: The Long Competitive Struggle to Reach the Moon* (Garden City, 1970).

VORYS, JOHN M(ARTIN)
b. June 16, 1896; Lancaster, Ohio.
d. Aug. 25, 1968, Columbus, Ohio.
Republican Representative, Ohio,
1938-59.

Vorys received his B.A. from Yale in 1918 and taught for a year in Changsha, China. During 1921-22 he was an assistant secretary of the American delegation to the conference on the Limitation of Arms and Pacific and Far East Affairs. He then studied law at Ohio State University, acquiring his degree in 1923. A Republican, Vorys served in the Ohio General Assembly during 1923-24 and from 1925 to 1926 sat in the Ohio State Senate. In 1938 Vorys won election to the U.S. House of Representatives on a platform opposing the New Deal.

As a member of the House Foreign Affairs Committee, Vorys initially supported isolationist policies. However, following the Japanese attack on Pearl Harbor, he modified his views and in 1943 supported the Fulbright Resolution, backing U.S. entry into a world body designed to further the cause of peace.

Vorys focused a large amount of his attention on foreign aid. During the Truman Administration he opposed foreign aid grants, recommending that assistance be made in the form of long-term loans. In 1951 he was the author of the Vorys Compromise, which won House permission for massive shipments of wheat to India in return for a long-term repayment plan. The following year his amendments to the Truman Administration's aid budget accounted for a substantial part of the $1.7 billion

eliminated from the request. Vorys was a strong supporter of Sen. Robert Taft (R, Ohio) [*q.v.*] for the Republican presidential nomination in 1952.

Vorys often acted as spokesman for the Eisenhower Administration and defender of presidential authority. On February 23, 1953 he introduced legislation containing a draft of the President's call for repudiation of secret agreements (specifically the Yalta and Potsdam agreements) that permitted the "enslavement" of people. Five days later the Foreign Affairs Committee unaminously approved the measure. The proposal was permitted to die following Stalin's death.

During 1953 Vorys opposed Taft's proposal for a congressional investigation of the Korean war. "I doubt if you can investigate the past conduct of a war that is going on without having the committee influence the current war," he said, "and I don't think a congressional committee can conduct a war." Two years later he pushed for approval for the Formosa Resolution, authorizing the President to use the U.S. Armed Forces to defend Formosa and the neighboring Pescardores Islands against a possible Communist Chinese invasion.

In 1956 Vorys opposed the Hardy amendment to the Mutual Security Act, which would have required the executive branch to refer relevant documents to Congress before spending foreign aid funds. Vorys said, "An executive cannot be independent if somebody else has the right to look not only at his mail but at every scrap of information." The amendment was defeated. In 1957 Vorys opposed the Senate version of the Eisenhower Doctrine, giving the President power to aid Middle Eastern nations threatened by Communism, because it deleted the House's authorization for the President to use troops "as he deemed necessary." However, Vorys said its acceptance was preferable to spending more time in debate.

Vorys was a key defender of the Administration's foreign aid program in the 1950s. According to the *New York Times*, the Congressman was a "trimmer" rather than a "slasher" of White House foreign aid budgets. In debate on the 1953 Mutual

Security Act, he urged approval of what he called the "smallest foreign aid bill in five years." Vorys attempted to keep congressional cuts to $500 million, but Congress shaved off $1 billion from the Administration's military and economic aid requests. The following year, under his management, the President's request was passed with a substantially smaller cut.

Vorys was appointed to the Commission on Foreign Economic Policy in 1953. In January 1954 the panel released its final report suggesting methods for improving the nation's international trade situation. These included a three-year extension of the Tariffs Agreement Act and other proposals to encourage international trade. It recommended reducing tariffs, reorienting U.S. foreign aid toward making loans instead of grants and increasing trade with Soviet satellites. Eisenhower submitted a program to Congress based on the Commission's recommendations, but most of the proposals were stalled on Capitol Hill during 1954. After a bitter struggle in 1955 he succeeded in getting approval of the extension of reciprocal trade agreements and implementation of tariff cuts over a three-year period.

Vorys retired from the House in 1959. In 1961 President John F. Kennedy appointed him to a commission studying the cost of political campaigns. He died of a respiratory ailment in Columbus, Ohio, in August 1968.

[ACD]

WADSWORTH, JAMES J(EREMIAH)
b. June 12, 1905; Groveland, N.Y.
Deputy U.S. Representative to the United Nations, February 1953-August 1960; Permanent Representative, September 1960-January 1961.

Wadsworth was born into a wealthy Hudson Valley family that traced its ancestry back to the colonial period. He was related to John Hay, Lincoln's private secretary and later Secretary of State. His father was a U.S. senator. Following his graduation from Yale in 1927, Wadsworth returned to

his family estate to manage his own dairy farm. From 1931 to 1941 he served in the New York Assembly. Wadsworth then resigned to become assistant manager of industrial relations at the Curtis-Wright Corp. in Buffalo, N.Y. In 1945 he was appointed director of the public service division of the War Assets Administration. Between 1946 and 1948 he was in charge of the governmental affairs department of the Air Transport Association. He soon became known as a skillful labor negotiator.

Wadsworth returned to government service in 1948. As special assistant to Paul G. Hoffman [q.v.], head of the Economic Cooperation Administration, he helped line up congressional support for the Marshall Plan. In June 1950 he became administrator of the civil defense office of the National Security Resources Board.

President Eisenhower appointed Wadsworth deputy representative to the U.N. in 1953. He sat on the Economic and Social Council and was an alternate representative to the U.N. Technical Assistance Conference. As a representative, Wadsworth had no policy-making role but served as spokesman for the Administration on many sensitive issues. He opposed the blanket admission of new members, which could lead to the entrance of Communist China to the international organization, and barred any negotiations on Korean unification until North Korea recognized the "authority of the United Nations in repelling the Communist invasion of South Korea." Wadsworth also urged the Security Council in 1955 to censure Israel for attacking the Gaza Strip. He advised the Arab nations to recognize the right of Israel to exist and recommended that they resettle Palestinian refugees from Israel permanently and regard them "not as temporary residents but as fellow citizens and co-sharers of the Near East's future."

During the same period Wadsworth, as deputy representative to the U.N. Disarmament Commission, became involved in negotiations for an arms reduction and atomic control program. Speaking before the General Assembly in October 1954, he voiced the Eisenhower Administration's policy that disarmament must be accompanied by an effective inspection system. "We cannot stop an arms race unless all the racers stop running," he said, "and we cannot know whether all the racers have stopped running if one of them insists on running on a concealed track. For the free world to stop arming while the Soviet Union keeps on increasing its strength would be an invitation to the very war we seek to avoid."

As U.S. representative to the Disarmament Commission's Subcommittee on Atomic Control, Wadsworth reiterated the Administration's demand for an end to secrecy in nuclear development and ready access to atomic installations for inspection purposes. In May 1955 he cautioned that Soviet proposals for a self-inspection system "still appear to fall short of the minimum safety requirements." In his own opinion, disarmament was plausible only when "inspectors can go everywhere and see everything necessary to make sure that forbidden munitions are not being manufactured." He responded unequivocally to Soviet Foreign Minister Andrei Y. Vishinsky's demand in October 1954 that the U.N. Security Council be given veto powers in any disarmament formula. Wadsworth believed that Vishinsky's proposal would make the Soviets the supreme arbiter in deciding which disarmament violations were to be punished.

Wadsworth gradually achieved a reputation as the Administration's "chief troubleshooter." His abilities as a negotiator earned him the praise of many of his colleagues in the U.N. During 1956 he handled the extremely delicate negotiations leading to the formulation of the Statute of the International Atomic Agency, establishing a 70-nation organization to further peaceful use of atomic energy. In October 1956 Dr. Joao Carlos Muniz of Brazil, chairman of the council which elaborated the fine points of the Statute, called it a "monument to Wadsworth."

In February 1958 Secretary of State John Foster Dulles [q.v.] appointed Wadsworth to replace Harold Stassen [q.v.] as chief U.S. disarmament negotiator. Wadsworth later replaced Henry Cabot Lodge [q.v.] in September 1960 as permanent U.S. representative to the U.N. He proved to be a

popular diplomat, known for his informal manner and ready laugh as well as his diplomatic expertise. The Russians who worked with him said privately that he was a "serious, not a cold warrior." Wadworth left his U.N. post in 1961. He served as a government consultant during the 1960s and was a member of the Federal Communications Commission from 1965 to 1969.

[ACD]

WAGNER, ROBERT F(ERDINAND), JR.

b. April 20, 1910; New York, N.Y.
Mayor, New York, N.Y., 1954-65.

The son of the popular liberal Sen. Robert F. Wagner, Sr. (D, N.Y.), Wagner attended Taft School and Yale University. After receiving his law degree in 1937, he ran successfully for a seat in the New York State Assembly. He resigned in 1941 to serve in the Air Corps in Europe. After World War II Wagner returned to New York to resume his political career. With the support of Tammany Hall, he advanced rapidly, serving as city tax commissioner, commissioner of housing and buildings and chairman of the city planning commission. In 1949 he was elected Manhattan borough president but lost his bid for the Democratic senatorial nomination in 1952.

In 1953 Tammany boss Carmine DeSapio [q.v.], disillusioned with Mayor Vincent Impellitteri and anxious to improve Tammany's image, chose Wagner as his candidate for the Democratic mayoral nomination. Although not a charismatic leader, Wagner's use of an excellent staff, his capacity for hard work and his ability to make well thought-out decisions earned him public recognition. His advocacy of school improvement gained him the support of the powerful Parent-Teachers Association, while his father's popularity further enhanced his standing. These factors and his ability to stay clear of the kind of scandals that had rocked the previous Democratic administrations, made him a strong candidate.

Wagner ran a primary campaign on a platform condemning the incumbent for rent, tax and transit fare increases. He particularly stressed the problem of overcrowded classrooms. With the support of unions and reformers anxious to rid the Party of the scandals of the Impellitteri years, Wagner won the primary by over 160,000 votes. He easily defeated Republican Harold Riegelman in the November general election.

As mayor, Wagner became known for the steady, methodical and cautious way in which he attacked the city's problems. An associate said his greatest assets were "a cast-iron behind and an awesomely retentive memory." He used his administrative abilities and impressive political skills to bring about important improvements in the city. Careful not to offend New York's many interest groups, Wagner often delayed decisions until assured of broad political support. His habit of delaying action generated criticism but kept him from making disastrous blunders.

During Wagner's first two terms he increased school construction, improved welfare services, opened new parks, modernized the city's building code to improve the plight of tenement dwellers and undertook a substantial program of housing and highway development. In an extremely popular move he hired 3,000 additional policemen, transferred others from desk jobs to street assignments and reduced major crime in the city by 21%. When a blue-ribbon panel suggested closing 30 fire houses to save $1 million a year, Wagner yielded to popular pressure and refused to shut them down.

Wagner also took important steps to improve city government. He created the office of city administrator to coordinate the activities of various departments and hired expert administrators for top-level posts. Although obligated to DeSapio and Tammany Hall for his election, he refused to put political hacks in policymaking positions. Yet aware of his need for Tammany support, he rarely took low-level jobs away from political appointees and did not interfere with established political practices and customs.

During the late-1950s Wagner pressed unsuccessfully for revision of the city charter to concentrate executive and administrative power in the hands of the mayor and legislative power in the City Council. The move was intended to simplify the government's structure, limit political rivalries and maneuvering, and unify the city administration. It was particularly designed to reduce the power of the City Council and Board of Estimate, often rivals of the mayor. In 1958 Wagner asked the state legislature to authorize a charter revision commission, but the measure was not passed. The following year he proposed a city law establishing the commission; the state responded by forming its own panel. The state commission's first report was essentially a political document criticizing the city administration. In February 1960 Wagner countered by creating a city panel of high-ranking municipal officials to recommend charter revision. Facing the prospect of two commissions preparing conflicting reports, the state legislature enlarged the committee and authorized the Mayor to appoint two of its 11 members. Wagner then dissolved his task force.

In 1961 voters approved the new charter. It gave the mayor greater power in preparing the capital budget and administering the expense budget, where the Board of Estimate had previously exercised total control. At the same time the power of the borough presidents was reduced, effectively limiting their patronage.

Yet, despite these accomplishments, the problems that beset all major urban areas during the 1950s continued to haunt Wagner. In 1957 New York experienced a seven-day subway strike. The following year Wagner extended union recognition to most municipal workers. With new-found power and the threat of a strike, the unions began to extract substantial wage and benefit increases which, according to some observers, laid the basis for the city's fiscal problems during the 1970s. Although Manhattan experienced a boom in the construction of office buildings and luxury housing, large residential areas decayed. Thousands of poor blacks and Hispanics moved into the city, while the white middle class fled to the suburbs. The presence of an ever increasing poor population was accompanied by a rising crime rate, school segregation and growing unemployment.

As mayor, Wagner sought to be both friendly with and independent of DeSapio. The Tammany leader was Wagner's chief political adviser and regularly counseled him on patronage matters. Wagner, himself, ran as the regular Democratic candidate for the Senate in 1956 only to lose to Jacob Javits [q.v.]. In 1957 Wagner ran his own reelection campaign, winning with a thunderous 72% of the vote. This victory gave him the opportunity to divorce himself from DeSapio, and during Wagner's second term the two became rivals. In 1961 Wagner broke with Tammany Hall, seeking his third term in the Democratic primary by running on a "No Bossism" platform. Supported by such Democratic reformers as Herbert Lehman [q.v.] and Eleanor Roosevelt [q.v.], Wagner defeated DeSapio's hand-picked candidate and went on to win reelection.

During his third term Wagner was increasingly called on to deal with racial violence and shortfalls of municipal revenues. He committed the city to borrowing at unprecedented levels to meet current expenses, thereby establishing a precedent that contributed to the city's fiscal crisis in the following decade. Wagner was succeeded by Rep. John V. Lindsay (R, N.Y.). He then returned to the practice law. [See KENNEDY, JOHNSON Volumes]

[JB]

WALTER, FRANCIS E(UGENE)
b. May 26, 1894; Easton, Pa.
d. May 31, 1963; Washington, D.C.
Democratic Representative, Pa., 1933-63; Chairman, Subcommittee on Immigration Affairs of the Judiciary Committee, 1955-63; Chairman, Un-American Activities Committee, 1955-63.

Walter received his LL.B. degree from Georgetown University in 1919 and returned to his native Easton, Pa., to practice law. In 1928 he was appointed county so-

licitor. After his election to the House in 1933, he built a record of qualified support for New Deal domestic policies. With the end of World War II, he supported congressional moves to combat Communist influence at home and abroad.

After World War II Walter became deeply involved in immigration affairs. In 1950 he proposed a bill to ease racial restrictions on immigrants. As a 1951 delegate to the International Committee for European Migration, he worked to place immigrants in many countries, mostly other than the U.S. But in 1952 he cosponsored the McCarran-Walter Act, a bill denounced by President Truman as discriminatory and vague. Passed over Truman's veto, the Act established immigration quotas based on 1920 census reports of Americans' national origins and had the practical effect of severely reducing the number of Eastern and Southern European and Asian immigrants. Critics attributed Walter's harsh legislation to his fear of Communist infiltration through foreign immigration. [See TRUMAN Volume]

During the next eight years, six of them as chairman of the Judiciary Committee's Subcommittee on Immigration Affairs, Walter consistently opposed President Dwight D. Eisenhower's efforts to reform the Act, sometimes supplementing his objections with warnings about the dangers of internal Communist subversion. In 1953 the President managed to secure passage of the Refugee Relief Act, designed to admit 200,000 non-quota immigrants over the next three years. In 1956 the State Department hired Edward Corsi [q.v.], a respected former immigration official, to administer the law. Walter forced the removal of Corsi from his post, in partly because Corsi had criticized the McCarran-Walter Act. Walter had also charged that Corsi had once been affiliated with Communist-front organizations but never substantiated his accusations. Eisenhower continued his struggle against Walter in 1956 by recommending major revisions in immigrations laws, including the removal of national origins quotas and liberalization of policies affecting Iron Curtain refugees. Again Walter was able to block major changes. Later in 1956, however, he amended his hardline views to propose the admission of 5,000 refugees of the Hungarian revolt. But one month later Walter was "thoroughly convinced" that many of the new refugees had been Communists in Hungary, and he urged that they be admitted as "parolees." In Eisenhower's final year Walter again thwarted the President's efforts to increase immigration and change admission procedures.

As a member of the House Un-American Activities Committee (HUAC) under chairman Harold Velde (R, Ill.) [*q.v.*] in 1953-54, Walter was widely regarded as one of the fairer, more temperate investigators of that panel, which searched out alleged Communist subversives. When he assumed the HUAC chairmanship in 1955, however, his own proclamations and actions took on a new stridency that intensified over the next nine years.

In 1955 HUAC investigated one of its familiar targets, the entertainment industry. Little new information turned up during the hearings, however. In the spring of 1956 the Committee began an investigation of alleged unauthorized use of U.S. passports. Walter was concerned with dissemination abroad of what he viewed as anti-American opinions. As a result of the hearings, HUAC issued eight contempt citations, none of which were upheld in the courts. The U.S. Supreme Court in 1958 ruled that the State Department had not been authorized by Congress to withhold passports on the basis of "beliefs and associations." Walter immediately pressed for tighter legislative controls on passports. In July of the same year, HUAC probed the Fund for the Republic, set up by the Ford Foundation. Commentator Walter Goodman wrote that Walter suspected the group of campaigning against his immigration law. Furthermore, the liberal foundation was committed to support the "elimination of restrictions on freedom of thought." At the center of the confrontation was the financing by the Fund of a critical report on blacklisting in the entertainment industry. During the hearings it became clear that while Walter would not admit to the existence of a blacklist, he backed the exclusion of Com-

munists from jobs. Walter attacked the Fund as a tax-exempt organization supporting dubious, anti-American activities. In the annual HUAC report of 1956, he declared that 200,000 people in the U.S., "the equivalent of 20 combat divisions of enemy troops," were aiding the subversion of U.S. political affairs. HUAC recommended tighter postal and passport controls and more severe punishment for individuals who "obstructed" congressional hearings.

In subsequent years HUAC chose targets that had been heavily investigated in previous congressional sessions, including the labor movement, churches and the entertainment industry. HUAC went to California in 1957 to investigate suspected Communists in the education system. In an unusual action the Committee released names to local school boards and delegated to them the authority to hear testimony that would be duly recorded for HUAC's later study. Numerous teachers lost their jobs, this time in the hands of local school board officials. Hearings in San Francisco in 1959 provoked demonstrations against HUAC. In 1960 the Committee produced a movie, *Operation Abolition*, which depicted the demonstrations as Communist-inspired and directed. The film was criticized by many as a blatantly deceptive and manipulative journalistic enterprise.

During the Kennedy Administration Walter continued to resist efforts to overhaul the McCarran-Walter Act and warned Congress of the dangers of imported subversion. On the other hand, he supported much of President Kennedy's domestic legislation and was a key operative for the President in numerous congressional votes. Walter's HUAC had a diminishing role in U.S. affairs during the early-1960s and did not regain some degree of sensational publicity until the civil rights movement and Vietnam War occupied the nation's attention. Walter died of leukemia in 1963. [See KENNEDY Volume]

[TGD]

For further information:
Walter Goodman, *The Committee* (New York, 1968).

WARREN, EARL

b. March 19, 1891; Los Angeles, Calif.
d. July 9, 1974; Washington, D.C.
Chief Justice of the United States,
1953-69.

The son of Scandinavian immigrants, Earl
Warren grew up in Bakersfield, Calif., and
attended the University of California,
where he received an undergraduate degree in 1912 and a law degree in 1914.
After five years as a deputy district attorney
in Alameda Co., Calif., Warren became
the district attorney in 1925 and over the
next 13 years built a reputation as an honest, efficient and fair-minded prosecutor.
He ran successfully for state attorney general in 1938 and in 1942 won the first of
three successive terms as governor.

A Republican who also won the Democratic gubernatorial endorsement in 1946,
Gov. Warren increased old age and unemployment benefits, overhauled the state
penal system and inaugurated a public
works program of new schools, highways,
hospitals and parks to meet the needs of
the state's rapidly expanding population.
He proposed a statewide compulsory health
insurance program and fought a loyalty oath
requirement for the state university's faculty. However, Warren also supported the
evacuation of Japanese Americans from the
West Coast during World War II, an action
he later said he regretted, favored a loyalty
pledge for all state employes and signed a
bill outlawing the Communist Party in
California. On balance, he was recognized
as a member of the liberal wing of the Republican Party and as a governor with an
open and independent mind and a socially
progressive record.

The Republican vice presidential candidate in 1948, Warren made a bid for the
Party's presidential nomination in 1952. At
the Republican National Convention that
July, the California delegation which Warren led voted at an important moment to
seat pro-Eisenhower delegates, and the
Governor campaigned for the General in
California that fall. [See TRUMAN Volume]

Following the election, according to Warren, Eisenhower promised him the first
Supreme Court vacancy. However, when
Chief Justice Fred Vinson [q.v.] died early
in September 1953, the President considered other possible appointees before settling on Warren. Eisenhower announced
Warren's nomination as Chief Justice on
Sept. 30, saying he had chosen the Califor-
nian for his unquestioned integrity,
middle-of-the-road philosophy and experience in government and law. Warren was
given a recess appointment and sworn in
less than a week later on Oct. 5, the day
the Court's new term started. The Senate
confirmed his nomination by a unanimous
voice vote on March 1, 1954.

In December 1953, soon after Warren
took his seat, the Court heard arguments in
five cases held over from its previous session which challenged the legality of racial
segregation in public schools. Contrary to
their usual practice, the justices did not
vote on the cases at their weekly conference following the argument but instead
continued to discuss the suits over the next
few months. After a vote was finally taken
in late February or March 1954, Warren
undertook the writing of the opinion himself. On May 17, 1954 he delivered his first
major opinion as Chief Justice in *Brown* v.
Board of Education and, in a deliberately
brief and low-key manner, stated that the
justices had unanimously decided that racially segregated public schools deprived
children of equal educational opportunities.
Citing sociological studies, Warren stated
that separate educational facilities were inherently unequal. Therefore, he ruled, they
violated the Constitution. He left open the
question of how this desegregation decision
should be implemented and called for further argument on this issue. A year later,
on May 31, 1955, Warren again spoke for a
unanimous Court to rule that school desegregation must proceed "with all deliberate speed."

The *Brown* decision was called the "supreme achievement" of the Warren Court
and it was unquestionably a momentous decree. It overturned the nearly 60-year-old
"separate-but-equal" doctrine, which had
held that segregated facilities were constitutional so long as blacks and whites received
equivalent treatment. In the next few years

the Court extended its judgment that racial barriers imposed by law were invalid to an array of public facilities including parks, playgrounds, transportation, courtrooms and public housing. *Brown* ended the legality of the South's Jim Crow system, helped set in motion major changes in American race relations and also led to the first major controversy over a Warren Court decision with many white Southerners denouncing the justices for their ruling.

Warren's special contribution in *Brown* may well have been his success in winning unanimity among the justices. Although several prior rulings strongly suggested that the Court would outlaw segregation in *Brown*, a unanimous decision was by no means assured. According to several fellow justices as well as some outside analysts of the cases, Warren contributed significantly to the Court's unity by his handling of the issue in conference, his discussion of the cases with individual justices and the moderate phrasing of the final opinion. Some supporters as well as opponents of the *Brown* decision, however, criticized Warren's opinion as being deficient in solid legal analysis and argument, and many civil rights advocates expressed dissatisfaction with the gradualist "all deliberate speed" formula adopted by the Court.

Aside from *Brown*, Warren in his first years on the bench was the moderate and rather cautious jurist most observers expected him to be when he was appointed. In his first term, for example, he voted to uphold a state gambling conviction based on illegally seized evidence and to sustain New York State medical authorities when they suspended a doctor's license to practice because he had refused to cooperate with a congressional investigation into Communism.

By mid-1956, however, Warren had moved away from the center and had aligned himself with the Court's more libertarian members. His shift was most evident in a series of controversial cases involving loyalty-security issues in which he consistently voted in favor of individual claimants and against the government, though on a variety of grounds. In April 1956 Warren's opinion for a six-man majority overturned a

state conviction for sedition against the U.S. on the grounds that Congress had preempted this field from the states with the 1940 Smith Act. In the *Watkins* decision of June 1957, the Chief Justice again spoke for the Court to reverse the contempt conviction of an individual who had refused to answer questions about former Communist Party associates before a subcommittee of the House Un-American Activities Committee. The subcommittee had failed, Warren said, to show the witness that the questions asked were pertinent to the subject under investigation, but he added to this narrow holding a lengthy essay which insisted that congressional committees were subject to constitutional limitations and that Congress had no power to expose the private beliefs and affairs of individuals solely for the sake of exposure.

In a companion case reversing a similar state contempt conviction, Warren's plurality opinion also discussed in broad terms the limits on state investigatory powers, but its actual holding was again fairly narrow. The language of both opinions led many people to believe that the Court had cut significantly into congressional and state authority to inquire into possible subversion, and they aroused considerable controversy. Two years later, however, in June 1959, the Court by a five-to-four vote upheld contempt convictions in two cases very similar to the 1957 suits, and the majority opinions emphasized the limits of the earlier rulings. The Chief Justice dissented from both of the later decisions. Warren's liberalism in these and other cases ultimately led President Eisenhower to call the appointment one of the biggest mistakes he made while in office.

During the 1960s, when new appointments created a liberal majority, Warren led an increasingly activist Court whose rulings were marked by a concern for protecting individual liberties and promoting equality. In a March 1962 case which Warren considered the most significant of his tenure, the justices ruled that federal courts could decide legislative apportionment issues; they later ordered reapportionment on a one-man, one-vote basis. The Warren Court expanded the rights of those suspected or accused of crime, overturned much of the loyalty-security apparatus of the 1950s, held prayer and Bible reading in public schools unconstitutional and expanded the scope of freedom of speech and of the press. By the time Warren retired in June 1969, the Court had wrought a constitutional revolution in several areas and its rulings had had a profound impact on American social and political life. [See KENNEDY, JOHNSON, NIXON/FORD Volumes]

Aside from those who objected to the outcome in particular cases, the Warren Court met criticism for allegedly reaching out to decide controversial issues and for being too result-oriented in its rulings. Even some supporters of the Court's decisions said that the justices acted more like legislators than judges in the way they made new policy. Warren's answer to these criticisms was that the Court had an obligation to decide all cases properly placed before it, however controversial the issues. In the judicial process, Warren also wrote, the "basic ingredient of decision is principle and it should not be compromised and parceled out a little in one case, a little more in another, until eventually someone receives the full benefit. If the principle is sound and constitutional, it is the birthright of every American" and should be accorded "to everyone in its entirety whenever it is brought into play." For Warren the Court's special function lay in guaranteeing the constitutional protections afforded the individual, especially for those least likely to receive them. Unless "the Court has the fiber to accord justice to the weakest member of society," he stated, "we never can achieve our goal of 'life, liberty and the pursuit of happiness' for everyone."

Warren was not a great legal scholar or judicial philosopher, but most analysts consider him to have been a preeminent Chief Justice. He could not have achieved the many legal changes of the Warren Court on his own, but as Anthony Lewis noted, he "saw the movement and put behind it the weight of his character and position and public reputation; they were essential in converting what might have been lost legal causes into the wave of the future." Under

Warren's leadership, according to Archibald Cox, the Court gave "creative and enduring impetus" to the "responsibility of government for equality among men, the openness of American society to change and reform and the decency of the administration of criminal justice."

[CAB]

For further information:
Alexander Bickel, *The Supreme Court and the Idea of Progress* (New York, 1970).
Archibald Cox, *The Warren Court* (Cambridge, Mass., 1968).
Richard Kluger, *Simple Justice* (New York, 1976).
Philip Kurland, *Politics, the Constitution and the Warren Court* (Chicago, 1970).
Anthony Lewis, "Earl Warren," in Leon Friedman and Fred L. Israel, eds. *The Justices of the U.S. Supreme Court, 1789-1969* (New York, 1969), Vol. 4.
Richard H. Sayler et al, eds., *The Warren Court* (New York, 1969).
Earl Warren, *The Memoirs of Chief Justice Earl Warren* (Garden City, 1977).

WATKINS, ARTHUR V(IVIAN)
b. Dec. 18; 1886; Midway, Utah
d. Sept. 1, 1973; Orem, Utah
Republican Senator, Utah, 1947-59.

A Mormon whose grandparents were among the early pioneers of Utah, Arthur Watkins studied at the Mormon sponsored Brigham Young University from 1904 to 1907. That year he left for New York City to serve two years as a missionary. He remained to earn a law degree from Columbia University in 1912 and then returned to Utah to set up a practice and edit a weekly newspaper. From 1919 to 1932 he also managed commercial orchards and a turkey farm in his home state. He served as judge for the fourth judicial district in Utah from 1928 to 1933. After an unsuccessful attempt to gain a House seat in 1936, he won the senatorial election in 1946.

Watkins soon established himself as a conservative supporter of the Republican Party's "Old Guard." Anxious to assert congressional control over foreign policy, he opposed the North Atlantic Treaty of 1949 because Congress would not have control over deployment of U.S. troops and weapons supplied to North Atlantic Treaty Organization allies. Later he criticized President Harry S. Truman's decision to send troops to Korea without congressional sanctions. Although a strong anti-Communist, Watkins remained noncommital on Sen. Joseph R. McCarthy's (R, Wisc.) [q.v.] anti-Communist crusade during the early-1950s.

Watkins played a key role in the events leading to the Senate's condemnation of McCarthy in late 1954. In July Sen. Ralph Flanders (R, Vt.) [q.v.] introduced a resolution to censure McCarthy for conduct "unbecoming a member of the U.S. Senate . . . contrary to senatorial traditions . . . and tending to bring the Senate into disrepute." Sens. William Fulbright (D, Ark.) [q.v.] and Wayne Morse (Ind. Ore.) [q.v.] later added 33 specific complaints against McCarthy. The issue quickly threatened to divide the Senate on partisan and ideological grounds. To prevent this the chamber chose six "neutral" senators to investigate the charges. These men, highly respected by their colleagues, were all members of the moderately conservative group that held the balance of power in both parties. None had taken a strong stand on McCarthy. Watkins, with his reputation as a dry, stern moralist devoted to order, propriety and the dignified traditions of the Senate, was chosen chairman.

When the Committee's hearings began on Aug. 31, Watkins clearly intended to exercise full control and not allow McCarthy to create a flambuoyant showcase for himself. Watkins advised reporters, "Let us get off the front pages and back among the obituaries." The Committee forbade smoking and television cameras in the hearing room, did not call witnesses McCarthy could abuse in his cross examination, and clamped down on McCarthy's celebrated tactics of disruption. According to journalist Richard Rovere [q.v.], Watkins, with an "almost parsonical mien," proved to be the man whose gavel "could play variations on the crack of doom." After being frustrated by Watkins's iron-fisted command of the proceedings, a flustered McCarthy said, "I think it's unheard of thing I ever heard of."

The Watkins Committee decided to consider 13 charges divided into five general categories, including abuse and contempt of the Senate, receipt of classified information, encouragement of federal employes to violate the law and abuse of Gen. Ralph W. Zwicker [q.v.], who had appeared before McCarthy's Government Operations Committee during its investigation of the Army. Through long hours of tedious recitation, the panel and an admittedly bored McCarthy heard a mass of evidence documenting the Wisconsin Senator's behavior. The Committee report, issued on Sept. 27, recommended censure on two counts: Contempt of the Senate for failing to appear before the Subcommittee on Privileges and Elections in 1952 and abuse of Gen. Zwicker. McCarthy's conduct was described as "contumacious, denunicatory, unworthy, inexcusable and reprehensible." A full Senate vote on the censure resolution was postponed until after the November elections. During the interim Sen. McCarthy denounced Watkins as "cowardly and stupid."

On the first day of debate, Nov. 10, Watkins presented his group's charges before the Senate. He was afflicted with a painful spastic abdominal muscle but did not weaken under attacks by McCarthy and his allies. In a speech inserted into the *Congressional Record* on Nov. 15, McCarthy accused the Committee of becoming a "unwitting handmaiden" of the Communists. Watkins then told the Senate that McCarthy should be censured for his attacks on the panel. This charge replaced the one dealing with the abuse of Zwicker. Later in the proceedings an angry Watkins elicited tears and applause from his colleagues when he described McCarthy's attack on the Select Committee as a blow against the Senate itself, and he challenged that body, "What are you going to do about it?"

When the final votes were counted on Dec. 2, the censure resolution passed by a 67-22 margin. Under the direction of Vice President Richard M. Nixon [q.v.], the word "censure" was stricken from the resolution's title, but there was no misinterpreting the Senate's forceful condemnation. McCarthy himself noted, "I wouldn't exactly call it a vote of confidence." Soon afterward President Eisenhower personally congratulated Watkins for his excellent work, a fact that provoked charges of "lynching" from McCarthy's remaining supporters.

After the McCarthy investigation Watkins receded from the public eye. He was defeated in the 1958 election when independent J. Bracken Lee [q.v.] split the Republican vote; Democrat Frank Moss was elected senator. Watkins was appointed an associate member of the Indian Claims Commission in 1959 and was named Chief Commissioner in 1960. After retiring he returned to Utah, where he died in 1973.

[TGD]

For further information:
Robert Griffith, *The Politics of Fear: Joseph R. McCarthy and the Senate* (Lexington, Ky., 1970).

WATSON, THOMAS J(OHN) JR.
b. Jan. 8, 1914; Dayton, Ohio.
President, International Business Machines Corporation, 1952-61.

The son of the founder of International Business Machines Corp. (IBM), Watson graduated from Brown University in 1937 and the same year joined IBM as a salesman. Following service in the Army Air Force during World War II, Watson returned to IBM, where he demonstrated managerial ability and a flair for salesmanship in the rapidly growing corporation whose principal source of profit was in the office automation field.

Watson rose quickly through the company's ranks and was appointed president in 1952. After the elder Watson died in 1956, his son became the major force behind the company. During the mid-1950s IBM introduced new computers which became increasingly valuable to offices, factories and transportation facilities. Under his direction the sales and profits of IBM skyrocketed. Its research division turned out more advanced models to meet the increasing demand for sophisticated equipment. Wat-

son's company also obtained lucrative defense contracts. By 1960 IBM had become one of the nation's leading corporations, holding a near monopoly on the production of computers. That years its profits reached over $168 million.

Unlike many of the important business executives of the period, Watson was not opposed to heavy government spending or to the high tax rates which the spending necessitated. In a speech before the National Association of Manufacturers (NAM) in 1959, he maintained that a liberal welfare state was necessary to achieve U.S. goals at home and abroad. He pointed out that the Soviet Union's success in raising its standard of living tremendously impressed underdeveloped nations which were often tempted to use it as an example. Watson thought that the U.S. economic system was an even more appealing model. He asked businessmen to realize that the nation must do everything in its power to help other countries adopt it.

Watson told his audience that business leaders should not complain about high taxes. "We can't do all the things necessary for the United States to do—in this country and abroad—and still proceed on the 'business as usual' basis." The American people desired a stronger nation, a balanced budget and the same or even lower taxes. "These three goals," Watson said, "are incompatible. One of our first sacrifices must be a willingness to accept higher taxes if necessary. . . . There are no easy solutions." Watson's speech received polite but restrained applause.

The following year Watson testified before a Senate subcommittee examining the economic and military threat posed by the Soviet Union. He said that although he disliked government controls of business, he accepted them as necessary in a cold war situation. He remarked, "I would rather have greater control by our government under the present system than to discover one day that business-as-usual has not been sufficient to win the battle." Here, as in his speech to the NAM, Watson stressed that only liberalism could prevent the spread of Communism. This set him apart from other business leaders who believed a balanced budget and a laissez-faire government were needed to offset radical change.

Watson became chairman of the board of IBM in 1961. During the 1960s and 1970s IBM grew to be one of the largest multinational corporations in the world. A close friend of President John F. Kennedy, Watson served on a number of important advisory committees, including the Committee on Labor Management Policy, the National Advisory Council for the Peace Corps and the Citizens Committee for International Development. In the late-1960s the government began numerous antitrust suits to break up the company's apparent computer monopoly. This highly complex litigation was still pending well into the 1970s. Watson became chairman of the executive committee of IBM in 1972. [See KENNEDY Volumes]

[JB]

WEEKS, SINCLAIR
b. June 15, 1893; West Newton, Mass.
d. Jan. 27, 1972; Lancaster, N.H.
Secretary of Commerce, January 1953-November 1958.

The son of Calvin Coolidge's Secretary of War, Sinclair Weeks graduated from Harvard in 1914 and served in the Army during World War I. He managed a silver works company before becoming mayor of Newton, Mass., in 1930. In 1936 he lost the Republican Senate nomination to Henry Cabot Lodge, Jr., [q.v.], but he soon took over the state's Republican Party chairmanship. From 1941 to 1944 Weeks served as treasurer for the Republican National Convention, and from 1949 to 1952 he was chairman of the Republican Finance Committee, where he served as liaison between the GOP and big business. During 1944 Weeks served in the U.S. Senate, taking the seat vacated by Lodge's resignation.

Weeks organized Dwight D. Eisenhower's primary drive, which gathered a record campaign fund. He then helped swing delegates to Eisenhower's candidacy during the Republican National Convention. At one point he even attempted to in-

fluence Sen. Robert Taft (R, Ohio) [q.v.] into dropping out of the race. In a much publicized statement Weeks told the Senator that his stepping down would be a "supreme act of self-denial" that could "electrify the nation, instantly unite the Party . . . guarantee victory and save the country." Taft, however, refused his plea. After the election Eisenhower approached Weeks about assuming the chairmanship of the Republican National Party, vacated when Arthur Summerfield [q.v.] resigned to become Postmaster General. However, Weeks expressed a strong interest in becoming Secretary of Commerce because he thought it would be an excellent position in which to use his management, financial and business abilities.

During the closing months of 1952, Weeks headed a panel formed to study the question of ending the wage and price controls imposed by the Truman Administration. The commission recommended reverting to a free market. Pointing out that historically controls had been able to cope only with the symptoms of inflation rather than its basic causes, the panel recommended they be reserved only for extreme emergencies and then used only for short periods of time. Weeks maintained that controls would "distort and impede our production effort." He conceded that removal might raise prices but maintained that the long-range effect would be salutary. Eisenhower followed Weeks's advice and in February ordered all wage and some price controls removed at once.

Weeks soon made it clear to other members of the Administration that he would vigorously "represent the business viewpoint even when that viewpoint is in the minority." He soon became involved in an intra-Administration debate over modifying the 1947 Taft-Hartley Act, opposed by labor because of its restrictions on unions. Secretary of Labor Martin Durkin [q.v.] was the principal proponent of revision. He wanted to drop the Act's provision requiring union leaders to sign non-Communist affidavits, abolish "right-to-work" laws, give unions more control over membership and liberalize the freedom to engage in secondary boycotts. Most importantly, he hoped to minimize the jurisdiction of state courts in labor disputes. Eisenhower rejected extreme revisions and supported amending the legislation only to eliminate those provisions that could be used to "smash unions." Weeks, on the other hand, saw the attempt at revision as an opportunity to strengthen the Act. He was particularly anxious to clarify the authority of states in labor disputes to prevent "erroneous" interpretations of the statutes.

The two Secretaries soon engaged in bitter clashes over the issues. Because they could not come to an agreement, presidential assistants Bernard Shanley [q.v.] and Gerald Morgan [q.v.] drew up a 19-point memorandum suggesting an Administration position. Most points were concessions to Durkin. The memorandum eventually became the basis for a draft message to Congress to be forwarded on July 31. However, Taft died that day, and because he had coauthored the original legislation, the White House delayed action. In the meantime Weeks, joined by Vice President Richard Nixon [q.v.], manuevered behind the scenes to kill the message. They convinced the President that alienating business and states rights advocates would be political suicide. During the early part of September, Eisenhower informed Durkin he could not accept the 19 points.

Weeks became involved in another well-publicized clash—this time within his own department. Dr. Allen V. Austin, head of the Bureau of Standards, ruled that a product advertised as giving longer life to storage batteries was totally ineffectual. On March 31 Weeks attempted to force Austin's resignation on the grounds that he had made a subjective judgment. However, public opposition to his action and feeling within the Bureau (400 employes threatened to resign) forced him to establish a panel of scientists to rule on the product. The committee not only backed Austin's conclusions but also insisted that he remain on the job. Recognizing his own mistake, Weeks retreated and eventually became Austin's friend.

The Secretary was liaison between the cabinet and various subcommittees during the planning stages of the St. Lawrence Seaway. He argued strongly in favor of the project, pointing out that soon American shippers would request aid for the development of harbors. Weeks also furthered the passage of the Federal Highway Aid Act of 1956. Eisenhower later wrote that "the great highway system would stand as a memorial to the man in my cabinet who headed the department responsible for it."

Weeks retired from the cabinet in November 1958 for personal and business reasons. At the time of his retirement, he could look back on a list of important accomplishments. Weeks had led the fight for lower tariffs and became a firm advocate of the reciprocal trade program. Known as a hardliner on Communism, he had nevertheless issued regulations in August 1957 permitting an increase in the export of "peaceful" goods to Poland. He had fought for U.S. membership in the anti-protectionist Organization of Trade Cooperation, broadened Weather Bureau services, modernized the air navigation system, furthered railroad assistance legislation, administered the nation's largest peacetime shipbuilding program for merchant ships, expanded the fair trade program and increased the Department's statistical activities. Weeks became known as an optimist for his positive views concerning future directions of the American economy.

In 1959 Weeks was reelected director of the First National Bank of Boston. Five years later he joined Hornblower & Weeks, Hemphill, Noyes, as a limited partner. Weeks died in January 1972 at the age of 78.

[GAD]

WELCH, JOSEPH N(YE)
b. Oct. 22, 1890: Primghar, Iowa
d. Oct. 6, 1960: Hyannis, Mass
Special Counsel, U.S. Army, 1954.

The son of poor English-born parents, Welch graduated from Grinnell College in Iowa and went to Harvard law school on a scholarship. After receiving his LL.B. in 1917, he established a highly successful practice in civil law and in 1923 became a partner in the Boston firm of Hale and Dorr.

In April 1954 Welch was appointed special counsel for the Army in its dispute with Sen. Joseph R. McCarthy (R, Wisc.) [q.v.]. He immediately filed 29 charges with the Senate Government Operations Committee's Permanent Investigations Subcommittee, chief among which was that McCarthy and his aide Roy M. Cohn [q.v.] "had improperly pressed the Army to promote Pvt. G. David Schine [q.v.]"—a former member of McCarthy's staff.

The hearings, which opened before the subcommittee on April 22, developed through a series of incidents rather than through a logical exploration of the charges. More often than not the issues were obscured by haggling over trivial matters and by McCarthy's violent personal attacks on the participants.

Throughout the proceedings Welch's dry wit, legal skill and self-composure gained him national sympathy. Towards the end of the 36-day hearings, however, the mounting personal animosity between him and his chief antagonist exploded in a celebrated exchange. During Welch's heated cross-examination of Cohn, McCarthy interrupted to charge the attorney with trying to "burlesque" the hearings. He did not believe, McCarthy added, that counsel had "any conception of the danger of the Communist Party," as indicated by the fact that a young member of Welch's law firm, Frederick G. Fisher, had once belonged to the Lawyers' Guild, an alleged Communist front. Visibly shaken, Welch explained that Fisher had been a member of the Guild only briefly, while in law school, and that he had since become an entirely respectable Republican lawyer. Although he had originally been chosen to help with the Army defense, Welch had sent Fisher back to Boston in order to avoid any possible controversy. Turning to McCarthy, he said, "Little did I dream you could be so reckless and so cruel as to do an injury to that lad. . . . If it were in my power to forgive you for your reckless cruelty, I [would] do so . . . but your forgiveness will have to come from some one other than me." When McCarthy persisted Welch cut him short demanding,

"Have you no sense of decency, sir, at long last. Have you left no sense of decency?" He then left the room to the applause of the spectators.

According to some observers, McCarthy's attack on Welch's associate was his single most damaging blunder during the hearings. It contributed to a growing sense of national outrage at the Senator's actions. More importantly, his rashness and general disregard for Senate procedures and decorum alienated a substantial bipartisan bloc in the upper house and led to his eventual condemnation by the Senate in December.

Welch returned to his law practice. As a result of the hearings, his popularity was so great that he was later called to appear on a number of television shows. In 1959 he played a judge in the film, *Anatomy of a Murder*.

[TLH]

WELKER, HERMAN
b. Dec. 11, 1906; Cambridge, Ida.
d. Oct. 30, 1957; Washington, D.C.
Republican Senator, Ida., 1951-57.

Welker grew up in rural Idaho and worked his way through the University of Idaho law school, where he received his LL.B. in 1929. While still attending college he was appointed the prosecuting attorney of Washington Co., Ida. In 1936 he left his home state for Los Angeles, where he set up private law practice. After serving in the Army Air Corps in 1943 and 1944, he established a law practice in Idaho and then won election to the state Senate in 1948. Two years later he won a U.S. Senate seat by the largest margin in Idaho since 1936. He credited his victory to the support and strength of his ally, Sen. Joseph R. McCarthy (R, Wisc.) [q.v.].

Welker, a virulent anti-Communist, was a member of the small ultraconservative group of Republicans in the Senate. He shared McCarthy's belief that most of the nation's problems were the result of Democratic appeasement and misgovernment. In 1955 he supported a complete ban on allied trade with the Soviet bloc. He also favored drastic cuts in foreign aid to Europe, which he regarded as the home of numerous left-wing groups. Welker was one of McCarthy's strongest supporters in the upper house. As a member of the Senate Subcommittee on Privileges and Elections, he attempted to delay the panel's investigation of McCarthy in 1952. [See TRUMAN Volume]

Welker remained on the extreme right of the Republican Party throughout the first Eisenhower Administration. On domestic issues he supported limited government intervention in the private sector. He voted to cut appropriations for the Tennesee Valley Authority and opposed wage and price controls and tax increases.

An extreme cold warrior, in 1953 Welker opposed the nomination of Charles Bohlen [q.v.] as ambassador to the Soviet Union because of the diplomat's role in what Welker termed the "Truman-Acheson policy of appeasement" towards the Soviet Union. Welker argued against the 1953 emergency immigration bill that was designed to admit increased numbers of East European refugees. In 1954 he vigorously opposed U.S. recognition of Communist China, saying that the Communist Chinese had shown no indication of altering their "course of hatred for the United States and the free world." In that year Welker accused Arthur H. Dean [q.v.], the U.S. negotiator of the Korean Armistice, of supporting appeasement and of collaborating with Communist China. He assailed Dean as an "ex-official spokesmen" of the Communist linked Institute of Pacific Relations. In 1954 he also supported the Bricker amendment, designed to limit the President's treaty-making power.

The Idaho Senator was known for his vitriolic style in debate. Reporter Richard Rovere [q.v.] said Welker was "capable of more hatred than McCarthy as well as more ideology." Welker served as McCarthy's self-appointed floor manager during the debate over the Senator's possible censure in the fall of 1954. He attacked the Watkins Committee's recommendation to censure McCarthy as indirectly promoting the aim of Communist conspirators.

In November 1954 Welker spent two days presenting a defense of McCarthy, in which he praised his friend as "one of the greatest living foes of Communist slavery." On Nov. 16 he said that the Constitution provided for punishing senators for "disorderly behavior but did not for the specification in the censure resolution—conduct unbecoming a senator or . . . contrary to senatorial traditions." The following day Welker said that there was no precedent for censuring McCarthy, that many senators had assailed colleagues with violent language without being censured. He predicted that he himself would be censured for defending McCarthy. Welker protested repeatedly that senators showed "disrespect" to McCarthy by their sparse attendance during Welker's speech. At one point in the hearings, McCarthy refused a backroom offer to compromise because his friends—Sen. Welker notable among them—had worked so hard for him. McCarthy insisted that he did not wish to disappoint them or their mission. On Dec. 2 the Senate condemned McCarthy by a 67-22 vote.

In 1955 Sen. McCarthy named Welker, with F.B.I. Director J. Edgar Hoover [q.v.], as "good candidates to replace Eisenhower as President." In 1956 Welker was defeated in a reelection bid by Frank Church. Welker died in Washington in the following year.

[TGD]

WHITTAKER, CHARLES E(VANS)
b. Feb. 22, 1901: Troy, Kan.
d. Nov. 26, 1973: Kansas City, Mo.
Associate Justice, U.S. Supreme Court, 1957-62.

Charles E. Whittaker worked his way through law school at the University of Kansas City, Mo., and passed the state bar exam in 1923, a year before his graduation. He joined a prestigious Kansas City law firm, eventually becoming a senior partner, where he specialized in litigation and business planning for a largely corporate clientele. Although not active politically, Whittaker was a Republican and a close friend of

President Eisenhower's brother Arthur, and he was well regarded by state political leaders. He was named to a federal district court judgeship in Kansas City in July 1954 and promoted to a seat on the Eighth Circuit Court of Appeals in June 1956. In both posts Whittaker demonstrated great industry and efficiency. Eisenhower nominated him to the Supreme Court in March 1957, and he was quickly confirmed by the Senate.

On the bench Whittaker soon aligned himself with the Court's more conservative members. In June 1957 he wrote the majority opinion in a case upholding a section of the 1952 McCarran Act, which resulted in the deportation of an alien for committing an offense that had not been grounds for deportation when he committed it. A year later Whittaker was part of a five-man majority that sustained the dismissal of a public school teacher who had refused to answer questions about possible Communist affiliations in the past. He also dissented in June 1958 when the Court ruled that Congress had not authorized the Secretary of State to refuse a citizen a passport because of his political beliefs. In two June 1959 cases the Justice voted to uphold the contempt convictions of witnesses who had refused to answer questions or produce records for congressional and state investigations of Communism.

Whittaker did occasionally vote with the Court's liberals in First Amendment and loyalty-security cases. His opinion for the Court in a January 1958 decision declared unconstitutional a local ordinance that required union organizers to obtain permits before they could solicit membership in a union. Whittaker also voted in two March 1958 cases to overturn federal statutes taking away the citizenship of wartime deserters or individuals who voted in a foreign election. Generally, however, he voted in a conservative vein, and in the 1959 and 1960 Court terms, the Justice had the lowest civil liberties record of any member of the Court.

In criminal rights cases Whittaker again leaned toward conservatism. He joined the majority in a March 1959 case that held that an individual acquitted in a federal court could then be tried for the same offense in a state court without violating the safeguard against double jeopardy. In many criminal cases, such as those involving an allegedly coerced confession, Whittaker was accused of inconsistency because he would vote opposite ways in largely similar cases without clearly explaining his reasons for doing so.

A modest, sincere man who worked extremely hard while on the Court, Whittaker has been considered by most commentators a failure as a justice. He had a very limited view of his role, was not outstanding either as a judicial thinker or legal craftsman and wrote almost no significant opinions. He articulated no judicial philosophy and "was not," according to Leon Friedman, "fitted intellectually or physically for the job" of a Supreme Court justice. He retired from the Court in March 1962 and died in 1973. [See KENNEDY Volume]

[CAB]

For further information:
Daniel M. Berman, "Mr. Justice Whittaker: A Preliminary Appraisal," *Missouri Law Review*, 24 (January, 1959), pp. 1-15.
Leon Friedman, "Charles Whittaker," in Leon Friedman and Fred L. Israel, eds., *The Justices of the United States Supreme Court, 1789-1969* (New York, 1969), Vol. 4.

WILEY, ALEXANDER
b. May 26, 1884; Chippewa Falls, Wisc.
d. Oct. 26, 1967; Philadelphia, Pa.
Republican Senator, Wisc., 1939-63.

Following graduation from the University of Michigan law school in 1907, Wiley returned to his Wisconsin home of Chippewa Falls. Over the next 32 years he was a successful lawyer, business man and dairy farmer. He also became active in Kiwanis International. As its state leader, he often toured Wisconsin making valuable contacts that eventually enabled him to win the Republican nomination for governor in 1936. The popular governor, Philip LaFollette, defeated him in the race, but two years later Wiley won a U.S. Senate seat as a conservative Republican.

The Senator was an opponent of Franklin D. Roosevelt's New Deal legislation and of U.S. entry into World War II. However, after Pearl Harbor he renounced his isolationist views and joined the international wing of the Republican Party led by Sen. Arthur Vandenberg (R, Mich.). In 1945 he became the second-ranking Republican member of the Foreign Relations Committee chaired by Vandenberg. Wiley supported American entry into the U.N. and worked closely with the Truman Administration to obtain passage of legislation implementing the North Atlantic Treaty and the Marshall Plan, the two cornerstones of the President's containment policy toward the Soviet Union. Wiley, however, broke with the Administration over its China policy. A member of the so-called China bloc in the Senate, he called for all-out aid to Chiang Kai-shek to win the civil war against the Communists.

Wiley opposed Sen. Joseph R. McCarthy (R. Wisc.) [q.v.] both on moral grounds and because of internal state politics. In the spring of 1952 Wiley delivered a speech defending Dean Acheson [q.v.], then under attack by the Republican Right. Alluding to McCarthy, Wiley said, "I will oppose, as a matter of principle not personality, the efforts of anyone within my own party, or any other party, who has the mistaken idea that simply because the other fellow recommended a policy it is necessarily wrong." Wiley's stand was opposed by the conservative *Chicago Tribune*, which pictured the Senator as a "Truman Republican and an Acheson stooge." The paper also maintained that he was an "expert on betrayal," as sinister as Alger Hiss. McCarthy supporters in the Senate also attacked Wiley, implying that Acheson had seduced an "illiterate country bumpkin inflated to the point of bombast." Despite the denunciation Wiley refused to retract his statement.

As chairman of the Foreign Relations Committee from 1953 to 1954 and as its ranking minority member from 1955 to 1960, Wiley was a major supporter of the Eisenhower Administration's foreign policy,

often defending it against challenges from the Republican Right. During 1953 he supported the appointment of Charles Bohlen [q.v.] as ambassador to the Soviet Union. The diplomat was strongly attacked by conservatives, who felt him too closely associated with the "Truman-Acheson policies of appeasement."

Wiley was a strong supporter of the North Atlantic Treaty Organization, and he favored a strong, rearmed West Germany as its leading European power. Although he believed that the U.S. should not recognize Communist China and should oppose its admission to the U.N., he refused to join Republican conservatives in criticizing the British and French governments for recognizing and trading with the Peking regime. He believed the attacks would play into Moscow's hands by splitting the alliance. Although he was deeply concerned about Communist electoral victories in Western Europe, he thought they reflected a discontent with existing governments rather than acceptance of Communist ideology.

Wiley led the Senate opposition to the Bricker amendment, which would have curbed the President's treaty-making powers. As a result, the McCarthy dominated Wisconsin Republican State Convention censured him in June 1953. On May 26, 1956, Wiley's 72nd birthday, it denied him renomination because of his internationalist position. The Convention chose Rep. Glen R. Davis, who had supported the Bricker amendment and advocated a reduction in foreign aid. Wiley, sobbing after leaving the hall, vowed to run anyway. He won the September primary by 9,700 votes out of more than 424,000 cast. His victory was attributed to a heavy lead in normally Democratic Milwaukee. Wiley then went on to win the general election.

Wiley served in the Senate until 1962, when Gov. Gaylord Nelson defeated him in his reelection bid. Throughout the early Kennedy period, he voted as a conservative on domestic legislation except civil rights. He also supported the President's diplomacy but called for a more aggressive action against Cuba. Wiley died of a stroke in October 1967. [See KENNEDY Volume]

[JB]

WILKINS, ROY
b. Aug. 30, 1901; St. Louis, Mo.
Executive Secretary, NAACP, 1955-64;
Executive Director, 1965-77.

Wilkins majored in sociology at the University of Minnesota and was secretary of the St. Paul, Minn., chapter of the NAACP in his senior year. After graduating in 1923 he began working as a reporter for the *Kansas City Call*, a weekly black newspaper, and eventually became its managing editor. In 1930 Wilkins worked against Senate confirmation of Judge John J. Parker, an allegedly racist Supreme Court nominee and the reelection of Kansas Sen. Henry J. Allen (R, Kan.), a segregationist. As a result of this activity, he was offered the post of assistant secretary of the national NAACP in New York City. In his new position he investigated conditions of black workers on the Mississippi levees in December 1931. During and after World War II, he ran the national office in the absence of Walter White, the organization's leader. In 1950 Wilkins organized an Emergency Civil Rights Mobilization in Washington, D.C., to lobby on behalf of civil rights legislation. In 1955 Executive Secretary White retired, and Wilkins replaced him as leader of the 240,000-member organization. The goal of the NAACP was the elimination of racial discrimination; its primary methods were legal suits and legislative lobbying.

Wilkins's major function was formulating the strategy of the NAACP's legal and legislative efforts. He also administered the national office, made speeches throughout the country, wrote pamphlets and raised funds. One of Wilkins's first activities after becoming NAACP executive secretary was to help raise money to support the Montgomery bus boycott led by Martin Luther King, Jr. [*q.v.*]. However, he focused his primary attention upon attempts to integrate Southern schools. In June 1955 the national office urged NAACP Southern chapters to petition local school boards for implementation of the Supreme Court's 1954 *Brown v. Board of Education* decision outlawing segregation in public schools.

In 1956 Wilkins attacked both major political parties for allegedly taking weak positions on civil rights. He criticized Democratic presidential aspirant Adlai E. Stevenson [*q.v.*] in February as favoring a go-slow approach in granting blacks their rights as citizens. In August Wilkins unsuccessfully urged the Republican Platform Committee to promise an amendment to Senate rules that would bar filibusters. Subsequently, he criticized both national party platforms as inadequate. Since the NAACP was a nonpartisan organization, Wilkins did not express a preference in the presidential race.

In February 1957 Wilkins, testifying before a subcommittee of the House Judiciary Committee, described the Administration's civil rights bill as "minimum legislation." Before its enactment by Congress, the Senate eliminated the crucial Part III, permitting the Attorney General to obtain court injunctions in all cases of civil rights violations. Nevertheless, Wilkins decided that the bill, which established a civil rights commission and gave blacks some protection in exercising their right to vote, was the best that could be obtained at the moment. He also concluded that it represented an historic breakthrough that would open the way for more far-reaching legislation in the future. Wilkins convinced the Leadership Conference on Civil Rights, a coalition of groups opposing racial discrimination, to back the measure.

On June 23, 1958 Wilkins, King, A. Philip Randolph [*q.v.*] and Lester B. Granger met with President Eisenhower to present a nine-point program to further civil rights. The plan included the organization of a White House conference on school desegregation; the granting of funds to officials and community groups seeking to promote the desegregation of schools; the denial of federal funds for segregated institutions; the assurance of federal protection against terrorist bombings in the South; and the enactment of Part III of the original 1957 civil rights bill. They received little more than a polite audience from the President.

Wilkins denounced the 1960 Civil Rights Act which extended the voting rights protection of the 1957 rights legislation. He declared, "The Negro has to pass more check points and more officials than he would if he were trying to get the United States gold reserves in Fort Knox. It's a fraud." In that year he again denounced both parties' civil rights planks as inadequate and participated in picketing the Democratic National Convention. He and other rights leaders believed that, among other things, the major parties should repudiate the segregationists within their ranks and, in accordance with the 14th Amendment, back a reduction of congressional representation in areas where blacks were denied the right to vote.

In 1960 Wilkins endorsed new, direct-action techniques to promote desegregation in the South. He announced in the spring that the NAACP would support student "sit-ins" at lunch counters and that the organization itself would stage "wade-ins" in the summer to integrate swimming facilities.

The legal and legislative activity of the NAACP under Wilkins helped to secure a 1962 executive order against housing discrimination in federally financed housing, the Civil Rights Act of 1964 and the Voting Rights Act of 1965. Wilkins participated in a number of Deep South civil rights marches in the mid-1960s. In 1965 the officficial title of his post was changed to executive director.

Wilkins opposed the call for "black power" raised by Stokeley Carmichael in 1966 and denounced the growing number of militant black nationalist and separatist groups. He condemned the black riots in many Northern cities during the summer of 1967. Unlike many civil rights activists who spoke out against the war in Vietnam, Wilkins believed that the civil rights and peace issues should be kept separate.

Wilkins's moderate stands made him a major target of criticism by black militants. Within the NAACP a group of militant Young Turks sought to enhance their power in 1967 and 1968. The failure of these efforts led to a number of resignations from the NAACP. In 1977 Wilkins retired as executive director. [See KENNEDY, JOHNSON Volumes]

[MLL]

WILLIAMS, G(ERHARD) MENNEN
b. Feb. 25, 1911: Detroit, Mich.
Governor, Michigan, 1949-61.

Williams was a product of one of Detroit's wealthy old families. His grandfather was a soap manufacturer and his father a pickle magnate. After attending the exclusive Salisbury school in Connecticut, Williams earned his B.A. from Princeton in 1933 and his law degree from the University of Michigan in 1936. He then surprised his family by joining the Democratic Party. In 1936 he went to Washington to serve as an attorney for the Social Security Board. The following year Michigan Gov. Frank Murphy appointed Williams assistant attorney general. When Murphy became U.S. Attorney General in 1939, Williams joined his staff as an administrative assistant. In 1942 he left the Justice Department to enlist in the Navy.

Following World War II Williams practiced law in Detroit and became active in Democratic politics. Supported by many young liberals, the youthful Williams ran for governor in 1948 on a platform that included demands for improved housing, education, civil rights, farm programs and veterans' benefits. With the support of blacks, ethnic voters and the United Automobile Workers, he won the election. Williams later went on to win five more terms in a state where Democrats had previously done poorly. [See TRUMAN Volume]

During the 1950s Williams earned a reputation as one of the most liberal governors in the nation. He modernized Michigan's courts, built more schools and reformed state prisons. To win public support for his programs, he formed bipartisan commissions of experts to study proposals. The panels were responsible for recommending legislation to aid the handicapped, improve the juvenile justice system and reform election procedures. Williams was also a strong supporter of civil rights. In 1948 he proposed a fair employment practices law, which the Republican-dominated legislature finally passed in 1955. The Governor also got the legislature to ban discrimination in the sale of real estate. Williams appointed many blacks to state offices, including positions in his cabinet and on the state courts.

The Governor lost his battle to introduce a more equitable tax system and raise adequate revenues for the state. Beginning in 1952 he unsuccessfully attempted to enact a corporate and personal income tax. In 1959 a temporary tax measure was passed to provide necessary funds until the adoption of a new state constitution in 1963. The difficult tax battle and the rising state debt were factors contributing to Williams's decision not to seek reelection in 1960.

As the prominent governor of one of the nation's largest states, Williams was constantly mentioned as a possible presidential or vice presidential candidate. He never denied interest in either office. At the 1952 Democratic National Convention the Governor was Michigan's favorite-son candidate. Williams supported Sen. Estes Kefauver (D, Tenn.) [q.v.] in the expectation that if the Senator obtained the presidential nomination he might be the vice presidential nominee.

Williams was once again mentioned as a presidential contender in 1956. However, his strong civil rights record and his belief that segregation must end throughout the nation made him unacceptable to the South. One incident particularly irritated Southerners. In 1955 Williams had been invited to speak at a Democratic fund-raising event in Birmingham, Ala. He initially accepted the invitation, but after finding out that blacks would be banned from the affair, Williams publicly refused to attend. In a 1957 article in The Nation, Williams again appealed to the Democratic Party to be more forceful on civil rights. The U.S., he warned, could not afford to face the world as a nation that did not adhere to the principles upon which it had been founded.

Although his name was once again mentioned, Williams was not a serious candidate for the 1960 Democratic nomination because of his civil rights stand. Williams expressed interest in Sen. John F. Kennedy's (D, Mass.) [q.v.] candidacy but was skeptical of his commitment to liberalism. However, after a meeting with Kennedy,

Williams endorsed him on the spot. At the National Convention the Governor spoke for Kennedy to the uncommitted states.

In 1961 Kennedy appointed Williams assistant secretary of state for African affairs, a position he held until 1966. Williams made an unsuccessful bid for the Senate in 1966. In November 1970 he won election to the Michigan Supreme Court. [See KENNEDY Volume]

[JB]

WILLIAMS, HARRISON A(RLINGTON), JR.
b. Dec. 10, 1919; Plainfield, N.J.
Democratic Representative, N.J., 1953-57; Democratic Senator, N.J., 1959-

Williams received a B.A. degree from Oberlin College in 1941 and then worked as a copy boy for the Washington Post. After service in the Army during World War II, he was employed as a steelworker in Lorain, Ohio. Williams enrolled in Columbia University law school in 1946 and received an LL.B. degree in 1948. He practiced law in New Hampshire for a year, returning subsequently to New Jersey, where he was admitted to the state bar in 1951. That year Williams made an unsuccessful race for the state Assembly; the following year he failed in an effort to win a seat on the Plainfield City Council.

In August 1953 Rep. Clifford P. Case [q.v.], a liberal Republican, resigned his seat from New Jersey's sixth district. The district, which encompassed Union Co. had been Republican-controlled since its creation in 1932. Williams ran as the Democratic candidate in the November 1953 special election for the seat. Because the party regarded the race as hopeless, he had to finance the campaign with his own money. But Williams, promising to follow in Case's political footsteps and benefiting from Democrat Robert Meyner's [q.v.] victorious gubernatorial campaign, defeated his opponent by a narrow margin. Running on a platform critical of Sen. Joseph R. McCarthy (R, Wisc.) [q.v.], Williams won by a more substantial margin in 1954.

Williams compiled a liberal record in the House, backing government-supported urban renewal and slum clearance and an extension of unemployment benefits in 1954. He favored the elimination of the national origins quota system for immigration in 1955 and supported the Powell amendment, stipulating that no federal school aid would go to segregated schools, in 1956. A strong critic of Communism, in 1955 he introduced a resolution condemning Soviet violations of its agreements with the U.S. and urging that measures be taken to inform the American people of such infractions. The following year Williams successfully offered an amendment to the Mutual Security Act terminating all aid to Yugoslavia unless the President declared such aid in the national interest.

In 1956 Williams, hampered by the coattail effect of President Dwight D. Eisenhower's landslide victory, lost his congressional seat. The next year he played a major role in Gov. Meyner's reelection campaign, serving as chairman of the Meyner for Governor Clubs. Meyner's 200,000-vote margin of victory revived Williams's political fortunes. The following year the Governor helped him win the state organization's endorsement for the Senate. As a result of Meyner's backing and the economic recession of 1958, Williams was elected by 85,000 votes. He thereby became the first Democratic senator from New Jersey since 1936.

During his first month in the Senate, Williams joined the chamber's liberals in backing Sen. Paul Douglas's (D, Ill.) [q.v.] proposal to enable a majority of senators to cut off a filibuster. The measure was defeated 28-67. In March 1960 he joined in an unsuccessful effort to end a Southern filibuster against an Administration civil rights bill. That same year he successfully offered an amendment to increase funds for housing for the elderly from $5 million to $50 million (the final bill provided $20 million). He also backed Sen. Patrick V. McNamara's (D, Mich.) [q.v.] abortive attempt to provide health care to the elderly through social security. In June 1960 the Labor and Public Welfare Committee's

Special Migratory Labor Subcommittee, chaired by Williams, recommended legislation providing for the extension of the minimum wage law and child labor provisions of the Fair Labor Standards Act to agriculture, the registration of farm labor contractors, and the establishment of matching federal grants to the states for migrant worker education and health programs. Most of these measures were adopted during the Kennedy and Johnson Administrations.

Williams consistently backed Kennedy and Johnson social welfare programs. He voted against the 1966 Vietnam war appropriation but did not take a clear-cut position against U.S. policies in Southeast Asia until 1969. According to journalist Franklin Pierce, Williams "undercut his own effectiveness for years by heavy drinking . . . until he finally went on the wagon around the end of 1968." [See KENNEDY, JOHNSON, NIXON/FORD Volumes]

[MLL]

WILLIAMS, JOHN J(AMES)
b. May 17, 1904; Frankford, Del.
Republican Senator, Del., 1947-71.

The ninth of 11 children, John Williams grew up on a farm in southern Delaware. After graduating from Frankford's high school, he moved to nearby Millsboro and set up a feed business with his brothers. Williams became an active Rotarian and in 1940 was elected to the town council.

Despite his obscurity, Williams entered the race for the U.S. Senate in 1946. Given little chance to win, he campaigned vigorously against government controls and big budgets and was swept into office on the Republican tide of that year. In the Senate he established an extremely conservative voting record. The most noteworthy accomplishment of Williams's first term was his investigation of corruption within the Internal Revenue Service (IRS). Congressional and Justice Department action followed his 1951 revelations; by November 1953 Sen. Williams reported that 380 IRS employes had been fired and over 200 indicted for crimes including bribery, extortion and embezzlement. [See TRUMAN Volume]

Throughout the 1950s and 1960s Williams continued to conduct his independent investigations of fraud, waste and mismanagement within the federal government. Operating without a staff and eschewing the fanfare of committee hearings, he relied on agency informants, the General Accounting Office (GAO) and his own dogged thoroughness. In the mid-1950s, for example, he criticized the government for paying over $2 million for radar equipment to a British manufacturer, then declaring the equipment surplus and selling it back for $114,000. In 1960 he criticized the Air Force for buying 272,710 screws for $1 each from a contractor who paid the manufacturer 5.5 cents each.

In addition to such waste Williams sought to expose and eliminate some of the perquisites enjoyed by government employes. His favorite targets were overseas trips taken by members and employes of Congress at public expense. In February 1957 he demanded that public accounting be made of "counterpart funds" (foreign currency supplied by U.S.-aided nations) spent by congressional employes on foreign travel. In May 1960 the Senate adopted, 68-0, a Williams amendment requiring members of Congress and congressional staff members to submit itemized public accountings of money spent on foreign travel. However, the amendment was dropped in a House-Senate conference. Williams's June 1958 amendment to prohibit government employes from traveling at a reduced rate on any American ship suffered a similar fate at the time, but it finally passed in June 1960 when attached to a shipbuilding subsidy bill. His campaigns against favoritism won him the sobriquet "the conscience of the Senate."

During the Eisenhower years Williams served on the Finance Committee and the Agriculture and Forestry Committee; in 1960 he left the latter for the Foreign Relations Committee. On the Finance Committee his general opposition to high taxation and big government found expression in actions such as his proposed amendment to the 1953 extension of the excess profits

tax. The amendment would have raised the amount of corporate income exempt from the tax from $25,000 to $100,000, but it was defeated, 52-34.

On the other hand, Williams strove to eliminate various tax loopholes favored by his fellow Republicans and conservative Finance Committee colleagues. Throughout the decade he tried and failed to lower the 27.5% oil depletion allowance. Williams also voted against various tax reductions. For example, in June 1958 he voted not to repeal the 3% excise tax on freight shipments and the 10% levy on passenger travel. He was the only one of 15 Senate Republicans seeking reelection to vote against the popular tax cuts.

Consistent with his free market beliefs, Williams supported the Eisenhower Administration's farm program intended to make price supports more flexible. He was a critic of rigid price supports, saying in June 1956 that they "continue to stimulate wasteful production." In the same month Williams said in opposition to additional airline subsidies: "Let us not fool ourselves; this is a little extra gravy for a special group that has already been riding the gravy train." He also sought to reduce subsidies to the maritime industry.

Williams consistently voted against social welfare legislation, and his overall voting record was one of the most conservative in the Senate. In 1959-60 he voted against a foreign aid authorization, federal aid to education, federal aid to depressed areas, an increase in the minimum wage, larger appropriations for housing and public works and the Democratic medicare plan. A moderate on civil rights questions, Williams favored the Civil Rights Acts of 1957 and 1960 but also voted for some restrictive amendments.

During the 1960s Williams continued to pursue his one-man investigations and to champion more stringent ethical requirements for Congress. His independent inquiry turned up important information in the Bobby Baker scandal of 1963-64. Williams retired from the Senate at the end of his fourth term in 1971. [See KENNEDY, JOHNSON Volumes]

[TO]

WILSON, CHARLES E(RWIN)
b. July 18, 1890; Minerva, Ohio
d. Sept. 26, 1961; Norwood, La.
Secretary of Defense, January 1953-
October 1957.

The son of a high school principal and a teacher, Charles Wilson graduated from the Carnegie Institute of Technology with a degree in electrical engineering in 1909. Wilson began work at Westinghouse Electric and was put in charge of all of Westinghouse's automobile electrical equipment engineering. In 1919 Wilson joined the Remy Electric Co. as chief engineer and sales manager; in 1929 he became a vice president of General Motors Corp. In 1941 he was elected president and took over wartime production, eventually manufacturing $12 billion worth of armaments. Soon after the War, Wilson went on record as opposing the closed shop on the grounds that it infringed upon workers' liberties. One of Wilson's most important contributions came in 1947, when he devised a concept known as the "cost-of-living wage formula," which called for pay raises beyond the cost of living based on worker productivity. The plan drew praise from labor leaders.

Dwight D. Eisenhower had first become impressed with Wilson when, as Army Chief of Staff, he consulted the executive on production and supply problems. Convinced that Wilson would not simply be a "yes man," and that the Secretary of Defense should be have expertise in management and procurement, President-elect Eisenhower offered him the position in late 1952.

Wilson almost immediately became a center of controversy. During hearings on his nomination, the Senate Armed Services Committee became concerned that his holdings of General Motors stock could constitute a conflict of interest because of the number of defense contracts held by the corporation. The panel, therefore asked him to sell his shares. Wilson objected and spoke in what the Senators felt an arrogant manner. The Committee asked if he might be able to make a decision that could be unfavorable to General Motors. To this Wilson answered, "For years, I thought what was good for the country was good for General Motors and vice versa." The remakr was circulated as "What's good for General Motors is good for the country." He agreed to sell all his stock on Jan. 22; the following day the Senate unanimously approved his nomination.

Wilson interpreted his role as mainly administrative and operational rather than policy forming. Eisenhower would formulate military policy and Secretary of State John Foster Dulles [q.v.] would give instructions on foreign affairs. By the first four months of his administration, the tenor of Wilson's approach became established. The Secretary cut nearly 40,000 civilian employes from the Defense Department staff, canceled or held up many military building programs and instituted the "narrow base" approach to mobilization (production restricted mainly to large corporate contracts). A Defense Department reorganization plan created several assistant secretaries. It facilitated implementation of the Secretary's decisions and improved communications. By the end of his first year, Wilson pared his immediate staff from 3,100 to 2,400.

Wilson never succeeded in smoothing over press relations. Known as a generally good natured, excellent man to work under, he nevertheless developed a habit of putting his foot in his mouth. Opposed to exploratory research, Wilson explained that he did not support, "finding out why the grass is green, things like that." On another occasion, asked his opinion about unemployment assistance, he stated that he preferred "hunting dogs to kennel-fed dogs because the hunting dogs or bird dogs would get out and hunt for what they wanted; whereas the kennel-fed dog would set back his haunches and yelp." Still another time Wilson stated that he wanted to cut back the National Guard, adding that the Guard is not much of a fighting force and consisted of individuals attempting to evade regular military service.

Regardless of his lack of verbal discretion, Wilson retained Eisenhower's confidence because of his support for the "New

Look" defense policy. This called for a reduction in the defense budget and reliance on strategic nuclear weapons rather than costly conventional forces for defense. Between December 1953 and June 1955, the Army's budget was slashed from nearly $13 billion to $7 billion; manpower was cut from 1.5 million to one million men. During the same period Navy and Marine manpower dropped from one million to 870,000 men. On the other hand, Air Force personnel rose from 950,000 in 1953 to 970,000 in 1955, with a budget climb from $16.4 billion in 1955 to $18 billion in fiscal 1957.

By 1955 many prominent military officials publicly opposed the Department's New Look. Wilson issued a "gag" directive to stop their writing. However, retiring Chief of Staff Gen. Matthew B. Ridgway [q.v.] leaked proof of Army discontent and published a series of articles in *Life* magazine. Even though Wilson issued a clarification concerning the jurisdiction and roles of the various services, squabbles continued, and an Army colonel was even arrested for allegedly leaking classified information concerning missiles to the press.

Wilson began to weary of the disputes and the pace. He submitted his resignation in August 1957 and told friends, "I'm leaving because I found myself making decisions from fatigue." He returned to his business activities. Wilson then served as a member of the board of directors of General Motors, a director of the National Bank of Detroit and chairman of the Michigan advisory committee to the U.S. Commission on Civil Rights. He died in 1961 at the age of 71.

[GAD]

For further information:
Carl W. Borklund, *Men of the Pentagon* (New York, 1966)

WILSON, SLOAN
b. May 8, 1920; Norwalk, Conn.
Author

The son of writers, Wilson was educated at Phillips Exeter Academy and entered Harvard College in 1938, where he majored in psychology and philosophy. Wilson interrupted his education in 1942 to join the Coast Guard. He commanded small sea craft before he was discharged as a lieutenant in 1945. The following year he returned to Harvard and received the B.A. degree. In 1946 Wilson published *Voyage to Somewhere*, his first novel dealing with wartime experiences. Following a brief stint as a newspaper reporter, he joined *Time* magazine as a researcher. In 1952 Wilson quit *Time* to become assistant professor of English at the University of Buffalo. As a result of his concern for the problems of American education, he was appointed as assistant director of the White House Conference on Education in 1955.

Wilson published *The Man in the Gray Flannel Suit* in July 1955. Following a clever marketing campaign, it became a best-seller. Not distinguished in style or composition, the novel's theme of the "alienated commuter" drew the interest of middle-class America. Wilson described a new type of American who arose to staff the growing media and advertising industries. Fleeing cities and their problems for a false sense of the good life in suburbia, utterly dependent on automobile or train and abundant cheap power to carry him the many miles to work, he found success illusory. Wilson's novel dealt with the malaise of this conformist, status-hungry male executive commuter. Working to produce an intangible product and living in a cultureless environment, he cut himself off from traditional values like heroism and saw no way to deal with his problems. Wilson resolved the book on a quietly optimistic note when his protagonist tried to face his problems bravely. In 1956 the novel was made into a movie starring Gregory Peck.

Wilson followed his first success with *A Summer Place*, published in 1958. Amplifying the unresolved negative strains of the man in gray flannel, Wilson's characters tried to resolve insecurities and establish personal worth through money and status. Wilson also satirized the racial and religious bigots he encountered as an educator fighting discrimination. The two books together were the first popular novels of the 1950s to question the American dream of personal happiness realizable through economic success. *A Summer Place* was sold through a high-powered advertising campaign and earned Wilson over a million dollars. However, many serious writers and critics were repelled by the crass hard-sell and spurned Sloan Wilson as greedy and commercial. Five subsequent novels were received indifferently. Wilson sank into depression and became an alcoholic. Helped from his psychological problems with the aid of drugs and finally overcoming his alcoholism with family help, he wrote *What Shall We Wear to This Party?* (1976), dealing with his life before and after the mid-1950s.

[MJS]

WOLFSON, LOUIS E(LWOOD)
b. Jan. 28, 1912; St. Louis, Mo.
Industrialist

The son of a junk dealer, Wolfson attended the University of Georgia, but he left after his junior year to work in his father's scrap yard in Jacksonville, Fla. Wolfson began his business career during the Depression as an officer for a Florida industrial pipe company. During World War II the business, which he had started with $10,000, had over $4.5 million in government contracts. After the War he extended his interests into real estate and shipbuilding along the East Coast, buying up companies whose book values far exceeded the value of their common stock. He then moved in with his own management and revived a number of firms that had been running deficits. In 1951 he became majority shareholder and board chairman of Capital Transit Co., which provided bus transit service for Washington, D.C.

Wolfson's manipulations drew government attention in 1955. In the summer a strike stopped Capital Transit operations for 51 days and crippled the city's transport system. On Aug. 1, 1955 Congress voted to purchase the company from Wolfson amid charges that he had acquired it (at five dollars per share) only for the purpose of selling it at a profit to the federal government.

(Wolfson had offered his holdings at $15 per share.)

Between 1954 and 1958 Wolfson attempted to win control of two major corporations: Montgomery Ward & Co., the nation's second largest mail-order and department store retailer, and American Motors Corp. (AMC), the fourth largest domestic auto producer. Wolfson's Ward campaign commenced in August 1954, when the financier and his associates began to purchase large blocs of Ward common stock. Management problems at Ward aided Wolfson's cause. Past his 80th birthday, board chairman Sewell Avery [q.v.] still single-handedly ran the company and had of late allowed it to stagnate. Despite a protracted eight-month struggle and a court-fight, Wolfson failed to acquire Ward; he secured just under 1% of the company's stock. Through his initiative, however, he won for himself and two allies places on the board of directors and forced Avery's retirement. Wolfson declared Avery's resignation to be a victory for his side which had "succeeded in infusing new blood into the Ward management." Curiously, Wolfson quit the board in January 1956.

A year later Wolfson attempted to gain control of AMC. Several auto concerns had merged in January 1954 to form that corporation. Wolfson had owned a large number of shares in one of these companys, Hudson, and used this bloc as the base for his acquisitions. In October 1956 Wolfson threatened AMC president George Romney [q.v.] with a stock takeover unless he partially liquidated some of AMC's assets. Unable to compete with the industry's three leaders and in desperate need of new financing, AMC management appeared vulnerable. Romney, however, persuaded Wolfson, by now the largest individual stockholder, to delay acting against management and not to demand a place on the board of directors. Wolfson issued a statement in support of Romney and dropped his campaign. Wolfson profited from his cooperation. By 1958 AMC had markedly improved its sales and earnings. As his stocks' value rose, Wolfson sold his holdings for a two million dollar profit.

Wolfson continued his financial manipulations into the 1960s. His ties to Supreme

Court Justice Abe Fortas contributed to Fortas's resignation in May 1969. Wolfson himself went to prison in 1969 for conspiracy, perjury and two counts of issuing false and misleading reports to the Securities and Exchange Commission. [See NIXON/FORD Volume]

[JLB]

WRIGHT, J(AMES) SKELLY
b. Jan. 14, 1911: New Orleans, La.
U.S. District Court Judge, 1949-62.

Wright, a native of New Orleans, graduated from Loyola University in 1931. While working as a high school English teacher, he attended Loyola University law school, from which he received his degree in 1934. After a year as a lecturer at Loyola, Wright became an assistant U.S. attorney for New Orleans: he remained at that post until 1946. Two years later he became U.S. attorney for the eastern district of Louisiana, which included New Orleans. In 1949 Wright became a U.S. district court judge for the eastern district.

During the 1950s Wright was involved in many Louisiana desegregation suits. In 1957 he ruled that laws designed to keep Louisiana State University and other state universities segregated were unconstitutional, and the following year he ordered the desegregation of New Orleans transportation facilities. In 1959 Wright ruled a law banning sports events between whites and blacks unconstitutional, and in 1960 he ordered Washington Parish, La., registrars to restore blacks to the voting rolls.

Wright was deeply involved in the effort to desegregate New Orleans public schools. In 1952 the NAACP filed a suit against the Orleans Parish School Board for the desegregation of the public schools. The suit made no progress until 1956, when the U.S. district court in New Orleans ruled that segregation was unconstitutional under the Supreme Court's 1954 *Brown* decision. Wright then ordered the School Board to make arrangements for integration "with all deliberate speed" but conceded that he did not require it be done "overnight" or "even in a year or more."

A series of appeals delayed action on the case, but in 1959 the NAACP got Wright to order the School Board to submit a desegregation plan by March 1960. When it refused Wright ordered integration to begin in September on a grade-per-year basis. In the face of this decision, Louisiana Gov. Jimmie Davis [q.v.] took control of the schools under a recently enacted statute in an attempt to close them and thus maintain segregation. Wright then issued restraining orders prohibiting the move. Integration was achieved in New Orleans on Nov. 14, when four blacks entered two previously white schools over the protests of taunting white mobs.

As U.S. circuit court judge during the 1960s, Wright continued to hand down important civil rights decisions, including the 1967 ruling that declared de facto segregation of blacks in the District of Columbia's public schools unconstitutional. In 1973 Wright was a member of the circuit court that ordered President Nixon to release the Watergate tapes [See KENNEDY, JOHNSON, NIXON/FORD Volumes]

[EWS]

For further information:
Edward Haas, *DeLesseps S. Morrison and the Image of Reform* (Baton Rouge, 1974).

YARBOROUGH, RALPH W(EBSTER)
b. June 8, 1903; Chandler, Tex.
Democratic Senator, Tex., 1957-71.

Yarborough received an LL.B. degree from the University of Texas in Austin in 1927 and was admitted to the Texas bar in the same year. From 1936 to 1941 he served as a judge of the 53rd judicial district. In 1938 Yarborough ran unsuccessfully for state attorney general. He served in the Army during World War II, and after his discharge in 1946 he returned to private law practice.

During the 1950s Yarborough gradually emerged as the leader of Texas's small band of liberal Democrats. In 1952 he entered his Party's Democratic primary against incumbent Gov. Allan Shivers [q.v.]. Shivers, the dominant figure in the Texas Party, was a conservative who led the state organization in its decision to back Republican presidential candidate Dwight D. Eisenhower. Yarborough, a neopopulist who supported social reform and opposed the powerful Texas business establishment, ran on an anti-machine platform and was soundly defeated, receiving 488,000 votes to Shivers's 833,000.

Two years later Yarborough, denouncing Shivers for his endorsement of Eisenhower, ran against the Governor again, this time losing by 90,000 votes. Both men campaigned on platforms directly or indirectly supporting segregation. Shivers directly appealed to racial prejudice. Yarborough, on the other hand, offered opposition to "forced" desegregation. Yarborough was aided by the growing cohesiveness of Texas's liberals, comprised of intellectuals, populist East Texas farmers, trade unions, blacks and Mexican-Americans. The previous year they had formed the Democratic Organizing Committee with the support of House Minority Leader Sam Rayburn (D, Tex.) [q.v.], who wanted to reestablish the loyalty of the state organization to the national Party. In 1956 Yarborough entered his third successive gubernatorial primary, facing U.S. Sen. Price Daniel (D, Tex.) [q.v.], who wanted to reestablish the loyalty of the state organization to the national Party. He lost by less than 4,000 votes.

In April 1957 a special primary was held to fill Daniel's Senate seat. The race was nonpartisan, and Yarborough won a plurality against a Democrat and a Republican who split the conservative vote. Seeking a full term in 1958, Yarborough defeated conservative William A. Blakeley in the Democratic primary and easily won the general election.

Like many legislators in the populist tradition, Yarborough compiled a generally liberal record during his early years in the Senate. He voted for liberal Democratic housing and area redevelopment bills in 1959 and supported unsuccessful efforts to override President Eisenhower's vetoes of those measures. He backed the Civil Rights Acts of 1957 and 1960. In the 86th Congress (1959-61), according to *Congressional*

Quarterly, Yarborough voted with the Southern Democratic-Republican conservative coalition on 23% of key roll call votes and against it on 67% of such votes.

Yarborough, however, joined the predominantly conservative Texas congressional delegation in defending the state's powerful oil interests. In March 1958, during a debate over a reciprocal trade bill, he stated that voluntary import quotas on foreign oil were not working and that "enforceable import quotas are critically needed." In June of the following year, he voted against a tax bill amendment offered by Sen. Paul H. Douglas (D, Ill.) [q.v.] to reduce the depletion allowance on oil and gas wells.

In the early-1960s an acrimonious relationship developed between Yarborough and Gov. John Connally, who was the leader of the state's moderate and conservative Democrats. During the mid and late 1960s, Yarborough voted for President Lyndon B. Johnson's civil rights and social welfare measures. In 1968 he endorsed antiwar candidate Sen. Eugene McCarthy (D, Minn.) [q.v.] for President. Two years later Lloyd Bentsen, Jr., a heavily-financed conservative, defeated Yarborough in the Democratic senatorial primary. [See KENNEDY, JOHNSON Volumes]

[MLL]

YATES, EUGENE A(DAMS)
b. Nov. 7, 1880; Elizabeth, N.J.
d. Oct. 6, 1957; New York, N.Y.
Chairman of the Board. The Southern Company, Inc., 1950-57.

Born in Elizabeth, N.J., Eugene Yates graduated from Rutgers University in 1902 with a B.S. in civil engineering. He became chairman of the board of The Southern Co., Inc., in 1950. In 1954 Yates joined Edgar H. Dixon in forming the Mississippi Valley Generating Co. to build a $107 million electric generating plant at West Memphis, Ark., to sell power to the Atomic Energy Commission. [See **DIXON, EDGAR H.**, Profile]

YORK, HERBERT F(RANK)

b. Nov. 24, 1921; Rochester, N.Y.
Chief Scientist, Advanced Research Projects Agency, Department of Defense, March 1958-February 1959; Director of Defense Research and Engineering, Department of Defense, February 1959-January 1961.

York graduated with honors in physics from the University of Rochester in 1942 and won an M.A. there the following year. During 1944-45 he participated in the electro-magnetic isotope separation program at Oak Ridge, Tenn., but left to study for a doctorate at the University of California at Berkeley. Awarded his Ph.D. in 1949, York then worked as a consultant at the Los Alamos, N.M., Scientific Laboratory. In 1951 he was appointed an assistant professor at the University of California and the following year became director of Livermore Radiation Laboratory. There he headed research programs in applied science and other classified projects underwritten by the Atomic Energy Commission until he took a leave of absence to become chief scientist of the Defense Department's Advanced Research Projects Agency (ARPA) in March 1958.

Coming in the wake of the Soviet *Sputniks* and the United State's only partially successful satellite launchings, York's appointment signaled an American effort to emphasize its space program. Soon after York joined the ARPA, the White House and Pentagon jointly announced that ARPA would undertake the coordination of plans for "lunar probes." In April 1958, before the House Select Committee on Astronautics and Space Exploration, York comprehensively outlined the ARPA space itinerary, which included the launching of five lunar probes, the sending aloft of one scientific satellite per month beginning January 1959 and especially the development of more powerful rocket engines to thrust larger satellites into orbit around the earth.

In December 1958 Eisenhower appointed York to the newly created post of director of defense research and engineering. While at that post York found himself involved in the military aspects of the space program and was often asked to defend its more controversial elements. In March 1959 a White House report prepared by the Science Advisory Committee made public details of the 1958 "Project Argus" nuclear tests in space. York denied that the project's three ionospheric bursts posed any danger of radioactive fallout, despite the fact that the tests had generated intense radioactivity, which was trapped in the earth's magnetic field.

York was also asked to explain Administration action on scientific projects. In July 1958 he backed the Administration's decision to halt the modification of some existing planes for use as atomic-powered aircraft, contending that such a makeshift project would divert funds and facilities which could be better used to develop a true atomic engine. The following month York announced the creation of a committee to expand U.S. research on the detection of underground nuclear explosions. In September York explained the Air Force's assumption of the prime space role in the U.S. missile and space program.

York eschewed the development of military-scientific projects simply for their own sake. In February 1961 Navy witnesses before the House Science and Astronautics Committee protested that York had slashed funds for the development of the "Sea Scout" solid-fueled rocket, based on the Polaris missile design and used as a satellite launching vehicle. York had opposed the rate of construction and funding of the entire Polaris missile system. In urging such restraint, York's main argument was that development of the Polaris missile ought to precede accelerated construction of the Polaris submarine.

After leaving the Pentagon in 1961, York became chancellor of the University of California at San Diego. President John F. Kennedy appointed him to the General Advisory Committee of the U.S. Arms Control and Disarmament Agency in 1962. During the 1960s and 1970s he consistently expressed his opposition to the U.S.-USSR arms race. In 1970 he published *Race to Oblivion: A Participant's View of the Arms Race*, which detailed his view of the weakness of the antiballistic missile. In 1972 York aided Sen. George McGovern's (D, S.D.) campaign as cochairman of its national security panel and supported the Senator's announced intention of reducing "wasteful and dangerous elements" in the defense budget.

[RJB]

YOUNG, MILTON R(UBEN)
b. Dec. 6, 1897: Berlin, N.D.
Republican Senator, N.D., 1945- .

After graduating from high school in 1915, Young studied at North Dakota Agricultural College and at Graceland College in Iowa. He subsequently became a grain farmer and real estate dealer in the southeastern area of his native state. In 1932 Young won a seat in the lower house of the state legislature, and two years later he was elected to the state Senate. He served in the upper house until March 1945, when he was appointed to a U.S. Senate vacancy. Young won a special election in June 1946 to complete the term, and in 1950 he was elected to a full term by a more than two-to-one majority. Generally conservative in his voting, Young supported the Taft-Hartley Act of 1947, the Internal Security Act of 1950 and the McCarran Act of 1952. As a senator from one of the nation's leading wheat-producing states, he was also one of the foremost advocates of high price supports for agricultural products. [See TRUMAN Volume]

Young was a strong critic of President Dwight D. Eisenhower's Secretary of Agriculture, Ezra Taft Benson [q.v.], who favored a flexible system of supports. In February 1953 Benson, anticipating the Administration's agricultural program, set off a storm of controversy when he declared that price supports "encourage uneconomic production" and should be used only as "disaster insurance." The following October Young called for Benson's resignation. During debate over the Administration's omnibus farm bill in 1954, Young asserted that "the lowering of price supports . . . will re-sult in drastically reduced prices received by farmers" and warned that it would "hurt the Republicans in farm states." He voted for a House-amended version of the bill setting the minimum support level at 80%, but he opposed the final conference bill, which set the minimum at 75%.

In 1956 Young successfully amended a farm bill to establish 90% support for millable varieties of wheat for that year. Three years later, during debate over a wheat bill, he warned that the Administration's plan for reducing supports would ruin all but large farmers and would cut the wheat support price in his state from $1.81 per bushel to $1.30. Young voted for a bill offering farmers the alternatives of 90% support and a 25% acreage reduction or 50% support and no restriction on acreage. The President, however, vetoed the measure.

On non-agricultural issues Young usually voted with the conservatives of his party. In February 1954 he voted for the Bricker amendment, which would have imposed limits on the President's treaty-making powers. The following December Young opposed the censure of Sen. Joseph R. McCarthy (R, Wisc.) [q.v.]. In June 1956 he joined a coalition of Southern Democrats and conservative Republicans to add $1.16 billion to the appropriations voted by the House for the Air Force.

In February 1956 Young voted for a bill to exempt independent gas producers from federal price regulation. President Eisenhower vetoed the measure the same month after it was revealed that gas lobbyists were exerting improper influence upon Congress. A North Dakota newspaper declared that Young had "sold out" by supporting the bill. Young, who faced an election later that year, demanded an investigation. The editor of the newspaper appeared in late May before a special Senate panel investigating corrupt practices and declared that the charge had not been meant literally. The probe was dropped, and Young was reelected the following November by 108,000 to 63,000 votes.

Young received national attention in 1961 when he declared that the John Birch Society was gaining influence within North

Dakota Republican circles. In 1962 he was the only Republican who voted for the Administration's bill providing for strict control of wheat and feed grain production. Young was reelected in 1962, 1968 and 1974. [See KENNEDY, JOHNSON NIXON/ FORD Volumes]

[MLL]

ZWICKER, RALPH W(ISE)
b. April 17, 1903
Army officer

A graduate of the U.S. Military Academy at West Point and a much-decorated veteran of World War II, Gen. Zwicker became a key figure in the 1954 events that brought the Eisenhower Administration into confrontation with Sen. Joseph R. McCarthy (R, Wisc.) [q.v.].

Beginning in the fall of 1953 the Senate Government Operations Committee's Permanent Investigations Subcommittee, chaired by McCarthy, intensified its investigations of alleged subversive activity in the Army. It demanded access to the Army's loyalty-security files and summoned officers for questioning. On Jan. 30, 1954 the panel questioned Maj. Irving Peress [q.v.], an Army dentist under Zwicker's command at Camp Kilmer, N.J., who had been promoted while his loyalty was in question. Three days later the Army granted Peress an honorable discharge. The action was taken in spite of McCarthy's demand that the Major, who he insisted was a Communist, be courtmartialed. On Feb. 18 the subcommittee asked Zwicker to name the officers responsible for Peress's discharge. When he refused, on the advice of Army counsel John G. Adams [q.v.], McCarthy denounced him as "not fit to wear that uniform" and lacking "the brains of a five-year-old."

The Army was furious over what it considered the ill treatment of Zwicker. On Feb. 20 Army Secretary Robert T. Stevens [q.v.] declared in a press statement that he had ordered the General not to appear for a scheduled second interrogation before the subcommittee because he was "unwilling to have so fine an officer . . . run the risk of further abuse." Four days later several Republican senators persuaded Stevens to agree that McCarthy had the right to question Zwicker and other Army officers. Faced with news reports terming the agreement a "capitulation" to McCarthy and under pressure from the White House, which feared that McCarthy was destroying the Army's morale, Stevens stated a week later that he would not permit officers to be "browbeaten or humiliated" by a congressional committee. McCarthy denied that he had abused Zwicker.

In July Sen. Ralph Flanders (R, Vt.) [q.v.] introduced a motion to censure McCarthy. It was based, in part, on the charge that McCarthy had exhibited "habitual contempt for people," as demonstrated in the questioning of Zwicker. This was referred to a select bipartisan committee which recommended in September that McCarthy be censured on two counts—contempt of the Senate and "reprehensible" treatment of Zwicker. During the subsequent debate, however, select committee member Sen. Francis Case (R, S.D.) announced that new evidence revealed that the Army had ignored McCarthy's urgent request to hold Peress for courtmartial before the dentist was discharged, and that, for this reason, McCarthy's treatment of Zwicker was the result of great "provocation." As a result, the Zwicker count was dropped from the final resolution approved by the Senate on Dec. 2.

Soon after his confrontation with McCarthy Zwicker was transferred to Japan, where he became assistant chief of staff for American military personnel in the Far East. In 1957, during hearings conducted by the Senate Armed Services Committee on his nomination to the rank of major general, Zwicker discussed his 1954 testimony. He admitted that he may have been uncooperative in order to avoid accidentally revealing classified information. The Committee ignored McCarthy's demand that Zwicker be indicted for perjury, and the nomination was approved with only McCarthy and Sen. George W. Malone (R, Nev.) dissenting.

[TLH]

Appendix

CHRONOLOGY

1951

OCT. 16—Sen. Robert A. Taft announces his candidacy for the Republican presidential nomination.

1952

JAN. 6—Sen. Henry Cabot Lodge enters Gen. Dwight D. Eisenhower's name in the New Hampshire Republican presidential primary.

JAN. 23—Sen. Estes Kefauver announces his candidacy for the Democratic presidential nomination.

MARCH 11—Eisenhower wins the New Hampshire Republican presidential primary with 50.4% of the vote. Taft garners 38.9%.

MARCH 18—In the Minnesota primary Eisenhower polls 108,692 write-in votes to 129,076 for favorite-son candidate Harold Stassen. The result convinces Eisenhower to seek the Republican presidential nomination.

MARCH 29—President Harry S. Truman announces he will not seek reelection.

APRIL 22—In the Pennsylvania primary Eisenhower receives over 847,420 votes, a figure larger than the combined totals of his Democratic and Republican opponents.

MAY 27—The Texas State GOP Convention selects rival Taft and Eisenhower delegations to the Republican National Convention despite wide majorities won by Eisenhower delegates in local party conventions.

JUNE 2—Eisenhower retires from the Army to campaign for the Republican presidential nomination.

JULY 2—At the Republican Governors Convention in Houston, Tex., 23 governors, including three Taft supporters, sign a manifesto urging that contested delegates be kept from voting on the seating of others at the National Convention. The move favors Eisenhower forces.

JULY 7—The Republican National Convention opens in Chicago. It is the first presidential nominating convention to be televised nationally.

JULY 9—In a key test of disputed delegates, the Republican National Convention votes to seat a Georgia delegation favoring Eisenhower. Eisenhower delegates from six other states, Texas, Florida, Mississippi, Kansas and Missouri are subsequently seated.

JULY 11—Eisenhower defeats Taft for the Republican presidential nomination on the first ballot. Sen. Richard M. Nixon is chosen the vice presidential candidate.

JULY 19—The Democratic National Committee approves a loyalty oath requiring each delegation to "exert every honorable means" to get the Party's nominees on its state ballot.

JULY 21—The Democratic National Convention opens in Chicago.

JULY 24-25—The Louisiana, South Carolina and Virginia delegations to the Democratic National Convention win full voting rights despite their refusal to take the loyalty pledge.

JULY 25—Puerto Rico becomes a U.S. commonwealth.

JULY 26—Gov. Adlai E. Stevenson is drafted as the Democratic presidential nominee on the third ballot. Sen. John J. Sparkman is chosen as the vice presidential candidate.

AUG. 22—At a Denver, Colo., news conference, Eisenhower says that he would not give blanket endorsement to Sen. Joseph R.

McCarthy, but he would back any Republican candidate for Congress.

AUG. 25—Eisenhower tells the American Legion Convention in New York that the U.S. should help the people of Communist countries "liberate" themselves. He omits a passage in his prepared text assailing "character assassins" and promoters of "witch hunts," a veiled reference to McCarthy.

SEPT. 23—In a nationally televised address, later known as the "Checkers Speech," Nixon defends himself against charges that he had accepted money from a secret political fund.

OCT. 3—Eisenhower delivers a campaign address in Milwaukee, Wisc., deleting a portion praising Gen. George C. Marshall, an old friend under attack by McCarthy.

OCT. 24—Eisenhower announces that he will go to Korea if elected.

NOV. 1—The U.S. tests the world's first hydrogen (fusion) bomb.

NOV. 4—Eisenhower defeats Stevenson in the presidential election by over six million votes and receives 442 of 531 electoral votes. The Republicans gain control of both houses of Congress by very narrow margins: 221 to 211 in the House and 48 to 47 in the Senate. There is one independent in each house.

DEC. 2-5—Fulfilling his campaign pledge, Eisenhower visits Korea.

1953

JAN. 20—Eisenhower is inaugurated 34th President of the U.S.

FEB. 2—In his State of the Union address, Eisenhower announces that there is no "sense or logic" in the U.S. assuming "defensive responsibilities on behalf of Chinese

Communists." He will therefore, withdraw the Seventh Fleet from the Formosa Strait between Taiwan and mainland China. He also announces that he will let wage and price controls end by April 30.

FEB. 4—McCarthy begins a loyalty-security probe of the State Department.

FEB. 11—Eisenhower refuses to grant executive clemency to Ethel and Julius Rosenberg, under death sentences for transmitting atomic secrets to the USSR.

FEB. 20—Dulles submits the Captive Peoples Resolution to Congress. It rejects "any interpretations or applications" of secret World War II agreements "which have been perverted to bring about the subjugation of free peoples" and deplores Soviet "totalitarian imperialism" in Eastern Europe.

FEB. 28—The Senate Permanent Investigations Subcommittee, chaired by McCarthy, opens televised hearings on subversion in the Voice of America.

MARCH 4—Dulles announces his acceptance of the resignation of State Department China expert John Carter Vincent, under attack by McCarthy.

MARCH 5—Marshal Josef Stalin dies.

MARCH 7—Congress shelves the Captive Peoples Resolution following the announcement of Stalin's death.

MARCH 9—Rep. Harold Velde suggests investigation of subversive influences among the clergy.

MARCH 27—Despite strong opposition, the Senate confirms Charles Bohlen as ambassador to the Soviet Union. Conservatives had accused Bohlen of being part of the "Truman-Acheson policy of appeasement" toward the USSR.

APRIL 2—Japan and the U.S. sign a 10-year treaty of friendship, commerce and navigation.

APRIL 4-21—McCarthy aides Roy Cohn

and G. David Schine tour Europe in search of subversive literature in U.S. Information Agency libraries.

APRIL 11—The Federal Security Agency is elevated to cabinet rank as the Department of Health, Education and Welfare.

APRIL 20—The Subversive Activities Control Board determines that the U.S. Communist Party is a subversive political organization controlled by the Soviet Union and orders it to register as such with the Attorney General.

APRIL 27—Eisenhower issues Executive Order 10450, instituting a strict loyalty-security program for the executive branch.

MAY 19—In a nationwide address, Eisenhower calls for a six month extension of the excess profits tax beyond June 30, 1953.

MAY 22—Eisenhower signs the Tidelands Oil bill, giving coastal states title to offshore oil.

JUNE 14—In a speech at Dartmouth College, Eisenhower assails "book burning," a reference to the Cohn and Schine European trip.

JUNE 17—Workers in East Germany riot to protest factory speedups and food shortages. Russian tanks are brought in to quell the uprising.

JUNE 19—The Rosenbergs are executed for giving atomic secrets to the USSR.

JULY 2—The Senate Foreign Relations Committee approves a resolution praising the East Germans' "patriotic defiance of Communist tyranny" and calling for German unification on the basis of free elections.

JULY 9—Eisenhower denounces an article

by McCarthy aide J.B. Matthews charging Protestant clergymen with forming "the largest single group supporting the Communist apparatus."

JULY 10—The Senate Permanent Investigations Subcommittee's three Democratic members, Sens. Henry Jackson, John McClellan and Stuart Symington, resign in protest after the panel votes to give McCarthy sole power to hire and fire staff members.

JULY 27—The U.S. and North Korea sign an armistice at Panmunjom. The treaty calls for a demilitarized zone along the 38th parallel and the voluntary repatriation of prisoners of war.

JULY 31—Taft dies of cancer.

AUG. 7—Eisenhower signs the refugee relief bill, permitting 214,000 over-quota refugees to enter the U.S. during the next three years.

AUG. 12—The USSR explodes its first hydrogen bomb.

AUG. 19—The House Un-American Activities Committee releases its report on organized Communism in the U.S. The report recommends that membership in the Communist Party be considered as prima facie evidence of violation of the Smith Act and urges legislation to prohibit misuse of the Bill of Rights to withhold information from congressional committees.

AUG. 19-22—A coup, engineered by the Central Intelligence Agency (CIA), overthrows the leftist government of Premier Mohammad Mossadegh in Iran and installs a pro-Western regime loyal to Shah Pahlevi.

AUG. 31—McCarthy begins an investigation of possible Communist infiltration in the Armed Forces.

SEPT. 10—Secretary of Labor Martin P. Durkin resigns because of the Administration's failure to revise the Taft-Hartley Act.

SEPT. 22—The American Federation of Labor expels the International Longshoremen's Association for failing to rid itself of corruption.

OCT. 5—Earl Warren is sworn in as Chief Justice of the U.S.

OCT. 23—The White House announces that in the first four months of its new security program, 1456 persons have been dropped from the federal payroll. (863 were dismissed and 593 resigned when notified of "unfavorable" reports about them.)

NOV. 6—Attorney General Herbert Brownell, Jr., charges that Truman promoted Harry Dexter White to U.S. executive director of the International Monetary Fund (IMF) in 1946, despite the fact that he knew White was a "Russian spy."

NOV. 16—In a nationwide radio-TV broadcast Truman defends his actions and charges that the Eisenhower Administration is "embracing McCarthyism for political advantage."

DEC. 3—Eisenhower orders Dr. J. Robert Oppenheimer's security clearance suspended pending a review.

DEC. 4-7—President Eisenhower, British Prime Minister Winston Churchill and French Premier Joseph Laniel confer in Bermuda on the exchange of atomic information.

DEC. 8—Eisenhower delivers his "Atoms for Peace" speech at the U.N., proposing the creation of an international atomic energy agency to pool resources for the peaceful development of nuclear energy.

1954

JAN. 11—Eisenhower sends Congress a controversial farm program recommending flexible price supports.

JAN. 12—Secretary of State John Foster Dulles announces a policy of "massive retaliation," the use of strategic nuclear weapons as America's primary line of defense.

JAN. 21—The Navy launches the first nuclear powered submarine the *S.S. Nautilus.*

JAN. 26—Sens. Jackson, McClellan and Symington resume membership in the Senate Permanent Investigations Subcommittee after McCarthy capitulates to their demands for a greater role in subcommittee investigations.

FEB. 2—McCarthy demands the courtmartial of Army dentist Irving Peress for his early affiliation with left-wing organizations.

FEB. 8—In *Irvine v. California*, the Supreme Court holds that evidence gained through electronic surveillance is admissible in jury trials.

FEB. 10—Eisenhower tells newsmen that he can conceive of no greater tragedy than for the U.S. to become involved in all-out war in Indochina.

FEB. 18—The Berlin Conference of foreign ministers fails to reach an agreement on the reunification of Germany.

FEB. 18—During an investigation of alleged subversion in the Army, McCarthy accuses the Army of "coddling Communists" and disparages Gen. Ralph W. Zwicker as "not fit to wear that uniform" and lacking "the brains of a five year old child."

FEB. 26—By a vote of 50-42, the Senate defeats the Bricker amendment, which would have limited the President's treaty-making powers.

MARCH 1—Firing from the House visitors' gallery, three Puerto Rican nationalists wound five congressmen.

MARCH 1—U.S. sets off its second hydrogen bomb at Bikini Atoll in the Pacific Ocean. The force of the explosion inadvertently exposes 379 persons to radiation, including 23 Japanese fishermen seriously burned on a ship 70-90 miles from the blast center.

MARCH 8—The U.S. and Japan sign a mutual defense treaty, providing for the gradual rearmament of Japan.

MARCH 9—On "See It Now," Edward R. Murrow accuses McCarthy of habitually using half-truths and of repeatedly stepping over the "line between investigating and persecuting."

MARCH 11—The Army releases a report listing the dates on which the status of Private G. David Schine was discussed by Army officials and the Senator or members of McCarthy's subcommittee staff. The next day McCarthy accuses the Army of "blackmail" and of "trying to use Schine as a hostage to pressure us to stop our hearings on the Army."

MARCH 13—The Organization of American States adopts a U.S. sponsored resolution calling for joint action against any Latin American state falling under Communist control.

MARCH 20—French Chief of Staff Gen. Paul Henry Ely flies to Washington seeking direct U.S. military aid for the beleaguered French garrison at Dien Bien Phu in northern Vietnam.

MARCH 24—Eisenhower announces that Southeast Asia is "of the most transcendent importance to the United States and the Free World."

MARCH 29—Dulles calls for united action in Indochina.

MARCH 31—Eisenhower signs a bill providing for an estimated $999 million annual reduction in federal excise taxes.

APRIL 14—The Army files formal charges with the Senate Permanent Investigations Subcommittee, accusing McCarthy and Cohn of trying to obtain preferential treatment for Schine "by improper means."

APRIL 20—McCarthy denounces Army charges against him and charges Assistant Secretary of Defense Struve Hensel with malfeasance and attempting to try to interfere with his subcommittee's investigation of the Army.

APRIL 22-JUNE 17—The Senate Permanent Investigations Subcommittee holds public hearings into conflicting charges made by the Army and McCarthy.

APRIL 26—The Geneva Conference on Korea and Indochina opens with foreign ministers of 19 nations, including Communist China, present.

MAY 4—Dulles withdraws from the Geneva Convention after his plan for a South Asian defense alliance fails.

MAY 7—The French garrison at Dien Bien Phu surrenders after a 55 day seige.

MAY 13—Eisenhower signs a bill authorizing the joint U.S.-Canadian construction of the St. Lawrence Seaway.

MAY 17—In *Brown v. Board of Education*, the Supreme Court unanimously rules that segregated schools are "inherently unequal."

MAY 24—The Supreme Court upholds a provision of the Internal Security Act of 1950 making past membership in the Communist Party grounds for deportation.

JUNE 9—Army counsel Joseph Welch reproaches McCarthy for "cruelty and recklessness" in trying to "assassinate" the reputation of Frederick Fisher, a member of Welch's Boston law firm.

JUNE 11—Sen. Ralph Flanders introduces a resolution to remove McCarthy from his committee chairmanships until he answers charges stemming from his action in the 1952 election.

JUNE 14—Eisenhower signs legislation to add the words "under God" to the Pledge of Allegiance to the Flag.

JUNE 18-25—A CIA implemented coup takes place in Guatemala, ousting the leftist government of Jacobo Arbenz.

JUNE 29—In a controversial 4-1 decision, the Atomic Energy Commission refuses to reinstate Dr. J. Robert Oppenheimer's security clearance for access to classified information on nuclear technology. The verdict is based on "proof of fundamental defects in his character" and his associations with Communists.

JULY 10—Eisenhower signs Public Law 480, providing for foreign disposal of surplus farm commodities.

JULY 21—The Geneva Conference on Indochina ends with the signing of the Geneva Accords, partitioning Vietnam at the 17th parallel and providing for unified elections within two years.

JULY 22—Eisenhower signs the Chemical Amendments of 1954 (Miller Act) designed to protect consumers from chemical residues left in food products by setting "poison residue tolerances."

JULY 30—Flanders introduces a resolution charging McCarthy with "personal contempt" of the Senate for refusing to answer questions about finances and for the "frivolous and irresponsible" conduct of his aides.

AUG. 2—Eisenhower signs the Housing Act of 1954 providing funds for 35,000 houses to serve families displaced by various urban redevelopment programs.

AUG. 2—The Senate votes to refer the Flanders resolution to a select bipartisan committee of "neutral" senators headed by Sen. Arthur V. Watkins.

AUG. 4—Eisenhower signs the Watershed Protection and Flood Prevention Act of 1954, authorizing federal aid in construction of small watershed projects to prevent floods and conserve soil.

AUG. 5—Eisenhower signs the Reed Act, establishing a $200 million loan fund from which states with high unemployment could draw to pay unemployment insurance.

AUG. 10—Eisenhower signs the Securities Information bill permitting greater distribution of information on new investment security issues.

AUG. 16—Eisenhower signs the Internal Revenue Code of 1954, cutting personal taxes by up to $1.36 billion and moving the deadline for personal income tax returns from March 15 to April 15.

AUG. 20—Eisenhower signs the Immunity Act of 1954, allowing congressional committees to grant immunity from prosecution to witnesses giving self-incriminatory testimony in security cases. Critics charge the measure forces witnesses to testify or go to jail.

AUG. 23—Eisenhower vetoes a bill providing a 5% increase in the salaries of federal employes.

AUG. 24—Eisenhower signs the communist control bill of 1954, outlawing the Communist Party and making its members subject to the provisions and penalties of the Internal Security Act of 1950.

AUG. 28—Eisenhower signs the 1954 agricultural bill, instituting a flexible scale of farm support prices to stem overproduction of surplus crops.

AUG. 30—Eisenhower signs the 1954 atomic energy bill, permitting private industry to use nuclear fuels and build and operate nuclear power plants.

AUG. 31-SEPT. 13—The Watkins Committee holds hearings on the censure of McCarthy.

SEPT. 3—Communist China begins heavy shelling of the Pescadores islands claimed by Nationalist China.

SEPT. 3—Eisenhower signs the espionage and sabotage bill of 1954, authorizing the death penalty for peacetime espionage and sabotage.

SEPT. 8—Australia, Great Britain, France, New Zealand, Pakistan, the Philippines, Thailand and the U.S. form the Southeast Asian Treaty Organization (SEATO), pledging joint action in defense of member nations. Nationalist China is excluded from the alliance.

SEPT. 27—The Watkins Committee unanimously recommends the censure of McCarthy for his conduct toward the Senate Subcommittee on Privileges and Elections during the 82nd Congress and for his treatment of Gen. Zwicker during the Army-McCarthy hearings.

NOV. 2—In mid-term elections, the Democrats gain control of Congress by 29 votes in the House and one in the Senate. They also oust Republicans from eight state governorships.

NOV. 5—Dulles announces the dismissal of career diplomat John Paton Davies, Jr., who had been attacked by McCarthy.

NOV. 11—The Atomic Energy Commission (AEC) signs the Dixon-Yates contract permitting a private utility combine to build a generating plant in the Tennessee Valley to feed power into the Tennessee Valley Authority system and supply the Atomic Energy Commission's installations in the area.

NOV. 23—The Dow Jones Industrial average regains its 1929 peak of 381.

DEC. 2—The U.S. and Nationalist China sign a mutual defense treaty, pledging American retaliation if Communist China attacks Formosa.

DEC. 2—The Senate votes, 67-22, to condemn McCarthy for obstructing the elections subcommittee in 1952, abusing Sen. Watkins and the Select Committee to Study Censure and insulting the Senate during the censure proceedings.

DEC. 11—Eisenhower creates a Council of Foreign Economic Policy, headed by Joseph M. Dodge, to coordinate foreign aid activities and develop foreign economic policies.

DEC. 28—Dulles indicates at a press conference that aggression in Western Europe would be met with tactical atomic weapons.

1955

JAN. 1—U.S. Foreign Operations Administration begins to supply direct financial aid to South Vietnam, Cambodia and Laos.

JAN. 10—Eisenhower asks Congress for new powers to reduce foreign trade barriers, including a three year extension of the Reciprocal Trade Agreements Act.

JAN. 13—Eisenhower asks Congress to inaugurate a military reserve plan, extend the Selective Service System and to raise military pay, allowances and benefits.

JAN. 28—Congress passes the Formosa Resolution, giving Eisenhower discretionary powers to use U.S. forces in the defense of Formosa and the Pescadores Islands. It is the first time Congress has granted a President such war-making powers in peacetime.

FEB. 8—Eisenhower proposes a 3-year $7 billion federal-state-local school construction program to Congress.

FEB. 18—Sen. Lister Hill accuses Adolphe Wenzell, a Bureau of the Budget consultant, of conflict of interest in connection with the Dixon-Yates contract. He also denounces Budget Director Rowland Hughes for concealing Wenzell's actions.

FEB. 23—Eisenhower states that the U.S. would stop testing atomic weapons only under a workable disarmament agreement with effective international inspection.

MARCH 23—By voice vote the House adopts a minimum standard of conduct for House Committee investigations. It bars "one-man hearings" and assures witnesses the right to counsel and the opportunity to rebut testimony tending to "defame, degrade or incriminate" them.

MARCH 31—Eisenhower signs a bill providing for an increase of $745 million annually in military pay and allowances.

APRIL 12—Scientists announce that the Salk vaccine is "safe, effective and potent" in preventing polio.

APRIL 20—During testimony before a Senate Judiciary subcommittee, dismissed State Department special adviser on refugees Edward J. Corsi charges that the management of the Refugee Relief Act of 1953 is "a national scandal" and that the emphasis on security investigation of refugees had made their admission incidental.

APRIL 21—The U.S. ends its occupation of Germany.

MAY 9—West Germany is admitted to full membership in the North Atlantic Treaty Organization (NATO).

MAY 15—The U.S., Great Britain, France and the USSR sign a peace treaty with Austria, granting it full independence in return for political neutrality.

MAY 26—The Senate Banking and Currency Committee issues its report on the rise of stock market prices in 1954. The panel describes an "increase in unhealthy speculative developments," and it recommends tightening existing federal regulations and undertaking further study of abuses.

MAY 31—In *Brown v. Board of Education,* the Supreme Court implements its earlier school desegregation decision placing the burden on local authorities to integrate the schools "with all deliberate speed."

JUNE 21—The reciprocal trade program is extended for 3 years.

JUNE 30—In his second U.N. speech, Eisenhower calls for a "new kind of peace," in which the atom will be used for productive purposes.

JUNE 30—A 12-hour steel strike of 600,000 workers is settled with an hourly wage increase averaging 15¢. Steel prices increase an average of $7.50 a ton.

JUNE 30—The Second Hoover Commission submits its final report, recommending that government not compete with the private sector.

JUNE 30—Eisenhower signs a bill authorizing an increase of $6 billion in the public debt.

JULY 1—Eisenhower signs a bill requiring the inscription "In God We Trust" on all currency.

JULY 11—Following an announcement that the city of Memphis has voted to build its own electrical generating plant, Eisenhower cancels the Dixon-Yates contract.

JULY 18-23—President Dwight D. Eisenhower, Premier Nikolai Bulganin, Prime Minister Winston Churchill and Premier Edgar Faure hold a summit conference at Geneva. The major topic is German unification.

JULY 21—Eisenhower submits his "Open Skies" proposal at the Geneva summit conference. He suggests that the USSR and the U.S. exchange military blueprints and allow mutual air reconnaissance over their military installations.

AUG. 1—Air Force Secretary Harold E. Talbott resigns following a Senate Permanent Investigations Subcommittee probe of his activities in promoting Defense Department contracts with the Paul Mulligan Co., of which he is part owner.

AUG. 4—Rejecting proposals for federal construction of a single high dam at Hell's Canyon on the Snake River, the Federal Power Commission grants the private Idaho Power Co. a 50-year license to build and operate three low hydroelectric dams in the same area.

AUG. 8—The first conference on the peaceful uses of atomic energy opens in Geneva. Seventy-three nations are represented.

AUG. 9—Eisenhower signs a bill creating a 12-member bipartisan commission to review the government's loyalty-security program.

AUG. 12—Eisenhower signs the poliomyelitis vaccination bill, providing free vaccine for children under 20 and pregnant women, regardless of ability to pay.

AUG. 28—Emmett Till, a 15-year-old black, is kidnapped after allegedly propositioning a white woman. Three days later his body is recovered from the Tallahatchie River. An all-white jury later acquits the two white men accused of the murder.

SEPT. 24—Eisenhower suffers a "moderately severe" heart attack.

SEPT. 30—Film actor James Dean, symbol of alienated youth, dies in a car crash.

OCT. 27—The foreign ministers of the U.S., Great Britain, France and the USSR meet in Geneva to discuss disarmament, German unification and East-West relations.

NOV. 15—Adlai Stevenson announces that he will be a candidate for the Democratic nomination for President in 1956.

NOV. 25—The Interstate Commerce Commission bans racial segregation on interstate trains and buses.

DEC. 1—Rosa Parks is arrested for refusing to give up her bus seat to a white man in Montgomery, Ala.

DEC. 5—Under the direction of Martin Luther King, Jr., Montgomery, Ala., blacks begin a 54-week boycott of city buses.

DEC. 5—The American Federation of Labor and the Congress of Industrial Organizations merge. George Meany becomes president of the new organization.

DEC. 16—Kefauver announces his candidacy for the Democratic presidential nomination.

1956

JAN. 5—In his State of the Union address, Eisenhower makes his first civil rights request, recommending the creation of a bipartisan commission to investigate denial of voting rights.

JAN. 13—Eisenhower names a panel of eight prominent citizens, headed by James Killian, to monitor the activities of the CIA.

JAN. 16—In a *Life* magazine interview, Dulles defends his "brinkmanship" policies, saying that the U.S. has gone "to the verge of war" to maintain peace. He states that "the ability to get to the verge without getting into the war is the necessary art." "We walked to the brink, and we looked it in the face."

JAN. 24—At a conference in Richmond, Va., four Southern governors endorse the doctrine of interposition. They pledge the use of state power to prevent desegregation by placing the "sovereignty of the state between local school board officials and federal courts."

FEB. 3—Autherine Lucy attempts to integrate formerly all-white University of Alabama. She is expelled four days later because her presence "threatens public order."

FEB. 6—General Services Administrator Edward Mansure resigns in the midst of a congressional probe of political influence in granting government contracts.

FEB. 17—Eisenhower vetoes a bill to free natural gas producers from direct federal rate control after Sen. Francis Case reveals that he received a $2,500 campaign contribution from persons favoring the measure.

FEB. 25—Eisenhower declares he will seek reelection.

MARCH 1—The national minimum wage is increased from 75¢ to $1 per hour.

MARCH 11—One hundred and one Southern senators and representatives issue a Declaration of Constitutional Principles, known as the "Southern Manifesto," denouncing the Supreme Court's desegregation decision and pledging to use all "lawful means" to resist it.

MARCH 13—Eisenhower and Kefauver win the New Hampshire presidential primaries. Nixon gets a heavy vote of confidence with over 22,000 write-in votes for his renomination.

MARCH 20—Kefauver scores an upset victory over Adlai E. Stevenson in the Minnesota presidential primary, winning by over 50,000 votes.

APRIL 2—In *Pennsylvania v. Nelson*, the Supreme Court rules that the Smith Act of 1940, the Internal Security Act of 1950 and the Communist Control Act of 1954 preempt state sedition laws.

APRIL 9—In *Slochower v. Board of Education*, the Supreme Court rules that a state cannot discharge an employe for invoking the Fifth Amendment before a congressional committee.

APRIL 11—The Senate rejects, 27-59, a proposal to establish a joint congressional committee to review the activities of the CIA and other intelligence operations.

APRIL 11—Eisenhower signs a bill authorizing the Upper Colorado River Project, one of the largest water projects undertaken by the federal government.

APRIL 18—The State Department announces agreement among 12 nations, including the USSR, to charter the International Atomic Energy Agency.

APRIL 26—Nixon announces that Eisenhower is "delighted" to have him on the ticket as the vice presidential candidate.

MAY 10—The Senate cites several newsmen for contempt of Congress because of their refusal to answer questions on Communism during an Internal Security Subcommittee probe into Communist penetration of the press.

MAY 28—Eisenhower signs the 1956 agricultural bill. It establishes the "Soil Bank" program to compensate farmers for land left fallow in attempts to reduce surpluses. Alternatively, farmers are permitted to contract with the Agriculture Department to convert productive land to specified conservation projects.

MAY 29—Stevenson narrowly defeats Kefauver in Florida's Democratic presidential primary.

JUNE 9—Eisenhower suffers an attack of ileitis and has emergency surgery.

JUNE 9—New York Gov. Averell Harriman announces his candidacy for the Democratic presidential nomination.

JUNE 11—In *Cole v. Young*, the Supreme Court rules that only government employes in "sensitive" positions can be dismissed as security risks.

JUNE 19—The House Special Government Activities Subcommittee files a report on its probe of the $43 million expansion of a government owned nickel project at Nicaro, Cuba. The Democratic majority finds "political and private influence" in the contract award.

JUNE 29—Eisenhower signs the highway bill of 1956, initiating the largest road-building program in U.S. history. The measure authorizes $32.4 billion for the construction of over 40,000 miles of controlled access road.

JULY 5—The House defeats a federal aid-to-education bill authorizing $1.6 billion for school construction. The defeat is, in part, attributed to a controversial Powell amendment, prohibiting aid to segregated schools.

JULY 19—At the close of fiscal year 1956, the U.S. budgetary surplus is $1.75 billion.

JULY 19—Dulles announces that the U.S. is withdrawing an offered $56 million grant for Egyptian construction of the proposed $1.3 billion Aswan High Dam.

JULY 23—The House passes an Administration civil rights bill focusing on the protection of voting rights. Parliamentary maneuvers prevent the bill from reaching the Senate floor.

JULY 23—Liberals, led by Stassen, recommend Mass. Gov. Christian A. Herter as the Republican vice presidential nominee replacing Nixon.

JULY 31—Kefauver withdraws from the race for the Democratic presidential nomination, throwing his support to Adlai Stevenson.

AUG. 16—Stevenson is selected as the Democratic Party's presidential nominee on the first ballot at the Chicago Convention. Stevenson unexpectedly throws the choice of a vice presidential running mate to the Convention.

AUG. 16—Liberals fail in an attempt to insert a strong civil rights plank in the Democratic National platform.

AUG. 17—Kefauver wins the Democratic vice presidential nomination in a dramatic two-ballot contest with Sen. John F. Kennedy.

AUG. 22—The Republican National Convention nominates Eisenhower and Nixon for reelection.

AUG. 23—The Federal Reserve Board raises the discount rate from 2¾% to 3%.

OCT. 9—Commerce and Labor Departments report that factory workers' average weekly wage is at a record $81 for the month of September, with average factory pay exceeding $2 an hour for the first time. Nonfarm employment is at a record 52,100,000; unemployment is down to 1,988,000, the lowest figure since November 1953.

OCT. 23—An armed revolt begins in Budapest, Hungary. As demanded by the rebels, the imprisoned Imre Nagy, a moderate Communist, is brought back to head the government.

OCT. 29—War breaks out in the Middle East as Israel invades the Gaza Strip and the Sinai Peninsula, driving toward the Suez Canal.

OCT. 30—A joint British-French ultimatum to Israel and Egypt demands immediate cessation of all fighting and withdrawal of military forces to positions at least 10 miles from the Suez Canal.

OCT. 31—As Anglo-French forces attack Egyptian installations around the Suez Canal Zone, Eisenhower declares himself opposed to the use of force to settle international disputes.

NOV. 2—The U.S. offers $20 million worth of food and medical supplies to Hungary.

NOV. 4—Khrushchev orders Soviet armored units to crush the Hungarian "fascists." Thirty thousand Hungarians and 7,000 Russians die in the ensuing conflict, which ends a year of unrest and dissent in the Soviet satellites.

NOV. 4—In a letter to Bulganin, Eisenhower urges "in the name of humanity and in the cause of peace" that the USSR halt the bloodshed in Hungary.

NOV. 5—The U.N. votes to organize a police force to restore peace in the Middle East.

NOV. 6—Eisenhower wins reelection in a landslide, defeating Stevenson by over nine million votes and capturing 457 out of 531 electoral votes.

NOV. 8—Eisenhower announces that he has directed the Refugee Relief Administration to speed the processing of Hungarian refugees.

NOV. 13—The Supreme Court unanimously rules the Montgomery, Ala., city ordinance requiring racial segregation in buses unconstitutional.

DEC. 6—Eisenhower orders an air and sea lift to bring 21,500 Hungarian refugees to the U.S. by Jan. 1, 1957 or shortly thereafter.

DEC. 10—Supreme Court rules that a union cannot be penalized because an officer files a false non-Communist affidavit with the National Labor Relations Board.

DEC. 31—Sociologist C. Wright Mills's book *The Power Elite* is published.

1957

JAN. 10-11—Martin Luther King, Jr., and 60 other black leaders from 10 Southern states meet in Atlanta, Ga., to form the Southern Christian Leadership Conference.

JAN. 21—Eisenhower is inaugurated as the first second term lame-duck President.

JAN. 30—The Senate adopts a resolution setting up the Select Committee on Improper Activities in the Labor or Management Field, chaired by John McClellan.

MARCH 7—Congress approves the Eisenhower Doctrine, giving the President the authority to use military force in the Middle East to preserve "the independence and integrity" of Middle Eastern nations and prevent "overt armed aggression from . . . international Communism."

MARCH 24—Eisenhower and British Prime Minister Harold Macmillan issue a joint communique, after four day conference at Bermuda, stating that the U.S. has agreed to supply guided missiles to Great Britain.

MARCH 26-27—Teamster Union President Dave Beck testifies before the McClellan Committee on Teamster links to organized crime.

APRIL 11—The House of Representatives votes to authorize $250,000 for a Special Subcommittee on Legislative Oversight to probe federal regulatory agencies.

APRIL 13—Postmaster General Arthur E. Summerfield halts Saturday Post Office operations because of Congress's failure to vote supplemental funds for the balance of the fiscal year.

APRIL 16—Normal Post Office service resumes after Eisenhower signs a $41 million supplemental appropiations bill.

APRIL 29—The Army's first nuclear power reactor is dedicated at Fort Belvoir, Va.

MAY 2—Sen. Joseph McCarthy dies of acute liver failure.

MAY 4—In testimony before the House Ways and Means Committee, Health, Education and Welfare Secretary Arthur S. Flemming proposes that the states set up federally subsidized medicare systems to provide health insurance for persons over 65.

MAY 14—The U.S. resumes military aid to Yogoslavia which had been halted because of Tito's reconciliation with the USSR.

JUNE 3—In *U.S. v. duPont*, the Supreme Court holds that duPont's acquisition of 23% of General Motors Co. stock violates the Clayton Antitrust Act.

JUNE 3—In *Jencks v. U.S.*, the Supreme Court rules that the government must permit defendants access to FBI reports forming the basis of witnesses' testimony in criminal trials.

JUNE 3-6—The U. S. formally joins the Military Committee of the Baghdad Pact at a meeting of the Council of Ministers in Karachi, Pakistan.

JUNE 17—In *Yates v. U.S.*, the Supreme Court rules that advocating an "abstract doctrine" of political revolution is not punishable under the Smith Act.

JUNE 17—In *Watkins v. U.S.* the Supreme Court overturns John Thomas Watkins's conviction for contempt of Congress. Watkins had refused to name others as Communists in testimony before the House Un-American Activities Committee.

JUNE 17—In *Sweezy v. New Hampshire*, the Supreme Court reverses the contempt conviction of a professor who had refused to answer questions concerning the content of his lectures and his earlier activities in the Progressive Party.

JULY 11—Twenty of 22 leading nuclear scientists attending a conference at Pugwash, Nova Scotia, warn that misuse of nuclear energy could lead to man's annihilation.

JULY 16—Secretary of Defense Charles Wilson orders the Armed Forces reduced by 100,000 men by the end of 1957.

JULY 20—The Southern Regional Council reports that in 11 Southern states only 25% of the eligible black voters are registered, compared with 60% of the white voters.

AUG. 12—Eisenhower signs a bill authorizing New York State to construct a $600 million power plant at Niagara Falls.

AUG. 13—The Senate Finance Committee approves a proposal, sponsored by Sen. Robert S. Kerr, under which the federal and state governments would share in paying medical expenses for needy aged persons.

AUG. 21—Eisenhower announces a U.S. offer to suspend nuclear weapons tests for two years in return for a Soviet agreement to halt production of fissionable material for weapons and to establish an inspection system.

AUG. 25—The Special Radiation Subcommittee of the Joint Atomic Energy Committee reports that the effect of radioactive fallout is negligible but might increase if atomic tests increase.

AUG. 28—Sen. Strom Thurmond stages a 24 hour 27 minute filibuster in an effort to prevent Senate passage of a civil rights bill.

AUG. 29—The Senate passes a civil rights bill focusing on voting rights.

SEPT. 1—Rev. Dr. Billy Graham's New York City crusade ends with a rally in Times Square. An estimated 2 million people attended his nightly meetings and 56,767 persons responded with "decisions for Christ."

SEPT. 4—Arkansas Gov. Orval E. Faubus orders National Guardsmen to bar nine black students from entering Little Rock's Central High School.

SEPT. 9—Eisenhower signs the 1957 Civil Rights Act, establishing a 6-man bipartisan commission with power to investigate the denial of voting rights and to study all aspects of the matter of "equal protections of the laws under the Constitution." It is the first civil rights act in 82 years.

SEPT. 14—Faubus and Eisenhower confer at Newport, R.I., on the question of school integration in Little Rock.

SEPT. 20—Faubus removes National Guardsmen from Little Rock Central High School in compliance with a federal court injunction.

SEPT. 23—Federal officers secretly escort the nine black students into the Little Rock high school building. With an enraged white mob outside and harassment of the students inside the school, they are removed after three hours.

SEPT. 24—Eisenhower federalizes the Arkansas National Guard and sends federal troops to Little Rock to enforce integration.

OCT. 4—The Soviet Union launches the first artificial earth satellite, *Sputnik*, into orbit. Americans fear a loss of world prestige.

OCT. 8—Eisenhower issues a statement expressing concern that the U.S. is no further advanced in production of intercontinental ballistic missiles.

OCT. 19—The Atomic Energy Commission reports that, according to current estimates, harm to Americans from H-bomb testing appears to be within "tolerable limits."

NOV. 7—In response to the Soviet space launching, Eisenhower appoints James Killian, president of the Massachusetts Insitute of Technology, to manage a program of scientific improvement in the U.S. defense program.

NOV. 7—The Gaither Report, leaked to the press, finds that because of increased Soviet spending, the USSR will achieve missile superiority over the U.S. by 1959. The group recommends increased military spending and the development of a fallout shelter program to meet the challenge.

NOV. 13—In a nationwide address Eisenhower proposes a considerable increase in defense appropriations to meet

the threat of scientific advances by the USSR.

NOV. 25—Sen. Lyndon Johnson's Preparedness Subcommittee of the Senate Armed Services Committee begins an inquiry into the history, status and future of the nation's missile and satellite programs.

NOV. 26—Eisenhower suffers a mild stroke.

DEC. 6—America's first attempt to launch a space satellite ends in failure as the Vanguard rocket explodes on its launch pad before a national TV audience.

DEC. 6—AFL-CIO votes overwhelmingly to expel the Teamsters Union on charges that it had failed to purge itself of corrupt leadership.

DEC. 15—Eisenhower rejects an appeal by Indian Prime Minister Jawaharlal Nehru for a halt in nuclear weapons tests.

DEC. 16-19—At the Paris NATO meeting, the U.S. convinces Great Britain, Italy and Turkey to station U.S. intermediate-range missiles on their territory.

DEC. 17—The U.S. successfully fires the Atlas, its first intercontinental ballistic missile.

DEC. 18—The first commercial nuclear electric generating plant goes into operation at Shippingport, Pa.

1958

JAN. 5—The Rockefeller Brothers Fund releases a report, prepared by Henry Kissinger, warning of massive Soviet success in improving technology and approaching military weapons parity with the U.S.

JAN. 7—Eisenhower requests Congress to appropriate an additional $1.4 billion to

speed up and expand missile and air defenses.

JAN. 9—Eisenhower's State of the Union message stresses the need for an accelerated defense effort and the reorganization of the Defense Department to curb interservice rivalry.

JAN. 12—In a letter to Bulganin Eisenhower urges that "outer space should used only for peaceful purposes."

JAN. 13—Eisenhower sends his fiscal 1959 budget to Congress. It provides for moderate increases in military spending and cutbacks in other areas.

JAN. 13—Linus Pauling releases a petition signed by 9,235 scientists, including 36 Nobel Prize laureates, calling for an international nuclear test ban.

JAN. 27—Eisenhower urges enactment of an "emergency" four year program to improve education, especially in mathematics and the sciences.

JAN. 30—Eisenhower requests Congress to extend the reciprocal trade program for five years.

JAN. 31—An Army rocket team, led by Dr. Wernher von Braun, sends the first U.S. satellite, Explorer I, into orbit.

FEB. 10—Bernard Schwartz is dismissed as chief counsel of the Special House Committee on Legislative Oversight after he accuses committee members of trying to whitewash the investigation of federal regulatory agencies.

FEB. 22—In a television address former President Harry S. Truman charges the Eisenhower Administration with bringing on the recession.

FEB. 27—Eisenhower signs a bill temporarily raising the national debt limit from $275 to $285 billion.

MARCH 5—Eisenhower vetoes a bill granting funds for the development of a nuclear powered airplane.

MARCH 31—The USSR announces a unilateral suspension of nuclear tests.

APRIL 1—Eisenhower signs the emergency housing bill to stimulate housing construction by calling for federal purchase of new home mortgages and providing additional money for federal loans on veterans' housing.

MAY 1—The Coast Guard arrests four pacifists attempting to sail their ship into the U.S. atomic testing site in the South Pacific. Protests against nuclear testing increase.

MAY 8—Eisenhower orders the removal of federalized National Guardsmen from Little Rock's Central High School.

MAY 15—Nixon returns from a stormy 18-day tour of eight South American republics. During the tour he was often assailed by anti-American mobs protesting U.S. alleged support of dictators.

MAY 20—Eisenhower delivers a nationwide radio-TV address stating that an economic upturn is in the making and promising an early decision on proposed tax reductions.

MAY 26—Eisenhower asks Congress to extend excise and corporation income taxes for one year.

JUNE 4—Eisenhower signs a bill extending unemployment benefits to counter the recession. Under the measure, the federal government grants financial aid to states to enable them to extend coverage for an average of eight weeks.

JUNE 5—The House Special Subcommittee on Legislative Oversight begins hearings on conflict-of-interest charges involving Sherman Adams.

JUNE 16—In *Kent v. Dulles*, the Supreme Court rules that the State Department cannot withhold passports to applicants because of their alleged Communist beliefs or associations.

JUNE 17—Adams denies before the House Special Subcommittee on Legislative Oversight that he had interceded with federal agencies on behalf of Bernard Goldfine. But Adams acknowledges he might have "acted more prudently" in inquiring about matters involving Goldfine.

JUNE 30—In *Crooker v. California*, the Supreme Court rejects the appeal of a man who had been forbidden to see his lawyer before giving the police a written confession.

JUNE 30—In *NAACP v. Alabama*, the Supreme Court holds that the NAACP has the right, by freedom of association, not to divulge its membership list.

JULY 1—Nuclear scientists representing the Western and Soviet blocs meet in Geneva to convene a "conference of experts to study the possibility of detecting violations of possible agreement on suspension of nuclear weapons tests."

JULY 15—Eisenhower orders U.S. Marines to Lebanon in response to an urgent request from President Camille Chamoun for assistance.

JULY 29—Eisenhower signs a bill creating the National Aeronautics and Space Administration (NASA) to direct U.S. nonmilitary space activities.

AUG. 1—New postal rates go into effect: Regular mail rises from 3¢ to 4¢ an ounce, domestic airmail from 6¢ to 7¢.

AUG. 6—Eisenhower signs a bill reorganizing the Defense Department. The measure strengthens the powers of the Secretary of Defense and creates a directorate of defense research and engineering.

AUG. 12—U.S. Marines begin withdrawing from Lebanon.

AUG. 22—Eisenhower offers to halt U.S. nuclear tests for one year. He also proposes that the nuclear powers meet in Geneva to seek an agreement on suspending nuclear tests and setting up an inspection system.

AUG. 23—Eisenhower signs a bill creating the Federal Aviation Agency to supervise air transportation safety.

AUG. 23—Communist China resumes shelling Quemoy and Matsu.

SEPT. 2—Eisenhower signs the National Defense Education Act, providing loans for college students and funds to encourage young people to enter teaching careers, particularly in higher education and the sciences.

SEPT. 2—Eisenhower signs the excise tax technical changes bill. The measure is the first important revision of the general excise tax provisions of the Internal Revenue code since 1932.

SEPT. 9—Eisenhower orders federal agencies to cut their employment levels by 2% in fiscal 1959 to absorb a pay raise voted by Congress.

SEPT. 11—On national TV Eisenhower reiterates the U.S.'s commitment to defend Quemoy and Matsu.

SEPT. 22—Accused of conflict of interest, Sherman Adams resigns as Eisenhower's chief aide.

SEPT. 25—A federal grand jury indicts former Federal Communications Commission member Richard A. Mack and Miami attorney Thurman Whiteside on charges of conspiracy to defraud the U.S.

SEPT. 27—In a state-wide referendum Arkansas voters reject school integration.

SEPT. 28—In *Cooper v. Aaron*, the Supreme Court denies a Little Rock, Ark., school board request for additional time to implement its integration plan.

OCT. 6—Peking announces a one week suspension of its bombardment of Quemoy.

OCT. 7—NASA initiates Project Mercury, its first program for manned space flight.

NOV. 4—In mid-term elections the Democrats increase their majorities in both houses of Congress. They control the Senate by 30 seats and the House by 128.

Democrats also win 26 gubernatorial races, leaving only 14 Republican governors in office.

NOV. 10—Khrushchev calls on the U.S., Great Britain and France to "give up the remnants of the occupation regime in Berlin" and implies that he will hand over USSR powers in Berlin to the East Germans if the Western allies do not withdraw troops from the city.

NOV. 11-DEC. 18—The U.S. and USSR hold an inconclusive conference on the Prevention of Surprise Attack in Geneva.

NOV. 22—The U.S. reaffirms its intention to "maintain the integrity" of West Berlin.

DEC. —The John Birch Society is founded.

DEC. 14—The U.S., Britain and France formally reject Soviet demands for their withdrawal from West Berlin.

1959

JAN. 1—Fidel Castro's guerrilla forces overthrow the Batista regime in Cuba. The revolution is greeted sympathetically in the U.S.

JAN. 2—The USSR achieves the world's first moon shot as *Lunik I* passes within a few thousand miles of the moon.

JAN. 3—Eisenhower proclaims Alaska the 49th state.

JAN. 5—The White House releases a statement by its science advisory committee questioning the reliability of techniques for detecting underground nuclear tests.

FEB. 2—Eisenhower outlines to Congress a 10-year space program to launch a satellite or space probe vehicle each month starting in mid-1959.

FEB. 5—In a special message to Congress, Eisenhower submits a seven-point civil rights program that includes support for school integration.

MARCH 23—The peacetime draft is extended until July 1, 1963.

MARCH 30—In *Abbatev v. U.S.* and *Bartkis v. Illinois*, the Supreme Court rules that a person may be tried for the same offense in federal and state courts, with no infringement on his freedom from double jeopardy.

APRIL 4—In an address at Gettysburg College, Eisenhower makes his first commitment to maintain South Vietnam as a separate national state.

APRIL 9—NASA selects seven astronauts for the Project Mercury.

APRIL 15—Suffering from terminal cancer, Dulles resigns as Secretary of State.

APRIL 25—The St. Lawrence Seaway opens.

MAY 11—The foreign ministers of the U.S., Great Britain, France and the USSR meet in Geneva to begin talks on the problems of Berlin, German reunification, an all-German peace treaty and European security.

MAY 24—Dulles dies of cancer.

JUNE 8—In *Barenblatt v. U.S.*, the Supreme Court reaffirms the right of Congress and the states to investigate Communism.

JUNE 8—Eisenhower asks Congress to abolish the interest ceiling on U.S. savings and treasury bonds and to raise the public debt limit to $295 billion.

JUNE 11—Postmaster General Arthur Summerfield bans a new unexpurgated edition of D.H. Lawrence's *Lady Chatterley's Lover* from the mails.

JUNE 17—Eisenhower refuses personal or federal agency intervention in steel industry wage negotiations.

JUNE 19—The Senate refuses to confirm Lewis Strauss as Secretary of Commerce. He is the first cabinet appointee rejected since 1925.

JUNE 27—The U.S. denounces Cuba before the Organization of American States for contributing to Caribbean tensions and for its slanderous attacks upon the U.S.

JUNE 29—In *Kingsley International Pictures v. Regents*, the Supreme Court unanimously legalizes showings of the film version of D.H. Lawrence's *Lady Chatterley's Lover*, but leaves the general question of obscenity unclear.

JUNE 30—The public debt limit is raised temporarily to $295 billion, permanently to $285 billion.

JULY 7—Sept. 10—The House Armed Services Committee holds hearings on the employment of retired military officers by industry.

JULY 15—Despite Eisenhower's call for further negotiations, 500,000 steelworkers go on strike against the 28 companies that normally produce 85%-90% of America's steel.

JULY 24—Nixon and Khrushchev engage in a political debate at a preview of the U.S. exhibition in Moscow. The discussion, held in the kitchen of a so-called typical American home, becomes known as the "kitchen debate."

AUG. 1—In a radio-TV address from Moscow, Nixon tells the Soviet people that they will continue to live in an era of fear, suspicion and tension if Khrushchev tries to promote the Communization of countries outside the USSR.

AUG. 12—Four Little Rock public high schools, closed since 1958 to avoid integration, reopen.

AUG. 21—Hawaii is officially proclaimed the 50th state.

AUG. 31—The Joint Atomic Energy Committee's Special Subcommittee on Radiation issues a report concluding that further nuclear tests could be hazardous and urging the establishment of a national civil defense system.

SEPT. 8—The Civil Rights Commission issues its first report on voting rights. It finds that only 25% of eligible black voters are registered in 10 Southern states and outlines a dozen specific legislative measures to assure blacks their full voting rights.

SEPT. 10—Congress overrides Eisenhower's veto of the 1959 public works bill.

SEPT. 14—Eisenhower signs a bill exempting TV and radio news from having to provide equal time to all competing political candidates in cases where one has appeared in a newscast or interview.

SEPT. 14—Eisenhower signs the Labor Management Reporting and Disclosure Act (Landrum-Griffin Act) designed to surpress corruption in unions. It also includes provisions protecting members from unfair actions by their unions and revises the ban on secondary boycotts.

SEPT. 15—Soviet Premier Khrushchev arrives in the U.S. on a good-will visit.

SEPT. 25-17—Agreements made during congenial talks between Khrushchev and Eisenhower at Camp David, Md., prepare the way for a summit meeting the following year.

OCT. 1—Federal taxes on gasoline are increased by 1¢ per gallon to finance the national highway program.

OCT. 12—The U.S. places an embargo on all exports to Cuba, except medical supplies and food.

OCT. 19—The U.S. Development Loan Fund releases a major policy statement announcing that future loans to underdeveloped countries must be spent on U.S. goods.

OCT. 21—District Judge Herbert Sorg signs an 80-day Taft-Hartley injunction ordering the United Steelworkers to halt their 99-day strike.

OCT. 26—Eisenhower announces his firm intention to defend the U.S. naval base at Guantanamo, Cuba.

NOV. 3—Panamanian nationalists riot over U.S. domination of the Panama Canal Zone.

NOV. 6—The Senate Subcommittee on Legislative Oversight concludes hearings on rigged TV quiz shows. No indictments are handed down although several contestants, including Charles Van Doren, testified that they were coached on answers and told when to lose.

NOV. 7—The Supreme Court upholds an 80-day Taft-Hartley injunction halting the 116-day steel strike.

DEC. 1—The U.S., USSR and 10 other nations sign the Antarctic Treaty, establishing a nuclear-free zone around the Antarctic ice mass and setting up inspection and enforcement procedures.

DEC. 3—Eisenhower embarks on an 11 nation good-will tour of Europe, Asia and North Africa.

DEC. 30—The Navy commissions the S.S. *George Washington*, the first nuclear powered submarine designed to fire Polaris missiles.

DEC. 30—Sen. Hubert Humphrey begins his campaign for the 1960 presidential nomination.

1960

JAN. 2—Kennedy announces his candidacy for the Democratic presidential nomination.

JAN. 4—Negotiators for the United Steelworkers and 11 major steel producers reach an agreement on a new contract.

JAN. 9—Nixon announces his candidacy for the Republican presidential nomination.

JAN. 19—The U.S. and Japan sign the Mutual Security Treaty under which both countries pledge to maintain and develop their capacities to resist armed attacks.

JAN. 26—Formally restating U.S. policy, Eisenhower reaffirms that there will be no reprisals against Cuba or intervention in its internal affairs.

FEB. 1—Black students quietly sit in at segregated lunch counters in Greensboro, N.C.

FEB. 22-MARCH 7—Eisenhower undertakes a four nation goodwill tour of Latin America.

MARCH 8—Kennedy wins the New Hampshire Democratic primary with a record 42,969 votes.

MARCH 10—Federal Communications Commission chairman John Charles Doerfer resigns effective March 14, as a result of conflict-of-interest charges raised by the Special House Subcommittee on Legislative Oversight.

MARCH 15—The Ten-Nation Disarmament Conference begins in Geneva.

MARCH 15—Eisenhower meets with West German Chancellor Konrad Adenauer at the White House, assuring him of U.S. support in maintaining the freedom of West Berlin.

MARCH 16—Eisenhower endorses Nixon as his successor.

MARCH 17—Eisenhower formally approves a CIA plan to train Cuban emigrés for an invasion of the island.

MARCH 31—The House Ways and Means Committee kills the Forand plan to provide hospital and nursing home care for the elderly, financed through Social Security.

APRIL 1—U.S. launches *Tiros I*, the first weather satellite, to receive televised pictures of cloud cover over the earth's surface.

APRIL 3—Daniel Bell's *The End of Ideology: On the Exhaustion of Political Ideas in the Fifties* is published.

APRIL 8—Senate, by a vote of 71-18, passes a civil rights bill that gives increased authority to the federal courts and Civil Rights Commission to prevent the intimidation of black voters in the South.

APRIL 22—In a television speech Castro charges that the U.S. is plotting to overthrow his government.

APRIL 26—Kennedy wins the Pennsylvania Democratic presidential primary by 49,838 votes.

MAY 1—Francis Gary Powers, on a U-2 reconnaissance flight for the CIA, is shot down over the USSR by a surface to air missile.

MAY 2—Caryl Chessman is executed for first degree rape at San Quentin prison, Calif., despite worldwide protests.

MAY 3—A spokesman for NASA announces that a U-2 "research airplane," gathering weather data for NASA and the Air Force Weather Service, had apparently crashed in Turkey.

MAY 5—Khrushchev reveals that an American aircraft has been shot down over Soviet air space and angrily declares it an act of "aggressive provocation." Two days later he produces Powers's confession and the U-2 plane.

MAY 7—Eisenhower announces that the U.S. will resume underground nuclear testing as part of research on detecting such blasts.

MAY 7—The State Department admits that the U-2 plane was "probably" endeavouring to obtain intelligence information.

MAY 9—Secretary of State Christian Herter strongly defends the need for the aerial intelligence program to counter the USSR's ability to prepare secretly for a surprise attack.

MAY 9—The Federal Drug Administration approves Enovid, an oral contraceptive for women, safe for public sale.

MAY 10—Kennedy defeats Humphrey in the West Virginia Democratic primary by 77,305 votes. Humphrey withdraws from the presidential race.

MAY 11—In his first public comment on the U-2 incident, Eisenhower accepts personal responsibility for the U-2 flights. It is the first time a head of state has ever openly admitted that his country was spying on others.

MAY 16—After three hours the Paris summit meeting collapses when Khrushchev vehemently demands that Eisenhower apologize for the U-2 flights, punish the culprits responsible and ban future flights.

He also revokes his invitation to Eisenhower to visit the USSR later in the spring.

MAY 27—Eisenhower announces the termination of U.S. economic aid to Cuba.

MAY 31—In *U.S. v. States of La., Tex., Miss., Ala., and Fla.*, the Supreme Court upholds the historical right of Texas and Florida, under the 1953 Tidelands Act, to submerged offshore oil and denies such claims by the other states.

JUNE 2—The Federal Reserve Board authorizes a reduction in the discount rate from 4 to 3½%.

JUNE 7—A Surgeon General's report on the mission of the Public Health Service underscores the growing danger of environmental health factors.

JUNE 8—Eisenhower signs legislation directing the Surgeon General to make a study of the effects of motor vehicle exhaust fumes on the public health.

JUNE 12—Eisenhower leaves on a two-week good-will tour of the 12 Far Eastern countries.

JUNE 16—Thousands of Japanese riot against the U.S.-Japanese security treaty. Eisenhower cancels his visit to Japan.

JUNE 20—In *Hannah v. Larche*, the Supreme Court upholds the right of the Civil Rights Commission, under the Civil Rights Act of 1957, to hold hearings in Louisiana and take measures to preserve the anonymity of informants.

JUNE 27—In *Elkins v. U.S.*, the Supreme Court rules that evidence obtained by state officers during an illegal search was inadmissible in federal courts.

JUNE 27—The 10-Nation Disarmament Conference ends with no movement on either side.

JULY 1—Congress overrides Eisenhower's veto of a bill providing pay increases for federal employes.

JULY 6—In retaliation for the seizure of millions of dollars worth of American property, the U.S. cuts Cuba's sugar import quota by 700,000 tons.

JULY 9—Eisenhower asserts that the U.S. will never permit the establishment of a Communist regime in the Western Hemisphere.

JULY 13—Kennedy wins the Democratic presidential nomination on the first ballot at the Los Angeles convention. The vote is 806 for Kennedy, 409 for his chief rival Lyndon Johnson. Johnson is chosen vice-presidential candidate at the following session.

JULY 22—Eisenhower orders a 3% reduction in the number of federal employes.

JULY 22-23—In a meeting with New York Gov. Nelson Rockefeller, Nixon agrees to a stronger platform on civil rights, defense and foreign policy in exchange for Rockefeller's support for the presidential nomination. The meeting is dubbed the "Treaty of Fifth Avenue" by the press.

JULY 25—Nixon easily wins the Republican presidential nomination on the first ballot in Chicago.

AUG. 19—A Soviet military tribunal sentences Powers to 10 years in prison for espionage.

AUG. 20—The U.S. joins other members of the Organization of American States in voting to sever diplomatic relations with the Dominican Republic and to impose economic sanctions and a complete arms embargo on it for its "acts of aggression" in participating in a plot to overthrow the Venezuelan government.

AUG. 24—In response to a reporter's query for an example of a major idea Nixon has contributed to Administration planning, Eisenhower replies, "If you give me a week, I might think of one. I don't remember."

SEPT. 11—The Inter-American Economic Conference adopts the "Act of Bogota," an extensive social and economic aid program for Latin America.

SEPT. 13—Eisenhower signs a bill making the fixing of TV quiz shows a federal crime and giving the Federal Communications Commission the powers to tighten restrictions on deceptive broadcasting practices.

SEPT. 22—Eisenhower addresses the U.N. General Assembly, proposing national self-determination for African colonies and a five-point program of economic and educational assistance to be administered through the U.N.

SEPT. 26—Kennedy and Nixon hold the first of four televised debates between the presidential candidates.

OCT. 17—National variety store chains: Woolworth, Kresge, W.T. Grant, and McCrory-McLellan announce that lunch counters in their stores have been integrated in more than 100 southern cities.

OCT. 24—U.S. church membership for 1959 is reported to have risen to a record 112,226,905 at year's end.

OCT. 28—The U.S. requests the Organization of American States to investigate reports that Cuba is receiving large shipments of arms from the Soviet bloc.

NOV. 1—Eisenhower announces that the U.S. would take "whatever steps" necessary to maintain the U.S. naval base at Guantanamo, Cuba.

NOV. 8—Kennedy defeats Nixon in the presidential election by 113,057 votes and receives 303 of the 537 electoral votes. The Democrats retain control of both the House and Senate.

NOV. 17—The CIA briefs Kennedy on its involvement in training Cuban exiles in Guatemala to overthrow Castro.

NOV. 18—Eisenhower orders U.S. naval units to patrol Central American waters to prevent Communist-led invasions of either Guatemala or Nicaragua.

NOV. 19—Eisenhower's science advisory committee urges the federal government and all other elements of the national community to assume a greater role in supporting, strengthening and expanding basic scientific research and graduate education in science.

NOV. 27—Eisenhower's Commission on National Goals issues a report calling for "extraordinary personal responsibility" and sustained "effort and sacrifice" from "every American" in the 1960s to help the U.S. achieve "high and difficult goals" in the period of "grave danger" ahead.

DEC. 5—The Supreme Court rules that racial discrimination in bus terminal restaurants serving interstate passengers is a violation of the Interstate Commerce Act.

DEC. 7—Kefauver's Senate Antitrust and Monopoly Subcommittee begins an investigation of pricing in the prescription drug industry.

DEC. 7—The Office of Education announces that a record 3.6 million students are pursuing college degrees.

DEC. 14—Western European nations, the U.S. and Canada sign an agreement in Paris creating an Organization for Economic Cooperation and Development.

1961

JAN. 17—Eisenhower delivers an eloquent farewell address to the nation in which he warns that America "must guard against . . . the unwarranted influence . . . of the military-industrial complex."

CONGRESS
1953-1960

SENATE

Alabama

Lister Hill (D) 1938-69
John J. Sparkman (D) 1946-

Alaska

E. L. Bartlett (D) 1959-69
Ernest Gruening (D) 1959-69

Arizona

Carl Hayden (D) 1927-69
Barry M. Goldwater (R) 1953-65; 1969-

Arkansas

J. William Fulbright (D) 1945-75
John L. McClellan (D) 1943-

California

Clair Engle (D) 1959-64
William F. Knowland (R) 1945-59
Thomas H. Kuchel (R) 1953-69

Colorado

John A. Carroll (D) 1957-63
Edwin C. Johnson (D) 1937-55
Gordon Allott (R) 1955-73
Eugene D. Millikin (R) 1941-57

Connecticut

Thomas J. Dodd (D) 1959-71
Prescott Bush (R) 1953-63
William A. Purtell (R) 1952-59

Delaware

J. Allen Frear, Jr. (D) 1949-61
John J. Williams (R) 1947-71

Florida

Spessard L. Holland (D) 1946-71
George P. Smathers (D) 1951-69

Georgia

Walter F. George (D) 1923-57
Richard B. Russell (D) 1933-71
Herman E. Talmadge (D) 1957-

Hawaii

Oren E. Long (D) 1959-63
Hiram Fong (R) 1959-77

Idaho

Frank Church (D) 1957-
Henry C. Dworshak (R) 1947-49; 1949-62
Herman Welker (R) 1951-57

Illinois

Paul H. Douglas (D) 1949-67
Everett M. Dirksen (R) 1951-69

Indiana

Vance Hartke (D) 1959-77
Homer E. Capehart (R) 1945-63
William E. Jenner (R) 1944-45; 1947-59

Iowa

Guy M. Gillette (D) 1936-45; 1949-55
Bourke B. Hickenlooper (R) 1945-69
Thomas E. Martin (R) 1955-61

Kansas

Frank Carlson (R) 1951-69
Andrew F. Schoeppel (R) 1949-62

Kentucky

Alben W. Barkley (D) 1927-49; 1955-56
Earle C. Clements (D) 1950-57
Robert Humphreys 1956-57
John Sherman Cooper (R) 1946-49; 1952-55; 1956-73
Thruston B. Morton (R) 1957-69

Louisiana

Allen J. Ellender (D) 1937-72
Russell B. Long (D) 1948-

Maine

Edmund S. Muskie (D) 1959-
Frederick G. Payne (R) 1953-59
Margeret Chase Smith (R) 1949-73

Maryland

J. Glenn Beall (R) 1953-65
John Marshall Butler (R) 1951-63

Massachusetts

John F. Kennedy (D) 1953-60
Leverett Saltonstall (R) 1945-67

Michigan

Philip A. Hart (D) 1959-76
Pat V. McNamara (D) 1955-66
Homer Ferguson (R) 1943-55
Charles E. Potter (R) 1953-59

Minnesota

Hubert H. Humphrey (D) 1949-64; 1971-
Eugene J. McCarthy (D) 1959-71
Edward J. Thye (R) 1947-59

Mississippi

James O. Eastland (D) 1941; 1943-
John C. Stennis (D) 1947-

Missouri

Thomas C. Hennings, Jr. (D) 1951-60
Stuart Symington (D) 1953-77

Montana

Mike Mansfield (D) 1953-77
James E. Murray (D) 1934-61

Nebraska

Hazel H. Abel (R) 1954
Eva K. Bowring (R) 1954
Hugh A. Butler (R) 1941-54
Carl T. Curtis (R) 1955-
Dwight P. Griswold (R) 1952-54
Roman L. Hruska (R) 1954-77
Sam W. Reynolds (R) 1954

Nevada

Alan Bible (D) 1954-75
Howard W. Cannon (D) 1959-
Pat McCarran (D) 1933-54
Ernest S. Brown (R) 1954
George W. Malone (R) 1947-59

New Hampshire

H. Styles Bridges (R) 1937-61
Norris Cotton (R) 1954-75
Charles W. Tobey (R) 1939-53
Robert W. Upton (R) 1953-54

New Jersey

Harrison A. Williams, Jr. (D) 1959-
Clifford P. Case (R) 1955-
Robert C. Hendrickson (R) 1949-55
H. Alexander Smith (R) 1944-59

New Mexico

Clinton P. Anderson (D) 1949-73
Dennis Chavez (D) 1935-62

New York

Herbert H. Lehman (D) 1949-57
Irving M. Ives (R) 1947-59
Jacob K. Javits (R) 1957-
Kenneth B. Keating (R) 1959-65

North Carolina

Sam J. Ervin, Jr. (D) 1954-75
Clyde R. Hoey (D) 1945-54
B. Everett Jordan (D) 1958-73
Alton Lennon (D) 1953-54
W. Kerr Scott (D) 1954-58
Willis Smith (D) 1950-53

North Dakota

Quentin N. Burdick (D) 1960-
C. Norman Brunsdale (R) 1960
William Langer (R) 1941-59
Milton R. Young (R) 1945-

Ohio

Thomas A. Burke (D) 1954
Frank J. Lausche (D) 1957-69
Stephen M. Young (D) 1959-71
George H. Bender (R) 1954-57
John W. Bricker (R) 1947-59
Robert A. Taft (R) 1939-53

Oklahoma

Robert S. Kerr (D) 1949-63
A. S. Mike Monroney (D) 1951-69

Oregon

Richard L. Neuberger (D) 1955-60
Guy Cordon (R) 1944-55
Wayne Morse (R) 1945-52; (Ind.) 1952-55;
(D) 1955-69

Pennsylvania

Joseph S. Clark (D) 1957-69
James H. Duff (R) 1951-57
Edward Martin (R) 1947-59
Hugh Scott (R) 1959-77

Rhode Island

Theodore Francis Green (D) 1937-61
John O. Pastore (D) 1950-77

South Carolina

Charles E. Daniel (D) 1954
Olin D. Johnston (D) 1945-65
Burnet R. Maybank (D) 1941-54
Strom Thurmond (D) 1954-56, 1956-64; (R) 1964-
Thomas A. Wofford (D) 1956

South Dakota

Francis Case (R) 1951-62
Karl E. Mundt (R) 1948-73

Tennessee

Albert Gore (D) 1953-71
Estes Kefauver (D) 1949-63

Texas

William A. Blakley (D) 1957
Price Daniel (D) 1953-57
Lyndon B. Johnson (D) 1949-61
Ralph W. Yarborough (D) 1957-71

Utah

Frank E. Moss (D) 1959-77
Wallace F. Bennett (R) 1951-75
Arthur V. Watkins (R) 1947-59

Vermont

George D. Aiken (R) 1941-75
Ralph E. Flanders (R) 1946-59
Winston L. Prouty (R) 1959-71

Virginia

Harry Flood Byrd (D) 1933-65
A. Willis Robertson (D) 1946-66

Washington

Henry M. Jackson (D) 1953-
Warren G. Magnuson (D) 1944-

West Virginia

Robert C. Byrd (D) 1959-

Harley M. Kilgore (D) 1941-56
William R. Laird, III (D) 1956
Matthew M. Neely (D) 1923-29; 1931-41;
1949-58
Jennings, Randolph (D) 1958-
John D. Hoblitzell, Jr. (R) 1958
Chapman Revercomb (R) 1943-49; 1956-59

Wisconsin

William Proxmire (D) 1957-
Joseph R. McCarthy (R) 1947-57
Alexander Wiley (R) 1939-63

Wyoming

Lester C. Hunt (D) 1949-54
Gale W. McGee (D) 1959-77
Joseph C. O'Mahoney (D) 1934-53; 1954-61
Edward D. Crippa (R) 1954
Frank A. Barrett (R) 1953-59

HOUSE OF REPRESENTATIVES

Alabama

George W. Andrews (D) 1944-71
Laurie C. Battle (D) 1947-55
Frank W. Boykin (D) 1935-63
Carl Elliott (D) 1949-65
George M. Grant (D) 1938-65
George Huddleston, Jr. (D) 1955-65
Robert E. Jones (D) 1947-77
Albert Rains (D) 1945-65
Kenneth A. Roberts (D) 1951-65
Armistead I. Selden, Jr. (D) 1953-69

Alaska

Ralph J. Rivers (D) 1959-67

Arizona

Harold A. Patten (D) 1949-55
Stewart L. Udall (D) 1955-61
John J. Rhodes (R) 1953-

Arkansas

Dale Alford (D) 1959-63
E. C. Gathings (D) 1939-69
Oren Harris (D) 1941-66
Brooks Hays (D) 1943-59
Wilbur D. Mills (D) 1939-77
W. F. Norrell (D) 1939-61
James W. Trimble (D) 1945-67

California

Jeffery Cohelan (D) 1959-71
Robert L. Condon (D) 1953-55
Clyde Doyle (D) 1945-47; 1949-63
Clair Engle (D) 1943-59
Harlan D. Hagen (D) 1953-67
Chet Holifield (D) 1943-75
Harold T. Johnson (D) 1959-
George A. Kasem (D) 1959-61
Cecil R. King (D) 1942-69
John J. McFall (D) 1957-
Clem Miller (D) 1959-62

George P. Miller (D) 1945-73
John E. Moss (D) 1953-
James Roosevelt (D) 1955-65
D. S. Saund (D) 1957-63
John F. Shelley (D) 1949-64
Harry R. Sheppard (D) 1937-65
B. F. Sisk (D) 1955-
Samuel W. Yorty (D) 1951-55
John J. Allen, Jr. (R) 1947-59
John F. Baldwin (R) 1955-66
Ernest K. Bramblett (R) 1947-55
Charles S. Gubser (R) 1953-75
Edgar W. Hiestand (R) 1953-63
Patrick J. Hillings (R) 1951-59
Carl Hinshaw (R) 1939-56
Joseph F. Holt, III (R) 1953-61
Craig Hosmer (R) 1953-75
Allan O. Hunter (R) 1951-55
Donald L. Jackson (R) 1947-61
J. Leroy Johnson (R) 1943-57
Glenard P. Lipscomb (R) 1953-70
Gordon L. McDonough (R) 1945-63
William S. Mailliard (R) 1953-74
John Phillips (R) 1943-57
Norris Poulson (R) 1943-45; 1947-53
Hubert B. Scudder (R) 1949-59
H. Allen Smith (R) 1957-73
Charles M. Teague (R) 1955-74
James B. Utt (R) 1953-70
Bob Wilson (R) 1953-
J. Arthur Younger (R) 1953-67

Colorado

Wayne N. Aspinall (D) 1949-73
Byron L. Johnson (D) 1959-61
Byron G. Rogers (D) 1951-71
J. Edgar Chenoweth (R) 1941-49; 1951-65
William S. Hill (R) 1941-59

Connecticut

Chester Bowles (D) 1959-61
Emilio Q. Daddario (D) 1959-71
Thomas J. Dodd (D) 1953-57
Robert N. Giaimo (D) 1959-
Donald J. Irwin (D) 1959-61; 1965-69
Frank Kowalski (D) 1959-63
John S. Monagan (D) 1959-73
Albert W. Cretella (R) 1953-59
Edwin H. May, Jr. (R) 1957-59
Albert P. Morano (R) 1951-59
James T. Patterson (R) 1947-59
Antoni N. Sadlak (R) 1947-59
Horace Seely-Brown, Jr. (R) 1947-49; 1951-59; 1961-63

Delaware

Harris B. McDowell, Jr. (D) 1955-57; 1959-67
Harry Haskell, Jr. (R) 1957-59
Herbert B. Warburton (R) 1953-55

Florida

Charles E. Bennett (D) 1949-
Courtney W. Campbell (D) 1953-55
Dante B. Fascell (D) 1955-
James A. Haley (D) 1953-
A. Sydney Herlong, Jr. (D) 1949-69
William C. Lantaff (D) 1951-55
Chester B. McMullen (D) 1951-53
D. R. (Billy) Matthews (D) 1953-67
Dwight L. Rogers (D) 1945-54
Paul G. Rogers (D) 1955-
Robert L. F. Sikes (D) 1941-44; 1945-
William C. Cramer (R) 1955-71

Georgia

Iris F. Blitch (D) 1955-63
Paul Brown (D) 1933-61
A. Sidney Camp (D) 1939-54
James C. Davis (D) 1947-63
John J. Flynt, Jr. (D) 1954-
E. L. Forrester (D) 1951-65
Phil M. Landrum (D) 1953-77
Henderson Lanham (D) 1947-57
Erwin Mitchell (D) 1958-61
J. L. Pilcher (D) 1953-65
Prince H. Preston, Jr. (D) 1947-61
Carl Vinson (D) 1914-65
W. M. Wheeler (D) 1947-55

Hawaii

Daniel K. Inouye (D) 1959-63

Idaho

Gracie Pfost (D) 1953-63
Hamer H. Budge (R) 1951-61

Illinois

James B. Bowler (D) 1953-57
Charles A. Boyle (D) 1955-59
William L. Dawson (D) 1943-70
Thomas S. Gordon (D) 1943-59

Kenneth J. Gray (D) 1955-75
John C. Kluczynski (D) 1951-75
Roland V. Libonati (D) 1957-65
Peter F. Mack, Jr. (D) 1949-63
William T. Murphy (D) 1959-71
James C. Murray (D) 1955-57
Thomas J. O'Brien (D) 1933-39; 1943-64
Barratt O'Hara (D) 1949-51; 1953-69
Melvin Price (D) 1945-
Roman C. Pucinski (D) 1959-73
Dan Rostenkowski (D) 1959-
George E. Shipley (D) 1959-
Sidney R. Yates (D) 1949-63; 1965-
Leo E. Allen (R) 1933-61
Leslie C. Arends (R) 1935-75
C. W. (Runt) Bishop (R) 1941-55
Fred E. Busbey (R) 1943-45; 1947-49; 1951-55
Emmet F. Byrne (R) 1957-59
Robert B. Chiperfield (R) 1939-63
Marguerite Stitt Church (R) 1951-63
Harold R. Collier (R) 1957-75
Edward J. Derwinski (R) 1959-
Elmer J. Hoffman (R) 1959-65
Richard W. Hoffman (R) 1949-57
Edgar A. Jonas (R) 1949-55
Russell W. Keeney (R) 1957-58
William E. McVey (R) 1951-58
Noah M. Mason (R) 1937-63
Robert H. Michel (R) 1957-
Chauncey W. Reed (R) 1935-56
Timothy P. Sheehan (R) 1951-59
Edna Oakes Simpson (R) 1959-61
Sid Simpson (R) 1943-58
William L. Springer (R) 1951-73
Harold H. Velde (R) 1949-57
Charles W. Vursell (R) 1943-59

Indiana

Joseph W. Barr (D) 1959-61
John Brademas (D) 1959-
Winfield K. Denton (D) 1949-53; 1955-67
Randall S. Harmon (D) 1959-61
Earl Hogan (D) 1959-61
Ray J. Madden (D) 1943-77
J. Edward Roush (D) 1959-69; 1971-77
Fred Wampler (D) 1959-61
E. Ross Adair (R) 1951-71
John V. Beamer (R) 1951-59
William G. Bray (R) 1951-75
Charles R. Brownson (R) 1951-59
Shepard J. Crumpacker, Jr. (R) 1951-57
Charles A. Halleck (R) 1935-69
Cecil M. Harden (R) 1949-59
Ralph Harvey (R) 1947-59; 1961-66
D. Bailey Merrill (R) 1953-55
F. Jay Nimtz (R) 1957-59
Earl Wilson (R) 1941-59; 1961-65

Iowa

Steven V. Carter (D) 1959
Merwin Coad (D) 1957-63
Neal Smith (D) 1959-
Leonard G. Wolf (D) 1959-61
Paul Cunningham (R) 1941-59
James I. Dolliver (R) 1945-57
H. R. Gross (R) 1949-75
Charles B. Hoeven (R) 1943-65
Ben F. Jensen (R) 1939-65
John H. Kyl (R) 1959-65; 1967-73
Karl M. LeCompte (R) 1939-59
Thomas E. Martin (R) 1939-55
Fred Schwengel (R) 1955-65; 1967-73
Henry O. Talle (R) 1939-59

Kansas

J. Floyd Breeding (D) 1957-63
Newell A. George (D) 1959-61
Denver D. Hargis (D) 1959-61
Howard S. Miller (D) 1953-55
William H. Avery (R) 1955-65
Myron V. George (R) 1950-59
Clifford R. Hope (R) 1927-57
Edward H. Rees (R) 1937-61
Errett P. Scrivner (R) 1943-59
Wint Smith (R) 1947-61

Kentucky

Frank W. Bruke (D) 1959-63
Frank Chelf (D) 1945-67
Noble J. Gregory (D) 1937-59
William H. Natcher (D) 1953-
Carl D. Perkins (D) 1949-
Brent Spence (D) 1931-63
Frank A. Stubblefield (D) 1959-75
John C. Watts (D) 1951-71
Garrett L. Withers (D) 1952-53
James S. Golden (R) 1949-55
John M. Robsion, Jr. (R) 1953-59
Eugene Siler (R) 1955-65

Louisiana

Hale Boggs (D) 1941-43; 1947-72
Overton Brooks (D) 1937-61
F. Edward Hebert (D) 1941-77
George S. Long (D) 1953-58

Harold B. McSween (D) 1959-63
James H. Morrison (D) 1943-67
Otto E. Passman (D) 1947-77
T. Ashton Thompson (D) 1953-65
Edwin E. Willis (D) 1949-69

Maine

Frank M. Coffin (D) 1957-61
James C. Oliver (D) 1937-43; 1959-61
Robert Hale (R) 1943-59
Clifford G. McIntire (R) 1952-65
Charles P. Nelson (R) 1949-57

Maryland

Daniel B. Brewster (D) 1959-62
George H. Fallon (D) 1945-71
John R. Foley (D) 1959-61
Samuel N. Friedel (D) 1953-71
Edward A. Garmatz (D) 1947-73
Thomas F. Johnson (D) 1959-63
Richard E. Lankford (D) 1955-65
James P. S. Devereux (R) 1951-59
DeWitt S. Hyde (R) 1953-59
Edward T. Miller (R) 1947-59
Frank Small, Jr. (R) 1953-55

Massachusetts

Edward P. Boland (D) 1953-
James A. Burke (D) 1959-
Harold D. Donohue (D) 1947-75
Thomas J. Lane (D) 1941-63
John W. McCormack (D) 1928-71
Torbert H. Macdonald (D) 1955-76
Thomas P. (Tip) O'Neill, Jr. (D) 1953-
Philip J. Philbin (D) 1943-71
William H. Bates (R) 1950-69
Silvio O. Conte (R) 1959-
Laurence Curtis (R) 1953-63
Angier L. Goodwin (R) 1943-55
John W. Heselton (R) 1945-59
Hastings Keith (R) 1959-73
Joseph W. Martin, Jr. (R) 1925-67
Donald W. Nicholson (R) 1947-59
Edith Nourse Rogers (R) 1925-60
Richard B. Wigglesworth (R) 1928-59

Michigan

Charles C. Diggs, Jr. (D) 1955-
John D. Dingell (D) 1933-55

John D. Dingell, Jr. (D) 1955-
Martha W. Griffiths (D) 1955-74
Donald Hayworth (D) 1955-57
John Lesinski, Jr. (D) 1951-65
Thaddeus M. Machrowicz (D) 1951-61
George D. O'Brien (D) 1937-39; 1941-47;
1949-55
James G. O'Hara (D) 1959-77
Louis C. Rabaut (D) 1935-47; 1949-61
John B. Bennett (R) 1943-45; 1947-64
Alvin M. Bentley (R) 1953-61
William S. Broomfield (R) 1957-
Elford A. Cederberg (R) 1953-
Charles E. Chamberlain (R) 1957-74
Kit Francis Clardy (R) 1953-55
George A. Dondero (R) 1933-57
Gerald R. Ford (R) 1949-73
Robert P. Griffin (R) 1957-66
Clare E. Hoffman (R) 1935-63
August E. Johansen (R) 1955-65
Victor A. Knox (R) 1953-65
Robert J. McIntosh (R) 1957-59
George Meader (R) 1951-65
Charles G. Oakman (R) 1953-55
Paul W. Shafer (R) 1937-54
Ruth Thompson (R) 1951-57
Jesse P. Wolcott (R) 1931-57

Minnesota

John A. Blatnik (D) 1947-74
Joseph E. Karth (D) 1959-77
Coya Knutson (D) 1955-59
Eugene J. McCarthy (D) 1949-59
Fred Marshall (D) 1949-63
Roy W. Wier (D) 1949-61
H. Carl Andersen (R) 1939-63
August H. Andresen (R) 1925-33; 1935-58
Harold C. Hagen (FL) 1943-45; (R) 1945-55
Walter H. Judd (R) 1943-63
Odin Langen (R) 1959-71
Ancher Nelsen (R) 1959-75
Joseph P. O'Hara (R) 1941-59
Albert H. Quie (R) 1958-

Mississippi

Thomas G. Abernethy (D) 1943-73
William M. Colmer (D) 1933-73
Frank E. Smith (D) 1951-62
Jamie L. Whitten (D) 1941-
John Bell Williams (D) 1947-68
W. Arthur Winstead (D) 1943-65

Missouri

Richard Bollin (D) 1949-
Charles H. Brown (D) 1957-61
Clarence Cannon (D) 1923-64
A. S. J. Carnahan (D) 1945-47; 1949-61
George H. Christopher (D) 1949-51; 1955-59
W. R. Hull, Jr. (D) 1955-73
Paul C. Jones (D) 1948-69
Frank M. Karsten (D) 1947-69
Morgan M. Moulder (D) 1949-63
William J. Randall (D) 1959-77
Leonor K. Sullivan (D) 1953-77
William C. Cole (R) 1943-49; 1953-55
Thomas B. Curtis (R) 1951-69
Jeffrey P. Hillelson (R) 1953-55
Dewey Short (R) 1929-31; 1935-57

Montana

LeRoy H. Anderson (D) 1957-61
Lee Metcalf (D) 1953-61
Wesley A. D'Ewart (R) 1945-55
Orvin B. Fjare (R) 1955-57

Nebraska

Lawrence Brock (D) 1959-61
Donald F. McGinley (D) 1959-61
Jackson B. Chase (R) 1955-57
Glenn Cunningham (R) 1957-71
Carl T. Curtis (R) 1939-54
Robert D. Harrison (R) 1951-59
Roman L. Hruska (R) 1953-54
A. L. Miller (R) 1943-59
Phil Weaver (R) 1955-63

Nevada

Walter S. Baring (D) 1949-53; 1957-73
C. Clifton Young (R) 1953-57

New Hampshire

Perkins Bass (R) 1955-63
Norris Cotton (R) 1947-54
Chester E. Merrow (R) 1943-63

New Jersey

Hugh J. Addonizio (D) 1949-62
Dominick V. Daniels (D) 1959-77

Cornelius E. Gallagher (D) 1959-73
Edward J. Hart (D) 1935-55
Charles R. Howell (D) 1949-55
Peter W. Rodino, Jr. (D) 1949-
Alfred D. Sieminski (D) 1951-59
Frank Thompson, Jr. (D) 1955-
T. James Tumulty (D) 1955-57
Harrison A. Williams (D) 1953-57
James C. Auchincloss (R) 1943-65
William T. Cahill (R) 1959-70
Gordon Canfield (R) 1941-61
Clifford P. Case (R) 1945-53
Vincent J. Dellay (R) 1957-58; (D) 1958-59
Florence P. Dwyer (R) 1957-73
Peter H. B. Frelinghuysen, Jr. (R) 1953-75
Milton W. Glenn (R) 1957-65
T. Millet Hand (R) 1945-56
Robert W. Kean (R) 1939-59
Frank C. Osmers, Jr. (R) 1939-43; 1951-65
George M. Wallhauser (R) 1959-65
William B. Widnall (R) 1950-74
Charles A. Wolverton (R) 1927-59

New Mexico

John J. Dempsey (D) 1935-41; 1951-58
Antonio M. Fernandez (D) 1943-56
Joseph M. Montoya (D) 1957-64
Thomas G. Morris (D) 1959-69

New York

Victor L. Anfuso (D) 1951-53; 1955-63
Charles A. Buckley (D) 1935-65
Emanuel Celler (D) 1923-73
Irwin D. Davidson (D) 1955-56
James J. Delaney (D) 1945-47; 1949-
Isidore Dollinger (D) 1949-60
James G. Donovan (D) 1951-57
Thaddeus J. Dulski (D) 1959-75
Leonard Farbstein (D) 1957-71
Sidney A. Fine (D) 1951-56
Jacob H. Gilbert (D) 1960-71
James C. Healey (D) 1956-65
Louis B. Heller (D) 1949-54
Lester Holtzman (D) 1953-61
Edna F. Kelly (D) 1949-69
Eugene J. Keogh (D) 1937-67
Arthur G. Klein (D) 1941-45; 1946-56
Abraham J. Multer (D) 1947-67
Leo W. O'Brien (D) 1952-67
Adam C. Powell, Jr. (D) 1945-67; 1969-71
John J. Rooney (D) 1944-74
Franklin D. Roosevelt, Jr. (L) 1949-51; (D) 1951-55
Alfred E. Santangelo (D) 1957-63

Samuel S. Stratton (D) 1959-
Ludwig Teller (D) 1957-61
Herbert Zelenko (D) 1955-63
Robert R. Barry (R) 1959-65
Frank J. Becker (R) 1953-65
Albert H. Bosch (R) 1953-60
W. Sterling Cole (R) 1935-57
Frederic R. Coudert, Jr. (R) 1947-59
Steven B. Derounian (R) 1953-65
Edwin B. Dooley (R) 1957-63
Francis E. Dorn (R) 1953-61
Paul A. Fino (R) 1953-68
Ralph A. Gamble (R) 1937-57
Charles E. Goodell (R) 1959-68
Ralph W. Gwinn (R) 1945-59
Seymour Halpern (R) 1959-73
Jacob K. Javits (R) 1947-54
Bernard W. (Pat) Kearney (R) 1943-59
Kenneth B. Keating (R) 1947-59
Clarence Kilburn (R) 1940-65
Henry J. Latham (R) 1945-58
John V. Lindsay (R) 1959-65
William E. Miller (R) 1951-65
Harold C. Ostertag (R) 1951-65
John R. Pillion (R) 1953-65
Alexander Pirnie (R) 1959-73
Edmund P. Radwan (R) 1951-59
John H. Ray (R) 1953-63
Daniel A. Reed (R) 1919-59
R. Walter Riehlman (R) 1947-65
Howard W. Robison (R) 1958-75
Katharine St. George (R) 1947-65
John Taber (R) 1923-63
Dean P. Taylor (R) 1943-61
Stuyvesant Wainwright (R) 1953-61
Jessica McC. Weis (R) 1959-63
J. Ernest Wharton (R) 1951-65
William R. Williams (R) 1951-59

North Carolina

Hugh Alexander (D) 1953-63
Graham A. Barden (D) 1935-61
Herbert C. Bonner (D) 1940-65
Frank E. Carlyle (D) 1949-57
Richard Thurmond Chatham (D) 1949-57
Harold D. Cooley (D) 1934-67
Charles B. Deane (D) 1947-57
Carl T. Durham (D) 1939-61
L. H. Fountain (D) 1953-
David M. Hall (D) 1959-60
Woodrow W. Jones (D) 1950-57
A. Paul Kitchin (D) 1957-63
Alton Lennon (D) 1957-73
Ralph J. Scott (D) 1957-67
George A. Shuford (D) 1953-59
Roy A. Taylor (D) 1960-77

Basil L. Whitener (D) 1957-69
Charles R. Jonas (R) 1953-73

North Dakota

Quentin N. Burdick (D) 1959-60
Usher L. Burdick (R) 1935-45; 1949-59
Otto Krueger (R) 1953-59
Don L. Short (R) 1959-65

Ohio

Thomas L. Ashley (D) 1955-
Robert E. Cook (D) 1959-63
Robert Crosser (D) 1913-19; 1923-55
Michael A. Feighan (D) 1943-71
Wayne L. Hays (D) 1949-76
Michael J. Kirwan (D) 1937-70
Robert W. Levering (D) 1959-61
Walter H. Moeller (D) 1959-63; 1965-67
James G. Polk (D) 1931-41; 1949-59
Robert T. Secrest (D) 1933-42; 1949-54; 1963-66
Charles A. Vanik (D) 1955-
William H. Ayres (R) 1951-71
A. D. Baumhart, Jr. (R) 1941-42; 1955-61
George H. Bender (R) 1939-49; 1951-54
Jackson E. Betts (R) 1951-73
Frances P. Bolton (R) 1940-69
Oliver P. Bolton (R) 1953-57; 1963-65
Frank T. Bow (R) 1951-72
Clarence J. Brown (R) 1939-65
Cliff Clevenger (R) 1939-59
David Dennison (R) 1957-59
Samuel L. Devine (R) 1959-
John E. Henderson (R) 1955-61
William E. Hess (R) 1929-37; 1939-49; 1951-61
Thomas A. Jenkins (R) 1925-59
Delbert L. Latta (R) 1959-
William M. McCulloch (R) 1947-73
J. Harry McGregor (R) 1940-58
Ward M. Miller (R) 1960-61
William E. Minshall (R) 1955-75
Paul F. Schenck (R) 1951-65
Gordon H. Scherer (R) 1953-63
John M. Vorys (R) 1939-59
Alvin F. Weichel (R) 1943-55
H. Frazier Reams (Ind.) 1951-55

Oklahoma

Carl Albert (D) 1947-77
Ed Edmondson (D) 1953-73
John Jarman (D) 1951-75; (R) 1975-77
Toby Morris (D) 1947-53; 1957-61
Tom Steed (D) 1949-

Victor Wickersham (D) 1941-47; 1949-57; 1961-65
Page Belcher (R) 1951-73

Oregon

Edith Green (D) 1955-74
Charles O. Porter (D) 1957-61
Al Ullman (D) 1957-
Homer D. Angell (R) 1939-55
Sam Coon (R) 1953-57
M. Harris Ellsworth (R) 1943-57
A. Walter Norblad (R) 1946-64

Pennsylvania

William A. Barrett (D) 1945-47; 1949-76
Vera D. Buchanan (D) 1951-55
James A. Byrne (D) 1953-73
Earl Chudoff (D) 1949-58
Frank M. Clark (D) 1955-74
John H. Dent (D) 1958-
Herman P. Eberharter (D) 1937-58
Daniel J. Flood (D) 1945-47; 1949-53; 1955-
Kathryn E. Granahan (D) 1956-63
William T. Granahan (D) 1945-47; 1949-56
William J. Green, Jr. (D) 1945-47; 1949-63
Elmer J. Holland (D) 1942-43; 1956-68
Augustine B. Kelley (D) 1941-57
William S. Moorhead (D) 1959-
Thomas E. Morgan (D) 1945-77
Robert N. C. Nix (D) 1958-
Stanley A. Prokop (D) 1959-61
James M. Quigley (D) 1955-57; 1959-61
George M. Rhodes (D) 1949-69
Herman Toll (D) 1959-67
Francis E. Walter (D) 1933-63
Edward J. Bonin (R) 1953-55
Alvin R. Bush (R) 1951-59
Joseph L. Carrigg (R) 1951-59
Robert J. Corbett (R) 1939-41; 1945-71
Willard S. Curtin (R) 1957-67
Paul B. Dague (R) 1947-67
Douglas H. Elliott (R) 1960
Ivor D. Fenton (R) 1939-63
James G. Fulton (R) 1945-71
Leon H. Gavin (R) 1943-63
Louis E. Graham (R) 1939-55
Benjamin F. James (R) 1949-59
Carroll D. Kearns (R) 1947-63
Karl C. King (R) 1951-57
John A. Lafore, Jr. (R) 1957-61
Samuel K. McConnell, Jr. (R) 1944-57
William H. Milliken, Jr. (R) 1959-65
Walter M. Mumma (R) 1951-61

John P. Saylor (R) 1949-73
Herman T. Schneebeli (R) 1960-77
Hugh Scott (R) 1941-45; 1947-59
Richard M. Simpson (R) 1937-60
S. Walter Stauffer (R) 1953-55; 1957-59
James E. Van Zandt (R) 1939-43; 1947-63
J. Irving Whalley (R) 1960-73

Rhode Island

John E. Fogarty (D) 1941-44; 1945-67
Aime J. Forand (D) 1937-39; 1941-61

South Carolina

Robert T. Ashmore (D) 1953-69
Joseph R. Bryson (D) 1939-53
W. J. Bryan Dorn (D) 1947-49; 1951-75
Robert W. Hemphill (D) 1957-64
John L. McMillan (D) 1939-73
James P. Richards (D) 1933-57
John J. Riley (D) 1945-49; 1951-62
L. Mendel Rivers (D) 1941-70

South Dakota

George S. McGovern (D) 1957-61
E. Y. Berry (R) 1951-71
Harold O. Lovre (R) 1949-57

Tennessee

Ross Bass (D) 1955-64
Jere Cooper (D) 1929-57
Clifford Davis (D) 1940-65
Robert A. Everett (D) 1958-69
Joe L. Evins (D) 1947-77
James B. Frazier, Jr. (D) 1949-63
J. Carlton Loser (D) 1957-63
Tom Murray (D) 1943-67
J. Percy Priest (D) 1941-56
Pat Sutton (D) 1949-55
Howard H. Baker (R) 1951-64
B. Carroll Reece (R) 1921-31; 1933-47; 1951-61

Texas

Lindley Beckworth (D) 1939-53; 1957-67
John J. Bell (D) 1955-57
Lloyd M. Bentsen, Jr. (D) 1948-55
Jack Brooks (D) 1953-
Omar Burleson (D) 1947-

Bob Casey (D) 1959-76
Martin Dies, Jr. (D) 1931-45; 1953-59
John Dowdy (D) 1952-73
O. C. Fisher (D) 1943-75
Brady Gentry (D) 1953-57
Frank Ikard (D) 1951-61
Paul J. Kilday (D) 1939-61
Joe M. Kilgore (D) 1955-65
Wingate H. Lucas (D) 1947-55
John E. Lyle (D) 1945-55
George H. Mahon (D) 1935-
Wright Patman (D) 1929-76
W. R. Poage (D) 1937-
Sam Rayburn (D) 1913-61
Kenneth Regan (D) 1947-55
Walter Rogers (D) 1951-67
J. T. Rutherford (D) 1955-63
Olin E. Teague (D) 1946-
Albert Thomas (D) 1937-66
Clark W. Thompson (D) 1933-35; 1947-66
W. Homer Thornberry (D) 1949-63
J. Franklin Wilson (D) 1947-55
James C. Wright (D) 1955-
John Young (D) 1957-
Bruce Alger (R) 1955-65

Utah

David S. King (D) 1959-63; 1965-67
William A. Dawson (R) 1947-49; 1953-59
Henry Aldous Dixon (R) 1955-61
Douglas R. Stringfellow (R) 1953-55

Vermont

William H. Meyer (D) 1959-61
Winston L. Prouty (R) 1951-59

Virginia

Watkins M. Abbitt (D) 1948-73
Thomas N. Downing (D) 1959-77
J. Vaughan Gary (D) 1945-65
Porter J. Hardy (D) 1947-69
Burr P. Harrison (D) 1946-63
W. Pat Jennings (D) 1955-67
Edward J. Robeson, Jr. (D) 1950-59
Howard W. Smith (D) 1931-67
Thomas B. Stanley (D) 1946-53
William M. Tuck (D) 1953-69
Joel T. Broyhill (R) 1953-74
Richard H. Poff (R) 1953-72
William C. Wampler (R) 1953-55; 1967-

Washington

Julia B. Hansen (D) 1960-74
Don Magnuson (D) 1953-63
Hal Holmes (R) 1943-59
Walt Horan (R) 1943-65
Russell V. Mack (R) 1947-60
Catherine May (R) 1959-71
Thomas M. Pelly (R) 1953-73
Thor C. Tollefson (R) 1947-65
Jack Westland (R) 1953-65

West Virginia

Cleveland M. Bailey (D) 1945-47; 1949-63
M. G. Burnside (D) 1949-53; 1955-57
Robert C. Byrd (D) 1953-59
Ken Hechler (D) 1959-77
M. Elizabeth Kee (D) 1951-65
Robert H. Mollohan (D) 1953-57; 1969-
John M. Slack, Jr. (D) 1959-
Harley O. Staggers (D) 1949-
Arch A. Moore, Jr. (R) 1957-69
Will E. Neal (R) 1953-55; 1957-59

Wisconsin

Gerald T. Flynn (D) 1959-61
Lester R. Johnson (D) 1953-65
Robert W. Kastenmeier (D) 1959-
Henry S. Reuss (D) 1955-
Clement J. Zablocki (D) 1949-
John W. Byrnes (R) 1945-73
Glenn R. Davis (R) 1947-57; 1965-74
Merlin Hull (R) 1929-31; (Prog.) 1935-47;
(R) 1947-53
Charles J. Kersten (R) 1947-49; 1951-55
Melvin R. Laird (R) 1953-69
Alvin E. O'Konski (R) 1943-73
Lawrence H. Smith (R) 1941-58
Donald E. Tewes (R) 1957-59
William K. Van Pelt (R) 1951-65
Gardner R. Withrow (R) 1931-35; (Prog.) 1935-
39; (R) 1949-61

Wyoming

William H. Harrison (R) 1951-55; 1961-65;
1967-69
E. Keith Thomson (R) 1955-60

SUPREME COURT

Fred M. Vinson, Chief Justice 1946-53
Earl Warren, Chief Justice 1953-69
Hugo L. Black 1937-71
William J. Brennan, Jr. 1956-
Harold H. Burton 1945-58
Tom C. Clark 1949-67
William O. Douglas 1939-75

Felix Frankfurter 1939-62
John Marshall Harlan 1955-71
Robert H. Jackson 1941-54
Sherman Minton 1949-56
Stanley F. Reed 1938-57
Potter Stewart 1958-
Charles E. Whittaker 1957-62

EXECUTIVE DEPARTMENTS

Department of Agriculture

Secretary of Agriculture
  Ezra Taft Benson, 1953-61

Undersecretary
  True D. Morse, 1953-61

Assistant Secretaries
  J. Earl Coke, 1953-54
  John H. Davis, 1953-54
  Ross Rizley, 1953-54
  Ervin L. Peterson, 1954-60
  Earl L. Butz, 1954-57
  James A. McConnell, 1955
  Marvin L. McLain, 1956-60
  Don Paarlberg, 1957-58
  Clarence L. Miller, 1958-61

Administrative Assistant Secretary
  Ralph S. Roberts, 1953-61

Department of Commerce

Secretary of Commerce
  Sinclair Weeks, 1953-58
  Lewis L. Strauss, (acting) 1958-59
  Frederick H. Mueller, 1959-61

Undersecretary
  Walter Williams, 1953-58
  Frederick H. Mueller, 1958-59
  Philip A. Ray, 1959-61

Undersecretary for Transportation
  Robert B. Murray, Jr. 1953-55
  Louis S. Rothschild, 1955-58
  John J. Allen, Jr., 1959-61

Assistant Secretary for Administration
  James C. Worthy, 1954-55
  George T. Moore, 1955-61

Assistant Secretary for International Affairs
  Samuel W. Anderson, 1953-55
  Harold C. McClellan, 1955-57
  Henry Kearns, 1957-60
  Bradley Fisk, 1960-61

Assistant Secretary for Domestic Affairs
  Craig R. Sheaffer, 1953
  Lothair Teetor, 1953-55
  Frederick H. Mueller, 1955-58
  Carl F. Oechsle, 1958-61

Department of Defense

Secretary of Defense
  Charles E. Wilson, 1953-57

Neil H. McElroy, 1957-59
Thomas S. Gates, Jr., 1959-61

Deputy Secretary of Defense
Roger M. Kyes, 1953-54
Robert B. Anderson, 1954-55
Reuben B. Robertson, Jr., 1955-57
Donald A. Quarles, 1957-59
Thomas S. Gates, Jr., 1959
James H. Douglas, Jr., 1959-61

Secretary of the Air Force
Harold Talbott, 1953-55
Donald A. Quarles, 1955-57
James H. Douglas, Jr., 1957-59
Dudley C. Sharp, 1959-61

Secretary of the Army
Robert T. Stevens, 1953-55
Wilbur M. Brucker, 1955-61

Secretary of the Navy
Robert B. Anderson, 1953-54
Charles S. Thomas, 1954-57
Thomas S. Gates, Jr., 1957-59
William B. Franke, 1959-61

Assistant Secretary of Defense
(Comptroller)
Wilfred J. McNeil, 1949-59
Franklin B. Lincoln, 1959-61

Assistant Secretary of Defense
(Engineering)
Frank D. Newbury, 1953-57
Reorganized under Assistant Secretary
(Research and Engineering), 1957

Assistant Secretary of Defense
(Health and Medical)
Dr. Melvin A. Casberg, 1953-54
Dr. Frank B. Berry, 1954-61
Reorganized under Assistant Secretary (Manpower) 1961

Assistant Secretary of Defense
(International Security Affairs)
Frank C. Nash, 1953-54

H. Struve Hensel, 1954-55
Gordon Gray, 1955-57
Mansfield D. Sprague, 1957-58
John N. Irwin, II, 1958-61

Assistant Secretary of Defense
(Legislative and Public Affairs)
Frederick A. Seaton, 1953-55
Robert Tripp Ross, 1955-57
Reorganized under Assistant Secretary
(Public Affairs), 1957

Assistant Secretary of Defense
(Manpower)
John A. Hannah, 1953-54
Carter L. Burgess, 1954-57
William H. Francis, Jr., 1957-58
Charles C. Finucane, 1958-61

Assistant Secretary of Defense
(Public Affairs)
Murray Snyder, 1957-61

Assistant Secretary of Defense
(Properties and Installations)
Franklin G. Floete, 1953-56
Floyd S. Bryant, 1956-61
Reorganized under Assistant Secretary
(Installations and Logistics), 1961

Assistant Secretary of Defense
(Research and Development)
Donald A. Quarles, 1953-55
Dr. Clifford C. Furnas, 1955-57
Reorganized under Assistant Secretary
(Research and Engineering), 1957

Assistant Secretary of Defense
(Research and Engineering)
Frank D. Newbury, 1957
Paul D. Foote, 1957-58
Reorganized under Directorate of Defense Research and Engineering, 1958

Assistant Secretary of Defense
(Supply and Logistics)
Charles S. Thomas, 1953-54
Thomas P. Pike, 1954-56

E. Perkins McGuire, 1956-61
  Reorganized under Assistant Secretary
  (Installations and Logistics), 1961

Director of Defense Research and Engineering*
  Herbert F. York, 1958-61
    *Created from the Assistant Secretariat
    of Defense (Research and En-
    gineering), 1958

Joint Chiefs of Staff

Chairman
  Gen. of the Army Omar N. Bradley,
    U.S. Army, 1949-53
  Adm. Arthur W. Radford, U.S. Navy,
    1953-57
  Gen. Nathan F. Twining, U.S. Air Force,
    1957-60
  Gen. Lyman L. Lemnitzer, U.S. Army,
    1960-62

Chief of Staff, U.S. Army
  Gen. J. Lawton Collins, 1949-53
  Gen Matthew B. Ridgeway, 1953-55
  Gen. Maxwell D. Taylor, 1955-59
  Gen. Lyman L. Lemnitzer, 1959-60
  Gen. George H. Decker, 1960-62

Chief of Naval Operations
  Adm. William M. Fechteler, 1951-53
  Adm. Robert B. Carney, 1953-55
  Adm. Arleigh A. Burke, 1955-61

Chief of Staff, U.S. Air Force
  Gen. Hoyt S. Vandenberg, 1948-53
  Gen. Nathan F. Twining, 1953-57
  Gen. Thomas D. White, 1957-61

Commandant of the Marine Corps
  Gen. Lemuel C. Shepherd, 1952-55
  Gen. Randolph McC. Pate, 1956-59
  Gen. David M. Shoup, 1960-63

Department of Health, Education and Welfare

Secretary
  Oveta Culp Hobby, 1953-55

Marion B. Folsom, 1955-58
Arthur S. Flemming, 1958-61

Undersecretary
  Nelson A. Rockefeller, 1953-54
  Harold C. Hunt, 1955-57
  John A. Perkins, 1957-58
  Bertha S. Adkins, 1958-61

Assistant Secretary
  Russell R. Larmon, 1953-55
  Bradshaw Mintener, 1955-57
  Edward Foss Wilson, 1957-60

Assistant Secretary for Program Analysis
  Roswell B. Perkins, 1954-57

Assistant Secretary for Legislation
  Elliot L. Richardson, 1957-59
  Robert A. Forsythe, 1960-61

Department of the Interior

Secretary of the Interior
  Douglas McKay, 1953-56
  Frederick A. Seaton, 1956-61

Undersecretary
  Ralph A. Tudor, 1953-54
  Clarence A. Davis, 1954-57
  Olin H. Chilson, 1957-58
  Elmer F. Bennett, 1958-61

Assistant Secretary—Fish and Wildlife
  Ross L. Leffler, 1957-61

Assistant Secretary—Mineral Resources
  Felix E. Wormser, 1953-57
  Royce A. Hardy, 1957-61

Assistant Secretary—Public Land
  Management
  Orme Lewis, 1953-55
  Wesley A. D'Ewart, 1955-56
  Olin H. Chilson, 1956-57
  Roger C. Ernst, 1957-60
  George W. Abbott, 1960-61

Assistant Secretary—Water and Power
  Development
  Fred G. Aandahl, 1953-61

Administrative Assistant Secretary
D. Otis Beasley, 1952-65

Department of Justice

Attorney General
Herbert Brownell, Jr., 1953-57
William P. Rogers, 1957-61

Deputy Attorney General
William P. Rogers, 1953-57
Lawrence E. Walsh, 1957-60

Solicitor General
Simon E. Sobeloff, 1954-55
J. Lee Rankin, 1956-61

Assistant Attorney General/Administration
S. A. Andretta, 1950-65

Assistant Attorney General/Antitrust
Division
Stanley N. Barnes, 1953-56
Victor R. Hansen, 1956-59
Robert A. Bicks, (acting) 1960-61

Assistant Attorney General/Civil Division
Warren E. Burger, 1953-56
George Cochran Doub, 1956-60

Assistant Attorney General/Civil Rights
Division
W. Wilson White, 1957-59
Joseph M. F. Ryan, Jr., (acting) 1959-60
Harold R. Tyler, Jr., 1960-61

Assistant Attorney General/Criminal
Division
Warren Olney, III, 1953-57
Malcolm Anderson, 1958-59
Malcolm R. Wilkey, 1959-61

Assistant Attorney General/Internal
Security Division
William F. Tompkins, 1954-58
J. Walter Yeahley, 1959-70

Assistant Attorney General/Lands Division
Perry W. Morton, 1953-61

Assistant Attorney General/Office of Alien
Property
Dallas S. Townsend, 1953-60

Assistant Attorney General/Office of Legal
Counsel
J. Lee Rankin, 1953-56
Malcolm R. Wilkey, 1958-59
Robert Kramer, 1959-61

Assistant Attorney General/Tax Division
H. Brian Holland, 1953-56
Charles K. Rice, 1956-61

Department of Labor

Secretary of Labor
Maurice J. Tobin, 1948-53
Martin P. Durkin, 1953
Lloyd A. Mashburn, (acting) 1953
James P. Mitchell, 1953-61

Undersecretary
Michael J. Galvin, 1949-53
Lloyd A. Mashburn, 1953
Arthur Larson, 1954-56
James T. O'Connell, 1957-61

Deputy Undersecretary
Millard Cass, 1955-71

Assistant Secretary for Labor-Management
Relations
John J. Gilhooley, 1957-61

Assistant Secretary for Employment and
Manpower
Rocco C. Siciliano, 1953-57
Newell Brown, 1957-60
Walter C. Wallace, 1960-61
Jerry R. Holleman, 1961-62

Assistant Secretary for International Labor
Affairs
Philip M. Kaiser, 1949-53
Spencer Miller, Jr., 1953-54
J. Ernest Wilkins, 1954-58
George C. Lodge, 1958-61
George L. P. Weaver, 1961-69

Assistant Secretary for Standards and Statistics
Harrison C. Hobart, 1953-54

Post Office Department

Postmaster General
Arthur E. Summerfield, 1947-61

Deputy Postmaster General
Charles R. Hook, Jr., 1953-55
Maurice H. Stans, 1955-57
Edson O. Sessions, 1957-59
John M. McKibbin, 1959-61

Assistant Postmaster General/Bureau of
Operations
Norman R. Abrams, 1953-57
John M. McKibbin, 1957-59
Bert B. Barnes, 1959-61

Assistant Postmaster General/Bureau of
Transportation
John C. Allen, 1953-54
E. George Siedle, 1954-59
George M. Moore, 1959-61

Assistant Postmaster General/Bureau of
Finance
Albert J. Robertson, 1953-56
Hyde Gillette, 1957-61

Assistant Postmaster General/Bureau of
Facilities
Ormonde A. Kieb, 1953-59
Rollin D. Barnard, 1959-61

Assistant Postmaster General/Bureau of
Personnel
Eugene J. Lyons, 1953-59
Frank E. Barr, 1960-61

State Department

Secretary of State
John Foster Dulles, 1953-59
Christian A. Herter, 1959-61

Undersecretary
Walter B. Smith, 1953-54

Herbert Hoover, Jr., 1954-57
Christian A. Herter, 1957-59
C. Douglas Dillon, 1959-61

Undersecretary for Administration
Donold B. Lourie, 1953-54
Charles E. Saltzman, 1954

Undersecretary for Economic Affairs
C. Douglas Dillon, 1958-59

Undersecretary for Political Affairs
Robert D. Murphy, 1959
Livingston T. Merchant, 1959-61

Deputy Undersecretary
H. Freeman Matthews, 1950-53

Deputy Undersecretary for Administration
Carlisle H. Humelsine, 1950-53
Loy W. Henderson, 1955-61

Deputy Undersecretary for Economic
Affairs
Samuel C. Waugh, 1955
Herbert V. Prochnow, 1955-56
C. Douglas Dillon, 1957-58

Deputy Undersecretary for Political Affairs
Robert D. Murphy, 1953-59
Livingston T. Merchant, 1959
Raymond A. Hare, 1960-61

Assistant Secretary for Administration
Edward T. Wailes, 1953-54
Isaac W. Carpenter, Jr., 1954-55, 1957
Walter K. Scott, 1958-59
Lane Dwinell, 1959-61

Assistant Secretary for African Affairs
Joseph C. Satterthwaite, 1958-61

Assistant Secretary for Congressional
Relations
Thruston B. Morton, 1953-56
Robert C. Hill, 1956-57
William B. Macomber, Jr., 1957-61

Assistant Secretary for Controller
Isaac W. Carpenter, Jr., 1955-57

Assistant Secretary for Economic Affairs
  Harold F. Linder, 1952-53
  Samuel C. Waugh, 1953-55
  Thorsten V. Kalijarvi, 1957
  Thomas C. Mann, 1957-60
  Edwin M. Martin, 1960-62

Assistant Secretary for European Affairs
  Livingston T. Merchant, 1953-56,
    1958-59
  C. Burke Elbrick, 1957-58
  Foy D. Kohler, 1959-62

Assistant Secretary for Far Eastern Affairs
  John M. Allison, 1952-53
  Walter S. Robertson, 1953-59
  J. Graham Parsons, 1959-61

Assistant Secretary for Inter-American
  Affairs
  John M. Cabot, 1953-54
  Henry F. Holland, 1954-56
  Roy R. Rubottom, Jr., 1957-60
  Thomas C. Mann, 1960-61

Assistant Secretary for International
  Organization Affairs
  David McK. Key, 1954-55
  Francis O. Wilcox, 1955-61

Assistant Secretary for Near Eastern, South
    Asian & African Affairs
  Henry A. Byroade, 1952-55
  George V. Allen, 1955-56
  William M. Rountree, 1956-59
    Reorganized as Near Eastern and
      South Asian Affairs, 1958
    G. Lewis Jones, 1959-61

Assistant Secretary for Policy Planning
  Robert R. Bowie, 1955-57
  Gerard C. Smith, 1957-61

Assistant Secretary for Public Affairs
  Carl W. McCardle, 1953-57
  Andrew H. Berding, 1957-61

Assistant Secretary for United Nations
  Affairs
  John D. Hickerson, 1949-53
  Robert D. Murphy, 1953
  David McK. Key, 1953-54
    Reorganized as International Organiza-
      tion Affairs, 1954

Department of the Treasury

Secretary of the Treasury
  George M. Humphrey, 1953-57
  Robert B. Anderson, 1957-61

Undersecretary
  Marion B. Folsom, 1953-55
  W. Randolph Burgess, 1955-57
  Fred C. Scribner, Jr., 1957-61

Undersecretary for Monetary Affairs
  W. Randolph Burgess, 1954-55
  H. Chapman Rose, 1955-56
  Julian B. Baird, 1957-61

Assistant Secretaries
  H. Chapman Rose, 1953-55
  Andrew N. Overby, 1952-57
  Laurence B. Robbins, 1954-61
  David W. Kendall, 1955-57
  A. Gilmore Flues, 1958-61
  Tom B. Coughran, 1957-58
  T. Graydon Upton, 1958-60

Assistant Secretary for Fiscal Affairs
  Edward F. Bartelt, 1945-55
  William T. Heffelfinger, 1955-62

Administrative Assistant Secretary
  William W. Parsons, 1950-59
  A. E. Weatherbee, 1959-70

REGULATORY COMMISSIONS
AND INDEPENDENT AGENCIES

Atomic Energy Commission

Joseph Campbell, 1953-54
Gordon E. Dean, 1949-53; Chairman,
  1950-53
John F. Floberg, 1957-60
John S. Graham, 1957-62
W. F. Libby, 1954-59
John A. McCone, 1958-61; Chairman,
  1958-61
Thomas E. Murray, 1950-57
Loren K. Olson, 1960-62
Henry D. Smyth, 1949-54
Lewis L. Strauss, 1946-50; Chairman,
  1953-58
Harold S. Vance, 1955-59
John Von Neumann, 1955-57
John H. Williams, 1959-60
Robert E. Wilson, 1960-64
Eugene M. Zuckert, 1952-54

Civil Aeronautics Board

Joseph P. Adams, 1951-56
Alan S. Boyd, 1959-65; Chairman, 1961-65
Harmar D. Denny, 1953-59
James R. Durfee, Chairman, 1956-60
Whitney Gillilland, 1959-
Chan Gurney, 1951-65; Chairman, 1954
Louis J. Hector, 1957-59
Josh Lee, 1945-55
G. Joseph Minetti, 1956-74
Ross Rizley, 1955-56; Chairman, 1955-56
Oswald Ryan, 1945-54; Chairman, 1953

Federal Communications Commission

Robert T. Bartley, 1952-72
T. A. M. Craven, 1956-63
John S. Cross, 1958-62
John C. Doerfer, 1953-60; Chairman,
  1957-60
Frederick W. Ford, 1957-65; Chairman,
  1960-61

Frieda B. Hennock, 1948-55
Rosel H. Hyde, 1946-69; Chairman,
  1953-54, 1966-69
Robert E. Lee, 1953-
Richard A. Mack, 1955-58
George C. McConnaughey, 1954-57;
  Chairman, 1954-57
Eugene H. Merrill, 1952-53
George E. Sterling, 1948-54
Paul A. Walker, 1945-53; Chairman,
  1952-53
Edward M. Webster, 1947-56

Federal Power Commission

Thomas C. Buchanan, 1948-53; Chairman,
  1952-53
William R. Connole, 1955-60
Seaborn L. Digby, 1953-58
Dale E. Doty, 1952-54
Claude L. Draper, 1945-56
John B. Hussey, 1958-60
Arthur Kline, 1956-61
Jerome K. Kuykendall, 1953-61; Chairman,
  1953-61
Nelson Lee Smith, 1945-55; Chairman,
  1947-50
Frederick Stueck, 1954-61
Paul A. Sweeny, 1960-61
Harrington Wimberly, 1945-53

Federal Reserve Board

C. Canby Balderston, 1954-66
Rudolph M. Evans, 1945-54
G. H. King, Jr., 1959-63
William McC. Martin, Jr., 1951-70;
  Chairman, 1951-70
Paul E. Miller, 1954
A. L. Mills, Jr., 1952-65
J. L. Robertson, 1952-73
Charles N. Shepardson, 1955-67
M. S. Szymczak, 1945-61
James K. Vardaman, Jr., 1946-58

Federal Trade Commission

Sigurd Anderson, 1955-64
Albert A. Carretta, 1952-54
John Carson, 1949-53
John W. Gwynne, 1953-59; Chairman,
    1955-59
Edward F. Howrey, 1953-55; Chairman,
    1953-55
William C. Kern, 1955-62
Earl W. Kintner, 1959-61; Chairman,
    1959-61
Lowell B. Mason, 1945-56; Chairman,
    1949-50
James M. Mead, 1949-55; Chairman,
    1950-53
Edward K. Mills, Jr., 1960-61
Robert T. Secrest, 1954-61
Stephen J. Spingarn, 1950-53
Edward T. Tait, 1956-60

Securities and Exchange Commission

Clarence H. Adams, 1952-56
J. Sinclair Armstrong, 1953-57; Chairman,
    1955-57
Donald C. Cook, 1949-53; Chairman,
    1952-53
Ralph H. Demmler, 1953-55; Chairman,
    1953-55
Edward N. Gadsby, 1957-61; Chairman,
    1957-61
A. Jackson Goodwin, Jr., 1953-55
Earl Freeman Hastings, 1956-61
Richard B. McEntire, 1946-53
Andrew Downey Orrick, 1955-60
Harold C. Patterson, 1955-60
Paul R. Rowen, 1948-55
James C. Sargent, 1956-60
Byron D. Woodside, 1960-67

GOVERNORS

Alabama

James E. Folsom (D) 1947-51; 1955-59
Gordon Persons (D) 1951-55
John Patterson (D) 1959-63

Alaska

William A. Egan (D) 1959-67

Arizona

Howard Pyle (R) 1951-55
Ernest W. McFarland (D) 1955-59
Paul Fannin (R) 1959-65

Arkansas

Francis Cherry (D) 1953-55
Orval E. Faubus (D) 1955-67

California

Earl Warren (R) 1943-53
Goodwin J. Knight (R) 1953-59
Edmund G. Brown (D) 1959-67

Colorado

Dan Thornton (R) 1951-55
Ed. C. Johnson (D) 1955-57
Stephen L. McNichols (D) 1957-63

Connecticut

John Davis Lodge (R) 1951-55
Abraham A. Ribicoff (D) 1955-61

Delaware

J. Cabel Boggs (R) 1953-60

Florida

Dan McCarty (D) 1953
Charley E. Johns (D) (acting) 1953-55
LeRoy Collins (D) 1955-61

Georgia

Herman Talmadge (D) 1948-55
Marvin Griffin (D) 1955-59
Ernest Vandiver (D) 1959-63

Hawaii

William F. Quinn (R) 1959-63

Idaho

Len B. Jordan (R) 1951-55
Robert E. Smylie (D) 1955-67

Illinois

William G. Stratton (R) 1953-61

Indiana

George N. Craig (R) 1953-57
Harold W. Handley (R) 1957-61

Iowa

William S. Beardsley (R) 1949-54
Leo A. Hoegh (R) 1954-57
Herschel C. Loveless (D) 1957-61

Kansas

Edward F. Arn (R) 1951-55
Fred Hall (R) 1955-57
George Docking (D) 1957-61

Kentucky

Lawrence W. Wetherby (D) 1950-56
Albert B. Chandler (D) 1956-59
Bert T. Combs (D) 1959-63

Louisiana

Robert F. Kennon (D) 1952-56
Earl K. Long (D) 1956-60
Jimmie H. Davis (D) 1960-64

Maine

Burton M. Cross (R) 1953-55
Edmund S. Muskie (D) 1955-59
Clinton A. Clauson (D) 1959
John H. Reed (R) 1960-67

Maryland

Theodore R. McKeldin, Jr. (R) 1951-59
J. Millard Tawes (D) 1959-67

Massachusetts

Christian A. Herter (R) 1953-57
Foster Furcolo (D) 1957-61

Michigan

G. Mennen Williams (D) 1949-61

Minnesota

C. Elmer Anderson (R) 1951-55
Orville L. Freeman (D) (FL) 1955-61

Mississippi

Hugh White (D) 1952-56
James P. Coleman (D) 1956-60
Ross R. Barnett (D) 1960-64

Missouri

Phil M. Donnelly (D) 1953-57
James T. Blair, Jr. (D) 1957-61

Montana

J. Hugo Aronson (R) 1953-61

Nebraska

Robert B. Crosby (R) 1953-55
Victor E. Anderson (R) 1955-59
Ralph G. Brooks (D) 1959-60

Nevada

Charles H. Russell (R) 1951-59
Grant Sawyer (D) 1959-67

New Hampshire

Hugh Gregg (R) 1953-55
Lane Dwinell (R) 1955-59
Wesley Powell (R) 1959-63

New Jersey

Alfred E. Driscoll (R) 1947-54
Robert B. Meyner (D) 1954-62

New Mexico

Edwin L. Mechem (R) 1951-55; 1957-59; 1961-62
John F. Simms, Jr. (D) 1955-57
John Burroughs (D) 1959-61

New York

Thomas E. Dewey (R) 1943-55
Averell Harriman (D) 1955-59

North Carolina

William B. Umstead (D) 1953-54
Luther H. Hodges (D) 1955-61

North Dakota

C. Norman Brunsdale (R) 1951-57
John E. Davis (R) 1957-61

Ohio

Frank J. Lausche (D) 1945-47; 1949-57
C. William O'Neill (R) 1957-59
Michael V. DiSalle (D) 1959-63

Oklahoma

Johnston Murray (D) 1951-55
Raymond Gary (D) 1955-59
J. Howard Edmondson (D) 1959-63

Oregon

Paul L. Patterson (R) 1952-56
Robert D. Holmes (D) 1957-59
Mark O. Hatfield (R) 1959-67

Pennsylvania

John S. Fine (R) 1951-55
George M. Leader (D) 1955-59
David L. Lawrence (D) 1959-63

Rhode Island

Dennis J. Roberts (D) 1951-59
Christopher Del Sesto (R) 1959-61

South Carolina

James F. Byrnes (D) 1951-55
George B. Timmerman, Jr. (D) 1955-59
Ernest F. Hollings (D) 1959-63

South Dakota

Sigurd Anderson (R) 1951-55
Joe J. Foss (R) 1955-59
Ralph Herseth (D) 1959-61

Tennessee

Frank G. Clement (D) 1953-59
Buford Ellington (D) 1959-63

Texas

Allan Shivers (D) (R) 1949-57
Price Daniel (D) 1957-63

Utah

J. Bracken Lee (R) 1949-57
George D. Clyde (R) 1957-65

Vermont

Lee E. Emerson (R) 1951-55
Joseph B. Johnson (R) 1955-59
Robert T. Stafford (R) 1959-61

Virginia

John S. Battle (D) 1950-54
Thomas B. Stanley (D) 1954-58
J. Lindsay Almond, Jr. (D) 1958-62

Washington

Arthur B. Langlie (R) 1949-57
Albert Rossellini (D) 1957-65

West Virginia

William C. Marland (D) 1953-57
Cecil H. Underwood (R) 1957-61

Wisconsin

Walter J. Kohler (R) 1951-57
Vernon W. Thomson (R) 1957-59
Gaylord A. Nelson (D) 1959-63

Wyoming

Frank A. Barrett (R) 1951-53
C. J. Rogers (R) 1953-55
Milward L. Simpson (R) 1955-59
J. J. Hickey (D) 1959-61

BIBLIOGRAPHY

THE EISENHOWER ERA

Very few historians have attempted to study the 1950s in depth. Charles C. Alexander, *Holding the Line: The Eisenhower Era, 1952-1961* (Bloomington, 1975) is a first-class, readable account of the decade and contains an exceptionally thorough annotated bibliography. For another excellent, readable account of the period see Eric Goldman, *The Crucial Decade* (New York, 1961) which covers the Truman as well as the Eisenhower periods. Broader in scope is William E. Leuchtenburg, *A Troubled Feast: American Society Since 1945* (Boston, 1973), which covers political and social trends over a quarter of a century. Robert Divine, *Since 1945: Politics and Diplomacy in Recent American History* (New York, 1975) contains an excellent summary of the period. Lawrence S. Wittner, *Cold War America: From Hiroshima to Watergate* (New York, 1975) provides a left-wing critique. The Facts on File *Yearbooks* contain a wealth of information indexed for easy reference.

THE PRESIDENCY AND THE ADMINISTRATION

Historians are only beginning to study the Eisenhower presidency. The best work is Herbert Parmet, *Eisenhower and the American Crusade* (New York, 1972). Robert J. Donovan, a member of the press corps who was permitted to sit in on cabinet meetings, relates his favorable impressions in *Eisenhower: The Inside Story* (New York, 1956), an excellent study of the first term. Merlo Pusey, *Eisenhower the President* (New York, 1956) is another sympathetic account. Liberal journalists, such as Richard Rovere, *Affairs of State* (New York, 1956) and Marquis Child *Eisenhower: The Captive Hero* (New York, 1958) are often critical of the President. Norman Graebner, a leading foreign policy specialist, and William V. Shannon, a popular journalist, wrote articles in *Current History* XXXIX (October, 1960) and *Commentary* XXVI (November, 1958) respectively critical of Eisenhower's leadership.

There are many valuable memoirs of those close to the President. White House speech writer, Emmet John Hughes, *The Ordeal of Power: A Political Memoir of the Eisenhower Period* (New York, 1963) is critical of Eisenhower, while Arthur Larson, *Eisenhower: The President Nobody Knows* (New York, 1968) is favorably impressed with the President. Sherman Adams, *First Hand Report: The Story of the Eisenhower Administration* (New York, 1961) is an extremely important work by the man considered the "second most powerful in Washington."

A number of scholars have focused on Eisenhower's use of presidential power. Arthur E. Schlesinger, Jr., in the *Imperial Presidency* (Boston, 1973), related the Eisenhower presidency to the continued expansion of White House power. Richard E. Neustadt, *Presidential Power: The Politics of Leadership* (New York, 1960) is critical of Eisenhower. Clinton Rossiter, *The American Presidency* (New York, 1960) uses the Eisenhower Administration to analyze the component parts of presidential power. For the contrast between Eisenhower's desire for morality in high office and political reality see David A. Frier, *Conflict of Interest in the Eisenhower Administration* (Ames, Iowa, 1969).

Recently Eisenhower's use of power has been praised in light of what some consider the excesses of the Johnson and Nixon presidencies. See Richard Rovere, "Eisenhower Revisited: A Political Genius? A Brilliant Man?" *New York Times Magazine* (Feb. 7, 1971) reprinted in Barton J. Bernstein and Allen J. Matuson, eds., *Twentieth Century America: Recent Interpretations* (New York, 1972) and Murrary Kempton, "The Underestimation of Dwight D. Eisenhower," *Esquire* (September, 1967), reprinted in Robert D. Marcus and David Burner, eds., *America Since 1945* (New York, 1972).

For Eisenhower's own observations of the period and his description of the events see his *The White House Years*, 2 vols. (Garden City, 1963-1965). Although self-justifying, they provide a wealth of information not usually found in presidential memoirs.

Other Works

Agar, Herbert, *The Price of Power* (Chicago, 1957).

Albertson, Dean, ed., *Eisenhower as President* (New York, 1963).

Alsop, Stewart, "Impact of Eisenhower," *The Saturday Evening Post* (November 9, 1963).

Branyan, Robert L., and Lawrence Glaser, eds., *The Eisenhower Administration, 1953-61, A Documentary History* (New York, 1971).

Brooks, John, *The Great Leap* (New York, 1966).

Burnham, Walter Dean, "Eisenhower as a Man, Eisenhower as Mystique," *Commonweal* (Dec. 27, 1963).

Crozier, Michel, *The Bureaucratic Phenomenon* (Chicago, 1964).

David, Paul T. ed., *The Presidential Election and Transition, 1960-61* (Washington, 1961).

Degler, Carl N., *Affluence and Anxiety* (Glenview, N.J. 1968).

Eisenhower, Dwight D., *At Ease: Stories I Tell My Friends* (Garden City, 1967).

Finer, Herman, *The Presidency: Crisis and Regeneration* (Chicago, 1960).

Gunther, John, *Eisenhower: The Man and the Symbol* (New York, 1951).

Howard, Nathaniel R., ed., *The Basic Papers of George M. Humphrey as Secretary of the Treasury* (Cleveland, 1965).

———, "Portrait of the President As World Leader," *New York Times Magazine* (Jan. 18, 1959).

Hyman, Sidney, "Inner Circles of the White House," *New York Times Magazine* (Jan. 5, 1958).

———, "Problems of a Lame Duck President," *New York Times Magazine* (Jan. 18, 1959).

Johnson, Walter, *1600 Pennsylvania Avenue* (Boston, 1963).

Krock, Arthur, "Impressions of the President and the Man," *New York Times Magazine* (June 23, 1957).

McCann, Kevin, *Man from Abilene* (New York, 1952).

Phillips, Cabell, "Eisenhower's Inner Circle," *New York Times Magazine* (Feb. 3, 1957).

———, "The New Look of the Presidency" *New York Times Magazine* (Aug. 16, 1959).

Reston, James, "Dilemma of the White House," *New York Times Magazine* (June 1, 1958).

Strauss, Lewis L., *Men and Decisions* (Garden City, 1962).

Sundquist, James L., *Politics and Policy: The Eisenhower, Kennedy and Johnson Years* (Washington, 1968).

Tugwell, Rexford G., *Off Course: From Truman to Nixon* (New York, 1971).

Ungar, Sanford J., *F.B.I.: An Uncensored Look Behind the Walls* (New York, 1975).

Wexler, Robert, *Dwight David Eisenhower 1890-1969* (Dobbs Ferry, 1970).

White, William S., "Eisenhower Opens the Last Act," *Harpers* (December, 1958).

———, "Evolution of Eisenhower As a Politician," *New York Times Magazine* (Sept. 23, 1956).

Williams, William Appelman, "Officers and Gentlemen," *New York Review of Books* (May 6, 1971).

NATIONAL POLITICS

For studies of Eisenhower's successful rise to the presidency see Herbert Parmet, *Eisenhower and the American Crusade* (New York, 1972) and James Patterson, *Mr. Republican: A Biography of Robert A. Taft* (Boston, 1972). Arthur M. Schlesinger, Jr., and Fred L. Israel, eds., *History of American Presidential Elections* (New York, 1971) Vol. 4 contains essays on the postwar elections. The most recent biography of Adlai Stevenson, Kenneth S. Davis, *The Politics of Honor: A Biography of Adlai E. Stevenson* (New York, 1967) covers the career of the President's chief rival. Stevenson's 1952 speeches are published in *Call To Greatness* (New York, 1956); for a more complete collection of his articles, letters and speeches see Walter Johnson, ed., *The Papers of Adlai E. Stevenson* (Boston, 1972). W. Bruce Gorman, *Kefauver: A Political Biography* (New York, 1971) is the only biography of Stevenson's major competitor. See Richard Nixon, *Six Crises* (Garden City, 1962) for the Vice President's view of his role in the period.

For studies of the American electorate's voting behavior see Angus Campbell and Philip E. Converse, et. al., *The American Voter* (New York, 1960) and Walter Dean Burnham, *Critical Elections and the Mainsprings of American Politics* (New York, 1970).

Herbert Parmet, *The Democrats* (New York, 1976) contains several excellent chapters on the Party in the 1950s. Clifton Brock's court history of the Americans for Democratic Action, *The A.D.A.* (New York, 1962) documents the difficulties liberals had in remaining united during the era of moderation. Joseph P. Lash, *Eleanor: The Years Alone* (New York, 1972), Mrs. Roosevelt's own memoir, *On My Own* (New York, 1958) and Chester Bowles, *Promises to Keep* (New York, 1971) also contain useful material about liberal Democrats. See Theodore S. White's award winning *The Making of A President 1960* (New York, 1961) for the preliminaries of the campaign in both parties.

For studies of several of the major controversies of the period see E. R. Bartley, *The Tidelands Oil Controversy* (Austin, 1953) and Aaron Wildavsky, *Dixon-Yates* (New Haven, 1962). David A. Frier, *Conflict of Interest in the Eisenhower Administration* (Ames, Iowa, 1969) is an excellent study of the many scandals which stirred national interest.

Other Works

Bean, Louis H., *Influences in the 1954 Mid-Term Elections* (Washington, 1954).

Brown, Stuart G., *Conscience in Politics* (Syracuse, 1961). Adlai Stevenson

Burns, James MacGregor, *The Deadlock of Democracy* (Englewood Cliffs, 1963).

Byrnes, James F., *All in One Lifetime* (New York, 1958).

Campbell, Angus, *Group Differences in Attitude and Votes* (Ann Arbor, 1956).

——, et al., *The Voter Decides* (Evanston, 1954).

Caridi, Ronald J., *The Korean War and American Politics: The Republican Party as a Case Study* (Philadelphia, 1969).

Cochran, Bert, *Adlai Stevenson: Patrician Among Politicians* (New York, 1969).

Dalfiume, Richard M., ed., *American Politics Since 1945* (New York, 1969).

Eaton, Herbert, *Presidential Timber: A History of Nominating Conventions 1868-1960* (New York, 1964).

Eulau, Heinz, *Class and Party in the Eisenhower Years: Class Roles in Perspective in the 1952 and 1956 Elections* (New York, 1962).

Harris, Louis, *Is There a Republican Majority?* (New York, 1954).

Howe, Irving and Lewis Coser, *The American Communist Party: A Critical History, 1919-1957* (Boston, 1957).

Johnson, Walter, *How We Drafted Stevenson* (New York, 1955).

Key, V. O. Jr., *Public Opinion and American Democracy* (New York, 1961).

———, *The Responsible Electorate* (Cambridge, Mass., 1966).

Lubell, Samuel, *Revolt of the Moderates* (New York, 1956).

Mazo, Earl, *Richard Nixon: A Political and Personal Portrait* (New York, 1959).

Mazo, Earl and Stephen Hess, *Nixon: A Political Portrait* (New York, 1958).

Miller, William J., *Henry Cabot Lodge* (New York, 1967).

Muller, Herbert J., *Adlai Stevenson* (New York, 1967).

Nixon, Richard, *The Challenge We Face* (New York, 1961).

Redding, Jack, *Inside the Democratic Party* (Indianapolis, 1958).

Richardson, Elmo, *Dams, Parks and Politics: Resource Development and Preservation in the Truman-Eisenhower Era* (Lexington, Ken., 1973).

Roseboom, Eugene H., *A History of American Presidential Elections from George Washington to Richard M. Nixon* (New York, 1970).

Rovere, Richard, *The American Establishment and Other Reports, Opinions and Speculations* (New York, 1962).

Shannon, David A., *The Decline of American Communism* (New York, 1959).

Soth, Lauren, *Farm Trouble in the Age of Plenty* (New York, 1957).

Starobin, Joseph R., *American Communism in Crisis, 1943-1957* (Cambridge, Mass., 1972).

Stevenson, Adlai E., *The New America* (New York, 1957).

———, *What I Think* (New York, 1956).

Stone, I. F., *The Haunted Fifties* (New York, 1963).

Theoharis, Athan, *The Yalta Myths: An Issue in U.S. Politics, 1945-1955* (Columbia, Mo., 1970).

Thomson, C. A. H. and F. N. Shattuck, *The 1956 Presidential Campaign* (Washington, 1960).

Thomson, Charles A. A. *Television and Presidential "Politics": The Experience in 1952 and the Problems Ahead* (Washington, 1956).

Tillet, Paul, ed., *Inside Politics: The National Conventions, 1960* (Dobbs Ferry, 1962).

Willoughby, William B., *The St. Lawrence Waterway: A Study in Politics and Diplomacy* (Madison, 1961).

Wills, Garry, *Nixon Agonistes: The Crisis of the Self-Made Man* (Boston, 1970).

Zinn, Howard, *Postwar America* (Indianapolis, 1973).

McCARTHYISM

For the past 25 years journalists, politicians, historians and social scientists have been searching for explanations for Sen. Joseph R. McCarthy's rise and the hysteria his charges produced. One of the most prominent studies written by contemporary journalist, Richard Rovere, *Senator Joe McCarthy* (New York, 1959), portrays him as a brilliant demagogue. Another important contemporary account is Daniel Bell, ed., *The New American Right* (New York, 1955), which sees McCarthy's support as coming from status anxiety. Eric Goldman, *The Crucial Decade and After* (New York, 1960) synthesizes the two interpretations into an excellent overview of the period.

Recently the status anxiety thesis has come under attack. Michael Paul Rogin, *The Intellectual and McCarthy* (Cambridge, Mass., 1967) questions Bell's thesis using statistical evidence. He contends that McCarthyism can be explained as an attempt by conservative Republicans to attain power. Earl Latham, *The Communist Controversy in Washington* (Cambridge, Mass., 1966) takes a similar approach for the Truman era. Richard Freeland, *The Truman Doctrine and the Ori-*

gins of McCarthyism (New York, 1970) and Athan Theoharis, Seeds of Repression (Chicago, 1971) hold the Truman Administration's anti-Communist rhetoric responsible for preparing the nation for McCarthyism. Robert Griffith, The Politics of Fear: Joseph McCarthy and the Senate (Lexington, Ky., 1970) and Richard Fried, Men Against McCarthy (New York, 1976) both focus on the political complexities in Washington that led to his rise and downfall. For defenses of McCarthy praising his goals and minimizing the consequences of his methods see William F. Buckley, Jr., and L. Brent Bozell, McCarthy and His Enemies: The Record and the Meaning (Chicago, 1954) and Roy Cohn, McCarthy (New York, 1968).

Many subjects of McCarthy's investigations have published their memoirs. See, for example, Lillian Hellman, Scoundrel Time (New York, 1976), Owen Lattimore, Ordeal by Slander (Boston, 1950), Harvey Matusow, False Witness (New York, 1955) and James Wechsler, The Age of Suspicion (New York, 1953). Civil libertarians, such as Henry Steele Commanger and Telford Taylor have deplored the disregard for civil liberties during this period. See their Freedom, Loyalty and Dissent (New York, 1954) and Grand Inquest: The Story of Congressional Investigations (New York, 1955) respectively. For an excellent study of the House Un-American Activities Committee see Walter Goodman, The Committee (New York, 1968).

Other Works

Anderson, Jack and Ronald May, McCarthy: The Man, The Senator and The -Ism (Boston, 1952).

Arnold, Thurmond, Fair Fights and Foul: A Dissenting Lawyer's Life (New York, 1965).

Bentley, Eric, Are You Now Or Have You Ever Been? (New York, 1972).

———, ed., Thirty Years of Treason (New York, 1971).

"Bowman, Alfred," [Miles McMillin] "The Man Behind McCarthy—Coleman of Wisconsin," Nation (March 24, 1954).

Brown, Ralph S., Jr., Loyalty and Security: Employment Tests in the U.S. (New Haven, 1958).

———, "Is McCarthy Slipping?" Reporter (Sept. 18, 1951).

Cater, Douglass, "A Senate Afternoon: the Red Hunt," Reporter (Oct. 10, 1950).

Caughey, John W., In Clear and Present Danger: The Crucial State of our Freedoms (Chicago, 1958).

Chambers, Whittaker, Odyssey of a Friend: Whittaker Chambers' Letters to William F. Buckley Jr. 1954-61 (New York, 1969).

———, Witness (New York, 1952).

Cook, Fred J., The Nightmare Decade: The Life and Times of Sen. Joseph McCarthy (New York, 1971).

Dorsen, Norman and John G. Simon, "McCarthy and the Army: A Fight on the Wrong Front" Columbia University Forum (Fall, 1964).

Flanders, Ralph E., Senator From Vermont (Boston, 1961).

Friendly, Alfred, "The Noble Crusade of Senator McCarthy," Harpers (August 1950).

Gore, Leroy, Joe Must Go (New York, 1954).

Griffith, Robert, "The Political Context of McCarthyism," Review of Politics (January 1971).

Griffith, Robert and Athan Theoharis, ed., The Specter: Original Essays on the Cold War and McCarthyism (New York, 1974).

Hiss, Alger, In the Court of Public Opinion (New York, 1957).

Hoving, John, "My Friend McCarthy," Reporter (April 25, 1950).

Kendrick, Frank J., "The Senate and Sen. Joseph R. McCarthy," Journal of the Minnesota Academy of Science (1964).

———, "McCarthy and the Senate," unpublished Ph.D. dissertation, University of Chicago, 1962.

Lasch, Christopher, "The Cultural Cold War" in Barton Bernstein, ed., *Towards a New Past* (New York, 1968).

Latham, Earl, ed., *The Meaning of McCarthyism* (Boston, 1965).

Luthin, Reinhard H., *American Demagogues: Twentieth Century* (Boston, 1954).

Matusow, Allen J., ed., *Joseph R. McCarthy* (Englewood Cliffs, 1970).

Nevins, Allen, *Herbert Lehman and His Era* (New York, 1963).

O'Brien, Michael, "Sen. Joseph R. McCarthy and Wisconsin, 1946-57," unpublished Ph.D. dissertation, University of Wisconsin, 1971.

Polsby, Nelson W., "Toward An Explanation of McCarthyism," *Political Studies* (October 1960).

Reeves, Thomas C., ed., *McCarthyism* (Hinsdale, Ill., 1973).

Rorty, James and Moshe Decter, *McCarthy and the Communists* (Boston, 1954).

Schlamm, William S., "Across McCarthy's Grave," *National Review* (May 18, 1957).

Shannon, David, *The Decline of American Communism* (New York, 1959).

Steinke, John M. and James Weinstein, "McCarthy and the Liberals," *Studies on the Left* (1962).

Straight, Michael, *Trial by Television* (Boston, 1954).

Thelen, Ester S. and David P., "Joe Must Go: The Movement to Recall Sen. Joseph R. McCarthy," *Wisconsin Magazine of History* (Spring, 1960).

Watkins, Arthur, *Enough Rope* (Englewood Cliffs, 1969).

Wiebe, G. D. "The Army-McCarthy Hearings and the Public Conscience," *Public Opinion Quarterly* (Winter 1958-59).

CONGRESS

The *Congressional Quarterly Almanac* (Washington, D.C., 1945-) is the most important source of information for examining Congress on an annual basis. The series contains information on legislation, committee assignments, roll call votes and legislators' support or opposition to important Administration legislation. Congress's most important activities are summarized in Congressional Quarterly Service, *Congress and the Nation 1945-1964* (Washington, D.C., 1964). This massive volume gives the history of congressional action on specific issues and records legislative investigations as well as votes on important measures.

For an analysis of the Senate see Donald R. Matthews, *U.S. Senators and Their World* (Chapel Hill, 1960) and Joseph S. Clark, *The Senate Establishment* (New York, 1963). *House Out of Order* (New York, 1966) is a study of the lower chamber by liberal congressman Richard Bolling. Two important critics of the legislature are Joseph S. Clark, *Congress: The Sapless Branch* (New York, 1967), which denounces its inefficiency and lack of democracy, and Drew Pearson, and Jack Anderson, *The Case Against Congress* (New York, 1968), a study in the muckraking genre.

There are numerous biographies and autobiographies of important congressional figures. The most important are Joseph B. Gorman, *Estes Kefauver* (New York, 1971), Alfred Steinberg, *Sam Rayburn* (New York, 1973), Joseph Martin, *My First Fifty Years in Politics* (New York, 1973). James Patterson, *Mr. Republican: A Biography of Robert A. Taft* (Boston, 1972) is a sympathetic account of the powerful Senator's career. Extremely useful studies of Lyndon B. Johnson are Rowland Evans and Robert Novak, *Lyndon B. Johnson: The Exercise of Power* (New York, 1966) and Doris Kearns, *Lyndon Johnson and the American Dream* (New York, 1976).

Other Works

Bowles, Chester, *Promises to Keep* (New York, 1971).

Burns, James MacGregor, *John Kennedy: A Political Profile* (New York, 1960).

Coffin, Tristram, *Senator Fulbright: Portrait of a Public Philosopher* (New York, 1966).

Douglas, Paul H., *In the Fullness of Time* (New York, 1972).

Evans, Rowland, Jr., "Louisiana's Passman: The Scourge of Foreign Aid," *Harper's* (January, 1962.

———, "The Sixth Sense of Carl Vinson," *The Reporter* (Jan. 4, 1962).

Flanders, Ralph E. *Senator from Vermont* (Boston, 1961).

Greenfield, Meg, "The Man Who Leads the Southern Senators," *The Reporter* (May 21, 1964). Sen. Richard B. Russell.

Gruening, Ernest H., *Many Battles* (New York, 1973).

Huitt, Ralph K. and Robert L. Peabody, eds., *Congress: Two Decades of Analysis* (New York, 1961).

Humphrey, Hubert H., *The Education of A Public Man: My Life and Politics* (New York, 1976).

Johnson, Haynes, and Bernard M. Gwertzman, *Fulbright: The Dissenter* (Garden City, 1968).

McAdams, Alan K., *Power and Politics in Labor Legislation* (New York, 1964).

McNeil, Neil, *Dirksen: Portrait of a Public Man* (New York, 1970).

Manley, John F., *The Politics of Finance: The House Ways and Means Committee* (Boston, 1970).

Nevins, Allen, *Herbert Lehman and His Era* (New York, 1963).

Ognibene, Peter I., *Scoop: The Life and Politics of Henry M. Jackson* (New York, 1975).

Potter, Charles, *Days of Shame* (New York, 1965).

Powell, Adam Clayton, *Adam by Adam* (New York, 1971).

Seib, Charles B. and Alan L. Otten, "Fulbright: the Arkansas Paradox," *Journal of Politics* (June, 1956).

Sheele, Henry Z., *Charlie Halleck* (New York, 1966).

Smith, A. Robert, *The Tiger in the Senate: The Biography of Wayne Morse* (Garden City, 1962).

Smith, Margaret Chase, *Declaration of Conscience* (New York, 1972).

Sykes, Jay G., *Proxmire* (Washington, 1972).

terHorst, J. F., *Gerald Ford* (New York, 1974).

Wellman, Paul I. *Stuart Symington: Portrait of a Man with a Mission* (Garden City, 1960).

White, William S., *Citadel: The Story of the United States Senate* (New York, 1956).

———, *The Taft Story* (New York, 1954).

Wilkinson, J. Harvie III, *Harry Byrd and the Changing Face of Virginia Politics, 1945-1966* (Charlottesville, 1968).

STATE AND LOCAL GOVERNMENT

The most thorough studies of state politics have been a series written by journalist Neal Peirce. These include, *The Border South States* (New York, 1975), *The Deep South States* (New York, 1974), *The Great Plains States* (New York, 1973), *The Mountain States* (New York, 1972), *The Pacific States* (New York, 1974) and *The Megastates* (New York, 1972). Other important regional studies are Robert Fenton, *Midwest Politics* (New York, 1966) and Robert Sherill, *Gothic Politics in the Deep South* (New York, 1968), which also contains important information on congressional figures. Numan Bartley, *The Rise of Massive Resistance* (Baton

Rouge, 1969) analyzes state governments' reactions to the Supreme Court's de-segregation decisions.

Deterioration of the central city and the flight to the suburbs characterized the Eisenhower era. See Mike Royko, *Boss: Richard Daley of Chicago* (New York, 1971) and Warren Moscow, *The Last of the Big-Time Bosses: The Life and Times of Carmine DeSapio and the Decline and Fall of Tammany Hall* (New York, 1971) for studies of how the urban political machines adjusted to the changes in their cities. Robert Caro, *The Power Broker: Robert Moses and the Fall of New York* (New York, 1974) and Allan R. Talbot, *The Mayor's Game: Richard Lee of New Haven and the Politics of Change* (New York, 1967) describe how two cities, through massive building programs, sought to survive. Edward F. Haas, *DeLesseps Morrison and the Image of Reform* (Baton Rouge, 1974) is an interesting study of how a public relations oriented mayor ran a modern city still deeply rooted in old southern values.

Other Works

Baggaley, Andrew R. "Religious Influence On Wisconsin Voting 1928-1960," *American Political Science Review* (March, 1962).

Bartley, Numan V., *From Thurmond to Wallace: Political Tendencies in Georgia, 1948-1968* (Baltimore, 1968).

———, *The Rise of Massive Resistance: Race and Politics in the South During the 1950's* (Baton Rouge, 1969).

Casdorph, Paul, *A History of the Republican Party in Texas, 1865-1965* (Austin, 1965).

Clark, Thomas D., *Kentucky: Land of Contrast* (New York, 1968).

Connery, Robert H., and Gerald Benjamin, eds., *Governing New York State: The Rockefeller Years* (New York, 1974).

Cooke, Edward F., and Edward G. Janosik, *Pennsylvania Politics* (New York, 1965).

Delmatier, Royce D., and C. McIntosh, eds., *The Rumble of California Politics, 1948-1970* (New York, 1970).

Doherty, Herbert L., "Liberal and Conservative Voting Patterns in Florida," *Journal of Politics* (August 1952).

Epstein, Leon D., *Politics in Wisconsin* (Madison, 1958).

Fenton, John H., *Politics in the Border States* (New Orleans, 1957).

———, *In Your Opinion . . .* (Boston, 1960).

Griffith, Robert, "The General and the Senator: Republican Politics and the 1952 Campaign in Wisconsin," *Wisconsin*

Magazine of History (Autumn, 1970).

Heard, Alexander, *A Two Party South?* (Chapel Hill, 1952).

Hinckley, John T., "The 1952 Elections in Wyoming," *Western Political Quarterly* (March, 1953).

Hoover, Edgar M., and Raymond Vernon, *Anatomy of a Metropolis* (New York, 1962).

Judah, Charles, "The 1952 Elections in New Mexico" *Western Political Quarterly* (March, 1953).

Karlen, Jules A., "The 1952 Elections in Montana," *Western Political Quarterly* (March, 1953).

Kelso, Paul A., "The 1952 Elections in Arizona," *Western Political Quarterly* (March, 1953).

Key, V. O., Jr., *American State Politics* (New York, 1956).

Kutz, Myer, *Rockefeller Power* (New York, 1974).

Litt, Edgar, *The Political Cultures of Massachusetts* (Cambridge, Mass., 1965).

Lowe, Jeanne, *Cities in a Race with Time; Progress and Poverty in America's Growing Cities* (New York, 1967).

McKelvey, Blake, *The Emergence of Metropolitan America, 1915-1966* (New Brunswick, 1968).

Merrill, M. R., "The 1952 Elections in Utah," *Western Political Quarterly* (March, 1953).

Morgan, Neil, *Westward Tilt: The American West Today* (New York, 1961).

Moscow, Warren, *What Have You Done for Me Lately? The Ins and Outs of New*

York City Politics (Englewood Cliffs, 1967).

Moses, Robert, Public Works: A Dangerous Trade (New York, 1970).

Nevins, Allan, Herbert H. Lehman and His Era (New York, 1963).

Ogden, Daniel, "The 1952 Elections in Washington," Western Political Quarterly (March, 1953).

Oshinsky, David M. Jr., "Wisconsin Labor and the Campaign of 1952," Wisconsin Magazine of History (Winter, 1972-73).

Ostrander, Gilman M., Nevada: The Great Rotten Borough 1895-1964 (New York, 1966).

Petshak, Kirk, The Challenge of Urban Reform: Policies and Programs in Philadelphia (Philadelphia, 1973).

Price, H. D., The Negro in Southern Politics: A Chapter of Florida History (May, 1955).

Ravitch, Diane, The Great School Wars, New York City, 1805-1973: A History of the Public Schools as Battlefield of Social Change (New York, 1974).

Silver, James W., Mississippi: The Closed Society (New York, 1964).

Sindler, Allen P., ed., Change in the Contemporary South (Durham, 1963).

Smith, C. G., "The 1952 Elections in Utah," Western Political Quarterly (March, 1953).

Turner, Wallace, The Mormon Establishment (Boston, 1966).

Wentworth, Evelyn L., "County Alignments in Maryland Elections 1934-1958," unpublished M.A. essay, University of Maryland, 1962.

FOREIGN POLICY

The largest portion of the literature dealing with the Eisenhower Administration focuses on the development and execution of foreign policy. The works on this subject can be divided very broadly into three categories: traditional, those that accept the Cold War policies of the Administration; realist, those that criticize Eisenhower's stand as too ideologically oriented and ignorant of these realities of big power politics; and revisionist, those that view the U.S. as a historically expansionist power and maintain that many of the crises of the period could have been avoided by more moderate action on the part of the Administration. For a traditionalist view of the period see, Paul Seabury, The Rise and Decline of the Cold War (New York, 1967) and Desmond Donnelly, Struggle for the World: The Cold War, 1917-1965 (New York, 1965). Realist interpretations include John Spanier, American Foreign Policy Since World War II (New York, 1971), Seyom Brown, The Faces of Power: Constancy and Change in United States Foreign Policy from Truman to Johnson (New York, 1968) and Louis J. Halle, The Cold War as History (New York, 1967). Revisionists have yet to give Eisenhower the attention they have devoted to the Truman Administration. Major studies in this school include William Appleman Williams, The Tragedy of American Diplomacy (New York, 1962), Walter LaFeber, America, Russia and the Cold War, 1945-66 (New York, 1967) and Stephen E. Ambrose, Rise to Globalism: American Foreign Policy, 1938-1970 (Baltimore, 1971).

The figure of John Foster Dulles dominated foreign policy during the period. For an early articulation of his views see his Life Magazine article, "A Policy of Boldness," (May 19, 1952) and "Policy for Security and Peace," Foreign Affairs, XXXII (1954). The Secretary of State unveiled his concept of "brinkmanship" in James Shepley, "How Dulles Averted War," Life (Jan. 16, 1956). Townsend Hoopes award winning biography of Dulles, The Devil and John Foster Dulles (Boston, 1973) is critical of his moralism and unilateralism, which Hoopes thinks often exacerbated diplomatic crises. Hoopes contrasts Eisenhower's realism with

Dulles's impulsive crusading zeal. The President emerges as the Administration's dominent foreign policy figure, restraining the Secretary of State. One of Dulles's leading critics from the academic world, Hans Morgenthau, wrote an essay in Norman Graebner, ed., *An Uncertain Tradition* (New York, 1961) that focuses on how the Secretary's fear of the Republican Right, and particularly Sen. Joseph McCarthy, shaped his diplomacy. For more sympathetic accounts of Dulles see Richard Goold-Adams, *The Time of Power: A Reappraisal of John Foster Dulles* (London, 1962), John Robinson Beal, *John Foster Dulles: A Biography* (New York, 1957) and Louis Gerson, *John Foster Dulles* (May, 1957). Dulles's successor, Christian A. Herter, is discussed in George B. Noble, *Christian A. Herter* (New York, 1970).

A large number of Administration critics have published important memoirs. See, in particular, George F. Kennan, *Memoirs* (Boston, 1972) dealing with Cold War policy and Chester Bowles, *Promises to Keep* (New York, 1971) focusing on relations with underdeveloped nations. Compare and contrast the columns of the *New York Times*'s two foremost columnists, James Reston and Arthur Krock for their appraisals of the Administration's diplomacy. Both have published anthologies of their best articles: James Reston, *Sketches in the Sand* (New York, 1967) and Arthur Krock, *In the Nation, 1932 to 1966* (New York, 1966). Walter Johnson, ed., *The Papers of Adlai Stevenson* (Boston, 1974-76) includes an excellent collection of speeches and articles critical of the Administration in volumes four through six.

There are numerous regional studies of American foreign policy during the Eisenhower era. For U.S. policy toward Europe see, Anatole Rapoport, *The Big Two: Soviet-American Perceptions of Foreign Policy* (New York, 1971) and Bennett Kovrig, *The Myth of Liberation: East-Central Europe in U.S. Diplomacy and Politics since 1941* (Baltimore, 1973). For studies of the North Atlantic Treaty Organization see Robert E. Osgood, *NATO: The Entangling Alliance* (Chicago, 1962) and Klaus Knorr, ed., *NATO and American Security* (Princeton, 1959). Contemporary writers advocating early relaxation of tension in Europe include, C. L. Sulzberger, *The Big Thaw* (New York, 1956), George Kennan, "Overdue Changes in Our American Foreign Policy," *Harper's Magazine* (August, 1956) and "Peaceful Coexistence: A Western View," *Foreign Affairs* (January 1960), and his most important, *Russia, The Atom, and the West* (New York, 1957). For an important justification of a hardline stand in Europe see Dean Acheson's interview in *U.S. News and World Report* (Jan. 17, 1958).

Valuable studies of the Berlin crisis include Jean E. Smith, *The Defense of Berlin* (Baltimore, 1963), Jack M. Schick, *The Berlin Crisis, 1958-1962* (Philadelphia, 1971) and Robert M. Slusser, *The Berlin Crisis of 1961* (Baltimore, 1973). For Eisenhower's diplomacy in the Middle East see John C. Campbell, *Defense of the Middle East* (New York, 1960), a good survey of the entire areas. Herman Finer, *Dulles over Suez* (Chicago, 1964) is critical of how the Secretary of State handled the crisis, while Carey B. Joynt, "John Foster Dulles and the Suez Crisis" in Gerald N. Grob, ed., *Statesmen and Statecraft of the Modern West* (Barre, Mass., 1967) defends the Secretary of State's performance.

Robert N. Burr, *Our Troubled Hemisphere: Perspectives in United States-Latin American Relations* (Washington, 1967) is an excellent overview of Latin American diplomacy during the Eisenhower Administration. Theodore Draper, *Castro's Revolution* (New York, 1962) attacks the Castro takeover while William Appleman Williams, *The U.S., Cuba and Castro* (New York, 1962) is more sympathetic to the new government.

There is an extensive literature on U.S. policy in the Far East, particularly in Vietnam. Foster Rhea Dulles, *American Foreign Policy Toward Communist China,*

1949-1969 (New York, 1972) includes chapters documenting the deterioration of relations between the two powers. For a discussion of early U.S. intervention in Vietnam see particularly Bernard B. Fall, *The Two Viet-Nams* (New York, 1963) and George M. Kahin and John W. Lewis, *The United States in Vietnam* (New York, 1969). For a detailed study of the events behind the 1954 Geneva Accords see Melvin Gurtov, *The First Vietnam Crisis: Chinese Communist Strategy and United States Involvement, 1953-1954* (New York, 1967), Philip Devillers and Jean Lacoutre, *End of a War: Indo-China, 1954* (New York, 1969) and Robert E. Bandle, *Geneva: 1954* (Princeton, 1969). Compare these works with the documents available in the *Pentagon Papers* (Boston, 1971).

The question of disarmament has been deeply analyzed. See particularly, Bernard G. Bechhoefer, *Postwar Negotiations for Arms Control* (Washington, 1961), a comprehensive treatment of the American disarmament program. Critics of the American stand during the period include Richard J. Barnet, *Who Wants Disarmament?* (Boston, 1960), Edgar M. Bottome, *The Balance of Terror: A Guide to the Arms Race* (Boston, 1971) and Joseph P. Murray, *From Yalta to Disarmament: Cold War Debate* (New York, 1961).

Other Works

Acheson, Dean, *Power and Diplomacy* (Cambridge, Mass., 1958).

Adler, Selig, *The Isolationist Impulse: Its Twentieth Century Reaction* (New York, 1957).

Baldwin, David, *Economic Development and American Foreign Policy, 1943-1962* (Chicago, 1966).

Berding, Andrew H., *Dulles on Diplomacy* (Princeton, 1965).

Bowles, Chester, *Ideas, People and Peace* (New York, 1958).

——, *The New Dimensions of Peace* (New York, 1950).

Cohen, Bernard C., *The Press and Foreign Policy* (Princeton, 1963).

Commanger, Henry Steel, "The Perilous Folly of Senator Bricker," *The Reporter* (October 13, 1953).

Dean, Arthur A., "The Bricker Amendment and Authority Over Foreign Affairs," *Foreign Affairs* (October, 1953).

Divine, Robert A., *Since 1945: Politics and Diplomacy in Recent American History* (New York, 1975).

Donelan, Michael, *The Ideas of American Foreign Policy* (London, 1963).

Drummond, Roscoe and Gaston Coblentz, *Duel at the Brink: John Foster Dulles' Command of American Power* (Garden City, 1960).

Dulles, Eleanor Lansing, *John Foster Dulles: The Last Year* (New York, 1963).

Elliot, William Y., et al., *The Political Economy of American Foreign Policy* (New York, 1955).

Feis, Herbert, *Foreign Aid and Foreign Policy* (New York, 1961).

Finletter, Thomas K., *Foreign Policy: The Next Phase* (New York, 1958).

——, *Power and Policy* (New York, 1954).

Graebner, Norman A., *The New Isolationism: A Study in Politics and Foreign Policy since 1950* (New York, 1956).

Gukin, Michael, *John Foster Dulles: A Statesman and His Times* (New York, 1972).

Hatch, Alden, *The Lodges of Massachusetts* (New York, 1973).

Henderson, John W., *The United States Information Agency* (New York, 1969).

Herz, John H., *International Politics in the Atomic Age* (New York, 1959).

Hoffman, Stanley, ed., *Contemporary Theory in International Relations* (Englewood Cliffs, 1960).

Hughes, Emmet J., *America the Vincible* (Garden City, 1959).

Johnson, Haynes and Bernard M. Gwertzman, *Fulbright: The Dissenter* (New York, 1968).

Kaplan, Morton, *System and Process in International Politics* (New York, 1957).

——, *Nuclear Weapons and Foreign Policy* (New York, 1957).

Kissinger, Henry A., *The Necessity for*

Choice: Prospects of American Foreign Policy (New York, 1960).

Kolko, Gabriel, Roots of American Foreign Policy (Boston, 1969).

Kolko, Joyce and Gabriel Kolko, The Limits of Power: The World and U.S. Foreign Policy 1945-1954 (New York, 1972).

Magdoff, Harry, The Age of Imperialism (New York, 1969).

May, Ernest R., "Eisenhower and After" in May, ed., The Ultimate Decision: The President as Commander-in-Chief (New York, 1960).

Medaris, John B., Countdown for Decision (New York, 1960).

Miller, William, Henry Cabot Lodge (New York, 1967).

Osgood, Robert E., Ideals and Self-Interest in America's Foreign Relations: The Great Transformation of the 20th Century (Chicago, 1953).

Osgood, Robert E., et al., America and the World: From the Truman Doctrine to Vietnam (Baltimore, 1970).

Padelford, Norman J. and George A. Lincoln, The Dynamics of International Politics (New York, 1962).

Pye, Lucian W., "Soviet and American Styles in Foreign Aid," Orbis IV (Summer, 1960).

Radosh, Ronald, American Labor and United States Foreign Policy (New York, 1970).

Rosenau, James N., ed., International Politics and Foreign Policy (New York, 1961).

Rostow, Walt W., The Diffusion of Power: An Essay in Recent History (New York, 1972).

——, The United States in the World Arena: An Essay in Recent History (New York, 1960).

Slessor, John, Strategy for the West (New York, 1954).

Smith, Merriman, A President's Odyssey (New York, 1961).

Sorensen, Thomas C., The Word War (New York, 1968).

Steel, Richard, Pax Americana (New York, 1967).

Thomas, Ann Van Wynen and A. J. Thomas Jr., Non-intervention: The Law and Its Import in the Americas (Dallas, 1966).

Vagts, Alfred, A History of Militarism: Civilian and Military (New York, 1959).

Wittner, Lawrence S., Rebels Against War: The American Peace Movement 1941-1960 (New York, 1969).

Asia

Bachrack, Stanley, D. The Committee of One Million: "China Lobby" Politics 1953-1971 (New York, 1976).

Barnet, Richard J., Roots of War (New York, 1972). Origins of Vietnam War.

Bator, Victor, Vietnam: A Diplomatic Tragedy: The Origins of the United States Involvement (Dobbs Ferry, 1965).

Cameron, Allan W., Vietnam Crisis: A Documentary History (Ithaca, 1971).

Clubb, Oliver E., "Formosa and the Offshore Islands in American Policy 1950-1955," Political Science Quarterly (December, 1959).

Cooper, Chester L., The Los Crusade: America in Vietnam (New York, 1970).

Dunn, Frederick S., Peacemaking and the Settlement with Japan (Princeton, 1963).

Halberstam, David, The Best and the Brightest (New York, 1972).

——, The Making of a Quagmire (New York, 1964).

Honey, P. J., ed., North Vietnam Today: Profile of a Communist Satellite (New York, 1962).

Jones, Howard P., Indonesia: The Possible Dream (New York, 1971).

Kalb, Marvin and Elie Abel, Roots of Involvement: The U.S. in Asia, 1784-1971 (New York, 1971).

Lansdale, Edward G., In the Midst of Wars: An American's Mission to Southeast Asia (New York, 1972).

Poole, Peter A., The U.S. and Indochina from FDR to Nixon (Hinsdale, Ill., 1973).

Rankin, Karl Lott, China Assignment (Seattle, 1964).

Reischauer, Edwin O., "The Broken Dialogue with Japan," Foreign Affairs (October, 1960).

Ridgway, Matthew B., The Korean War (New York, 1967).

Schlesinger, Arthur M. Jr., The Bitter

Heritage: Vietnam and American Democracy, 1941-1968 (Boston, 1968).

Shaplen, Robert, *The Lost Revolution: Twenty Years of Neglected Opportunities in Vietnam and of American Failures to Foster Democracy There* (New York, 1965).

Steele, A. T., *The American People and China* (New York, 1966).

Stevenson, Charles A., *The End of Nowhere, American Policy Toward Laos Since 1954* (Boston, 1972).

Europe and the Cold War

Acheson, Dean, "The Illusion of Disengagement," *Foreign Affairs*, XXXVI (April, 1958).

Crankshaw, Edward, *Khrushchev: A Career* (New York, 1966).

Duchacek, Ivo, "Czechoslovakia," in Stephen D. Kertesz, ed., *The Fate of East Central Europe* (Notre Dame, 1956).

Dulles, Eleanor L., *The Wall: A Tragedy in Three Acts* (Columbia, S.C., 1972).

Fontaine, André, *History of the Cold War* (New York, 1970).

Gelber, Lionel, *America in Britain's Place: The Leadership of the West and Anglo-American Unity* (New York, 1961).

Graebner, Norman, *Cold War Diplomacy* (New York, 1962).

———, ed., *The Cold War: A Conflict of Ideology and Power* (New York, 1976).

Hammond, Paul Y., *Cold War and Detente* (New York, 1975).

Harriman, W. Averell, *America and Russia in a Changing World: A Half Century of Personal Observations* (Garden City, 1971).

Horowitz, David, ed., *Containment and Revolution* (Boston, 1967).

Houghton, Nealie Doyle, ed., *Struggle Against History: U.S. Foreign Policy in the Age of Revolution* (New York, 1968).

Kaplan, Lawrence S. "The U.S. and the Atlantic Community: The First Generation," in John Braeman and David Brody, eds., *Twentieth Century American Foreign Policy* (Columbus, 1971).

Kennan, George F., *Realities of American Foreign Policy* (Princeton, 1954).

Lukacs, John, *A New History of the Cold War* (Garden City, 1966).

Neustadt, Richard E., *Alliance Politics* (New York, 1970).

Planek, Charles R., *The Changing Status of German Reunification in Western Diplomacy, 1955-1966* (Baltimore, 1967).

Plishcke, Elmer, "Eisenhower's 'Correspondence Diplomacy' with the Kremlin: Case Study in Summit Diplomatics," *Journal of Politics* (February 1968).

Schwartz, Harry, *The Red Phoenix: Russia Since World War II* (New York, 1961).

Tatu, Michel, *Power in the Kremlin: From Krushchev to Kosygin* (New York, 1969).

Theoharis, Athan, G., *The Yalta Myths* (Columbia, Mo., 1970).

Ulam, Adam B., *Expansion and Coexistence: The History of Soviet Foreign Policy, 1917-1967* (New York, 1968).

———, *The Rivals: America and Russia since World War II* (New York, 1971).

Vigneras, Marcel, *Rearming the French* (Washington, 1957).

Latin America

Berle, Adolf A., Jr., *Latin America: Diplomacy and Reality* (New York, 1962).

Bonsal, Philip W., *Cuba, Castro and the United States* (Pittsburgh, 1971).

Dozer, Donald M., *We Good Neighbors? Three Decades of Inter-American Relations, 1930-1960* (Gainesville, Fla., 1959).

Eisenhower, Milton, *The Wine is Bitter* (Garden City, 1963).

Gillin, John and K. H. Silvert, "Ambiguities in Guatemala," *Foreign Affairs*, XXXIV (April, 1956).

Lewis, Gordon K., *Puerto Rico: Freedom and Power in the Caribbean* (New York, 1963).

McClellan, Grant S., ed., *U.S. Policy in Latin America* (New York, 1963).

Mecham, J. Lloyd, *The United States and Inter-American Security, 1889-1960* (Austin, 1961).

Mezerik, A. G., *Cuba and the United States* (New York, 1963).

Pike, Frederick B., "Guatemala, the United States, and Communism in the Americas," *Review of Politics*, XVII (April, 1955).

Ronning, C. Neale, *Law and Politics in Inter-American Diplomacy* (New York, 1963).

Taylor, Philip B., Jr., "The Guatemala Affair: A Critique of United States Foreign Policy," *American Political Science Review*, L (September, 1956).

Middle East and Africa

Bowles, Chester, *Africa's Challenge to the Americans* (Berkeley, 1957).

Dougherty, James E., "The Aswan Decision in Perspective," *Political Science Quarterly* (March, 1959).

Eden, Anthony, *The Suez Crisis of 1956* (Boston, 1966).

Emerson, Rupert, "American Policy in Africa," *Foreign Affairs* (January 1962).

Engler, Robert, *The Politics of Oil* (Chicago, 1961).

Fitzsimmons, M. A., "The Suez Crisis and the Containment Policy," *Review of Politics* (October, 1957).

Hammond, Paul Y. and Sidney S. Alexander, *Political Dynamics in the Middle East* (New York, 1972).

Nutting, Anthony, *No End of the Lesson* (London, 1967). Middle East.

Polk, William R., *The United States and the Arab World* (Cambridge, Mass., 1969).

Robertson, Terrence, *Crisis: The Inside Story of the Suez Conspiracy* (London, 1964).

Smolansky, O.M., "Moscow and the Suez Crisis, 1956: A Reappraisal," *Political Science Quarterly* (December, 1965).

Weissman, Stephen R., *American Foreign Policy in the Congo: 1960-1964* (Ithaca, 1974).

Disarmament

Brennan, Donald G., ed., *Arms Control, Disarmament and National Security* (New York, 1961).

Bull, Hedley, *The Control of the Arms Race* (New York, 1961).

Dean, Arthur H., *Test Ban and Disarmament: The Path of Negotiation* (New York, 1966).

Gettleman, Marvin, *A Summary of Disarmament Documents, 1945-1962* (San Francisco, n.d.).

Levine, Robert A., *The Arms Debate* (Cambridge, Mass., 1963).

Nogee, Joseph L., *Soviet Policy Toward International Control of Atomic Energy* (Notre Dame, 1961).

Roberts, Chalmers M., *The Nuclear Years: The Arms Race and Arms Control, 1945-1970* (New York, 1970).

Schelling, Thomas C. and Morton H. Halperin, *Strategy and Arms Control* (New Haven, 1961).

Spanier, John W. and Joseph L. Nogee, *The Politics of Disarmament: A Study in Soviet-American Gamesmanship* (New York, 1962).

The Central Intelligence Agency

Agee, Philip, *Inside the Company: CIA Diary* (New York, 1975).

Berman, Jerry J., and Morton H. Halperin, eds., *The Abuses of the Intelligence Agencies* (Washington, 1975).

Dulles, Allen W., *The Craft of Intelligence* (New York, 1963).

Marchetti, Victor, and John D. Marks, *The CIA and the Cult of Intelligence* (New York, 1974).

Powers, Francis Gary and Curt Gentry, *Operation Overflight* (New York, 1970).

Ransom, Harry H., *Central Intelligence and National Security* (Cambridge, Mass., 1958).

U.S. Commission on CIA Activities within the United States, *Report to the President by the Commission on CIA Activities within the United States* (Washington, 1975).

U.S. Senate, Select Committee on Intelligence Activities, *Alleged Assassination Plots Involving Foreign Leaders* (Washington, 1975).

———, *Intelligence Activities and the Rights of Americans* (Washington, 1976).

Wise, David, and Thomas B. Ross, *The Invisible Government* (New York, 1964).

DEFENSE

Eisenhower's adoption of a "New Look" policy, with its emphasis on strategic nuclear weapons and economy in defense spending, was considered a dramatic departure in defense at the time. For a description of the program see Warner Schilling, Paul Y. Hammond and Glenn Snyder, *Strategy, Politics and Defense Budget* (New York, 1962). Samuel P. Huntington, *The Common Defense: Strategic Programs in National Politics* (New York, 1961) is the best overall assessment of the defense program. Richard Aliano, *American Defense Policy from Eisenhower to Kennedy, 1957-1961* (Athens, Ohio, 1975) focuses closely on the policy debate during Eisenhower's second Administration.

The policy produced a great debate within the Pentagon, where a large number of prominent military officers criticized the Administration. Matthew D. Ridgway, *Soldier* (New York, 1956) and Maxwell Taylor, *Swords into Plowshares* (New York, 1972) emphasize the need for a more varied defense capable of fighting conventional as well as nuclear war. James Gavin, *War and Peace in the Space Age* (New York, 1958) echoes this demand and contains a plea for the development of missiles. Curtis LeMay with McKinley Kantor, *Mission with LeMay: My Story* (New York, 1965) traces the life of the chief advocate of reliance on strategic bombers. Military officials were not the only people calling for a change in Administration policy. Under Henry Kissinger's direction, the Council on Foreign Relations produced a popular and extremely influential study, *Nuclear Weapons and Foreign Policy* (Garden City, 1958), calling for a more diversified defense policy and increased development of missiles.

During the last years of the decade, a debate raged over whether a "missile gap" existed between the U.S. and the Soviet Union. The controversy was prompted by the successful launching of the Soviet satellite *Sputnik* and the leaking of the Gaither Report to the press in the fall of 1957. For material on the Gaither Report see Morton H. Halperin, "The Gaither Committee and the Policy Process," *World Politics* (April, 1961). Edgar M. Bottome, *The Missile Gap: A Study of the Formation of Political and Military Policy* (Rutherford, 1971) and Roy E. Licklider, "The Missile Gap Controversy," *Political Science Quarterly* XVIII both discuss the controversy which became an issue in the 1960 presidential campaign. For a discussion of intragovernment maneuvering that slowed down missile development see Edmund Beard, *Developing the ICBM: A Study in Bureaucratic Politics* (New York, 1976).

During the Eisenhower Administration the space program grew out of the Defense Department's missile program. For studies of the early space program see Robert L. Rosholt, *An Administrative History of NASA, 1958-1963* (Washington, 1966) and Loyd S. Swenson, Jr., James M. Grumwood and Charles C. Alexander, *This New Ocean: A History of Project Mercury* (Washington, 1966).

In his farewell address, President Eisenhower warned of the growth of the "miliatry-industrial complex . . . the conjunction of an immense military establishment and a large arms industry." The dangers of the association became the theme of a large body of literature. See especially Fred J. Cook, *The Warfare State* (New York, 1962), Richard J. Barnet, *The Economy of Death* (New York, 1969), and Sidney Lens, *The Military-Industrial Complex* (Philadelphia, 1970). Seymour Melman, a Columbia University professor of engineering, became one of the most conspicuous critics of the association. See his *Pentagon Capitalism: The Political Economy of War* (New York, 1970) and the earlier *Our Depleted Society* (New York, 1965).

Other Works

Aron, Raymond, *The Great Debate: Theories of Nuclear Strategy* (Garden City, 1965).

Baldwin, Hanson W., *The Great Arms Race: A Comparison in U.S. and Soviet Power Today* (New York, 1958).

Barclay, C. N., *The New Warfare* (New York, 1954).

Borklund, C. W., *The Department of Defense* (New York, 1968).

———, *Men of the Pentagon: From Forrestal to McNamara* (New York, 1966).

Brodie, Bernard, *Strategy in the Missile Age* (Princeton, 1959).

Caraley, Demetrios, *The Politics of Military Unification* (New York, 1966).

Coffin, Tristram, *The Armed Society: Militarism in Modern America* (Baltimore, 1964).

Dietchman, Seymour, *Limited War and American Defense Policy* (Cambridge, Mass., 1964).

Dinerstein, H. S., *War and the Soviet Union: Nuclear Weapons and the Revolution in Soviet Military and Political Thinking* (New York, 1962).

Duscha, Julius, *Arms, Money and Politics* (New York, 1964).

Fryklund, Richard, *One Hundred Million Lives: Maximum Survival in a Nuclear War* (New York, 1962).

Gilpin, Robert, *American Scientists and Nuclear Weapons Policy* (Princeton, 1962).

Glines, Carroll, V., Jr., *The Compact History of the United States Air Force* (New York, 1973).

Goldwin, Robert A., ed., *America Armed: Essays in U.S. Military Policy* (Chicago, 1963).

Hahn, Walter F. and John C. Neff, eds., *American Strategy for the Nuclear Age* (New York, 1960).

Halperin, Morton H., *Limited War in the Nuclear Age* (New York, 1960).

Hammond, Paul Y., *Organizing for the Defense: The American Military Establishment in the Twentieth Century* (Princeton, 1961).

Hersh, Seymour M., *Chemical and Biological Warfare: America's Hidden Arsenal* (Garden City, 1969).

Huntington, Samuel, *Changing Patterns of Military Politics* (New York, 1962).

———, *The Soldier and the State: The Theory and Politics of Civil-Military Relations* (New York, 1957).

Huszar, George B. de, ed., *National Strategy in an Age of Revolutions: Addresses and Panel Discussions of the Fourth National Military-Industrial Conference* (New York, 1959).

Kahn, Herman, *On Thermonuclear War* (Princeton, 1960).

Kaufmann, William W., ed., *Military Policy and National Security* (Princeton, 1956).

———, *The Requirements of Deterrence, Memorandum No. 7* (Princeton, 1954).

Knorr, Klaus and Thornton Read, *Limited Strategic War* (New York, 1962).

Kolodziej, Edward A., *The Uncommon Defense and Congress, 1945-1963* (Columbus, 1966).

Lansdale, Edward G., *In the Midst of Wars: An American's Mission to Southeast Asia* (New York, 1972).

Miksche, F. O., *The Failure of Atomic Strategy and a New Proposal for the Defense of the West* (New York, 1958).

Mills, Walter, *Arms and Men: A Study in American Military History* (New York, 1956).

Morgenstern, Oskar, *The Question of National Defense* (New York, 1959).

Osgood, Robert E., *Limited War: The Challenge to American Security* (Chicago, 1957).

Parry, Albert, *Russia's Rockets and Missiles* (Garden City, 1960).

Schwartz, Urs, *American Strategy: A New Perspective* (Garden City, 1966).

Schwiebert, Ernest G., *A History of Air Force Ballistic Missiles* (New York, 1965).

Smith, Bruce L. R., *The Rand Corporation: Case Study of A Nonprofit Advisory Agency* (Cambridge, Mass., 1966).

Snyder, Glenn H., *Deterrence and Defense: Toward a Strategy of National Security* (Princeton, 1961).

Turner, Gordon G. and Richard D. Challenger, eds., *National Security in the Nuclear Age: Basic Facts and Theories* (New York, 1960).

Twining, Nathan F., *Neither Liberty nor Safety: A Hard Look at U.S. Military Policy and Strategy* (New York, 1966).

Waskow, Arthur I., ed., *The Debate over Thermonuclear Strategy* (Boston, 1965).

Weigley, Russell F., *History of the United States Army* (New York, 1967).

Yarmolinsky, Adam, *The Military Establishment: Its Impact on American Society* (New York, 1971).

Space

Bates, David R., ed., *Space Research and Exploration* (New York, 1958).

Bergaust, Erik, *Reaching for the Stars* (Garden City, 1960).

Bloomfield, Lincoln, ed., *Outer Space* (Englewood Cliffs, 1962).

Boyd, Robert Lewis, *Space Research By Rocket and Satellite* (New York, 1960).

Cox, Donald, *The Space Race: from Sputnik to Apollo* (Philadelphia, 1962).

Emme, Eugene M., ed., *The History of Rocket Technology: Essays on Research, Development and Utility* (Detroit, 1964).

Etzioni, Amitai, *The Moondoggle* (New York, 1964).

Gantz, Kenneth Franklin, *Man In Space* (Washington, 1959).

Green, Constance McLaughlin, and Milton Lomask, *Vanguard: A History* (Washington, 1971).

Haley, Andrew G., *Rocketry and Space Exploration* (Princeton, 1958).

Hayes, E. Nelson, *Trackers of the Skies* (Cambridge, Mass., 1968).

Kenman, Erland, and Edmund H. Harvey Jr., *Mission to the Moon: A Critical Examination of NASA and the Space Program* (New York, 1969).

Lapp, Ralph E., *Man and Space: The Next Decade* (New York, 1961).

Schwiebert, Ernest G., et al., *A History of the U.S. Air Force Ballistic Missiles* (New York, 1965).

Shelton, William, *American Space Exploration: The First Decade* (Boston, 1967).

Sobel, Lester A., *Space: From Sputnik to Gemini* (New York, 1965).

Swenson, Loyd S., Jr., et al., *The New Ocean: A History of Project Mercury* (Washington, 1966).

Van Dyke, Vernon, *Pride and Power: The Rationale of the Space Program* (Urbana, 1964).

Witkin, Richard, ed., *The Challenge of Sputnik* (Garden City, 1958).

BUSINESS, LABOR AND THE ECONOMY

Harold G. Vatter, *The American Economy in the 1950s* (New York, 1963) is the most comprehensive survey of the Eisenhower period. Robert Sobel, *The Age of Giant Corporations: A Microeconomic History of American Business, 1914-1970* (Westport, Conn., 1972) includes useful material on the growth of major corporations during the period. See John Kenneth Galbraith, *The Affluent Society* (Boston, 1958) and his earlier *American Capitalism: The Concept of Countervailing Power* (Boston, 1952) for critiques of conservative economics. For a later liberal work consult Bernard D. Nessiter, *The Mythmakers: An Essay on Power and Wealth* (Boston, 1964). Ronald L. Mighell, *American Agriculture: Its Structure and Place in the Economy* (New York, 1955) describes the plight of the farmers in the 1950s.

In *People of Plenty* (Chicago, 1954) historian David Potter asserts that the American people had been successful because of the nation's unlimited wealth. Contrast his thesis with Michael Harrington, *The Other American* (New York, 1962), one of the first studies of poverty in the 1950s. Eli Chinoy, *Automobile Workers and the American Dream* (New York, 1955) is a sociological case study of factory workers, whose attitudes are less optimistic than Potter's.

Joseph C. Goulden, *Meany* (New York, 1972) is a good biography of the AFL-CIO leader that is particularly useful on the merger of the AFL and CIO in 1955 and on Meany's futile attempts to purge unions of underworld elements. The reformist zeal of many unionists remained in the 1950s. It is best shown in Victor G. Reuther, *The Brothers Reuther* (Boston, 1976) and David Dubinsky, *A Life with Labor* (New York, 1977). For the most thorough study of union corruption see Walter Sheridan, *The Fall and Rise of Jimmy Hoffa* (New York, 1973). Ronald Radosh, *American Labor and United States Foreign Policy* (New York, 1969) discusses the Cold War militancy of national unions.

Other Works

Adams, Walter, ed., *The Structure of American Industry* (New York, 1961).

Aronowitz, Stanley, *False Promises* (New York, 1973).

Baldwin, David A., *Economic Development and American Foreign Policy, 1943-1962* (Chicago, 1966).

Barber, Richard J., *The Politics of Research* (Washington, 1966).

Bauer, Raymond A., Ithiel de Sola Pool and Lewis A. Dexter, *American Business and Public Policy; The Politics of Foreign Trade* (New York, 1963).

Benoit, Emile and Kenneth Boulding, eds., *Disarmament and the Economy* (New York, 1963).

Berle, Adolf A., *The Twentieth Century Capitalist Revolution* (New York, 1954).

———, *The American Economic Republic* (New York, 1963).

Blough, Roger, *The Washington Embrace of Business* (New York, 1976).

Domhoff, G. William, *Who Rules America?* (Englewood Cliffs, 1967).

Elliot, William Y., et al., *The Political Economy of American Foreign Policy* (New York, 1955).

Freeman, Ralph E., ed., *Postwar Economic Trends in the U.S.* (New York, 1960).

Gerber, Albert B., *Bashful Billionaire* (New York, 1967). Howard Hughes.

Gillam, Richard, ed., *Power in Postwar America* (New York, 1971).

Goulden, Joseph C., *Meany: The Unchallenged Strongman of American Labor* (New York, 1972).

Harrington, Michael, *Labor in a Free Society* (Berkeley, 1959).

Hession, Charles H., *John Kenneth Galbraith and his Critics* (New York, 1972).

Holmans, A. E., *United States Fiscal Policy, 1945-1959* (New York, 1961).

James, Ralph C. and Estelle, *James Hoffa and the Teamsters: A Study of Union Power* (Princeton, 1965).

Kaplan, A. D. H., *Big Enterprise in a Competitive System* (Washington, 1964).

Kendrick, John, *Productivity Trends in the United States* (New York, 1961).

Kolko, Gabriel, *Wealth and Power in America* (New York, 1962).

Kutz, Meyer, *Rockefeller Power* (New York, 1974).

Lampman, Robert, *The Share of Top Wealth-Holders* (New York, 1962).

Larrowe, Charles P., *Harry Bridges, The Rise and Fall of Radical Labor in the United States* (New York, 1972).

Lewis, Wilfred, Jr., *Federal Fiscal Policy in the Postwar Recessions* (Washington, 1962).

Lilienthal, David E., *Big Business: A New Era* (New York, 1954).

MacDonald, Dwight, "Our Invisible Poor" *New Yorker* (Jan. 19, 1963).

Miller, Herman, *Rich Man, Poor Man* (New York, 1964).

Monsen, R. Joseph, Jr., *Modern American Capitalism, Ideologies and Issues* (Boston, 1963).

Radosh, Ronald, *American Labor and United States Foreign Policy* (New York, 1970).

Reagan, Michael, *The Managed Economy* (New York, 1963).

Shappard, Harold, *Poverty and Wealth in America* (Chicago, 1970).

Stern, Philip, *The Great Treasury Raid* (New York, 1964).

Sutton, Francis Xavier, et al., *The American Business Creed* (Cambridge, Mass., 1956).

Trebing, Harry M., ed., *The Corporation and the American Economy* (New York, 1970).

Triflin, Robert, *Gold and the Dollar Crisis* (New Haven, 1961).

Wallich, Henry C., *The Cost of Freedom: Conservation and Modern Capitalism* (New York, 1962).

Warner, W. Lloyd and James Abegglen, *Big Business Leaders in America* (New York, 1955).

White, Lawrence J., *The Automobile Industry since 1945* (Cambridge, Mass., 1971).

SUPREME COURT

During the Eisenhower Administration the Court moved in a liberal direction, particularly in regard to civil liberties and civil rights. For an excellent summary chapter covering this transformation in judicial philosophy see Paul L. Murphy, *The Constitution in Crisis Time, 1918-1969* (New York, 1972). C. H. Pritchett, *The Political Offender and the Warren Court* (New York, 1958) is the best contemporary study of the Court. For a more recent one see Archibald Cox, *The Warren Court: Constitutional Decisions as an Instrument of Reform* (Cambridge, Mass., 1968) and Samuel Krislov, *The Supreme Court and Personal Freedom* (New York, 1968). Leon Friedman and Fred L. Israel, eds., *The Justices of the United States Supreme Court, 1789-1969* (New York, 1969) contains biographical articles and representative opinions of each justice.

Other Works

Berman, Daniel M., "Constitutional Issues and the Warren Court," *American Political Science Review*, LIII (1959).

Bickel, Alexander, *Politics and the Warren Court* (New York, 1965).

Bioff, Allan L., "Watkins v. United States as a Limitation on Power of Congressional Investigating Committees," *Michigan Law Review*, LVI (1957).

Black, Hugo, "The Bill of Rights," *New York University Law Review*, (April, 1960).

Brennan, William J., *An Affair With Freedom* (New York, 1967).

Chase, Harold W., "The Warren Court and Congress," *Minnesota Law Review*, XLIV (1960).

Cramton, Roger C., "The Supreme Court and State Power to Deal with Subversion and Loyalty," *Minnesota Law Review*, XLIII (1959).

Hunt, Allan R., "Federal Supremacy and State Legislation," *Michigan Law Review* (1955).

Kemper, Donald J., *Decade of Fear: Senator Hennings and Civil Liberties* (Columbia, Mo., 1965).

Lewis, Anthony, "The Supreme Court and Its Critics," *Minnesota Law Review*, XLV (1965).

Lytle, Clifford M., *The Warren Court and Its Critics* (Tucson, 1968).

Magrath, C. Peter, "The Obscenity Cases: Grapes of Roth," in Philip B. Kurland, ed., *Supreme Court Review* (1966).

Mollan, Robert, "Smith Act Prosecutions: The Effect of the Dennis and Yates Decisions," *University of Pittsburgh Law Review*, XXVI (June, 1965).

Murphy, Terrence J., *Censorship: Government and Obscenity* (Baltimore, 1963).

Murphy, Walter F., *Congress and the Court: A Case Study in the American Political Process* (Chicago, 1962).

Nelson, Steve, *The 13th Juror: The Inside Story of My Trial* (New York, 1955).

Paul, James C. N. and Murray L. Schwartz, *Federal Censorship: Obscenity in the Mail* (New York, 1961).

Pritchett, C. H., *Congress versus the Supreme Court, 1957 to 1960* (New York, 1961).

Sayler, Richard H. et al., eds., *The Warren Court: A Critical Analysis* (New York, 1969).

Weaver, James D., *Warren, The Man, the Court, the Era* (Boston, 1967).

CIVIL RIGHTS

Much of the literature on civil rights in the 1950s deals with the Supreme Court's ruling in *Brown v. Board of Education*. Richard Kluger, *Simple Justice* (New York, 1975) is a brilliant account of the arguments behind the case. For a concise description of the Court's ruling and the reaction to it see Paul L. Murphy, *The Constitution in Crisis Time* (New York, 1972). Southern attempts to obstruct the Court's ruling are masterfully chronicled in Numan V. Bartley, *The Rise of Massive Resistance* (Baton Rouge, 1969). Consult his lengthy bibliography for a listing of specific studies in the South's response to the decision.

Herbert Parmet, *Eisenhower and the American Crusade* (New York, 1972) and Kenneth Davis, *The Politics of Honor: A Biography of Adlai E. Stevenson* (New York, 1967) give respective accounts of how the two rivals in the 1956 campaign dealt with the school desegregation issue. John W. Anderson, *Eisenhower, Brownell, and the Congress: The Tangled Origin of the Civil Rights Bill of 1956-1957* (Montgomery, 1964) discusses the problems of getting the Civil Rights Act of 1957 passed. Richard Neustadt, *Presidential Power* (New York, 1963) contains an illuminating case study of how Eisenhower handled the 1957 Little Rock crisis.

For a general overview of the civil rights struggle during the 1950s see, Anthony Lewis, *Portrait of a Decade* (New York, 1964) and Thomas R. Brooks, *Walls Come Tumbling Down: A History of the Civil Rights Movement* (Englewood Cliffs, 1974). There are a number of biographies of leading civil rights leaders. David Lewis, *King: A Critical Biography* (New York, 1970) is still the best study of Dr. King. Jervis Anderson, *A. Philip Randolph* (New York, 1973) contains a useful section on the black labor leader's futile struggle to force the AFL-CIO to desegregate its member unions. For background information on militant organizations see August Meier and Elliot Rudwick, *CORE: A Study of the Civil Rights Movement, 1942-1968* (New York, 1973).

Other Works

Baldwin, James, *The Fire Next Time* (New York, 1963).

Bates, Daisy, *Long Shadow of Little Rock* (New York, 1962).

Bendiner, Robert, "The Compromise on Civil Rights—I" *Reporter* (Sept. 6, 1956).

Brown, Sterling Allen, *The Negro in Washington* (New York, 1969).

Clark, Thomas D., *The Emerging South* (New York, 1961).

Dulles, Foster Rhea, *The Civil Rights Commission, 1957-1965* (East Lansing, Mich., 1968).

Fenderson, Lewis H., *Thurgood Marshall: Fighter for Justice* (New York, 1969).

Franklin, John Hope, *From Slavery to Freedom* (New York, 1974).

Friedman, Leon ed., *Argument: The Oral Argument Before the Supreme Court in Brown v. Board of Education of Topeka, 1952-1955* (New York, 1969).

Ginzberg, Eli, *The Negro Potential* (New York, 1956).

Hane, Walton, Jr., *The Political Philosophy of Martin Luther King, Jr.* (Westport, Conn., 1972).

Harbaugh, William Henry, *Lawyer's Lawyer: The Life and Times of John W. Davis* (New York, 1973).

Harding, Vincent, "Black Radicalism: The Road from Montgomery," in Alfred E. Young, ed., *Dissent: Explorations in the History of American Radicalism* (DeKalb, Ill., 1968).

Hays, Brooks, *A Southern Moderate Speaks* (Chapel Hill, N.C., 1959).

Hickey, Neil and Ed Edwin, *Adam Clayton Powell and the Politics of Race* (New York, 1966).

King, Coretta Scott, *My Life With Martin Luther King, Jr.* (New York, 1969).

King, Martin Luther, Jr., *Stride Toward Freedom: The Montgomery Boycott* (New York, 1958).

Lincoln, C. Eric, ed., *Martin Luther King, Jr.: A Profile* (New York, 1970).

Lomax, Louis, *The Negro Revolt* (New York, 1962).

L'Moore, Alford, *The Case of the Sleeping People* (Little Rock, 1959).

McPherson, James M., et al., *Black in America* (Garden City, 1971).

Malcolm X, *Autobiography of Malcolm X* (New York, 1965).

Martin, John Bartlow, *The South Says "Never"* (New York, 1957).

Meier, August and Francis L. Broderick, *Negro Protest Thought in the Twentieth Century* (Indianapolis, 1966).

Muse, Benjamin, *Ten Years of Prelude: The Story of Integration Since the Supreme Court's 1954 Decision* (New York, 1961).

Newby, I. A., *Challenge to the Court: Social Scientists and the Defense of Segregation, 1954-1966* (Baton Rouge, 1969).

Powell, Adam Clayton, Jr., *Adam by Adam* (New York, 1971).

Rischin, Moses, *Our Own Kind: Voting by Race, Creed or National Origin* (Santa Barbara, 1960).

Rovere, Richard, "The Civil Rights Bill," *The New Yorker* (Aug. 31, 1957).

Rustin, Bayard, *Down the Line* (New York, 1971).

Sarratt, Reed, *The Ordeal of Desegregation: The First Decade* (New York, 1966).

Silberman, Charles E., *Crisis in Black and White* (New York, 1964).

Silverman, Corinne, *The Little Rock Story* (University, Ala., 1959).

Smith, Bob, *They Closed Their Schools: Prince Edward County, Virginia, 1951-1964* (Chapel Hill, 1965).

Steinkraus, Warren E., "Martin Luther King's Personalism," *Journal of the History of Ideas* (Jan.-March 1973).

Wolk, Allan, *The Presidency and Black Civil Rights: Eisenhower to Nixon* (Rutherford, 1971).

Workman, William D. Jr., *The Case for the South* (New York, 1960).

MEDIA

The *New York Times* and Time, Inc., are the subjects of detailed studies: Gay Talese, *The New York Times: The Kingdom and the Power* (New York, 1966) and W. A. Swanberg, *Luce and His Empire* (New York, 1972). The liberal columnist of the *New York Times*, James Reston, has edited his best columns in *Sketches in the Sand* (New York, 1967). Contrast his opinions to those of his more conservative colleague, Arthur Krock, who published his own anthology, *In The Nation 1932-1966* (New York, 1966). For a summary of Walter Lippmann's views see his *Conversations with Walter Lippmann* (New York, 1960).

Erik Barnouw, *A History of Broadcasting in the United States* (New York, 1966-70) includes a great deal of material on television. For a study of television and politics see Edward W. Chester, *Radio, Television and American Politics* (New York, 1969). Alexander Kendrick's biography of Edward R. Murrow, *Prime Time* (New York, 1969), focuses on the top news broadcaster of the period.

Other Works

Abell, Tyler, ed., *Drew Pearson Diaries, 1949-1959* (New York, 1974).

Alsop, Joseph and Stewart, *The Reporter's Trade* (New York, 1958).

Aronson, James, *The Press and the Cold War* (Indianapolis, 1970).

Bliss, Edward, ed., *In Search of Light: The Broadcasts of Edward R. Murrow, 1938-1961* (New York, 1967).

Boorstin, Daniel J., *The Image: A Guide to Pseudo-Events in America* (New York, 1961).

Cash, Kevin, *Who the hell is William Loeb?* (Manchester, 1975).

Kendrick, Alexander, *Prime Time: The Life of Edward R. Murrow* (Boston, 1969).

Krock, Arthur, *Sixty Years on the Firing Line* (New York, 1968).

Lawrence, Bill, *Six Presidents, Too Many Wars* (New York, 1971).

Markmann, Charles Lam, *The Buckleys* (New York, 1973).

Metz, Robert, *C.B.S.: Reflections in a Bloodshot Eye* (New York, 1970).

Michie, Allan A., *Voices Through the Iron Curtain: The Radio Free Europe Story* (New York, 1963).

Pilat, Oliver, *Drew Pearson* (New York, 1973).

Sulzberger, C. L., *The Last of the Giants* (New York, 1970).

————, *A Long Row of Candles: Memoirs and Diaries, 1934-1954* (New York, 1969).

TOPICAL INDEX

The following is a list of individuals profiled in the *Eisenhower Years* according to their most important public political activity. In some cases names appear under two or more categories.

House of Representatives

Albert, Carl (D, Okla.)
Allen, Leo (R, Ill.)
Anderson, William R. (D, Tenn.)
Arends, Leslie C. (R, Ill.)
Ayres, William H. (R, Ohio)
Barden, Graham A. (D, N.C.)
Boggs, Thomas H. (D, La.)
Bowles, Chester B. (D, Conn.)
Brown, Clarence J. (R, Ohio)
Burns, John A. (D, Hawaii)
Byrnes, John W. (R, Wisc.)
Cannon, Clarence A. (D, Mo.)
Celler, Emanuel (D, N.Y.)
Cooper, Jere (D, Tenn.)
Curtis, Thomas B. (R, Mo.)
Dawson, William L. (R, Ill.)
Ford, Gerald R. Jr. (R, Mich.)
Green, Edith (D, Ore.)
Griffin, Robert P. (R, Mich.)
Gross, H. R. (R, Iowa)
Halleck, Charles A. (R, Ind.)
Harris, Oren (D, Ark.)
Hays, Lawrence B. (D, Ark.)
Hays, Wayne L. (D, Ohio)
Hebert, Felix E. (D, La.)
Hoffman, Clare E. (R, Mich.)
Holifield, Chet (D, Calif.)
Hope, Clifford R. (R, Kan.)
Judd, Walter (R, Minn.)
Keating, Kenneth B. (R, N.Y.)
Landrum, Phillip (D, Ga.)
McCormack, John W. (D, Mass.)
Mahon, George H. (D, Texas)

Martin, Joseph J. (R, N.C.)
Metcalf, Lee (D, Mont.)
Mills, Wilbur D. (D, Ark.)
Passman, Otto E. (D, La.)
Patman, Wright (D, Texas)
Powell, Adam Clayton, Jr. (D, N.Y.)
Rayburn, Sam (D, Texas)
Reed, Daniel A. (D, Va.)
Richards, James P. (D, S.C.)
Rivers, Mendel L. (D, N.Y.)
Rooney, John J. (D, N.Y.)
Scott, Hugh D. Jr. (R, Pa.)
Short, Dewey J. (R, Mo.)

Senate

Aiken, George (R, Vt.)
Allott, Gordon L. (R, Colo.)
Anderson, Clinton P. (D, N.M.)
Bennett, Wallace F. (R, Utah)
Benton, William (D, Conn.)
Bible, Alan H. (D, Nev.)
Bonner, Herbert (D, N.C.)
Bricker, John W. (R, Ohio)
Bridge, Styles (R, N.H.)
Bush, Prescott S. (R, Conn.)
Byrd, Harry (D, Va.)
Byrd, Robert C. (D, W. Va.)
Cannon, Howard W. (D, Nev.)
Capehart, Homer E. (R, Ind.)
Carlson, Frank (R, Kan.)
Carroll, John (D, Colo.)
Case, Clifford P. (R, N.J.)
Chavez, Dennis (D, N.M.)

National Politics, Organizations and Issues

McCarthy

Flanders, Ralph
Hensel, Strove
McCarthy, Joseph
Matthews, J. B.
Peress, Irving
Schine, G. David
Stevens, Robert
Watkins, Arthur
Zwicker, Ralph

State And Local Politics

Almond, Lindsay
Boggs, J. Caleb
Byrnes, James
Chandler, Albert
Clement, Frank
Coleman, James
Collins, LeRoy
Daley, Richard
Davis, Jimmie
DeSapio, Carmine
Dilworth, Richardson
DiSalle, Michael
Egan, William
Faubus, Orval
Finletter, Thomas
Folsom, James
Freeman, Orville
Griffin, Marvin
Harriman, Averell
Hogen, Frank
Kennon, Robert Floyd
Knight, Goodwin
Leader, George
Lee, J. Braken
Lee, Richard
Long, Earl
McKeldin, Theodore
Meyner, Robert
Morrison, DeLesseps
Munoz Marin, Luis
Patterson, John
Poulson, Norris
Ribicoff, Abraham
Rockefeller, Nelson
Roosevelt, Eleanor
Rose, Alex
Shivers, Allen
Smylie, Robert
Stanley, Thomas
Timmerman, George, Jr.
Wagner, Robert
Williams, G. Mennen

Judiciary

Black, Hugo
Brennan, William
Burton, Harold
Clark, Thomas C.
Douglas, William
Frankfurter, Felix
Harlan, John Marshall
Hoffman, Walter
Jackson, Robert
Johnson, Frank
Minton, Sherman
Prettyman, E. Barrett
Reed, Stanley
Soboloff, Simon
Stewart, Potter
Timmerman, George Sr.
Vinson, Fredrick
Warren, Earl
Whittaker, Charles
Wright, J. Skelly

White House and Executive Branch

Adams, Sherman
Anderson, Robert
Benson, Ezra Taft
Brownell, Herbert
Burns, Arthur
Cherry, Francis
Corsi, Edward
DeLoach, Deke
Dodge, Joseph
Dulles, John Foster
Durkin, Martin
Eisenhower, Dwight D.
Eisenhower, Milton
Fleming, Arthur
Folsom, Marion
Goodpaster, Andrew
Hagerty, James
Harlow, Bryce
Hobby, Ovetta Culp
Hodges, Luther
Hoover, J. Edgar
Hughes, J. Emmet
Hughes, Rowland
Humphrey, George
Jackson, D. C.
Ladejinsky, Wolf
McElroy, Neil
McKay, Douglas
McLeod, Scott
Mack, Richard

Mansure, Edmund
Mitchell, James P.
Morgan, Gerard
Morrow, Frederic
Nixon, Richard
Persons, Wilton
Rogers, William
Saulnier, Raymond
Seaton, Frederick
Shanley, Bernard
Stephens, Thomas
Summerfield, Arthur
Weeks, Sinclair
Wilson, Charles

Foreign Affairs

Acheson, Dean
Aldrich, Winthrop
Allen, George
Allison, John
Armour, Norman
Bissell, Richard
Black, Eugene
Bohlen, Charles
Bowie, Robert
Braden, Sprille
Brown, Winthrop
Bruce, David
Bunche, Ralph
Cabot, John
Clay, Lucius
Collins, J. Lawton
Corsi, Edward
Dean, Arthur
Dillon, Douglas
Dowling, Walter
Dulles, John F.
Eaton, Frederick
Farland, Joseph
Foster, William
Harris, Reed
Herter, Christian
Hill, Robert
Hollister, John
Hoover, Herbert II
Houghton, Amory
Jones, Howard
Kennan, George
Kohlberg, Alfred
Kohler, Foy
Lansdale, E. H.
Lodge, Henry C.
Lovett, Robert
Luce, Clare
MacArthur, Douglas II
Mann, Thomas

Merchant, Livingston
Murphy, Robert
Parson, J. Graham
Rankin, Karl
Roosevelt, Kermit
Smith, Earle
Smith, W. Bedell
Streibert, Theodore Arthur
Thompson, Llewellyn
Wadsworth, James

Defense Department and Military

Brucker, William
Burke, Arleigh
Clark, Mark
Gaither, H. Rowan
Gardner, Trevor
Gates, Thomas
Gavin, James
Harrison, William
Hensel, Strove
LeMay, Curtis
McElroy, Neil
Norstad, Lauris
Quarles, Donald
Radford, Arthur
Rickover, Hyman
Ridgway, Mathew
Ross, Robert Tripp
Stevens, Robert
Talbott, Harold
Taylor, Maxwell
Thomas, Charles
Twining, Nathan
Vandenberg, Hoyt
Wilson, Charles
York, Herbert
Zwicker, Ralph

Science

Bethe, Hans
Bush, Vannevar
Conant, James
Dryden, Hugh
Einstein, Albert
Killian, James
Kistiakowsky, George
Oppenheimer, J. Robert
Pauling, Linus
Salk, Jonas
Seaborg, Glenn

Strauss, Lewis
Teller, Edward
Von Braun, Wernher

Treasury, Economic Policy and Regulatory Commissions

Black, Eugene
Brundage, Percival
Burns. Arthur
Cross, Hugh
Davis, Clarence
Dodge, Joseph
Doerfer, John C.
Funston, Keith
Galbraith, John Kenneth
Hughes, Rowland
Humphrey, George
Mack, Richard
Mansure, Edmund
Martin, William McChesney
Saulnier, Raymond

Business and Labor

Avery, Sewell
Biemiller, Andrew
Boulware, Lemuel
Brewster, Frank
Bridges, Harry
Carey, James
Coleman, John S.
Curran, Joseph
Curtice, Harlow
Dubinsky, David
Eaton, Cyrus
Fairless, Benjamin
Ford, Henry
Gleason, Thomas
Gold, Ben
Goldberg, Arthur
Greenwalt, Crawford
Hoffa, James
Hughes, Howard
Hutcheson, Maurice
Kohler, Herbert
Lewis, John L.
Lovestone, Jay
McDonald, David
Meany, George
Pace, Frank
Percy, Charles
Randolph, A. Phillip
Reuther, Walter
Romney, George
Watson, Thomas

Wolfson, Louis
Yates, Eugene

Civil Rights, Social Protest, and Political Dissent

Abernathy, Ralph
Bates, Mrs. Lucius (Daisey Getson)
Battle, John S.
Blossom, Virgil
Hannah, John
King, Martin Luther
Lury, Autherine
Marshall, Thurgood
Mitchell, Clarence
Muste, A. J.
Rankin, J. Lee
Rustin, Bayard
Shuttleworth, F.
Till, Emmet
Wilkins, Roy

Intellectuals, Writers and Churchman

Alsop, Joseph
Alsop, Stewart
Arendt, Hannah
Ashmore, Harry
Bell, Daniel
Blake, Eugene
Bruce, Lenny
Buckley, William
Burnham, James
Chambers, Whittaker
Cousins, Norman
Drucker, Pete
Eastman, Max
Fast, Howard
Fiedier, Leslie
Ginzburg, Alan
Graham, Billy
Herberg, Will
Hofstadter, Richard
Hook, Sidney
Kerouac, Jack
Kerr, Clark
Kinsey, Albert
Kirk, Russell
Kissinger, Henry
Lippmann, Walter
Lipset, Seymour Martin
Luce, Henry
Miller, Arthur
Mills, C. Wright

Murrow, Edward R.
Niebuhr, Reinhold
Packard, Vance
Parsons, Talcott
Peale, Norman Vincent
Pearson, Drew
Pusey, Nathan
Rand, Ayn
Reisman, David
Reston, James

Salisbury, Harrison
Sarnoff, David
Schlesinger, Arthur Jr.
Sheen, Fulton J.
Smith, Gerald L. F.
Spellman, Francis
Sulzburger, C.
Viereck, Peter
Wilson, Sloan

Index

Index

740—Eisenhower

and area redevelopment 122, 154-155, 399; program for Army base desegregation 271; warns against "bookburners" 114; fiscal 1958 budget 76; opposes investigation of Bunche 78; and civil rights legislation 194, 547; meets with civil rights leaders 337, 642; and defense spending 597; and Dirksen 145; and Dixon-Yates contract 147, 269, 294, 435, 587; and aid to segregated schools 238; and farm policy 34-38, 193, 608, 653; vetoes federal employee salary increase 351; fiscal policy views 150; backs Halleck for minority leadership 415; endorses Hawaii statehood 244; and highway program 112; and Second Hoover Commission report 287; and J. Hoover 289-290; vetoes housing legislation 93-94, 451, 515, 570; and labor reform legislation 171, 242, 419, 636-637; and Little Rock school desegregation controversy 29, 73, 75, 200, 241, 260, 273, 440; loyalty-security program of 23, 134, 463; and McCarran-Walter Act reform 382, 629-630; and J. McCarthy 246, 291, 303, 387, 417, 482, 579, 635; S. Mitchell attacks policies of 435; vetoes natural gas price deregulation bill 133, 205, 374, 653; Neuberger criticizes on civil rights 451; suspends Oppenheimer security clearance 86, 463, 548; expresses concern over National Park System 403; and Powell amendment 438; signs witness immunity bill 308; vetos public works bill 451; and quiz show scandal 616; Rauh criticizes 499; rejects clemency for Rosenbergs 527; on Reston 506; on Senate Republican leadership struggle 351; opposes social security increases 513; and space program 343; and 1959 steel strike 50; and tax policy 259, 503; and tidelands oil dispute 329, 497; and urban renewal 489; on Velde's subpeonas 618; ends wage and price controls 258, 636

1952 Election Campaign—advisers to 70, 302, 440; Aldrich raises funds for 11; Clay role in 112; "draft Eisenhower" movement 141-142; Hague role in 258; P. Hoffman role in 277-278; E. Hughes role in 291; issues 105-106, 181, 382, 456; J. Lee and 360; Lodge role in 371; J. McCarthy and 386; "Morning-

side Heights" agreement 596; Morse and 441; Persons role in 482; Roberts's role in 514; Seaton role in 549; Summerfield role in 591; support for 90, 96, 205, 209, 271; 290, 329, 368, 377, 378, 455, 478, 513, 515, 540, 548, 551, 553, 631; Weeks role in 636

1956 Election Campaign—issues 583; Nixon renomination 246; support for 329, 478, 486, 513, 554

Foreign Affairs—and Atoms-for-peace program 303, 587; and dissemination of atomic information 397, 471; Blatnik criticizes 48; authorizes military training of Cuban refugees 163; and Castro 267; and Development Loan Fund 22; J. Dulles and 165-170; and Eisenhower Doctrine for the Middle East 234; ends Korean war 166, 555; sends Murphy to Lebanon 447; and Lumumba assassination 162; and nuclear peace ship 55; and nuclear test ban 397; conflict with Passman on 1957 foreign aid budget 470; general foreign policy of 165; policy on Quemoy and Matsu 318, 493, 498, 512; criticizes Radford 493; urges U.S.-Soviet cooperation 3, 303; supports 1955 summit conference 167; urges Trujillo overthrow 162; takes responsibility for U-2 flights 487; opposes U.S. intervention in Vietnam 493, 512, 565; and resolution condemning Yalta and Potsdam agreements 268;

EISENHOWER, Milton S.—Profile **190-193**

EISENHOWER Doctrine for the Middle East—Dulles and 170; Eisenhower requests 187; Flanders opposes Democratic amendments to 205; Humphrey-Mansfield amendment to 411; opposition to 217-218, 276, 625; support for 55, 260, 308, 443, 523, 569, 608

EISENHOWER'S Six Great Decisions (book)—565

El SALVADOR—270, 409

ELLENDER Sen. Allen—Profile **193-194; 51**

ELITCHER, Max—566

ELKINS, James B.—62

ELLINGTON, Buford—113

ELY, Gen. Paul Henry—492, 564

END of Ideology: On The Exhaustion of Political Ideas in the Fifties, The (book)—32

END to Innocence, An (book)—201, 202

ENGLE, Sen. Clair—Profile **194-195; 344, 606-607**

ERVIN, Sen. Sam J., Jr.—Profile **195-196; 395, 434, 606**

EUROPEAN Coal and Steel Community (ECSC)—74

EUROPEAN Defense Community (EDC)—74, 142, 166-167

EUROPEAN Iron and Steel Community—166

EXPORT-Import Bank—92, 142

F

FACTS Forum—261

FAIRLESS, Benjamin F.—Profile **196-197**

FAMILY, Socialization and Interaction Process (book)—469

FARLAND, Joseph S.—Profile **197-198**

FARLEY, John L.—403

FARM Credit Administration—290

FAST, Howard—Profile **198-199; 425**

FAUBUS, Gov. Orval—Profile **199-200;** defeats Cherry for Arkansas governorship 104; and Little Rock desegregation controversy 28-29, 73, 187, 273, 413

FEDERAL Aviation Agency (FAA)—191

FEDERAL Bureau of Investigation (FBI)—139-140, 288-290, 404, 523, 547

FEDERAL Communications Commission (FCC)—Doerfer as member of 150-151; R. Lee nominated to 436; and Miami television license scandal 479; action on quiz show scandals 151; 1958 Mack scandal 10; Special Subcommittee on Legislative Oversight probe of 253-254, 406, 546

FEDERAL Council on Science and Technology—191

FEDERAL Highway Aid Act (1956)—235, 637

FEDERAL Power Commission (FPC)—253, 402, 441, 546

FEDERAL Reserve Board—82, 218, 236, 416-417, 472-473, 542

FEDERAL Security Agency—271, 517

FEDERAL Trade Commission (FTC)—231, 254, 546

FEDERAL Trade Union Committee—375

G

FBI implements 289; in HEW 271; Judiciary Committee rejects extension of 195; McLeod and 404; Ladejinsky dismissed under 574; and Navy 601; Nixon praises Administration on 457; and Peters dismissal 567; Schlesinger opposes 545; Senate Constitutional Rights Subcommittee investigates 263; Service dismissed under 550-551; N. Thomas criticizes 75, 602; and USIA 588-589; Vincent dismissed under 620; See also **OPPENHEIMER, J. Robert, SUPREME Court**
INTERNATIONAL Atomic Energy Agency—587, 627
INTERNATIONAL Bank for Reconstruction and Development—45
INTERNATIONAL Brotherhood of Longshoremen—128, 418
INTERNATIONAL Brotherhood of Teamsters (IBT)—and AFL-CIO 420; expelled from AFL-CIO 161, 230, 508, 526; Beck as president of 31-32; Brewster and 61, 62; Curran and 128; Dorfman and 152; Hoffa and 273-275; R. Kennedy investigates 328; Senate probe of 196, 232, 394, 444; and United Mine Workers 366
INTERNATIONAL Business Machines Corp. (IBM)—635
INTERNATIONAL Confederation of Free Trade Unions—419-420
INTERNATIONAL Cooperation Administration (ICA)—191, 284;
INTERNATIONAL Development Association (IDA)—436, 595
INTERNATIONAL Fur and Leather Workers Union of the United States and Canada (IFLWU)—229
INTERNATIONAL Information Administration—254-255, 543
INTERNATIONAL Ladies Garment Workers Union (ILGWU)—160-161, 363
INTERNATIONAL Longshoremen's Association (ILA)—Curran and 128; expelled from AFL 161, 418, 507; Hoffa connections with 274; New York City Anti-Crime Committee probes 59; pact with Teamsters 61; racial discrimination in 496
INTERNATIONAL Longshoremen's and Warehousemen's Union (ILWU)—65-66

INTERNATIONAL Monetary Fund (IMF)—142
"INTERNATIONAL Security: The Military Aspect" (report)—517-518
INTERNATIONAL Typographical Union—370
INTERNATIONAL Union of Electrical, Radio and Machine Workers (IUE)—56, 95, 96
INTERSTATE Commerce Commission—115, 126, 329
IRAN—25, 162, 287-288
IRELAND—404
ISRAEL—78, 308, 319, 523, 524, 626
ITALY—377, 447, 604
IVES, Sen. Irving M.—Profile **301-302**; 205, 252, 275

J

JACK, Hulan—486
JACKSON, C(harles) D(ouglas)—Profile **302-303**; 291
JACKSON, Sen. Henry M.—Profile **303-306**; 87, 114, 327, 544, 401, 421
JACKSON, Justice Robert H.—Profile **306-307**; See also **SUPREME Court**
JAGAN, Prime Minister Cheddi—375
JAPAN—13-14, 157, 245, 381, 495
JAVITS, Sen. Jacob K.—Profile **308**; 241, 547, 629
JENCKS v. U.S.—60, 195
JENKINS, Ray—390
JENNER, Sen. William E.—Profile **309-311**; 8, 569, 596
JOHNS, Gov. Charley E.—118
JOHNSON, Frank M., Jr.—Profile **311-312**
JOHNSON, Jim—199
JOHNSON, Sen. Lyndon B.—Profile **312-316**; R. Anderson and 22; Biemiller and 43; action on cloture rule 94, 451; and civil rights 107, 174, 236; and Harlow 250; and cuts in 1959 omnibus housing bill 570; and H. Humphrey 298; and Lausche 358; challenges to the leadership of 109, 203, 236, 258, 489, 613; liberals criticize 499; on McCarthy 195, 387; selects Mansfield as majority whip 411; Meany and 421; urges speed up in missile production 401; 1960 presidential bid 502, 594; as protege of Rayburn 502; Rowe

advises to speak against Administration 533; Smathers as aide to 558; chosen 1960 vice presidential candidate 215, 305, 326, 400, 509, 526
JONES, Bobby—435
JONES, Howard P.—Profile **316-317**
JONES, Theodore—138
JOUHAUX, Leon—527
JUDD, Rep. Walter H.—Profile **317-318**; 185, 352
JUNO I (missile)—See **MISSILES**
JUPITER (missile)—See **MISSILES**
JUSTICE, Dept. of—Brownell as Attorney General 70-73; creation of civil rights division in 520, dismisses Gold indictment 229; racketeering unit established 520, Rogers as Attorney General 520; and Talbott case 598; declines to invene in Till case 608; on loyalty-security procedures in 567

K

KAPPEL, Frederick—72
KARTIGANER Hat Corp.—526
KASAVUBU, President Joseph—78
KATANGA—See **CONGO**
KATZENTINE, A. Frank—406
KAUFMAN, Judge Irving—566
KEAN, Winthrop—552
KEATING, Rep. Kenneth B.—Profile **318-319**, 149, 281, 547
KEESHIN, John—126
KEFAUVER, Sen. Estes—Profile **319-322**; proposes code for congressional committees 363; member of Democratic Advisory Council 613; investigates Dixon-Yates contract 147; calls for anti-lynching legislation 608-609; 1952 presidential bid 501, 580, 644; 1956 presidential bid 215, 252, 424, 582; wins 1956 vice presidential nomination 146, 236, 326, 582; opposes "Southern Manifesto" 236; voting record 235
KELLY, Rep. A. D.—42
KENNAN, George F.—Profile **323-324**; 3, 135, 165, 453
KENNEDY or Nixon? (book)—545
KENNEDY, Sen. John F.—Profile **324-327**; Bowles and 58; views on defense 188, 225, 305, 599; attacks Federal Reserve tight

money policies 416; and labor reform legislation 196, 242, 302, 394, 395, 433-434; defeats Lodge 371; Morse on 442; sponsors social security medical care plan 333; Stevenson opinion of 584; 1956 vice presidential bid 236, 321, 502, 510; warns on U.S. intervention in Vietnam 576

1960 Presidential Campaign—advisers to 256, 328, 362, 545; Daley role in 132; chooses Johnson as running mate 215, 305, 315; Luce views on 379; debates Nixon 573; Peale views on 478; primary campaign 298-299, 315, 499, 584; results 132, 460; support for 43, 116, 215, 221, 230, 369, 399, 400, 421, 474, 510, 526, 603, 604, 644

KENNEDY, Joseph P.—287
KENNEDY, ROBERT F.—Profile 327-328; questions Anastasia 19; and Beck probe 31; and Brewster probe 62; and Dorfman probe 152; and Hoffa probe 274; favors H. Jackson as 1960 vice presidential nominee 305; and Kerr-Mills Act 429; role in labor corruption probe 232; as counsel to Permanent Investigations Subcommittee 304, 393; and United Auto Workers 130, 444, 509
KENNELLY, Mayor Martin—132, 138
KENNON, Gov. Robert F.—Profile 328-329
KENNY, John V.—424
KENTUCKY—102, 583
KEROUAC, Jack—Profile 329-330; 228
KERR, Clark—Profile 330-331
KERR, Sen. Robert—Profile 331-332
KERR-MILLS Act (1960)—429
KEYSERLING, Leon—Profile 333-334
KHRUSHCHEV, Premier Nikita S.—meets with L. Collins 119; meets Curran 128, meets with C. Eaton 177; meets with Harriman 252; Nixon engages in "kitchen debate" 457-458; meets Pace 465; Poulson debates 485; on Quemoy and Matsu 170; meets with Reuther 509; meets with E. Roosevelt 524; meets Stevenson 583; reaction to U-2 flight 487; 1958 ultimatum on Berlin 187, 266; 1959 visit to U.S. 155, 379
KILLIAN, James R.—Profile 334-335; 188, 343

KING Martin Luther, Jr.—Profile 335-338; relations with Abernathy 1-2; meets with Eisenhower on civil rights 642; role in Montgomery bus boycott 1, 311, 466; relations with Shuttlesworth 557-558
KING, Gov. Samuel—64-65
KINSEY, Alfred—Profile 338-339
KIRK, Russel—Profile 545-546
KISHI, Prime Minister Nobusuke—381
KISSINGER, Henry A.—Profile 341-342; 324, 517-518
KISTIAKOWSKY, George B.—Profile 342-343
KLINE, Albert—556
KNIGHT, Gov. Goodwin—Profile 343-344; 194, 346, 351
KNOWLAND, Sen. William—Profile 345-346; and California Republican politics 68, 344, 351; and Chotiner 106; views on Communist China 54, 122, 227, 555; introduces loyalty-security bill 125; succeeds Taft as majority leader 597; opposes aid to Yugoslavia 145
KOHLBERG, Alfred—Profile 346-347
KOHLER, Herbert—Profile 347-348
KOHLER, Gov. Walter—386, 489
KOHLER Co.—347-348, 444, 509
KONG Le, Capt.—69, 467-468
KOREA, North—157
KOREA, South—138, 157, 257
KOREAN War—Dulles role in ending 166; Eisenhower role in ending 183; Flanders opposes armistice 204; Harrison role in peace negotiations 256-257; Rovere lauds U.S. intervention in 532; Stevenson defends Truman policies 581; as 1952 presidential campaign issue 181
KOREAN Mutual Defence Treaty (1954)—374
KROCK, Arthur—Profile 349-350; 505
KUCHEL, Sen. Thomas H.—Profile 350-351; 145
KU Klux Klan—89, 473

L

LABOR, Organized—and automation 400; Boulwarism collective bargaining technique 55-56; Brownell charges Communist infiltration of unions 72;

congressional probes of 394, 617; Dilworth defends rights of unions 143; Durkin and 171-172; Goldwater as foe of 232-233; H. Jackson and 305; Mundt opposed to 444; Passman favors curbs on 469; and right-to-work legislation 146, 358; See also specific individuals and unions
LABOR, Dept. of—128, 171-172, 243, 433
LADEJINSKY, Wolf—Profile 351-352; 574
LADY Chatterley's Lover (book)—174, 585, 592
LAIT, Jack—563
LAMB, Edward—150-151
LANDRUM, Rep. Phillip—Profile 352-353; 242, 395
LANDRUM-Griffin Act (1959)—H. Bridges defies 65; Halleck's role in passage of 247; legislative history of 420-421, 434; provisions of 242, 275, 353, 395; opposition to 230; support for 54, 233
LANDY, Eugene W.—601
LANGER, Sen. William—Profile 354-355
LANSDALE, Edward G.—Profile 354-355; 162, 169
LAOS—69-70, 380, 467-468
LARSON, Arthur—Profile 357
LATIN America—59, 92, 142, 189, 409-410, 446; See also specific countries
LATTIMORE, Owen—345, 488
LAUSCHE, Sen. Frank—Profile 358; 146
LAWRENCE, Mayor David L.—359
LAWRENCE Radiation Laboratory—549
LEADER, Gov. George—Profile 359; 547
LEBANON—187, 234, 447, 614
LEE, Gov. J. Bracken—Profile 360; 635
LEE, Mayor Richard—Profile 360-361
LEE, Robert E.—8, 436
LEHMAN, Sen. Herbert H.—Profile 362-363; 8, 203, 520
LeMAY, Gen. Curtis—Profile 363-365; 593
LEVITT, Arthur—141, 204
LEVITTOWN, Pa.—359
LEWIS, John L.—Profile 365-366; 403
LIBERAL Hour, The (book)—221
LIBERAL Party (N.Y.)—526
LIBERATION (magazine)—449
LIEBMAN, Marvin—Profile 367
LIFE is Worth Living (book)—553

Eisenhower policy toward 184, 187; Jenner views on 311; Knowland views on 346; Lippmann views on 369; K. Rankin recommendations on 498; Ridgway recommendations on 512; H. Smith views on 561; Twining recommendations on 614; as 1960 campaign issue 459

QUIET American, The (book)—357

R

RABB, Maxwell—78, 106, 440
RADDOCK, Max—299
RADFORD, Adm. Arthur—Profile 492-493; 57, 167-168, 169, 512
RADIO Corporation of America (RCA)—541, 598
RADIO Free Europe—541
RADULOVICH, Lt. Milo—448
RAILROAD Transfer Service Inc.—126
RAINACH, Willie—135, 373
RAND, Ayn—Profile 493-494; 340
RANDALL, Clarence—Profile 494-495
RANDOLPH, A. Philip—Profile 495-496; 421, 642
RANKIN, J. Lee—Profile 497
RANKIN, Karl—Profile 498
RARICK, Donald—400
RAUH, Joseph L.—Profile 498-500; 310
RAYBURN, Rep. Sam—Profile 500-503; and S. Adams probe 131; and Albert 8; and R. Anderson 22, and the Democratic Advisory Council 203, 613; and foreign aid budget 470; defeats Administration health insurance plan 42; Halleck limits effectiveness of 247; and Harlow 250; and O. Harris 253; aids 1960 Johnson presidential bid 315; urges formation of legislative oversight panel 253, 546; and E. McCarthy 382; and McCormack 398; and J. Martin 247, 415; S. Mitchell strengthens Stevenson's ties with 436; opposes 1954 tax bill 121; and Texas Democratic politics 554, 651; describes C. Vinson 621
RECIPROCAL Trade—R. Byrd views on 89; Commission on Foreign Economic Policy report on 494, 626; Milliken views on 426; J. Martin and 414; opposition to 243, 332, 503-504; support for 52, 121, 142; 236, 247, 428, 429, 443, 480, 501, 637
RECLAMATION, Bureau of—550

RECONSTRUCTION Finance Corp.—76, 182
REDSTONE (missile)—See MISSILES
REECE, Rep. B. Carroll—261, 534
REED, Rep. Daniel—Profile 503-504; 13, 91, 414, 426
REED, Justice Stanley F.—Profile 504; 505; See also SUPREME Court
REFLECTIONS on the Failure of Socialism (book)—175-176
REFUGEE Relief Act (1953)—123-124, 404, 607, 629
REPUBLICAN Looks at His Party, A (book)—357
REPUBLICAN National Committee—10, 181, 246, 514, 589, 591
REPUBLICAN National Convention (1952)—Brownell role in 70; delegate struggle at 67, 181, 371, 519; Dirksen role in 144; M. Eisenhower role in 191; W. Hoffman and 278; McKay role in 402; Stassen role in 14, 574; Summerfield role in 591; Weeks role in 636
REPUBLICAN National Convention (1956)—10, 102, 266, 287, 578
REPUBLICAN National Convention (1960)—210, 233, 287, 318, 443, 575
REPUBLICAN National Finance Committee—559, 601
REPUBLICAN Party—Alcorn strategy for 10; and 1952 election 181; Larson analyzes 357; Morse resigns from 441; McCarthy and 246; Morton a National Chairman of 443; and 1954 election 246; Schlesinger on 544; and 1958 election 10
RESTON, James—Profile 505-506; 181, 522
REUTHER, Victor—163
REUTHER, Walter P.—Profile 506-509; Beck and 31; Curtice opposes profitsharing suggestion of 129; Ford Motor Co. and 211; feud with Goldwater 232-233; Kohler on 348; feud with McDonald 399; Meany and 418, 419, 421; Romney criticizes 521; as president of United Auto Workers 444
RHEE, President Syngman—157, 166, 571
RIBICOFF, Gov. Abraham A.—Profile 509-510; 40, 58
RICHARDS, Rep. James P.—54
RICKOVER, Adm. Hyman G.—Profile 511; 305

RIDGWAY, Gen. Matthew—Profile 511-512; 169, 188, 492, 512, 598
RIVERCOMB, Sen. Chapman—89
RIVERS, Rep. L. Mendel—Profile 513-514
ROBERTS, C. Wesley—Profile 514; 245
ROBERTSON, Sen. A. Willis—Profile 515-516
ROBERTSON, Walter—493
ROBESON, Paul—Profile 516-517
ROCKEFELLER, Gov. Nelson A.—Profile 517-519; Dulles attitude toward 165; Goldwater attacks 233; appoints Kissinger director of Special Studies Project 341; wins 1958 New York gubernatorial nomination 252; as member of PACGO 191; 1960 Republican platform and 459, 481
ROCKEFELLER, Winthrop—199
ROCKEFELLER Brothers Fund—341-342, 517-518, 600
ROCKEFELLER Foundation—219, 339, 530, 534
ROGERS, William—Profile 519-520; 20, 458, 497
ROMNEY, George—Profile 520-521; 649
ROMUALDI, Serafino—375
ROONEY, Rep. John J.—Profile 522-523; 140
ROOSEVELT, Eleanor—Profile 523-524; as member of the Democratic Advisory Council 613; on Brown decision 499; role in DeSapio decline 203; J. E. Hoover reports to Eisenhower on 289; appears before Internal Security Subcommittee 449; urges Murrow to run for Senate 449; and National Council for Industrial Peace 363; and the formation of the New York Committee for Democratic Voters 203, 363; criticizes Powell Amendment 485
ROOSEVELT, Rep. Franklin D., Jr.—54, 252, 299, 308, 617
ROOSEVELT, Kermit—Profile 525; 12, 162
ROSE, Alex—Profile 525-526
ROSENBERG, Ethel—Profile 526-528; Brownell supports execution of 71; Einstein urges clemency for 179; the FBI and 289; Fiedler on 202; C. Jackson urges clemency for 303; Sobell tried with 566; the Supreme Court and 156, 620
ROSENBERG, Julius—Profile 528
ROSS, Robert Tripp—Profile 528-530; 328

tion 33; Finance Committee: Douglas as member of 236, rejects foreign investment bill 52, Gore as member of 236, R. Kerr as member of 333, R. Long as member of 374, Milliken as chairman of 227, 426; Foreign Relations Committee: receives letters supporting Bohlen nomination 25, and Eisenhower Doctrine 411, Engle testifies before 194, restores foreign aid cuts 227, Fulbright becomes chairman of 239, Green and 239, Gore as member of 236, J. Kennedy as member of 326, confirms C. Luce nomination 377, Streibert testifies before 589, and Yalta and Potsdam agreements 239, 268; Foreign Relations Committee, Disarmament Subcommittee 41, 255-256, 298; Government Operations Committee, Permanent Investigations Subcommittee; 578-579, probes Army 388, 389, 481, probes Armed Forces Army-McCarthy hearings 114-115, 264, 579, 638, Carr as executive staff director of 97, investigates Chotiner 106, Cohn as chief counsel to 114-115, investigates Cross 126, probes Defense Dept. 388, 393, 394, Democratic minority resigns from 388, 417, Dworshak and 172-173, investigates R. Harris 255, Hollister refuses open testimony before 284, J. Kennedy as member of 325, R. Kennedy and 31, 327-328, J. McCarthy becomes chairman of 386, J. B. Matthews as executive director of 388, 417, McClellan and 393, Mundt as member of 444, Potter as member of 483, investigates Ross 529, Schine as chief consultant to 543, Symington as member of 593, investigates Talbott 598, probes Voice of America 198, Zwicker testifies before 654; Judiciary Committee 73, 174, 249, 355, 363; Judiciary Committee, Antitrust and Monopolies Subcommittee 129, 150, 294, 354, 521; Judiciary Committee, Constitutional Rights Subcommittee 263; Judiciary Committee Internal Security Subcommittee: Eastland as chairman of 174, questions Hutchins 301, Muste testifies before 449, lists Pauling as Communist supporter 476, investigates Communist influence in the press 174, 263, E. Smith testifies before 559-560,

probes test ban movement 149, probes H. White appointment 71, 289; Interior and Insular Affairs Committee 304, 329, 426, 565; Interstate and Foreign Commerce Committee 194, 407; Interstate and Foreign Commerce Committee, Aviation Subcommittee 436; Labor and Public Welfare Committee 232, 269, 271-272, 394, 645; Post Office and Civil Service Committee 96; Public Works Committee 103, 332, 606; Rules and Administration Committee 239, 263, 423; Rules and Administration Committee, Elections Subcommittee 130; Select Committee on Improper Activities in the Labor or Management Field: investigates Beck 31, hears charges against Capehart 95, investigates Dorfman 152, investigates Dubinsky 161, Genovese testifies before 226, investigates Hoffa 274-275, investigates Hutcheson 299, J. Kennedy as member of 326, R. Kennedy as chief counsel to 328, probes Kohler strike 444, probes labor union corruption 196, 230, 242, 302, J. McCarthy as member of 392, McClellan as chairman of 394, recommendations of 394, Reuther supports 508, Probes United Auto Workers 130, 323, 509; Select Committee to Study Censure: Carlson role in 96, Jenner denounces 310, McCarran assails 382, procedures of 391, recommendations of 66, 391, 634, Stennis as member of 576, Watkins as chairman of 634; Small Business Committee 194, 569; Special Committee on Unemployment Problems 383

SENATOR Joe McCarthy (book)—531

SERVICE, John S.—Profile 550-551; 347

SEXUAL Behavior in the Human Female (book)—339

SEXUAL Behavior in the Human Male (book)—338

SHANLEY, Bernard—Profile 551-552; 172, 637

SHARFMAN, Herbert—151

SHARP, Dudley C.—47

SHAW, Artie—617

SHEEN, Fulton J.—Profile 552-553; 265

SHIELDS, Julius—497

SHIVERS, Gov. Allan—Profile 553-554; 15-16, 133-134, 314, 501, 502, 650-651

SHORT, Rep. Dewey—Profile 554-556

SHUMAN, Charles B.—Profile 556

SHUTTLESWORTH, Fred L.—Profile 557-558

SIMPSON, Rep. Richard—429

SMALL Business Administration (SBA)—94, 472, 515

SMALL Watershed Act (1954)—8

SMATHERS, Sen. George A.—Profile 558-559

SMITH, Dana—455

SMITH, Earl T. A.—Profile 559-560

SMITH, Gerald—Profile 560-561

SMITH, Sen. H. Alexander—Profile 561-562; 380

SMITH, Rep. Howard—Profile 562-563

SMITH, Sen. Margaret Chase—Profile 563-564; 355

SMITH, W. Bedell—Profile 564-565; 168, 387, 404

SMYLIE, Gov. Robert E.—Profile 565

SNARE Corp., Frederick—246, 412

SOBELL, Helen—566

SOBELL, Morton—Profile 566-567; 527

SOBELOFF, Judge Simon—Profile 567-568; 71-72, 516

SOCIAL Security—T. Curtis supports private control of 131; L. Johnson favors strengthening system 313; R. Long supports expansion of 374; Patton favors extension of 475; Rivers favors increase in 513; 1954 bill extends 130; 1956 amendment to aid disabled workers 228

SOCIALIST Party—602

SOCIETY for the Propagation of the Faith—553

SOCIOLOGICAL Imagination, The (book)—428

SORENSEN, Theodore—325

SOURWINE, Julian G.—308

SOUTHEAST Asia Collective Defense Treaty (1954)—380

SOUTHEAST Asia Conference (1954)—411

SOUTHEAST Asia Treaty Organization (SEATO)—155, 169, 411, 565

SOUTHERN Christian Leadership Conference (SCLC)—1-2, 336, 557

SOUTHERN Governors Conference (1957)—119

SOUTHERN Governors Conference (1959)—474

SOUTHERN Manifesto—drafting of 133, 228, 606; Fulbright supports revised version of 217; O.

XYZ

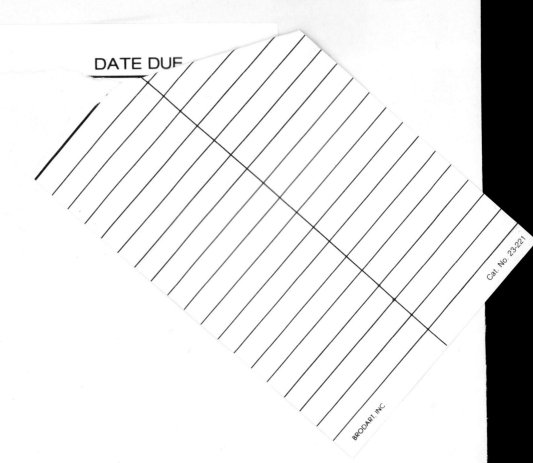